Contents

Introduction

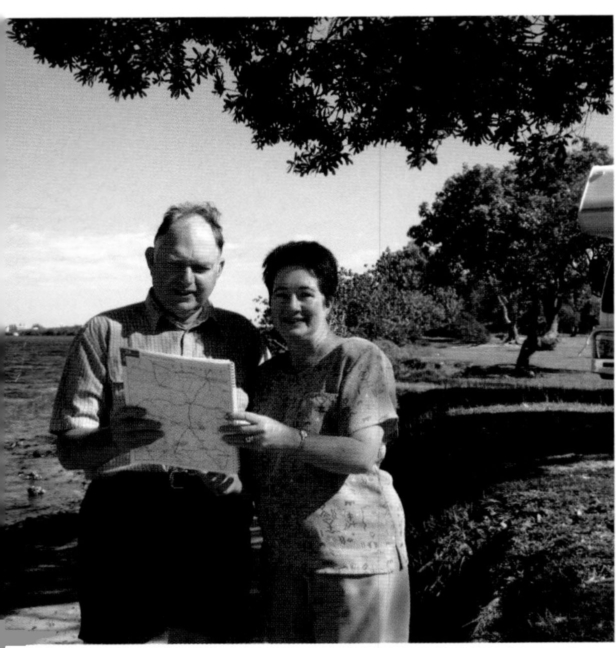

About the authors

Evon and Peter Anderson's travelling experience spans well over 40 years, firstly by car or hired motorhome. For many of those years they travelled with their three children. After early retirement in 1997 they purchased a motorhome and were able to devote more time to exploring Australia. They have always lived in Brisbane and use their home there as a base.

After several years of travelling and writing travel articles, Evon and Peter decided to undertake a much more ambitious project – writing a travel guidebook. Two editions of *Around Australia* have now been successfully launched into the marketplace by the Publisher, Hema Maps.

Evon and Peter are often asked about caravans and motorhomes and many of the practical aspects of travelling. It quickly became apparent that most people embarking on this travelling lifestyle literally do not know where to start, and this can result in some expensive mistakes. Well over a year's research went into all aspects of the vehicles used for travelling and what people need to know to enjoy a trouble-free lifestyle. This information has been collated and illustrated with photos they have taken on their travels.

Peter is a keen amateur astronomer and has his own observatory, although with a lot of time spent travelling there has not been as much time to devote to astronomy as he would like. Peter's other lifelong interest, photography, has complemented their travel writing.

Authors' tip:

Often when people start travelling they assume they will always stay in caravan parks. Later, some people regret not having a more self-contained vehicle that gives them the freedom to choose – as well as saving a considerable amount of money on overnight camping fees.

The freedom lifestyle

Many Australians dream of exploring our great country, but rather than just thinking about it, we urge you to make the dream a reality. Discover the 'Freedom Lifestyle' – travel as and when you want. You might start with small trips before undertaking the ultimate adventure of touring around the continent.

The around Australia trip is not as massive an undertaking as it might sound, and thousands set off every year. If you ask several travellers how long it would take, you will probably get a different answer from each one. Many go around mainland Australia, seeing all the highlights, in five or six months, while others can take a year or two. This is part of the Freedom Lifestyle – you travel as it suits you. Most travellers are busy planning their next adventure as soon as they finish their current journey.

There has never been a wider selection of caravans and motorhomes to choose from, and they all give you a precious gift – the freedom to travel at your own pace and decide where and when you want to go. Don't rush your purchase because the vehicle you choose will be an important element in your enjoyment of travelling. When deciding what suits you, look at all the options, keeping in mind whether you will be taking short or long trips and also where you intend to travel.

If you are planning a big trip, research what you would like to see and do before you set off. It might sound romantic to just 'hit the road' and travel as the whim takes you, but in reality it will mean that you will miss a lot, unless you have unlimited time and money to keep back-tracking.

Tourist information offices can tell you all about their local area, but you cannot get this information until you arrive in their town and then only if they are open. Staff at tourist information offices are always very helpful, but in their attempt to 'sell' their area they will often tell you everything is fantastic. You will then have to sort through a mountain of brochures to work out what you want to see and do. It is better to do some research before you go, use a guidebook as you travel and seek local information when you need that little bit more. Note – The travel guide book *Around Australia*, written by the authors of this publication, is a complete guide book not only for the big trip, but for short trips as well.

We encourage you to take to the road to experience for yourself all this incredible country has to offer – its scenery, plants and animals, and people. One of the joys of travelling is the people you meet, either locals or those you share a campfire with, and sometimes lifelong friendships can result from such chance meetings. It is a special experience to swap tales of your journeys and the great places you have found with other travellers.

The most difficult step to take is the first one: we urge you to take that step and join us in a very special lifestyle. Experience the freedom of independent travel – but be careful, you might find, like many thousands of others, that this lifestyle is addictive.

Motorhome near Swansea, Tasmania Photo: Rob Boegheim

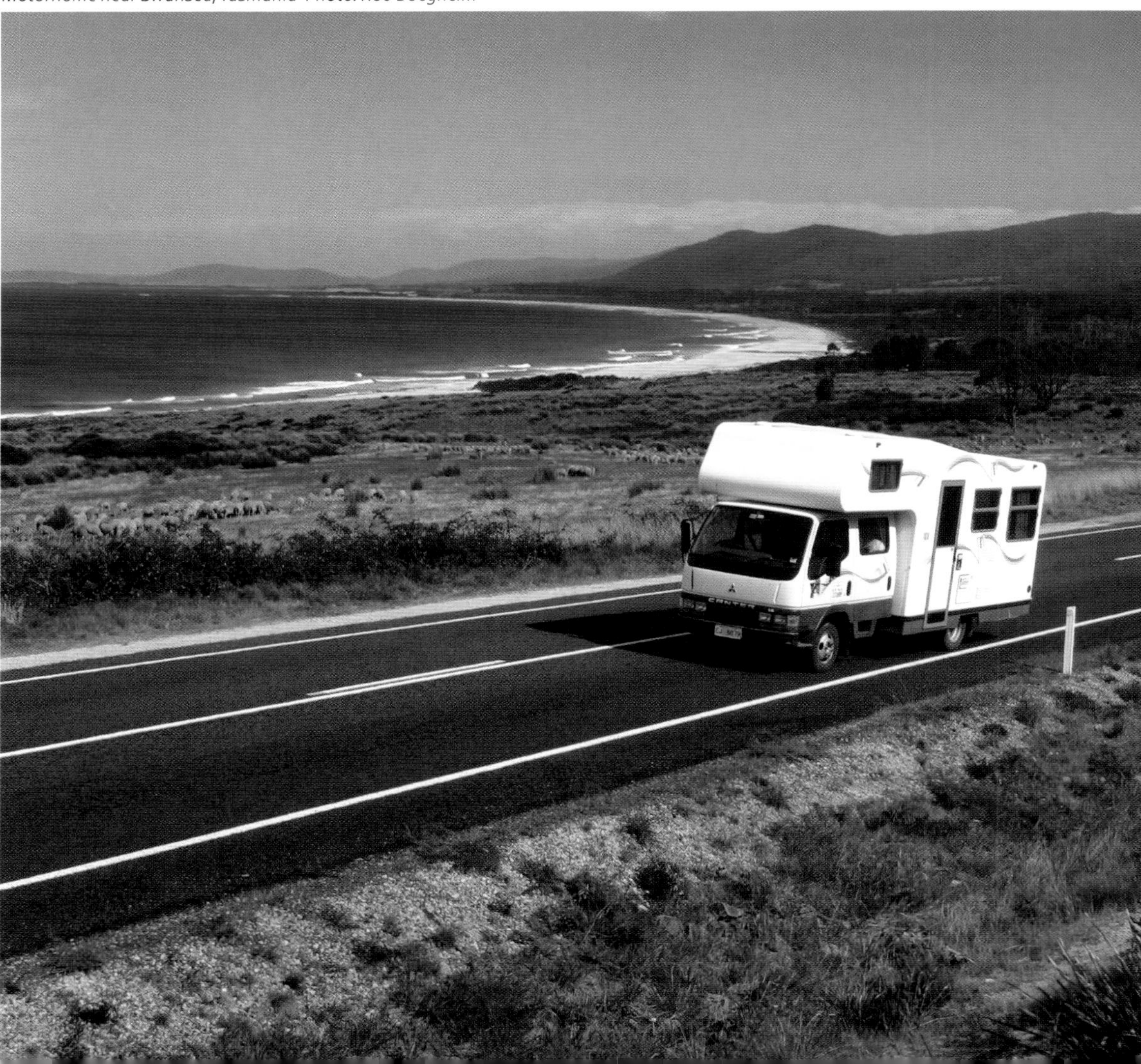

Frequently asked questions

Question – *What is best – a caravan, motorhome or camper trailer?*

Answer – There are advantages and disadvantages with all options, but you have to consider where and how you wish to travel. If you plan to stay in one place for a period of time and use it as a base, a caravan or fifth-wheeler could be best. If you plan to just keep on travelling, even if it is only a small distance each day, a motorhome or campervan would probably be more convenient. If you want to travel in remote areas on unsealed roads, a camper trailer might best suit the conditions. *Refer to Choosing Your Recreational Vehicle p44 for more details.*

Question – *With the current high price of fuel, does it cost too much to travel?*

Answer – Fuel is only one component of your travelling costs, and there is no point in waiting for the price to come down significantly. An example is the authors' mid-size motorhome that has fuel consumption of 7.1km per litre when travelling at 85kph. When fuel is $1.25 per litre the fuel cost is $17.61 per 100km, at $1.50 per litre it costs $21.13 and at $1.75 the cost is $24.65. With an increase in fuel price from $1.25 per litre to $1.75 per litre, someone travelling an average of 200km per day would pay an extra $14.08 per day. Other vehicle costs (tyres, repairs and servicing), entrance fees to attractions, food, camping fees and other personal costs far outweigh the extra cost of fuel.

Question – *Should I consider fuel consumption when choosing a caravan or motorhome?*

Answer – Most definitely. There is a significant difference in fuel consumption between different vehicles and different car/caravan combinations. With a motorhome or campervan, the weight and aerodynamics of the vehicle impact heavily on fuel consumption, as do the specifications and capacity of the motor. If you plan to tow a caravan or camper trailer, it is not only the specifications of the tow vehicle that determine fuel consumption, but also the weight and aerodynamics of the towed unit.

Question – *What are the advantages of different fuels – petrol, diesel or LPG?*

Answer – A vehicle will travel further on a litre of diesel than on a litre of any other fuel. LPG (liquefied petroleum gas) is cheaper per litre, but it is less efficient than petrol, both in terms of the distance you can drive and the power of the engine. *Refer to Fuel p80 for more details.*

Question – *Are supplies of petrol, diesel and LPG gas readily available?*

Answer – Petrol and diesel are both readily available on the highways, however, supplies of LPG are not as widespread. In some very remote regions diesel is the only fuel available (see the Atlas section), although a replacement for unleaded fuel, known as Opal, is becoming available in some Aboriginal communities that previously only had diesel.

Question – *Do you need long-range fuel tanks or extra fuel in jerry cans to travel around Australia?*

Answer – No. Unless you are travelling in remote desert regions, there is never more than a couple of hundred kilometres between service stations. It is not worth adding to the weight of your rig by carrying extra fuel, and the transportation of fuel, particularly petrol, in cans presents an unnecessary danger.

Question – *If I am travelling in a remote area, how can I carry fuel safely?*

Answer – Fuel can only be transported in containers designed for the purpose and cannot be carried within the passenger compartment of a vehicle, or the accommodation area of a motorhome or campervan. Take a funnel to help pour fuel into the tank.

Travellers enjoying a barbecue

Question – *Can I travel around Australia driving only on bitumen roads?*

Answer – Yes. Most of the popular attractions are accessible on sealed roads, and the few that are not can be visited on a local tour. Unless you have a 4WD, consider paying for a tour rather than taking a vehicle not designed for off-road travel on a badly corrugated road. In addition to possible damage to the vehicle, tyres and contents, it can be very stressful for a driver not used to these conditions, and after all, you are meant to be having fun.

Question – *If I want to travel around Australia, which direction should I go?*

Answer – Most travellers favour anti-clockwise. There are two main reasons: you can be in each area when the weather should be at its best, and you should have the advantage of tail winds on the Barkly Tableland and the Nullarbor Plain. Tail winds can reduce fuel consumption dramatically.

Question – *When should I go?*

Answer – Follow the weather reports so you arrive in north Queensland after the Wet has finished. Sometimes there is a short Wet (January/February) so by April the weather should be great, but in other years the Wet can extend as late as May. Continue on to the Northern Territory in May/June. This is long enough after the Wet for floodwaters to have subsided, but before the countryside becomes dry and dusty. Travel on to the Kimberley around early July. Western Australian wildflowers come into bloom in the north in July, and as you travel south the weather will warm up and a new montage of colourful flowers will come into bloom. In the midlands, the wildflowers are at their best in September. The southern part of Australia has cold, wet winters, so explore the southern part of Western Australia, South Australia, Victoria and Tasmania in the summer.

Question – *How can I travel more economically?*

Answer – Reduce the weight of your rig by not carrying unnecessary heavy items, and reduce your travelling speed. Fuel consumption of the authors' vehicle driven at 85kph is 7.1km per litre, while increasing the speed to a little over 90kph results in fuel consumption of 6.5km per litre. Fuel economy decreases even more at higher speeds. You can also save money on accommodation costs. Try bush camping, or if you prefer to stay in caravan parks, seek out smaller, less expensive ones in country towns rather than fancy resort-style ones in tourist areas.

Question – *Do I have to stay in caravan parks?*

Answer – No. There are thousands of low-cost or free campsites available and many publications list them. *Camps Australia Wide* is the most popular of these books. It is your choice how often you stay in caravan parks, although in some tourist areas there won't be any other alternative. If you plan to camp where you do not have access to 240 volt power you should set up your caravan or motorhome accordingly. *See Refrigeration (p66) for more details.*

Question – *Is bush camping safe?*

Answer – Yes. Very rarely do campers feel threatened when bush camping. In all our years of travelling we have never felt even remotely uneasy when bush camping. If you are unsure at first, camp near other travellers. *See Bush Camping (p112) for more details.*

Question – *Is it safe for a single person to travel alone?*

Answer – Yes. Hundreds of single people travel alone, many of them on the road permanently. For companionship, many travel with another single person, or even a few people, each in their own vehicle.

Question – *Can I travel with school-age children?*

Answer – Yes. Many families sell or rent their home and travel for a year or two, or even permanently, while the children undertake schooling by Distance Education supervised by a parent. This is probably easier with primary school age children rather than high school. Parents say that their children learn far more than they would have in a normal school, and that their children are generally more mature than others their age. Travelling together is a fantastic bonding experience for a family. A disadvantage can be that it is hard for children to establish friendships with a wide group of their peers as happens at school, although they will meet other young people while they travel, then they can keep in contact by email. *See Travelling full-time with children (p117) for more details.*

Question – *Can I travel with a pet?*

Answer – Yes, but there are places you cannot take a pet. *See Travelling with pets (p118 for more details).*

Terms used in caravans and motorhomes

- **Black water** is toilet waste.
- **Black-water tank** stores toilet waste that is emptied into a dump point.
- **Cassette toilet** is an in-built unit that uses minimal water and has a cassette that is removed to empty.
- **Dump point** is an access point to a sewer or underground tank, designed for the emptying of toilet waste.
- **Fridges** –
  - **All electric fridge** (compressor type) operates on 240 volt, 24 volt or 12 volt (or a combination).
  - **Three-way fridge** (absorption fridge) operates on gas, 240 volt or 12 volt.
  - **Two-way fridge** (absorption fridge) operates on gas and 240 volt, but does not operate on 12 volt.
- **Gas** used for cooking and refrigeration is propane gas stored in cylinders.
- **Grey water** is waste water from a shower or sink.
- **Grey-water tank** holds waste water until it can be emptied where it will not cause offence.
- **Porta-Potti toilet** is a portable unit similar to a cassette toilet. Porta Potti is a brand name and is just one of the several portable toilets available. *See Toilets (p69 for more details).*

Caravan Parks

1 - Site number

This arbitrary number has been allocated to enable you to find each site on the atlas page, and conversely to find a site's details from the atlas page.
Discounts: (Abbreviations – DP = Dump point; p or pen = pension; s or snr = senior; off-pk or o-p = off peak; week = week stay; multi-nt, multi or m-nt = multi-night stay; auto = auto club; FPA = Family Parks of Australia; TT = Top Tourist; CMCA = Campervan and Motorhome Club of Aust)

* A minimum booking period applies at peak times.

Site facilities

✓ - Author recommended
These are the parks that particularly appealed to the authors. It may have been the friendly welcome, great location or little 'service' extras. Some are smaller parks with a possible AAA rating of only two stars, whilst others may be more expensive 'upmarket' four or five star rated. Whilst the authors' personal taste may not be your 'cup of tea', they believe these camps usually offer something a little extra, and are worth checking out.

- **Drive through sites**
- **Long vehicle sites**
- **Wastewater disposal facilities**
- **Swimming pool**
- **Disabled facilities** (shower and toilet)
- **Public phones**
- **Shop or small kiosk**
- **Kitchen facilities**
- **LPG refill** (noted if swap only)
- **Internet**
- **Pets allowed** (conditions may apply – always phone for details)

Unless otherwise stated these caravan parks have laundry facilities, town water and cabin accommodation.

AAA star rating system

★ - ★★★★★
For more information about the AAA Star Rating System please visit: www.aaatourism.com.au

$ - $$$$ - Price range
Specific prices are not noted as all prices will go up with time. The number of $ symbols gives an indication of the type of cost visitors can expect to pay. A + symbol means a higher price applies at peak times.

Map ref **- Hema Atlas Map Reference**
All of the sites listed in this book are shown in the Hema Maps' Atlas pages that are included in this book. Simply use the reference, along with the site number, to find the site on the relevant Hema Atlas page.

Queensland

No.	Site	Rating / Price / Map ref
1	**Agnes Water**, Discovery Coast Caravan & Camping Park, Rocky Crossing Rd Ph: 07 4974 7547 **Notes:** long vehicle to 8m; no cabin accomm; eco-friendly; filtered water	★★★ $ Map ref 11 J12
2	**Airlie Beach**, BIG 4 Airlie Cove Resort, Cnr Shute Harbour & Ferntree Rds Ph: 07 4946 6727 **Discounts:** BIG4 **Notes:** few long vehicle sites; LPG swap only; restaurant; some ensuite sites	★★★★ $$$+ Map ref 11 B8
3	**Airlie Beach**, Island Gateway Holiday Park, Shute Harbour Rd (1.2km from PO) Ph: 1800 466 528 **Discounts:** Top Tourist; CMCA; snr **Notes:** long vehicle to 12m; mini golf; tennis; walk to CBD; some ensuites	★★★☆ $$$$+ Map ref 11 B8
4	**Alpha** Caravan & Villa Park, Hooper St, Alpha (500m E of Gateway R'house) Ph: 07 4985 1337 **Discounts:** week **Notes:** public ph, shop & LPG refill close; peaceful; walk to town centre	★★★ $$ Map ref 10 H4
5	**Aratula** Village Caravan Park, Cunningham Hwy, Aratula Ph: 07 5463 8161 **Notes:** shady areas; motel units & onsite vans	★★ $ Map ref 6 F6
6	**Atherton** Halloran's Leisure Park, Robert St, Atherton Ph: 07 4091 4144 **Discounts:** snr; 2 night stay **Notes:** on 6.5 acres, close to town & hospital	★★★☆ $$ Map ref 14 F3
7	**Atherton** BIG4 Woodlands Tourist Park, Herberton Rd, A therton (1km S of PO) Ph: 1800 041 441 **Discounts:** BIG4; week (off-pk) **Notes:** shop close; gardens; birds; close to Platypus Park	★★★★ $$$+ Map ref 14 F3
8	**Atkinsons Dam** Waterfront Caravan Park, Atkinsons Dam Rd, Coominya Ph: 07 5426 4151 **Discounts:** week **Notes:** lakefront park; boat ramp	★★★ $ Map ref 6 A5
9	**Augathella** Caravan Park, BP Roadhouse, Landsborough Hwy, Augathella Ph: 07 4654 5177 **Notes:** public ph & shop close; good for overnight stop	$ Map ref 8 C1
10	**Ayr**, BIG4 Ayr Silver Link Caravan Village, Northam Rd, Ayr Ph: 07 4783 3933 **Discounts:** BIG4 **Notes:** LPG swap only; birds permitted; playground & spa	★★★★ $$$ Map ref 10 A6
11	**Ayr**, Burdekin Cascades Caravan Park, Queen St, Ayr Ph: 07 4783 1429 **Notes:** pulic ph, shop & LPG refill close; shady; close to town centre	★★★☆ $ Map ref 10 A6
12	**Barcaldine**, Homestead Caravan Park, Box St (Matilda Hwy), Barcaldine Ph: 07 4651 1308 **Discounts:** week **Notes:** swimming pool & public ph close; discount fuel; entertainment	★★★ $ Map ref 10 H3
13	**Barcaldine** Tourist Park, 51-65 Box St (Matilda Hwy), Barcaldine Ph: 07 4651 6066 **Discounts:** Top Tourist; CMCA **Notes:** ph for long vehicle info; grass sites; free washing machine	★★★☆ $$ Map ref 10 H3
14	**Bargara**, Absolute Oceanfront Tourist Park, Woongarra Scenic Dr, Bargara Ph: 07 4159 2436 **Discounts:** week **Notes:** few drive thru & long vehicle sites; public ph close; oceanfront park; shady sites; fishing	★★★☆ $$$ Map ref 9 A12
15	**Bargara**, Turtle Sands Tourist Park, Mon Repos (14km NE of Bundaberg) Ph: 07 4159 2340 **Discounts:** week **Notes:** long vehicle to 7m; beachfront; near turtle rookery; rain water	★★☆ $$ Map ref 9 A12
16	**Beachmere**, Lions Club Caravan Park, Biggs Ave, Beachmere Ph: 07 5496 8077 **Notes:** long vehicle to 9m; public ph close; across road from beach	$ Map ref 5 H10
17	**Beaudesert** Caravan & Tourist Park, Albert St, Beaudesert Ph: 07 5541 1368 **Discounts:** week **Notes:** public ph & shop close; shaded sites; close to town	$ Map ref 7 G9
18	**Beerburrum**, Glasshouse Mountains Tourist Park, Steve Irwin Way (1.5km N of PO) Ph: 07 5496 0151 **Discounts:** week **Notes:** superb mountain view	★★★☆ $$ Map ref 5 F9
19	**Bell**, Bells & Whistles Caravan Park, Bunya Hwy, Bell Ph: 07 4663 1265 **Discounts:** week **Notes:** public ph & shop close; gateway to Bunya Mts	$$ Map ref 9 E10
20	**Benaraby**, Greenacres Motel Van Park, Bruce Hwy, Benaraby (N end of town) Ph: 07 4975 0136 **Discounts:** Oz Parks; CMCA; week **Notes:** good for overnight stop	★★★ $$ Map ref 11 J11

21 **Benaraby**, Discovery Parks - Benaraby, Bruce Hwy (20km S of Gladstone) Ph: 07 4975 0163
Discounts: BIG4; CMCA **Notes:** shop close; on Boyne River; some ensuites; boat ramp
★★★★ $$$ Map ref 11 J11

22 **Biloela** Caravan Park, Dawson Hwy, Biloela Ph: 07 4992 1211
Notes: close to shops
★★★ $$ Map ref 11 J11

23 **Biloela**, Discovery Holiday Park (White Cockatoo), Valentine Plains Rd, Biloela Ph: 07 4992 2618
Discounts: CMCA, week **Notes:** all ensuite sites; snooker/pool table
$$ Map ref 11 J11

24 **Birdsville** Caravan Park, Florence St, Birdsville Ph: 07 4656 3214
Discounts: week **Notes:** close to everything in town
$$+ Map ref 16 K3

25 **Blackall** Caravan Park, Garden St, Blackall (300m E of PO) Ph: 07 4657 4816
Discounts: multi-night stay **Notes:** public ph close; camp oven meals in winter
★★★ $ Map ref 10 J3

26 **Blackwater,** Bottletree Motel & Caravan Park, Littlefield St, Blackwater Ph: 07 4982 5611
Discounts: CMCA **Notes:** feed wild birds at 4pm daily
$$ Map ref 11 H8

27 **Bororen** Caravan Park, Bruce Hwy, Bororen (100m S of PO) Ph: 07 4974 4200
Discounts: week **Notes:** one long vehicle site; public ph, shop & LPG refill close; grassy sites; 100m to town
★★★ $ Map ref 11 J11

28 **Boulia** Caravan Park, Winton Rd, Boulia Ph: 07 4746 3320
Notes: close to town
$ Map ref 16 D4

29 **Bowen** Discovery Holiday Parks - Bowen, Cnr Soldiers & Horseshoe Bay Rds Ph: 07 4785 1262
Discounts: BIG4; CMCA; week **Notes:** long vehicle to 10m; birds permitted; beachfront park; no unpowered sites
★★★★☆ $$$+* Map ref 10 B7

30 **Bowen** Village Caravan Park, Bruce Hwy, Bowen (1km N of Info Centre) Ph: 07 4786 1366
Discounts: CMCA, snr; off-pk **Notes:** some ensuite sites
★★★☆ $$ Map ref 10 B7

31 **Boyne Island** Caravan Park, Jacaranda Dr, Boyne Island Ph: 07 4973 8888
Notes: long vehicle to 8m; playground; boat ramp, close to bowls & golf
★★★ $$ Map ref 11 J12

32 **Bribie Island**, Bongaree Caravan Park, Welsby Pde, Bongaree (500m from PO) Ph: 07 3408 1054
Discounts: week **Notes:** long vehicle to 8m; close to water & boat ramp
★★★☆ $$+* Map ref 5 G11

33 **Bribie Island** Caravan Park, Jacana Ave, Woorim (E side of island) Ph: 1800 649 831
Discounts: Top Tourist **Notes:** long vehicle to 7m; shop close; mini golf; half court tennis; recreation room
★★★★ $$+ Map ref 5 G11

34 **Brisbane**, BIG4 Brisbane Northside Caravan Village, Zillmere Rd, Aspley Ph: 1800 060 797
Discounts: BIG4 **Notes:** one drive thru site; LPG swap only; tennis; some ensuite sites
★★★★ $$$$+* Map ref 3 B3

35 **Brisbane** Holiday Village, Holmead Rd, Eight Mile Plains Ph: 07 3341 6133
Discounts: Top Tourist; week **Notes:** long vehicle to 8m; some ensuite sites; resort style park
★★★★☆ $$$$$* Map ref 3 H5

36 **Brisbane**, Newmarket Gardens Caravan Park, Ashgrove Ave, Newmarket Ph: 07 3356 1458
Discounts: CMCA; snr; week **Notes:** few drive thru sites; cassette DP; public ph close; close to shops & bus route
★★★☆ $$$ Map ref 3 D3

37 **Bundaberg,** Apollo Gardens Caravan Park, Princess St, Bundaberg East Ph: 07 4152 8899
Notes: close to Rum Distillery; bus at door
★★★☆ $$$$+ Map ref 9 A12

38 **Bundaberg,** BIG4 Cane Village Holiday Park, Twyford St, Bundaberg Ph: 07 4155 1022
Discounts: BIG4 **Notes:** award-winning gardens
$$ Map ref 9 A13

39 **Bundaberg**, Glenlodge Caravan Village, Goodwood Rd, Thabeban Ph: 07 4153 1515
Discounts: Top Tourist; week **Notes:** some ensuite sites
★★★★ $$$+ Map ref 9 A13

40 **Burke Developmental Rd**, Burke & Wills Roadhouse, Junction Wills Developmental Rd Ph: 07 4742 5909
Notes: meals & bar; van parking visit Lawn Hill
$ Map ref 12 H5

41 **Burketown** Caravan Park, Sloman St, Burketown Ph: 07 4745 5118
Discounts: week **Notes:** swimming pool, public ph, LPG refill & internet close; close to town
$$ Map ref 12 E4

42 **Burnett Heads**, Lighthouse Caravan Park, Paul Mittleheuser St, Burnett Heads Ph: 07 4159 4313
Discounts: week **Notes:** ph for long vehicle info; shop, LPG refill & internet close; boat ramp close; no cabin accommodation
★★★☆ $+ Map ref 9 A12

43 **Burrum Heads** Beachfront Tourist Park, Burrum St, Burrum Heads Ph: 07 4129 5138
Discounts: week (off-pk) **Notes:** public ph & shop close; riverfront; boat ramp
★★★☆ $$+ Map ref 9 B12

44 **Burrum Heads**, Hillcrest Holiday Park, Howard St, Burrum Heads Ph: 07 4129 5179
Discounts: month stay **Notes:** waterfront park, grass & trees
★★★ $+ Map ref 9 B12

45 **Caboolture** Caravan Park, Burnett Rd, Caboolture (2.5km NE of PO) Ph: 07 5495 1041
Notes: boat ramp river
★★★ $$+ Map ref 5 G9

46 **Cairns**, Cool Waters Caravan Park, Brinsmead Rd, Brinsmead (7km NW of Cairns) Ph: 07 4034 1949
Discounts: snr, week, auto club **Notes:** hand feed turtles and fish
★★★★ $$$+ Map ref 14 E6

47 **Cairns**, First City Caravilla Caravan Park, Kelly St, Earlville (3km S of Cairns PO) Ph: 07 4054 1403
Discounts: Top Tourist **Notes:** mini golf & playground
★★★☆ $$$+ Map ref 14 E6

48 **Cairns**, Lake Placid Tourist Park, Lake Placid Rd, Lake Placid Ph: 07 4039 2509
Discounts: Top Tourist **Notes:** ph re pets; some ensuite sites
★★★★ $$$+ Map ref 14 E6

49 **Cairns** Sunland Leisure Park, Little Pease St (4km W of Cairns PO) Ph: 07 4053 6888
Notes: long vehicle to 9m; shady; 4km to town centre
★★★★ $$$+ Map ref 14 E6

50 **Cairns area**, Barrier Reef Tourist Park, Bruce Hwy, Edmonton (12km S of Cairns) Ph: 07 4055 4544
Discounts: Top Tourist **Notes:** shop & LPG refill close; dogs permitted; large ensuites on all sites; close to shops
★★★☆ $$$$ Map ref 14 E5

51 **Calen**, St Helens Gardens Caravan Park, Bruce Hwy, Kolijo (1km S of PO) Ph: 07 4958 8152
Discounts: week **Notes:** few long vehicle sites; public ph & shop close; some covered sites
★★★☆ $ Map ref 11 C8

52 **Calliope** Caravan Park, Stowe Rd, Calliope Ph: 07 4975 7472
Discounts: snr/pen; week **Notes:** quiet park opposite golf course
★★★ $ Map ref 11 J11

53 **Camooweal** Roadhouse Caravan Park, Barkly Hwy (Shell Roadhouse) Ph: 07 4748 2155
Discounts: CMCA; week **Notes:** good for overnight stop
★★☆ $ Map ref 12 J2

54 **Cania Gorge** Tourist Retreat, 1253 Cania Rd (24km NW of Monto) Ph: 07 4167 8110
Discounts: Top Tourist; week **Notes:** wildlife; close to National Park
★★★★ $$ Map ref 9 A10

55 **Cape Hillsborough** Nature Resort, Cape Hillsborough (43km NW of Mackay) Ph: 07 4959 0152
Discounts: week (not sch hols) **Notes:** long vehicle to 8m; wildlife; located in National Park
★★★☆ $$ Map ref 11 C8

56 **Cape Tribulation** Rainforest Village, Cape Tribulation Rd (18km N of ferry) Ph: 07 4098 9015
Notes: bore water; no cabin accommodation
★★★ $$ Map ref 13 B13

57 **Capella** Van Park, Langton St, Capella (1km N of PO) Ph: 07 4984 9615
Discounts: CMCA; week **Notes:** public ph close; adjacent to bowls club
★★★☆ $ Map ref 10 G6

58 **Cardwell**, Discovery Holiday Parks - Cardwell, Marine Pde (1.5km N of PO) Ph: 1800 005 633
Discounts: CMCA; Top Tourist; week **Notes:** public ph & shop close; restaurant; on esplanade
★★★☆ $$$ Map ref 13 F13

59 **Cardwell**, Kookaburra Holiday Park, Bruce Hwy, Cardwell (800m N of PO) Ph: 07 4066 8648
Discounts: Family Parks; snr **Notes:** 3 acres tropical gardens; 250m to beach
★★★☆ $$$ Map ref 13 F13

60 **Carnarvon Gorge**-Takarakka Resort, Carnarvon Gorge Rd Ph: 07 4984 4535
Notes: river water; close NP; accommodation is tents
$$$$ Map ref 8 A4

61 **Cecil Plains** Retreat Caravan Park, Taylor St (enter via Warfield St), Cecil Plains Ph: 07 4668 0822
Discounts: discount 3rd night **Notes:** public ph, shop & LPG refill close; economical; no cabins; close to town centre
$ Map ref 9 G9

62 **Charleville,** Bailey Bar Caravan Park, King St, Charleville Ph: 07 4654 1744
Discounts: Top Tourist **Notes:** long vehicle to 10m; winter camp oven dinners
★★★☆ $$ Map ref 19 D13

63 **Charters Towers,** BIG4 Aussie Outback Van Village, Dr George Ellis Dr Ph: 07 4787 8722
Discounts: BIG4; week **Notes:** spacious sites; jumping pillow
★★★★ $$$ Map ref 13 J13

64 **Charters Towers** Tourist Park, Mt Leyshon Rd, Charters Towers Ph: 07 4787 7944
Discounts: Top Tourist **Notes:** ph for long vehicle info; some ensuite sites
★★★☆ $$ Map ref 13 J13

65 **Childers,** Sugar Bowl Caravan Park, Bruce Hwy, Childers (1.5km N of PO) Ph: 07 4126 1521
Notes: few drive thru & long vehicle sites; shady sites
★★★ $$ Map ref 9 B11

66 **Chillagoe** Tourist Village, Queen St, Chillagoe Ph: 07 4094 7177
Discounts: week **Notes:** café; takeaways; ice & fuel
$$ Map ref 13 D11

67 **Chinchilla,** Cypress Pines Caravan Park, Villiers St, Chinchilla (500m NW of PO) Ph: 07 4662 7741
Discounts: CMCA; week **Notes:** one drive thru site; ph for long vehicle info; swimming pool & public ph close; walk to shops
★★★☆ $ Map ref 9 E8

68 **Clairview** Beach Holiday Park, Colonial Dr, Clairview Ph: 07 4956 0190
Notes: rain water; close to boat ramp
$ Map ref 11 E8

69 **Clermont** Caravan Park, Haig St, Clermont (500m S E of PO) Ph: 07 4983 1927
Discounts: week **Notes:** shady sites; recreation room
★★★☆ $$ Map ref 10 G6

70 **Clifton,** Spring Creek Caravan Park, New England Hwy (9km N of Allora) Ph: 07 4697 3397
Discounts: very economical **Notes:** 9km from town
★★☆ $ Map ref 6 F1

71 **Cloncurry,** Gilbert Park Tourist Village, McIlwraith St (Matilda Hwy), Cloncurry Ph: 07 4742 2300
Discounts: Top Tourist
★★★☆ $$$ Map ref 12 K5

72 **Conway Beach** Tourist Park Whitsunday, Daniels St, Conway Beach Ph: 07 4947 3147
Discounts: week **Notes:** playground; rec room; lic bar; bore water
★★★☆ $$$+ Map ref 11 C8

73 **Cooktown** Caravan Park, Howard St, Cooktown (1km S of PO) Ph: 07 4069 5536
Discounts: off-pk **Notes:** bushland with shade; no sandflies
★★★☆ $$$ Map ref 13 A13

74 **Cooktown** Peninsula Caravan Park, Howard St, Cooktown Ph: 07 4069 5107
Notes: shop close; playground; book in peak season
★★★ $$$ Map ref 13 A13

75 **Crows Nest** Caravan Park, New England Hwy, Crows Nest (1km S of PO) Ph: 07 4698 1269
Discounts: week **Notes:** licensed restaurant
★★★★ $$ Map ref 4 J1

76 **Croydon** Gold Caravan Park, Aldridge St, Croydon Ph: 07 4745 6238
Discounts: week **Notes:** public ph & shop close; close to town centre
$$ Map ref 12 F7

77 **Cunnamulla,** Jack Tonkin Caravan Park, Watson St, Cunnamulla Ph: 07 4655 1421
Discounts: CMCA; mult-night stay **Notes:** shop close; quiet off-highway location
★★★ $ Map ref 19 H12

78 **Dalby,** Pioneer Caravan Village, Black St, Dalby Ph: 07 4662 1811
Discounts: week **Notes:** 2km to town
$$ Map ref 9 F10

79 **Dalby** Tourist Park, Myall St, Dalby (opposite RSL Club) Ph: 07 4662 4793
Notes: shop close; centrally located; some ensuite sites
★★★☆ $$ Map ref 9 F10

80 **Eidsvold** Caravan Park, Esplanade St, Eidsvold (500m from PO) Ph: 07 4165 1168
Discounts: very economical **Notes:** public ph & shop close; close to shops & 9 hole golf
★★★ $ Map ref 9 B9

81 **Elliott Heads** Caravan Park, Lihs St, Elliott Heads (at surf life saving club) Ph: 07 4159 6193
Discounts: week **Notes:** public ph & shop close; LPG swap only; close patrolled beach
★★★ $$+ Map ref 9 A12

82 **Ellis Beach** Oceanfront Bungalows & Caravan Park, Captain Cook Hwy Ph: 1800 637 036
Discounts: week (off-pk) **Notes:** internet access close; absolute beachfront
★★★☆ $$$+ Map ref 14 C5

83 **Emerald,** Discovery Holiday Parks - Lake Maraboon, Fairbairn Dam Access Rd Ph: 1800 627 226
Discounts: Top Tourist; CMCA; week **Notes:** swimming pool close; lakefront park; boat hire; boat ramp
★★★★ $$$ Map ref 10 H6

84 **Emu Park,** Bell Park Caravan Park, Pattison St, Emu Park Ph: 07 4939 6202
Discounts: week **Notes:** swimming pool & shop close; beachfront park
★★★☆ $$ Map ref 11 H11

85 **Esk** Caravan Park, Hassall St, Esk Ph: 1800 462 375
Discounts: Top Tourist; pen **Notes:** public ph & shop close; quiet park; some ensuite sites
★★★☆ $ Map ref 4 J4

86 **Eungella** Holiday Park, North St, Eungella Ph: 07 4958 4590
Discounts: CMCA **Notes:** public ph close; LPG swap only; spring water; base for Nat Pk
$ Map ref 10 D7

87 **Fishery Falls** Caravan Park, Bruce Hwy, Fishery Falls Ph: 07 4067 5283
Discounts: week **Notes:** public ph close; quiet park; good as a base
★★★☆ $$ Map ref 14 F6

88 **Forsayth** Tourist Park & Store, First St, Forsayth Ph: 07 4062 5324
Discounts: economical; week **Notes:** public ph & internet access close; in town; licensed restaurant
★★★☆ $ Map ref 13 G9

89 **Gatton** Caravan Park, Helidon Rd, Gatton Ph: 07 5462 1198
Discounts: week **Notes:** close to shops
$ Map ref 6 C4

90 **Gayndah**, Riverview Caravan Park, Barrow St, Gayndah (1km N of PO) Ph: 07 4161 1280
Discounts: snr; week **Notes:** riverfront park
★★★☆ $ Map ref 9 C10

91 **Georgetown**, Midway Caravan Park, North St, Georgetown (500m W of PO) Ph: 07 4062 1219
Discounts: week; CMCA **Notes:** grass & shade; meals available
★★★ $ Map ref 13 F10

92 **Gin Gin**, Lake Monduran Holiday Park, Claude Wharton Dr (20km N of Gin Gin) Ph: 07 4157 3881
Notes: adjacent to dam; boat ramp
★★★☆ $$$+ Map ref 9 A11

93 **Gladstone**, Kin Kora Village Tourist Park, Olsen Av, Kin Kora (off Dawson Hwy) Ph: 07 4978 5461
Notes: few long vehicle sites; shop close; near shops; some ensuite sites
★★★★☆ $$ Map ref 11 H12

94 **Gladstone**, Barney Beach Seabreeze Caravan Park, Friend St, Barney Point Ph: 07 4972 1366
Discounts: week **Notes:** shop close; 80m to beach
★★★★ $$$ Map ref 11 H12

95 **Glass House Mountains** Holiday Village, Steve Irwin Way (3km S of PO) Ph: 07 5496 9338
Discounts: week **Notes:** close to Glass House Mtns
★★★ $$ Map ref 5 F9

96 **Gold Coast, Biggera Waters**, Treasure Island Holiday Park, 117 Brisbane Rd Ph: 07 5500 8699
Discounts: BIG4, auto club; services **Notes:** long vehicle to 7.5m; mini golf; jumping pillow; restaurant.
★★★★☆ $$$$+* Map ref 7 F12

97 **Gold Coast, Burleigh Heads**, Burleigh Beach Tourist Park, Goodwin Tce Ph: 07 5581 7755
Discounts: week **Notes:** long vehicle to 8m; swimming pool soon; beachfront
★★★★ $$$$+* Map ref 7 G14

98 **Gold Coast, Helensvale**, Gold Coast Holiday Park, Siganto Dr, Helensvale Ph: 07 5573 1185
Discounts: Top Tourist; CMCA **Notes:** near theme parks; some ensuite sites
★★★★ $$$+* Map ref 7 F12

99 **Gold Coast, Kirra** Beach Tourist Park, Charlotte St (off Coolangatta Rd) Kirra Ph: 07 5581 7744
Discounts: Top Tourist; week **Notes:** long vehicle to 11m; 600m to beach
★★★★ $$$+* Map ref 7 H13

100 **Gold Coast, Southport**, Broadwater Tourist Park, Gold Coast Hwy, Southport Ph: 1800 444 474
Discounts: Top Tourist; week (off-pk) **Notes:** waterfront park (Broadwater)
★★★★☆ $$$$+ Map ref 7 F13

101 **Goondiwindi**, AAAGundy Star Tourist Van Park, Old Cunningham Hwy Ph: 07 4671 2900
Discounts: Family Parks **Notes:** free damper and tea (winter)
★★★★ $$$ Map ref 9 J8

102 **Goondiwindi** Top Tourist Park, Hungerford St, Goondiwindi Ph: 07 4671 2566
Discounts: Top Tourist **Notes:** 20 acre park; some ensuite sites
★★★★ $$ Map ref 9 J8

103 **Greenvale** Caravan Park & Cabins, Kylee Court, Greenvale Ph: 07 4788 4155
Discounts: CMCA **Notes:** few long vehicle sites; swimming pool & public ph close; native trees & birds
$ Map ref 13 G11

104 **Gympie** Caravan Park, Jane St, Gympie (1km W of PO) Ph: 07 5483 6800
Discounts: multi-night stay; pen **Notes:** close to town; some ensuite sites
★★★☆ $$ Map ref 9 D13

105 **Hebel** Caravan Park, behind the General Store, Hebel Ph: 07 4625 0920
Discounts: economical; week **Notes:** in town; restaurant
$ Map ref 8 K3

106 **Hervey Bay, Scarness**, Australiana Top Tourist Park, Boat Harbour Dr Ph: 07 4128 2762
Discounts: Top Tourist; week (off-pk) **Notes:** some ensuite sites; table tennis; snooker
★★★★☆ $$$+* Map ref 9 B13

107 **Hervey Bay, Torquay**, Fraser Lodge Holiday Park, Fraser St, Torquay Ph: 1800 641 444
Discounts: BIG4 **Notes:** long vehicle to 8m; some ensuites; close beach; playground; tennis
★★★★☆ $$$+* Map ref 9 B13

108 **Hervey Bay, Torquay**, Palms Caravan Park, Truro St, Torquay Ph: 07 4125 1704
Discounts: CMCA; week **Notes:** 300m to beach; tour bookings
★★★ $$$+ Map ref 9 B13

109 **Hervey Bay, Urangan**, Hervey Bay Caravan Park, Margaret St, Urangan Ph: 07 4128 9553
Discounts: Oz Parks; CMCA **Notes:** public ph close; adjacent to bowls club
★★★★ $$$$ Map ref 9 B13

110 **Howard**, Burrum River Caravan Park, Old Bruce Hwy, Howard Ph: 07 4129 4859
Discounts: CMCA; snr **Notes:** riverfront park; boat ramp
★★★☆ $$ Map ref 9 B12

111 **Hughenden** Allan Terry Caravan Park, Resolution St, Hughenden Ph: 07 4741 1190
Notes: DP, swimming pool, public ph & shop close; grass and shade
★★★ $ Map ref 10 C1

112 **Ingham**, Palm Tree Caravan Park, Bruce Hwy, Ingham (3km S of PO) Ph: 07 4776 2403
Discounts: CMCA; week **Notes:** lots of birds; shady sites
★★★☆ $$ Map ref 13 G14

113 **Inglewood**, Lake Coolmunda Caravan Park, Cunningham Hwy (13km E of PO) Ph: 07 4652 4171
Discounts: week **Notes:** public ph, shop & LPG refill close; lakefront; fishing; birdwatching
★★★ $$ Map ref 9 J9

114 **Injune** Caravan Park, Third Ave, Injune (behind Information Centre) Ph: 07 4626 1053
Discounts: economical price **Notes:** few drive thru; DP, swimming pool, public ph, shop, LPG refill & internet access close
$ Map ref 8 C4

115 **Innisfail**, August Moon Caravan Park, Bruce Hwy, Innisfail (4km S of PO) Ph: 07 4063 2211
Discounts: Top Tourist, week **Notes:** on 10 acres; TV room & playground
★★★☆ $$$+* Map ref 14 H7

116 **Innisfail** Flying Fish Point Caravan Park, Elizabeth St, Flying Fish Point Ph: 07 4061 3131
Discounts: Family Parks **Notes:** beachfront park
★★★★ $$$+* Map ref 14 H7

117 **Innot Hot Springs** Leisure Park, Kennedy Hwy, Innot Hot Springs Ph: 07 4097 0136
Discounts: CMCA; snr **Notes:** six thermal pools
$$$ Map ref 14 J2

118 **Ipswich** Caravan Village, Mt Crosby Rd, Ipswich (4km N of PO) Ph: 07 3281 7951
Notes: long vehicle to 8m; shop close; bus at the door
★★★ $$$ Map ref 6 C7

119 **Jandowae** Accommodation Park, High St, Jandowae Ph: 07 4668 5071
Discounts: CMCA; week **Notes:** swimming pool close; close bowls; tennis; squash; shop
$+ Map ref 9 E9

120 **Julia Creek** Caravan Park, Old Normanton Rd, Julia Creek (500m from PO) Ph: 07 4746 7108
Discounts: economical **Notes:** artesian spa; accomm is on-site vans
$ Map ref 12 K7

121 **Karumba**, Gulf Country Caravan Park, Yappar St, Karumba (100m to PO) Ph: 07 4745 9148
Discounts: CMCA **Notes:** long vehicle to 9m; shop close; close to shops and boat ramp
★★★ $$ Map ref 12 E6

122 **Kilcoy**, Lake Somerset Park Esk-Kilcoy Rd, Kilcoy (10km S of PO) Ph: 07 5497 1093
Discounts: FPA; caravan clubs **Notes:** boat ramp; one cabin only
★★★ $$$+* Map ref 4 F6

123 **Killarney**, Queen Mary Falls Caravan Park, Spring Creek Rd (10km E of Killarney) Ph: 07 4664 7151
Discounts: week **Notes:** opposite waterfall; café
★★★ $$+ Map ref 6 K4

124 **Kingaroy** Holiday Park, D'Aguilar Hwy, Kingaroy (1.7km E of PO) Ph: 1800 502 218
Discounts: BIG4 **Notes:** few drive thru sites; DP close; close to restaurant
★★★☆ $$+ Map ref 9 E10

125 **Kinka Beach**, Coolwaters Holiday Village, Scenic Hwy, Kinka Beach Ph: 1800 266 556
Notes: few drive thru sites; lake; across road from ocean
★★★★ $$$* Map ref 11 G10

126 **Kuranda** Rainforest Accomm Park, Kuranda Heights Rd (2km N of PO) Ph: 07 4093 7316
Notes: long vehicle to 9m; restaurant
★★★ $$$ Map ref 14 D4

127 **Kurrimine**, King Reef Resort Van Park, Jacobs Rd, Kurrimine Beach (opp PO) Ph: 07 4065 6144
Discounts: week **Notes:** shop close; beachfront park; close to boat ramp
★★★☆ $$$ Map ref 14 J7

128 **Kynuna** Roadhouse Caravan Park, Matilda Hwy, Kynuna Ph: 07 4746 8683
Discounts: very economical **Notes:** public ph close; licensed restaurant; large sites
$ Map ref 16 B7

129 **Laidley** Caravan Park, Campbell St, Laidley (600m NE of PO) Ph: 07 5465 3506
Notes: dogs permitted; no cabin accommodation
★★★ $ Map ref 6 C5

130 **Lake Moogerah** Caravan Park, off Cunningham Hwy near Aratula Ph: 07 5463 0141
Discounts: CMCA; snr **Notes:** lake; boat ramp; spacious grassy
$$ Map ref 6 G6

131 **Lakeland** Caravan Park, Sesame St, Lakeland Ph: 07 4060 2033
Discounts: CMCA, service veterans **Notes:** public ph close; lush green park close to town
$$ Map ref 13 B11

132 **Landsborough** Pines Caravan Park, Glasshouse Mountains Tourist Dr Ph: 07 5494 1207
Discounts: week **Notes:** few drive thru & long vehicle sites; public ph & shop close; 300m to train; all sites powered
★★★☆ $$+ Map ref 5 E9

133 **Longreach** Caravan Park, Ibis St, Longreach Ph: 07 4658 1770
Discounts: CMCA; pen **Notes:** internet access soon; free morning & afternoon tea
★★★ $$ Map ref 10 H1

134 **Longreach**, Discovery Holiday Parks - Longreach, Thrush Rd (1km E of PO) Ph: 1800 356 099
Discounts: CMCA **Notes:** restaurant, entertainment
★★★☆ $$$ Map ref 10 H2

135 **Lucinda**, Wanderers Holiday Village, Bruce Pde, Lucinda (200m from PO) Ph: 1800 629 450
Discounts: week **Notes:** drive thru sites avail off-pk; shop close; LPG swap only; close to beach; fish cleaning
★★★☆ $$$ Map ref 13 F14

136 **Mackay**, Andergrove Caravan Park, Beaconsfield Rd, Mackay Ph: 1800 424 922
Discounts: Top Tourist; snr; week **Notes:** few long vehicle sites; some ensuite sites
★★★★ $$$ Map ref 11 D9

137 **Mackay**, Central Tourist Park, Malcomson St, Mackay (300m N of PO) Ph: 07 4957 6141
Notes: long vehicle to 10m; shop & internet access close; playground; walk to shops
$$ Map ref 11 D9

138 **Malanda** Falls Caravan Park, Park Ave, Malanda Ph: 07 4096 5314
Discounts: week **Notes:** close to town and waterfall
★★★☆ $$ Map ref 14 G4

139 **Maleny**, Ocean View Caravan Park, Landsborough-Maleny Rd, Mt Mellum Ph: 1300 769 443
Discounts: Top Tourist; week(off-pk) **Notes:** long vehicle to 10m; superb views; rain water
★★★☆ $$$ Map ref 5 D8

140 **Mapleton**, Lilyponds Holiday Park, Warruga St, Mapleton (300m NW of PO) Ph: 1800 003 764
Discounts: week **Notes:** public ph & shop close; birdwatching; spring water
★★★★ $$$* Map ref 5 C8

141 **Mareeba** Country Caravan Park, Emerald End Rd, Mareeba (via Hastie Rd) Ph: 07 4092 3281
Discounts: CMCA
★★☆ $$ Map ref 14 E3

142 **Marlborough** Caravan Park, Bruce Hwy, Marlborough Ph: 07 4935 6112
Notes: licensed restaurant
★★★ $$ Map ref 11 G9

143 **Maryborough**, Huntsville Caravan Park, Gympie Rd, Maryborough Ph: 07 4121 4075
Discounts: Oz Parks; CMCA **Notes:** long vehicle to 12m; shop close; some ensuite sites; shops close
★★★★ $$ Map ref 9 C13

144 **Maryborough**, Wallace Caravan Park, Ferry St, Maryborough (1km SW of PO) Ph: 07 4121 3970
Discounts: week **Notes:** some ensuite sites
★★★★ $$ Map ref 9 C13

145 **Mena Creek**, Paronella Park, Japoonvale Rd (old Bruce Hwy) (19km S of Innisfail) Ph: 07 4065 3225
Discounts: 1 night free with pk entry **Notes:** long vehicle to 8m; public ph & shop close; no cabin accomm; adjoins Paronella Park
★★☆ $$ Map ref 14 J6

146 **Midge Point** Travellers Rest Caravan Park, Jackson St, Midge Point Ph: 1800 772 341
Discounts: Top Tourist; week **Notes:** shop close; rainforest park; close to beach
★★★ $$$ Map ref 11 C8

147 **Miles**, Possum Park Tourist Park, Leichhardt Hwy, Miles (20km N of Miles) Ph: 07 4627 1651
Discounts: CMCA; week **Notes:** DP soon; bore water; bushland; some ensuite sites
★★★☆ $$ Map ref 8 D7

148 **Millaa Millaa** Tourist Park, Cnr Malanda Rd & Lodge Ave, Millaa Millaa Ph: 07 4097 2290
Discounts: CMCA; 3 night stay **Notes:** tropical rainforest; birds & butterflies
$$ Map ref 14 H4

No.	Park	Rating / Price / Map
149	**Millmerran** Village Caravan Park, Bruce Rd, Millmerran (700m NW of PO) Ph: 07 4695 2020 **Discounts:** CMCA; pen **Notes:** public ph & shop close	★★★☆ $ Map ref 9 H9
150	**Mission Beach area** Beachcomber Coconut Caravan Village, Mission Beach Sth Ph: 1800 008 129 **Discounts:** BIG4 **Notes:** across road from beach	★★★★ $$$$+ Map ref 14 K7
151	**Mission Beach area** Tropical Hibiscus Park, Cassowary Dr, Wongalong Beach Ph: 07 4068 8138 **Notes:** public ph, shop, LPG refill & internet close; rainforest garden; close to shops	★★★☆ $$ Map ref 14 K7
152	**Mitchell**, Major Mitchell Caravan Park, Warrego Hwy (E entrance to Mitchell) Ph: 07 4623 8177 **Discounts:** 3 night discount **Notes:** public ph close; some ensuite sites	$$ Map ref 8 D4
153	**Monto** Caravan Park, Flinders St (Burnett Hwy) NW entrance to Monto Ph: 07 4166 1492 **Discounts:** CMCA; snr **Notes:** public ph & shop close; opposite hospital	$$ Map ref 9 A9
154	**Mossman area, Newell Beach** Caravan Park, Marine Pde, Newell Beach Ph: 07 4098 1331 **Discounts:** CMCA; week **Notes:** few drive thru & long vehicle sites; across road from beach	★★★ $$ Map ref 14 B3
155	**Mt Carbine** Caravan Park, Mulligan Hwy, Mt Carbine (300m SE of roadhouse) Ph: 07 4094 3160 **Discounts:** for ex-servicemen **Notes:** close to hotel; caravan storage available	★★★☆ $ Map ref 14 B2
156	**Mt Isa** Caravan Park, Marian St, Mt Isa (900m E of Information Centre) Ph: 07 4743 3252 **Discounts:** Oz Parks; CMCA **Notes:** few long vehicle sites; playground	★★★☆ $$ Map ref 12 K3
157	**Mt Isa**, Copper City Caravan Park, West St, Mt Isa (2km N of PO) Ph: 07 4743 4676 **Discounts:** Family Parks **Notes:** some ensuite sites	★★★☆ $$$ Map ref 12 K3
158	**Mt Isa**, Riverside Tourist Caravan Park, West St, Mt Isa Ph: 07 4743 3904 **Discounts:** Family Parks **Notes:** long vehicle to 8m; huge inground pool	★★★☆ $$$ Map ref 12 K3
159	**Mt Isa**, Sunset Top Caravan Park, Sunset Dr, Winston (1.6km N of PO) Ph: 1800 786 738 **Discounts:** Top Tourist **Notes:** spacious shady sites; TV room	★★★☆ $$$ Map ref 12 K3
160	**Mt Morgan**, Silver Wattle Caravan Park, Burnett Hwy (1km W of CBD) Ph: 07 4938 1550 **Notes:** owner-operated; economical prices	★★★☆ $ Map ref 11 H10
161	**Mt Surprise**, Bedrock Village Caravan Park, Garnet St, Mt Surprise Ph: 07 4062 3193 **Discounts:** CMCA; snr; week **Notes:** DP & public ph close; tours; pet minding; mini golf	★★★☆ $$$ Map ref 13 F11
162	**Mt Tamborine** Caravan & Camping, Tamborine Mountain Rd, Mt Tamborine Ph: 07 5545 0034 **Notes:** tennis; creek water; no cabins	★★☆ $$ Map ref 7 G11
163	**Mundubbera**, Three Rivers Park, Strathdee St, Mundubbera Ph: 07 4165 3000 **Discounts:** BIG4; pen **Notes:** close to town and golf	★★★★ $$$ Map ref 9 B9
164	**Murgon**, Barambah Bush Caravan Park, Cnr Barambah Rd & Borcherts Hill Rd Ph: 07 4168 1085 **Discounts:** CMCA; week **Notes:** treated dam water	★★★☆ $$ Map ref 9 D11
165	**Nambour** Rainforest Holiday Village, Nambour Connection Rd (2.5km S of PO) Ph: 07 5442 1153 **Notes:** off-leash dog area.	★★★☆ $$$+ Map ref 5 C9
166	**Nanango**, Twin Gums Caravan Park, Cnr Scott St & Arthur St, Nanango Ph: 07 4163 1376 **Discounts:** week **Notes:** few long vehicle sites; public ph close; birdlife in park; economical prices	★★★ $ Map ref 4 C1
167	**Normanton** Tourist Park, Brown St, Normanton (80m from PO) Ph: 07 4745 1121 **Discounts:** week **Notes:** shop close; artesian spa; resort pool	$$ Map ref 12 E6
168	**Pittsworth**, Shady Rest Caravan Park, Cnr Yandilla St & McIntyre St, Pittsworth Ph: 07 4693 1440 **Notes:** close to town centre	$$ Map ref 9 G10
169	**Poona** Palms Caravan Park, Cnr Owen Cox St & Borona Dr, Poona Ph: 07 4129 8167 **Discounts:** week **Notes:** close to boat ramp (tidal)	★★★ $$ Map ref 9 C13
170	**Port Douglas**, Pandanus Van Park, Davidson St, Port Douglas Ph: 07 4099 5944 **Notes:** public ph close; 5 minute walk to beach	$$$ Map ref 14 B4
171	**Port Douglas** Glengarry Holiday Park, Mowbray River Rd (8km S of PO) Ph: 1800 888 134 **Discounts:** BIG4; week (off-pk) **Notes:** some ensuite sites; gardens; spring water	★★★★ $$$$ Map ref 14 B4
172	**Proserpine**, O'Connell River Whitsunday Tourist Park, Bruce Hwy, Proserpine Ph: 07 4947 5148 **Discounts:** solo travellers; week **Notes:** grassed and slab sites	$ Map ref 10 C7
173	**Quilpie**, Channel Country Caravan Park, Chipu St, Quilpie Ph: 07 4656 2087 **Notes:** public ph & shop close; bore water; opal fossicking; artesian spas	★★★ $$ Map ref 19 D10
174	**Rainbow Beach** Holiday Village, Rainbow Beach Rd, Rainbow Beach Ph: 07 5486 3222 **Discounts:** Top Tourist **Notes:** close to town & ocean	★★★☆ $$$+ Map ref 9 C14
175	**Richmond**, Lakeview Caravan Park, Flinders Hwy, Richmond Ph: 07 4741 3772 **Discounts:** CMCA **Notes:** public ph & shop close; bore water	$$+ Map ref 13 K9
176	**Rockhampton**, Parkhurst Motel & Caravan Pk, Bruce Hwy, Parkhurst (8km N of PO) Ph: 07 4936 1126 **Discounts:** week **Notes:** public ph close; some ensuite sites	★★★ $ Map ref 11 H11
177	**Rockhampton**, Southside Holiday Village, Lower Dawson Rd, Allenstown Ph: 07 4927 3013 **Discounts:** Top Tourist; week **Notes:** some ensuite sites	★★★★☆ $$$+ Map ref 11 H11
178	**Rockhampton**, Discovery Holiday Parks - Rockhampton, Yaamba Rd (2km N of PO) Ph: 1800 815 563 **Discounts:** BIG4; CMCA **Notes:** long vehicle to 14m; award-winning gardens	★★★★☆ $$$$+ Map ref 11 H11
179	**Rolleston** Caravan Park, 46 Comet St, Rolleston Ph: 07 4984 3145 **Discounts:** week **Notes:** dogs permitted; close to town	$ Map ref 10 J7
180	**Rollingstone** Beach Caravan Resort, Hencamp Creek Rd, Rollingstone Ph: 07 4770 7277 **Discounts:** BIG4 **Notes:** LPG swap only; beachfront; resort pool; some ensuite sites	★★★★ $$$+ Map ref 13 G14

No.	Park	Rating, price, map ref
181	**Roma** Aussie Tourist Park, Bowen St, Roma (1km E of PO) Ph: 07 4622 6464 **Discounts:** Family Parks **Notes:** DP & public ph close; grassed with trees	★★★☆ $$$ Map ref 8 D5
182	**Roma**, BIG4 Villa Holiday Park, Northern Rd (Injune Rd), Roma Ph: 1800 116 117 **Discounts:** BIG4; week **Notes:** shop close; some ensuite sites; adjoins winery	★★★★ $$$ Map ref 8 D5
183	**Rubyvale**, Bedford Gardens Caravan Park, Vane-Tempest Rd (300m NW of PO) Ph: 07 4985 4175 **Discounts:** week & seasonal **Notes:** shop close; close to gemfields	★★★ $$ Map ref 10 H6
184	**Sarina**, Tropicana Caravan Park, Range Rd, Sarina Ph: 07 4956 1480 **Notes:** long vehicle to 9m; cassette DP; no unpowered sites; owner-operated park	★★★ $ Map ref 11 D9
185	**Seventeen Seventy** Camping Grounds, Captain Cook Dr, Seventeen Seventy Ph: 07 4974 9286 **Discounts:** week **Notes:** DP close; waterfront park	★★★ $$$+ Map ref 11 J13
186	**Shute Harbour**, Flametree Tourist Village, Shute Harbour Rd (5km from Airlie Bch PO) Ph: 1800 069 388 **Discounts:** week (off-pk) **Notes:** newly renovated facilities	★★★☆ $$+ Map ref 11 C8
187	**St George**, Pelican Rest Tourist Park, Carnarvon Hwy (2km N of PO) Ph: 07 4625 3398 **Discounts:** CMCA; week **Notes:** public ph close; spacious quiet park	★★★★ $ Map ref 8 H4
188	**Stanthorpe** Top of Town Accomm Village, High St, Stanthorpe (1.5km N of PO) Ph: 1800 030 123 **Discounts:** CMCA; week **Notes:** some ensuite sites; café; table tennis	★★★★ $$ Map ref 9 K10
189	**Sunshine Coast, Caloundra**, Golden Beach Holiday Park, Onslow St, Golden Beach Ph: 07 5492 4811 **Discounts:** week **Notes:** shop close; compact older park; no unpowered sites	★★★☆ $$$+ Map ref 5 E11
190	**Sunshine Coast, Caloundra**, Dicky Beach Family Holiday Park, Beerburrum St Ph: 07 5491 3342 **Discounts:** week **Notes:** close to ocean beach & shops	★★★★ $$$$+* Map ref 5 D11
191	**Sunshine Coast, Coolum Beach** Caravan Park, David Low Way, Coolum Beach Ph: 07 5446 1474 **Discounts:** FPA; week **Notes:** shop close; beachfront park; near SLSC	★★★☆ $$$$+* Map ref 5 B11
192	**Sunshine Coast, Maroochydore**, Cotton Tree Caravan Park, Cotton Tree Pde Ph: 1800 461 253 **Discounts:** FPA; week **Notes:** long vehicle to 9m; public ph & shop close; park is beach and river front	★★★☆ $$$$+* Map ref 5 C11
193	**Sunshine Coast, Maroochydore**, Maroochy Palms Holiday Village, Bradman Ave Ph: 1800 623 316 **Discounts:** BIG4; week; off-pk **Notes:** long vehicle to 9m; shop close; across from river; close to shops	★★★★☆ $$$$$+* Map ref 5 C11
194	**Sunshine Coast, Noosaville**, Noosa River Caravan Park, Russell St, Munna Point Ph: 07 5449 7050 **Notes:** public ph & internet access close; riverfront; boat ramp; no cabin accommodation	★★★☆ $$$$+ Map ref 5 A9
195	**Sunshine Coast, Tewantin**, Noosa Bougainvillia Holiday Park, Cooroy-Noosa Rd Ph: 1800 041 444 **Discounts:** BIG4; week **Notes:** shop close; opposite golf course; some ensuite sites	$$$$+* Map ref 5 A9
196	**Tannum Sands**, Tannum Beach Caravan Village, The Esplanade, Tannum Sands Ph: 07 4973 7201 **Discounts:** week **Notes:** close to beach; some ensuite sites	★★★★☆ $$$ Map ref 11 J12
197	**Taylors Beach** Holiday Park, John Dory St, Taylors Beach Ph: 07 4777 8560 **Discounts:** week **Notes:** public ph close; 300m from beach	★★★ $$ Map ref 13 G14
198	**Thargomindah**, BIG4 Explorers Caravan Park, Dowling St (200m W of PO) Ph: 1800 820 890 **Discounts:** BIG4 **Notes:** LPG refill close; close to town & swimming pool	★★★★ $$ Map ref 19 H9
199	**Tin Can Bay**, Kingfisher Caravan Park, Esplanade, Tin Can Bay Ph: 07 5486 4198 **Discounts:** week (off-pk) **Notes:** few drive thru sites; long vehicle to 8m; public ph & shop close; LPG swap only; waterfront park; older style park	★★ $+ Map ref 9 C12
200	**Tin Can Bay** Tourist Park, Trevally St, Tin Can Bay (1.5km S of PO) Ph: 07 5486 4411 **Discounts:** Top Tourist; week (off-pk) **Notes:** book long vehicle sites; walk to town; some ensuite sites	★★★☆ $$+ Map ref 9 C12
201	**Tinaroo**, Discovery Holiday Parks - Lake Tinaroo (14.5km NE of Atherton PO) Ph: 1300 727 044 **Discounts:** Top Tourist, CMCA, week **Notes:** takeaways; canoes; jumping pillow	★★★★ $$$ Map ref 14 F4
202	**Toorbul** Caravan Park, off The Esplanade, Toorbul (12km NE of Caboolture) Ph: 07 5498 8701 **Notes:** public ph, shop & LPG refill close; good fishing	★★★ $+ Map ref 5 G10
203	**Toowoomba** Garden City Holiday Park, Eiser St, Harristown (3km S of PO) Ph: 1800 333 667 **Discounts:** BIG4; week **Notes:** ph for long vehicle info; public ph close; some ensuite sites	★★★★ $$+ Map ref 6 C1
204	**Toowoomba**, Jolly Swagman Caravan Park, Kitchener St, East Toowoomba Ph: 07 4632 8735 **Discounts:** week **Notes:** internet access close; close to shops	★★★★ $$ Map ref 6 C1
205	**Toowoomba** Motor Village Caravan Park, Ruthven St, Kearneys Spring (2.5km S) Ph: 1800 675 105 **Discounts:** Top Tourist; week **Notes:** shop close; parkland with walking & bike tracks	★★★★ $$ Map ref 6 C1
206	**Townsville**, Bluewater Caravan Park, Bruce Hwy (26km N of Townsville) Ph: 07 4778 6118 **Discounts:** snr **Notes:** bush golf course	★★★ $$ Map ref 10 A5
207	**Townsville**, Rowes Bay Caravan Park, Heatleys Pde, Coral Bay Ph: 07 4771 3576 **Discounts:** week **Notes:** on esplanade	★★★☆ $$$ Map ref 10 A6
208	**Townsville**, BIG4 Townsville Woodlands Holiday Park, 548 Bruce Hwy, Deeragun Ph: 1800 251 485 **Discounts:** BIG4; CMCA; week **Notes:** 15km N of Townsville CBD	★★★★ $$$ Map ref 10 A5
209	**Tully Heads**, Googarra Beach Caravan Park, Tully Heads Rd (16km E of Tully) Ph: 07 4066 9325 **Discounts:** week **Notes:** close to beach; landscaped gardens	★★★☆ $$ Map ref 13 F14
210	**Undara (Nat Pk)** Experience, Savannah Way (53km E of Mt Surprise) Ph: 1800 990 992 **Discounts:** family discount **Notes:** wildlife; tours of lava tubes	★★★ $$$ Map ref 13 F11
211	**Warwick**, Kahlers Oasis Caravan Park, New England Hwy, Warwick (2km S) Ph: 07 4661 2874 **Discounts:** BIG4 **Notes:** large spacious park	★★★★ $$$ Map ref 6 J2

212	**Warwick**, Rose City Caravan Park, New England Hwy, Warwick Ph: 07 4661 1662 **Discounts:** week **Notes:** long vehicle to 8m; public ph & shop close; close to golf course	★★★☆	$$	Map ref 6 J2
213	**Weipa** Camping Ground, Newbold Dr, Weipa Ph: 07 4069 7871 **Notes:** waterfront park	★★★	$$$	Map ref 15 E1
214	**Willows**, Gem Air Village Caravan Park and Cabins, Village Rd, Willows Ph: 07 4985 5124 **Discounts:** Top Tourist; week **Notes:** rain water; sapphire fossicking	★★★	$$	Map ref 10 H6
215	**Winton**, Matilda Country Tourist Park, Chirnside St, Winton Ph: 07 4657 1607 **Discounts:** Top Tourist; CMCA; week **Notes:** few drive thru sites; internet access soon; bush poet in winter	★★★☆	$$$	Map ref 17 D9
216	**Wonga Beach**, Pinnacle Village Holiday Park, Vixies Rd (22km N of Mossman) Ph: 1800 222 728 **Discounts:** Top Tourist; week **Notes:** cassette DP; beachfront park; close to Daintree NP	★★★★	$$$+	Map ref 14 A4
217	**Woodgate** Beach Tourist Park, The Esplanade, Woodgate Ph: 07 4126 8802 **Discounts:** week (off-pk) **Notes:** across road from beach	★★★☆	$$+	Map ref 9 B12
218	**Yarraman** Caravan Park, D'Aguilar Hwy, Yarraman (1km N of PO) Ph: 1800 288 560 **Discounts:** week **Notes:** walk to town & forest; some ensuite sites	★★★☆	$$	Map ref 4 E1
219	**Yeppoon**, Poinciana Tourist Park, Scenic Hwy, Cooee Bay Ph: 07 4939 1601 **Discounts:** week **Notes:** shop & internet access close; LPG swap only; 200m to beach	★★★☆	$$$	Map ref 11 G11
220	**Yeppoon**, Discovery Holiday Parks - Capricorn Coast, Mulambin (7km S of Yeppoon) Ph: 1800 068 703 **Discounts:** BIG4 **Notes:** recreation and TV room	★★★★	$$$+	Map ref 11 G11

New South Wales

221	**Albury** All Seasons Tourist Park, Wagga Rd, Lavington (6km N of Albury PO) Ph: 02 6025 1619 **Discounts:** Family Parks **Notes:** public ph close; playground; grass & trees	★★★★	$$$+*	Map ref 33 K13
222	**Albury**, Trek-31 Tourist Park, Cnr Wagga Rd & Catherine Cres, Lavington Ph: 02 6025 4355 **Discounts:** multi-night stay **Notes:** some ensuite sites	★★★☆	$$$+*	Map ref 33 K13
223	**Albury**, Lake Hume Tourist Park, Riverina Hwy, Lake Hume Village (14km E of Albury) Ph: 02 6049 8100 **Discounts:** Family Parks **Notes:** lakefront park; waterslide & playground	★★★☆	$$+*	Map ref 33 K13
224	**Albury area Bowna**, Wymah Valley Retreat, Wymah Rd (35km N of Albury) Ph: 1800 776 523 **Discounts:** CMCA; pen **Notes:** rural setting; lakefront	★★★★	$$+*	Map ref 33 K13
225	**Anglers Reach** Caravan Park, Peninsula Rd (14km W of Adaminaby PO) Ph: 02 6454 2223 **Notes:** dogs permitted; on Lake Eucumbene; playground; tennis	★★★	$$	Map ref 34 F2
226	**Armidale**, Highlander Van Village, Glen Innes Rd, Armidale Ph: 02 6772 4768 **Discounts:** CMCA **Notes:** games and TV room	★★★☆	$	Map ref 29 G9
227	**Arrawarra**, Darlington Beach Holiday Park, Eggins Dr (6km N of Woolgoolga) Ph: 02 6640 7499 **Discounts:** BIG4; auto club; services **Notes:** long vehicle to 7m; beachfront; some ensuites; waterslides; sports fac.	★★★★☆	$$$$+*	Map ref 29 F13
228	**Arrawarra**, Lorikeet Tourist Park, Old Pacific Hwy, Arrawarra Ph: 1800 555 858 **Discounts:** Top Tourist; week (off-pk) **Notes:** resort park; some ensuite sites	★★★★☆	$$$+*	Map ref 29 F13
229	**Ballina** Central Caravan Park, River St, Ballina (1km E of PO) Ph: 02 6686 2220 **Discounts:** BIG4 **Notes:** opposite river & pool; close to CBD	★★★★	$$$+*	Map ref 29 C14
230	**Ballina** Seabreeze Holiday Park, South Ballina Beach Rd, South Ballina Ph: 02 6686 3900 **Discounts:** week (off-pk) **Notes:** rain water; bushland setting	★★★	$$+	Map ref 29 C14
231	**Ballina**, Shaws Bay Caravan Park, Brighton St, East Ballina (1km E of PO) Ph: 02 6686 2326 **Notes:** on Richmond River; close to beach	★★★	$$$+*	Map ref 29 C14
232	**Ballina area**, Sandalwood Van Park, 978 Pimlico Rd, Wardell (12km S of Ballina) Ph: 02 6683 4221 **Discounts:** week **Notes:** filtered water; quiet; spacious	★★★☆	$	Map ref 29 C14
233	**Balranald** Caravan Park, Court St, Balranald (800 E of PO) Ph: 03 5020 1321 **Discounts:** CMCA; week **Notes:** public ph close; riverfront park; close to town	★★★★	$$	Map ref 32 G6
234	**Bargo**, Avon Caravan Village, Avon Dam Rd (1.6km off Bargo exit off Hume Hwy) Ph: 02 4684 1026	★★★	$$	Map ref 25 J8
235	**Barham** Caravan & Tourist Park, Noorong St, Barham (adjacent to RSL) Ph: 03 5453 2553 **Discounts:** 2nd night; week **Notes:** riverfront park; in town; some ensuite sites	★★★★	$$$+*	Map ref 32 J7
236	**Barham** Lakes Murray View Caravan Park, East Barham Rd (1km E of PO) Ph: 03 5453 2009 **Discounts:** Family Parks; week **Notes:** playground; tennis; some ensuite sites	★★★☆	$+	Map ref 32 J7
237	**Barooga**, Cobram Barooga Golf Resort, Golf Course Rd (1.2km W of PO) Ph: 1800 062 334 **Discounts:** week **Notes:** golf; tennis; volleyball; playground	★★★★	$$+	Map ref 33 K10
238	**Bateau Bay**, Blue Lagoon Beach Resort, Bateau Bay Rd, Bateau Bay Ph: 1800 680 036 **Discounts:** week **Notes:** ph for long vehicle info; beachfront park; restaurant; tennis	★★★	$$$$$+*	Map ref 23 H6
239	**Batehaven**, Pleasurelea Tourist Resort, Beach Rd, Sunshine Bay (5km S of PO) Ph: 1800 639 396 **Discounts:** Top Tourist; pen; snr; week **Notes:** some ensuite sites; tennis; playground	★★★★	$$$+*	Map ref 34 F6
240	**Batemans Bay**, East's Riverside Holiday Park, Wharf Rd, Batemans Bay Ph: 1800 132 787 **Discounts:** BIG4; week (off-pk) **Notes:** riverfront park; some ensuite sites	★★★★	$$$+*	Map ref 34 F5

241 **Batemans Bay North** Tourist Park, Princes Hwy, North Batemans Bay Ph: 02 4478 6060
Discounts: week (off-pk) **Notes:** public ph close; dam water; quiet bush setting
$$$+ Map ref 34 F5

242 **Bathurst**, BIG4 Panorama Holiday Park, 250 Sydney Rd, Kelso Ph: 1800 669 911
Discounts: BIG4; week **Notes:** long vehicle to 12m; some ensuite sites
★★★☆ $$$+* Map ref 26 F6

243 **Bawley Point**, Racecourse Beach Tourist Park, Murramarang Rd (10km E Termeil PO) Ph: 02 4457 1078
Notes: beachfront with trees & wildlife
★★★☆ $$+* Map ref 35 E6

244 **Bega** Caravan Park, 256 Princes Hwy, Bega (2km S of Bega PO) Ph: 02 6492 2303
Discounts: week (off-pk) **Notes:** close to national parks
★★★ $$+ Map ref 34 H5

245 **Bendalong** Point Tourist Park, Red Point Rd, Bendalong Ph: 1300 733 026
Discounts: pen (off-pk) **Notes:** public ph & LPG refill close; close surf beach; ensuites; natural area; playground
★★★★ $$$$+ Map ref 34 D7

246 **Bermagui**, Zane Grey Park, Lamont St, Bermagui Ph: 02 6493 4382
Discounts: singles; snr; week **Notes:** shop close; 100m to beach
★★★ $$+* Map ref 35 J4

247 **Bingara** Riverside Caravan Park, Keera Rd, Bingara (near bridge) Ph: 02 6724 1209
Discounts: CMCA; pen; week **Notes:** swimming pool close; close to town
★★★ $ Map ref 28 E7

248 **Blue Mountains, Blackheath** Caravan Park, Prince Edward St (500m S of PO) Ph: 02 4787 8101
Discounts: week **Notes:** close to pool & playground
★★★ $$$+* Map ref 24 D3

249 **Blue Mountains, Katoomba** Falls Caravan Park, Katoomba Falls Rd (2km S of PO) Ph: 02 4782 1835
Discounts: week (off-pk) **Notes:** public ph close; close to walks & scenic attractions
★★★ $$$$+* Map ref 24 E4

250 **Blue Mountains, Oberon**, Jenolan Caravan Park, Cunynghame St, Oberon Ph: 02 6336 0344
Discounts: week (off-pk) **Notes:** public ph & shop close; 29km from Jenolan Caves
★★★ $$+ Map ref 24 E1

251 **Bombala** Park Caravan Park, Monaro Hwy, Bombala (adjacent to bridge) Ph: 02 6458 3270
Discounts: week **Notes:** close to town
★★★☆ $$ Map ref 34 J3

252 **Bonny Hills**, Rainbow Beach Holiday Village, Beach St (500m N of surf club) Ph: 1800 045 520
Discounts: Family Parks **Notes:** direct beach access; mini golf
★★★★ $$$+* Map ref 27 A14

253 **Boorowa** Caravan Park, Brial St, Boorowa (1km N of PO) Ph: 02 6385 3658
Notes: DP close; beside river; close to town
★★★ $ Map ref 26 J3

254 **Broadwater** Stopover Tourist Park, Pacific Hwy (1.6km S of Old PO) Ph: 1300 850 054
Notes: shop close; adjacent to koala sanctuary & boat ramp
★★★☆ $+ Map ref 29 C14

255 **Broken Hill** City Caravan Park, Rakow St (Adelaide Rd), Broken Hill Ph: 08 8087 3841
Discounts: Top Tourist **Notes:** solar-heated pool
★★★★ $$$ Map ref 30 K1

256 **Broken Hill**, Lake View Broken Hill Caravan Park, Mann St, Broken Hill Ph: 08 8088 2250
Notes: some ensuite sites; playground
★★★ $$ Map ref 30 K1

257 **Brooms Head** Caravan Park, Ocean Rd, Brooms Head Ph: 02 6646 7144
Discounts: CMCA; pen; week **Notes:** waterfront park; boat ramp; playground
★★★ $$+ Map ref 29 E14

258 **Broulee** Beach Holiday Park, Lyttle St, Broulee (500m S of PO) Ph: 1800 633 590
Discounts: BIG4; week (off-pk) **Notes:** ph for long vehicle info; shop close; beachfront; no unpowered sites; playground
★★★★ $$$+* Map ref 35 G5

259 **Brunswick Heads**, Ferry Reserve Holiday Park, Pacific Hwy (2km N of PO) Ph: 02 6685 1872
Discounts: Family Parks; week (off-pk) **Notes:** boat ramp
★★★☆ $$+* Map ref 29 B14

260 **Brunswick Heads**, Massey Greene Holiday Park, Tweed St (1km N of PO) Ph: 02 6685 1329
Discounts: week (off-pk) **Notes:** shop close; riverfront; close to town; playground
★★★☆ $$$+* Map ref 29 B14

261 **Brunswick Heads**, Terrace Reserve Holiday Park, Fingal St (50m E of PO) Ph: 02 6685 1233
Discounts: Top Tourist; week (off-pk) **Notes:** shop close; riverfront park; close to town
★★★★ $$$+* Map ref 29 B14

262 **Buckenderra** Holiday Village, Buckenderra Rd, Buckenderra Ph: 1800 339 461
Discounts: week **Notes:** lakefront park; mini golf; playground
★★★ $$ Map ref 34 G2

263 **Budgewoi** Holiday Park, Weemala St, Budgewoi Ph: 1800 241 342
Discounts: week (off-pk) **Notes:** lakefront park; close to beach & boat ramp
★★★☆ $+ Map ref 23 F7

264 **Byron Bay**, Clarkes Beach Holiday Park, off Lighthouse Rd (2km E of PO) Ph: 02 6685 6496
Discounts: week (off-pk) **Notes:** long vehicle to 7m; public ph close; beachfront park; 10 min walk to town
★★★☆ $$$$+* Map ref 29 B14

265 **Byron Bay**, First Sun Holiday Park, Lawson St, Byron Bay (200m N of PO) Ph: 02 6685 6544
Discounts: week **Notes:** on beach; close to town centre
★★★☆ $$$$$+* Map ref 29 B14

266 **Byron Bay**, Glen Villa Resort, Butler St, Byron Bay (400m W of PO) Ph: 02 6685 7382
Discounts: week **Notes:** 400m from town centre
★★★ $$$$+ Map ref 29 B14

267 **Byron Bay area, Broken Head** Holiday Park, Beach Rd (8.5km S of Byron Bay) Ph: 1800 450 036
Discounts: Top Tourist; week (off-pk) **Notes:** beachfront park in national park
★★★☆ $$$+* Map ref 29 B14

268 **Byron Bay area, Suffolk Park** Holiday Park, Alcorn St, Suffolk Park (6km S) Ph: 02 6685 3353
Discounts: week (off-pk) **Notes:** LPG refill close; beachfront park
★★★☆ $$$+* Map ref 29 B14

269 **Casino**, Casino Village RV Resort, Light St, Casino Ph: 02 6662 1069
Discounts: CMCA **Notes:** shop close; activities
$$ Map ref 29 C13

270 **Cessnock**, BIG4 Valley Vineyard Tourist Park, Mt View Rd (2km NW of PO) Ph: 1800 649 156
Discounts: BIG4; week **Notes:** some ensuite sites; close to wineries & gardens
★★★☆ $$$+ Map ref 23 C3

271 **Chinderah** Village, Chinderah Bay Dr (5km S of Tweed Heads S PO) Ph: 02 6674 1536
Discounts: week (off-pk) **Notes:** public ph & shop close; close to river; some ensuite sites
★★★★ $$+ Map ref 29 A14

272 **Cobar** Caravan Park, 101 Barrier Hwy, Cobar (1km W of PO) Ph: 02 6836 2425
Discounts: CMCA; pension; week **Notes:** grass and shade
★★★☆ $$ Map ref 31 H10

273 **Coffs Harbour**, Bananacoast Caravan Park, 429 Pacific Hwy, Coffs Harbour Ph: 02 6652 2868
Discounts: pen **Notes:** few drive thru sites; bore water; close to Big Banana
★★★★ $$$+ Map ref 29 G14

274 **Coffs Harbour**, Park Beach Holiday Park, Ocean Parade, Coffs Harbour Ph: 1800 200 111
Discounts: Top Tourist; week (off-pk) **Notes:** across from beach; some ensuite sites
★★★★☆ $$$+* Map ref 29 G14

275 **Coffs Harbour area, Emerald Beach** Holiday Park, Fishermans Dr (18km N) Ph: 1800 681 521
Discounts: BIG4; specials **Notes:** shop close; beachfront; some ensuite sites; jumping pillow
★★★★ $$$+* Map ref 29 G14

276 **Coffs Harbour area, Moonee Beach** Holiday Park, Moonee Beach Rd (12km N) Ph: 1800 184 120
Discounts: Top Tourist; week **Notes:** beachfront park; ocean views
★★★☆ $$+* Map ref 29 G14

277 **Condobolin**, Riverview Caravan Park, Diggers Ave, Condobolin (1km S of PO) Ph: 02 6895 2611
Discounts: economical; 3 nights **Notes:** public ph & shop close; riverfront park; grassed shady sites
★★★☆ $ Map ref 33 C13

278 **Coolah**, Cunningham Caravan Park, Cunningham St, Coolah (300m E of PO) Ph: 02 6377 1338
Discounts: pen; snr; week **Notes:** swimming pool & public ph close; riverfront park; close to town
★★★☆ $ Map ref 26 B6

279 **Cooma**, Snowtels Caravan Park, Snowy Mountains Hwy (1.6km W of Info Centre) Ph: 02 6452 1828
Discounts: snr; week **Notes:** ski hire; tennis; mini golf
★★★☆ $$ Map ref 34 G3

280 **Coonabarabran**, Getaway Tourist Park, Newell Hwy (2km S of PO) Ph: 02 6842 1773
Discounts: week **Notes:** bushland setting; playground
★★☆ $$ Map ref 28 J4

281 **Coonamble** Riverside Caravan Park, Castlereagh Hwy (1km S of PO) Ph: 02 6822 1926
Discounts: CMCA; pen; snr **Notes:** shop close; quiet park with grass & trees
★★★ $ Map ref 28 H2

282 **Cootamundra** Caravan Park, Mackay St, Cootamundra (500m W of PO) Ph: 02 6942 1080
Discounts: week **Notes:** park located in town
★★★ $$ Map ref 34 B1

283 **Corindi Beach** Holiday Park, 93 Pacific St (32km N of Coffs Harbour) Ph: 02 6649 2803
Discounts: week (off-pk) **Notes:** public ph & shop close; park has absolute ocean frontage
★★☆ $$+ Map ref 29 F13

284 **Corowa**, Ball Park Caravan Park, Bridge Rd, Corowa (500m from PO) Ph: 02 6033 1426
Discounts: Family Parks; week **Notes:** swimming pool close; riverfront park; boat ramp; close to CBD
★★★ $+ Map ref 33 K11

285 **Cowra** Holiday Park, Mid Western Hwy, Cowra (4km E of PO) Ph: 02 6342 2666
Discounts: Family Parks; CMCA **Notes:** bore water
★★★☆ $$ Map ref 26 H4

286 **Cowra** Van Park, Lachlan St (off Kendal St), Cowra (1km W of PO) Ph: 02 6340 2110
Discounts: week **Notes:** public ph & shop close; close to main shopping centre
★★★☆ $$ Map ref 26 H4

287 **Crescent Head** Holiday Park, Pacific St, Crescent Head (400m E of PO) Ph: 02 6566 0261
Discounts: pen; snr **Notes:** beachfront park; close to town centre
★★★☆ $$+* Map ref 29 J13

288 **Cudmirrah**, Swan Lake Tourist Village, Goonawarra Dr, Cudmirrah Ph: 1300 555 517
Discounts: pen; week **Notes:** tennis; playground; canoe hire; rec room
★★★★ $$$$+* Map ref 35 D6

289 **Culburra**, Crookhaven Heads Tourist Park, Prince Edward Ave (20km E of Nowra) Ph: 02 4447 2849
Discounts: pen **Notes:** close to beach
★★★★ $$$$* Map ref 34 C7

290 **Currarong** Beachside Tourist Park, Nowra Rd, Currarong (800m W of PO) Ph: 1300 555 515
Discounts: week **Notes:** beachfront; grassed sites; boat ramp; creek access
★★★☆ $$$+ Map ref 34 D7

291 **Dareton**, Coomealla Club Caravan Park Resort, Silver City Hwy (400m NW of PO) Ph: 1800 854 737
Notes: public ph & shop close; adjacent to club; some ensuite sites
★★★★ $$ Map ref 32 F3

292 **Darlington Point** Riverside Caravan Park, Kidman Way (200m E of PO) Ph: 02 6968 4237
Discounts: Family Parks **Notes:** riverfront park; shady sites
★★★ $+ Map ref 33 G10

293 **Deniliquin** McLean Beach Caravan Park, Butler St, Deniliquin (1.5km W of PO) Ph: 03 5881 2448
Discounts: week **Notes:** close to river
★★★★ $$+* Map ref 33 J8

294 **Deniliquin** Riverside Caravan Park, Davidson St (Cobb Hwy), Deniliquin Ph: 03 5881 1284
Discounts: Family Parks **Notes:** shop close; boat ramp
★★★★ $$ Map ref 33 J8

295 **Denman** Van Village, Macauley St, Denman (700m S of PO) Ph: 02 6547 2590
Notes: shop close; all ensuite sites; 6 acres bushland
★★☆ $$ Map ref 27 C8

296 **Dubbo** City Caravan Park, Whylandra St, Dubbo (2km W of PO) Ph: 1800 824 820
Discounts: Top Tourist **Notes:** public ph close; playground
★★★★ $$+ Map ref 26 C4

297 **Dubbo**, Midstate Motor Park, Bourke St, Dubbo (1km N of PO) Ph: 02 6882 1155
Discounts: CMCA; week **Notes:** long vehicle to 15m; putt putt golf; playground
★★★☆ $$ Map ref 26 C4

298 **Dubbo**, Westview Tourist Caravan Park, Mitchell Hwy, Dubbo Ph: 02 6882 1339
Discounts: Family Parks; week **Notes:** playground
★★★☆ $$ Map ref 26 C4

299 **Dungog**, Riverwood Downs Mountain Valley Resort, Upper Monkerai Rd, Monkerai Ph: 02 4994 7112
Discounts: mid-week **Notes:** LPG swap only; 35km S of Gloucester, near Nat Pk
★★☆ $$$$+ Map ref 27 D11

300 **Eden**, Discovery Holiday Parks - Eden, Princes Hwy (4.5km S of PO) Ph: 1800 111 419
Discounts: CMCA **Notes:** LPG swap only; beach; tennis; jumping pillow; playground
★★★☆ $+* Map ref 34 J5

301 **Eden** Tourist Park, Aslings Beach Rd, Eden (2km E of PO) Ph: 02 6496 1139
Discounts: snr; week **Notes:** across road from beach; lake
★★★☆ $$+ Map ref 34 J5

302 **Eden**, Twofold Bay Beach Resort, 731 Princes Hwy, Eden (7km S of PO) Ph: 1800 631 006
Discounts: BIG4; CMCA; snr **Notes:** beachfront; ensuites; playground; jumping pilllow
★★★★ $$+* Map ref 34 J5

303	**Evans Head**, Silver Sands Caravan & Camping Reserve, Park St, Evans Head Ph: 02 6682 4212 **Discounts:** week **Notes:** shop, LPG refill & internet access close; close to beach & town; some ensuite sites	★★★☆ $+* Map ref 29 C14
304	**Fingal** Holiday Park, Prince St, Fingal (10km NE of PO) Ph: 07 5524 2208 **Discounts:** week **Notes:** beachfront park	★★★★ $$$+* Map ref 29 A14
305	**Finley**, Lakeside Caravan Park, Newell Hwy, Finley (2km N of PO) Ph: 03 5883 1170 **Discounts:** CMCA **Notes:** DP, swimming pool & shop close; lakefront park	★★★ $ Map ref 33 J10
306	**Forbes**, Country Club Caravan Park, Sam St (off Newell Hwy), Forbes Ph: 02 6852 1957 **Discounts:** Family Parks; CMCA **Notes:** walk to town & golf club	★★★ $$ Map ref 26 F2
307	**Forbes** River Meadows Caravan Park, Cnr Newell Hwy & River Rd (1.5km Sth of PO) Ph: 02 6852 2694 **Discounts:** week **Notes:** horses allowed	★★★☆ $+ Map ref 26 F2
308	**Forster** Beach Caravan Park, Reserve Rd, Forster (200m W of PO) Ph: 1800 240 632 **Discounts:** CMCA; week **Notes:** shop close; adjacent to main beach & lake	★★★☆ $$+* Map ref 27 C13
309	**Forster**, Lakeside Resort Forster, Tea Tree Rd, Forster (5km S of PO) Ph: 02 6555 5511 **Discounts:** Family Parks; week (off-pk) **Notes:** waterfront park; some ensuite sites	★★★☆ $$$+* Map ref 27 C13
310	**Forster**, Smugglers Cove Holiday Village, The Lakes Way, Forster Ph: 02 6554 6666 **Discounts:** BIG4 **Notes:** resort-style park	★★★★☆ $$$+* Map ref 27 C13
311	**Gerringong**, Werri Beach Holiday Park, Bridges Rd (off Fern St) Ph: 1800 655 819 **Discounts:** pen; week; off-pk **Notes:** public ph close; playground; half court tennis	★★★☆ $$$$+* Map ref 35 B7
312	**Gerroa**, Discovery Holiday Parks - Gerroa, Crooked River Rd (300m W of PO) Ph: 02 4234 12233 **Discounts:** snr **Notes:** riverfront park; café in grounds	★★★☆ $$+* Map ref 35 B7
313	**Gerroa**, Seven Mile Beach Holiday Park, Crooked River Rd, Gerroa Ph: 1800 666 665 **Discounts:** pen **Notes:** some ensuite sites; playground; tennis; spa	★★★★ $$+* Map ref 35 B7
314	**Gilgandra** Rotary Caravan Park, Newell Hwy, Gilgandra (300m N of bridge) Ph: 02 6847 2423 **Notes:** shop close; shady sites	★★★☆ $$ Map ref 26 B3
315	**Glen Innes**, Fossicker Caravan Park, Church St, Glen Innes (750m S of PO) Ph: 1300 300 207 **Discounts:** Top Tourist **Notes:** LPG swap only; 200m to town centre	★★★☆ $$ Map ref 29 E9
316	**Glen Innes**, Poplar Caravan Park, Church St (New England Hwy) Glen Innes Ph: 02 6732 1514 **Discounts:** CMCA **Notes:** takeaways available	★★★☆ $ Map ref 29 E10
317	**Gloucester** Holiday Park, Denison St, Gloucester (700m W of PO) Ph: 02 6558 1720 **Discounts:** Family Parks; CMCA **Notes:** swimming pool close; mini golf	★★★ $$$ Map ref 27 C11
318	**Goulburn South** Caravan Park, Hume St, Goulburn (3km S of PO) Ph: 02 4821 3233 **Discounts:** week **Notes:** trees & prolific birdlife	★★★ $$ Map ref 35 B3
319	**Grafton**, Glenwood Tourist Park & Motel, Heber St, South Grafton Ph: 02 6642 3466 **Discounts:** pen; snr **Notes:** grass, trees & lovely gardens	★★★☆ $$ Map ref 29 E12
320	**Grassy Head** Holiday Park, Reserve Rd, Grassy Head (4km N of PO) Ph: 02 6569 0742 **Discounts:** pen; snr **Notes:** secluded beach; birds & wildlife	★★☆ $$+* Map ref 29 H12
321	**Grenfell** Caravan Park, Grafton St, Grenfell (1.5km W of PO) Ph: 02 6343 1194 **Discounts:** pen; week **Notes:** public ph close; small park; close to town	★★★ $$ Map ref 26 H2
322	**Griffith** Tourist Caravan Park, Willandra Avenue, Griffith (2km S of PO) Ph: 02 6964 2144 **Discounts:** week **Notes:** some covered & ensuite sites; tennis	★★★★ $$ Map ref 33 F10
323	**Gulgong**, Henry Lawson Caravan Park, Mayne St, Gulgong (1.5km W of PO) Ph: 02 6374 1294 **Discounts:** week **Notes:** ph for long vehicle info; close to town; playground	★★★☆ $$ Map ref 26 C5
324	**Gundagai** Tourist Park, Nangus Rd, Gundagai (400m S of Info Centre) Ph: 1300 722 906 **Discounts:** Top Tourist; week **Notes:** swimming pool & shop close; some undercover & ensuite sites	★★★★ $$$ Map ref 34 D1
325	**Gunnedah** Tourist Caravan Park, Henry St, Gunnedah (500m E of PO) Ph: 1800 007 142 **Discounts:** Top Tourist **Notes:** ph for long vehicle info; close to restaurant and clubs	★★★☆ $$ Map ref 28 H5
326	**Guyra** Summit Caravan Park, New England Hwy, Guyra (1.8km S of PO) Ph: 02 6779 1241 **Discounts:** week **Notes:** highest caravan park in Australia	$ Map ref 29 F9
327	**Hallidays Poin**t, Beachfront Holiday Resort, Redhead Rd, Hallidays Point Ph: 1800 888 706 **Discounts:** BIG4 **Notes:** resort-style park	★★★★☆ $$$+* Map ref 27 C13
328	**Harrington**, BIG4 Harrington Beach Holiday Park, Crowdy Rd (300m NE of PO) Ph: 1300 666 369 **Discounts:** BIG4 **Notes:** public ph & shop close; close patrolled beach; playground	★★★★ $$$+* Map ref 27 B13
329	**Harrington**, Colonial Leisure Village, Harrington Rd, Harrington (3km W of PO) Ph: 02 6556 3312 **Discounts:** week **Notes:** long vehicle to 8m; table tennis; pool table; rec room	★★★☆ $$+* Map ref 27 B13
330	**Hastings Point** Holiday Park, Tweed Coast Rd, Hastings Point (50m N of PO) Ph: 02 6676 1049 **Discounts:** week **Notes:** shop close; beachfront park; no cabin accomodation	★★☆ $$+* Map ref 29 A14
331	**Hat Head** Holiday Park, Straight St, Hat Head (500m E of PO) Ph: 1800 006 600 **Discounts:** pen/snr; winter **Notes:** boat ramp	★★★☆ $$+* Map ref 29 J12
332	**Hawks Nest** Beach Caravan Park, Booner St, Hawks Nest (1km E of PO) Ph: 1800 072 244 **Discounts:** week **Notes:** LPG swap only; internet access close; beachfront park; no unpowered sites	★★★☆ $$+ Map ref 27 D12
333	**Hay** Plains Holiday Park, Nailor St, Hay (1km SW of PO) Ph: 02 6993 1875 **Discounts:** BIG4 **Notes:** shade; some ensuite sites; TV room	★★★★ $$ Map ref 33 F8

334	**Hillston** Caravan Park, Cnr Oxley Avenue & High St, Hillston (1km N of PO) Ph: 02 6967 2575 **Discounts:** CMCA **Notes:** swimming pool close; close to lake	★★★	$$	Map ref 33 D10
335	**Holbrook** Motor Village, Cnr Hume Hwy & Bardwell St, Holbrook (800m S of PO) Ph: 1800 131 101 **Discounts:** Top Tourist; CMCA; auto club **Notes:** playground; close to shops	★★★★	$$+	Map ref 33 J13
336	**Howlong** Caravan Park, Hume St, Howlong (600m E of PO) Ph: 02 6026 5304 **Discounts:** Family Parks; week (off-pk) **Notes:** close to river & to wineries	★★★	$$+*	Map ref 33 K12
337	**Huskisson** Beach Tourist Resort, Beach St, Huskisson (1km from PO) Ph: 1300 733 027 **Discounts:** pen (off-pk) **Notes:** public ph close; beachfront; ensuites; close to town; playground	★★★☆	$$$$+	Map ref 35 C6
338	**Huskisson**, Jervis Bay Cabins & Camping, Goodlands Rd (4km W of PO) Ph: 02 4441 5809 **Discounts:** singles; pen; snr; wk; off-pk **Notes:** long vehicle to 10m; riverfront park; wildlife & birds; canoe hire	★★★	$$$+	Map ref 35 C6
339	**Huskisson** White Sands Tourist Park, Cnr Nowra St & Beach St (1km SE of PO) Ph: 1300 733 028 **Discounts:** pen (off-pk) **Notes:** swimming pool, public ph, shop, LPG refill & internet access close; close to town; waterfront powered sites	★★★☆	$$$$+	Map ref 35 C7
340	**Iluka**, Anchorage Holiday Park, Marandowie Dr, Iluka (2km N of PO) Ph: 02 6646 6210 **Discounts:** Top Tourist; week **Notes:** ph for long vehicle info; close to beach & river; boat ramp	★★★★	$$$+*	Map ref 29 D14
341	**Inverell**, Fossickers Rest Caravan Park, Lake Inverell Dr (3km E of PO) Ph: 02 6722 2261 **Discounts:** CMCA **Notes:** some ensuite sites; on-site gem fossicking	★★★★	$$+	Map ref 29 E8
342	**Jerilderie** Motel and Caravan Park, Newell Hwy, Jerilderie (1km NE of PO) Ph: 03 5886 1366 **Discounts:** week **Notes:** swimming pool, LPG refill & internet access close; grass & shade; adjacent to golf & pool	★★★☆	$$	Map ref 33 H10
343	**Jindabyne** Discovery Holiday Park, Kosciuszko Rd & Alpine Way (2km S of PO) Ph: 1800 248 148 **Discounts:** BIG4; CMCA; multi-night **Notes:** long vehicle to 8m; spa; lakefront park; lake water; ski hire	★★★★☆	$$$$+	Map ref 34 H2
344	**Jindabyne** Holiday Park, Kosciuszko Rd, Jindabyne (150m NW of PO) Ph: 02 6456 2249 **Discounts:** week **Notes:** lakefront park	★★★☆	$$$+*	Map ref 34 H2
345	**Junee** Caravan Park, Sunnyside Lane, Junee (1.5km NW of PO) Ph: 1800 003 464 **Discounts:** Top Tourist; CMCA **Notes:** shop close; open & roomy with shade	★★★★	$$	Map ref 33 G14
346	**Kangaroo Valley** Glenmack Park, Moss Vale Rd, Kangaroo Valley Ph: 02 4465 1372 **Discounts:** CMCA; week **Notes:** mini golf, tennis	★★★☆	$+	Map ref 35 B6
347	**Kangaroo Valley** Tourist Park, Moss Vale Rd, Kangaroo Valley (1km N of PO) Ph: 02 4465 1310 **Discounts:** pen **Notes:** long vehicle to 7m; public ph, LPG refill & internet access close; riverfront; close to town; grassed sites	★★★	$$$+	Map ref 35 B6
348	**Kempsey** Tourist Village, 325 Pacific Hwy, South Kempsey (3km S of PO) Ph: 02 6562 7666 **Discounts:** snr **Notes:** close to golf course	★★★☆	$$	Map ref 29 J13
349	**Kempsey South**, Tall Timbers Caravan Park, 425 Pacific Hwy, Kempsey Ph: 02 6562 4544 **Discounts:** CMCA; snr **Notes:** cassette DP; bush setting	★★★	$$	Map ref 29 J13
350	**Khancoban** Lakeside Caravan Resort, Alpine Way, Khancoban (1km E of PO) Ph: 02 6076 9488 **Discounts:** 2nd night; snr; auto club **Notes:** swimming pool close; table tennis; playground; birdlife	★★★	$$$+	Map ref 33 K14
351	**Kiama**, Kendalls on the Beach Holiday Park, Bonaira St, Kiama (2km S of PO) Ph: 1800 111 224 **Discounts:** pen/snr; week **Notes:** beachfront park; playground	★★★★	$$+*	Map ref 35 B7
352	**Kiama**, Surf Beach Holiday Park, Bourrool St, Kiama (1km S of PO) Ph: 02 4232 1791 **Discounts:** snr; week (off-pk) **Notes:** long vehicle to 9m; close to patrolled beach	★★★★	$$$+*	Map ref 35 B7
353	**Kingscliff** Beach Holiday Park, Marine Parade, Kingscliff (500m NE of PO) Ph: 02 6674 1311 **Discounts:** week **Notes:** shop close; beachfront park	★★★	$$$+*	Map ref 29 A14
354	**Kingscliff** North Holiday Park, Marine Parade, Kingscliff (2km N of PO) Ph: 02 6674 1071 **Discounts:** week **Notes:** public ph close; beachfront park; accomm is safari tents	★★★	$$+*	Map ref 29 A14
355	**Kioloa** Beach Holiday Park, Murramarang Rd, Kioloa (11km E of Termeil) Ph: 02 4457 1072 **Discounts:** week & pen (off-pk) **Notes:** LPG refill close; beachfront park; rain water; playground	★★★☆	$+*	Map ref 35 F5
356	**Kootingal** Country Caravan Park, New England Hwy, Kootingal (1km from PO) Ph: 02 6760 3902 **Notes:** restaurant & takeaways	★★★☆	$	Map ref 29 J8
357	**Kyogle** Gardens Caravan Park, Summerland Way, Kyogle (300m N of PO) Ph: 02 6632 1204 **Notes:** close to town & tennis court	★★☆	$	Map ref 29 B13
358	**Lake Cargelligo**, Lake View Caravan Park, Naradhan & Womboyn Sts (1.5km SE) Ph: 02 6898 1077 **Discounts:** economical; 4th night **Notes:** close to lake	★★★	$	Map ref 33 D11
359	**Lake Conjola** Entrance Tourist Park, Lake Conjola Entrance Rd (200m E of PO) Ph: 1300 133 395 **Discounts:** pen (off-pk) **Notes:** public ph & LPG refill close; lakefront & beachfront; playgrounds	★★★★	$$$+	Map ref 34 D7
360	**Lake Macquarie**, Belmont Bayview Park, Gerald St, Belmont Ph: 02 4945 3653 **Discounts:** snr **Notes:** long vehicle to 7m; shop close; close to lake, shops & clubs	★★★☆	$+	Map ref 23 D7
361	**Lake Macquarie**, Blacksmiths Beachside Holiday Park, Blacksmiths Beach Ph: 02 4971 2858 **Discounts:** CMCA; snr & week off-pk **Notes:** some ensuite sites; tennis court	★★★★	$+*	Map ref 23 D7
362	**Lake Macquarie**, Wangi Point Lakeside Holiday Park, Watkins Rd, Wangi Wangi Ph: 02 4975 1889 **Discounts:** CMCA; pen & week off-pk **Notes:** shop close; lakefront park; boat ramp; playground	★★★☆	$$+*	Map ref 23 D6
363	**Lake Tabourie** Tourist Park, Princes Hwy, Lake Tabourie (12km S of Ulladulla) Ph: 1300 559 966 **Discounts:** week **Notes:** grassed beachfront sites; spa cabins	★★★★	$$$+	Map ref 34 E7
364	**Leeton**, An Oasis Caravan Park, Corbie Hill Rd, Leeton (2km SE of PO) Ph: 02 6953 3882 **Discounts:** week **Notes:** bush setting	★★★☆	$$	Map ref 33 G11

365 **Lennox Head**, Lake Ainsworth Holiday Park, Pacific Parade (800m N of PO) Ph: 02 6687 7249
Discounts: snr **Notes:** lakeside; across from beach
★★★☆ $$$+* Map ref 29 B14

366 **Lightning Ridge** Hotel Motel Caravan Park, Onyx St (500m W of PO) Ph: 02 6829 0304
Notes: shop & LPG refill close; restaurant; bottle shop
★★☆ $$ Map ref 31 C14

367 **Lismore** Palms Caravan Park, Brunswick St, Lismore (1km N of PO) Ph: 02 6621 7067
Discounts: pen **Notes:** riverfront park; freshwater fishing
★★★ $$ Map ref 29 B13

368 **Macksville**, Nambucca River Tourist Park, Nursery Rd, Macksville Ph: 02 6568 1850
Discounts: week **Notes:** dogs permitted; boat ramp; tennis; spa
★★★☆ $$+ Map ref 29 H13

369 **Maclean** Riverside Caravan Park, River St, Maclean (1km N of PO) Ph: 02 6645 2987
Notes: long vehicle to 7m; shop & LPG refill close; close to the river
★★★☆ $$+ Map ref 29 D13

370 **Manilla**, River Gums Caravan Park, Strafford St, Manilla (2km E of PO) Ph: 02 6785 1166
Discounts: CMCA; snr; week **Notes:** riverfront park; fishing
★★★☆ $ Map ref 28 H7

371 **Manning Point**, East's Ocean Shores Holiday Park, Manning St, Manning Point Ph: 02 6553 2624
Discounts: BIG4; week (off-pk) **Notes:** close to beach
★★★★☆ $$$+ Map ref 27 B13

372 **Manning Point**, Weeroona Holiday Park, Main Rd, Manning Point Ph: 02 6553 2635
Discounts: week (off-pk) **Notes:** internet access close; beachfront park; 10 shady acres
★★★★ $$+* Map ref 27 B13

373 **Merimbula** Beach Holiday Park, Short Point Rd, Merimbula (1.5km NW of PO) Ph: 02 6495 1269
Discounts: BIG4; auto clubs **Notes:** long vehicle to 8m; public ph close; close to beach; some ensuite sites; tennis
★★★★☆ $$$+* Map ref 34 J5

374 **Milton** Tourist Park, Princes Hwy, Milton (2km SE of PO) Ph: 02 4455 2028
Discounts: CMCA; week **Notes:** ph for long vehicle info; playground
★★★☆ $$$+* Map ref 35 D5

375 **Mittagong** Caravan Park, Old Hume Hwy, Mittagong (1km N of PO) Ph: 02 4871 1574
Discounts: pen/snr, week **Notes:** swimming pool & public ph close; close to shops & golf course
★★★☆ $$+* Map ref 35 A6

376 **Moama**, Maiden's Inn Holiday Park, Chanter St, Moama (1.5km E of PO) Ph: 1800 825 235
Discounts: BIG4 **Notes:** LPG swap only; riverfront park; boat ramp; some ensuite sites
★★★★ $$$+ Map ref 33 K8

377 **Moree**, Gwydir Carapark, Cnr Newell Hwy & Amaroo Dr (3km S of PO) Ph: 02 6752 2723
Discounts: Family Parks; week **Notes:** few long vehicle sites; thermal pools on site
★★★☆ $$$ Map ref 28 D5

378 **Moruya**, River Breeze Tourist Park, Princes Hwy, Moruya (500m N of PO) Ph: 1800 467 730
Discounts: Top Tourist; CMCA; snr; week **Notes:** shop & LPG refill close; riverfront park; close to town centre
★★★★ $$$+* Map ref 35 G4

379 **Moss Vale** Village Caravan Park, Willow Dr, Moss Vale (2km S of PO) Ph: 02 4868 1099
Discounts: week **Notes:** spacious; putting/golf practice
★★★★ $$+ Map ref 35 A5

380 **Mudgee** Riverside Caravan & Tourist Park, Short St (behind Info Office) Ph: 02 6372 2531
Discounts: CMCA **Notes:** riverfront park
★★★☆ $$ Map ref 26 D6

381 **Mulwala**, Lake Mulwala Holiday Park, Melbourne St, Mulwala Ph: 03 5744 1050
Discounts: Family Parks **Notes:** lakefront park, boat ramp, marina
★★★☆ $$$+* Map ref 33 K11

382 **Murwillumbah**, Greenhills Caravan Park, Tweed Valley Way (1.5km S of rail station) Ph: 02 6672 2035
Notes: public ph close; close to national parks
★★★★ $$+ Map ref 29 A14

383 **Muswellbrook**, Pinaroo Leisure Park, New England Hwy (3.2km S of PO) Ph: 02 6543 3905
Notes: tennis; adjacent to golf course
★★★☆ $$ Map ref 27 C9

384 **Nambucca Heads**, White Albatross Holiday Centre, Wellington Dr (1km E of PO) Ph: 1800 152 505
Discounts: week (off-pk) **Notes:** cassette DP; beach, tidal lagoon; some ensuite sites
★★★★☆ $$$$+ Map ref 29 H13

385 **Nambucca Hds** area, Valla Beach Resort, Regatta Dr, Valla Beach Ph: 02 6569 5555
Discounts: CMCA **Notes:** beach access
$$+ Map ref 29 H13

386 **Narooma**, East's Narooma Shores Holiday Park, Princes Hwy, Narooma Ph: 1800 332 787
Discounts: BIG4 **Notes:** long vehicle to 8m; shop close; waterfront; rec/TV room; some ensuite sites
★★★★ $$$+* Map ref 35 J5

387 **Narooma**, Island View Beach Resort, Princes Hwy, Narooma (5km S of PO) Ph: 1800 465 432
Discounts: BIG4; week (off-pk) **Notes:** beachfront park; tennis, games room
★★★★☆ $$$+* Map ref 35 J5

388 **Narrabri**, Highway Tourist Village, Cooma Rd, Narrabri (2km S of PO) Ph: 1800 674 253
Discounts: Top Tourist; week **Notes:** shop close; LPG swap only; some ensuite sites
★★★☆ $$$ Map ref 28 G5

389 **Narrandera** Caravan Park, junction of Sturt & Newell Hwys (2km S of PO) Ph: 02 6959 2955
Discounts: Oz Parks; CMCA **Notes:** long vehicle to 8m; filtered bore water
★★★★ $$+ Map ref 33 G11

390 **Narrandera**, Lake Talbot Tourist Park, Gordon St, Narrandera (2km SE of PO) Ph: 1800 106 601
Discounts: Top Tourist; CMCA; snr; week **Notes:** swimming pool close; lakeside park; boat ramp
★★★★ $$+ Map ref 33 G11

391 **Narromine** Tourist Park, Mitchell Hwy, Narromine (2km NW of PO) Ph: 02 6889 2129
Discounts: week **Notes:** quiet and spacious
★★★ $$+ Map ref 26 C2

392 **Newcastle area,** Stockton Beach Tourist Park, Pitt St, Stockton (1km SW of PO) Ph: 02 4928 1393
Discounts: Family Parks; week; mid wk **Notes:** few drive thru & long vehicle sites; swimming pool close; LPG swap only; beachfront park; situated N of Newcastle
★★★☆ $$$+* Map ref 23 B7

393 **Norah Head** Holiday Park, Victoria St, Norah Head (800m W of lighthouse) Ph: 1800 241 342
Discounts: Family Parks; week (off-pk) **Notes:** walk to beach; situated north of The Entrance
★★★☆ $$+ Map ref 23 G7

394 **North Haven**, Jacaranda Caravan Park, The Parade, North Haven (1km E of PO) Ph: 1800 088 765
Discounts: Top Tourist; week (off-pk) **Notes:** few long vehicle sites; shop close; 400m to beach
★★★★☆ $$$+* Map ref 27 B14

395 **North Haven**, Beachfront Caravan Park, The Parade, North Haven (3km from PO) Ph: 02 6559 9193
Discounts: pen/snr **Notes:** close to water
★★★☆ $$+ Map ref 27 B14

396 **Nowra**, Shoalhaven Caravan Village, Terara Rd, Nowra (1km E of PO) Ph: 02 4423 0770
Discounts: week **Notes:** riverfront park; boat ramp; tennis
★★★☆ $$+ Map ref 35 C6

397 **Nundle**, Fossickers Tourist Park, Jenkins St, Nundle (100m N of PO) Ph: 1300 366 676
Discounts: Top Tourist; CMCA **Notes:** swimming pool, public ph & shop close; LPG swap only; fossicking close by
★★★☆ $$+ Map ref 27 A9

398 **Nyngan**, Riverside Caravan Park, Junction of Barrier & Mitchell Hwys, Nyngan Ph: 02 6832 1729
Discounts: CMCA; multi-night stay **Notes:** boat ramp; some ensuite sites
★★★☆ $$ Map ref 31 H13

399 **Old Adaminaby**, Rainbow Pines Tourist Park, Lucas St (7km S of Snowy Mtn Hwy) Ph: 02 6454 2317
Notes: long vehicle to 8m; public ph close; lakefront park; some ensuite sites
$$ Map ref 34 F2

400 **Orange**, Colour City Caravan Park, Margaret St, Orange (2km N of PO) Ph: 02 6362 7254
Discounts: week **Notes:** few long vehicle sites; shop & LPG refill close; grass & many European trees
★★★☆ $ Map ref 26 F4

401 **Pambula Beach**, Discovery Holiday Parks Pambula Beach, Pambula Beach Rd (3km E hwy) Ph: 1800 677 808
Discounts: BIG4; CMCA; week **Notes:** beachfront; some ensuite sites; indoor pool
★★★★☆ $$$$+* Map ref 34 J5

402 **Parkes**, Currajong Cara-Park, Newell Hwy, Parkes (200m N of info centre) Ph: 02 6862 3400
Discounts: singles **Notes:** no unpowered sites; walk to town
$$ Map ref 26 E2

403 **Peak Hill** Caravan Park, Ween St, Peak Hill (350m N of PO) Ph: 02 6869 1422
Discounts: CMCA;ACC; 2nd night **Notes:** close to shops & clubs
★★★☆ $ Map ref 26 D2

404 **Port Macquarie**, Edgewater Holiday Park, Hastings River Dr (3km W of PO) Ph: 1800 228 800
Discounts: week **Notes:** waterfront park; some ensuite sites; mini golf
★★★★ $$+* Map ref 27 A14

405 **Port Macquarie**, Sundowner Breakwall Tourist Park, Munster St (200m N of PO) Ph: 1800 636 452
Discounts: BIG4; week **Notes:** shop close; close to town & breakwall
★★★☆ $$$$+* Map ref 27 A14

406 **Port Macquarie area Telegraph Point**, Stoney Park, Hacks Ferry Rd (20km NW) Ph: 02 6585 0080
Discounts: CMCA; week **Notes:** on manmade lakes; adjacent to boat ramp
★★★☆ $$+ Map ref 27 A14

407 **Port Stephens, Anna Bay**, Bays Holiday Park, Port Stephens Dr (3km N of PO) Ph: 02 4982 1438
Discounts: Family Parks **Notes:** long vehicle to 9m; treated water; trees; koalas
★★★★ $$$+* Map ref 27 E11

408 **Port Stephens, Fingal Bay** Holiday Park, Marine Dr, Fingal Bay Ph: 1800 600 203
Discounts: snr; week **Notes:** public ph & shop close; beachfront park; playground
★★★★ $$$+* Map ref 27 E11

409 **Port Stephens, Karuah** Jetty Village Resort, Holdom Rd, Karuah (1km NE of PO) Ph: 1800 005 552
Discounts: BIG4; week **Notes:** riverfront park; boat ramp
★★★☆ $$+* Map ref 27 D11

410 **Port Stephens, Lemon Tree Passage**, Discovery Parks Port Stephens (3km S of PO) Ph: 02 4982 4401
Discounts: BIG4; CMCA; off-pk **Notes:** long vehicle to 10m; some ensuite sites; boat ramp; activities
★★★★☆ $$$$+ Map ref 27 E11

411 **Port Stephens, Nelson Bay**, Halifax Holiday Park, Beach Rd (2km E of PO) Ph: 1800 600 201
Notes: close to beaches; boat ramp
★★★★ $$$+* Map ref 27 E12

412 **Port Stephens, Shoal Bay** Holiday Park, Shoal Bay Rd, Shoal Bay Ph: 1800 600 200
Discounts: week, snr (not holidays) **Notes:** public ph & shop close; beachfront; some ensuite sites; half court tennis
★★★★ $$$+* Map ref 27 E12

413 **Port Stephens, Soldiers Point** Holiday Park, Ridgeway Ave (7km NW Nelson Bay) Ph: 1800 827 300
Discounts: week; loyalty program **Notes:** public ph & shop close; beachfront park
★★★★ $$$+* Map ref 27 E11

414 **Pottsville** North Holiday Park, Tweed Coast Rd, Pottsville (1km N of PO) Ph: 1800 234 121
Discounts: week **Notes:** riverfront park; volleyball; basketball
★★★★ $$+* Map ref 29 A14

415 **Pottsville** South Holiday Park, Tweed Coast Rd, Pottsville (200m E of PO) Ph: 1800 234 121
Notes: DP & shop close; beachfront park; volleyball; basketball
★★★☆ $$$+* Map ref 29 A14

416 **Queanbeyan** Riverside Tourist Park, Morrisett St, Queanbeyan (200m E of PO) Ph: 02 6297 4749
Notes: public ph & shop close; riverfront park; close to town centre
★★★ $$ Map ref 37 G7

417 **Rankin Springs** Caravan Park, Mid Western Hwy, Rankin Springs Ph: 02 6966 1346
Discounts: CMCA **Notes:** public ph & shop close; pleasant park, grassed sites
$ Map ref 33 E11

418 **Raymond Terrace**, Bellhaven Caravan Park, Old Pacific Hwy (2km S of PO) Ph: 02 4987 2423
Discounts: week **Notes:** public ph, shop & LPG refill close; convenient to highway
★★☆ $ Map ref 23 A6

419 **Sandy Hollow** Tourist Park, Golden Hwy, Sandy Hollow Ph: 02 6547 4575
Discounts: CMCA **Notes:** public ph close; motel units
★★★☆ $$ Map ref 27 C8

420 **Sawtell** Beach Caravan Park, Lyons Rd, Sawtell (200m S of PO) Ph: 02 6653 1379
Discounts: Top Tourist; week **Notes:** close to ocean & shops
★★★☆ $$$+* Map ref 29 G13

421 **Scone** Caravan Park, Kelly St (New England Hwy), Scone (1km N of PO) Ph: 02 6545 2024
Discounts: week **Notes:** few drive thru sites; some ensuite sites
★★★ $$ Map ref 27 C9

422 **Scone**, Lake Glenbawn State Park, Glenbawn Rd, Scone (14km SE of Scone) Ph: 02 6543 7193
Discounts: week **Notes:** dam water; fishing; boat ramp
$ Map ref 27 C9

423 **Scotts Head** Holiday Park, Short St, Scotts Head Ph: 02 6569 8122
Discounts: week (off-pk) **Notes:** shop & LPG refill close; beachfront park; fishing, swimming
★★★☆ $$$+* Map ref 29 H12

424 **Shellharbour** Beachside Tourist Park, John St, Shellharbour (1km S of PO) Ph: 02 4295 1123
Discounts: snr; week (off-pk) **Notes:** swimming pool, public ph, shop & internet access close; beachfront park; close to shops
★★★☆ $$+* Map ref 35 A7

425 **Shoalhaven Heads** Tourist Park, Shoalhaven Heads Rd, Shoalhaven Heads Ph: 1300 782 222
Discounts: pen; snr; week (off-pk) **Notes:** swimming pool, shop & LPG refill close; some ensuite sites; close to boat ramp
★★★★ $$$+* Map ref 35 C7

426 **Singleton** Caracourt Caravan Pk, Bridgman Rd & New England Hwy (1.5km NW of PO) Ph: 02 6572 2886
Discounts: week **Notes:** some ensuite sites; close to town & vineyards
★★★☆ $+ Map ref 23 A1

427 **South Durras** Holiday Park, Beagle Bay Rd (16km N of Batemans Bay) Ph: 1800 558 718
Discounts: BIG4; auto club **Notes:** few long vehicle sites; bore water
★★★★ $$+* Map ref 35 F5

428 **South West Rocks** Tourist Park, Gordon Young Dr, South West Rocks Ph: 1800 666 264
Discounts: Top Tourist **Notes:** waterfront park; some ensuite sites
★★★★ $$$+* Map ref 29 J13

429 **Stuarts Point** Holiday Park, Marine Pde, Stuarts Point (500m from PO) Ph: 1800 006 600
Discounts: pen/snr; winter **Notes:** riverfront sites available; walk to shops
★★★☆ $$+* Map ref 29 H13

430 **Sussex Inlet**, Riverside Caravan Park, Sussex Rd, Sussex Inlet (2km S of PO) Ph: 02 4441 2163
Discounts: snr/pen for wk off-pk **Notes:** riverfront; moorings & boat storage avail
★★★ $$+* Map ref 34 D6

431 **Sutton**, Capital Country Holiday Village, Bridges Rd, Sutton Ph: 02 6230 3433
Discounts: Family Parks **Notes:** bore water; 14km NE Canberra
★★★☆ $$$ Map ref 38 A6

432 **Sutton**, Eaglehawk Holiday Park, Federal Hwy, Sutton Ph: 02 6241 6411
Discounts: auto clubs **Notes:** some ensuite sites; tennis court
★★★★ $$$+* Map ref 38 A6

433 **Swansea** Gardens Lakeside Holiday Park, Wallarah St, Swansea (2km W of PO) Ph: 02 4971 2869
Discounts: snr (off-pk only) **Notes:** boat ramp; tennis
★★★☆ $$+ Map ref 23 E6

434 **Sydney, Dural**, Sydney-Hills Holiday Park, New Line Rd (35km N of Sydney) Ph: 1300 135 296
Discounts: Top Tourist; snr; week off-pk **Notes:** some ensuite sites; tennis court
★★★★☆ $$$$+* Map ref 22 B2

435 **Sydney, Narrabeen**, Sydney Lakeside Holiday Park, off Pittwater Rd (26km N) Ph: 1800 008 845
Discounts: BIG4; CMCA; snr **Notes:** swimming pool & shop close; on lake, close to beach; some ensuite sites
★★★★☆ $$$$$$+ Map ref 22 B7

436 **Sydney, North Ryde**, Lane Cove River Tourist Park, Plassey Rd (10km NW) Ph: 1300 729 133
Discounts: CMCA; snr; week **Notes:** lovely bush setting
★★★☆ $$$$$ Map ref 22 E5

437 **Sydney, Parklea**, Sydney Gateway Holiday Park, Majestic Dr (38km NW) Ph: 1800 080 117
Discounts: BIG4, auto clubs, services **Notes:** some ensuite sites; large spa
★★★★ $$$$+* Map ref 25 C9

438 **Sydney, Sans Souci**, Grand Pines Tourist Park Ramsgate Beach, Grand Parade Ph: 02 9529 7329
Notes: shop close; close to bay; no tents accepted
★★★☆ $$$$$+* Map ref 22 H5

439 **Tamworth**, City Lights Caravan Park, New England Hwy, Tamworth (6km S of PO) Ph: 02 6765 7664
Notes: surcharge during Music Festival
★★★☆ $$+ Map ref 28 J7

440 **Tamworth** North Holiday Park, New England Hwy & Somerset Pl (6km E of PO) Ph: 02 6760 9356
Discounts: CMCA; snr **Notes:** quiet park; close to town
★★★ $$+ Map ref 28 J7

441 **Tamworth**, Paradise Tourist Park, Peel St, Tamworth (1km S of PO) Ph: 02 6766 3120
Discounts: BIG4; week **Notes:** riverfront; closest park to town; some ensuites
★★★☆ $$$+* Map ref 28 J7

442 **Tamworth area, Lake Keepit** State Park, Lake Keepit Rd (57km NW Tamworth) Ph: 02 6769 7605
Discounts: 2nd night **Notes:** few drive thru sites; LPG swap only; treated water; boat ramp
★★★☆ $+* Map ref 28 H7

443 **Taree**, Dawson River Tourist Park, Manning River Dr, Taree (5km N of PO) Ph: 02 6553 9237
Notes: LPG swap only; riverfront; 3km off hwy; boat ramp
★★★☆ $$+ Map ref 27 B13

444 **Tathra**, Countryside Caravan Park, Old Wallagoot Rd, Kalaru (5km W of PO) Ph: 02 6494 1417
Discounts: Family Parks; CMCA; snr; week **Notes:** dogs permitted; some ensuite sites; takeaways; playground
★★★☆ $$+ Map ref 34 H5

445 **Tathra**, Seabreeze Holiday Park, Andy Poole Dr, Tathra (1km N of PO) Ph: 1800 614 444
Discounts: BIG4; week **Notes:** shop close; close to beach; some ensuite sites
★★★★☆ $$$+* Map ref 34 H5

446 **Tenterfield**, Craigs Caravan Park, Rouse St (New England Hwy) (800m S of PO) Ph: 02 6736 1585
Discounts: week **Notes:** shop close; spacious sites with shade
★★★ $ Map ref 29 C10

447 **The Entrance**, Dunleith Tourist Park, Hutton Rd (100m SE of N end of bridge) Ph: 1300 133 60
Discounts: Top Tourist **Notes:** few long vehicle sites; waterfront park; boat ramp
★★★☆ $$$$+* Map ref 23 G7

448 **The Entrance**, Two Shores Holiday Village, Wilfred Barrett Dr (3km N of PO) Ph: 1300 653 602
Discounts: Family Parks; week (off-pk) **Notes:** public ph close; lakefront park; close to fishing area
★★★ $$$+* Map ref 23 G7

449 **The Entrance area, Toowoon Bay** Holiday Park, Koongara St (1km S of PO) Ph: 1800 241 342
Discounts: week (off-pk) **Notes:** waterfront park; fishing
★★★☆ $$+* Map ref 23 H6

450 **Tocumwal**, Boomerang Way Tourist Park, Murray St (500m N of info centre) Ph: 1800 888 987
Discounts: Top Tourist; week (off-pk) **Notes:** some ensuite sites
★★★☆ $$$+* Map ref 33 J10

451 **Tomakin** River Tourist Park, Sunpatch Pde, Tomakin (12km SE of Batemans Bay) Ph: 02 4771 7235
Discounts: week **Notes:** shop close; riverfront park; 1km from beach
★★★ $$+ Map ref 34 F6

452 **Tooleybuc** Caravan Park, Murray St, Tooleybuc (50m N of PO) Ph: 03 5030 5025
Notes: public ph & shop close; walk to clubs
★★★☆ $$ Map ref 32 H6

453 **Toronto**, Paradise Palms Carey Bay, Ambrose St, Carey Bay (1.6km SE Toronto PO) Ph: 02 4959 1271
Notes: public ph, shop & LPG refill close; waterfront park; boat ramp & jetty
★★★ $$$+ Map ref 23 D6

454 **Toukley**, Canton Beach Holiday Park, Oleander St, Canton Beach (3km S of PO) Ph: 1800 241 342
Notes: located on Tuggerah Lake
★★★☆ $+ Map ref 23 F6

455 **Trangie**, Tandara Caravan Park, John St, Trangie (1km S of PO) Ph: 02 6888 7330
Discounts: CMCA; snr; 3rd night **Notes:** LPG swap only; shady sites
$ Map ref 26 B2

456 **Tumbarumba** Creek Caravan Park, Lauder St (behind showgrounds) Ph: 02 6948 3330
Discounts: week **Notes:** swimming pool, public ph & shop close; close to shops
★★★☆ $$ Map ref 34 E1

457 **Tumut**, Riverglade Caravan Park, Snowy Mountains Hwy, Tumut (1km N of PO) Ph: 02 6947 2528
Discounts: Family Parks **Notes:** shop close; riverfront park; some ensuite sites
★★★☆ $$+ Map ref 34 D1

458 **Tuncurry** Beach Caravan Park, Beach St, Tuncurry (800m E of PO) Ph: 1800 227 275
Discounts: snr (not school hols) **Notes:** public ph close; adjacent to beach & rock pool; close to shops
★★★★ $$+* Map ref 27 C13

459 **Tuncurry**, Wallamba River Holiday Park, Aquatic Rd, N Tuncurry Ph: 02 6554 3123
Discounts: Top Tourist; CMCA; snr **Notes:** riverfront park; fishing, water skiing
★★★☆ $+* Map ref 27 C13

460 **Tuross Head**, Tuross Lakeside Tourist Park, Hector McWilliam Dr (2km S of PO) Ph: 02 4473 8181
Discounts: 3rd night (off-pk) **Notes:** few drive thru sites; long vehicle to 9m; internet access soon; lakefront park; boat ramp
★★★☆ $$+* Map ref 35 H5

461 **Tweed Heads**, Boyds Bay Holiday Park, Dry Dock Rd, Tweed Heads Ph: 07 5524 3306
Discounts: week **Notes:** riverfront park; some ensuite sites
★★★★ $$$+* Map ref 29 A14

462 **Tweed Heads**, Pyramid Holiday Park, Kennedy Dr, Tweed Hds (3km NW of PO) Ph: 07 5536 3666
Discounts: Family Parks; week **Notes:** some ensuite sites
★★★★☆ $$$$+* Map ref 29 A14

463 **Tweed Heads**, Tweed Billabong Holiday Park, Holden St, Tweed Heads South Ph: 07 5524 2444
Discounts: BIG4 **Notes:** some ensuite sites
★★★★☆ $$$$+* Map ref 29 A14

464 **Ulladulla**, Beach Haven Holiday Resort, Princes Hwy, Ulladulla (2km S of PO) Ph: 02 4455 2110
Discounts: snr **Notes:** shop close; beachfront; playground; jumping pillow; sauna; spa
★★★★ $$$+* Map ref 35 E6

465 **Ulladulla** Headland Tourist Park, South St, Ulladulla (1km E of PO) Ph: 1300 733 021
Discounts: pen; snr; 4th night **Notes:** public ph & LPG refill close; some ensuite sites
★★★★ $$$+* Map ref 35 E6

466 **Ulladulla area, Burrill Lake** Tourist Park, Princess Ave (4km S of Ulladulla PO) Ph: 1300 555 525
Discounts: pen (off-pk) **Notes:** public ph & LPG refill close; lakefront park; beach access; playground
★★★☆ $$$+ Map ref 34 E7

467 **Umina**, Ocean Beach Holiday Park, Sydney Ave, Umina (86km N of Sydney) Ph: 1800 611 522
Discounts: BIG4; auto clubs; services **Notes:** long vehicle to 7m; public ph close; LPG swap only; beachfront; ensuites; spa, waterslides & playground
★★★★ $$$$+* Map ref 23 K5

468 **Uralla**, Country Road Caravan Park, New England Hwy, Uralla (1.5km S of PO) Ph: 02 6778 4563
Discounts: Family Parks **Notes:** some ensuite sites
★★★☆ $$ Map ref 29 H9

469 **Urana** Caravan Park & Aquatic Centre, Corowa Rd, Urana (1.5km S of PO) Ph: 02 6920 8192
Discounts: economical; pen **Notes:** dogs permitted; lakefront park; birdwatching; boat ramp
★★★ $ Map ref 33 H11

470 **Urunga** Heads Holiday Park, Morgo St, Urunga Ph: 1800 638 039
Discounts: Top Tourist; week (off-pk) **Notes:** public ph & shop close; lakefront park; walk to shops & restaurants
★★★☆ $$$+ Map ref 29 G13

471 **Wagga Wagga** Beach Caravan Park, Johnston St, Wagga Wagga (500m from PO) Ph: 02 6931 0603
Notes: river; beachfront
★★★☆ $$ Map ref 33 H13

472 **Wagga Wagga**, Horseshoe Motor Village Caravan Pk, Horseshoe Rd (5km N PO) Ph: 02 6921 6033
Discounts: Family Parks **Notes:** 200m off Olympic Hwy; some ensuites; playground
★★★☆ $$$+ Map ref 33 H13

473 **Walcha** Caravan Park, Middle St, Walcha (1km N E of PO) Ph: 02 6777 2501
Discounts: week **Notes:** shop close; heated floors in amenities
★★★★ $$ Map ref 29 J9

474 **Wallaga Lake**, Ocean Lake Caravan Park, Wallago Lake Rd (7km N of Bermagui) Ph: 02 6493 4055
Discounts: week (off-pk) **Notes:** lakefront park; boat ramp; petrol; playground
★★★☆ $$+* Map ref 34 G6

475 **Wallaga Lake** Park, Wallaga Lake Rd, Wallaga Lake (7km N of Bermagui) Ph: 02 6493 4655
Discounts: week (off-pk) **Notes:** long vehicle to 7m; LPG swap only; jumping pillow; tennis
★★★ $$$+ Map ref 34 G6

476 **Warialda** Caravan Park, Cnr Gwydir Hwy & Holden St, Warialda (1km W of PO) Ph: 02 6729 3000
Discounts: pen; week **Notes:** swimming pool & public ph close; walk to town
★★☆ $ Map ref 28 D7

477 **Warren**, Macquarie Caravan Park, Hospital Rd, Warren (1km N of PO) Ph: 02 6847 4706
Discounts: CMCA; week **Notes:** shop close; shady grassed sites; playground
★★★☆ $ Map ref 26 A2

478 **Wellington** Caves Caravan Park, Caves Rd, Wellington (6km S of PO) Ph: 02 6845 2970
Discounts: Family Parks **Notes:** adjacent to caves
★★★ $$* Map ref 26 D4

479 **Wentworth**, Willow Bend Caravan Park, Darling St, Wentworth (200m from PO) Ph: 03 5027 3213
Discounts: CMCA; auto club **Notes:** shop close; riverfront park; walk to shops & clubs
★★★ $ Map ref 32 F3

480 **West Wyalong**, Ace Caravan Park, Newell Hwy, West Wyalong (500 W of PO) Ph: 02 6972 3061
Discounts: Family Parks; week **Notes:** shady sites; close town centre
★★★☆ $$ Map ref 33 E13

481 **West Wyalong** Caravan Park, Main St, West Wyalong (turn at BP service station) Ph: 02 6972 3133
Discounts: CMCA; week **Notes:** close to shops & clubs
★★★☆ $$ Map ref 33 E13

482 **White Cliffs**, Opal Pioneer Tourist Park, Johnston St (200m N of PO) Ph: 08 8091 6688
Discounts: week **Notes:** basic facilities; 1 cabin, BYO bed linen
★★☆ $ Map ref 30 G5

483 **Windeyer**, Bushlands Tourist Park, Mudgee St, Windeyer Ph: 02 6373 8252
Discounts: week **Notes:** next to hotel; playground
★★★☆ $ Map ref 26 E5

484 **Wollongong**, Bulli Beach Tourist Park, Farrell Rd, Bulli Beach (1.2km E of PO) Ph: 02 4285 5677
Discounts: CMCA; snr & wk off-pk **Notes:** adjoins patrolled beach
★★★★ $$+* Map ref 25 J11

485 **Wollongong**, Corrimal Beach Tourist Park, Lake Pde, Corrimal (800m SW of PO) Ph: 02 4285 5688
Discounts: CMCA; snr & wk off-pk **Notes:** fronts patrolled beach
★★★☆ $$+* Map ref 25 K11

486 **Wollongong**, Windang Beach Tourist Park, Fern St, Windang (500m NE of bridge) Ph: 02 4297 3166
Discounts: CMCA; snr & wk off-pk **Notes:** adjoins Lake Illawarra
★★★☆ $$+* Map ref 35 A7

487 **Wombeyan Caves** Caravan/Camping Res, Wombeyan Caves Rd (32km NE of Taralga) Ph: 02 4843 5976
Notes: long vehicle to 9m; no mobile phone service; playground; swimming
★★★ $$$ Map ref 26 J6

488 **Woolgoolga** Beach Caravan Park, Beach St, Woolgoolga (50m from PO) Ph: 02 6654 1373
Discounts: week **Notes:** shop close; beachfront park; no unpowered sites
★★★ $$+* Map ref 29 F14

489 **Woolgoolga**, Lakeside Caravan Park, Lake Rd, Woolgoolga Ph: 02 6654 1210
Discounts: week **Notes:** park is beachfront & lakefront
$$+* Map ref 29 F14

490 **Wyangala Dam**, Wyangala Waters State Park, (40km E of Cowra) Ph: 02 6345 0877
Discounts: week **Notes:** walking trails; waterslide
★★★ $ Map ref 26 H4

491 **Yamba**, Blue Dolphin Holiday Resort, Yamba Rd, Yamba (2.2km W of PO) Ph: 02 6646 2194
Notes: long vehicle to 8m; riverfront; some ensuites; boat ramp & fishing
★★★★☆ $$$+* Map ref 29 D14

492 **Yamba**, Calypso Holiday Park Yamba, Harbour St, Yamba Ph: 02 6646 8847
Discounts: snr; week **Notes:** few long vehicle sites; shop close; riverfront park; close to town & beach
★★★☆ $$$+* Map ref 29 D14

493 **Yamba** Waters Holiday Park, Golding St, Yamba (2.5km W of PO) Ph: 02 6646 2930
Discounts: BIG4 **Notes:** long vehicle to 10m; LPG swap only; surrounded by lagoon; close to river; ensuites
★★★★ $$$$+* Map ref 29 D14

494 **Yass** Caravan Park, Cnr Old Hume Hwy & Grampian St, Yass Ph: 02 6226 1173
Discounts: week **Notes:** swimming pool & public ph close; close to town centre
★★★ $$ Map ref 34 C3

495 **Young** Tourist Park, Zouch St, Young (650m N of PO, on Olympic Hwy) Ph: 02 6382 2190
Discounts: 3rd night **Notes:** some ensuite sites
★★★★ $$ Map ref 34 A1

Australian Capital Territory

Refer also to New South Wales parks in Queanbeyan and Sutton

496 **Canberra** Carotel Motel & Caravan Park, Federal Hwy (7km N of Canberra CBD) Ph: 02 6241 1377
Notes: 22 acre park
★★☆ $$$+ Map ref 37 C5

497 **Canberra** Motor Village, Kunzea St, (3km W of Canberra visitor centre) Ph: 02 6247 5466
Notes: long vehicle to 8m; tennis & playground
★★★☆ $$$+* Map ref 37 D4

498 **Canberra** South Motor Park, Canberra Ave, Symonston (5km S of Parliament House) Ph: 02 6280 6176
Notes: spacious; convenient location
★★★☆ $$$+ Map ref 37 F6

Victoria

499 **Alexandra** Tourist Park, Maroondah Hwy, Alexandra (1km W of PO) Ph: 03 5772 1222
Notes: long vehicle to 12m; swimming pool & internet access close; grassed sites; adventure playground
★★★☆ $$$+* Map ref 48 G5

500 **Anglesea** Beachfront Family Caravan Park, Cameron Rd (800m SE of PO) Ph: 03 5263 1583
Discounts: Top Tourist **Notes:** beach & riverfront; no unpowered sites
★★★★☆ $$$+* Map ref 42 K2

501 **Apollo Bay**, Pisces Holiday Park, Great Ocean Rd (1.4km NE of PO) Ph: 03 5237 6749
Discounts: week **Notes:** opposite beach; some ensuites; TV/games room
★★★★ $$$+* Map ref 45 K10

502 **Apollo Bay** Recreation Res Caravan & Camping Park, Great Ocean Rd (1.1km S PO) Ph: 03 5237 6577
Discounts: snr; pen; week **Notes:** close to surf beach, town & golf course
★★ $$+* Map ref 45 K10

503 **Ararat**, Pyrenees Caravan Park, Pyrenees Hwy, Ararat (2km NE of PO) Ph: 03 5352 1309
Discounts: CMCA **Notes:** bush setting; some ensuite sites
★★★☆ $$ Map ref 44 D7

504 **Avoca** Caravan Park, Liebig St, Avoca (1.2km W of PO) Ph: 03 5465 3073
Discounts: CMCA; pen/snr **Notes:** long vehicle to 10m; quiet park beside golf club
★★☆ $ Map ref 45 C9

505 **Bacchus Marsh** Caravan Park, Main St (800m W of Main St roundabout) Ph: 03 5367 2775
Discounts: Family Parks **Notes:** swimming pool, public ph & shop close; playground
★★★☆ $$$ Map ref 42 B3

506 **Bairnsdale** Holiday Park, Princes Hwy, Bairnsdale East (1.2km E of Mitchell River) Ph: 03 5152 4066
Discounts: BIG4 **Notes:** long vehicle to 10m; LPG swap only; some ensuites; tennnis; mini golf; playground
★★★★☆ $$$+* Map ref 49 K11

507 **Bairnsdale**, Mitchell Gardens Caravan Park, Princes Hwy (600m E of PO) Ph: 03 5152 4654
Discounts: Oz Parks; CMCA; week **Notes:** riverfront park; lawns; walk to town
★★★ $$+* Map ref 49 K11

508 **Ballarat**, Eureka Stockade Caravan Park, Stawell St, Ballarat (3.1km E of PO) Ph: 03 5331 2281
Discounts: Family Parks; snr **Notes:** LPG swap only; ensuites; playground; waterslide (summer)
★★★☆ $$$* Map ref 45 E10

509 **Ballarat** Goldfields Holiday Park, Clayton St, Golden Point Ph: 1800 632 237
Discounts: BIG4 **Notes:** shop close; 300m Sovereign Hill; some ensuite sites
$$$$+* Map ref 45 E10

510 **Ballarat,** Shady Acres Accommodation Caravan Park, Western Hwy (5km E of PO) Ph: 03 5334 7233
Discounts: CMCA **Notes:** shop close; some ensuite sites; bush setting
$$ Map ref 45 E11

511 **Ballarat area, Lake Burrumbeet** Caravan Park, Western Hwy (15km NW Ballarat) Ph: 03 5344 0583
Discounts: Oz Parks; CMCA **Notes:** shady grassed sites
★★★ $ Map ref 45 E10

512 **Barwon Heads** Caravan Park, Ewing Blyth Dr, Barwon Heads (200m S of PO) Ph: 03 5254 1115
Notes: shop, LPG refill & internet access close; park is river & ocean front; close to town
★★★★ $$$+* Map ref 42 H4

513 **Beaufort** Lake Caravan Park, Park Rd (Skipton Rd), Beaufort (800m S of PO) Ph: 03 5349 2196
Discounts: week (off-pk) **Notes:** some ensuites; tennis; boat ramp; playground
★★★ $ Map ref 45 E9

514 **Beechworth** Silver Creek Caravan Park, Stanley Rd (2.3km SE of PO) Ph: 03 5728 1597
Notes: easy access to walks
★★★☆ $+* Map ref 49 C8

515 **Benalla** Leisure Park, Benalla-Winton Rd, Benalla (2.7km N E of PO) Ph: 1800 888 548
Discounts: Top Tourist; week **Notes:** some ensuite sites; spacious; rec room
★★★☆ $$$ Map ref 48 D5

516 **Bendigo**, Central City Caravan Park, Calder Hwy, Bendigo (2.5km S of PO) Ph: 1800 500 475
Discounts: snr **Notes:** LPG swap only; close to public transport
★★★★ $$$+* Map ref 45 B12

517 **Bendigo**, Gold Nugget Tourist Park, Midland Hwy, Epsom (8.1km N of Bendigo) Ph: 1800 637 176
Discounts: Top Tourist **Notes:** some ensuite sites; mini golf; games room
★★★★☆ $$$+* Map ref 45 A12

518 **Bendigo area, Marong** Caravan & Cabin Village, Calder Hwy, Marong (15.5km NW) Ph: 1800 642 329
Discounts: Family Parks; CMCA; week **Notes:** some ensuite sites
★★★☆ $$+ Map ref 45 B11

519 **Blackwood** Mineral Springs Caravan Park, Golden Point Rd (1km E of PO) Ph: 03 5368 6539
Discounts: snr **Notes:** dogs permitted; lovely walks; accomm is onsite vans
★★★ $$ Map ref 45 E12

520 **Bonnie Doon**'s Lakeside Leisure Resort, Hutchinsons Rd (3km S of bridge) Ph: 1800 266 643
Notes: LPG swap only; boat ramp; petrol
★★★☆ $$+* Map ref 48 F5

521 **Boort** Lakes Caravan Park, Durham Ox Rd, Boort (1km E of PO) Ph: 03 5455 2064
Notes: shop close; grassed lakefront park
★★★ $ Map ref 47 J10

522 **Boundary Bend**, Murray River Caravan Park, Murray Valley Hwy (270m W of PO) Ph: 03 5026 8201
Notes: on bend of river; rain water
$+ Map ref 47 C8

523 **Bridgewater** Public Caravan Park, Park St, Bridgewater (800m SW of PO) Ph: 03 5437 3086
Discounts: pen **Notes:** shop close; boat ramp; near water-ski club
★★★ $+ Map ref 45 A11

524 **Bright** Caravan Park, Cherry Ave, Bright (900m E of PO) Ph: 03 5755 1141
Discounts: week (off-pk) 10% **Notes:** long vehicle to 9m; shop close; playground; close to town
★★★★ $$$+* Map ref 49 E9

525 **Bright** Riverside Holiday Park, Toorak Ave, Bright (400m N of PO) Ph: 03 5755 1118
Discounts: Family Parks; week **Notes:** long vehicle to 8m; LPG swap only; riverfront park; shade, playground
★★★★ $$$+* Map ref 49 E9

526 **Bright**, Freeburgh Cabins & Caravan Park, Great Alpine Rd (9.7km SE of Bright) Ph: 03 5750 1306
Discounts: snr **Notes:** riverfront; tennis; playground; bore water
★★★★ $+ Map ref 49 E9

527 **Bright area Wandiligong** Holiday Village, School Rd (6km S of Bright PO) Ph: 03 5755 1848
Discounts: CMCA; pen **Notes:** bush setting; spring water
$$ Map ref 49 E9

528 **Buchan** Caves Reserve, Caves Rd, Buchan (300m W of PO) Ph: 03 5162 1900
Notes: few long vehicle sites; shop close; adjacent to caves
★★★ $+ Map ref 51 C8

529 **Camperdown**, Lakes & Craters Holiday Park, Park Rd (3.4km from PO) Ph: 03 5593 1253
Discounts: week **Notes:** overlooking lake
★★☆ $$ Map ref 45 H9

530 **Cape Otway**, Bimbi Park, Manna Gum Dr, Cape Otway Ph: 03 5237 9246
Discounts: Family Parks **Notes:** spring water; 2km to beach
★★★ $$+* Map ref 45 K9

531 **Castlemaine** Gardens Caravan Park, Doran Ave, Castlemaine (1.5km N of PO) Ph: 03 5472 1125
Discounts: pen; snr **Notes:** swimming pool & shop close; next to botanic gardens
★★★☆ $$* Map ref 45 C11

532 **Chiltern**, Lake Anderson Caravan Park, Alliance St, Chiltern (500m E of PO) Ph: 03 5726 1298
Notes: long vehicle to 10m; shop close; lakefront park; birdwatching
★★★☆ $$ Map ref 49 B8

533 **Cobram** Oasis Tourist Park, Cnr Koonoomoo & Racecourse Rds (1.7km W of PO) Ph: 03 5871 2010
Discounts: week **Notes:** some ensuite sites; tennis; golf driving range
★★★★ $$$+* Map ref 48 A5

534 **Cobram**, RACV Cobram Resort, Campbell Rd, Cobram (2km E of PO) Ph: 03 5872 2467
Discounts: auto club members 20% **Notes:** some ensuite sites; recreation facilities
★★★★☆ $$$$+* Map ref 48 A5

535 **Cohuna** Waterfront Holiday Park, Island Rd (1km N of PO on Gunbower Is) Ph: 03 5456 2562
Notes: riverfront park; boat ramp
★★★★ $$+* Map ref 47 H12

536 **Colac** Caravan & Cabin Park, Princes Hwy, Colac (2.5km W of high school) Ph: 03 5231 5337
Discounts: week **Notes:** spacious; peaceful rural setting
★★★☆ $ Map ref 45 H10

537 **Corryong**, Colac Colac (Clack Clack) Caravan Park, Murray Valley Hwy (7km S of PO) Ph: 02 6076 1520
Discounts: Family Parks; CMCA **Notes:** riverfront park; food & alcohol; river water
★★★☆ $$$+* Map ref 49 C12

538 **Creswick** Calembeen Lake Caravan Park, Cushing Ave (900m NW of PO) Ph: 03 5345 2411
Discounts: CMCA; pen; snr **Notes:** swimming pool & shop close; lakefront park; playground
★★★☆ $$+ Map ref 45 D10

539 **Daylesford**, Jubilee Lake Caravan Park, Lake Rd, Daylesford (3km SE of PO) Ph: 03 5348 2186
Notes: lakefront park; canoe hire
★★★ $$+* Map ref 45 D11

540 **Dimboola** Caravan Park, Wimmera St, Dimboola (200m S of PO) Ph: 03 5389 1416
Discounts: Family Parks; week **Notes:** public ph & shop close; some ensuite sites
★★★ $$ Map ref 44 A4

541 **Dromana**, Kangerong Holiday Park, Point Nepean Rd, Dromana (1km E of PO) Ph: 1800 670 859
Discounts: BIG4 **Notes:** long vehicle to 6m; shop close; opposite beach; no unpowered sites
★★★★ $$$+* Map ref 42 J7

542 **Drouin**, El Paso Caravan Park, Princes Way, Drouin (2.3km W of PO) Ph: 03 5625 1710
Discounts: week **Notes:** shady sites
★★★☆ $ Map ref 43 G14

543 **Eagle Point** Caravan Park, Camp Park Rd, Eagle Point (12km S of Bairnsdale) Ph: 03 5156 6232
Notes: public ph close; cats permitted; close lake; licensed kiosk
★★★★ $+* Map ref 50 E6

544 **Echuca** Caravan Park, Crofton St, Echuca (1km NW of PO) Ph: 03 5482 2157
Discounts: Top Tourist; week (off-pk) **Notes:** LPG swap only; close to historic port
★★★★ $$+* Map ref 48 B1

545 **Echuca**, Yarraby Holiday & Tourist Park, River Ave (4km E of water tower) Ph: 1800 222 052
Discounts: Top Tourist; CMCA; snr **Notes:** LPG swap only; riverfront park; mini golf; some ensuite sites
★★★★☆ $$$$+* Map ref 48 B1

546 **Edenhope** Lakeside Tourist Park, Lake St, Edenhope (100m N of PO) Ph: 03 5585 1659
Discounts: week **Notes:** swimming pool close; lakefront park; close to lawn bowls
★★★★ $$ Map ref 44 C2

547 **Eildon**, Blue Gums Caravan Park, Back Eildon Rd, Eildon (5km W of PO) Ph: 03 5774 2567
Discounts: snr/pen (off-pk) **Notes:** few drive thru & long vehicle sites; riverfront park; river water
★★★☆ $$+* Map ref 48 G5

548 **Eldorado**, Gemstone Caravan Park, Main St, Eldorado (300m E of PO) Ph: 03 5725 1745
Discounts: week **Notes:** public ph, shop & LPG refill close; bush-type park; playground
★★★ $* Map ref 48 C7

549 **Eppalock**, Moorabbee Lodge Caravan Park, off McIvor Hwy (11km NW of Heathcote) Ph: 03 5439 1231
Discounts: Family Parks; closed June-Aug 1 **Notes:** LPG swap only; lakefront, bush setting; playground
★★☆ $$ Map ref 45 B13

550 **Euroa** Caravan & Tourist Park, Kirkland Avenue, Euroa (1km E of PO) Ph: 03 5795 2160
Discounts: Family Parks; week **Notes:** parkland setting; walk town
★★★☆ $$ Map ref 48 E4

551 **Everton** Gardens Caravan Village, Great Alpine Rd (22km SE of Wangaratta) Ph: 03 5727 0365
Discounts: week **Notes:** some ensuites; tennis; on bike & rail trails
★★★ $$ Map ref 48 D7

552 **Flinders** Caravan Park, The Avenue, Flinders (1km NE of PO) Ph: 03 5989 0458
Discounts: pen & week (off-pk) **Notes:** tennis; playground; recreation room; boat park
★★★ $$$+ Map ref 43 K8

553 **Foster**, Prom Central Caravan Park, Nelson St, Foster (500m E of PO) Ph: 03 5682 2440
Discounts: Family Parks; CMCA; auto clubs **Notes:** few drive thru sites; good base to visit nat parks
★★★☆ $$+ Map ref 52 G7

554 **Geelong**, Barwon Caravan & Tourist Park, Barrabool Rd, Belmont Ph: 1800 657 955
Discounts: Top Tourist **Notes:** some ensuites, no unpowered; close to shops
★★★★ $$$+ Map ref 42 G3

555 **Geelong**, Riverglen Holiday Park, Barrabool Rd, Belmont (800m W of bridge) Ph: 03 5243 5505
Discounts: Family Parks; week **Notes:** some ensuite sites, no unpowered
★★★★ $$+ Map ref 42 G3

556 **Geelong**, BIG4 Geelong Riverview Tourist Pk, Barrabool Rd (1km W Barwon River bridge) Ph: 1800 336 225
Discounts: BIG4; snr **Notes:** public ph close; riverfront; grassed sites; some ensuite sites
★★★★☆ $$+* Map ref 42 G3

557 **Geelong** Surf Coast Hwy Holiday Park, Torquay Rd, Mt Duneed (10km S Geelong) Ph: 03 5264 1243
Discounts: Family Parks; week **Notes:** all sites ensuite with power
★★★☆ $$+* Map ref 42 H3

558 **Gellibrand**, Otways Tourist Park, Main Rd, Gellibrand (200m S of PO) Ph: 03 5235 8357
Discounts: week/pen/snr (off-pk) **Notes:** LPG swap only; playground; recreation room; walk/bike trail
★★★★ $$$+* Map ref 45 J10

559 **Glenrowan** Warby Range Tourist Park, Old Hume Hwy Glenrowan (2.2km N of PO) Ph: 03 5766 2288
Discounts: week **Notes:** playground; 36 acres with walk tracks; wildlife
★★ $ Map ref 48 D6

560 **Goughs Bay** Caravan Park, Bayside Blvd, Goughs Bay (900m S of PO) Ph: 03 5777 3572
Discounts: CMCA; pen; snr **Notes:** few drive thru sites; takeaways; lake water; boat ramp
★★★☆ $* Map ref 48 G6

561 **Grantville**, French View Caravan Park, Pier Rd, Grantville (100m W of PO) Ph: 03 5678 8232
Notes: close to shops; next to boat ramp & jetty
★★★ $+ Map ref 43 J11

562 **Gunbower** Caravan Park, Murray Valley Hwy, Gunbower (400m N of PO) Ph: 03 5487 1412
Discounts: CMCA; week **Notes:** shop close; playground
★★★ $+* Map ref 47 H12

563 **Halls Gap** Caravan Park, Grampians Rd, Halls Gap (100m S of PO) Ph: 03 5356 4251
Discounts: week **Notes:** shop close; tennis; close to shops
★★★☆ $$+* Map ref 44 C6

564 **Halls Gap**, Takaru Bush Resorts, Grampians (Lakeside) Tymna Dr (4km S of PO) Ph: 1800 100 478
Discounts: Top Tourist **Notes:** close to lake; playground
★★★☆ $$+* Map ref 44 C6

565 **Hamilton** Caravan Park, Shakespeare St, Hamilton (1.7km NW of PO) Ph: 03 5572 4235
Discounts: pen; week **Notes:** swimming pool close; walk to town; adjacent Aquatic Centre
★★★☆ $$ Map ref 44 F5

566 **Hamilton**, Lake Hamilton Motor Village & Caravan Park, Glenelg Hwy Ph: 03 5572 3855
Discounts: Top Tourist **Notes:** close to lake; all sites powered with ensuite
★★★★ $$$+* Map ref 44 F5

567 **Hastings**, Marina View Van Village, Salmon St, Hastings (1.3km S of PO) Ph: 03 5979 2322
Discounts: Family Parks **Notes:** few long vehicle sites; shop close; overlooking bay; no unpowered sites
★★★☆ $$+* Map ref 43 J9

568 **Healesville**, BIG4 Badger Creek Holiday Park, Don Rd (5km SE of PO) Ph: 03 5962 4328
Discounts: BIG4 **Notes:** long vehicle to 9m; LPG swap only; some ensuite sites; tennis; playgrounds
★★★★ $$$+* Map ref 43 B11

569 **Heathcote** Queen's Meadow Caravan Park, Barrack St (500m S of PO) Ph: 03 5433 2304
Discounts: week **Notes:** swimming pool & shop close; recreation room; playground
$ Map ref 45 B13

570 **Horsham** Caravan Park, Firebrace St, Horsham (1.1km S of PO) Ph: 1800 032 217
Discounts: CMCA; snr; week; auto club **Notes:** swimming pool close; close gardens & CBD; some ensuite sites
★★★☆ $$+ Map ref 44 B5

571 **Howqua** Valley Caravan Park, Mansfield-Jamieson Rd, Howqua Ph: 03 5777 3588
Discounts: week (off-pk) **Notes:** lake water; boat ramp; hire boats
★★★★ $$$$+* Map ref 48 G6

572 **Inverloch** Holiday Park, Cuttriss St, Inverloch (1km E of PO) Ph: 03 5674 1447
Discounts: BIG4 **Notes:** close to beach; some ensuites sites
★★★★ $$$$+* Map ref 52 G5

573 **Johnsonville**, Lealow Caravan Park, Punt Rd (W of Swan Reach) Ph: 03 5156 4237
Discounts: week **Notes:** shop close; some ensuite sites, no unpowered; 9 hole golf
$$ Map ref 50 D6

574 **Kennett River** Caravan Park, Great Ocean Rd, Kennett River Ph: 1300 664 417
Discounts: Top Tourist; week **Notes:** close to beach: river water
★★★☆ $$$+* Map ref 45 K11

575 **Kerang**, Ibis Caravan Park, Murray Valley Hwy, Kerang (3km S of PO) Ph: 03 5452 2232
Discounts: Oz Parks; CMCA **Notes:** LPG swap only; bird watching; rain water
★★★★ $ Map ref 47G10

576 **Kilcunda** Oceanview Holiday Retreat, Bass Hwy, Kilcunda (100m S of PO) Ph: 03 5678 7260
Discounts: pen **Notes:** shop close; oceanfront park; rec room
$$+* Map ref 52 G4

577 **Kilmore** Caravan Park, 110 Northern Hwy, Kilmore (400m N of PO) Ph: 03 5782 1508
Discounts: week **Notes:** shop close; close to town; playground
★★★ $$ Map ref 48 H2

578 **Koondrook** Caravan Park, Keene St, Koondrook (150m N of PO) Ph: 03 5453 2103
Discounts: week 10% **Notes:** swimming pool, public ph & shop close; some ensuite sites; playground; boat park
★★★☆ $$+* Map ref 47 G11

579	**Koroit**, Koroit-Tower Hill Caravan Park, High St, Koroit Ph: 03 5565 7926 **Discounts:** CMCA; pen/snr **Notes:** long vehicle to 15m; shop close; close to shops	$ Map ref 44 H6
580	**Korumburra** Tourist Park, Bourke St, Korumburra (1.2km N of PO) Ph: 03 5655 2326 **Discounts:** CMCA; pen; week **Notes:** few drive thru sites; LPG swap only; basketball; tennis; playground	★★★★ $$ Map ref 43 K13
581	**Kyabram** Caravan Park, Anderson St, Kyabram (1.2km E of PO) Ph: 03 5852 2153 **Discounts:** week **Notes:** few long vehicle sites; public ph & shop close; walk to town	★★★ $ Map ref 48 C2
582	**Kyabram,** Western Gums Caravan Park, McEwen Rd (1.8km W of PO) Ph: 03 5852 3310 **Discounts:** week **Notes:** every site has ensuite & free laundry	★★★☆ $$ Map ref 48 C2
583	**Laanecoorie** Lakeside Park, Brownbill Reserve Rd, Laanecoorie (adjacent to weir) Ph: 03 5435 7303 **Discounts:** Family Parks **Notes:** LPG refill only; lakefront park; boat ramp; rain water	★★★☆ $$+* Map ref 45 B10
584	**Lake Boga** Caravan Park, Murray Valley Hwy, Lake Boga Ph: 03 5037 2386 **Discounts:** week; pen **Notes:** public ph & shop close; lakefront park	$$+ Map ref 47 F9
585	**Lake Bolac** Caravan & Tourist Park, Frontage Rd, Lake Bolac (1.6km S of PO) Ph: 03 5350 2329 **Discounts:** pen **Notes:** lakefront park; boat park; playground	★★★ $$+ Map ref 44 F7
586	**Lake Charm**, Pelican Waters Tourist Park, Boat Ramp Rd (1km NE of PO) Ph: 03 5457 9318 **Discounts:** CMCA; pen/snr **Notes:** lakefront park	★★★☆ $$ Map ref 47 G10
587	**Lakes Entrance**, Eastern Beach Tourist Park, Eastern Beach Rd (2.9km E of PO) Ph: 03 5155 1581 **Discounts:** week **Notes:** some ensuite sites; no cabin accomm	★★★☆ $$$+ Map ref 50 E7
588	**Lakes Entrance**, Echo Beach Tourist Park, Roadknight St (400m E of footbridge) Ph: 03 5155 2238 **Discounts:** Family Parks **Notes:** public ph close; indoor spa; games room; playground	★★★★ $$$+* Map ref 50 E7
589	**Lakes Entrance** Tourist Park, Princes Hwy (2km E of traffic lights) Ph: 03 5155 1159 **Discounts:** Oz Parks; CMCA **Notes:** playground; heated pool; boat park	★★★★ $$+* Map ref 50 E7
590	**Lakes Entrance**, Waters Edge Holiday Park, Esplanade (300m E of footbridge) Ph: 1800 679 327 **Discounts:** BIG4 **Notes:** few drive thru sites; long vehicle to 10m; public ph close; no unpowered sites; close to lake	★★★★ $$$+* Map ref 50 E7
591	**Lake Tyers** Beachfront Holiday Retreat, Lake Tyers Beach Rd, Lake Tyers Ph: 03 5156 5582 **Discounts:** Family Parks; week (off-pk) **Notes:** oceanfront park, but steep walk to beach	★★★★ $$$+* Map ref 50 E7
592	**Lake Tyers** Camp and Caravan Park, Lake Tyers Beach Rd, Lake Tyers Ph: 03 5156 5530 **Discounts:** pen/snr; 4 night stay **Notes:** beachfront park; church owned	★★★ $$+ Map ref 50 E7
593	**Leongatha** Apex Caravan Park, Turner St, Leongatha (800m N of PO) Ph: 03 5662 2753 **Discounts:** week **Notes:** swimming pool close; close to town centre	★★★☆ $$ Map ref 43 K14
594	**Loch Sport**, 90 Mile Beach Holiday Retreat, 10 Seacombe Rd, Loch Sport Ph: 03 5146 0320 **Discounts:** pen (off-pk) **Notes:** unique 338 acre beachfront; wildlife	★★★ $$$+ Map ref 50 E6
595	**Lorne** Foreshore Reserves, Great Ocean Rd, Lorne (650m N of PO) Ph: 03 5289 1382 **Notes:** public ph close; across road from beach	★★★ $$+* Map ref 45 J11
596	**Macedon** Caravan Park, Cnr McBean Ave & Blackforest Dr (1.6km S of PO) Ph: 03 5426 1528 **Discounts:** Family Parks **Notes:** spacious park	★★★☆ $$ Map ref 45 D13
597	**Maldon** Caravan & Camping Park, Hospital St, Maldon (600m NW of PO) Ph: 03 5475 2344 **Discounts:** week **Notes:** one long vehicle site; swimming pool, public ph & shop close; close to town, rec room	★★★☆ $$* Map ref 45 C11
598	**Mallacoota** Foreshore Camp Park, Allan Dr, Mallacoota Ph: 03 5158 0300 **Discounts:** 4 weeks off-pk **Notes:** public ph close; waterfront park; no cabin accomm	★★★ $$+ Map ref 51 D13
599	**Mansfield**, High Country Holiday Park, Ultimo St, Mansfield (400m W of PO) Ph: 03 5775 2705 **Notes:** few drive thru sites; one long vehicle site; shop close; good base to visit Mt Buller	★★★☆ $$+* Map ref 48 F6
600	**Marlo** Caravan Park, Argyle Pde, Marlo (50m from PO) Ph: 03 5154 8226 **Discounts:** 4 nights (off-pk) **Notes:** shop close; no unpowered sites; 200m to boat ramp	$$+ Map ref 51 D9
601	**Marlo** Ocean View Caravan & Camping Park, Marine Pde, Marlo (800m E of PO) Ph: 03 5154 8268 **Discounts:** week **Notes:** public ph close; 13 acre site close to beach	★★★ $$+ Map ref 51 D9
602	**Maryborough** Caravan Park, Holyrood St, Maryborough (1km N of PO) Ph: 03 5460 4848 **Discounts:** CMCA; prospectors; week **Notes:** swimming pool & shop close; LPG swap only; gold prospecting area	★★★☆ $$ Map ref 45 C10
603	**Marysville** Caravan and Holiday Park, Buxton Rd, Marysville (300m N of PO) Ph: 03 5963 3443 **Discounts:** Family Parks **Notes:** close to town centre	★★★☆ $$$$+* Map ref 43 A13
604	**Melbourne, Braybrook,** Melbourne Ashley Gardens, Ashley St (150m S of hway) Ph: 1800 061 444 **Discounts:** BIG4; snr **Notes:** shop close; some ensuite sites; tennis; spa; playground	★★★★☆ $$$$+* Map ref 41 C2
605	**Melbourne, Carrum Downs,** Discovery Holiday Park, 1165 Frankston-Dandenong Rd Ph: 1800 337 045 **Discounts:** CMCA **Notes:** LPG swap only; close to beach	★★★☆ $$$ Map ref 41 J6
606	**Melbourne, Chelsea,** Discovery Holiday Parks, Broadway, Bonbeach (3km E of PO) Ph: 03 9772 2485 **Discounts:** CMCA; pensioner off-pk **Notes:** long vehicle to 7m; no unpowered sites; walk to train	★★★★ $$$+ Map ref 41 J6
607	**Melbourne, Coburg,** Melbourne BIG4 Holiday Park, 265 Elizabeth St (2km off hwy) Ph: 1800 802 678 **Discounts:** BIG4 **Notes:** one drive thru site; close to public transport; some ensuite sites	$$$$+* Map ref 41 B3
608	**Melbourne, Craigieburn,** Apollo Gardens Caravan Park, 290 Hume Hwy Ph: 1800 886 352 **Discounts:** Top Tourist; multi-night stay **Notes:** long vehicle to 10m; close to public transport; some ensuite sites	★★★★☆ $$$$+ Map ref 42 B7
609	**Melbourne, Doncaster East,** Discovery Holiday Parks,182 Heidelberg-Warrandyte Rd Ph: 03 9844 3637 **Discounts:** Family Parks; CMCA **Notes:** birds and wildlife; bus to city	★★★☆ $$$$+ Map ref 41 C6

610 **Melbourne, Frankston**, Discovery Holiday Parks, 1324 Frankston-Dandenong Rd Ph: 1800 701 661
Discounts: week **Notes:** centrally located park; some ensuite sites
$$$+* Map ref 41 K6

611 **Melbourne, Frankston** Holiday Village, Robinsons Rd (5km S of PO) Ph: 1800 623 491
Discounts: BIG4 **Notes:** some ensuites; recreation room; public transport
★★★★ $$$+* Map ref 43 G9

612 **Melbourne, Tullamarine**, Discovery Holiday Parks, Ardlie St (off Mickleham Rd) Ph: 1800 808 114
Discounts: CMCA; auto club **Notes:** long vehicle to 9m; close to shopping centre; no unpowered sites
★★★☆ $$$ Map ref 41 A2

613 **Merbein** Caravan Park, Box St, Merbein (1km N W of PO) Ph: 03 5025 2198
Notes: swimming pool close; near bowls club
★★★ $ Map ref 46 A5

614 **Mildura**, Apex River Beach Holiday Park, Chaffey Bend (4.4km W of PO) Ph: 03 5023 6879
Discounts: Family Parks; week **Notes:** beach (swimming); boat ramp
★★★☆ $$+ Map ref 46 A5

615 **Mildura**, Calder Tourist Park, Calder Hwy, Mildura (300m E of Plaza PO) Ph: 1800 231 310
Discounts: Top Tourist; pen **Notes:** long vehicle to 6m; public ph & shop close; no unpowered sites; pancakes on Sunday
★★★★☆ $$+* Map ref 46 A5

616 **Mildura**, Golden River Holiday Resort, Flora Ave, Mildura (4.5km NW of PO) Ph: 1800 621 262
Discounts: snr **Notes:** riverfront; some ensuites; playground; games/TV room
★★★★☆ $$$+ Map ref 46 A5

617 **Mildura**, Sunraysia Holiday Park, Cnr Sturt Hwy & Walnut Ave (8km SW of Mildura) Ph: 03 5023 1914
Discounts: very economical **Notes:** air-con backpackers accommodation
★★★☆ $+ Map ref 46 A5

618 **Moe** Gardens Caravan Park, Mitchells Rd, Moe (1.6km W of PO) Ph: 03 5127 3072
Discounts: CMCA **Notes:** close to town centre
★★★ $$ Map ref 50 F1

619 **Mooroopna**, Acacia Gardens Mooroopna Caravan Park, Midland Hwy (3km W of PO) Ph: 03 5825 2793
Discounts: week **Notes:** spacious sites
★★★ $ Map ref 48 C3

620 **Mornington** Gardens Holiday Village, Bungower Rd (1km E of highway) Ph: 03 5975 7373
Discounts: winter discount **Notes:** long vehicle to 8m; some ensuite sites
★★★★ $$$ Map ref 42 H7

621 **Mt Beauty** Holiday Centre, Kiewa Valley Hwy, Tawonga Sth (800m NW of PO) Ph: 03 5754 4396
Discounts: CMCA; week **Notes:** spa; shop close; riverfront park; mini golf; tennis
★★★☆ $+* Map ref 49 E9

622 **Myrtleford**, Arderns Caravan Park, Willow Grove, Myrtleford (1km E of PO) Ph: 03 5752 1394
Notes: one drive thru site; few long vehicle sites; tennis; playground; close to Mt Buffalo
★★★ $$* Map ref 49 D8

623 **Nagambie** Caravan Park, Goulburn Valley Hwy, Nagambie (1.5km S of PO) Ph: 03 5794 2681
Discounts: week (off-pk) **Notes:** few drive thru sites; close to CBD & wineries
$* Map ref 48 E2

624 **Nangiloc** Caravan Park, Nangiloc Rd, Nangiloc (44km SE of Mildura) Ph: 03 5029 1407
Discounts: very economical **Notes:** playground
★★★ $ Map ref 46 B5

625 **Narbethong**, Black Spur Motel & Caravan Park, Maroondah Hwy (4km S of Marysville) Ph: 03 5963 7153
Discounts: week (off-pk) **Notes:** long vehicle to 9m; public ph, shop & LPG refill close; playground; mini golf; spring water
★★★ $$+ Map ref 43 A12

626 **Narrawong** Holiday Park, off Princes Hwy, Narrawong Ph: 1800 005 066
Discounts: Top Tourist; week; caravan clubs **Notes:** park is river & beach front; bore water
★★★★ $$+ Map ref 44 H4

627 **Nathalia**, Riverbank Caravan Park Nathalia, Park St, Nathalia (800m E of PO) Ph: 03 5866 2615
Discounts: week **Notes:** public ph & shop close; close to town; playground
★★☆ $+* Map ref 47 J14

628 **Nelson**, Kywong Caravan Park, North Nelson Rd, Nelson (1km N of bridge) Ph: 08 8738 4174
Discounts: week (May to Oct) **Notes:** shop close; bush setting; rain & bore water
★★★☆ $ Map ref 44 G2

629 **Nhill** Caravan Park, Western Hwy, Nhill (1km SW of PO) Ph: 03 5391 1683
Discounts: week **Notes:** some ensuites; playground; walks; birdwatching
$$ Map ref 46 K3

630 **Nicholson**, Lakes Bushland Caravan Park, Stephenson Rd (4.7km N of PO) Ph: 03 5156 8422
Discounts: CMCA; pen, wk off-pk **Notes:** golf; tennis; playground
★★★☆ $$+ Map ref 50 D6

631 **Numurkah** Caravan Park, Melville St, Numurkah (400m S of PO) Ph: 03 5862 1526
Discounts: pen; snr **Notes:** swimming pool & shop close; some ensuite sites
★★★ $$ Map ref 48 B3

632 **Ocean Grove**, Riverview Family Caravan Park, Barwon Heads Rd (1km SW of PO) Ph: 03 5256 1600
Discounts: week **Notes:** shop avail seasonally; adjacent to beach & river; boat ramp
★★★★ $$$+* Map ref 42 H4

633 **Omeo** Caravan Park, Old Omeo Hwy, Omeo (2km N of PO) Ph: 03 5159 1351
Notes: LPG swap only; special area for self-sufficient campers
★★★ $$+ Map ref 50 A6

634 **Orbost** Caravan Park on the Snowy Mountain, Lochiel St, Orbost Ph: 03 5092 1426
Discounts: week **Notes:** shop close; close to town; fishing; boat park
★★★ $$+ Map ref 49 J14

635 **Ouyen** Caravan Park, Calder Hwy, Ouyen (300m S of railway station) Ph: 03 5092 1426
Discounts: CMCA; week **Notes:** birdwatching; 4WDing
★★★☆ $$ Map ref 46 E6

636 **Pakenham** Caravan Park, Cnr Princes Hwy & Racecourse Rd (500m N of racecourse) Ph: 03 5941 2004
Notes: two long vehicle sites; quiet park; close to town
★★★ $$$ Map ref 43 F11

637 **Paynesville**, Resthaven Caravan Park, Gilsenan St, Paynesville (400m W of PO) Ph: 03 5156 6342
Discounts: Top Tourist **Notes:** long vehicle to 8m; LPG swap only; walk to lake & shops
★★★☆ $$$+* Map ref 50 E6

638 **Peterborough**, Great Ocean Rd Tourist Park, Great Ocean Rd (150m N of PO) Ph: 03 5598 5477
Discounts: Top Tourist **Notes:** close to river & beach; boat ramp
★★★☆ $$$+* Map ref 44 J7

639 **Phillip Is, Cowes**, A Maze 'N Things Holiday Park, Phillip Is Rd (4km SE of PO) Ph: 03 5952 2020
Discounts: Oz Parks; CMCA **Notes:** award-winning park; playground
★★★☆ $+* Map ref 43 K9

640 **Phillip Is, Cowes** Caravan Park, Church St, Cowes (1km W of PO) Ph: 03 5952 2211
Discounts: Family Parks; CMCA; pen; off-pk **Notes:** shop close; beachfront park
★★★★ $$$+* Map ref 43 K9

641 **Phillip Is, Newhaven,** Phillip Island Caravan Park, Old Bridge Dr, Newhaven Ph: 1800 990 090
Discounts: BIG4; week (off-pk) **Notes:** few drive thru & long vehicle sites; public ph & shop close; LPG swap only; close to beach
★★★★ $$$+* Map ref 52 G3

642 **Porepunkah** Bridge Caravan Park, Mt Buffalo Rd (800m SW of PO) Ph: 1800 552 380
Discounts: CMCA: week (off-pk) **Notes:** riverfront park; close to Mt Buffalo
★★★☆ $$+* Map ref 49 E9

643 **Porepunkah,** Riverview Caravan Park, Junction Rd (1.8km SW of PO) Ph: 03 5756 2290
Discounts: Family Parks; week (off-pk) **Notes:** riverfront park; tennis, close Mt Buffalo
★★★☆ $$+* Map ref 49 E9

644 **Port Albert** Seabank Caravan Park, Old Port Rd, Port Albert Ph: 03 5183 2315
Discounts: week (off-pk) **Notes:** waterfront park; mini golf
★★★☆ $$+ Map ref 50 H3

645 **Port Campbell** Caravan Park, Morris St, Port Campbell (100m N of PO) Ph: 03 5598 6492
Discounts: winter specials **Notes:** few drive thru sites; shop close; LPG swap only; close to beach & river
★★★ $$$+* Map ref 45 J8

646 **Port Fairy** Gardens Caravan Park, Griffith St, Port Fairy (700m NE of PO) Ph: 03 5568 1060
Discounts: snr **Notes:** shop close; 100m to surf beach club
★★★☆ $$$+* Map ref 44 J5

647 **Port Fairy,** Gum Tree Caravan Park, Toolong Rd, Port Fairy (4km NE of PO) Ph: 03 5568 1462
Discounts: CMCA; pen/snr (cash) **Notes:** quiet bushland park
★★★☆ $$+* Map ref 44 J5

648 **Port Welshpool,** Long Jetty Caravan Park, Port Welshpool Rd, Port Welshpool Ph: 03 5688 1233
Notes: on foreshore; close to shop
$+* Map ref 50 H2

649 **Portarlington** Seaside Resort, Boat Rd (off Sproat St) (500m W of PO) Ph: 03 5259 2764
Notes: LPG swap only; some ensuites; playground; boat ramp & park
★★★★ $$+* Map ref 42 G5

650 **Portland,** Centenary Caravan Park, Bentinck St, Portland (1km NE of PO) Ph: 03 5523 1487
Discounts: week **Notes:** near beach; playground
★★★☆ $$+ Map ref 44 H4

651 **Portland,** Henty Bay Beachfront Van and Cabin Park, Dutton Way (6km NE of PO) Ph: 03 5523 3716
Discounts: Family Parks; week **Notes:** cassette DP; close to beach; some ensuite sites; rain water
★★★★ $$+ Map ref 44 H4

652 **Princetown,** Apostles Camping Park and Cabins, Post Office Rd, Princetown Ph: 03 5598 8119
Notes: few drive thru & long vehicle sites; public ph close; LPG swap only; fishing, birdwatching; bore water
★★★ $$+ Map ref 45 K8

653 **Queenscliff,** BIG4 Beacon Resort, Bellarine Hwy (3.5km W of PO) Ph: 1800 351 152
Discounts: BIG4 **Notes:** long vehicle to 8m; public ph & shop close; some ensuite sites; kids' activities
★★★★☆ $$$$+* Map ref 42 H5

654 **Queenscliff** Tourist Parks, Hesse St, Queenscliff Recreation Res (600m S of PO) Ph: 03 5258 1765
Discounts: CMCA; snr; week off-pk **Notes:** few long vehicle sites; beachfront park; playground; tennis
★★★☆ $$$+* Map ref 42 H5

655 **Red Cliffs** Caravan Park, Calder Hwy, Red Cliffs (500m N of PO) Ph: 03 5024 2261
Discounts: Top Tourist; snr; auto club **Notes:** close to town; ensuites; playground; boat park
★★★ $$+* Map ref 46 B5

656 **Robinvale** Riverside Caravan Park, Riverside Dr, Robinvale (1km N of PO) Ph: 03 5026 4646
Discounts: Family Parks; week (off-pk) **Notes:** waterfront park; boat ramp
★★★☆ $$+* Map ref 46 C7

657 **Rochester** Caravan & Camping Park, Church St, Rochester (400m E of PO) Ph: 03 5484 1622
Discounts: CMCA; week **Notes:** shop close; some ensuite sites
★★★☆ $$ Map ref 48 C1

658 **Rushworth,** Lake Waranga Caravan Park and Holiday Camp, Waranga Basin Rd Ph: 03 5856 1243
Discounts: Family Parks; snr; week off-pk **Notes:** lakefront park; 4km off Rushworth-Tatura Rd
★★★ $$* Map ref 48 D2

659 **Rutherglen** Caravan & Tourist Park, Murray St, Rutherglen (700m SW of PO) Ph: 02 6032 8577
Discounts: Oz; CMCA; 2 night **Notes:** swimming pool close; lakefront park; close to golf & bowls
★★★★ $$+* Map ref 48 B7

660 **Sale** Motor Village, Princes Hwy, Sale (1km W of PO) Ph: 03 5144 1366
Discounts: Top Tourist **Notes:** swimming pool close; close to town; some ensuite sites; playground
★★★★ $$+ Map ref 50 F4

661 **Seymour,** Highlands Caravan Park, Emily St (500m SW of police station) Ph: 03 5792 2124
Discounts: Family Parks; CMCA **Notes:** walk to town centre
★★★ $$ Map ref 48 F3

662 **Shepparton** BIG4 East Holiday Park, Cnr Midland Hwy & Orrvale Rd, Orrvale Ph: 1800 022 345
Discounts: BIG4; week (winter) **Notes:** ensuites; tennis; playground; jumping pillow
★★★★ $$$+* Map ref 48 C4

663 **Shepparton,** Victoria Lake Holiday Park, Goulburn Valley Hwy (1km S of PO) Ph: 1800 880 070
Discounts: Top Tourist; week (off-pk) **Notes:** disabled facilities soon; shop close; lakefront park; some ensuite sites
★★★ $$+* Map ref 48 C4

664 **Somers** Holiday Village, Camp Hill Rd, Somers (50m N of PO) Ph: 03 5983 5538
Discounts: week **Notes:** public ph close; playground; walk to beach
★★★ $$+* Map ref 43 J9

665 **Somerville,** Western Port Harbour Caravan Park, Lumeah Rd (9km from PO) Ph: 03 5977 3344
Discounts: snr; week **Notes:** public ph close; dogs permitted; playground
★★★★ $$ Map ref 43 H9

666 **St Arnaud** Caravan Park, Cnr Dundas & Alma Sts, St Arnaud (400m N of PO) Ph: 03 5495 1447
Discounts: CMCA; snr **Notes:** close to town
★★☆ $ Map ref 45 A9

667 **Stawell** Park Caravan Park, Western Hwy, Stawell (4.7km E of info centre) Ph: 03 5358 2709
Discounts: CMCA; snr; week **Notes:** LPG swap only; sell alcohol; close to golf course
★★★★ $ Map ref 44 C7

668 **Stratford** Top Tourist Park, McMillan St, Stratford (400m S of PO) Ph: 1800 787 275
Discounts: Top Tourist; week (off-pk) **Notes:** shop close; riverfront park; playground
★★★★ $$ Map ref 50 E4

669 **Strathmerton,** Murray River Hideaway Holiday Park, Wasers Rd (17km NW of PO) Ph: 03 5868 2259
Discounts: week **Notes:** LPG swap only; close to river; tennis; playground
★★★ $$+* Map ref 48 A4

670 **Swan Hill** Holiday Park, Murray Valley Hwy, Swan Hill (3km S of PO) Ph: 03 5032 4112
Discounts: Family Parks; CMCA; week off-pk **Notes:** large sites; games room
★★★★ $$+* Map ref 47 F9

671 **Swan Hill** Pioneer City Tourist Park, Murray Valley Hwy (1.5km N of PO) Ph: 1800 990 389
Discounts: BIG4; week (off-pk) **Notes:** some ensuite sites; tennis; playground
★★★★☆ $$$+ Map ref 47 F9

672 **Swan Hill** Riverside Caravan Park, Monash Dr, Swan Hill (600m SE of PO) Ph: 1800 101 012
Discounts: Top Tourist; week (off-pk) **Notes:** riverside park; some ensuite sites
★★★★☆ $$$+* Map ref 47 F9

673 **Swan Reach** Gardens, Princes Hwy, Swan Reach (600m E of bridge) Ph: 03 5156 4366
Discounts: Top Tourist; week (off-pk) **Notes:** LPG swap only; close to river; no unpowered sites
★★★★☆ $$+* Map ref 50 D7

674 **Taggerty**, Yarrolyn Holiday Park, Maroondah Hwy, Taggerty (400m N of PO) Ph: 1800 880 895
Discounts: BIG4; week; snr **Notes:** riverfront park; mini golf; tennis; jumping pillow
★★★★ $$+* Map ref 48 H4

675 **Tarra Valley** 'Fernholme' Tourist Park, Tarra Valley Rd (19km N of Yarram) Ph: 03 5186 1283
Discounts: Oz Parks; CMCA; pen; week **Notes:** river water; caravans drive via Yarram
$$$ Map ref 50 G2

676 **Tatura**, Country Gardens Caravan Park, Winter Rd, Tatura (2km W of PO) Ph: 03 5824 2652
Discounts: pen **Notes:** few drive thru sites; some ensuite sites; no credit card facility
★★★ $ Map ref 48 D3

677 **Tawonga** Caravan Park, Mountain Creek Rd, Tawonga (1km E of Kiewa Hwy) Ph: 03 5754 4428
Discounts: pen; snr **Notes:** few long vehicle sites; riverfront park; base for snow area
★★★☆ $+* Map ref 49 E10

678 **Tongala** Caravan Park, Finlay Rd, Tongala Ph: 03 5859 0725
Discounts: CMCA; pen/snr **Notes:** spacious park; playground; games room
★★★★ $+ Map ref 48 C2

679 **Toora** Tourist Park, South Gippsland Hwy, Toora (200m NE of PO) Ph: 03 5686 2257
Discounts: Top Tourist; 5th night (off-pk) **Notes:** shop close; some ensuites; no unpowered sites; playground
★★★★ $$+* Map ref 52 G7

680 **Torquay** Holiday Resort, Surfcoast Hwy, Torquay Ph: 03 5261 2493
Discounts: week (off-pk) **Notes:** LPG swap only; jumping pillow; tennis; mini golf
★★★☆ $$$+* Map ref 42 J3

681 **Torrumbarry** Weir Holiday Park, Weir Rd, Torrumbarry (8km N of highway) Ph: 03 5487 7277
Notes: riverfront park; fishing & water skiing
★★★★ $+* Map ref 47 H12

682 **Traralgon**, Park Lane Tourist Park, Princes Hwy, Traralgon (3.5km W of PO) Ph: 1800 440 000
Discounts: Top Tourist **Notes:** jumping pillow; rec room; sport facilities; ensuites
★★★★☆ $$$* Map ref 50 F2

683 **Venus Bay** Caravan Park, Jupiter Boulevarde, Venus Bay Ph: 03 5663 7728
Discounts: Family Parks; week (off-pk) **Notes:** some ensuites, no unpowered sites; bore water
★★★★ $$$+* Map ref 52 H5

684 **Violet Town**, Honeysuckle Caravan Village, High St, Violet Town Ph: 03 5798 1223
Discounts: week **Notes:** LPG swap only; takeaways; covered sites
$$ Map ref 48 D4

685 **Wangaratta**, Painters Island Caravan Park, Pinkerton Cr (900m N of PO) Ph: 03 5721 3380
Discounts: Family Parks; week **Notes:** close to town; tennis; playground
★★★★ $$ Map ref 48 C6

686 **Warburton** Caravan & Camping Park, Woods Point Rd (1.5km E of PO) Ph: 03 5966 2277
Notes: ph for long vehicle info; swimming pool close; riverfront park; close to Mt Donna Buang
★★★ $$+ Map ref 43 C13

687 **Warracknabeal** Caravan Park, Lyle St, Warracknabeal (1km SW of PO) Ph: 03 5398 0100
Discounts: economical; week **Notes:** few long vehicle sites; shop close; some ensuite sites; no cabin accommodation
★★☆ $ Map ref 46 J6

688 **Warragul** Gardens Holiday Park, Burke St, Warragul (500m S of PO) Ph: 03 5623 2707
Discounts: week **Notes:** close to town centre; playground
★★★★ $$$+ Map ref 43 G14

689 **Warrnambool**, Discovery Holiday Parks Warrnambool, Perobe Rd (1.8km S of PO) Ph: 1800 808 130
Discounts: BIG4; CMCA; week off-pk **Notes:** some ensuite, no unpowered sites; heated pool
★★★★ $$$+* Map ref 44 J6

690 **Warrnambool**, Fig Tree Holiday Village, Lava St, Warrnambool (1km E of PO) Ph: 1800 611 233
Discounts: Top Tourist **Notes:** shop close; some ensuites; no unpowered sites; indoor pool
★★★★ $$$+* Map ref 44 J6

691 **Warrnambool** Holiday Park, Simpson St, Warrnambool (2.5km E of info centre) Ph: 1800 650 441
Discounts: Top Tourist **Notes:** long vehicle to 9m; some ensuite sites; heated pool; tennis
★★★★ $$$$+* Map ref 44 J6

692 **Warrnambool**, Surfside Holiday Park, Pertobe Rd (900m S of PO) Ph: 03 5559 4700
Discounts: Family Parks; pen/wk (off-pk) **Notes:** beach access; close to town & playground
★★★☆ $$$+* Map ref 44 J6

693 **Wedderburn** Pioneer Caravan Park, Hospital St, Wedderburn (1.2km E of PO) Ph: 03 5494 3301
Notes: spacious sites
★★★ $$ Map ref 47 K10

694 **Werribee South** Caravan Park, Beach Rd (11km S of Werribee PO) Ph: 03 9742 1755
Discounts: week **Notes:** public ph & shop close; ocean views; close to boat ramp
★★★☆ $$+* Map ref 42 E5

695 **Whitfield**, Valley View Caravan Park, Valley View Dr (opposite PO) Ph: 03 5729 8350
Discounts: pen; week **Notes:** public ph, shop & LPG refill close; accomm is onsite vans
★★★ $$ Map ref 48 E7

696 **Wodonga**, Boathaven Holiday Park Boathaven Rd, Ebden (13km E of Wodonga) Ph: 1800 352 982
Discounts: BIG4; snr **Notes:** long vehicle to 10m; lakefront park; some ensuite sites; boat ramp
★★★★☆ $$$+* Map ref 49 B8

697 **Wodonga**, Borderland Holiday Park, McKoy St, West Wodonga (3.5km W of PO) Ph: 02 6024 3906
Discounts: BIG4 **Notes:** public ph close; quiet off-highway location
★★★★ $$$ Map ref 49 B8

698 **Wodonga** Caravan & Cabin Park, Melbourne Rd, Wodonga (2.4km W of PO) Ph: 02 6024 2598
Discounts: week **Notes:** playground; 2km from town
★★★☆ $$ Map ref 49 B8

699 **Woodside** Beach Caravan Park, Woodside Beach Rd (10km E of PO) Ph: 03 5187 1214
Discounts: CMCA; snr week (off-pk) **Notes:** long vehicle to 8m; LPG swap only; close to patrolled beach; bore water
★★★☆ $$+* Map ref 50 G3

700 **Wye River** Tourist Park, Great Ocean Rd, Wye River (adjacent to PO) Ph: 03 5289 0241
Discounts: BIG4 **Notes:** close to beach; playground
★★★★ $$$$+* Map ref 45 J11

701 **Yackandandah** Holiday Park, Taymac Dr, Yackandandah (500m S of PO) Ph: 02 6027 1380
Notes: internet access close; quiet park, close to town
★★★ $$+* Map ref 49 C8

702 **Yanakie**, Shallow Inlet Caravan Park, Lester Rd, Yanakie (7.7km NW of PO) Ph: 03 5687 1385
Discounts: week (off-pk) **Notes:** beachfront park; fishing; rain water
★★★☆ $$+ Map ref 52 H7

703 **Yarram** Rosebank Tourist Park, Commercial Rd (South Gippsland Hwy) Yarram Ph: 03 5182 5063
Discounts: week (off-pk) **Notes:** shop close; close to town
★★★☆ $$+* Map ref 50 H3

704 **Yarrawonga** Holiday Park, Piper St, Yarrawonga (500m W of PO) Ph: 03 5744 3420
Discounts: week (off-pk) **Notes:** shop close; riverfront; boat ramp; bowls & putting greens
★★★☆ $$$+* Map ref 48 B5

705 **Yea** Family Caravan Park, Court St, Yea (800m E of PO) Ph: 03 5797 2972
Discounts: Family Parks; week **Notes:** shop close; half court tennis; rec room
★★★☆ $$* Map ref 48 G3

Tasmania

706 **Beauty Point** Tourist Park, West Arm Rd, Beauty Point (1km N of PO) Ph: 03 6383 4536
Discounts: week (off-pk) **Notes:** waterfront park; tennis; close to town
★★★☆ $$$ Map ref 55 D2

707 **Bicheno** Caravan Park, Burgess St, Bicheno (200m SW of PO) Ph: 03 6375 1280
Discounts: week (off-pk) **Notes:** public ph close; close to town
★★★☆ $ Map ref 59 A14

708 **Bicheno** East Coast Holiday Park, Champ St, Bicheno (300m W of PO) Ph: 03 6375 1999
Discounts: Family Parks **Notes:** public ph close; in town; opposite beach; playground
★★★☆ $$$* Map ref 59 A14

709 **Bruny Is,** Captain James Cook Memorial Caravan Park, Adventure Bay Ph: 03 6293 1128
Notes: public ph & shop close; waterfront park; fishing charter; spring water
★★★☆ $$* Map ref 59 J10

710 **Burnie** Holiday Caravan Park, Bass Hwy, Cooee (3km W of Burnie PO) Ph: 03 6431 1925
Discounts: long term stay **Notes:** indoor heated pool
★★★☆ $+ Map ref 60 D5

711 **Cradle Mountain,** Discovery Holiday Parks - Cradle Mountain, Cradle Mountain Rd Ph: 03 6492 1395
Discounts: CMCA **Notes:** long vehicle to 7m; adjacent to National Park; limited spring water
$$$$+ Map ref 60 G5

712 **Devonport,** Bay View Holiday Village, North Caroline St (1km N of PO) Ph: 03 6427 0499
Discounts: Family Parks **Notes:** shop close; close to ferry; all sites powered with ensuite
★★★ $$$ Map ref 60 D7

713 **Devonport,** Discovery Holiday Parks - Devonport, Tarleton St, Devonport Ph: 03 6498 6333
Discounts: BIG4; week **Notes:** waterfront park; spectacular views
★★★★ $$$+ Map ref 60 D7

714 **Devonport** Vacation Village, North Caroline St, East Devonport (1km NE of PO) Ph: 03 6427 8886
Notes: shop close; some ensuite sites; takeaways; playground
★★★ $$$ Map ref 60 D7

715 **Devonport area,** Latrobe Mersey River Caravan Pk, River Rd (off Bells Pde, 7km S of ferry) Ph: 03 6426 1944
Notes: close to town centre & ferry terminal
$$ Map ref 60 E7

716 **Dover** Beachside Tourist Park, Kent Beach Rd, Dover (1km SE of PO) Ph: 03 6298 1301
Discounts: week (off-pk) **Notes:** long vehicle to 11m; shop close; beachfront park; swimming & fishing
★★★☆ $$$ Map ref 59 J9

717 **Greens Beach** Caravan & Holiday Park, Greens Beach Rd, Greens Beach Ph: 03 6383 9222
Discounts: CMCA; week **Notes:** next to golf course, national park & beach
★★☆ $+ Map ref 55 C1

718 **Gunns Plains,** Wings Wildlife Park, Winduss Rd, Gunns Plains Ph: 03 6429 1335
Discounts: very economical **Notes:** wildlife park; river water
$ Map ref 60 E6

719 **Hadspen,** Discovery Holiday Parks - Hadspen, Bass Hwy (12km SW of PO) Ph: 03 6393 6391
Discounts: week **Notes:** games & rec room; close to town
★★★☆ $$$+ Map ref 55 H4

720 **Hobart, Berriedale,** Treasure Island Caravan Park, Alcorso Dr (11km NW of Hobart PO) Ph: 03 6249 2379
Notes: riverfront park; some ensuite sites
★★★☆ $$$+ Map ref 56 B5

721 **Hobart, Cambridge,** Barilla Holiday Park, Richmond Rd, Cambridge Ph: 03 6248 5453
Discounts: BIG4; CMCA **Notes:** long vehicle to 12m; takeaways; hot spa; mini golf
★★★☆ $$+ Map ref 56 B7

722 **Hobart, Risdon,** Discovery Holiday Parks, 673 East Derwent Hwy (12km NE of Hobart) Ph: 03 6243 9879
Discounts: CMCA **Notes:** long vehicle to 8m; all sites have power & ensuite
$$$+ Map ref 56 B6

723 **Kelso** Sands Holiday Park, Paranaple Rd, Kelso (15km N of Beaconsfield) Ph: 1800 664 826
Discounts: BIG4; CMCA **Notes:** few drive thru sites; LPG swap only; bush setting riverfront; 6 hole golf
★★★★ $$$ Map ref 55 C2

724 **Launceston,** Treasure Island Caravan Park, Glen Dhu St (2km S of PO) Ph: 03 6344 2600
Notes: shop close; 7 acres, lawn & English trees
★★★☆ $$$ Map ref 55 G5

725 **Launceston area, Legana,** Launceston Holiday Park, West Tamar Hwy Ph: 03 6330 1714
Discounts: Family Parks **Notes:** few long vehicle sites; bush setting
★★★☆ $$$ Map ref 55 F4

726 **Longford** Riverside Caravan Park, 2A Archer St, Longford (1km NE of PO) Ph: 03 6391 1470
Notes: heritage walks; fishing & boating
★★★☆ $$ Map ref 55 J5

727 **Low Head** Tourist Park, Low Head Rd, Low Head Ph: 03 6382 1573
Discounts: Family Parks; CMCA **Notes:** few drive thru sites; some ensuite sites; opposite Tamar River
★★★★ $$+ Map ref 55 B2

728 **New Norfolk** Caravan Park, The Esplanade, New Norfolk (1.5km N of PO) Ph: 03 6261 1268
Discounts: winter **Notes:** swimming pool & shop close; riverfront park; boat ramp; walk to town
★★★☆ $$ Map ref 56 A2

729 **Nubeena area,** White Beach Tourist Park, White Beach Rd (10km W of Port Arthur) Ph: 03 6250 2142
Discounts: Family Parks **Notes:** beachfront park; playground; dam water
★★★★ $$+ Map ref 57 H11

730 **Port Arthur** Caravan and Cabin Park, Garden Point, Port Arthur (1km N of PO) Ph: 1800 620 708
Discounts: week (off-pk) **Notes:** 1km to Port Arthur; some ensuites; playground
★★★★ $$ Map ref 57 H12

731 **Port Sorell** Lions Caravan Park, Meredith St, Port Sorell Ph: 03 6428 7267
Discounts: week; unpowered $12 **Notes:** shop close; pets off-pk only; beachfront park; playground
$$ Map ref 61 E8

732 **Queenstown** Cabin & Tourist Park, Grafton St, Queenstown Ph: 03 6471 1332
Discounts: CMCA; week **Notes:** public ph & shop close; convenient to scenic railway
$$$ Map ref 58 B4

No.	Park	Rating / Price / Map ref
733	**Rosebery** Cabin & Tourist Park, Park St, Rosebery (700m NW of PO) Ph: 03 6473 1366 **Discounts:** CMCA **Notes:** long vehicle to 15m	$$ Map ref 58 A4
734	**Ross** Caravan Park (check in at Ross Motel, High St, Ross) Ph: 03 6381 5224 **Notes:** swimming pool, public ph & shop close; close to town & historic sites	$ Map ref 59 B11
735	**Snug** Beach Cabin and Caravan Park, Beach Rd, Snug (1km SE of PO) Ph: 03 6267 9138 **Notes:** few drive thru sites; public ph & shop close; close to beach	★★★☆ $$+ Map ref 56 G5
736	**Somerset** Beachside Cabin and Caravan Park, Bass Hwy (1km W of PO) Ph: 03 6435 2322 **Discounts:** CMCA; week **Notes:** café; gift shop	★★★ $$ Map ref 60 D5
737	**Southport** Settlement Tavern and Caravan Park, Huon Hwy, Southport Ph: 03 6298 3144 **Discounts:** CMCA **Notes:** most southerly park in Australia	★★ $$ Map ref 59 J9
738	**St Helens** Caravan Park, Penelope St, St Helens (1.5km S of PO) Ph: 1300 559 734 **Discounts:** BIG4 **Notes:** some ensuite sites	★★★★ $$$+* Map ref 61 F13
739	**St Helens**, Hillcrest Tourist Park, Chimney Heights Rd (7km S of PO) Ph: 03 6376 3298 **Discounts:** CMCA; week **Notes:** on St Helens Point; beach access	★★★ $$ Map ref 61 F14
740	**Stanley** Cabin and Tourist Park, Wharf Rd, Stanley Ph: 1800 444 818 **Notes:** shop close; waterfront park; close to town centre	★★★★ $$+* Map ref 60 C3
741	**Strahan**, Discovery Holiday Parks - Strahan, Andrews & Innes Sts (800m W of PO) Ph: 1800 454 292 **Discounts:** CMCA; pen; snr **Notes:** public ph & shop close; close to water; playground	★★★ $$$+ Map ref 58 C3
742	**Swansea** Beach Chalets, Shaw St, Swansea (500m N of PO) Ph: 03 6257 8177 **Discounts:** enquire when booking **Notes:** one drive thru site; public ph close; waterfront park; heated pool; games room	★★★☆ $+ Map ref 59 C13
743	**Tarraleah** Highland Caravan Park, The Edge, Tarraleah Ph: 03 6289 0111 **Discounts:** unpowered sites $15 **Notes:** LPG swap only	$$$ Map ref 58 D7
744	**Triabunna** Cabin and Caravan Park, Vicary St, Triabunna (100m S of PO) Ph: 03 6257 3575 **Notes:** few drive thru sites; public ph & LPG refills close; close Maria Island ferry & town	★★★☆ $$ Map ref 59 E12
745	**Ulverstone** Holiday Park, Water St, Ulverstone (1km NE of PO) Ph: 1800 008 028 **Discounts:** BIG4 **Notes:** shop close; beachfront park; playground	★★★★ $$$+ Map ref 60 E6
746	**Wayatinah** Lakeside Caravan Park, Wayatinah (1km off Lyall Hwy) Ph: 03 6289 3317 **Notes:** close to shop, tavern, golf & fishing	$ Map ref 58 D7
747	**Wynyard**, Leisure Ville Holiday Centre, Old Bass Hwy (3km E of PO) Ph: 03 6442 2291 **Discounts:** Family Parks **Notes:** shop close; some ensuite sites; indoor pool; tennis	★★★☆ $$+ Map ref 60 D5
748	**Zeehan**, Treasure Island Caravan Park, Hurst St, Zeehan (500m NE of PO) Ph: 03 6471 6633 **Notes:** playground	★★☆ $+ Map ref 58 A3

South Australia

No.	Park	Rating / Price / Map ref
749	**Adelaide, Bedford Park**, Marion Holiday Park, 323 Sturt Rd (12km S of PO) Ph: 1800 063 193 **Discounts:** BIG4; week (off-pk) **Notes:** long vehicle to 8m; some ensuites; close to wineries, shops & beach	★★★★ $$$+* Map ref 64 K3
750	**Adelaide, Hackney**, Adelaide Caravan Park, Richmond St (2km NE of PO) Ph: 08 8363 1566 **Discounts:** Top Tourist **Notes:** shop close; close to CBD and public transport	★★★ $$$+* Map ref 63 B3
751	**Adelaide, Kingston Park**, Brighton Caravan Park & Holiday Village, Burnham Rd (17km SW) Ph: 03 8377 0833 **Discounts:** Family Parks; week **Notes:** beachfront; close transport; no unpowered sites	★★★★ $$$+* Map ref 64 K2
752	**Adelaide, Mitcham**, Brownhill Creek Tourist Park, Brownhill Ck Rd (7km S of GPO) Ph: 1800 626 493 **Discounts:** Top Tourist; snr; week (off-pk) **Notes:** LPG swap only; some ensuite sites; playground; tennis	★★★★ $$$+* Map ref 64 J5
753	**Adelaide, Semaphore**, Discovery Holiday Parks - Adelaide Beachfront, Military Rd Ph: 1800 810 140 **Discounts:** Top Tourist; CMCA **Notes:** beachfront; some ensuites; no unpowered sites	★★★★ $$$+* Map ref 64 E1
754	**Adelaide, Walkerville**, Levi Park Caravan Park, Lansdowne Tce (5km N of PO) Ph: 1800 442 209 **Discounts:** BIG4; week(off-pk) **Notes:** long vehicle to 8m; close to CBD; playground	★★★★ $$$$+* Map ref 64 F5
755	**Adelaide area, Aldinga**, Beach Woods Eco Tourist Park, Tuit Rd (3km N of PO) Ph: 08 8556 6113 **Discounts:** Family Parks; CMCA; auto clubs **Notes:** close to beach; games room; tennis	★★★★ $$$* Map ref 66 C4
756	**Ardrossan** Caravan Park, Park Tce, Ardrossan (300m from PO) Ph: 08 8837 3262 **Discounts:** pen; snr; week off-pk **Notes:** long vehicle to 11m; public ph & shop close; close to town; some ensuite sites	★★★☆ $+* Map ref 68 F5
757	**Arkaroola** Wilderness Sanctuary, Northern Flinders Ranges Ph: 08 8648 4848 **Notes:** fuel & repairs; tours; restaurant	$ Map ref 73 J11
758	**Arno Bay** Foreshore Tourist Park, Park Lane, Arno Bay (1km S of PO) Ph: 08 8628 0157 **Discounts:** week (off-pk) **Notes:** cassette DP; shop close; beachfront park; swimming & fishing	★★★☆ $+ Map ref 68 E3
759	**Barmera**, Discovery Holiday Parks -Lake Bonney, Lakeside Dr (1.5km W of PO) Ph: 1800 034 828 **Discounts:** Family Parks; CMCA **Notes:** lakefront; hire bikes & canoes; jumping pillow	★★★☆ $$+* Map ref 69 A6
760	**Barossa Valley, Lyndoch**, Barossa Caravan Park, Barossa Valley Hwy (2km NW of PO) Ph: 08 8524 4262 **Discounts:** CMCA; week **Notes:** long vehicle to 10m; shady grassed sites; playground	★★★ $$ Map ref 65 D5
761	**Barossa Valley, Nuriootpa**, Barossa Valley SA Tourist Park, Penrice Rd Ph: 1800 251 634 **Discounts:** Top Tourist; week **Notes:** shade & grass; walk trails; lake	★★★★ $$+ Map ref 65 B6
762	**Barossa Valley, Tanunda** Caravan and Tourist Park, Barossa Valley Way Ph: 08 8563 2784 **Discounts:** Family Parks; pen **Notes:** grassy sites; bicycles; basketball	★★★★ $$ Map ref 65 C6

763 **Beachport**'s Southern Ocean Tourist Park, Somerville St Beachport (500m to PO) Ph: 08 8735 8153
Discounts: CMCA; pen; week **Notes:** swimming pool & shop close; close to beach & jetty; playground
★★★☆ $$ Map ref 69 J5

764 **Berri** Riverside Caravan Park, Riverview Dr, Berri (2km from PO) Ph: 1800 332 255
Discounts: Top Tourist **Notes:** shop close; LPG swap only; riverfront park; some ensuite sites; boat ramp
★★★★ $$* Map ref 69 A7

765 **Bordertown** Caravan Park, Penny Tce, Bordertown Ph: 08 8752 1752
Notes: shop close; shady grassed sites
★★★☆ $$ Map ref 69 F7

766 **Burra** Caravan & Camping Park, Bridge Terrace, Burra Ph: 08 8892 2442
Discounts: week **Notes:** close to town & playground; accomm is onsite vans
★★★☆ $ Map ref 68 D7

767 **Carrieton**, Horseshoe View Caravan Park, Carrieton (36km N of Orroroo) Ph: 08 8658 9090
Discounts: CMCA; 3rd night free **Notes:** public ph & shop close; spacious shady sites
$ Map ref 68 A7

768 **Ceduna** Airport Caravan Park & Restaurant, Hwy 1 (2km E of PO) Ph: 08 8625 2416
Discounts: Oz Parks; CMCA **Notes:** spacious, quiet park; restaurant
★★ $$ Map ref 70 C2

769 **Ceduna** Foreshore Caravan Park, Poynton St, Ceduna (50m E of PO) Ph: 1300 666 290
Discounts: Top Tourist **Notes:** two drive thru sites; shop close; close to bay; fish cleaning facility
★★★☆ $$* Map ref 70 C2

770 **Ceduna** Shelly Beach Caravan Park, Decres Bay Rd, Ceduna (3km E of PO) Ph: 08 8625 2012
Discounts: Family Parks **Notes:** beachfront park; some ensuite sites
★★★★☆ $$ Map ref 70 C2

771 **Clare** Caravan Park, Main North Rd, Clare (4km S of PO) Ph: 08 8842 2724
Discounts: Top Tourist **Notes:** LPG swap only; close to walking trail; playground
★★★★ $$$ Map ref 68 E7

772 **Cobdogla** Station Caravan Park, Shuear Rd (Old Sturt Hwy) (500m W of PO) Ph: 1300 666 623
Discounts: Oz Parks; CMCA; week **Notes:** shop close; LPG swap only; jetty; fishing; canoe hire; playground
★★★☆ $$$ Map ref 69 A6

773 **Coffin Bay** Caravan & Camping Park, The Esplanade, Coffin Bay (50m NE of PO) Ph: 08 8685 4170
Discounts: pen; snr; week off-pk **Notes:** shop, LPG refill & internet access close; across road from water
★★★☆ $$+* Map ref 70 H5

774 **Coober Pedy**, Stuart Range Caravan Park, Hutchison St (800m S of PO) Ph: 08 8672 5179
Discounts: Family Parks **Notes:** pizza available; playground
★★★★ $$ Map ref 72 G4

775 **Coober Pedy**, Oasis Tourist Park, Hutchison St, Coober Pedy (800m N of PO) Ph: 1800 060 541
Discounts: BIG4 **Notes:** some ensuite sites; mine tour bookings
★★★ $$+ Map ref 72 G4

776 **Coober Pedy**, Opal Inn Caravan Park, Hutchison St (200m S of PO) Ph: 1800 088 523
Discounts: Top Tourist; pen; week **Notes:** swimming pool, public ph, shop, LPG refill & internet access close; discount opal sales & mine tours
★★★ $$$ Map ref 72 G4

777 **Coobowie** Caravan Park, Beach Rd, Coobowie (400m S of PO) Ph: 08 8852 8132
Discounts: Top Tourist; CMCA; pen **Notes:** shop close; beachfront park; shady lawn sites
★★★☆ $+ Map ref 69 C1

778 **Corny Point** Caravan Park, Main Rd, Corny Point (2km E of general store) Ph: 08 8855 3368
Discounts: pen; snr; week off-pk **Notes:** close to beach; rain water
★★★☆ $+* Map ref 68 G4

779 **Cowell** Foreshore Caravan Park & Holiday Units, The Esplanade (200m SW of PO) Ph: 08 8629 2307
Discounts: week (10%) **Notes:** waterfront park; no unpowered sites; boat ramp
★★★☆ $$+* Map ref 68 D3

780 **Edithburgh** Caravan Park and Tourist Park, O'Halloran Parade, Edithburgh Ph: 1800 500 356
Discounts: pen; week **Notes:** swimming pool & shop close; waterfront park; playground; close to boat ramp
★★★☆ $$+ Map ref 68 H5

781 **Elliston** Waterloo Bay Tourist Park, Beach Tce, Elliston (200m NW of PO) Ph: 1800 798 888
Discounts: Top Tourist; week (off-pk) **Notes:** close to beach & town
★★★☆ $$* Map ref 70 G4

782 **Gladstone** Caravan Park, West Tce, Gladstone (1km W of PO) Ph: 08 8662 2522
Discounts: return visits **Notes:** swimming pool, shop & internet access close; in Southern Flinders Ranges
★★★☆ $ Map ref 68 C6

783 **Goolwa** Camping & Tourist Park, Kessell Rd, Goolwa (1km NW of PO) Ph: 08 8555 2144
Discounts: Family Parks **Notes:** public ph & shop close; close to town & historic wharf
★★★ $$+ Map ref 67 G8

784 **Goolwa** Caravan Park, Noble Ave, Goolwa (3km N of PO) Ph: 1800 130 353
Discounts: Top Tourist **Notes:** ph for long vehicle info; mini golf; playground; spa; boat ramp
★★★☆ $$+* Map ref 67 G8

785 **Hawker**, Flinders Ranges Caravan Park, Hawker-Leigh Creek Rd, Hawker Ph: 08 8648 4266
Discounts: Family Parks **Notes:** LPG swap only; internet access close; some ensuite sites; rec room
★★★★☆ $$ Map ref 71 C10

786 **Jamestown** Country Retreat Caravan Park, Cnr Ayr & Bute Sts, Jamestown Ph: 08 8664 0077
Notes: swimming pool & shop close; shady sites; close to CBD
★★★ $$ Map ref 68 C7

787 **Kangaroo Is**, Western KI Caravan Park & Wildlife Reserve, South Coast Rd Ph: 08 8559 7201
Notes: close to Nat Park; rain water
★★★☆ $$ Map ref 68 K3

788 **Kangaroo Is**, Kingscote Nepean Bay Tourist Park, First St, Brownlow (3km SW PO) Ph: 08 8553 2394
Discounts: pen; snr **Notes:** public ph close; beachfront park; close to golf course
★★☆ $$+ Map ref 68 J5

789 **Keith** Caravan Park, Eyre Hwy, Keith (1km W of PO) Ph: 08 8755 1957
Discounts: pen; snr **Notes:** swimming pool, shop, LPG refill & internet access close; close to town; ensuites; rain & bore water
★★☆ $ Map ref 69 E6

790 **Kimba** Caravan Park Motel, Eyre Hwy, Kimba (1km W of PO) Ph: 1300 663 024
Discounts: Top Tourist; CMCA; snr **Notes:** licensed restaurant
★★ $ Map ref 68 C2

791 **Kingston** Caravan Park, Marine Pde, Kingston (2km from PO) Ph: 08 8767 2050
Discounts: Oz Parks; CMCA; pen/snr/week **Notes:** close to beach & boat ramp; playground
★★★☆ $$$+ Map ref 69 G4

792 **Kingston on Murray** Caravan Park, River Tce, Kingston on Murray (200m E of PO) Ph: 08 8583 0209
Discounts: CMCA **Notes:** long vehicle to 10m; boat ramp & jetty; rain water
★★★☆ $$+* Map ref 69 A6

793 **Leigh Creek area, Copley** Caravan Park, Railway Terrace, Copley (100m S of PO) Ph: 08 8675 2288
Discounts: CMCA **Notes:** public ph close; close to Flinders Ranges; campfires
★★★ $$ Map ref 71 A10

794 **Loxton** Riverfront Caravan Park, Sophie Edington Dr, Loxton (2km NW of PO) Ph: 1800 887 733
Discounts: BIG4; week **Notes:** LPG swap only; some ensuite sites; playground; golf
★★★☆ $$+* Map ref 69 A7

795 **Mannum** Caravan Park, Purnong Rd, Mannum (adjacent to ferry) Ph: 08 8569 1402
Discounts: CMCA; pen/snr off-pk **Notes:** LPG swap only; riverfront; boat ramp; rec room; tennis
★★★★ $$ Map ref 69 B4

796 **Marion Bay** Caravan Park, Willyama Dr, Marion Bay Ph: 08 8854 4094
Notes: few drive thru sites; public ph & shop close; close to beach; no unpowered sites
★★★☆ $$ Map ref 68 H4

797 **Marla** Travellers Rest Caravan Park, Stuart Hwy, Marla Ph: 08 8670 7001
Discounts: CMCA **Notes:** good for overnight stop
$ Map ref 72 C2

798 **Melrose** Caravan Park, Joes Rd, Melrose Ph: 08 8666 2060
Discounts: CMCA; pen/snr off-pk **Notes:** public ph, shop, LPG refill & internet access close; on creek; close to Mt Remarkable NP
★★★ $ Map ref 68 B6

799 **Meningie**, Lake Albert Caravan Park, Narrung Rd, Meningie (1km W of PO) Ph: 08 8575 1411
Discounts: Top Tourist; week off-pk **Notes:** internet access close; lakefront park; boat ramp
★★★★ $$+* Map ref 67 J13

800 **Middleton** Caravan Park, Goolwa Rd, Middleton (adjacent to general store) Ph: 08 8554 2383
Discounts: week (off-pk) **Notes:** long vehicle sites in off-pk; shop close; shady grass sites; close to beach
★★★☆ $$$ Map ref 66 G7

801 **Milang** Lakeside Caravan Park, Daranda Terrace, Milang Ph: 08 8537 0282
Discounts: Oz Parks; CMCA **Notes:** public ph, shop & internet access close; lakefront park; boat ramp; shady grass
★★★ $ Map ref 67 E9

802 **Millicent**, Hillview Caravan Park, Dalton St, Millicent (2.6km SE of PO) Ph: 08 8733 2806
Discounts: CMCA; snr; multi-night; solos **Notes:** shop close; quiet park beside pine forest
★★★☆ $ Map ref 69 J6

803 **Minlaton** Caravan Park, Cnr Bluff & Maitland Rds, Minlaton Ph: 08 8853 2435
Discounts: CMCA **Notes:** shady lawn areas
★★★ $ Map ref 68 G5

804 **Moonta** Bay Caravan Park, Tossell St, Moonta Bay (3km from PO) Ph: 1800 666 682
Discounts: Top Tourist; pen (off-pk) **Notes:** shop close; waterfront park; close to jetty; fishing
★★★☆ $$$+* Map ref 68 E4

805 **Morgan** Riverside Caravan Park, Main Rd, Morgan (adjacent to ferry) Ph: 08 8540 2207
Discounts: Top Tourist; week **Notes:** playground; mini golf; canoe hire
★★★ $$+* Map ref 71 G11

806 **Mt Barker** Caravan & Tourist Park, Cameron Rd, Mt Barker (300m N of PO) Ph: 08 8391 0384
Discounts: week (10%) **Notes:** shop close; playground
★★★ $$ Map ref 65 K5

807 **Mt Compass** Caravan Park, Heysen Boulevarde, Mt Compass (4km S of PO) Ph: 08 8556 8600
Notes: some ensuites; close to restaurant & golf
★★★★ $$ Map ref 66 E6

808 **Mt Gambier**, Blue Lake Holiday Park, Bay Rd, Mt Gambier (2km SW of PO) Ph: 1800 676 028
Discounts: BIG4; week (10%) **Notes:** close to lake & golf; some ensuites; playground
★★★★ $$$+* Map ref 69 K6

809 **Mt Gambier**, Central Caravan Park, Krummel St, Mt Gambier (900m SE of PO) Ph: 08 8725 4427
Discounts: Family Parks **Notes:** rec room, playground
★★★☆ $$+* Map ref 69 K6

810 **Mt Gambier**, Kalganyi Holiday Park, Cnr Penola & Bishop Rds (3km N of PO) Ph: 1800 651 746
Discounts: Top Tourist **Notes:** some ensuites; heated pool; sports facilities
★★★★ $$$ Map ref 69 K6

811 **Mt Gambier**, Pine Country Caravan Park, Port MacDonnell Rd, Mt Gambier Ph: 1300 720 115
Discounts: Oz Parks; CMCA **Notes:** public ph close; some ensuite sites; playground; tennis
★★★☆ $$ Map ref 69 K6

812 **Murray Bridge**, Long Island Caravan Park, Roper Rd (3km S of PO) Ph: 08 8532 6900
Discounts: Family Parks; week **Notes:** riverfront; some ensuites; no unpowered sites
★★★☆ $$* Map ref 67 B13

813 **Murray Bridge**, Princes Hwy Caravan Park, Adelaide Rd (5km W of PO) Ph: 08 8532 2860
Discounts: Oz Parks; CMCA **Notes:** quiet, shady park
★★★ $$ Map ref 67 B13

814 **Naracoorte** Holiday Park, Park Tce, Naracoorte (1km N of PO, adjacent to lake) Ph: 08 8762 2128
Discounts: BIG4 **Notes:** swimming pool close; close to town; mini golf; playground
★★★☆ $$$ Map ref 69 G6

815 **Normanville**, Beachside Caravan Park, Cape Jervis Rd (1.6km S of PO) Ph: 08 8558 2458
Discounts: Top Tourist **Notes:** internet access close; beachfront park; fishing; playground
★★★☆ $$* Map ref 66 F2

816 **Orroroo** Caravan Park, Second St, Orroroo (200m W of PO) Ph: 08 8658 1444
Discounts: CMCA **Notes:** swimming pool, public ph, shop & LPG refill close; close to town centre; campfire
★★★☆ $ Map ref 68 B7

817 **Padthaway** Caravan Park, Beeamma Rd, Padthaway (1km E of PO) Ph: 08 8765 5212
Discounts: week **Notes:** quiet; shade grass & gardens
★★★☆ $$ Map ref 69 G6

818 **Paringa** Caravan Park, Sturt Hwy, Paringa (200m S of PO) Ph: 08 8595 5178
Discounts: week **Notes:** long vehicle to 8m; public ph & shop close; close to town centre; no unpowered sites
★★★☆ $$ Map ref 69 A7

819 **Penola** Caravan Park, Cnr Riddoch Hwy & South Tce, Penola (900m S of PO) Ph: 08 8737 2381
Discounts: pen/snr; week **Notes:** shop close; close to town; some ensuite sites
★★★ $$ Map ref 69 J7

820 **Penong** Caravan Park, Siggants Rd, Penong (300m off Eyre Hwy) Ph: 08 8625 1111
Discounts: CMCA **Notes:** free washing machine; rain water
★★☆ $$ Map ref 70 C1

821 **Peterborough** Caravan Park, Grove St, Peterborough (1km S of PO) Ph: 08 8651 2545
Discounts: CMCA; snr; week **Notes:** swimming pool close; mini golf, playground
★★★ $$ Map ref 68 C7

822 **Pine Point** Caravan Park, Main Coast Rd, Pine Point Ph: 08 8838 2239
Discounts: week **Notes:** public ph & shop close; close to beach; playground; accomm is onsite vans
★★★ $ Map ref 68 G5

823 **Point Turton** Caravan Park, Bayview Rd, Point Turton (adj to jetty & boat ramp) Ph: 08 8854 5222
Discounts: very economical **Notes:** ph for long vehicle info; close to beach; boat ramp; bore water
★★★☆ $+* Map ref 68 H4

824 **Port Augusta** Big4 Holiday Park, Cnr Hwy 1 & Stokes Tce (1.5km W of PO) Ph: 1800 833 444
Discounts: BIG4; CMCA **Notes:** close to shops; some ensuites; playground
★★★★☆ $$$ Map ref 68 A5

825 **Port Augusta**, Shoreline Caravan Park, Gardiner Ave (1.5km W of PO) Ph: 1800 422 965
Discounts: Top Tourist **Notes:** waterfront park; some ensuite sites; playground
★★★☆ $$ Map ref 68 A5

826 **Port Broughton** Caravan Park, Barker St, Port Broughton (1km S of PO) Ph: 08 8635 2188
Discounts: Family Parks; CMCA; snr; week **Notes:** waterfront park; playground
★★★★ $$* Map ref 68 D5

827 **Port Clinton** Progress Assoc Caravan Park, The Parade (200m S of PO) Ph: 08 8837 7003
Discounts: economical price; week **Notes:** public ph, shop & LPG refill close; beachfront park; crab cooking facility
★★★ $ Map ref 68 F6

828 **Port Hughes** Tourist Village, South Terrace, Port Hughes (3.5km from PO) Ph: 08 8825 2106
Discounts: pen **Notes:** few drive thru sites; shop & LPG refill close; waterfront park; some ensuite sites
★★★☆ $$$ Map ref 68 E4

829 **Port Lincoln** Tourist Park, Hindmarsh St, Port Lincoln (3km E of PO) Ph: 08 8621 4444
Discounts: Top Tourist; pen; snr **Notes:** LPG swap only; waterfront park; boat ramp; playground
★★★★ $$$ Map ref 68 G1

830 **Port Macdonnell** Foreshore Tourist Park, Sea Parade (1.5km SE of PO) Ph: 08 8738 2095
Discounts: week (off-pk) **Notes:** internet access close; beachfront park; boat ramp; playground
★★★☆ $+ Map ref 69 K6

831 **Port Pirie** Beach Caravan Park, Beach Rd, Port Pirie (1.5km E of PO) Ph: 1800 819 323
Discounts: Family Parks **Notes:** shop close; riverfront park; close to town centre
★★★☆ $$$ Map ref 68 C5

832 **Port Pirie**, Range View Caravan and Cabin Park, Hwy 1 (5km E of PO) Ph: 08 8634 4221
Discounts: Oz Parks; CMCA **Notes:** off-leash area for dogs
★★★ $ Map ref 68 C5

833 **Port Rickaby** Caravan Park, Waimana Ct, Port Rickaby Ph: 08 8853 1177
Discounts: Family Parks; week off-pk **Notes:** beachfront park; close to jetty
★★★ $$+ Map ref 68 G4

834 **Port Victoria**, Gulfhaven Caravan Park, Davies Tce, Port Victoria Ph: 08 8834 2012
Discounts: Top Tourist; week **Notes:** shop close; beachfront park; close to jetty & fishing
★★★☆ $$+ Map ref 68 F4

835 **Port Vincent** Foreshore Caravan Park, Marine Pde (500m NE of PO) Ph: 08 8853 7073
Discounts: Family Parks; week (off-pk) **Notes:** long vehicle to 8m; shop close; waterfront park; no unpowered sites
★★★★ $$+ Map ref 68 G5

836 **Port Wakefield** Caravan Park, Wakefield St, Port Wakefield Ph: 08 8867 1151
Discounts: CMCA; week **Notes:** tidal pool (swimming); close to playground
$$ Map ref 68 F6

837 **Quorn** Caravan Park, Silo Rd, Quorn (100m NW of Pichi Richi railway station) Ph: 08 8648 6206
Discounts: week **Notes:** situated in town
★★★☆ $$ Map ref 68 A6

838 **Renmark**, BIG4 Renmark Riverfront Holiday Park, Sturt Hwy (2km E of PO) Ph: 1300 664 612
Discounts: BIG4 **Notes:** riverfront park; canoe hire; playground
$$$+* Map ref 69 A7

839 **Renmark**, Riverbend Caravan Park, Sturt Hwy, Renmark (3km E of PO) Ph: 1800 552 451
Discounts: Top Tourist **Notes:** shop close; riverfront park; canoe hire; river water
★★★☆ $$$+* Map ref 69 A7

840 **Riverton** Caravan Park, Cnr Oxford Tce & Torrens Rd, Riverton Ph: 08 8847 2419
Discounts: week **Notes:** shop close; playground; tennis; close to bike trail
★★★☆ $ Map ref 68 F7

841 **Robe**, BIG4 Robe Long Beach Holiday Park, The Esplanade (2km E of PO) Ph: 1800 106 106
Discounts: BIG4; CMCA **Notes:** long vehicle to 8m; close to beach; indoor heated pool
★★★★☆ $$$+ Map ref 69 H4

842 **Robe**, Lakeside Tourist Park, Squire Dr, Robe (1km E of PO) Ph: 1300 135 012
Discounts: Top Tourist **Notes:** lakefront park; close to town; playground
★★★★ $$$+* Map ref 69 H4

843 **Robe**, Sea Vu Caravan Park, Squire Dr, Robe (1km E of PO) Ph: 08 8768 2273
Discounts: Family Parks **Notes:** beachfront park; close to town; playground
★★★★ $$$+* Map ref 69 H4

844 **Roxby Downs**, Myall Grove Holiday Park, Burgoyne St, Roxby Downs Ph: 1800 356 103
Discounts: snr **Notes:** swimming pool & shop close; near opal field; mine & wildlife tours
★★★ $$ Map ref 70 A7

845 **Smoky Bay** Caravan Park, South Terrace, Smoky Bay (270m S of PO) Ph: 08 8625 7030
Discounts: week (off-pk) **Notes:** public ph & shop close; close to water; seafood on sale
★★★☆ $$ Map ref 70 D2

846 **Southend** on Sea Tourist Park, Eyre St, Southend (opposite PO) Ph: 08 8735 6035
Discounts: CMCA; pen/snr/wk off-pk **Notes:** beachfront park; boat ramp; jetty
★★★ $$* Map ref 69 J5

847 **Stansbury** Progress Assoc Foreshore Caravan Park, Anzac Pde, Stansbury Ph: 08 8852 4171
Discounts: Family Parks; CMCA; pen/snr/wk **Notes:** beachfront park; no unpowered sites; playground
★★★☆ $$+ Map ref 68 H5

848 **Streaky Bay** Foreshore Tourist Park, Wells St (1.5km W of PO) Ph: 08 8626 1666
Discounts: Family Parks; pen; snr **Notes:** waterfront park; fishing & crabbing
★★★★ $$ Map ref 70 E3

849 **Tailem Bend**, Rivers Edge Caravan Park, Princes Hwy (2km NW of PO) Ph: 08 8572 3307
Discounts: CMCA **Notes:** public ph & shop close; riverfront park; boat ramp; rain water
★★ $ Map ref 67 C14

850 **Tumby Bay** Caravan Park, Tumby Tce, Tumby Bay (1.5km S of PO) Ph: 1800 800 320
Discounts: Top Tourist; week (10%) **Notes:** pets permitted off-pk; beachfront park; boat ramp; playground
★★★☆ $$+ Map ref 68 F2

851 **Venus Bay** Caravan Park, Matson Tce, Venus Bay Ph: 08 8625 5073
Discounts: concession cards **Notes:** public ph close; beachfront park
★★★ $$ Map ref 70 F4

852 **Victor Harbor** Beachfront Caravan Park, Victoria St (1.5km W of PO) Ph: 1800 620 100
Discounts: Top Tourist **Notes:** shop close; LPG swap only; some ensuite sites, no unpowered sites
★★★☆ $$+ Map ref 66 G6

853 **Victor Harbor** Holiday & Cabin Park, Bay Rd, Victor Harbor (2km W of PO) Ph: 08 8552 1949
Discounts: Family Parks; CMCA **Notes:** playground; games room; quiet park
★★★☆ $$+* Map ref 66 G6

854 **Waikerie** Caravan Park, Peake Tce, Waikerie (700m W of PO) Ph: 1300 668 151
Discounts: Top Tourist; week (off-pk) **Notes:** public ph close; close to river, fauna park & playground
★★★☆ $$* Map ref 69 A6

855 **Wallaroo** North Beach Tourist Park, Pamir Ct (3km NW of PO) Ph: 08 8823 2531
Discounts: CMCA; pen; week **Notes:** beachfront park; rec room; playground
★★★☆ $$* Map ref 68 E4

856 **Wellington** Caravan Park, Main Rd, Wellington (12km S of Tailem Bend) Ph: 08 8572 7302
Discounts: week **Notes:** quiet; close to river; rain water
★★★ $* Map ref 67 E14

857 **Whyalla** Caravan Park, Mullaquana Rd, Mullaquana (5km SW of PO) Ph: 1800 828 012
Discounts: Top Tourist; CMCA; week **Notes:** quiet, friendly, spacious park
★★★☆ $$ Map ref 68 C5

858 **Whyalla**, Discovery Holiday Parks - Whyalla, Broadbent Tce (1km SW of PO) Ph: 1800 352 966
Discounts: Family Parks **Notes:** playground; boat ramp & jetty; jumping pillow
★★★☆ $$+ Map ref 68 C5

859 **Wilmington**, Beautiful Valley Caravan Park, Main North Rd (1km S of PO) Ph: 08 8667 5197
Discounts: week **Notes:** rec room; playground; spa
★★★☆ $$* Map ref 68 B6

860 **Wilpena** Pound Camping and Caravan Park, Wilpena, Flinders Ranges Nat Park Ph: 1800 805 802
Discounts: CMCA; snr; week **Notes:** adjacent to Wilpena Pound
★★☆ $$$ Map ref 71 B10

861 **Wilpena**, Rawnsley Park Station, Wilpena Rd (21km S of Wilpena Pound) Ph: 08 8648 0008
Discounts: Top Tourist; pen (off-pk) **Notes:** close to Flinders Ranges NP; rain water
★★★★ $$$ Map ref 71 C10

862 **Woomera** Travellers Village, Old Pimba Rd, Woomera Ph: 08 8673 7800
Notes: licensed bar; cabins, motel rooms, backpackers
$$ Map ref 70 B7

863 **Yorketown** Caravan Park, Memorial Dr, Yorketown (500m E of PO) Ph: 08 8852 1731
Discounts: week **Notes:** public ph & shop close; close to town
★★★ $ Map ref 68 H5

Western Australia

864 **Albany**, Emu Beach Holiday Park, Medcalf Pde, Emu Point (6km NE of PO) Ph: 1800 984 411
Discounts: Top Tourist **Notes:** public ph close; mini golf; close to beach
★★★★☆ $$$$+* Map ref 81 J12

865 **Albany** Holiday Park, 550 Albany Hwy, Albany (4km N of PO) Ph: 08 9841 7800
Discounts: Family Parks; 3rd night **Notes:** shop & LPG refill close; no unpowered sites; rural outlook
★★★☆ $$$+ Map ref 81 J12

866 **Albany**, Kalgan River Chalets & Caravan Park, Nanarup Rd, Kalgan (14km E of PO) Ph: 08 9844 7937
Notes: cassette DP; boat ramp, canoes, boats; golf; tennis; wildlife
★★★☆ $$ Map ref 81 J12

867 **Albany**, Middleton Beach Holiday Park, Flinders Parade (3km SE of PO) Ph: 1800 644 674
Discounts: BIG4; week (off-pk) **Notes:** beachfront; some ensuites; spa; playground
★★★★☆ $$$$+ Map ref 81 J12

868 **Albany**, Rose Garden Beachside Holiday Park, Mermaid Ave, Emu Point (8km NE PO) Ph: 1800 889 999
Discounts: off-pk **Notes:** beachfront park; shady sites; café
★★★★ $$$+ Map ref 81 J12

869 **Augusta**, Molloy Caravan Park, Fishers Rd, Augusta (8km E of Bussell Hwy) Ph: 08 9758 4515
Discounts: pen **Notes:** riverfront park; boat ramp; canoe hire
★★★☆ $$+ Map ref 80 G2

870 **Augusta**, Turner Caravan Park, 1 Blackwood Ave, Augusta Ph: 08 9758 1593
Discounts: CMCA; pen off-pk **Notes:** shop close; riverfront park; boat ramp; no cabin accomm
★★★☆ $$$ Map ref 80 G2

871 **Auski** Tourist Village, Great Northern Hwy, Munjina Ph: 08 9176 6988
Notes: quiet location 100m behind roadhouse
★★★ $$$ Map ref 87 E8

872 **Australind**, Leschenault Inlet Caravan Park, Cathedral Ave (2km NW of shop centre) Ph: 08 9797 1095
Notes: located on estuary; bore water
★★★ $ Map ref 80 B4

873 **Balladonia** Caravan Facility, Balladonia Roadhouse, Eyre Hwy Ph: 08 9039 3453
Discounts: CMCA **Notes:** no laundry; rain water
★★★ $$ Map ref 91 H2

874 **Boulder**, Discovery Holiday Parks - Boulder, Lane St, Boulder (800m S of PO) Ph: 1800 001 266
Discounts: Family Parks; CMCA **Notes:** medium length vehicles only; cassette DP; some ensuite sites
★★★☆ $$$ Map ref 85 H12

875 **Bremer Bay** Beaches Tourist Park, Wellstead Rd (3km S of PO) Ph: 08 9837 4290
Discounts: off-pk **Notes:** some ensuite sites; cafe; close to ocean
★★★★ $$+ Map ref 83 H9

876 **Broome**, Cable Beach Caravan Park, Millington St (5km NW of PO) Ph: 08 9192 2066
Discounts: week (off-pk) **Notes:** bookings for minimum of 1 week
★★★★ $$$$+* Map ref 88 G3

877 **Broome** Caravan Park, Wattle Dr, Broome Ph: 08 9192 1776
Notes: located off highway into town
★★★☆ $$$+ Map ref 88 G3

878 **Broome** Vacation Village, Port Dr, Broome (4km SW of PO) Ph: 08 9192 1057
Discounts: Family Parks **Notes:** powered sites closed Nov-Easter
★★★☆ $$$+ Map ref 88 G3

879 **Bunbury** Glade Caravan Park, Bussell Hwy, Bunbury (4km S of PO) Ph: 1800 113 800
Discounts: BIG4 **Notes:** long vehicle to 8m; public ph close; LPG swap only; on bus route; playground; rec room
★★★★ $$$* Map ref 80 B3

880 **Bunbury**, Discovery Holiday Park -Koombana, Koombana Dr (1km NE of PO) Ph: 1800 003 367
Discounts: BIG4; CMCA **Notes:** close to beach; some ensuites; jumping pillow
★★★★ $$$$+ Map ref 80 B3

881 **Bunbury**, Discovery Holiday Parks -Bunbury, Bussell Hwy/Washington Ave (6km S of PO) Ph: 1800 007 100
Discounts: Top Tourist; CMCA; snr, auto clubs **Notes:** cassette DP; mini golf; tennis; spa; playground
★★★★ $$$+* Map ref 80 B3

882 **Busselton**, Kookaburra Caravan Park, Marine Tce, Busselton (700m N of PO) Ph: 08 9752 1516
Discounts: pen/snr; week **Notes:** few drive thru sites; public ph & shop close; close to town & beach; no unpowered sites
★★★★ $$$+ Map ref 80 C2

883 **Busselton**, Mandalay Holiday Resort, Mandalay Entrance (4km W of PO) Ph: 1800 248 231
Discounts: Top Tourist; week (off-pk) **Notes:** long vehicle to 9m; pets permitted off-pk; no unpowered sites; playground
★★★★☆ $$$$+* Map ref 80 C3

884 **Busselton**, Peppermint Park Eco Village, 97 Caves Rd, Busselton Ph: 08 9755 4241
Discounts: BIG4; week (off-pk) **Notes:** LPG swap only; close to beach; wildlife; playground
★★★★☆ $$$+* Map ref 80 C3

885 **Busselton area**, Four Seasons Holiday Resort, Caves Rd (14km W of Busselton) Ph: 08 9755 4082
Discounts: Oz Parks **Notes:** LPG swap only; large shady park close to beach
★★★ $$+ Map ref 80 C2

886 **Carnarvon**, Capricorn Holiday Park, North West Coastal Hwy (5km E of PO) Ph: 08 9941 8153
Discounts: Family Parks; off-pk **Notes:** conveniently located on highway
★★★ $$ Map ref 86 J1

887 **Carnarvon**, Coral Coast Tourist Park, Robinson St (700m E of PO) Ph: 08 9941 1438
Discounts: snr; week **Notes:** shop close; some ensuite sites; walk to town centre
★★★☆ $$ Map ref 86 J1

888 **Carnarvon**, Marloo Retiree Senior Tourist Caravan Park, Wise St (3km E of PO) Ph: 08 9941 1439
Discounts: snr; week **Notes:** tranquil secure haven
★★★★ $$$ Map ref 86 J1

889 **Carnarvon**, Norwesta Caravan Park, Cnr Robinson & Angelo Sts, Carnarvon Ph: 1800 851 964
Discounts: CMCA; week **Notes:** shop close; large grass sites; accomm is onsite vans
$$ Map ref 86 J1

890 **Cervantes** Pinnacles Caravan Park, Aragon St, Cervantes (500m N of PO) Ph: 08 9652 7060
Discounts: CMCA; snr **Notes:** close to water
★★★ $$$+ Map ref 84 H4

891 **Cheynes Beach** Caravan Park, Cheynes (68km E of Albany) Ph: 08 9846 1247
Discounts: Family Parks; week (off-pk) **Notes:** close to beach; no unpowered sites; bore water
★★★★ $$$* Map ref 81 J14

892 **Collie** River Valley Tourist Park, 1 Porter St, Collie (2km W of PO) Ph: 08 9734 5088
Discounts: CMCA; pen; snr; week **Notes:** public ph close; quiet, clean & friendly
★★★☆ $$ Map ref 80 B6

893 **Coorow** Caravan Park, Long St, Coorow Ph: 08 9952 0100
Discounts: CMCA; economical **Notes:** swimming pool, public ph & shop close; wildflower area in spring
$ Map ref 84 G5

894 **Coral Bay**, Bayview Caravan Park, Robinson St, Coral Bay Ph: 08 9385 6655
Discounts: week **Notes:** long vehicle to 8m; LPG refill & internet access close; bore water; tennis; playground
★★★ $$$+* Map ref 86 F1

895 **Corrigin** Caravan Park, Kirkwood St, Corrigin (500m SE of PO) Ph: 0427 632 515
Discounts: week **Notes:** swimming pool & shop close; close to town
★★★ $$ Map ref 79 F12

896 **Denham** Seaside Tourist Village, Stella Rowley Dr, Denham (500m W of PO) Ph: 1300 133 733
Discounts: Top Tourist; snr; week (off-pk) **Notes:** beachfront park; close to town CBD
★★★☆ $$$ Map ref 84 A1

897 **Denmark** Rivermouth Caravan Park, Inlet Dr, Denmark (1km S of PO) Ph: 08 9848 1262
Discounts: seasonal discounts **Notes:** boat ramp
★★★ $$+* Map ref 81 J10

898 **Derby**, Kimberley Entrance Caravan Park, Rowan St, Derby Ph: 08 9193 1055
Notes: close to CBD; no cabin accomm
$$$ Map ref 88 F6

899 **Dongara** Denison Beach Holiday Park, Ocean Dr, Dongara (3km S of PO) Ph: 1800 600 776
Discounts: BIG4 **Notes:** shop close; beachfront; some ensuite sites; no unpowered
★★★★ $$$+ Map ref 84 F3

900 **Dongara**, Seaspray Caravan Park, 79 Church St, Dongara (1km W of PO) Ph: 08 9927 1165
Discounts: pen; week **Notes:** ensuites, no unpowered; playground & water playground
★★★ $$$+ Map ref 84 F3

901 **Dongara** Tourist Park, George St, Port Denison (3km S of PO) Ph: 08 9927 1210
Discounts: Top Tourist; snr (off-pk) **Notes:** beachfront park, ocean views; playground
★★★☆ $$$+ Map ref 84 F3

902 **Dwellingup** Chalets & Caravan Park, Delpark Rd (600m W of PO) Ph: 08 9538 1157
Discounts: snr **Notes:** few drive thru sites; no unpowered sites
★★★ $$ Map ref 78 H5

903 **Eighty Mile Beach** Caravan Park, Eighty Mile Beach Rd, Eighty Mile Beach Ph: 08 9176 5941
Notes: beachfront park; fishing; bore water
★★★☆ $$$$ Map ref 87 A11

904 **Eneabba area,** Western Flora Caravan Park, Brand Hway (22km N of Eneabba) Ph: 08 9955 2030
Discounts: CMCA **Notes:** wildflowers; rain water
★★★☆ $$ Map ref 84 G4

905 **Esperance**, Bathers Paradise, Westamacott St, Esperance (3km NE of PO) Ph: 08 9071 1014
Discounts: Oz Parks; CMCA; week **Notes:** public ph & shop close; close to beach
★★★ $+ Map ref 83 G13

906 **Esperance** Bay Holiday Park, Dempster St, Esperance (1km S of PO) Ph: 1800 999 923
Discounts: Top Tourist **Notes:** shop close; close to beach; playground
★★★★ $$+ Map ref 83 G13

907 **Esperance, Chadwick**, Crokers Park Holiday Resort, Harbour Rd (3km N of PO) Ph: 1800 001 466
Discounts: loyalty program (off-pk); week **Notes:** parkland setting
★★★★ $$$+* Map ref 83 G13

908 **Esperance**, Pink Lake Tourist Park, Pink Lake Rd (2km W of PO) Ph: 1800 011 311
Discounts: Family Parks; week (off-pk) **Notes:** shady grassed sites; playground; jumping pillow
★★★★ $$+ Map ref 83 G14

909 **Eucla** Caravan Park, Eyre Hwy, Eucla (100m E of Eucla Travellers Cross) Ph: 08 9039 3468
Notes: motel units; playground; rain water
★★★ $ Map ref 91 H7

910 **Exmouth** Cape Holiday Park, Cnr Truscott Cr & Murat Rd (1.5km S of PO) Ph: 1800 621 101
Discounts: BIG4; snr **Notes:** long vehicle to 9m; public ph close; some ensuite sites
★★★☆ $$$ Map ref 86 D2

911 **Exmouth,** Ningaloo Caravan & Holiday Resort, Murat Rd (opposite Info centre) Ph: 1800 652 665
Discounts: Top Tourist, CMCA, week **Notes:** LPG refill close; playground; close to restaurant & dive shops
★★★★ $$$+ Map ref 86 D2

912 **Fitzroy Crossing,** Fitzroy River Lodge, Great Northern Hwy (2km SE of town) Ph: 08 9191 5141
Discounts: CMCA **Notes:** spacious grass sites; bore water
★★★★ $$$ Map ref 89 H9

913 **Fraser Range** Sheep Station, Eyre Hwy, 100km E of Norseman Ph: 08 9039 3210
Discounts: extra people at no cost **Notes:** operating sheep station; wildlife; rain water
★★★☆ $$ Map ref 91 H2

914 **Fremantle** Village, 1 Cockburn Rd, South Fremantle (3km S of PO) Ph: 1800 999 938
Discounts: CMCA; pen **Notes:** shop close; close to public transport
★★★★ $$$+ Map ref 77 K1

915 **Fremantle**, Coogee Beach Holiday Park, Cockburn Rd, Coogee (5km S of Fremantle) Ph: 1800 817 016
Discounts: CMCA; snr **Notes:** long vehicle to 9m; direct beach access
★★★ $$$+* Map ref 77 K2

916 **Fremantle**, Woodman Point Holiday Park, 132 Cockburn Rd (10km S of Fremantle) Ph: 1800 244 133
Discounts: snr **Notes:** beach access; rec room; transport
★★★★ $$$+* Map ref 78 E4

917 **Geraldton,** Belair Gardens Caravan Park, Marine Tce (2km W of PO) Ph: 1800 240 938
Discounts: BIG4; pen **Notes:** close to beach; some ensuite sites; playground
★★★☆ $$$ Map ref 84 E3

918 **Geraldton,** Sunset Beach Holiday Park, Bosley St, Sunset Beach (5km N of PO) Ph: 1800 353 389
Discounts: BIG4; week **Notes:** beachfront park; some ensuite sites; playground
★★★★ $$$+ Map ref 84 E3

919 **Geraldton area,** Drummond Cove Holiday Park, NW Coastal Hwy (13km N of PO) Ph: 1800 992 524
Discounts: Top Tourist; week (5%) **Notes:** close to beach; no unpowered sites
★★★☆ $$ Map ref 84 E3

920 **Goomalling** Caravan Park, Throssell St, Goomalling (1km SE of PO) Ph: 08 9629 1183
Discounts: CMCA; pen/snr/week **Notes:** swimming pool, public ph, shop, LPG refill & internet access close; close to town
★★★ $ Map ref 79 B8

921 **Greenough** Rivermouth Caravan Park, Hull St (10km S of Geraldton) Ph: 1800 800 580
Discounts: CMCA; snr; week **Notes:** park is river & ocean front; playground; tennis
$$ Map ref 84 F3

922 **Gregory,** Port Gregory Caravan Park, 13 Sanford St, Gregory Ph: 08 9935 1052
Discounts: pen/snr; week **Notes:** close to beach, 4WD access
★★★ $$ Map ref 84 E2

923 **Guilderton** Caravan Park, Dewar St, Guilderton (500m S of PO) Ph: 08 9577 1021
Notes: public ph & shop close; close to river & boat ramp
★★★★ $$$+ Map ref 78 B3

924 **Harvey** Rainbow Caravan Park, Kennedy St, Harvey (1km NE of PO) Ph: 08 9729 2239
Discounts: CMCA; pen; week **Notes:** free tea & scones on arrival
★★★☆ $$ Map ref 78 K5

925 **Hopetoun** Caravan Park, Esplanade St, Hopetoun (400m W of PO) Ph: 08 9838 3096
Discounts: seasonal discounts **Notes:** shop close; beachfront park close to town; playground
★★★ $$ Map ref 83 G10

926 **Horrocks** Beach Caravan Park, opposite Horrocks Post Office Ph: 08 9934 3039
Discounts: Family Parks; week (off-pk) **Notes:** public ph & shop close; close to beach & golf course
★★★ $$$+ Map ref 84 E3

927 **Hyden,** Wave Rock Resort & Caravan Park, Wave Rock Rd (5km E of PO) Ph: 08 9880 5022
Notes: adjacent to Wave Rock
★★★ $$$ Map ref 83 D8

928 **Jurien Bay** Tourist Park, Roberts St, Jurien Bay (50m N of PO) Ph: 08 9652 1595
Discounts: Top Tourist; CMCA **Notes:** public ph & shop close; close to ocean; jumping pillow
★★★☆ $$$+ Map ref 84 H3

929 **Kalbarri** Anchorage Caravan Park, River Rd, Kalbarri (next door to PO) Ph: 08 9937 1181
Discounts: CMCA; week (off-pk) **Notes:** public ph, shop & internet access close; across road from the water
$$$ Map ref 84 D2

930 **Kalbarri,** Murchison Park Caravan Park, Grey St, Kalbarri (300m NE of PO) Ph: 1300 851 555
Discounts: Top Tourist; pen; senior; week **Notes:** public internet & shop close; overlooking river & ocean; playground
★★★☆ $$$ Map ref 84 D2

931 **Kalgoorlie,** Discovery Holiday Parks -Kalgoorlie, Burt St (2km W of Boulder PO) Ph: 1800 004 800
Discounts: Top Tourist; CMCA; snr **Notes:** playground; tour desk
★★★★ $$$+ Map ref 83 A11

932 **Kalgoorlie,** Goldminer Tourist Caravan Park, Great Eastern Hwy (3.5km W of PO) Ph: 08 9021 3713
Notes: some ensuite sites
★★★ $$$ Map ref 83 A11

933 **Kalgoorlie,** Prospector Holiday Park, Great Eastern Hwy (3km SW of PO) Ph: 1800 800 907
Notes: shop close; closest park to Kalgoorlie CBD
★★★★ $$$$+ Map ref 83 A11

934 **Karlgarin,** Tressie's Museum & Caravan Pk, Kondinin-Hyden Hwy (600m from PO) Ph: 08 9889 5043
Discounts: CMCA; week **Notes:** shop close; accomm is budget rooms
★★★★ $ Map ref 83 E8

935 **Karratha** Caravan Park, Moonligunn Rd, Karratha (3km S of PO) Ph: 08 9185 1012
Discounts: Family Parks **Notes:** grassed sites
$$$$ Map ref 86 B6

936 **Karratha,** Pilbara Holiday Park, Rosemary St (4km SW of PO) Ph: 1800 451 855
Discounts: BIG4; CMCA; snr **Notes:** long vehicle to 9m; some ensuite sites; no unpowered sites
★★★★ $$$$$$ Map ref 86 B6

937 **Kojonup** Caravan Park, Newstead Rd, Kojonup (1km E of PO) Ph: 08 9831 1127
Discounts: CMCA; pen/snr; 3rd nght **Notes:** LPG swap only; shady, quiet and peaceful
★★★ $$ Map ref 81 D9

938 **Kondinin** Caravan Park, Cnr Graham & Gordon Sts, Kondinin Ph: 08 9889 1006
Discounts: economical; week **Notes:** swimming pool, public ph, shop, LPG refill & internet access close; close to town centre; no cabin accommodation
$ Map ref 79 G14

939 **Kununurra,** Ivanhoe Village Caravan Resort, Ivanhoe/Coolibah Dr (700m W of PO) Ph: 1800 668 367
Discounts: BIG4 **Notes:** long vehicle to 10m; shop close; some ensuite sites; spa; playground
5 $$$+ Map ref 89 D13

940 **Kununurra,** Discovery Holiday Park - Lake Kununurra, Lakeview Dr (1.8km W of PO) Ph: 1800 648 112
Discounts: CMCA **Notes:** few long vehicle sites; lakefront park with grass; bore water
★★★★ $$$ Map ref 89 D13

941 **Kununurra** Lakeside Resort Caravan Park, Casuarina Way (2km SE of PO) Ph: 08 9169 1092
Discounts: Family Parks **Notes:** few long vehicle sites; boat ramp & jetty; restaurant
★★★☆ $$$ Map ref 89 D14

942 **Lake Grace** Caravan Park, Mather St, Lake Grace (300m N of PO) Ph: 08 9865 1263
Discounts: week **Notes:** swimming pool, public ph, shop & internet access close; park is in town; budget accomm only
★★★ $ Map ref 79 K14

943 **Lake King** Caravan Park, Critchley Ave, Lake King Ph: 08 9838 0052
Discounts: week **Notes:** wildflower area in spring
★★★ $ Map ref 83 F9

944 **Ledge Point** Holiday Park, Ledge Point Rd, adjacent to golf course Ph: 1300 856 088
Discounts: BIG4; CMCA; snr **Notes:** close to beach, golf & lawn bowls
$$$+* Map ref 78 A2

945 **Leonora** Caravan Park, Rochester St, Leonora Ph: 08 9037 6568
Discounts: week **Notes:** spacious sites, large lawn area
$$ Map ref 85 F12

946 **Mandurah** Caravan & Tourist Park, Pinjarra Rd, Furnissdale (5km E of PO) Ph: 1800 332 221
Discounts: Top Tourist; week **Notes:** some ensuites; playground; jumping pillow
★★★★ $$$$+* Map ref 78 G3

947 **Manjimup,** Warren Way Caravan Park, South Western Hwy, Manjimup Ph: 08 9771 1060
Discounts: CMCA; week; pen **Notes:** meals available; fuel available
★★☆ $$ Map ref 80 F6

948 **Margaret River** Tourist Park, Station Rd, Margaret River (1km E of PO) Ph: 08 9757 2180
Discounts: Family Parks **Notes:** long vehicle to 9m; walk to town; some ensuite sites
★★★★ $$+ Map ref 80 E2

949 **Margaret River**, Taunton Farm Holiday Park, Bussell Hwy (5km N) Ph: 1800 248 777
Discounts: BIG4 **Notes:** shady grassed sites; playground
★★★★ $$$+* Map ref 80 E2

950 **Margaret River area, Gracetown** Caravan Park, Cowaramup Bay Rd (3km E ofPO) Ph: 1800 555 818
Discounts: Top Tourist; snr; week **Notes:** bushland; tennis spring water
★★★☆ $$+ Map ref 80 D1

951 **Merredin** Caravan Park & Av-A-Rest Village, Cnr Hwy & Oats St, Merredin Ph: 08 9041 1535
Discounts: CMCA; week **Notes:** shop & LPG refill close; 4 star villas; playground
★★★★ $$ Map ref 79 B13

952 **Monkey Mia** Dolphin Resort via Denham Ph: 08 9948 1320
Discounts: CMCA; snr; auto clubs; wk **Notes:** de-salinated & bore water; restaurant; tennis
★★★ $$$$ Map ref 84 A2

953 **Mount Barker** Caravan Park, Albany Hwy, Mt Barker (1km N of PO) Ph: 08 9851 1691
Notes: close to town, wineries & wildflower areas
★★★ $$$+* Map ref 81 H11

954 **Muckinbudin** Caravan Park, Cruickshank Rd, Mukinbudin (700m SW of PO) Ph: 08 9047 1103
Discounts: very economical; week **Notes:** in town next to recreation centre
★★★☆ $ Map ref 82 A7

955 **Newdegate**, Myriadena Motel & Caravan Park, North Newdegate Rd Ph: 08 9871 1685
Discounts: CMCA; snr/pen **Notes:** public ph close; shady & quiet; accomm is onsite vans
$$ Map ref 83 F8

956 **Newman**, Dearlove's Caravan Park, Cowra Dr, Newman Ph: 08 9175 2802
Discounts: pen; snr **Notes:** shop close; accomm is 'dongas'
$$ Map ref 87 F9

957 **Norseman**, Gateway Caravan Park, Prinsep St (1km N of PO) Ph: 08 9039 1500
Notes: shop close; 1km from town centre
★★★☆ $$$ Map ref 83 D13

958 **Northam** Caravan Park, Yilgarn Ave, Northam Ph: 08 9622 1620
Discounts: CMCA; week **Notes:** some ensuite sites
$$ Map ref 79 C8

959 **Northcliffe**, A Round Tu-It Eco Caravan Park, Muirillup Rd (1.5km E of PO) Ph: 08 9776 7276
Notes: public ph close; accomm is B&B & onsite vans; wildlife
★★★ $$ Map ref 80 H6

960 **Onslow**, Ocean View Caravan Park, Second Ave, Onslow Ph: 08 9184 6053
Discounts: week **Notes:** shop & internet access close; beachfront park; close to boat ramp
$$$ Map ref 86 D3

961 **Pemberton** Caravan Park, Pump Hill Rd, Pemberton (700m W of PO) Ph: 08 9776 1300
Discounts: week **Notes:** swimming pool close; nestled in kauri forest; playground
★★★☆ $$+* Map ref 80 G5

962 **Perth, Caversham**, Perth Vineyards Holiday Parks, Benara Rd (14km NE of GPO) Ph: 1800 679 992
Discounts: BIG4; CMCA **Notes:** long vehicle to 9m; close to train; some ensuite sites
★★★★ $$$$ Map ref 77 D6

963 **Perth, Forrestfield**, Discovery Holiday Parks - Perth, 186 Hale Rd (18km E of Perth) Ph: 08 9453 6677
Discounts: BIG4; CMCA **Notes:** some ensuites; recreation room; takeaways
★★★★☆ $$$$ Map ref 77 G7

964 **Perth, Gwelup**, Karrinyup Waters Resort, 467 North Beach Rd (14km NW of GPO) Ph: 1800 633 665
Discounts: Top Tourist **Notes:** long vehicle to 12m; spa; playground; jumping pillow
★★★★ $$$$ Map ref 77 D2

965 **Perth, Madeley**, Kingsway Tourist & Caravan Park, Cnr Kingsway & Wanneroo Rds Ph: 1800 119 988
Discounts: Acclaim Parks **Notes:** close to shopping centre
★★★★ $$$$+ Map ref 77 C3

966 **Perth, West Swan**, Swan Valley Tourist Park, 6581 West Swan Rd (16km NE) Ph: 1800 999 190
Discounts: Acclaim Parks **Notes:** shop close; near wineries
★★★☆ $$$$+ Map ref 77 C6

967 **Pinjarra** Caravan Park, Pinjarra Rd, Pinjarra (2km W of PO) Ph: 08 9531 1374
Discounts: week **Notes:** LPG swap only; recreation room
★★★ $$ Map ref 78 H4

968 **Port Hedland**, Cooke Point Holiday Park, Cnr Athol & Taylor Sts (8km E of PO) Ph: 1800 459 999
Discounts: snr **Notes:** long vehicle to 7m; playground; pool/snooker; cable TV access
★★★★ $$$$$ Map ref 87 B8

969 **Ravensthorpe** Caravan Park, South Coast Hwy (600m E of PO) Ph: 08 9838 1050
Discounts: CMCA; snr **Notes:** close to wildflower area
★★ $$ Map ref 83 F10

970 **Southern Cross** Caravan Park & Motor Lodge, Great Eastern Hwy (opp hospital) Ph: 08 9049 1212
Notes: close to town; rec room
★★★☆ $$ Map ref 83 B8

971 **Stirling Range** Retreat, Cnr Bluff Knoll & Chester Pass Rds, Stirling Range Ph: 08 9827 9229
Discounts: week (off-pk) **Notes:** eco-tourism park; rain water
★★★★ $$$ Map ref 81 F13

972 **Tom Price** Tourist Park, Mount Nameless Rd, Tom Price Ph: 08 9189 1515
Notes: book national park tours
$$$$ Map ref 86 E7

973 **Toodyay** Caravan Park - Avon Banks, Railway Rd, Toodyay (1.5km NW of PO) Ph: 08 9574 2612
Discounts: CMCA; week **Notes:** boat ramp; playground
★★★☆ $$$+ Map ref 78 C7

974 **Toodyay**, Moondyne Caravan Park, Racecourse Rd (adjacent to racecourse) Ph: 08 9574 2534
Discounts: CMCA; week **Notes:** 25 acres of bushland
★★☆ $$$+ Map ref 78 C7

975 **Walpole**, Coalmine Beach Holiday Park, Coalmine Beach Rd (3km SE of PO) Ph: 1800 670 026
Discounts: Top Tourist; week (10%) **Notes:** cassette DP; birds permitted; beachfront park; boat ramp; playground
★★★★ $$$ Map ref 81 J8

976 **Warmun (Turkey Creek)** Caravan Park, Great Northern Hwy Ph: 08 9168 7882
Notes: meals; tours of Bungle Bungle
$$$ Map ref 89 F13

977 **Williams**, Shady Acre Caravan Park, Williams St (behind BP roadhouse) Ph: 08 9885 1192
Discounts: CMCA; pen/snr; week **Notes:** public ph & shop close; motel accomm
$ Map ref 79 J8

978 **Wongan Hills** Caravan Park, Wongan Rd, Wongan Hills (500m N of PO) Ph: 08 9671 1009
Discounts: week **Notes:** close to town
★★★ $ Map ref 82 A4

979 **Yallingup** Beach Holiday Park, Valley Rd, Yallingup (1.5km NW of PO) Ph: 1800 220 002
Discounts: Top Tourist; snr **Notes:** public ph close; across from beach
★★★☆ $$$+ Map ref 80 C1

980 **York** Caravan Park, Eighth Rd, York (3km N of town, turn left into Bland Rd) Ph: 08 9641 1421
Discounts: CMCA **Notes:** cassette DP; spacious park
$$$ Map ref 79 D8

Northern Territory

981 **Alice Springs**, MacDonnell Range Holiday Park, Palm Pl, Alice Springs Ph: 1800 808 373
Discounts: BIG4 **Notes:** some ensuites sites; free Sunday breakfast
★★★★☆ $$$$+ Map ref 101 F8

982 **Alice Springs**, Wintersun Cabin & Caravan Park, North Stuart Hwy Ph: 08 8952 4080
Discounts: Top Tourist **Notes:** long vehicle to 9m; DP soon; shop close; spacious park, shade & grass
★★★★ $$$ Map ref 101 F8

983 **Alice Springs**, Heavitree Gap Outback Lodge, Palm Cct (5km SW of PO) Ph: 08 8950 4444
Discounts: CMCA; snr **Notes:** bar & bistro; motel rooms
★★★ $$ Map ref 101 F8

984 **Barkly Homestead** Caravan Park, Junction of Barkly & Tablelands Hwys Ph: 08 8964 4549
Notes: located behind roadhouse; bore water
$$ Map ref 99 H11

985 **Batchelor** Resort Caravillage, Rum Jungle Rd, Batchelor Ph: 08 8976 0166
Discounts: BIG4 **Notes:** some ensuite sites; mini golf; takeaways
★★★☆ $$$$ Map ref 95 E2

986 **Berry Springs** Lakes Holiday Parks, Doris Rd (off Cox Peninsula Rd, 2.4km E of Nature Pk) Ph: 08 8988 6277
Discounts: snr; week **Notes:** waterslide; canoes; boat ramp
★★★☆ $$+ Map ref 95 D2

987 **Cooinda**, Gadudju Lodge Cooinda Caravan Park/Campground, off Kakadu Hwy(56km S Jabiru) Ph: 08 8979 0145
Notes: meals,; tours; fishing; boat ramp
★★★☆ $$$+ Map ref 95 D6

988 **Daly River area**, Woolianna on the Daly Tourist Park, Woolianna Rd (17km NW) Ph: 08 8978 2478
Discounts: 2 week **Notes:** closed Wet; individual pontoons; bore water; 5 star units
★★☆ $$$$ Map ref 95 F1

989 **Daly Waters** Hi-Way Inn, Junction of Stuart & Carpentaria Hwys Ph: 08 8975 9925
Discounts: CMCA **Notes:** bore water
$ Map ref 98 B7

990 **Daly Waters** Pub Caravan Park, Daly Waters (beside Daly Waters pub) Ph: 08 8975 9927
Discounts: week **Notes:** bore water; meals available
$ Map ref 98 B7

991 **Darwin, Berrimah**, FreeSpirit Resort, 901 Stuart Hwy, Berrimah Ph: 1800 350 888
Discounts: BIG4 **Notes:** resort-style park; bistro
★★★★ $$$+* Map ref 95 C2

992 **Darwin, Berrimah**, Hidden Valley Tourist Park, 25 Hidden Valley Rd (12km S of PO) Ph: 08 8984 2888
Notes: tour desk
★★★★ $$$+* Map ref 94 G7

993 **Darwin, Virginia**, Coolalinga Caravan Park, Stuart Hwy (26km SW of PO) Ph: 08 8983 1026
Discounts: Family Parks; CMCA **Notes:** roomy park; shade; rec room
★★★★ $$$ Map ref 95 D2

994 **Darwin, Virginia**, Darwin Boomerang Motel & Caravan Park, 30 Virginia Rd Ph: 08 8983 1202
Discounts: Top Tourist **Notes:** playground; tavern next door
★★★★ $$+ Map ref 95 C2

995 **Douglas Daly** Tourist Park, Oolloo Rd (Turnoff 8km S of Hot Springs turnoff) Ph: 08 8978 2479
Discounts: BIG4; Top Tourist; Family Parks **Notes:** filtered bore water
★★★☆ $$$ Map ref 95 G3

996 **Dunmarra** Wayside Inn Caravan Park, Stuart Hwy (318km S of Katherine) Ph: 08 8975 9922
Discounts: CMCA **Notes:** fuel and meals; bore water
$ Map ref 98 B7

997 **Erldunda**, Desert Oaks Caravan Park, Cnr Stuart & Lasseter Hwys (200m S of PO) Ph: 08 8956 0984
Notes: playground; motel rooms & backpackers accomm
★★★☆ $$$ Map ref 100 H7

998 **Glen Helen** Resort, Namatjira Dr (132km W of Alice Springs) Ph: 08 8956 7489
Discounts: 4 night stay **Notes:** walks; waterhole; live entertainment
$$ Map ref 100 F6

999 **Jabiru**, Kakadu Lodge, Jabiru Dr, Jabiru (500m W of PO) Ph: 1800 811 154
Discounts: CMCA; pen/snr **Notes:** DP close; bar/bistro; resort-style pool
★★★☆ $$$$ Map ref 95 D7

1000 **Katherine**, Takaru Bush Resorts, Low Level Caravan Pk, Shadforth Rd (5km W of PO) Ph: 08 8972 3962
Discounts: BIG4 **Notes:** bistro May-Oct; bore water
★★★★ $$$ Map ref 95 J5

1001 **Katherine**, Red Gum Tourist Park, Victoria Hwy, Katherine (1km W of CBD) Ph: 08 8972 2239
Discounts: CMCA **Notes:** closest park to town; alcohol licence
$$$ Map ref 95 J5

1002 **Kings Canyon** Resort Camp Ground, Luritja Rd, Watarrka National Park Ph: 1300 134 044
Notes: bore water; sunset viewing
★★★★ $$$$ Map ref 100 G5

1003 **Mataranka** Homestead Caravan Park, Homestead Rd, Mataranka Ph: 08 8975 4544
Discounts: week; pen (off-pk) **Notes:** thermal pool; restaurant; bore water; card phone only
$$ Map ref 96 G7

1004 **Tennant Creek**, Outback Caravan Park, Peko Rd (1km E of PO) Ph: 08 8962 2459
Discounts: 3-night stay **Notes:** bar; entertainment
★★★★ $$$ Map ref 99 G8

1005 **Threeways** Roadhouse Caravan Park, junction of Stuart & Barkly Hwys Ph: 08 8962 2744
Discounts: CMCA **Notes:** fuel & meals; dam water
$$ Map ref 99 G9

1006 **Ti Tree** Roadhouse Caravan Park, Stuart Hwy (190km N of Alice Springs) Ph: 08 8956 9741
Notes: grassy sites; accomm is in bunkhouse
★★★ $ Map ref 100 C7

1007 **Victoria River** Roadhouse Caravan Park, Victoria Hwy, Victoria River Ph: 08 8975 0744
Discounts: CMCA **Notes:** fuel & meals; bore water
$ Map ref 96 H4

1008 **Wycliffe Well** Holiday Park, Stuart Hwy, Wycliffe Well Ph: 1800 222 195
Discounts: BIG4; CMCA; singles **Notes:** bore water
★★★★ $$$ Map ref 99 J9

1009 **Yulara**, Ayers Rock Campground, Yulara Dr, Yulara Ph: 08 8957 7001
Notes: petrol sales
★★★★ $$$$$ Map ref 100 H4

Wastewater disposal sites

Many caravan parks have dump points, and these are not included in this list unless they are available to the travelling public rather than being restricted to park residents. A small fee may be charged to non-residents, but there will be no additional charge for park residents who use the facility. Many of the parks in the caravan park directory in this book also have dump points, but they may only be for park residents. (This listing has been carefully researched to be as accurate as possible at the time of preparation in late 2008. Please be aware that conditions change and some existing dump points may close, shift or no be longer available, while new ones will open.)

Cassette toilets or black-water holding tanks cannot be emptied into small septic systems, particularly if the old-style formaldehyde-based chemicals are used. If in doubt, check with park management or the relevant authority. We have checked, where possible, whether each dump point can be used to empty black water tanks, but cannot guarantee that every one will be suitable for the discharge arrangements for all types of black-water tanks. Where access or inlet height issues have been advised that would prevent discharge from black-water tanks, the notation 'cassette only' appears.

Queensland, South of Tropic of Capricorn

No.	Site	Map	Latitude	Longitude
1	**Barcaldine** Showgrounds, Pine St North; 2 dump points: a. behind grandstand near swimming pool clubhouse b. SE corner of toilet block near rodeo arena	(Map 10 H3)	23° 33' 06.5"S	145° 17' 35.2"E
2	**Barcaldine area** – Lloyd Jones Weir, 15km SW of Barcaldine	(Map 10 H2)	23° 38' 59.5"S	145° 12' 55.5"E
3	**Biggenden** – Isis Hwy, opposite BP service station, adj to caravan park	(Map 9 B11)	25° 30' 56.5"S	152° 02'12.5"E
4	**Biloela** – SILO Info Centre (Primary Industries), Exhibition Ave; open 9am-4pm 7 days; (07) 4992 2400	(Map 11 J11)	24° 24' 15.5"S	150° 30' 04.5"E
5	**Blackall** – cnr Blackall-Isisford Rd & Coronation Dr (near Garden St), 500m from info centre; (07) 4657 4637	(Map 10 J3)	24° 25' 30.4"S	145° 27' 45.4"E
6	**Blackall** Showgrounds, Salvia St	(Map 10 J3)	24° 25' 33"S	145° 28' 28.5"E
7	**Bollon** – William St, behind fire brigade; (07) 4620 8888 - Cassette only	(Map 8 H2)	28° 01' 51.8"S	147° 28' 39.1"E
8	**Boonah** Showgrounds, Caravan Park & Camping Grounds, Melbourne St; DP open 24/7; (07) 5463 1124	(Map 6 G7)	27° 59' 52.4"S	152° 41' 05.3"E
9	**Bribie Island area** near boat ramp, Kal Ma Kuta Drive, off Caboolture-Bribie Road near Bridge, Sandstone Point - Cassette only	(Map 5 G10)	27° 04' 06.95"S	153° 08' 00.4"E
10	**Bundaberg** – Hinkler Lions Park, cnr Childers Hwy & University Dr; key at waste transfer station	(Map 9 A13)	24° 53' 51.7"S	152° 18' 50.7"E
11	**Cecil Plains** Rural Retreat Caravan Park, Taylor St, enter via Warfield St; (07) 4695 1399	(Map 9 G9)	27° 31' 58.4"S	151° 11' 42.7"E
12	**Cecil Plains** – beside council depot shed, 26 Cheetham St, near water tower; (07) 4695 1399	(Map 9 G9)	27° 31' 51.2"S	151° 11' 39.8"E
13	**Charleville** – Mitchell Hwy, then turn left along Qantas Dr for 240m towards airport; (07) 4656 8355	(Map 17 K13)	Entry at 26° 24' 59"S	146° 15' 06.7"E
14	**Childers** rest area, Crescent St, behind PO; 24hr access; (07) 4192 1000	(Map 9 B11)	25° 14' 06.3"S	152° 16' 45.4"E
15	**Chinchilla** – Park St (Wondai Rd), next to toilets, opposite rec res; (07) 4662 7056	(Map 9 E8)	26° 44' 07.45"S	150° 37' 50.5"E
16	**Clifton** Showgrounds, Morton St; (07) 4697 4222; $10 fee if not staying - Cassette only	(Map 6 F1)	27° 55' 35"S	151° 54' 43.2"E
17	**Coombabah** – Shelter Rd, opp dog pound	(Map 7 F12)	27° 54' 55"S	153° 21' 56"E
18	**Cunnamulla** – William St, outside showground; (07) 4655 8400	(Map 19 H12)	28° 04' 07.7"S	145° 41' 48.7"E
19	**Dirranbandi** – Theodore St, beside showgrounds; (07) 4620 8844 - Cassette only	(Map 8 J4)	28° 34' 33.5"S	148° 13' 58"E
20	**Eidsvold** – in truck park, cnr Esplanade & Hodgkinson Sts (Burnett Hwy); (07) 4166 9918 or 4165 7214	(Map 9 B10)	25° 22' 16.7"S	151° 07' 25.5"E
21	**Emerald** – near info centre, Capricorn Hwy; (07) 4982 8367 - Cassette only	(Map 10 H7)	23° 31' 29"S	148° 09' 23"E
22	**Esk** Caravan Park, 26 Hassell St; small fee; (07) 5424 1466	(Map 4 J4)	27° 14' 20"S	152° 25' 22.8"E
23	**Gatton** Showgrounds, Spencer St, behind toilet block; (07) 5462 2577	(Map 6 C4)	27° 33' 30.5"S	152° 16' 50.8"E
24	**Gayndah** – Zonhoven Park, Burnett Hwy, near Tableland Rd junction; (07) 4161 1377	(Map 9 C10)	25 37' 44.7"S	151 37' 33.5"E
25	**Gin Gin** – Opposite Mobil service station on N side of town; (07) 4133 2000	(Map 9 A11)	24° 59' 01.6"S	151° 57' 02.9"E
26	**Gin Gin area** – Fred Haigh Dam (Lake Monduran Rec Res)	(Map 9 A11)	24° 52' 29"S	151° 51' 09.2"E
27	**Gladstone area** – Benaraby 20km S, Willowgrove on the River Holiday Park, on E side of Bruce Hwy 250m N of Boyne River bridge; small fee; (07) 4975 0613 (Mark)	(Map 11 J11)	24° 00' 22"S	151° 20'11"E
28	**Goondiwindi** – Caltex service station, Boundary Rd; (07) 4671 0999	(Map 9 J8)	28° 31' 45"S	150° 18' 36.8"E
29	**Goondiwindi** Showgrounds, Boundary Rd, enter main entrance, turn right, drive to tin shed toilets then turn right again; Caretaker (07) 4671 1596	(Map 9 J8)	28° 31' 51.5"S	150° 19'11.3"E
30	**Gympie** – Archery Park, cnr Bruce Hwy & Cross St, 4km N of town; (07) 5481 0800	(Map 9 D13)	26° 11' 19"S	152° 39'13"E
31	**Gympie** – Six Mile Rest Area, Bruce Hwy S of Gympie; (07) 5481 0800	(Map 9 D13)	26° 13' 51.6"S	152° 41' 50.5"E
32	**Hebel** – Main St, near hotel & opposite children's playground	(Map 8 K3)	28° 58' 20.4"S	147° 47' 44.6"E
33	**Ilfracombe**- Murray St; Council (07) 4658 2233 or 0427 582 232	(Map 10 H1)	23° 29' 25.6"S	144° 30' 37.5"E
34	**Inglewood** – Lions Park, Brooks St; Shire office (07) 4652 1444	(Map 9 J9)	28° 24' 51.4"S	151° 05' 01.5"E
35	**Injune** – truck wash area in Flower St, turn at Shell Rdhouse; (07) 4626 1581	(Map 8 C4)	25° 50' 26.5"S	148° 34' 05"E
36	**Isisford** – off St Frances St, beside toilet block in camping area; no fee; (07) 4658 8900	(Map 10 J1)	24° 15' 31"S	144° 26' 39"E
37	**Kilcoy** – Council overnight campsite, cnr D'Aguilar Hwy & Seib St; (07) 5422 4900	(Map 4 F6)	26° 56' 34"S	152° 34' 03.9"E
38	**Kingaroy** – Lions Park, cnr Kingaroy & Baron Sts; open 7am-7pm; (07) 4162 6230 - Cassette only	(Map 9 E10)	26° 32' 47.5"S	151° 50' 17"E
39	**Kingaroy** Showgrounds Caravan Park, Youngman St; (07) 4162 5037	(Map 9 E10)	26° 32' 51.3"S	151° 49' 52.6"E
40	**Longreach** Showgrounds, Sandpiper St; caution: remove grate over inlet; Caretaker 0427 581 303	(Map 10 H2)	23° 26' 19"S	144° 14' 54.5"E
41	**Manly** Boat Harbour, Royal Esplanade, at toilets near boat ramp, entry point S of Britannia St - Cassette only, unit is off-ground	(Map 3 E7)	27° 27' 42"S	153° 11' 22"E
42	**Maroochydore** – Maroochy Shire Sewerage Plant, cnr Commercial & Fisherman's Rds; call into office, 230m from corner in Commercial Rd, for keys & directions; Mon-Fri 8am-4pm; (07) 5475 8501	(Map 5 C10)	Office at 26° 39' 09.3"S	153° 03' 28.55"E
43	**Maryborough** Showgrounds, Bruce Hwy; (07) 4123 5311	(Map 9 C14)	Entry at 25° 30' 12"S	152° 40' 03"E
44	**Maryborough** – near airport, 2km from town on road to Hervey Bay, turn right just past Woodrow St, DP is behind sheds	(Map 9 C14)	25° 31' 06"S	152° 42' 30.5"E
45	**Meandarra** – Leo Gordon Apex Park, near cnr Meandarra, Dillon & Osler Sts	(Map 8 F7)	27° 19' 19.2"S	149° 52' 47"E
46	**Miles** – off Leichhardt Hwy, 700m S of Warrego Hwy, via Waterworks Rd	(Map 8 E7)	26° 39' 59.7"S	150° 11' 07.8"E
47	**Millmerran** – pump station cnr Charles & Walpole Sts, opposite Jaycees rest area; (07) 4695 1399	(Map 9 H10)	27° 52' 17"S	151° 16' 28.1"E
48	**Mitchell** – Alice St, 1km SE from Warrego Hwy intersection	(Map 8 D4)	26° 29' 47.6"S	147° 58' 45.1"E
49	**Monto** Showgrounds, Oxley St, adj to cattle wash area; (07) 4166 9999	(Map 9 A10)	24° 51' 57"S	151° 07' 01.5"E
50	**Moura** – Bauhinia Road (Dawson Hwy), 2km SW of town; (07) 4997 2084	(Map 11 K9)	24° 35' 18"S	149° 57' 31"E
51	**Nanango** – D'Aguilar Hwy on Yarraman side, in Lions Park next to BP servo, opposite Arthur St East	(Map 4 C2)	26° 40' 47"S	151° 59' 49.7"E
52	**Petrie** – Wylie Park, Gympie Rd, near railway overpass; gates open 8am-6pm; (07) 3840 6582	(Map 5 J9)	27° 16' 22.5"S	152° 58' 51"E
53	**Proston** – Lake Boondooma Caravan Park; (07) 4168 9694	(Map 9 C10)	26° 06' 08.2"S	151° 27' 04.6"E
54	**Quilpie** – cnr Quarrion & Chipu Sts, in park behind toilet block	(Map 19 D10)	26° 37' 57.5"S	144° 15' 47"E

No.	Location	Map	Latitude	Longitude
55	**Rainbow Beach** – N of town, Clarkson Dr, opposite road to beach near Inskip Pt campers water point; (07) 5486 3160	(Map 9 C14)	25° 54' 03.4"S	153° 05' 18.7"E
56	**Redcliffe** Showground, Scarborough Rd; daylight hrs; (07) 3283 0233	(Map 5 J10)	27° 13' 30"S	153° 06' 22.2"E
57	**Rolleston** – Beazley Park, Dawson Hwy, centre of town	(Map 10 J7)	24° 27' 47.5"S	148° 37' 26.8"E
58	**Roma** – Station St between Lewis & Major Sts, outside council depot; (07) 4622 1266	(Map 8 D5)	26° 34' 33.7"S	148° 47' 46"E
59	**Roma** – Bassett Park Showgrounds, Northern Rd (road to Injune); 0408 988 002 - Unit is off ground	(Map 8 D5)	26° 33' 07.1"S	148° 47' 04.5"E
60	**St George** – McGahan St, behind Showgrounds; (07) 4620 8844	(Map 8 H4)	28° 01' 39"S	148° 35' 28"E
61	**Scarborough** – toilet block at W end of Thurecht Pde beside Redcliffe Coastguard - Off ground, cassette only	(Map 5 H10)	27° 11' 39.5"S	153° 06' 15.8"E
62	**Seventeen Seventy** – council depot on Agnes Water-1770 Rd, DP 70m on right from entry	(Map 11 J13)	24° 10' 52.3"S	151° 53' 00.6"E
63	**Shorncliffe** – Sinbad St, Cabbage Tree Ck, at toilet block near boat ramp - Off ground, cassette only	(Map 3 B5)	27° 20' 01.3"S	153° 04' 51"E
64	**Springsure** – Cnr William & Eclipse Sts, toilet block in park; (07) 4984 1551 - Cassette only	(Map 10 J7)	24° 07' 04.5"S	148° 05'17.8"E
65	**Springsure** Showgrounds, Barcoo St; (07) 4984 1551	(Map 10 J7)	24° 07' 19.5"S	148° 05' 03"E
66	**Stanthorpe** – Apex Park, cnr Folkestone & Creek Sts, beside toilets; 0419 783 622	(Map 9 K10)	28° 39' 28.7"S	151° 55' 55.4"E
67	**Stonehenge** (64km N of Jundah) – DP adjacent to hotel and hall	(Map 17 G9)	~ 24° 21' 13.4"S	143° 17' 12.5"E
68	**Stonehenge area** – junction of Thompson Dev & Isisford-Bimera Rds	(Map 17 G9)	24° 14' 16.5"S	143° 33' 22"E
69	**Surat** – Fishermans Park, 1km N on Balonne R; (07) 4626 5058	(Map 8 F5)	27° 08' 57.5"S	149° 04' 24.5"E
70	**Tara** – Lagoon Rest Area, Showgrounds Rd	(Map 9 F8)	27° 16' 19.7"S	150° 27' 37.5"E
71	**Taroom** – end of Wolsey St, between North & Rose Sts, next to Council workshop; (07) 4628 9555	(Map 8 C7)	25° 38' 02.5"S	149° 47' 56.3"E
72	**Texas** – Flemming St, S of Mingoola Rd, behind old Riverside Freezing works; (07) 4652 1444	(Map 9 K10)	28° 51' 29.4"S	151° 10' 21.9"E
73	**Theodore** – near tennis courts, Eastern Lane via 7th Ave; (07) 4992 9500	(Map 8 A7)	24° 56' 39.5"S	150° 04' 31.5"E
74	**Tin Can Bay** – Sewerage Pump Stn, Wes Mitchell Park on Esplanade; (07)5481 0800	(Map 9 C13)	25° 54' 58.8"S	153° 00' 20.8"E
75	**Tin Can Bay** – Snapper Creek Rd, Tin Can Bay (go on to tip to turn)	(Map 9 D13)	25° 55' 24"S	152° 59' 28"E
76	**Toowoomba** Showgrounds, Glenvale Rd; 8am-5pm Mon-Fri; (07) 4634 7400	(Map 6 C1)	27° 33' 36.2"S	151° 53' 06"E
77	**Toowoomba** Motor Village, 821 Ruthven St; ph (07) 4635 8186 first	(Map 6 C1)	27° 35' 17.7"S	151° 56' 54.9"E
78	**Wandoan** – Jerrard St near water tower; (07) 4627 5227	(Map 8 D7)	26° 07' 21.8"S	149° 57' 35.5"E
79	**Windorah** – on left just before entering town from the NE (road from Quilpie); info centre (07) 4656 3063	(Map 17 J8)	25° 25' 04.5"S	142° 39' 33"E
80	**Windorah area** – rest area, junction Diamantina & Birdsville Dev Rds (189km W), DP behind toilet - Chemical restrictions	(Map 18 B5)	25° 22' 53.5"S	141° 37' 06.5"E

Queensland, North of Tropic of Capricorn

No.	Location	Map	Latitude	Longitude
81	**Aramac** – Council caravan park, Booker St - Cassette only	(Map 10 G2)	22° 58' 03.5"S	145° 14' 21.5"E
82	**Atherton** sewerage treatment plant, Grove St; 9am-4pm week days; (07) 4091 0700	(Map 14 F3)	17° 15' 16"S	145° 28' 48"E
83	**Atherton** – Big4 Woodlands Tourist Park, 141 Herberton Rd; ring first (07) 4091 1407	(Map 14 F3)	17° 16' 55"S	145° 28' 10.9"E
84	**Ayr** – Burdekin Cascades Caravan Park, 228 Queen St; small fee; (07) 4783 1429	(Map 10 A6)	19° 34' 48.5"S	147° 24' 05.5"E
85	**Babinda** – Rotary Park, on ck bank, Howard Kennedy Dr (~600m SE); key at info centre; (07) 4067 1008	(Map 14 G6)	17° 20' 55.5"S	145° 55' 32.4"E
86	**Babinda area** (20km N) – Fishery Falls Van Park, Bruce Hwy; small fee; (07) 4067 5283	(Map 14 F6)	17° 10' 54.9"S	145° 53' 09.2"E
87	**Bowen** Showgrounds, rear of caretaker's cottage, Mt Nutt Rd; (07) 4786 5353	(Map 10 B7)	19° 59' 42.5"S	148° 13' 41"E
88	**Cairns** – Wastewater Depot, 40 Macnamara St, near Anderson St; business hrs, key at lab office next door	(Map 14 E5)	16° 54' 46.1"S	145° 45' 00"E
89	**Cairns** – Wastewater Treatment Plant, Kate St, Woree off Ray Jones Dr; open office hours but with trucks & plant operation, access & use may be delayed so it is preferable to use Macnamara St Depot	(Map 14 E6)	16° 57' 13"S	145° 45' 11"E
90	**Capella** – Bridgeman Park, 36 Hibernia Rd; (07) 4988 7200	(Map 10 G6)	23° 05' 13.5"S	148° 01' 02"E
91	**Carmila Beach** – on Esplanade, 5km E of Carmila; 2 DPs at toilet blocks at beach – 200m and 350m south of junction with Carmila Beach Rd, sandy road; (07) 4964 5400	(Map 11 E9)	a. 21° 54' 47"S b. 21° 54' 51.5"S	149° 27' 49"E 149° 27' 49.5"E
92	**Charters Towers** Showground, Mary St; get key from Council chambers; (07) 4787 1999	(Map 10 B3)	20° 04' 22"S	146° 15' 12.7"E
93	**Charters Towers** – Columbia Mine, Poppet Head, cnr New Queen Rd & Devereux St	(Map 10 B3)	20° 04' 21.9"S	146° 16' 35.6"E
94	**Clermont** – 2 DPs a. Lime Street next to bowls club (between Karmoo & East Sts) b. sewerage works, off Cheeseborough Rd; business hours; (07) 4983 1133	(Map 10 G6)	a. 22° 49' 09"S b. 22° 49' 01"S	147° 38' 39.8"E 147° 39' 18"E
95	**Clermont area** – Theresa Creek Dam, 22km SW of Clermont - 300mm above ground, cassette only	(Map 10 G6)	22° 58' 10"S	147° 33' 14"E
96	**Cloncurry** Caravan Park Oasis, McIlwraith St (Flinders Hwy), cnr Railway St, park on E closest to town; (07) 4742 1313	(Map 12 K5)	20° 42' 25.1"S	140° 31' 02.4"E
97	**Cloncurry area** – rest area Matilda Hwy, 79km N of Cloncurry, 103km S of Burke & Wills Roadhouse	(Map 12 J5)	20° 04' 51.2"S	140° 13' 39.9"E
98	**Cooktown** – beside old Council chambers, Charlotte St, S of Green St corner; (07) 4069 5444	(Map 13 A13)	15° 27' 58.5"S	145° 14' 59.4"E
99	**Croydon** – Gulf Dev Rd, in park opp Club Hotel - No vehicle access, cassette only	(Map 12 F7)	18° 12' 12"S	142° 14' 33"E
100	**Hughenden** – McLaren St, outside Ergon Energy depot; (07) 4741 1288	(Map 10 C1)	20° 51' 03.5"S	144° 11' 34.4"E
101	**Ingham** – Bruce Hwy at Tyto Visitor Info Centre, S side of town, cnr Cooper St; (07) 4776 5211	(Map 13 G14)	18° 39' 20.1"S	146° 09' 13.1"E
102	**Innisfail** – Bruce Hwy (River Ave), between Eslick St & Scullen Ave, opposite Barrier Reef Motel; (07) 4030 2222, Ext 297	(Map 14 H7)	17° 32' 00.5"S	146° 01' 47"E
103	**Julia Creek** Caravan Park, cnr Hickman St & Old Normanton Rd; (07) 4746 7108	(Map 12 K7)	20° 39' 09.4"S	141° 44' 41.1"E
104	**Julia Creek** – Hickman St, 90m on right from CP entrance	(Map 12 K7)	20° 39' 09.5"S	141° 44' 37.9"E
105	**Karumba** Truck Stop, in Bypass Rd near cnr Yappar St	(Map 12 E5)	17°29' 26.5"S	140° 50' 10"E
106	**Mackay** – BP Macs Truck Stop, 21km S of Mackay; (07) 4956 4218	(Map 11 D8)	21° 17' 52.3"S	149° 10' 11"E
107	**Mareeba** – Doyle St, opposite Leagues Club & Davies Park; (07) 4092 5674	(Map 14 E3)	16° 59' 42.3"S	145° 24' 50.7"E
108	**Mareeba** Rodeo Grounds, 3km W on Dimbulah Rd; small fee; open Apr to Nov, not wet season; Jim or Shirley (07) 4092 1583 or 4092 1654	(Map 14 E3)	16° 59' 38"S	145° 23' 45.2"E
109	**Mossman** – Riverside Leisure Park, cnr Captain Cook Hwy & Park St, at entry to park; (07) 4098 2627	(Map 14 B4)	16° 27' 19.3"S	145° 22' 20.5"E
110	**Mt Isa** – Arline St, at rear of Riversleigh Fossil Centre; (07) 4747 3200	(Map 12 K3)	20° 43' 41.3"S	139° 29' 54.3"E
111	**Mt Isa area** – WWII airstrip rest area, Barkly Hwy 57km NW of Mt Isa	(Map 12 K3)	20° 22' 20.7"S	139° 15' 52.1"E
112	**Mt Molloy** – Rifle Creek rest area, 1.2km N of Mt Molloy - Cassette only	(Map 14 C3)	16° 39' 55.2"S	145° 19' 41.5"E
113	**Mt Surprise** – public toilets on Gulf Dev Road	(Map 13 F11)	18° 08' 50.8"S	144° 19' 02.6"E
114	**Normanton** – Philp St, adjacent Council depot; business hrs; (07) 4745 2240 - Suitable for cass, length of hose required for BW tank	(Map 12 E6)	17° 40' 50.8"S	141° 04' 35.4"E

115	**Normanton area** – rest area 107.4km S of Normanton, 90km N of Burke & Wills Rdhouse	(Map 12 G5)	18° 31' 35"S	140° 39' 11.3"E
116	**Proserpine** Council Caravan Park, 55-79 Anzac Rd, junction Barry St; small fee; (07) 4945 1554	(Map 10 C7)	20° 24' 14.4"S	148° 34' 18.7"E
117	**Ravenshoe** – outside sewerage works, 26 Ascham St; (07) 4096 2244	(Map 14 J4)	17° 36' 54"S	145° 28' 51.5"E
118	**Richmond** – Lakeview Caravan Park, 109 Goldring St (Flinders Hwy); small fee; (07) 4741 3772	(Map 13 K9)	20° 44' 06"S	143° 08' 44.1"E
119	**St Lawrence** Rec Grounds, on St Lawrence Connection Rd, behind toilet block, approx 1km SW of town; (07) 4964 5400	(Map 11 F9)	22° 20' 57.5"S	149° 31' 16.3"E
120	**Sapphire** Res, Flagon Alley via Rifle Range Rd, near public toilets; (07) 4982 8318 - Hose needed for BW tank	(Map 10 H6)	23° 27' 56"S	147° 43' 09.5"E
121	**Townsville area** – entrance to Ross River Dam Park, Upper Ross River Rd, Thuringowa	(Map 13 H14)	19° 24' 27.5"S	146° 44' 00.5"E
122	**Townsville –** Woodlands Holiday Village, 548 Bruce Hwy, on NW side of Townsville; small fee; (07) 4751 6955 - No chemicals	(Map 10 A6)	19° 14' 22.3"S	146° 39' 52"E
123	**Townsville** – Caltex Service Station, 900 Ingham Rd, Bohle, Townsville; (07) 4774 5899	(Map 10 A6)	19° 15' 41.5"S	146° 42' 53"E
124	**Winton** Rec Ground, Vindex St, near skate park; (07) 4657 1188 - Cassette only	(Map 17 D9)	22° 23' 13.3"S	143° 01' 55.8"E

New South Wales

125	**Aberdeen** – Taylor Park, near golf club, New England Hwy	(Map 27 C8)	32° 09' 37.4"S	150° 53' 17"E
126	**Adelong** – Travers St, 40m off Snowy Mtns Hwy	(Map 34 D1)	35° 18' 24"S	148° 03' 41.4 "E
127	**Ballina** Central Holiday Park, 1 River St; small fee; (02) 6686 2220 - Cassette only	(Map 29 C14)	28° 52' 22.8"S	153° 33' 59.5"E
128	**Ballina** – Shaws Bay Holiday Park, cnr Hill & Water Sts, East Ballina; small fee; (02) 6686 2326	(Map 29 C14)	28° 52' 00.1"S	153° 34' 46.4"E
129	**Ballina area** – Wardell (12km SE), Sandalwood Van & Leisure Park, 978 Pimlico Rd; small fee; (02) 6683 4221	(Map 29 C14)	28° 56' 29.2"S	153° 28' 20.8"E
130	**Balranald** – Church St, in car park next to swimming pool; (03) 5020 1599	(Map 32 G6)	34° 38' 08.2"S	143° 33' 42"E
131	**Batehaven** – Beach Rd, in Park opp shops, N of junction with Edward Rd	(Map 35 F5)	35° 43' 53.6"S	150° 11' 55.6"E
132	**Bathurst** – Morriset St (near Commonwealth St), inside Council Depot	(Map 26 F6)	33° 24' 10"S	149° 34' 26"E
133	**Batlow** – Memorial Ave, opposite and just W of Wakehurst Ave junction; 0429 491 327	(Map 33 J14)	35° 31' 12.3"S	148° 09' 00.7"E
134	**Belmont area** – Australian Motorhomes, Pacific Hwy, Bennetts Green; enter via The Groves Rd, right into Statham St, 2nd driveway on right, 2 dump points; 8am-4pm Mon-Fri; (02) 4948 0433	(Map 23 D6)	32° 59' 50.3"S	151° 41' 25.8"E
135	**Berrigan** – near Berrigan Caravan Park, Jerilderie St; (03) 5888 5100	(Map 33 J10)	35° 39' 37.7"S	145° 48' 49"E
136	**Berry** Showgrounds in Alexandra St, near camping area; (02) 4448 6053	(Map 35 B6)	34° 46' 42.8"S	150° 41' 45.7"E
137	**Bingara** Showgrounds, Bowen St, at entrance gate; contact Gwydir Shire Council, (02) 6724 200	(Map 28 E7)	29° 52' 00"S	150° 33' 19.5"E
138	**Bingara** – Junction St, 50m S of corner of Cunningham St; (02) 6724 2025	(Map 28 E7)	29° 52' 06.6"S	150° 34' 27"E
139	**Blayney** – Henry St, between Martin & Burns Sts; (02) 6368 2104	(Map 26 G5)	33° 31' 59"S	149° 15' 22.6"E
140	**Bookham area** – Burrunjuck Waters State Park, Burrunjuck Dam, 30km from town; (02) 6227 8114 - Septic tank	(Map 34 C2)	34° 58' 48"S	148° 37' 18"E
141	**Boorowa** – Park St, next to caravan park	(Map 34 B2)	34° 26' 01.9"S	148° 43' 12.9"E
142	**Bourke** Visitors Info Centre, Anson St; (02) 6872 1222	(Map 31 E11)	30° 05' 38"S	145° 56' 07.2"E
143	**Braidwood** – Bicentennial Park, Mackellar St; 1300 735 025	(Map 35 E3)	35° 26' 23.8"S	149° 48' 05.7"E
144	**Broken Hill** – rear of info centre, cnr Bromide & Blende Sts, enter via Blende St	(Map 30 K1)	31° 57' 36"S	141° 27' 37.1"E
145	**Broken Hill** – Racecourse, St Patrick's Racing Club	(Map 30 K2)	31° 54' 54"S	141° 28' 48"E
146	**Casino** – Showgrounds & Racecourse, Grafton Rd (Summerland Way), just S of Casino; (02) 6660 0300	(Map 29 C13)	28° 53' 01.3"S	153° 02' 40.1"E
147	**Casino** Village RV Resort Ltd, Light St; no charge; (02) 6662 1069	(Map 29 C13)	28° 52' 28"S	153° 02' 58.5"E
148	**Cobar** Visitor Info Centre, Marshall St; (02) 6836 2448	(Map 31 H10)	31° 29' 53"S	145° 50' 33.5"E
149	**Coleambally** Lions Park, near Big Excavator; (02) 6954 4179 - Cassette only	(Map 33 G10)	34° 47' 52.1"S	145° 52' 47.6"E
150	**Condobolin** River View Caravan Park, Diggers Ave; no charge; (02) 6895 2611,	(Map 33 C13)	33° 05' 38.8"S	147° 08' 45"E
151	**Coolamon** Caravan Park, Bruce St, between Loughnan & Mann Sts; no charge; (02) 6927 3206	(Map 33 G13)	34° 48' 49"S	147° 12' 10"E
152	**Coonamble** – in front of Riverside Caravan Park, Castlereagh Hwy; no charge; (02) 6822 1926	(Map 28 H2)	30° 57' 48.5"S	148° 23' 23.2"E
153	**Corowa** – Rowers Park, near Ball Park Caravan Park, Bridge Rd; deposit required for key; CP entry 80m S; contact kiosk at Ball Park CP (02) 6033 1426	(Map 33 K11)	36° 00' 14.4"S	146° 23' 37.1"E
154	**Cowra** – Edgell Park, Lachlan Valley Hwy; (02) 6342 4333	(Map 26 H4)	33° 50' 12.1"S	148° 40' 54.5"E
155	**Darlington Point** – Lions Park, cnr Darlington St; (02) 6954 4179 - Cassette only	(Map 33 F10)	34° 33' 59.2"S	146° 00' 31"E
156	**Deniliquin** – rest area, Davidson St (Cobb Hwy), near Morris St	(Map 33 J9)	35° 31' 30"S	144° 58' 39.7"E
157	**Dorrigo** – 1km W of Dorrigo on Waterfall Way, just past Oak St; (02) 6657 2486	(Map 29 G12)	30° 20' 28.7"S	152° 42' 02.3"E
158	**Dubbo** Showgrounds, Wingeewarra St; (02) 6884 8845 or 0418 634 020	(Map 26 C4)	32° 15' 03"S	148° 36' 52.6"E
159	**Euston** – cnr Murray Tce & Nixon St, drive between Euston Club Motel and Euston Bowl & Rec Club, 70m to river; ask at Club for key; (03) 5026 4244	(Map 32 G4)	34° 34' 47.4"S	142° 44' 41.5"E
160	**Evans Head** Airport, Memorial Rd (opp Winjeel Dr), near Council Depot; (02) 6682 4392	(Map 29 C14)	29° 06' 17.3"S	153° 25' 22.1"E
161	**Finley –** Endeavour St, from Main St follow sign for caravan park, (03) 5888 5100	(Map 33 J10)	35° 38' 51.5"S	145° 34' 31"E
162	**Forbes** – Shire Works, Newell Hwy, S side of town, opp Back Marsden Rd near Warrul Rd; open Mon-Fri 8-5, w'ends 7-10; 0418 972 446 on w'ends	(Map 26 F2)	33° 24' 07.9"S	147° 59' 05.5"E
163	**Forster** Beach Caravan Park, cnr Reserve Rd & Oyster Pde, adjacent amenities bldg; no charge; 1800 240 632	(Map 27 C13)	32° 10' 43.4"S	152° 30' 34.2"E
164	**Forster** Lakeside Resort, 13 Tea Tree Rd; small fee; (02) 6555 5511	(Map 27 C13)	32° 13' 21.5"S	152° 31' 50.5"E
165	**Glen Innes** – Lions Park, East Ave	(Map 29 E10)	29° 44' 05.3"S	151° 44' 04.2"E
166	**Grafton** Greyhound Racing Club, Cranworth St, at Caravan Park entry between Dobie & Eggins Sts; (02) 6642 3713	(Map 29 E13)	29° 40' 27"S	152° 55' 30.9"E
167	**Grenfell** – West St, 2nd driveway from cnr Camp St, near old railway station; (02) 6343 1212	(Map 26 H2)	33° 53' 43.1"S	148° 09' 21.9"E
168	**Griffith** – Willow Park toilet block, via Walla Ave near Kookora St; 1800 681 141 - Cassette only	(Map 33 F10)	turnoff 34° 17' 18.5"S	146° 01' 56"E
169	**Gulgong** – Saleyards Lane (ext Station St) & cnr Spring Creek Rd, in front of Shire Depot; (02) 6374 1202,	(Map 26 C5)	32° 21' 30"S	149° 32' 45.2"E
170	**Gulgong** – Henry Lawson Caravan Park, Mayne St; small fee; (02) 6374 1294	(Map 26 C6)	32° 21' 57.2"S	149° 31' 30.7"E
171	**Gunnedah** Showgrounds, South St (Oxley Hwy), just inside main entrance on left; (02) 6740 2125	(Map 28 J5)	30° 58' 48"S	150° 14' 53"E
172	**Hay** – Showground Rd (Dunera Way), north end of Hay; (02) 6993 1003	(Map 33 F8)	34° 29' 50.8"S	144° 50' 01.7"E
173	**Howlong –** Riverina Hwy between High & Larmer Sts, near toilet block in Lowe Square Rec Res; key at Howlong Trading Post, Shell servo, Riverina Hwy, between Townsend & Read Sts; deposit required for key; (02) 6033 8999	(Map 33 K12)	35° 58' 53.7"S	146° 38' 01.7"E
174	**Inverell** Showgrounds, Clyde St (later Tingha Rd), near Medora St; (02) 6728 8161	(Map 29 E8)	29° 46' 57.7"S	151° 07' 07.1"E

No.	Location	Map	Latitude	Longitude
175	**Jerilderie** – in car park, Newell Hwy, 100m N of Conargo Rd, W of Uniting Church	(Map 33 H10)	35° 21' 19.7"S	145° 43' 22.3"E
176	**Jindabyne** – Kosciusko Rd, on left on road to Jindabyne tip; (02) 6450 5195	(Map 34 H2)	turnoff 36° 25' 48"S	148° 37' 25.6"E
177	**Junee** – Willow Park in Park Lane, 70m N in park from entry; (02) 6924 8100	(Map 33 G14)	34° 51' 37"S	147° 34' 25.1"E
178	**Karuah** – Australian Motorhomes Tourist Park, 4406 Pacific Hwy, 12 Mile Ck, S of Karuah, opp The Bucketts Way; (02) 4987 017	(Map 27 D11)	32° 39' 09.4"S	151° 52' 08.9"E
179	**Kempsey area** – Kundabung rest area, Pacific Hwy, 15km S of Kempsey	(Map 29 J12)	31° 12' 13"S	152° 49' 23"E
180	**Khancoban** – Scott St, near cnr Mitchell Ave & near Parks & Wildlife Info Centre; (02) 6076 9373	(Map 34 G1)	36° 13' 00.1"S	148° 07' 24.2"E
181	**Lake George** – Charles Anderson VC memorial rest area, 7km N of Bungendore Rd turnoff, just off Federal Hwy on shore of Lake George	(Map 35 C2)	entry 35° 06' 03.6"S	149° 22' 27.6"E
182	**Lake Keepit** State Park, near Gunnedah/Tamworth, directions at Park office; (02) 6769 7605	(Map 28 H6)	entry at Park Office 30° 54' 14.5"S	150° 30' 37.5"E
183	**Leeton** Showgrounds, Racecourse Rd; (02) 6953 2213	(Map 33 G11)	34° 33' 40.4"S	146° 24' 04.4"E
184	**Lennox Head** – Lake Ainsworth Caravan Park, cnr Ross St & Pacific Pde, enter from Ross St; small fee; (02) 6687 7249	(Map 29 B14)	28° 47' 11.3"S	153° 35' 33.4"E
185	**Lightning Ridge** Visitor Info Centre, Lions Park, Morilla St, on approach to town from the west; (02) 6829 1670	(Map 31 C14)	29° 25' 52"S	147° 58'17.3"E
186	**Lithgow** Showgrounds, George Coates Ave, turn off Great Western Hwy at info centre to avoid low underpass and then right into Barton St and left into showgrounds; gate unlocked daylight hours; (02) 6353 1775	(Map 24 C2)	33° 28' 54.65"S	150° 08' 31.7"E
187	**Lockhart** Caravan Park, Green St, just West of Urana St intersection; no charge; 0458 205 303 or (02) 6920 5131	(Map 33 H12)	35° 13' 14.3"S	146° 42' 46.6"E
188	**Maitland area –** Clarence Town, Bridge Res; (02) 4984 2680	(Map 27 D11)	entry 32° 34' 58.5"S	151° 46' 55"E
189	**Mathoura** – E side Mathoura St, between Steven & Mitchell Sts, behind bowling club; (03) 5884 3730	(Map 33 J8)	35° 48' 33.8"S	144° 53' 55.1 "E
190	**Merriwa** Tourist Welcoming Centre, Bow St, laneway behind RSL, DP in 2nd car park; (02) 6548 2607	(Map 26 C7)	entry 32° 08' 16.95"S	150° 21' 13"E
191	**Morisset** Showgrounds, Ourimbah St; (02) 4973 2670	(Map 23 E5)	33° 06' 29.8"S	151° 28' 47.5"E
192	**Moruya** – Riverside Park, access is by foot from Church St (near John St) or unnamed St parallel to Church St on the riverside; in grassed parkland halfway between the two streets and 55m N of Church St position -35° 54'35.65" +150° 05'08.5" (-35.9099 +150.0857)	(Map 35 G4)	35° 54' 33.8"S	150° 05' 08.5"E
193	**Moulamein** Lakeside Caravan Park, Brougham St; (03) 5887 5206	(Map 32 H7)	35° 05' 07.9"S	144° 02' 05"E
194	**Mudgee** Showgrounds, Douro St best entry, 200m from cnr Nicholson St, DP behind toilets; phone (02) 6372 3828 first	(Map 26 D6)	entry 32° 36' 10.2"S	149° 34' 53.4"E
195	**Mulwala** – Purtle Park, Melbourne St; key at newsagent; (03) 5744 3376 - Chemical restriction	(Map 33 K11)	35° 59' 08"S	146° 00' 33.1"E
196	**Narrandera** Showgrounds, cnr Elizabeth St & Victoria Ave (entry Elizabeth St); (02) 6959 2190 - Cassette only	(Map 33 G11)	34 44' 57.9"S	146 33' 51"E
197	**Nowra** Showgrounds, W end of Junction St, behind grandstand	(Map 35 C6)	34° 52' 22.5"S	150° 35' 27.7"E
198	**Oberon** – Jenolan Caravan Park, Cunynghame St; small fee; (02) 6336 0344	(Map 24 E1)	33° 42' 06"S	149° 51' 28.5"E
199	**Orange** – 68 Bathurst Rd, rear Naughton's Shell service station, 250m W of McDonalds; (02) 6393 8109	(Map 26 F5)	33° 17' 26.8"S	149° 06' 35.5"E
200	**Rylstone** Caravan Park, 5 Carwell St, entry opp Piper St; small fee; 0409 873 340	(Map 26 E7)	32° 48' 03.2"S	149° 58' 04.6"E
201	**Sydney** – North Ryde, Lane Cove River Tourist Park, Plassey Rd; daylight hours; small fee; (02) 9888 9133	(Map 22 D5)	33° 47' 22.3"S	151° 08' 35"E
202	**Talbingo** – on N side Murray Jackson Dr (New Dam Rd) when entering town from E between Bridle and Lampe Sts	(Map 34 E1)	35° 34' 44.5"S	148° 17' 59.3"E
203	**Tamworth** – Rotary Park, 3km N of Tamworth on New England Hwy; (02) 6755 4555	(Map 28 J7)	entry 31° 06' 28.6"S	150° 57' 14.8"E
204	**Taree** – Rotary Park, adjacent info centre; (02) 6552 1900	(Map 27 B13)	31° 53' 57.8"S	152° 29' 27.5"E
205	**Temora** – Airport St, past the airport; (02) 6980 1100	(Map 26 J1)	34° 25' 19.1"S	147° 31' 04.9"E
206	**Tenterfield** Showground, Miles St entrance, DP near gate; (02) 6736 4547	(Map 29 C10)	29° 03' 25.1"S	152° 00' 55.7"E
207	**Tocumwal** Tourist Park, 9 Bruton St; small fee; (03) 5874 2768	(Map 33 J10)	35° 48' 33"S	145° 33' 58"E
208	**Tocumwal** Foreshore Res, Town Beach Rd (dirt road), entry at W end of Hennessy St	(Map 33 J10)	35° 48' 48.5"S	145° 33' 55.5"E
209	**Tumbarumba** – cnr Cape & Bridge Sts, 100m from visitor centre; (02) 6948 3333	(Map 33 J14)	35° 46' 37.2"S	148° 00' 33"E
210	**Tumut** – Elm Dr, 120m off Snowy Mtns Hwy; (02) 6941 2555	(Map 34 D1)	35° 18' 11.3"S	148° 13' 42"E
211	**Tumut –** Riverglade Caravan Park, Snowy Mtns Hwy; (02) 6947 2528	(Map 34 D1)	35° 17' 44.8"S	148° 13' 16.8"E
212	**Tuncurry** Beach Caravan Park, Beach St, entry opp Wallis St, DP just inside entry, see office first; no fee; (02) 6554 6440 - Long hose reqd for BW tank	(Map 27 C13)	32° 10' 18.1"S	152° 30' 13.2"E
213	**Urana** Caravan Park & Aquatic Centre, Corowa Rd, 1.5km S; substantial fee; (02) 6920 8192	(Map 33 H11)	35° 20' 17"S	146° 16' 24.3"E
214	**Urunga** – Hungry Head Rd, S end of town	(Map 29 G13)	30° 30' 06.1"S	153° 01' 16.5"E
215	**Wagga Wagga** Showgrounds, Bourke St; 8am to 5pm; small fee; (02) 6925 2180	(Map 33 H13)	35° 07' 31.2"S	147° 21' 16.2"E
216	**Walgett –** Alex Trevallion Park, Castlereagh Hwy, Walgett; (02) 6828 1399	(Map 28 F1)	30° 02' 03.9"S	148° 06' 55.1"E
217	**Woodburn** – NW of Woodburn-Coraki Rd & Pacific Hwy, near bridge; (02) 6660 0227 - Cassette only	(Map 29 C13)	29° 04' 26"S	153° 20' 19"E
218	**Woodenbong** – campground W of town, near swim pool; key at service station, cnr Macpherson & Unumgar Sts; (02) 6662 0900,	(Map 29 A12)	28° 23' 17.5"S	152° 36' 24.5"E
219	**Wyangala Dam** – Wyangala Waters State Park (access via Cowra), directions at Park office; (02) 6345 0877	(Map 26 H4)	Park Office 33° 57' 46.4"S	148° 57' 17.6"E
220	**Wyong** – Caltex Service Station, F3 freeway (north bound), near bus parking area; (02) 4352 3621	(Map 23 G5)	entry 33° 15' 28.8"S	151° 24' 11.9"E
221	**Wyong** – Caltex Service Station F3 freeway (south bound), near bus parking area; (02) 4352 3626	(Map 23 G5)	entry 33° 15' 05"S	151° 24'17.2"E
222	**Young** Showgrounds, Whiteman Ave; (02) 6382 5433	(Map 34 A2)	34° 18' 59.5"S	148° 18' 51.9"E

Australian Capital Territory

No.	Location	Map	Latitude	Longitude
223	**Canberra** – EPIC Exhibition Park, Flemington Rd, off Federal Hwy (when grounds vacant); (02) 6241 3022	(Map 37 C5)	35° 13' 56.2"S	149° 08' 41.9"E

Victoria

No.	Location	Map	Latitude	Longitude
224	**Ararat** – Alexandra Ave; (03) 5355 0281	(Map 44 D7)	37° 16' 49.7"S	142° 55' 58"E
225	**Bairnsdale** Holiday Park, 139 Princes Hwy, East Bairnsdale; (03) 5152 4066 - Cassette only	(Map 49 K11)	37° 49' 10"S	147° 39' 21.5"E
226	**Bruthen** Caravan Park, 1 Tambo Upper Rd, just over bridge; small fee; (03) 5157 5753	(Map 49 K12)	entry 37° 42' 44.1"S	147° 50' 09.3"E
227	**Charlton** – Travellers Rest Ensuite Caravan Park, John Curtin Dr, off High St, adj to St Arnaud Rd junction; (03) 5491 1647	(Map 47 J9)	36° 16' 05.8"S	143° 21' 03"E
228	**Colac** – Central Caravan Park, Showgrounds, 50 Bruce St; (03) 5231 3586	(Map 45 H10)	38° 20' 08.5"S	143° 36' 12"E
229	**Corryong** Saleyards, Donaldson St, cnr Stock Route Rd, Corryong, N of town, DP at toilet; (02) 6076 2160	(Map 49 C12)	36° 11' 18.3"S	147° 53' 59"E
230	**Dimboola** Riverside Caravan Park, Wimmera St; small fee; (03) 5389 1416 - Cassette only	(Map 44 A4)	36° 27' 23.3"S	142° 01' 31.5"E
231	**Dunkeld** Caravan Park, cnr Glenelg Hwy & Templeton St; small fee; (03) 5577 2578	(Map 44 F6)	37° 38' 59.2"S	142° 20' 43.8"E

No.	Location	Map	Latitude	Longitude
232	**Girgaree** – Morgan Cres via Winter Rd and Olympic St or Station St, at back of local hall opp PO	(Map 47 K14)	36° 23' 51"S	144° 58' 48.4"E
233	**Heathcote** – Queens Meadow Caravan Park, Barrack St; (03) 5433 2304	(Map 45 B13)	36° 55' 24.5"S	144° 42' 46.7"E
234	**Hollands Landing** near Sale – Hollands Landing Rd; (03) 5142 3422 - Cassette only	(Map 50 F5)	38° 03' 15.2 "S	147° 27' 36.3"E
235	**Horsham** – Firebrace St, outside Horsham Caravan Park; (03) 5382 3476	(Map 44 B6)	36° 43' 21.8"S	142° 11' 58.7"E
236	**Kerang** Caravan & Tourist Park, 21 Museum Dr, off Murray Valley Hwy, beside toilets; (03) 5452 1161	(Map 47 G10)	35° 44' 14"S	143° 54' 50.5"E
237	**Lakes Entrance** – Bullock Is Spit, Bullock Island Rd boat ramp, opp visitors centre; (03) 5153 9500 - Cassette only	(Map 49 K13)	37° 52' 58.5"S	147° 58' 18.5"E
238	**Mallacoota** – Lakeside Dr, on water side of toilet block near jetty; (03) 5158 0800 - Cassette only	(Map 51 D13)	37° 32' 12.8"S	149° 44' 38.7"E
239	**Marong** Caravan & Cabin Village, 1449 Calder Hwy, near Torrens St, NW side of town; small fee; (03) 5435 2329	(Map 45 B11)	36° 43' 58.2"S	144° 07' 47.75"E
240	**Metung** – Chinamans Creek, cnr Metung & Rosherville Rd, at jetty; (03) 5153 9500 - Cassette only	(Map 49 K12)	37° 52' 43.3"S	147° 51' 29"E
241	**Mildura** – Benetook Depot, 1174 Benetook Ave, opp Sunraysia TAFE; (03) 5018 8450	(Map 46 A5)	34° 12' 17.3"S	142° 10' 07"E
242	**Nicholson** River Reserve, Boat Ramp near toilet; (03) 5153 9500 - Cassette only	(Map 49 K12)	37° 49' 01.2"S	147° 44' 23.5"E
243	**Paynesville** – Progress Jetty, toilet block on esplanade; (03) 5153 9500 - Cassette only	(Map 50 E6)	37° 55' 08.4"S	147° 43' 10.8"E
244	**Port Campbell** Holiday Park, Morris St near cnr Tregea St; small fee; (03) 5598 6492	(Map 45 J8)	entry 38° 37' 06.5"S	142° 59' 44.1"E
245	**Portland** – Henty Bay Beachfront Van & Cabin Park, 342 Dutton Way, past Ocean St; (03) 5523 3716	(Map 44 H4)	38° 17' 57.2"S	141° 37' 13"E
246	**St Arnaud** – Dunstan St, off Charlton-St Arnaud Rd, N side of town, back of sports club	(Map 45 A9)	36° 36' 32.8"S	143° 15' 35.05"E
247	**Sale** Showground, Sale Maffra Rd; enter at -38° 05'30.9" +147° 04'00" (-38.09191 +147.06666) & turn right 125m for DP; (03) 5144 2603	(Map 50 F4)	38° 05' 28.6"S	147° 03' 55.3"E
248	**Sale** – Port of Sale, Canal Rd, behind Council office, water side of toilet block); (03) 5142 3422 - Cassette only (access difficulties)	(Map 50 F4)	38° 06' 44.5"S	147° 03' 46.5"E
249	**Swan Hill** Showgrounds, Stradbroke Ave, entry 120m N of roundabout	(Map 47 F9)	35° 20' 20.5"S	143° 33' 04"E
250	**Tatura** Park, entry via Hastie St, opp Davy St; (03) 5832 9700	(Map 48 D3)	36° 26' 44.5"S	145° 13' 57.7"E
251	**Wangaratta** – Painters Island Caravan Park, Pinkerton Cr; small fee; (03) 5721 3380	(Map 48 C6)	36° 21' 01.3"S	146° 19' 46.3"E
252	**Warrnambool** – near sewerage treatment works off Elliott St; 0417 338 688 bus hrs	(Map 44 J6)	38° 23' 20"S	142° 27' 48"E
253	**Warrnambool** – near old tourist info Kepler St, 50m N of KFC; key from Flagstaff Hill Visitor Centre, Merri St	(Map 44 J6)	38° 22' 44"S	142° 29' 03"E
254	**Warrnambool** – Surf Side Holiday Park, Pertrobe Rd; no charge; (03) 5559 4700	(Map 44 J6)	38° 23' 31.2"S	142° 29' 00.4"E
255	**Wulgulmerang** Rec Res, Snowy River Rd, 4km N of McKillops Rd turnoff to Little River Gorge	(Map 49 G13)	37° 04' 06.8"S	148° 15' 39.1"E
256	**Yackandandah** Holiday Park, Taymac Dr, off 1 Dederang Rd; no motorhomes over 8m; small fee; (02) 6027 138	(Map 49 C8)	entry 36° 18' 53.9"S	146° 50' 24.7"E

Tasmania

No.	Location	Map	Latitude	Longitude
257	**Arthur River** – at end of Airey St, 2nd on right south of bridge; (03) 6457 1225 - Cassette only	(Map 60 D1)	41° 03' 27.2"S	144° 39' 38"E
258	**Beaconsfield** Showground, York St, off Grubb St, adjacent toilet block; overnight stay OK; 1800 637 989	(Map 55 D2)	41° 11' 54"S	146° 49'15"E
259	**Bicheno** – 2 Jetty Rd, 100m from hwy, adjacent toilet block; (03) 6375 1500 - Cassette only	(Map 59 A14)	41° 52' 22.7"S	148° 18' 05.4"E
260	**Bothwell** – Market Place, inside Council Caravan Park, behind Golf Museum; (03) 6259 5503	(Map 59 D9)	42° 22' 59"S	147° 00' 28.8"E
261	**Brighton** – Pontville Park, Midlands Hwy, S of Pontville Bridge, enter beside Memorial Hall; daylight hours Mon-Fri, DP at rear; (03) 6268 7000 - Cassette only	(Map 59 F10)	entry 42° 41' 14"S	147° 15' 49.3"E
262	**Burnie** – wastewater treatment plant, 3km W on Cooee Point Rd (at end); (03) 6430 5700	(Map 60 D6)	41 02' 15"S	145 52' 31"E
263	**Burnie** – toilets on Esplanade, near Reeve St	(Map 60 D6)	41° 03' 44.5"S	145° 54' 54.3"E
264	**Cambridge** Memorial Oval, 1000 Cambridge Rd; DP on SE border of oval; (03) 6245 8600 - Cassette only, posts around unit	(Map 56 B7)	42° 50' 11.6"S	147° 26' 34"E
265	**Campbell Town** – King St, past Glenelg St, turn next left, then drive 100m	(Map 59 B11)	41° 55' 48.5"S	147° 29' 16.8"E
266	**Cygnet** – Burtons Res, adjacent to toilets; (03) 6264 0300	(Map 56 H3)	43° 09' 47.9"S	147° 04' 54.6"E
267	**Deloraine** – Racecourse Crescent Dr, adjacent to tennis courts; (03) 6393 5300	(Map 55 H1)	41° 31' 20.9"S	146° 39' 39"E
268	**Devonport East** – Girdlestone Park car park, cnr Caroline & John Sts, entry John St; (03) 6424 0551	(Map 60 E7)	41° 11' 11"S	146° 22' 45.2"E
269	**Dover** Beachside Tourist Park, 27 Kent Beach Rd; small fee; (03) 6298 1301	(Map 59 J9)	43° 18' 55.25"S	147° 01' 28.5"E
270	**Evandale** – Morven Park, Barclay St; (03) 6397 7303	(Map 55 J6)	41° 34' 06.1"S	147° 14' 48.3"E
271	**Fingal** – in main street, beside public toilets, near info booth; (03) 6376 1866 - Cassette only	(Map 61 G13)	41° 38' 18.4"S	147° 58' 06.6"E
272	**Franklin** – foreshore res adj to toilet block, nearly opp Walpole Lane; (03) 6264 8448	(Map 56 G2)	43° 05' 35.5"S	147° 00' 32.7"E
273	**George Town** – Main Rd (East Tamar Hwy) , near cnr Victoria St, behind info centre; (03) 6382 1700	(Map 55 C2)	41° 06' 32.8"S	146° 50' 17.5"E
274	**Hamilton** – River St, via Tarleton St, in park on right just past Council Chambers; (03) 6286 3202	(Map 59 E9)	42° 33' 34.2"S	146° 49' 51"E
275	**Hobart** – BP service station, 200 Brooker Hwy; (03) 6234 3549 - Cassette only	(Map 54 B2)	42° 52' 12.3"S	147° 19' 18.3"E
276	**Hobart –** Montrose Bay Res, off Foreshore Rd, Glenorchy, near yacht & rowing clubs	(Map 56 B5)	42° 49' 17.4"S	147° 16' 07.8"E
277	**Hobart** Showgrounds, Howard Rd, Glenorchy; (03) 6272 6812	(Map 56 C5)	42° 49' 52.7"S	147° 17' 16.3"E
278	**Hobart** – wastewater treatment, Rosny Esplanade, Rosny; (03) 6245 8600	(Map 54 B4)	42° 52' 24.1"S	147° 21' 22.4"E
279	**Kempton** – Victoria Memorial Hall, cnr Main St & Old Hunting Ground Rd, next to toilets; (03) 6259 3011 - Cassette only	(Map 59 E10)	42° 31' 54.2"S	147° 12' 01"E
280	**Kingston** – entrance to wetland res Channel Hwy; (03) 6211 8242	(Map 56 E6)	42° 58' 28"S	147° 18' 50.6"E
281	**Latrobe** – entry via unnamed road W of Weld St, off Cotton St; (03) 6426 2099	(Map 60 E7)	41° 14' 12.4"S	146° 24' 36.9"E
282	**Latrobe** Caravan Park, River Rd, between Madeline & Last Sts: (03) 6426 1944	(Map 60 E7)	41° 13 58' 6"S	146° 24' 09.25"E
283	**Narawntapu National Park**, Bakers Beach, nth coast between Devonport & George Town; 2 DPs, enquire at Park HQ; (03) 6428 6277	(Map 61 E8)	Park HQ 41° 08' 57.1"S	146° 36' 11.4"E
284	**New Norfolk** Caravan Park, Esplanade via Alfred, Montagu, Ferry, Page Ave, adj to public toilets; no charge; (03) 6261 1268 - Chemical restrictions	(Map 56 A3)	42° 46' 34"S	147° 08' 58.5"E
285	**Nubeena** – opp police station in Nubeena Rd; (03) 6251 2400	(Map 57 G11)	43° 05' 43.8"S	147° 44' 36.6"E
286	**Oatlands** – cnr William & Wellington Sts, outside Council yard; (03) 6254 5000	(Map 59 C10)	42° 17' 52"S	147° 21' 58.5"E
287	**Penguin** – Johnsons Beach Rd, near cnr Main Rd; (03) 6437 1421	(Map 60 D6)	41° 06' 35.2"S	146° 04' 09.4"E
288	**Port Huon** – Shipwright's Point, on side of toilet block in informal camping area; (03) 6264 0300	(Map 56 H1)	turnoff 43° 09' 29.2"S	146° 58' 44.2"E
289	**Port Sorell** – a. Very northern end of Darling St (jetty), opp caravan park; (03) 6428 7267 b. Camp Boomerang, enter via 22 Kermode St, next to caravan park; (03) 6428 7226 daylight hrs, 0418 178 093 a/hrs	(Map 61 E8)	a. 41° 09' 51"S b. 41° 09' 52.5"S	146° 33' 22.8"E 146° 32' 54.4"E
290	**Queenstown** – Batchelor St (Lyell Hwy), near cnr Mary St & beside Council works building	(Map 58 B4)	42° 04' 38"S	145° 33' 35.4"E
291	**Ross** Caravan Park, end of Esplanade, off High St; no fee; (03) 6381 5224	(Map 59 B11)	42° 01' 48.2"S	147° 29' 27"E

292	**St Helens** – at sports Grounds, 110 Tully St, 1st entrance on left in Tully St; (03) 6376 1866	(Map 61 F14)	41° 18' 58.1"S	148° 14' 03.5"E
293	**Scottsdale** – Northeast Park Rest Area, Ringarooma Rd (Tasman Hwy), 1km SE of town; (03) 6352 6500	(Map 61 E11)	41° 09' 54.5"S	147° 31' 21.8"E
294	**Sheffield** – West Nook Rd, W of town, 160m from Sheffield Rd intersection; (03) 6491 2500	(Map 60 F7)	41° 22' 41.1"S	146° 19' 06.2"E
295	**Sisters Beach** – cnr Honeysuckle Ave & Cumming St, behind fire station	(Map 60 C4)	40° 55' 05"S	145° 33' 53"E
296	**Smithton** – West Esplanade, W side of town, over Duck River Bridge, 60m on right	(Map 60 C3)	40° 50' 20.4"S	145° 07'12.8"E
297	**Sorell** – Council Depot, 30 Montague St; open 7am to 5pm weekdays, (03) 6265 6400 - Cassettes only	(Map 57 B9)	42° 47' 04.9"S	147° 33' 07.9"E
298	**Stanley** – Henry Hellyer Res (adj toilet block), Wharf St, past Stanley Caravan Park; (03) 6458 126	(Map 60 C4)	40° 45' 49.7"S	145° 17' 46.7"E
299	**Strahan** – Ocean Beach Rd (Harvey St), outside Council Depot	(Map 58 C3)	42° 08' 59.6"S	145° 18' 48.9"E
300	**Swansea** – boat ramp car park Jetty Rd, opp PO; (03) 6257 8155	(Map 59 C13)	42° 07' 25.7"S	148° 04' 38.7"E
301	**Triabunna** Visitor Info Centre, Charles St, 40m from info centre, W on Esplanade; (03) 6257 4772	(Map 59 E12)	42° 30' 34.9"S	147° 54' 52.6"E
302	**Ulverstone** – cnr Victoria St & Beach Rd, in car park next to archway	(Map 60 E6)	41° 09' 06.15"S	146° 10' 27.9"E
303	**Ulverstone** – Apex Caravan Park, Queen St; (03) 6425 2935	(Map 60 E6)	41° 08' 41.7 "S	146° 09' 39.3"E
304	**Waratah** – Annie St, opp Council Works; (03) 6443 8342	(Map 60 F4)	41° 26' 37.2"S	145° 31' 50.5"E
305	**Westbury** – behind Andy's Bakery, 43 Meander Valley Rd; overnight OK; (03) 6393 1846	(Map 55 H2)	41° 31' 33.9"S	146° 50' 39.7"E
306	**Wynyard** waste transfer station, 170 Goldie St; open 8.30am-5pm; (03) 6443 8342	(Map 60 D5)	40° 59' 32.3"S	145° 43' 05"E
307	**Zeehan** – Mulcahy-Packer St, on E side, 250m from Zeehan Hwy junction	(Map 58 A3)	41° 53' 25.4"S	145° 20' 44.4"E

South Australia

308	**Ardrossan** – West Tce, near cnr Second Street, behind tennis club shed	(Map 68 F6)	34° 25' 27.6"S	137° 54' 51.4"E
309	**Bordertown** – near toilets beside recreation lake, via North Tce, Woolshed St, Golf Course Rd, & 1st right after railway	(Map 69 F7)	36° 18' 21.2"S	140° 46' 31.4"E
310	**Cadell** Recreation & Camp Ground, Dalzell Rd	(Map 71 G12)	34° 02' 15"S	139° 45' 25"E
311	**Carrieton** – Horseshoe View Caravan Park, Fourth St; travelling N, turn right into Second St, right again into Fourth St; donation req; (08) 8658 9090 - Chemical restrictions	(Map 68 A7)	32° 25' 29.6"S	138° 31' 55"E
312	**Ceduna** – adj BP Roadhouse, Eyre Hwy, W side of town; (08) 8625 3407	(Map 70 C3)	32° 06' 47.3"S	133° 40' 22.6"E
313	**Cleve** – field day site, Rudall Rd (Birdseye Hwy), 1.7km W of town centre	(Map 68 D3)	entry 33° 41' 52.5"S	136° 28' 32.2"E
314	**Coffin Bay** – near toilet block at boat ramp, enter from Esplanade opposite Greenly Ave junction	(Map 70 H5)	entry 34° 36' 58.8"S	135° 27' 46.15"E
315	**Coober Pedy** – Hutchison St, on right past Umina St junction, drive-in theatre, and just past Country Fire Service shed; (08) 8672 4600	(Map 72 G4)	29° 00' 16.7"S	134° 45' 21.8"E
316	**Cowell** Sportsground, Brooks Dr, 80m from corner North Tce; (08) 8629 2019 - Chemical restrictions	(Map 68 D4)	33° 40' 51.3"S	136° 55' 33.6"E
317	**Cummins** Caravan Park, Roe St	(Map 68 F1)	34° 16' 15.4"S	135° 43' 23.7"E
318	**Gladstone** Caravan Park, cnr Main North Rd & West Tce; no charge; (08) 8662 2522	(Map 68 C7)	33° 16' 08.4"S	138° 21' 04.4"E
319	**Jamestown** – Ayr St, outside Jamestown Country Retreat Caravan Park (CP is cnr Ayr & Bute Sts); (08) 8664 0077	(Map 68 C7)	33° 12' 18.8"S	138° 36' 03"E
320	**Kadina** – near cnr Eliza St & Doswell Tce, a little off the road; (08) 8821 1600	(Map 68 E5)	33° 57' 31.9"S	137° 43' 15"E
321	**Kangaroo Island** (Kingscote area) – Third St, Brownlow adj to the Kingscote Nepean Bay Tourist Park	(Map 68 J5)	35° 40' 16.3"S	137° 36' 42.1"E
322	**Kangaroo Island** (Penneshaw) – Christmas Cove, Christmas St - Cassette only	(Map 68 K5)	35° 43' 09.5"S	137° 56' 02.3"E
323	**Kangaroo Island** – Western KI Caravan Park, South Coast Rd, 3km from junction with West End Hwy; small fee; (08) 8559 7201	(Map 68 K3)	35° 57' 40"S	136° 48' 27.7"E
324	**Kimba** Rec Res, Buckleboo Rd (extension of North Tce), through 'Kimba Pioneer Memorial' archway	(Map 68 C2)	33° 08' 05.6"S	136° 24' 54.1"E
325	**Lameroo** Caravan Park, N side of Mallee Hwy, just E of town between Bews Tce & Leckie Ave; enquiries through hotel (08) 8576 3006	(Map 69 C6)	entry road 35° 19' 42.7"S	140° 31' 17.5"E
326	**Laura** Caravan Park, Mill St, DP on roadside ~50m E on North Tce from junction with Main North Rd; no charge; (08) 8663 2296, 0428 632 296	(Map 68 C6)	33° 10' 54.4"S	138° 18' 03.4"E
327	**Loxton** – West Traeger Dr, near cnr Coral & Pine Sts, outside Loxton Motorhome Res	(Map 69 A7)	34° 27' 05.8"S	140° 34' 42.2"E
328	**Maitland** Showgrounds, Rogers Tce, turn right around shed inside	(Map 68 F5)	entry 34° 22' 20.4"S	137° 40' 37.8"E
329	**Mannum** Caravan Park, Purnong Rd; small fee; (08) 8569 1402	(Map 69 B4)	34° 54' 30.5"S	139° 19' 01.7"E
330	**Mannum** – Mary Ann Res (at riverside, southern end), River Lane; (08) 8569 0100 - Cassette only	(Map 69 B4)	34° 54' 58.1"S	139° 18' 39"E
331	**Melrose** Showground, Main North Rd, 2km N of Melrose; (08) 8666 2158	(Map 68 B6)	entry road 32° 48' 40.7"S	138° 11' 51"E
332	**Mt Gambier** Showgrounds, Pick Ave, showground entry opp deli & bakery; small fee; get key (deposit req) at Mobil servo, 85m north in Pick Ave; 0408 492 182	(Map 69 K6)	entry 37° 50' 16.4"S	140° 47' 50.75"E
333	**Mt Pleasant** – Talunga Park Oval Complex, Melrose St; ph in advance (08) 8568 2045 or 0429 682 045	(Map 65 F7)	34° 46' 34.3"S	139° 02' 34.2"E
334	**Murray Bridge** – Railway Tce, just north of railway station near First St junction; (08) 8539 1142 (or 1143)	(Map 67 B13)	35° 06' 57.9"S	139° 16' 25.15"E
335	**Normanville** Jetty Caravan Park, Jetty Rd; (08) 8558 2038	(Map 66 F3)	entry 35° 26' 45.35"S	138° 18' 35.4"E
336	**Orroroo** Caravan Park, Wilmington-Orroroo Rd; small fee; (08) 8658 1444	(Map 68 B7)	32° 43' 56.5"S	138° 36' 38.3"E
337	**Port Augusta** Motorhome Park, Old Power Station Rd, 1st left after causeway into town; small fee; (08) 8642 4122	(Map 68 A5)	32° 30' 40.8"S	137° 47' 10.5"E
338	**Port Broughton** – NE cnr Bute & Mundoora Rds, in front of Council Depot; open 24/7; (08) 8635 2107	(Map 68 D5)	33° 36' 09.7"S	137° 56' 09"E
339	**Port Vincent** Foreshore Caravan Park, Marine Pde, near junction Curramulka Rd; no charge; (08) 8853 7073 - Cassette only, waist-high unit	(Map 68 G5)	34° 46' 40.9"S	137° 51' 46.2"E
340	**Stansbury** Foreshore Caravan Park, Oyster Point Dr, on the point; (08) 8852 4171	(Map 68 H5)	34° 54' 45.4"S	137° 48' 13.5"E
341	**Streaky Bay** – Lions Park, East Tce between Flinders Hwy and Mudge Tce	(Map 70 E3)	32° 47' 42.5"S	134° 13' 05.7"E
342	**Tanunda** Caravan & Tourist Park, Barossa Valley Way; small fee; (08) 8563 2784	(Map 65 C6)	34° 31' 55.7"S	138° 57' 00.3"E
343	**Tumby Bay** Motorhome Facility, 8 Lipson Rd, opp cemetery (northern access road); (08) 8688 2101	(Map 68 F2)	34° 21' 33.4"S	136° 05' 59.7"E
344	**Victor Harbor** Beachfront Holiday Park, Victoria St; small fee; (08) 8552 1111	(Map 66 G7)	35° 33' 30.7"S	138° 36' 46.7"E
345	**Wallaroo** – cnr Hughes & Victoria Sts, opp Santo Tce, beside Mobil service station; (08) 8823 2023	(Map 68 E5)	33° 56' 03.7"S	137° 37' 53.8"E
346	**Whyalla** – off N side of Lincoln Hwy, 250m W of McDouall Stuart Ave, 6km W CBD	(Map 68 C5)	33° 02' 46"S	137° 31' 34.5"E
347	**Whyalla area** – Port Lowly, turn S from Port Bonython Rd, 1km past the Port Bonython installation turnoff, DP on road to beach	(Map 68 C5)	32° 59' 25.8"S	137° 46' 40.7' "E
348	**Wudinna** – behind Gawler Ranges Motel, 72 Eyre Hwy, E end of town; (08) 8680 2090	(Map 70 E5)	33° 03' 19.8"S	135° 28' 03"E

Western Australia

349	**Albany** – Amity Quays next to Princess Royal Dr, near Brig Amity; (08) 9841 9377	(Map 81 K12)	35° 01' 46.5"S	117° 52' 43.3"E
350	**Albany** – information bay, Albany Hwy N side, S of Drome Rd; (08) 9841 9377	(Map 81 J12)	entry 34° 59' 27.5"S	117° 51' 21.05"E
351	**Albany** – information bay, on South Coast Hwy (between Charles St & Link Rd), 7km from central Albany; (08) 9841 9377	(Map 81 J12)	34° 59' 53.5"S	117° 49' 03.5"E
352	**Arrowsmith** – rest area 30km N of Eneabba on Brand Hwy (50km S of Dongara)	(Map 84 G4)	29° 34' 40.8"S	115° 08' 09.1"E
353	**Barradale** – Yannarie River rest area, North West Coastal Hwy	(Map 86 F3)	22° 51' 51.8"S	114° 57' 14.3"E
354	**Beasley River** Rest Area, between Tom Price and Nanutarra Rdhouse, 185km E of Nanutarra	(Map 86 F6)	turnoff 22° 56' 47.4"S	116° 58' 24"E
355	**Bridgetown** Caravan Park, on South Western Hwy just south of town; (08) 9761 1900 - Cassette only	(Map 80 E5)	33° 58' 20"S	116° 08' 08.5"E
356	**Broome** – BP Central service station, cnr Frederick & Coghlan Sts; (08) 9193 5517 - Long hose req for BW tanks	(Map 88 G4)	17° 57' 20"S	122° 14' 13.5"E
357	**Broomehill** Caravan Park, Morgan Rd, via Journal St - Chemical restrictions	(Map 81 D11)	33° 50' 54.2"S	117° 38' 09.3"E
358	**Bruce Rock** Caravan Park, 4 Dunstal St, between Railway Pde & Lethlean St; (08) 9061 1377	(Map 79 D13)	31° 52' 26.4"S	118° 09' 04.8"E
359	**Brunswick Junction** Showgrounds, end of Ridley St and turn right inside showgrounds; key at EZIWAY supermarket, cnr Ridley St & South Western Hwy, shop hours; (08) 9726 1244	(Map 80 A4)	entry 33° 15' 11.1"S	115° 50' 13.4"E
360	**Busselton** – Kookaburra Caravan Park, 66 Marine Tce, cnr Brown St, entry via Brown St; fee; (08) 9752 1516	(Map 80 C3)	33° 38' 44.9"S	115° 20' 53.5"E
361	**Carnarvon** – toilet block near Piyarli Yardi Aboriginal Cultural Centre; (08) 9941 1146	(Map 86 J1)	entry 24° 52' 36.7"S	113° 39' 45.5"E
362	**Carnarvon** – Babbage Is Rd, on left 150m from Robinson St, in car park next to swim pool near building; (08) 9941 0000	(Map 86 J1)	24° 52' 36.4"S	113° 39' 37.4"E
363	**Cervantes** – waste transfer stn, 613 Cervantes Rd; open 7 days; phone first (08) 9652 0800	(Map 84 H4)	30° 29' 42.5"S	115° 04' 44.5"E
364	**Coronation Beach** – (08) 9920 5011 - Cassette only	(Map 84 E3)	28° 33' 07.7"S	114° 33' 53.7"E
365	**Corrigin** – Walton St, opp Campbell St, behind toilet block; (08) 9063 2203	(Map 79 F12)	32° 19' 51.5"S	117° 52' 24.5"E
366	**Derby** – Kimberley Entrance Caravan Park, Rowan St; 2 DPs; small fee; (08) 9193 1055	(Map 88 F6)	17° 18' 24.5"S	123° 37' 46.5"E
367	**Dowerin area** – Minnivale 16km E on Goomalling-Wyalkatchem Rd, then 5km N on Cunderin-Minnivale Rd, near old tennis courts near Hughes St/Berry Rd cnr; (08) 9631 1202	(Map 79 A9)	31° 08' 18.37"S	117° 11' 07.45"E
368	**Esperance** Seafront Caravan Park, cnr Goldfield & Norseman Rds; substantial fee; (08) 9071 1251	(Map 83 G13)	33° 50' 45.7"S	121° 54' 09.2"E
369	**Exmouth** – Murat Rd, back of rec centre at main sportsground, entry nearly opp Maidstone Cr; (08) 9949 1176	(Map 86 D2)	21° 55' 57.1"S	114° 07' 40.6"E
370	**Forty Mile Beach** – part way along the beach section of the road	(Map 86 C5)	20° 50' 45.5"S	116° 21' 45.5"E
371	**Forty Mile Beach** – at the end of the beach section of the road	(Map 86 C5)	20° 50' 28.7"S	116° 20' 52"E
372	**Fremantle** – Woodman Point Holiday Park, 132 Cockburn Rd, entry via Magazine Ct; small fee; (08) 9434 1433	(Map 78 E4)	32° 07' 44.7"S	115° 46' 05"E
373	**Galena Bridge** – Murchison R Rest Area, 13km N of Kalbarri turnoff on NW Coastal Hwy	(Map 84 D3)	S turnoff 27° 50' 00.5"S N turnoff 27° 49' 19.6"S	114° 41' 18.5"E 114° 41' 22.8"E
374	**Geraldton area** – Ellendale Pool, SE of Geraldton via Walkaway - Chemical restrictions	(Map 84 F3)	28° 51' 39"S	114° 58' 21.7"E
375	**Gingin area** – Regan's Ford Rest Area, 50km N on Brand Hwy	(Map 84 J5)	turnoff 30° 58' 58.1"S	115° 42' 13.4"E
376	**Goomalling** Caravan Park, Throssell St; small fee; (08) 9629 1183 - Need hose for BW tank	(Map 79 B8)	31° 17' 57.9"S	116° 49' 56.6"E
377	**Hopetoun** – cnr Esplanade & Veal St, at groyne; (08) 9838 1001	(Map 83 G10)	33° 57' 05"S	120° 07' 35"E
378	**Kununurra** – BP Ord River Roadhouse, 5 Messmate Way, cnr Bandicoot Dr; small fee or free with fuel; (08) 9169 1188	(Map 89 D14)	15° 46' 42.35"S	128° 44' 25.2"E
379	**Kununurra** Showgrounds, Coolibah Dr, entry in NW part of loop near Ivanhoe Dr	(Map 89 D14)	15° 46' 16.7"S	128° 43' 52.7"E
380	**Lyndon River** Rest Area on the Minilya-Exmouth Rd, N of Minilya	(Map 86 G2)	23° 32' 32"S	113° 57' 47.9"E
381	**Manjimup** – Warren Way Caravan Park, South Western Hwy, 1km N of town; (08) 9771 1060 - Eco only, no chemicals	(Map 80 F6)	34° 13' 20.5"S	116° 09' 08"E
382	**Menzies area** – Niagara Dam, turnoff is 9km SW of Kookynie on Kookynie-Mt Remarkable Rd, Dam is 3km from turnoff	(Map 85 F12)	29° 24' 13.3"S	121° 25' 39.6"E
383	**Moora** – Roberts St, in parking area beside Moora Caravan Park, opp IGA; (08) 9651 1401	(Map 82 A3)	30° 38' 16.5"S	116° 00' 19.4"E
384	**Norseman** Visitor Centre, Welcome Park, 68 Roberts St, opp Sinclair St, in car park beside visitors centre; small fee; (08) 9039 1071	(Map 83 D13)	32° 11' 45.1"S	121° 46' 49.6"E
385	**Northam** – Peel Tce, near Duke St, opp Caltex service station, S side of roadway; (08) 9622 2100	(Map 79 C8)	31° 38' 58.6"S	116° 40' 37.7"E
386	**Northampton** – behind memorial gardens, N of centre of town via Essex St	(Map 84 E3)	28° 20' 53"S	114° 37' 50"E
387	**Onslow** – Cameron Ave, near public toilets at basketball courts - Chemical restrictions	(Map 86 D3)	21° 38' 28.5"S	115° 06' 46.6"E
388	**Perenjori** – Council waste depot, Carnamah Rd, 9km from Perenjori; (08) 9973 1002	(Map 84 F5)	29° 27' 21.2"S	116° 12' 02.1"E
389	**Perth** Vineyards Holiday Park, 91 Benara Rd, Caversham; small fee; (08) 9279 6700	(Map 77 D6)	31° 52' 32.5"S	115° 57' 53.9"E
390	**Perth** (west) – Advent Park, 345 Kalamunda Rd, near David St, Maida Vale, trees beside driveway; fee; essential ph first (08) 9454 5341	(Map 77 F7)	entry 31° 56' 40.6"S	116° 01' 09"E
391	**Quinninup** Eco-Tourist Park, Wheatley Coast Rd, turnoff beside general store; fee; (08) 9773 1329 - Chemical restrictions	(Map 80 G6)	turnoff 34° 26' 11.5"S	116° 15' 00.7"E
392	**Ravensthorpe** – Queen St in rest area, near cnr Morgans St (Sth Coast Hwy), future access may be from Morgans St; (08) 9839 0000	(Map 83 F10)	Queen St entry 33° 34' 56.05"S	120° 02' 40.6"E
393	**Robe River** Rest Area, North West Coastal Hwy, 147km S of Karratha turnoff	(Map 86 D4)	entry 21° 36' 50.8"S	115° 55' 25.5"E
394	**Southern Cross area** – Koorarawalyee rest area, 68km E on Great Eastern Hwy	(Map 83 B10)	entry 31° 16' 05.4"S	120° 01' 04.4"E
395	**Wagin** Caravan Park, Scaddan St, near cnr Arthur Rd; 0419 611 057,	(Map 81 B10)	33° 18' 38.6"S	117° 20' 01.3"E
396	**Wongan Hills** – Wongan Hills Rd, near cnr Quinlan St, beside public toilets at tourist info; (08) 9671 1973	(Map 82 A4)	30° 53' 36.2"S	116° 43' 01.5"E
397	**Wyalkatchem** Caravan Park, Goomalling Merredin Rd (Hands Dr), W of Riches St junction; (08) 9681 1166	(Map 79 A10)	31° 10' 58.5"S	117° 22' 47"E

Northern Territory

398	**Alice Springs** – Commonage Rd, just S of The Gap, near waste transfer; (08) 8952 5800 or 1800 645 199	(Map 101 F8)	23° 43' 56.8"S	133° 51' 36.7"E
399	**Borroloola** – Tamarind Park, near gate to airport; 1800 245 091 - Cassette only	(Map 97 J12)	16° 04' 20.2"S	136° 18' 24"E
400	**Darwin** – Greyhound Club grounds, Hook Rd, Winnellie; (08) 8936 2499, 13 888 608	(Map 94 F5)	12° 25' 40.8"S	130° 53' 38.3"E
401	**Jabiru** – Jabiru Dr, 300m past tourist info board; (08) 8979 9444	(Map 95 D7)	12° 39' 51.2"S	132° 50' 17.8"E
402	**Katherine** – Lindsay St, off Stuart Hwy, near visitor info centre, entry nearly opp Second St; (08) 8972 2650	(Map 95 J5)	14° 27' 53"S	132° 16' 01.5"E
403	**Pine Creek** – Ward St, on footpath outside Council yard; 1800 245 091	(Map 95 G4)	13° 49' 27.5"S	131° 49' 56"E
404	**Tennant Creek** – Purkiss Memorial Res, 82 Ambrose St, via Peko Rd or Stuart St, DP entry between Davidson & Stuart Sts; 1800 500 879 - Cassette only	(Map 99 G8)	19° 38' 36.5"S	134° 11' 33.5"E
405	**Yulara** – industrial area, cnr Tuit Cr & Berry Rd, behind AAT Kings depot; 1800 245 091	(Map 100 H4)	25° 13' 24.2"S	130° 58' 32.8"E

The first step: your recreational vehicle

Choosing your recreational vehicle

Caravans have been the traditional recreational vehicle in Australia since the 1950s. However, in the last couple of decades **campervans** and **motorhomes** have become an important sector in the market. In the last few years, the 'new kid on the block' is the **fifth-wheeler**: a concept from the USA, where there are very few caravans. Many adventurous Australians who want to experience outback tracks buy a **camper trailer**, particularly as their first travelling vehicle. After they have visited the outback areas, some people change to a caravan or motorhome where they have more comfort.

Camping near Palm Valley, Northern Territory

Both caravans and motorhomes involve **compromise**: everyone would like them to be bigger on the inside and smaller on the outside. Even without taking the budget into account, a buyer usually has to decide **priorities**. Some people want all the comforts of home, while other travellers are happy with just the necessities. If you intend to live permanently on the road, your needs will be different from someone travelling occasionally or for short periods.

With the key word 'compromise' in mind, you have to choose a vehicle where, for you, the advantages **outweigh the disadvantages**. Other buyers might come to a different conclusion because they will place more importance on certain aspects than you do. Research the market thoroughly to avoid buying a unit that is not right for you – particularly if it is your first purchase – and don't rush your decision. **Allow plenty of time** so you do not feel pressured to buy 'second best' just because it is available immediately.

There are numerous manufacturers, with many of the larger ones selling through dealers, while some smaller manufacturers sell direct. They may not all be near your home town, but most exhibit at the **caravan, camping and holiday shows** held annually in several major cities. Many manufacturers will make-to-order or customise one of their designs, but this can entail a wait of several months.

Comparing motorhomes with caravans and fifth-wheelers

Many people initially plan to buy a caravan simply because that is what they have seen all their lives. To make sure you select what is best for you, keep an open mind and look at everything available.

If you plan to:

- use your van only a few weeks a year – a caravan could be a better choice than a motorhome
- stay in one place for a week or two at a time – a caravan or fifth-wheeler will allow you to travel around in your tow vehicle
- travel several days each week, even if it is only a hundred kilometres – a motorhome will be more convenient

Advantages of motorhomes over caravans and fifth-wheelers

- You **don't need a suitable tow vehicle**: this will be a considerable extra expense if you need to purchase one for a caravan or fifth-wheeler.
- Motorhomes are **easy to handle** and **do not suffer from sway**, a potentially dangerous problem.
- A campervan or motorhome is **only one unit to register and insure**.
- A motorhome up to 6m or so in length **can be parked in a normal parking space**. For vehicles exceeding 4.5 tonnes GVM and/or with a combined length over 7.5m, there are legal restrictions on parking and travelling. These restrictions will only apply to large motorhomes, but all car/caravan combinations and fifth-wheelers are classified as long vehicles.
- The **effect of side winds is minimal** as all the weight of the vehicle is one unit. Wind pushed in front of a semitrailer travelling in the opposite direction has a much greater effect on lighter-weight units such as caravans and, to a much lesser extent, fifth-wheelers.
- In virtually all motorhomes and campervans, you can **access the driving cab without going outside**: which gives peace of mind regarding security and is also very convenient in bad weather.
- Campervans and motorhomes usually have **seating in the 'house' section for passengers** to use while travelling.
- Most motorhomes have **facilities that give total freedom** and allow travellers to bush camp (shower/toilet, grey-water storage). Although many caravans have a shower and toilet, not many have a grey-water holding tank. Many caravanners prefer to book into a caravan park to have a secure place to leave the van while they go sightseeing whereas a motorhomer can bush camp if they wish.
- In a motorhome your **facilities are always available**. So when you go sightseeing for the day, the kitchen facilities are available for morning tea and lunch, whereas if you have left the caravan behind you'll have to pack a picnic basket and take a cooler box.
- Often caravanners leave their van in a caravan park and go out on day trips, which requires back-tracking at the end of the day. However motorhomers can do their sightseeing and continue on their way. So, on a long trip, for instance around Australia, motorhomers would usually **travel a much shorter distance** in total than someone towing a caravan.

Authors' tip:

Don't believe that a motorhomer has to pack everything up just to buy a bottle of milk. In all our years of travelling in a motorhome, there have only been a few occasions where a separate car would have been useful. However, our style of travelling is to 'travel on' and we rarely stay in one place for more than a couple of days. We do our shopping during the day when we drive through a town. If a caravanner has to go out for a bottle of milk, they usually have to unhitch the van anyway.

Advantages of caravans and fifth-wheelers over motorhomes

- A caravanner has a **separate vehicle for short trips**, so they do not have to take their 'house' with them everywhere.
- A caravanner has **a vehicle to use as the family car** whereas with anything other than a small campervan, motorhome owners usually require a second vehicle to use when they are not travelling.
- Some bush tracks are not suitable for mid-size or larger motorhomes because of their height and width, and there are corrugated roads most motorhome/campervan owners will not take their vehicle over. If you tow a caravan with a 4WD, you can **go to many less accessible places**, including some popular national parks.

Authors' tip:

Before you start looking at vehicles, decide where you want to travel and how much you intend to spend.

Early morning at the Devils Marbles campground, Northern Territory

Points to consider before you buy

Consider and discuss these questions before you start looking at vehicles. Even if you want to buy a secondhand unit it is still worth looking at new ones to see what is available and help you work out what you want.

- **What is your budget?** This is the most important factor.
- **Do you intend to keep the vehicle** for several years or do you plan to sell after you have done a couple of trips?
- **When will you be travelling** – in cool or cold weather as well as summer? Check out the insulation.
- **Do you want an in-built shower and/or toilet**, or do you intend to rely on facilities at caravan parks? If you want the freedom to bush camp, shower and toilet facilities are very desirable.

> **Authors' tip:**
>
> Often when people start travelling they assume they will always stay in caravan parks.. Later, some people regret not having a more self-contained vehicle that gives them the freedom to choose – as well as saving a considerable amount of money on overnight camping fees.

- **Are you prepared to make up your bed every night** or do you want a bed you can leave made up?
- **Do you need an extra sleeping place** for family members to travel with you, even occasionally? Maybe a lounge that converts to a bed would be suitable.
- **How many people do you need to seat at the dining table?**
- **Do you want to take a boat?** You can use a boat loader to carry a tinnie on top of a tow vehicle or camper trailer, or a collapsible boat can be strapped to the side of a caravan or motorhome.

What to consider when you are looking

Accommodation area

The accommodation areas of caravans and motorhomes have a lot in common, so check out the following aspects:

- Look at the **general spaciousness** of the interior. If you are particularly tall, is there sufficient headroom? Can you live and move around in the 'house'?
- If there is a bathroom, is it large enough for you to shower, and is there **sufficient headroom**? Note – There is often less head height in the bathroom, because the floor is raised to allow space for drainage pipes underneath.
- If the bathroom has a small shower/bath, make sure you can step in and out of the **shower** because the side is approximately knee height. These baths are handy to bathe a small child, but are rather difficult for an adult to use. Try it!
- Is there a curtain or door to prevent the toilet getting wet when you use the shower?
- **Type of toilet** –
    - The most common is a built-in unit with a cassette that is removed for emptying.
    - Smaller vehicles often have a portable toilet similar to a cassette toilet, but not built in.
    - Vacuum marine-style toilets flush either to a cassette or holding tank.
    - Flush toilets empty into a black-water holding tank. *See Toilets (p69) for more details.*

> **Authors' tip:**
>
> We have used portable toilets, cassettes and also a flush toilet with a black-water tank, and find the cassette toilet the most convenient.

- Make sure the **bed** is wide and long enough for you. If you need a particularly long bed, you may be able to fit an extending section. Also check that the bed is comfortable. A foam mattress on a solid base might be somewhat hard, but you can make it softer by adding a mattress overlay. The foam 'egg carton' style overlay is very effective.
- **Floor covering** – vinyl flooring is much more practical than carpet, and it is easy to add a couple of mats that can be washed or replaced as necessary.
- Check that there is enough **storage, working spaces, power points and lights** for your particular needs. Do you need space for a computer or hobby/craft equipment? If you want to take bulky items such as golf clubs or fishing rods, where will you store them?
- Is there a **'house' battery** to run 12 volt lighting when it is not plugged into 240 volt power?

Windows and ventilation

Windows

- Windows can be either **glass or acrylic**. Polycarbonate windows weigh less and do not break as easily as glass, however they scratch easily, even when cleaning.
- Check that windows are **placed** where you would like them and that they are large enough.
- There are three **different styles** of windows – louvres, sliding and wind-out/push-out.
    - Louvres are effective in allowing good ventilation, and rain does not enter unless it is wind-driven.
    - Wind-out windows provide good rain protection and reasonable ventilation, but large windows of this style bring security problems because they provide a point of access. *Dometic* wind-out windows are double-glazed for insulation (both heat and sound) and come with a pull down fly screen made out of white mesh.
    - With a sliding window, less than 50% of the window is available for ventilation, and rain can easily enter.

Devils Marbles, Northern Territory

Boat loader for carrying a dinghy on a 4WD or even on a motorhome

Travelling in Western Australia

Authors' tip:

It is very pleasant to have a large window beside the table so you can enjoy the view during meals. We believe that louvres are the best style of window and there is absolutely no problem with rattling or dust entering when driving because they lock tight for travelling.

Air conditioning

- Do you want air conditioning in the accommodation area? You can only use this when connected to 240 volt power or when using a generator large enough for the purpose.

Roof hatches

- A **Four Seasons hatch** provides excellent ventilation when fully open. It can be set to keep out rain while still allowing some air in, and because it has a solid roof it does not transmit any heat.
- A **large opening roof hatch** (called a 'shooters hatch' or 'European hatch') provides a point of access, thereby creating a security issue. They usually have a clear or translucent panel that allows both light and heat through. Although there is a pull-across screen to keep direct sunlight out, it is not very effective against heat. Extra light is desirable, but in our climate, additional heat is not. Some travellers with one of these roof hatches have small insulating screens that attach with suction cups to try to reduce the heat transmitted.
- Any **'flap' style hatch** has drawbacks – rain enters easily when it is open, and wind can catch the flap.
- **Roof vents** are available with a fan and a 'rain sensor' so they close in the event of rain. These are more expensive and have to be connected to the 12 volt electrical system.

Authors' tip:

We recommend the Four Seasons hatch and had one installed in our Winnebago. We would not have a hatch with a clear or translucent panel because they transmit too much heat into the 'house'.

Four Seasons Hatch

'Shooters' Hatch

Kitchen

- If there is a microwave, is it installed at a convenient height? It is easy to have an accident with hot food if the microwave is too high, but if it is too low it can be inconvenient too.
- Is there enough working space for food preparation and enough storage space?
- How many gas burners does the stove have? If you plan to bush camp without a generator you will not be able to use a microwave oven or electric frypan so you will probably need three burners on your cooktop.
- Do you need an oven or a grill?
- What type is the fridge: all electric or three-way? And is it large enough?

See Refrigeration (p66) for more information.

Authors' tip:

We recommend that you get the largest fridge that will fit. No-one ever says their fridge is too large! We have a 150 litre 3-way Dometic (model RM 2553) and are very happy with it.

What next?

When you have narrowed the options down to a 'short list', spend some time sitting in each and move about as you would when living in it. Consider how you will live in the confined space for a period of time. Although, in good weather you will probably spend a lot of time outdoors, you will most likely spend your evenings inside.

If you cannot find a unit that exactly fits all your requirements, consider having a caravan or motorhome customised. Many companies are happy to do this and will work with you to achieve the best result. Usually a smaller manufacturer will find it easier to accommodate changes, as a large manufacturer might find it uneconomic to interrupt their production line.

Hatch with rain sensor

As a starting point, find a company whose vans or motorhomes are the appropriate size with the major features you want, particularly items that would be difficult or expensive to change – including the general layout and bathroom. Minor changes or additions will obviously cost less than major alterations. You will have your own ideas on what you want, but listen to the manufacturer as well. After years in the industry they will have a good idea of what works and what doesn't. You don't want to end up with a unit customised with impractical design features that will make it hard to sell at a later date.

Before purchasing a caravan or camper trailer

When considering a caravan the following factors are important. (Some also apply to camper trailers.)

Tow vehicle

- Consider whether you will use your present vehicle to tow the caravan or camper trailer. Check your vehicle's manual to ascertain the **weight it can safely tow**.
- If you are planning to buy a tow vehicle, consider whether you want to drive extensively off-road and whether it is worth buying a large **4WD**.
- With a caravan, **weight and towing capacity** need to be considered – so choose the caravan and tow vehicle as a 'matched set'.
- Ideally, the loaded caravan should weigh less than the tow vehicle.

Weight

This is the most important factor. Allow not only for the weight of the caravan, but for a **realistic amount of belongings**. A rule of thumb to cover housekeeping essentials and personal belongings for two people is at least 300kg in a small caravan, and at least 400–500kg in a larger tandem axle unit. It seems to be human nature that if people have extra space, they will find more and more things they absolutely cannot travel without.

Authors' tip:

A luxury 22 foot-long caravan will weigh more than a 'budget' caravan of the same length. Don't just take the salesman's word for it that your vehicle will tow a 22 foot van. Check out the weight/towing issue thoroughly to avoid making an expensive and potentially dangerous mistake. Do not buy a caravan that is at the upper limit of what your vehicle can tow.

Campers enjoying an early morning cup of coffee on a cold morning while camped on the Nullarbor

Definitions

- **Gross Vehicle Mass (GVM)** is the maximum allowable weight of a vehicle and its load including driver and passengers.
- **Gross Trailer Mass (GTM)** is the weight of a caravan or trailer and its payload, but does not include the mass supported by the tow ball.
- **Aggregate Trailer Mass (ATM)** is the total weight of a caravan or trailer plus its payload and the tow ball mass.

Tandem axle caravan camped on the banks of the Gregory River in Queensland

Driver's licence

A standard C class licence is required to drive any vehicle weighing less than 4.5 tonnes GVM (Gross Vehicle Mass) and when towing a caravan or trailer weighing less than 9 tonnes GVM. Caravans do not weigh 9 tonnes, so unless you are going to use an unusually large truck (over 4.5 tonnes GVM) as a tow vehicle, a standard licence is all that is required.

Driving speed limits

For vehicles towing a trailer with a GTM (Gross Trailer Mass) of less than 4.5 tonnes, **the posted speed limits apply** (except in Western Australia) unless the manufacturer of the towing vehicle has stipulated a lower towing speed limit. In this case, you are legally bound to keep within those limits. In Western Australia the maximum speed limit is 100kph for vehicles towing a trailer with an ATM (Aggregate Trailer Mass) over 750kg.

Towing

A well-designed caravan or camper trailer has **weight distributed evenly over the axle** with approximately 10% transferred to the tow ball. Before buying, you can get a good indication of the ball weight by placing the jockey wheel on a set of bathroom scales. Place a piece of plywood on the scales to spread the weight evenly, and gently lower the jockey wheel into the centre. You might have to buy or borrow scales that will register heavier weights. *See Towing (p87) for more details.*

Authors' tip:

If the axle is placed too far back (to meet internal design preference regarding the position of the door) there could be too much weight in front which can drag the towball down. If the axle is placed too far forward, the unit can be out of balance and unstable to tow.

Shower/toilet

Some people feel that if they plan to stay solely in caravan parks, it is a waste of space to duplicate facilities available there. However, others consider an on-board shower and toilet to be essential. Over the last five years there has been a dramatic increase in the number of caravans with in-built shower and toilet.

Authors' tip:

We believe an on-board toilet is very convenient, both for use while on the road and when camping.

12 volt system

A battery is required to store power for the internal lights, water pump and cassette toilet. Many caravans, particularly those with in-built shower/toilet, come with a battery pack as standard, while others have provision for one to be installed as an optional extra. *See 12 Volt Power (p61) for more details.*

Gas cylinder/s

See if there are one or two cylinders and what size they are. Also remember to consider where the gas cylinders are placed. Gas cylinders over 2.25kg must be stored outside the accommodation area. *See Gas Cylinders (p58) for more details.*

Tandem axles

Caravans over 17 or 18 feet usually have tandem axles, however the weight of the unit also has to be considered when deciding whether to build on one or two axles.

Advantages of tandem axles:

- A more stable ride. A shorter rear overhang (section extending past the axle) reduces sway or snaking.
- Better braking. If only the front axle is braked and there is a brake lockup on a slippery surface, the rear wheels keep steering the van straight. If brakes are fitted on both axles, set the rear axle brakes to brake less to give the same effect.
- Safer stopping after a tyre failure because you can safely slow down by travelling on the other tyre.

Disadvantages of tandem axles:

- Sluggish cornering.
- Difficulty when hand manoeuvreing using a jockey wheel.

Factors to consider when choosing a caravan

- **Size and weight.**
- **Budget.**
- **Ground clearance** – If you want to travel even on short unsealed access roads to national parks, you will need good ground clearance on the caravan and the tow vehicle. If you want to do extensive off-road travel, look at an off-road camper and a 'serious' 4WD tow vehicle.
- **Caravan frame** – Welded aluminium (durable and also rugged for dirt road driving), pop-riveted aluminium (durable), or timber (flexes slightly for dirt road driving but is subject to rot if water gets in any joints). It is debatable which type of frame is better and the quality of manufacture is the important factor.
- **Aluminium cladding or fibreglass** – Aluminium is lighter in weight, but fibreglass has better insulation properties and is not easily damaged by hail.
- **Electrics** – If you do not want to be reliant on 240 volt power, you will need a battery (for internal lighting) and a battery charger. Unless you are connected to 240 volt power, if you do not have a battery system there is no electrical power available in the caravan when you turn off the ignition of the tow vehicle.
- **Battery** – Check what battery and transformer/charger are supplied with the van. How long will it take to recharge the van battery from 240 volt power?
- **Lights** – If the lights in the van are 240 volt/12 volt, are they bright enough when used on 12 volt? It is rather difficult to assess this on a bright, sunny day.
- Examine the **quality of workmanship**, underneath as well as inside and out.
- Water tanks, plumbing and wiring underneath the van should have some form of **stone protection**.
- **Draw bar** – Is it a reasonable length for the van? A 2m draw bar makes reverse parking easier than a short drawbar.
- Check the specifications of the van for the **ball weight**, to ensure your tow vehicle can tow the van you are considering buying. *See Couplings (p88) for more details.*
- **Kitchen** facilities and layout. *See Kitchen fittings (p68) for more details.*
- **Pressure hatch** – This can be opened for travelling to increase air pressure inside the van and reduce the chance of dust entering.
- **Layout** and **fittings** – Many manufacturers will vary these within constraints imposed by such things as wheel arches, so we have deliberately put this one last.

Types of caravans available

- Traditional **hard roof**, full height caravans in a variety of sizes.
- **Pop-top** caravans that have an extendable vinyl-sided section at the top.
- **Off-road** caravans are ruggedly constructed on a more solid chassis to cope with unsealed roads.
- **Solid 'folding'** caravans made for off road. These are a cross-over between a caravan and a camper trailer.
- **'Folding'** caravans made for conventional use.
- **Camper** caravans have a solid roof and an interior set-up similar to a caravan. The extending section is canvas that folds down to half height for travelling.

Note – Slide-ons are covered in the campervan section later in this chapter.

This owner-built caravan has an extreme departure angle

Signs warning of the condition of the road into the Purnululu National Park (Bungle Bungle)

Authors' tip:

Although owners of off-road caravans take them on roads such as the Tanami Track and to Cape York, it is our opinion that a camper trailer or a folding caravan like a Kimberley Kamper or an Eco-Tourer would be more suitable. The most challenging road we have come across is the access road into Purnululu National Park (Bungle Bungle). With 27 creek crossings and non-stop corrugations, the 51km to the ranger station takes at least a couple of hours (after that the road is not so bad). Anything 'less' than a rugged off-road camper would be shaken to pieces. Unless you have a suitable vehicle, take a tour either by air from Kununurra or by road from Turkey Creek. We recommend the tour from Turkey Creek.

Advantages & disadvantages of different types of caravans

	Hard roof	Pop-top	Off-road	'Folding'	Camper
Advantages	• Usually very well appointed inside. • The walls are full height, so there are plenty of cupboards. • If there is a bathroom, it will have full height solid walls. • Insulation (affecting both temperature and noise) is more effective than in a pop-top or a camper which has canvas or vinyl sections in the walls. • Solid walls are more durable than a style with sections of vinyl or canvas.	• The low profile reduces wind resistance when driving and the adverse effect on fuel consumption is less than with a full height caravan. • The low profile results in less buffeting from passing trucks. • An advantage over a camper is that, even with the roof down, you can get inside to put away grocery shopping, make a cup of tea or get a drink of water.	• They are built to cope with vibrations caused by driving on corrugated roads, so these vans can be taken on roads that would defeat conventional caravans. • They have higher clearance, so can travel on tracks with deep wheel ruts that would cause conventional caravans to 'bottom out'. • Usually have a steep 'departure angle' that enables them to negotiate the upwards slope after crossing a creek without the rear end hitting the ground. • Have wiring and piping under the floor secured out of the way so they do not catch on obstacles.	• Kimberley Kampers and Eco-Tourers are no higher or wider than a tow vehicle (usually a 4WD). • The low profile reduces wind resistance and therefore does not greatly increase fuel consumption. • Off-road folding caravans offer a higher level of comfort than a camper trailer, but can access the same locations. • With solid walls, there is some insulation, and in high winds there is no flapping noise from canvas as with a camper trailer.	• The very low profile makes towing easier. • Less wind resistance and less weight improve fuel economy. • The low profile means there is not an excessive amount of buffeting from cross winds or when large trucks pass. • A camper caravan is much simpler to erect than a camper trailer and offers a higher degree of comfort.
Disadvantages	• Wind resistance from the height of the van – this increases fuel consumption and wind buffeting. • A full height caravan is not suitable for many bush tracks. Depending on your tow vehicle, you could take it on unsealed roads, but we would not recommend taking a conventional caravan on corrugated roads for hundreds of kilometres.	• A disadvantage compared with a full-height caravan is loss of cupboard storage space because of lower walls. • The vinyl section has ventilation panels, however they are not as durable as solid walls. • Insulation (both for heat and noise) is not as effective as with a full height caravan. • When camping in a high wind area the vinyl section can produce a noise and in extreme weather conditions a pop-top could possibly lose its roof.	• There is additional weight caused by heavier construction. • Floor space can be lost because of the 'departure angle' which restricts internal layout. • The van is higher off the ground, requiring more steps. • Compared with a camper trailer, an off-road is higher and wider. If you plan to travel on bush tracks, you will have to go where the usual vehicle is a 4WD but you will be towing a much higher and wider caravan that is likely to brush against bushes and may not get through in some areas.	• 'A' van folding caravans fold flat to half height or less, thereby reducing wind drag and fuel consumption, but can't be considered off-road. • You need a cooler box or car fridge in the tow vehicle to use for meal breaks while you are travelling or to keep your food purchases cold until you have access to your main fridge.	• The canvas walls provide virtually no insulation and can flap in high winds. • Some people might find the kitchen benches rather low. • When the camper is packed for travelling you cannot access any items inside (even water) or put shopping away and you need to carry supplies in the tow vehicle for use when travelling.

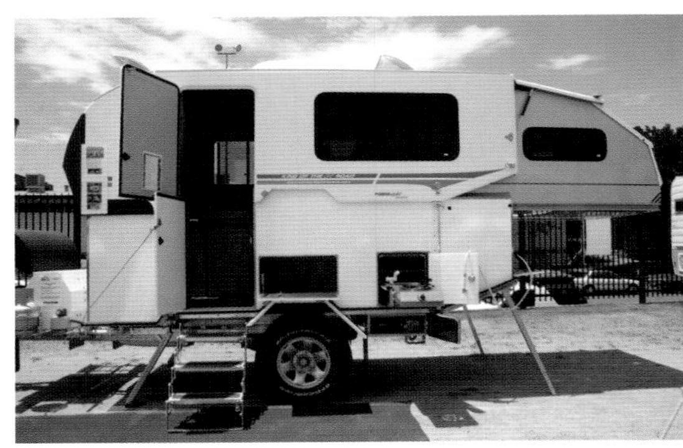

Kimberley Kamper opened up for camping

Pop-top caravan camped on the banks of the Gregory River, North Queensland

Coromal van folds flat for travelling

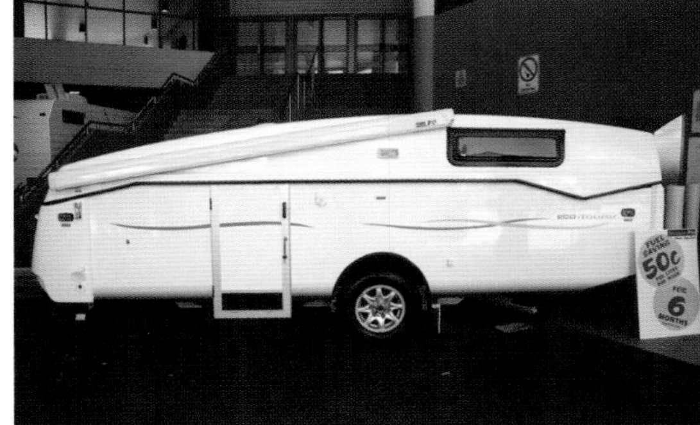

Eco Tourer in travelling mode

A Van folds flat for travelling and opens to an 'A' frame shape when camped

Camper Caravan in an idyllic spot at Bingil Bay, North Queensland

Geographe Bay, near Meelup WA, photo: Pelusey Photography

Hard floor camper trailer with an interesting stone deflector

Car top camper in the Pilbara, Western Australia

Hard floor camper trailer at Orroroo, South Australia

Camper trailers and car-top camping units

Camper trailers are increasingly popular, particularly with travellers who want to explore areas of the country where they could not reasonably take a conventional caravan or motorhome. There is a wide range of designs and fittings available but, broadly, they fall into two main types - 'hard floor' and 'soft floor'. The most common camper trailers are constructed totally of canvas and the walls and roof fold into a trailer for travelling.

The sleeping area is 'upstairs' on the trailer, and the kitchen and living area are 'downstairs'.

In a '**hard floor**' or '**flip top**' design the living section flips over to the rear of the camper and becomes a solid floor a couple of inches off the ground.

With a '**soft floor**' unit, the living area has a sewn-in soft floor that lies on the ground.

Car-top campers are a small section of the camping market. The sleeping tent is stored on top of the vehicle for travelling, and opens up to make a tent on top of the car for sleeping.

Exodus, Tvan and *The Ultimate Off-Road Camper* are designed for off-road travel but still have the conveniences found in conventional camper trailers.

Car top camper at the Jardine River, Cape York

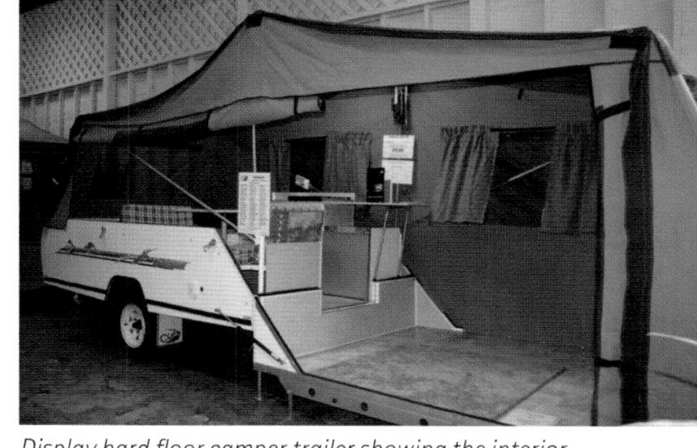

Display hard floor camper trailer showing the interior

Authors' tip:

If you buy a camper trailer, practice setting it up in the yard at home several times. It is better to do this when you are not tired from travelling and also without the audience that will probably be present in a campground or caravan park.

Authors' tip:

We believe a tent for sleeping would probably be a better option than a car-top camper.

Ready to cook breakfast at Cobar

	Camper trailers	Car-top campers
Advantages	• Ideal for real off-road travel, provided the tow vehicle is suited to the conditions. They have a higher road clearance than conventional caravans so are better suited to unsealed roads. • They do not have as many breakable items (microwave, TV). • Usually, the kitchen equipment rolls out from the side of the trailer so it can be used easily for road-side stops. • The low profile and light weight do not impact too heavily on fuel economy. • Buying a camper trailer does not break the budget. • A boat loader is often available as an optional extra.	• You do not have to tow anything – provided you can fit all your camping equipment inside the vehicle. • Weight is less than other camping units so the only detrimental effect on fuel consumption will be from wind resistance of the load on the roof of the vehicle.
Disadvantages	• It can take quite some time to erect a camper trailer, although with practice this becomes easier. The effort of setting up and disassembling is a disadvantage if you are travelling and camping only for one night. • Even in fine weather, you would probably want to wait until dew has dried off the canvas before packing up in the morning. • Lack of insulation. • The canvas can flap in high winds. • A lack of security: when you leave your campsite you cannot lock the tent, and someone intent on getting in can cut the canvas.	• The inconvenience of climbing a steep ladder to access the sleeping compartment. • Every time you move about in bed, the vehicle will rock to some degree. • When travelling, the weight added to the top of the vehicle will raise the centre of gravity (not good on uneven terrain). • You will still need to carry other camping equipment.

Camper trailer kitchen

Tvan in travelling mode

Tvan set up for camping at Fitzroy Crossing, Western Australia

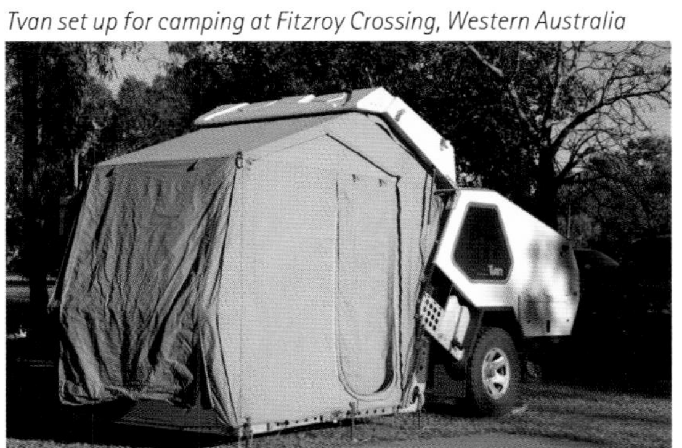

Campervans & motorhomes

This category ranges from small delivery-type vans to large luxury units with every comfort imaginable.

Try before you buy

If you have never travelled in a motorhome, you can hire one before buying so you can work out what size suits you and what facilities you require for comfortable living. At first glance, the cost of hiring might look like money wasted, but consider it as research. It is cheaper than buying a vehicle that does not suit your needs and then having to upgrade, or to downsize to one that is easier for you to handle. Keep in mind that the vehicle you hire may not have all the added extras you can add to your own vehicle.

Some dealers who have a rental fleet as well as selling motorhomes will refund the hire fee if you later buy from them. By buying a secondhand motorhome you can try the lifestyle and also the particular type of vehicle, and then if it is not for you, you may be able to sell it without incurring a large financial loss.

Authors' tip:

Before making a final decision, take the motorhome for a test drive. It will handle differently from a normal sedan, but most drivers quickly become accustomed to the larger vehicle.

Slide-out section of fifth-wheeler

Motorcamper at Maleny overlooking the Glasshouse Mountains, Queensland

Before purchasing a campervan or motorhome

When considering a campervan or motorhome the following factors are important.

Base vehicle

The variables you should consider in the base vehicle are:

- **Length** and **width** of the motorhome, and also the wheel base. If you have a garage or carport where you plan to store the vehicle? Does it fit?
- Is it **manual** or **automatic** and are the number and ratio of the **gears** appropriate to your needs?
- Is the size, type and power, torque and fuel economy of the motor suitable for your needs?
- What is the **availability of service, support and parts** for the vehicle?
- What are the **registration and insurance costs** of the vehicle and its weight?
- Ensure you are happy with the **layout and comfort of the driving cab** because you will spend a considerable amount of your time there. Is there enough leg room and head height? Check that there is sufficient storage space for maps, mobile phone etc.

Things to look out for

- Check the vehicle compliance plate for the **tare weight** and **GVM (Gross Vehicle Mass)**. Ensure there is enough lee-way between them to allow for the weight of water, fuel, household equipment and personal belongings as well as the driver and passenger/s themselves. A reasonable rule of thumb for the weight of household and personal items for two people is at least 300kg in a campervan and at least 400–500kg in a larger motorhome. Usually people take more belongings if they have the space to fit them. Add to this the weight of the driver and passenger.
- Check that the **length of overhang** past the rear axle does not exceed the legal limit of 60% of the wheelbase to a maximum of 3.7m. If there is a rear storage box or bike rack, it must be included in this measurement. With tandem axles, the measurement is from the point centrally between the two axles.
- Check the **compliance plate** to see if the unit is certified as 'second stage of manufacture compliant'. This covers only new vehicles made into motorhomes or campers, and does not include vehicles that have already been used for another purpose (eg as a bus). Check the website http://rvcs-prodweb.dot.gov.au specifying the category of vehicle (NA for trucks up to 3.5 tonnes GVM; NB1 between 3.5 and 4.5 tonnes, and NB2 between 4.5 and 12 tonnes).

Authors' tip:

We suggest you check the three important aspects mentioned above, and do not just assume that a vehicle complies.

Terms used in motorhomes and campervans

- **'A' Class motorhome** – built on a truck, coach or bus chassis. It usually has no driver's or passenger's doors – just one in the passenger's side of the house section. The whole unit has a flat floor, and the driver's and passenger's seats usually swivel to form part of the living section of the motorhome. There is a permanent bed at floor level, usually in a separate bedroom at the rear. These motorhomes are usually longer than 7m.
- **'B' Class motorhome** – built on a cab chassis unit (a truck chassis with the driver's cab built on, but no truck body). Sleeping and living areas are all on floor level and there is no bed over the cab, giving a sleeker looking exterior than a 'C' class. Being more streamlined, there is less wind resistance when travelling and this helps with fuel economy.
- **'C' Class motorhome** – built on a truck cab chassis, usually with a bed over the driving cab. There is usually an additional sleeping space in the main part of the motorhome, often achieved by converting a dinette to a double bed. The space over the cab is sometimes used as storage space or for an entertainment unit, in which case the main bed is on floor level, usually at the rear.
- **Motorcamper** – a larger van conversion, such as Ducato, Mercedes Sprinter or VW. It is a larger version of a campervan and includes a shower and toilet.
- **Campervan** – a small van fitted with sleeping and kitchen facilities but no show er or toilet.
- **Pop-top** – a campervan with a section of roof that extends to allow extra head height when parked, but can be secured in a lower configuration for travelling.
- **'Whizz-bang'** – a small campervan with a sliding side door. The name comes from the noise made when the side door is closed. Whizz-bangs often have a pop-top roof.
- **Fifth-wheeler** – a similar configuration to a semi-trailer. The living area is hitched to the towing vehicle by means of a turntable-style hitch installed on the flat bed of a utility or light truck above the rear axle. See p56 for more details.
- **Slide-on** – a small campervan-type unit secured on the back of a utility or tray-top truck. It can be removed to stand independently on legs so the vehicle can be driven away. A slide-in is a similar unit that slides into the rear of a fixed side utility truck.
- **Slide-out** – a section of wall that slides out taking with it a section of roof and floor, together with furniture and fittings. This extra bay is usually about 2m long and extends between 300-900mm, giving much more living space and a very spacious look. Some luxurious units have two or more slide-outs.

A class motorhome

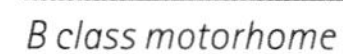

B class motorhome

C class motorhome

House section

There is an incredibly wide range of options available in the house section and these have been listed earlier in this section. There are a couple of extra points that apply to motorhomes.

- Check **ease of access to the driver's cab** from the house. In many flat floor motorhomes you can walk through, and sometimes the front seats swivel around to double as lounge chairs, increasing the living area significantly.
- **Slide-outs** increase the living area, but also the cost.
- 'A' class motorhomes often do not have **doors** in the driver's cab, and the only way out is through a door in the house section. A disadvantage is that every time you want to get out (at a service station) you have to walk back to that door. Some mid-size converted buses have a front driver's door but no front passenger door.
- Check out the type and size of **fridge**.
- Does it have one or two **gas cylinders**?
- **Walk around** inside as if you are living in it.
- If you have to construct the **bed** using cushions, how easy is it?
- If there is a bed over the cab, how easy is it for you to climb up and down and are you comfortable with the headroom. Try it out.
- If you are looking at a DIY or non-factory fit-out, check that it complies with **Australian Design Rules**.

Pop-top 'whizz bang' campervan

Diesel vs petrol engines

Overview

Diesel vehicles have gained popularity mainly because of lower fuel consumption. Official laboratory fuel figures indicate that vehicles with a turbo-diesel motor can travel between 20% and 40% further than petrol fuelled vehicles on a measured amount of fuel. Although diesel is the most expensive fuel per litre at the pump, it is still the most economical when you look at the overall picture. Diesel-powered vehicles cost more than petrol vehicles, mainly because of the increased strength built into diesel engines, however this is more than offset by long-term economy and reduced maintenance.

The characteristics of a diesel engine are different from those of a petrol engine. Traditionally, diesel engines are noisier but have more desirable torque characteristics. Peak power is attained at lower engine speeds, and because of the design and nature of combustion, these engines are very durable.

Fuel efficiency

A diesel engine compresses at a far higher ratio than a petrol engine, giving it greater fuel efficiency. A diesel engine compresses at a ratio of 14:1 to 25:1, while a petrol engine compresses at a ratio of 8:1 to 12:1. Diesel fuel also has a higher energy rating than petrol – 38.4 MJ/per litre compared with 34.85 MJ/per litre for petrol.

Lower maintenance and more reliability

Because diesel engines do not use electricity to ignite the fuel they do not need the complex ignition systems (spark plugs, coils, HT leads, distributor etc) associated with petrol engines. Petrol engines also require a carburettor or injection system to mix the fuel and air, but diesel engines do not need them. This means there is far less to go wrong with a diesel engine. Diesel fuel itself acts as a lubricant, so there is less wear on piston rings than in a petrol engine.

Environmental issues

Compared with petrol motors, diesel motors are lower producers of carbon dioxide (CO^2) – the gas responsible for greenhouse warming – and also less nitric oxide (NO). They do produce more particulate matter (PM) emissions (soot) that are considered carcinogenic (cancer causing) and also contribute to smog. With the introduction in 2006 of ultra-low sulphur diesel (ULSD), diesel motors have become more environmentally friendly. Ultra-low sulphur diesel aids the effectiveness of diesel particulate filters that are seen as essential in lowering these emissions, but not all diesel vehicles have these filters.

Authors' tip:

Name-brand motorhomes and campervans usually have a good resale value, and this is particularly relevant if you are planning to keep the vehicle only for a couple of years before selling.

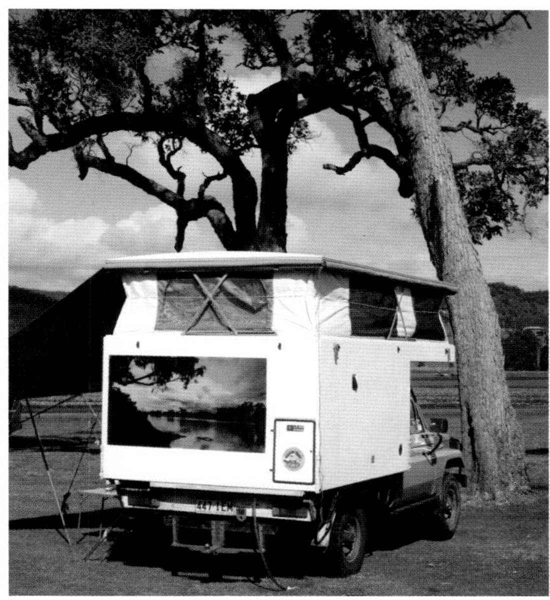

Pop-top motorhome camped at Mulgowie, Queensland

Advantages & disadvantages of motorhomes and campervans

	Larger motorhomes	Mid-size motorhomes (6-7m)	Small bus conversions	Motor campers	Small campervans & pop-tops
Advantages	• Extra space. • Bed is permanently made up. • Usually equipped with shower and toilet. • There is much more space inside, which is, particularly important in bad weather or at night.	• Bed is permanently made up. • Usually equipped with shower and toilet. • There is much more space inside, which is, particularly important in bad weather or at night. • It is fairly easy to find somewhere to park a motorhome or campervan up to 7m in length.	• There are many small buses available secondhand, so prices are reasonable. • Bed is permanently made up. • Usually equipped with shower and toilet. • There is much more space inside, which is, particularly important in bad weather or at night.	• They are easy to drive, manoeuvre and park.	• Relatively inexpensive to purchase and economical to drive. • Easy to drive and manoeuvre and even easier to park than a mid-size motorhome. • Ideal for one person.
Disadvantages	• Initial cost. • Fuel cost. • They are more difficult to drive, manoeuvre and park. • In some caravan parks an extra fee applies to very large units, and some places cannot accommodate big rigs.		• Unless the roof has been raised, head height is around six feet, so these buses will not suit tall people. • Width inside is around six feet, so a crossways bed (the usual layout) will not suit tall people. • Many do not have a bathroom, and if there is one, it will be compact.	• These are more compact than the small bus conversions, and have similar size disadvantages.	• The bed usually has to be set up each night. • Internal space is very limited, especially for two people; however, many owners of these vehicles spend most of their time outside under their awning. • There is limited storage space. • No bathroom or toilet.

Advantages & disadvantages of demountable units and 4WD motorhomes

	Demountable units (slide-ons and slide-ins)	4WD motorhomes
Advantages	• The vehicle has many other uses. (They are particularly suited to tradesmen who can use the truck during the week and add the camper for weekends away.) • They handle more like a motorhome than a caravan and are not affected by crosswinds or buffeting like a caravan. • Vehicle registration costs are low because fees are charged only on the truck. The slide-on or slide-in is legally classified as a load and therefore is not registered as a vehicle.	• In 4WD mode, they can cope better with slippery, boggy or sandy roads and campsites. • They are more ruggedly built and have higher ground clearance. • There are places you can travel to where you could not reasonably go in a 2WD campervan, motorhome or with a caravan.
Disadvantages	• It is not possible to access the driver's cabin from the house to leave in an emergency. • It is higher off the ground than a motorhome, thereby necessitating more steps for entry. • It is rather top-heavy and this affects the handling. • The extra weight may require strengthening the suspension of the carrying vehicle. • Passenger numbers are limited to the seating in the cab as it is not legal for anyone to travel in the camper section. • Unloading and reloading the unit is quite difficult on sloping or uneven ground, although it is relatively straightforward on a level surface. • There are no under-floor storage bins. • Slide-in units are generally smaller than slide-ons because their base can be no wider than the width of the tailgate of the fixed side utility. Consequently, they have very little available space at floor level. • With some insurance companies, the slide-on or slide-in unit has to be separately insured.	• A 4WD vehicle is considerably more expensive. • Because of the higher ground clearance, more steps are needed to access the accommodation section. • They have a higher centre of gravity and are likely to be a little less manoeuvrable than their 2WD cousins.

Slide-on campervan secured on truck for travelling

Free-standing slide-on campervan

Motorhome 'Xanadu' before conversion

4WD motorhome 'Xanadu'

Slide-on units

There are some unusual slide-on units that combine elements of a camper trailer, but built as a slide-on. *Innovan* makes a compact slide-on; *Piggy Back Campers* have a roof that swings over to form a queen-size bed; and the *Trayon Camper* opens up like a hard-floor camper trailer.

Traditionally, slide-on or slide-in units have not retained their value for resale as much as campervans or motorhomes, however they seem to be gaining in popularity.

4WD motorhomes

Generally, the terms 4WD and motorhome are mutually exclusive. With a few exceptions, like a 4WD Oka motorhome and a few 4WD trucks that have been converted to motorhomes, you can't do serious four-wheel driving in a motorhome, even an off-road model. Most owners like a few home comforts such as a microwave oven, TV or similar appliances, and these do not respond well to badly corrugated roads. Even though a 4WD motorhome may be able to handle the surface of a bush track, there are restrictions where it can go because of height and width compared with other traffic that uses these tracks.

Beautifully crafted recreational vehicle built in the style of a bygone era

4WD motorhome with a penthouse bedroom

Motorhome showing bed raised to the ceiling

Do-it-yourself motorhome conversions

Some people with the skill and time, undertake the mammoth job of building or fitting-out a campervan or motorhome. Anyone attempting this should obtain a copy of the Australian Design Rules and ensure their motorhome complies; otherwise it will not be registered to drive on the road. It is better to get it right the first time, rather than having to fix up aspects that do not comply.

Manuka Campground, north west Tasmania Photo: Rob Boegheim

Imported motorhomes

Importing a motorhome

A motorhome can only be imported if it was built before January 1 1989 or if you are eligible to import it under the 'Personal Imports' classification (see below). For more information contact the Department of Transport and Regional Services, Vehicle Safety Standard section, GPO Box 594, Canberra 2601 or phone 1800 815 272.

Before buying a vehicle, check the specific points listed in the checklist above to ensure it conforms to Australian Design Rules (ADRs). Examine it for excessive rust. This is often a problem in USA and Canada where salt is often laid on snow-covered roads to improve traction. After a period of time the salt causes damage to the vehicles. Do not buy a vehicle over the internet without inspecting it. Some people who have bought one sight unseen, have found they have a unit that cannot be imported into Australia and that is virtually unsaleable in its country of origin.

- There are several different eligibility criteria when importing a vehicle, and the most relevant are set out below. For registration purposes a 'vehicle' is a motorised unit such as a motorhome or bus. Fifth-wheelers and caravans are regarded as 'trailers'.
- Vehicles built before 1st January 1989 may be imported to Australia without restriction. The vehicle has to comply with ADRs and an Import Approval is required. State or Territory registration requirements still apply.
- Trucks less than 12 tonnes GVM and buses with less than 12 seating positions, must meet the ADRs applicable at the date of original manufacture. Trucks and buses over that capacity need to meet the ADRs applicable when the Used Import plate was fitted.
- To be eligible to be considered a personal import, the vehicle must have been owned and used by the applicant for a continuous period of at least 12 months, and extensive documentation supporting this claim must be supplied. The applicant must be an Australian citizen or an Australian permanent resident and be of an age to hold a licence to drive the vehicle. There are provisions for holders of 410 and 457 visas and also New Zealand citizens.

Import approval

This must be obtained for a vehicle to gain customs clearance at its point of entry to Australia, and this approval should be obtained before shipping the vehicle. Vehicles that arrive in Australia without such approval generally incur significant storage costs until an Import Approval is issued.

Tax payable

In addition to the cost of freight, in most cases there will be tax and GST to pay. Tax is calculated at a rate of 10% of the purchase price, while GST is 10% of the total of the purchase price, tax and freight. (For example: a $100 000 motorhome would have freight/insurance costs of $10 000. Tax would be $10 000 and GST would be an additional $12 000.) Additional costs would be quarantine inspection, port handling charges and customs agent fees. Luxury Car Tax does not apply to motorhomes and campervans. Vehicles over 30 years old are exempt from the 10% tax, but 10% GST still applies.

Aspects you should check:

- **Width** – maximum allowed is 2.5m to the extreme edges (lights, bumper bar or furled awning – whatever protrudes the most).
- **Maximum rear overhang** (section of the body that extends past the axle) – cannot be more than 60% of the wheelbase and is not to measure more than 3.7m. This is measured from the rear of the bumper bar to the centre of the rear axle or, if there are tandem rear axles, the half-way point between the two.
- **Access** – must have a door on the left-hand (passenger) side.
- **Ground clearance** – must be adequate.
- **Electrical system** and **electrical appliances** – the USA electrical system is 110 volt while the Australian electrical supply is 240 volt. The two are not compatible and the wiring may need attention.
- **Gas pipes** – often do not comply. You need an Australian Gas Certificate and Australian Gas Compliance Plate. Check the origin of gas appliances.
- **Gas heating system** – is not legal unless it draws air from outside and also vents through the hull.
- **Gas tank** – built-in gas tanks used to fuel appliances are not legal in Australia. These are used in USA where automotive gas is 100% propane, while in Australia it is usually a mixture of propane and butane.
- **Right-hand-drive conversion** – must be in accordance with Vehicle Standards Bulletin 6 (www.infrastructure.gov.au/roads/vehicle_regulation/bulletin/index.aspx) for vehicles over 4.5 tonnes GVM.
- **Windscreen tinting** – Australian regulations stipulate that only the section of windscreen above the top of the windscreen wiper blade arc or the top 10% (whichever is the lesser) can be tinted. Tinting on other glass (side or rear glass) must have a light transmission factor no less than 35%.
- **Weight of vehicle** – weigh the vehicle on a weighbridge and compare this with the GVM shown on the Australian compliance plate. If the vehicle is not loaded with your personal items when it is weighed, allow at least 500kg. Allow for the weight of fresh and grey water and also fuel in the case of a motorhome.

Dealers are aware of the areas where an imported vehicle may not conform to Australian standards and will likely have these altered to comply, but a private seller might not. Do not assume that just because a vehicle is already registered it must be okay, because aspects that do not comply might not have been picked up prior to its previous registration. If anomalies are found, the vehicle may require uneconomic modifications to meet Australian Standards and, unless it complies, it cannot be registered and driven on the road. Check the information contained in Vehicle Standards Bulletin 10 (www.infrastructure.gov.au/roads/vehicle_regulation/bulletin/index.aspx).

If you are buying a motorhome that was imported as a used vehicle (eg a bus) and then fitted out locally, you should check that it complies with Australian Design Rules (www.infrastructure.gov.au/roads/motor/design/index.aspx). If the vehicle originally had less than 12 seating positions or a GVM less than 12 tonnes, the date of manufacture determines which Australian Design Rules (ADRs) apply. For vehicles that had more than 12 seating positions or a GVM over 12 tonnes, the ADRs applicable are those in force on the date the used import compliance plate was fitted to the vehicle.

Fifth-wheelers

A fifth-wheeler is similar to a semitrailer and has the accommodation section in a detachable trailer. The house section extends over the back of the towing truck and this is where the bedroom is usually located. The sitting area is usually at the rear, with the kitchen and bathroom placed centrally. The interior has much in common with a caravan or motorhome. The fifth-wheeler couples to a turntable or ball fitting on the bed of the truck, usually just in front of the rear axle.

Weight of fifth-wheelers

The overall weight of the trailer and tow vehicle is limited to the Gross Combined Mass (GCM) stipulated for the tow vehicle. If the GCM is 4.5 tonnes and the GVM of the tow vehicle is 2 tonnes, the maximum weight of the loaded trailer must not exceed 2.5 tonnes (including equipment, water and belongings).

Driver's licence

The class of licence is determined by the GVM of the towing vehicle, so unless you are going to use a large truck with a GVM in excess of 4.5 tonnes to tow your fifth-wheeler, a standard licence is all that is required.

Buying an imported fifth-wheeler

Some fifth-wheelers on the Australian market have been manufactured in the USA to Australian Design Rules and they should comply, but before purchase you should check the vehicle thoroughly. Refer to the section on imported motorhomes above for points that you should check.

Some imported fifth-wheelers have the original US layout with the main entry door on the righthand side and a small emergency door located on the lefthand side to comply with Australian Design Rules. This extra door is often not conveniently placed and therefore is not very useable. There are practical difficulties using a fifth-wheeler with the main door on the driver's side.

Importing a fifth-wheeler

It is fairly easy to import a fifth-wheeler because it is regarded as a trailer for importation and registration purposes. The restrictions that apply to importing newer motorhomes do not apply to fifth-wheelers.

Trailers up to 4.5 tonnes ATM must be modified according to Vehicle Standards Bulletin 1 (www.infrastructure.gov.au/roads/vehicle_regulation/bulletin/index.aspx). Trailers with an ATM greater than 4.5 tonnes must comply with the ADRs applicable at the date they are first supplied to the market in Australia and have an identification plate fitted.

Advantages and disadvantages of a fifth-wheeler

	Compared with a motorhome	Compared with a caravan
Advantages	• Having a separate vehicle for local transport after unhooking the trailer. 	• Overall length – when hooked-up, a fifth-wheeler is around 3m shorter than a caravan with the same length of living space because it overlaps the tow vehicle by around 1m, and does not have a draw bar. • Handling is dramatically better with less pitching and swaying (snaking) because of the location of the hitch and because the weight is transferred to the rear wheels of the tow vehicle. A fifth-wheeler places around 25% of its weight on the rear wheels, whereas caravans place 10% onto the towball that is located a distance behind the rear wheels. The weight of a caravan pressing down on the back of the tow vehicle will tend to reduce the weight on the front wheels thereby reducing stability unless a load distribution hitch is used. By placing weight directly over the rear axle, a fifth-wheeler does not have this effect. • Reversing is much easier. • It is not buffeted by side winds or gusts from passing trucks to the same degree.
Disadvantages	• Cannot move directly from the house to the driving cabin. • Total length makes parking difficult and classifies the combination as a 'long vehicle'. • Passenger numbers are limited to the seating in the cab of the towing vehicle, as it is not legal for anyone to travel in the accommodation section. • The towing truck and the accommodation section have to be registered separately, although they can be insured as one unit with some insurance companies. • It is not possible to tow a trailer (eg for a boat) behind the fifth-wheeler.	• Cannot move directly from the house to the driving cabin. • Total length makes parking difficult and classifies the combination as a 'long vehicle'. • Passenger numbers are limited to the seating in the cab of the towing vehicle, as it is not legal for anyone to travel in the accommodation section. • The towing truck and the accommodation section have to be registered separately, although they can be insured as one unit with some insurance companies. • It is not possible to tow a trailer (eg for a boat) behind the fifth-wheeler.

Driving from Busselton to Cape Naturaliste, WA Photo: Pelusey Photography

Fifth-wheeler motorhome

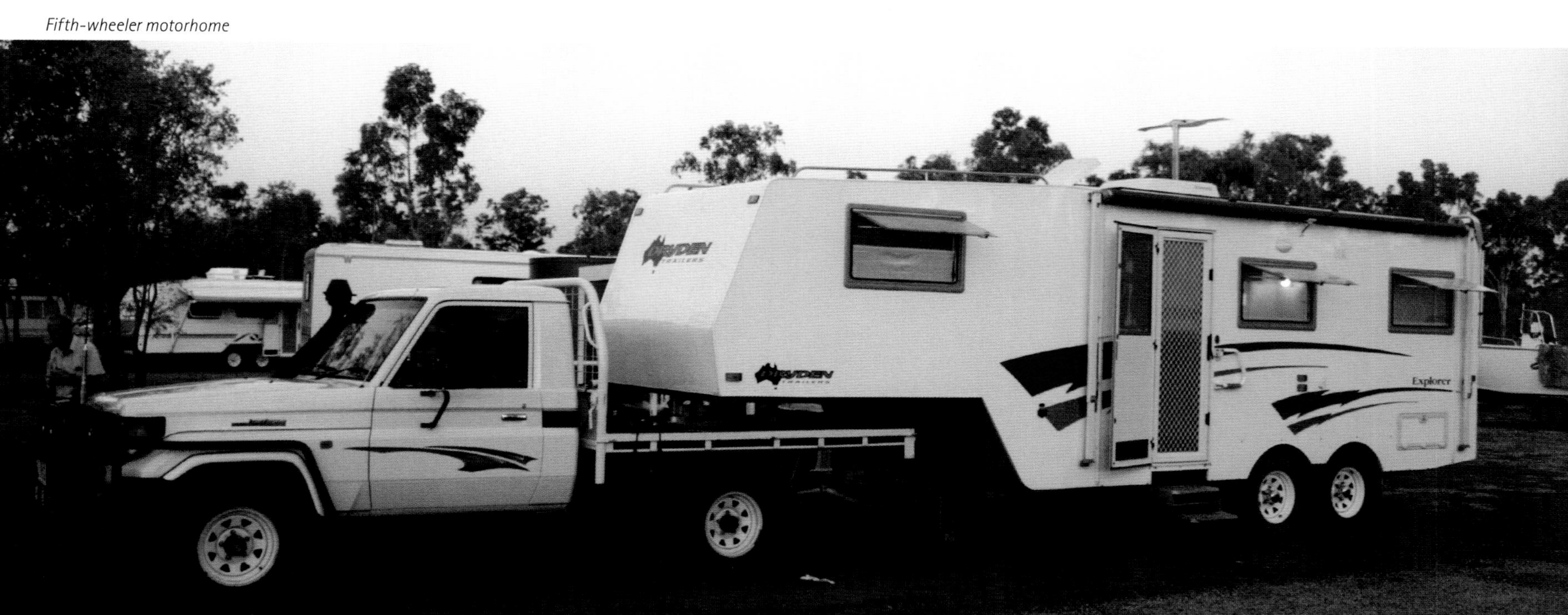

Purchasing a secondhand caravan, campervan or motorhome

Safety or roadworthiness certificate

Any vehicle (including campervans and motorhomes) registered to travel on the road that is offered for sale must have a current Safety Certificate (or Certificate of Roadworthiness). This should be obtained by the person offering it for sale. This certificate must be displayed at the time the vehicle is offered for sale, but an intending purchaser should be aware it is not a guarantee that a vehicle is mechanically sound. The safety certificate covers the following points:

- Tyres
- Suspension
- Brakes
- Body
- Steering
- Windscreen
- Suspension
- Lights

A Safety Certificate is no longer valid after three months have elapsed or if the vehicle has travelled more than 1000km since the certificate was obtained.

New vehicles do not need a Safety Certificate because they are registered for the first time in the new owner's name after they have been sold. A vehicle that is sold unregistered also does not need a Safety Certificate – the buyer takes the risk. A certificate is also not required for a vehicle being sold or traded-in to a motor dealer.

Gas certificate

A current gas certificate is required by law when a caravan, motorhome, campervan or similar unit is offered for sale, whether privately or by a dealer. A qualified gas fitter must certify that the gas installation is safe and in accordance with regulations. The certificate is only valid if it is issued less than 30 days before the transfer. It is the seller's responsibility to obtain a certificate, except when trading-in to a dealer. Any work carried out on gas lines or equipment can only be done by a qualified gas fitter.

Gas tanks on gas-powered vehicles must be inspected every ten years, so if you are considering such a vehicle, check how soon the tank will need inspecting.

Authors' tip:

Your first trip should be a short 'shake-down' trip before you head off on a major adventure. You will probably find you have items on board that you do not need and you will undoubtedly think of more things you should have taken with you.

Inspecting a secondhand unit

When you find a caravan, campervan or motorhome that appeals to you and is reasonably priced, be prepared to spend time checking it thoroughly, both inside and out.

- **Outside walls** – Start by walking around the outside, sighting down the side, examining window seals and checking weatherproofing strips and corner joints for wear. If it has a steel body, look carefully for signs of rust, particularly in the roof and around the windows. If it has been newly painted, examine it very carefully in case the work camouflages an area where rust has been sandpapered rather than cut out. If a motorhome has rubber sheeting on the roof, check it for scratches and tears. If it has a pop-top roof, examine the extending section for cracks or mould. Check that the clamps will securely hold the roof down when travelling.
- **Underneath** – Use a torch to inspect underneath. Excessive stone damage indicates it has travelled many kilometres on unsealed roads. Look for serious scrapes, bending damage or corrosion. If there is a shower fitted, check if there are signs of water damage to the underside of the floor. Look for signs of age-related damage if the caravan or motorhome has been sitting unused for a period of time, particularly if it has not been under cover. Look at the tyres for age, tread wear and general condition.
- **Roof** – Use a ladder to check out the roof for damage and scrapes. If there is an air-conditioner on the roof, sight along the roof to make sure there is no sagging. Have a look at seals around roof hatches.
- **Inside walls and ceiling** – Common forms of construction include: an aluminium outer skin over a timber or metal framework, a fibreglass 'sandwich' wall construction or a fibreglass shell. Carefully check the interior ceiling and walls for discolouration, swelling or 'sponginess' that would indicate that water has entered the wall panels. Look particularly around the roof vents, where the ceiling meets the walls and below the windows. Take extra care checking for water damage if the vehicle has been stored outside for a long period of time. If water has entered the sandwich construction of the wall panels there could be damage that is expensive to repair. If you suspect there could be a leak, ask the owner if you can try testing the exterior by directing water from a hose around the (closed) windows and roof vents. Someone watching inside may see if there are significant leaks.
- **Roof vents and windows** – Make sure that the door, windows and hatches all operate correctly. Any scraping, with the door in particular, could suggest a problem with the square of the frame. Enquire from the owner when the seals around the roof vents, seals on the beading along the top edges and around the windows have last been renewed or checked.
- **Internal fittings**
  - Caravans, campervans or motorhomes with gas installed must have a certificate from a qualified gas fitter.
  - If the unit has been a non-factory fit-out, confirm that all 240 volt electrical work has been done by a qualified electrician. It is probably worth having an electrician check over the unit.
  - Inspect the shower carefully for leaks, particularly if it was not built as a one-piece unit.
  - Check the lights, stove and fridge. If you are keen, you could ask the salesman or owner to turn on the fridge when you first arrive so by the time you have completed your detailed inspection you should be able to detect cooling in the freezer compartment. With an all-electric fridge this will take 15 minutes or so, but with a three-way fridge it will take around an hour before the freezer feels cold, even when it is operating on 240 volt power.
  - Don't be too worried about the cosmetics as you can quickly 'freshen up' a secondhand unit by replacing the curtains and seat covers and maybe the mattress.

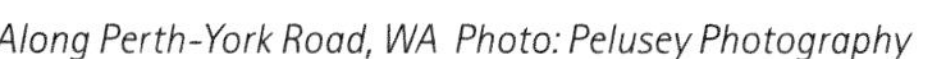

Along Perth-York Road, WA Photo: Pelusey Photography

Camping at Green Point, Tasmania

Power sources

- LPG (propane gas) is usually used for cooking and often for refrigeration.
- 240 volt mains power is used to run appliances and also to recharge batteries through a battery charger.
- 12 volt (or 24 volt) power from batteries is used for appliances and lighting.
- An inverter will enable 240 volt appliances to run from batteries.
- A generator can be used to recharge batteries or supply power directly to appliances.
- Solar panels can be used to supply energy to the house batteries.
- Diesel can be used to run a heater or cooktop.

LPG (propane gas)

Commonly referred to as LPG, propane gas is used for cooking and often for refrigeration and heating water. Unless you plan to operate your gas fridge while travelling (unwise in a campervan or motorhome) turn off the valve on top of the gas cylinder before you start to drive. This is not essential, but it is a wise safety measure.

Automotive LPG

Liquid Petroleum Gas used to power vehicles is usually a mixture of propane and butane, with the percentage of propane being anywhere between 50% and 100%. Butane has higher energy content than propane (28.61 megajoules per litre compared with 25.49 megajoules per litre). There is no way of knowing when you buy gas what the butane component is, and it will not necessarily be the same on your next purchase, even if you return to the same retailer. Because of the butane content, automotive gas must never be used to power on-board appliances.

To use gas from a cylinder it must vaporise before being piped to appliances. Butane and propane vaporise at different temperatures: propane will vaporise down to -42°C but butane will not vaporise below -1°C. If a cylinder has a propane/butane mixture, the propane will vaporise more easily than the butane, leaving a higher concentration of butane in the cylinder. This does not happen with vehicle engines because the gas is piped in its liquid form to the engine.

Gas cylinders

Propane gas is stored in heavy steel cylinders capable of withstanding the high pressure required to maintain propane in a liquid state, and it remains in liquid form only while it is under pressure. Gas cylinders must be installed upright and securely fastened with the valve uppermost to ensure the inlet to the safety valve always remains in the vapour space clear of the liquid content of the cylinder.

Cylinders are usually fitted with a safety relief valve designed to release gas if the pressure within the cylinder becomes too high. This can happen as a result of very high temperatures. When installing a cylinder on the drawbar or front wall of a caravan, place it so the relief valve is pointing away from both the caravan and the tow vehicle.

There are different types of gas cylinders available, and the regulations do not specify that any particular type should be used for a specific purpose or stored in a set location. Cylinders are marked as follows:

- #1 cylinders are galvanised steel and are considered the premium quality;
- #2 cylinders are steel with a polyester epoxy coating, usually powder coated, and are very robust;
- #3 cylinders are steel treated with a zinc rich paint and finishing coats;
- #4 cylinders are steel painted conventionally using approved metal primer and finishing coats – it is not advisable to use this type of container where it is subject to rain and weather, because the exterior would soon deteriorate; and
- fibre reinforced polymer cylinders. Popular with yacht owners, these are top of the range. This type of cylinder is many times the price of steel bottles.

When cylinders reach their marked expiry date they cannot be refilled unless they have been re-inspected and re-certified. Cylinders can still be refilled at some service stations, large hardware stores and caravan parks, or you can use a 'swap and go' exchange service. If you use the exchange system, check that the time left before the expiry date on the replacement cylinder is not less than your old one, and check the number marked on the bottle to ensure that you are taking a cylinder of the same standard.

Two gas cylinders are preferable to a single cylinder, particularly if you use gas to run a three-way fridge.

Where to install gas cylinders

- Cylinders larger than 2.25kg must be housed in an approved manner outside the accommodation area.
- With caravans, the cylinder can be installed on the draw bar or in a similarly secured location on the caravan wall that would normally face the towing vehicle.
- Cylinders can be installed in a fully open recess within the profile of the caravan or motorhome. This recess must be vapour-proof from the living quarters.
- Briefly, the gas regulations state that a gas cylinder compartment must:
  - House the cylinder(s) and associated equipment only.
  - Not have access from the inside of the caravan or motorhome.
  - Be sealed to prevent gas vapour from entering the caravan or motorhome.
  - A compartment with a door must be accessible without the use of a tool if there is an emergency. Under the regulations a key is not considered a tool so it is legal to have the compartment locked, although it would be wise to keep it unlocked while gas is being used.
  - The compartment must be identified with an approved, durable, red label with white lettering stating 'LP Gas Storage' and a 'Flammable Gas 2' logo.

For full details refer to AS5601 (www.standards.org.au or www.saiglobal.com).

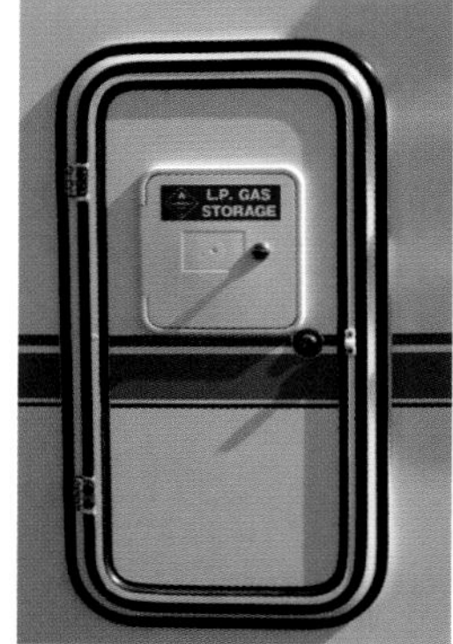

Ingenious gas compartment door with a small flap to access the gas cylinder.

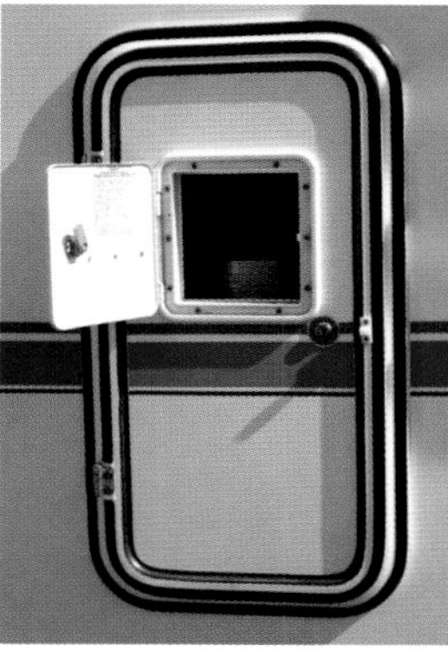
Flap in gas door opened so cylinder valve can be turned off quickly while the main door remains locked.

Authors' tip:

If you have only one cylinder, it is probably prudent to have the cylinder re-filled at a convenient time, even though it might not be totally empty. The loss of a couple of dollars worth of gas is better than having the gas run out when you are cooking a meal and there is nowhere nearby to have the cylinder refilled.

Changing a gas cylinder

Close the valve on the empty cylinder before disconnecting it and do not open the valve on the new cylinder until it is securely connected. The thread to connect or disconnect the cylinder is a left-hand thread – it turns the opposite way to most other Australian threads.

Transporting gas cylinders

There is a limit on the size of gas cylinders that can be transported in an enclosed vehicle. A 9kg cylinder falls within this limit, but a 13.5kg cylinder is too large. Cylinders should be carried upright and secured, preferably in the boot. Ensure that the valves are tightly turned off, and for added safety, fit a screwed plug (sometimes called a 'mouse') to the cylinder outlet. No more than two cylinders should be carried at any one time.

Gas regulator

A regulator controls and lowers the pressure at which gas flows from a cylinder to appliances. Never attempt to use gas from a cylinder that is not fitted with a regulator. If the flames on a burner reduce significantly when you light a second burner, it indicates that the regulator is faulty and it should be replaced immediately.

If the gas cylinder is stored outside, the regulator should be covered to prevent water damage and checked regularly to make sure there is no corrosion. Cover the regulator so wasps cannot enter and make a nest.

Gas leakage and repairs

For safety, a smell has been deliberately added to propane, and most people can detect a gas leak by its 'garlic' smell. Propane is heavier than air, and will pool in the lowest area if it is released. To allow gas to escape from an enclosed caravan in the event of a gas leak, air vents are built in the bottom of the door or the step well. Each gas appliance (fridge or stove) has its own isolation valve, in addition to the main valve on top of the gas cylinder. Any work carried out on gas lines or equipment can only be done by a qualified gas fitter.

Gas certificate

Vehicles fitted with LPG gas must have a compliance plate attached, certifying that the fuel system complies with the relevant Australian Standards. By law, secondhand caravans, motorhomes or similar units with gas installed must have a current gas certificate when offered for sale, whether privately or by a dealer. The certificate is only valid if it is issued less than 30 days before the transfer. It is the seller's responsibility to obtain a certificate, except when trading in to a dealer.

Gas tanks require inspection every ten years and this costs between $500 and $1000.

240 volt mains power

Consider carefully the amount of power that you will use. Firstly, determine whether you have 15 amps or 10 amps available by checking the power source, sockets, electrical lead and vehicle electrical system. If you use a standard 15 amp 'caravan' lead plugged into a 15 amp socket (standard in caravan parks) your system will be 15 amp, provided your caravan or motorhome is wired for 15 amps. (Check your circuit breaker – many motorhomes have a 16 amp circuit breaker.) If any of the components in the system are 10 amps (like when you are plugged into a domestic power point) then that is the limit of power available.

Using 240 volts on a 10 amp system, the maximum power that you may safely use is 2400 watts. With a 15 amp system it is 3600 watts.

To determine what appliances you can use, you need to work out how many amps (or amperes) these units will draw.

The formula is 'watts = volts x amperes'.

- To determine the number of amps you are using with a particular appliance, the formula is turned the other way around – divide the watts of a large toaster (1800) by the volts (240) = power consumption of 7.5amps.
- If you attempt to use more power than the 10 or 15 amps that your system can carry, the circuit breaker should automatically shut off the power to prevent damage to the electrical circuit. In these circumstances, turn off one appliance, then flip the switch of the circuit breaker and power should be restored.

Power-hungry appliances that can contribute to the problem include air conditioners, electric kettles and heaters. For example, an electric kettle commonly uses 2400 watts or 10 amps, so you should not run it simultaneously with another power-hungry appliance. If you have a refrigerator operating on 240 volt and an in-built battery charger, combined they will likely draw up to a couple of amps (depending on the models) when you first plug into the 240 volt power source. You need to allow for this usage when you consider what other appliances you can use.

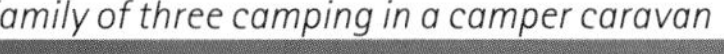

Family of three camping in a camper caravan

Authors' tip:

My simple rule is not to use any other electrical appliance (like the microwave) while the electric jug is on.

Some caravans and motorhomes have a separate electrical circuit for their air conditioning unit so they can connect leads to two separate power points. This could be difficult in a caravan park where there is usually one power point for each site. If you do have two separate power sources available and two separate circuits in your caravan or motorhome, this will double the power available for use.

Electrical leads

The Australian Standard applying to electrical supply to caravans and motorhomes stipulates that supply leads are to be in a single length. It is no longer acceptable to join leads. Joining leads may result in a circuit breaker failing to operate in time to prevent electrocution.

'Caravan' electrical leads have a 15 amp plug that will not fit into an ordinary household 10 amp socket. Many travellers have a 15 amp lead with a 15 amp socket and a 10 amp plug, thereby enabling them to plug into home power to recharge batteries. The maximum demand for this type of lead is not to exceed 10 amps (2400 watts) of power and its length is not to exceed 25m. For safety reasons these leads are to have a built-in 10 amp circuit breaker and can only be assembled by a licensed electrician.

Because of voltage drop, the longer the lead, the heavier the cabling has to be. The maximum length of lead permitted is 40m, but it must have a 4sq mm conductor. That makes it very heavy and also expensive. If your lead is much longer than required to reach the power point, you should not leave the excess length of cable coiled as it can overheat when in use. A lead that is not lying flat on the ground can present a hazard to an unwary pedestrian too.

If you notice wear or exposed wires on a power lead or the power cord of an appliance, discard it or have it repaired by an electrician. Do not use electrical equipment that is in an unsafe condition.

Power points

It is usual to have a couple of 240 volt power points in motorhomes and caravans, together with a 12 volt point in a location suitable for a TV. Household power points, known as general purpose outlets (GPOs) are usually rated at 10 amps, so power usage on one power point should be restricted to 10 amps. Although they use minimal power, most chargers for mobile phones, camera batteries etc are too bulky to allow usage of the second outlet on a double power point. A multi-point power board will allow you to use two or more such chargers simultaneously. An external 240 volt power point on a caravan or motorhome is often useful.

Authors' tip:

We suggest you have two 15 amp leads: one 10m in length and one 20m. They are available from hardware stores in lengths up to 25m.

Lighting

Lighting is usually 12 volt, powered from the 'house' battery. Some caravans are also equipped with 240 volt lights that can be used when connected to mains power.

The following different types of lighting are used:

- **Incandescent bulbs** are not energy efficient, as they work by heating a filament that glows and produces light and also a small amount of heat.
- **Fluorescent tubes** are very energy efficien, using about one quarter of the energy of conventional incandescent bulbs, and about half that of halogen globes. With fluorescent lights, electricity is used to generate ultraviolet light that causes a phosphor coating to fluoresce and give off light.
- **Light emitting diodes** (LEDs) are the most energy efficient lighting available, and although they are more expensive initially, they have a very long life. If you intend to bush camp extensively, it may be worthwhile replacing incandescent bulbs with LEDs.

12 volt power

While travelling, a 12 volt fridge should operate well because it will be receiving power from the vehicle's alternator at up to 14.2 volts. When the vehicle stops, the fridge will draw power from the house battery, which puts out between 12.8 volts and 12 volts when it is nearly flat. This is sufficient to run a fridge, provided the cable connecting the fridge to its power source is adequate. Inevitably, voltage will drop in a length of electrical cable, and in an undersized cable can easily drop below the voltage required for a fridge to operate. For most fridges this is around 11.5 volts. This common problem can be alleviated by installing a thicker cable – 13.5mm cross-sectional area is suggested.

Batteries

Batteries used in the house

Motorhomes and campervans – All except small campervans have a dual battery system with an automotive battery to start the engine and a deep cycle battery to power the house. The batteries are connected to a diode isolator and both batteries are automatically recharged while driving. If you have a battery charger, the house battery will be recharged when the motorhome/campervan is connected to 240 volt power. Many motorhomes have two or more batteries in parallel for extra capacity, and some motorhomes have a 24 volt system.

Caravans – Most caravans have 12 volt lighting, but some have 240 volt lights or dual 240 volt/12 volt lighting. Most caravans have a house battery that is recharged by the alternator of the tow vehicle or by an in-built charger when connected to 240 volt mains power. If a trickle-charge transformer is used, it will make recharging a very slow process from 240 volt, so it would be advantageous to install a faster charger. If there is no battery, the 12 volt lighting is powered by a transformer when connected to 240 volt mains power. When the van is not connected to 240 volt power, there is no power available unless the vehicle ignition is turned on.

Choosing a battery

In all batteries (automotive, marine or deep cycle) there are different types of construction:

- **Conventional flooded lead acid** (low maintenance) batteries are the most common type, probably because they are well-suited to Australian conditions, i.e. high under-bonnet and ambient temperatures, and also being shaken on corrugated roads. They are fairly tolerant of a range of charging rates and depths of discharge, but leaving them stand in a discharged state can cause irreparable damage. The electrolyte level should be checked periodically and topped up with distilled water. Usually older batteries need topping up more often.
- **Flooded lead acid** batteries in a maintenance-free sealed design. The calcium-alloy plates of sealed batteries are prone to irreversible sulphation when completely discharged, and that is a death sentence to the battery.
- **Valve regulated lead-acid (VRLA)** batteries are either gel cell or absorbed glass mat (AGM) and are totally maintenance free. They deliver the cranking power required for a starter motor, and have a faster recovery than a conventional flooded lead acid battery. Both gel and AGM batteries are sealed so acid cannot spill if they are broken. Because there is no risk of spillage of acid and no venting of explosive hydrogen gas, they are commonly used in marine applications or in wheelchairs, and can be installed on their side. AGMs are around twice the price of conventional deep cycle batteries of the same nominal capacity, but their useable capacity is much greater and they should last longer. They are not prone to sulphation in the way a sealed flooded battery is.

Types of batteries

The different types of batteries used in motor vehicles and caravans/motorhomes are designed to give optimum performance in different situations.

- An **automotive starter battery** can deliver the high cranking amps (usually 200 to 400 amps for five to 15 seconds) required to power a starter motor. Starter batteries are rated by their cold cranking current, i.e. the amount of current (amps) that the battery will deliver for 30 seconds. It will deliver around 4000 – 5000 shallow discharge cycles over a lifetime, but if it was deep cycled, these plates would probably fail after 30 – 150 cycles because the plates are more porous and thinner than in a deep cycle battery.
- A **marine battery** is part way between an automotive battery and a deep cycle battery. It is designed to supply sufficient cranking amps for a starter motor, and has the versatility to allow a greater depth of discharge than an automotive battery, but it cannot discharge as much as a deep cycle battery. The separator plates are designed with further separation than in a conventional automotive battery, so it can withstand jarring caused by impact from waves. These batteries are sometimes installed in off-road caravans because they can withstand the vibrations caused by driving over corrugated roads.
- **Deep cycle batteries** are constructed with thicker grids of antimony lead alloy and a denser paste of active material than conventional batteries. Deep cycle batteries are rated in ampere hours. They are designed to deliver sustained power with low current drain for extended periods of time but are not designed for high current discharges. Although they will withstand 400 to 500 cycles up to about 60% to 80% depth of discharge, the deeper the cycle, the shorter life the battery will have. Once a deep cycle battery is flattened it will take a long time to charge it from the vehicle alternator. They are ideal for solar power systems.

Commonly used battery terms

- **Ampere (amp)** – unit of measurement for the electron flow or current through a circuit.
- **Ampere Hours (AH)** – unit of measurement for a battery's electrical storage capacity, calculated by multiplying the current in amperes by the time in hours (amps x hours = amp hours). Example – 5 amps for 20 hours provides 100 AH of capacity.
- **Cell** – the basic current-producing unit in a battery. A wet cell's nominal voltage is 2 volts, and a 12 volt battery has six cells.
- **Cold Cranking Amps (CCA)** – rating used for automotive (starting) batteries.
- **Cranking battery** – battery used to start an automobile.
- **Current** – the flow rate of energy from the battery, measured in amps.
- **Cycle** – one complete discharge plus one recharge.
- **Depth of Discharge (DOD)** – the percentage of capacity actually removed from a battery compared with the total rated capacity.
- **Electrolyte** – a dilute solution of sulphuric acid and water contained within the battery.
- **Flooded cell battery** (the most common type) – has electrolyte solution of acid and water 'flooding' the plates.
- **Voltage** – the potential available between the terminals of a battery that, for a fully charged battery, would be 12.7 – 12.8 volts.

Authors' tip:

If you are buying a caravan, check to see what battery and charger are included.

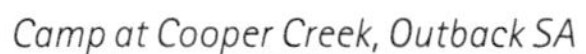

Camp at Cooper Creek, Outback SA

Differences between gel and AGM batteries

Gel batteries	AGM batteries
Gel batteries contain acid that has been 'gelled' by the addition of silica gel, turning the acid into a solid mass similar to jelly. • One of the disadvantages is that the battery cannot be fast-charged on a conventional automotive charger because excess gas can damage the cells. This is not a problem with solar electric systems, but if an auxiliary generator or inverter bulk charger is used, the current must be limited to the manufacturer's specifications. • If a gel battery is overcharged, voids can develop in the gel causing permanent loss in battery capacity. • The voltage at which gel batteries are charged is important, and it is recommended this should not exceed 14 volts. • In hot climates, water loss can be enough over 2 to 4 years to cause premature battery death.	Absorbed glass mat (AGM) batteries consist of acid suspended in a special glass mat separator. AGM batteries are sometimes called 'dry' because the fibreglass mat is only 95% saturated with sulphuric acid and there is no excess liquid. • They have the advantages of gel batteries, but none of the disadvantages mentioned here. • They also have a low discharge rate while in storage, an extended life-cycle durability and an ability to withstand shock and vibration better than any standard battery. Their hydrogen emission is well below the 4% maximum specified for aircraft and enclosed spaces.

What to look for when buying batteries

- **Age of battery** – If you are buying a conventional flooded lead acid battery, do not buy one that has been sitting on the shelf unless it has been recharged periodically – and that is unlikely on a retailer's premises. Buy from a retailer who has a good turnover, and if you have to blow dust off the battery, it has been sitting on the shelf far too long. This is not a problem with AGM batteries as they have a very low discharge rate when sitting unused. Reputable brands of batteries carry a letter/number code imprinted on the lid or a terminal that indicates their date of dispatch from the factory. The letter component of the code shows the month: A – January, B – February, C – March, D – April, E – May, F – June, G – July, H – August, J – September, K – October, L – November, M – December. The year is shown as follows: 7 – 2007, 8 – 2008 and so on. Example: A battery coded G8 was dispatched in July 2008.
- **Deep cycle battery** – The most important consideration is the ampere-hour (AH) or reserve capacity (or reserve minutes) rating that will meet or exceed your requirements. The next factor is how much the battery weighs. A battery with more ampere hours or reserve capacity will tend to have a longer life but it will also weigh more because of thicker plates and more lead. You will need to weigh up (pardon the pun) the extra weight and longer life expectancy against the cost.

Authors' tip:

Go to a battery specialist who will help you select the best battery for your requirements. The information above should help you make sense of any recommendations.

Battery compartment

All batteries should have some **ventilation**, and this is essential with flooded lead acid batteries. They give off hydrogen and must always be housed in a compartment with ventilation holes at the bottom (for fresh air) and at the top for gas to vent to the outdoors. Without ventilation there is the chance of an explosion.

Getting the most life out of your battery

The life of a battery will vary considerably depending on how it is used, temperature, and how it is maintained and charged. Batteries like to be kept cool, but not ice cold. A battery discharged by only 10% of its capacity will last about five times as long as one cycled to 50% **DOD (depth of discharge)**. However, a battery cycled to 50% DOD should last about twice as long as one discharged by 80% DOD. It is obviously not practical to have a bank of batteries and use each in turn just to limit the DOD, but an ideal to aim for is 50% discharge between recharges. However, the single greatest cause of battery failure is leaving the battery in a discharged state for a prolonged period of time. If a battery is not recharged to full capacity quickly, it can lead to permanent loss of part of its capacity.

A **temperature compensation device** can be used to limit the charge that goes to a battery in high temperatures and prevent over-charging. This device is connected to both the regulator and the battery, and controls the rate of charge as the ambient temperature rises and falls.

Batteries that are **stored for long periods** will eventually lose all their charge, and the rate varies according to battery type, age and temperature. It can range between 1% and 15% per month, with a higher rate in higher temperatures. A battery stored at 35°C will self discharge twice as quickly as one stored at 24°C. Inactivity can be extremely harmful to a battery, so if it is not in use, keep it on a continual trickle charge. Leaving a battery stored in a partly or fully discharged state for a few months is very damaging.

In situations where multiple batteries are connected in series, parallel or series/parallel, they should all be the same **size, type and manufacturer**. Do not put a new battery into a series that is more than three months old or that has had more than 75 cycles. Either replace all with new batteries, or obtain a good used battery.

Authors' tip:

It is a myth that lead acid batteries should be fully discharged before recharging. This will lead to premature battery failure.

A device called a **Megapulse** can be used with lead-acid batteries, and it is claimed it can reduce or even reverse excessive sulphation.

Measuring how much power is left in a battery

After a battery has been rested (no load and no charging) for several hours, a voltmeter can be used to give an indication of battery condition.

Alternatively, a **battery monitor** can be used to measure battery voltage and amps flowing into and out of a battery. It can calculate the amp hours used during discharging and compute the amp hours returned to the battery during charging. By displaying this information, a monitor will help you manage your battery usage and get the maximum life span out of your batteries.

Camping area near Stanley, Tasmania Photo: Rob Boegheim

Maintenance of flooded batteries

During the charging process the electrolyte solution bubbles producing hydrogen, and some water is lost. Batteries need to be checked every eight to ten weeks to ensure the electrolyte solution remains at the correct level. Procedure:

- Remove the water vent caps and **check the electrolyte level**. The minimum level is to the top of the plates, and these should never be exposed to air. For safety reasons, you should wear spectacles or safety goggles when topping up a battery in case there is an acid splash.
- **Top up with distilled water**. Use only a non-metallic container and take care not to overfill.
- If there is no electrolyte visible, add just enough water to cover the plates. Replace and tighten all vent caps and put the battery on a complete charge before adding any more water.
- If you accidentally come into contact with battery acid, wash the skin immediately with soap and water.
- **Replace and tighten all vent caps**.
- **Clean the battery terminals externally**.
- If you need to top up with water often, then you are over-charging.

Working with batteries

- Never disconnect a battery cable from a vehicle with the engine running. Turn off all electrical switches and components, turn off the ignition and then disconnect the battery.
- Always disconnect the negative conductor (black) first, then the positive conductor (red).
- Reconnect the positive conductor (red) first then the negative conductor (black). A small spark may be produced.

Temperature effects on batteries

Battery capacity (how many amp hours it can hold) is reduced as temperature goes down and is increased as the temperature goes up. At zero degrees, battery capacity is reduced by 20%. This is why an automobile battery approaching the end of its life often fails in winter.

Battery life is also affected by temperature. At higher temperatures, battery life is shortened, while in a cold climate battery life is longer. As most batteries will have periods of high temperatures and also periods of lower temperatures, it will tend to even out.

Increasing your battery system power

Two or more batteries can be connected to boost your system's voltage and/or capacity. Always use matching batteries, i.e. same age, brand and capacity.

- To increase voltage, connect two deep cycle batteries in **series** (positive to negative). This will result in a 24 volt system instead of a 12 volt system.
- To increase amp hour capacity, connect two deep cycle batteries in **parallel** (positive to positive, negative to negative).
- To increase both voltage and amp hour capacity, connect four deep cycle batteries in **series/parallel**.

Battery charger

Most motorhomes, and some caravans, are equipped with a battery charger so the house batteries can be charged when connected to 240 volt mains power.

A battery charger has three key functions:

- **Charging** – getting the charge into the battery;
- **Stabilising** – optimising the charging rate; and
- **Terminating** – knowing when to stop.

Determining when the battery is fully charged and terminating the charging process at that time is critical in preserving battery life. This is particularly important with fast chargers where the danger of overcharging and overheating the battery is greater. During **fast charging** it is possible to pump electrical energy into a battery faster than the chemical process within the battery can react to it, with damaging results.

If you are buying or replacing a charger, buy a good one. Three stage (or three step) chargers work as follows:

- First stage – bulk charge mode until it reaches a factory-set (or programmable) level;
- Second stage – absorption mode; and
- Third stage – float (or trickle) charge when the battery is fully charged.

Trickle charging is designed to compensate for the self-discharge of a battery with a continuous charge. This long-term constant current charging is not suitable for some battery chemistries, e.g. NiMH and lithium batteries are susceptible to damage from overcharging. Nicad batteries are the most robust type and can be left on trickle charge for very long periods. However; it is still preferable to take a nicad battery off the charger. Lead acid batteries can tolerate a short duration trickle charge but flooded batteries tend to use up their water.

Fast chargers and **quick chargers** must be designed for specific cell chemistries and it is not normally possible to charge one cell type in a charger designed for another type of cell chemistry.

Universal chargers able to charge all cell types must have sensing devices to identify the cell type and apply the appropriate charging profile.

Pulse charging is becoming more common because it is claimed to charge batteries more efficiently and in less time than conventional charging. Negative pulse (or burp) charging schemes generally consist of one or more of the following charging sequences:

- A positive charging pulse;
- A rest period with no charging; and
- A discharge pulse (or burp).

The sequencing, duration and repetition rate of each of the above sequences can vary.

Travellers who want to recharge AA or AAA batteries for a camera or other equipment from the cigarette lighter socket of a vehicle, can use a 'Smart Quick Charger for Battery' that is quite inexpensive.

Inverters

An inverter is an electronic device that converts 12 volt direct current (DC) power from a battery into standard 240 volt alternating current (AC) power for household use. When you do not have access to 240 volt power, an inverter can convert stored 12 volt battery power to run normal 240 volt household appliances. Be warned, appliances that involve heating are power hungry, e.g. electric jug, microwave or toaster.

Before purchasing an inverter, consider what **equipment you intend to power** through it, because it is a matter of 'you get what you pay for'. It is advisable to buy an inverter that is larger than you think you will need, because it is likely you will want to power extra equipment once you have it.

Decide what appliances you will want to power simultaneously. Check the data plate on the larger appliances and work out the maximum power requirement (in watts) at any one time. If the data plate only states the power in amps, convert to watts by using the formula: volts (240) x amps = watts.

Types of inverters

Modified square wave inverters (sometimes called modified sine wave inverters) are the standard, and manufacturers claim they will safely power many appliances including most TVs, blenders, toasters, fridges, fans, hair driers, laptop computers and bubble jet printers.

Appliances are designed to operate on 240 volt AC power – a pure sine wave voltage that changes up and down in a smooth wave-like pattern. A modified square wave inverter changes up and down far quicker and with a square wave rather than a curving wave. Some simple electric appliances will operate on this power, but you should exercise caution if you want to use equipment with electronic components. It is possible equipment could shut down when it detects an unusual form of power but it is also possible that damage could occur. Before buying or using a modified square wave inverter, check the instruction books or contact the manufacturer/distributor of the equipment you plan to power.

True (or pure) **sine wave inverters** are more expensive and are required for laser computer printers, laser fax, breadmakers, some microwave ovens, most NiCad chargers, many electric shavers and almost anything that has an inbuilt electric clock.

All inverters that are safe will be marked **'electrically isolated'** – you should not buy or use one that is not so marked.

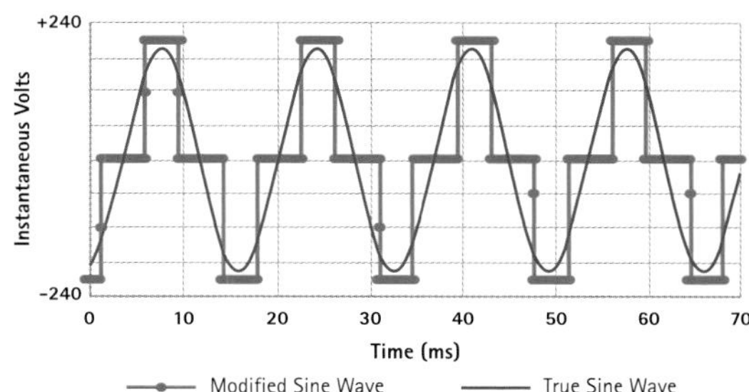

How long can you run the inverter?

The capacity of a battery is specified in amp hours, so you need to work out how many amp hours of power your appliance will consume.

For example: a 500 watt breadmaker powered from a 200 amp hour battery.

- Divide the watts needed for the breadmaker (500) by 10 – so the result is 50 amp hours. (The 'rule of thumb' is 10 not 12 because of power loss .)
- Then divide the amp hours needed (50) into the capacity of the battery (200 amp hours) and the result is four hours.
- So theoretically you can power the breadmaker for four hours, but this is not a realistic expectation. It wouldn't merely flatten the battery, it would 'kill' it.

To run major appliances you would be well advised to install a solar system to charge the battery or batteries, or use a generator, otherwise you will run out of battery power rather quickly. If you only want to operate a few small items (eg phone, camera battery charger, fan, or electric shaver) a small inverter plugged into the 'house' battery system will provide sufficient amp hours.

Before buying a generator, consider:

- **What do you want to power** with the generator? Heavy users of power are air-conditioning units, electric fridges and microwave ovens. A unit large enough to run an air-conditioner, electric fridge and microwave is heavy and costs a considerable amount. Don't economise and buy one that is too small for what you want to power.
- If you want to run an air conditioner, make sure the generator has enough capacity to cope with the heavy load of starting it.
- The **additional weight** added to the vehicle.
- Where the generator would be stored and, if you have to move it before use, can you easily lift and carry it. If you have an under-floor storage bin with outside access, you can secure the generator to a sliding shelf installed within the storage bin. In this way the generator is well ventilated while in use and yet the owner does not have to lift it out before use or put a chain and padlock around it to secure it at campgrounds. If you plan to use the generator inside a storage bin, check that fumes will not leak into the living space. If you use the generator on the ground, secure it with a solid chain and padlock to the bull bar or draw bar to prevent theft, even while you are using it.
- You will have to **carry a supply of petrol (or diesel)** to fuel the generator.
- Check on the **running cost** (fuel consumption per hour) and servicing costs. Fuel consumption will vary depending on the brand and size of generator and also on the load. For example a 2400 watt generator uses one litre per hour whereas a small 1000 watt model used to charge batteries uses less than a quarter of a litre per hour under low load.
- Good quality, four-stroke generators are much **quieter**, and produce more power using less fuel with lower emissions when compared with cheap two-stroke models.
- A **noisy generator can be annoying** for fellow campers. Considerate generator owners try to camp away from others and restrict the hours they run the machine. Position it so exhaust fumes do not blow into your neighbour's caravan or motorhome, or your own. There are some campgrounds, particularly in national parks, where you are not permitted to use a generator at all.
- **Do you really need to use appliances** such as a microwave and air conditioner, and watch television for extended hours when you bush camp? You may decide you do not need a generator at all.

Authors' tip:

Cheaper generators are often much heavier than good quality ones. If you only use the air-conditioner and microwave when you have 240 volt power and install a three-way fridge, you probably do not need a generator. However if you decide you 'must' have one, go for quality.

Generators

Generators are powered by either petrol or diesel and vary in the types of power they produce. Some produce only 240 volt AC power, some produce a small amount of 12 volt DC in addition, and others produce only 12 volt or 24 volt DC. To choose between these, consider not only your anticipated use, but also storage of the energy. With **240 volt AC**, power is only available when the generator is operating (unless you use a battery charger to store this power in a battery) but in that process you lose about 30% of the power you convert. If **DC power** is generated, it can be stored in batteries and used directly to run DC appliances, or used via an inverter to power 240 volt AC appliances. With this latter method, power is available as needed.

Fuel cells

With further development, fuel cells are **likely to become the most efficient energy source** for travellers. A fuel cell is an electrochemical conversion device that produces electricity from various external quantities of fuel (on the anode side) and an oxidant (on the cathode side). Since the conversion of the fuel to energy takes place via an electrochemical process, not combustion, the process is clean, quiet and highly efficient. Fuel cells are different from batteries in that they consume reactant, which must be replenished, whereas batteries store electrical energy chemically in a closed system.

Some fuel cells use hydrogen and oxygen and convert these chemicals into water, and in the process produce electricity. Other fuel cells use methanol to power the unit, however the difficulty is in the transportation of the fuel.

A German company, Truma VeGA, is developing a fuel cell powered by LPG (propane/butane mix) specifically for the recreational vehicle market. It is expected to be available in 2010. This unit will produce cheap, clean, power from a readily available fuel.

Solar power

As a source of power, an array of solar panels is more **environmentally friendly** than a generator. The panels are usually installed on the roof and can be either fixed flat-mounted or the newer mobile units that follow the position of the sun. The solar panels charge the house batteries and this will reduce or may even remove your reliance on 240 volt mains power.

As part of the 'going solar' exercise, you should examine what power you currently use, and whether this can be reduced. The appliances that use the most power are the air conditioning unit, microwave oven and electric fridge. If you have a gas fridge, your electricity requirements can easily be handled by a small to moderate size solar system if you are prepared to forego an air conditioner and a microwave. Lighting is an area where you can save some power, with fluorescent tubes using about 75% less power than incandescent light bulbs, and LEDs being even more efficient.

Generator on slide-out tray ready for use

Generator secured in storage bin

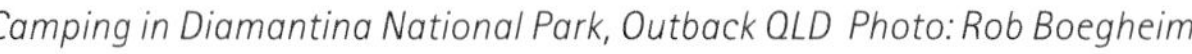

Camping in Diamantina National Park, Outback QLD Photo: Rob Boegheim

How solar power works

Solar modules **convert sunlight to DC electricity** and this energy can be stored by charging a battery during the day. The rate of battery charging depends on the solar module and the intensity of the sunlight: the brighter the sunlight, the more effective charging. Solar modules like bright sun, not hot sun. Even on cloudy days a solar module will charge a battery, but the current will be reduced. Ideally, solar modules should be placed in a shadow-free position, although more recent models are more shadow tolerant and more efficient than earlier models.

For optimum performance, the solar module/s should be angled at **90° toward the sun** and be shifted, either manually or electronically, to follow the path of the sun across the sky during the day. On a sunny day, maximum charging occurs in five to six peak sun hours during the main part of the day, although this varies with different locations.

The power rating is measured in watts. A number of modules can be mounted together to form a **solar array**. A solar system will consist of one or more solar modules, a regulator and a battery or batteries. The input voltage coming from the solar panels will vary depending on the intensity of the sun, the prevalence of cloud and whether the solar array is at the correct angle to the sun. A **regulator** is required to control the voltage going to the battery to the optimum level. A three-step regulator will start off with a 'bulk charge' to a pre-set voltage, move into the absorption stage, then continue on a float charge.

To determine the amps of power generated: check the solar panel manufacturer's net rated output. In theory, to ascertain the energy stored (amp hours) you should be able to divide the number of watts of the solar panel (e.g. 60) by the voltage (12) and multiply by the number of charging hours (say 6) to result in about 30 amp hours. In practice, the actual output is often somewhat lower than the manufacturer's stated output. An example provided is a 120 watt system that produces 7.1 amps instead of 10 amps as may be expected.

Small portable solar panel

How many solar modules do you need?

You should list the 12-volt appliances you want to use, estimate how long you will use each and calculate the energy they will consume (watt hours). Each appliance should have the power it draws (watts) marked on it. Multiply this by the expected time it will be used, expressed as a proportion of an hour. As an example – a colour TV that draws 36 watts is used for 2½ hours. Multiply 36 (watts) by 2.5 (hours) to find that you will use 90 watt hours. In this example, add a few hours' use of fluorescent lighting and use of a water pump and the total can easily be in the vicinity of 130 watt hours. Divide by 12 (12 volt battery) and a figure of 11 amp hours is reached.

When calculating the size of a solar array needed to provide sufficient electricity, assume that not every day will be clear and sunny. For efficient charging, the panels should be washed regularly to remove dust build-up. Solar panels come with a twenty or twenty-five year warranty.

Another critical factor in going solar is to ensure you have appropriate storage capacity in your batteries for the energy produced by your solar array. *Please refer to the earlier section on batteries in this Chapter.*

Wind generators

A wind generator might seem to be an ideal way to charge batteries, however the equipment cannot be used while travelling because the units are not designed to work at the wind speeds generated while driving. A roof-mounted unit, even when switched off, would have a detrimental effect on fuel consumption because of wind resistance. A wind generator is only practical in a stationary situation or on a boat where it can operate while the craft is travelling.

Authors' tip:

Probably the best option is to install a solar system and have a small (1000 watt) generator to charge the batteries when you encounter a period of cloudy or wet weather. This set-up would not allow you to use power-hungry appliances.

Maximum power point tracking controller

You can have a much more efficient system by using a maximum power point tracking controller (MPPT). This device takes the varying voltage (due to levels of light and temperature) and current from the panels and converts this DC to high frequency AC. It then rectifies to the best DC voltage to get maximum amps into the battery, actually getting an increase in amps due to the design of the process. Example: power (volts x amps) 18V x 10A = 180W converts to 14V x 12.5A = 175W losing only 3% of power but putting an additional 2.5 amps into the batteries.

MPPT controllers can be expensive, and it may be cheaper to buy an additional solar cell to provide more amps. However these controllers, like all new technology, are decreasing in price and may become a cost-effective option.

Authors' tip:

You will need professional advice to help you decide whether to 'go solar', and if so, what you need. If you are new to this field, take care not to underestimate the size and cost of the panels required to generate the electricity needed for the equipment you plan to use.

Disadvantages of solar

The initial cost and the fact that the van or motorhome needs to be parked in the sun to enable roof-mounted panels to charge the batteries at peak efficiency can be disadvantages.

Alternatively, you can use mobile panels that can be placed in full sun while the van or motorhome is parked in the shade. Disadvantages of this are that you may have to keep shifting the panels to keep them in the sun; the equipment has to be stored when travelling; and precautions have to be taken to prevent theft. If you use a long connecting cable, it is important to locate the regulator at the battery end because of the voltage drop in the cable. It is only practical to have a small system of mobile panels, and this will supply only limited battery power.

Is it worth the extra cost to have a system that tracks the sun?

In recent years solar systems that 'track' the sun have become available where formerly flat-mounted roof models were the standard. To achieve the maximum input, solar panels need to face in the general direction of the sun.

In summer, over all of Australia, the sun is high enough in the sky during the five to six peak sun hours that the gain from tracking would be minimal. In winter, in northern Australia, the sun is still high enough in the sky to effectively charge flat-mounted modules and there would only be a modest gain from tracking.

On the other hand, in Tasmania in winter the sun is fairly low in the sky so it is shining at an oblique angle onto flat-mounted solar modules. In these circumstances, there would be an appreciable gain if the modules were tilted. So unless you are travelling in Tasmania in winter, there is generally not much to be gained by installing a tracking system. It is probably cheaper and simpler to buy an extra solar module.

Camping near Red Bluff, WA Photo: Pelusey Photography

Equipment for inside

Before adding any equipment, consider the anticipated usage against cost, space and weight. This applies particularly to motorhomes, many of which are underpowered, and many, when fully packed and provisioned, are near their weight limit. There is more information about this in later chapters, but you should always keep in mind that extra weight means higher fuel consumption. It also increases your stopping distance in an emergency.

Refrigeration

Technically, there are two types of fridges – compressor (electric fridges) and absorption (fridges that can operate on gas or electricity). Power is supplied by 240 volt mains power, 12 volt/24 volt battery, or propane gas: but most likely a combination of these. The most important factor when choosing a fridge is how you will power it. Consider the length of time you intend to camp away from 240 volt power and whether you will have solar panels or a generator as an alternative energy source.

Chest-style fridges are more efficient than upright models because cold air is heavier than warm air, and with a front-opening fridge cold air comes out every time you open the door. An advantage of a front-opening fridge is that you do not lose valuable bench space.

Authors' tip:

If you have a gas fridge that hasn't run on gas for some time, when you first light the gas it will take a few seconds to flow through.

Advantages and disadvantages of a three-way fridge

- Most suitable type if you want to camp **without being dependent on electricity**.
- Totally silent when running, and this is important in a confined space.
- It is **sensitive to slope**, although current models are significantly more tolerant than models produced several years ago. Depending on the model, they will work at between 3° and 6° off level (and you would not want to be camped on such an angle anyway).
- A three-way fridge **takes about three hours to chill** when it is first turned on whereas a small all-electric fridge will chill in 15 minutes or so. However after the initial cooling period, there is little difference between the two.

Authors' tip:

If you hear stories of an inefficient fridge, the likelihood is that the problem is not the fridge itself, but the way it is installed.

Authors' tip:

Rather than the cost and hassle of powering an all-electric fridge when you do not have 240 volt power all the time, we believe it is simpler to install a three-way fridge, even if the absorption design is not as energy-efficient as a compressor fridge.

Powering an electric fridge

A 12 volt or 12 volt/240 volt compressor fridge will operate on power from the vehicle's alternator when you are driving. If you intend to camp without access to mains power, you can use either solar energy or a generator, but most likely you would need a combination of these. To power a reasonable size fridge from solar panels, you would need an extensive array of solar panels and a sizeable bank of batteries to store the energy. Even then, you would need a generator for back-up during the inevitable periods of cloudy or wet weather. A generator is not an efficient power source for a fridge because a generator runs continuously while a fridge will only require power periodically as it cycles on and off during the whole 24 hours in the day. Meanwhile you are paying for fuel at probably $1 to $1.50 an hour.

Powering a fridge on 12 volt

The 12 volt cabling of some installations may be inadequate to supply sufficient power to properly operate the fridge on 12 volt. With the inevitable drop in voltage in a length of cable, the voltage in an under-sized cable can easily drop below the minimum at which the fridge will operate. This is usually around 11.5 volts. Not only will the fridge not operate properly, but the wiring may overheat. The solution is to replace the cable. *Refer to p61 for more details.*

Modifications that can improve fridge performance include:

- A hinged door in the side wall behind the fridge to allow additional ventilation.
- A small shade cover to prevent direct sun hitting the outside wall behind the fridge.
- Installation of a computer fan to aid air circulation behind the fridge.

12 volt fridges and freezers

Fridges and freezers that are solely 12 volt are mainly portable units ideal for campers who don't have the facilities available in a caravan or motorhome. These fridges are also very useful as a 'car fridge' to run off the cigarette lighter. Some caravanners have one in their tow vehicle as an auxiliary fridge, and also use it instead of a cooler box while they travel. Some camper-trailer owners have a 12 volt freezer in the camper and a portable 12 volt fridge that runs off the cigarette lighter in the tow vehicle. When they camp, provided they have solar power or a generator, they have both a fridge and freezer.

Types of fridges

- **240 volt refrigerator** – Even though these are relatively inexpensive to purchase and operating costs are low, they are not very popular because of their limitations. When camping away from 240 volt power, an alternative source of power is required. An inverter can be installed to run the fridge while driving.
- **240 volt/12 volt or 12 volt refrigerators** – Due to the efficiency of their small compressors, there is adequate power for a 12 volt fridge when the vehicle engine is running. However, if you camp without mains power the house batteries can only run a fridge for a day or two before they flatten unless you have either a generator or a solar array. An automatic isolator switch ensures that usage of power in the house does not flatten the vehicle battery.
- **240 volt/12 volt/gas refrigerators (three-way)** – These are very popular. Although they are more expensive to purchase than an all-electric compressor fridge, three-way units will enable you to bush camp without using a generator or solar power. When camped, the fridge operates well on either 240 volt mains power or gas. When driving, it operates on 12 volt power from the house battery that is constantly charged from the vehicle's alternator, but when the engine isn't running, it will quickly flatten the house battery. It draws more power than leaving the headlights switched on. The cost of running a fridge on gas is generally calculated at around $1.50 per day. Some caravanners who don't install a cable to charge the house battery from the tow vehicle alternator operate the three-way fridge on gas while driving. This is legal, but definitely inadvisable in a motorhome or campervan.
- **240 volt/gas refrigerator** – As this type of fridge does not have the capacity to operate on 12 volt, there are three alternatives while travelling. One is to treat the fridge like an esky, but the unit will not remain as cold as it should, thereby limiting the amount of food you can carry and how long you can safely store it. The second alternative is to install an inverter to run the fridge from the battery while the engine is running. The third alternative is to operate the fridge on gas while driving, although this is not recommended for a caravan and is dangerous for a campervan or motorhome.

The latest models of three-way refrigerator with **automatic energy selection (AES)** do not need the controls switched to the type of power required. The fridge senses what power source is available and automatically selects the power, in the pre-programmed priority order as follows:

- 240 volt electricity if it is available;
- 12 volt electricity if the motor is running and the house batteries are being charged from the vehicle's alternator; or
- gas (that will be ignited automatically).

The AES facility can be bypassed to have the fridge run on gas.

Fridge efficiency

- **Ventilation** (mentioned right) is critically important.
- Whether it is an all-electric fridge or a three-way, inadequate **12 volt wiring** will reduce the efficiency of a fridge, and the longer the cable, the heavier it is required to be. This is unlikely to be an issue in caravans or motorhomes produced by major manufacturers, but if you are having new wiring installed, use heavier wiring because it will improve fridge efficiency.
- **Seals on the fridge** door may need replacing.
- Do not put **hot food** into the fridge, and if possible buy items that are already cold.
- **Thaw frozen food in the fridge** – it helps keep the fridge cold as it thaws.
- **A nearly empty fridge is less efficient** than a full one. To fill the spaces, put in square food storage containers or plastic soft-drink bottles filled with water, or use frozen 'cooler' blocks. However, do not fill the fridge to the extent that you have to push the door and hold it closed to do up the catch. In that case, it is likely the bottom edge of the door would not be firmly closed and cold air would flow out.
- **Open the door as infrequently as possible** – plan what items you will need and get them out promptly. When putting food away after a meal, have it all close by and open the fridge door only once.
- When placing food in the fridge, be aware that **the warmest part of the unit is the top shelf of the door**. This area is not suitable for food that might spoil if not kept at a low enough temperature.
- Ideally, the **temperature** in a refrigerator should be 3°C or 4°C and -15°C to -18°C in a freezer. This can be monitored with a fridge thermometer. One style of thermometer is placed in the fridge and you have to open the door to check the temperature – rather counter-productive. A better style has a sensor that is placed in the fridge, connected by a fine wire to the read-out unit placed outside the fridge. Don't become obsessed with the temperature your fridge is maintaining. As long as the milk doesn't go off and the drinks are cold, what more do you want!

Factors in selecting a fridge

- **Size** – After considering what type of fridge will suit your planned style of travelling, the next point to consider is size. In general terms, we recommend that you buy the largest fridge that will fit in your caravan or motorhome – within reasonable limits. If applicable, the weight of the fridge should be considered if you do not have much leeway before reaching the gross vehicle mass (GVM) of the vehicle. Very large fridges need heavier 12 volt cabling but there is not much cost involved in this.
- **Insulation** – Check the insulation rating of the fridge: indicated by 'climate class'. Three-way fridges with a 'T' rating are designed to be efficient with outside temperatures up to 42°C. The next rating down the scale is 'ST', and these fridges are still quite efficient. Fridges designated 'N', 'SN' or with no rating are designed to operate with a maximum ambient temperature of 32°C. No matter what fridge you have, the most important factors are proper installation and adequate ventilation.
- **Ventilation** – This is the most important factor in the efficient operation of a fridge, particularly a three-way. Air has to pass through the cooling fins on the back of the fridge to take heat produced by the fridge away from the unit. For this to occur efficiently, there should be ventilation at floor level below the fridge cooling fins, and, because hot air rises, there needs to be a second vent above the top of the fridge cooling fins. The fridge needs to be sealed around the sides and top to encourage a flow of air to follow the path desired, exiting via the top vent. The result is similar to a fireplace chimney. The most effective way to vent the warm air is through the roof using a unit called a 'tropical vent'. An alternative is a ventilation panel in the sidewall above the top of the fridge cooling fins, with a 'chimney' constructed to funnel the warm air. With effective ventilation a fridge can operate well, even in hot conditions, and also be more energy efficient.

Authors' tip:

A simple home-made cooler block can be made by freezing a container of water with a liberal addition of salt. It freezes at a lower temperature than pure water, so will remain frozen longer.

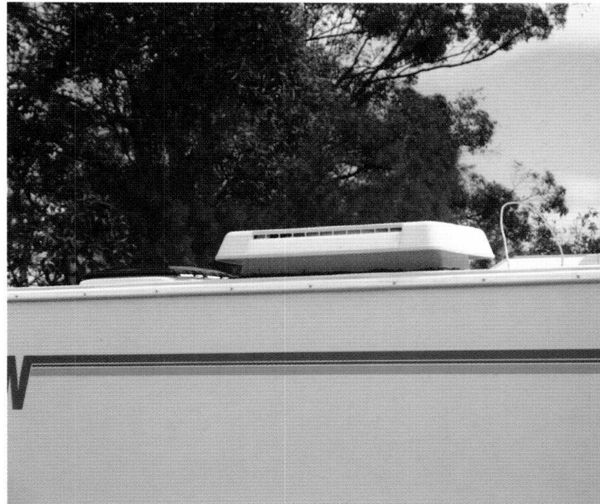

Tropical vent for fridge ventilation on roof of the motorhome

Cooking

Most vans and motorhomes use **LPG** for cooking, and this is considered an efficient and safe energy source. For quite a few years gas stoves have been built with a flame failure safety cut-out (a **thermocouple**) that only allows gas to flow while it senses heat from a flame. If the flame is blown out, the gas on that burner will be cut off. When you light a gas point that has a thermocouple you have to hold the knob down for several seconds until the device heats sufficiently to let the flow of gas continue. If the gas continually goes out immediately or will only stay alight for a few seconds it is likely the thermocouple is malfunctioning. If you use a stove without this safety feature, it should only be used in a well-ventilated area, and greater care should be exercised.

If you have not used the cooktop for some time, when you first turn a point on it will take several seconds for the gas to flow through.

When choosing your cooktop, keep in mind that if you bush camp without a generator as a power source, you cannot use an electric frypan or microwave oven. Unless you use a barbecue or campfire you will probably want to use up to three burners on occasions because all the cooking has to be done on the stove.

Dual fuel cooktops are available with a combination of two or three gas burners and one electric hot plate. The benefit of this model is that you can use the electric hot plate if you are in a caravan park and connected to 240 volt power, thereby saving your gas.

Some cooktops have a glass lid that closes flush with the benchtop, giving you more working space when the points are not being used. The *Spinflo* models have a device that automatically cuts off the gas immediately the glass lid is closed.

'Household' electrical appliances require an external 240 volt power source, a large generator or an expensive battery system. If you plan to have access to 240 volt power on a regular basis, you may decide to have a microwave oven and smaller appliances such as an electric frypan, kettle and toaster. *Please refer to the information on 'Use of 240 volt power' in this chapter for limitations on usage.*

For travellers who don't want to install gas, *Webasto* has a diesel-powered ceramic cooktop with one cooking element and one simmer element. The fuel source can be the vehicle's main diesel fuel tank or an auxiliary 12 litre or 24 litre fuel tank. Exhaust fumes are discharged via a through-hull exhaust pipe.

> **Authors' tip:**
>
> We have a Smev four burner gas stove. The points are a bit close together, particularly when using a frying pan or large saucepan. I would prefer a larger cooktop or one that has three burners laid out in a triangular design; however my first choice would be a dual fuel cooktop.

Some small campervans have a marine-type stove that operates on methylated spirit. Portable camping stoves powered by butane or propane canisters, or the dual-fuel versions powered by unleaded petrol and gas must not be used in the enclosed space of a van or motorhome. Gas canisters should not be stored within the accommodation space of the vehicle. Do not attempt to refill propane canisters, and dispose of used canisters properly.

Cooktops or barbecues connected to a gas cylinder can only be used outside the accommodation area where there is sufficient ventilation (under the awning is fine). Gas cylinders over 2.25kg must be stored outside the accommodation area.

Kitchen appliances

Kitchen appliances used in your home can also be used in your travelling home.

- **Microwave oven** – these are usually 240 volt. Make sure it is installed at a convenient height and secured in place.
- **Exhaust fan** over the cooktop – these 12 volt exhaust fans effectively remove cooking smells, but they are usually noisy in operation.
- **240 volt household appliances** – for e.g. toaster, electric kettle, blender, food processor, electric frypan and breadmaker.
- **12 volt kitchen appliances** – 12/24 volt microwaves are available, but they are much more expensive than 240 volt models. They are very power-hungry so would need to be separately wired and powered by a sizeable solar array linked to a bank of batteries. Even then, it would be advisable to use the microwave for only a few minutes at a time because of the power it draws. Other 12 volt appliances available include kettles, blenders and coffee makers.

> **Authors' tip:**
>
> Be warned that 12 volt microwave ovens are probably too power-hungry to be practical. Other 12 volt appliances may not be as effective as 240 volt appliances. Note that heavier 12 volt cabling may be necessary, depending on the power consumption of the appliance.

Kitchen fittings

If you are buying a caravan or motorhome, the kitchen will be fully fitted out, but if you are having a unit built or are renovating one you have a choice. Sinks and stoves are now available with an unbreakable **glass lid** that, when closed, will give you additional working space. See the range from *Thetford Australia.*

Consider a **roll-out pantry unit** because it is an exceptionally efficient use of space. The shelves should have bars to prevent items from falling off shelves. If the kitchen cupboards are across the back of the caravan or motorhome, every time you brake sharply, the contents of the cupboard will move forward against the cupboard door. So place a sheet of non-slip plastic on the floor of the cupboard and make sure the latches work effectively.

Tables

There are several styles available:

- **Dinette tables** usually slot into a track on the wall and have a leg that folds down to support the outer edge of the table. This table is used as a base to convert the dinette to a bed. A disadvantage with a support leg is that someone inevitably kicks it and the table can drop down unless someone else is quick enough to grab it.
- Some caravans or motorhomes have a separate **free-standing table with a single leg** that slots into a fitting on the floor. This avoids the problem that the table leg can be kicked, but the table has to be dismantled and put away when not in use.
- Some tables **slot down into a storage unit** when not in use. A disadvantage is that the size of the table is limited by the size of the storage unit, and also because it does not have a leg for support.
- If you are making a table or altering one you have more options available. Consider having one or more extensions that fold out using piano hinges.

Hot water

If you are connected to 240 volt power, you can use an electric jug or microwave to heat water for kitchen use, but otherwise the most economical way is to use a kettle on the stove. A hot water system is an expensive way to heat water for washing up.

To heat water for showers

- **Gas hot water systems** are the most common. An electric start with an inside switch is more convenient than having to light the hot water system outside the vehicle, often in the dark.
- A **dual-fuel heater** that works on either 240 volt or gas. The unit is more expensive to purchase, but it could be worth considering if you plan to spend a lot of time with access to mains power but prefer to use your own shower rather than an amenities block.
- **Water heaters** are available that work solely from 240 volt electricity and heat water as required. These heaters require 240 volt mains electricity or a sizeable solar and battery set-up.
- **A heat exchange system** uses heat from the vehicle engine, often with a small 240 volt element as an additional energy source.
- A **diesel-powered hot water system** also has an electric heating element.
- A **black plastic solar hot water bag** is available from camping shops. The bag filled with water can be left on the dashboard of the vehicle in the sun to heat while you travel.

> **Authors' tip:**
>
> We operate our gas hot water system just long enough to heat water for the two of us to shower. We have worked out that it takes from 7 to 20 minutes depending on the temperature of the previous 24 hours. *Refer to p85 for information on maintenance of a hot water system.*

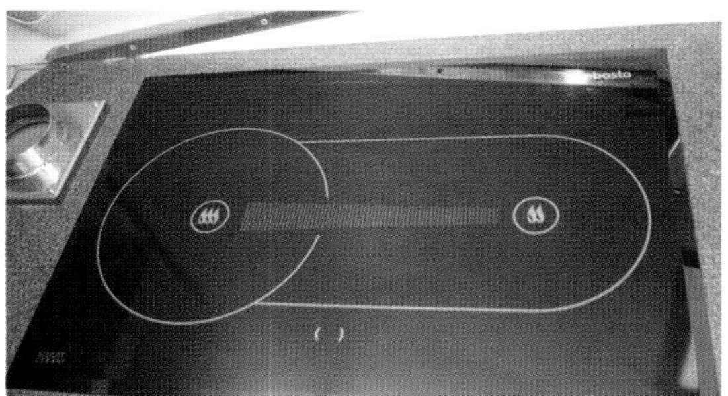

Diesel powered cooktop

Gas/electric cooktop

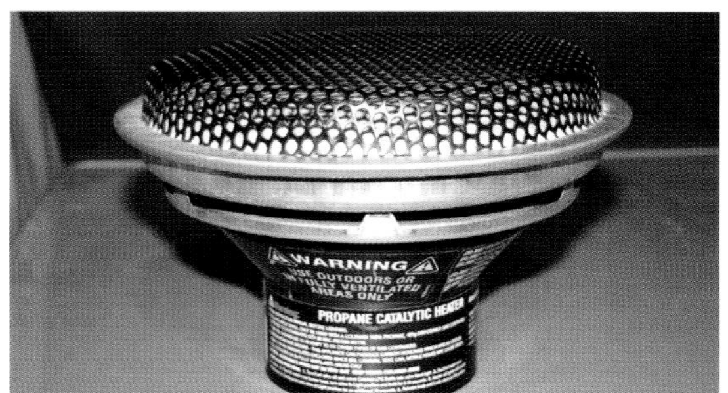

Catalytic heater

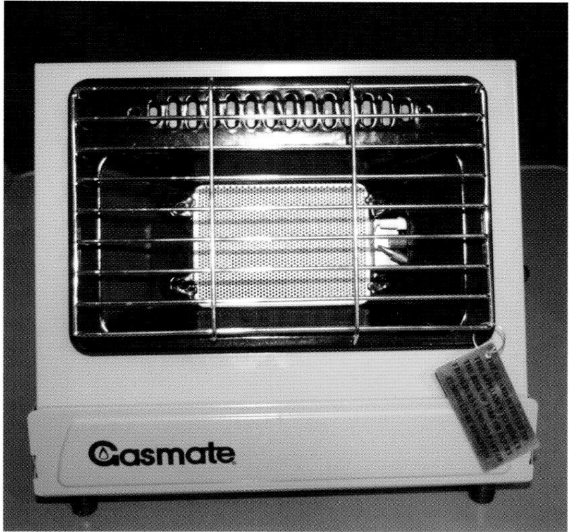

Catalytic heater that cannot be used indoors

Room heater

- **Catalytic heaters** – These heaters are dangerous and illegal in an enclosed space and come with a clear warning that they can only be used in a well-ventilated location. They produce unacceptably high levels of carbon monoxide that pollute the air in an enclosed living space because they do not draw air from outside nor vent gasses through the hull. Because the gas is colourless and odourless, it can prove fatal. If you are asleep there will be no warning – you simply won't wake up. Catalytic heaters operate on a propane gas canister and are sold as camping heaters.
- **Fan heater** – A small inexpensive 240 volt fan heater is very effective however it should be kept at least one metre from combustible material. These heaters work by a fan blowing air over a heated coil. Ensure you buy one that has a thermostat and an automatic cut-off switch that operates if it is knocked over.
- **Ceramic heater** – These 240 volt heaters have a fan blowing air over a heated ceramic plate. They are some-what quieter and safer than the cheaper coil fan heaters.
- **Under floor and ducted propane heating systems** – Although similar to those systems used in the USA and Europe, they are only legal in Australia if they draw air from outside and vent back outside. These systems must be fitted by a qualified gas fitter. If you have an imported fifth-wheeler or motorhome with a gas furnace heater, check that the appliance complies with Australian regulations (AS 5601 – 2004, Sections 5 and 6).
- **Diesel heaters** – These heaters are totally safe and very effective. The diesel fuel is either from the vehicle fuel tank or a specially installed small tank, and consumption is approximately one litre of fuel every five hours. For all round heating, even in the bathroom, the system can be installed with ducting. Gases from the unit vent through the hull to outside.

Warning

Do not use the gas stove (either the cook top or the oven) to heat the living space because the dangers are similar to those from catalytic heaters mentioned above. There is no danger from the stove for the limited time it operates to cook, but if it is used for an extended period of time it depletes the atmosphere of oxygen and the carbon monoxide it produces can rise to dangerous levels. Anyway, a stove is not very efficient at heating the living space and will only increase the temperature by a few degrees.

Authors' tip:

Friends with diesel heaters have told us they are delighted with them. If you travel often in cold conditions the cost could be warranted.

Cooling systems

Obviously **air conditioning** in the cab of a motorhome only operates when the engine is running. Some converted buses also have an air conditioning unit in the main section of the vehicle that operates in the same way as normal cab air conditioning. 'House' air conditioners can be powered by either 240 volt mains power or a generator. Reverse cycle units have the ability to heat as well as cool.

An **evaporative cooler** that runs on 12 volt or 24 volt battery power can be installed on the roof of a van or motorhome. This system is water-based and runs without noise. It is more efficient in areas of low humidity than in hot and humid conditions.

A small, inexpensive **240 volt** fan can be effective and is not power hungry. If you are not connected to mains power, a 240 volt fan can run through an inverter using power from the 'house' batteries. An alternative is a **12 volt fan**, but they are quite expensive. Cheaper models can be noisy.

Authors' tip:

For the same money you would spend on a good quality 12 volt fan, you can buy a 240 volt fan and an inverter to run it. The inverter will also have other uses.

Toilets

- **Cassette toilets** – The most common type of toilet is a built-in cassette style. These come in two different versions: bench type and swivel. With the bench type, water with a deodorising additive is stored in the top tank and is used to flush. The swivel style of toilet swivels out of the way when not in use and uses water from the motorhome's fresh water tank. An additive is also put in the waste tank (cassette) and, depending on usage, this would need to be emptied every four to five days. The cassette is accessed from outside. Some tanks have wheels and a retractable handle to allow for ease of handling. An alternative is to strap the tank onto a light luggage trolley.
- **Portable toilets** – Smaller vehicles may have a portable toilet that is very similar to a cassette toilet, but not built in. To empty it, the lower section of the toilet is detached and carried outside to be emptied. Brands of portable toilet are *Fiamma Bi Pot*, *Porta Potti* and *Sanipottie*.

Practical considerations for the portable toilet

- Where you would store it and where you would **place it for use**?
- **Can you lift the unit** out of its storage place easily? The weight can be up to 20kg, although this is less if you do not fill the top tank totally, and empty it more often. A portable toilet **can be installed onto a base with castors** so it moves easily out of a storage space.
- The low **height** of a portable toilet can present difficulties for people with mobility problems. A simple solution is to place the toilet on a *Fiamma* caravan step with a sheet of non-slip material on top.

Additives for cassette or portable toilets

The old-style formaldehyde based additives are very effective, however a toilet with these chemicals should not be emptied into a septic toilet system and definitely not into any long drop or environmental toilet. Systems are now available that are more natural and therefore environmentally friendly. *Refer to p85 for more details.*

Additive-free toilet system

The German-made **SOG ventilation system** operates totally additive or chemical free. It has a fan that automatically operates when the blade valve of the toilet is open. The down-flow of fresh air prevents smells from the cassette coming back into the bathroom and this air is vented outside. The decomposition process of the waste is accelerated by the increased flow of oxygen. Ordinary toilet paper should be used. The SOG system can be installed on some *Thetford* and *Dometic* cassette toilets as well as portable toilets. Power consumption is a very low 0.43watts.

Authors' tip:

A friend who has this SOG unit assures us that there are no noticeable smells outside the motorhome when the toilet is in use. We have also been told that if there is a strong wind blowing onto the outside vent, the fan may not be strong enough to prevent some smells from blowing back into the bathroom.

Vacuum marine-style toilets

These can empty to either a cassette or a black-water holding tank. A disadvantage is the noise it makes when it is flushed. It is claimed that you will not need to use additives in the cassette or holding tank, but if you do not, the build-up of gas can be very noticeable when you empty it.

Flushing toilets

These empty to a black-water tank. Advantages of this system are that the toilet seems more like a 'normal' house toilet, and it only needs emptying about every ten days. A disadvantage is that not all dump points can be used because the vehicle has to be positioned close to the inlet, so unless a pump is used, it has to be higher.

Macerator pump

The design of some dump points makes it difficult to empty a black-water tank unless you use a pump. A macerator pump is often used to grind up the contents of the tank for ease of emptying.

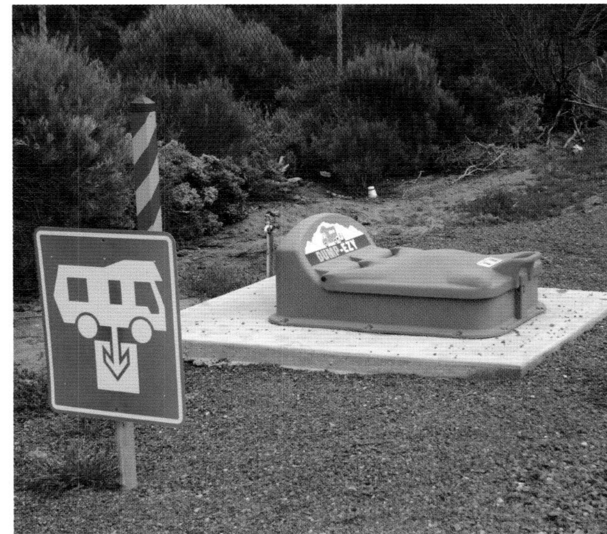
Dump point in Whyalla for toilet waste

Along the road near Point Moore Lighthouse, Geraldton photo: Pelusey Photography

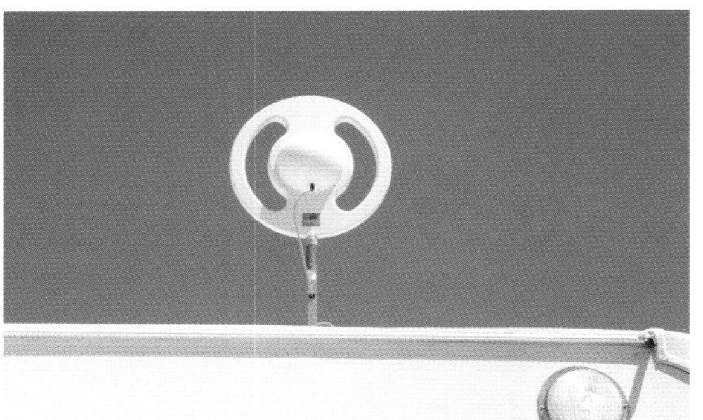

This is a very effective type of antenna

Above: Roof-mounted satellite TV dish
Top: Mobile satellite TV dish

Television

These can be either normal 240 volt or a more expensive 240 volt/12 volt unit. Without access to 240 volt mains power, or an alternative energy source, you may have to limit your use of the television, but if you have solar panels or a generator there should be little restriction on usage.

Operating on 12 volt power, a typical 34cm set uses no more power than one headlight and an LCD screen is even more energy-efficient. Other advantages of an LCD television are that they are very thin and lightweight and with wall-mounted brackets and rear mount capability the screen can be swivelled when in use and locked away for travelling.

Antennas

Some television antennas are more effective than others. If you have a style that needs adjusting to achieve a good picture, it is convenient to have one that can be adjusted from inside. This makes it a simple one-person job. Many systems have an electronic signal booster.

Many people with a 240 volt/12 volt televison find that they rarely use it on 12 volt because when they are in the bush, they are usually out of range of most channels unless they have satellite television.

Satellite television

In many areas of Australia, television reception is limited or non-existent so travellers who are keen viewers can still watch their favourite programmes by buying a satellite set-up. The signal is broadcast in digital format and has excellent clarity.

ABC, SBS and commercial television networks are available, and each has a licenced area:

- **Australia-wide**: ABC has five separate television broadcasts available; and SBS (Special Broadcasting Service) has multi-language programmes as well as English.
- **Remote areas of NSW, TAS, VIC, SA, QLD and NT**: Southern Cross Broadcasting (SCB – formerly Seven Central); and Imparja (based in Alice Springs, takes programming from the Nine and Ten networks).
- **Remote areas of WA**: Golden West (GWN) an independent channel based in Bunbury; and WIN Television.
- Educational TV Services such as Westlink are also available.

Start by purchasing the correct equipment from a company specialising in satellite television for travellers, and have it properly configured for the services you wish to view. A traveller should purchase an *Optus Aurora Smartcard* then apply by fax, phone or email for authorisation. Access to remote area commercial broadcasters is given to travellers for the period they are within the particular licence area. Broadcasters regularly update codes to combat piracy so your card may lose authorisation if it is not used for some time. This is usually not an issue under a couple of months, but if services are lost or scrambled messages appear, leave it on overnight to regain services.

Positioning the satellite dish

The satellite dish needs to have a clear view without obstructions. In Eastern Australia the dish should point just east of north, while in Western Australia it should be just north of east. The angle of altitude varies between 70 degrees at Cape York to 35 degrees in southwest Western Australia. The alignment of the dish can be checked using a small test meter.

Mattress

- **Motorhome bed over cab** (foam mattress) – In some circumstances, foam mattresses can develop mildew caused by condensation, and to prevent this, allow air ventilation under the mattress. Either install timber slats under the mattress (which would reduce the height above the bed) or place a sheet of specially made ventilation material (*Hypervent*) under the mattress. Using solarscreens on the windscreen and windows of the cab will help by keeping the air in the cab warm and reducing condensation.
- **Caravans and motorhomes** (innerspring mattress) – Innerspring mattresses are very popular and can be made in any shape. Mattresses designed for caravans and motorhomes weigh less than standard mattresses and have side air vents to prevent the moisture problems previously mentioned. Another feature is additional side supports because the bed is often used as a seat as well as for sleeping.

Photo: Pelusey Photography

Additional equipment for caravans and motorhomes

You will not necessarily need all of the following items.

- **Fire blanket** and **smoke detector**.
  See p95 for more details.
- **Torch**.
- **UHF radio**.
- **GPS** (global positioning system).
  See p117 for more details.
- **Electric step**. Be cautious about installing one if the door is close to either the front or the back. Mud and stones that can be thrown up by your own wheels may cause a problem with the step's electric motor. The step can be operated either by a door contact or by the ignition. A disadvantage with the door contact version is that every time you open or close the door, the step will extend or retract using battery power each time. An accident can result if the step malfunctions and someone steps out assuming it is in place.
- Small **spirit level** to determine if the vehicle is parked reasonably level. The 'T' shaped variety will give you a reading both sideways and front to back. For a motorhome or campervan, the spirit level can be placed (or stuck with double-sided tape) in the driver's cab so you can quickly check the levels when setting up camp. Some people can tell this by 'feel' and don't need a spirit level.
- A **water filtration system** will ensure your water is free of bacteria and will also remove any unpleasant taste.
- An electronic device is available that indicates the level in the water storage tank.
- With a home food **dehydrator** you can preserve food and retain over 96% of its original nutrients.
- A **vacuum packing system** will allow you to slow the deterioration of food and extend the shelf life of many fresh or dehydrated foods. Vacuum-sealed raw meat will keep in the fridge for eight to nine days while fruit and vegetables and many other foods will keep three times longer than usual.
- If you like to cook on campground barbecues, a **non-stick hotplate liner** will give you a clean and hygienic cooking surface. Just wipe it clean, roll up and store when you have finished cooking. It is also great for using on your own barbecue or electric frypan because it is easy to clean.
- **Water-saving heads** are available for taps and showers.
- **Gas leak detector**. *See p96 for more details.*
- An electronic device can be installed in the fridge to automatically switch it to 12 volt when the vehicle moves.
- **Small washing machine**. Front loading machines use less water than top loading models, and *Dometic* have a Swedish machine that will handle laundry loads up to 3kg. Before installing one though consider the weight, power source and amount of water you will need to run it. A small bucket washing machine powered by 12 volt or 240 volt is also available. These machines are more effective than bucket-washers that work with a hand-operated plunger.

Washing machine stored in shower recess

- Alternative clothes washing – A simple and cost-effective washing method is to place clothes, water and detergent in a bucket with a tight-fitting lid. The clothes are washed by movement of the water while you drive. Make sure the bucket is securely wedged in a corner, preferably in the shower. Place towels around the bucket so it does not scratch the shower. Washing by this method is more effective in a caravan than a motorhome because there is usually more movement in a caravan.
- **Security doors** that incorporate fly mesh are available to fit most caravans or motorhomes.
- If you are concerned about the security of your valuables, you can install a **safe** in your van or motorhome. The small ones will hold cash, credit cards and jewellery, while the larger sizes will hold bigger items like a laptop computer and camera as well.
- If you have a towbar, a **tiny safe** can be installed within the towbar to hold spare keys and very small items. It is opened by a combination.
- If you have only a cassette player built into your motorhome (or tow vehicle) and you would like to listen to CDs or an MP3 player while you drive, you can use a **cassette adaptor** and car power adaptor. The power adaptor plugs into the cigarette lighter socket and the CD player or MP3 player transmits the music through a 'dummy' cassette inserted into the tape deck.

Authors' tip:

Many people have reported that they do not find their hand bucket-washer very effective.

Authors' tip:

This is an inexpensive way to convert to CDs or MP3s rather than having a new system installed. If you do not want to have the expense of buying batteries, make sure you buy the adaptor that includes a cigarette lighter fitting.

Extra equipment for motorhomes

- Some motorhomers with a bed over the cab take a **ladder** (larger than that supplied) for easier access to the bed. The ladder can be stored on the bed when travelling, and can also be useful if you need to access the roof.
- **Seat covers** on driver's and passenger's seats. If you have soft upholstery, covers will add to the life of the original seat covers, and if you have vinyl seats, covers will add to your comfort level in summer.
- When camping, **insulation screens** attached to the inside of the windscreen and side windows of a motorhome dramatically reduce heat build-up as well as heat loss in cold climates.

Authors' tip:

We find our Solarscreens are very effective when we are camped in both hot and cold conditions. By using the screens instead of curtains to the front cab, the motorhome looks much more spacious inside while giving us complete privacy. We can easily reach items placed out of the way on the passenger seat yet these items are also not on public view.

Solar Screens on windscreen and side windows

Security door

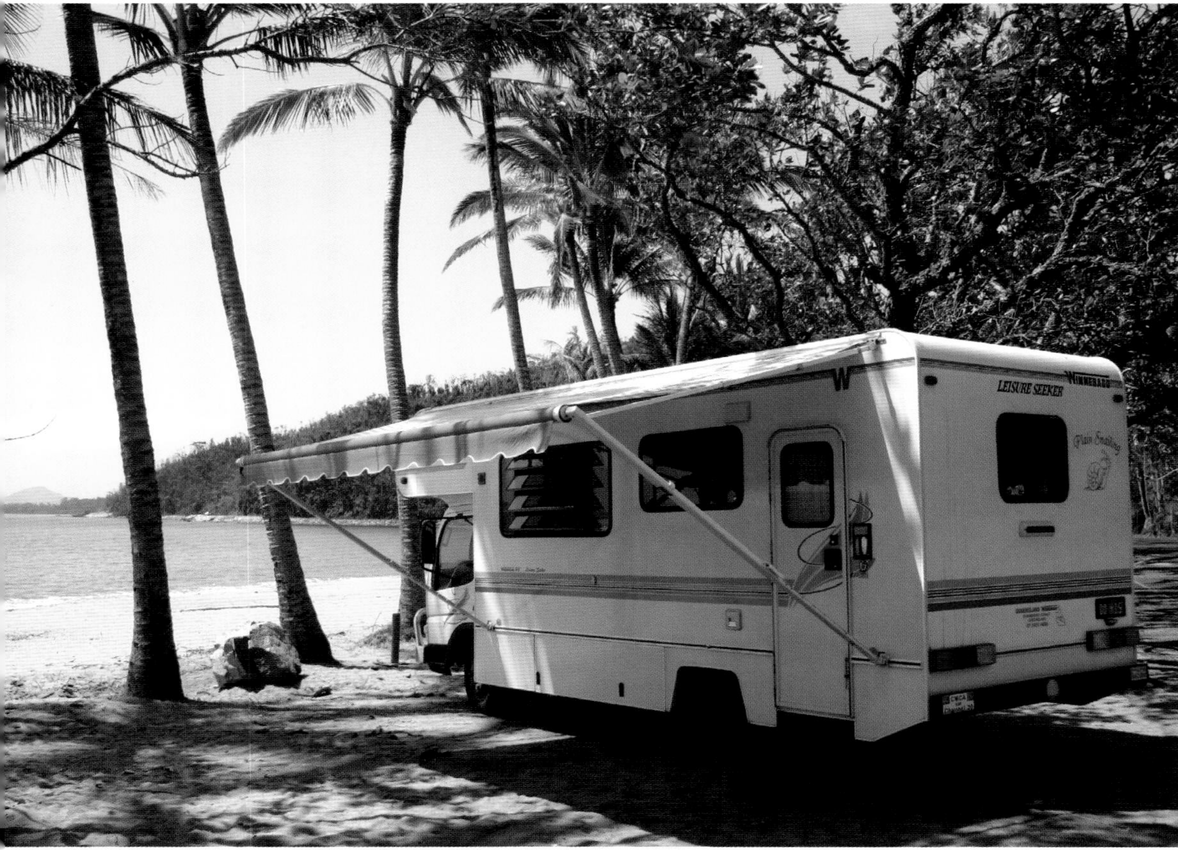
Motorhome parked at beautiful Bingil Bay, North Queensland

Authors' tip:

We strongly advise people planning to drive extensively in the country to have a bull bar. On our previous vehicle, we found that, when we turned our headlights on, the light reflected back into our eyes from the top cross-member of the bull bar. To stop this, we covered this section with black tape.

Awning clip to reduce flapping

Equipment for outside

Before adding any equipment to your caravan or motorhome that will increase its width, length or height, you should measure the vehicle carefully to ensure it remains within legal limits. The maximum height of 4.3m is not usually a problem, however many caravans and motorhomes are built very close to the legal width limit of 2.5m, including all projections. For a caravan, the maximum length allowed past the rear axle is 3.7m and for a motorhome it is 60% of the wheelbase to a maximum of 3.7m. For units with tandem axles the measurement is taken from the centre point between the two axles.

Awning

This is an essential item because it provides a lot of **extra space** and enables travellers to **enjoy the outdoors while still having shelter**. An extra benefit is that extending an awning will shade the side of the caravan or motorhome and help **keep the interior cooler**. Usually the awning shelters the door, and this helps to **keep the floor dry and clean in wet weather**.

Points to consider on awnings and annexes

- They are made either of vinyl or canvas. Vinyl weighs about twice as much as canvas and is more expensive. Durability is about the same, but vinyl is usually used for appearance reasons.
- Canvas copes better than vinyl with extreme cold when vinyl can crack.
- Roll out awnings are usually made of vinyl. These awnings roll up for storage on the side of a caravan or motorhome so they are constantly exposed to rain and weather. Canvas is not suitable for roll-out awnings because water could soak in and mildew would develop because the fabric would not dry out while it remained rolled.
- Walls, if required, are usually made from canvas because it weighs less and is easier to repair. Damage to canvas can be repaired by sewing, while vinyl must be welded to prevent leakage.
- Conventional annexes are made out of canvas or canvas with a vinyl roof.
- With canvas annexes, usually 12-ounce canvas is used for the roof, and 10-ounce for the walls.
- A full annexe will provide an extra room, but if you want to insect proof it, you will need a 'skirt' for the side wall of your caravan or motorhome to stop insects entering.
- If you are thinking about a full annexe, consider the weight and also where you will store it when travelling. Another factor is that it will reduce the light and breeze coming into the living area.
- If you are considering annexe walls simply to reduce wind, blowing rain or direct sunlight, maybe one or two walls made from shade cloth will achieve the desired result. These are reasonably compact and lightweight, as well as being economical.
- Even if you have a style of awning that does not have to be tied down, it is advisable to use ropes and pegs to keep the corners steady if there is any wind at all or if you are camping for a number of days.

Using an awning or annexe

- To erect an awning so it is level, the locking pin in each support arm needs to be set in the same position. You may find it convenient to mark your preferred points with a pen or a spot of paint. This will save the bother of counting the number of locking-pin holes on each support arm.
- In wet weather, lower the outer edge of the awning so it is angled more steeply. This will help the water run off faster and prevent it pooling. If a significant amount of water is trapped on the awning, the increased weight can cause damage to the awning struts.
- An anti-flap kit is available to stop the annoying noise of awning fabric flapping against the metal arms, or rattling the whole structure when there is wind. The full-length clamp of the anti-flap kit can be used to attach walls. In light to moderate winds, a simple option to reduce flapping is to use plastic clips that secure the awning to the metal support arms. In strong winds most travellers roll their awning up and secure it for safety.
- When an awning is rolled up for travel, it is important to lock it securely into position so it cannot roll down while you are driving.

Care of awnings

- Do not leave the awning exposed to the elements unnecessarily, and if possible, it should be dry before being stowed.
- If you have to roll an awning up wet, dry it out at the earliest convenient opportunity.
- Do not let bird droppings, leaves or other material remain on the awning for a period of time.
- All awnings and annexes erected for long periods require regular maintenance.
- **Canvas awnings**
  - Brush down both inside and out with a soft brush and hose it occasionally, but do not use soap, detergent or cleaning fluid. Do not allow cleaning fluids, insecticides, petrol, oil, solvents, kerosene or similar fluids to come in contact with the canvas.
  - Do not use aerosols such as hairspray and deodorants in the vicinity of the canvas.
  - If mildew spots appear these should be gently brushed off immediately. Persistent mould or mildew growth should be brushed with a solution of four parts water to one part liquid bleach (White King or similar), allow to stand for 15 minutes. Brush it gently with a soft brush then wash off with clean water. Canvas that has been cleaned in this way may need to be re-proofed.
- **Vinyl awnings**
  - Clean with mild soapy solution and warm water, then rinse with clean water.
  - Lubricate hardware with silicone spray, not grease because this will catch dust and dirt.

Authors' tip:

The best type of awning is one that can be erected quickly and preferably by one person. When you have selected the awning and the salesperson has demonstrated how to erect it, do it yourself with the salesperson watching.

Bull bar

Many caravan tow vehicles, campervans and motorhomes have a bull bar as a frontal protection system for the following reasons:

- To minimise damage to the vehicle in the event of a collision with other vehicles or animals.
- To reduce the chance of the vehicle being immobilised as a result of a minor collision.
- To provide mounting points for a winch, communication aerials, and additional driving or fog lights.

Some bull bars replace the original bumper bar, while other more lightweight types fit over the original bumper. Obtain expert advice about which bull bars meet the current Australian standards.

On the Eyre Highway near the Nullarbor Roadhouse

Miscellaneous items to carry

- Comfortable folding **chairs** to enjoy the travelling lifestyle.
- **Small folding table**. Decide if you want a table large enough to use for meals outside.
- **Mat** for under the awning. Start at least with a small one for outside the door. Shade cloth with hemmed edges makes a lightweight and cost-effective mat that does not absorb water, but it tends to curl on the edges, particularly if it is not hemmed and pegged down.
- A **barbecue** will enable you to enjoy the outdoors while you cook. In addition to frying, these units can be used to cook a roast or bake a cake. Cooking outdoors keeps the smells outside and prevents grease build-up in the living area. Easy to clean units are made of stainless steel and most are gas powered.
- A **spade** can be handy if you become bogged or, in some circumstances, if you need to change a tyre by digging around it if the jack can't raise it high enough. Folding camping spades are compact and easy to pack.
- A couple of **pieces of timber** can be used under a wheel to level the unit on very uneven ground, or to put under a jack to increase height or to provide a solid base. Look for a piece of thick plywood or a lightweight option like pine.
- A short length of **hose** to fill the water tank. Buy the drinking water type of hose and not the garden variety. If you want to hook up to the water supply in caravan parks you will need a longer hose. Consider a flat hose that comes on a storage reel. This is a compact unit that is easy to store.
- A **sullage hose** is required if you want to empty the grey water directly into a caravan park drainage system. The best type has a corrugated exterior and a smooth internal bore. Hoses with corrugated internal ribs will trap particles from the grey water that will end up causing an unpleasant smell. If you don't use a sullage hose, place a bucket under the outlet and dispose of the water where it won't cause a problem. (Storage of the sullage hose – It is not a good idea to store a sullage hose inside an enclosed van boot or motorhome storage bin because any residue in the hose can cause bad odours. Consider installing a storage pipe, with locking caps, across the bumper bar or underneath the van.)
- A one-metre length of **metal pipe** can be used to give extra leverage by slipping it over the end of the wheel brace when you are trying to undo tight wheel nuts. A commercial device is also available that enables even elderly and infirm people to undo stubborn wheel nuts very easily.

Authors' tip:

Before storing any hose you need to empty it of water, and this can be difficult with some hoses.

- Many travellers carry their own **tyre pressure gauge** because those at service stations are often inconsistent in their readings. Some pressure gauges only register to around 50 psi and you may need to purchase a truck gauge. A gauge is essential if you plan to vary tyre pressures for driving on sandy or rocky surfaces.
- A **tyre pressure monitoring system** will allow the driver to monitor tyre pressures from the driver's seat.
- If you plan to drive on sandy or rocky surfaces where lower tyre pressures are required, **a pump or 12 volt air compressor** is needed to inflate tyres to normal pressure to resume road travel.
- **Portable warning signs** to use in the event of a breakdown on the road.
- A small **tomahawk or machete** may come in handy.
- A **piece of mesh** attached across the front grille or bull bar will stop locusts and other insects entering in large numbers and blocking the vehicle's cooling system. This protection is particularly relevant in areas where there can be plagues of locusts. Caution – Make sure the mesh is open-weave so it will not impede the flow of air to the radiator. Check occasionally to ensure it does not become clogged.
- Animals on the road present a danger on country roads, with kangaroos particularly active at dusk and dawn and on heavily overcast days. A **high frequency vehicle protection device** called *Shu-Roo* alerts the animals and hopefully they will move off the road in time.
- Extra insulation can be easily added to your van or motorhome by applying a coat of **insulating paint**.
- A **cover** for your caravan or motorhome will protect it from the elements if you have to store it outside.
- **Roll-out sunshades** can be made for motorhome or caravan windows.
- A **mini clothes hoist** will enable you to hang your washing close to your campsite. The hoists are lightweight and portable, with over 20m of line space.
- If you have a caravan or small campervan without an on-board shower, you might consider a pop-up **ensuite tent.** These are erected very quickly, and can be purchased from camping goods suppliers.
- **Bicycle carrier racks** can be fitted to the back of a motorhome or caravan.
- **Roof top luggage carriers** provide a weather-proof storage space, but will increase the height (and wind resistance) of the vehicle. If heavy items are carried on the roof of a vehicle, stability could be noticeably affected.
- Clear plastic **stone shields** on headlights – these are much cheaper than having to replace a headlight.
- **Jerry can holders** are available to safely carry fuel cans on the back of a motorhome or caravan.
- A **boat loader** that can be operated by one person to load a 'tinnie' on top of a 4WD, however it cannot work on a lower vehicle like a station wagon. Check the load-carrying capacity of the roof of the vehicle too.
- In some cases, the venting hot gas from the water heater may discolour the external wall above the unit. A small piece of metal can be fitted to deflect the heat and prevent damage.
- A few **basic tools** such as screwdrivers, pliers, small shifting spanner, multigrips, scissors, duct tape, tube of glue and household oil can come in handy for small running repairs and adjustments. Keep a few **spare fuses and globes**.

Window shades for small windows

Shower tent used by motorhomers

Bicycle rack on rear of motorhome

Additional equipment for caravans

For information on towbars, hitches and caravan brakes, refer to the section on towing p86.

Extended mirrors

Caravans are invariably wider than the tow vehicle, and to give a driver the legally-required view to the rear, extended mirrors are required. They should be solidly mounted and easy to install and remove. If you have limited mobility in your hands consider how easily this can be done.

Towing mirrors fit into three categories:

- **Low-cost strap-ons** that are really only useful for short hauls at low speed and on good road surfaces. Lower priced versions are liable to being blown off by the draught from passing trucks.
- **Braced strap-ons** attach to the standard mirror and are stabilised by an adjustable rod that runs at an angle from the mirror arm down to the door where it is secured by a magnetic pad or suction cup.
- **Separate mirrors** fitted to a brace that runs across the bonnet. This style will not fit all vehicles.

Windscreen stone shield

Stone shield

Used to protect the front of the caravan. Gravel and stones will be thrown up by the tow vehicle's wheels and can damage the front of the caravan and also the rear of the tow vehicle if the stones ricochet off the caravan. The deflection angle of a stone shield is important to prevent damage to the tow vehicle. If the stone shield is made from a soft material like shadecloth on a frame, it will absorb much of the flicked-up stone's energy. If gas cylinders are carried on the drawbar, it is simple to protect them from stone damage with the same stone shield.

Mud flaps

Larger than normal mud flaps can be the first line of defence against stones that might be thrown towards the caravan. Make sure the flaps sit clear of the road when the vehicle is loaded and with the caravan hitched on.

Towtector make a mud flap 'skirt' with bristles similar to a broom. This should sit 75mm to 100mm above the road, when the vehicle is fully loaded.

Off-road tracks often have a hump in the middle, and your mud flaps should be clear of this hump.

RV underskirt

An RV underskirt will take the place of both the stone shield and mud flaps by filling in the gap between the bumper bar of the tow vehicle and the front of the caravan or towed car. The *Blue Ox* underskirt is made from a lightweight sturdy woven mesh, and is distributed in Australia by Northcoach on the Gold Coast.

Stone deflector on caravan draw bar

Stabilisers

Caravans are fitted with stabilisers at the rear that are lowered to the ground when camped so the unit does not rock as people move about inside. The usual stabiliser is a straight-leg style that folds to the back of the unit when not in use. It is preferable to fit stabilisers that have a small wheel so when the caravan negotiates a slope the wheel runs on the ground rather than having the stabiliser leg gouge into the surface of the road or driveway. Another alternative is a stabiliser that folds to the front when not in use.

Jockey wheels

Your caravan will come with a simple jockey wheel to enable you to manoeuvre it to couple to the towbar. If the jockey wheel is removable, once the van is hitched, stow it securely and re-tighten the holding clamp bolt. More expensive wheels are available that will make it easier to handle the unit. *Trail-a-Mate* make a hydraulic jockey wheel that converts to a hydraulic jack and this makes handling heavier caravans much easier.

Caravans are even easier to move and also park in a tight spot using a motorised system instead of manually moving using a jockey wheel. These devices are not inexpensive, but could be worth the outlay for a driver who has difficulty manually manoeuvring a caravan or who has to park it in a very tight space. Power it from either the caravan's battery or its own separately installed battery.

- With the *Aussie Wheel* unit the caravan is hitched to a wheeled unit that is operated by hand controls on a removable handle. The unit weighs between 30kg and 37kg and is unhitched and stowed when not in use.
- The *Move Control* device is permanently installed onto the caravan chassis with clamps and is suitable for single axle or tandem axle vans. A hand-held remote control is used to control the caravan as it moves on its own wheels.

Tyre pressure monitoring

A simple device can be fitted to a caravan axle to warn of loss of tyre pressure. An alarm will sound if a caravan tyre loses sufficient pressure for the sensing device to touch the ground.

Jack

Try your tow vehicle's jack to see if it will effectively lift your caravan to change a wheel. Don't wait until you are caught with a flat caravan tyre.

Authors' tip:

With a heavy jockey wheel or motorised system, consider where you would stow it and also how easy it would be for you to carry to its storage location.

Camping in the Margaret River region, WA Photo: Pelusey Photography

Additional equipment for motorhomes

Wheel-levelling ramps

Unless you have an upmarket motorhome with hydraulic levelling rams, you will need wheel-levelling ramps when your campsite is not level. Either commercially produced ramps or pieces of timber can do the job, and the most effective type is wedge-shaped, allowing the vehicle to be driven as far up the ramp as required. It is important that the ramps are large enough to cover the whole footprint of the wheel, and in the case of dual wheels, both should be on the ramp (or ramps). Some ramps are advertised as having 'wells' that can be filled with water so ants cannot access the motorhome via the wheels.

Wheel levelling ramps used on dual wheels

Authors' tip:

We use wheel-levelling ramps quite often, even occasionally in caravan parks. So far we haven't had a problem with ants climbing in via our wedge-shaped plastic ramps.

Driving beside Horseshoe Bay, Queensland

Storage boxes

A storage box seems to be an easy way to gain additional storage space, but there are several factors that need to be checked.

- Before buying a storage box, check that the weight of the vehicle with passengers, fully loaded and provisioned does not exceed the GVM (gross vehicle mass) shown on the compliance plate.
- Check that the length of the overhang past the rear axle (including the storage box) does not exceed 60% of the wheelbase or 3.7m. If your vehicle is found to exceed these limits, it can be put off the road until it complies, and you could also be in a difficult position if you have an insurance claim following an accident.
- If you do add a storage box, use it for lightweight items so handling of the vehicle is not adversely affected by excessive weight behind the rear axle.
- The same comments apply if you carry a heavy and bulky item such as a motorbike on the back.

Warning signs

Vehicles with a GVM in excess of 12 tonnes are required to carry and use warning triangles in the case of breakdown. One is to be placed between 50m and 150m in front of the vehicle, one between 50m and 150m behind the vehicle, and one at the side in a position that gives sufficient warning to other road users.

Extra items you might wish to consider:

- In some motorhomes, the 'house' batteries are fitted in a side bin with a sliding tray that requires some effort to extend when you need to top up the batteries. A **rolling device** can be fitted to make this easier.
- Some motorhomers transport a **small motorbike** on the back of their motorhome. Make sure the overhang (distance behind the back axle) is still within legal limits.
- **Stone guard** for the front windshield.

Aiding the view to the rear

- If your motorhome has normal, and not **wide angle, side-mounted mirrors**, cheap and effective wide angle 'stick on' mirrors available from auto accessory shops can be added hese are very handy for filling in blind spots.
- As visibility to the rear of a campervan or motorhome leaves a lot to be desired, many people fit a **small camera** at the rear with a screen mounted on the dashboard. The camera tends to distort distances so it may not be very useful when parking. A simple alternative when parking or reversing is to have the passenger directing the driver by voice instructions over a hand-held UHF radio.
- If a campervan or motorhome has a 'straight through' rear view, a **wide-angle plastic lens** stuck on the inside of the rear window will give an excellent view, although distances will be distorted. These inexpensive lenses are around 20cm x 25cm in size and are available from auto accessory outlets. Because of the height of an average motorhome, without such a lens your rear view is often that of the distant horizon or sky.

Authors' tip:

Value for money, this lens could be the best add-on you can buy for your motorhome.

Hinged storage box that allows access to boot of motorhome.

Motorbike ramp at rear of motorhome

Motorbike ramp at rear of motorhome

Tyres

For a vehicle to accelerate, brake and steer safely, there needs to be the correct contact between the tyre and the road. Important factors include:

- having the most appropriate tyres;
- correct inflation; and
- depth of tread and general condition of the tyre.

Understanding tyre codes

The tyre and wheel sizes fitted to your vehicle as original equipment were chosen by the manufacturer and the recommended sizes, speed and load ratings will be shown in the owner's handbook. Specifications of passenger vehicle tyres including the size, construction, load and speed rating are shown in a series of codes on the sidewall of the tyre.

Example: A tyre with the codes **185/60 R 14 82 H**.

- '**185**' – the **section width of the tyre in millimetres** at its widest point when inflated.
- '**60**' – the **profile** (or aspect ratio) of the tyre. This is the height of the sidewall divided by the tyre's width. For passenger vehicles this is typically between 60 and 75.
- '**R**' – the **construction** of the tyre; in this case radial.
- '**14**' – the **nominal rim diameter** to which the tyre must be fitted expressed in inches.
- '**82**' – the **load index**. A chart indicates the maximum load the tyre can carry at the speed indicated by its speed symbol. In this case it is 475kg per tyre.
- '**H**' – the **speed rating** of the tyre. This is the most common for passenger vehicles.
- Markings on some tyres also indicate its expected life and durability by showing a comparative rating for wear, traction and temperature resistance. The example tyre:
- 'Treadwear 260'. A tyre marked 160 would give only half the life of one that is marked 320. The relative performance will vary due to driving habits, service practices and differences in road surface.
- 'Traction AA' which is the highest rating. Lower ratings in descending order are A, B and C. This is the tyre's ability to stop on a wet road, measured under controlled conditions.
- 'Temperature A' is the highest rating, followed by B and C. This rating represents the tyre's resistance to the generation of heat.

Tyres also have their **date of manufacture** moulded into the sidewall with the first two numbers indicating the calendar week and the next two numbers the year it was made. Our sample tyre shows '1305' indicating it was made in the 13th week of 2005. For tyres made before 2000, there are only three numbers: '238' is the 23rd week of 1998, or maybe 1988.

Tyre codes

Correct tyres

Present day **steel radial tyres** have advantages of greater strength, durability and lighter weight than their predecessor – **bias-ply tyres**. With bias-ply tyres the load-carrying capacity was increased by adding more layers of cotton, or plies, giving a 4, 6, 8, 10 or 12 ply tyre. Radial tyres are rated by their equivalent in bias-ply tyres.

Radials have less rolling resistance than cross-plies, letting the vehicle move more easily on the road. As the engine doesn't have to work quite as hard, it also consumes slightly less fuel. It is illegal to mix radial tyres with cross-ply tyres on the same axle as the greater adhesion of radials could cause the vehicle to spin when braking hard.

Some steel radial tyres used for passenger vehicles have nylon used in construction of the side walls, while an **all steel radial tyre** has steel in both the casing and the tread. These details will be shown on markings on the side wall. All steel radials offer a long life, but you should avoid putting extra stress on the side walls as this could damage the steel wires that give the tyre its strength.

When using wheel-levelling ramps, ensure the weight of the vehicle is supported by all tyres. If, for example, a ramp is placed under only one tyre of a dual set, that tyre will be holding all the weight on that corner of the vehicle, putting too much strain on the side walls of that tyre. The levelling ramp should sit under the full 'footprint' of the tyre, and not just half its width.

Tyres used in a dual configuration should be matched in diameter. It is also advisable to have the tyres on the front steering axle matched due to varying grip between different brands, tyre type and tread patterns. If one tyre has had considerably more wear than the other, or sometimes if they are from different manufacturers, the diameter may not be consistent. Two new tyres on one side of the vehicle and two old ones on the other can cause a spin, particularly in the wet.

Tyres are also rated for their maximum carrying capacity – calculated when the tyre is inflated to the recommended pressure. Check your vehicle's manual to determine what tyres you should use.

Inflation

The standard of measurement for tyre pressure has always been 'pounds per square inch' (**psi**), but the metric standard is 'kilopascals', abbreviated as **kPa**. Tyre pressure gauges usually show both measurements. A simple way to convert psi to kPa is to multiply by seven, but the exact figure is 6.8948.

If tyres are not inflated correctly, the stability and ride of the vehicle can be affected, and more importantly, the life of the tyre will be shortened. If under-inflated it will reduce fuel economy, and there is a danger of overheating and possible blow-out. A tyre has to be inflated to its maximum recommended pressure before the load rating of the tyre can be achieved.

Tyre pressure should be **checked when tyres are cold** as heat build-up caused by normal flexing when travelling increases the pressure significantly. Never let air out of a hot tyre just to bring it back to the pressure recommended for a cold tyre. If you can only check the tyre pressure when the tyres are hot, allow an extra 2psi (13.8 kPa) to the pressure recommended for a cold tyre.

Authors' tip:

It is worth carrying your own tyre pressure gauge because those at service stations will not all give a consistent reading.

Typical maximum pressures for radial passenger or 'P' tyres are 36 psi (248 kPa) for a 4 ply or standard load tyre and 40 psi (276 kPa) for a 6 ply or extra load tyre. Light truck or 'LT' tyres have a typical maximum inflation pressure of 50 psi (345 kPa) if they have a 6-ply rating and 65 psi (448 kPa) for 8 ply, 80 psi (552 kPa) for 10 ply, and 87 psi (600 kPa) for 12 ply. These will vary depending upon the dimensions and construction of the individual tyre. If the inflation pressure of the tyre is less, the load carrying capacity will be lower. Note – Many light truck type tyres are identified by the letter 'C' (for example 195 R 14 C).

Recommended tyre pressures shown on the driver's door pillar or in your vehicle's manual are based on the load the manufacturer expects the vehicle will carry. It is usually recommended that you use the same pressure for all tyres on the same axle, although some drivers whose vehicle has more weight on one side than the other put a pound or two more pressure in the tyre carrying extra weight. Don't forget to check the pressure on the spare.

When a radial tyre is correctly inflated, the tread will be flat on the road and the sidewall will be bowed out slightly. If it is **over-inflated** the outer edges of the tread will not be in proper contact with the road and the sidewalls will be bowed only very slightly. When **under-inflated**, tyres will bulge out noticeably and when driving the sidewalls will flex abnormally, causing an excessive build-up of heat and irregular wear. It can even result in structural damage and tyre failure. The effect on a tyre of under-inflation is the same as loading it with excessive weight.

Authors' tip:

If you are uncertain what the correct tyre pressure is, opt for a slightly higher pressure, not lower.

Nitrogen v compressed air

Tyres have traditionally been inflated with compressed air, however there are advantages in using nitrogen.

Advantages of nitrogen

Slower rate of pressure loss. The rubber used for tubes and inner liners in tubeless tyres is not 100% impermeable and the air in the tyre slowly 'bleeds', resulting in loss of pressure. Due to its molecular structure, nitrogen bleeds through the rubber at a slower rate, although pressure can still be lost through a puncture or damage to the tyre valve.

Cooler running temperatures of a tyre inflated with nitrogen will increase tread life. (However, some sources suggest it's only likely to be of benefit when the tyres are operating at or near their maximum load and/or speed capacities.)

As the tyres are cooler, **pressure does not build-up as much** as tyres filled with compressed air. When the pressure increases above recommended levels, the area of rubber in contact with the road surface is reduced and therefore the tyre has reduced grip. (Again some sources suggest the greatest benefits are likely under heavy load.)

In summary, proponents say by maintaining correct tyre pressure, using nitrogen improves the **life of the tyres, fuel consumption and handling**.

Disadvantages of nitrogen

While there is no cost to use compressed air at a service station, there is a **charge for nitrogen** (usually between $5 and $10 per tyre).

If you do need to adjust the pressure in the tyres, nitrogen is required to maintain the advantages of using this gas. While nitrogen is available at tyre outlets, the general **availability** and hours you can buy the product are limited compared with compressed air, which is always available at every service station and roadhouse.

Wear

When a vehicle is travelling at 80kph the average tyre rotates 40 000 times in an hour, so proper care of the tyres is an important factor in ensuring a trouble-free journey. It is recommended that tyres are rotated about every 10 000km, but check this with your tyre supplier as warranty conditions may apply. The driving wheels will wear faster than the others, so swapping tyres around (usually referred to as rotation) will even out the wear. You may also notice that the inner and outer edges of the front tyres wear a little more due to the extra work in steering.

Tyres wear from use and also from natural aging but you can try to avoid premature or uneven tyre wear caused by under-inflation, overloading, or defects such as a bent axle or wheels out of alignment.

Tips to achieve the maximum life out of your tyres

- **Keep the pressure at the maximum recommended**. Damage to tyres is progressive and cumulative, and under inflation by (say) 10% is much more damaging than over inflation by the same amount.
- **Avoid under inflation** because the excessive heat that builds up from the flexing of an under-inflated tyre can cause the rubber compound to break down and result in structural damage and failure of the tyre.
- **Driving at 100kph** and over will wear tyres faster than driving at 80kph because driving at a higher speed causes the tyres to flex more and generates excessive heat that can damage the tyres.

Over-inflated tyres will wear more in the centre of the tyre, while under-inflated tyres will wear rapidly on the outside edges. If your tyres appear to be wearing faster than you would expect, or if the wear is uneven, consult a tyre specialist.

This tyre shows excessive tread wear on one side only caused by incorrect wheel alignment

Types of tyre wear

- **Excessive wear on shoulders or outer edges** – under inflation, lack of rotation or high speed cornering.
- **Excessive wear on centre section** – over inflation or lack of rotation.
- **Excessive wear on one side of the tread** – needs wheel alignment because of excessive camber.
- **Feathered or saw-tooth tread** – incorrect toe-in.
- **Irregular depressions or spots** – unbalanced tyre and wheel or defective tyre.
- **Cupped or scalloped depressions** – lack of rotation, improper alignment, worn or damaged steering or suspension parts.
- **Cracked ribs** – overloading, high speed driving or alternate over and under inflation.

Wheel alignment

Badly-aligned suspension will wear tyres more rapidly and affect the vehicle's handling.
Principles in wheel alignment:

- **Camber** is the measurement in degrees of the angle of the tyre from vertical when seen from the front or rear. It is normal to have a slight positive camber (ie outward at the top) when stationary. This will straighten up when the vehicle is in motion.
- **Castor** is the relationship between the steering axis and true vertical. When the steering axis is tilted backwards (by far the most common design) it has positive castor. Unequal castor from side to side causes steering pull to the side that has the least amount of positive castor.
- **'Toe in'** is the difference between the front of the wheels and the rear of the wheels. Most vehicles have slight inward pointing when stationary, but the wheels become approximately parallel when the vehicle is in motion.
- If there is excessive or uneven wear on your tyres, or if you feel by looking at them that the angles do not look right, have the alignment checked. When you purchase new tyres it is worth having a wheel alignment done.

Aging of tyres

Tyres usually have a 'life expectancy' of five to seven years and you should check the condition of older tyres for signs of aging. To determine the age of a tyre, refer to the explanation of tyre codes earlier in this section. (Be wary of tyres with only three numbers, e.g. '238' – it means they were made before 2000 and are too old.)

- Tyres that are used on a regular basis will have a longer life than those that sit unused for long periods because the flexing caused by normal use keeps the rubber supple.
- Don't use products to polish the sidewalls of your tyres to enhance the appearance.
- Exposure to ultraviolet rays in sunlight has a detrimental effect, so if you have to store your motorhome or caravan outside for periods of time, cover the wheels.

Blow out

A front axle blow out may be felt in the steering wheel, while a rear axle blow out is usually felt through the driver's seat. Tyre companies recommend briefly using the accelerator to regain control, then letting the vehicle glide to a stop or gently decelerating by changing to a lower gear or using compression braking.

4WD tyres

Most 4WDs start out fitted with **highway terrain (HT) tyres** as standard. These provide a quiet, comfortable ride and handle well on sealed surfaces, and are suited to a driver who spends limited time (maybe 10%) off-road, but they will not stand up very well to severe off-road use.

All terrain (AT) tyres are more robust and are suited to approximately 50% off-road use.

Drivers who spend at least 80% of their time off road are advised to consider **mud terrain (MT) tyres**. However, they will generally wear faster, are much noisier and will perform less well on bitumen.

Caravan tyres

As they carry a much greater load when towing, the rear tyres on the tow vehicle should be inflated to near their maximum. Front tyres of the tow vehicle will need an extra 4 psi (27.5 kPa) above normal. It is generally considered unwise to inflate caravan tyres above 45 psi (310 kPa) as it may affect the ride of the van.

It is difficult for the driver to notice loss of pressure in a caravan tyre before it becomes too late, and risks include a tyre blow out, shredded tyres or even a rollover. A simple mechanical sensing device can be fitted that will **warn the driver if there is a significant deflation of a tyre**. *See p74 for more details.*

Tyre tips for varying uses

Tyre design involves a huge number of variables including tread pattern, sidewall construction, tyre shape, cord ply type and rubber compounding. Owners usually expect their vehicle to handle a wide range of road conditions, and optimum performance in one area may adversely affect another. When choosing the most suitable tyres, consider how much off-road driving you intend to do and seek the advice of a tyre expert.

Tyre after a blow-out

If a caravan is going to sit unused for a period of time, **remove some of the weight off the tyres** and suspension. Place blocks under the chassis behind the wheels, use the jockey wheel to raise the front of the van and place blocks under the point where the drawbar attaches to the chassis.

Motorhome tyres

Most motorhomes are likely to need a much higher tyre pressure than a family car, and tyres should be carefully monitored. An easy way to do this is to install an electronic **tyre pressure monitoring system** that allows the driver to monitor tyre pressure with information transmitted from each tyre by small radio transmitters.

When using **levelling blocks**, the tyre (or tyres) should be fully on a block and not have just a portion of the tyre on the block and supporting the full load. Dual wheels should have a block for each wheel or one large block that both wheels will fit on so they both continue to hold the load.

Alternative spare tyres

Approximately 65% of all new cars sold in Australia are equipped with a **full-size spare wheel**, while others have a **temporary-use or a space saver** tyre. These are smaller than the standard tyres on the vehicle, and usually carry a warning sticker advising that the vehicle should not exceed a certain speed (usually 80kph) when the temporary tyre is being used. Space saver tyres are made of a softer compound than normal tyres and can adversely affect handling and braking.

Another alternative is **'runflat'** tyres, which must be used in conjunction with a tyre pressure monitoring system. Runflats have stiff sidewalls that will allow flat-tyre driving at 80kph for up to 250km (or less, depending on the vehicle's load). These tyres are more expensive than conventional tyres, cannot be repaired and are unlikely to be available immediately in country areas. Runflat tyres should only be fitted to vehicles that come with runflat tyres as original equipment.

Authors' tip:

Tyres such as runflats that are designed for the autobahns of Germany could be more susceptible to damage on our rough roads.

Practical matters: Using your RV

Motorhome under 4.5 tonnes GVM with three axles can be driven on a C class licence.

Operating a motorhome or caravan

Driver's licences

Australia has a uniform driver licencing system that sets out the class of licence required to drive a particular class of vehicle, depending on its Gross Vehicle Mass (GVM).

- A vehicle with a GVM **less than 4.5 tonnes** and that carries up to 12 adults including the driver can be driven on a **'C' (car) class licence**.
- A vehicle with a GVM **between 4.5 tonnes and 8 tonnes** requires a **Light Rigid (LR) truck licence**.
- With vehicles up to 8 tonnes the licence class is dependent on the GVM and it is irrelevant whether the vehicle has two or three axles. A vehicle over **8 tonnes with two axles** requires a **Medium Rigid (MR) licence, and with three axles, a Heavy Rigid (HR) licence.**
- When towing a caravan or fifth wheeler (GVM less than 9 tonnes) the driver's licence class is dependent on the GVM of the tow vehicle.
- If a towed trailer has a GVM over **9 tonnes a Heavy Combination (HC)** licence is required.

To upgrade your licence

You must have held an open or provisional licence for at least one year before you can have your licence upgraded. The procedure in each State is as follows:

- **Australian Capital Territory** – Pass a practical driving assessment. (www.rego.act.gov.au)
- **New South Wales** – Undertake a Heavy Vehicle Competency Based Assessment with an RTA accredited assessor. If you are outside of the Sydney, Central Coast and Newcastle regions you can undertake a driving test instead. (www.rta.nsw.gov.au)
- **Northern Territory** – Complete an approved training course or pass the practical and theory tests (only the practical test is required for LR class). (www.nt.gov.au/transport/mvr)
- **Queensland** – Pass a practical driving test at a Driver Licensing Centre. (www.transport.qld.gov.au)
- **South Australia** – Take either a Vehicle-On-Road-Test (VORT) or complete a Competency Based Training (CBT) course. (www.transport.sa.gov.au)
- **Tasmania** – Take either a prescribed training course with an approved organisation or complete a driving test with an approved External Service Provider. (www.transport.tas.gov.au)
- **Victoria** – Pass a knowledge test and a heavy vehicle driving test. (www.vicroads.vic.gov.au)
- **Western Australia** - Pass a practical driving assessment. (www.dpi.wa.gov.au/licensing)

Renewing a driver's licence

- **Australian Capital Territory** licences must be renewed in person at any ACT Government Shopfront or the Civic Driver Licence Service. If you are interstate or overseas you can renew by mail. (www.rego.act.gov.au)
- **New South Wales** licences are for one, three or five years. If you are interstate when the licence is due for renewal, phone RTA on 132 213 to obtain a Photo Kit. (www.rta.nsw.gov.au)
- **Northern Territory** licences can be renewed online, by phone or mail, or at customer service centres. (www.nt.gov.au/transport/mvr)
- **Queensland** licences can be for a period between one and five years and you can apply up to six weeks before expiry. Provided it has not already expired, a licence can be renewed online if you do not need a new photo (photos are valid for ten years). Drivers renewing online receive a sticker to attach to their old licence. (www.transport.qld.gov.au)
- **South Australia** licences are for up to ten years. You can apply at a customer service centre, selected Australia Post offices, or by mail (if applying by mail you must still personally attend a photo point location). If it is due for renewal when you are interstate, phone the Customer Service Centre on 13 10 84. (www.transport.sa.gov.au)
- **Tasmania** licences are issued for a period of one to five years and can be renewed within six months of expiry. You can apply at Service Tasmania shops and some police stations. Photo kits are available if you are travelling interstate or overseas when the licence expires. Drivers over 65 years only pay a small fee for the photo-card. (www.transport.tas.gov.au)
- **Victoria** licences are normally for a period of ten years, however a three-year licence can be requested. Drivers over 75 years of age are only issued with a three-year licence. Licences can be renewed in person at a Photo Point or VicRoads customer service centre, or by Bpay, telephone or mail if a recent digital image is held. (www.vicroads.vic.gov.au)
- **Western Australia** licences are for a period of from one to four years. If a new photo is not required you can renew online or by phone. If a photo is required you must attend a licensing centre or agent, or an Australia Post office. If you are interstate or overseas when the licence expires you can arrange for a Photo Kit. (www.dpi.wa.gov.au/licensing)

Older drivers and medical issues

- In the **Australian Capital Territory** drivers with any permanent or long-term medical conditions that affect their ability to drive, and advanced age drivers may be required to have medical examinations.
- In **New South Wales** all drivers over the age of 75 are required to have an annual medical checkup. Over the age of 80 heavy vehicle drivers in licence classes LR, MR, HR and HC need to undertake annual driving assessments. Drivers are required to report any permanent and long-term medical conditions that will affect their ability to drive. Regular medical examinations and/or an annual driving test may be required depending upon the condition.
- In the **Northern Territory** drivers are required to report any permanent and long-term medical conditions that will affect their ability to drive. If there are medical issues, a medical assessment on the person's fitness to drive must be carried out by a health professional.
- **Queensland** drivers are required to immediately report any permanent and long-term medical conditions that will affect their ability to drive. From the age of 75, drivers are required to have a medical certificate and to carry this with them at all times.
- In **South Australia** drivers are required to immediately report any permanent and long-term medical conditions that will affect their ability to drive. Drivers with certain medical conditions or who are over 70 years of age must have a medical certificate showing their fitness to drive completed annually.
- In **Tasmania** drivers 75 years of age and over must have a medical examination every year, and from age 85 they must also undertake an annual driving test to keep their five-year licence valid.
- In **Victoria** drivers must report any medical condition that affects their ability to drive. Drivers over 75 years of age are only issued with a licence for three years.
- In **Western Australia**, when reaching 75 years of age drivers must complete a Seniors Declaration Form and undertake a medical examination. At 78 and 80 they must again complete the form and have a medical examination. From 80 this is undertaken every year, and from 85 they must also undertake a practical driving assessment every year. Drivers are also required to report any permanent and long-term medical conditions that will affect their ability to drive.

Moving interstate

If you move interstate permanently you must transfer your driver's licence to your new address within the following period:

- Within 30 days of moving to Queensland.
- Within 3 months of moving to New South Wales, the Northern Territory, the Australian Capital Territory, South Australia, Tasmania or Victoria.
- In Western Australia you can drive on your interstate licence until it expires.

Vehicle registration

Registration class

In nearly all cases, registration fees are determined by the weight (GVM) and class of the vehicle. An exception is Tasmania where campervans and motorhomes are considered to be light vehicles for the purposes of registration fees. Even if they weigh more, they are placed in the category up to 4.5 tonnes GVM, however the driver is still required to hold a driver's licence appropriate for the weight of the vehicle. The definition of a 'campervan or motorhome' is a motor vehicle that has been constructed or permanently modified for use as a temporary dwelling and does not include a slide-on with removable living quarters. The actual GVM of the vehicle needs to be recorded on the Motor Registry System.

Garage address

To register a vehicle a person usually has to provide evidence that they reside in the State or establish a 'garage address' i.e. the address where the vehicle is normally garaged when it is not travelling. This can be difficult for people who are on the road permanently (itinerants). Evidence normally required includes driver's licence, rates notice, or a gas, electricity or phone bill. Permanent caravan park residents can submit a statement from the owner/manager of the park, as well as their driver's licence. Details applying in each State:

- **Australian Capital Territory** – Proof of identity and residency; and proof that the vehicle is normally kept or 'garaged' in the ACT. (www.rego.act.gov.au)
- **New South Wales** – Provide evidence of an NSW address. No provision for itinerants. (www.rta.nsw.gov.au)
- **Northern Territory** – Itinerants can apply for a Long Term Travellers Permit. (www.nt.gov.au/transport/mvr)
- **Queensland** – Itinerants can nominate a relative or friend or an organisation to receive their mail. A letter or other form of confirmation from that person or organisation is required. (www.transport.qld.gov.au)
- **South Australia** – A current SA driver's licence and a residential address are required. A caravan park address is acceptable. (www.transport.sa.gov.au)
- **Tasmania** – A residential address and proof of residency are required. There is no provision for itinerants. (www.transport.tas.gov.au)
- **Victoria** – A garage address within Victoria is required (this can be the last or next accommodation address, accommodation receipts are acceptable), and also evidence of an Australian contact address (postal address is acceptable). (www.vicroads.vic.gov.au)
- **Western Australia** – Permanent travellers can use the address of a relative or friend in the State. (www.dpi.wa.gov.au/licensing)

Changing registration to another State

If you have moved permanently to another State you must change the registration within the following period:

- Within 14 days of moving to Queensland.
- Within 3 months of moving to New South Wales, the Australian Capital Territory, the Northern Territory, South Australia or Western Australia.
- In Tasmania or Victoria it is when a permanent residence is established.

With all States you can apply for a refund of the unexpired portion of an interstate registration. Destroy the windscreen label and hand the interstate registration number plates to the transport authority in the State to which you have moved. A receipt will be issued. Send this receipt to the relevant interstate authority together with a statement that you have destroyed the windscreen sticker and ask for a refund.

Inspection of vehicles (mechanical)

In some States regular inspections are required for renewal of registration. If a vehicle has been modified (eg converted to LPG or a bus converted to a motorhome) or if registration is transferred from another State, inspection may be required.

AUSTRALIAN CAPITAL TERRITORY (www.rego.act.gov.au)

Vehicles weighing more than 4.5 tonnes are required to be inspected at the time of renewal. For initial registration after moving from another State an inspection will be required, and if the vehicle is gas powered you will be required to supply a gas certificate from an ACT authorised gas fitter too.

NEW SOUTH WALES (www.rta.nsw.gov.au)

Most vehicles more than five years old require an e-Safety Check every registration renewal (this replaces the old Safety Inspection Report – pink slip). Caravans weighing up to 410kg and trailers weighing up to 250kg are exempt. The registration renewal notice will advise if your vehicle needs an inspection.

NORTHERN TERRITORY (www.nt.gov.au/transport/mvr)

Regular inspections by a Motor Vehicle Registry inspector or an authorised inspector are required. If an inspection becomes due while you are travelling outside the Territory, this can be done by someone authorised in that State to carry out Roadworthiness or Safety inspections. Their certificate should be sent to the Motor Vehicle Registry with your registration renewal. You are permitted only one interstate inspection and the next one must be done in the Territory.

- Vehicles with a GVM of 4.5 tonnes or more must be inspected every year.
- Vehicles under 4.5 tonnes GVM need the following inspections:
  - New vehicles do not need to be inspected for the first three years.
  - After the first three years, inspections are required every two years until the vehicle is 10 years old.
  - Vehicles over 10 years old must be inspected every year.

QUEENSLAND (www.transport.qld.gov.au)

Vehicles with a GVM of 4.5 tonnes or more require annual inspections. Vehicles weighing less than 4.5 tonnes are exempt.

SOUTH AUSTRALIA (www.transport.sa.gov.au)

Private cars, caravans and motorhomes do not need regular inspections, however an identity inspection will be required for initial registration after moving from another State. Vehicles converted to run on LPG must be inspected, and the certificate carried in the vehicle.

TASMANIA, VICTORIA & WESTERN AUSTRALIA

No regular inspections are required.

Note – For information on gas inspections see p57

Restrictions – long or heavy vehicles

Driver's blood alcohol content

In Queensland and Tasmania drivers of vehicles with a GVM exceeding 4.5 tonnes must have a **zero** blood alcohol content. In the Australian Capital Territory the limit is **0.02** for drivers of vehicles with a GVM exceeding 4.5 tonnes. In all other States and the Northern Territory the limit is **0.05** (the same as for drivers of vehicles weighing less than 4.5 tonnes GVM), provided the driver is not on a learner's or provisional driving licence.

Restrictions

Vehicles over 4.5 tonnes GVM or exceeding 7.5m in length (combined length of vehicle and trailer or caravan) are classified as long vehicles. Therefore any car/caravan combination, a motorhome towing a trailer or a fifth-wheeler is classified as a long vehicle and the following restrictions apply:

- On roads outside built-up areas that do not have more than one lane in the direction you are driving, a long vehicle must remain at least 60m from another long vehicle, and in areas where there are road trains, there must be at least 200m between long vehicles. The exception is when you are overtaking.
- Long vehicles are not permitted to stop on a road outside a built-up area except on a hard shoulder or in a truck bay or other area set aside for parking of goods vehicles.
- Long vehicles are not permitted to park in a built-up area for more than one hour unless otherwise signed by the local authority. The exception is if you are picking up or delivering goods.

Authors' tip:

You cannot get around this by taking up two parking spaces and putting money in two parking meters!

Signs for long vehicles

The following signs are optional:

- DO NOT OVERTAKE TURNING VEHICLE sign can only be used by vehicles (or combinations) with an overall length of 7.5m or more. If this sign is attached to the rear of the vehicle (or combination), other traffic must give way if the long vehicle, when turning, takes up more than one traffic lane. It is an offence to straddle lanes when turning if this sign is not displayed. The sign cannot be affixed to vehicles with a combined length less than 7.5m.
- VEHICLE UNDER TOW sign is required in New South Wales when flat-towing (or using an 'A' frame), but in other States the sign is not mandatory. *See p93 for details of the sign.*

Road train warning sign

Stuck behind a road train

Fuel

Available fuels

Fuels used to power vehicles are: petrol, ethanol/petrol blends, diesel, biodiesel or LPG. It is important to consider, not only the cost per litre of a particular fuel, but how much energy it produces, i.e. how far you can drive on that litre. Also consider fuel availability – petrol and diesel are widely available, but with only around 3000 outlets stocking LPG, it can be difficult to find in the outback. To ascertain if LPG is available where you will be travelling, phone LPG Australia on (02) 9319 4733 or access the website www.lpgaustralia.com.au. Electric-powered cars are not practical as recreational vehicles because of the limited distance they can drive before the batteries require recharging.

The unit of measurement used for energy that fuel produces is Mega Joules per litre (MJ/pl). Fuels are rated by a Research Octane Number (RON), a figure that is usually referred to simply as octane, however with blended fuels, the octane rating does not indicate the energy produced. Although a petrol/ethanol blend might have an octane rating of 95, it does not produce as much energy as 95 octane premium petrol.

A comparison of fuels

- Petrol – Regular unleaded (91 octane) produces 34.85 MJ/pl; premium unleaded (95 octane) produces 35.61 MJ/pl; and high performance unleaded (98 octane) produces 38.58 MJ/pl.
- Petrol blended with ethanol in 10% ratio produces 33.5 MJ/pl. (Pure ethanol has a rating of 21.1 MJ/pl).
- Diesel fuel produces approximately 38.4 MJ/pl.
- 100% biodiesel produces 10% less energy than petroleum diesel: B20 (20% biodiesel/80% petroleum diesel) produces approximately 37.63 MJ/pl of energy.
- LPG – propane alone produces 25.49 MJ/pl; butane alone produces 28.61 MJ/pl. LPG is usually a mixture of propane and butane with the butane proportion being up to 60%.

Regular unleaded petrol is the most commonly sold petrol, and is suitable for the vast majority of vehicles. Petrol is also available with a higher octane rating. Oil companies use different names for their products, and this can cause some hesitation when trying to select the correct fuel. Check your vehicle owner's manual for the manufacturer's recommendations.

Although the brand names fuel companies give their products vary, the octane ratings are basically the same. (Some types of fuel are not available at all sites – check with the relevant company's website.)

	ULP – 91 octane	ULP – 95 octane	ULP – 98 octane	Diesel	Biodiesel	LPG
BP	Unleaded 91 Opal (replacement for ULP in some remote communities)	Unleaded 95 (formerly Premium Unleaded)	Ultimate Unleaded	Ultra Low Sulphur Diesel BP Winter Diesel BP Ultimate Diesel (available in Perth only)		LPG
Caltex	Regular unleaded Bio E10* Unleaded (93/94 octane)	Vortex Premium	Vortex 98	Vortex Premium Diesel Low Sulphur Diesel Ultra Low Sulphur Diesel	New Generation Diesel (2%)	Vitalgas
Freedom	Unleaded 91	Unleaded Elite 95 (E10*)	Premium Elite 98 (E10*)		Elite Diesel (up to 20%)	
Gull WA	Unleaded	Premium Unleaded		Xtra low sulfur diesel	Gull Bio-D (up to 20%)	LPG
Liberty	Unleaded Unleaded 94 ™ (94 octane E10*)	Premium Unleaded PremiuMAX TM (96 octane blend of 95 PULP with an additive)	PremiuMAX 98 TM* (98 octane blend of 96 PremiuMAX with 10% ethanol)		ULS Diesel (5%) B20 Diesel (20%)	
Matilda	Unleaded	Premium Unleaded		Diesel		LPG
Mobil	Synergy 2000	Synergy 6000	Synergy 8000	Diesel (ultra low sulphur)		LPG
Neumann	Unleaded	Premium Unleaded E-Gen 95 (E10*)	E-Gen 98 (E10*)	Diesel	B20 Bio Diesel (20%)	Unigas
Shell	Unleaded Unleaded E10*	Premium Unleaded	V-Power V-Power Racing* (100 octane with 5% ethanol)	Diesel 50 (ultra low sulphur)		Shell AutoGas
United	Unleaded	Premium PLUS Unleaded (E10*)	Premium98 Boost 98 (E10*) Premium100* (100 octane)	Diesel		LPG

* Petrol is unleaded petrol blended with ethanol – usually in a concentration of 10% ethanol (see below).

A 'knocking' sound can occur if you use the incorrect petrol for your engine. This is caused by unwanted detonation of the fuel mixture, however this is not usually a problem with modern engines because they have an electronic device that makes adjustments in the engine. Most vehicles do not require fuel with an octane rating of 98 or even 95, and will operate very well on standard unleaded petrol (91 octane). High octane fuel is often recommended for higher performance engines. Check your vehicle owner's manual for the manufacturer's recommendations.

Volatility characteristics of petrol vary on a monthly basis to provide good cold weather starting in winter and to prevent vapour lock in summer. This is one reason why petrol should not be stored for long periods.

Opal petrol

Opal has been produced specifically by BP for some areas of central Australia to combat the problem of some young people getting high after sniffing petrol. Tests have proven that motorists can safely use this fuel and they will not notice any difference in performance or any long-term effects. The energy rating of Opal unleaded petrol is 1.5Mj/pl lower than ordinary fuel: too low to be noticeable or significant. Shell has started distributing 'Low Aromatic Unleaded' in Alice Springs.

Lead-replacement fuel

Owners of pre-1986 vehicles with petrol motors need to ensure that they use the correct fuel and additive for their vehicle to protect the engine against valve seat recession. Some vehicles can use unleaded or premium unleaded petrol (a full list is available on the Australian Institute of Petroleum website (www.aip.com.au/health/lead_guide.htm). Other pre-1986 vehicles should use premium unleaded petrol plus a lead replacement additive, which is available from most service stations. Manufacturers tend to recommend not using ethanol blends in cars made prior to 1986.

Petrol/ethanol blends

Ethanol is a renewable fuel that reduces our reliance on fossil fuels and also reduces harmful exhaust emissions. Ethanol (or ethyl alcohol) is derived mainly from sorghum, corn, wheat and sugar cane. Pure ethanol has a higher octane rating than petrol, but only about 60% of its energy content, therefore any petrol/ethanol blend will have a lower energy content than petrol. This means you cannot drive as far on a tank full of ethanol blend fuel as you can on pure petrol.

All petrol/ethanol blends with more than 1% ethanol must be labelled, however a blended fuel may be labelled '95' RON E10, i.e. 90% standard unleaded fuel/10% ethanol. Vehicle manufacturers advise that blended fuel will not damage engines, but performance could be affected at higher revs and fuel consumption may increase by around 3%. Experts also suggest that regular vehicle maintenance is particularly important if you use ethanol-blended petrol. Check your vehicle owner's manual for the manufacturer's recommendations.

Re-fuelling your vehicle

These following points are probably well known to every driver, but, in the interests of safety, we will re-state them. After stopping at the appropriate fuel pump, follow these steps:

- Turn off the vehicle's ignition.
- If your gas fridge is operating you should have already turned it off before driving up to the re-fuelling area.
- Take care to select the correct fuel as you might use different fuels in different vehicles you drive.
- Do not overfill the tank.

Water front camping near Exmouth, WA

Diesel

Diesel produces more energy than any other fuel available, so you will be able to drive further on a litre of diesel than on any other fuel. In January 2006 Government regulations tightened specifications for diesel to lower the sulphur content from 500 parts per million to 50 ppm. In the future this will be reduced further to 10 ppm. The lower sulphur content does not affect performance of the motor or fuel consumption, but it significantly reduces emissions that could be harmful to the environment.

Another major step in reducing emissions from diesel engines is the use of a diesel particulate filter that removes between 85% and 90% of the particulate matter (soot) contained in the gas emitted by the engine. A diesel-powered vehicle with a filter installed will emit no visible smoke from its exhaust pipe.

In addition to the diesel bowsers situated with petrol bowsers, truck stops often have 'high flow' diesel bowsers designed for faster filling of trucks. Unless your vehicle has been designed to accommodate this higher flow rate, there will be 'blowback' causing the automatic cut-off on the fuel nozzle to operate every few seconds. With constant stopping, fuelling will be tedious and the only solution is to avoid high flow bowsers.

Biodiesel

Biodiesel is made by enhancing the chemical composition of vegetable or animal oils or fats such as canola, soy, palm or coconut oil. Used cooking oils or animal tallow can also be used. These oils are too thick to use directly in modern fuel injection systems, so they are processed to separate the glycerine from the methyl esters (the chemical name for biodiesel). Biodiesel is usually blended with conventional petroleum diesel at concentrations of up to 20%. At this ratio it will produce 2% less energy than 100% petroleum diesel.

Caution on biodiesel – Before using biodiesel you MUST check with your vehicle's manufacturer for their recommendations. Manufacturers of some popular vehicles advise that using biodiesel will void the vehicle warranty, some will approve of its use in a ratio of 5% (B5), while others state that they will neither approve nor disapprove of biodiesel.

Using biodiesel – Biodiesel can be mixed with conventional (petroleum) diesel that may remain in the tank. With biodiesel there is a dramatic reduction in harmful emissions of carbon dioxide, carbon monoxide and particulate matter (soot).

No engine modifications are required before using biodiesel, however after biodiesel has been used for a couple of hundred kilometres it may be necessary to replace the fuel filter. Because biodiesel is more viscous than petroleum diesel it will tend to clean any soot particles and these will accumulate on the fuel filter. These particles are from the petroleum diesel that had been used previously, not from the biodiesel. Because it is more viscous than petroleum diesel, in particularly cold conditions biodiesel can become too thick for the engine to operate.

LPG – Liquid Petroleum Gas

Although they are both commonly referred to as LPG, the gas used for appliances is propane, whereas autogas is usually a mixture of propane and butane. Butane has a higher energy content than propane (28.61 Mj/pl to 25.49 Mj/pl) and the percentage of butane in autogas can range up to 60%. There is no way of knowing when you buy autogas what the butane component is, and it will not necessarily always be the same from a particular retailer.

At present prices, LPG is more economical than other fuels. Currently there is no Government excise on LPG but there is on petrol and diesel. From 1 July 2011 excise of 2.5 cents per litre will be imposed on LPG used to fuel vehicles, and this will increase each year until it reaches 12.5 cents per litre on 1 July 2015.

Currently LPG is not available in all areas in Australia, so a gas-only vehicle would not be practical for travelling in outback areas. (To ascertain if LPG is available where you will be travelling, phone LPG Australia on (02) 9319 4733 or access the website www.lpgaustralia.com.au.) Dual-fuel vehicles must be operated on petrol occasionally.

Gas tanks must be inspected every ten years and there is a significant cost involved because the tank has to be removed from the vehicle. The cost was quoted at between $500 and $1000.

Warning signs to help motorists avoid running out of fuel

Converting a vehicle to LPG

Many petrol vehicles have been converted to a dual-fuel system that will run on gas or petrol. The Federal Government pays a subsidy of $2000 towards the conversion of privately registered petrol-powered vehicles with a GVM less than 3.5 tonnes. This applies to petrol vehicles converted to dual fuel and to diesel vehicles that have a gas injection system installed. (For full details contact the AusIndustry Hotline on 13 28 46 or visit the website www.ausindustry.gov.au/EnergyandFuels/LPGVehicleScheme.) Gas is stored in a liquid state in a specially installed tank under pressure and piped to the engine. A disadvantage of conversion is the loss of valuable boot space to store a bulky gas tank. If the engine is under manufacturer's warranty, check if it will be affected by the installation of LPG.

All LPG installations must comply with the technical requirements of Australian Standard AS 1425 current at the time of conversion and be fitted with an acceptable LPG compliance plate if converted to operate on LPG on or after 1st February 1993. The structural integrity of the vehicle and its continued compliance with the Standards for Registration must not be adversely affected. The owner/operator of the vehicle should supply details of the LPG conversion to the motor vehicle registry in their State. A vehicle fitted with an LPG system should have an LPG label attached to the vehicle's number plates.

Handling fuel (petrol and diesel)

Accidentally adding petrol to a diesel tank

This has the potential to be a very expensive mistake unless handled properly. Modern diesel engines have a system where the diesel fuel-injection equipment relies on the diesel fuel for lubrication. Petrol is a solvent that can strip lubricant from moving parts allowing metal-to-metal contact, resulting in damage to precisely machined components. The extent of damage and the cost of repair will depend on the type of vehicle and how long it has operated on the wrong fuel.

What to do

Do not turn the ignition on as the electric fuel pump will circulate the fuel through the system. Even starting the engine to move the vehicle away from the bowser will greatly increase the repair costs.

Phone your motoring club (if your vehicle is not over their weight for towing) or insurer (if you have coverage for towing after a breakdown) and **have the vehicle towed to a repairer** who can drain the petrol from the system. If you have to move the vehicle out of the way while waiting for a tow truck, ask other motorists to help you push the vehicle.

Accidentally adding diesel to a petrol tank

A petrol motor will not run on 100% diesel, but if you have added only a small amount of diesel to a petrol tank, the motor will run, but not efficiently. It will knock or ping, and blow clouds of smoke. The severity of the problem will depend on the proportion of diesel to petrol in the tank, and also on your particular motor. If there is regular 'pinging' you should stop as the pistons can be damaged. If you have filled a nearly empty petrol tank with diesel, don't even start the motor. **Drain the tank then refill with petrol.**

Carrying extra fuel

If you plan to travel only on major roads it is not necessary to carry additional fuel because there is never more than a few hundred kilometres between service stations. If there is a particularly long distance to the next available fuel, warning signs beside the road indicate the distance. (Note – the longest stretches on major highways are 323km in northwest Western Australia between Roebuck Plains Roadhouse and Sandfire Roadhouse, or 371km in Northern Territory on a less travelled route between Barkly Homestead and Cape Crawford. Travellers using the Plenty Highway will need fuel to cover the 472km stretch between Jervois Station in Northern Territory and Boulia in Queensland.)

If you do carry fuel, it must be in an **approved container** that must not be stowed inside the motorhome or tow vehicle. Petrol is particularly volatile, and you should check with your insurer whether carrying extra fuel will affect your coverage. As a alternative, you might consider increasing the fuel capacity of the vehicle by adding an **extra fuel tank**.

When travelling on long stretches of highway (e.g. Plenty Highway, northwest Western Australia, the Nullarbor, the Barkly Tableland) top up your fuel tank rather than risk running out of fuel. Be aware of headwinds that will cause your vehicle to consume more fuel than otherwise would be the case. If you are towing, consider the extra fuel consumption caused by the additional load.

Running out of fuel

If you run out of fuel with a modern diesel motor or a fuel-injected petrol motor, often it is not simply a matter of pouring fuel into the tank to get you going. You will likely need professional assistance before you can get under way. There are too many vehicles on the market to detail what is required in every circumstance – suffice to say prevention is best.

Storing fuel

Petrol can only be stored in containers designed for the purpose that allow for 10% expansion without pressurising the container, and possibly causing it to leak. Petrol should not be stored for long periods and ideally should be used within two months, but six months is the recommended maximum storage time.

Petrol/ethanol blends can absorb water from humid air that can eventually cause the mixture to separate. A container used to store blended petrol must be sealed very well, and the fuel should not be stored for long periods.

Diesel can be stored from six months to one year if kept in cool and dry conditions.

Winterised fuel

In areas that routinely experience very cold winter temperatures in winter, fuel is 'winterised', so if you are travelling to the snow, fuel up when you arrive so you have the appropriate fuel.

Increasing engine efficiency

Turbo charging a diesel motor

Fitting a turbo system will give increased power and torque for hills and towing. Investigate how much you can increase the power and efficiency of the motor and whether it may shorten the life of the engine and other components. Some motorhomes and 4WDs have factory-fitted turbo.

Adding gas to a diesel motor

It is claimed that installing a computer-controlled gas additive system will increase combustion efficiency, power and torque, and reduce emissions. It allows a small amount of LPG into the engine via the air intake system to increase combustion ensuring all diesel injected is burnt.

Increasing flow of air

Some motorhomers increase the flow of air to the motor by installing an air 'scoop' to force more airflow past the air intake of the engine to give better fuel economy.

A more technological solution is a device that fits inside the air filter housing or in the air hose on EFI or diesel vehicles. It changes the flow of air into the combustion chamber so the fuel is used more efficiently, resulting in more power and less pollution.

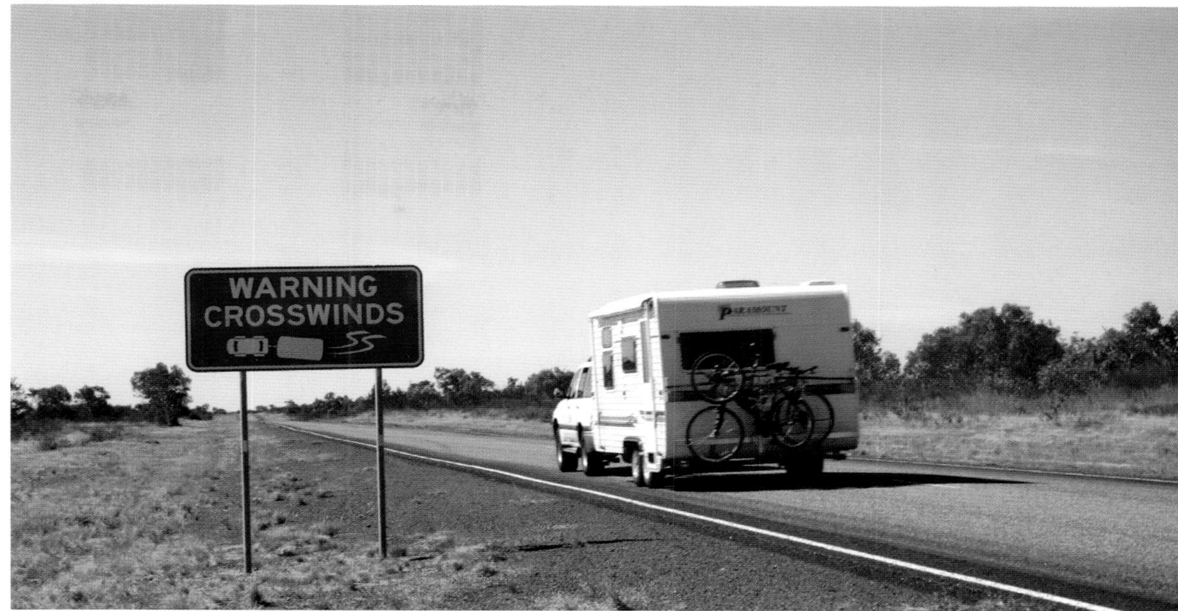

Warning sign, particularly relevant for caravanners

Caravans

Weight

The maximum total combined legal weight of the tow vehicle and the fully laden caravan is the **Gross Combination Mass (GCM)**. The GCM is determined by the specifications of the tow vehicle and can usually be found in the owner's manual. To work out the maximum weight you can tow, deduct the Gross Vehicle Mass (GVM) of the tow vehicle from the GCM.

To work out what extra weight of household equipment and personal items you can add and still remain within the GCM, ascertain the tare (or unladen) weight of the caravan. A rule of thumb for the weight of goods for two people is at least 300kg in a small van and up to 500kg in a larger unit. People tend to pack more 'stuff' if they have space for it. It is preferable to have a tow vehicle that allows a reasonable amount of leeway.

When driving, take care with the following:

- **Posts and trees close to the edge of the road** can cause a problem where the camber slopes towards the gutter. The camber will cause the top edge of the van to angle closer to any nearby posts and trees.
- If you are parked with a **post or parking meter very close to the back of the van** you should pull out gradually so the rear of the van does not hit the post. The section behind the rear wheels will swing in as you pull out.
- Your caravan is probably wider than the towing vehicle so you need to be conscious of this extra width at all times. Your **towing mirrors will be the widest part of the combination**.
- When turning you must **take the corner wider** than you would otherwise because the caravan will cut the corner short. If you are turning left the van could easily hit the edge of the gutter. Watch how semitrailer drivers negotiate a corner.
- The cornering characteristics of the combination will be much poorer than the towing vehicle alone, and **corners have to be taken at lower speed**.

Authors' tip:

When reversing, where possible have the caravan turning to the driver's right-hand side so the van remains within the driver's sight so he/she can monitor what is happening. If the van is being turned to the passenger's side it is out of sight of the driver.

Driving tips

- **Night driving** – Dim headlights if you are following within 200m of another vehicle, when you are 200m from an approaching vehicle, and just before a crest if you can see the glow of approaching headlights. Do not use fog lights unless you are in fog.
- **Descending mountains** – Maintain a safe speed by changing to a lower gear and only use the brakes from time to time as required. Brakes can overheat if you maintain a light pressure all the way down a hill. Use exhaust brakes if they are fitted to your vehicle.
- **Driving in rain, fog, dust or smoke** – Turn on the headlights, decrease driving speed and increase the following distance.
- **Snow** – Check that the appropriate tyres are fitted to your vehicle and that they are in good condition. When you arrive in the snow country, hire chains and find out how to put them on. If your vehicle has dual rear wheels it needs chains on one tyre in each set of duals. Turn on the headlights, decrease driving speed and increase the following distance.

- **Both acceleration and braking will be much slower** when you are towing a van.
- Large trucks push air in front of them and this will have a noticeable effect particularly on full-height caravans. Drivers need to **keep as far away from oncoming trucks as reasonably possible**. When you feel the buffeting effect on your vehicle, avoid overreacting and making excessive steering wheel corrections.
- **Crosswinds** will be very noticeable when towing a van, so be prepared in high wind areas. These places are usually signposted.

See p87 for more detailed information.

Smoke across road

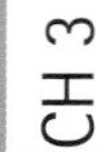

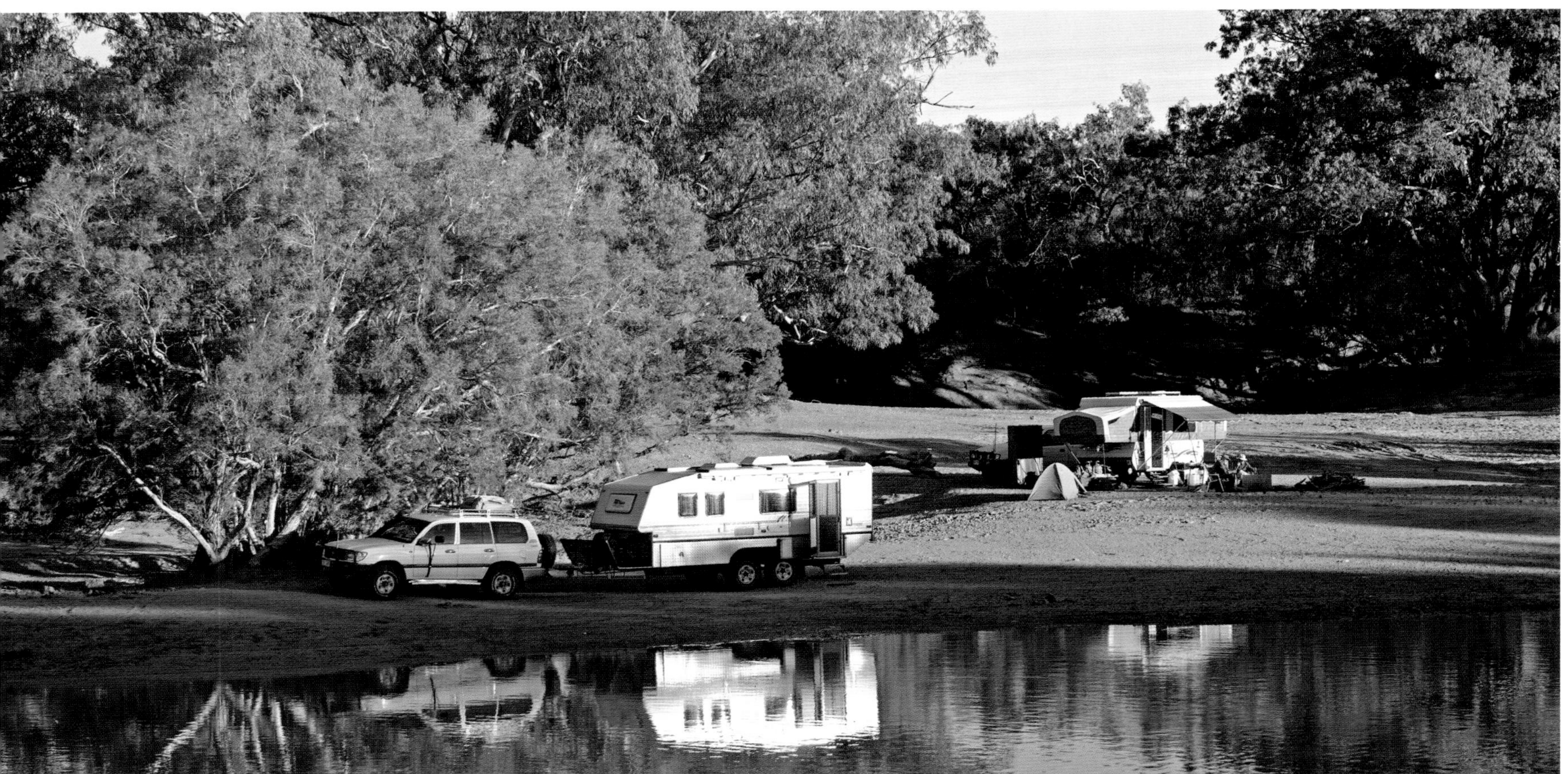

Camping on the banks of Cooper Creek, Windorah, QLD photo: splitimage

Motorhomes or campervans

Weight

Excess weight in motorhomes can lead to an increased risk of mechanical and tyre failure as well as the possibility of being put off the road if the vehicle is found to be overweight. Before adding extra equipment, ensure that there is sufficient leeway between the Tare (unladen) Weight and the legal maximum loaded weight, the Gross Vehicle Mass (GVM).

The **Tare Weight** is the weight of an unoccupied and unladen vehicle with ten litres of fuel and full fluid reservoirs (oil and coolants), but does not include extras added after manufacture, weight of stored water and personal belongings. It is usually calculated that two people in a small campervan will have in excess of 300kg of household equipment and personal belongings, and that this weight will be 400kg to 500kg in larger motorhomes where people tend to carry more 'stuff'. To this amount add the weight of the after-manufacture additions (eg microwave, TV), plus water and the weight of the driver and passenger.

Check other paperwork with the vehicle for the **GAWR (Gross Axle Weight)**. If you are concerned that the total weight of your laden motorhome might exceed the GVM, check it on a weighbridge.

- Fill the water and fuel tanks and stock up the motorhome.
- Firstly weigh the whole vehicle, allowing for the weight of its usual driver and passengers.
- Secondly, ensure that the weight on each axle does not exceed the GAWR for that axle.
- Then weigh each wheel so you can try to achieve a reasonably even side to side weight distribution. Weigh motorhomes equipped with air suspension by individual wheel positions.

If you tow a trailer, the **ball weight** (usually 10% of the total weight of the trailer) has to be added to the weighbridge reading to find the total weight of the motorhome. If this exceeds the GVM or the axle weights exceed the GAWR, you will have to shed some equipment. If found to be overweight, some vehicles may be able to be modified and re-certified.

Water weighs 1kg per litre so empty the grey water tank often, and if you are in an area where you can easily obtain good water every day, just keep a couple of days' supply in the clean water tank. Petrol weighs .74kg per litre and diesel weighs .85kg per litre, so if your vehicle is loaded to near its maximum weight, do not travel with a full fuel tank unless you are driving in a remote area.

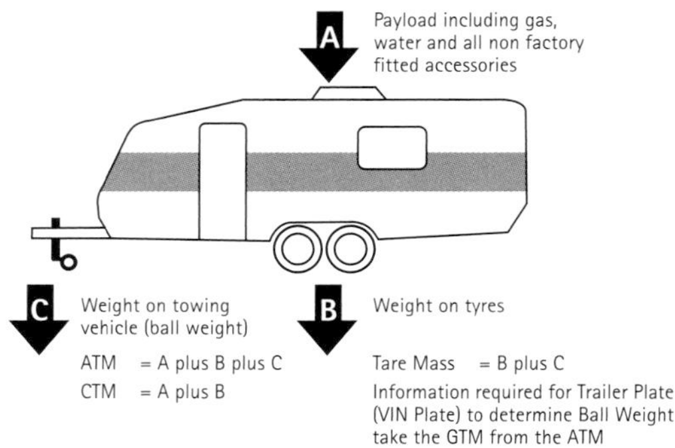

Restrictions of size

As campervans and motorhomes are considerably larger than the cars we have been accustomed to driving, it is imperative that you remain conscious of the height and width of the vehicle. You should **know the exact height** measured to the top of the roof vents, air conditioning unit or other projections. As a reminder, attach a sticker displaying the height dimension to the dashboard or back of the sun visor for ready reference. **Keep the width of the vehicle in mind.** The passenger side of the vehicle usually has protrusions (awning and/or outside light), and these will be the first to be damaged against posts.

In particular:

- Watch out for **service station awnings**. A sign indicating the height clearance may not be accurate and if there is any doubt, have the passenger outside the vehicle watching as you approach. If it looks close, don't do it! The line of sight is deceptive, and the clearance would be less than it appears, particularly as the vents and air conditioning unit are usually well back on the roof and not easily seen when standing in front.
- Take care with **low branches** on trees. Generally if you are travelling on a route used by buses and/or semi-trailers, the trees will be high enough to give you clearance, but that is not the case in rest areas and camping areas.
- Watch for **posts, shop awnings and trees close to the edge of the road** where the camber slopes towards the gutter. The camber will tilt the motorhome causing the top edge to angle closer to any nearby posts and trees.
- The **side-mounted rear vision mirrors are the widest** part of the vehicle.
- If you are parked on a street where a **post or parking meter is very close to the back** of the motorhome you may have to pull out gradually so the rear of the vehicle does not hit the post. When making a turn, the overhang (body extension behind the rear axle) initially moves opposite to the turn before quickly following the vehicle through the turn.

Braking, acceleration and handling

The following aspects will become apparent when driving a large vehicle:

- The **driver's position is generally considerably higher** than in a family car.
- **Both acceleration and braking are likely to be poorer** than a family car.
- When turning a corner in a vehicle with a wheelbase longer than you are used to, **take the corner a little wider**. A good example is how bus drivers negotiate a corner.
- Cornering characteristics will be much poorer than a car, and **corners should be taken at lower speed.**
- **Crosswinds** are more noticeable when driving a motorhome than a car.
- Large trucks push air in front of them and this will have a noticeable **buffeting effect** on many motorhomes. Smaller campervans and motorhomes with aerodynamic body shape will not be unduly affected.

Living in your caravan or motorhome

Gas stove & fridge

- LPG gas flames produce water vapour and high levels of carbon monoxide. This is not a problem when the stove is used for the time required for cooking, but if used for an extended period it can become dangerous. **Always have a window or roof vent open when using a gas stove.**
- If the stove gas jets are lower than normal, and when you turn a second point on the first one reduces, it is likely the **gas regulator** has developed a fault (unless the valve to the stove has been partly turned off). See a licensed Gas Fitter.
- If the gas flame continually extinguishes after it has been properly lit, the **thermocouple device** may be malfunctioning.

Refrigerator

Although it is legal to operate a fridge on gas while driving, it is unwise in a motorhome or campervan because the fuel tank is close to the ignition source. This is dangerous with a petrol-fuelled motor because gas from the petrol can be ignited. **Note** – The Australian Standards states "the minimum clearance between a fuel filler cap or fuel tank vent and an appliance flue or combustion air intake shall be one metre (except for vehicles fuelled by diesel)".

It is not so dangerous in a caravan where several metres separate the fridge from the fuel tank. With a caravan, the main danger would occur in the event of an accident. Where the gas fridge in a caravan is left running while travelling, it should be turned off before entering a service station driveway. Gas fridges must be turned off before boarding a vehicular ferry. *See p97.*

Water

Refilling water tank

When you are travelling, **check the quality of the local water** before adding any to your water tank. Towns in Western Queensland, northwest New South Wales and northeast South Australia draw their water from the Great Artesian Basin, and in some areas this water is very alkaline and not pleasant to drink, but in other areas it is excellent. Some towns in the area reticulate treated river or dam water. If possible, avoid bore water unless you taste test it. If you have to use bore water that has a smell, fill a container and let it stand for several hours. You might find it improves somewhat.

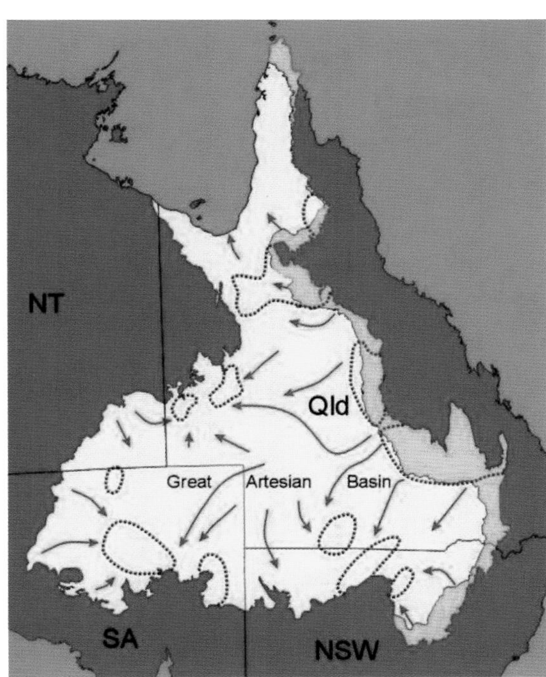

Map showing the extent of the Great Artesian Basin

Water tank

If you are concerned that your water storage tank may not be clean, a commercial product such as *Tank Fresh* or *Tank Clean* can be used and *Pure Tabs* added to the drinking water to maintain this cleanliness.

> **Authors' tip:**
>
> If you are heading into an area where only bore water will be available, it is probably worth filling some plastic bottles with good water beforehand, and keep that for drinking.

Hot water system

Gas hot water systems have a **sacrificial anode**, usually made of magnesium or aluminium, that helps prevent corrosion of the metal tank. Electrolysis eats away the metal anode instead of the metal of the tank, but once the anode is gone, the tank itself begins to corrode. The anode should be checked regularly and replaced to prolong the life of the tank. Some water, particularly bore water, can wear away the sacrificial anode at a greater rate.

When the hot water system is unused for a period of time, bacteria can react with the anode causing **hydrogen sulphide (rotten egg gas)** that will be obvious when you turn on the hot water tap. You can avoid having this smell by draining and flushing out the hot water system before a trip, or letting a couple of buckets of water flow through the hot water tap (without turning the heater on). A regular flow of water through the hot water system will prevent the gas from building up.

Water pump

Always turn off the water pump when it is not in use. Before driving, release the water in the pipes so they are not filled with water at full pressure when subjected to bumping and jarring from travelling.

Toilets

Emptying holding tanks

- A black-water tank can be emptied either **by gravity or pump**. The valve and hose are usually 75mm in diameter to allow all material in the holding tank to be evacuated.
- An electric (12 volt or 24 volt) **macerator pump** can be installed to grind the waste into small particles that can be evacuated through a 25mm garden hose. The advantage is that you do not have to be located directly over or next to a dump point to empty the tank. Carry a standard 75mm hose in case something goes wrong with the macerator.
- Unless you have a pump, a black-water tank can only be emptied into a **dump point that is low enough to allow drainage by gravity**.
- Whichever method you use, obviously the **hose will need flushing out after use**.

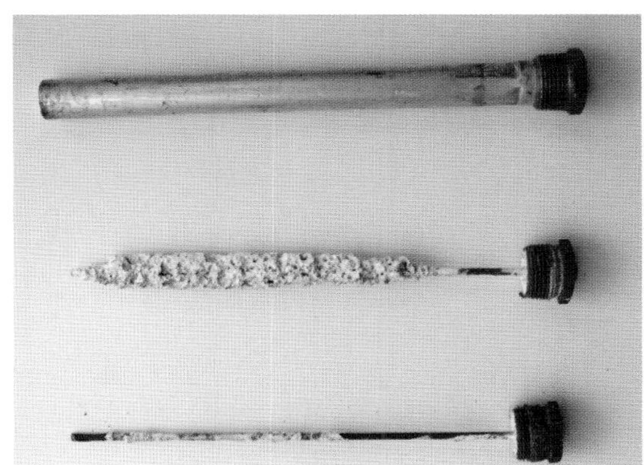

Hot water system anodes – new anode, anode that requires replacement and one that is long past its use-by date

Dump point in Bourke for motorhome and caravan toilet waste

Styles of toilets and black-water storage facilities

- **Built-in cassette** toilets are the most common, and can be either built into a bench or have a bowl that swivels out of the way when not in use. To flush, bench-style toilets use water from a small tank that is part of the toilet installation, while the swivel type uses water from the main water storage tank. Cassette toilets need emptying every three to five days, depending on usage. The cassette is removed through a small door in the sidewall of the motorhome or caravan directly beneath the toilet installation.
- **Portable toilet** – Small campervans or caravans often have a portable unit with a tank that detaches for emptying. This needs to be done about every three to four days.
- Toilet waste can be stored in a **black-water holding tank**. This needs emptying only every ten days or so, but can only be emptied into a dump point. Not all dump points can be accessed to empty a black-water tank.
- **Vacuum toilets** have a ceramic bowl, but are very noisy when flushed. The unit can be positioned metres away from the cassette or black-water tank. Although it is claimed that chemicals or other additives are not required, the job of emptying the unit will be less unpleasant if additives have been used.
- **A ventilated toilet system (SOG)** eliminates the need for any toilet treatment by using a fan to add fresh air and vent any odour to the outside. It can work on both cassette and black-water tanks, however the simplest installation is to a cassette unit where the ventilation is installed through the external door to the cassette compartment.

Options to treat toilet waste

Unless you have a ventilated toilet system, you need to consider what type of waste treatment to use. The priorities will probably be for an odour-free toilet and one that does not harm the environment when it is emptied.

You can use either chemicals or natural products. Chemicals will kill the bacteria in the waste and effectively prevent odour, but the waste can only be emptied into a large sewer system where it will be quickly diluted. The waste can be emptied into dump point, but not in environmental toilets, 'long drops' or septic systems. Natural products are designed to use naturally occurring bacteria to convert the waste quickly into safe end products. Waste treated with natural products can be emptied into natural waste systems, septic tanks or small sewer systems.

Authors' tip:

It is suggested you use the toilet with the flap to the cassette or holding tank in the closed position to prevent fumes entering the toilet compartment.

Natural toilet treatments

- *BioMagic* is an industrial bio-stimulant that is nonhazardous and completely biodegradable. Its properties allow for instant odour elimination upon contact with malodorous molecules and can be used in the treatment of liquid and solid organic waste. The formula is designed to hyper-accelerate the activity of indigenous microbes, mainly facultative anaerobes, inhabiting waste stream environments by providing an abundance of oxygen (electron acceptor) for metabolism to occur.
- *Odour-B-Gone* is an environmentally friendly treatment in tablet form.

Chemicals used to treat toilet waste

- **Formaldehyde** is toxic and will kill and retard all bacterial growth. It is a widely used chemical, marketed as a blue perfumed liquid.
- **Paraformaldehyde** releases formaldehyde when it is heated, and it is very toxic. It is usually packaged in dry powder sachets.
- **Benzaldehyde** does not contain formaldehyde, but it is in the same chemical family and acts the same way.
- **Bronopol** is a bacterial pesticide that when added to sewerage releases formaldehyde.
- **Dowicil** is a bacterial pesticide that will damage any waste system.
- **Ammonium** compounds are bacterial pesticides.
- **Sodium Perborate** when added to water releases hydrogen peroxide that kills bacteria.

Hints

- Where possible use **dump points to empty toilet waste**, and this is particularly important if you are using chemicals. Dump points are listed in this publication (see p39-43), and virtually all are free of charge. Most caravan parks have a dump point for use by park guests, and some will allow non-guests to use it, usually for a fee.

To keep the seals of cassette toilets pliable and operating properly, occasionally spray a small amount of olive oil around the area of the seal when you have emptied the unit and are reinstalling it. A light spray inside the toilet bowl helps cleaning.

- If you find that the low level of a portable toilet makes it difficult to use, place the toilet on a Fiamma caravan step with a sheet of non-slip material on top.
- If you use either environmentally friendly additives, or no additives, it is often suggested that you use Marine & RV toilet paper, however inexpensive single ply toilet paper breaks down just as easily. Do not use thick soft paper.

Hints for inside

Following are some ideas that come from years of travelling experience.

- **Weight distribution** – Pack heavy items in low cupboards or in under-floor storage bins to keep the centre of gravity as low as possible. Heavy items should be placed between the axles in a campervan or motorhome, and close to the axle in a caravan. Consider the location of in-built heavy items such as the fridge and water tanks to achieve an even weight distribution across the vehicle.

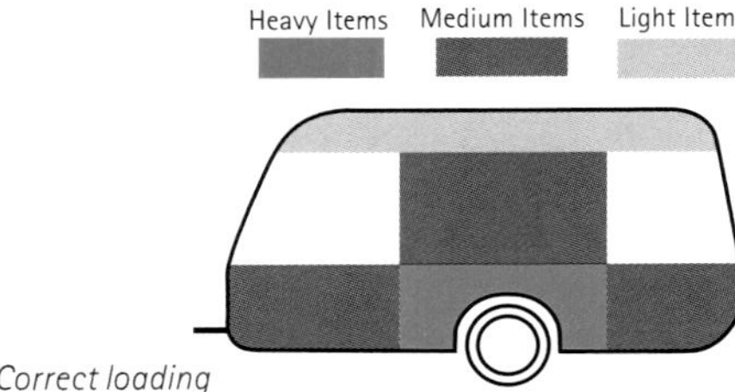

Correct loading

- **Stove** – If the gas stove is near the door of the motorhome or caravan, the wind can extinguish the flame. Campers use various ingenious (flameproof) devices as wind shields. To prevent the wire rack on the cooktop from rattling when the vehicle is moving, place a folded tea towel under the glass cover.
- **Refrigerator** – The door shelves, particularly the top one, are the warmest part of the fridge. If you are travelling in hot weather, or if your fridge is not very efficient, do not store milk or meat in the door. If a milk bottle has been opened, close it securely and lay it down on a shelf, but put it in a plastic bag to catch any stray drops that might leak. If you stand opened milk bottles in a door shelf, fill the shelf so the bottle does not tip over and leak when you are travelling. If you only have a few items in the fridge (probably an unlikely scenario) fill some of the empty space with plastic containers or bottles filled with water or ice (made before you leave home). Select containers with securely fitting lids to prevent spillage. Do not overfill the fridge to the extent that you have to hold the door closed to do up the catch because it is likely the bottom edge of the door will not be fitting tight, and cold air will seep out. *Refer to the section on Fridge Efficiency on p67.*
- **Condensation** – The air around us contains water in vapour form that is measured as relative humidity. In the confined space of a caravan or motorhome extra water vapour is added to the air by many sources, such as boiling pots, gas stoves and even our breath. When this water vapour is more than the air can support, the excess will condense when it comes in contact with a cold surface. When the condensation occurs on windows or even the ceiling it will not cause a problem, however it can develop into mildew if it occurs in areas such as under beds, or in cupboards or wardrobes. Condensation cannot be eliminated, but it can be minimised or reduced:
  - Open windows to improve ventilation, although this will not be desirable in cold weather when condensation is more likely to occur.
  - Raise the temperature of the air because warmer air can support more moisture.
  - When cooking, put lids on saucepans.
  - Do not leave a kettle or saucepan boiling longer than necessary.
  - If you have an exhaust fan over the stove use it to vent the moist air from cooking.
  - Try to avoid drying wet clothes inside the caravan or motorhome.
  - Leave wet items such as umbrellas and coats outside under the awning so you do not add extra moisture into the closed living space.
  - If moisture condenses on the windows, wipe it off with a sponge or small cloth that can be wrung out. Do not use a towel that is then spread out to dry. This is simply recycling the water.
  - Condensation can occur under the mattress of a bed over the cab because the cab gets cold by losing heat through the glass of the windscreen and windows. In cold weather use solar screens to retain heat in the cab and consequently keep the bed over the cab warmer.
- **Morning tea** – When you are travelling, it will save time at morning tea time if you prepare a thermos flask of hot water at breakfast. Stainless steel flasks are ideal because they will not break in a mishap.
- **Stopping a tablecloth from blowing off** – Sew the corners of the tablecloth so it slips down over the table like a fitted bed sheet. Alternatively, place a circle of elastic around the table and cloth just under the tabletop. Commercial products are available: plastic clips that hold the cloth to the tabletop or weights that attach to the cloth. The latter are not ideal because in very windy conditions the cloth, with weights attached, can blow upwards and break something on the table.
- **Carrying china plates** – Just because you are travelling, it doesn't mean that you have to eat off plastic. China plates can be transported easily if the stacked plates are separated by a piece of non-slip sheeting. Rolls of this material can be purchased from camping stores and cut to size.
- **Carrying glassware safely** – You can still use your favourite crystal glasses. Each glass should have a small bag made out of thick fabric (maybe part of a worn-out towel), with a drawstring top or a bag long enough to tuck the top half inside the glass. A simpler but less attractive solution is to use old socks.
- **Food** – Where possible take dehydrated food rather than canned, because it weighs much less. In small towns shops may not have extended trading hours so keep some long life milk and cans of chunky soup for emergencies. When stocking up with fresh fruit and vegetables, remember the quarantine zones. *Refer p99 or the Atlas for details.* If you are planning to drive on rough or corrugated roads, take extra care packing food items because vibrations can cause bottles and cans to move around and break, resulting in quite a mess. Put some form of padding (towelling or non-slip plastic) in the bottom of the shelf or drawer and use some protection (bubble wrap or a few layers of newspaper held with a rubber band) around individual items. Lay a folded towel across the top.
- **Carrying drinking water or wine casks** – Wine casks should be carried with the valve upwards, and it is wise to carry them in a plastic tub because the bladder can wear through with rubbing when travelling. (Remember to consider alcohol restrictions if you are travelling in areas where these apply, for example Cape York and Central Australia.) Any other plastic water containers should also be carried in a plastic tub or icecream container in case of leakage.
- **Linen** – Thin towels, either well-worn or cheaper ones, will dry faster than thick fluffy ones. Microfibre towels have gained popularity because they dry exceptionally quickly. If you have the space, take extra towels and sheets so laundry can be done when convenient.
- **Clothes** – The usual advice to travellers is to take half the clothes they planned to pack and twice the money – the same applies to a caravan or motorhome holiday. Don't even think about taking items that will require ironing. Many travellers wash their underwear and socks daily so only carry three sets (an extra set in case the washing doesn't dry quickly). Take a warm jacket because it gets cool at night in the inland, and in southern Australia it can be cold even in summer.
- **A tip for keeping clothes on the rail** – If the van or motorhome has a wardrobe at the back, it is likely some of the hangers will 'jump off' the rail if you strike a large bump. If the hanging rail is the cut out metal variety, try stretching a short octopus strap between the last cut-out hole at either end to prevent movement of the hangers when driving. If your clothes hang on a bar, you could attach a strap to an anchor point on each sidewall with the octopus strap immediately above the hanging bar to try to stop the hangers jumping off the rail.
- **Keeping the floor clean in wet weather** – Take some old bath towels to put on the floor immediately inside the door so anyone entering can dry their feet.

Towing

Drivers have a legal responsibility to other road users to drive safely to suit the conditions, and towing requires additional skills and safety precautions. Some vehicle manufacturers stipulate a speed when towing, and if this is the case with your vehicle, you are legally obliged to follow the recommendation. Check your owner's manual for towing recommendations.

In Western Australia a vehicle towing a caravan or trailer of any kind is limited to a maximum speed of 100kph, although other traffic can travel at 110kph in some areas.

Legal requirements

(Regulations can change from time to time – check with relevant State authorities.)

- The tow vehicle and caravan or trailer must comply with all relevant **standards for registration**.
- The tow vehicle and caravan or trailer must be in a **roadworthy and safe condition**.
- The total weight of the tow vehicle and trailer cannot exceed the **Gross Combination Mass (GCM)** for the tow vehicle.
- The combined length of the tow vehicle and trailer **cannot exceed 19m**.
- All caravans or trailers must be fitted with **a rear numberplate** and a **registration label** fixed to the left side or rear of the body, with the label facing outward.
- Towbars and couplings must **not obscure the tow vehicle's numberplate or rear lights** when the caravan or trailer is not connected.
- **Towing more than one trailer is prohibited**. For example, a trailer cannot be towed behind a caravan or fifth-wheeler.
- **People are not permitted to ride** in caravans, trailers or cars under tow by an 'A' frame.
- Vehicle combinations exceeding **7.5m in length are classified as long vehicles**. See p79 for restrictions.
- A **Safety Certificate (or Roadworthiness Certificate)** is required for a caravan or trailer with an ATM between 750kg and 3500kg when it is offered for sale or given away, re-registered or transferred from interstate registration except when selling or trading in to a dealer.

Definitions

- **Aggregate Trailer Mass (ATM)** is the total mass of a laden trailer when carrying the maximum load recommended by the manufacturer. This includes the tow ball mass.
- **Gross Trailer Mass (GTM)** is the mass transmitted to the ground by the axle or axles of a trailer when coupled to a towing vehicle and carrying its maximum load approximately uniformly distributed over the load bearing area. This does not include the tow ball mass.
- **Gross Combination Mass (GCM)** is the total weight of a tow vehicle and its load plus the trailer and its load.
- **Tare weight or Kerb weight** refers to an empty trailer or caravan or an unladen vehicle with only oil and radiator coolant and 10 litres of fuel.
- **Trailer axle capacity** is determined by the manufacturer, taking into account suspension, springs, axle strength and wheels.

Information sign on towing speed in WA

Obvious differences when towing

- Increased fuel consumption.
- Increased length – Allow for this length when overtaking and turning corners.
- Slower acceleration – This is particularly relevant when overtaking and when pulling into a line of traffic.
- Slower braking performance – You need to take additional care and maintain greater clearance between your vehicle and the vehicle in front.
- Reduced vehicle control – This can result in jack-knifing or a rollover.
- Reduced vehicle manoeuvrability.
- It will be much more difficult to find a parking place long enough for the combined rig. There are legal limitations on where long vehicles can park. *See p79.*

These effects become more pronounced on your vehicle as the trailer size and the mass of the load increase.

Authors' tip:

A driver of a Land Cruiser told us that when he towed a van the same height as his vehicle, the fuel consumption rose by 2 to 3 litres per 100km. When towing a low height camper trailer that weighs less and has less wind resistance, his fuel consumption increased by only 1.5 litres per 100km.

Tow vehicle

If you are buying a caravan or considering towing a car behind a motorhome you should determine your **vehicle's towing specifications**. Vehicle manufacturers publish Towing Guides for their vehicles, and the most critical point to consider is weight. The Towing Guide may not factor in the weight of goods and passengers in the tow vehicle that will add to its load and thereby reduce the weight it can safely tow. If you plan to tow a fifth-wheeler you will have to include the weight of the hitch assembly when calculating the load you can carry.

National Towing Regulations limit the mass a vehicle can tow as follows:

'A motor vehicle with a Gross Vehicle Mass (GVM) not exceeding 4.5 tonnes must not, without approval of the authorities, tow a trailer with a mass (including any load) exceeding:

- *the capacity of the towing equipment fitted to the vehicle; or*
- *the maximum towing capacity specified by the vehicle manufacturer.'*

If the vehicle manufacturer has not stipulated a recommended tow mass, then the vehicle may tow one and a half times its own unladen mass if the trailer has brakes. If the trailer does not have brakes fitted, then a one-to-one ratio applies.' (Please note that all trailers and caravans weighing over 750kg must have brakes.)

Authors' tip:

It is suggested that drivers not used to towing should start with a caravan considerably lighter than the weight of their tow vehicle, and it is also preferable to have one well under the vehicle's towing limit.

The construction of the body of the tow vehicle must be sturdy enough to attach a towbar, and some vehicles require **structural reinforcement** and/or **special suspension** to tow heavy loads.

Generally a rear wheel drive vehicle is more suitable to tow a caravan, although in most situations a weight distribution hitch will significantly improve the towing ability of front wheel drive vehicles. *See section below on weight distribution hitches.*

Modifications required to all tow vehicles

- Fit **electrical sockets for lighting**. A seven pin connector provides power to operate the trailer lights as well as the electrical brakes that are fitted to some caravans and heavy trailers.
- Fit a **suitable brake controller and connection** if the trailer has a GTM of 750kg or more.
- **Wide mirrors** are likely to be needed to give a clear and unobstructed view of the road.
- Automatic transmission vehicles may require an **extra transmission** oil cooler. This is standard on some late model vehicles.

Drivers should

- Refer to the owner's manual for **towing speed limitations** imposed by the vehicle manufacturer. It is your legal responsibility to follow these restrictions.
- **Limit heavy items** placed behind the rear axle of the tow vehicle.

Couplings

Weight distribution

For maximum safety, stability and vehicle control, both the caravan (trailer) and tow vehicle should be **level**. If the back of the tow vehicle is dragged down there is not sufficient weight on the front wheels, and this will adversely affect steering. This situation is particularly dangerous with a front-wheel drive vehicle on a steep up-hill slope where gravity will cause the weight to be transferred further backwards, resulting in loss of traction on the driving wheels.

If the caravan or trailer is not riding level, one of the following could be the reason:

- Incorrect tow ball height compared with the trailer coupling height.
- 'Ball weight' exceeding the recommended 10%, usually caused by incorrect weight distribution.
- Inadequate towing equipment.

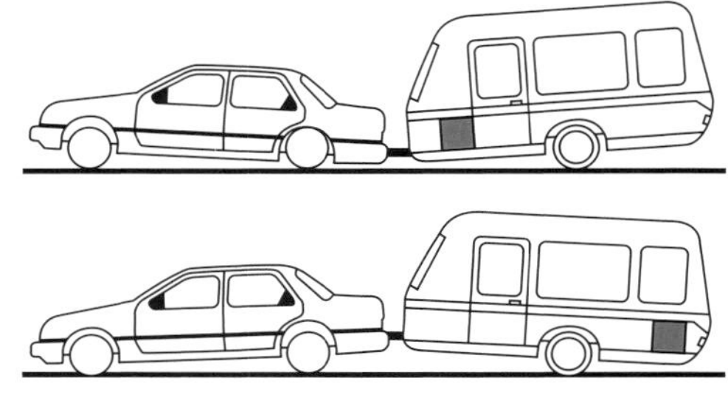

Incorrect loading

The towbar

If you buy a vehicle with a towbar already fitted, do not assume it matches the towing capabilities of the vehicle, or that it is designed for the load you want to tow. It is your responsibility to check it out. If you have kept your tow vehicle, but bought another caravan, have the towing equipment checked and re-adjusted to match the new van.

For safe towing, a properly designed and fitted towbar with an **adequate weight rating** is essential. All towbars manufactured after 1 July 1988 must clearly display the maximum load rated capacity plus the make and model of vehicle for which it is intended. Alternatively, it could display the manufacturer's name, trade mark and part number so you can ascertain whether the towbar suits your needs.

The towbar must have a towing and ball weight **capacity equal to or higher than the loaded weight (GTM)** of the caravan or trailer, and it must be suitable for use with the towing vehicle. There are two classes of towbar used generally – standard class 2 and heavy duty class 4. If you are planning to use a weight distribution system it is important to have a suitable towbar, and a heavy duty model is usually recommended.

The ball mount or tongue

This is the section of the towbar to which the tow ball is attached. It is usually a flat 75mm wide, 16mm to 20mm thick steel bar that may be either straight or curved to achieve the correct coupling height. If the ball mount obscures the number plate it must be removed from the towbar when the trailer is not attached.

The tow ball

Tow balls suitable for weights up to 3500kg must be **50mm in diameter** and should comply with **Australian Standard 4177-2**. The tow ball must be a one-piece element, and the shank should be 22.2mm in diameter. The top face of the sphere should be clearly stamped with the capacity (3.5t) and the tow ball diameter (50). The tow ball unit must be fitted to the vehicle with a locking washer and an appropriately sized nut. In accordance with Australian Standard 4177.2, the manufacturer's name or trademark must be stamped on the flange of the tow ball.

To tow properly and safely, the tow ball needs to be at the **same height as the coupling body** on the caravan drawbar. To determine the correct ball height, start by positioning the caravan on level ground. Measure the distance from the ground to the bottom of the coupling and also the distance from the ground to the base of the tow ball. If these are not very nearly the same, the ball mount (or tongue) may need to be adjusted or altered.

The coupling body

This is the section that is attached to the drawbar or 'A' frame of the trailer. It forms a socket for the tow ball and provides the necessary pivot point between the trailer and the towing vehicle. Coupling bodies used on trailers and caravans with an ATM up to 3.5 tonnes must comply with **Australian Standard 4177.3-1994**. Coupling bodies commonly in use can range in capacity from 750kg to 3500kg, and they must be marked with their load rating (750kg, 2000kg or 3500kg). Markings will also show the manufacturer's name or trademark if Australian made; the mark '50' indicating the size in mm and a code to indicate the serial number, batch and production date. If the coupling body is manufactured from cast iron or other non-weldable material, it will have the words 'do not weld'. It is important that the coupling body's capacity exceeds, or is at least equal to the fully laden weight of the trailer.

The traditional 50mm tow ball compatible coupling body fitted to the vast majority of trailers, boat trailers and caravans has its limitations when travelling on rough terrain. **Ball couplings** with swivels between the coupling body and the mounting plate on the trailer drawbar have more rough ground tolerance than fixed types.

The trailer's drawbar or 'A' frame

This is the front section of the trailer or caravan chassis to which the coupling body is attached with nuts, bolts and locking washers. Welding the coupling body is permitted on trailers under 1000kg. Under Australian Design Rules, the drawbar is required to be of sufficient strength for the specified trailer ATM (Aggregate Trailer Mass). Do not add additional heavy items (such as a spare wheel or storage bin) that will increase the load on the drawbar.

Safety chains

Safety chains are compulsory, and they must be strong enough to hold the trailer should the trailer coupling fail or become disconnected. Chains must comply with **AS4177-4** and have a size designation at least equal to the trailer ATM. A chain must be stamped with its capacity, the manufacturer's identification and the digits 4177.

Chain specifications

Towed vehicle GVM	Minimum number of chains	Nominal material size
0 to 1000 kg	1	6.3
Up to 1600kg	1	8.0
Up to 2500kg	1	10.0
Up to 3500kg	2	13.0

For specifications relating to towing vehicles weighing in excess of 3.5 tonnes, refer to **AS 2321-2001** *Short-Link chain for lifting purposes.*

The chains attach the drawbar of the trailer to the main towbar framework on the vehicle. The chain/s **must be permanently attached** to the trailer and **shackles are not permitted at the trailer connection**. Safety chains on trailers up to 3.5 tonnes ATM can be attached by welding provided the weld extends around half of the circumference of the link. The adjoining link must have free movement.

It is vital that the chains are attached to the main towbar framework and not to a detachable ball mount or tongue. The safety chain attachments must be mounted adjacent to the tow coupling and arranged so as to maintain the direction of a trailer in the event of coupling failure or disconnection.

The **length** of the safety chain/s must prevent the trailer's drawbar striking the ground if the trailer is detached from the towing vehicle. The chains should be as short as possible but there has to be enough slack to permit tight turns. If using two chains, attach them in an X-shape under the trailer tongue to prevent the forward end of the drawbar from hitting the ground if the coupling becomes disconnected.

Authors' tip:

We have heard of a couple of instances where a trailer has become detached on hitting a bump, but because there were two fairly short chains the drawbar did not spear into the road and there was no damage.

Load distribution hitches and suspension

Some caravanners feel it is necessary to fit stronger springs to the back of their tow vehicle because it goes down when the caravan is attached to the tow ball. However, if the suspension height is only altered because of the weight of the caravan or trailer then a weight distribution hitch could take care of the problem. All shock absorbers on the tow vehicle should be in good condition to help prevent instability when towing and you should ensure that the ball weight and suspension of the vehicle are appropriate to the combination.

A load distribution hitch should not be used to correct poor weight distribution in the caravan, however it will help to **level out the vehicle/trailer combination** by redistributing some of the load placed on the rear of the tow vehicle to its front axle. This sounds like magic, but it is really simple. The more tension that is placed on the weight distribution bars, the more weight is transferred forward onto the front wheels of the tow vehicle. Some of the ball weight is also transferred back to the axle of the caravan. If your vehicle manufacturer stipulates that this type of hitch is to be used with your vehicle when towing, you are legally obliged to do so. On some vehicles it is virtually essential to use a weight distribution hitch.

If you are towing a large (and heavy) caravan or trailer you should definitely consider using a load distribution hitch. If you already have a towbar, consult the manufacturer before using this equipment as it may overload the towbar and its components. Heavy duty towbars and attachments should usually be used with load distribution hitches.

Caravan hitch with load distribution device

Two basic types of load distributing hitches

- **Spring bar models** are rated for the actual tongue weight of the caravan or trailer. If the bars are set with too much tension, there would be loss of traction on the rear wheels, particularly when braking. If they are set with too little tension and therefore not transferring sufficient weight to the forward axle, towing stability will not be improved as much as it should be.
- **Non-spring bar models** use springs contained within the hitch. As well as distributing tongue weight forward, the spring action controls the upward and downward movement of the hitch.

Sway controls

An anti-sway device will **improve towing stability**, particularly if you tow a large van, by helping to minimise the sideways pivotal movement that occurs when a truck passes or overtakes. Air pushed ahead of an overtaking truck moves the unpowered caravan sideways making 'the tail wag the dog'. Sway controls also reduce sway caused by cross winds.

Different types of sway controls

- **Friction activated** – Swaying motion of the caravan activates a friction bar that will help control this movement. This type of sway control device requires ongoing adjustment and occasional overhaul or replacement.
- **Cam Sway Control Device** – Dual cam sway controls are applied to the spring bars of the caravan to reduce sway. This type of control device does not require ongoing adjustments to be made.
- **Electronic Sway Control System** – This system will electronically sense caravan or trailer sway and use the brake controller to apply the trailer brakes asymmetrically to offset any sway. This is a very effective system.

Ball weight

The ball weight is a proportion of the weight of the caravan (or trailer) that is transferred via the drawbar to the tow ball. A well-designed caravan or properly loaded trailer will have the weight balanced evenly over the axle so that no more than 10% of its GTM (Gross Trailer Mass) is supported by the tow ball. This weight should not exceed the load capacity of the towbar. If the ball weight is not heavy enough, towing will not be stable and the van may bounce about on the road. If the ball weight is too heavy, it can impose additional strain on the rear suspension of the tow vehicle. It also reduces the weight on the vehicle's front wheels, reducing driving stability.

The ball weight can be checked on a weighbridge after unhitching the tow vehicle follow these steps:

- Weigh the caravan or trailer with the wheels and the jockey wheel on the scales.
- Move the caravan's wheels off the weighbridge and weigh only the jockey wheel while it is supporting the draw bar.
- The weight registered for the jockey wheel is a good approximation of the ball weight, even though it is not at the point where the coupling body attaches to the towball.
- If the ball weight exceeds 10%, weight distribution within the caravan or trailer should be examined and items moved to achieve the desired result.

Touring near Bright Photo: Rob Boegheim

Braking systems

- Single-axled trailers with GTM not exceeding 750kg do not require brakes. Two axles with centres spaced less than 1 metre apart are regarded as a single axle.
- All trailers except single-axled trailers with GTM not exceeding 750kg must be fitted with an efficient braking system.
- Trailers weighing between 751kg and 2 tonnes GTM should have brakes operating on the wheels on at least one axle. For caravans and trailers exceeding 1000kg, independent brakes are strongly recommended, with electric brakes being the most common used.
- Trailers over 2 tonnes GTM must have brakes operating on all wheels.
- All brakes must be operable from the driver's seat of the towing vehicle except for overrun brakes.
- Overrun brakes may be used on trailers up to 2 tonnes GTM.

For more information refer to Standards Bulletin VSB1 issued by the Department of Infrastructure, Transport, Regional Development and Local Government, Canberra (www.infrastructure.gov.au).

Types of braking systems

- **Electronically controlled electric brakes** have a controlling device fitted in the tow vehicle to exercise automatic or manual control over the trailer brakes. This control module is fitted under the dash of the tow vehicle and wired to the car's battery, the stop light circuit and also to the seven-point socket into which the caravan plug connects. Its installation is virtually independent of the vehicle's electrical circuit and has no conflict with a car computer or anti-lock braking system (ABS). There are several different controllers available.
- **Hydraulic-controlled electric brakes** operate via a hydraulic controller connected to the tow vehicle's brakes. As the driver applies pressure to the brake pedal of the tow vehicle, the brakes of the trailer are also applied.
- **Hydraulic override brakes** operate with a master cylinder mounted on the trailer tongue. The forward momentum of the moving trailer pushing against the decelerating tow vehicle activates the master cylinder that produces hydraulic pressure to the trailer brakes. Brakes can be either drum or disc type.
- **Air brakes** are a very efficient system and operate with an 'air kit' fitted to the tow vehicle that supplies the air pressure required to operate the air brakes. The system is operated by depressing the brake pedal in the tow vehicle, resulting in proportional braking of the trailer. These brakes are usually only used on very large motorhomes.

Electric brakes are fairly simple, effective and low cost, although they do not meet Australian Standards for trailers over 4.5 tonnes GTM (loaded weight). Electric brakes are drum brakes, not disc, and can be controlled either electronically or hydraulically. These brakes are by far the most common type of brakes fitted to caravans and trailers and are very effective.

Brake controller

All electric or electric/hydraulic trailer brake systems need a controller to activate the brakes of the trailer. The controller allows the driver to set the ratio of braking between the car and the trailer, and applies the trailer brakes when the tow vehicle's brakes are applied. It also enables the trailer brakes to be applied manually.

Most brake controllers are attached under the dashboard of the towing vehicle. The controller is wired to the vehicle battery, the stop light circuit and the seven-point socket into which the trailer plug connects.

Features to look for in a brake controller

- Simple to set
- Easy access to all adjustments
- Full trailer braking will occur when the manual brake lever is operated
- It should sense the deceleration rate of the vehicle combination for safe and effective braking

Types of brake controllers

- **Time Delay Activated or 'solid state' controllers** apply a gradual voltage to the trailer's brakes using a Time Delay Circuit activated by applying the brakes in the tow vehicle.
- **Inertia Activated or Pendulum Style controllers** sense the stopping motion of the tow vehicle and the Pendulum Circuit applies a proportional voltage to the trailer's brakes. The Pendulum Circuit is enabled by depressing the brake pedal of the towing vehicle. When the control is properly adjusted, the trailer will decelerate at the same speed as the towing vehicle. Caution – Careful adjustment of the control module is very important. If the control module loses power from the vehicle battery, the stored data in memory will be lost and erratic operation may result. Set-up and readjustment will be required. The pendulum is a deceleration sensor and it can momentarily energise the trailer brakes under bumpy or adverse road conditions. The controller can be desensitised to this condition by adjusting the pendulum levelling arm to a slightly delayed position.

Caravan hitch with break-away brake system

Towing training course

A nationally accredited towing course is available in all capital cities and some major regional centres. This one-day course covers State regulations and focuses on practical hands-on training and should help you avoid some of the pitfalls, as well as teaching you how to get out of trouble if things start to go wrong.

Authors' tip:

This course should be considered a 'must' and could end up saving you a lot of money and heartache if you have an accident caused by inexperience. Even very experienced drivers who take their partners to the course so they can learn about towing, say they themselves learned a lot also.

Boat trailers

When loading a boat on a trailer, it should be placed so it does not extend further behind the axle than it does in front of the axle so the load is evenly distributed.

Towing a caravan

Firstly **check your vehicle owner's manual** for the manufacturer's recommendations regarding the weight you can tow, allowing for the weight you will add to the caravan. It is estimated that household necessities and personal belongings for two people will add at least 300kg to the weight of a small van, while in large caravans it could be 400kg to 500kg. People tend to pack more into a larger van.

When you are looking at caravans, be aware that not all caravans are created equal. A 22' van at the top end of the market is likely to weigh more than a 22' van in the lower price bracket.

Authors' tip:

A broad comment of "Sure, you can tow a 22 foot van with your vehicle" is not good enough. Check it out to avoid an expensive, and potentially dangerous, mistake. It is recommended that the loaded caravan should weigh less than the tow vehicle.

To get an unbiased opinion on the weight of caravan you can safely tow, **talk to a towbar manufacturer** who has no stake in selling you either a new tow vehicle or a caravan. Do not tow a van that is at the upper limit of the towing capacity of the tow vehicle. Either choose a lighter caravan or upgrade your tow vehicle.

You will need **towing mirrors wide enough to provide a clear and safe view**.

Mud flaps are already fitted to most vehicles, but you might consider **heavy-duty mudflaps** to help protect the front of the caravan. *See p74 for more details.*

Controlling a caravan

When towing a caravan, particularly a heavy one, the two main difficulties that may be encountered are 'pitching' and 'swaying' or 'snaking'. Neither situation is good, but the two together are even worse.

Pitching

This is the up-and-down movement of the rear of the tow vehicle that reduces the grip of the front wheels on the road. There are a number of reasons a caravan will exert excessive downward pressure on the towbar, and because this point is a considerable distance behind the rear axle, the downward pressure is 'magnified'. This causes the front of the tow vehicle to lift and the effect continues and grows more pronounced.

Suggestions to help avoid pitching:

- When attached, the **caravan should be riding level** and not be down at the front. This can be caused by the towball not being at the correct height.
- It is better if the tow vehicle **does not have an excess overhang behind the rear axle.**
- **Do not load heavy items in the rear** of the tow vehicle.
- Check that the **suspension of the tow vehicle is adequate** for the load it will carry.
- **Ball weight should be around 10%** – this indicates a well-designed van, but don't cause problems for yourself by incorrect loading.
- **Do not carry heavy items on the draw bar** (such as a spare wheel). The further forward a heavy item is located, the more weight it will transfer to the tow ball.
- **Do not store heavy items in the front or rear boot** of the caravan.
- When loading the van **place heavy items close to floor level near the axle.**
- **Install a weight distribution hitch.** *See section p88.*

Sway or snaking

This is the **side-to-side movement of a caravan** that can start when one van wheel encounters a dip or hump or runs off the bitumen. Other triggering factors can be a wet or slippery road, or a gust of wind caused by a passing truck. This swaying motion can quickly increase to a dangerous level where the van tries to spin the tow vehicle. As the wheels slide on the road surface, the result can be jack-knifing. **Factors in the caravan that can cause simple events to result in dangerous sway:**

- Unsuitable tow **vehicle and caravan/trailer combination.**
- Poorly designed caravan with the **axle located too far forward** leaving too much overhang behind the van axle.
- **Excess weight** at the back of the van.
- **Under inflated tyres.**
- **Incorrect tow ball height.**

Under inflated tyres and incorrect weight distribution are the easiest problems to correct.

Heavy items should be concentrated close to floor level and towards the centre of the van or trailer. Only light items should be stored in the front or rear lockers of a caravan. Try relocating movable heavy items to a position where they will balance in-built heavy equipment such as the refrigerator and water tank. Incorrect ball height can be corrected. If either a poorly designed caravan or a mismatched combination is the problem, the simplest solution is to fit an anti-sway device. Some drivers who travel regularly in areas with high winds (either natural or from passing road trains) find anti-sway devices helpful.

For details on correct tow ball height and anti-sway devices, see the section on Couplings p88.

Koorda Hotel, WA Photo: Pelusey Photography

Safety tips

- Ensure **you do not exceed the Aggregate Trailer Mass** specified by the trailer manufacturer, or the capacities of the tyres or tow coupling.
- **Attach two safety chains** in an X-shape under the towbar and ensure they do not drag on the ground. Even if the regulations do not require you to have two chains, it is a safer option.
- To make sure that the 12 volt power cable between the tow vehicle and caravan cannot drag on the ground, **pass the cable through the coupling handle.**
- **Never attempt to load a trailer** until it is hitched securely onto the tow vehicle.
- If you are towing a car on a trailer, **always unload the car before unhitching the trailer.**
- When hitching or unhitching a caravan or trailer (whatever type), either **apply the trailer handbrake** or **place blocks under the wheels** so the caravan or trailer is unable to move on its own.
- **Have someone guide you while reversing** – a hand-held UHF radio is helpful to communicate directions.
- Check the caravan or trailer **tyres** for proper inflation.
- Attach the electrical cable and check that all **lights and turn indicators** are working correctly.
- Although the speed limit when towing is the same as for other traffic (except in WA where it is 100kph) you must **adhere to the maximum speed recommended in your vehicle's manual.** Obviously you must also remain within the legal speed limit.
- When driving, **apply the accelerator, brakes and steering smoothly** and gently to avoid sway especially in wet or slippery conditions.
- **Avoid applying the towing vehicle's brakes if the trailer begins to sway or snake.** If the trailer is fitted with brakes that can be operated independently, apply the manual control firmly. Otherwise, continue at a steady speed or accelerate slightly at a gradually increasing speed until the sway stops.
- **When travelling downhill**, engage a lower gear in both manual or automatic vehicles to increase vehicle control and reduce brake strain.
- **Maintain a space of at least 60m** between your vehicle and the vehicle in front.
- When entering or leaving a service station driveway, drive slowly to avoid having the tow assembly or the rear of the caravan coming into contact with the bitumen and being damaged.
- When you stop for a break, **check the caravan or trailer coupling and safety chain/s** are still fastened securely. Also check the tyres.

Unusual way to transport a small car on a truck towing a fifthwheeler

Authors' tip:

People who change over to 'A' frame towing are amazed at how easy it is compared with towing by other means.

Towing a car behind a motorhome

Research indicates that around 12% of motorhomers tow a small car. To decide whether it is worth the expense and bother, consider how you plan to travel. Do you plan to stay in one place for a length of time when a car would be a great advantage? Some travellers have worked out other ways to take a car with them instead of towing.

Winching the bed to the side-wall to create a garage

Car after it is driven into the garage in the back of the motorhome

Factors to investigate

- Check that your **motorhome is suitable to tow** because some that have an extended chassis cannot do so legally. If you have a secondhand motorhome with a towbar fitted, don't assume that it must be legal. Check with the manufacturer or an engineer.
- If you are planning to use a standard trailer, check **what weight the trailer can carry**.
- If towing a car in other than a totally enclosed trailer, you need to **prevent windscreen, headlight and panel damage by stones** thrown up by the motorhome's wheels.
- **Check your trailer insurance policy** to ensure it covers 'accidents' at any time, whether or not the trailer is attached to your vehicle. You need to be insured, not only for damage to the trailer, but also for any damage it may cause to someone else's property.
- The length of the combination will exceed 7.5m so it is **regarded as a long vehicle**. *See p79.*

A multi-purpose car trailer that also carries a boat on top and bicycles on the back.

Different ways to tow a car behind a motorhome

- Carried on (or in) a **car trailer**. The car has no wheels on the ground.
- Using a **'car dolly'** where two wheels are on a trailer and the other two run on the road.
- Using an **'A' frame** where all wheels of the car are on the road and the car is connected to the towbar of the towing vehicle by a triangular shaped frame commonly known as an 'A' frame.

If you use a car trailer or car dolly, regulations regarding trailer weight and brakes apply (please see above).

A 4WD is winched onto the sloping ramp of the trailer for travelling

Standard trailer

- Around **10% of the total weight of the loaded trailer is carried by the tow ball** and this needs to be taken into account when working out the amount of gear that can be carried within the motorhome before exceeding the legal GV M.
- The **trailer must have tail lights, turn indicators, stop lights** and clearance lights if appropriate.
- Weighing around 300kg, a **tilting trailer is lighter** than a standard trailer and it requires no additional ramps.

Car trailer with ramps

Car on tilting trailer

Tow dolly

- Much **less than 5% of the weight of the loaded trailer will be transferred to the tow ball**. Examples: A Nissan Navara weighing 2 tonnes added 70kg to the tow ball, and a Magna station wagon weighing 1.7 tonnes added 50kg to the tow ball.
- With the front wheels of the vehicle on the trailer, the **majority of the weight is over the axle** of the dolly, helping with trailer stability.
- Check that the vehicle you are planning to tow is suitable for towing by this method.
- **Braking is on the wheels of the tow dolly** and not directly to the brakes of the towed car as with an 'A' frame device (see below).
- You **cannot reverse safely** as you can with a standard trailer.
- The vehicle **must be secured firmly** with nylon straps. Check them regularly for wear and tear.
- **Ensure the tilt bed dolly is securely locked** in the towing position after loading.

Tow Dolly

Tow Dolly with car secured

Braking systems of standard trailers and tow dollies

The braking systems required vary according to the Gross Trailer Mass (GTM) of the particular trailer as follows:

- Trailers up to and including 750kg do not require brakes.
- Trailers weighing between 750kg and 2000kg must be fitted with an efficient braking system operating on the wheels on at least one axle. The brake controller must be placed where it can easily be operated from the driver's seated position.
- Trailers weighing over 2000kg GTM require a brake system (breakaway brakes) that automatically applies if the trailer becomes detached from the towing vehicle. Trailers over 2000kg GTM must have brakes operating on all wheels.

'A' frame (or flat towing)

Section 294 (1) of the Australian Road Rules states:

The driver of a motor vehicle must not tow another motor vehicle unless:

a. *either:*

i. *the driver can control the movement of the towed vehicle; or*

ii. *the brakes and steering of the towed vehicle are in working order and a person who is licensed to drive the towed vehicle is sitting in the driver's seat of the towed vehicle, and is in control of its brakes and steering; and*

b. *it is safe to tow the vehicle.*

By using an 'A' frame device, the driver of the towing vehicle has control of the towed vehicle as required by Section 294(1)(a)(i) set out above. Although 'A' frame towing is legal Australia-wide, the regulations are not consistent, so if you plan to travel in every State in Australia at some time using an 'A' frame towing system, it will have to comply with the regulations in every State.

In New South Wales the 'A' frame towing regulations on braking differ significantly from those of the other States. If you drive in New South Wales using an 'A' frame device that does not comply with the Roads and Traffic Authority (RTA) regulations you are liable to receive a ticket. Refer below for a summary of important information from Vehicle Standards Information bulletin 41 (Guidelines for A-frame towing).

Discussions are planned to try to standardise regulations, but it is considered unlikely that all States will adopt the same rules. We have been advised that New South Wales RTA does not plan to change their regulations in the near future. We suggest you obtain a copy of your State's regulations and carry them with you, together with details of any certification you may be required to obtain.

You should get advice from a professional on whether your motorhome can tow, whether the vehicle you wish to tow is suitable for 'A' frame towing, and the equipment you will require. Two specialist companies are Hitch-n-Go (www.hitchngo.com.au) and Northcoach (www.northcoach.com.au).

Advantages of 'A' frame towing

- Very little weight (if any) is added to the towing motorhome.
- When the car is disconnected from the towing motorhome, only the 'A' frame towing device has to be stored, not a bulky trailer or tow dolly.

Disadvantages of 'A' frame towing

- The car cannot be seen by the driver of the motorhome unless a reversing camera or a stick-on wide-angle lens is used on the rear window.
- Reversing an 'A' frame combination is not recommended due to lack of directional control over the towed vehicle.
- The odometer of some towed vehicles will tick over when it is being towed, although later model cars with an electronic speedo will not accumulate kilometres while the ignition is off.
- If the combination is 7.5m long or longer, legal limitations apply. *See p79.*

Using A frame device to tow a car behind a motorhome

A frame towing equipment

Regulations for 'A' frame towing

Following is a guide to towing a vehicle that weighs less than 4.5 tonnes. If you wish to tow a heavier vehicle you should contact the relevant authority in your State.

Regulations that apply in all States:

- The loaded mass of the towed vehicle must not exceed the maximum capacity of any towing attachment fitted to the towed or towing vehicle including the 'A' frame, towbar and towball.
- If the tow vehicle has a GVM under 4.5 tonnes, the weight of the towed vehicle must not exceed the maximum towing mass specified by the towing vehicle's manufacturer. When the towing vehicle has a GVM exceeding 4.5 tonnes, it may tow a loaded vehicle up to, but not exceeding the towing vehicle's GVM provided the GCM is not exceeded.
- The overall length of the combination must not exceed 19m.
- No-one can ride in the towed vehicle.
- Towbars and safety chains must comply with AS 4177.4. *Please refer to the details on p87.*
- The loaded mass of the towed vehicle must not exceed the towing capacity of any component in the combination.
- The parking brake of the towing vehicle must be able to hold the combination stationary on a 12% gradient.

The 'A' frame coupling must:

- Be designed and constructed with sufficient strength to hold the vehicles together in tow and must comply with Australian Design Rule 62 (Mechanical connections between vehicles) relevant to the laden mass of the towed vehicle.
- Permit an adequate amount of angular movement between the towing and towed vehicles to cater for road undulations.
- Be secured to a substantial body member of the towed vehicle such as a sub-frame or chassis member.
- The coupling and towbar must not obscure the numberplate or lights on the rear of the towing vehicle when the towed vehicle is not attached.
- The 'A' frame and any attachment that could constitute a dangerous projection must be removed from the towed vehicle before it is driven on public roads.

Steering an 'A' frame combination:

- The 'A' frame towing system must provide safe and adequate steering control for both vehicles whilst being towed in combination.
- The vehicle combination must be capable of turning within a 25m diameter circle, measured at the outer wheel track.
- When travelling in a straight line on a level smooth surface, the towed vehicle must track in the path of the towing vehicle without shifting or swerving more than 100mm either side.

Differences in regulations:

- In all States except Victoria, the towed vehicle must be **registered**.
- Northern Territory, Queensland, South Australian, Victorian and Western Australian regulations specify that the **space between the vehicles** is not to exceed 2m when towing. Tasmanian regulations specify that there should be 'less than 4m' between the two vehicles and in New South Wales the space between the two vehicles is 'not to exceed 4m when towing'.
- In New South Wales a removable sign must be displayed at the rear of the towed vehicle with the words '**VEHICLE UNDER TOW**' in characters at least 75mm high on a contrasting background i.e. red on white, or black on yellow. In no other State are you required to display such a sign, although you may do so.
- New South Wales regulations require that a copy of the **engineer's certificate and a copy of VSI 41** must be kept with the vehicle combination at all times. All other States and the Northern Territory recommend that their Information Sheet, together with any reports and approvals, be carried with the vehicle.
- Northern Territory and Western Australian regulations require that the 'A' frame coupling must be marked with the **VIN/chassis numbers** of both the towing vehicle and the towed vehicle as well as the manufacturer's name or trademark and the rated capacity. All other States require that it be marked with manufacturer's name or trademark and the rated capacity.
- In Western Australia and South Australia the **maximum** speed when 'A' frame towing is 100kph or the posted speed limit, whichever is the lesser. In other States and the Northern Territory, the posted speed limit applies.

Braking of 'A' frames

The weight of the towing vehicle compared with the weight of the loaded towed vehicle (including the weight of the 'A' frame) is the combination's **Towed Mass Ratio**. (*Note*: The usual term is 'Towed Mass Ratio', however New South Wales regulations use the term '*Towing Ratio*' and Tasmanian regulations use the term '*Towing Mass Ratio*'.) Example – If the tow vehicle weighs 3.5 tonnes and the loaded towed vehicle weighs 1 tonne, the combination's Towed Mass Ratio is 3.5 to 1. In New South Wales and Tasmania the ratio is calculated using the loaded weight (or GVM) of the towing vehicle, while in the other States and the Northern Territory the tare (or unladen) weight of the towing vehicle is used.

The Towed Mass Ratio must be at least 3.5:1 (as in the example above) to provide adequate towing stability and braking performance, but it is highly recommended that the ratio be greater than this (eg at least 4:1) for improved handling, control and braking.

All States have the following braking requirements that must apply, irrespective of the Towed Mass Ratio:

- Combination Gross Mass under 2.5 tonnes when driving at 35kph must stop in 12.5m.
- Combination Gross Mass in excess of 2.5 tonnes when driving at 35kph must stop in 16.5m.

Specific regulations on braking of 'A' frames

New South Wales – If the towed vehicle's overall mass or its rated GVM is less than 750kg, operating its brakes is not mandatory, however if the GVM of the towed vehicle exceeds 750kg, the brakes must be operable from the driver's seated position in the towing vehicle. The towed vehicle must have emergency breakaway system or safety chain/s or cable/s, with the material size of the chain and number of safety chains dependent on the weight of the towed vehicle. Any vehicle driving in New South Wales using an 'A' frame device must comply with these regulations.

All other States and NT – Where the Towed Mass Ratio exceeds 3.5:1 there is no requirement for the brakes of the towed vehicle to be operable. Where the Towed Mass Ratio of the combination is *not* more than 3.5:1 the brakes on at least one axle of the towed vehicle must operate when the driver of the towing vehicle applies the brakes of the towing vehicle. It is not acceptable to utilise the park brake of the towed vehicle to achieve this.

Authors' tip:

It is our opinion that travellers who want to tow a vehicle using an 'A' frame device should consider installing a brake system even if it is not required in their own State. Some brake systems are not expensive. Not only does it make the towing safer, it keeps you within the law in New South Wales so you don't have to worry when you cross the border.

Lighting when towing with an 'A' frame

The following lamps must be fitted to the rear of the towed vehicle and must be operational whilst under tow:

- Two turn signal lamps showing yellow (or amber) light to the rear.
- Two stop lamps showing red light to the rear.
- Two reverse lamps showing white light to the rear.
- Two tail lamps showing red light to the rear that operate effectively at night or in hazardous weather conditions.
- One registration plate lamp at the rear of the towed vehicle to illuminate the registration plate.

These lamps may be arranged on a portable lamp bar providing it is securely fastened to the rear of the towed vehicle.

Inspection and certification regulations

NEW SOUTH WALES

Persons contemplating the use of an 'A' frame towing device must obtain an engineering certificate from an RTA recognised signatory.

1. The engineer's certificate must include details of:
   a. The towing & towed vehicles.
   b. The critical components of the 'A' frame and braking system.
   c A copy of a completed checklist found on page five of the information sheet.
   d. A statement of compliance with the requirements of VSI No. 41.
2. The engineer's certificate and a copy of Information Sheet VSI 41 must be kept with the vehicle combination at all times while 'A' frame towing, and must be presented to an authorised RTA officer or police on request.'

Note – This regulation applies not only to New South Wales registered vehicles, but also to interstate vehicles travelling in the State and towing using an 'A' frame device.

NORTHERN TERRITORY

Unless the 'A' frame is a proprietary item that has been designed and is appropriately marked as being suitable for the make and model of the towed vehicle, the 'A' frames and connecting hardware, including the connection of the 'A' frame and safety chains to the towed vehicle must be certified by a recognised engineering signatory.

QUEENSLAND

Persons wishing to tow a vehicle weighing less than 4.5 tonnes GVM may need to seek advice from a registered professional engineer to ensure that the 'A' frame device that is intended for use meets the technical requirements set down by Queensland Transport.

SOUTH AUSTRALIA

Persons wishing to undertake 'A' frame towing may need to seek advice from a Recognised Engineering Signatory or a Chartered Professional Engineer to ensure the 'A' frame device meets the relevant technical requirements.

TASMANIA

Unless it's already certified and fitted with a plate, it is necessary to have an 'A' frame coupling inspected and certified by either a qualified engineer or an Engineering Signatory to confirm that it meets ADR 62. Certification will involve inspection of both vehicles. A modification plate will be issued for attachment to approved and certified 'A' frames.

VICTORIA

Persons wishing to undertake 'A' frame towing may need to seek advice from a Vehicle Assessment Signatory Scheme (VASS) Signatory to ensure the 'A' frame device they intend to use meets the relevant technical requirements.

WESTERN AUSTRALIA

Persons wishing to undertake 'A' frame towing may need to seek advice from a recognised engineering signatory or a professional Chartered Engineer to ensure the 'A' frame meets the relevant technical requirements.

Vehicle compatibility

Most manual transmission vehicles can be towed with an 'A' frame, however automatics may require a transmission lube pump or axle disconnects. Some vehicles are not suitable for towing by this method, specifically the following constant 4WD vehicles: Suzuki Jimny, Toyota RAV 4, Honda CRV and Holden Cruz. Refer to the owner's manual for specific information on your vehicle. With some cars the bull bar and nudge bar may have to be removed or modified to allow the 'A' frame equipment to be fitted.

The steering wheel locking mechanism of the towed vehicle must be placed in the 'unlock' position when it is under tow by an 'A' frame. With most vehicles this requires the key to remain in the 'accessories' position and therefore a second car key is needed to lock the door.

'A' frame equipment

- The cheapest and simplest is a **metal triangle with a coupling** at the peak where it connects to the tow ball, and two fixed connection points on the arms to connect to the vehicle being towed. With this type of connection, the car has to be driven to the exact spot to enable the 'A' frame device to be connected to the car. It is a two-person job.
- A more expensive type of 'A' frame has **adjustable telescopic side arms** that collapse and extend. This makes connecting much easier because the car does not have to be precisely positioned.
- There is also a **folding 'A' frame** that does not have to be disconnected from the rear of the motorhome when it is not being used.
- A **base plate** (also called an adaptor or mounting) will need to be attached to the front of the towed vehicle.

Carrying a load in the towed vehicle

- You can legally carry a load in the towed vehicle provided the **loaded mass of the towed vehicle does not exceed the capacity of any component** in the combination.
- Any load should be **placed as low and as centrally as possible**, so it does not adversely affect handling of the combination.
- The tare mass of the towing vehicle must remain greater than **3.5 times the mass of the towed vehicle** when the vehicle is loaded.

Authors' tip:

If you are towing a car on an 'A' frame, as a precaution you can ask the passenger to stay outside as you pull out. He/she should watch to see that the wheels of the car are turning, indicating that the brakes have been released, and that the front wheels follow the direction of the tow vehicle indicating that the steering wheel lock has been released.

Towing a fifth-wheeler trailer

A turn-table hitch is located on the flat bed of a utility or truck, and for optimum handling it should be located in front of the axle. If the bed of the truck is not long enough to allow the trailer to make tight turns with the hitch in this position, a sliding hitch can be installed.

When the fifth-wheeler trailer is attached, around 25% of the trailer's weight is transferred to the tow vehicle. By placing the hitch even 50mm in front of the rear axle, this weight is directly over the suspension of the tow vehicle and a small proportion is transferred onto the front wheels. Handling of the rig is vastly improved compared with a caravan where the added weight is on a tow ball behind the rear bumper.

If the truck is not carrying between 20% and 30% of the weight, it could mean the hitch is too high, transferring too much weight backwards. The weight is then carried on the axle of the trailer causing excessive load on both axle and tyres, and resulting in poor handling.

You can check if the hitch is carrying the correct proportion of weight by weighing the rig at a weighbridge. Follow this procedure:

- Weigh the tow vehicle while the trailer is attached (but not weighing the trailer) = A
- Weigh both the truck and trailer = B
- Weigh the truck alone = C

Deduct the weight of the truck alone (C) from the weight of truck and trailer (B) to give you the weight of the trailer (D). Deduct weight of the truck (C) from weight (A) to give you the weight carried on the hitch. The result should be 20% to 30% of the weight of the trailer (D).

Static fifth wheeler hitch

Maintenance

Vehicle maintenance

Before setting out check:

- oil
- radiator water
- other fluid levels
- batteries
- tyres

Make sure these are working correctly:

- headlights
- turn indicators
- running lights
- tail and brake lights

Ensure you have onboard a couple of spare globes (including interior globes) and fuses, because they may not be readily available in some areas.

Tyres

It is very important that **tyre pressures** are checked regularly, as driving with tyres either under inflated, or to a lesser extent over inflated, will lessen their life and can seriously affect handling. Check the specifications of your vehicle (usually on the driver's door pillar) for the manufacturer's recommended tyre pressures. *See p76 for further details.*

Monitor the **condition and depth of tread**, and rotate (swap around) the tyres periodically, including the spare tyre, so all tyres wear evenly. Tyres deteriorate with age as well as wear, so you will get the maximum use out of them if you rotate all the tyres. Keep your spare properly inflated because you never know when you might need it, and it is useless if it is flat.

Tips for tyres on motorhomes

- If you have dual rear wheels, the quick daily check of inflation of the inner rear tyre can be carried out by lightly tapping it with a hammer or other object, and it should produce a musical note when inflated.
- If changing a wheel, you may need a block of wood in addition to a jack, because sometimes the jack cannot raise the vehicle high enough to change the wheel.
- A second jack may be needed if the corner of the vehicle with the flat tyre is sitting too low to allow the principal jack to be inserted.
- If the vehicle is on soft soil and you can't raise the vehicle high enough with the jack to remove the wheel, you can dig around the flat tyre so that it can be more easily removed. A piece of flat solid wood can be useful to prevent the jack sinking into soft ground under the weight of the vehicle.
- You may not be able to undo the wheel nuts using just the wheel brace. A simple solution is a length of galvanised pipe, around a metre long, to slip over the handle of the wheel brace for extra leverage.
- A small mechanical pump or 12 volt compressor can be used to attend to those 'slow leaks' where an immediate change of tyre may not be essential.

Sliding fifth wheeler hitch

Battery

Whilst all batteries fluid levels need careful monitoring, experts advise that 'house batteries' in particular require more frequent topping up in view of the regular substantial re-charging they receive. *See p61 for more information.*

Servicing and warranty

If you are buying a vehicle, check the warranty, and also check the owner's manual for services specified. Regular servicing and maintaining records of them is important.

With a new vehicle, only dealers can repair faults covered under the manufacturer's warranty. Although manufacturers prefer that you return the vehicle to their dealer network for maintenance, this is not essential to maintain your warranty provided servicing is done in accordance with the manufacturer's requirements. You would usually save a considerable amount by having regular servicing done by an independent mechanic, although it is recommended that genuine parts be used if the vehicle is still under new-car warranty. Read your warranty carefully and be careful not to miss a scheduled service.

If you do experience problems with a new vehicle, keep a record of the time, date, place, speed you were travelling and odometer reading each time the problem occurs. This record will be invaluable if it later turns out that the problem is recurring.

House maintenance

Your 'mobile home' is much more complex than the chassis or vehicle it is built upon. The house part needs regular maintenance, and this will vary according to the type of vehicle and facilities on board. The obvious points that need attention are:

- Inspect and re-caulk as appropriate any **exterior joins** in the body, particularly on the roof and around hatches and windows. Watch for any discolouration of the interior roof or walls indicating that water has entered, and then act quickly to avoid major damage. Check regularly if the vehicle is stored in the open.
- Check all **appliances** to ensure their safety, and check **gas, plumbing and electrical systems and lines**.
- **Dry powder fire extinguishers** need a couple of minutes' maintenance every month or so as the powder tends to settle and compact within the unit.
  - Remove and invert the extinguisher and gently bump the base against the palm of your hand.
  - Gently move it back and forth sideways to free the compacted powder until you can feel it moving freely.
  - Check the gauge on the extinguisher to ensure it is fully charged.
- Check that the **smoke alarm** is still operating and that the batteries have not gone flat while the caravan or motorhome has been waiting for its next trip.
- If you have a **gas hot water system**, at least annually inspect, and if necessary replace, the 'sacrificial anode'. *See p85 for details.*

Whilst the owner can do these jobs themselves, dealers and service organisations can perform this service professionally as part of a standard motorhome or caravan service. Work on gas equipment or 240 volt electrics can only be performed by licensed tradesmen. No qualifications are required to work on 12 volt electrics, but unless you are sure what you are doing, leave it to the experts.

Storage

Fridge

After emptying the fridge and wiping it out with a cloth or sponge dipped in vinegar, leave the door propped open to prevent mould. If there is mould on the rubber door seal, scrub it with an old toothbrush dipped in methylated spirits or bleach. Rinse the brush, then scrub the seal using warm soap suds.

Caravans and motorhomes

In areas with high humidity, mould can occur in poorly ventilated areas. If possible, leave roof vents open so there is some movement of air. Place some open containers of silica gel to absorb some of the moisture from the air.

Authors' tip:

An economical alternative to silica gel is the silica-type cat litter placed in a couple of trays or old ice-cream containers.

It is highly preferable to store all vehicles out of the weather, but not everyone has a garage to house their motorhome or caravan. Covers are available as an alternative.

Measures to minimise deterioration of caravans or motorhomes stored outdoors

- **Cover the gas cylinder** if housed externally to prevent moisture affecting the regulator or causing corrosion of the cylinder. Alternatively, remove the cylinder and store it under cover. Ensure that you protect the regulator, particularly against hornets building a nest inside.
- If the caravan or motorhome is not going to be used for a couple of months, **connect the battery to a charger on trickle charge**. You may wish to disconnect the battery.
- **Wash the roof and check sealant** along joints and edges for cracks and around hatches and windows, and if necessary replace the sealant. Take care that you do not dent the roof by kneeling on it. Place a sheet of plywood on the roof so your weight is spread and not concentrated in one area.

For caravans stored outdoors

- **Cover the coupling body and brake master cylinder** if fitted. A large plastic bag is suitable, but make sure there is airflow in the bottom so condensation does not build up on the inside of the plastic.
- **Paint the caravan drawbar and any other exposed parts** of the chassis. Use either silver paint or good quality exterior enamel and prepare the surface as directed by the paint manufacturer. Pay particular attention to areas that have chips and marks from stones being thrown up.
- Ideally the **wheels should be removed and stored** in a cool dark area. An alternative is to cover the tyres to prevent sun damage.
- The caravan can be **raised on blocks** placed under the chassis and the drawbar so the full weight is not resting on the tyres.
- As appropriate, apply a good quality **automotive polish** to protect the exterior.

Safety

Fire

Because there is both a 'house' and a 'motor vehicle' (either in one unit with a motorhome, or two separate units with a fifth-wheeler or car/caravan combination) there are different causes and ways to handle each event.

Causes of fire in any vehicle

- **Fire in the engine compartment** – Make sure there are no combustible materials such as grass or an oily rag in the engine compartment.
- **Overheated tyres** – A dragging brake can cause enough friction to heat a tyre to the point of self-ignition. If you have work done on the suspension or brakes of your vehicle, next time you travel check each wheel for excessive heat by touch.
- **Hot brakes** – Overheating of brakes can present a fire hazard. Overheating can occur from brake malfunctions or in mountainous areas when brakes are used instead of slowing the vehicle by gears. Exercising caution, touch your hand to the centre of each wheel to check for excessive temperature.
- **Engine exhaust** – With prolonged idling, an overheated exhaust can ignite dry grasses. If you have driven through long dry grass some strands may have caught around the exhaust pipe and these can ignite.
- **Rubber fuel lines** – Deteriorated or damaged rubber fuel lines can spring a leak, and fuel spraying onto the hot motor can cause a fire. This problem is more likely if the vehicle has a low number of kilometres for its age and has been in storage.

Authors' tip:

Clean up all fuel spills. Diesel fuel is less volatile than petrol, however it dissipates more slowly and provides a longer lasting fuel hazard.

Fire classifications

- Class 'A' – combustibles include furnishings, fittings, upholstery and bedding
- Class 'B' – petrol or diesel fuel and propane while it is contained within the pressurised cylinder
- Class 'C' – flammable gas, such as propane after it has passed through the regulator
- Class 'D' – combustible metals
- Class 'E' – electrical equipment and wiring
- Class 'F' – cooking oil and fat

Fire detection or fire fighting equipment

- By law, all motorhomes, campervans and caravans in Australia are required to have a **powder type fire extinguisher**. It should be placed in an easily accessible location, preferably near the door. An extinguisher with a hose is preferable because it would enable you to spray onto a fire (for example) by only lifting the bonnet of a vehicle slightly to access a fire in the engine compartment. If the bonnet is raised fully the inrush of fresh air would cause a fire to flare up. An extinguisher equipped with a hose is versatile in how a spray may be directed into hard to access places. See p94 for details on fire extinguisher maintenance.
- Install a **smoke alarm** and replace batteries as necessary. If your caravan or motorhome has been unused for a period of time, check that the batteries have not flattened. Some detectors have a 'sleep' mode enabling

North of Broome, WA Photo: Pelusey Photography

you to deactivate it for 15 minutes while you are cooking. A new type of smoke detector combines both an ionisation and photoelectric sensor. The former detects fast-flaming fires that consume materials rapidly and spread quickly, while the latter is more useful for detecting slow fires that smoulder before bursting into flames.
- Install a **fire blanket** to the side of the stove, not over the stove because you would have to reach over flames on the stove to get it. If you do not have a fire blanket, you can use a woollen blanket.

Fire blanket and extinguisher placed near the cooktop

Types of fire extinguishers

- **Red with white band or label** – This type of powder fire extinguisher is required by law to be fitted to all recreational vehicles in Australia. They are suitable for **class A, B, C and E fires** and may have limited effectiveness on class F fires. They are not considered effective on class D fires.
- **Red with a blue band or label (older models are solid blue)** – foam extinguisher suitable for **class A and B fires**, and with limited effectiveness on class F fires.
- **Solid red** – water extinguishers suitable on class A fires, but not effective on class B or C fires. It is dangerous if used on E and F class fires.
- **Red with black band or label** – carbon dioxide extinguisher suitable for fighting **class E fires**, but has limited effectiveness on class A, B, C and F fires.
- **Red with yellow band or label** – vaporising liquid extinguisher suitable for fighting **class A and E fires**, but has limited effectiveness on **class B and C fires**. Not effective on class F fires.
- **Red with oatmeal band or label (older models are solid oatmeal)** – wet chemical extinguisher suitable to fight **class A and F fires**, but not effective on class B or C fires. It is dangerous if used on class E fires.

Travelling on the Victoria Highway, Northern Territory

Precautions to avoid fire in a motorhome or caravan

(Precautions are similar to those required at home.)

- Never smoke in bed.
- Don't run too many electrical appliances from one power socket.
- Replace worn electrical cables.
- NEVER – EVER leave the kitchen area while cooking. If you are on hand a small problem can be attended to before it becomes a major incident.
- Never leave a heated pan of oil unattended.
- Never use pressure pack cans such as cooking spray or insecticide near a gas flame.
- Keep combustible materials such as curtains, tea towels and dishcloths well away from the flames of the stove.
- Wear short or tight fitting sleeves and avoid reaching across the flames.
- Position handles of saucepans inward to prevent them being knocked over.
- Don't drape towels or clothing over a heater to dry.

Authors' tip:

Use a 'long-nosed' lighter for the stove rather than matches so your hand and sleeve are further from the flame.

What to do in the event of a fire

- If a small fire breaks out, act immediately. Have someone else call the fire brigade.
- Extra people and pets should leave immediately. Possessions can be replaced but people cannot.
- Immediately disconnect 240 volt power and turn off the gas at the cylinder (if you can reach it safely).
- If you can, have someone spray water on the gas cylinder to keep it cool.
- Never pour water on a fat fire because it will splatter. If you have a fat or other fire on the stove, place a fire blanket over the flames immediately and leave it there. Do NOT lift up the edge of the blanket to 'see how the fire is going' because the rush of oxygen will cause flames to flare up, possibly causing facial burns.
- If you do not have a fire blanket or pure wool blanket to smother the flames, you should use a dry-powder fire extinguisher. These extinguishers contain sodium bicarbonate (bicarbonate of soda).
- If you have to use a fire extinguisher, stand on the doorside of the flames so you are not caught in a corner.
- Never attempt to fight a major fire with the limited fire fighting equipment available to you. Leave it to the professionals.

Electricity

The 12 volt DC system (in some cases 24 volt) operating from batteries powers the lights and other items in the 'house'. Most caravans and motorhomes have a dual system, with 240 volt AC electricity wired through the unit for the refrigerator and also to power points where appliances can be plugged in. This 240 volt system presents similar dangers to those in the home situation.

If a person comes into contact with 240 volt wires or a faulty appliance, there is a chance of electrocution. Electrical current will always seek the path of least resistance to earth, and if you touch a live wire or faulty appliance, that path will be through your body. If this happens, a bystander should:

- **Turn off** the electricity.
- If the electricity cannot be turned off immediately, **push the person away from the power** source using a piece of wood such as a broom handle or other non-conductive object.
- **Call for medical assistance** if the person appears to be injured, and start CPR if required.

A **safety switch** will automatically cut off when it detects an earth leakage and forestall such an event.

Gas

If you smell the distinctive 'garlic' odour of gas:

- **Extinguish** any open flame.
- **Turn off any appliance** currently operating on gas such as the fridge and water heater.
- **Shut off the valve** on the gas cylinder.
- **Don't touch** electrical switches.
- If the gas smell is inside, **open the windows**.
- As a final safety measure, **consider closing the valve to any appliances** connected to gas – cooktop, fridge and gas hot water system.
- Immediately **call a licensed gas fitter**.

Never use a gas stove to heat the interior

You will notice an appreciable warming of the living space when the stove is being used, however it should never be used to heat the room. Propane flames produce water vapour and high levels of carbon monoxide and will quickly deplete the oxygen in the enclosed space, particularly as the windows are likely to be closed to keep the room warm.

Safety with gas when driving a motorhome or campervan

Although it is legal to operate a fridge on gas while driving, it is unwise in a motorhome or campervan, particularly if the vehicle has a petrol motor. Petrol is more volatile than diesel, and there is a risk that petrol fumes will become ignited because of the fuel tank's proximity to the fridge. It is advisable to shut off the valve on top of the gas cylinder before driving as a safety measure in case of a traffic accident. This is not such an issue in a caravan where the fuel tank and fridge are a long distance apart.

If you travel with a gas fridge operating and the flame is accidentally extinguished, an in-built cut-off switch should stop the flow of gas thereby removing the danger of leaking gas.

Safety with gas when towing a caravan

- If you travel with a gas fridge operating, you should **extinguish it before entering a service station** driveway because of the risk of igniting petrol fumes that could remain from a previous fuel spill.
- The fridge must also be **turned off before boarding a vehicular ferry**. If you do not run a gas fridge while driving, turn off the gas cylinder valve before you set off driving for the day.
- In hot conditions, it is a good idea to **provide some shelter for the gas cylinders** because overheating will cause gas to expand and vent through the safety valve. If the cylinders are in the sun in the hottest part of the day, drape wet towels or bags over them.

Additional safety devices

- All vans and motorhomes should have their electrical system fitted with a **mechanical breaker/ residual current device**. Manufactured caravans and motorhomes would already have this device fitted and DIY motorhome builders should ensure that they do not overlook this important safety device.
- **Propane leak detector** (optional). Because gas is heavier than air a detector can be placed at floor level in the kitchen area. Gas escape vents are built into the door or step well, and also in roof hatches.
- **Carbon Monoxide (CO) detector** (optional). Used to detect gas from the engine or generator exhaust. Carbon monoxide is colourless, odourless and tasteless, but deadly, and it is wise to install such a detector if you use a generator.

Carbon monoxide gas from generator

A generator cannot be operated inside a caravan or motorhome accommodation area. If it is operated in a storage compartment of a motorhome, the compartment should be properly vented so highly toxic carbon monoxide gas does not enter the accommodation area. Before using a generator, position the exhaust so the gases are not expelled or drift towards your own or a neighbour's van or motorhome.

Fuel

Fuel vapours are flammable, but the liquid fuel is not, and petrol is more volatile than diesel. Petrol vaporises at 'normal' temperatures, while diesel requires a temperature of 65.5°C.

If a significant amount of petrol is spilt when refuelling:

- If your fridge is operating on gas, turn it off immediately at the cylinder. (You should have turned it off before entering the service station driveway.)
- Instruct all passengers to vacate the vehicle and take any pets with them.
- Notify the service station operator.

A diesel spill is not as dangerous as a petrol spill, but you should still advise the fuel station attendant if a significant amount is spilt. Spilt diesel can be slippery and dangerous underfoot.

Carrying extra fuel

Unless you plan to travel on remote desert tracks there is no generally need to carry extra fuel in cans, and it is not recommended. Extra fuel adds to the weight of your rig, thereby increasing fuel consumption, and it is very dangerous. Diesel fuel is a combustible liquid, however petrol is much more volatile, and extra care has to be taken during transportation.

On the highways and main roads there are fuel supplies at least every two to three hundred kilometres. The highways with the longest stretches without fuel are in north-west Western Australia between Roebuck Plains Roadhouse and Sandfire Roadhouse (323km), and in the Northern Territory between the less travelled highway between Barkly Homestead and Cape Crawford (371km). Travellers using the Plenty Highway will need fuel to cover the 472km stretch between Jervois Station in Northern Territory and Boulia in Queensland. Roadside signs will indicate if there is a long distance to the next fuel stop. Refer to the atlas for the details of fuel available in remote regions.

By law, petrol can only be carried in a **container approved for the purpose** and designed to prevent overfilling by leaving space for the fuel to expand without seeping out of the cap. Any container that has contained petrol and is now empty will still contain enough residual fumes to make it a potential bomb if ignited. If you must carry additional fuel because you are travelling where there are no supplies, you must not carry it in a passenger vehicle or in the driving compartment or living area of a motorhome. Petrol fumes are heavier than air and will 'pool' in a contained space.

If you want to carry fuel containers at the rear of a motorhome or caravan, consider encasing them in an **impact-resistant cage well above the bumper bar** level to prevent damage in a rear end collision. This cage should have an open mesh floor so any spilled fuel will not remain contained within the cage with the potential to cause an explosion. Secure them to the cage with a chain looped through the handle of the container.

Containers must be removed from the vehicle and placed **on the ground before filling** due to safety concerns with static electricity and ignition sources within the vehicle.

Travelling on the *Spirit of Tasmania*

- You are **not permitted to take an 'empty' gas cylinder on board**, however full cylinders, or those currently in use are OK.
- **Gas fridges must be turned off** before boarding.
- You will **not be permitted to access your vehicle** during the voyage so have the items you need during the trip ready to hand when you drive on.
- As you leave the vehicle deck, **take note of the deck number, doorway and stairwell** you use so you can find your vehicle prior to disembarkation. Vehicles start driving off the ship very soon after arrival, and it would be embarrassing to delay others because you couldn't find your vehicle. This is not as unlikely as it sounds, because the decks and doorways can be confusing.

Spirit of Tasmania vehicular ferry

Motorhomes driving on the Barkly Tableland

Insurance

Some insurance companies have concerns with coverage of vehicles carrying petrol in other than a vehicle's petrol tank. If you are considering carrying petrol, you should check with your insurer.

How much fuel you can carry

Where petrol carried for personal or recreational use totals less than 250 litres, the provisions of the **Dangerous Goods Regulation** do not apply. However, if one vehicle in a private convoy is designated to carry the petrol supplies, that vehicle is deemed to be operating as a goods transport vehicle, and the provisions of the Dangerous Goods Regulation do apply. This requires dangerous goods shipping documents and signage. (The Australian Dangerous Goods Code is available to download from the National Transport Commission website – www.ntc.gov.au.)

Fuel in a motorcycle or boat

An empty fuel container is more dangerous than a full one because residual fumes make it a potential bomb. The fuel tank of a motorcycle or boat should be transported filled to 90% capacity, leaving room for expansion of the fuel to avoid spillage.

General safety points

Systems in the house section require inspection and checking because the vibration of travelling may cause faults to develop.

- **Exterior and interior electrical wiring** both 12 volt and 240 volt. Check circuit breakers etc and give particular attention to the area surrounding 12 volt batteries.
- **Gas fittings and lines.**

Safety factors relating to motorhomes

A motorhome is effectively two units in one. There is the base vehicle that should be maintained in the usual manner, and there is the accommodation section. Listed are some specific areas that a motorhome owner should be aware of.

Weight

- Some motorhomers have discovered to their consternation that their **vehicle is over weight**. This is a problem, not only for the performance, handling and safety of the vehicle, but also could have insurance and legal implications. Occasions may well arise where the weight of the vehicle exceeds its registration class and it may also require a different class of license to drive. A 'C' class standard licence is valid only for vehicles weighing less than 4.5 tonnes. *See p78 for details on licences.*
- It is important that the **loading of each axle does not exceed that specified by the manufacturer**. If you have any doubts, check the load on each axle and check the total weight. If a specific axle load is a problem, you may be able to solve it by relocating some of your cargo.
- Consider also the **even distribution of weight**, not only from front to rear, but also from side to side.
- For any weight problems not easily solved, **seek professional help**.
- The suspension (and tyres) on some vehicles can be upgraded and, of course there is the upgrading of vehicle registration, possibly upgrade driver's licence, and advise your insurer of the changes.
- Seriously overweight vehicles can cause premature aging and failure of tyres, wear wheel bearings and suspension components, as well as poor handling and ineffective braking.
- If you become concerned about the weight of your vehicle, inflate the tyres to the maximum recommended by your vehicle's manufacturer, keeping within their load and pressure limitations. Avoid rough roads and travel slowly, certainly not over 80kph because at lower speeds the tyres will be under less stress. Empty the grey-water tank and do not fill the fresh-water tank (or just leave the minimum amount) to reduce the weight further because at 1kg per litre this can make a significant difference. By not filling the fuel tank to capacity, you will also reduce the weight.
- **Work out a permanent solution** to any suspected 'over weight' problem. If you become aware that your vehicle is overweight, you have the legal obligation to correct it before driving the vehicle.
- Unlike a family car or a truck that only carries its load part of the time, a motorhome is fully loaded all the time so **work on the suspension may be required** in a shorter time frame than would apply with other vehicles.

Safety factors relating to caravans

Tyres

Because the driver is not in direct control of a caravan or trailer, it may not be immediately evident if a problem such as a leaking valve or a tyre blow out occurs. With the tow vehicle's windows closed because of air conditioning, and maybe an audio system playing, a driver may not be aware of a tyre failure and may continue for several kilometres running on a tyre rim. Even a lost wheel may not be immediately apparent. A simple warning system is available that will sound an alarm in the tow vehicle when a sensor detects a significant reduction in the height of any tyre.

Personal safety

Fear of crime by the elderly and women in particular, is a perception generated by sensationalised media crime reporting, when in fact young people are more likely to become victims of crime. Statistics show that those aged between 19 and 25 are more susceptible to violent acts in public places due to excessive alcohol, illicit drugs and misadventure. People in the older age group are not often involved in street crime. Most assaults are perpetrated by someone the victim knows, even a member of his or her own family, and it is unlikely someone will break into your home, motorhome or caravan to assault or rob you.

Even though assault is extremely unlikely, it is prudent to exercise some basic measures:

- Avoid using an ATM at night if you are alone.
- Keep your wallet out of sight and your purse under your arm with the strap looped around your arm.
- Walk confidently to avoid appearing an easy target.
- If you see a couple of people nearby who you feel may present a threat, do your best not to appear intimidated. Don't stare in a challenging manner but let your gaze travel casually across them. If they get the impression you are not concerned by their presence, they are less likely to categorise you as an easy target.

Vehicle security

Many of the precautions you should follow are common sense ones that you probably exercise in your day to day activities, while others are more pertinent to travellers.

- **Do not leave items of value in view** when you leave your vehicle.
- **Always lock your vehicle** when you leave it.
- Have an **engine disabler** fitted so the vehicle cannot be started easily by a potential thief.
- Have a **vehicle alarm** fitted.
- Everyone knows a motorhome or caravan has a lot of equipment inside, and some of it will be valuable. When you leave your vehicle parked, **close the curtains** so it is not immediately obvious that the vehicle is empty. Maybe leave a battery-powered radio playing.
- A **security door** will enable you to see who is outside and talk to them without venturing out, and also will allow extra air circulation in total security. The door is constructed of heavy mesh and has three locking points into the door frame.
- Motorhomes like ours have a very secure double lock on the door to the house, and louvre windows that would not easily permit entry. The easiest access is through the doors to the front cab and from there through to the 'house' section of the motorhome. When we leave the vehicle parked for a length of time we **chain the two front doors together**, so even if a door lock is forced, a potential thief will not be able to open the door. Hopefully, a clearly visible chain will deter someone from trying to break in and they will go elsewhere for easier pickings.

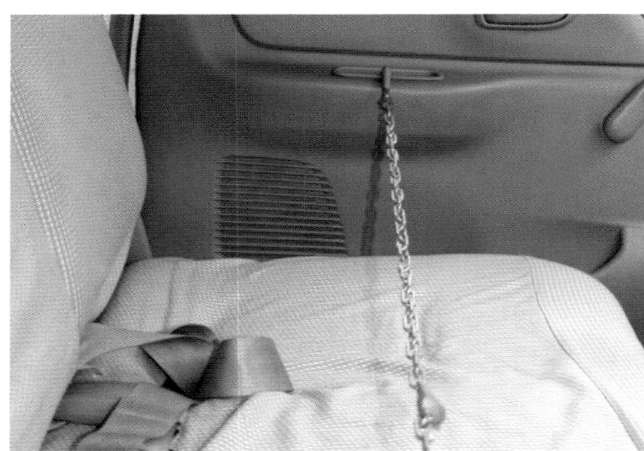

Security chain between the front doors

Great Ocean Road, Victoria

Pre-trip & moving off checklists

Pre-trip list

If your caravan or motorhome has not been used for a while, check the following:

- Is there **enough gas** in the cylinders?
- Is the **battery in the smoke alarm** still operating?
- Make sure spiders or wasps have not made a home in the **air vents** or around the **gas regulator**.
- **House batteries** – general maintenance check.
- **Tyres** – Check the air pressure and inspect the condition of the tyres.
- Maybe clean and flush the **water tank**. Refill.
- Flush water from the **hot water tank**, or run a couple of buckets of water through the system to eliminate bad-smelling water.
- Re-stock the **pantry**.

Moving off list for caravans

- After attaching the coupling body to the tow ball, attach the safety chain/s.
- Remove the jockey wheel from its clamp and store, or if it is of the swivel mount variety, lock it in the travelling position.
- Raise front and rear stabilisers.
- Attach electrical cable and check that lights on the van are operating.
- Ensure the hand brake of the caravan/trailer has been correctly released.
- Check the stone shield is securely fastened.
- If you have a pop-top, ensure it is securely fastened.

Moving off list for caravans, camper vans and motorhomes

- Roll up and secure **awning**
- Store all **outside furniture and doormat**
- Shut all **windows** and close **roof vents**
- Put **TV aerial** down
- Check in **bathroom** and close door
- Close and lock all **cupboard doors/drawers**
- Check there are no **loose items** inside
- Turn off **water pump** and release pressure in water pipes
- Turn off **12 volt power** (if not needed to power the fridge)
- Turn off **fridge** (or change to 12 volt)
- Disconnect and store **electric lead**
- Remove **grey-water drainage hose** from sullage, drain and store
- Turn **gas supply** off at cylinder
- Put up/store the **step/s**
- Roll off **levelling ramps**; remove and store
- Close **outside bins**
- Take a quick walk around check **outside** – tyres, anything loose etc, and look under the vehicle for the item you put there 'out of the way'
- Check on **route of exit** (slope/clearance etc)

Travelling

Information for travelling

Preparing to travel

So you don't have to worry about essential bills going unpaid while you travel, arrange automatic payment from your bank account of property rates, electricity, gas and telephone accounts. Check when insurance premiums (house, vehicle and life policies), vehicle registration and driver's licence renewal will become due.

Arrange for someone to collect your mail (or organise for your mail to be held by Australia Post) and also junk mail. If you have newspapers delivered, cancel them for the time you will be away. Uncollected items in your letterbox or several newspapers lying on the lawn clearly indicate that no-one is home.

Quarantine

Restrictions apply to each state and territory for the movement of fruit and vegetables. Penalties apply, so check the requirements for carrying items into any state, or declared quarantine areas within a state, with Quarantine Domestic (www.quarantinedomestic.gov.au, 1800 084 881) or the state's quarantine authorities. Remember, requirements may change as new pests, diseases and weeds are detected so it always pays to check for the latest information.

State quarantine authorities

Australian Capital Territory –
Environment Protection and Heritage Licensing & Compliance Unit:
www.act.gov.au, (02) 6207 9777

New South Wales –
Department of Primary Industries: www.dpi.nsw.gov.au, (02) 6391 3100

Northern Territory –
Department of Primary Industry, Fisheries and Mines:
www.nt.gov.au/dpifm,
(08) 8999 2138

Queensland –
Department of Primary Industries and Fisheries:
www.dpi.qld.gov.au, (07) 3404 6999

South Australia –
Primary Industries and Resources: www.pir.sa.gov.au,
1300 666 010

Tasmania –
Department of Primary Industries and Water:
www.dpiw.tas.gov.au/quarantine, (03) 6233 3352

Victoria –
Department of Primary Industries:
www.dpi.vic.gov.au/psb, (03) 8371 3500

Western Australia – Department Agriculture & Food:
www.agric.wa.gov.au, (08) 9334 1800

Quarantine inspection station on WA/NT border

Fruit Fly Exclusion Zone (FFEZ)

The FFEZ covers a large area of New South Wales, northern Victoria and the Riverland area of eastern South Australia. It includes Broken Hill in the northwest, Griffith and Narrandera in the east and Shepparton, Swan Hill and Waikerie on its southern boundary. This area is marked on the atlas. No raw fruit and vegetables, containers that have previously held fruit and vegetables, honey or plants can be taken into this area. (See www.fruitfly.net.au or www.quarantinedomestic.gov.au or 1800 084 881 for more information.)

The Greater Sunraysia Pest Free Area is located within the existing Fruit Fly Exclusion Zone (FFEZ). Do not bring host fruit or vegetables into the Pest Free Area. (For more information see www.pestfreearea.com.au.)

Queensland

The only permanent quarantine checkpoint is for southbound travellers on Cape York north of Coen to prevent fresh fruit and vegetables from the Torres Strait islands and the northern part of the Cape being taken south. If localised pests that could become a danger to agriculture are found, a temporary quarantine area may be established. There is a vehicle inspection station at Coen (Coen DPI office 07 4060 1135).

South Australia

These restrictions apply even to travellers coming from the FFEZ in Victoria:

- No fresh fruit, except pineapple.
- Potatoes and root vegetables are permitted provided they have been thoroughly washed and are soil free.
- Allium family (onions, garlic, spring onions and leeks) must be topped, tailed and the outer skin removed to inner flesh.
- Leaf vegetables are permitted if they are thoroughly washed and soil free. If you are entering from Western Australia, leaf vegetables are not permitted.
- Used fruit and vegetable cartons are permitted as packing containers provided they are clean and free of soil.

There are checkpoints in South Australia:

- on the Barrier Highway at Oodla Wirra
- on the Sturt Highway at Yamba near Renmar
- on the Mallee Highway between Murrayville and Pinnaroo
- on the Eyre Highway near Ceduna

Tasmania

No raw fruit and vegetables, containers that have previously held fruit and vegetables, honey or plants can be taken into Tasmania. Vehicles are checked at the ferry terminal.

Western Australia

Honey is not permitted, and neither are containers that have previously contained honey or fruit or vegetables. A small amount of some fruit and vegetables is permitted for personal consumption but you must declare it. The following is permitted:

- Potatoes – less than 1kg provided they are deep peeled to eliminate all eyes on tubers.
- Onions – less than 1kg provided they are peeled, topped and tailed.
- Other root vegetables such as carrots, sweet potato, radish or ginger – allowed if clean and tops removed.
- Fruit salad – up to 1kg cut into bite sized pieces. Grapes and berries do not need to be cut but must be mixed with other fruit that is cut.
- Vegetable salad – Up to 1kg cut up and washed. Cherry tomatoes must be cut into halves.
- All thoroughly cooked fruit and vegetables.

Vehicles crossing into Western Australia on the major highways will be inspected. There are checkpoints on the WA/NT border near Kununurra and on the Eyre Highway at the WA/SA border.

Toll roads

There are no toll roads in the Northern Territory, South Australia, Tasmania or Western Australia. Details of toll roads in the other States:

New South Wales

There are ten toll roads in the Sydney area, and the Cross City Tunnel, Sydney Harbour Bridge, Sydney Harbour Tunnel, Westlink M7 and Lane Cove Tunnel are fully electronic (payment is by an electronic tag or e-pass, no cash). Electronic tags work on all motorways in Sydney and interstate. If you travel on a toll road without paying, payment can be made within 48 hours. Etags/e-passes are available through RTA E-Toll (www.myrta.com, 131 865), E-way (www.tollpay.com.au, 1300 555 833), Roam Express (www.roamexpress.com.au, 13 76 26) and Roam (www.roam.com.au, 13 86 55). For details access the website www.sydneymotorways.com.

Queensland

Roads around Brisbane where tolls apply are the Gateway Bridge, Gateway Motorway Extension and Logan Motorway. The North-South Bypass Tunnel from Woolloongabba to Bowen Hills will also be a toll road.

With the introduction of free-flow tolling in July 2009, there will be no toll booths to collect road tolls. To pay their toll, drivers need to set up an Etag account and obtain a transponder from Queensland Motorways (www.etoll.com.au, 1300 038 655). The Queensland Etag will also work on all interstate motorways where a toll applies.

Drivers without a Etag account can buy a casual day pass at major service stations. If you drive on a toll road without an Etag or casual pass, you can pay the toll (plus a nominal fee) by credit card over the phone within the next couple of days.

Victoria

A system of freeways in and around Melbourne has been combined in the CityLink project that utilises a system of free-flow tolling. To travel on CityLink you need either a CityLink account or a CityLink pass because there are no toll booths to collect money. A pass can be purchased either prior to using the toll road or within three days AFTER the trip. Various passes are available and include a 24-hour pass, a weekend pass or those that specify up to 2 toll sections or more than 2 toll sections. Toll tickets can be purchased from Coles Express Shell Service Stations, Post Offices and some newsagencies. Alternatively, tickets can be purchased by phone or on the internet by quoting a credit card number. For information phone 13 26 29 or visit www.citylink.com.au.

The EastLink is a free-flow tolling road that links Melbourne's northeast, through Dandenong, to Frankston in the southeast. Breeze tag accounts and non-tag accounts are available as well as EastLink Trip Passes. Breeze tags operate on all Australian motorways, including CityLink. (You can open a Breeze pre-paid tag account or non-tag account online at www.Breeze.com.au.) For casual users one EastLink Trip Pass will pay for a single trip on EastLink, in one direction. For further information on EastLink visit www.eastlink.com.au or phone 13 54 65.

Time zones

New South Wales (except Broken Hill), Victoria, Queensland, Tasmania and the Australian Capital Territory operate on **Australian Eastern Standard Time (AEST)**.

South Australia, the Northern Territory and Broken Hill in far western New South Wales are on **Australian Central Standard Time (ACST)**, that is 30 minutes 'behind' AEST.

Western Australia is on **Australian Western Standard Time (AWST)** that is two hours behind AEST.

Daylight saving

The situation becomes more complicated when daylight saving time comes into force in some States, putting the clock ahead by one hour. The policy for daylight saving in each State is as follows:

- New South Wales/ACT, South Australia, Tasmania and Victoria – Daylight saving commences at 2am on the first Sunday in October and ends at 2am on the first Sunday in April in the following year.
- Northern Territory and Queensland – no daylight saving.
- Western Australia – no daylight saving. After a three-year trial, a referendum in May 2009 voted against daylight saving.

Fuel

High fuel prices have made it more important to try to lower fuel consumption. Some points to help:

- **Driving speed** is critical, particularly with a vehicle that is not aerodynamically streamlined. The most fuel-efficient speed on the highway is probably well under 80kph, but as we share the roads with other traffic and we want to get to our destination in a reasonable time, many caravanners and motorhomers choose to drive around 85kph. Naturally you have to give faster drivers an opportunity to overtake. An example of how to partially offset recent increases in fuel prices by driving slower on a 400km drive:
  - At 85kph with fuel consumption of 7.1km per litre uses 56.3 litres and takes 4¾ hours.
  - At 95kph with fuel consumption of 6.2km per litre uses 64.5 litres and takes 4¼ hours.
  - On a fuel cost of $1.75 per litre, the saving is $14.35 and it has taken an extra 30 minutes.

The saving by reducing your speed by 10kph is roughly equivalent to half the amount that fuel has risen in the last couple of years, and driving even slower will produce greater savings.

- Keep the **total weight** of your vehicle to a reasonable minimum. Remove items you rarely use. If you have a grey water tank, it should be emptied frequently; and only fill the water storage tank completely if you are heading into an area where good water will be difficult to find.
- Look ahead in the traffic and **drive smoothly** so you do not accelerate then slow down. Avoid fast acceleration unless it is necessary in an emergency.
- If you can, **avoid peak hour traffic**.
- **Avoid prolonged idling** where possible. Switch off the engine if lengthy delays are expected.
- **Use the air conditioner sparingly**.
- Whether or not you have air conditioning, it is more economical to **drive with the windows up**. Driving with the windows down increases **wind resistance** and thus fuel consumption.
- Attachments to the outside of the vehicle such as roof racks also increase **wind resistance**.
- Check that the **engine is in good condition** and tuned correctly.
- **Tyre pressure** should be kept at the maximum recommended by the vehicle manufacturer unless you are driving in soft sand or on rocky terrain when the pressure should be lowered. *See p102.*
- Try to drive at a speed that corresponds with the **peak of the torque curve** of the engine. An experienced driver can usually gauge this by the sound of the engine, but if your vehicle is fitted with a tachometer you can monitor your revs more accurately. Most diesel motors perform best within the 2000 to 2400 rpm range, but it is best to check on the recommendations of the manufacturer shown in the driver's manual.
- In hilly terrain, the use of a **cruise control** can increase fuel consumption because the engine is working hard to maintain the set speed. On reasonably flat country, a cruise control will help maintain smooth driving.
- **Headwinds** dramatically increase fuel consumption. On long stretches like the Nullarbor or the Barkly Tableland, some travellers with time to spare prefer to camp for a few days until the wind drops or changes direction, rather than drive into strong headwinds. If you have access to a weather map you can work out how the winds are likely to change. In the southern hemisphere, winds around a low pressure system move in a clockwise direction while winds around a high pressure system move in an anticlockwise direction. Most weather patterns in southern Australia move from west to east.
- As the **temperature increases**, fuel will expand up to 10% so when you buy fuel that has been stored in an area where it may have increased in temperature, you may get less for your dollar. In hot areas, try to avoid buying fuel late in the day when the fuel could have heated.
- Fuel (particularly petrol) **deteriorates after several months**, so you should not store it for long periods. When buying fuel, it is prudent to buy from service stations that have a regular turnover of stock.

Health issues

Driver fatigue is an important health issue. *See p106.*

Health emergencies & preventative measures

Carry a **first aid kit**. These are available from St John Ambulance or you can seek advice at your local pharmacy. Travellers spend much of their time out of reach of immediate medical help so you should consider doing either a St John first aid course or at least learning how to apply cardiopulmonary resuscitation (CPR). If you learnt this procedure some years ago, you should upgrade your skills because the techniques have been changed to make CPR more effective. (Visit www.stjohn.org.au for details of first aid kits and training.)

Sunburn

Everyone spending time outdoors should apply **sunscreen** to exposed areas of skin and wear a broad-brimmed **hat** and **sunglasses** to protect against sun damage. Sunburn and damage to the cornea and lens of the eye can result from exposure to the UVB component of ultraviolet light from the sun. UV levels are at their highest between 10am and 3pm, although you can get sunburnt at other times of the day, or even in overcast conditions. Unless your windscreen has a **UV filter** you will be exposed to UVB rays when you are driving during the day. Apply sunscreen to your face and arms, and wear sunglasses.

Under Australian law, windscreens can only be tinted in the top 10% or to the upper point of the windscreen wiper arc, whichever is the lesser. Tinting of other windows is limited to 35% light transmission and would usually include a UV filter. Most windscreens currently available have a UV filter built in.

> **Authors' tip:**
>
> We had a UV filter applied to the side windows and find it very effective.

Insects

Annoying insects can spoil your enjoyment of the outdoors, but even worse, some insect bites, particularly those from March flies and sand flies (midges) can cause itching and discomfort for days. Such an allergic reaction might be alleviated by taking an antihistamine tablet, but you should discuss this with a pharmacist.

Big fat March flies are slow-moving and easy to swat but they are particularly vicious, so much so that they have been described as "teeth with wings". Although bites are painful and can leave temporary red spots, March flies do not transmit illness and they are only active during the day. Some insect repellents are not effective in repelling March flies.

Although mosquito bites are not painful, they are potentially serious because some mosquitoes can transmit illnesses such as dengue fever, Ross River fever or Barmah Forest fever. Mosquitos are most active at night, particularly at dusk, and the best way to avoid being bitten is to wear long pants and a long-sleeved shirt, however that is not always convenient. As an alternative, use an insect repellent, the most effective being those containing the active ingredient DEET (diethyltoluamide): the higher the percentage of DEET, the more effective the repellent is.

> **Authors' tip:**
>
> Bushman Repellent will repel virtually all insects, including sandflies and March flies, and lasts for 15 hours. It is available as an aerosol (20% DEET) and gel (80% DEET). It is also available in combination with a sunscreen.

Prescription medicines

If you take prescription medicine, check your supplies and make sure you have enough for your trip, or at least for several weeks. You will have to plan ahead for this because repeats on most medicines are not usually filled within 20 days. If you need the medication sooner, advise the pharmacist that you will be travelling and an exception will probably be made, although that purchase will not go towards your 'Safety Net' qualifying amount. On the other hand, it is not wise to stockpile too much medicine because your doctor may change your prescription, and some medications deteriorate if not kept under ideal conditions.

Having prescriptions filled while travelling can sometimes be difficult as it might not be available immediately at every pharmacy. Some small centres only have a depot pharmacy where medications are ordered for pick-up a few days later, but this would not be convenient for someone wanting to keep travelling.

Make a list of the medicines you take, including the strength of each medication. Do it now (while you are well and unstressed). If you take several medications, or have a serious medical condition, ask your doctor to prepare a report, or give you a copy of your relevant medical records. If you need to see a doctor while you are travelling, full details will assist in diagnosis and treatment. You may need to pay a small charge for photocopying your medical records, but this is minor compared with the value of the information if you need medical help. It could save you the cost of having additional tests or x-rays as well as speeding up diagnosis because the doctor would not have to wait for test results.

> **Authors' tip:**
>
> The PBS section of Medicare interprets the term 'within 20 days' as being '20 days or less' therefore it is actually 21 days.

Dental problems

Dental problems such as a broken filling, broken or loosened teeth can occur at the most inconvenient times. In remote areas, or even small towns, it would usually not be possible to find a dentist at short notice, however some dental problems can be managed anytime, anywhere with the help of a 'Dentist in a Box' dental emergency kit. The kit is about the size of a CD case and contains temporary dental filling material, mouth mirror, applicators and easy to follow directions.

Driving situations

Blow out

A blow out of a front tyre will usually be felt through the steering wheel, while a blow out of a rear tyre can be felt through the driver's seat. If a blow out occurs, you should not brake hard, but slow gradually while keeping the vehicle travelling straight ahead. Gradually pull off the road where it is safe. If one tyre of a set of duals fails, you can drive slowly on the remaining tyre to a place where it is safe to change the failed tyre.

Safaris

If the group involves vehicles travelling together on a two-lane highway, it is considerate to leave a 60m gap so other vehicles can overtake.

Long vehicles (over 4.5 tonnes or a combined length of 7.5m) are legally required to leave such a gap. *See p79.* Better still, if the group involves several long or slower-moving vehicles, split up by a kilometre or two and maintain contact by UHF radio.

Speed

Many motorhome drivers or caravanners prefer to maintain a speed of around 85kph for economical fuel consumption and also for comfortable handling of the vehicle. If you travel at this speed you should be conscious of other traffic on the highway and do your best not to hold them up. At times this may mean travelling a few kilometres an hour faster than you would choose to. If traffic builds up behind you, pull off the road when safe and let them go past. It is not helpful for a caravanner or motorhomer to pull partly off the road and keep driving on the verge where they are likely to throw up stones at someone overtaking.

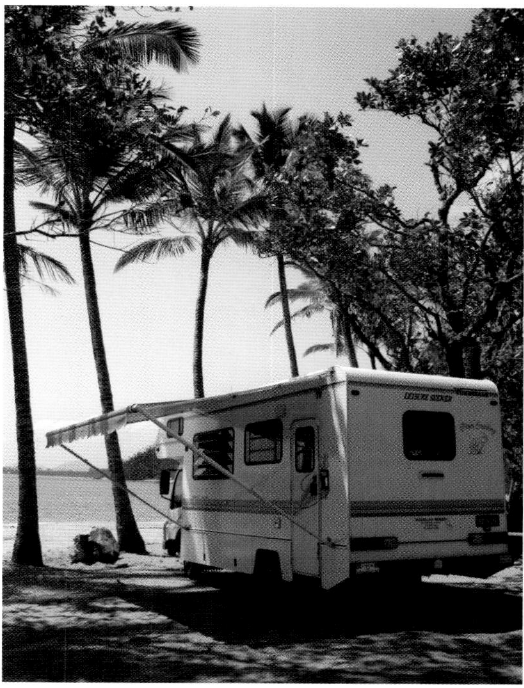

Sharing the road with trucks and road trains

The caravanner or motorhomer should be especially considerate and try not to delay other road users, especially professional truck drivers who have tight schedules to keep. If you follow these procedures it will make travelling easier and safer for both truckies and other drivers.

- **Braking** – Due to its size and weight, the handling of a truck is very restrictive. Do not pull out in front of a moving truck and do not cut in front as you approach traffic lights. Allow safe road space for the truck to pull up because a loaded truck will need much more distance than you will to stop.
- **Following distance** – Do not tailgate a truck. Unless you can see the driver's mirrors, he can't see you and you can't see what is happening ahead. If he has to brake suddenly, you will have nowhere to go.
- **Lights** – High beam glare contributes to night driving fatigue. Dip your lights when you are within 200m of another vehicle, or before reaching a crest or curve. Truck mirrors are much larger than those on cars, and they have no anti-glare position. When overtaking do not switch to high beam until you are past the truck's rear vision mirrors. Only use fog lights in fog.
- **Overtaking**
    - If it appears that a truck driver wants to overtake and you have a UHF radio, you may be able to contact him on channel 40 to ask him if he wants to overtake. He probably knows the road very well and will know the best place to do this. If you have a sticker on the back of your vehicle indicating what UHF channel you are using, often a truckie will call you up before overtaking.
    - If it appears a driver behind you is looking for a place to overtake, find a wider spot, slow down and pull over so he can overtake. It is not helpful if you pull half off the bitumen and continue driving because your vehicle can throw stones up at the overtaking vehicle.
    - If a long road train wants to overtake you, allow him plenty of room because the last trailer will probably move around more than the trailer closer to the prime mover. If you can, pull off the road completely to let him pass.
    - If someone is overtaking you, do not allow your speed to increase as this only makes the passing manoeuvre more difficult. Ease off the accelerator, let him pass, and give him a single flash of your headlights to indicate when it is safe for him to move over in front of you.
    - To overtake a road train you need a clear view for at least several hundred metres because they can be up to 55m long. Stay back a distance so you have a better view and so you can accelerate well before the clear area comes up that will allow you to overtake. It is too dangerous for a road train to pull off the road to let you past, so on a narrow strip of bitumen you may have to pull partly off. Do not pull back in front of the truck until you see both the truck's headlights. This allows a safe space. Maintain your speed – don't overtake and then slow directly in front of the truck.
    - Because of the weight of their load, trucks often slow down on hills, and then drive at their maximum speed on downhill and flat sections of highway. This is probably faster than most caravanners or motorhomers like to travel. If you overtake a truck when he slows on a hill, it is likely he will try to overtake you on the down hill run. Slow down behind him on the uphill section and then let him get away and continue with his day's work.
- **Passing** (a vehicle going in the other direction)
    - If a large truck passes in the other direction, allow for the effects of cross winds and also the possible sideways movement of either your own or the other vehicle on an uneven road surface. Bumps on the road can make a road train trailer swing, and the last trailer of a long road train will move about more than the first trailer. Keep as far to the left as you reasonably can so a sideswipe does not occur and also to lessen the buffeting effects of the wind a large truck pushes in front of it.
    - On a narrow bitumen road, if you stay on the road the other vehicle is forced to move off and can shower you with stones. Slow down and move off a little to encourage the other driver to stay on the bitumen. Even if he also pulls off, the two vehicles will be far enough apart that stones thrown up are less likely to cause a problem.
- **Rest areas** – Do not use rest areas that are signposted for trucks only. In rest areas available for all travellers, park to the side so other traffic can get past.
- **Road positioning** – On many roads trucks need all of their lane space, so if there is approaching traffic do not travel right on the centre line. If stopped or broken down, if possible park well clear of the roadway. Ideally, there should be a clear metre between your vehicle and the edge of the travelling lane, usually marked with an unbroken white line.
- **Turning** – Long vehicles displaying a 'DO NOT OVERTAKE TURNING VEHICLE' sign can legally turn left from the second or even third lane of a multiple lane road. Other traffic must give way and not try to squeeze through in the left-hand lane. Large trucks need the whole roadway to negotiate a roundabout. Slow down and let the truck make the turn without trying to squeeze past him.

Road train warning sign

Roadtrain parked at Turkey Creek Roadhouse, Western Australia

Braking distance

Several factors come into play to determine the braking distance of a vehicle, but the most important is the weight of the vehicle. Others are the condition of the tyres and brake components, the road surface, whether the road is wet or dry and the reaction time of the driver. Whereas a car travelling at 100kph will stop in around 40m to 45m, a motorhome will take around 60m and a motorhome towing a car or a car/caravan combination will take considerably longer. Keep in mind that a heavily laden truck or road train needs an even longer distance to stop.

A rear-end collision is usually regarded as the fault of the following driver, not the driver who may have stopped suddenly, thereby causing a heavier vehicle to run into the back because they could not stop in time. If you are travelling behind a vehicle (maybe a truck or a caravan) that obscures your view of the traffic ahead, do not follow too closely. Leave yourself room to stop in an emergency because you will not get much advance warning if you cannot see what is happening further ahead.

A. Stekelenburg

Rear end collision where a 4WD towing a loaded trailer ran into the back of a caravan that had slowed for merging traffic lanes

Wet brakes

In adverse weather conditions, water can splash onto the brakes and reduce their effectiveness. This is more common with drum brakes than with disc brakes. If you are travelling in wet weather or have driven through water, apply the brakes gently to see how they respond. If the braking ability is reduced, apply light pressure on the brake pedal a couple of times. The brakes will heat slightly and dry out and then operate normally.

Wheels leaving the roadway

Many country highways are narrow, and inevitably there will be occasions when the left-hand wheels of the caravan or motorhome will leave the bitumen. Particularly with a caravan, it is imperative not to over react and jerk the steering wheel to bring the van back onto the road quickly. It is important not to swerve, but to maintain a steady gradual line. If there is a 'drop-off' between the bitumen and road shoulder you will have to slow down before bringing the wheels gradually back onto the roadway.

Difficult road surfaces

Unsealed roads

Dust entering the vehicle while travelling on unsealed roads is often a concern. Cars and buses can usually be sealed but caravans and motorhomes have permanent refrigerator and gas safety vents.

In the normal course of events, when you travel on unsealed roads, dust will be sucked inside because the air pressure inside is lower than the air pressure outside. This low pressure effect also occurs immediately behind a vehicle while it is travelling, and the result is evident with a dust build-up on the back. If you increase the air pressure inside the vehicle while you are travelling, dust will not be sucked in. If you have a caravan, open the small pressure hatch, and if you have a motorhome, leave a vent (such as the back quarter of a *Four Seasons* hatch) open slightly. Alternatively, drive a motorhome or campervan with the air conditioning or ventilation on 'fresh air', but switch the control briefly to recirculated air if a vehicle passes and raises dust. Experiment with your own vehicle to find the best way to prevent dust entering.

On roads with fine **'bull dust'** drive at a cautious speed and take care not to drive into deep sections of dust. Slow down as much as possible if you see another vehicle approaching, particularly a road train, and note whether their dust cloud travels across the road. Visibility will drop to virtually zero if you have to drive into a cloud of dust. Drop your speed so you do not raise too much dust and reduce visibility to danger levels for the other driver.

Inland roads in either black soil or bull dust areas become **impassable after rain**, even to 4WD vehicles. Please heed the signs warning 'dry weather road only' because driving on these roads in wet conditions can damage the road and you can be fined.

Graphic warning sign, Lincoln National Park, South Australia

Warning sign on the Gibb River Road, Western Australia

Authors' tip:

We had a slide-on that had a rear door with permanent vents that could have allowed dust to enter. We travelled with the rear quarter of the Four Seasons roof hatch open on the 'rain' setting and no dust entered even though the back of the vehicle was coated with dust.

Corrugated roads

There are two speeds that work well on badly corrugated roads. Drivers of 4WD vehicles can ride over the top of the corrugations at 80kph to 85kph, but to do this without risking tyre damage, reduce the tyre pressure by 4 to 6 psi. Lowering tyre pressures will also ease the comfort of the ride and aid traction.

It goes without saying that drivers must remain very alert for wash outs and corners that will present a hazard, particularly if they are encountered at fairly high speed.

Many travellers with a caravan or motorhome don't want to tackle corrugations at 80kph because they are concerned about damage to their vehicle or the contents. The alternative is to crawl over the worst sections at around 15kph to avoid excessive vibration.

Some drivers have remarked that they cannot enjoy driving on badly corrugated roads because all their attention has to be riveted on the road looking for wash outs, potholes and corrugations and they cannot glance up even for a moment. Other drivers revel in the challenge.

Authors' tip:

We have observed that corrugations are worse where drivers apply their brakes – on the inside curve of bends and just before a bridge or culvert. Take extra care as you approach these.

Sandy or rough rocky terrain

If you are planning to drive on uneven terrain or in sand, it is very important to keep the **centre of gravity of the vehicle as low as possible** by packing heavy items low, and definitely not on the roof.

Whether you are driving in sand or on rocky terrain, it is recommended that you **lower tyre pressures** by up to 30%. Driving on rocky terrain with fully or overinflated tyres can result in tyre casing damage that can cause a blow out. If you drive in sand with fully inflated tyres it is virtually guaranteed that you will get bogged. Lowering tyre pressure is made easier by using a device known as a Tyre Deflator that is screwed into the tyre valve and enables the operator to quickly lower tyre pressures to a pre-set level. Tyres must be reinflated before resuming normal driving to avoid tyre damage. *See p76.*

On rocky terrain you will have to **drive slowly**. Driving in sand should only be attempted if you have a 4WD, and a realistic speed in soft sand is 15kph. If you are driving on the beach, be alert for areas of soft sand. Follow close to the tyre tracks of other vehicles.

Becoming bogged in sand

Dig out in front of all wheels and compact the sand, then lower tyre pressures further. To aid traction, peg down whatever is available over the sand – hessian bags, mats etc. Alternatively, wet the sand and attempt to reverse out slowly after the water has soaked in, but before the sand has dried. Drive slowly until you are out of the soft sand area and can reinflate your tyres.

Emergency help

Ambulance or police

Dial **000** and even if your phone does not have service, if there is another phone company operating in the area it will handle the call. The 000 service will operate on prepaid mobiles, even if the account has a nil balance. Because you are calling from a mobile phone and not a landline, the Emergency Services operator will not be aware of your location. Answer the operator's questions calmly and give specific directions, including the State you are located in to avoid confusion and delay. For more information, refer below.

Breakdown

If you are a member of an automobile club refer to the section below for full details. Alternatively, phone Sensis (Yellow Pages telephone directory) on **1234** and ask for the nearest mechanic, tow truck or whatever you need.

Help via UHF radio

If you do not have mobile phone coverage and you have a UHF radio, call for help on the radio. Try channels 18 (for caravans), 20 (for motorhomes and camper vans) or 40, maybe 29, (for truck drivers).

Ambulance

Although we all hope we will not need to call on the services of an ambulance, a circumstance can arise, usually without warning. It is helpful for you to know if you will have to pay the charges personally because these are high. Ambulance services are State-based, so the cost and entitlement to free service varies. Obviously in a serious emergency, you would have no alternative but to call an ambulance, regardless of cost.

A brief summary of ambulance cover in each State.

- Pensioner residents of all states except Tasmania and Northern Territory are looked after Australia-wide. Western Australian pensioners must be in receipt of a full pension or DVA pension to be covered for costs.
- Tasmanian pensioners travelling to Queensland in particular should consider insurance through a health fund.
- Northern Territory pensioners travelling to Queensland should subscribe to their Ambulance Service.
- Travellers (other than Queensland residents) who do not hold a concession card should consider either subscribing to their Ambulance Service or adding an ambulance cover to their private health insurance.

For detailed information refer below.

Motoring clubs

Australia's motoring clubs offer information on road conditions, maps, breakdown assistance and towing if necessary after a breakdown. These state-based clubs have reciprocal agreements with their sister clubs so you only have to join one organisation to be covered Australia-wide. Conditions and restrictions apply to roadside service and towing, but unfortunately these are not consistent.

Wherever you are in Australia when you require assistance, if you have 'basic' club membership phone **13 11 11**. The call will be directed to the local call centre and you will be looked after, within the limitations shown below. If you have just a 'basic' club membership you may find that the assistance will be limited to that provided by the local club, rather than what you would be entitled to with your own club. If you have paid for a higher level of membership, telephone the number designated to receive your extra entitlements.

Car and caravan under tow at the Wooramel Roadhouse, WA

If you are towing a caravan or camper trailer and your tow vehicle is immobilised, it is possible the caravan will have to be left beside the road, or you will have to pay for a second tow truck. In some cases, the tow truck operator will be able to put your vehicle on the tray of the tow truck and tow the caravan, provided it is under the length limit (usually 5.5m including the draw bar). Before phoning the auto club, stop and consider whether you should be phoning them or your insurance company.

> **Authors' tip:**
>
> We came across a car that had been immobilised after hitting an emu on the road. The driver and his passenger had nearly 24 hours' wait beside the road for a tow truck because initially he sent a message to the auto club instead of his insurer. Hitting an animal is an accident, not a breakdown. The situation was complicated because there was no mobile phone coverage in the area.

Details of ambulance services

ACT residents are covered for emergency ambulance services within the ACT through the road rescue fee levied on vehicle registration. Residents with private health cover are covered for emergency ambulance service outside the ACT, but there is an additional charge for every kilometre travelled outside the ACT. ACT Pensioner Concession and Health Care Card holders are entitled to free emergency and non-emergency ambulance services within the ACT. When interstate, ACT Pensioner Concession and Health Care Card holders are entitled to free emergency ambulance services only if that state participates in reciprocal arrangements with the ACT. It is recommended that you check your entitlements prior to travelling interstate.

New South Wales residents receiving a Centrelink or DVA (Department of Veterans Affairs) pension, holders of a Commonwealth Seniors Card or Health Care Concession Card are exempt from fees for emergency transport to the nearest hospital in NSW. NSW residents who do not have one of the concession cards listed have to pay for ambulance service unless they have hospital cover through a health fund or have other insurance. Reciprocal agreements cover NSW concession card holders (listed above) for emergency use of an ambulance when travelling interstate with some exceptions. Holders of a Health Care Card are not covered in Western Australia, and holders of a Commonwealth Seniors Health Card are not covered in Victoria. There are no reciprocal agreements in place with Queensland and South Australia. Concession card holders who receive an invoice for service from an interstate ambulance should send a copy to the NSW Ambulance Service with a claim for reimbursement.

Northern Territory pensioners and holders of a Health Care Card receive free ambulance service in the Territory and also interstate with the exception of Queensland. Residents who subscribe to the NT Ambulance Service are covered in the Territory and also when in Queensland. Non-subscribers who do not have a Centrelink concession card or DVA pension are responsible for the bill themselves.

Queensland residents are covered nation-wide for the use of an ambulance. Accounts received for use of an interstate ambulance should be sent for payment to the Department of Emergency Services together with proof of Queensland residency. Other people eligible for free ambulance service in Queensland are Veterans' Affairs gold card-holders, ambulance subscribers from Victoria, ACT, Northern Territory and South Australia, pensioners from Victoria, ACT and Western Australian, and people living near the Queensland border where a cross-border arrangement applies.

South Australia residents receiving a Centrelink or DVA pension, or holders of a Health Care Card are exempt from fees for use of an ambulance Australia-wide. Commonwealth Seniors Card does not give exemption from fees. SA residents (other than pensioners and Health Care Card holders) have to pay for use of an ambulance unless they subscribe to the South Australian Ambulance Service. SA does not have reciprocal agreements with other States, so residents will receive an account if they use an ambulance interstate. SA concession card holders or South Australian Ambulance subscribers should send the account to the Ambulance Service for payment. Other SA residents are responsible for payment themselves, whether the service was in South Australia or interstate.

The **Tasmanian** Ambulance Service provides a free service to all Tasmanian residents, except in the case of an accident where insurance arrangements cover costs. DVA meets the cost for veterans. Tasmanian residents travelling interstate are covered by reciprocal arrangements except in South Australia and Queensland where charges apply. Private health insurance or travel insurance can be taken out to cover this eventuality.

Victorian residents in receipt of a Centrelink or DVA pension, or holders of a Health Care Card are exempt from fees to use an ambulance, but a Commonwealth Seniors Card does not give exemption. Victorian residents who do not hold a concession card listed above must pay to use the Ambulance Service unless they pay a subscription. When travelling interstate, Victorian concession card holders are only eligible for emergency transport to the nearest hospital. Reciprocal agreements covering pensioners, Health Care Card holders and Victorian Ambulance subscribers apply except with Queensland and South Australia. Concession card holders and subscribers who receive an account for use of a Queensland or South Australian ambulance should forward it to the Victorian Ambulance Service for settlement. Other Victorian residents are responsible for payment themselves, whether the service was in Victoria or interstate.

Western Australia pensioners (full Centrelink or Department of Veterans Affairs pension) receive free ambulance service Australia-wide. A reciprocal agreement takes care of the charges for pensioners in all states except South Australia and Queensland where charges will apply, however, these accounts should be passed on to the Western Australian Ambulance Service. Western Australian residents aged over 65 who do not receive a full pension are entitled to a 50% subsidy on the cost of using an ambulance in Western Australia, but this subsidy does not apply interstate. Other residents are required to pay the full fee for ambulance service unless they have insurance with a private health fund or St John Ambulance. Check that this will cover you Australia-wide.

Definitions

* **Breakdown** – a vehicle being disabled due to unexpected mechanical or electrical failure. Roadside Assistance does not cover regular maintenance or permanent repairs that should normally be carried out in a repair workshop. It does not cover damage following an accident, theft, impact damage, vandalism or any insurable incident.
* **Impact damage** – a single vehicle incident where a vehicle runs off the road or impacts with an animal or an inanimate object such as a rock or a tree is regarded as an accident, not a breakdown. Incidents such as these will not be covered under Roadside Assistance, but would require entitlement to separate Accident Assistance.
* **Recovery** – transporting a disabled vehicle between two centres, usually by a vehicle carrier.
* **Roadside Assistance** – primary assistance provided by a Patrol Officer to attempt to restore the mobility of the vehicle at the breakdown location.
* **Towing** – the vehicle's removal from a breakdown site to another location.

Important restrictions

In most states, heavy vehicles (in excess of either 2 tonnes or 4 tonnes depending on the club) and caravans over 5.5m total length are not eligible for roadside assistance and/or towing. Check this out carefully.

Although there are upgraded levels of membership at an additional price, these usually do not give you additional benefits if your vehicle is oversize. With some clubs, higher levels of membership are claimed to cover the member, regardless of the vehicle they are driving, but beware, elsewhere in the brochure it states that vehicles over a particular size and weight are not eligible for service. This means that a member is covered only if they are driving an eligible vehicle. It does not matter what level of membership you have, heavy vehicles are excluded from roadside assistance and towing (except in South Australia).

Caravan towing – Other than having the tow vehicle disabled, the main causes of a caravan being disabled are a broken axle or damaged wheel bearing. In both instances the caravan would have to be transported on a tilt tray, and this would usually be categorised as requiring 'special towing equipment'. Check your entitlement.

Only one tow is available per breakdown incident, except for the RAC of Western Australia and Premium Membership of RAA of South Australia.

If you are entitled to assistance in changing a flat tyre, the club's representative will only do this if your spare is considered to be in a roadworthy condition.

We have not included all the entitlements and restrictions of each level of membership, but have summarised the main features that apply to travellers. Before buying a particular membership package, read the terms and conditions carefully. The highest level of membership entitles the member to be towed for a greater distance than with the basic membership and there are also many other additional benefits. You should join the Club in the state where you reside.

Authors' tip:

If your vehicle is outside the size or weight limitations for towing by your motoring club, check your insurance policy to see if you are covered for towing after a breakdown as well as after an accident.

Summary of auto club membership and restrictions

NEW SOUTH WALES & ACT (NRMA)

NRMA subscription packages (subject to the exclusions shown below) –

- Premium Care has the most generous benefits. Your nominated vehicle and any trailer attached to it are entitled to Roadside Assistance, but the trailer (or caravan) must not exceed 2 tonnes GVM 5.5m in length including the draw bar, 2.5m in width or 2.6m in height. Call the special hotline on 13 29 00 from anywhere in Australia to access your increased benefits.
- Classic Care. Your nominated vehicle (but not the trailer) is entitled to Roadside Assistance.
- Basic Care. Your nominated vehicle (but not the trailer) is entitled to Roadside Assistance, and this is limited to four call-outs per subscription year.
- Traveller Care. This is available to a member who is also a member of the Royal Automobile Club of Australia or who is entitled to receive Roadside Assistance through a manufacturer's warranty programme. Traveller Care does not include Roadside Assistance, but does include towing and some other benefits to the same level as Premium Care. Call the special hotline on 13 29 00 from anywhere in Australia.
- Club Care does not entitle a member to Roadside Assistance or towing.

Exclusions (Extracts from the NRMA Terms and Conditions)

- Emergency roadside assistance – 'We will make every effort to provide roadside assistance to vehicles over 2.5 tonnes GVM. However, there may be circumstances where we are unable to mobilise such a vehicle. In these cases we will assist you to make alternative arrangements at your own expense.'
- *Wheel changing* – 'We will assist in changing a wheel with a flat tyre provided you have a roadworthy spare and your vehicle is under 2.5 tonnes GVM. We will also try to assist vehicles over 2.5 tonnes GVM.'
- *Towing of nominated vehicles* – 'The location of the breakdown and your subscription package, will determine the towing benefits which can be provided.' Following are some of the exclusions:
  - Vehicles weighing over 2.5 tonnes or exceeding 5.5m in length.
  - Trailers (or caravans) that exceed the size and weight limitations shown above.
  - A vehicle damaged as a result of an accident, flood, theft, fire or malicious damage.
  - A vehicle bogged in a location inaccessible to normal two-wheel drive vehicles.
  - If your vehicle has pulled to the side of the road and become bogged without being involved in an accident, NRMA will attempt to salvage the vehicle without calling for a tow truck. If towing equipment is required, this will be at your expense.

NORTHERN TERRITORY (AANT)

Road service is available to AANT members for any vehicle they are driving at the time of breakdown, provided the member is present with the vehicle and shows their membership card. AANT offers three levels of membership, with more generous benefits available to Plus and Premium levels. With all levels of membership there is no limit on the size of vehicle eligible for roadside service.

Memberships available:

- Premium Membership has unlimited service call outs per year. The weight limit for towing is 4 tonnes except that "recreational mobile homes" exceeding that weight are covered to a maximum of $220 per annum.
- Plus Membership has unlimited service call outs per year. The weight limit for towing is 2 tonnes.
- Standard Membership includes towing for vehicles less than 2 tonnes.

Caravan Towing

With both Premium and Plus memberships, if you are towing a caravan or trailer and your vehicle breaks down, AANT will tow the vehicle and the towed unit to a place of repair or safety. If special equipment is required due to the size of the caravan, there may be an additional charge.

Wheel changing

Vehicles exceeding 2 tonnes gross weight are not eligible.

Vehicle recovery exclusion – Vehicles or caravans over 5.5m long (including the draw bar), 2.3m wide, 2m high, wheel span over 1.8m or weighing more than 2 tonnes.

QUEENSLAND (RACQ)

RACQ membership is available in the following levels, with more generous benefits available to Ultra and Plus Members:

Ultra Care covers any driver of the nominated vehicle or the member when driving any eligible vehicle (plus a caravan or trailer). For assistance phone 1800 777 917 anytime from anywhere in Australia.

Plus Care covers any driver of the nominated vehicle (plus a caravan or trailer). For assistance phone 1800 777 917 anytime from anywhere in Australia.

Club Care covers any driver of the nominated vehicle for towing. Many of the additional benefits listed for Ultra and Plus are available at the member's cost.

Gold Membership – members of the Club for over 25 years. A member receives benefits when driving any eligible vehicle. A 25% discount applies to Ultra and Plus Care membership.

Roadside Assistance

Only vehicles with a GVM under 4 tonnes are eligible for road service, regardless of the level of membership (Club, Plus, Ultra or Gold Card) of the driver. For all members driving an eligible vehicle, free roadside assistance is available up to 40km from the nearest available RACQ contractor's premises.

Wheel changing

Free attendance up to 40km from the nearest available RACQ contractor's premises. Where the weight of the wheel and tyre assembly is beyond the safe lifting capacity of a single person it will attract a service fee for additional assistance.

Caravan and trailer entitlements applicable to all levels of membership – Free minor repairs and/or adjustments and replacement of a faulty tyre/wheel up to 40km from the nearest available contractor's premises.

If you are in an area where a contractor is not available to attend to your call, you are advised to call any nearby garage, pay the charges and then apply to the Club for consideration of an ex-gratia payment.

Towing

Regardless of the level of membership the following vehicles will **not** be towed:

- Vehicles weighing over 2.5 tonnes (loaded or unloaded). Vehicles weighing up to 4 tonnes may be towed if the contractor handling the job has a large enough tow truck, although a fee may apply.
- Vehicles weighing over 4 tonnes will not be towed.
- Vehicles longer than 5.5m, wider than 2.3m or higher than 2m.
- 'Motorised Homes' means campervans and motorhomes over the weight and dimensions limit. We are advised that a camper van under 2.5 tonnes in weight would be regarded as a normal vehicle.
- Fifth-wheelers.
- Caravans or trailers exceeding 7m in length including the draw bar or exceeding 4 tonnes gross weight.

SOUTH AUSTRALIA (RAA)

RAA membership comes in three levels:

- Premium membership includes a caravan or trailer. Towing of vehicles is normally limited to 2 tonnes, however for vehicles weighing between 2 tonnes and 4 tonnes (or those requiring specialised equipment), RAA will contribute $220 towards the cost of towing. The limit of 4 tonnes does NOT apply to 'recreational mobile homes'. Phone 1800 888 522 Australia wide to access your benefits.
- Plus membership includes caravans and trailers that weigh less than 2 tonnes and measure less than 5.5m long (including draw bar), 2.3m wide, 2m high or wheel span of 1.8m. Phone 1800 888 522 to access benefits.
- Standard membership is limited to vehicles weighing less than 2 tonnes and with the size limitations shown for 'Plus' membership.

Road service terms and conditions

- RAA membership is personal and the member must be present with the vehicle and show a membership card.
- Recovery of vehicles exceeding 5.5m in length, 2.3m in width, 2m in height, 1.8m wheel span or weigh more than 2 tonnes is not covered. Recovery of caravans, trailers or similar is not covered.
- Vehicles over 2 tonnes, modified vehicles and some caravans/trailers are excluded from towing in metropolitan and country serviced areas, however with Premium membership the limit is 4 tonnes.
- Except with Premium membership, towing of large vehicles is not covered. The limit is 5.5m in length, 2.3m in width, 2m in height or wheel span of 1.8m.
- Wheel changing is excluded for vehicles exceeding 2 tonnes gross weight.
- Service or towing is not provided to vehicles, caravans and trailers involved in an accident, fire or theft whether insured or not.

TASMANIA (RACT)

RACT membership is available in two levels:

- Ultimate membership covers vehicles weighing between 2 tonnes and 4.5 tonnes with no limit to towing within Tasmania, however there are limits interstate. If a vehicle over the size and weight limits shown below requires towing, RACT will contribute up to $200 towards the cost. If wheel changing is required RACT will contribute up to $150. *Caravan cover* – If your tow vehicle requires towing, a caravan up to 2 tonnes is eligible for towing. If your caravan is damaged and needs to be recovered, RACT will arrange this and contribute up to $200.
- Advantage membership covers vehicles only up to 2 tonnes and does not cover towing of caravans or trailers.

With both Advantage and Ultimate membership the following applies:

- Service eligibility applies to the member personally, and is not limited to a particular vehicle.
- Vehicles exceeding 2 tonnes as loaded are not eligible for free towing.
- Vehicles exceeding 2 tonnes but not exceeding 4.5 tonnes as loaded, are entitled to service but not wheel changing or any service involving lifting, hoisting or towing. Service for 24 volt electrical systems in vehicles is subject to available equipment.
- Roadside assistance and/or towing are not available for vehicles that weigh more than 4.5 tonnes, that are longer than 5.5m, wider than 2.3m or higher than 2m.
- RACT service and towing are not provided for vehicles involved in any form of accident or with broken windscreens or that have been stolen.

VICTORIA (RACV)

Benefits apply to all levels of membership, although the dollar value of service and the distance a vehicle will be towed varies with the different membership levels:

- 'Total Care' membership covers a member whilst driving any eligible vehicle, and also the member's nominated vehicle regardless of who is driving. There is assistance with wheel changing, however if special equipment is needed due to weight restrictions, RACV will pay up to $300 towards such cost. If interstate phone 1800 333 300 for service.
- 'Extra Care' membership applies to a nominated vehicle. RACV will pay up to $220 for the cost of special equipment needed to tow your vehicle. There is assistance with wheel changing, however if special equipment is needed due to weight restrictions, RACV will pay up to $300 towards such cost. When travelling interstate phone 1800 333 300 for service.
- 'Roadside Care' applies to a nominated vehicle.

Restrictions apply to vehicles exceeding 2.5 tonnes GVM.

- 'Total Care' and 'Extra Care' – Vehicles weighing between 2.5 tonnes and 4 tonnes are entitled to towing up to $500 per service call, wheel changing up to $300 per service call, and vehicle recovery. Members will incur commercial charges for towing a vehicle over 4 tonnes GVM.
- 'Roadside Care' Membership – Vehicles exceeding 2.5 tonnes GVM but not exceeding 4 tonnes are entitled to roadside service not requiring wheel changing or lifting, hoisting or towing. Service is not available for vehicles exceeding 4 tonnes GVM. Towing is not available to vehicles exceeding 2.5 tonnes GVM, however RACV can organise a commercial tow at the member's cost.

Caravan and trailer coverage

An eligible trailer (or caravan) is less than 6.7m in length, 2.3m in width, 2.7m in height or 3.9 tonnes gross weight. Larger trailers or caravans will be subject to commercial arrangements. An eligible trailer is entitled to assistance after becoming disabled through mechanical failure only if it is being towed by an eligible vehicle. For members with Roadside Care, only trailers weighing less than 2.5 tonnes are eligible for wheel changing. Service is not available for permanent on-site caravans. RACV will not tow trailers carrying livestock.

WESTERN AUSTRALIA (RAC)

There are three levels of membership:

- 'Ultimate' membership covers the nominated vehicle and also the member no matter which (eligible) vehicle he/she is driving. An eligible caravan or trailer (within the limits below) will be towed up to 100km in metropolitan or regional areas, and in country areas back to the town of the attending service provider. There is a limit to the 'dollar value' of benefits that can be claimed in any one year, and this amount increases over the first five years of membership.
- 'Classic' covers a nominated vehicle and eligible trailer or caravan. Roadside assistance and towing are the same as for 'Ultimate' membership except for caravans and trailers where the towing limit is less. The annual limit on benefits increases over the first five years of membership, however the value is less than with Ultimate membership.
- 'Standard' covers a nominated vehicle, but does not include roadside assistance or towing of a caravan or trailer. Benefits are less than with Ultimate and Classic membership.

Note – The guaranteed service areas are Perth metropolitan area and 10km radius from the GPO of the following towns: Albany, Bunbury, Geraldton, Kalgoorlie and Mandurah. The rest of WA is a non-guaranteed service area.

Ultimate or Classic members should phone 1800 999 036 (if more than 100km from home).

Exclusions

Breakdown service will not apply to vehicles exceeding 4 tonnes GVM or length of 5.5m.

Also excluded are trailers that exceed 2 tonnes gross weight, 5.5m long (including the draw bar), 2.5m wide or 2.6m high or those being used other than for private or recreational purposes.

Authors' tip:

We are advised by the RAC that, even if your vehicle is outside the size and weight limits listed above, they will send a Patrol Officer who will attempt to help.

Towing

If a vehicle weighing over 2 tonnes requires towing, an extra charge will apply.

Caravans and trailers

Only Ultimate and Classic memberships cover trailers and caravans (within the size and weight limitations above). Service is available for a trailer only when it is being towed by a vehicle driven by the member or towed by a nominated vehicle that suffers breakdown. The trailer or caravan will receive the same towing benefits as the tow vehicle, however if special equipment is required for a disabled caravan or trailer, additional costs for time and equipment are at the member's expense.

RAC members travelling interstate

Towing may only be provided up to the limit of the local club's standard membership, and you will have to pay for any additional towing including that of a caravan or trailer. Keep the receipt and check with the RAC on your return home to see if you are entitled to a refund.

Caravan immediately after a jack-knife and rollover incident

Dangers when travelling

Health

Driver fatigue

Probably the most dangerous element in the equation is the driver. Avoid alcohol and start off rested. Plan your trip so you drive when you would normally be awake. Avoid driving at night because not only will you be tired, but other drivers will also.

If you think you are experiencing any of the following danger signs you should stop immediately:

- You feel tired or have to consciously try to keep your eyes open.
- Lack of alertness or delayed reactions.
- Your vision becomes fuzzy or dim or you start seeing things.
- Unintentional changes in speed or fumbling gear changes.
- Vehicle wandering across the road.

Some suggestions to avoid fatigue

- When planning your trip, be realistic about how far you can drive in a day.
- Make sure the driver's seat is properly adjusted and that you are comfortable. If the seats are not well-designed you may need to add a lumbar support cushion.
- Talk to your passenger, listen to music or sing along.
- Adjust the ventilation system so there is cold air blowing on your face.
- Have a supply of drinking water close by and take a drink about every hour to make sure you do not become dehydrated. The first sign of dehydration is usually a headache – easi ly reversed by drinking a lot of water, otherwise the headache will be followed by more debilitating symptoms.
- Stop every two hours for a break. Get out of the vehicle and have some refreshments. This is a good time to check the vehicle – tyres and, if you are towing, the connections to the towed vehicle.
- When you stop for a break, both the driver and passenger should walk around. Sitting in the one place for a few hours can cause deep vein thrombosis, and this condition can become serious, even fatal. We have all heard of this occurring after a long flight, but it can happen much closer to home too.
- If at all possible, the passenger should also be qualified (and comfortable) to drive the vehicle, and on long travelling days both occupants can take a turn.
- If you are sleepy have a short nap or change drivers.

Authors' tip:

We find that reasonably up-tempo music is more effective than classical that might tend to lull you to sleep.

Water

In addition to drinking sufficient water to prevent dehydration, you should ensure that your drinking water is safe and clean. Buying bottled water is not the only option – there is a considerable cost, and storing the additional water takes up valuable space. If you rely on unfiltered water from your water storage tank, you are totally reliant on the quality of water you put in your tank and also on the tank's cleanliness.

Options:

- Keep drinking water separate from the tank that is used for washing up and bathing.
- Boil water for at least a minute to remove any bacteria. Allow the water to cool and store in bottles.
- Use a carbon filtration system that will remove any dirt and unpleasant taste. Cartridges usually have to be replaced every six to 12 months. Filtration systems should comply with Australian Standard 4348.

Food

We are all aware of safe food handling practices from our home kitchens, but cooking with limited facilities and equipment in a caravan or motorhome kitchen presents additional challenges.

- The fridge is smaller and probably not as efficient as your home fridge, so you should monitor the temperature. If margarine or butter is soft it is a clear indication the fridge is not cold enough.
- Store meat in the bottom of the fridge, definitely not in the door. Do not allow meat juices to drip onto other food.
- Do not try to store meat for a long period in the fridge.
- Before freezing, pack meat or cooked meals in meal-sized portions so you can thaw just what you need.
- Occasionally check meat in the freezer to make sure it is totally frozen and stays that way all day.
- Thaw frozen meat or meals in the fridge, not on the bench or sink during the day. This prevents bacteria multiplying in the food in hot conditions, and an additional bonus is that while the food thaws it helps keep the fridge cold.
- With limited working space and utensils causing practical difficulties, make sure there is no cross-contamination between raw meats and salads or other food ready to eat. If you have sufficient equipment, use different knives and different cutting boards. If this is not possible, clean the utensils well after cutting raw meat and before re-using. This is particularly important if you are cutting food (i.e. salad or garnish) that will be eaten raw.
- After you cook meat, place it on a clean plate and not on the same plate that held the raw meat.

Driving

- **Size**: If you are driving anything larger than a small campervan, the size of the vechicle or combination has to be continually taken into account. Where the camber on the road tilts the top of the caravan or motorhome outwards, watch out for power poles close to the edge of the road and for shop awnings. If you are driving a high vehicle, check the height of older style service station awnings and tree branches in rest areas and caravan parks.
- **Acceleration and braking**: Both these will be considerably reduced compared to small passenger vehicles.
- **Cornering**: Be very cautious until you have experience with the vehicle. Make a wider turn into corners, particularly if you are towing a caravan and be prepared to negotiate corners more slowly.
- **Speed**: Because fuel consumption increases markedly as speed increases, many caravan and motorhome drivers travel around 85kph to 90kph.

Fishing at campground, Coopers Creek, Windorah, QLD

Windscreen damage

Windscreens can easily be damaged by stones thrown up by overtaking or passing vehicles. It is not possible to totally avoid stones, and sometimes they are thrown up at unexpected times. Consider installing a windscreen stone shield and stone guards over the headlights.

Repairs

Stone impact damage to a windscreen can often be repaired and extend the life of the windscreen, but it may not be economic to repair major damage, particularly if your vehicle insurance has a nil excess. If your windscreen is damaged put sticky tape or a stick-on patch over the pit or crack as soon as you can. By keeping out dust and moisture, the repair will be more successful. A crack up to about 10cm in length can be repaired by drilling to stop it extending further, then injecting liquid resin that will run along the crack to seal it. The resin is hardened under UV light. Star breaks and pits in the windscreen are filled with liquid resin and when the job is complete, the damage is hard to see. If there is noticeable damage directly in the driver's view, it is probably better to replace the windscreen because irregularities directly in front of the driver can be distracting. If you are going to have repairs done, do it as soon as possible before the damage becomes worse.

External dangers

Road rage

Unfortunately bad behaviour by some drivers has become a more common occurrence in recent years. Usually road rage is avoidable if you adopt a defensive driving attitude and try to avoid a direct confrontation with other drivers. Some suggestions:

- Do not travel in the right-hand lane of a multiple lane highway unless you are prepared to travel near the speed limit.
- If you are driving in the right-hand lane and it appears that other drivers want to travel faster, move over and let them go. Don't stay in front of them deliberately to keep them within the speed limit.
- Indicate before changing lanes and do not cut in front of another vehicle.
- When two lanes of slow-moving traffic have to merge and a driver in the other lane moves ahead of you out of turn – let him go. It makes little difference in the scheme of things.
- Most importantly – do not honk your horn to show displeasure at someone else's bad driving or discourtesy.
- Do not retaliate against another driver honking or gesturing at you. If possible, avoid eye contact. Ignore them and just consider how their blood pressure must have risen and how they are spoiling their day. Don't let them spoil yours as well.

Bush fires

If you are camped or travelling during summer in areas that are susceptible to bush fires, listen to the news each day and talk to locals or other travellers. If there is a bush fire nearby it is better to evacuate well ahead of the dangerous time. If you stay until the last minute you could be putting yourself in danger as well as others who might try to help you.

Difficult road conditions

Narrow tracks

If you are towing a caravan or driving a motorhome, before you enter narrow tracks or a campsite where there isn't a clear view, make sure that you will have room to turn. We had difficulty negotiating the track through the Pinnacles that in places is virtually the same width as our motorhome.

Driving very slowly and carefully through the Pinnacles, WA

Poor visibility

If visibility is reduced due to heavy rain, fog or smoke, slow down and turn on the headlights.

Water over the road

Before driving into water, check how deep it is. Unless you can estimate the depth by watching other traffic travel through, park your vehicle out of the way and walk through. Do not attempt to cross a swiftly-flowing current either on foot or in your vehicle.

Crossing Fletchers Creek, a tributary of the Ord River, on the Great Northern Highway, Western Australia

Wide loads

Large equipment is often transported on country roads, and by law there will be an accompanying escort vehicle with flashing lights. If an escort driver signals you to pull over he is escorting a vehicle that needs nearly the full width of the road.

Wide vehicles are often encountered on country highways

Animals on the road

Animals can be on the road at any time of the day, but particularly near dawn and dusk and in heavily overcast conditions. At these times, lower light levels make them more difficult to see. Take any action necessary to avoid an animal, but don't swerve violently and risk running off the road or overturning. You would be putting your own and other people's lives at risk. It is much safer to brake firmly and smoothly and try to keep your vehicle in a straight line.

If you collide with an animal, try to lessen any suffering the animal may experience or take it to the nearest vet or animal shelter. Some native animals may have babies in their pouch, and if this is the case, contact an animal shelter if possible. If the animal has died, try to drag it a couple of metres off the road so birds feeding on the carcass are not hit by passing traffic. Secondary road kills are particularly upsetting because they are usually avoidable.

Warning signs on the Eyre Highway across the Nullarbor

Kangaroos and **wallabies** are unpredictable and can easily jump in front of a vehicle instead of heading for the bush. If one kangaroo or wallaby jumps across the road, slow down immediately as it is possible others will follow it to 'safety'.

Wedge-tailed eagles feeding on road kill are very protective of their food source so are reluctant to leave it when a competitor (you) arrives on the scene. Because of their size they are very slow to take off, so if you see a large bird feeding on road kill, slow down to give it a chance to get away. Wedge-tailed eagles usually take off into the wind, so if you are aware of the wind's direction, you will have an idea which way the bird is likely to go.

A wedge-tailed eagle starting to take off as we approach

Some country roads travel through unfenced **sheep** and **cattle** properties and stock wander freely across the road. Keep an eye on animals near the road because they can bolt across the road at the last minute, particularly if a mother and her young have become separated. Take extra care if you drive through unfenced cattle properties at night because dark-coloured cattle are very difficult to see in the dark.

Warning of stock on the road, Gibb River Road

Emus can dash across the road or even try to outrun you by running directly in front.

An emu dashing across the road, South Australia

Other animal dangers

Crocodiles

Two different species of crocodiles inhabit many waterways in northern Australia. Dangerous *estuarine (saltwater) crocodiles* have a blunt snout whereas the less dangerous *freshwater crocodiles* have a thinner snout and a smaller body. Warning signs have been erected in areas that these reptiles are known to inhabit, but it is wise to assume any river, billabong or waterhole in the north could have estuarine crocodiles in residence.

There are simple precautions:

- Do not swim if there is any possibility of a crocodile being in the area.
- Stay well back from the water's edge when fishing.
- If you are in a boat keep your arms and legs inside.
- Do not clean fish at boat ramps.
- If you are sleeping on ground level in a crocodile area make sure your camp is at least 50m from any waterway.
- Keep your food stocks secure and do not leave food scraps lying around.
- Do not feed crocodiles or interfere with them.

Crocodile warning signs appear throughout northern Australia

Estuarine crocodile on the banks of the Victoria River near Timber Creek, NT

Freshwater crocodile in the Ord River, WA.

Dingoes

Dingoes should not be fed, and food stores must be kept secure. If dingoes could be in the area, children should be accompanied at all times. This applies particularly when visiting Fraser Island. Fines apply on Fraser Island for feeding dingoes or disturbing them in any way. (Dingo-safe procedures are outlined in the QPWS visitor guide and signage on the island.)

Dingo looking for a feed at the Devils Marbles Campground, NT

Snakes

There are several species of poisonous snakes in Australia, although few are aggressive. If you see a snake leave it alone. Many people have been bitten when they try to catch or kill a snake and it turns to defend itself. If you are walking in long grass wear enclosed footwear and make some noise. If there is a snake in the vicinity it will usually head the other way because they are more frightened of you than you are of them. If someone is bitten, don't wash the venom off the skin because it can help identify the snake species so the correct antivenene can be used. Immobilise the limb with tight bandaging to slow the spread of the venom through the bloodstream. Note the time when the bite occurred and seek urgent medical attention.

Sharks

It is estimated that there are about 90 species of sharks present in Australian waters and fortunately they are not all dangerous to man. Research has shown that sharks are more active in warmer water, but unfortunately so are people. It is wise to exercise caution when swimming in salt water and assume there could be a dangerous shark in the vicinity. The safest area to swim is between the flags at a patrolled beach. Do not swim at dusk or at night. If lifesavers detect a shark in the area a siren will sound to alert swimmers to leave the water immediately.

Marine stingers

Box jellyfish and irukandji jellyfish can be found in tropical waters between November and April. It is unlikely you will encounter them, but it is helpful to know what they look like, how serious a sting is and what to do as emergency first aid. Bluebottles are more common and are found over a wider area, but are not dangerous.

- Box jellyfish (*Chironex fleckeri*) – This most dangerous marine stinger is shaped like an upturned square flowerpot measuring up to 30cm with dozens of ribbon-like tentacles that can be over 4m in length. It is usually found in waters close to the coast. Contact with the tentacles results in a severe and potentially life-threatening sting that immediately causes severe burning skin pain. Often the tentacles remain on the sting, but attempting to wipe them away or pull them off will cause more venom to be discharged and make the sting worse. Pour vinegar onto the sting for at least 30 seconds and call for medical help if it is available. On many beaches where there is the possibility of marine stingers the local council has placed containers of vinegar is to be used as first aid. A severe sting may cause the victim's breathing to cease or heart to stop, so apply CPR if required while waiting for medical attention. Antivenom is available to help treat a box jellyfish sting, and even if the sting is to only a small area of skin, a victim should receive medical attention to minimise scarring.
- Irukandji jellyfish (*Carukia barnesi*) – This tiny transparent jellyfish is shaped like the top of a thumb, measures only 1-2cm across and has four very long thin tentacles. It is often found in deep water, but can be washed inshore. Contact with the tentacles causes an initial minor stinging sensation to the skin, followed 20 to 40 minutes later by severe generalised muscular pain, headache, vomiting and sweating. In some cases it can cause life threatening high blood pressure. These symptoms are known as 'Irukandji Syndrome'. Vinegar should be poured on the area of the sting for at least 30 seconds to stop any further venom being discharged into the skin. Reassure the victim and take him or her to hospital or an ambulance station immediately and do not wait for symptoms to manifest themselves.

Marine Stinger warning sign, North Queensland

Containers of vinegar are located on many beaches

- Irukandji jellyfish (*Morbakka fenneri*) – A larger relative of the tiny irukandji jellyfish described above was identified and named late in 2008. It measures up to 15cm high with four tentacles up to a metre in length and can be found in coastal waters as far south as Sydney. A sting from this jellyfish is not typically fatal. Symptoms and treatment are similar to a sting from the smaller irukandji jellyfish.
- Blue bottles can inflict a painful sting, but this is not life threatening. If you see these little blue 'bladder-like' creatures washed up on the beach, it is likely they are also floating in the water. Contact with a tentacle will result in a sting that causes burning pain that can last an hour. Immerse the area of the sting in hot water (as hot as can be tolerated). Vinegar will not help, and the traditional remedy of ice packs will help only marginally.

In tropical areas in summer, when the weather is hot and the water is most inviting, you should observe the following precautions to avoid being stung by box jellyfish or irukandji.

- Observe warning signs and do not enter the water if the beach is closed.
- Swim only at patrolled beaches and stay between the red and yellow flags.
- Swim in stinger-resistant enclosures where these have been installed. These are not necessarily stinger-proof.
- Wear a full lycra stinger suit or wetsuit.

Coral cuts

Coral formations are sharp and rigid, and accidental contact can result in a cut with a small amount of animal protein and calcareous material in the wound. Without proper treatment, a small harmless-looking cut can quickly develop into an infected wound. Scrub the cut with soap and water and flush with fresh water. If the wound stings, rinse with vinegar. Flush the wound with a 50/50 mix of water and peroxide. Rinse daily and apply antibiotic ointment.

Rainforest dangers

Ticks

Ticks can become attached to your body when you walk though tall grass or dense undergrowth. Wear long pants tucked into your socks and also a long-sleeved shirt. Check your body thoroughly after walking in forested areas. If you find a tick remove it, and if you suffer an allergic reaction causing headache and nausea, seek medical attention. If you have a pet with you, check its body thoroughly because a tick can kill a dog or cat.

Leeches

Leeches can be found in wet areas, and spraying repellent around the top of your socks usually prevents them from attaching themselves. You will not feel a leech bite, so if you are not wearing fully enclosed shoes, check your feet, especially under and around your toes. If one has become attached, sprinkle salt on it and it will drop off. The leech injects its saliva into the bite and this has an anticoagulant and anaesthetic effect. When you remove the leech the wound will bleed, the extent dependent on how long the leech has been attached. Although unpleasant, a leech bite is generally harmless and should not cause concern.

Stinging plants

When bushwalking don't touch or brush against foliage. One unpleasant stinging plant has large heart-shaped leaves covered with tiny fine hairs that break off in the skin and cause extreme pain for days or weeks.

Vines and palms

Lawyer vine or wait-a-while is an attractive climbing palm with tendrils that hook into your clothing as you brush past. Vicious-hairy-Mary is a rattan palm with prickles that become embedded in the skin of anyone who touches or grabs the palm fronds.

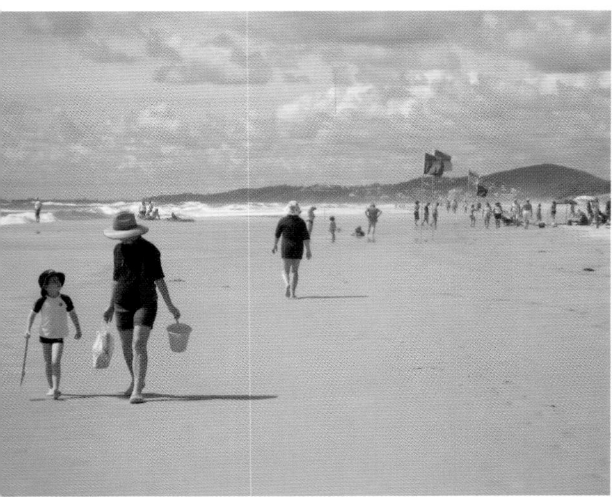

Patrolled surf beach, Peregian Beach, Sunshine Coast Queensland

Other external dangers

Surf

The surf can conceal a rip that can drag unwary swimmers out of their depth, particularly on an out-going tide. Lifesavers understand the local surf conditions and choose a safe location for swimming, marked with red and yellow flags. Read the information board (on most patrolled beaches) where lifesavers detail beach and surf conditions. It is extremely rare for someone to drown in a patrolled area, but unfortunately an average of 60 people drown every year when swimming in unpatrolled areas. If the conditions are calm and you simply can't resist having a swim even though the area is not patrolled, remain in very shallow water. However, if there is the possibility of marine stingers, confine your swimming to the pool.

Valuable information for swimmers and board riders

Bushwalking

If you are considering hiking in a national park, ask the rangers for advice on walks, taking your physical capabilities into account. Consider possible adverse weather conditions and extreme temperatures. Take plenty of water, a hat and sunglasses and use sunscreen (reapply as directed).

> **Authors' tip:**
>
> When you are considering a long walk or hike in a national park, think about your physical fitness compared with the park rangers. Walkers of average fitness should allow 15 minutes per kilometre on a reasonably level path. Allow extra time for an occasional break, and photo stops.

Extreme weather conditions

Cyclones

If you are travelling in tropical regions in summer, you should be aware of the possibility of a cyclone. Follow weather reports because cyclone alerts are usually issued a couple of days in advance of danger. If there is news of a cyclone approaching but there is no rain and wind, do not be lulled into a false sense of security because sometimes the effects of a cyclone are not felt until the storm centre gets close. Some cyclones can be small in area, but intense, so do not underestimate the risk if you hear a cyclone described as 'small'. The important information is the cyclone's intensity or rating that is determined from the barometric pressure at the centre of the cyclone. It gives a clear indication of wind speed and the risk of damage.

In **Queensland** and **Northern Territory**, cyclones are rated from category 1 to category 5 (the most dangerous).

- Category 1 – winds speed 125kph, damage to crops, trees and caravans.
- Category 2 – winds 125-169 kph, minor house damage, significant damage to trees and caravans, risk of power failure.
- Category 3 – winds 170-224 kph, roof and structural damage, some caravans destroyed.
- Category 4 – winds 225-279 kph, significant roof loss and structural damage. Many caravans destroyed and blown away. Dangerous airborne debris.
- Category 5 – winds in excess of 280kpm, extremely dangerous with widespread destruction.

In **Western Australia** cyclone alerts are colour-coded.

- Blue Alert – a cyclone may affect the area within 48 hours.
- Yellow Alert – the cyclone is moving close and appears inevitable within 12 hours. Strong winds are likely to occur in affected ares.
- Red Alert – destructive winds are imminent and you should seek shelter.

If you are travelling and there is a cyclone alert affecting the area where you are, it is advisable to leave and go inland because cyclones lose intensity as soon as they cross the coast. Areas well inland will receive heavy rain but are unlikely to suffer from destructive winds to the same degree as coastal areas.

Thunderstorms

Severe thunderstorms can occur at any time of the year. In northern Australia they are very rare during the dry winter months and most strike between September and March when the supply of solar energy is greatest. In the southwest of Western Australia and southeast South Australia severe winter storms linked to cold fronts are common. Storms can produce hail, lightning, strong wind gusts, flash floods, or even tornadoes.

If a severe storm approaches your campsite, take down the awning or annexe and stow moveable objects such as chairs. Examine your immediate surroundings to ensure there are no large trees close enough to come down on your caravan or motorhome. If a very severe storm is approaching and you are camped in a camper caravan, camper trailer or tent, pack up as you would for travelling and sit in your tow vehicle while you wait for the storm to pass. Take these safety measures well before the storm hits your camp.

If you see a storm approaching while you are travelling, look for a relatively sheltered spot where you can park away from large trees, power lines and areas that could appear liable to flash flood. Ensure that you pull well off the road, preferably into a rest area, so traffic does not run into the back of your vehicle due to poor visibility in heavy rain. If heavy rain is blowing from one particular direction, try to park with the side of the caravan or motorhome with permanent vents (for the fridge) away from the wind.

Strong wind gusts can very easily blow the pop-top roof off a caravan or camper, and as a precaution, it is wise to lower the pop-top section. If there is a very high wind warning, tie the pop-top section down if possible.

Lightning kills between five and ten people in Australia and injures over 100 people each year. To estimate the distance (in kilometres) to a lightning strike, divide the time delay (in seconds) between the flash and the thunder by three. If the time delay is less than 30 seconds you should consider looking for shelter.

Shelter in a solid building or 'hard-top' vehicle (caravan, campervan or motorhome) however you should not touch metal sections of the vehicle while there is a chance of a lightning strike. Camper caravans, camper trailers or tents do not provide adequate protection against lightning, so if you are camped in this style of accommodation you will be safer in your tow vehicle until the storm passes. If you cannot reach shelter, crouch in a hollow with your feet together but do not stretch out flat. If not, huddle with other people. Do not shelter under trees, and avoid being the highest object in the vicinity. Remove metal objects from your head and body and stay away from metal poles, fences and clotheslines. Do not handle fishing rods, umbrellas or golf clubs. If boating, go ashore to shelter as soon as possible.

Hail, **flash floods** and **tornadoes** are not common occurrences. Do not continue driving during a hailstorm because the speed of your vehicle will increase the impact velocity of the hail and increase the damage to your vehicle. A flash flood can sometimes occur when a storm moves slowly dumping a heavy downfall on a small area and this run off is funnelled by creeks and gullies. If there is sustained torrential rain, keep clear of areas that are likely to flood. Tornadoes, the rarest and most violent of thunderstorm phenomena, contain very damaging winds that may reach more than 450kph. The tornado vortex ranges in width from a few metres to hundreds of metres. Luckily, they are extremely rare in Australia, but not totally unknown.

> **Authors' tip:**
>
> If you are camped near a stream and there is heavy rain in the catchment area monitor the level of the water. If in doubt, move to higher ground.

Cold weather conditions

Ice

In southern regions in winter there may be a chance of ice on the road, particularly early in the morning. Danger areas are on bridges or overpasses, and on areas of roadway that the sun has not yet reached. Ice will have a dramatic effect on traction, so you should decrease driving speed and increase following distance.

Snow

If you plan to travel in snow areas in winter, you should carry chains that can be hired in towns near the snow resorts. Motorhomes with dual rear wheels require chains for one of the duals on each side of the vehicle. Decrease travelling speed and drive with vehicle lights on to increase visibility. In general, driving on snow has many of the characteristics of driving on sand or black soil.

Travelling on Cape York

Camping and environmental awareness

Caravan parks

Many travellers prefer the security of staying in a caravan park, and also the convenience of using the facilities. If you have a large caravan or motorhome, mention this to the staff at check-in to make sure you are given an appropriate site.

If you have not stayed in the particular park previously take the time to walk into the park and check out the site they have offered.

- Look for **low branches** and be cautious about **overhanging trees**. They can drop sap and are often home to birds that leave droppings on your vehicle or awning roof. Check that there is enough height to extend a TV antenna.
- How **level** is the site and is there a **steep gutter** to negotiate?
- For caravan owners particularly, **drive-through sites** are the most convenient, but if one is not available, check out how easy the site is to reverse into. If you have a large caravan, is there enough room for you to swing the van when reversing. If you need to use part of the adjacent site to reverse into your own, you have to assume that it may not be vacant and available for you to use when you are driving out.
- If you are connecting to electricity, check where the **power** is located to see if you have a lead long enough to reach without joining. Check that the power point looks to be in good condition. If the power socket shows signs of damage report it to park management and do not use it.
- If you intend to connect to the **water supply**, check where the tap is located and consider whether you have hose long enough to reach. If you are doubtful on the quality of the water, ask the park management or a nearby camper. See if there is a sullage point for your site.
- If you need to empty a toilet cassette or portable toilet, ask if the park has a **dump point**. You are usually not permitted to empty portable toilets in the toilets.
- Check out the **bathroom facilities**. Ask at the office whether you need a key for the amenities block or if there is a combination lock on the door.
- If you have a camper trailer with a kitchen at the back, a site that backs onto a fence will give you privacy.
- If you intend to use a house air conditioner, check if there is an extra fee.
- If you have additional people with you, check what the extra fee is.
- If you have to pay a deposit for a key to the amenities, or an electronic gate opener and you plan to leave early in the morning, check what time the office will be open for a refund.

Driving onto your site

This is where you need your 'co-pilot' giving directions, using a hand-held UHF radio. You do not need an in-built UHF in your tow vehicle: a second hand-held will do because the driver only has to listen to the directions, not debate them. If your site has a concrete annexe pad higher than the surrounding grass, take care when reversing on to the site so you do not run your wheels into the corner of the pad. If you have difficulty reversing your caravan onto a site, for whatever reason, most park managers will help you park or even do it for you.

Remote area travel

There are some simple basic steps you can take to avoid getting into trouble, and others that can help you if you get stuck in a remote area.

- **Inform a responsible person** of your planned itinerary and your vehicle registration number.
- **Keep in touch** with your contact person on a regular basis so if you do not make a scheduled phone call, they can call for help.
- **Check your vehicle carefully** and take a few spares – fan belt, extra fuel and some tools.
- Take a **tarp, blanket, spade and matches**.
- Take **additional food**, and more importantly plenty of **extra drinking water**. You can survive without food for a couple of weeks, but water is essential. The minimum requirement is two litres per person per day. Take plenty of extra water in case you are delayed or break down.
- Consider taking the following equipment – compass, GPS (and spare batteries), satellite phone, HF radio or an EPIRB (Emergency Position Indicating Radio Beacon).
- Consider taking an **orange 'V' sheet** used in marine situations to signal for help. In an emergency, this can be tied across the roof of the vehicle where it can be seen from the air.

If your vehicle breaks down

- Remain with it. A vehicle can easily be found, but a person on foot is very hard to find.
- Use the vehicle and tarp to provide shade, and try to keep as cool as possible. The ground is likely to be hot, so if you have chairs use them, but otherwise sit on a blanket.
- Drink your water sparingly. Do not overlook food that might contain water (fruit, vegetables, canned food). Do not drink alcohol as this will dehydrate you further.
- Collect brush and dry timber and set up a fire, ready to light if you hear an aircraft or another vehicle.

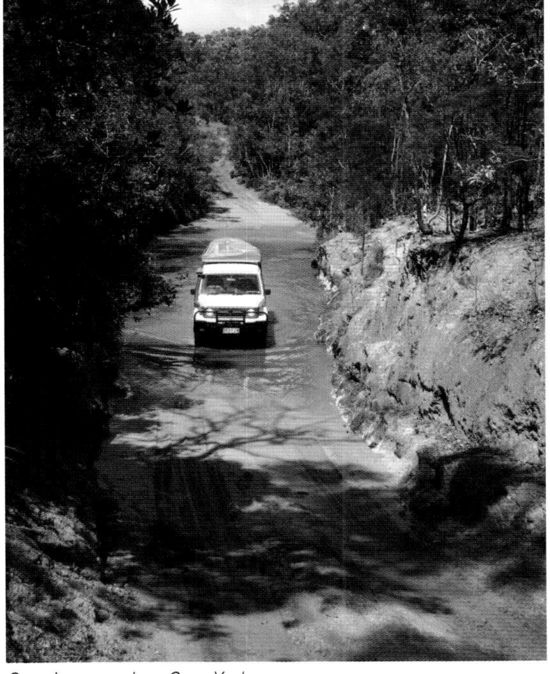

Crossing a creek on Cape York

If you decide you must leave your vehicle

- Leave a note telling rescuers when you left and the direction in which you will be walking.
- Take your map, GPS if you have one, compass, matches and obviously, all your water.
- If you do not have a compass you can work out where north is by using a watch. Position the watch with the '12' pointing at the sun. North is half way between the '12' and the hour hand.
- Keep your body as well covered as possible and wear a hat. Take additional coverings such as towels.
- Rest frequently by sitting down in shade if possible. Prop your feet up but do not take your shoes off because you might have difficulty getting them back on.

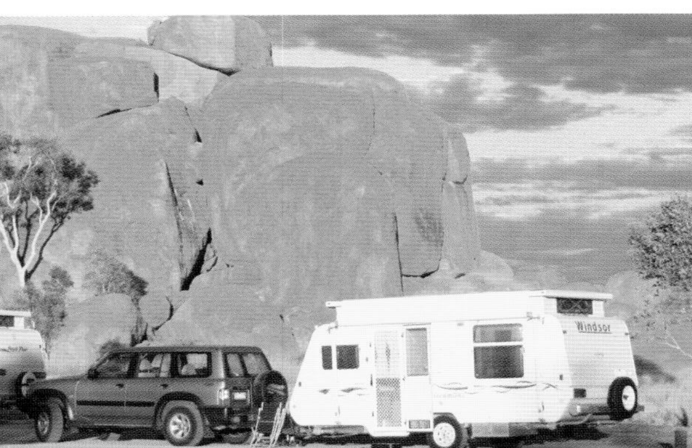

Devils Marbles campground, Northern Territory

Staying in a caravan park

Showers

To avoid contracting a fungal foot infection such as tinea in the showers, wear rubber thongs or use your own rubber mat. Do not stand bare-foot on the shower floor. Because many showers do not have shower curtains, your clothes can become wet unless you keep them in a large plastic bag while you are showering.

Security

Even if you are staying in a caravan park you need to be aware of security. Just as most of us would not go out and leave our home unlocked, we should lock our caravan or motorhome and not leave valuables unattended in the annexe. Despite the best efforts of caravan park management, unfortunately, on occasions people can come into a park at night, and walk out with items left in the open.

Security tips:

- When you leave your van – lock it.
- Even when you are in your van or close by, have your wallet, purse and valuables out of clear view.
- Don't have valuables in view in your tow vehicle or motorhome cab.
- Don't leave valuable items such as camera, laptop computer or mobile phone unattended in the annexe.
- At night put away easily transportable items such as BBQ, fishing rod, wetsuit and maybe even chairs.

Bush camping

As well as spending time at caravan parks, some travellers park overnight in rest areas or camp for a few days at a bush campsite. 'Overnight parking' is when a caravan or motorhome stops overnight so the occupants can rest, but no camping equipment is placed outside the vehicle. 'Bush camping' usually means that you put out some camping equipment. Many travellers with an onboard shower and toilet bush camp almost exclusively, and the degree of comfort depends on the facilities in the vehicle. Whether you are parking overnight or camping for a couple of days, the following items are applicable.

- Never stay overnight or camp in an area with a 'no camping' sign.
- Always observe the 'maximum stay' limit.
- Park out of direct sight of the road if possible.
- Avoid overhanging trees and especially dead tree branches – look up and live! Some trees, particularly river red gums, can drop branches even when there is no wind, and a large branch can seriously damage a van or motorhome. More minor annoyances are sap or gum that can drop onto your vehicle leaving a stain, or light branches that can scratch against it and keep you awake at night.
- If there are a lot of fast food wrappers and empty drink containers lying about and wheel 'do-nuts' in the dirt it is an indication it might not be a quiet campsite.
- Be cautious of camping close to a town, particularly on Friday and Saturday nights when there is more likelihood of noisy young people arriving to party.
- Do not park too close to other campers because they might start up a noisy generator when you want to enjoy the peace and quiet of the bush. If they were there first you cannot really object if they do use a generator.
- Check the area where you plan to camp for ant nests. These critters can enter your caravan or motorhome by climbing the awning guy ropes or even long grass or bushes that touch the vehicle. Once inside, the ants establish a nest and you will have them travelling with you for a long time. If you see a nest at your campsite, sprinkle ant powder or talcum powder around any points that the ants might use to access the vehicle.
- If there are other campers, go over and say "hello". The usual etiquette is not to disturb campers who are inside their vehicle with the door closed, unless you know them personally.
- Be considerate of others using the area if you are using a generator or playing music.
- If you have washing to dry, keep it close to the van or motorhome, preferably under the awning. Laundry flapping on a line between trees is not a pretty sight.
- If you decide to light a campfire use a fireplace if there is one nearby. If not, preferably build the fire where other people have previously lit one. Clear away any dry grass or other combustible material near the fire. Ensure that the smoke does not cause a nuisance for others.

Security

Security is one of the problems cited against staying overnight in a rest area, though in reality, hardly any travellers have a problem.

Simple steps can be taken for peace of mind:

- In choosing a spot to park, try to be away from the access road.
- Park facing outward so you can drive out easily.
- Do not leave the awning out, and pack away outside furniture and mats.
- Have the vehicle ready to leave in the unlikely event of a situation arising.
- Keep your ignition key readily accessible (or even in the ignition of a motorhome) so you can leave without delay.
- Do not store excess items on the driver's seat.
- As you probably do at home, lock the doors before you settle down for the night, and if anyone knocks, check who it is before you open the door.
- If your names are painted on the outside of your caravan or motorhome, just because someone calls you by name it does not mean they know you. Ask who it is before you open the door.
- In the unlikely event of someone bothering you, do not step outside the vehicle. Do not respond verbally as this can inflame the situation.
- A security door will enable you to see who is outside and talk to them without venturing out, and also will allow extra air circulation in total security. These doors are constructed of heavy mesh with three locking points into the doorframe.

Camp fires

- Take note of fire **bans**. Do not light a fire in hot dry windy conditions.
- If you are permitted to light a fire, it is preferable to use a **fireplace** if one is available. If not, try to use a bare patch of earth where other people have previously had a fire, but do not make a ring of stones to surround your fire. Ensure the fire does not get out of control by removing leaf litter or long or dry grass close to the fire.
- Keep your fire **small**.
- If you need wood for a fire, try not to collect wood that might provide a home for native animals. In national parks you are not permitted to collect wood for this reason. Do not break limbs from trees or shrubs.
- Do not try to burn household rubbish on the campfire, particularly plastic items.
- If you do have a fire, before retiring for the night **extinguish it thoroughly**, preferably by pouring water on the coals. Do not cover the coals with soil or sand because heat is retained underneath the covering soil and anyone who walks on the area can be burnt, possibly severely. Children are at particular risk.
- If your fire was not in a fireplace, you should aim to **remove all trace of the fire**. Next morning, check that the coals are cold before scattering them. Rake soil and leaves over the area.

Rubbish

- Do not leave your rubbish in an overflowing bin in a picnic area or rest area. These bins are usually emptied weekly and often by a contractor who has to drive quite a distance. Travellers can take their rubbish with them to put in a bin that is serviced more regularly.
- If rubbish overflows from a bin, animals can be drawn to the area and possibly ingest harmful items and also make the mess worse.
- Do not try to dispose of your rubbish on a campfire.
- Do not bury food scraps, sanitary pads, tampons or disposable nappies. Animals might dig them up.
- To safeguard our right to use bush camps, always leave them at least as clean as when you arrived. Many rest areas have been abused and littered with rubbish, resulting in closure.

Bush camping in Western Australia

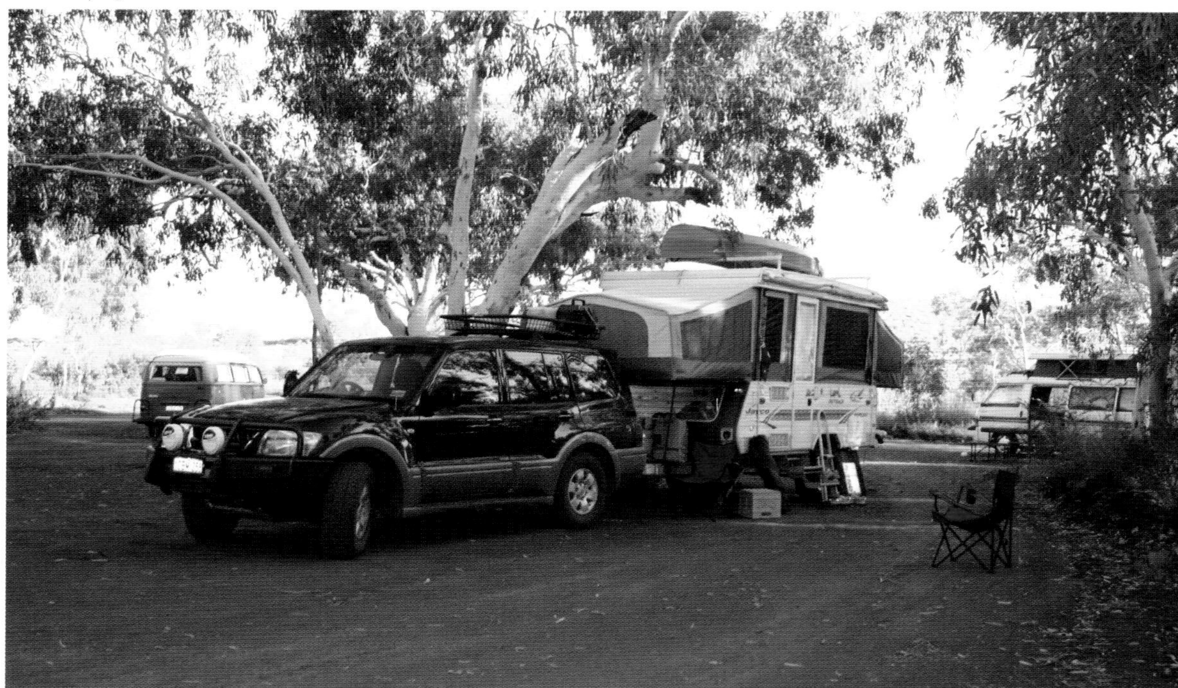

Toilets

- Use environmentally friendly products in an onboard toilet.
- Cassettes or black water tanks should be emptied in dump points. These are available at some highway rest areas, in many towns and in caravan parks. Refer to the list of dump points – pp 37-43
- You should never ever empty a toilet cassette that contains chemical additives in to a 'long drop' or 'environmental toilet' or a septic system because the chemicals will destroy the bacteria that enable those systems to work. *See p69.*
- If you do not have your own toilet and are concerned you might be 'caught short' carry a small spade to dig a bush toilet. This should not be close to a stream or creek.

Grey water

- If you don't have a grey-water tank to hold waste shower and kitchen water, let it flow into a bucket then pour on nearby trees or bushes that will benefit from a drink. Don't let it run onto the ground and leave muddy patches that other people might have to walk through. If you are in a caravan park, waste water should be emptied down a sullage inlet.
- Do not empty grey-water tanks close to a stream. The grey water will probably contain detergent and soap.
- If you use a portable shower tent, do not erect it very close to a stream.

Lawn Hill Gorge, Queensland

Kangaroo in a campground

Caring for the environment

There are several measures you can adopt to lessen your impact on the environment:

- As with any vehicle, keep the engine of your tow vehicle, campervan or motorhome well maintained to reduce air pollution.
- Avoid carrying out vehicle maintenance in rest areas or national park campgrounds.
- If you change the oil in your vehicle, do not pour the used oil on the ground or down the drain. Use a container and drip tray and where possible, recycle waste oil.
- Because caravanners and motorhomers travel widely, the vehicles can inadvertently carry weed seeds in mud on the vehicle and pests such as cane toads in storage bins. Check the vehicle, and wash off accumulated mud.
- Heed restrictions on carrying fruit, vegetables and honey into specific areas. *See p99.*
- Avoid driving at night because many species of wildlife are nocturnal and there is much more chance of hitting an animal between late afternoon and early morning. Many animals are particularly active at dusk and dawn.
- Do not feed birds and animals around a campsite because they may become dependent on handouts and become a nuisance to other travellers. Another problem can be that the food might be harmful.
- If you travel with a dog or cat, ensure that it does not disturb wildlife. Clean up after your pet.
- Avoid driving on dirt roads in wet weather because the road surface can be easily damaged.
- The travellers' motto should be: take only photographs and leave only footprints (or maybe tyre prints).

Caring for the bush

- If you are driving off-road, stay on existing tracks.
- When you are bushwalking, stay on the trails so you do not trample sensitive vegetation.
- If you must walk in an area without a trail, watch where you put your feet and avoid stepping on plants.
- Do not pick wildflowers. Admire and leave them for someone else to enjoy. By leaving the flowers, there is a chance their seeds will become the next generation of plants.

Banksia Menziesii, north of Perth, WA

Mother possum with her baby

Indian Head Falls, Cape York, QLD photo: Rob Boegheim

Social interaction & recreational activities

Social interaction

With local communities

- Country tracks often travel through cattle or sheep properties. Any gates you come across should be left as you find them.
- Travellers should not be impatient when they come across slow moving farm machinery travelling on the road.
- Slow down and drive carefully if sheep or cattle are feeding beside the road.
- If sheep or cattle are being herded across the road, stop your vehicle and let them go before proceeding.

With indigenous communities

- If you are travelling through an Aboriginal community, take note of restrictions that may apply to the carriage of alcohol or the consumption or supply of alcohol.
- Do not photograph anyone without his or her permission. Everyone should be treated with respect and not regarded as a 'tourist attraction'.
- Respect the spiritual and cultural significance of particular areas. Comply with signs that request that you do not enter a particular area or photograph a natural feature.
- Do not touch or interfere with indigenous relics such as paintings, rock carvings or middens.

Recreational activities

National parks

Most of the truly beautiful natural wonders of Australia are contained within our national parks. A small number of parks are 'wilderness parks' but the majority have facilities for day visitors and often for campers.

Some national parks do not have an indication of the length of time it will take to complete the walks, but will show a distance. A reasonable rule of thumb for people of average fitness and wearing appropriate footwear would be 15 to 20 minutes per kilometre. This would be on a constructed track without steep slopes. Don't start out on a hike if you are not sure you can complete it before dark. Take water, a hat, sunscreen and possibly insect repellent. If you are in a mountainous region where the weather could change, take warm clothing and rain protection.

National park fees

NEW SOUTH WALES – www.environment.nsw.gov.au

A daily entry fee of $7 is payable at 40 of the state's most popular national parks, and a few other parks have a higher entry fee. At Budderoo, Ku-ring-gai Chase and Royal national parks the fee is $11, and at Kosciuszko National Park it is $16 per day in summer and $27 per day in winter (from the start of the June long weekend to the end of the October long weekend). An access permit is required for two areas of Oxley Wild Rivers National Park, and a fee applies. If you are planning to visit several parks, it may be economic to purchase an annual pass that costs $190 and gives unlimited entry to all national parks in the state (or $65 for all parks except Kosciuszko). Pensioners resident in NSW are entitled to free entry into all national parks and reserves in the state, and they need to apply for an exemption card. New South Wales Senior Card holders are entitled to a 20% discount on all annual passes.

NORTHERN TERRITORY – www.nt.gov.au/nreta/parks

No entry fees apply to parks administered by the Northern Territory Government. An entry fee applies to Uluru-Kata Tjuta National Park, administered by Parks Australia. The pass costs $25 per person and is valid for three consecutive days. There is no charge to enter Kakadu National Park, also administered by Parks Australia.

There are several areas of Aboriginal land where visitors require a permit, and these are marked on the atlas. To obtain a permit to drive on the Mereenie Loop Road, contact the Central Land Council in Alice Springs. (Phone 08 8951 6211.) A permit is required to enter the Garig Gunak Barlu National Park on the Cobourg Peninsula by road. This costs $232.10 and allows camping for seven nights for a maximum of five people. Contact the Cobourg Peninsula Sanctuary and Marine Park Board in Palmerston. (Phone 08 8999 4814.)

QUEENSLAND – www.epa.qld.gov.au/parks_and_forests

There is free entry into all national parks. A vehicle permit is required to drive on Fraser Island and Bribie Island National Park. A Bribie Island National Park permit can be obtained from either the Environmental Protection Agency (phone 1300 130 372 in business hours) or the Bongaree Caravan Park on Bribie Island (phone 07 3408 1054). The cost is $35.50 for one week or $110.80 for one year. Fraser Island permits can be purchased online, and cost $37.10 for one month or $185.80 for one year.

SOUTH AUSTRALIA – www.environment.sa.gov.au/parks

Many national parks have an entry fee: in most cases $7.50 ($6 for concession card holders) per vehicle. There are a number of parks passes available that might be more economical. A Holiday Parks Pass valid for two months costs $30 ($24 concession) per vehicle and covers national parks in the State with the exception of Kangaroo Island and the desert parks. A Multi Parks Pass (excludes the desert parks and Kangaroo Island) is valid for one year and costs $67 ($54 concession). A Desert Parks Pass valid for 12 months costs $105 per vehicle and comes with an information booklet, park information and maps. This pass is required to visit parks and reserves north of the Gammon Ranges. Phone 1800 816 078 for information on Desert Parks passes. A Kangaroo Island Pass covering entry fees and some tours costs $46.50 per person ($36.50 for concession, $26.50 for children).

TASMANIA – www.parks.tas.gov.au

An entry fee applies to many national parks, whether there is a collection booth or not. A 24 hour pass to any number of parks costs $22 for a vehicle with up to eight people, or $11 per person. An eight-week Holiday Vehicle Pass costs $56 per vehicle (for up to eight people) and allows entry into all parks. A Holiday Person Pass costs $28 per person and is valid for up to eight weeks. An annual All Parks Pass if purchased between May 1 and October 30 costs $66 ($53 concession) and if purchased between November 1 and April 30 costs $90 (or $72 concession). Passes can be purchased onboard the ferries to Tasmania and at major national park visitor centres.

VICTORIA – www.parkweb.vic.gov.au

Most parks in Victoria have free entry, but a small number of parks have a daily entry fee.

- Baw Baw National Park entry fee is $10.30 per vehicle;
- Mornington Peninsula National Park (excluding Point Nepean National Park) entry fee is $4.40 per vehicle. Point Nepean National Park only is $7.90 per adult and $3.80 child or pensioner.
- Mt Buffalo National Park vehicle entry fee varies with the seasons -
  - When ski lifts are not operating the entry fee is $10.30 for one day; $16.20 for two consecutive days; and $20.50 for three consecutive days.
  - When ski lifts are operating the entry fee is $14.40 for one day; $22.00 for two consecutive days; $28.20 for three consecutive days.
- Wilsons Promontory National Park has a vehicle entry fee of $10.20 for one day, $16.20 for two consecutive days, $30.50 for five consecutive days. In holidays seasons a ballot is held for camping sites.
- Yarra Ranges National Park entry fee is $8 per vehicle.

A National Parks Pass costing $72.50 allows entry for one year into all parks, with the exception of the Point Nepean section of the Mornington Peninsula National Park. Phone 13 19 63 for details.

WESTERN AUSTRALIA – www.dec.wa.gov.au

Of the state's 63 national parks, 24 of the most popular have an entry fee. These cover a vehicle with up to eight people. A day pass into one or more parks costs $10 per day ($5 if the driver has a pension card, a senior's card or carer's card). A Holiday Pass valid for four weeks costs $35 (no concession available) and an Annual All Parks Pass costs $75 ($50 concession). Additional charges apply for the Tree Top Walk, Geikie Gorge boat trip, Dryandra Woodland guided night tours and Monkey Mia Reserve.

If you have a concession card we advise you to consider how many parks you intend to visit to work out if it is more economical to pay as you go rather than buy a pass. The following national parks have day visitor fees:

- Near Perth – Yanchep, John Forrest, Serpentine, Walyunga and Avon Valley national parks.
- North of Perth – Nambung National Park (Pinnacles).
- Mid West & Pilbara – Kalbarri, François Peron, Cape Range, Millstream-Chichester and Karijini national parks.
- Kimberley – Purnululu and Mirima national parks.
- Near Albany – Porongurup, Stirling Range and Fitzgerald River national parks.
- Near Esperance – Cape Le Grand, Cape Arid and Stokes national parks.

Fishing

Many travellers and campers enjoy fishing, but you need to check whether you need a fishing licence.

NEW SOUTH WALES

For both freshwater and saltwater fishing, you are required to pay the Recreational Fishing Fee and carry the receipt issued. This applies when spear fishing, hand lining, hand gathering, trapping, bait collecting and prawn netting or when in possession of fishing gear in, on or adjacent to waters. Permits are available for three days, one month, a year or three years. The fee can be paid online, by phone 1300 369 365, at most Kmart stores in NSW and from hundreds of standard and gold fishing fee agents. For more information visit the NSW Department of Primary Industries website www.dpi.nsw.gov.au/fisheries.

NORTHERN TERRITORY

Anglers require a temporary fishing permit from the Northern Land Council. There is no charge. The Northern Land Council handles all recreational fishing licences and permits for tidal Aboriginal waters on a behalf of the Anindilyakwa, Nothern, and Tiwi land councils. Ph: 1800 645 299 or visit the NLC website www.nlc.org.au.

QUEENSLAND

No licence is required to fish in salt water or freshwater rivers and streams, although size and bag limits apply. New limits were introduced in March 2009. A Stocked Impoundment Permit is required for 33 freshwater dams and a fee applies. Phone the Department of Primary Industries on 13 25 23 or refer to the website www.dpi.qld.gov.au. Spearfishing for barramundi is prohibited between 6pm and 6am. Shark species that are fully protected are the grey nurse shark, great white shark, speartooth shark, whale shark and all sawfish.

SOUTH AUSTRALIA

No licence is required for recreational fishing using fishing rods or handlines, but a licence is required to use rock lobster pots. Minimum lengths, and bag and boat limits apply. Phone (08) 8347 5100 or access the website www.pir.sa.gov.au.

TASMANIA

Fishing licences are not required for saltwater or marine fishing with a rod and line, but a licence is required for any fishing in inland waters including some river mouths and estuaries. Licences are available from major fishing tackle and sports stores and are valid from August 1 to July 31. (For more information visit www.ifs.tas.gov.au.) There are substantial discounts for pensioners and holders of a seniors card. A Recreational Sea Fishing Licence is required for abalone, rock lobster dives, rock lobster pots, rock lobster rings, graball nets, mullet nets, beach seine nets and scallop dives. Licences are valid from November 1 to October 31. For information phone (03) 6233 7042 or visit www.dpiw.tas.gov.au.

VICTORIA

A Recreational Fishing Licence is required for all recreational fishing in Victoria's marine, estuarine and fresh waters. Fees apply. Exemptions to licences are made for those under 18 or over 70 years of age, and holders of a Victorian seniors card, Veteran Affairs pension card or Centrelink pension card. Licences are available online, or through many DPI offices and many retail businesses including most retail fishing tackle stores. For more information visit www.dpi.vic.gov.au.

WESTERN AUSTRALIA

A Recreational Fishing Licence is only required for abalone, rock lobster, marron, net fishing and freshwater angling. Fees apply. A licence is required for each category, or you can buy a combined licence. Licences are available online, by post or in person at any Department of Fisheries' office. For more information visit www.fish.wa.gov.au.

Broome sunset

Bicycles

If you plan to stay in one place for a while, bicycles can be a cheap way to get around country towns while you leave your caravan or motorhome in the caravan park. Since the early 1990s it has been compulsory for cyclists to wear a protective bicycle helmet. Helmets should comply with Australian standard AS 2063:1996.

If you carry bicycles on an outside bicycle rack, consider putting a weatherproof cover over the bikes. Chain the wheels to the bicycle frame and also the bike to the rack so it cannot be removed when you are parked.

The usual way to carry bikes is on a rack attached to the rear of the van or motorhome. Before doing this, check whether your van or motorhome is already at its maximum length making it illegal to add anything to the rear. Fittings added, such as a bicycle rack, are included in the maximum overhang allowed to the rear of the axle. Maximum overhang on a caravan is 3.7m from the axle (or the centre point between tandem axles). With a motorhome the maximum is 60% of the wheelbase to a maximum of 3.7m. A disadvantage in carrying bicycles at the back is that they will become covered in dust that can damage the mechanics. They would have to be cleaned before being ridden. Take care that the bikes do not chafe against the wall of the caravan or motorhome.

With a caravan, a bicycle rack can be mounted on the draw bar of the caravan or on a carrier attached to a bracket on the tow bar at the rear of the tow vehicle. Both options will add weight that may affect towing stability.

Folding bikes are easier to transport than full-size bikes, however weight limitations apply to riders.

Digital photography

Travellers who use a digital camera need to decide on a few important points – how they will extract the data from the camera, where to store the digital images, and a back-up system.

Options:

- Visit a photographic shop to have photos printed and a CD burned as a back-up. Carry extra memory cards because it is unlikely country photo shops will be open seven days a week.
- If you have a computer, download the images to the hard drive. We recommend burning a CD as a back-up.
- Download from the camera to an external hard disc (eg iPod). Check compatibility between the camera and hard disc device. The advantages are that you do not require a computer or 240 volt power. When possible, make a back-up by having a CD burned.
- Buy a photo printer. This does not require a computer, however, unless you back-up your images (CD or iPod) you will not be able to reprint photos once you clear the camera memory chip.

If you decide to use one of the more technical options, try it out at home before you travel. You will need sufficient data storage available and a convenient method of retrieval, so you are not restricted in your photo taking.

Coolamunda Dam near Inglewood, QLD

Communications & GPS

Mobile telephone

Mobile phone service is available in heavily populated areas and country towns, but only about 5% of the outback has mobile phone service. We have found that coverage is particularly poor in Western Australia. Travellers planning to travel in remote areas off the main highways should consider a satellite phone, but the costs are high. An alternative is HF radio but this also costs a considerable amount.

A phone fitted into a vehicle with an outside antenna can achieve a much wider range than when using a hand-held unit. To give maximum range, the antenna should be fitted where it is clear of the body of the vehicle.

It is illegal for a driver to use a hand-held phone while driving, and talking on a phone using a hands-free kit can be a distraction. Have the passenger attend to phone calls, and if you need to take a call, pull over when you can do so safely. If you are travelling alone, let the incoming call go to message bank then return the call when you can stop safely.

Calls from a landline to 1800 numbers are free and calls to 1300 numbers cost 30 cents. These same calls made on a mobile phone are charged at the normal contract rate for your phone. If you want to save money when calling 1800 or 1300 numbers, use a public telephone.

Emergency phone calls

In an emergency, dial 000. If your phone company does not have service in the area but another company does, an emergency call will still operate. Emergency calls will operate on prepaid mobiles, even if the account has a nil balance.

Because your mobile phone is not linked to a street address, the emergency service operator will not automatically have your address as they do when you phone from a landline. Answer the operator's questions calmly, and tell him/her where you are, including the state you are in to avoid confusion and delay in responding to your call.

Networks

Telstra

Telstra has replaced its CDMA network with an enhanced mobile phone system known as '**Next G**' (short for generation). It has greatly increased speed, particularly important if you use the system for internet connection. Telstra claims it coves 98% of the Australian population with less 'black spots' than CDMA.

A **GSM network** phone will not be much use if you plan to travel and use your phone outside the main centres of population and main highways on the eastern seaboard of Australia. It is planned that the current GSM network will be shut down in 2012.

Optus

Optus is constantly implementing new base stations on its **GSM network** around the country Australia and it currently reaches more than 96% of the Australian population.

The **Optus 3G** (Third Generation) network can now reach 84% of the population, concentrating on the major cities. Optus has announced that the network will be upgraded, with a target completion date of December 2009. It is claimed that it will then reach 98% of the population, making it a competitor with Telstra for travellers. 3G is much faster than GSM, and gives a wider range of services. A 3G phone is required to use these services, however when travelling outside the 3G network, the phone will access and use the normal Optus GSM network.

Other networks

Vodafone operate GSM and 3G networks. They claim coverage of 99.53% of Australia's metropolitan areas, and with National Roaming activated, they claim the coverage is increased to 94.52% of the population.

AAPT and **3** also operate GSM and 3G networks.

Phone plans

There are a wide range of plans available, including some where you pay off the cost of the phone. If you own the phone and do not make a lot of calls, a pre-paid system could be the best option.

Authors' tip:

We have always used a Telstra mobile (in the last few years CDMA then Next G) and have noticed we have service in many areas when people using other phone companies do not. If you are planning country travelling, you should compare maps from each company showing their coverage Australia wide.

Email

There are several ways travellers can stay in touch electronically with family and friends.

Without a computer

- Use email facilities at libraries (often free of charge) or at 'internet cafes'.
- Send and receive emails on a suitable mobile phone. You can also view attachments and browse the internet.
- With a Pocketmail device, messages are typed on a small keyboard and displayed on an inbuilt screen before being despatched via an 1800 number. It will not send or receive attachments such as document files and images. The device is held against a phone handset, but most mobile phones and landline cordless phones are physically too small for it to work.

With a computer

Several companies operate wireless hotspots that allow access to the internet at high speed and at a reasonable cost, with no set up charges and no ongoing expenses. In some places there may be free access.

- Telstra Wireless Hotspots have been installed at many locations including McDonalds restaurants, shopping centres and many caravan parks. Charges accrue to your BigPond account. You need:
  - BigPond Username and Password
  - Wireless adaptor device – either a Wi-Fi- enabled laptop or a Wireless Adaptor (for older laptops)
  - Phone Telstra on 1800 050 381 for information
- Optus has more than 500 Wireless Hotspots that you can use if you have Wi-Fi technology on your laptop.
- Access the internet on NextG or 3G Wireless Broadband networks via a USB wireless modem. Both Telstra and Optus offer pre-paid data packs and contracts. Telstra NextG network is by far the most extensive, covering 99% of the population. Broadband is available wherever there is mobile phone service. Other companies do not have such an extensive network, and some would not be suited to the traveller. You can also use your mobile phone as a modem (if it has inbuilt Wi-Fi), using a data pack attached to your phone account, but this could be expensive.
- Connect your computer to your mobile phone, but unless you have a data pack it is expensive because you are paying for the time you are online at mobile phone rates.
- Satellite technology can be used to access broadband Australia-wide, however the equipment is very expensive.

Authors' tip:

Whichever system you use, ask friends not to send big files of jokes or photos!

UHF/VHF radio

Ultra High Frequency (UHF) radio units are very useful for communication, particularly between two mobile units, but you must be aware that the conversation is not private. It is fairly certain that several other people will be tuned in to the same channel. Always use moderate language and avoid making statements that could be offensive to others.

No user licences are required to use a UHF radio. Most caravanners use channel 18, motorhomers usually use channel 20, and most truckies use channels 40 or 29. Inexpensive battery-powered handheld UHF radios have a range of 3-8km depending on the power of the unit and local conditions. Because UHF signals travel in a straight line, the terrain plays an important part in the range of the unit.

Radio antenna

If you have a UHF radio built into your vehicle with an outside aerial you can expect a range of 20km and possibly up to 40km, dependent on your aerial and the topography. Generally, the higher you mount the antenna, the better. Do not position it where the signal will be blocked by part of your own vehicle.

UHF repeaters

These are special transmitting/receiving stations usually located in high areas to provide extended coverage, and these are spread throughout Australia. The repeater stations are usually owned by businesses, clubs and local councils, and other UHF users can utilise repeaters to extend their range.

To use the repeater, press your microphone button with the 'Duplex or Repeater' button selected also. You must transmit between channels 1 to 8 and the Duplex or Repeater selection on your UHF will add 30 channels and transmit to channels 31 to 38 on the repeater. After collecting your signal, the repeater then switches to its output channel 1 to 8 to transmit simultaneously to another radio receiver out of range. You must not transmit on channels 31 to 38. If using a repeater, please keep your communications relatively short because the repeater has been erected and is maintained by a private individual or a company or council.

UHF channels

Listed are the channels available for communicating with other travellers, and those reserved for special use:

- 1 to 8 can be used when sending a signal to a repeater
- 5 can only be used in an emergency situation
- 9 is available for conversations
- 10 is used by 4WD enthusiasts and clubs and in national parks
- 11 is a calling channel used to call and locate another station – both parties are then required to switch to another channel to continue their conversation
- 12 to 21 are available for conversations
- 22 and 23 are reserved for data transmissions – voice transmissions are not permitted
- 24 to 30 are available for conversations
- 29 is used by some truck drivers
- 31 to 38 are received by a repeater and re-transmitted on channels 1 to 8
- 35 can be used in case of an emergency situation
- 39 and 40 are available for conversations – channel 40 is often used by truck drivers

Authors' tip:

We suggest you start off with a hand-held UHF and decide later if you want to install a larger unit. If you have two hand-held units you can relay directions to the driver from the 'co-pilot' when reversing or parking. It saves misunderstanding hand signals that could be followed by a heated domestic debate.

HF radio

The most reliable and cost-effective way to maintain contact when travelling in very remote areas is by using an HF radio. This equipment is much more expensive than UHF, but it has a much greater range.

The VKS-737 Radio Network was established in 1993 to provide improved safety communications for members of that network and other travellers, particularly in rural and remote areas of Australia. By joining the Network, travellers do not require an ACMA Mobile Outport Licence (commonly referred to as an RFDS licence) to access the Network frequencies. Annual membership costs $95, with a reduced charge for holders of a concession card and members of several organisations. Contact VKS-737 Radio Network at PO Box 2101 Elizabeth Park SA 5113, by phone on (08) 8287 6222, or through the website www.vks737.on.net.

Using frequencies in the range of two to 25MHz, HF radio users have free radio contact over thousands of kilometres with each other and also base stations located all around Australia that relay messages. Depending on the selected frequency, power output and time of day, it is possible to make contact with other radio operators world-wide.

With an HF radio, travellers can contact Royal Flying Doctor Service bases for assistance in an emergency. Everyone travelling in the vehicle, even children, should know how to use the radio and should be familiar with the procedure involved in case an emergency arises.

Mail forwarding services

If you don't have a relative or friend to forward your mail while you are travelling, use a mail-forwarding service. Have your mail re-directed by Australia Post to the mail forwarding service who will send it on to you as requested. Advantages are that your mail does not sit in your mailbox, possibly getting wet, and also advertising the fact that there is no-one at home. It is a good security measure to have your addressed mail re-directed and put up an 'Addressed Mail Only' sign on your mail box to stop junk mail clogging it up.

GPS (global positioning system)

A GPS enables drivers, hikers and boaties to determine their position very accurately by using a small device that receives signals from a network of satellites. It can tell you where you are within a few metres by measuring the time it takes for signals to travel from the GPS unit to whatever satellites are available to it at the time. This can be as few as three satellites or could be as many as twelve.

GPS units are small held-held devices, or larger dash-mounted units, that operate on batteries or are connected to the vehicle's electrical system. Most now come preloaded with a comprehensive range of Australian maps covering country roads, as well as cities. In addition to supplying directions, some units will advise you of toll roads, speed cameras and school speed zones. Some GPS units will instruct you turn-by-turn with voice directions, whereas others will display directions on a screen.

The new Hema Navigator is the ultimate in GPS units because it has detailed maps for off-road travel as well as street maps.

Travelling with children

Child seat belts

Random inspections of vehicles indicate that only about one quarter of children travelling in motor vehicles are in a properly fitted child restraint appropriate for their size. Children should remain in either a booster seat or harness until they weigh at least 26kg, when they can progress to an adult seatbelt. They should not sit in the front seat until they reach the age of 12.

Holidays with children

For many years the authors travelled during school holidays with three children, starting when they were tiny, and continued until they were young adults. The following ideas might help make the travelling experience more enjoyable for both parents and children.

- Show the children photos and brochures and include them in the planning phase.
- Research where you are going, plan the route and include some attractions that will appeal to children. Interactive places appeal more than looking at scenery. Examples are wildlife parks, water parks or science museums. Simple (and free) activities that will appeal include feeding bread to ducks or swans that you might find in a park.
- Don't travel too far each day and travel only in daylight hours.
- Plan breaks every two hours, and if you have young children try to stop where there is a playground or somewhere the children can run around and burn off excess energy while you sit back and relax.
- Take plenty of snacks such as muesli bars and fruit and have a separate water bottle (with straw) for each child. Don't give children foods with a high sugar content and steer away from food or drinks with artificial colours if there is a chance it could make your children over active.
- Take moist towelettes and travel sickness remedies.
- Let each child take a few favourite toys, games and books. If you have young children take a stable table, colouring book and coloured pencils for each child.
- If possible let the children take their own photos.
- Encourage older children to write a journal about the trip and illustrate it with pictures cut out of tourist brochures or their own photos.
- MP3 or CD players with earphones for their favourite music.

As you travel, the key to keeping children happy is to have interactive activities with variety that do not wear out the adults too much. Some suggestions:

- Obviously hand-held game machines are great, as long as each child has his or her favourite to avoid fights!
- Some of the old favourites work well. Try I Spy or a memory game like I went shopping and I bought ....
- Another is Car Bingo. Make lists of passing objects that the children have to spot and tick off, e.g. cars of a particular colour, road signs, or a particular farm animal.
- Word game – Spot something that starts with the last letter of the previous word. Obviously these word games only work with older children.
- Number plate game – Think of a word with the letters of the number plate of a car you see. The letters have to be in the same order.
- If you are staying in caravan parks with facilities such as a pool or games room, stop early enough in the day that the children can enjoy some of these activities.

Travelling full-time with children

Many families spend a year or two, or even longer travelling. The children usually continue their education with one of the state schools of distance education or by home schooling. Distance education schools cater for children from preschool to grade 12.

The experience of families who travel full time is positive. Parents find that the children are not disadvantaged scholastically when compared with their peers in mainstream schools. As with most things in life, there are advantages and disadvantages. The children are exposed to many more experiences than they would be at home, and usually have a more mature outlook. This is probably because they spend virtually all their time with their parents and other adults rather than spending the vast majority of their waking hours with friends of their own age. Of course that can also be a disadvantage. Without exception, families who adopt this lifestyle are very close-knit. Maybe if they weren't, living together 24-7 would not work.

Most families find it preferable to complete their nomadic travelling before the eldest child enters grade 8 or 9. Discuss this with the School of Distance Education or the Home Schooling administrators.

Kids studying while they travel Australia

A motorhomer's tiny dog

Travelling with pets

Pets are not permitted within national parks, not even in the parking area. Some caravan parks do not allow pets, particularly resort-style caravan parks in tourist areas. Some caravan parks, even if they are shown as not accepting pets, will let you stay with a pet if you phone and ask. This is more likely in off-peak times, and it only applies to caravan sites, not to cabins. Refer to the caravan park directory in this publication for a caravan park that will allow pets. If you cannot find one, try the local show-grounds, because many allow travellers to stay and pets are nearly always accepted.

Obviously, an animal that starts travelling when it is young will usually take to the travelling lifestyle better than an older animal. Whilst there are some restrictions to the type of travel and places that may be visited, the responsible pet owner should not find things too difficult. Many people who travel with a dog claim that the companionship they enjoy with their pet more than compensates for the restrictions. A pet is also a good 'conversation starter' with other campers or walkers.

Some very organised travellers with pets find kennels or dog-sitters in the vicinity of a national park they want to visit, so they know their companion is being looked after. Take your pet's vaccination certificates in case you need to put it in a kennel. Sometimes a couple of travellers with pets travel together and take turns in looking after the animals while the other pet owner visits a national park. We have heard that sometimes other campers will look after (or keep an eye on) someone's pet while they go on an excursion.

Another option to consider is an organisation called Pet Places. This is a network of people who will look after your pet in their own home. This would suit pet owners who, for whatever reason, feel their pet would be happier in a home environment rather than in a kennel/cattery. There is a modest annual joining fee to access the contact details of pet sitters. Read about the service on www.petplaces.com.au or telephone (03) 6432 1517. Pet Places also have recommendations of pet friendly caravan parks and accommodation.

There are many products available that will add to your pet's comfort and probably make life easier for you, the pet owner. These include a pop-up/zip-up kennel or 'mobile home' for your pet.

Pet owners need to be considerate and aware of issues that may concern others – cleaning up droppings, barking or howling dogs, and the possibility the pet might attack or bite. Don't take your dog to the shower block.

If you are camped or walking in a country area with a small dog or cat, keep the animal close by on a hand-held lead. Otherwise, keep your pet under your awning. We know of a couple of cases where a wedge-tailed eagle has swooped and picked up a small pet. If you are close enough you can probably frighten the bird to drop your pet, but we have heard of an occasion where an eagle flew away with a silky terrier.

Insurance

Free seniors' travel insurance

The ANZ Bank has introduced a free Seniors Privilege Domestic Travel Insurance for customers aged between 60 and 80 years of age who hold an Access Advantage or Access Deeming account opened on or after 1 October 2007 at the time of travel. The policy covers interstate and intrastate journeys involving overnight stays, up to a maximum of three months' duration. Claims can be made in the following circumstances:

- if your journey is rescheduled, delayed or cancelled;
- if your luggage or travel documents are damaged or stolen;
- if you die or become permanently disabled;
- the insurance excess if your hire vehicle is damaged;
- return of a hire vehicle if you become unable to drive; or
- you have a liability claim made against you.

If you bank with another company, enquire if they also offer free domestic travel insurance. At the current time, this does not appear to be the case.

Levels of vehicle insurance

- **Compulsory Third Party** insurance paid with the vehicle registration will pay claims for death or injury of people in your vehicle other than the driver and for other people involved in an accident. The driver who is considered to be at fault is not entitled to any payment under Compulsory Third Party insurance, although some CTP insurers offer a small amount of cover for injury known as 'At Fault Driver Injury Insurance'.
- **Third Party Property** will pay for damage you may cause to other people's property, but does not cover you for damage to your own vehicle.
- **Third Party Property (Fire and Theft)** in addition to protecting you for damage you may cause to other people's property (the Third Party Property part of the policy), also covers damage to your own vehicle from fire or loss through theft.
- **Comprehensive** insurance protects you against damage to other people's property and also covers the repair of your own vehicle, regardless of fault.

It is worth having either comprehensive insurance, or at least third Party Property insurance, because if you are unfortunate enough to have an accident your insurer will follow it through. Don't think an accident cannot happen to you because a situation could arise involving another vehicle or an animal on the road, where it is not possible to avoid an accident.

Comprehensive insurance

It is very important to insure your caravan, motorhome or campervan for its full value, because unfortunately it can be damaged so badly that repair is not economical. Usually comprehensive insurance will include a basic amount for contents, but it is likely that this will not cover what you carry with you. Make a list of the contents of your vehicle with approximate values and you will probably be surprised at the total. Check what amount is included in your policy for contents, and increase it if necessary. Leave that list of contents at home or with a family member in case of total loss of your caravan or motorhome.

Motorhome overturned near Broome, Western Australia

Larger motorhomes like this are not eligible for towing by automobile clubs

In the event of a total write-off of your vehicle, the pay-out will be either the vehicle's market value or an agreed value, plus towing costs. If you have borrowed a substantial part of the purchase price of your vehicle, it is possible that the market value will be less than the amount outstanding on the loan. If you have a substantial loan, investigate Gap insurance.

What does your insurance policy cover?

For example 'rating one protection', excess, new for old on contents; towing after breakdown as well as accident; hire car/accommodation in the event of a major incident. Compare insurance policies offered by different companies, and choose the one that suits your needs. Caravanners or motorhomers usually travel on country highways, so it is important to have insurance coverage for towing of the vehicle in country areas. Check whether a vehicle the size (and weight) of yours can be towed, as well as how far it will be towed without charge. If the policy includes a non-removable excess of $500, it will mean that you will likely have to pay for towing because it is generally less than this amount. You will also pay for minor damage such as replacing the windscreen. This type of policy is obviously much cheaper than one with no excess. Talk to other travellers and find out how easy the company is to deal with if you have a claim. Keep a copy of your policy with you as you travel.

Authors' tip:

It is important to have comprehensive insurance cover that includes towing for your vehicle (whatever its size) following breakdown as well as an accident.

Restrictions on large vehicles

If you drive a large vehicle, do not expect that your motoring club will be able to help you with roadside service or towing. Automobile clubs have restrictions on the size of vehicles eligible for service, and even if your membership says you are covered for 'any vehicle you drive', you are actually covered only 'for any **eligible** vehicle you drive'. *See p104.* If your vehicle is outside the limits, try to get an insurance policy that includes towing following a breakdown as well as an accident.

If you are towing a caravan or camper trailer and your tow vehicle is disabled, it is possible the caravan will have to be left beside the road unless you pay for a second tow truck. If the tow truck operator has a truck that is large enough, he may be able to put your vehicle on the tray and tow the caravan, provided it is under the 5.5m or other specified limit.

Public liability

Obviously, if you are at fault in an accident while driving, your compulsory Third Party Insurance covers injury to other people, but it does not cover you when you are camped. For most of us there is a simple way to be insured for the possibility that an action of ours causes injury to someone else. A Contents Policy on your home will include a personal liability cover of between $1 million and $20 million, and this cover is usually portable. This means that wherever you go, whether down the street or across Australia in your caravan or motorhome, you are insured for any injury you may inadvertently cause to someone else (other than when you are driving). We are advised that "all major insurance companies include this in their policies" but you should check with your own household contents insurer.

Driving under the influence of alcohol

You should be aware that your insurance policy will not cover you if you are over the legal limit of alcohol or if you give permission to someone who exceeds the legal alcohol limit to drive your vehicle.

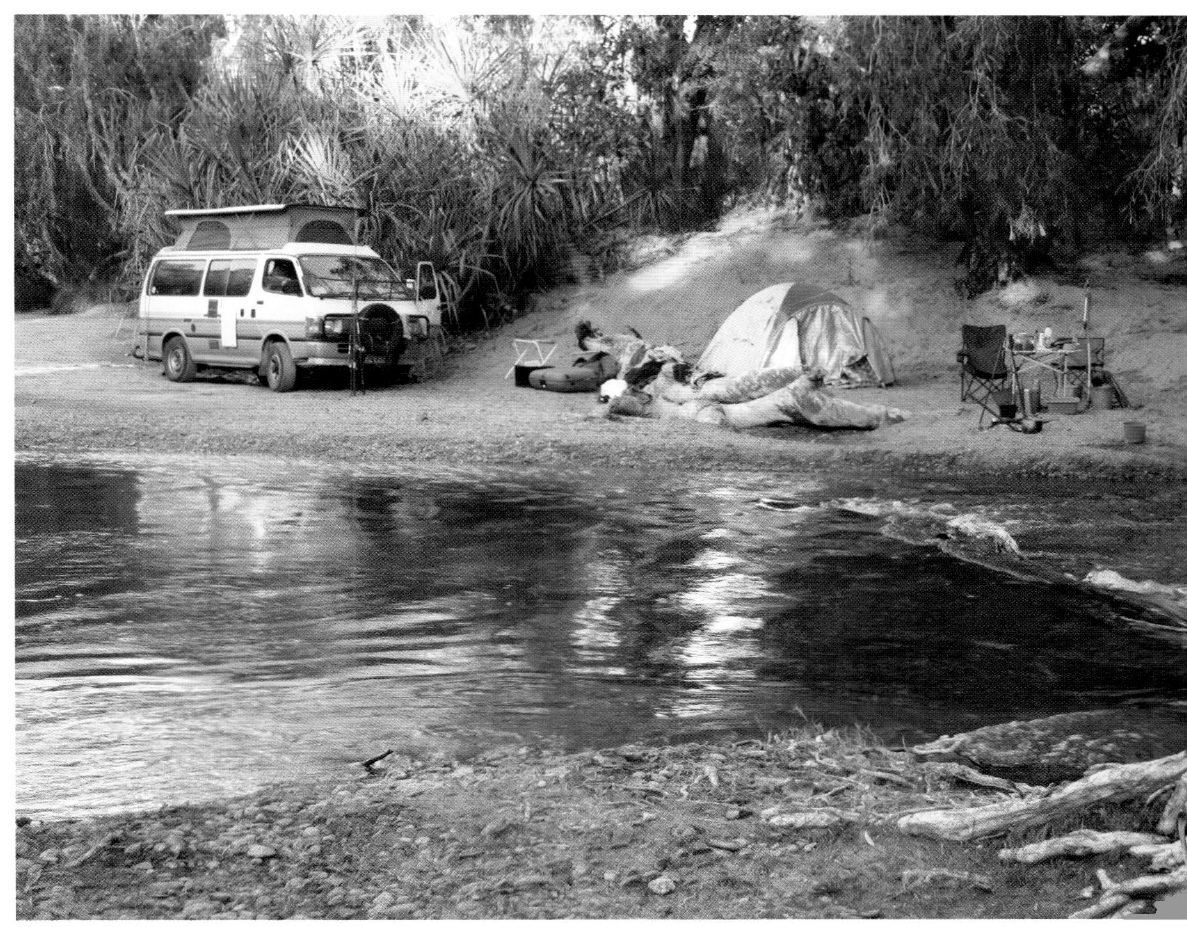

Camping beside the Gregory River, QLD

In the event of a road accident

If you are the first to arrive at the scene of an accident you should stop, but not immediately at the site of the accident. Leave room for emergency vehicles to park next to the damaged vehicles.

- You should approach damaged vehicles with caution to avoid personal risk. Check for hazards such as fallen power lines, toxic fumes, leaking fuel and gas. Watch for passing traffic. Do NOT endanger yourself.
- Turn off ignition switches and do not smoke or use naked flames.
- Look in and around the vehicles to see if anyone is injured. If someone is injured you must call the police. Check how many are injured and quickly assess how serious the injuries appear.
- If no one is injured, assess how serious the damage is and decide if the police should be notified.
- Dial 000 to request assistance from the Ambulance Service and/or Police. If your phone does not have service where you are, the emergency call will be picked up by any company that does have service in the area. The emergency service operator will know what information is required so you should answer these questions calmly. They will need to know how many people are injured, how serious the injuries appear and whether there is leaking fuel. Give accurate information on the location (including the state you are in) to avoid delays. The emergency service operator will assess what assistance is required and instruct the appropriate authorities immediately.
- If someone is injured, render all reasonable assistance and apply CPR if required. If you are not trained in first aid, call for help from bystanders.
- Only remove injured people from vehicles if they are in danger from fire or explosion. It is safer to leave injured people where they are than move them with the possibility of causing further injury. Direct traffic around the damaged vehicles.
- A motorcycle helmet should NOT be removed unless it is absolutely necessary, i.e. if it is obstructing an unconscious person's breathing. A conscious person may be able to safely remove the helmet themselves.
- If the accident is serious, or if someone is injured, it is advisable not to move the vehicle from the point of impact until the police arrive. At the appropriate time they will direct the vehicle to be moved.

If you are involved in an accident

- If you are involved in any way in an accident you MUST stop. If your vehicle has not come to a stop as a result of the accident, pull over in a safe location close to the site of the accident.
- Refer to the above recommendations that also apply in this situation.
- If your vehicle cannot be moved, turn on the hazard lights or place warning triangles. Alternatively, ask a bystander to warn approaching traffic of the hazard, but this person must have regard for his/her own safety.
- Ask any witnesses to wait until you can get their names and addresses.
- Assess the damage to both vehicles and decide whether it is serious enough to ask police to come to the scene. Even if it is not, the accident may still need to be reported to police, unless the damage is very minor. This should be done within 24 hours. Note down the officer's name and number and the station where he/she is attached.
- Call the police immediately if a person fails to stop or exchange information or if you believe the driver may be under the influence of alcohol or drugs.
- If there is only minor damage and your vehicle is obstructing traffic, note its position before you move it.
- Report the accident to your insurance company as soon as you can.

If you are involved in a minor accident and the police are not present you should follow this course of action:

- Do not admit liability. Your insurance company prefers that you make no such statement.
- Ask any possible witnesses if they would give you their name, address and phone number. Attend to this as quickly as possible before they leave the scene.
- Note down the full name and address of the driver(s) and owner(s) of the vehicle(s) as well as the driver's licence number and expiry date. They are required to supply this information. Ask the other driver(s) for the name of their insurance company and what level of insurance cover they have. Note down the make and model of any other vehicles involved and also their registration number(s).
- Give your details to anyone who has reasonable grounds to ask for them, i.e. other drivers involved in the accident or the owner of any property damaged as a result of the accident.
- Write down details of the accident – date, time and place, road and weather conditions at the time, estimated speed of vehicles, and description of the damage to both vehicles. If possible take photographs of the road with vehicles still in place as well as close-up photos of the damage to any vehicles involved. Draw a diagram showing the positions of the vehicles before and after the collision (you will have to put this on your insurance claim).
- While it is still fresh in your mind, note down what the other driver said. Did he/she admit fault?
- Remove all debris from the road. You might need to sweep up broken glass. If possible have a bystander warn approaching traffic to avoid injury to the person cleaning up.

See p103 for information on contacting an ambulance for medical assistance or a motoring club to arrange for towing.

Information

Members of a CMCA Chapter enjoying a game of disc bowls

Sources of information

Guidebooks & atlases

- *Around Australia Atlas and Guide: The Ultimate Guide to the Ultimate Trip* – Includes full Hema Road Atlas
- *Bush Camping with Dogs* – 1100 campsites in over 500 parks, reserves etc catering for dogs
- *Camps Australia Wide* – A guide for the budget conscious traveller with over 4000 listings, also available in a larger format that includes campsite photographs.
- *Hema Road Atlases* – Available in a range of sizes, including the new larger 'Easy Read', all available in either spiral or stapled versions.
- *Holidaying with Dogs* – List of over 2000 caravan parks, motels and other accommodation facilities that welcome guests with dogs.

Working as you travel

Contact the National Harvest Labour Information Service for the most up-to-date information about working the Harvest trail. Phone 1800 062 332 or visit the website www.harvesttrail.gov.au.

Refer to the publication **Workabout Australia** that details a variety of casual work.

Towing training

Driving a car/caravan or car/camper trailer combination requires different skills from simply driving the family sedan. No special class of licence is required to tow a caravan or camper trailer, so most people venture out with their new recreational vehicle and learn as they go. Often there are no problems, but if a difficult situation arises before the driver is fully competent, an accident can result.

There are practical courses available where the principal driver and the alternate driver can both acquire the necessary skills. Keep in mind that if a difficult situation arises, it will not necessarily be when the principal driver is behind the wheel. Tow-Ed operates accredited training courses in a number of venues across Australia.

Clubs for travellers

Motorhomes, camper vans and fifth-wheelers

Owners of motorhomes, campervans, fifth-wheelers, and slide-on campers (classified as 'qualifying vehicles') are eligible for ordinary membership of the **Campervan and Motorhome Club of Australia Limited**. The CMCA is the largest recreational vehicle club in Australia with over 53,000 members. It is very active in promoting the motorhoming and travelling lifestyle, and anyone interested can join as an Associate Member even if they do not own a qualifying vehicle.

The major benefits of club membership are:

- An excellent insurance scheme with tremendous benefits.
- A top quality monthly magazine The Wanderer with technical and travelling information.
- A very extensive network of caravan parks where members receive a significant discount.
- Discounts at many businesses.
- Over 90 Chapters around Australia that provide the social arm of the Club. Chapters usually meet once a month, and all CMCA Members are welcome at any Chapter event.
- Two large Rallies each year.
- Special Interest Groups, a major one catering for Solos – members who travel without a partner.

Anyone interested in the CMCA should contact the Club on (02) 4978 8788 during office hours or email membership@cmca.net.au. The Club website address is www.cmca.net.au.

Caravans and camper trailers

There are over a hundred separate **local caravan clubs** in Australia, many affiliated with the National Association of Caravan Clubs Inc. Members of these clubs enjoy friendship and fellowship with fellow travellers. The clubs hold State Rallies every year and the National Association has a Rally every three years.

If you would like information on a caravan club in your area, you can contact the Secretary of the relevant State organisation. Office-holders change periodically, but listed are the details of the current State secretaries:

- Australian Capital Territory – Mrs Maureen Taylor (02) 6286 2134, www.canberracaravanclub.org.au
- New South Wales – Mrs Lorraine Perry (02) 4393 9564
- Queensland – Mrs Barbara Rutherford (07) 3263 7340
- South Australia – Mrs Eva Warwick (08) 8837 9274
- Tasmania – Mrs Pam Skromanis (Southern Tasmanian Caravan Club Inc.) (03) 6267 2766
- Victoria – Mr Ray Stevens (03) 9870 9715
- Western Australia – Mr Eddy Tamlin (08) 9384 5460

The **Australian Caravan Club** is an Australia-wide club for caravan owners. To enquire about the club phone 1800 734 493 or access their website www.australiancaravanclub.com.au.

The **Australian Touring Caravan, Motorhome & Camping Club Inc.** caters for all campers. For more information visit their website www.atcmcc.org.au. Write to PO Box 298, Croydon Victoria 3136, or email atcmcc@optus.net.com.

Authors' tip:

We strongly recommend that caravanners should contact one (or more) of the caravan clubs and see what suits them. You don't know how much fun you are missing out on!

Members of the Suncoast Caravanning Club Qld Inc enjoying a weekend

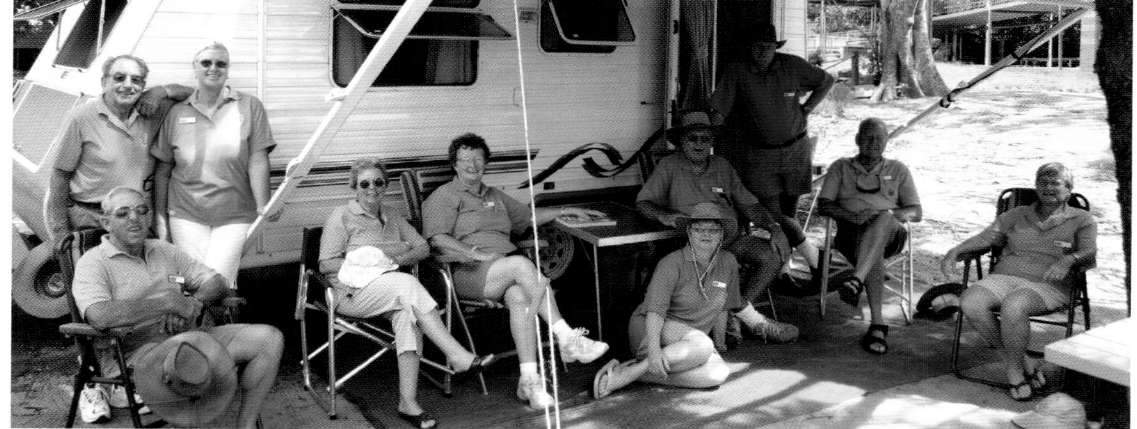

QUEENSLAND Key Map

POPULATION: 4 million
AREA: 1,730,648 sq km
CAPITAL CITY: Brisbane

Distances are shown in kilometres and follow the most direct major sealed route

	Birdsville	Brisbane	Bundaberg	Cairns	Charleville	Goondiwindi	Longreach	Mackay	Mount Isa	Rockhampton	Roma	Toowoomba	Townsville	Winton
Bamaga	2628	2646	2333	939	2574	2633	2063	1677	2188	2011	2297	2689	1283	1883
Birdsville		1589	1763	1685	847	1435	705	1493	686	1378	1112	1461	1335	745
Brisbane			361	1713	742	350	1172	969	1819	635	477	128	1363	1352
Bundaberg				1400	916	591	995	656	1642	322	651	412	1050	1175
Cairns					1631	1725	1120	744	1245	1078	1354	1715	350	940
Charleville						588	511	1039	1158	833	265	614	1281	691
Goondiwindi							1018	981	1665	647	336	222	1375	1198
Longreach								788	647	673	695	1044	770	180
Mackay									1289	334	774	971	394	968
Mount Isa										1320	1342	1691	895	467
Rockhampton											568	637	728	853
Roma												349	1004	875
Toowoomba													1365	1224
Townsville														590
Winton														

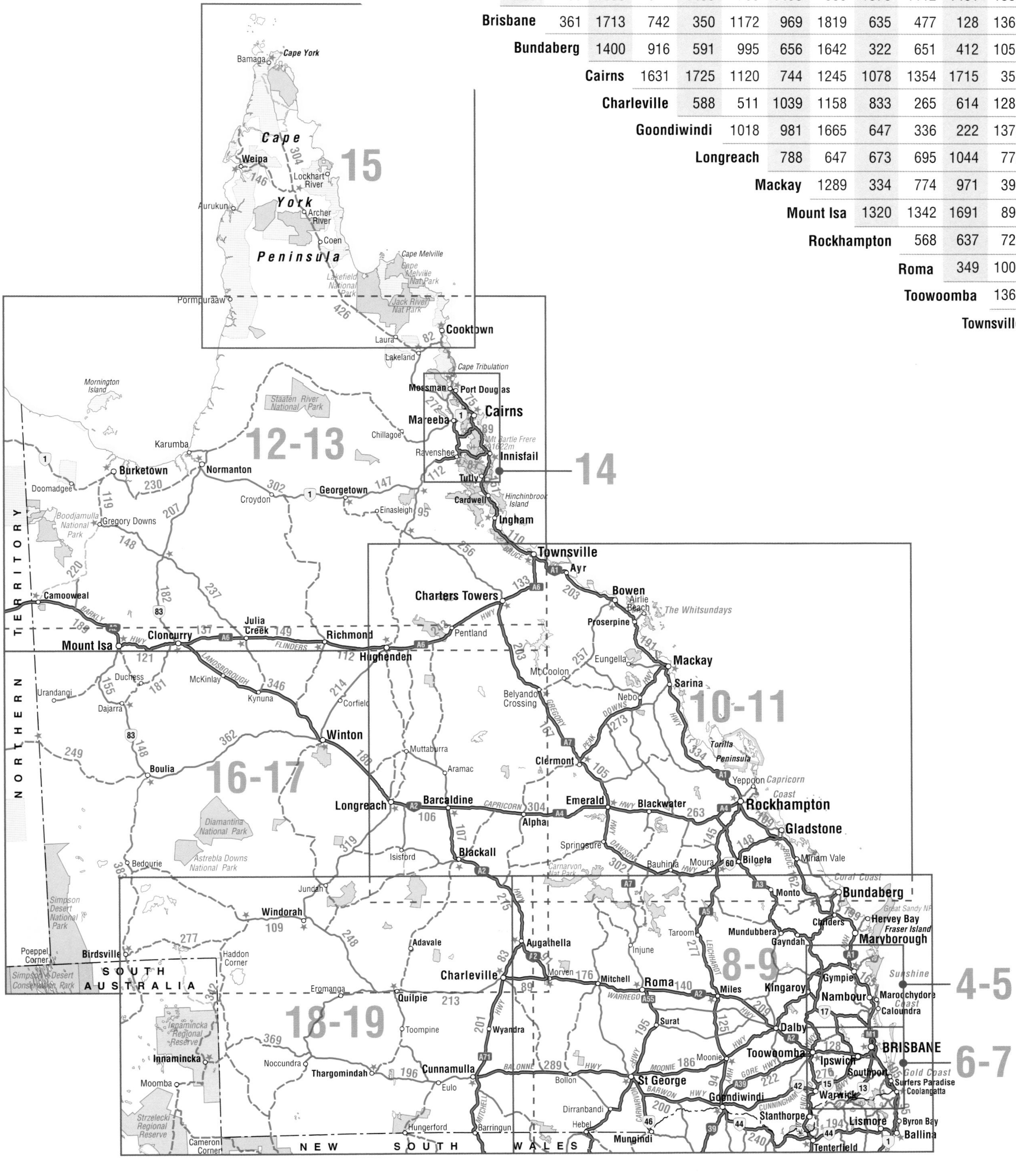

15 · 12-13 · 14 · 10-11 · 16-17 · 18-19 · 8-9 · 4-5 · 6-7

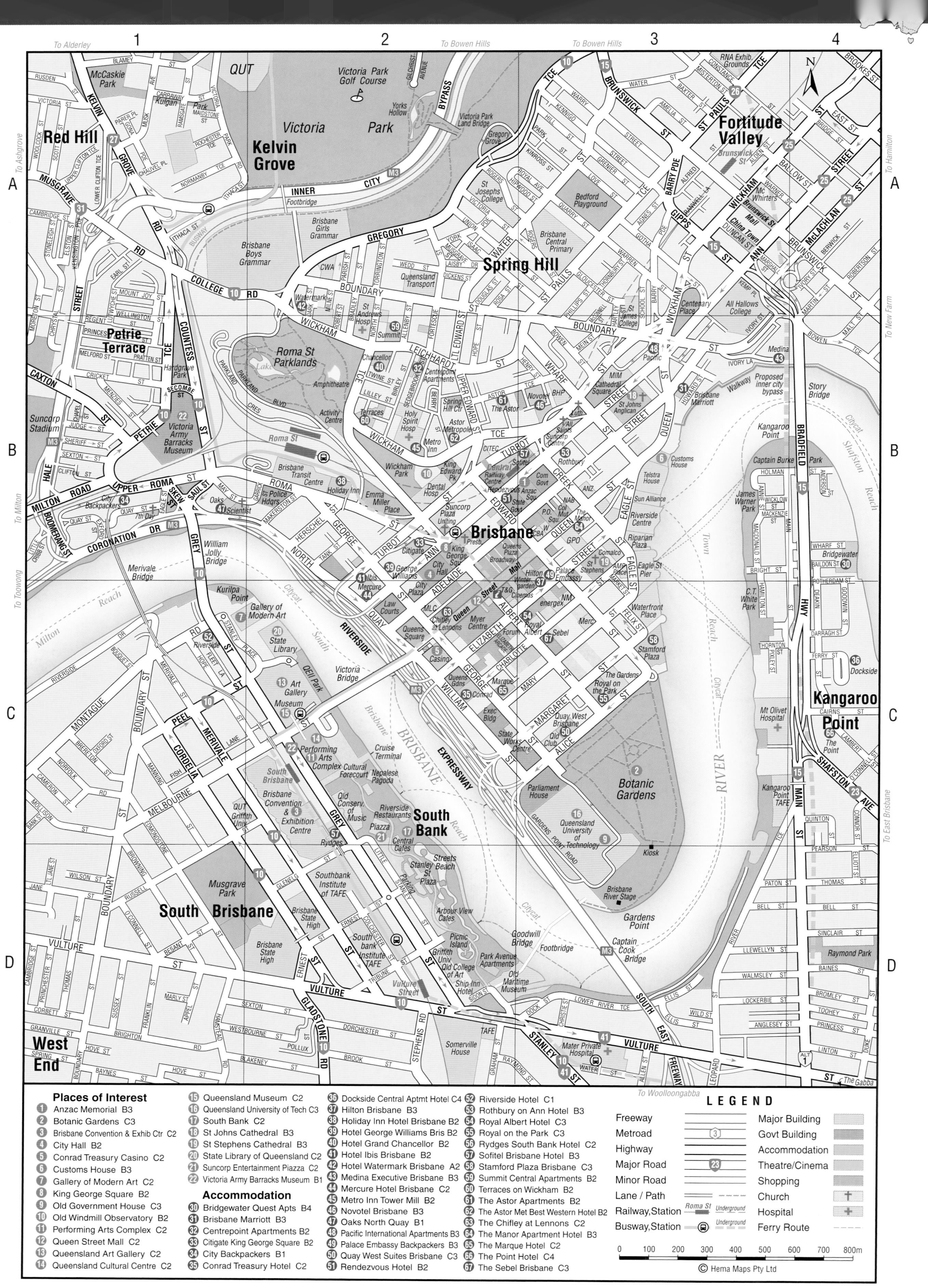

1
2
3
4
A
B
C
D
To Alderley
To Bowen Hills
To Bowen Hills
To Ashgrove
To Hamilton
To New Farm
To Milton
To Toowong
To East Brisbane
To Woolloongabba
Red Hill
Kelvin Grove
Victoria Park
Victoria Park Golf Course
QUT
Fortitude Valley
Spring Hill
Petrie Terrace
Roma St Parklands
Brisbane
Kangaroo Point
South Bank
South Brisbane
West End
Botanic Gardens
Musgrave Park
Suncorp Stadium
Story Bridge
Victoria Bridge
William Jolly Bridge
Merivale Bridge
Goodwill Bridge
Captain Cook Bridge
BRISBANE RIVER
Places of Interest
1 Anzac Memorial B3
2 Botanic Gardens C3
3 Brisbane Convention & Exhib Ctr C2
4 City Hall B2
5 Conrad Treasury Casino C2
6 Customs House B3
7 Gallery of Modern Art C2
8 King George Square B2
9 Old Government House C3
10 Old Windmill Observatory B2
11 Performing Arts Complex C2
12 Queen Street Mall C2
13 Queensland Art Gallery C2
14 Queensland Cultural Centre C2
15 Queensland Museum C2
16 Queensland University of Tech C3
17 South Bank C2
18 St Johns Cathedral B3
19 St Stephens Cathedral B3
20 State Library of Queensland C2
21 Suncorp Entertainment Piazza C2
22 Victoria Army Barracks Museum B1
Accommodation
30 Bridgewater Quest Apts B4
31 Brisbane Marriott B3
32 Centrepoint Apartments B2
33 Citigate King George Square B2
34 City Backpackers B1
35 Conrad Treasury Hotel C2
36 Dockside Central Aptmt Hotel C4
37 Hilton Brisbane B3
38 Holiday Inn Hotel Brisbane B2
39 Hotel George Williams Bris B2
40 Hotel Grand Chancellor B2
41 Hotel Ibis Brisbane B2
42 Hotel Watermark Brisbane A2
43 Medina Executive Brisbane B3
44 Mercure Hotel Brisbane C2
45 Metro Inn Tower Mill B2
46 Novotel Brisbane B3
47 Oaks North Quay B1
48 Pacific International Apartments B3
49 Palace Embassy Backpackers B3
50 Quay West Suites Brisbane C3
51 Rendezvous Hotel B2
52 Riverside Hotel C1
53 Rothbury on Ann Hotel B3
54 Royal Albert Hotel C3
55 Royal on the Park C3
56 Rydges South Bank Hotel C2
57 Sofitel Brisbane Hotel B3
58 Stamford Plaza Brisbane C3
59 Summit Central Apartments B2
60 Terraces on Wickham B2
61 The Astor Apartments B2
62 The Astor Met Best Western Hotel B2
63 The Chifley at Lennons C2
64 The Manor Apartment Hotel B3
65 The Marque Hotel C2
66 The Point Hotel C4
67 The Sebel Brisbane C3
LEGEND
Freeway
Metroad
Highway
Major Road
Minor Road
Lane / Path
Railway,Station
Busway,Station
Roma St
Underground
Major Building
Govt Building
Accommodation
Theatre/Cinema
Shopping
Church
Hospital
Ferry Route
0 100 200 300 400 500 600 700 800m
© Hema Maps Pty Ltd

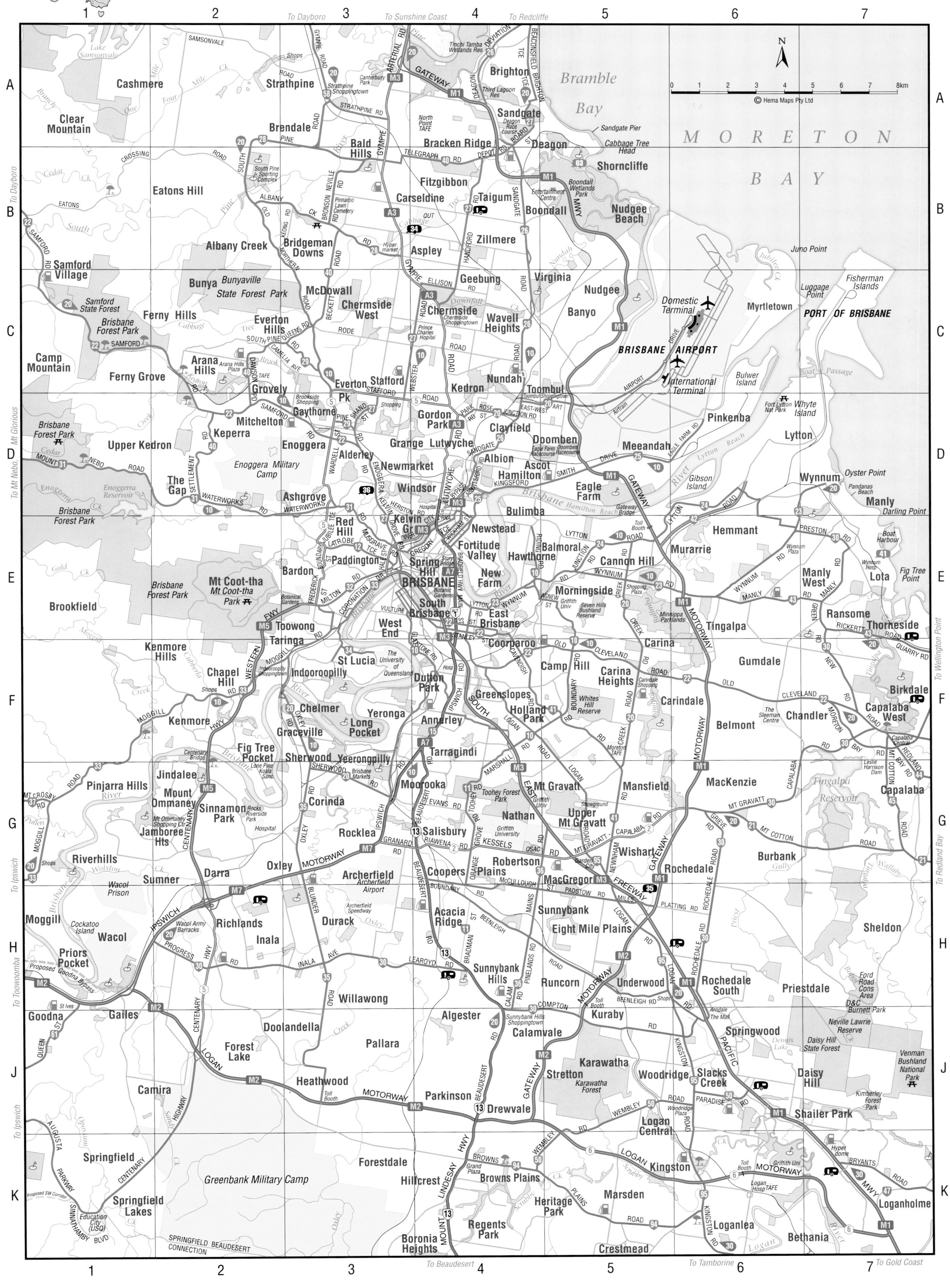

Brisbane Throughroads

© Hema Maps Pty Ltd

MORETON BAY

Bramble Bay

Cashmere, Strathpine, Brighton, Clear Mountain, Brendale, Sandgate, Bald Hills, Bracken Ridge, Deagon, Shorncliffe, Eatons Hill, Fitzgibbon, Carseldine, Taigum, Boondall, Nudgee Beach, Albany Creek, Bridgeman Downs, Aspley, Zillmere, Samford Village, Bunya, McDowall, Geebung, Virginia, Nudgee, Chermside West, Chermside, Wavell Heights, Banyo, Myrtletown, Ferny Hills, Everton Hills, Port of Brisbane, Brisbane Airport, Camp Mountain, Arana Hills, Ferny Grove, Everton Park, Stafford, Kedron, Nundah, Toombul, Grovely, Gaythorne, Gordon Park, Clayfield, Pinkenba, Mitchelton, Keperra, Upper Kedron, Enoggera, Grange, Lutwyche, Lytton, Alderley, Newmarket, Albion, Hooomben, Meeandah, Ascot, Hamilton, Wynnum, The Gap, Windsor, Eagle Farm, Ashgrove, Bulimba, Manly, Red Hill, Kelvin Grove, Newstead, Hemmant, Paddington, Fortitude Valley, Balmoral, Hawthorne, Cannon Hill, Murarrie, Bardon, Spring Hill, New Farm, Manly West, Lota, Mt Coot-tha, Brisbane, Morningside, Brookfield, South Brisbane, East Brisbane, Ransome, Thorneside, Toowong, West End, Tingalpa, Taringa, Coorparoo, Carina, Kenmore Hills, St Lucia, Gumdale, Chapel Hill, Indooroopilly, Dutton Park, Camp Hill, Carina Heights, Birkdale, Greenslopes, Carindale, Chelmer, Yeronga, Holland Park, Capalaba West, Kenmore, Long Pocket, Annerley, Chandler, Belmont, Graceville, Fig Tree Pocket, Sherwood, Yeerongpilly, Tarragindi, Jindalee, Pinjarra Hills, Moorooka, Mt Gravatt, Mansfield, MacKenzie, Capalaba, Mount Ommaney, Corinda, Sinnamon Park, Nathan, Upper Mt Gravatt, Jamboree Hts, Rocklea, Salisbury, Riverhills, Wishart, Burbank, Oxley, Robertson, Coopers Plains, Rochedale, Archerfield, Darra, Sumner, MacGregor, Moggill, Richlands, Acacia Ridge, Sunnybank, Durack, Wacol, Eight Mile Plains, Sheldon, Inala, Priors Pocket, Sunnybank Hills, Runcorn, Underwood, Rochedale South, Priestdale, Willawong, Goodna, Gailes, Algester, Kuraby, Doolandella, Springwood, Forest Lake, Pallara, Calamvale, Karawatha, Stretton, Woodridge, Slacks Creek, Daisy Hill, Camira, Heathwood, Parkinson, Drewvale, Shailer Park, Logan Central, Springfield, Forestdale, Kingston, Hillcrest, Browns Plains, Marsden, Loganholme, Springfield Lakes, Heritage Park, Regents Park, Loganlea, Bethania, Boronia Heights, Crestmead

To Dayboro · To Sunshine Coast · To Redcliffe · To Mt Glorious · To Mt Nebo · To Ipswich · To Toowoomba · To Wellington Point · To Redland Bay · To Beaudesert · To Tamborine · To Gold Coast

Brisbane Region, Queensland

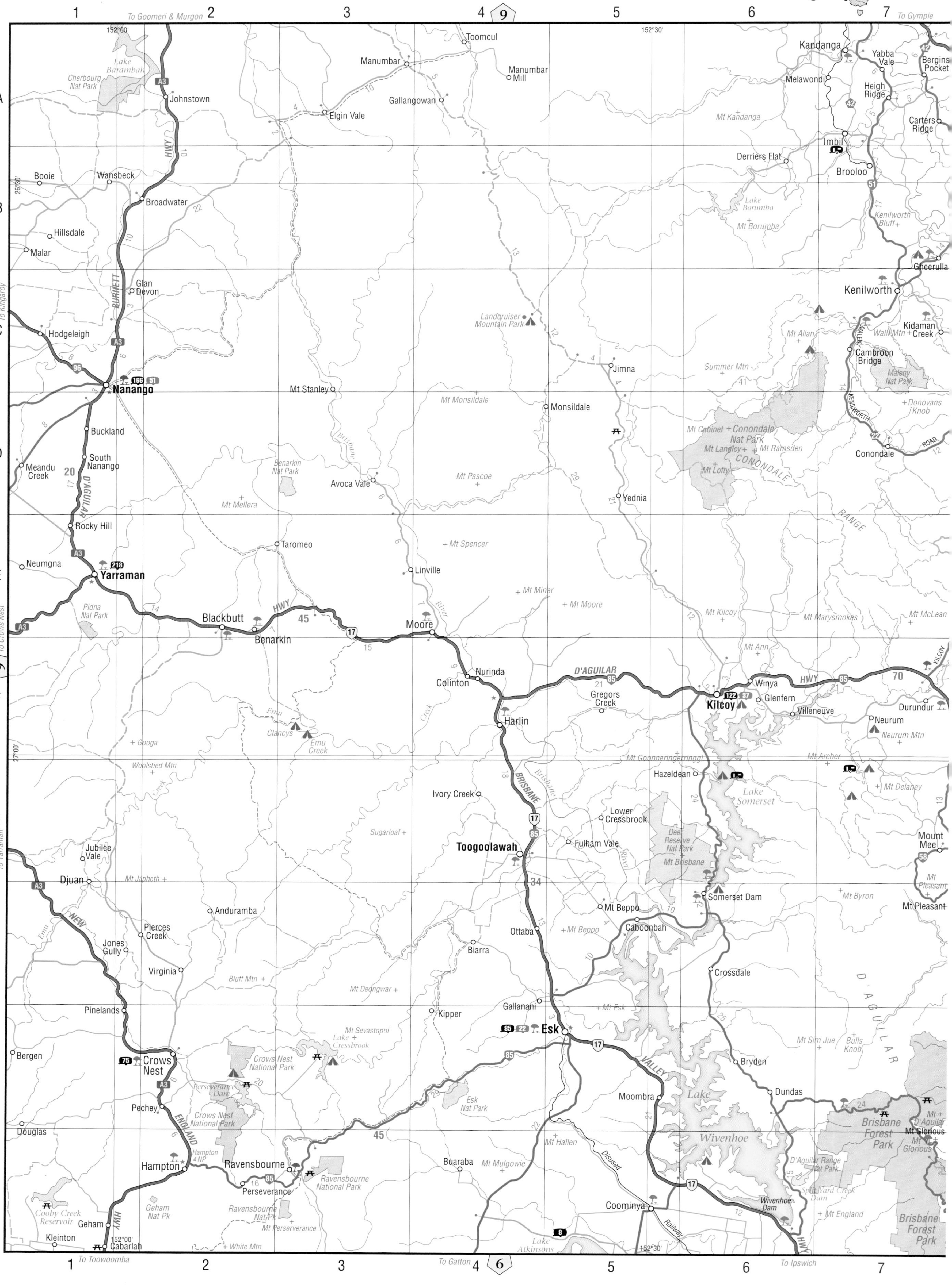

To Goomeri & Murgon · To Gympie · To Kingaroy · To Crows Nest · To Yarraman · To Kilcoy · To Toowoomba · To Gatton · To Ipswich

Toomcul
Manumbar
Manumbar Mill
Gallangowan
Elgin Vale
Johnstown
Lake Barambah
Cherbourg Nat Park
Kandanga
Yabba Vale
Bergins Pocket
Melawondi
Heigh Ridge
Carters Ridge
Mt Kandanga
Imbil
Derriers Flat
Brooloo
Booie
Wansbeck
Broadwater
Hillsdale
Malar
Lake Borumba
Mt Borumba
Kenilworth Bluff
Gheerulla
Kenilworth
Glan Devon
Hodgeleigh
Landcruiser Mountain Park
Mt Allan
Kidaman Creek
Walli Mtn
Cambroon Bridge
Maleny Nat Park
Jimna
Summer Mtn
Nanango
Mt Stanley
Mt Monsildale
Monsildale
Donovans Knob
Buckland
South Nanango
Meandu Creek
Mt Cabinet
Conondale Nat Park
Mt Langley
Mt Ramsden
Mt Lofty
Conondale
Benarkin Nat Park
Avoca Vale
Mt Pascoe
Mt Mellera
Yednia
Rocky Hill
Taromeo
Mt Spencer
Neumgna
Yarraman
Linville
Mt Miner
Mt Moore
Pidna Nat Park
Blackbutt
Benarkin
Moore
Mt Kilcoy
Mt Marysmokes
Mt McLean
Mt Ann
Nurinda
Colinton
Gregors Creek
Winya
Kilcoy
Glenfern
Durundur
Villeneuve
Neurum
Neurum Mtn
Harlin
Clancys
Emu Creek
Googa
Mt Goonneringerringgi
Mt Archer
Woolshed Mtn
Hazeldean
Lake Somerset
Mt Delaney
Ivory Creek
Lower Cressbrook
Sugarloaf
Toogoolawah
Fulham Vale
Deer Reserve Nat Park
Mt Brisbane
Jubilee Vale
Mount Mee
Djuan
Mt Japheth
Mt Pleasant
Somerset Dam
Mt Byron
Anduramba
Mt Beppo
Pierces Creek
Caboonbah
Ottaba
Jones Gully
Biarra
Virginia
Crossdale
Bluff Mtn
Mt Deongwar
Pinelands
Kipper
Gallanani
Mt Esk
Mt Sevastopol
Lake Cressbrook
Esk
Mt Sim Jue
Bulls Knob
Bergen
Crows Nest
Crows Nest National Park
Bryden
Perseverance Dam
Moombra
Dundas
Esk Nat Park
Pechey
Crows Nest National Park
Lake Wivenhoe
Brisbane Forest Park
Mt D'Aguilar
Mt Glorious
Douglas
Mt Hallen
Hampton
Hampton NP
Ravensbourne
Buaraba
Mt Mulgowie
D'Aguilar Range Nat Park
Ravensbourne National Park
Perseverance
Splityard Creek Dam
Cooby Creek Reservoir
Geham Nat Park
Ravensbourne Nat Pk
Cominya
Wivenhoe Dam
Mt England
Geham
Mt Perseverance
Brisbane Forest Park
Kleinton
Cabarlah
White Mtn
Lake Atkinson

BURNETT HWY · D'AGUILAR HWY · BRISBANE VALLEY HWY · NEW ENGLAND HWY · CONONDALE RANGE · D'AGUILAR RANGE · KENILWORTH ROAD · MALENY · Brisbane River · Emu Creek · Disused Railway

152°00' · 152°30' · 26°30' · 27°00'

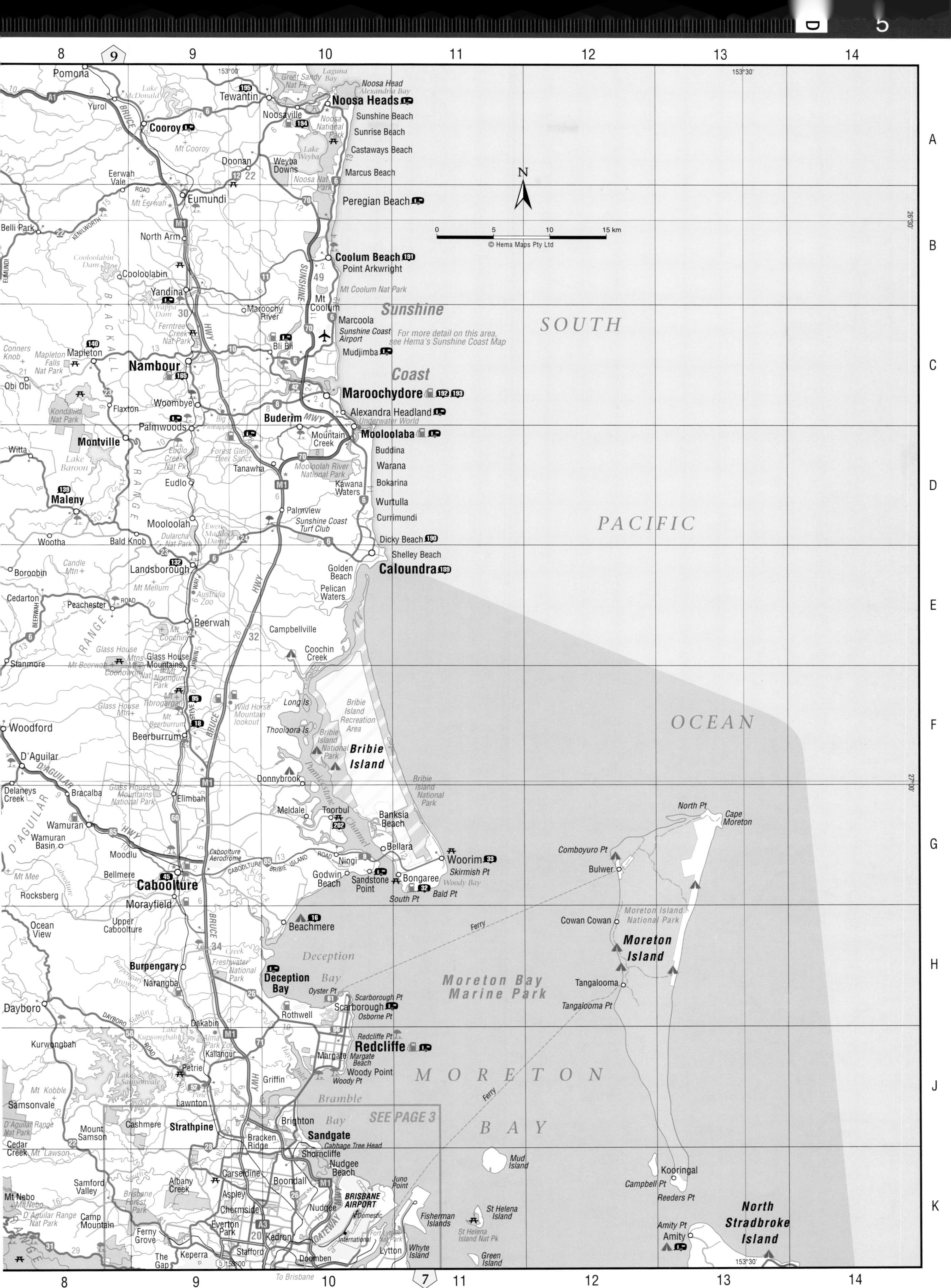

8
9
10
11
12
13
14
A
B
C
D
E
F
G
H
J
K
153°00'
153°30'
26°30'
27°00'
Pomona
Yurol
Lake McDonald
Tewantin
Great Sandy Nat Pk
Laguna Bay
Noosa Head
Alexandria Bay
Noosa Heads
Noosaville
Sunshine Beach
Noosa National Park
Sunrise Beach
Cooroy
Mt Cooroy
Lake Weyba
Castaways Beach
Doonan
Weyba Downs
Noosa Nat Park
Marcus Beach
Eerwah Vale
Eumundi
Mt Eerwah
Peregian Beach
Belli Park
Kenilworth
North Arm
Coolum Beach
Point Arkwright
Cooloolabin Dam
Cooloolabin
Mt Coolum Nat Park
Yandina
Wappa Dam
Mt Coolum
Maroochy River
Sunshine
Marcoola
Sunshine Coast Airport
Mudjimba
Ferntree Creek Nat Park
Conners Knob
Mapleton Falls Nat Park
Mapleton
Nambour
Bli Bli
For more detail on this area, see Hema's Sunshine Coast Map
Coast
SOUTH
Obi Obi
Flaxton
Woombye
Maroochydore
Alexandra Headland
Underwater World
Kondalilla Nat Park
Buderim
Palmwoods
Big Pineapple
Mooloolaba
Mountain Creek
Montville
Witta
Lake Baroon
Buddina
Forest Glen Deer Sanct.
Eudlo Creek Nat Pk
Tanawha
Warana
Mooloolah River National Park
Bokarina
Maleny
Eudlo
Kawana Waters
Wurtulla
Palmview
Currimundi
Mooloolah
Sunshine Coast Turf Club
Wootha
Bald Knob
Dularcha Nat Park
Ewen Maddock Dam
Dicky Beach
PACIFIC
Shelley Beach
Candle Mtn
Boroobin
Landsborough
Golden Beach
Caloundra
Mt Mellum
Australia Zoo
Pelican Waters
Cedarton
Peachester
Beerwah
Campbellville
Mt Coochin
Glass House
Glass House Mountains
Coochin Creek
Stanmore
Mt Beerwah
Mt Coonowrin
Mt Ngungun Nat Park
Mt Tibrogargan
Glass House Mtn
Wild Horse Mountain lookout
Long Is
Bribie Island Recreation Area
Woodford
Mt Beerburrum
Beerburrum
Thooloora Is
Bribie Island National Park
OCEAN
Bribie Island
D'Aguilar
Pumicestone Channel
Donnybrook
Delaneys Creek
Bracalba
Glass House Mountains National Park
Elimbah
Bribie Island National Park
North Pt
Cape Moreton
Meldale
Toorbul
Banksia Beach
Wamuran
Wamuran Basin
Comboyuro Pt
Moodlu
Caboolture Aerodrome
Bellara
Woorim
Bulwer
Bellmere
Ningi
Skirmish Pt
Caboolture
Godwin Beach
Sandstone Point
Bongaree
Woody Bay
Rocksberg
Morayfield
Bald Pt
South Pt
Mt Mee
Beachmere
Moreton Island National Park
Cowan Cowan
Ocean View
Upper Caboolture
Ferry
Moreton Island
Deception
Burpengary
Freshwater National Park
Bay
Deception Bay
Moreton Bay Marine Park
Tangalooma
Narangba
Oyster Pt
Scarborough Pt
Scarborough
Tangalooma Pt
Dayboro
Osborne Pt
Rothwell
Dakabin
Redcliffe Pt
Kurwongbah
Lake Kurwongbah
Alma Park Zoo
Kallangur
Redcliffe
Margate
Margate Beach
Woody Point
MORETON
Petrie
Lake Samsonvale
Griffin
Woody Pt
Mt Kobble
Samsonvale
Lawnton
Bramble
Ferry
Hays Inlet
SEE PAGE 3
Bay
BAY
Mount Samson
Cashmere
Strathpine
Brighton
Sandgate
D'Aguilar Range Nat Park
Bracken Ridge
Cabbage Tree Head
Cedar Creek
Mt Lawson
Shorncliffe
Mud Island
Nudgee Beach
Kooringal
Carseldine
Samford Valley
Albany Creek
Boondall
Juno Point
Campbell Pt
Mt Nebo
Aspley
BRISBANE AIRPORT
Reeders Pt
Brisbane Forest Park
Chermside
Nudgee
Domestic
Fisherman Islands
St Helena Island
North Stradbroke Island
D'Aguilar Range Nat Park
Camp Mountain
Everton Park
Kedron
Amity Pt
Ferny Grove
Amity
St Helena Island Nat Pk
International
Fort Lytton Nat Park
Stafford
Lytton
Whyte Island
Green Island
The Gap
Keperra
Doomben
To Brisbane
BRUCE HWY
SUNSHINE MWY
GATEWAY
BLACKALL RANGE
D'AGUILAR HWY
D'AGUILAR RANGE
CABOOLTURE BRIBIE ISLAND ROAD
DAYBORO ROAD
STEVE IRWIN WAY
KENILWORTH ROAD
0
5
10
15 km
© Hema Maps Pty Ltd
N

Brisbane Region, Queensland

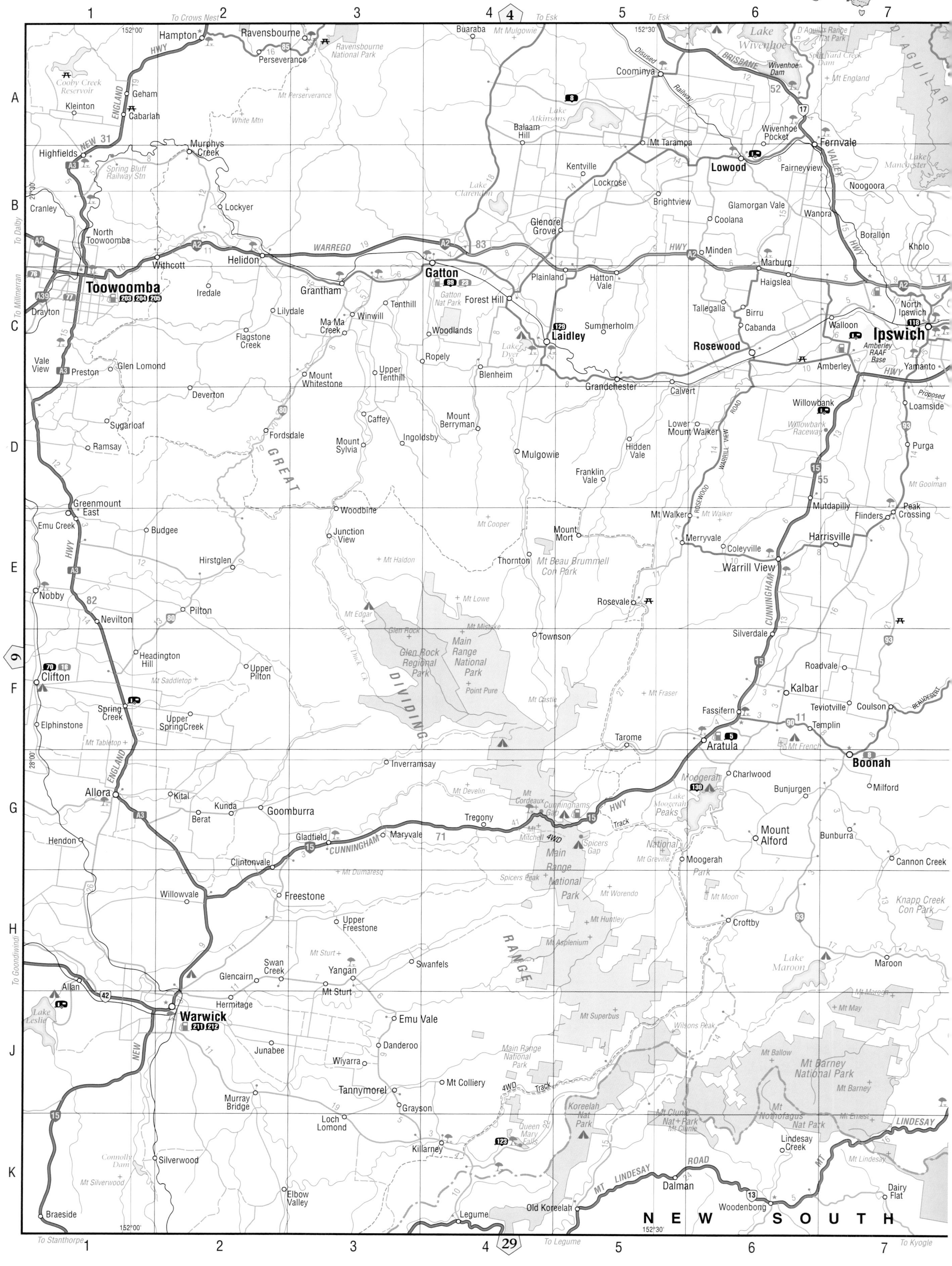

To Crows Nest
To Esk
To Dalby
To Millmerran
To Goondiwindi
To Stanthorpe
To Legume
To Kyogle

Hampton
Ravensbourne
Ravensbourne National Park
Perseverance
Buaraba
Mt Mulgowie
Lake Wivenhoe
D'Aguilar Range Nat Park
Wivenhoe Dam
Splityard Creek Dam
Mt England
D'AGUILAR
Cooby Creek Reservoir
Geham
Kleinton
Cabarlah
NEW ENGLAND HWY
Mt Perseverance
White Mtn
Coominya
Disused Brisbane Railway
Lake Atkinson
Balaam Hill
Mt Tarampa
Wivenhoe Pocket
Fernvale
Lowood
Fairneyview
Highfields
Murphys Creek
Spring Bluff Railway Stn
Kentville
Lockrose
Lake Manchester
Noogoora
Cranley
Lockyer
Lake Clarendon
Brightview
Glamorgan Vale
Wanora
Coolana
North Toowoomba
Glenore Grove
Borallon
Kholo
WARREGO HWY
Minden
Withcott
Helidon
Gatton
Marburg
Haigslea
Toowoomba
Iredale
Grantham
Plainland
Hatton Vale
Drayton
Tenthill
Gatton Nat Park
Forest Hill
North Ipswich
Lilydale
Winwill
Tallegalla
Birru
Ma Ma Creek
Flagstone Creek
Woodlands
Laidley
Summerholm
Cabanda
Walloon
Ipswich
Lake Dyer
Rosewood
Amberley RAAF Base
Vale View
Preston
Glen Lomond
Upper Tenthill
Ropely
Blenheim
Amberley
Yamanto
Mount Whitestone
Deverton
Grandchester
Calvert
Proposed
Willowbank
Loamside
Willowbank Raceway
Caffey
Mount Berryman
Lower Mount Walker
Sugarloaf
Fordsdale
Ingoldsby
Mount Sylvia
Mulgowie
Hidden Vale
Purga
Ramsay
GREAT DIVIDING RANGE
Franklin Vale
Mt Goolman
Greenmount East
Woodbine
Mutdapilly
Peak Crossing
Flinders
Emu Creek
Mt Cooper
Mt Walker
Budgee
Junction View
Mount Mort
Merryvale
Coleyville
Harrisville
Mt Haldon
Hirstglen
Thornton
Mt Beau Brummell Con Park
Warrill View
Nobby
Mt Lowe
Rosevale
Pilton
Mt Edgar
Nevilton
Mt Mistake
Glen Rock
Main Range National Park
Glen Rock Regional Park
Townson
Silverdale
Headington Hill
Point Pure
Upper Pilton
Roadvale
Clifton
Mt Saddletop
Mt Fraser
Kalbar
Mt Castle
Spring Creek
Upper Spring Creek
Teviotville
Coulson
BEAUDESERT
Elphinstone
Fassifern
Templin
Mt Tabletop
Tarome
Aratula
Mt French
Boonah
Inverramsay
Charlwood
Allora
Moogerah
Bunjurgen
Milford
Mt Devellin
Kital
Mt Cordeaux
Cunninghams Gap
Lake Moogerah
Peaks
Kunda
Goomburra
Berat
Tregony
Mount Alford
Bunburra
Mt Mitchell
Hendon
Gladfield
Maryvale
CUNNINGHAM HWY
Spicers Gap
National
Moogerah Park
Cannon Creek
Mt Greville
Clintonvale
Mt Dumaresq
Spicers Peak
Willowvale
Freestone
Mt Worendo
Mt Moon
Knapp Creek Con Park
Upper Freestone
Croftby
Mt Huntley
Mt Asplenium
Mt Sturt
Lake Maroon
Maroon
Swan Creek
Yangan
Swanfels
Glencairn
Allan
Mt Sturt
Hermitage
Mt Maroon
Lake Leslie
Mt May
Warwick
Emu Vale
Mt Superbus
Wilsons Peak
Junabee
Danderoo
Mt Ballow
Mt Barney National Park
Wiyarra
Main Range National Park
Mt Barney
Tannymorel
Mt Colliery
4WD Track
Murray Bridge
Grayson
Koreelah Nat Park
Mt Clunie Nat Park
Mt Nothofagus Nat Park
Mt Ernest
LINDESAY
Loch Lomond
Queen Mary Falls
Lindesay Creek
Killarney
Connolly Dam
Silverwood
Mt Lindesay
Mt Silverwood
MT LINDESAY ROAD
Dalman
Elbow Valley
Dairy Flat
Braeside
Legume
Old Koreelah
Woodenbong
NEW SOUTH

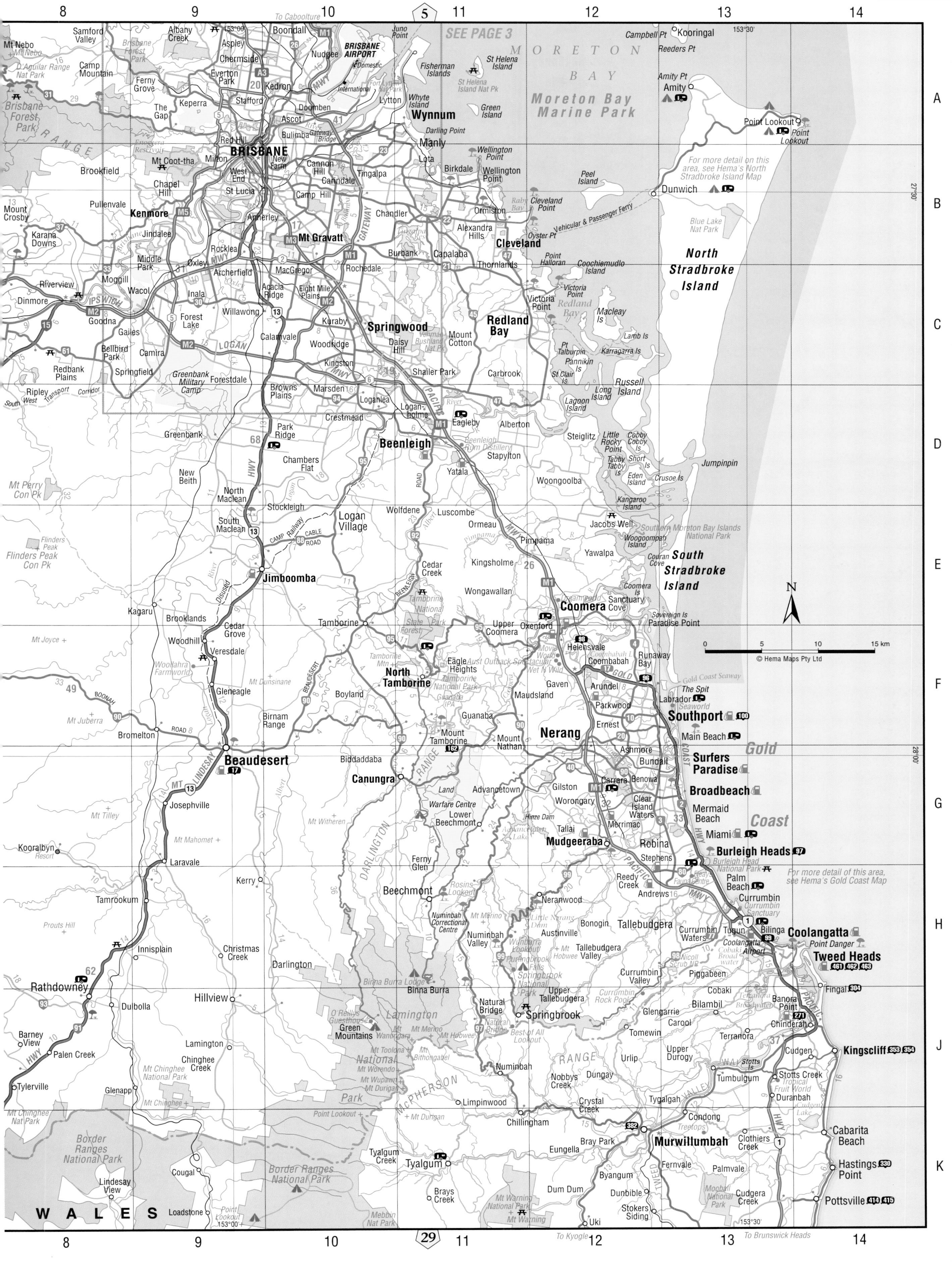

8 9 10 5 11 12 13 14

A B C D E F G H J K

SEE PAGE 3

To Caboolture

Mt Nebo, Samford Valley, Albany Creek, Aspley, Boondall, Nudgee, BRISBANE AIRPORT, Domestic, International, Juno Point, Fisherman Islands, St Helena Island, St Helena Island Nat Pk, Campbell Pt, Kooringal, Reeders Pt, Amity Pt, Amity

D'Aguilar Range Nat Park, Camp Mountain, Ferny Grove, Chermside, Everton Park, Kedron, Stafford, Keperra, The Gap, Doomben, Lytton, Whyte Island, Wynnum, Green Island, Darling Point, Manly, Lota

MORETON BAY

Moreton Bay Marine Park

Brisbane Forest Park, RANGE, Mt Coot-tha, Red Hill, BRISBANE, Milton, Ascot, Bulimba, Gateway Bridge, New Farm, Cannon Hill, Carindale, Tingalpa, Birkdale, Wellington Point, Point Lookout

Brookfield, West End, St Lucia, Chapel Hill, Camp Hill, Chandler, Ormiston, Raby Bay, Cleveland Point, Peel Island, Dunwich

For more detail on this area, see Hema's North Stradbroke Island Map

Mount Crosby, Pullenvale, Kenmore, Annerley, Alexandra Hills, Oyster Pt, Vehicular & Passenger Ferry, Blue Lake Nat Park

Karana Downs, Jindalee, Rocklea, Mt Gravatt, Burbank, Capalaba, Cleveland, Point Halloran, Coochiemudlo Island

North Stradbroke Island

Middle Park, Oxley, Archerfield, MacGregor, Rochedale, Thornlands, Victoria Point, Redland Bay, Macleay Is

Riverview, Moggill, Dinmore, Wacol, Inala, Acacia Ridge, Eight Mile Plains, IPSWICH, Goodna, Gailes, Forest Lake, Willawong, Kuraby, Springwood, Mount Cotton, Redland Bay, Lamb Is

Bellbird Park, Camira, LOGAN, Calamvale, Woodridge, Daisy Hill, Venman Bushland Nat Pk, Pt Talburpin, Karragarra Is, Pannikin Is

Redbank Plains, Springfield, Greenbank Military Camp, Forestdale, Kingston, Shailer Park, Carbrook, St Clair Is, Russell Island

Ripley, South West Transport Corridor, Browns Plains, Marsden, Loganlea, Loganholme, Lagoon Island, Long Island

Crestmead, Eagleby, Alberton, Greenbank, Park Ridge, Beenleigh, Beenleigh Rum Distillery, Stapylton, Steiglitz, Little Rocky Point, Cobby Cobby Is, Tabby Tabby Is, Short Is, Jumpinpin

New Beith, Chambers Flat, Yatala, Woongoolba, Eden Island, Crusoe Is, Mt Perry Con Pk, North Maclean, Stockleigh, Logan Village, Wolffdene, Luscombe, Ormeau, Kangaroo Island, Jacobs Well

South Maclean, CAMP CABLE ROAD, Pimpama, Southern Moreton Bay Islands National Park, Woogoompah Island, Flinders Peak, Flinders Peak Con Pk, Cedar Creek, Kingsholme, Yawalpa, Couran Cove, South Stradbroke Island

Jimboomba, Disused, Wongawallan, Coomera Is, Sanctuary Cove, Kagaru, Tamborine National Park, Coomera, Sovereign Is, Paradise Point

Brooklands, Cedar Grove, Tamborine, Upper Coomera, Oxenford, Mt Joyce, Woodhill, Veresdale, State Forest, Tamborine Mtn, Eagle Heights, Aust Outback Spectacular, Wet N Wild, Helensvale, Coombabah, Runaway Bay

Woollahra Farmworld, North Tamborine, Tamborine National Park, Gold Coast Seaway, The Spit, BOONAH, Mt Dunsinane, Gleneagle, BEAUDESERT, Boyland, Guanaba IPA, Gaven, Maudsland, Arundel, Labrador, Seaworld, Parkwood

Mt Juberta, Bromelton, ROAD, Birnam Range, Guanaba, Southport, Main Beach, Mount Tamborine, Mount Nathan, Nerang, Ernest, Ashmore, Gold Coast

Beaudesert, Biddaddaba, Canungra, RANGE, Bundall, Surfers Paradise, Benowa, Carrara, Lindesay Hwy, Advancetown, Gilston, Broadbeach

Josephville, Land Warfare Centre, Lower Beechmont, Worongary, Clear Island Waters, Mermaid Beach, Mt Tilley, Mt Witheren, Hinze Dam, Advancetown Lake, Tallai, Merrimac, Miami, Coast

Mt Mahomet, Kooralbyn Resort, DARLINGTON, Mudgeeraba, Robina, Burleigh Heads, Laravale, Ferny Glen, Stephens, Burleigh Head National Park, Reedy Creek, Palm Beach, Fleay Fauna Centre, Kerry, Beechmont, Rosins Lookout, Andrews

For more detail of this area, see Hema's Gold Coast Map

Tamrookum, Neranwood, Currumbin, Currumbin Sanctuary, Prouts Hill, Numinbah Correctional Centre, Mt Marino, Little Nerang Dam, Bonogin, Tallebudgera, Currumbin Waters, Tugun, Bilinga, Coolangatta, Point Danger, Innisplain, Christmas Creek, Darlington, Numinbah Valley, Wunburra Lookout, Mt Hobwee, Tallebudgera Valley, Coolangatta Airport, Cobaki Broadwater, Tweed Heads

Rathdowney, Binna Burra Lodge, Binna Burra, Purlingbrook Falls, Springbrook National Park, Currumbin Valley, Nicoll Scrub NP, Piggabeen, Cobaki, Fingal

Hillview, Dulbolla, O'Reilly's Guesthouse, Lamington, Natural Bridge, Upper Tallebudgera, Currumbin Rock Pool, Springbrook, Glengarrie, Bilambil, Terranora Broadwater, Banora Point, Chinderah

Barney View, Green Mountains, Mt Merino, Mt Hobwee, Natural Bridge, Best of All Lookout, Carool, Tomewin, Terranora, Kingscliff, Palen Creek, Lamington, Mt Toolona, Mt Bithongabel, Upper Duroby, Urlip, Cudgen

Tylerville, Chinghee Creek, Mt Chinghee National Park, National Park, Mt Worendo, Mt Wupawn, Mt Durigan, Numinbah, RANGE, Nobbys Creek, Dungay, Tumbulgum, Stotts Is, Stotts Creek, Tropical Fruit World, Duranbah, Cudgen Lake

Glenapp, Mt Chinghee, McPHERSON, Park, Limpinwood, Crystal Creek, Tygalgah, VALLEY, Mt Chinghee Nat Park, Point Lookout, Mt Durigan, Chillingham, Condong, Treetops

Border Ranges National Park, Tyalgum Creek, Tyalgum, Eungella, Bray Park, Murwillumbah, Clothiers Creek, Cabarita Beach

Lindesay View, Cougal, Border Ranges National Park, Fernvale, Palmvale, Hastings Point, TWEED, Byangum, Mooball National Park, Cudgera Creek

WALES, Loadstone, Point Lookout, Brays Creek, Mt Warning National Park, Mt Warning, Dum Dum, Dunbible, Stokers Siding, Pottsville, Mebbin Nat Park, Uki

153°00', 153°30', 27°30', 28°00'

0 5 10 15 km

© Hema Maps Pty Ltd

N

To Kyogle, To Brunswick Heads

29

8 9 10 11 12 13 14

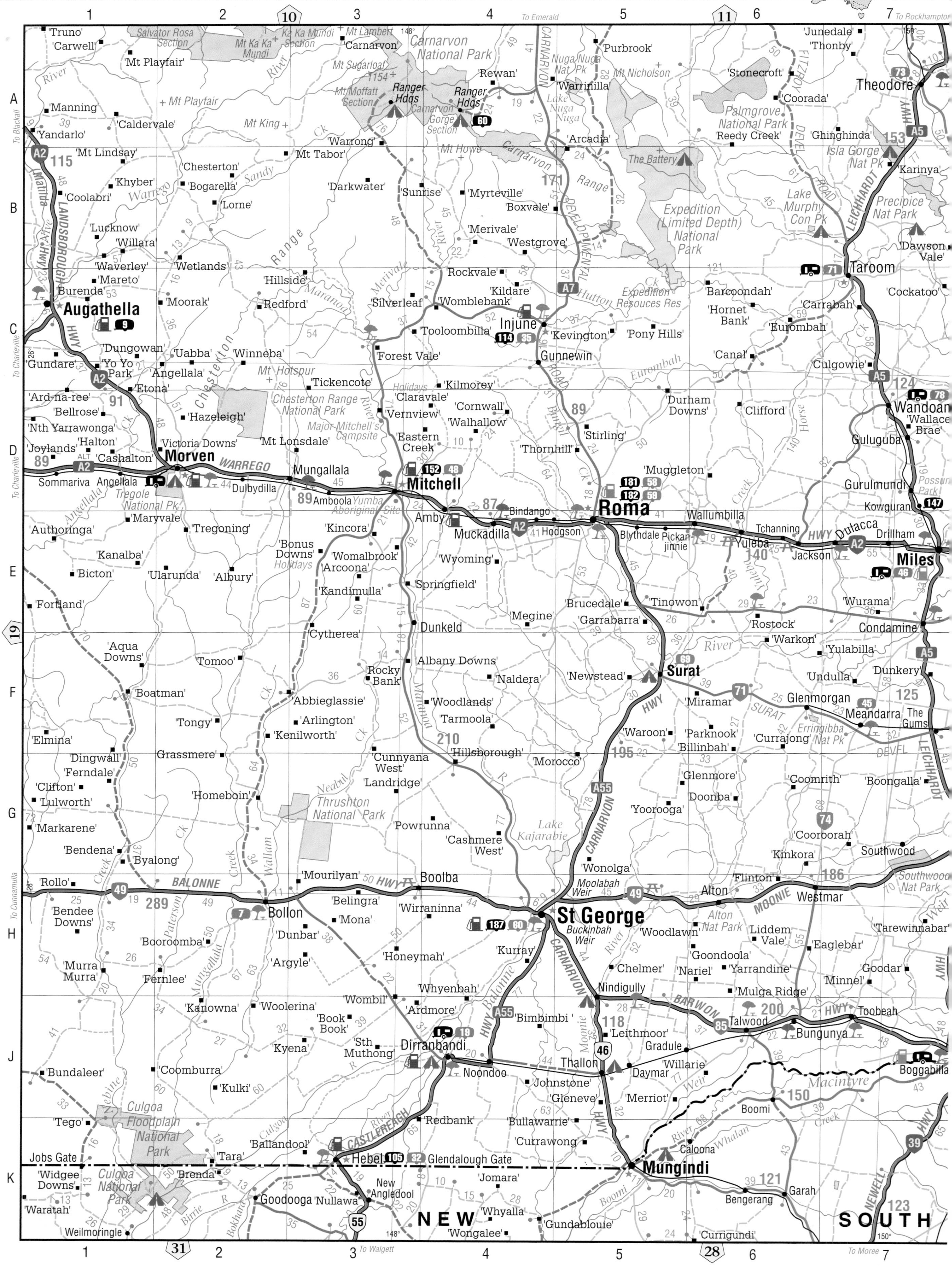

South-East Queensland

1 2 10 3 4 To Emerald 5 11 6 7 To Rockhampton

A
'Truno' 'Carwell' Salvator Rosa Section Mt Ka Ka Mundi Ka Ka Mundi Section Mt Lambert 'Carnarvon' Carnarvon National Park 'Purbrook' 'Junedale' 'Thonby'
'Mt Playfair' Mt Sugarloaf 1154 'Rewan' Nuga Nuga Nat Pk Mt Nicholson 'Stonecroft' Theodore
'Manning' Mt Playfair Mt Moffatt Section Ranger Hdqs Ranger Hdqs 'Warrinilla' Lake Nuga Nuga 'Coorada'
'Caldervale' Mt King Carnarvon Gorge Section Palmgrove National Park
'Yandarlo' 'Warrong' 'Arcadia' 'Reedy Creek' 'Ghinghinda' Isla Gorge Nat Pk
To Blackall

B
115 'Mt Lindsay' 'Mt Tabor' Mt Howe Carnarvon Range 171 The Battery 153 'Karinya'
'Chesterton' 'Khyber' 'Bogarella' 'Darkwater' 'Sunrise' 'Myrteville' Lake Murphy Con Pk Precipice Nat Park
'Coolabri' 'Lorne' 'Boxvale' Expedition (Limited Depth) National Park
'Lucknow' 'Merivale' 'Westgrove' 'Dawson Vale'
'Willara' 'Wetlands' 'Waverley' 'Mareto' 'Hillside' 'Rockvale' Taroom
LANDSBOROUGH HWY DEVELOPMENTAL ROAD LEICHHARDT HWY

C
'Burenda' Augathella 'Moorak' 'Redford' Silverleaf 'Womblebank' 'Kildare' Expedition Resouces Res 'Barcoondah' 'Hornet Bank' 'Cockatoo'
Injune 'Kevington' 'Pony Hills' 'Carrabah' 'Eurombah'
'Tooloombilla' Gunnewin 'Canal'
'Gundare' 'Dungowan' 'Uabba' 'Winneba' 'Forest Vale' 'Culgowie'
'Yo Yo Park' 'Angellala' Mt Hotspur To Charleville

D
'Ard-na-ree' 'Etona' 'Tickencote' 'Kilmorey' 124 Wandoan
91 'Bellrose' 'Hazeleigh' Chesterton Range National Park 'Claravale' 'Cornwall' 'Durham Downs' 'Clifford' 'Wallace Brae'
'Nth Yarrawonga' 'Vernview' 'Walhallow' 'Stirling' Guluguba
'Halton' Major Mitchell's Campsite 'Eastern Creek' 'Thornhill'
'Joylands' 'Victoria Downs' 'Mt Lonsdale'
89 'Cashalton' Morven WARREGO Mungallala 'Muggleton' Gurulmundi
Sommariva Angellala Dulbydilla Mitchell Roma Possum Park
Tregole National Pk 89 Amboola Yumba Aboriginal Site 87 Bindango Kowguran 147

E
'Maryvale' Amby Wallumbilla Tchanning Dulacca Drillham
'Authoringa' 'Tregoning' 'Kincora' Muckadilla Hodgson Blythdale Pickanjinnie Yuleba Jackson Miles
'Bonus Downs' Holidays 'Womalbrook' 140
'Kanalba' 'Arcoona' 'Wyoming'
'Bicton' 'Ularunda' 'Albury' 'Springfield'
'Kandimulla' 'Brucedale' 'Tinowon' 'Wurama'
'Fortland' 'Megine' 'Garrabarra' 'Rostock' Condamine
19 Dunkeld 'Warkon'
'Cytherea' 'Yulabilla'

F
'Aqua Downs' 'Tomoo' 'Albany Downs' Surat 'Dunkery'
'Rocky Bank' 'Naldera' 'Newstead' 'Undulla'
'Boatman' 'Abbieglassie' 'Woodlands' 'Miramar' Glenmorgan 125
'Tongy' 'Arlington' 'Tarmoola' SURAT Meandarra The Gums
'Kenilworth' 'Waroon' 'Parknook' 'Currajong' Erringibba Nat Pk
'Elmina' 210 195 'Billinbah'
'Dingwall' Grassmere 'Hillsborough' 'Morocco' DEVEL
'Cunnyana West'

G
'Ferndale' 'Landridge' 'Glenmore' 'Coomrith' 'Boongalla'
'Clifton' 'Homeboin' 'Doonba'
'Lulworth' Thrushton National Park 'Yoorooga'
'Markarene' 'Powrunna' Lake Kajarabie 'Cooroorah'
'Bendena' 'Cashmere West' 'Kinkora' Southwood
'Byalong' 'Wonolga'

H
'Rollo' BALONNE 'Mourilyan' Boolba Moolabah Weir 'Flinton' 186 Southwood Nat Park
'Bendee Downs' 289 'Belingra' Alton Westmar
Bollon 'Mona' 'Wirraninna' St George Alton Nat Park MOONIE 'Tarewinnabar'
'Dunbar' Buckinbah Weir 'Woodlawn' 'Liddem Vale'
'Booroomba' 'Honeymah' 'Kurray' 'Eaglebar'
'Murra Murra' 'Argyle' 'Goondoola' 'Goodar'
'Fernlee' 'Chelmer' 'Nariel' 'Yarrandine'
'Whyenbah' Nindigully 'Minnel'
'Kanowna' 'Woolerina' 'Wombil' 'Ardmore' 'Mulga Ridge'

J
'Book Book' 'Bimbimbi' 118 BARWON 200 Toobeah
'Leithmoor' Talwood Bungunya
'Kyena' 'Sth Muthong' Dirranbandi Gradule
'Bundaleer' 'Coomburra' Noondoo Thallon Daymar 'Willarie' Boggabilla
'Kulki' 'Johnstone' Macintyre
'Gleneve' 'Merriot' 150
Culgoa Floodplain National Park Boomi
'Tego' 'Redbank' 'Bullawarrie'

K
'Ballandool' CASTLEREAGH 'Currawong' Caloona
Jobs Gate 'Tara' Hebel 105 Glendalough Gate Mungindi 39
'Widgee Downs' Culgoa National Park 'Brenda' 'Jomara' 121 Garah
New Angledool Bengerang 123
'Waratah' Goodooga 'Nullawa' 'Whyalla'
Weilmoringle N E W 'Gundablouie' S O U T H
'Wongalee' 'Currigundi'

1 31 2 3 To Walgett 4 5 28 6 To Moree 7

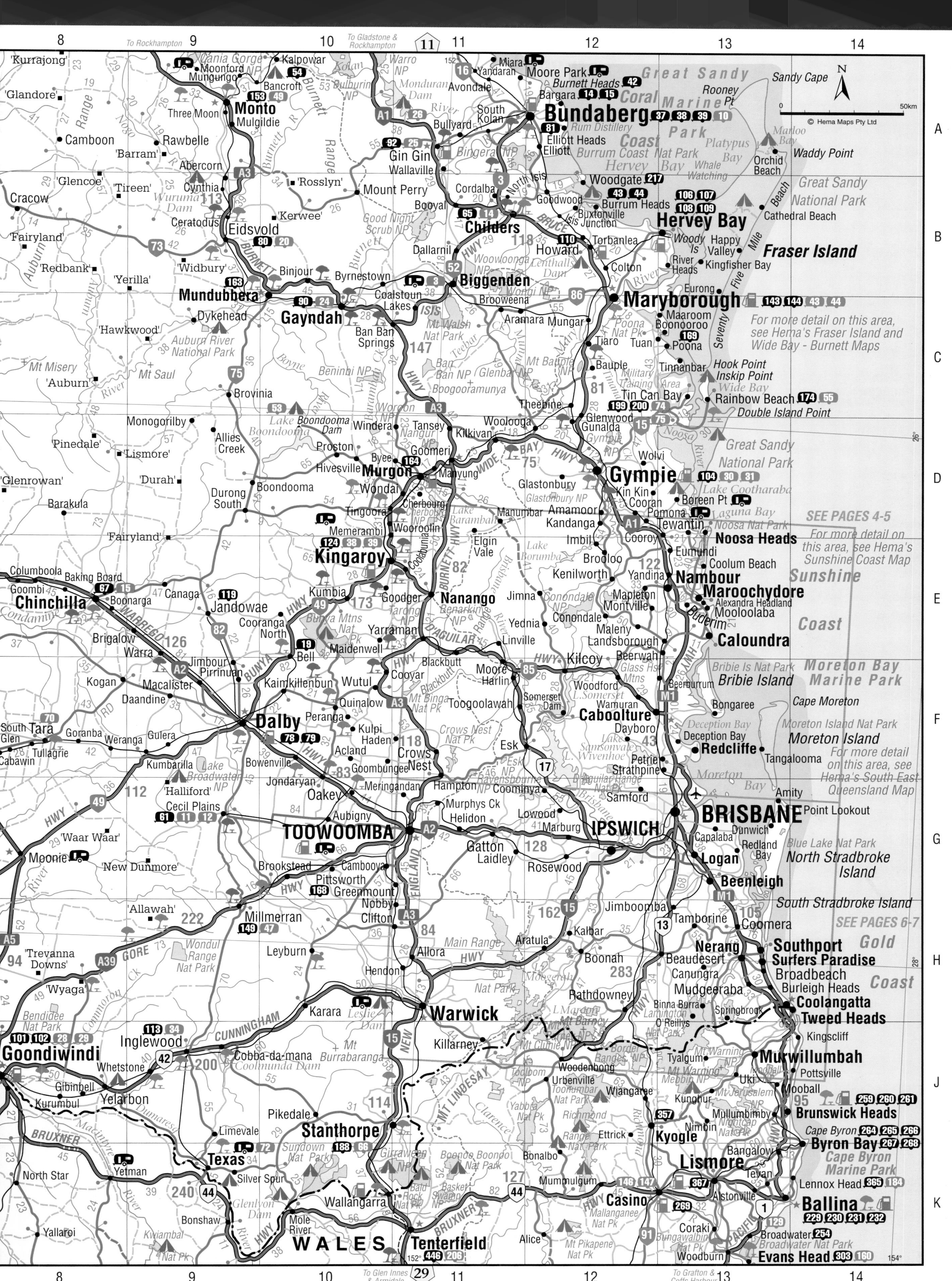
8
To Rockhampton
9
10
To Gladstone & Rockhampton
11
12
13
14
A
B
C
D
E
F
G
H
J
K
Sandy Cape
N
0
50km
© Hema Maps Pty Ltd
'Kurrajong'
'Glandore'
Range
Camboon
'Barram'
Rawbelle
Three Moon
Monto
Mulgildie
Moonford
Mungungo
Cania Gorge NP
Kalpowar
Bancroft
Burnett
'Glencoe'
'Tireen'
Cracow
Cynthia
Abercorn
Wuruma Dam
Ceratodus
Eidsvold
'Kerwee'
'Rosslyn'
Mount Perry
'Fairyland'
'Redbank'
'Widbury'
'Yerilla'
Auburn
Mundubbera
Dykehead
Gayndah
Binjour
Byrnestown
'Hawkwood'
Auburn River National Park
Mt Misery
'Auburn'
Mt Saul
Brovinia
Monogorilby
Allies Creek
Lake Boondooma
Boondooma Dam
'Pinedale'
'Lismore'
'Glenrowan'
'Durah'
Boondooma
Durong South
Barakula
'Fairyland'
Columboola
Baking Board
Goombi
Chinchilla
Boonarga
Canaga
Jandowae
Condamine
Brigalow
Warra
Kogan
Jimbour
Pirrinuan
Macalister
Daandine
South Glen
Tara
Goranba
Weranga
Gulera
Tullagrie
Cabawin
Kumbarilla
Lake Broadwater NP
'Halliford'
Cecil Plains
'Waar Waar'
Moonie
'New Dunmore'
'Allawah'
Millmerran
'Trevanna Downs'
Wondul Range Nat Park
'Wyaga'
Bendidee Nat Park
Goondiwindi
Inglewood
Whetstone
Gibinbell
Kurumbul
Yelarbon
Cobba-da-mana
Coolmunda Dam
Limevale
Texas
Yetman
North Star
Silver Spur
Bonshaw
Glenlyon Dam
Yallaroi
Kwiambal Nat Pk
BRUXNER
Dalby
Kaimkillenbun
Wutul
Bell
Kumbia
Maidenwell
Bunya Mtns Nat Pk
Cooranga North
Jondaryan
Oakey
Bowenville
Acland
Goombungee
Crows Nest
Haden
Kulpi
Peranga
Quinalow
Cooyar
Aubigny
Meringandan
TOOWOOMBA
Brookstead
Pittsworth
Cambooya
Greenmount
Nobby
Clifton
Leyburn
Allora
Hendon
Karara
Warwick
Killarney
Leslie Dam
Mt Burrabaranga
Pikedale
Stanthorpe
Sundown Nat Park
Girraween NP
Wallangarra
Mole River
WALES
Tenterfield
To Glen Innes & Armidale
29
Miara
Moore Park
Yandaran
Burnett Heads
Bargara
Avondale
Monduran Dam
Bulburin NP
Warro NP
Kolan
South Kolan
Bundaberg
Rum Distillery
Elliott Heads
Elliott
Bullyard
Gin Gin
Wallaville
Bingera NP
Cordalba
Booyal
Good Night Scrub NP
Childers
Dallarnil
Woowoonga NP
Biggenden
Coalstoun Lakes
Brooweena
Aramara
Mungar
Mt Walsh Nat Park
Ban Ban Springs
Beninbi NP
Boogooramunya
Woroon NP
Windera
Tansey
Kilkivan
Wooloowa
Proston
Byee
Goomeri
Hivesville
Murgon
Manyung
Wondai
Cherbourg
Tingoora
Memerambi
Wooroolin
Kingaroy
Coolabunia
Lake Barambah
Elgin Vale
Manumbar
Goodger
Nanango
Tarong NP
Yarraman
Benarkin NP
Blackbutt
Moore
Harlin
Toogoolawah
Esk
Hampton
Murphys Ck
Helidon
Gatton
Laidley
Ravensbourne NP
Coominya
Lowood
Marburg
IPSWICH
Rosewood
Main Range
Aratula
Kalbar
Boonah
Mt Lindesay
Great Sandy Coral Marine Park
Coast
Burrum Coast Nat Park
Hervey Bay
Platypus Bay
Whale Watching
Rooney Pt
Waddy Point
Orchid Beach
Woodgate
Goodwood
North Isis
Burrum Heads
Buxtonville
Isis Junction
Torbanlea
Howard
Hervey Bay
Woody Is
Happy Valley
Kingfisher Bay
River Heads
Great Sandy National Park
Cathedral Beach
Fraser Island
Seventy Five Mile Beach
Colton
Eurong
Maryborough
Maaroom
Boonooroo
Poona
Tuan
Tiaro
For more detail on this area, see Hema's Fraser Island and Wide Bay - Burnett Maps
Bauple
Tinnanbar
Hook Point
Inskip Point
Wide Bay
Tin Can Bay
Rainbow Beach
Double Island Point
Theebine
Glenwood
Gunalda
Gympie
Wolvi
Great Sandy National Park
Lake Cootharaba
Glastonbury
Kin Kin
Cooran
Boreen Pt
Pomona
Amamoor
Kandanga
Imbil
Cooroy
Tewantin
Laguna Bay
Noosa Nat Park
Noosa Heads
SEE PAGES 4-5
For more detail on this area, see Hema's Sunshine Coast Map
Eumundi
Coolum Beach
Brooloo
Kenilworth
Yandina
Nambour
Sunshine Coast
Jimna
Conondale NP
Mapleton
Montville
Maroochydore
Alexandra Headland
Mooloolaba
Buderim
Yednia
Conondale
Maleny
Landsborough
Caloundra
Linville
Kilcoy
Beerwah
Glass Hse Mtns
Bribie Is Nat Park
Bribie Island
Moreton Bay Marine Park
Beerburrum
Somerset Dam
Woodford
L. Somerset
Wamuran
Caboolture
Bongaree
Cape Moreton
Deception Bay
Dayboro
Moreton Island Nat Park
Moreton Island
Redcliffe
Tangalooma
For more detail on this area, see Hema's South East Queensland Map
Petrie
Strathpine
Samford
Moreton Bay
Amity
BRISBANE
Point Lookout
Dunwich
Capalaba
Redland Bay
Blue Lake Nat Park
North Stradbroke Island
Logan
Beenleigh
South Stradbroke Island
Jimboomba
Tamborine
Coomera
SEE PAGES 6-7
Gold Coast
Nerang
Southport
Surfers Paradise
Broadbeach
Beaudesert
Canungra
Mudgeeraba
Burleigh Heads
Rathdowney
Binna Burra
Lamington
O'Reillys
Springbrook
Coolangatta
Tweed Heads
Kingscliff
Border Ranges NP
Mt Warning
Murwillumbah
Tyalgum
Pottsville
Woodenbong
Urbenville
Wiangaree
Uki
Mooball
Mt Jerusalem NP
Kunghur
Mullumbimby
Brunswick Heads
Nimbin
Nightcap Nat Pk
Cape Byron
Byron Bay
Cape Byron Marine Park
Richmond Range Nat Park
Ettrick
Kyogle
Bangalow
Bonalbo
Mummulgum
Lismore
Tevan
Lennox Head
Casino
Alstonville
Ballina
Mallanganee Nat Pk
Coraki
Broadwater
Broadwater Nat Park
Alice
Mt Pikapene Nat Pk
Bungawalbin Nat Pk
Woodburn
Evans Head
To Grafton & Coffs Harbour
Toonumbar Nat Park
Yabbra Nat Pk
Clarence
Boonoo Boonoo Nat Park
Basket Swamp NP
Bald Rock Nat Pk
CUNNINGHAM
NEW ENGLAND
WARREGO
BUNYA HWY
D'AGUILAR
BRUCE HWY
PACIFIC HWY
GORE HWY
MT LINDESAY
ISIS HWY
BURNETT HWY
WIDE BAY HWY

Central-East Queensland

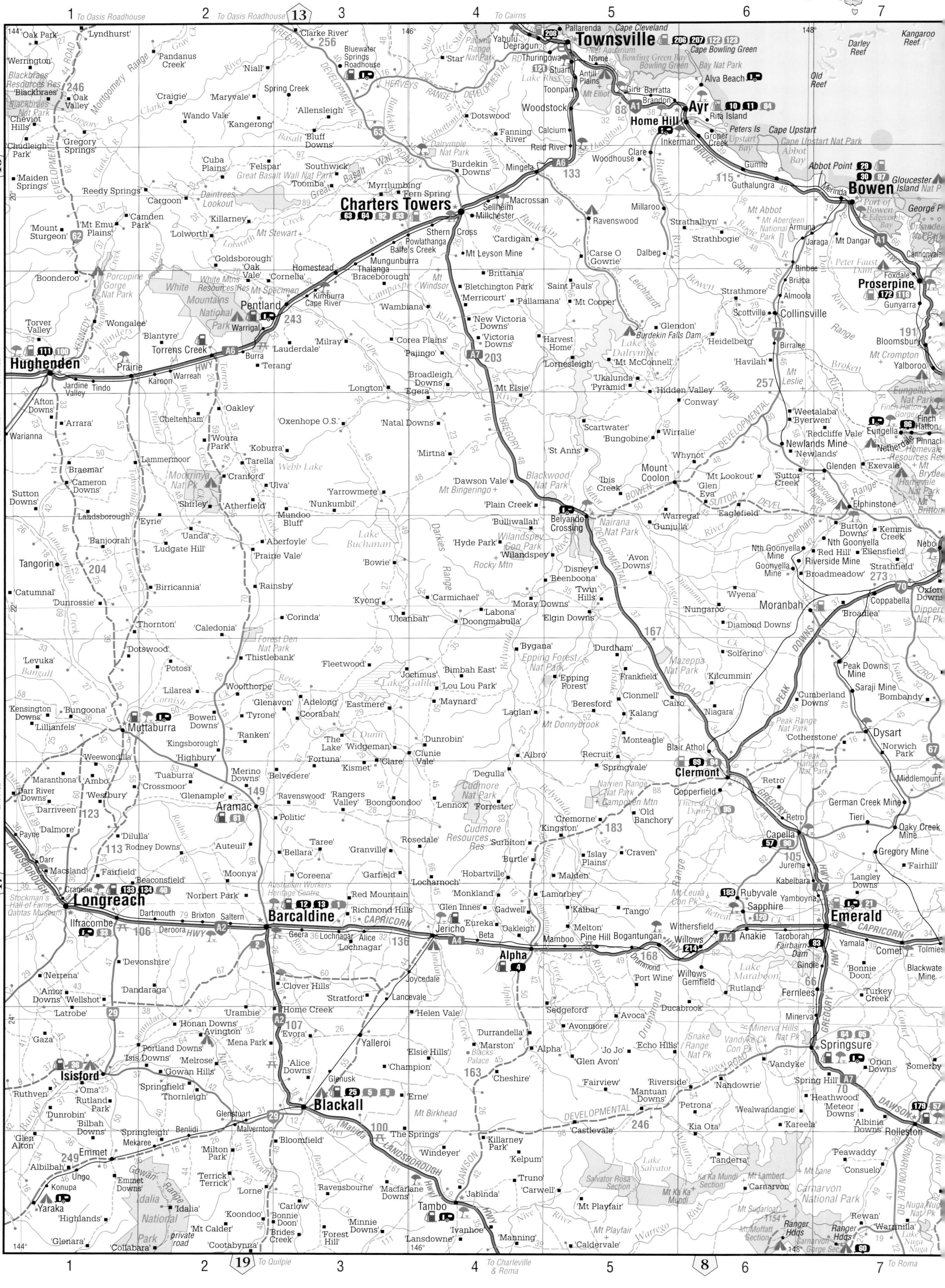

1 To Oasis Roadhouse 2 To Oasis Roadhouse 13 3 4 To Cairns 5 6 7

'Oak Park' 'Lyndhurst' 'Werrington' 'Pandanus Creek' Blackbraes Resources Res 246 Blackbraes 'Oak Valley' 'Cheviot Hills' 'Chudleigh Park' 'Gregory Springs' 'Maiden Springs' 'Mount Sturgeon' 'Mt Emu Plains' 'Camden Park' 'Lolworth' 'Craigie' 'Wando Vale' 'Maryvale' 'Kangerong' 'Niall' 'Clarke River' 256 Bluewater Springs Roadhouse Spring Creek 'Allensleigh' 'Bluff Downs' 'Cuba Plains' 'Felspar' 'Southwick' Great Basalt Wall Nat Park 'Toomba' 'Reedy Springs' 'Cargoon' Daintrees Lookout 'Killarney' Mt Stewart 'Myrrlumbing' 'Fern Spring' Charters Towers 'Star' Paluma Range Nat Park Yabulu Deeragun Thuringowa Stuart Pallarenda Cape Cleveland Townsville Reef Aquarium Bowling Green Bay Nat Park Cape Bowling Green Nome Antill Plains Lake Ross Toonpan Mt Elliot Giru Barratta Brandon Alva Beach Old Reef Ayr Home Hill Rita Island Inkerman Peters Is Cape Upstart Cape Upstart Nat Park Groper Creek Abbot Bay Abbot Point Gumlu Guthalungra Bowen Gloucester Island Nat Park Port of Bowen Darley Reef Kangaroo Reef George Point Woodstock Calcium 'Dotswood' 'Fanning River' Reid River Dalrymple Nat Park 'Burdekin Downs' Mingela 133 Clare Woodhouse 115 Macrossan Sellheim Millchester 'Cardigan' Ravenswood Millaroo Mt Abbot Mt Aberdeen National Park 'Strathalbyn' 'Strathbogie' Armuna Jaraga Mt Dangar Cannonvale Stern Cross Powlathanga Balfe's Creek Mungunburra Thalanga 'Goldsborough' 'Oak Vale' 'Cornelia' Homestead 'Braceborough' Mt Leyson Mine 'Carse O Gowrie' Dalbeg Peter Faust Dam Foxdale Proserpine Gunyarra Binbee Briaba Almoola 'Boonderoo' Porcupine Gorge Nat Park White Mountains National Park White Mtns Resources Res Mt Specimen Pentland Kimburra Cape River 243 Warrigal Mt Windsor 'Brittania' 'Bletchington Park' 'Merricourt' 'Pallamana' 'Saint Pauls' 'Mt Cooper' 'Strathmore' 'Scottville' Collinsville 'Torver Valley' 'Wongalee' 'Blantyre' Torrens Creek 'Wambiana' 'New Victoria Downs' 'Victoria Downs' 'Corea Plains' 'Milray' 'Lauderdale' 'Pajingo' 'Glendon' Burdekin Falls Dam 'Heidelberg' Harvest Home Lake Dalrymple 'Mt McConnell' 'Lornesleigh' 191 Bloomsbury Birralee Mt Crompton Yalboroo Hughenden Prairie Burra 'Terang' Warreah Karoon Jardine Valley Tindo 203 'Havilah' 'Broadleigh Downs' 'Egera' 'Longton' 'Mt Elsie' 'Ukalunda' 'Pyramid' 'Hidden Valley' 'Conway' 257 Mt Leslie Eungella Nat Park Finch Hatton Gorge

'Afton Downs' 'Arrara' Warianna 'Oakley' 'Cheltenham' 'Woura Park' 'Oxenhope O.S.' 'Natal Downs' 'Koburra' 'Tarella' Webb Lake 'Mirtna' 'Scartwater' 'Bungobine' 'Wirralie' 'Weetalaba' 'Byerwen' Eungella Finch Hatton Netherdale 'Redcliffe Vale' Newlands Mine 'Newlands' Pinnacle 'Lammermoor' Moorrinya Nat Pk 'Cranford' 'Ulva' 'St Anns' 'Whynot' Homevale Resources Res 'Braemar' 'Cameron Downs' 'Sutton Downs' 'Shirley' 'Atherfield' 'Yarrowmere' 'Nunkumbil' 'Dawson Vale' Mt Bingeringo Blackwood Nat Park 'Ibis Creek' Mount Coolon 'Mt Lookout' 'Glen Eva' 'Suttor Creek' Glenden 'Exevale' Mt Bryde Homevale Nat Park Elphinstone Mt Britton 'Landsborough' 'Eyrie' 'Mundoo Bluff' 'Plain Creek' Belyando Crossing 'Bulliwallah' Nairana Nat Park 'Warregal' 'Gunjulla' 'Eaglefield' 'Burton Downs' 'Kemmis Creek' 'Banjoorah' 'Uanda' 'Ludgate Hill' 'Aberfoyle' 'Prairie Vale' Lake Buchanan 'Hyde Park' Wilandspey Con Park 'Wilandspey' Rocky Mtn 'Avon Downs' Nth Goonyella Mine 'Red Hill' 'Ellensfield' Nth Goonyella Riverside Mine Goonyella Mine 'Broadmeadow' 'Strathfield' 273 Nebo Tangorin 204 'Bowie' 'Disney' 'Beenboona' 'Catumnal' 'Birricannia' 'Rainsby' 'Kyong' 'Carmichael' 'Twin Hills' 'Wyena' Moranbah 'Coppabella' 'Oxford Downs' Dipperu Nat Pk 'Dunrossie' 'Corinda' 'Labona' 'Moray Downs' 'Ulcanbah' 'Doongmabulla' 'Elgin Downs' 'Nungaroo' 'Diamond Downs' 'Broadlea' 'Thornton' 'Caledonia' Forest Den Nat Park 'Thistlebank' 167

'Levuka' 'Dotswood' 'Potosi' 'Fleetwood' 'Bygana' Epping Forest Nat Park 'Durdham' Mazeppa Nat Park 'Solferino' Peak Downs Mine Saraji Mine 'Bombandy' 'Lilarea' 'Woolthorpe' 'Jochmus' Lake Galilee 'Bimbah East' 'Lou Lou Park' 'Epping Forest' 'Frankfield' 'Kilcummin' 'Clonmell' 'Cumberland Downs' 'Kensington Downs' 'Bungoona' 'Lillianfels' Muttaburra 'Bowen Downs' 'Glenavon' 'Tyrone' 'Adelong' 'Coorabah' 'Eastmere' 'Maynard' 'Beresford' 'Laglan' Mt Donnybrook 'Cairo' 'Kalang' 'Niagara' Peak Range Nat Park 'Cotherstone' Dysart 'Norwich Park' 'Ranken' 'Kingsborough' 'Dunrobin' 'Monteagle' 'The Lake' 'Widgeman' 'Clunie Vale' 'Highbury' 'Fortuna' 'Kismet' 'Clare' 'Albro' 'Recruit' Blair Athol Clermont 'Springvale' Peak Range Nat Park 'Weewondilla' 'Maranthona' 'Ambo' 'Tuaburra' 'Crossmoor' 'Merino Downs' 149 'Belvedere' 'Degulla' Cudmore Nat Park 'Retro' Middlemount 'Darr River Downs' 'Westbury' 'Glenample' Aramac 'Ravenswood' 'Rangers Valley' 'Boongoondoo' 'Lennox' 'Forrester' Narrien Range Nat Park Campoyen Mtn 'Old Banchory' Copperfield Theresa Ck Dam German Creek Mine 'Darriveen' 123 'Politic' Tieri 'Dalmore' Payne 'Dilulla' 113 'Rodney Downs' 'Auteuil' 'Taree' 'Bellara' 'Granville' 'Rosedale' Cudmore Resources Res 'Surbiton' 'Cremorne' Kingston 183 Retro Capella Oaky Creek Mine Gregory Mine 'Fairhill' Darr 'Macsland' 'Fairfield' 'Moonya' 'Coreena' 'Garfield' 'Locharnoch' 'Hobartville' 'Burtle' 'Malden' 'Islay Plains' 'Craven' 105 Jurema 'Langley Downs' Kabelbara

Cramsie Beaconsfield Longreach Stockman's Hall of Fame Qantas Museum 'Norbert Park' Australian Workers Heritage Centre Red Mountain 'Richmond Hills' 'Monkland' 'Lamorbey' Rubyvale Sapphire Yamboyna Emerald Ilfracombe Dartmouth Brixton Saltern Barcaldine 'Glen Innes' 'Gadwell' 'Kalbar' 'Tango' Mt Leura Con Pk Retreat 'Eureka' 'Oakleigh' 106 Deroora 'Geera' Lochnagar Alice 'Lochnagar' 136 Jericho Beta Alpha 'Melton' Mamboo Pine Hill Bogantungan 168 Drummond Withersfield Willows Anakie Taroborah Fairbairn Dam Yamala Comet Tolmies 'Devonshire' 'Nerrena' 'Amor Downs' 'Wellshot' 'Dandaraga' 'Clover Hills' Joycedale Lancevale 'Stratford' 'Port Wine' Willows Gemfield Lake Maraboon 'Rutland' Gindie 'Bonnie Doon' 'Turkey Creek' Blackwater Mine Fernlees 'Latrobe' 'Urambie' Home Creek 'Helen Vale' 'Sedgeford' 'Avoca' 'Ducabrook' Minerva 'Gaza' 'Honan Downs' Avington 107 'Evora' 'Durrandella' 'Avonmore' Snake Range Nat Pk Minerva Hills Nat Park Vandyke Ck Con Pk Springsure 'Portland Downs' 'Mena Park' Yalleroi 'Elsie Hills' 'Marston' Blacks Palace 'Alpha' 'Jo Jo' 'Echo Hills' 'Glen Avon' 'Vandyke' 'Orion Downs' 'Somerby' Isisford 'Isis Downs' 'Gowan Hills' 'Alice Downs' 'Champion' 163 'Cheshire' 'Fairview' 'Riverside' 'Nandowrie' 'Spring Hill' 'Oma' 'Springfield' 'Thornleigh' Glenusk 'Erne' 'Mantuan Downs' 'Heathwood' 'Ruthven' 'Rutland Park' Blackall Mt Birkhead 'Petrona' 'Wealwandangie' 'Meteor Downs' 'Dunrobin' 'Bilbah Downs' Glenstuart 'Springleigh' Benlidi Malverton 'Bloomfield' 100 The Springs 'Castlevale' 246 'Kia Ora' 'Kareela' 'Albinia Downs' Rolleston 'Glen Alton' Emmet 249 Mekaree 'Milton Park' 'Windeyer' 'Killarney Park' 'Kelpum' 'Tanderra' 'Peawaddy' 'Consuelo' 'Albilbah' Ungo Konupa 'Emmet Downs' Idalia National Park 'Terrick Terrick' 'Ravensbourne' 'Macfarlane Downs' 'Jabinda' 'Truno' 'Carwell' Lake Salvator Salvator Rosa Section Ka Ka Mundi Section Mt Ka Ka Mundi Mt Lambert 'Carnarvon' Carnarvon National Park Mt Lane Yaraka 'Highlands' 'Idalia' 'Lorne' 'Carlow' 'Bonnie Doon' 'Brides Creek' Tambo 'Mt Playfair' Mt Sugarloaf Ranger Hdqs 'Rewan' 'Warrnilla' Nuga Nuga Nat Pk 'Koondoo' 'Minnie Downs' 'Forest Hill' Ivanhoe Mt Playfair Mt Moffatt Section Lake Nuga Nuga 'Glenara' 'Collabara' private road 'Mt Calder' 'Cootabynna' 'Lansdowne' 'Manning' 'Caldervale' Carnarvon Gorge Sec

1 2 19 To Quilpie 3 4 To Charleville & Roma 5 8 6 7 To Roma

A B C D E F G H J K

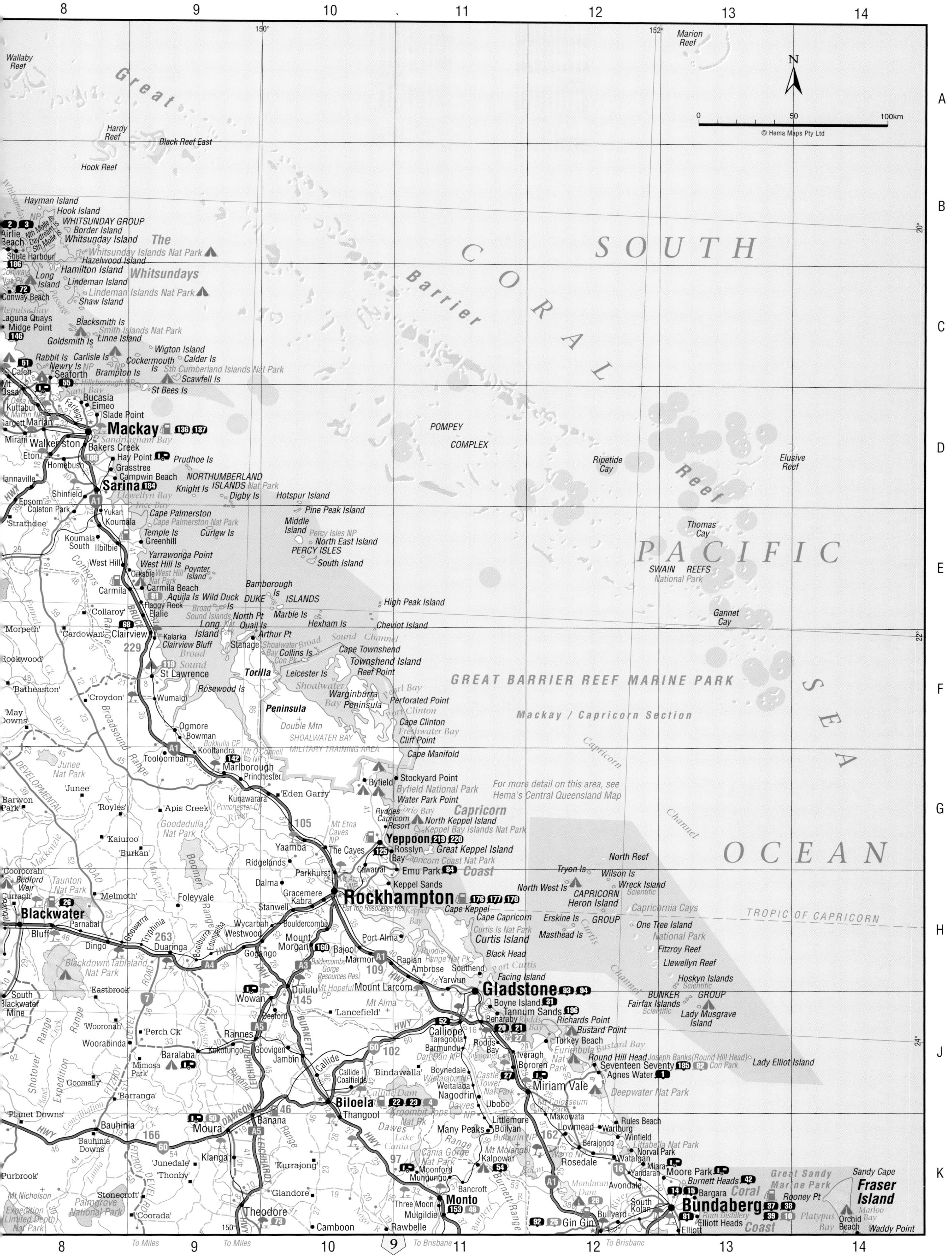

8 9 10 11 12 13 14

A

Wallaby Reef
Great Barrier Reef
Hardy Reef
Black Reef East
Hook Reef
Marion Reef
150°
152°
N
0 50 100km
© Hema Maps Pty Ltd

B

Hayman Island
Hook Island
WHITSUNDAY GROUP
Border Island
Whitsunday Island
Nth Molle Is
Daydream Is
Sth Molle Is
Airlie Beach
Shute Harbour
The Whitsundays
Whitsunday Islands Nat Park
Hazelwood Island
Hamilton Island
SOUTH
CORAL
20°

C

Conway Nat Park
Long Island
Lindeman Island
Lindeman Islands Nat Park
Conway Beach
Shaw Island
Repulse Bay
Laguna Quays
Midge Point
Blacksmith Is
Smith Islands Nat Park
Goldsmith Is
Linne Island
Wigton Island
Rabbit Is
Carlisle Is
Cockermouth Is
Calder Is
Newry Is NP
Cape Hillsborough NP
Sth Cumberland Islands Nat Park
Cafen
Seaforth
Brampton Is
Scawfell Is
Mt Ossa
Sand Bay
St Bees Is

D

Bucasia
Eimeo
Kuttabul
Slade Point
Mt Martin NP
Farleigh
Marian
Mackay 136 137
Mirani
Walkerston
Sandringham Bay
Bakers Creek
Eton
Hay Point
Prudhoe Is
Homebush
Grasstree
Campwin Beach
NORTHUMBERLAND ISLANDS Nat Park
Hannaville
Knight Is
Digby Is
Shinfield
Sarina 184
Llewellyn Bay
Hotspur Island
Epsom
Colston Park
Yukan
Inca Bay
Koumala
POMPEY COMPLEX
Ripetide Cay
Elusive Reef
Reef

E

'Strathdee'
Cape Palmerston
Cape Palmerston Nat Park
Pine Peak Island
Middle Island
Percy Isles NP
North East Island
PERCY ISLES
South Island
Temple Is
Greenhill
Curlew Is
Koumala South
Ilbilbie
Yarrawonga Point
West Hill
West Hill Is
Poynter Island
Orkable
West Hill Nat Park
Carmila
Carmila Beach
Aquila Is
Wild Duck Is
Bamborough Is
DUKE ISLANDS
Flaggy Rock
Broad Sound Islands Nat Park
North Pt
Marble Is
Connors
'Collaroy'
Funnel Ck
Elalie
Long Island
Quail Is
Hexham Is
Cheviot Island
High Peak Island
Thomas Cay
PACIFIC
SWAIN REEFS National Park
Gannet Cay

F

'Morpeth'
'Cardowan'
Clairview
Kalarka
Clairview Bluff
Arthur Pt
Stanage
Broad Sound
Shoalwater Bay
Collins Is
Con Pk
Cape Townshend
Townshend Island
Reef Point
'Rookwood'
229
St Lawrence
Torilla
Leicester Is
'Batheaston'
'Croydon'
Wumalgi
Rosewood Is
Shoalwater Bay
Warginburra Peninsula
Pearl Bay
Perforated Point
Port Clinton
Cape Clinton
Freshwater Bay
Cliff Point
Peninsula
Double Mtn
SHOALWATER BAY MILITARY TRAINING AREA
'May Downs'
Broadsound Range
Ogmore
Bowman
Bukkulla CP
Mt O'Connell NP
Kooltandra
GREAT BARRIER REEF MARINE PARK
Mackay / Capricorn Section
Capricorn Channel
22°
SEA

G

Junee Nat Park
Tooloombah
Marlborough
Princhester
DEVELOPMENTAL
'Junee'
Cape Manifold
Stockyard Point
Byfield
Byfield National Park
Water Park Point
For more detail on this area, see Hema's Central Queensland Map
Barwon Park
'Royles'
'Eden Garry'
Kunawarra
'Apis Creek'
Princhester Ck
Goodedulla Nat Park
105
Mt Etna Caves NP
Rydges Capricorn Resort
Corio Bay
North Keppel Island
Keppel Bay Islands Nat Park
Capricorn
'Kaiuroo'
'Burkan'
Yeppoon 219 220
Great Keppel Island
Yaamba
The Caves
Rosslyn Bay
Capricorn Coast Nat Park
Ridgelands
Emu Park
Coast
'Cooroorah'
Bedford Weir
Taunton Nat Park
Parkhurst
Cawarral
North Reef
Tryon Is
Wilson Is
Wreck Island Scientific
OCEAN
Channel

H

Curragh
Blackwater 28
'Melmoth'
Foleyvale
Boomer Range
Dalma
Gracemere
Kabra
Rockhampton 176 177 178
Flat Top Resources Res
Keppel Sands
North West Is
CAPRICORN Heron Island GROUP
Capricornia Cays
One Tree Island National Park
TROPIC OF CAPRICORN
Stanwell
Cape Keppel
Keppel Bay
Cape Capricorn
Curtis Is Nat Park
Erskine Is
Masthead Is
Curtis Island
Fitzroy Reef
Parnabal
Bluff
Dingo
Goowarra
Tryphinia
263
Duaringa
Boolburra
Edungalba
Wycarbah
Westwood
Bouldercombe
Mount Morgan 160
Gogango
Bajool
Port Alma
Rundle Range Nat Pk
Black Head
Narrows
Blackdown Tableland Nat Park
Marmor
109
Raglan
Ambrose
Southend
Port Curtis
Llewelyn Reef
Yarwun
Facing Island
Hoskyn Islands Scientific
Baldercombe Gorge Resources Res
Mt Hopeful CP
Mount Larcom
Gladstone 83 84
BUNKER GROUP
Fairfax Islands Scientific

J

South Blackwater Mine
'Eastbrook'
'Wooronah'
Wowan
Dululu
145
Mt Alma
'Lancefield'
Boyne Island
Tannum Sands 196
Lady Musgrave Island
Woorabinda
'Perch Ck'
Beeford
Benaraby
Richards Point
Rannes
Calliope
Rodds Bay
Bustard Point
Turkey Beach
Bustard Bay
Baralaba
Kokotungo
Goovigen
Jambin
102
Taragoola
Barmundu
Dan Dan NP
Eurimbula Nat Park
Round Hill Head
Joseph Banks (Round Hill Head) Con Park
Iveragh
Bororen
Seventeen Seventy
Lady Elliot Island
'Mimosa Park'
'Bindawalla'
Callide Coalfields
Boynedale
Castle Tower NP
Agnes Water
'Goomally'
Callide Dam
Westralaba
Weitalaba
Nagoorin
Miriam Vale
Deepwater Nat Park
'Barranga'
Biloela 22 23
Kroombit Tops NP
Ubobo
Mt Colosseum Nat Park
24°

K

'Planet Downs'
Moura
Banana
46
Thangool
Dawes Nat Park
Littlemore
Makowata
Rules Beach
Bauhinia
166
Many Peaks
Builyan
Lowmead
Wartburg
Winfield
Bauhinia Downs
Dawes Range
Lake Cania
Cania Gorge Nat Park
Mt Mongo Nat Park
Bulburin NP
162
Berajondo
Littabella Nat Park
Norval Park
'Junedale'
'Thonby'
Klanga
'Kurrajong'
Kalpowar
Rosedale
Watalgan
Miara
Yandaran
Moore Park
Great Sandy Marine Park
Sandy Cape
Fraser Island
'Purbrook'
97
Moonford
Mungungo
Burnett Heads
Bargara
Coral
Rooney Pt
Mt Nicholson
'Stonecroft'
'Glandore'
Bancroft
Monduran Dam
Avondale
Palmgrove National Park
Three Moon
Monto 153
Burnett Range
South Kolan
Bundaberg 37 38 39 10
Rum Distillery
Platypus Bay
Marloo Bay
Orchid Beach
Expedition (Limited Depth) Nat Park
'Coorada'
Theodore
Mulgildie
Bullyard
Elliott Heads
Coast
Waddy Point
Camboon
Rawbelle
Gin Gin
Elliott
150°
152°

North Queensland

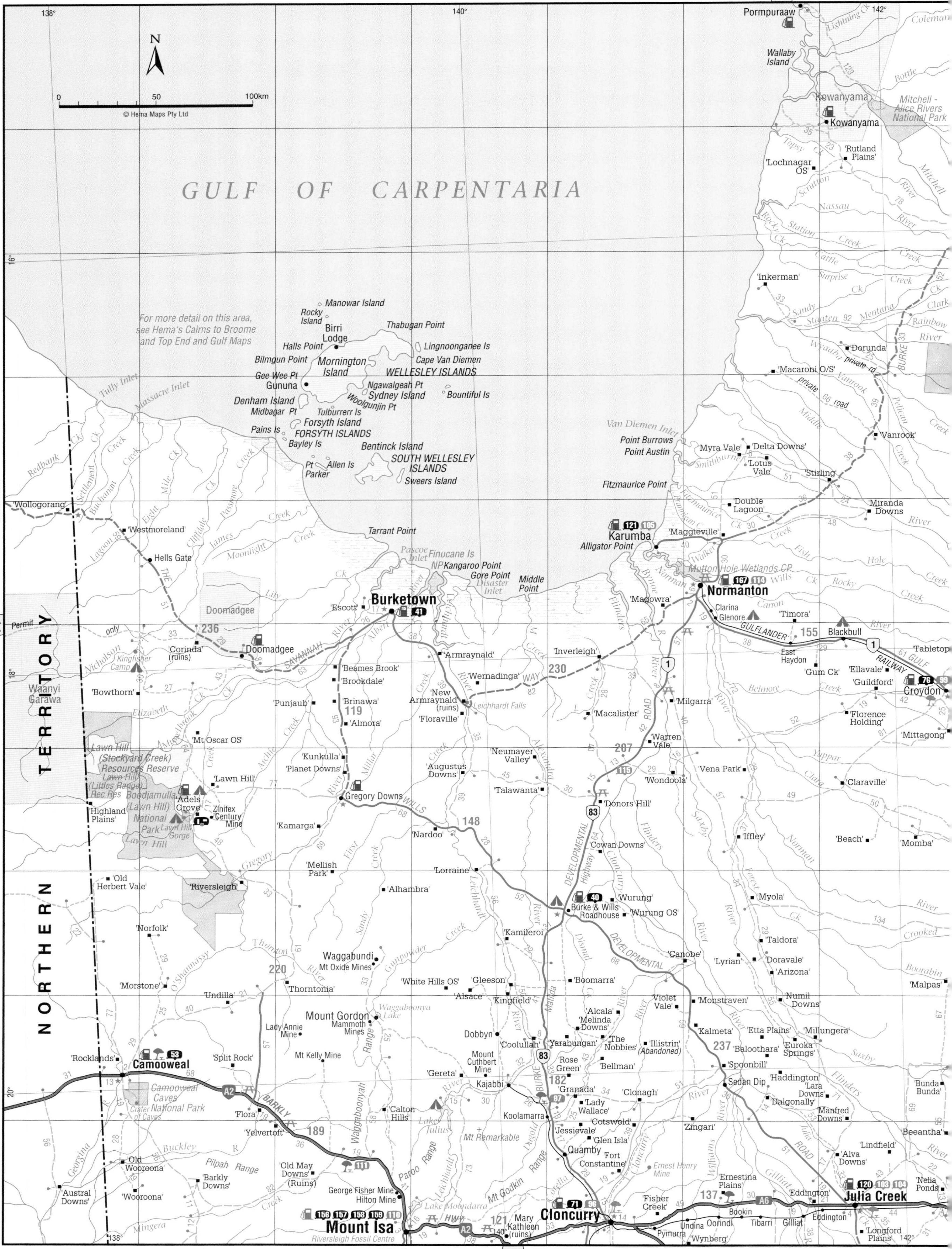

GULF OF CARPENTARIA

For more detail on this area, see Hema's Cairns to Broome and Top End and Gulf Maps

© Hema Maps Pty Ltd

Pormpuraaw
Wallaby Island
Kowanyama
Mitchell - Alice Rivers National Park
'Lochnagar OS'
'Rutland Plains'
'Inkerman'
'Dorunda'
'Macaroni O/S'
'Vanrook'
Manowar Island
Rocky Island
Birri Lodge
Thabugan Point
Halls Point
Lingnoonganee Is
Bilmgun Point
Mornington Island
Cape Van Diemen
WELLESLEY ISLANDS
Gee Wee Pt
Gununa
Ngawalgeah Pt
Sydney Island
Bountiful Is
Denham Island
Midbagar Pt
Woolgunjin Pt
Tulburrerr Is
Forsyth Island
FORSYTH ISLANDS
Pains Is
Bayley Is
Bentinck Island
SOUTH WELLESLEY ISLANDS
Allen Is
Pt Parker
Sweers Island
Van Diemen Inlet
Point Burrows
Point Austin
Myra Vale'
'Delta Downs'
'Lotus Vale'
'Stirling'
Fitzmaurice Point
'Double Lagoon'
'Miranda Downs'
'Wollogorang'
'Westmoreland'
Hells Gate
Tarrant Point
Karumba
Alligator Point
'Maggieville'
Pascoe Inlet
Finucane Is NP
Kangaroo Point
Gore Point
Disaster Inlet
Middle Point
Mutton Hole Wetlands CP
Normanton
Burketown
'Escott'
'Magowra'
Clarina Glenore
'Timora'
Blackbull
'Tabletop'
Doomadgee
'Corinda' (ruins)
Kingfisher Camp
'Armraynald'
'Inverleigh'
East Haydon
'Gum Ck'
'Ellavale'
'Guildford'
Croydon
Waanyi Garawa
'Beames Brook'
'Brookdale'
'Wernadinga'
'Bowthorn'
'Punjaub'
'Brinawa'
'Almora'
'New Armraynald' (ruins)
Leichhardt Falls
'Floraville'
'Macalister'
'Milgarra'
'Florence Holding'
'Mittagong'
'Mt Oscar OS'
Lawn Hill (Stockyard Creek) Resources Reserve
Lawn Hill (Littles Range) Rec Res
'Kunkulla'
'Planet Downs'
'Neumayer Valley'
'Augustus Downs'
'Warren Vale'
'Wondoola'
'Vena Park'
'Claraville'
'Lawn Hill'
Boodjamulla (Lawn Hill) National Park
Lawn Hill Gorge
Adels Grove
Zinifex Century Mine
'Highland Plains'
Gregory Downs
'Talawanta'
'Donors Hill'
'Kamarga'
'Nardoo'
'Iffley'
'Beach'
'Momba'
'Cowan Downs'
'Mellish Park'
'Lorraine'
'Old Herbert Vale'
'Riversleigh'
'Alhambra'
'Wurung'
Burke & Wills Roadhouse
'Wurung OS'
'Myola'
'Norfolk'
'Kamileroi'
'Taldora'
Waggabundi
Mt Oxide Mines
'Canobe'
'Lyrian'
'Doravale'
'Arizona'
'Malpas'
'Morstone'
'Thorntonia'
'White Hills OS'
'Gleeson'
'Alsace'
'Kingfield'
'Boomarra'
'Undilla'
'Violet Vale'
'Monstraven'
'Numil Downs'
Mount Gordon
Mammoth Mines
Lady Annie Mine
'Alcala'
'Melinda Downs'
Dobbyn
'Coolullah'
'Yarabungan'
'The Nobbies'
'Illistrin' (Abandoned)
'Kalmeta'
'Etta Plains'
'Millungera'
'Rocklands'
Camooweal
'Split Rock'
Mt Kelly Mine
Mount Cuthbert Mine
'Rose Green'
'Bellman'
'Baloothara'
'Euroka Springs'
'Spoonbill'
'Gereta'
Kajabbi
'Granada'
'Clonagh'
Sedan Dip
'Haddington'
'Lara Downs'
'Dalgonally'
'Bunda Bunda'
Camooweal Caves National Park
Crater of Caves
'Flora'
'Calton Hills'
Lake Julius
Mt Remarkable
Koolamarra
'Lady Wallace'
'Cotswold'
'Zingari'
'Manfred Downs'
'Beeantha'
'Yelvertoft'
'Jessievale'
'Glen Isla'
Quamby
'Fort Constantine'
'Lindfield'
'Alva Downs'
'Old Wooroona'
'Barkly Downs'
'Old May Downs' (Ruins)
Ernest Henry Mine
'Ernestina Plains'
'Nelia Ponds'
'Austral Downs'
'Wooroona'
George Fisher Mine
Hilton Mine
Lake Moondarra
Mt Godkin
'Fisher Creek'
'Eddington'
Julia Creek
Mount Isa
Riversleigh Fossil Centre
Mary Kathleen (ruins)
Cloncurry
Undina
Oorindi
Bookin
Tibarri
Gilliat
Eddington
Pymurra
'Wynberg'
'Longford Plains'

NORTHERN TERRITORY

To Borroloola
To Tennant Creek & Darwin
To Boulia
To Winton & Rockhampton

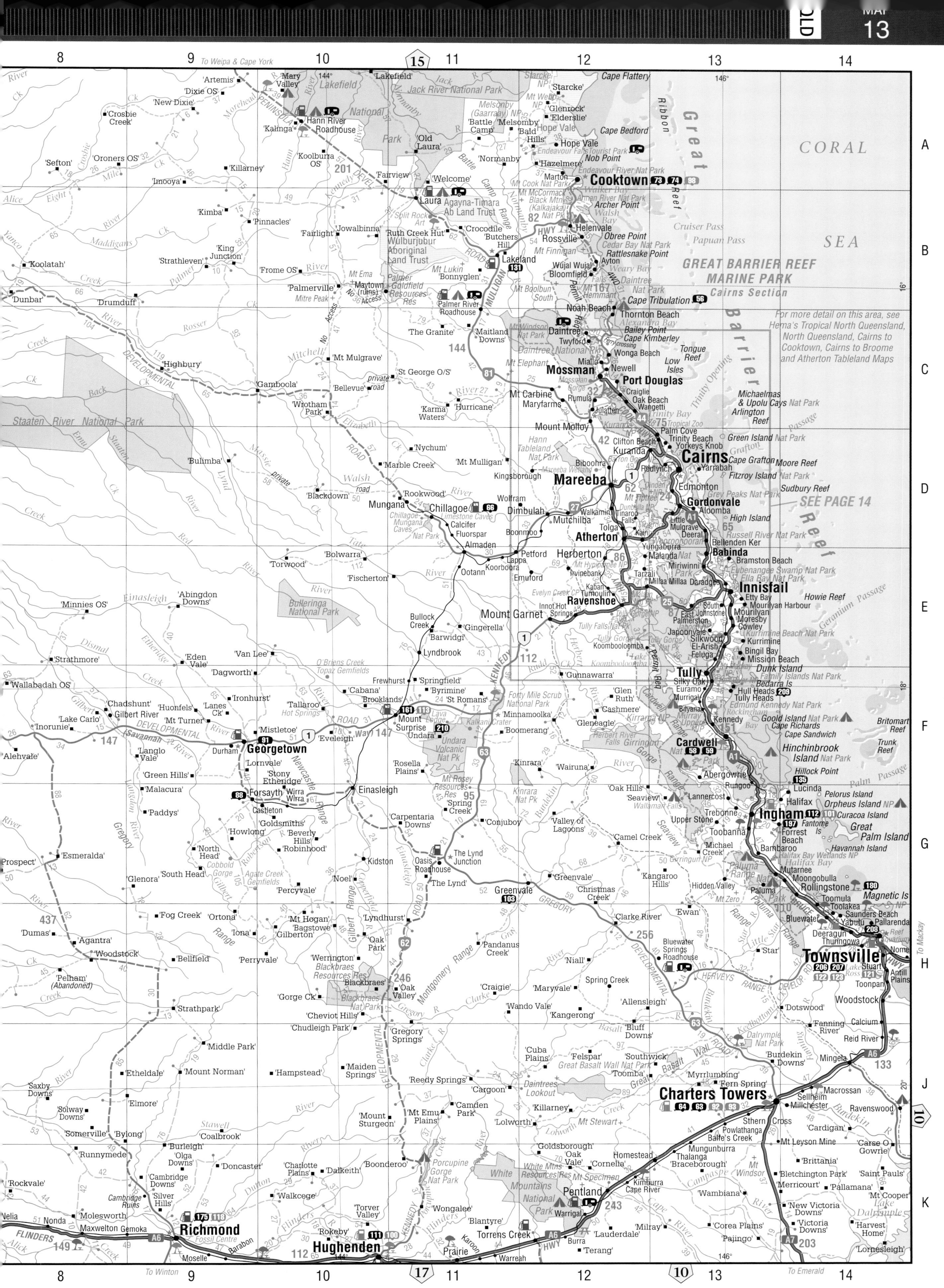
To Weipa & Cape York
CORAL
SEA
GREAT BARRIER REEF
MARINE PARK
Cairns Section
Great Barrier Reef
Ribbon Reef
Cape Flattery
Starcke
Cape Bedford
Hope Vale
Cooktown
Lakefield
Jack River National Park
Lakefield National Park
Hann River Roadhouse
Laura
Lakeland
Helenvale
Rossville
Cape Tribulation
Daintree
Mossman
Port Douglas
Mt Carbine
Mount Molloy
Kuranda
Cairns
Mareeba
Gordonvale
Atherton
Herberton
Babinda
Innisfail
Ravenshoe
Mount Garnet
Chillagoe
Mungana
Dimbulah
Almaden
Tully
Mission Beach
Dunk Island
Cardwell
Hinchinbrook Island
Ingham
Orpheus Island
Great Palm Island
Magnetic Is
Townsville
Rollingstone
Paluma
Woodstock
Charters Towers
Ravenswood
Pentland
Torrens Creek
Prairie
Hughenden
Richmond
Maxwelton
Nonda
Georgetown
Forsayth
Einasleigh
Mount Surprise
Undara Volcanic Nat Pk
The Lynd
Greenvale
Staaten River National Park
Bulleringa National Park
Great Basalt Wall Nat Park
White Mountains National Park
Porcupine Gorge Nat Park
For more detail on this area, see Hema's Tropical North Queensland, North Queensland, Cairns to Cooktown, Cairns to Broome and Atherton Tableland Maps
SEE PAGE 14
To Winton
To Emerald
To Mackay
FLINDERS HWY
GREGORY
KENNEDY
DEVELOPMENTAL ROAD
MULLIGAN HWY
PENINSULA DEVELOPMENTAL ROAD

Cairns Region, Queensland

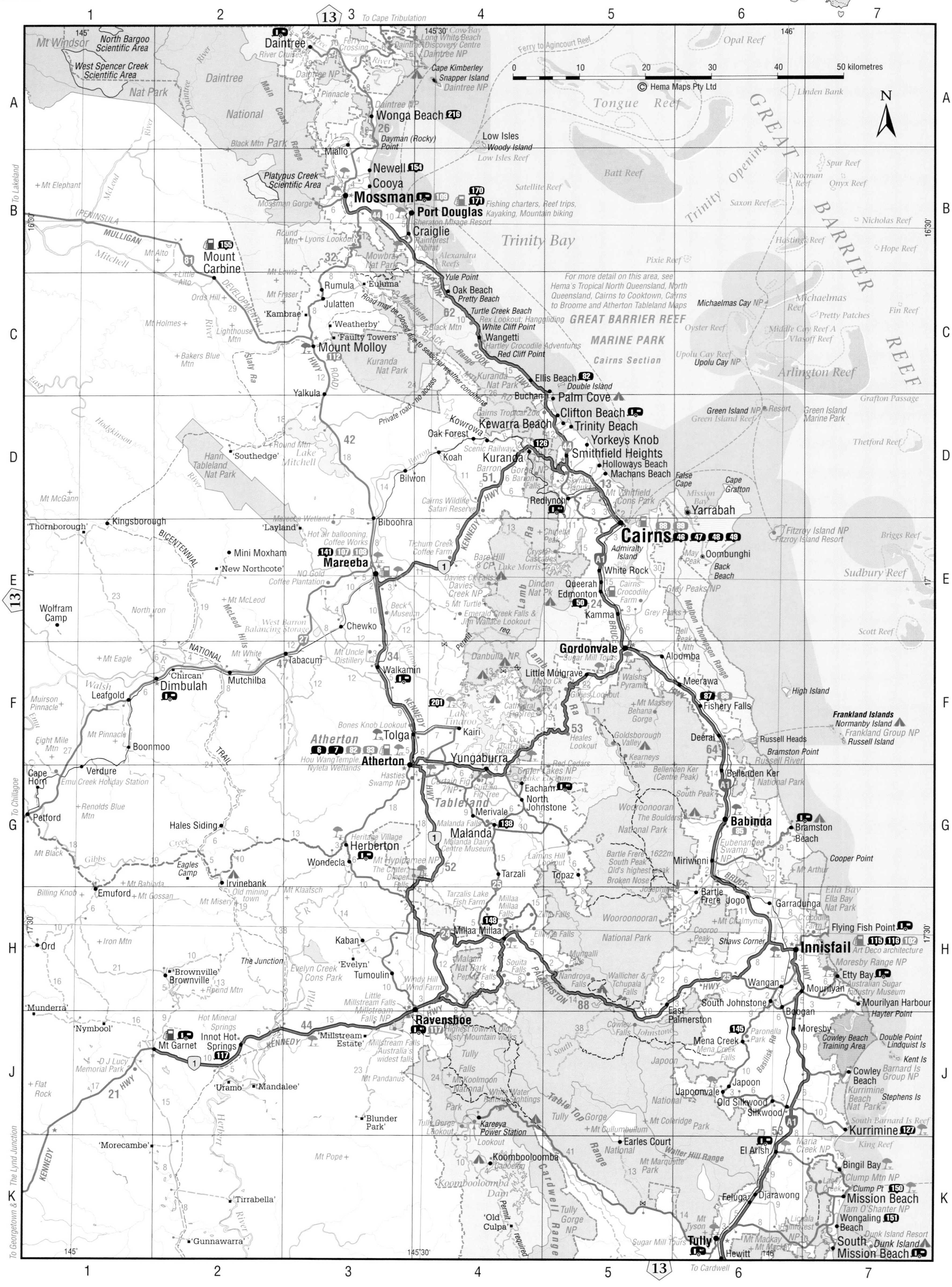

13 To Cape Tribulation

Ferry to Agincourt Reef

0 10 20 30 40 50 kilometres

© Hema Maps Pty Ltd

Mt Windsor
North Bargoo Scientific Area
West Spencer Creek Scientific Area
Daintree National Park
Daintree
Daintree River Cruises
Ferry Crossing
Daintree NP
Cow Bay
Long White Beach
Daintree Discovery Centre
Daintree NP
Cape Kimberley
Snapper Island
Daintree NP
Opal Reef
Pinnacle
Main Coast Range
Wonga Beach 216
Dayman (Rocky) Point
Tongue Reef
Linden Bank
Low Isles
Woody Island
Low Isles Reef
Black Mtn Park
Mt Elephant
Platypus Creek Scientific Area
Mossman Gorge
Mowbray Nat Park
Mt Alto
Mount Carbine 155
Little Alto
Mitchell
Mt Lewis
Mt Fraser
Ords Hill
Mt Holmes
Lighthouse Mtn
Rumula
Julatten
'Euluma'
'Kambrae'
'Weatherby'
'Faulty Towers'
Mount Molloy 112
Bakers Blue Mtn
Slaty Ra
Newell 154
Cooya
Mossman 109
Port Douglas 170 171
Fishing charters, Reef trips, Kayaking, Mountain biking
Sheraton Mirage Resort
Craiglie
Rainforest Habitat
Round Mtn
Lyons Lookout
Alexandra Reefs
Yule Point
Oak Beach
Pretty Beach
Turtle Creek Beach
Rex Lookout; Hanggliding
White Cliff Point
Wangetti
Hartley Crocodile Adventures
Red Cliff Point
Black Mtn
Road may be closed due to seasonal weather conditions
Private road - no access
Kuranda Nat Park
Ellis Beach 82
Double Island
Buchan Pt
Palm Cove
Clifton Beach
Trinity Beach
Yorkeys Knob
Smithfield Heights
Holloways Beach
Machans Beach
Kewarra Beach
Cairns Tropical Zoo
Kowrowa
Oak Forest
Koah
Scenic Railway
Kuranda 126
Barron Gorge NP
Barron Falls
Skyrail
Redlynch
Bilwon
Yalkula
Lake Mitchell
Round Mtn
'Southedge'
Hann Tableland Nat Park
Mt McGann
Satellite Reef
Batt Reef
Trinity Bay
Trinity Opening
Pixie Reef
Saxon Reef
Norman Reef
Spur Reef
Onyx Reef
Nicholas Reef
Hastings Reef
Hope Reef
GREAT BARRIER REEF
For more detail on this area, see Hema's Tropical North Queensland, North Queensland, Cairns to Cooktown, Cairns to Broome and Atherton Tableland Maps
GREAT BARRIER REEF MARINE PARK
Cairns Section
Michaelmas Cay NP
Michaelmas Reef
Pretty Patches
Fin Reef
Oyster Reef
Middle Cay Reef
Vlasoff Reef
Upolu Cay Reef
Upolu Cay NP
Arlington Reef
Green Island NP
Resort
Green Island Reef
Green Island Marine Park
Grafton Passage
Thetford Reef
False Cape
Cape Grafton
Mission Bay
Yarrabah
Mt Whitfield Cons Park
Cairns 46 47 48 49 88 89
Admiralty Island
Fitzroy Island NP
Fitzroy Island Resort
Briggs Reef
Oombunghi
May Peak
Back Beach
White Rock
Sudbury Reef
Cairns Crocodile Farm
Queerah
Edmonton 50
Grey Peaks NP
Grey Peaks
Kamma
Malbon Thompson Range
Scott Reef
'Thornborough'
Kingsborough
Mareeba Wetland
'Layland'
Biboohra
Hot air ballooning, Coffee Works
Cairns Wildlife Safari Reserve
Tichum Creek Coffee Farm
Mini Moxham
'New Northcote'
Mareeba 141 107 108
NQ Gold Coffee Plantation
Bare Hill CP
Lake Morris
Crystal Cascades
Davies Ck Falls
Davies Creek NP
Mt Turtle
Dinden Nat Pk
Lamb Ra
Emerald Creek Falls & Jim Wallace Lookout
Wolfram Camp
Mt McLeod
North Iron
McLeod Hills
West Barron Balancing Storage
Chewko
Beck Museum
Mt Eagle
Mt White
Tabacum
Mt Uncle Distillery
Walkamin
'Chircan'
Dimbulah
Mutchilba
Leafgold
Muirson Pinnacle
Mt Pinnacle
Eight Mile Mtn
Boonmoo
Cape Horn
Verdure
Emu Creek Holiday Station
Renolds Blue Mtn
Petford
Hales Siding
Mt Black
Gibbs
Eagles Camp
Irvinebank
Mt Bahinda
Billing Knob
Emuford
Mt Gossan
Mt Misery
Old mining town
Mt Klaatsch
Ord
Iron Mtn
'Brownville'
Brownville
Round Mtn
'Munderra'
'Nymbool'
Mt Garnet
Innot Hot Springs 117
Hot Mineral Springs
D J Lucy Memorial Park
Flat Rock
'Uramo'
'Mandalee'
'Morecambe'
'Tirrabella'
'Gunnawarra'
Danbulla NP
Lamb Ra
Gordonvale
Sugar Mill Tours
Aloomba
Little Mulgrave
Mobo Ck Crater
Walsh's Pyramid
Meerawa
Fishery Falls 87 86
Gillies Lookout
Mt Massey
Behana Gorge
Cathedral Fig Tree
Lake Tinaroo
201
Bones Knob Lookout
Tolga
Kairi
Atherton 6 7 82 83
Hou Wang Temple, Nyleta Wetlands
Yungaburra
Heales Lookout
Goldsborough Valley
Kearneys Falls
Deeral
Russell Heads
Bramston Point
Russell River
High Island
Frankland Islands
Normanby Island
Frankland Group NP
Russell Island
Hasties Swamp NP
Curtain Fig NP
Crater Lakes NP
Lake Eacham
Eacham
Red Cedars
Bellenden Ker (Centre Peak)
Bellenden Ker
National Park
South Peak
Tableland
North Johnstone
Merivale
Malanda Falls 138
Malanda
Malanda Dairy Centre Museum
Wooroonooran
The Boulders
National Park
Babinda
Bramston Beach
Eubenangee Swamp NP
Miriwinni
Cooper Point
Heritage Village
Herberton
Wondecla
Mt Hypipamee NP
The Crater
Dinner Falls
52
Tarzali
Lamins Hill Lookout
Topaz
Bartle Frere 1622m South Peak Qld's highest peak
Broken Nose
Josephine Falls
Bartle Frere
Jogo
Garradunga
Mt Arthur
Ella Bay
Ella Bay Nat Park
Tarzalis Lake Fish Farm
Millaa Millaa Falls
Millaa Millaa 148
Zillie Falls
Ellinjaa Falls
Wooroonooran National Park
Mt Chalmynia
Cooroo Peak
Shaws Corner
Flying Fish Point
Innisfail 115 116 102
Art Deco architecture
Moresby Range NP
Etty Bay
Mourilyan
Australian Sugar Industry Museum
Mourilyan Harbour
Hayter Point
Kaban
'Evelyn'
Evelyn Creek Cons Park
The Junction
Tumoulin
Windy Hill Wind Farm
Malanda Nat Park
Pepina Falls
Souita Falls
Mungalli Falls
Nandroya Falls
Wallicher & Tchupala Falls
Palmerston
Wangan
South Johnstone
Boogan
East Palmerston
Little Millstream Falls
Millstream Falls NP
Ravenshoe 117
Highest town in Qld
Misty Mountain Walks
'Millstream Estate'
Millstream Falls Australia's widest falls
Cowley Falls
Mena Creek 145
Mena Creek Falls
Paronella Park
Moresby
Cowley Beach Training Area
Double Point
Lindquist Is
Kent Is
Barnard Is Group NP
Cowley Beach
Kurrimine Beach Nat Park
Stephens Is
Tully Falls
Mt Koolmoon
National Park
White Water Rafting Sightings
Mt Pandanus
Japoon
Basilisk Ra
Japoonvale
Old Silkwood
Silkwood
South Barnard Is Reef
Kurrimine 127
'Blunder Park'
Tully Gorge Lookout
Kareeya Power Station
Tully Gorge National Park
Table Top Range
Mt Coleridge
Mt Cullumbullum
Earles Court
Walter Hill Range
Mt Marquette Park
El Arish
Maria Creek NP
King Reef
Mt Pope
Koombooloomba
Canoeing
Koombooloomba Dam
Cardwell Range
Bingil Bay
Clump Mtn NP
Clump Pt 150
Feluga
Djarawong
Mission Beach
Tam O'Shanter NP
Wongaling 151
Beach
Licuala Rainforest
South Mission Beach
Dunk Island Resort
Dunk Island
'Old Culpa'
Permit required
Tully Gorge NP
Sugar Mill Tours
Mt Tyson
Tully
Mt Mackay NP
Hewitt

PENINSULA MULLIGAN DEVELOPMENTAL HWY
Mt Molloy Road
CAPTAIN COOK HWY
KENNEDY HWY
BICENTENNIAL NATIONAL TRAIL
BRUCE HWY
PALMERSTON HWY
KENNEDY
21 HWY

To Lakeland
To Chillagoe
To Georgetown & The Lynd Junction
13 To Cardwell

145° 145°30' 146° 16°30' 17° 17°30'

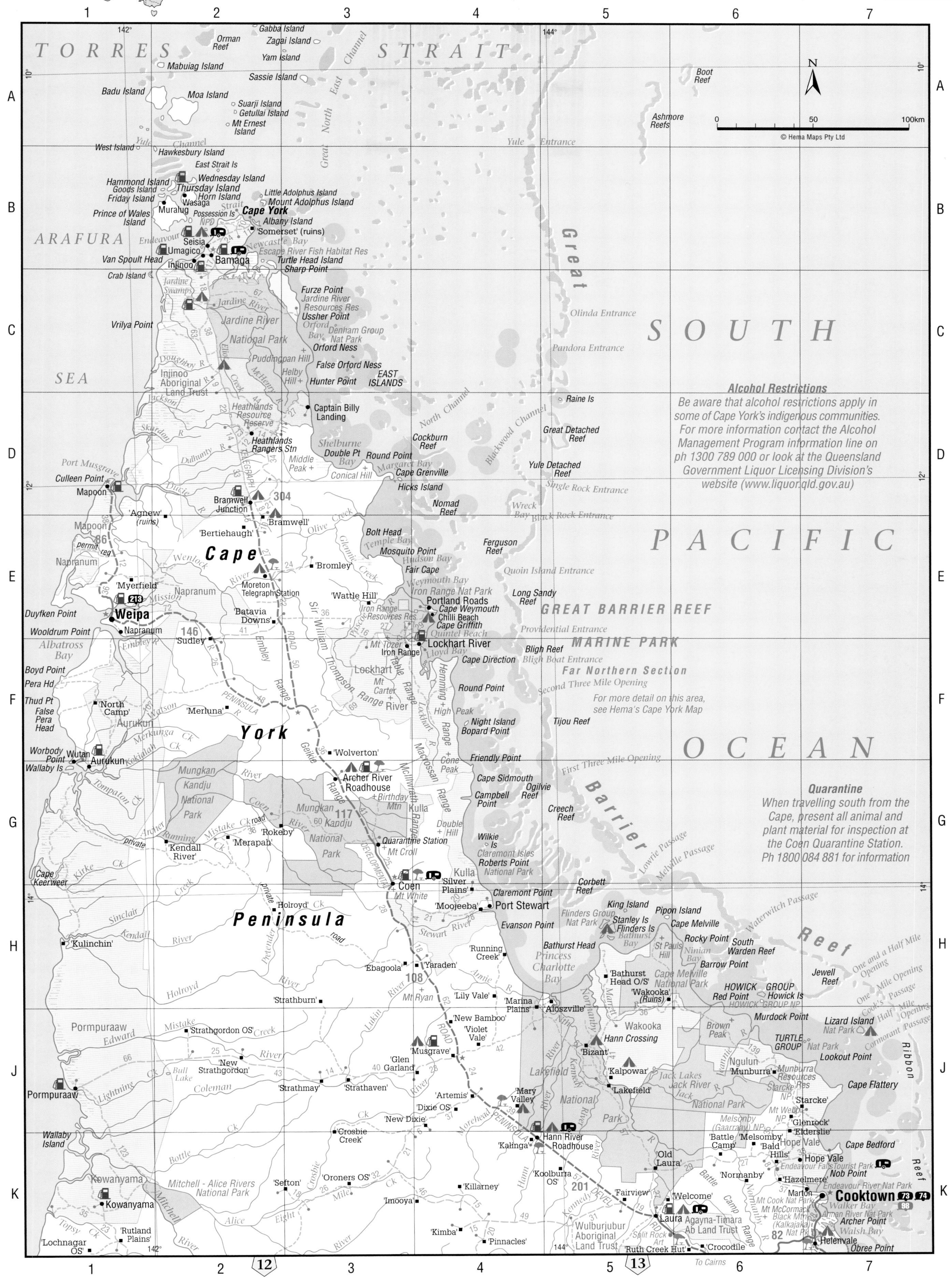

Alcohol Restrictions

Be aware that alcohol restrictions apply in some of Cape York's indigenous communities. For more information contact the Alcohol Management Program information line on ph 1300 789 000 or look at the Queensland Government Liquor Licensing Division's website (www.liquor.qld.gov.au)

Quarantine

When travelling south from the Cape, present all animal and plant material for inspection at the Coen Quarantine Station. Ph 1800 084 881 for information

For more detail on this area, see Hema's Cape York Map

0 50 100km

© Hema Maps Pty Ltd

TORRES STRAIT
ARAFURA SEA
SOUTH PACIFIC OCEAN
GREAT BARRIER REEF MARINE PARK
Far Northern Section
Great Barrier Reef
Cape York Peninsula

Gabba Island
Zagai Island
Orman Reef
Yam Island
Mabuiag Island
Sassie Island
Badu Island
Moa Island
Suarji Island
Getullai Island
Mt Ernest Island
Great North East Channel
Boot Reef
Ashmore Reefs
Yule Channel
Yule Entrance
West Island
Hawkesbury Island
East Strait Is
Hammond Island
Wednesday Island
Goods Island
Thursday Island
Friday Island
Horn Island
Wasaga
Little Adolphus Island
Mount Adolphus Island
Prince of Wales Island
Muralug
Possession Is NPD
Cape York
Albany Island
'Somerset' (ruins)
Endeavour Strait
Seisia
Newcastle Bay
Umagico
Escape River Fish Habitat Res
Van Spoult Head
Injinoo
Bamaga
Turtle Head Island
Sharp Point
Crab Island
Jardine Swamps
Furze Point
Jardine River Resources Res
Ussher Point
Olinda Entrance
Jardine River National Park
Vrilya Point
Orford Bay
Denham Group Nat Park
Orford Ness
Pandora Entrance
Puddingpan Hill
False Orford Ness
Helby Hill
Hunter Point
EAST ISLANDS
Doughboy R
Injinoo Aboriginal Land Trust
Elliot Creek
McHenry R
Jackson R
Raine Is
Captain Billy Landing
North Channel
Blackwood Channel
Heathlands Resource Reserve
Skardon R
Heathlands Rangers Stn
Great Detached Reef
Cockburn Reef
Shelburne Bay
Port Musgrave
Dulhunty R
Double Pt
Round Point
Middle Peak
Margaret Bay
Cape Grenville
Conical Hill
Yule Detached Reef
Culleen Point
Mapoon
Ducie R
TELEGRAPH
Hicks Island
Single Rock Entrance
Bramwell Junction
Nomad Reef
Wreck Bay
Black Rock Entrance
'Agnew' (ruins)
'Bramwell'
Olive Creek
Mapoon
'Bertiehaugh'
Bolt Head
Ferguson Reef
Temple Bay
Permit reg
Wenlock
Mosquito Point
Hudson Bay
Glennie Creek
Napranum
'Bromley'
Fair Cape
Quoin Island Entrance
Weymouth Bay
'Myerfield'
Napranum
Mission R
Moreton Telegraph Station
River
Iron Range Nat Park
Portland Roads
Long Sandy Reef
'Wattle Hill'
Duyfken Point
Weipa
'Batavia Downs'
Iron Range Resources Res
Cape Weymouth
Chilli Beach
Cape Griffith
Quintel Beach
Providential Entrance
Wooldrum Point
Napranum
Sudley
Pascoe R
Mt Tozer
Iron Range
Lockhart River
Lloyd Bay
Albatross Bay
Embley R
Embley R
ROAD
Sir William Thompson Range
Bligh Reef
Bligh Boat Entrance
Boyd Point
Cape Direction
Pera Hd
Lockhart
Mt Carter
Table Range
Hemming Range
Round Point
Second Three Mile Opening
Thud Pt
'North Camp'
PENINSULA
False Pera Head
Watson
'Merluna'
Range River
High Peak
Night Island
Bopard Point
Tijou Reef
Aurukun
Merkunga Ck
Geikie
Macrossan
Worbody Point
Kokialah
Ck
'Wolverton'
Friendly Point
Cone Peak
Wutan
Aurukun
Wallaby Is
Mungkan Kandju National Park
Archer River Roadhouse
Birthday Mtn
First Three Mile Opening
Cape Sidmouth
Ogilvie Reef
Tompaton Ck
Coen River
McIlwraith Range
Kulla
Campbell Point
Creech Reef
Mungkan Kandju National Park
Double Hill
Archer
Running
Mistake Ck
road
'Rokeby'
Quarantine Station
Mt Croll
Wilkie Is
Lowrie Passage
Melville Passage
private
'Kendall River'
'Merapah'
Claremont Isles
Roberts Point
National Park
Cape Keerweer
Kirke Ck
Coen
Kulla
'Silver Plains'
Claremont Point
Corbett Reef
Mt White
DEVELOPMENTAL
private
'Holroyd'
Creek
'Moojeeba'
Port Stewart
King Island
Pipon Island
Waterwitch Passage
Sinclair
Evanson Point
Flinders Group Nat Park
Stanley Is
Flinders Is
Cape Melville
Kendall
Peninsula
road
Stewart River
Bathurst Bay
St Pauls Hill
Rocky Point
South Warden Reef
'Kulinchin'
River
Pretender
Bathurst Head
Princess Charlotte Bay
Ninian Bay
Barrow Point
One and a Half Mile Opening
Jewell Reef
'Running Creek'
'Ebagoola'
'Yaraden'
Holroyd
River
Annie R
'Bathurst Head O/S'
Cape Melville National Park
HOWICK GROUP
Howick Is
One Mile Opening
'Strathburn'
Mt Ryan
'Lily Vale'
'Marina Plains'
'Aloszville'
'Wakooka' (Ruins)
Red Point
HOWICK GROUP NP
Cook's Passage
Pormpuraaw
Mistake Creek
Lukin
'New Bamboo'
Normanby
Marrett
Wakooka
Murdock Point
Half Mile Opening
Edward
'Strathgordon OS'
'Violet Vale'
Hann Crossing
Brown Peak
Lizard Island Nat Park
Cormorant Passage
River
'Musgrave'
ROAD
'Bizant'
TURTLE GROUP Nat Park
'New Strathgordon'
Bull Lake
'Glen Garland'
Kennedy
Jeannie R
Ngulun
'Munburra'
Lookout Point
Lightning Ck
Coleman
'Kalpowar'
Munburra Resources Res
Ribbon
Pormpuraaw
'Strathmay'
'Strathaven'
'Artemis'
Lakefield
Jack Lakes
Jack River
Jack National Park
Cape Flattery
'Mary Valley'
'Lakefield'
Starcke
'Starcke'
'Dixie OS'
National Park
NP
Ck
'New Dixie'
Morehead
PENINSULA
Melsonby (Gaarraay) NP
Mt Webb NP
'Glenrock'
'Elderslie'
Wallaby Island
'Crosbie Creek'
Bottle
Ck
Hann River Roadhouse
R
'Battle Camp'
'Melsomby'
Hope Vale
'Bald Hills'
Cape Bedford
'Kalinga'
'Old Laura'
Hope Vale
Endeavour Falls Tourist Park
Nob Point
Kowanyama
Mitchell - Alice Rivers National Park
'Sefton'
Crosbie
'Oroners OS'
'Koolburra OS'
'Normanby'
'Hazelmere'
Endeavour River Nat Park
Reef
Kowanyama
Mitchell
Mile
Ck
'Killarney'
Hann
DEVEL
'Fairview'
'Welcome'
Battle Camp Range
Normanby
Mt Cook Nat Park
Cooktown
Walker Bay
'Imooya'
Laura
Agayna-Timara Ab Land Trust
Mt McCormack
Archer River Nat Park
Archer Point
Black Mtns (Kalkajaka) Nat Pk
Walsh Bay
Topsy Ck
'Rutland Plains'
Alice
Eight
'Kimba'
Wulburjubur Aboriginal Land Trust
Split Rock Art
Helenvale
'Lochnagar OS'
River
River
'Pinnacles'
Ruth Creek Hut
'Crocodile'
Obree Point
To Cairns

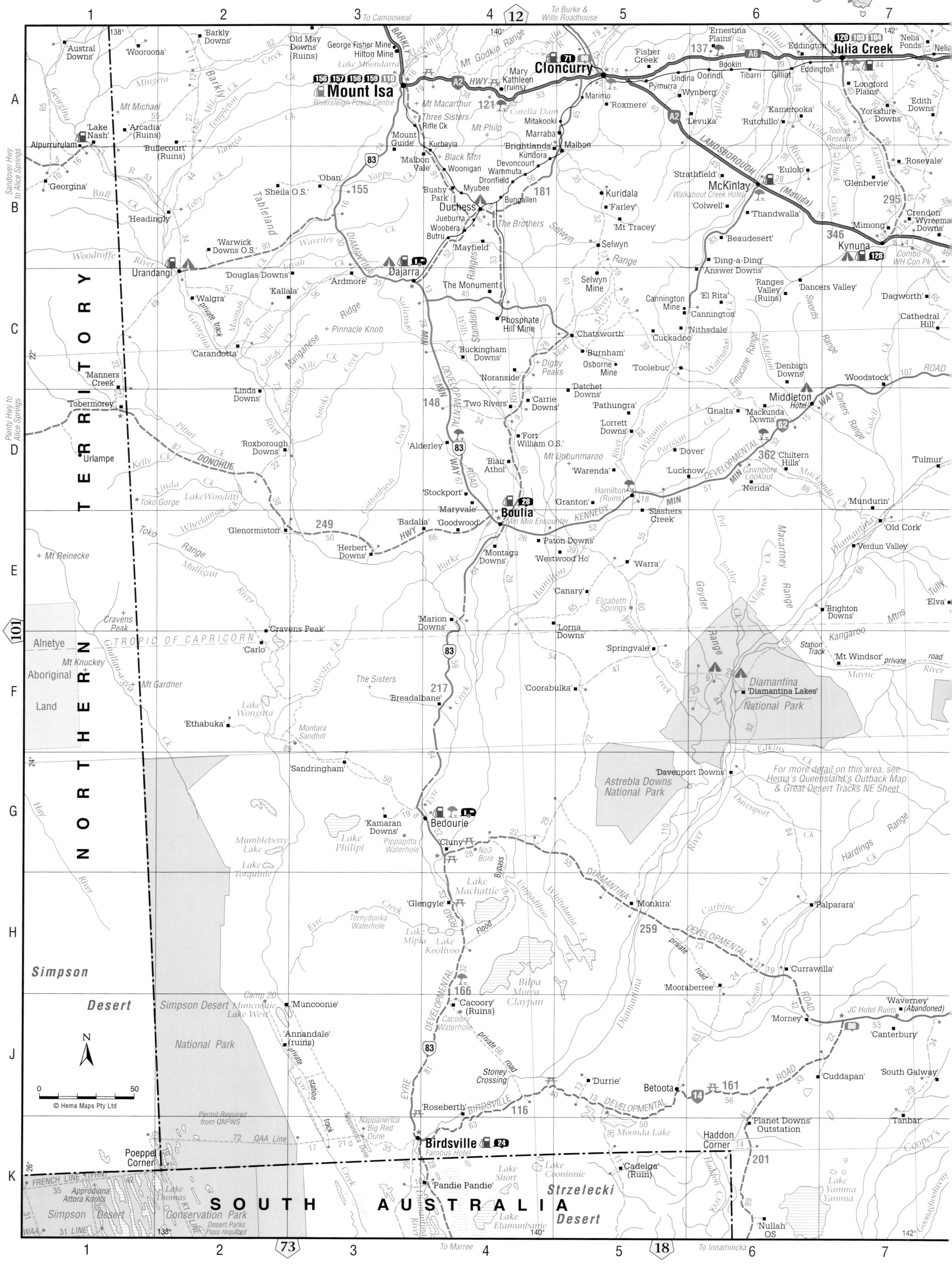

Outback Queensland

1 2 3 4 5 6 7

To Camooweal
To Burke & Wills Roadhouse

'Austral Downs'
'Wooroona'
'Barkly Downs'
'Old May Downs' (Ruins)
George Fisher Mine
Hilton Mine
Lake Moondarra
Mount Isa
Riversleigh Fossil Centre
Mt Godkin Range
Mary Kathleen (ruins)
Cloncurry
'Fisher Creek'
'Ernestina Plains'
Julia Creek
'Nelia Ponds'
Eddington
Gilliat
Tibarri
Bookin
Oorindi
Undina
Pymurra
Wynberg
'Levuka'
'Roxmere'
Marimo
Mt Michael
'Arcadia' (Ruins)
'Lake Nash'
Alpurrurulam
'Bullecourt' (Ruins)
Mt Macarthur
Three Sisters
Rifle Ck
Corella Dam
Mt Philp
Mitakooki
Marraba
Malbon
Brightlands
Kundora
Devoncourt
Wammuta
Dronfield
'Mount Guide'
Kurbayia
Black Mtn
'Malbon Vale'
Woonigan
Myubee
'Longford Plains'
'Kamerooka'
'Rutchillo'
'Yorkshire Downs'
'Edith Downs'
'Rosevale'
Toorak Research Station
LANDSBOROUGH (Matilda)
'Strathfield'
McKinlay
'Eulolo'
Walkabout Creek Hotel
'Colwell'
'Thandwalla'
'Glenbervie'
'Mimong'
'Crendon'
'Wyreema Downs'
Kynuna
Combo WH Con Pk
'Beaudesert'
'Georgina'
Sandover Hwy to Alice Springs
'Oban'
'Sheila O.S.'
Tableland
'Headingly'
'Bushy Park'
Duchess
Jueburra
Woobera
Butru
Bungallen
The Brothers
Selwyn
Kuridala
'Farley'
'Mt Tracey'
'Warwick Downs O.S.'
'Mayfield'
Woodroffe River
Urandangi
'Douglas Downs'
'Ardmore'
Dajarra
DIAMANTINA
Ranges
Range
'Ding-a-Ding'
'Answer Downs'
'Ranges Valley' (Ruins)
'Dancers Valley'
'Dagworth'
'Walgra'
'Kallala'
The Monument
Selwyn Mine
'El Rita'
Cannington Mine
'Cannington'
'Nithsdale'
'Cathedral Hill'
Pinnacle Knob
Manganese Ridge
Phosphate Hill Mine
'Chatsworth'
'Cuckadoo'
'Carandotta'
'Buckingham Downs'
'Burnham'
Digby Peaks
Osborne Mine
'Toolebuc'
'Denbigh Downs'
'Woodstock'
ROAD
'Manners Creek'
'Linda Downs'
'Noranside'
'Datchet Downs'
Middleton
Hotel
'Tobermorey'
Plenty Hwy to Alice Springs
Two Rivers
'Carrie Downs'
'Pathungra'
'Gnalta'
'Mackunda Downs'
Carters Range
'Lorrett Downs'
'Fort William O.S.'
Mt Upbunmaroo
'Dover'
'Chiltern Hills'
'Roxborough Downs'
'Alderley'
DEVELOPMENTAL
'Warenda'
'Lucknow'
Cawnpore Lookout
'Nerida'
'Tulmur'
Urlampe
DONOHUE
'Blair Athol'
'Stockport'
Boulia
Hamilton (Ruins)
'Granton'
Slashers Creek
'Mundurin'
Toko Gorge
Lake Wonditti
'Maryvale'
Min Min Encounter
KENNEDY
MIN
'Old Cork'
'Glenormiston'
'Badalia'
'Goodwood'
'Paton Downs'
'Verdun Valley'
Toko Range
'Herbert Downs'
HWY
'Montagu Downs'
'Westwood Ho'
'Warra'
Mt Reinecke
Mulligan River
Burke
Hamilton
'Canary'
Macartney Range
Goyder Range
Elizabeth Springs
'Elva'
'Brighton Downs'
Mtns
Kangaroo
Cravens Peak
'Cravens Peak'
'Marion Downs'
'Lorna Downs'
'Springvale'
Alnetye Aboriginal Land
TROPIC OF CAPRICORN
'Carlo'
Mt Knuckey
Mt Gardner
The Sisters
'Coorabulka'
Station Track
'Mt Windsor'
private road
Mayne River
'Breadalbane'
Diamantina National Park
'Diamantina Lakes'
Lake Wongitta
'Ethabuka'
Montara Sandhill
'Sandringham'
'Davenport Downs'
Edkins Ck
For more detail on this area, see Hema's Queensland's Outback Map & Great Desert Tracks NE Sheet
Astrebla Downs National Park
NORTHERN TERRITORY
'Kamaran Downs'
Bedourie
Lake Philipi
Pippagitta Waterhole
Mumbleberry Lake
Lake Torquinie
'Cluny'
No3 Bore
Bypass
Davenport
Hardings Range
DIAMANTINA
Lake Machattie
Unpadiboo
Whitulania Ck
'Glengyle'
'Monkira'
'Palparara'
Tomydonka Waterhole
Eyre Creek
Lake Mipia
Lake Koolivoo
Flood
Carbine
DEVELOPMENTAL
private road
'Currawilla'
Simpson Desert
Camp 20
Muncoonie Lake West
'Muncoonie'
Bilpa Morea Claypan
'Mooraberree'
Farrars
ROAD
'Cacoory' (Ruins)
Cacoory Waterhole
'Waverney' (Abandoned)
JC Hotel Ruins
'Morney'
'Canterbury'
Simpson Desert National Park
'Annandale' (ruins)
private station track
private road
Stoney Crossing
'Durrie'
Betoota
'Cuddapan'
'South Galway'
'Roseberth'
BIRDSVILLE
DEVELOPMENTAL
Permit Required from QNPWS
Nappanerica 'Big Red' Dune
QAA Line
Birdsville
Famous Hotel
Moonda Lake
'Planet Downs' Outstation
Haddon Corner
'Tanbar'
Cooper's
Poeppel Corner
FRENCH LINE (FH)
Approdinna Attora Knolls
Lake Thomas
K1 LINE
Simpson Desert Conservation Park
Desert Parks Pass required
WAA
31 LINE
SOUTH AUSTRALIA
'Pandie Pandie'
Lake Short
Lake Cooninnie
'Cadelga' (Ruin)
Strzelecki Desert
Lake Etamunbanie
Lake Yamma Yamma
Goonaghooeeny
'Nullah' OS

© Hema Maps Pty Ltd

To Marree
To Innamincka

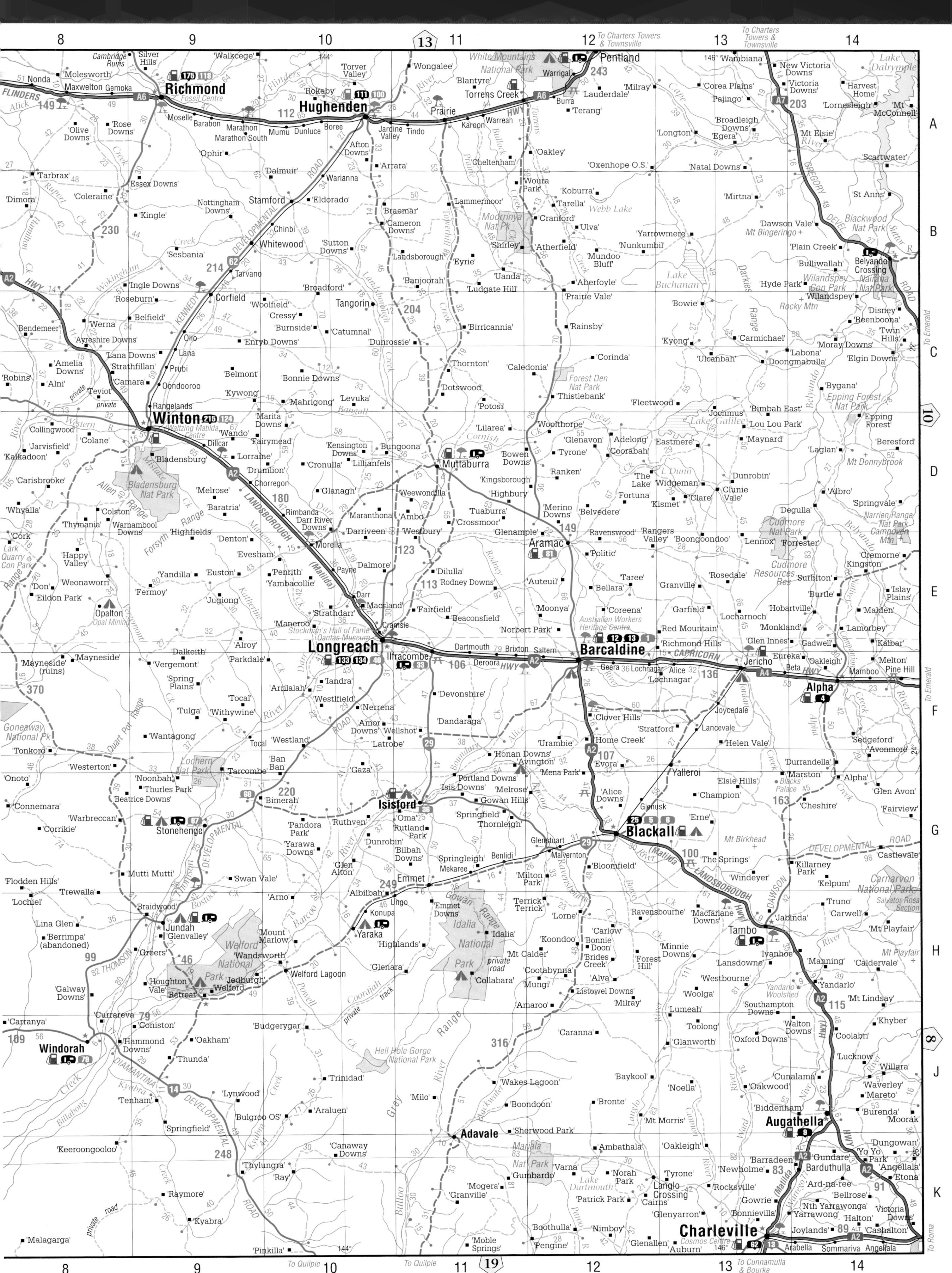

8
9
10
13
11
12
To Charters Towers & Townsville
13
To Charters Towers & Townsville
14
Cambridge Ruins
'Silver Hills'
'Walkcege'
144°
'Torver Valley'
'Wongalee'
White Mountains National Park
Warrigal
Pentland
243
146°
'Wambiana'
'New Victoria Downs'
'Victoria Downs'
Lake Dalrymple
'Harvest Home'
'Lornesleigh'
'Mt McConnell'
Nonda
'Molesworth'
Maxwelton
Gemoka
Richmond
Fossil Centre
FLINDERS
149
'Rokeby'
Hughenden
'Blantyre'
Torrens Creek
'Milroy'
'Corea Plains'
'Pajingo'
'Lauderdale'
'Terang'
Burra
203
A
'Olive Downs'
'Rose Downs'
Moselle
Barabon
Marathon
Marathon South
112
Mumu
Dunluce
Boree
Jardine Valley
Tindo
Prairie
Karoon
Warreah
HWY
'Broadleigh Downs'
'Egera'
'Longton'
'Mt Elsie'
'Ophir'
'Afton Downs'
'Oakley'
'Scartwater'
'Tarbrax'
'Essex Downs'
'Dalmuir'
'Arrara'
'Cheltenham'
'Oxenhope O.S.'
'Natal Downs'
'Dimora'
'Coleraine'
Warianna
'Woura Park'
'Koburra'
'Mirtna'
'St Anns'
Stamford
'Eldorado'
'Nottingham Downs'
'Lammermoor'
'Tarella'
Webb Lake
'Kingle'
'Braemar'
'Cameron Downs'
Moorrinya Nat Pk
'Cranford'
'Ulva'
'Dawson Vale'
Mt Bingeringo
Blackwood Nat Park
230
Chinbi
Whitewood
'Sutton Downs'
'Shirley'
'Atherfield'
'Yarrowmere'
'Nunkumbil'
B
'Sesbania'
'Landsborough'
'Eyrie'
'Mundoo Bluff'
'Plain Creek'
'Bulliwallah'
Belyando Crossing
214
Tarvano
'Uanda'
'Aberfoyle'
Lake Buchanan
'Hyde Park'
Wilandspey Con Park
Nairana Nat Park
'Ingle Downs'
'Banjoorah'
'Ludgate Hill'
'Prairie Vale'
'Wilandspey'
'Roseburn'
Corfield
'Broadford'
'Woolfield'
Tangorin
204
'Bowie'
Rocky Mtn
'Disney'
'Beenboona'
'Cressy'
'Belfield'
'Burnside'
'Catumnal'
'Birricannia'
'Rainsby'
'Twin Hills'
To Emerald
'Werna'
'Bendemeer'
'Ayrshire Downs'
Olio
'Enryb Downs'
'Dunrossie'
'Carmichael'
'Kyong'
'Moray Downs'
'Labona'
'Elgin Downs'
C
'Lana Downs'
'Strathfillan'
Lana
Prubi
'Amelia Downs'
'Thornton'
'Corinda'
'Ulcanbah'
'Doongmabulla'
'Caledonia'
'Robins'
'Alni'
'Camara'
Oondooroo
'Belmont'
'Bonnie Downs'
Forest Den Nat Park
'Bygana'
Epping Forest Nat Park
'Teviot'
private
'Kywong'
'Levuka'
'Dotswood'
'Thistlebank'
'Fleetwood'
Rangelands
'Mahrigong'
'Potosi'
'Jochmus'
'Bimbah East'
Winton
Waltzing Matilda Centre
'Marita Downs'
'Wando'
'Lilarea'
'Woolthorpe'
Lake Galilee
'Lou Lou Park'
'Epping Forest'
10
'Collingwood'
'Jarvisfield'
'Colane'
Dillcar
'Fairymead'
'Kensington Downs'
'Bungoona'
'Adelong'
'Glenavon'
'Eastmere'
'Maynard'
'Beresford'
'Kalkadoon'
'Bladensburg'
'Lorraine'
'Cronulla'
'Lillianfels'
Muttaburra
'Bowen Downs'
'Tyrone'
'Coorabah'
'Laglan'
Mt Donnybrook
'Carisbrooke'
'Drumlion'
'Ranken'
'The Lake'
'Dunrobin'
D
Bladensburg Nat Park
Chorregon
'Glanagh'
'Kingsborough'
'Widgeman'
'Clunie Vale'
'Melrose'
180
'Weewondilla'
'Highbury'
'Fortuna'
'Clare'
'Albro'
'Whyalla'
'Baratria'
Rimbanda
'Darr River Downs'
'Maranthona'
'Ambo'
'Tuaburra'
'Merino Downs'
'Belvedere'
'Kismet'
'Springvale'
'Colston'
'Thymania'
'Warnambool Downs'
'Highfields'
'Crossmoor'
'Degulla'
Cudmore Nat Park
Narrien Range Nat Park
Campoven Mtn
'Cork'
'Denton'
'Darriveen'
'Westbury'
'Glenample'
Aramac
149
'Ravenswood'
'Rangers Valley'
'Boongoondoo'
'Lennox'
'Forrester'
Lark Quarry Con Park
'Happy Valley'
'Evesham'
Morella
123
'Politic'
'Cremorne'
Kingston
'Yandilla'
'Euston'
'Penrith'
'Yambacollie'
Payne
'Dalmore'
'Dilulla'
'Rodney Downs'
113
'Auteuil'
'Taree'
'Granville'
'Rosedale'
Cudmore Resources Res
'Surbiton'
'Islay Plains'
'Don'
'Weonaworri'
'Fermoy'
'Jugiong'
Darr
'Macsland'
'Bellara'
E
'Eildon Park'
Opalton
Opal Mining
'Fairfield'
'Moonya'
'Coreena'
'Garfield'
'Hobartville'
'Burtle'
'Malden'
'Strathdarr'
'Beaconsfield'
Australian Workers Heritage Centre
'Locharnoch'
'Monkland'
'Maneroo'
Stockman's Hall of Fame
Qantas Museum
Cramsie
'Norbert Park'
'Red Mountain'
'Lamorbey'
'Alroy'
Longreach
Dartmouth
Brixton
Saltern
Barcaldine
'Richmond Hills'
'Glen Innes'
'Gadwell'
'Kalbar'
'Mayneside'
'Mayneside' (ruins)
'Dalkeith'
'Vergemont'
'Parkdale'
Ilfracombe
106
Deroora
HWY
Geera
Lochnagar
Alice
CAPRICORN
'Eureka'
Jericho
'Oakleigh'
'Melton'
Pine Hill
Mamboo
370
'Spring Plains'
'Iandra'
'Lochnagar'
136
Beta
HWY
Alpha
'Arrilalah'
'Westfield'
'Devonshire'
Joycedale
'Tocal'
'Withywine'
'Nerrena'
To Emerald
F
Goneaway National Pk
'Tulga'
Amor Downs'
'Wellshot'
'Dandaraga'
'Clover Hills'
'Stratford'
Lancevale
'Sedgeford'
'Avonmore'
'Wantagong'
Tocal
'Westland'
'Latrobe'
'Urambie'
'Home Creek'
'Helen Vale'
'Tonkoro'
'Honan Downs'
107
'Evora'
'Durrandella'
Lochern Nat Park
'Ban Ban'
'Gaza'
'Avington'
'Westerton'
'Tarcombe'
'Mena Park'
Yalleroi
'Marston'
'Alpha'
'Onoto'
'Noonbah'
'Portland Downs'
'Elsie Hills'
Blacks Palace
'Thurles Park'
220
'Isis Downs'
'Melrose'
'Alice Downs'
'Champion'
163
'Glen Avon'
'Beatrice Downs'
'Bimerah'
Isisford
'Gowan Hills'
Glenusk
'Cheshire'
'Fairview'
'Connemara'
'Warbreccan'
'Oma'
'Springfield'
'Erne'
Stonehenge
'Pandora Park'
'Ruthven'
'Rutland Park'
'Thornleigh'
Blackall
Mt Birkhead
G
'Corrikie'
'Yarawa Downs'
'Dunrobin'
Glenstuart
Malvernton
100
DEVELOPMENTAL
ROAD
'Castlevale'
'Bilbah Downs'
'Springleigh'
Mekaree
Benlidi
'Bloomfield'
'The Springs'
'Killarney Park'
'Mutti Mutti'
'Glen Alton'
'Milton Park'
'Windeyer'
'Flodden Hills'
'Swan Vale'
Emmet
249
'Kelpum'
Carnarvon National Park
Salvator Rosa Section
'Trewalla'
Albilbah
'Emmet Downs'
LANDSBOROUGH
'Arno'
Ungo
'Terrick Terrick'
'Truno'
'Lochiel'
Braidwood
Konupa
'Ravensbourne'
'Macfarlane Downs'
Jabinda
'Carwell'
Jundah
'Lorne'
'Lina Glen'
'Glenvalley'
'Mount Marlow'
Yaraka
Idalia National Park
'Idalia'
'Carlow'
Tambo
'Mt Playfair'
H
'Berrimpa' (abandoned)
'Highlands'
'Koondoo'
'Bonnie Doon'
'Minnie Downs'
'Ivanhoe'
Mt Playfair
Welford National Park
'Greers'
'Wandsworth'
'Brides Creek'
'Forest Hill'
'Lansdowne'
'Manning'
'Caldervale'
99
THOMSON
46
'Glenara'
'Mt Calder'
private road
'Westbourne'
'Houghton Vale'
'Retreat'
'Jedburgh'
'Welford'
Welford Lagoon
'Cootabynna'
'Alva'
'Yandarlo'
'Collabara'
'Mungi'
'Woolga'
Yandaro Woolshed
'Galway Downs'
'Listowel Downs'
'Milray'
'Mt Lindsay'
'Amaroo'
'Southampton Downs'
115
'Lumeah'
private track
'Carranya'
'Curraveva'
79
'Coniston'
'Budgerygar'
'Toolong'
'Walton Downs'
'Khyber'
109
'Hammond Downs'
'Oakham'
'Caranna'
'Glanworth'
'Oxford Downs'
'Coolabri'
8
Windorah
'Thunda'
Hell Hole Gorge National Park
316
'Lucknow'
J
'Baykool'
'Cunalama'
'Willara'
'Trinidad'
'Waverley'
'Lynwood'
'Wakes Lagoon'
'Noella'
'Oakwood'
'Mareto'
'Tenham'
'Araluen'
'Milo'
'Boondoon'
'Bronte'
'Biddenham'
'Burenda'
'Bulgroo OS'
'Mt Morris'
Augathella
'Moorak'
'Springfield'
Adavale
'Sherwood Park'
'Dungowan'
'Keeroongooloo'
248
'Canaway Downs'
'Ambathala'
'Oakleigh'
Yo Yo Park
'Barradeen'
'Gundare'
Mariala Nat Park
83
Barduthulla
'Angellala'
'Thylungra'
'Varna'
Lake Dartmouth
'Norah Park'
'Tyrone'
'Newholme'
'Etona'
'Ray'
'Gumbardo'
Langlo Crossing
91
'Mogera'
'Rocksville'
Ard-na-ree
K
'Raymore'
'Granville'
'Patrick Park'
'Cairns'
'Gowrie'
'Bellrose'
'Nth Yarrawonga'
'Victoria Downs'
private road
'Kyabra'
'Glenyarron'
'Bonnievilla'
'Yarrawong'
'Halton'
'Boothulla'
'Nimboy'
Charleville
Joylands
89
'Cashalton'
'Malagarga'
'Mobie Springs'
'Pengine'
'Glenallen'
Cosmos Centre
'Auburn'
Arabella
Sommariva
Angellala
'Pinkilla'
144°
146°
To Roma
8
9
To Quilpie
10
To Quilpie
11
19
12
13
To Cunnamulla & Bourke
14

South-West Queensland

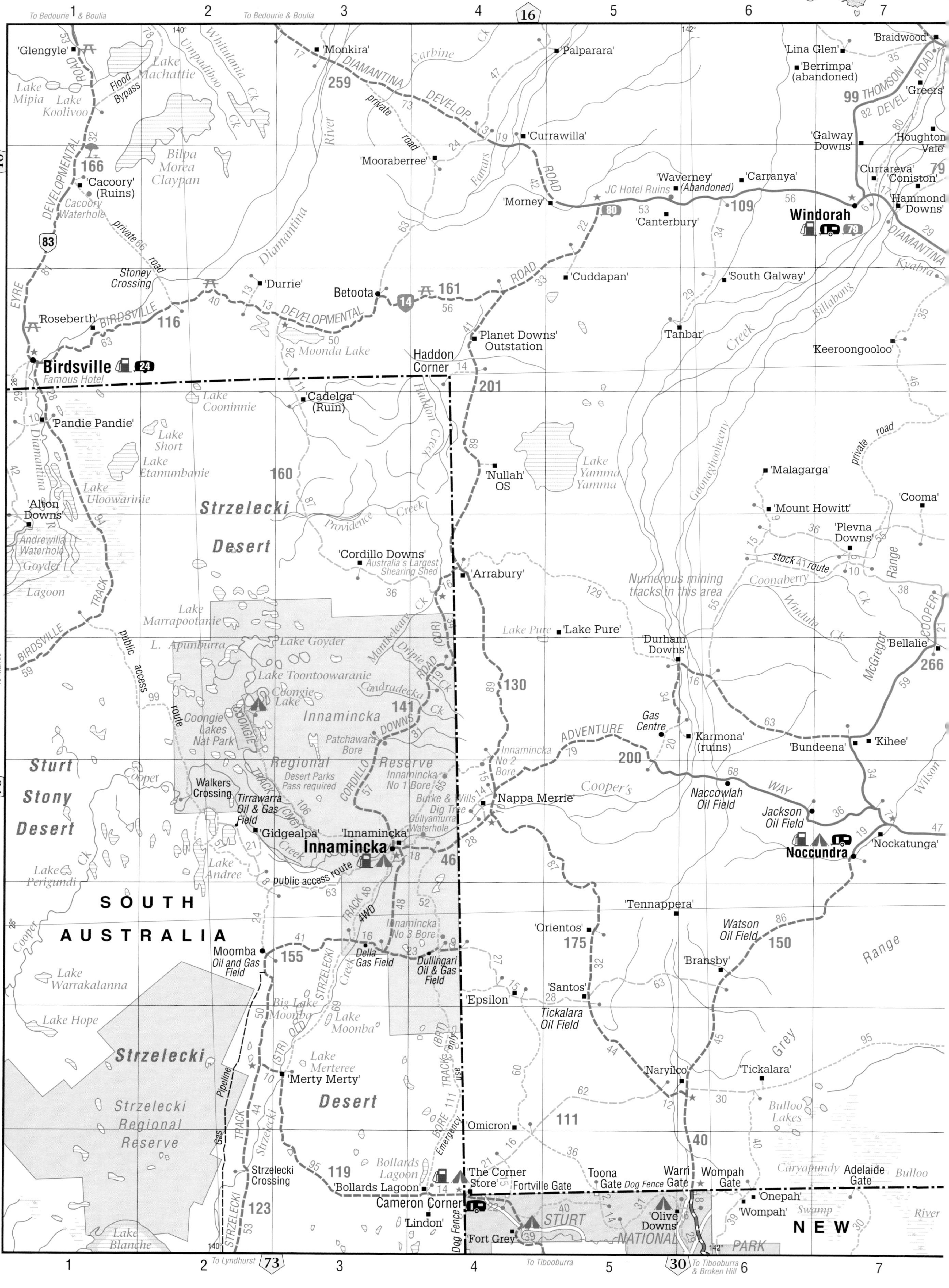

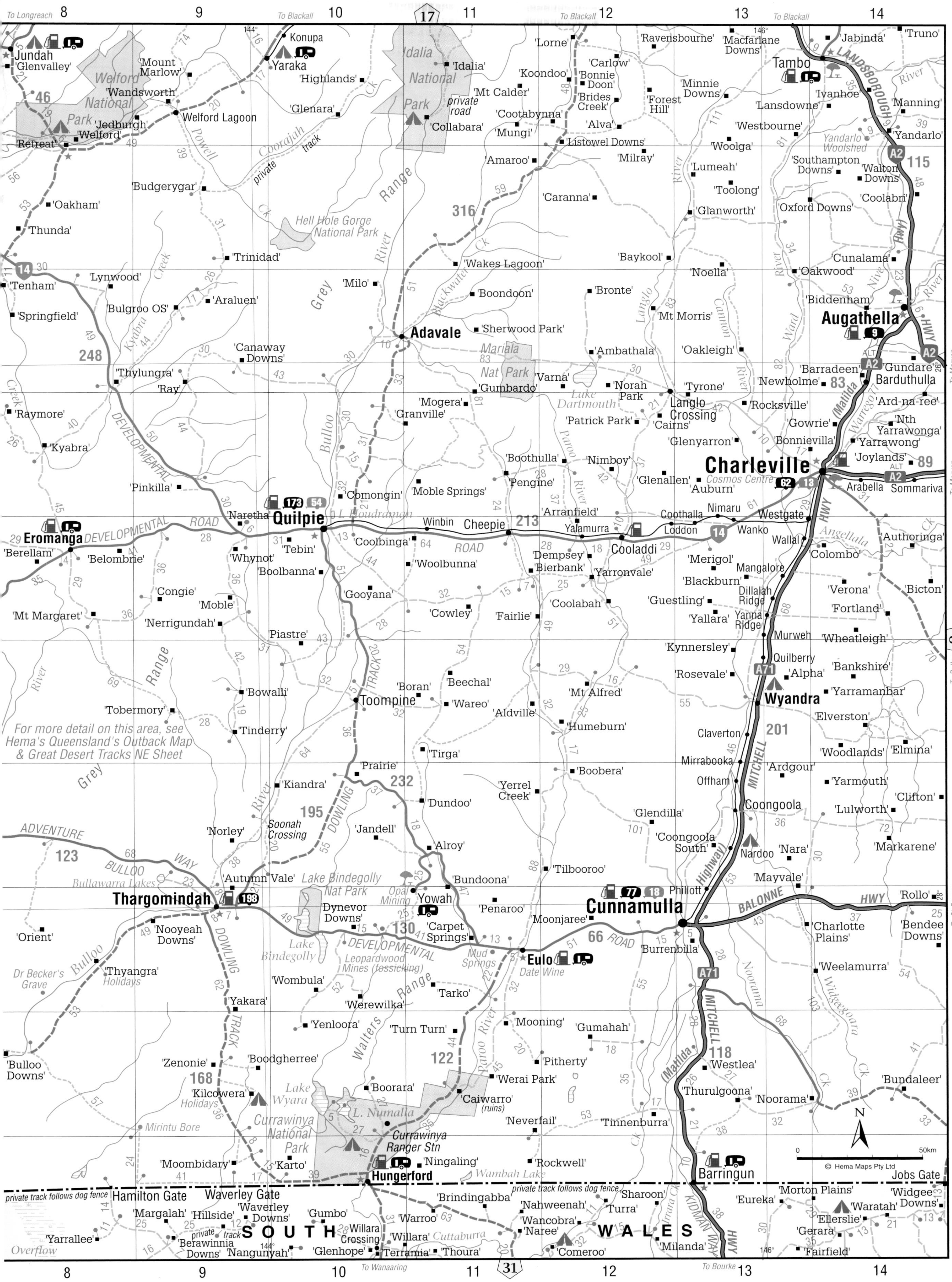

To Longreach 8 9 To Blackall 10 17 11 To Blackall 12 13 To Blackall 14

A
Jundah
'Glenvalley'
Welford National Park
'Mount Marlow'
'Wandsworth'
'Jedburgh'
'Welford'
'Retreat'
Konupa
Yaraka
Welford Lagoon
Powell
Coorajah private track
'Highlands'
'Glenara'
Idalia National Park
'Idalia'
'Mt Calder'
private road
'Collabara'
'Lorne'
'Koondoo'
'Cootabynna'
'Mungi'
'Carlow'
'Bonnie Doon'
'Brides Creek'
'Alva'
'Listowel Downs'
'Ravensbourne'
'Forest Hill'
'Macfarlane Downs'
'Minnie Downs'
'Lansdowne'
'Westbourne'
Tambo
'Jabinda'
'Truno'
LANDSBOROUGH
'Ivanhoe'
'Manning'
'Yandarlo'
Yandarlo Woolshed

B
'Budgerygar'
'Oakham'
'Thunda'
'Trinidad'
Hell Hole Gorge National Park
Range
'Amaroo'
'Caranna'
'Milray'
'Woolga'
'Lumeah'
'Toolong'
'Glanworth'
'Southampton Downs'
'Walton Downs'
'Oxford Downs'
'Coolabri'
'Baykool'
'Cunalama'
'Wakes Lagoon'
Ck

C
'Tenham'
'Lynwood'
'Springfield'
'Bulgroo OS'
'Araluen'
Kyabra
Creek
Grey
River
'Milo'
Blackwater Ck
'Boondoon'
'Bronte'
'Mt Morris'
Langlo
Cannon
Ward
'Noella'
'Oakwood'
'Biddenham'
Nive
Augathella
'Canaway Downs'
Adavale
'Sherwood Park'
Mariala Nat Park
'Ambathala'
'Oakleigh'
'Barradeen'
'Gundare'
Barduthulla
To Morven & Brisbane
'Thylungra'
'Ray'
'Varna'
'Gumbardo'
'Norah Park'
'Tyrone'
'Newholme'

D
'Raymore'
'Kyabra'
DEVELOPMENTAL
'Mogera'
'Granville'
Bulloo
Lake Dartmouth
Langlo Crossing
'Cairns'
'Patrick Park'
'Rocksville'
'Ard-na-ree'
'Gowrie'
'Nth Yarrawonga'
'Glenyarron'
'Bonnievilla'
'Yarrawong'
'Boothulla'
'Nimboy'
Paroo
River
'Pengine'
'Glenallen'
Charleville
Cosmos Centre
'Auburn'
'Joylands'
Arabella
Sommariva
To Morven & Brisbane
'Pinkilla'
'Comongin'
'Moble Springs'
'Arranfield'

E
Eromanga
DEVELOPMENTAL ROAD
'Berellam'
'Belombrie'
'Naretha'
Quilpie
L. Houdraman
Winbin
Cheepie
Yalamurra
Coothalla
Loddon
Nimaru
Westgate
Wanko
'Authoringa'
'Whynot'
'Tebin'
'Coolbinga'
'Woolbunna'
ROAD
'Dempsey'
'Bierbank'
Cooladdi
'Yarronvale'
'Merigol'
Mangalore
'Colombo'
Angellala Ck
Wallal
'Boolbanna'
'Blackburn'
Dillalah Ridge
'Congie'
'Moble'
'Gooyana'
'Cowley'
'Fairlie'
'Coolabah'
'Guestling'
'Yallara'
Yanna Ridge
'Verona'
'Bicton'
'Fortland'
'Mt Margaret'
'Nerrigundah'
'Piastre'
Murweh
'Wheatleigh'
To Bollon

F
River
Range
'Kynnersley'
Quilberry
'Alpha'
'Bankshire'
'Rosevale'
'Bowalli'
TRACK
'Boran'
'Beechal'
'Mt Alfred'
Wyandra
'Yarramanbar'
'Tobermory'
'Toompine'
'Wareo'
'Aldville'
'Humeburn'
'Elverston'
'Tinderry'
Claverton
'Woodlands'
'Elmina'
For more detail on this area, see Hema's Queensland's Outback Map & Great Desert Tracks NE Sheet
'Tirga'
Mirrabooka
MITCHELL
'Ardgour'
Grey
'Prairie'
'Boobera'
Offham
'Yarmouth'
'Kiandra'
'Dundoo'
'Yerrel Creek'
Coongoola
'Clifton'
'Lulworth'

G
ADVENTURE
'Norley'
Soonah Crossing
DOWLING
'Jandell'
'Glendilla'
'Markarene'
BULLOO
WAY
'Alroy'
'Coongoola South'
Highway
Nardoo
'Nara'
Bullawarra Lakes
'Autumn Vale'
Lake Bindegolly Nat Park
Opal Mining
'Bundoona'
'Tilbooroo'
'Mayvale'

H
Thargomindah
Yowah
'Dynevor Downs'
'Penaroo'
Cunnamulla
Phillott
BALONNE
HWY
'Rollo'
To St George
'Orient'
'Nooyeah Downs'
'Carpet Springs'
'Moonjaree'
ROAD
'Charlotte Plains'
'Bendee Downs'
Lake Bindegolly
DEVELOPMENTAL
Leopardwood Mines (fossicking)
Mud Springs
Eulo
Date Wine
'Burrenbilla'
'Weelamurra'
Dr Becker's Grave
Bulloo
'Thyangra' Holidays
'Wombula'
Range
'Tarko'
Noorama
Widgeegoara
'Yakara'
'Werewilka'

J
'Yenloora'
Walters
'Turn Turn'
Paroo River
'Mooning'
'Gumahah'
'Bulloo Downs'
'Zenonie'
TRACK
'Boodgherree'
'Pitherty'
Westlea'
Ck
'Bundaleer'
'Kilcowera' Holidays
Lake Wyara
'Boorara'
'Werai Park'
(Matilda)
'Thurulgoona'
'Noorama'
'Caiwarro' (ruins)
L. Numalla
Currawinya National Park
Mirintu Bore
'Neverfail'
'Tinnenburra'
Currawinya Ranger Stn
'Ningaling'
'Rockwell'
'Moombidary'
'Karto'
Hungerford
Wambah Lake
Barringun
Jobs Gate
0 50km
© Hema Maps Pty Ltd

K
private track follows dog fence
Hamilton Gate
Waverley Gate
private track follows dog fence
'Sharoon'
'Morton Plains'
'Widgee Downs'
'Margalah'
'Hillside'
'Waverley Downs'
'Gumbo'
'Brindingabba'
'Nahweenah'
'Turra'
'Eureka'
'Waratah'
'Yarrallee'
private track
'Berawinnia Downs'
SOUTH
Willara Crossing
'Warroo'
'Wancobra'
'Naree'
WALES
'Ellerslie'
'Gerara'
Overflow
'Nangunyah'
'Glenhope'
'Terramia'
'Willara'
'Thoura'
Cuttaburra
'Comeroo'
'Milanda'
KIDMAN WAY
HWY
'Fairfield'

8 9 10 To Wanaaring 11 31 12 To Bourke 13 14

NEW SOUTH WALES Key Map

POPULATION: 7 million
AREA: 800,642 sq km
CAPITAL CITY: Sydney

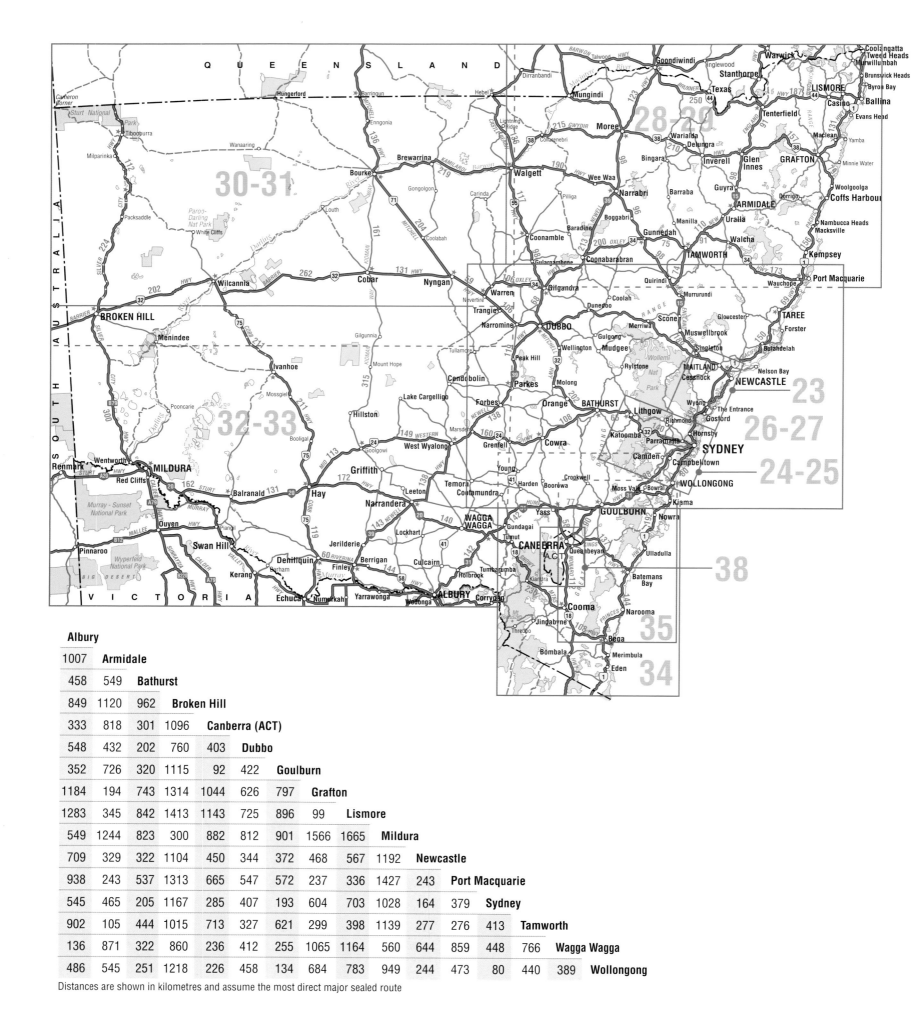

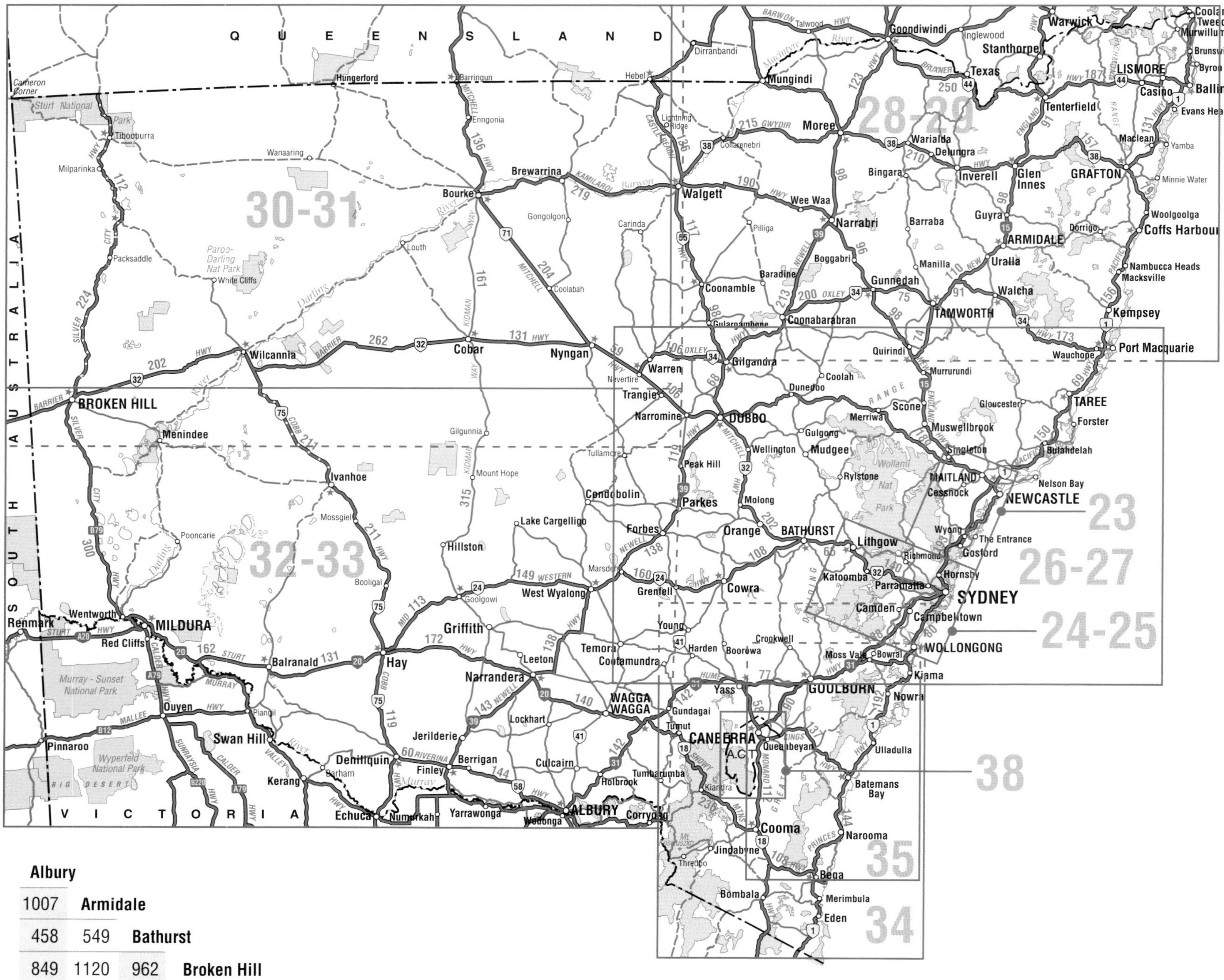

	Albury	Armidale	Bathurst	Broken Hill	Canberra (ACT)	Dubbo	Goulburn	Grafton	Lismore	Mildura	Newcastle	Port Macquarie	Sydney	Tamworth	Wagga Wagga
Albury															
Armidale	1007														
Bathurst	458	549													
Broken Hill	849	1120	962												
Canberra (ACT)	333	818	301	1096											
Dubbo	548	432	202	760	403										
Goulburn	352	726	320	1115	92	422									
Grafton	1184	194	743	1314	1044	626	797								
Lismore	1283	345	842	1413	1143	725	896	99							
Mildura	549	1244	823	300	882	812	901	1566	1665						
Newcastle	709	329	322	1104	450	344	372	468	567	1192					
Port Macquarie	938	243	537	1313	665	547	572	237	336	1427	243				
Sydney	545	465	205	1167	285	407	193	604	703	1028	164	379			
Tamworth	902	105	444	1015	713	327	621	299	398	1139	277	276	413		
Wagga Wagga	136	871	322	860	236	412	255	1065	1164	560	644	859	448	766	
Wollongong	486	545	251	1218	226	458	134	684	783	949	244	473	80	440	389

Distances are shown in kilometres and assume the most direct major sealed route

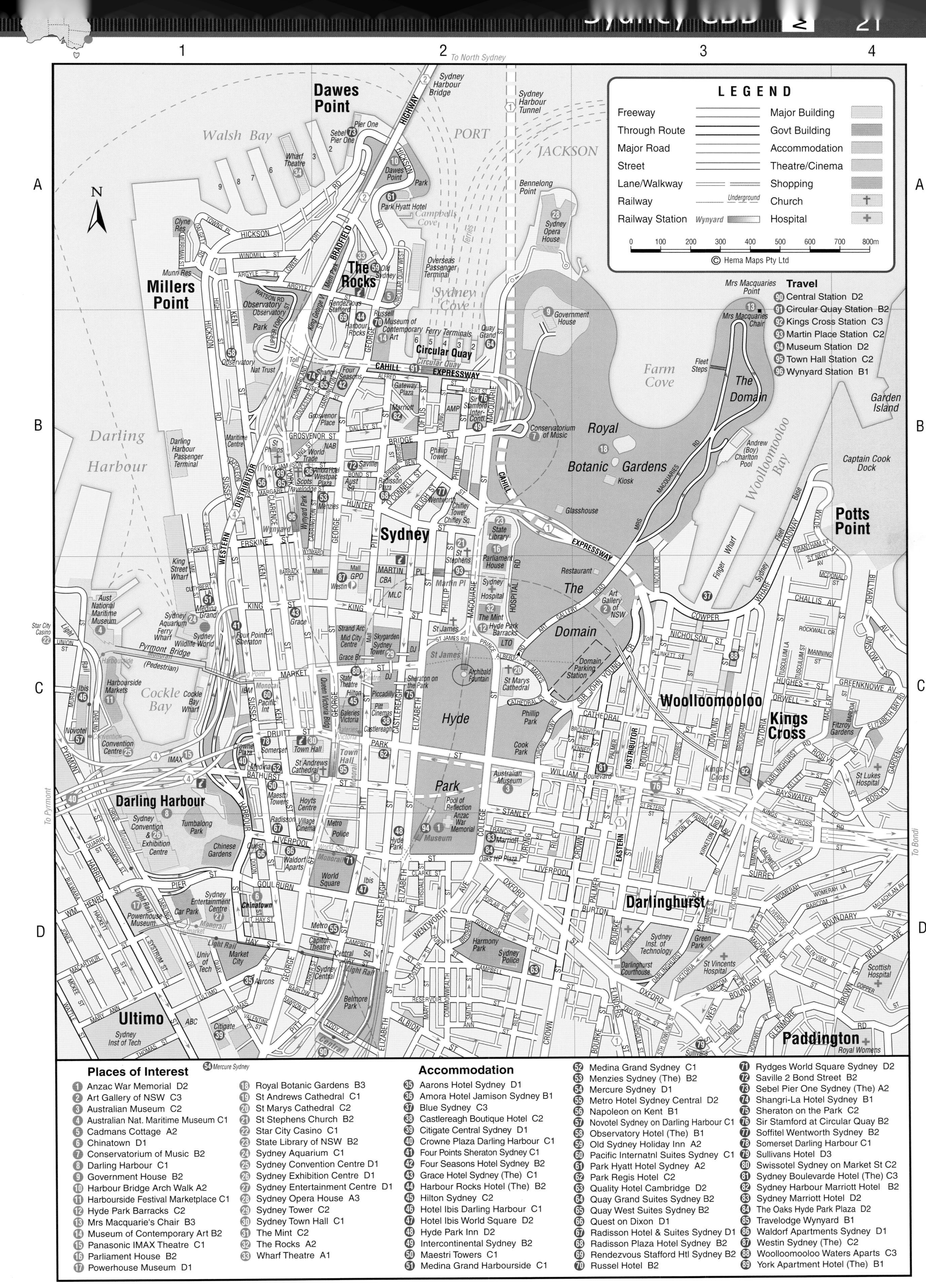
LEGEND
Freeway
Through Route
Major Road
Street
Lane/Walkway
Railway
Underground
Railway Station
Wynyard
Major Building
Govt Building
Accommodation
Theatre/Cinema
Shopping
Church
Hospital
0 100 200 300 400 500 600 700 800m
© Hema Maps Pty Ltd
Travel
90 Central Station D2
91 Circular Quay Station B2
92 Kings Cross Station C3
93 Martin Place Station C2
94 Museum Station D2
95 Town Hall Station C2
96 Wynyard Station B1
Dawes Point
Walsh Bay
PORT JACKSON
Millers Point
The Rocks
Sydney Cove
Circular Quay
Farm Cove
The Domain
Royal Botanic Gardens
Woolloomooloo Bay
Garden Island
Potts Point
Darling Harbour
Cockle Bay
Sydney
Hyde Park
Woolloomooloo
Kings Cross
Darlinghurst
Ultimo
Paddington
To North Sydney
To Pyrmont
To Bondi
Places of Interest
1 Anzac War Memorial D2
2 Art Gallery of NSW C3
3 Australian Museum C2
4 Australian Nat. Maritime Museum C1
5 Cadmans Cottage A2
6 Chinatown D1
7 Conservatorium of Music B2
8 Darling Harbour C1
9 Government House B2
10 Harbour Bridge Arch Walk A2
11 Harbourside Festival Marketplace C1
12 Hyde Park Barracks C2
13 Mrs Macquarie's Chair B3
14 Museum of Contemporary Art B2
15 Panasonic IMAX Theatre C1
16 Parliament House B2
17 Powerhouse Museum D1
18 Royal Botanic Gardens B3
19 St Andrews Cathedral C1
20 St Marys Cathedral C2
21 St Stephens Church B2
22 Star City Casino C1
23 State Library of NSW B2
24 Sydney Aquarium C1
25 Sydney Convention Centre D1
26 Sydney Exhibition Centre D1
27 Sydney Entertainment Centre D1
28 Sydney Opera House A3
29 Sydney Tower C2
30 Sydney Town Hall C1
31 The Mint C2
32 The Rocks A2
33 Wharf Theatre A1
Accommodation
35 Aarons Hotel Sydney D1
36 Amora Hotel Jamison Sydney B1
37 Blue Sydney C3
38 Castlereagh Boutique Hotel C2
39 Citigate Central Sydney D1
40 Crowne Plaza Darling Harbour C1
41 Four Points Sheraton Sydney C1
42 Four Seasons Hotel Sydney B2
43 Grace Hotel Sydney (The) C1
44 Harbour Rocks Hotel (The) B2
45 Hilton Sydney C2
46 Hotel Ibis Darling Harbour C1
47 Hotel Ibis World Square D2
48 Hyde Park Inn D2
49 Intercontinental Sydney B2
50 Maestri Towers C1
51 Medina Grand Harbourside C1
52 Medina Grand Sydney C1
53 Menzies Sydney (The) B2
54 Mercure Sydney D1
55 Metro Hotel Sydney Central D2
56 Napoleon on Kent B1
57 Novotel Sydney on Darling Harbour C1
58 Observatory Hotel (The) B1
59 Old Sydney Holiday Inn A2
60 Pacific Internatnl Suites Sydney C1
61 Park Hyatt Hotel Sydney A2
62 Park Regis Hotel C2
63 Quality Hotel Cambridge D2
64 Quay Grand Suites Sydney B2
65 Quay West Suites Sydney B2
66 Quest on Dixon D1
67 Radisson Hotel & Suites Sydney D1
68 Radisson Plaza Hotel Sydney B2
69 Rendezvous Stafford Htl Sydney B2
70 Russel Hotel B2
71 Rydges World Square Sydney D2
72 Saville 2 Bond Street B2
73 Sebel Pier One Sydney (The) A2
74 Shangri-La Hotel Sydney B1
75 Sheraton on the Park C2
76 Sir Stamford at Circular Quay B2
77 Soffitel Wentworth Sydney B2
78 Somerset Darling Harbour C1
79 Sullivans Hotel D3
80 Swissotel Sydney on Market St C2
81 Sydney Boulevarde Hotel (The) C3
82 Sydney Harbour Marriott Hotel B2
83 Sydney Marriott Hotel D2
84 The Oaks Hyde Park Plaza D2
85 Travelodge Wynyard B1
86 Waldorf Apartments Sydney D1
87 Westin Sydney (The) C2
88 Woolloomooloo Waters Aparts C3
89 York Apartment Hotel (The) B1

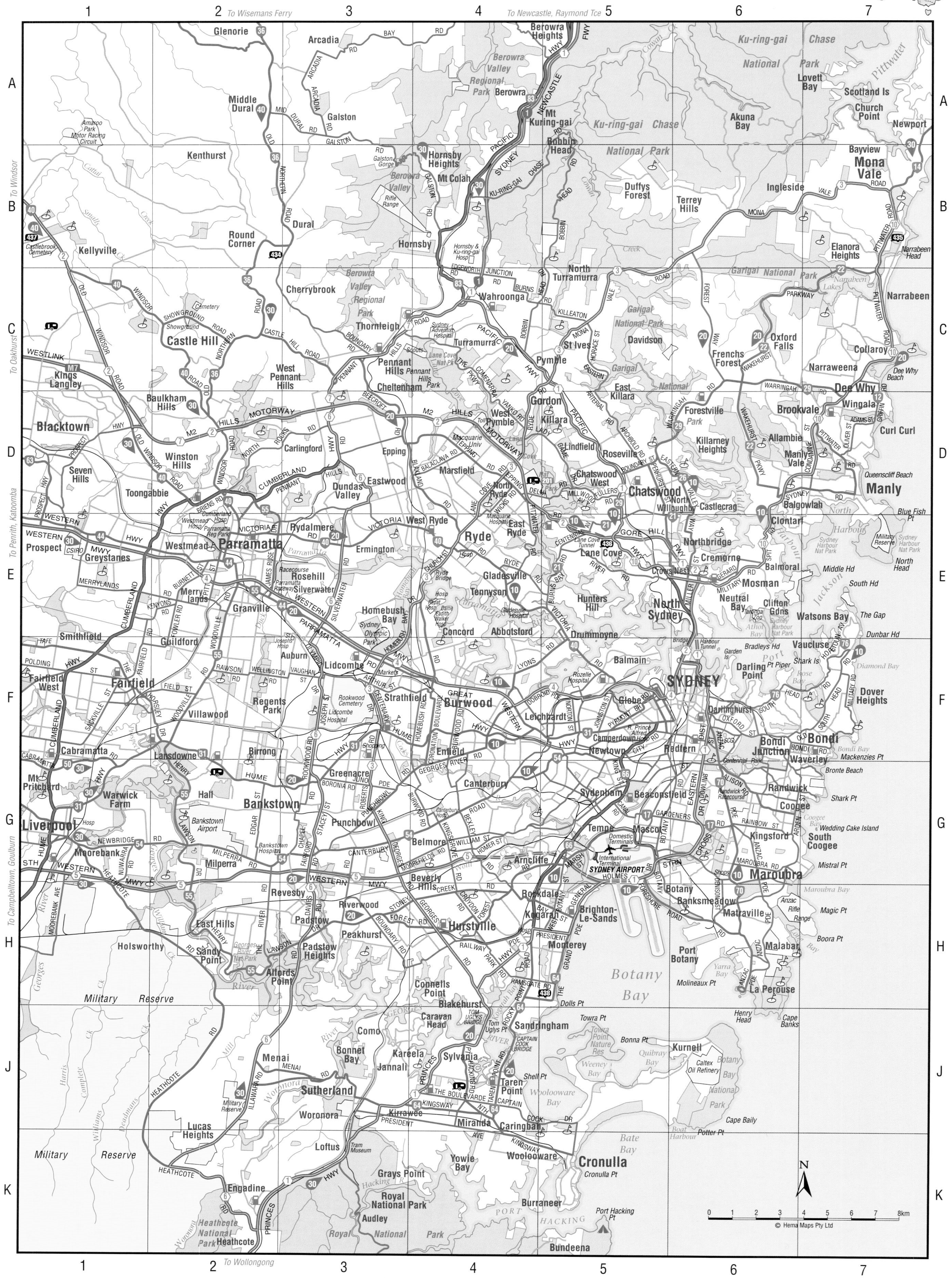

Sydney Throughroads

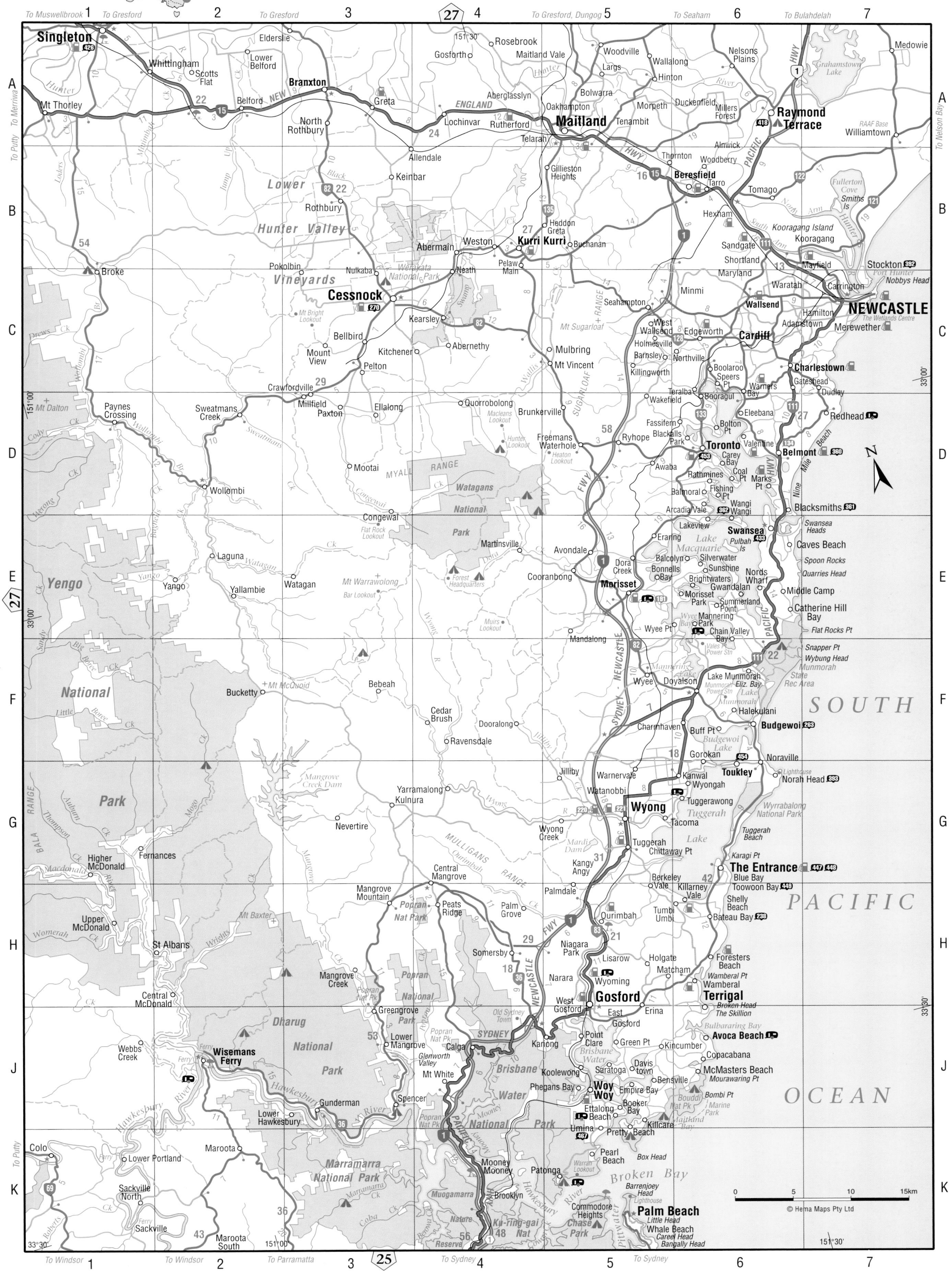

To Muswellbrook 1 To Gresford 2 To Gresford 3 27 4 To Gresford, Dungog 5 To Seaham 6 To Bulahdelah 7

Singleton
Whittingham
Scotts Flat
Elderslie
Lower Belford
Belford
Branxton
Greta
Mt Thorley
North Rothbury
Lochinvar
Allendale
Rosebrook
Gosforth
Maitland Vale
Aberglasslyn
Oakhampton
Rutherford
Maitland
Telarah
Woodville
Largs
Bolwarra
Wallalong
Hinton
Morpeth
Tenambit
Nelsons Plains
Duckenfield
Millers Forest
Raymond Terrace
Medowie
Grahamstown Lake
RAAF Base Williamtown
NEW ENGLAND HWY
Lower Hunter Valley Vineyards
Keinbar
Rothbury
Gillieston Heights
Heddon Greta
Kurri Kurri
Buchanan
Thornton
Beresfield
Tarro
Woodberry
Alnwick
Tomago
Fullerton Cove
Smiths Is
Hexham
Kooragang Island
Kooragang
Sandgate
Shortland
Maryland
Stockton
Mayfield
Port Hunter
Nobbys Head
Carrington
NEWCASTLE
Waratah
Wallsend
Hamilton
Adamstown
Merewether
The Wetlands Centre
Minmi
Broke
Pokolbin
Nulkaba
Werakata National Park
Abermain
Weston
Neath
Pelaw Main
Cessnock
Mt Bright Lookout
Bellbird
Kearsley
Abernethy
Kitchener
Mount View
Pelton
Seahampton
Mt Sugarloaf
West Wallsend
Holmesville
Edgeworth
Cardiff
Barnsley
Northville
Killingworth
Mulbring
Mt Vincent
Boolaroo
Speers Pt
Charlestown
Gateshead
Warners Bay
Dudley
Teralba
Booragul
Wakefield
Eleebana
Redhead
Mt Dalton
Paynes Crossing
Sweatmans Creek
Crawfordville
Millfield
Paxton
Ellalong
Quorrobolong
Macleans Lookout
Brunkerville
SUGARLOAF RANGE
Hunter Lookout
Freemans Waterhole
Heaton Lookout
Ryhope
Fassifern
Blackalls Park
Bolton Pt
Toronto
Valentine
Belmont
Carey Bay
Awaba
Rathmines
Coal Pt
Marks Pt
Mootai
MYALL RANGE
Watagans National Park
Wollombi
Congewai
Flat Rock Lookout
Balmoral
Fishing Pt
Arcadia Vale
Wangi Wangi
Nine Mile Beach
Blacksmiths
Lakeview
Eraring
Lake Macquarie
Swansea
Swansea Heads
Pulbah Is
Caves Beach
Laguna
Martinsville
Avondale
Dora Creek
Balcolyn
Silverwater
Bonnells Bay
Sunshine
Spoon Rocks
Quarries Head
Yengo
Yango
Yallambie
Watagan
Mt Warrawolong
Bar Lookout
Forest Headquarters
Cooranbong
Morisset
Brightwaters
Gwandalan
Nords Wharf
Middle Camp
Morisset Park
Summerland Point
Catherine Hill Bay
Mannering Park
Muirs Lookout
Mandalong
Wyee Pt
Chain Valley Bay
Flat Rocks Pt
Vales Pt Power Stn
Snapper Pt
Wybung Head
Munmorah State Rec Area
Bucketty
Mt McQuoid
Bebeah
Wyee
Doyalson
Lake Munmorah
Munmorah Power Stn
Eliz. Bay
Lake Munmorah
Halekulani
National
Little Boree Ck
Cedar Brush
Dooralong
Ravensdale
Charmhaven
Buff Pt
Budgewoi
Budgewoi Lake
Gorokan
Noraville
SOUTH
Mangrove Creek Dam
Jilliby
Warnervale
Kanwal
Toukley
Lighthouse
Norah Head
Yarramalong
Kulnura
Watanobbi
Wyongah
Tuggerawong
Wyong
Tacoma
Tuggerah Lake
Wyrrabalong National Park
Park
BALA RANGE
Nevertire
Wyong Creek
Mardi Dam
Tuggerah
Chittaway Pt
Tuggerah Beach
Karagi Pt
Fernances
Higher McDonald
MULLIGANS RANGE
Kangy Angy
The Entrance
Blue Bay
Central Mangrove
Berkeley Vale
Killarney Vale
Toowoon Bay
Mangrove Mountain
Popran Nat Park
Peats Ridge
Palmdale
Palm Grove
Shelly Beach
Tumbi Umbi
PACIFIC
Bateau Bay
Upper McDonald
Mt Baxter
Ourimbah
St Albans
Somersby
Niagara Park
Lisarow
Holgate
Matcham
Foresters Beach
Wamberal Pt
Wamberal
Mangrove Creek
Popran National Park
Narara
Wyoming
Terrigal
Central McDonald
Dharug National Park
Greengrove
Old Sydney Town
West Gosford
Gosford
Erina
East Gosford
Broken Head
The Skillion
Bulbararing Bay
Avoca Beach
Lower Mangrove
Popran Nat Pk
Kariong
Point Clare
Green Pt
Kincumber
Copacabana
Webbs Creek
Wisemans Ferry
Glenworth Valley
Calga
Brisbane Water
Koolewong
Saratoga
Davis town
MacMasters Beach
Mourawaring Pt
Mt White
Bensville
Phegans Bay
Woy Woy
Empire Bay
Bouddi Nat Pk
Bombi Pt
Marine Park
OCEAN
Gunderman
Spencer
Lower Hawkesbury
Hawkesbury River
Brisbane Water National Park
Ettalong Beach
Booker Bay
Killcare
Maitland Bay
Umina
Pretty Beach
Colo
Lower Portland
Maroota
Pearl Beach
Box Head
Marramarra National Park
Mooney Mooney
Patonga
Warrah Lookout
Broken Bay
Barrenjoey Head
Lighthouse
Sackville North
Muogamarra Nature Reserve
Brooklyn
Commodore Heights
Palm Beach
Little Head
Whale Beach
Careel Head
Bangally Head
Sackville
Maroota South
Ku-ring-gai Chase Nat Park
Pittwater
Hema Maps Pty Ltd

To Windsor 1 To Windsor 2 To Parramatta 3 25 To Sydney 4 5 To Sydney 6 7

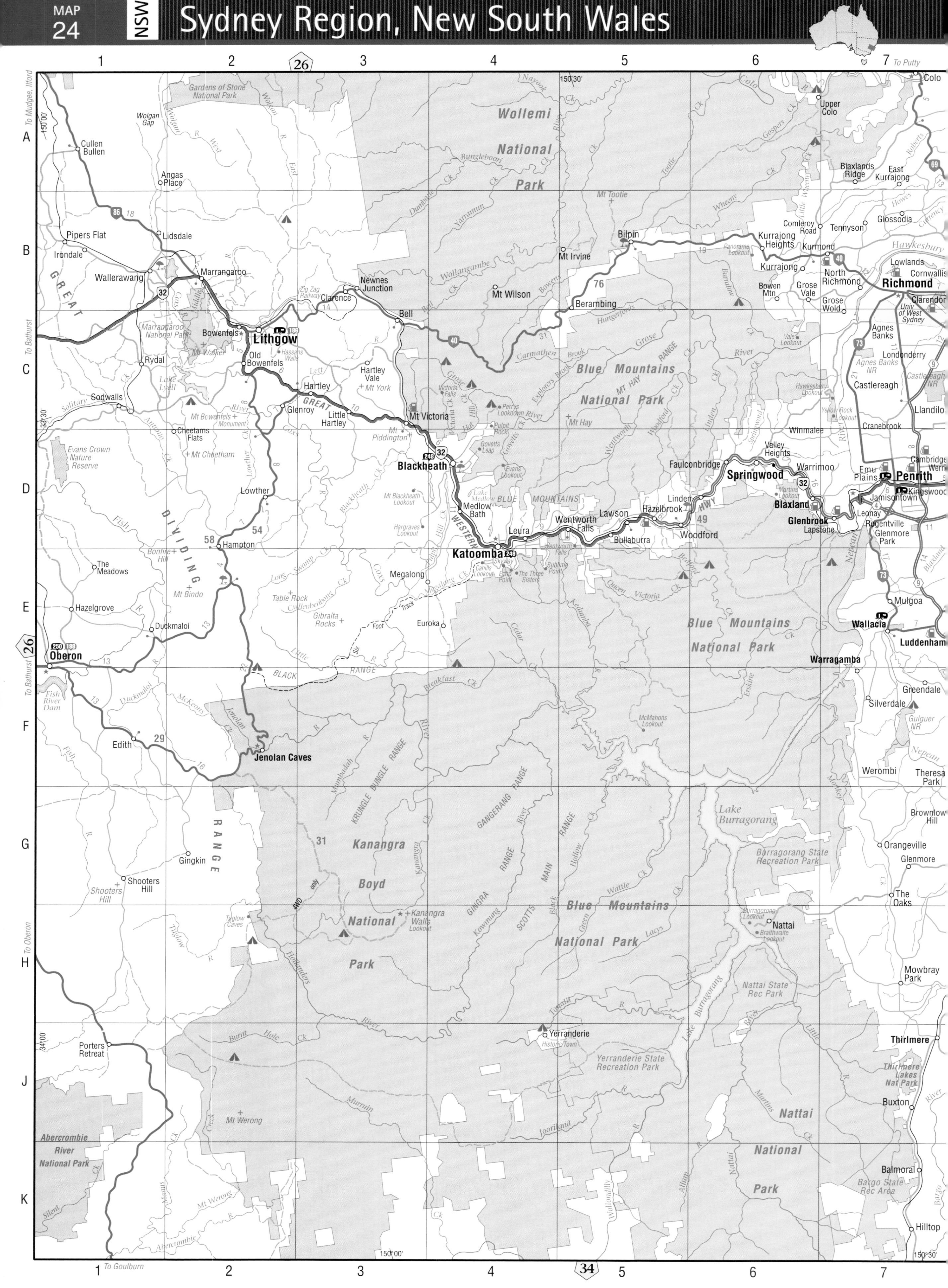
Wollemi National Park
Blue Mountains National Park
Kanangra Boyd National Park
Nattai National Park
Lithgow
Katoomba
Blackheath
Springwood
Penrith
Richmond
Oberon
Jenolan Caves
Wentworth Falls
Leura
Lawson
Hazelbrook
Woodford
Blaxland
Glenbrook
Lapstone
Mt Victoria
Medlow Bath
Bilpin
Kurrajong
Kurrajong Heights
North Richmond
Wallacia
Warragamba
Lake Burragorang
Yerranderie
Thirlmere
Buxton
Balmoral
Hilltop
Hartley
Little Hartley
Bowenfels
Marrangaroo
Wallerawang
Pipers Flat
Lidsdale
Cullen Bullen
Hampton
Lowther
Duckmaloi
Edith
Porters Retreat
Abercrombie River National Park
Mt Wilson
Mt Irvine
Berambing
Bell
Clarence
Newnes Junction
Megalong
Euroka
Gardens of Stone National Park
GREAT DIVIDING RANGE
To Putty
To Goulburn
To Bathurst
To Oberon
To Mudgee, Ilford

To Wisemans Ferry
To Gosford
Lower Portland
Sackville North
Sackville
Marramarra National Park
Muogamarra
Mooney Mooney
Patonga
Pearl Beach
Broken Bay
Barrenjoey Head
Palm Beach
Whale Beach
Brooklyn
Commodore Heights
Maroota South
Cattai
Ebenezer
Wilberforce
Cowan
Berowra Waters
Ku-ring-gai Chase
Clareville
Avalon
Bilgola
Newport
Forest Glen
Glenorie
Berrilee
Berowra
Cottage Point
Church Point
Bayview
Freemans Reach
Pitt Town
Windsor
Scheyville
McGraths Hill
Fiddletown
Arcadia
Galston
Mt Kuring-gai
Bobbin Head
Duffys Forest
Mona Vale
Ingleside
Warriewood
Terrey Hills
Elanora Heights
Narrabeen
Collaroy
Oakville
Vineyard
Mulgrave
Nelson
Box Hill
Bligh Park
Windsor Downs
Rouse Hill
Round Corner
Dural
Hornsby
Asquith
Mt Colah
St Ives Chase
North St Ives
Belrose
Oxford Falls
Narraweena
Dee Why
Curl Curl
Queenscliff
Manly
Riverstone
Schofields
Kellyville
Glenhaven
Castle Hill
Cherrybrook
Normanhurst
Thornleigh
Wahroonga
Warrawee
Turramurra
Pymble
Gordon
Killara
Lindfield
Roseville
Chatswood
Forestville
Killarney Heights
Seaforth
Balgowlah
Clontarf
Marsden Park
Colebee
Dean Park
Quakers Hill
Glenwood
Baulkham Hills
Pennant Hills
Beecroft
Cheltenham
West Pymble
West Killara
Epping
Carlingford
Eastwood
Marsfield
North Ryde
Ryde
Lane Cove
Artarmon
St Leonards
Balmoral
Mosman
Cremorne
Watsons Bay
Vaucluse
Dover Heights
North Bondi
Bondi
Bronte
Clovelly
Coogee
Oakhurst
Marayong
Plumpton
Doonside
Rooty Hill
Blacktown
Lalor Park
Seven Hills
Toongabbie
Girraween
Winston Hills
Oatlands
Dundas
Rydalmere
Parramatta
Ermington
Rhodes
Hunters Hill
Greenwich
Nth Sydney
SYDNEY
Rose Bay
Kings Cross
Edgecliff
Woollahra
Pad'ton
Waverley
Randwick
St Marys
Mt Druitt
Colyton
Eastern Creek
Prospect
Greystanes
Merrylands
Granville
Auburn
Lidcombe
Homebush
Strathfield
Burwood
Concord
Drummoyne
Rozelle
Balmain
Glebe
Leichhardt
Redfern
Camperdown
Hewitt
St Clair
Erskine Park
Woodpark
Smithfield
Guildford
Yennora
Berala
Regents Pk
Enfield
Ashfield
Marrickville
Enmore
St Peters
Kensington
Kingsford
Wetherill Park
Horsley Park
Bossley Park
Fairfield
Carramar
Chester Hill
Sefton
Yagoona
Bass Hill
Greenacre
Belmore
Canterbury
Earlwood
Sydenham
Mascot
Sydney Airport
Botany
Pagewood
Matraville
Maroubra
Chifley
Mt Vernon
Kemps Creek
Abbotsbury
Edensor Park
Cabramatta
Lansvale
Georges Hall
Condell Park
Bankstown
Lakemba
Punchbowl
Beverly Hills
Bexley
Rockdale
Brighton-Le-Sands
Monterey
Ramsgate
Phillip Bay
La Perouse
Little Bay
Cecil Park
Bonnyrigg
Mt Pritchard
Chipping Norton
Milperra
Liverpool
Riverwood
Hurstville
Badgerys Creek
Green Valley
Cartwright
Moorebank
Revesby
Padstow
Mortdale
Oatley
Hoxton Park
Miller
Austral
West Hoxton
Carnes Hill
Lurnea
Casula
Wattle Grove
East Hills
Holsworthy
Lugarno
Blakehurst
Sans Souci
Taren Pt
Kurnell
Botany Bay National Park
Bringelly
Rossmore
Leppington
Edmondson Park
Glenfield
Macquarie Fields
Ingleburn
Menai
Bangor
Como
Oyster Bay
Kareela
Sylvania
Caringbah
Gymea
Miranda
Cronulla
Sutherland
Lucas Heights
Loftus
Lilli Pilli
Port Hacking Point
Bundeena
Maianbar
Audley
Catherine Field
Oran Park
Raby
Minto
Eagle Vale
Leumeah
Kentlyn
Ruse
Cobbity
Smeaton Grange
MILITARY RESERVE
Engadine
Heathcote
Royal National Park
Wattamolla
Marley Head
Providential Head
Camden
Narellan
Narellan Vale
Mt Annan
Spring Farm
Camden South
Campbelltown
Bradbury
Ambarvale
Rosemeadow
Gilead
Menangle Park
Menangle
Mt Hunter
Cawdor
Wedderburn
Waterfall
Heathcote National Park
Garie
Woronora Reservoir
Helensburgh
Lilyvale
Otford
Stanwell Park
Darkes Forest
Dharawal SRA
Douglas Park
Appin
Coalcliff
Clifton
Scarborough
Wombarra
Coledale
Austinmer
Thirroul
Bulli Pt
Bulli
Woonona
Bellambi
Corrimal
Russell Vale
Balgownie
Towradgi
Fairy Meadow
North Wollongong
WOLLONGONG
Coniston
Fig Tree
Port Kembla
Unanderra
Kembla Heights
Mt Keira
Picton
Maldon
Tahmoor
Wilton
Bargo
Yanderra
Yerrinbool
Cataract Reservoir
Cordeaux Reservoir
Avon Reservoir
Nepean Reservoir
SEE PAGE 22
SOUTH PACIFIC OCEAN
TASMAN SEA
N
0 5 10 15 20km
© Hema Maps Pty Ltd
To Goulburn
To Kiama & Moss Vale
8 9 10 11 12 13 14
A B C D E F G H J K

Central-East New South Wales

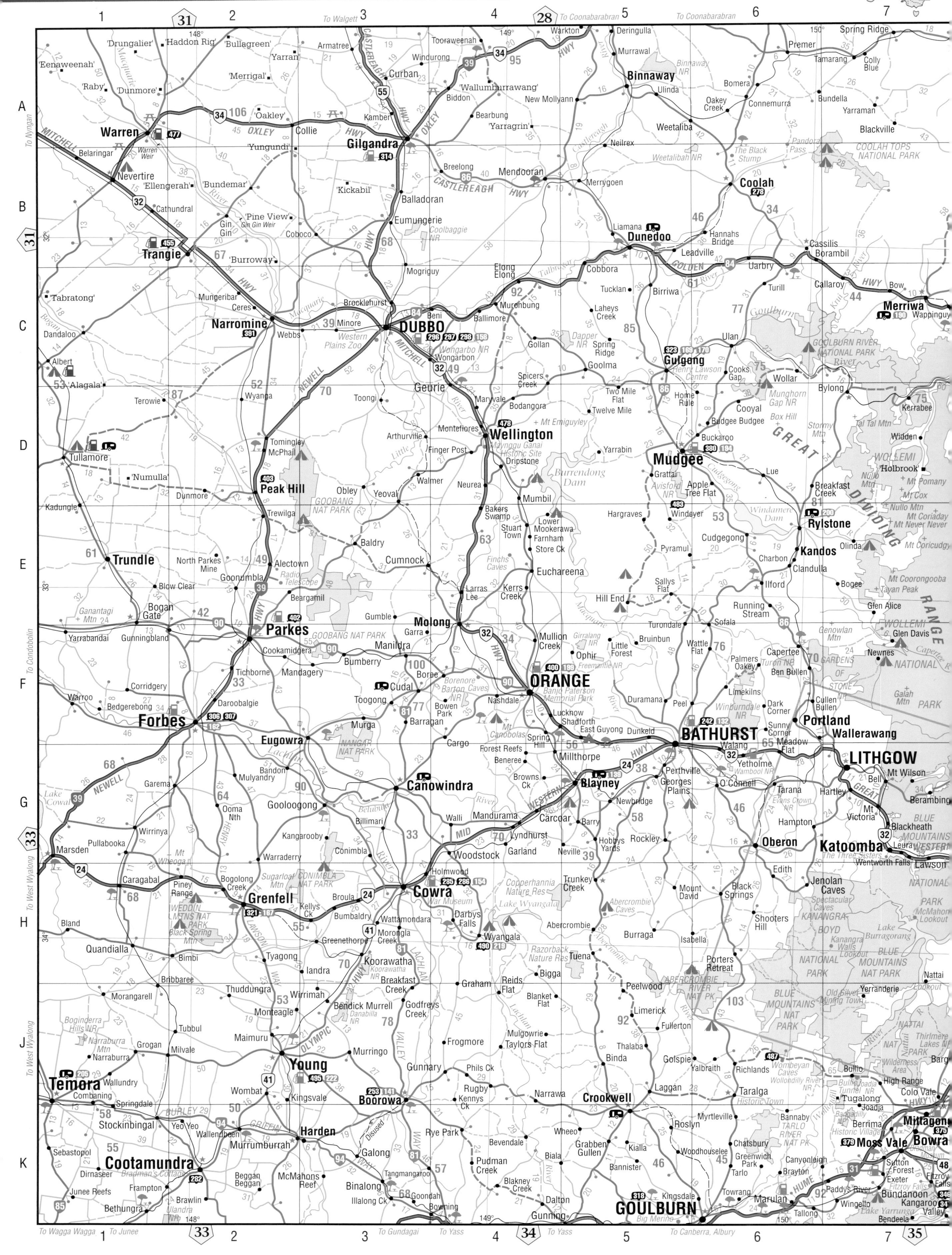

1 2 3 4 5 6 7

A B C D E F G H J K

To Walgett · To Coonabarabran · To Coonabarabran · To Nyngan · To Condobolin · To West Wyalong · To West Wyalong · To Wagga Wagga · To Junee · To Gundagai · To Yass · To Yass · To Canberra, Albury

'Drungalier' 'Haddon Rig' 'Bullagreen' Armatree Tooraweenah Warkton Deringulla Spring Ridge Premer 'Eenaweenah' 'Yarran' Windurong Murrawal Tamarang Colly Blue 'Merrigal' Curban Binnaway Binnaway NR 'Raby' 'Dunmore' 'Wallumburrawang' Ulinda Bomera Biddon New Mollyann Oakey Creek Connemurra Bundella Yarraman 'Oakley' Kamber Bearbung 'Yarragrin' Weetaliba Blackville Warren Collie Gilgandra Castlereagh Neilrex Pandora Pass COOLAH TOPS NATIONAL PARK Belaringar Warren Weir 'Yungundi' The Black Stump Weetaliba NR Nevertire 'Ellengerah' 'Bundemar' Breelong Mendooran Merrygoen Coolah 'Kickabil' Balladoran Cathundral 'Pine View' Gin Gin Gin Gin Weir Eumungerie Coolbaggie NR Liamana Dunedoo Hannahs Bridge Coboco Cassilis Borambil Trangie 'Burroway' Leadville Mogriguy Elong Elong Cobbora Uarbry Turill Callaroy Bow Merriwa Wappinguy 'Tabratong' Mungeribar Ceres Brocklehurst Tucklan Birriwa Laheys Creek Narromine Minore DUBBO Beni Ballimore Muronbung Goulburn River Dandaloo Webbs Western Plains Zoo Wongarbo NR Wongarbon Gollan Dapper NR Spring Ridge Ulan GOULBURN RIVER NATIONAL PARK Albert Gulgong Henry Lawson Centre Cooks Gap Wollar 'Alagala' Geurie Spicers Creek Goolma Terowie Wyanga Toongi Maryvale Bodangora Two Mile Flat Twelve Mile Home Rule Munghorn Gap NR Bylong Kerrabee Box Hill Cooyal Budgee Budgee Stormy Mtn Tal Tal Mtn Mt Emiguyley Montefiores Wellington Arthurville Tomingley Widden Tullamore McPhail Finger Post Maynggu Ganai Historic Site Dripstone Yarrabin Buckaroo Mudgee WOLLEMI 'Holbrook' Mt Pomany 'Numulla' Burrendong Dam Grattai Avisford NR Lue Nullo Mtn Breakfast Creek Mt Cox Dunmore Peak Hill Obley Walmer Yeoval Neurea Mumbil Apple Tree Flat Kadungle GOOBANG NAT PARK Trewilga Bakers Swamp Lower Mookerawa Hargraves Windeyer Windamere Dam Nullo Mtn Rylstone Mt Coriaday Mt Never Never Stuart Town Farnham Baldry Cudgegong Olinda Mt Coricudgy Trundle North Parkes Mine Goonumbla Alectown Cumnock Store Ck Pyramul Charbon Kandos Clandulla Finchs Caves Eucharenna Radio Telescope Blow Clear Sallys Flat Ilford Mt Coorongooba Bogee Tayan Peak Larras Lee Kerrs Creek Hill End Beargamil Running Stream Glen Alice Ganantagi Mtn Bogan Gate Gumble Molong Turondale Sofala Genowlan Mtn Glen Davis Yarrabandai Gunningbland Parkes Garra Mullion Creek Girralang NR Little Forest Bruinbun Wattle Flat GOOBANG NAT PARK Manildra Ophir Freemantle NR Capertee Turon NR Newnes Cookamidgera Bumberry Palmers Oakey Ben Bullen GARDENS OF STONE NATIONAL Tichborne Mandagery Borenore Barton Caves NR Borenore Cudal ORANGE Banjo Paterson Memorial Park Limekilns Corridgery Gallah Mtn PARK Warroo Bedgerebong Daroobalgie Toogong Bowen Park Nashdale Duramana Peel Winburndale NR Dark Corner Cullen Bullen Portland Forbes Barragan Mt Canobolas Lucknow Shadforth East Guyong Dunkeld BATHURST Sunny Corner Wallerawang Eugowra Murga Cargo Spring Hill Forest Reefs Meadow Flat Walang LITHGOW Nangar Nat Park Lachlan Millthorpe Perthville Yetholme Wambool NR Mt Wilson Bandon Mulyandry Benerce Browns Ck Blayney Georges Plains O'Connell Tarana Bell Garema Canowindra Evans Crown NR Hartley Berambing Lake Cowal Ooma Nth Gooloogong Belubula Mandurama Carcoar Newbridge Mt Victoria Blackheath Walli Barry Hampton BLUE MOUNTAINS Wirrinya Billimari Kangarooby Lyndhurst Hobbys Yards Rockley Oberon Katoomba Leura WESTERN Marsden Pullabooka Conimbla Garland Neville The Three Sisters Wentworth Falls Lawson Mt Wheoga Warraderry Woodstock Edith NATIONAL Caragabal Piney Range Bogolong Creek Sugarloaf Mtn CONIMBLA NAT PARK Holmwood Trunkey Creek Jenolan Caves Grenfell Cowra Copperhannia Nature Res Black Springs Spectacular Caves PARK WEDDIN MTNS NAT PARK Kellys Ck Broula War Museum Mount David McMahon Lookout KANANGRA Bland Bumbaldry Wattamondara Darbys Falls Lake Wyangala Abercrombie Caves Shooters Hill BOYD Lake Burragorang Black Spring Mtn Morongla Creek Greenethorpe Wyangala Abercrombie Burraga Kanangra Walls Lookout Quandialla Bimbi Tyagong Koorawatha Koorawatha NR Razorback Nature Res Tuena Isabella Porters Retreat NATIONAL PARK BLUE MOUNTAINS NAT PARK Iandra Biggal Nattai Bribbaree Breakfast Creek Graham Reids Flat ABERCROMBIE RIVER NAT PK Morangarell Thuddungra Wirrimah Blanket Flat Peelwood Old Silver Mining Town BLUE MOUNTAINS NAT PARK Yerranderie Lookout Boginderra Hills NR Monteagle Bendick Murrell Danabilla NR Godfreys Creek Limerick NATTAI Narraburra Mtn Tubbul Maimuru Mulgowrie Taylors Flat Fullerton Thirlmere Lakes NAT PARK Narraburra Grogan Milvale Young Murringo Frogmore Thalaba Binda Golspie Yalbraith Wombeyan Caves Wollondilly River NR Bullio Wilderness Area Barg Temora Wallundry Gunnary Phils Ck Richlands Joadja Tunnel NR High Range Colo Vale Combaning Springdale Wombat Kingsvale Boorowa Rugby Kennys Ck Narrawa Crookwell Laggan Taralga Historic Town 'Tugalong' Joadja Stockinbingal Yeo Yeo Wallendbeen Harden Rye Park Wheeo Roslyn Myrtleville Bannaby TARLO RIVER NAT PK Berrima Historic Village Mittagong Cootamundra Murrumburrah Galong Bevendale Grabben Gullen Kialla Chatsbury Moss Vale Bowral Sebastopol Dirnaseer Bradman's Cottage Beggan Beggan McMahons Reef Tangmangaroo Pudman Creek Biala Woodhouselee Greenwich Park Canyonleigh Exeter Sutton Forest Fitzroy Falls Frampton Binalong Blakney Creek Bannister Tarlo Brayton Junee Reefs Illalong Ck Goondah Dalton Kingsdale Towrang Paddys River Bundanoon Kangaroo Valley Bethungra Brawlin Ulandra NR Bowning Gunning GOULBURN Big Merino Marulan Wingello Tallong Fitzroy Falls Lake Yarrunga Bendeela

GREAT DIVIDING RANGE · MITCHELL HWY · OXLEY HWY · CASTLEREAGH HWY · NEWELL HWY · GOLDEN HWY · MID WESTERN HWY · GREAT WESTERN HWY · OLYMPIC WAY · LACHLAN VALLEY WAY · BURLEY GRIFFIN WAY · HUME HWY · Macquarie River · Bogan River · Lachlan River · Talbragar River · Cudgegong River · Turon River · Abercrombie River · Wollondilly River · Goulburn River · Little River · Belubula River · Lawson Way · Henry

148° · 149° · 150° · 32° · 33° · 34°

To Narrabri 8 To Tamworth 9 10 To Walcha 29 11 12 13 To Kempsey 14

Quirindi, Willow Tree, Murrurundi, Scone, Aberdeen, Muswellbrook, Denman, Singleton, Branxton, Cessnock, Maitland, Kurri Kurri, Raymond Terrace, Newcastle, Belmont, Swansea, Toronto, Morisset, Wyong, The Entrance, Gosford, Terrigal, Hornsby, Penrith, Parramatta, Liverpool, Sydney, Campbelltown, Camden, Picton, Wollongong, Port Kembla, Shellharbour, Kiama, Gerringong

Gloucester, Dungog, Stroud, Bulahdelah, Nelson Bay, Forster, Tuncurry, Taree, Wingham, Wauchope, Port Macquarie, Laurieton, Harrington, Old Bar, Pacific Palms, Hawks Nest, Tea Gardens, Karuah

GREAT DIVIDING RANGE

LIVERPOOL RANGE

BARRINGTON TOPS NAT PARK

MYALL LAKES NATIONAL PARK

YENGO NATIONAL PARK

ROYAL NATIONAL PARK

CROWDY BAY NATIONAL PARK

Opera House, Powerhouse Museum, Sydney Aquarium, Beautiful Harbour, Taronga Zoo, Sydney Tower, The Rocks, Darling Harbour.

For more details on this area, see Hema's Sydney to Brisbane Map

SEE PAGE 23

SEE PAGES 24-25

SOUTH PACIFIC OCEAN

TASMAN SEA

0 10 20 30 40 50 60km

1 2 3 4 5 6 7
A B C D E F G H J K

To St George
8
To Dalby
To Toowoomba
QUEENSLAND
149°
150°
151°
29°
30°
31°

'Whyenbah'
'Ardmore'
Balonne R
A55
HWY
Nindigully
CARNARVON
'Nariel'
'Mulga Ridge'
'Minnel'
A5
A39
Bendidee Nat Park
Commoron Ck
Bimbimbi'
118
46
'Leithmoor'
BARWON
Bungunya
Talwood
85
21 HWY
Toobeah
200
Dirranbandi
19
Noondoo
Thallon
Moonie R
Gradule
Goondiwindi
90
Yelarbon
101 102 28 29
Gibinbell
Kurumbul
'Johnstone'
Daymar
'Willarie'
Macintyre
River
Boggabilla
CASTLEREAGH
'Gleneve'
Boomi
Boomi NR
150
Boomi West NR
Boronga NR
Creek
39
'Redbank'
'Bullawarrie'
'Merriot'
Whalan
'Osterley'
44
116
Yetman
'Currawong'
North Star
BRUXNER
Glendalough Gate
Mungindi
Weemelah
'Jomara'
Creek
'Kiga'
Gil Gil
Boomi
CARNARVON
Garah
Careunga NR
123
Mt Mitchell
Yallaroi
Mt Russell
Croppa Creek
Planchonella NR
Mt Pleasant
'Whyalla'
'Gundablouie'
'Wongalee'
'Gingham'
121
NEWELL
'Birrah'
106
'Currigundi'
HWY
Crooble
Coolatai
Wallangra
'Banarway'
River
Gwydir
Ashley
Midkin NR
Milguy
Arakoola NR
95
'Dunumbral'
'Wandoona'
The Big Plane
'Manchester'
Bullarah
GWYDIR
38
Moree
'Myall Park'
377
'Warrinilla'
141
'Bundabarina'
Collarenebri
Pallamallawa
Balfours Peak
Graman
To Hebel
'Heathfield'
HWY
Biniguy
Gravesend Mtn
476
Warialda
Pokataroo
'Telleraga'
'Courallie'
Hadleigh
'Lourney'
Tycannah
Gragin Peak
'Poison Gate'
Gravesend
GWYDIR
Koloona
80
'Dungalear'
74
Barwon
Wah Wah Ck
Mt Jerrybang
Delungra
Mount Russel
'Bairnkine'
Merrywinebone
'Moomin'
Slaughterhouse
Kirramingly NR
Pinnacle
Mt Rodd
63
GWYDIR
38
Gurley
Cap & Bonnet Mtn
Elcombe
Rowena
128
'Thalaba'
Millie
98
Coffin Hill
Terry Hie Hie
Horton
Pian Creek
247 137 138
Bingara
'Eumanbah'
Wilminda
Bellata
Haystack Mtn
31
KAMILAROI
Cryon
Doreen
103
Dinoga
Walgett
216
Bugilbone
Nowley
River
Keera
Hot Spa Baths
Burren Junction
190
'Boolcarrol'
Mt Waa
Caroda
Grattai Mtn
Rocky Creek
Upper Bingara
CASTLEREAGH
'River View'
29
Castle Top Mtn
Grattai Wilderness Area
Edgeroi
Goangra
'Towrie'
Cubbaroo
Merah North
'Myall Vale'
Nandewar Wilderness Area
Mt Lindesay
'Trevallyn'
Upper Horton
To Bourke
Namoi
HWY
MT KAPUTAR NATIONAL PARK
Mt Drummond
Wee Waa
39
Mt Kaputar
Blue Nobby Mtn
Gull Ck
101
'Bugilbone'
'Drilldool'
Culgoora
388
Cobbadah
River
Australia Telescope
Narrabri
Mt Coryah
Mt Dowe
'The Furnace'
'Rocky Glen'
'Barlow'
'Bungle Gully'
Pilliga
Cuttabri
98
Narrabri West
Australian Cotton Centre
Rusden Wilderness Area
Come-By-Chance
Annual Picnic Races
Milchomi
Deriah Mtn
55
Woods Reef
Ironbark NR
Combogolong
'Yarrie Lake'
HWY
Turrawan
Barraba
Linton NR
117
KAMILAROI
Crow Mtn
Castlereagh
'Cubbo'
Mt Byar
'Wingadee'
Lucky Flat
Waterloo Pinnacle
Crow Mountain
Split Rock Dam
Warrabah NP
Gwabegar
Baan Baa
96
Goonbri Mtn
'Hobden'
'Gunyillah'
76
Mt Lowry
NEWELL
Upper Manilla
'Beanbah'
'Billeroy'
'Mayfield'
118
Boggabri
'Edale'
Merebene
'Halls Creek'
Gilgooma
370
Manilla
River
'Urawilkey'
Kenebri
37
Mt Binalong
Kelvin
Moonaran
Mundowey
Lake Keepit
Namoi
'Nebea'
67
Teridgerie
Emerald Hill
442
'Pine Grove'
Carroll Gap
MOONBI
Baradine
Pilliga Nature Reserve
325 171
182
Somerton
Attunga
Coonamble
Gunnedah
34
HWY
Tooloon
CASTLEREAGH
'Borah'
'Goohi'
Carroll
75
Moore Creek
'Blue Hills'
Wittenbra
King Jack Mtn
'Goorianawah'
45
Rocky Glen
OXLEY
Haystack Mtn
Mooki
Melville Range NR
Combara
Bugaldie
105
Mullaley
Sollys Mtn
Curlewis
439 440 441 209
'Budgeon'
Pilliga Nature Reserve
WARRUMBUNGLE
Yearinan
34
'Garrawilla'
'Allawah'
TAMWORTH
Country Music Capital
Nemingha
Mt Tenandra
'Brigalow'
'Mt Tenandra'
Bulga Mt
Nea
HWY
Piallaway
'Merri Merri'
Warrumbungle
Siding Spring Observatory
280
Mt Nombi
Duri Mtn
Duri
55
98
Gummin Gummin
Coonabarabran
Breeza
'Bourbah'
Mt Cenn Cruaich
WARRUMBUNGLE NATIONAL PARK
Ulamambri
'Currajong'
98
Currabubula
Gular
Gulargambone
Purlewaugh
'Ashgrove'
Goonoo Goonoo
Pine Clump
'Long Ridge'
Tambar Springs
Spring Ridge
37
Werris Creek
To Warren
Warkton
Deringulla
RANGE
Quirindi
74
'Bullagreen'
Armatree
Tooraweenah
Premer
Caroona
Quipolly
'Yarran'
Windurong
34
95
HWY
Murrawal
Castlereagh
Binnaway NR
Tamarang
Colly Blue
Quirindi
15
'Merrigal'
HWY
Curban
39
Binnaway
Pine Ridge
'The Ranch'
'Wallumburrawang'
Bomera
Castle Mtn
Wallabadah
Biddon
Ulinda
Bundella
Braefield
New Mollyann
Oakey Creek
Connemurra
Wallabadah NR
'Oakley'
Bearbung
Kamber
OXLEY
Weetaliba
Yarraman
To Dubbo
26
To Newcastle

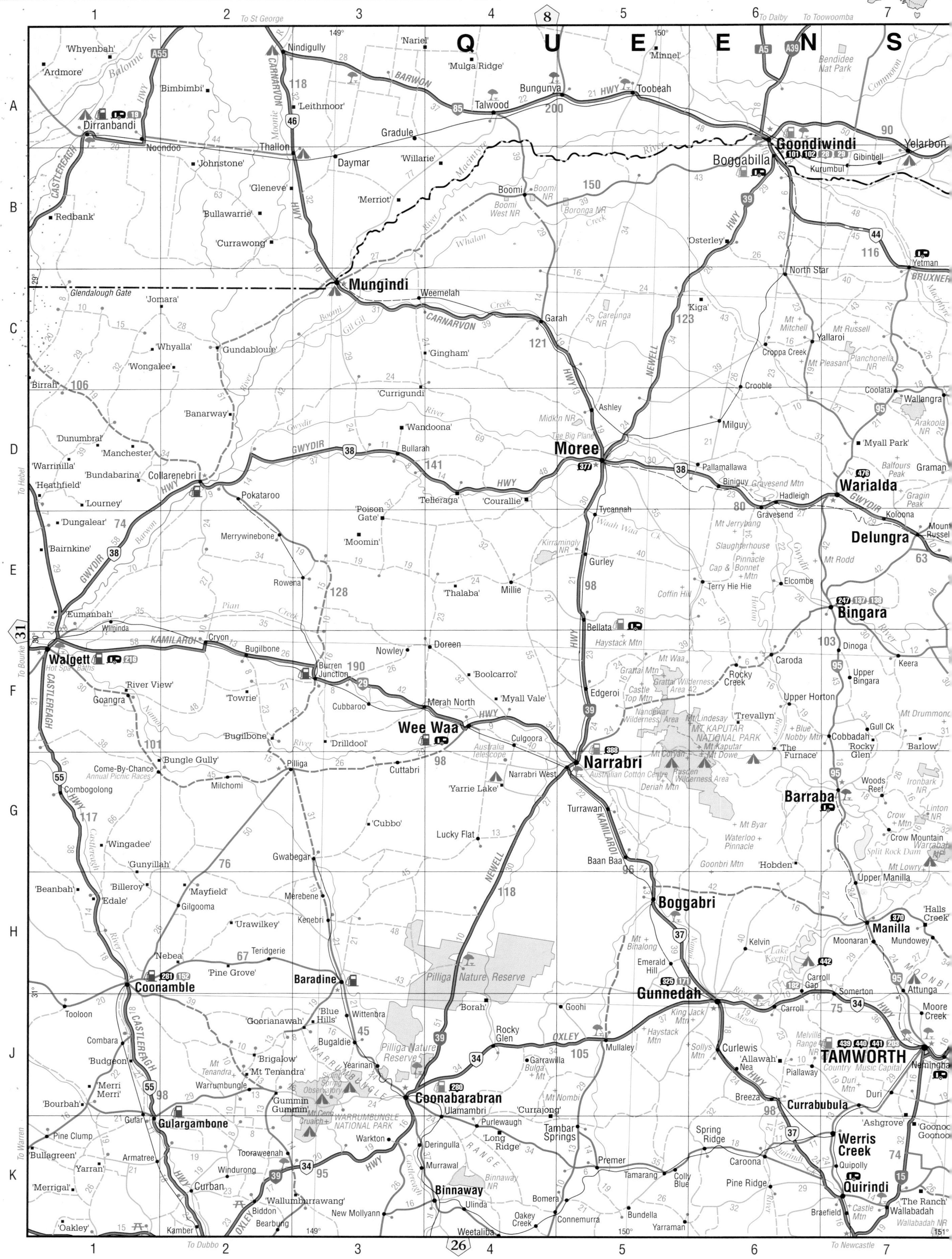

8
9
10
11
12
13
14
To Toowoomba, Brisbane
To Brisbane
To Brisbane, Surfers Paradise
L A N D
A
B
C
D
E
F
G
H
J
K
SOUTH
PACIFIC
OCEAN
Warwick
Stanthorpe
Texas
Inglewood
Whetstone
Karara
Tenterfield
Glen Innes
Inverell
Guyra
ARMIDALE
Uralla
Walcha
Coolangatta
Tweed Heads
Kingscliff
Murwillumbah
Pottsville
Mullumbimby
Brunswick Heads
Byron Bay
Lennox Head
Ballina
LISMORE
Casino
Kyogle
Woodenbong
Killarney
Rathdowney
Evans Head
Woodburn
Coraki
Maclean
Yamba
Iluka
GRAFTON
Ulmarra
Wooli
Woolgoolga
Coffs Harbour
Sawtell
Bellingen
Dorrigo
Urunga
Nambucca Heads
Macksville
South West Rocks
Kempsey
Crescent Head
Port Macquarie
Wauchope
Lake Cathie
Telegraph Point
Tingha
Bundarra
Ashford
Deepwater
Emmaville
Bonshaw
Mingoola
Drake
Tabulam
Bonalbo
Urbenville
Kootingal
Moonbi
Bendemeer
Nundle
Barry
Ellenborough
Yarras
Nowendoc
Tia
Yarrowitch
Kindee
Long Flat
Ebor
Jackadgery
Copmanhurst
Cangai
Newton Boyd
Nymboida
Glenreagh
Coramba
Frederickton
Smithtown
Gladstone
Hat Head
Kundabung
For more details on this area, see Hema's North East New South Wales Map
0 10 20 30 40 50km
© Hema Maps Pty Ltd

North-West New South Wales

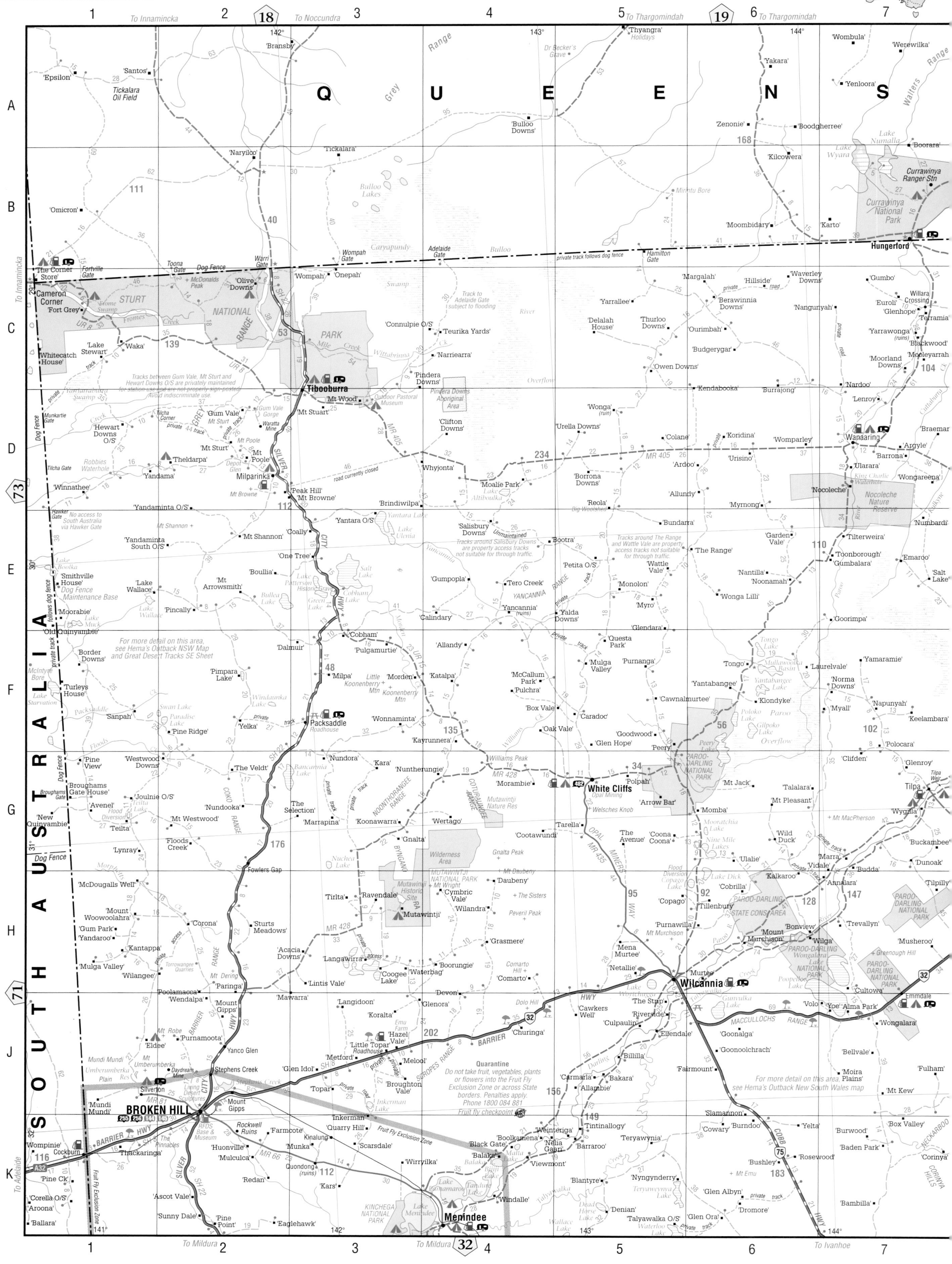

To Innamincka
To Noccundra
To Thargomindah
To Thargomindah
QUEENSLAND
'Epsilon'
'Santos'
Tickalara Oil Field
'Bransby'
Grey Range
'Thyangra' Holidays
Dr Becker's Grave
'Yakara'
'Wombula'
'Werewilka'
'Yenloora'
Walters Range
'Bulloo Downs'
'Zenonie'
'Boodgheree'
Lake Numalla
'Boorara'
'Naryilco'
'Tickalara'
'Kilcowera'
Lake Wyara
Currawinya Ranger Stn
Bulloo Lakes
Mirintu Bore
Currawinya National Park
'Omicron'
'Moombidary'
'Karto'
Hungerford
Cameron Corner
The Corner Store
Fortville Gate
Toona Gate
Dog Fence
Warri Gate
Wompah Gate
Caryapundy Swamp
Adelaide Gate
Bulloo
private track follows dog fence
Hamilton Gate
McDonalds Peak
'Olive Downs'
'Wompah'
'Onepah'
'Margalah'
'Hillside'
'Waverley Downs'
'Gumbo'
Willara Crossing
'Fort Grey'
Frome Swamp
STURT NATIONAL PARK
Track to Adelaide Gate subject to flooding
'Yarrallee'
'Berawinnia Downs'
'Euroli'
'Glenhope'
'Tarramia'
'Nangunyah'
'Connulpie O/S'
'Teurika Yards'
River
'Delalah House'
'Thurloo Downs'
'Ourimbah'
'Yarrawonga' (ruins)
'Blackwood'
'Lake Stewart'
'Waka'
'Budgeygar'
'Moorland Downs'
'Mooleyarrah'
Whitecatch House
'Narriearra'
Wittabrinna
'Owen Downs'
'Pindera Downs'
Overflow
Tracks between Gum Vale, Mt Sturt and Hewart Downs O/S are privately maintained for station use and are not properly sign-posted. Avoid indiscriminate use.
Tiboobura
'Mt Wood'
Outdoor Pastoral Museum
Pindera Downs Aboriginal Area
'Kendabooka'
'Burrajong'
'Nardoo'
'Lenroy'
Munkartie Gate
'Hewart Downs O/S'
Tilcha Corner
'Gum Vale'
Gum Vale Gorge
Waratta Mine
'Mt Stuart'
Mt Sturt
Mt Poole
'Mt Sturt'
'Clifton Downs'
'Wonga' (ruin)
'Urella Downs'
'Colane'
'Koridina'
'Womparley'
Wanaaring
'Braemar'
'Argyle'
'Barrona'
Robbies Waterhole
'Theldarpa'
'Mt Poole'
Depot Glen
Milparinka
road currently closed
'Whyjonta'
MR 405
'Ardoo'
'Urisino'
'Ularara'
'Wongareena'
Tilcha Gate
'Yandama'
'Winnathee'
'Peak Hill'
'Mt Browne'
Mt Browne
'Moalie Park'
Moalie Lake
Altiboulka
'Borrona Downs'
'Allundy'
'Mymong'
'Nocoleche'
Nocoleche Nature Reserve
King Charlie Waterhole
'Yandaminta O/S'
'Brindiwilpa'
'Reola'
Big Woolshed
Hawker Gate
No access to South Australia via Hawker Gate
Mt Shannon
'Yantara O/S'
Yantara Lake
Lake Ulenia
'Salisbury Downs'
Unmaintained
'Bundarra'
'Numbardi'
'Yandaminta South O/S'
'Mt Shannon'
'Coally'
Tracks around Salisbury Downs are property access tracks not suitable for through traffic.
'Bootra'
Tracks around The Range and Wattle Vale are property access tracks not suitable for through traffic.
'Garden Vale'
'Tilterweira'
Lake Bookia
'One Tree'
Yancannia
'Petita O/S'
'The Range'
'Toonborough'
'Gumbalara'
'Emaroo'
'Smithville House'
Dog Fence Maintenance Base
'Boullia'
Salt Lake
'Wattle Vale'
'Nantilla'
'Noonamah'
'Salt Lake'
'Lake Wallace'
'Mt Arrowsmith'
Lake Patterson Historic Grave
Bulleah Lake
Cobham Lake
Green Lake
'Gumpopla'
'Tero Creek'
YANCANNIA RANGE
'Monolon'
'Wonga Lilli'
'Moorabie'
Lake Wallace
'Pincally'
'Calindary'
'Yancannia' (ruins)
'Yalda Downs'
'Myro'
Lake Muck
'Old Quinyambie'
'Cobham'
'Glendara'
'Goorimpa'
For more detail on this area, see Hema's Outback NSW Map and Great Desert Tracks SE Sheet
'Questa Park'
'Border Downs'
'Dalmuir'
'Pulgamurtie'
'Allandy'
Tongo Lake
'Yamaramie'
McIntyre Bore
'Mulga Valley'
'Purnanga'
'Tongo'
Mullawoolka Basin
'Laurelvale'
'Pimpara Lake'
'Milpa'
Little Koonenberry Mtn
'Morden'
Koonenberry Mtn
'Katalpa'
'McCallum Park'
'Pulchra'
'Yantabangee'
Yantabangee Lake
'Norma Downs'
'Turleys House'
Lake Starvation
Windalanka Lake
'Cawnalmurtee'
'Klondyke'
'Napunyah'
'Myall'
'Sanpah'
Swan Lake
Paradise Lake
'Yelka'
Packsaddle Roadhouse
'Wonnaminta'
'Box Vale'
'Caradoc'
Poloko Lake
Paroo
'Keelambara'
'Pine Ridge'
'Kayrunnera'
'Oak Vale'
Gilpoko Lake
Overflow
'Goodwood'
'Glen Hope'
'Peery'
Peery Lake
'Polocara'
'Pine View'
'Westwood Downs'
'Nundora'
Williams Peak
'Clifden'
'Glenroy'
'Broughams Gate House'
'Kara'
Bancannia Lake
'The Veldt'
'Nuntherungie'
MR 428
NOONTHERANGEE RANGE
COTURAUNDEE RANGE
'Morambie'
White Cliffs
Opal Mining
'Polpah'
PAROO-DARLING NATIONAL PARK
'Mt Jack'
Tilpa
Tilpa Weir
'Avenel'
'Joulnie O/S'
Teilta Lake
'Nundooka'
CORONA RANGE
'The Selection'
Mutawintji Nature Res
Welsches Knob
'Arrow Bar'
'Talalara'
'Mt Pleasant'
'New Quinyambie'
Flood Diversion
'Teilta'
'Mt Westwood'
'Marrapina'
'Koonawarra'
'Wertago'
'Tarella'
'Momba'
Mooratchia Lake
Mt MacPherson
'Wyggilla'
'Floods Creek'
'Lynray'
Dog Fence
176
'Gnalta'
'Cootawundi'
'The Avenue'
'Coona Coona'
Nine Mile Lakes
'Wild Duck'
'Buckambee'
Nuchea Lake
BYNGANO RANGE
Wilderness Area
Gnalta Peak
OPAL MINERS WAY
MR 435
'Ulalie'
'Marra'
'Vidale'
'Budda'
'Dunoak'
Fowlers Gap
MUTAWINTJI NATIONAL PARK
Mt Daubeny
Flood Diversion
Lake Dick
Copago Lake
'Kalkaroo'
'McDougalls Well'
'Daubeny'
'Cobrilla'
'Annalara'
'Tilpilly'
'Tirlta'
'Ravendale'
Mutawintji Historic Site
Mt Wright
'Cymbric Vale'
The Sisters
'Copago'
'Tillenbury'
PAROO-DARLING STATE CONS AREA
PAROO-DARLING NATIONAL PARK
'Mount Woowoolahra'
'Mutawintji'
'Wilandra'
Peveril Peak
'Corona'
'Sturts Meadows'
'Gum Park'
'Yandaroo'
'Purnawilla'
Mt Murchison
'Bonview'
'Trevallyn'
'Mount Murchison'
'Wilga'
'Musheroo'
'Grasmere'
'Mena Murtee'
'Kantappa'
'Acacia Downs'
'Langawirra'
Torrowangee Quarries
Paroo
PAROO-DARLING Wongalara Lake NATIONAL PARK
Greenough Hill
PAROO-DARLING NATIONAL PARK
'Mulga Valley'
'Wilangee'
Mt Dering
'Paringa'
'Lintis Vale'
'Coogee Lake'
'Waterbag'
'Booringie'
Comarto Hill
'Comarto'
'Netallie'
'Murtee'
Wilcannia
Poopelloe Lake
'Cultowa'
'Poolamacca'
'Wendalpa'
'Mount Gipps'
'Mawarra'
'Langidoon'
'Devon'
Dolo Hill
Lake Wytchaqua
'Cawkers Well'
'The Stup'
'Riverside'
Gunvulka Lake
'Volo'
'Yoe'
'Alma Park'
Emmdale
'Koralta'
'Glenora'
Emu Farm
'Churinga'
MACCULLOCHS RANGE
'Wongalara'
Mt Robe
'Purnamoota'
BARRIER RANGE
'Hazel Vale'
'Little Topar' Roadhouse
202
'Culpaulin'
'Ellendale'
'Goonalga'
'Eldee'
Yanco Glen
'Metford'
'Meloof'
SCROPES RANGE
'Goonoolchrach'
'Bellvale'
Mundi Mundi
Mt Umberumberka
Daydream Mine
Umberumberka Res
'Glen Idol'
Quarantine
Do not carry fruit, vegetables, plants or flowers into the Fruit Fly Exclusion Zone across State borders. Penalties apply. Phone 1800 084 881
'Billilla'
'Fairmount'
'Moira Plains'
'Fulham'
Stephens Creek
Living Desert Sculptures
Silverton
'Broughton Vale'
'Carmarla'
'Bakara'
For more detail on this area, see Hema's Outback New South Wales map
'Mt Kew'
'Mundi Mundi'
BROKEN HILL
'Topar'
Inkerman Lake
'Allambie'
156
Mount Gipps
Fruit Fly checkpoint
'Inkerman'
'Quarry Hill'
149
'Slamannon'
'Box Valley'
RFDS Base & Museum
Rockwell Ruins
'Farmcote'
'Tintinallogy'
'Teryawynia'
'Coway'
'Burndoo'
'Yelta'
'Burwood'
'Wompinie'
Cockburn
'Thackaringa'
The Pinnacles
'Huonville'
Kinalung
'Munka'
'Scarsdale'
Fruit Fly Exclusion Zone
'Bookamena'
'Weinteriga'
'Nelia Gaari'
'Barraroo'
COBB HWY
'Baden Park'
NECKARBOO RANGE
'Mulculca'
MR 66
Quondong (ruins)
'Wirryilka'
Black Gate
'Balaka'
Balaka Lake
Malta Lake
'Viewmont'
'Bushley'
'Rosewood'
'Corinya'
CORINYA HILLS
'Pine Ck'
'Redan'
Lake Tandure
Lake Menamara
'Blantyre'
'Nyngynderry'
Mt Emu
'Corella O/S'
'Aroona'
'Ascot Vale'
'Kars'
'Windale'
Teryawynia Lake
'Glen Albyn'
'Dromore'
'Bambilla'
Dead Horse Lake
'Denian'
KINCHEGA NATIONAL PARK
Lake Menindee
'Sunny Dale'
'Pine Point'
Menindee
Wallace Lake
'Talyawalka O/S'
Waterloo Lake
'Glen Ora'
'Ballara'
'Eaglehawk'
Fruit Fly Exclusion Zone
To Adelaide
To Mildura
To Mildura
To Ivanhoe
SOUTH AUSTRALIA
SILVER CITY HWY
BARRIER HWY
A32
1 2 3 4 5 6 7
A B C D E F G H J K

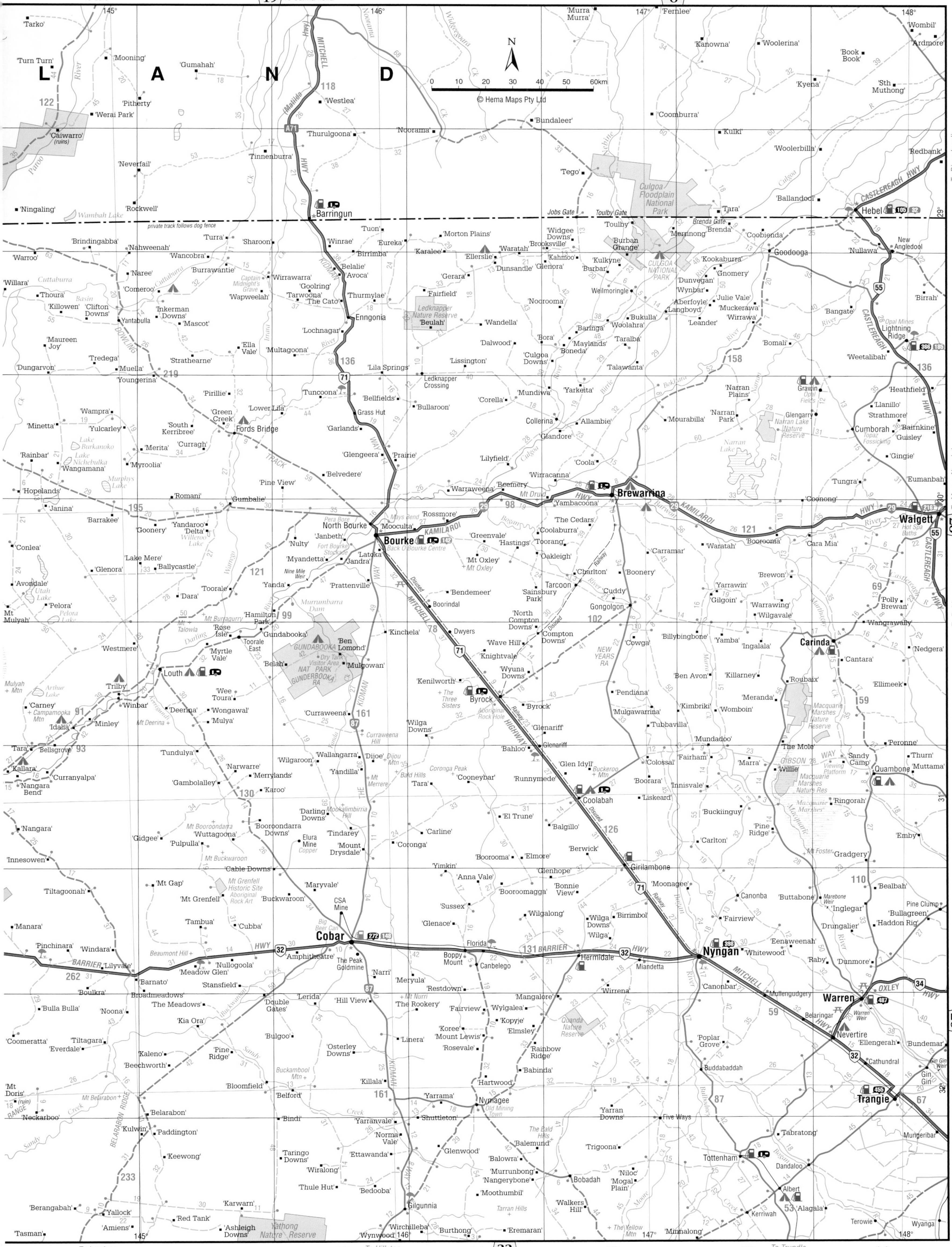

8 To Eulo 9 19 To Cunnamulla 10 11 12 8 13 14

145° 146° 147° 148°

Row A:
'Tarko' 'Turn Turn' 'Mooning' 'Gumahah' L A N D 'Pitherty' 'Werai Park' 'Caiwarro' (ruins) 122 118 'Westlea' 'Thurulgoona' Matilda Hwy MITCHELL HWY 'Noorama' 'Bundaleer' 'Murra Murra' 'Fernlee' 'Kanowna' 'Woolerina' 'Book Book' 'Wombil' 'Ardmore' 'Kyena' 'Sth Muthong' 'Coomburra' 'Kulki' 0 10 20 30 40 50 60km © Hema Maps Pty Ltd

Row B:
'Neverfail' 'Tinnenburra' 'Ningaling' 'Rockwell' Wambah Lake Barringun 'Tego' Culgoa Floodplain National Park Jobs Gate Toulby Gate 'Tara' 'Woolerbilla' 'Redbank' 'Ballandool' Hebel 105 CASTLEREAGH HWY To Dirranbandi private track follows dog fence

Row C:
'Brindingabba' 'Warroo' 'Willara' 'Nahweenah' 'Wancobra' 'Turra' 'Sharoon' 'Tuon' 'Eureka' 'Winrae' 'Birrimba' 'Morton Plains' 'Karalee' 'Ellerslie' 'Waratah' 'Widgee Downs' 'Brooksville' 'Dunsandle' 'Kahmoo' 'Glenora' 'Toulby' 'Burban Grange' 'Brenda' 'Merrinong' 'Coobienda' Goodooga 'Nullawa' New Angledool 'Naree' 'Burrawantie' 'Wirrawarra' 'Belalie' 'Avoca' 'Gerara' 'Kulkyne' 'Burbar' Culgoa National Park 'Kookaburra' 'Gnomery' 'Dunvegan' 'Wynbar' 'Thoura' 'Comeroo' 'Goolring' 'Tarwoona' 'Thurmylae' 'Fairfield' Weilmoringle 'Julie Vale' 'Birrah' 'Killowen' 'Clifton Downs' Yantabulla 'Inkerman Downs' 'Mascot' 'Wapweelah' 'The Cato' Enngonia Ledknapper Nature Reserve 'Beulah' 'Noorooma' 'Aberfoyle' 'Langboyd' 'Muckerawa' 'Wirrawa' 'Leander' 'Bangate' 'Wandella' 'Bukulla' 'Woolahra' 'Baringa' 'Maureen Joy' 'Lochnagar' 'Dalwood' 'Bora' 'Maylands' 'Boneda' 'Taralba' 'Bomali' Lightning Ridge Opal Mines 'Ella Vale' 'Multagoona' 'Tredega' 'Strathearne' 136 'Lissington' 'Culgoa Downs' 'Talawanta' 158 'Weetalibah' 'Dungarvon' 'Muella' 'Youngerina' 219 'Lila Springs' Ledknapper Crossing 136

Row D:
'Pirillie' 'Wampra' 'Yulcarley' 'Minetta' 'Lower Lila' 'Green Creek' Fords Bridge 'South Kerribree' 'Curragh' 'Merita' 'Tuncoona' 'Bellfields' 'Grass Hut' 'Bullaroon' 'Corella' 'Mundiwa' 'Yarkeita' 'Narran Plains' Grawin Opal Fields 'Heathfield' 'Llanillo' 'Strathmore' Glengarry 'Narran Park' Narran Lake Nature Reserve 'Mourabilla' 'Allambie' Collerina Glandore Cumborah 'Bairnkine' 'Guisley' 'Garlands' 'Glengeera' 'Prairie' 'Lilyfield' 'Coola' Narran Lake 'Gingie' 'Rainbar' Lake Burkanoko Lake Nichebulka 'Wangamana' 'Myroolia' 'Belvedere' 'Wirracanna' 'Hopelands' Murphys Lake 'Pine View' 'Romani' 'Gumbalie' 'Warraweena' 'Beemery' Mt Druid Brewarrina 'Tungra' 'Eumanbah' 'Janina' 195

Row E:
'Barrakee' 'Goonery' 'Yandaroo' 'Delta' Willeroo Lake 'Rossmore' North Bourke 'Mooculta' 'Yambacoona' 'The Cedars' 'Coonong' KAMILAROI HWY 121 'Walgett' Hot Spa Baths 'Conlea' 'Nulty' 'Janbeth' Bourke Back O'Bourke Centre 'Greenvale' 'Hastings' 'Toorang' 'Coolabarra' 'Booroona' 'Waratah' 'Cara Mia' 'Carramar' 'Lake Mere' 'Ballycastle' 'Myandetta' 'Latoka' 'Jandra' 'Mt Oxley' 'Oakleigh' 'Glenora' 121 'Charlton' 'Booney' 'Brewon' 'Avondale' Utah Lake 'Toorale' 'Yanda' Nine Mile Weir 'Prattenville' 'Bendemeer' 'Sainsbury Park' Tarcoon 'Cuddy' 'Yarrawin' 'Gilgoin' 69 'Polly Brewan' 'Pelora' Pelora Lake 'Dara' Murrumbarra Dam Boorindal 'North Compton Downs' Gongolgon 102 'Warrawing' 'Wilgavale' 'Mt Mulyah' 'Hamilton Park' 99 Mt Burragurry

Row F:
'Rose Isle' 'Gundabooka' 'Kinchela' Dwyers 'Wave Hill' 'Compton Downs' 'Billybingbone' 'Yamba' 'Ingalala' Carinda 'Cantara' 'Nedgera' 'Wangrawally' 'Westmere' Toorale East 'Myrtle Vale' Gundabooka Nat Park 'Ben Lomond' 'Belah' 'Mulgowan' 'Knightvale' 'Wyuna Downs' NEW YEARS RA 'Cowga' 'Ben Avon' 'Killarney' 'Roubaix' 'Ellimeek' Louth 'Trilby' 'Wee Toura' 'Kenilworth' The Three Sisters Byrock Aboriginal Rock Hole 'Byrock' 'Pendiana' 'Meranda' Macquarie Marshes Nature Reserve 'Carney' Campamoka Mtn 'Winbar' 'Deerina' 'Wongawal' 'Mulya' 'Minley' 'Idalia' 91 'Curraweena' 161 'Wilga Downs' 'Glenariff' 'Mulgawarrina' 'Kimbriki' 'Womboin' 159 'Tubbavilla'

Row G:
'Tara' 'Bellsgrove' 93 'Kallara' 'Curranyalpa' 'Nangara Bend' 'Tundulya' 'Narwarre' 'Merrylands' 'Wilgaroon' 'Wallangarra' 'Dijoe' 'Yandilla' Glenariff 'Bahloo' 'Mundadoo' The Mole 'Peronne' 'Thurn' 'Muttama' 'Fairham' 'Colossal' 'Marra' 'Willie' Sandy Camp Quambong 'Gambolalley' 130 'Karoo' 'Tara' Coronga Peak 'Cooneybar' 'Runnymede' 'Glen Idyll' Buckeroo Mtn 'Boorara' 'Innisvale' Macquarie Marshes Nature Res 'Ringorah' Coolabah 'Liskeard' 'Nangara' 'Booroondarra Downs' Mt Booroondarra 'Wuttagoona' 'Darling Downs' Mookalimbirria Hill 'El Trune' 'Buckiinguy' 'Gidgee' 'Pulpulla' Elura Mine Copper 'Tindarey' 'Carline' 'Balgillo' 'Pine Ridge' 'Emby' 'Innesowen' Mt Buckwaroon 'Mount Drysdale' 'Coronga' 126 'Carlton' 'Berwick' Mt Foster 'Gradgery' 'Booroomba' 'Elmore' 'Yimkin' Girilambone

Row H:
'Cable Downs' 'Tiltagoonah' 'Mt Gap' Mt Grenfell Historic Site Aboriginal Rock Art 'Mt Grenfell' 'Buckwaroon' 'Maryvale' 'Anna Vale' 'Glenhope' 'Booroomagga' 'Bonnie View' 'Moonagee' 110 'Bealbah' 'Canonba' 'Buttabone' Marebone Weir 'Inglegar' 'Pine Clump' 'Bullagreen' 'Haddon Rig' CSA Mine 'Sussex' 'Wilgalong' 'Birrimbol' 'Wilga Downs' 'Fairview' 'Drungalier' 'Manara' 'Tambua' 'Cubba' 'Glenace' 'Wilga' 'Pinchinara' 'Windara' Cobar Big Bear Can 'Eenaweenah' 'Whitewood' Nyngan 'Raby' 'Dunmore' Amphitheatre The Peak Goldmine Florida Boppy Mount Canbelego 131 BARRIER HWY Hermidale Miandetta BARRIER HWY 'Lilyvale' 262 Beaumont Hill 'Meadow Glen' 'Nullogoola' 'Barnato' 'Narri' 'Stansfield'

Row J:
'Boulkra' Broadmeadows 'The Meadows' 'Meryula' 'Restdown' Mangalore 'Wirrena' Canonbar 'Mullengudgery' OXLEY HWY Warren 'Bulla Bulla' 'Noona' 'Double Gates' 'Lerida' 'Hill View' Mt Nurri 'The Rookery' 'Fairview' 'Wylgalea' Quanda Nature Reserve 59 Belaringar Warren Weir Nevertire 'Ellengerah' 'Bundemar' 'Kia Ora' 'Kopyje' 'Elmsley' 'Coomeratta' 'Tiltagara' 'Everdale' 'Bulgoo' 'Koree' 'Mount Lewis' 'Linera' 'Poplar Grove' 'Kaleno' 'Pine Ridge' 'Osterley Downs' 'Rosevale' 'Rainbow Ridge' Cathundral Gin Gin Weir 'Beechworth' Buckambool Mtn 'Babinda' Buddabaddah 'Mt Doris' (ruin) 'Bloomfield' 'Killala' 'Hartwood' 87 Trangie 67 RANGE Mt Belarabon 'Belford' 161 'Yarrama' Nymagee Old Mining Town 'Yarran Downs' 'Neckarboo' 'Belarabon' BELARABON RIDGE 'Bindi' 'Yarranvale' 'Shuttleton' Five Ways 'Tabratong' 'Mungeribar'

Row K:
'Kulwin' 'Paddington' 'Norma Vale' The Bald Hills 'Balemund' 'Trigoona' Tottenham Dandaloo 'Keewong' 'Taringo Downs' 'Ettawanda' 'Glenwood' 'Balowra' 'Niloc' 'Mogal Plain' 233 'Wiralong' 'Murrunbong' 'Nangerybone' Bobadah Albert 'Thule Hut' 'Bedooba' 'Moothumbil' 53 'Alagala' 'Berangabah' 'Yallock' 'Karwarn' Gilgunnia Tarran Hills 'Walkers Hill' Kerriwah 'Red Tank' 'Amiens' 'Ashleigh Downs' Yathong Nature Reserve 'Wirchilleba' 'Burthong' 'Eremaran' The Yellow Mtn 'Minnalong' Terowie Wyanga 'Tasman' 'Wynwood'

Right margin: To Dirranbandi, To Moree, Narrabri, 28, To Dubbo, To Gilgandra, 26, To Dubbo
A B C D E F G H J K

8 To Ivanhoe 9 10 To Hillston 11 33 12 13 To Trundle 14

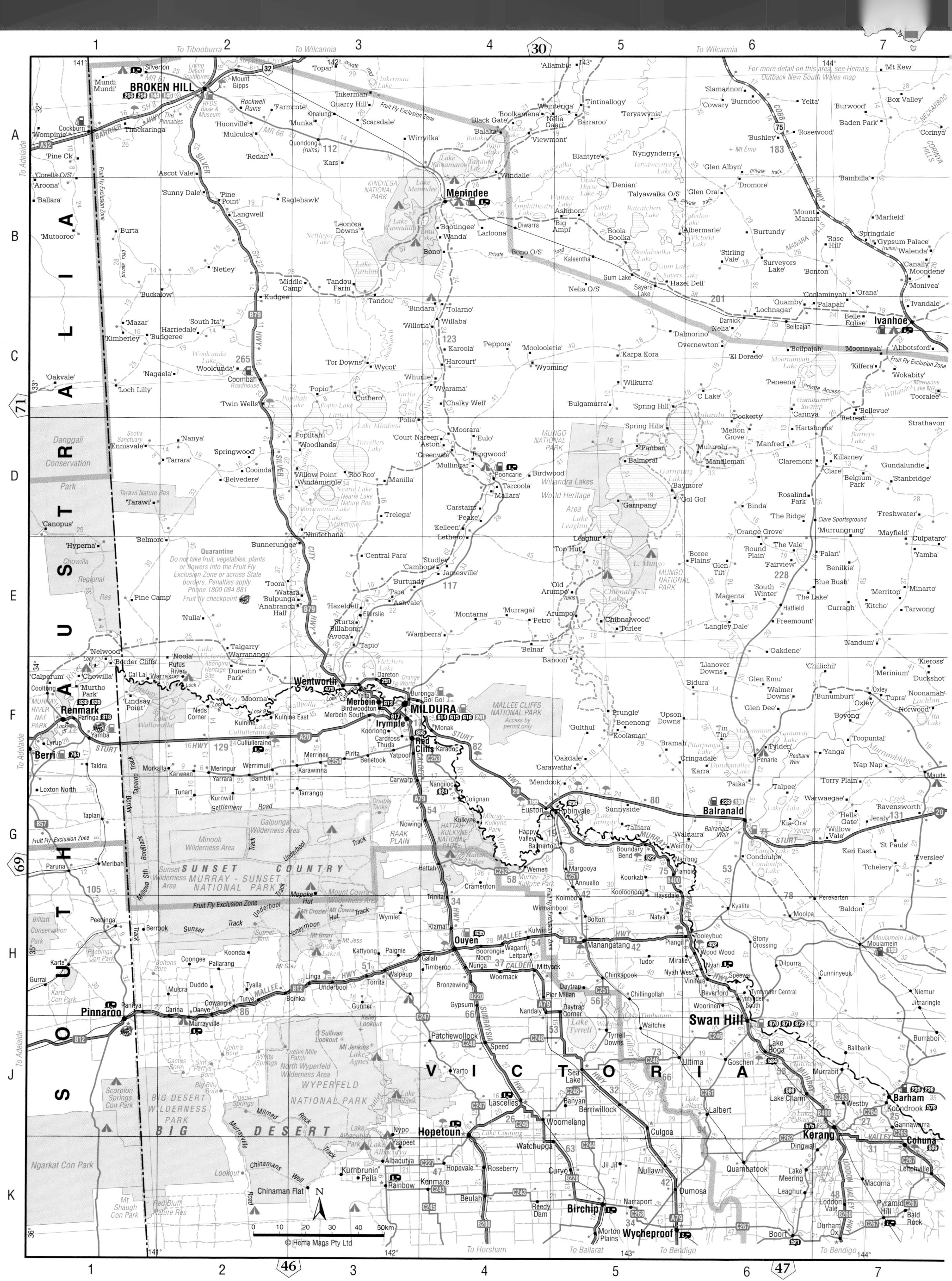

To Tibooburra
To Wilcannia
To Wilcannia
30
For more detail on this area, see Hema's Outback New South Wales map
BROKEN HILL
Silverton
Mundi Mundi
Mount Gipps
Rockwell Ruins
RFDS Base & Museum
The Pinnacles
Thackaringa
Cockburn
Wompinie
Pine Ck
Corella O/S
Aroona
Ballara
Mutooroo
Burta
Farmcote
Huonville
Mulculca
Redan
Quondong (ruins)
Kars
Topar
Inkerman
Quarry Hill
Kinalung
Munka
Scarsdale
Fruit Fly Exclusion Zone
Wirryilka
Ascot Vale
Sunny Dale
Pine Point
Eaglehawk
Langwell
Netley
Buckalow
Kudgee
Middle Camp
Tandou Farm
Tandou
Leonora Downs
KINCHEGA NATIONAL PARK
Lake Menindee
Lake Cawndilla
Menindee
Bootingee
Wanda
Bono
Larloona
Diwarra
Bono O/S
Allambie
Weinteriga
Bookkamena
Nelia Gaari
Tintinallogy
Barraroo
Teryawynia
Black Gate
Balaka
Viewmont
Windalle
Blantyre
Nyngynderry
Denian
Talyawalka O/S
Ashmont
Big Ampi
Kaleentha
Boola Boolka
Albermarle
Glen Oral
Glen Albyn
Dromore
Slamannon
Cowary
Burndoo
Yelta
Burwood
Box Valley
Mt Kew
Baden Park
Corinya
Bushley
Rosewood
Bambilla
Mount Manara
Marfield
Burtundy
Stirling Vale
Surveyors Lake
Bonton
Rose Hill
Springdale
Gypsum Palace
Walenda
Canally
Moondene
Monivea
Hazel Dell
Gum Lake
Sayers Lake
Nelia O/S
Coolaminyah
Orana
Quamby
Palapah
Lochnagar
Ivandale
Darnick
Nelia
Belle Eglise
Beilpajah
Ivanhoe
Dalmorino
Overnewton
El Dorado
Moorinyah
Abbotsford
Kilfera
Wokabity
Toorale
Mazar
Kimberley
South Ita
Harriedale
Budgeree
Woolcunda
Coombah Roadhouse
Nagaela
Loch Lilly
Oakvale
Bindara
Tolarno
Willaba
Willotia
Karoola
Peppora
Mooloolerie
Wyoming
Karpa Kora
Tor Downs
Wycot
Harcourt
Whurlie
Wyarama
Chalky Well
Popio
Cuthero
Twin Wells
Wilkurra
Bulgamurra
Spring Hill
C Lake
Peneena
Carinya
Bellevue
Retreat
Strathavon
Polia
Moorara
Eulo
Court Nareen
Aston
Greenvale
Ringwood
Mullingar
Pooncarie
Birdwood
Tarcoola
Mallara
MUNGO NATIONAL PARK
Willandra Lakes World Heritage Area
Spring Hills
Panban
Balmoral
Mulurulu
Mandleman
Baymore
Gol Gol
Garnpang
Melton Grove
Dockerty
Manfred
Hartshoms
Claremont
Killarney
Clare
Gundalundie
Belgium Park
Stanbridge
Rosalind Park
Binda
The Ridge
Clare Sportsground
Freshwater
Orange Grove
Murrungrung
Mayfield
Culpataro
Nanya
Scotia Sanctuary
Ennisvale
Tarrara
Springwood
Cooinda
Belvedere
Popiltah
Woodlands
Willow Point
Windamingle
Roo Roo
Manilla
Trelega
Carstairs
Peake
Kelleen
Lethero
Leaghur
Top Hut
Danggali Conservation Park
Tarawi Nature Res
Tarawi
Canopus
Hyperna
Chowilla Regional Res
Belmore
Quarantine
Do not take fruit, vegetables, plants or flowers into the Fruit Fly Exclusion Zone or across State borders. Penalties apply. Phone 1800 084 881
Fruit fly checkpoint
Bunnerungee
Nindethana
Central Para
Studley
Camborn
Jamesville
Boree Plains
Glen Tilt
The Vale
Round Plain
Fairview
Palari
Yamba
Benilkie
Pine Camp
Toora
Watara
Bulpunga
Anabranch Hall
Burtundy
Para
Ashvale
Old Arumpo
Arumpo
L. Mungo
Chibnalwood Lakes
Magenta
South Winter
The Lake
Blue Bush
Merritop
Minarto
Kitcho
Tarwong
Curragh
Hatfield
Freemount
Langley Dale
Nulla
Hazeldell
Ellerslie
Sturts Billabong
Avoca
Tapio
Wamberra
Montarna
Murragai
Petro
Chibnalwood
Turlee
Belnar
Banoon
Nandum
Oakdene
Kieross
Duckshot
Nelwood
Border Cliffs
Noola
Talgarry
Warrananga
Rufus River
Dunedin Park
Calperum
Chowilla
Cooltong
Murtho Park
Renmark
Paringa
Lyrup
Yamba
Berri
Lindsay Point
Wentworth
Dareton
Moorna
Neds Corner
Kulnine
Kulnine East
Merbein
Birdwoodton
Merbein South
Buronga
Gol Gol
MILDURA
MALLEE CLIFFS NATIONAL PARK
Access by permit only
Irymple
Koorlong
Cardross
Thurla
Red Cliffs
Yatpool
Karadoc
Monak
Sturt
Llanover Downs
Bidura
Prungle
Benenong
Upson Downs
Gulthul
Koolaman
Bramah
Oakdale
Carawatha
Cringadale
Karra
Glen Emu
Walmer Downs
Glen Dee
Tin Tin
Tylden
Penarie
Redbank Weir
Chillichil
Merinium
Oxley
Noonamah
Tupra
Norwood
Bunumburt
Boyong
Toopuntal
Yanga
Nap Nap
Torry Plain
Maude
Talpee
Paika
Warwaegae
Ravensworth
Jeraly
Hells Gate
Willow Vale
Kia-Ora
Yanga NP
Keri East
St Pauls
Tchelery
Everslee
Condoulpe
Taldra
Loxton North
Morkalla
Meringur
Karween
Werrimull
Yarrara
Bambill
Merrinee
Karawinna
Pirlta
Benetook
Carwarp
Tarrango
Kurnwill
Tunart
Settlement Road
Cullulleraine
Nangiloc
Colignan
Mendook
Euston
Robinvale
Sunnyside
Balranald
Taplan
Galpunga Wilderness Area
Minook Wilderness Area
Nowingi
RAAK PLAIN
HATTAH-KULKYNE NATIONAL PARK
Kulkyne
Murray-Kulkyne Park
Happy Valley
Bannerton
Talliara
Waldaira
Balranald Weir
Weimby
Boundary Bend
Narrung
Tol Tol
Hattah
Wemen
Margooya
Annuello
Koorkab
Piambie
Cramenton
Meribah
Paruna
SUNSET COUNTRY
MURRAY - SUNSET NATIONAL PARK
Sunset Wilderness Area
Mopoke Hut
Mt Crozier
Mt Cowra Hut
Mount Cowra Wilderness Area
Honeymoon Track
Underbool Track
Sunset Track
Berrook
Billiatt Conservation Park
Peebinga
Peebinga Con Park
Karte
Karte Con Park
Gurrai
Koonda
Coongee
Pallarang
Kattyong
Paignie
Wymlet
Mt Jess
Mt Gnarr
Pink Lakes
Trinita
Klamat
Kolmbo
Winnambool
Bolton
Koolooonong
Haysdale
Natya
Kyalite
Perekerten
Baldon
Moolpa
Ouyen
Mallee Hwy
Kulwin
Manangatang
Boorongie North
Wagant
Leitpar
Galah
Timberoo
Nunga
Calder
Woornack
Mittyack
Piangil
Tooleybuc
Wood Wood
Tudor
Miralie
Nyah
Nyah West
Vinifera
Speewa
Stony Crossing
Moulamein
Moulamein Lake
Dilpurra
Cunninyeuk
Niemur
Jimaringle
Duddo
Mulcra
Tyalla
Tutye
Linga
Torrita
Walpeup
Underbool
Bronzewing
Gypsum
Chinkapook
Chillingollah
Pier Millan
Daytrap
Daytrap Corner
Nandaly
Beverford
Tyntynder Central
Tyntynder South
Woorinen
Swan Hill
Pinnaroo
Parilla
Carina
Danyo
Cowangie
Murrayville
Boinka
Gunner
Kelley Lookout
Patchewollock
Speed
Lake Tyrrell
Tyrrell Downs
Waitchie
Lake Timboram
Ultima
Goschen
Lake Boga
Murrabit
Ballbank
Burraboi
O'Sullivan Lookout
Mt Jenkins
Lake Agnes
Twelve Mile Patch
North Wyperfeld Wilderness Area
WYPERFELD NATIONAL PARK
Yarto
VICTORIA
SOUTH AUSTRALIA
Sea Lake
Banyan
Berriwillock
Lalbert
Lake Charm
Westby
Koondrook
Gannawarra
Barham
Kerang
Cohuna
Scorpion Springs Con Park
BIG DESERT WILDERNESS PARK
BIG DESERT
Pigeon Springs
Milmed Rock
Murrayville Track
Lake Albacutya
Albacutya Park
Nypo
Yaapeet
Albacutya
Hopetoun
Lascelles
Woomelang
Culgoa
Watchupga
Dingwall
Quambatook
Leitchville
Lake Meering
Leaghur
Macorna
Ngarkat Con Park
Lookout
Chinamans Well
Chinaman Flat
Kurnbrunin
Pella
Rainbow
Hopevale
Roseberry
Kenmare
Beulah
Curyo
Jil Jil
Nullawil
Dumosa
Birchip
Narraport
Reedy Dam
Wycheproof
Morton Plains
Boort
Loddon Vale
Pyramid Hill
Bald Rock
Durham Ox
Mt Shaugh Con Park
Red Bluff Nature Res
0 10 20 30 40 50km
© Hema Maps Pty Ltd
To Adelaide
To Horsham
To Ballarat
To Bendigo
To Bendigo
141°
142°
143°
144°
32°
33°
34°
35°
36°
1 2 3 4 5 6 7
A B C D E F G H J K
46
47
69
71

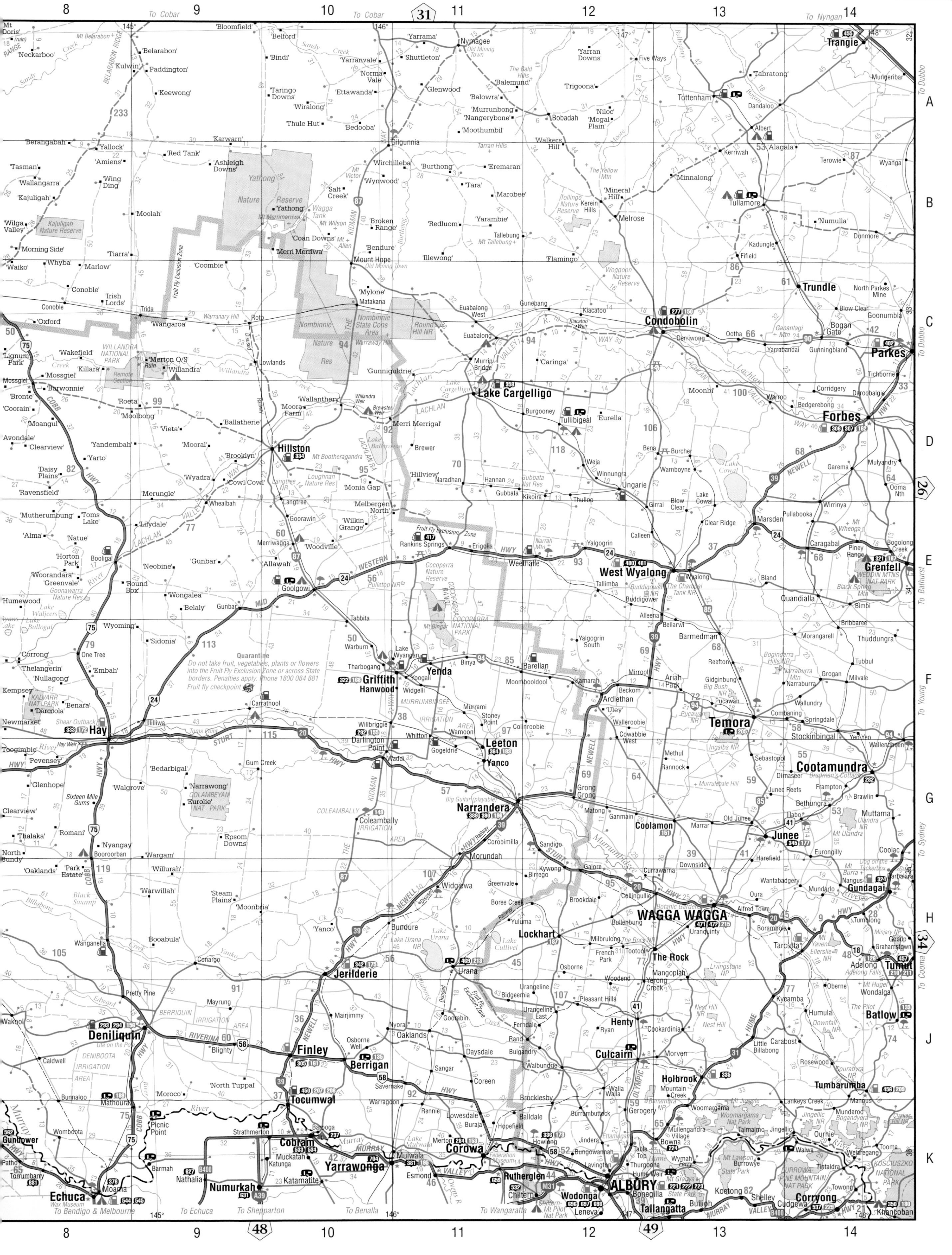

8 9 10 11 12 13 14

To Cobar
To Cobar
31
To Nyngan

A B C D E F G H J K

Trangie
Tottenham
Tullamore
Trundle
Condobolin
Parkes
Forbes
Lake Cargelligo
Hillston
West Wyalong
Grenfell
Ungarie
Temora
Griffith
Hanwood
Yenda
Leeton
Yanco
Narrandera
Hay
Cootamundra
Junee
Coolamon
Gundagai
WAGGA WAGGA
Lockhart
The Rock
Tumut
Jerilderie
Deniliquin
Finley
Berrigan
Culcairn
Holbrook
Henty
Batlow
Tumbarumba
Tocumwal
Cobram
Yarrawonga
Corowa
Rutherglen
ALBURY
Wodonga
Tallangatta
Corryong
Numurkah
Echuca
Moama
Mathoura
Nymagee
Gilgunnia
Mount Hope
Rankins Springs
Goolgowi
Darlington Point
Whitton
Coleambally
Urana
Oaklands
Walla Walla
Khancoban

To Dubbo
To Bathurst
To Young
To Sydney
To Cooma
To Bendigo & Melbourne
To Echuca
To Shepparton
To Benalla
To Wangaratta

Do not take fruit, vegetables, plants or flowers into the Fruit Fly Exclusion Zone or across State borders. Penalties apply. Phone 1800 084 881
Fruit fly checkpoint

48
49
26
34

South-East New South Wales

1 2 3 4 5 6 7

To Cowra · To Sydney · To Wagga Wagga, Albury · To Albury · To Orbost · To Cann River · To Cann River

SEE PAGES 24-25

SEE PAGE 38

Tyagong, Iandra, Thuddungra, Koorawatha NR, Breakfast Creek, Wirrimah, Monteagle, Bendick Murrell, Danabilla NR, Godfreys Creek, Maimuru, Young, Murringo, Wombat, Kingsvale, Boorowa, Burley Griffin Way, Wallendbeen, Murrumburrah, Harden, Galong, Rye Park, Cootamundra, Bradman's Cottage, McMahons Reef, Beggan Beggan, Binalong, Illalong Ck, Tangmangaroo, Goondah, Brawlin, Muttama, Jugiong, Hume, Bowning, Bookham, Yass, Woolgarlo, Good Hope, Talmo, Childowlah, Coolac, Dog on the Tuckerbox, Gobarralong, Burrinjuck, Burrinjuck NR, Darbalara, Black Andrew NR, Burrinjuck Dam, Oak Creek NR, Carey's Cave, Gundagai, Adjungbilly, Wee Jasper, Wee Jasper NR, Brungle, Mudjarn NR, Tumorrama, Minjary NR, Gocup, Grahamstown, Tumut, Lacmalac, Adelong, Adelong Falls, Wondalga, Blowering Res, Brindabella, Bogong Peaks Wilderness Area, Goobarragandra Wilderness Area, Batlow, Talbingo, Tumut 3 PS, Yarrangobilly, Bimbari Peak, Tantangara Res, Talbingo Reservoir, Yarrangobilly Caves, Rules Pt, Tumbarumba, Ravine, Mt Selwyn, Kiandra, Clarkes Hill NR, Tumut 2 PS, Bogandyera NR, Cabramurra, Australia's Highest Town, Tooma, Tumut 1 PS, Tumut Pond Res, Old Adaminaby, Adaminaby, Tooma Res, Jagungal Wilderness Area, Mt Jagungal 2060m, Eucumbene Cove, Lake Eucumbene, Buckenderra, Nimmo NR, Middingbank, Khancoban, Murray 1 PS, Khancoban Dam, Kosciuszko National Park, Geehi Res, Guthega, Island Bend, Lake Jindabyne, Olsens Lookout, Geehi, Charlotte Pass, Perisher, Smiggin Holes, Skitube, Jindabyne, Mt Kosciuszko 2229m, Australia's Highest Mountain, Thredbo, Dead Horse Gap, Tom Groggin, Pilot Lookout, Moonbah, Ngadang NR, Beloka, Paupong NR, Paupong, Ingebirah, Pilot Wilderness Area, The Pilot 1829m, Byadbo Wilderness Area, Byadbo Mtn 1236m, Alpine National Park, Cobberas Wilderness Area, Willis, Tingaringy Wilderness Area, Delegate River, Bonang, Snowy River National Park, Goongerah, Errinundra National Park

Graham, Reids Flat, Bigga, Razorback Nature Res, Blanket Flat, Lachlan, Mulgowrie, Taylors Flat, Frogmore, Gunnary, Phils Ck, Rugby, Kennys Ck, Narrawa, Crookwell, Wheeo, Bevendale, Grabben Gullen, Kialla, Biala, Pudman Creek, Blakney Creek, Bannister, Dalton, Gunning, Jerrawa, Breadalbane, Cullerin, Mundoonen NR, Collector, Bellmount Forest, Murrumbateman, Barton Hwy, Gundaroo, Cavan, Currawang, Lake Bathurst, Tarago, Lake George, Sutton, Hall, Ginninderra Falls, Belconnen, Bywong, Gooroowang NR, CANBERRA, Parliament House, National Gallery, Science & Technology Centre, Mint, War Memorial, National Aquarium, QUEANBEYAN, Kings Hwy, Cuumbeun NR, Bungendore, Scott NR, Tuggeranong, Bendoura Dam, Australian Capital Territory, Corin Dam, Tharwa, Royalla, Burra Ck NR, Burra, Williamsdale, Namadgi Wilderness, Namadgi National Park, Tourist Railway, Tinderry NR, Michelago, Scabby Range NR, Yaouk, Yaouk NR, Colinton, Shannons Flat, Bredbo, Mt Dowling NR, Peak View, Mt Clifford NR, Chakola, Tourist Railway, Coornartha NR, Numeralla, Bunyan, Binjura NR, Cooma, Countegany, Rock Flat, Berridale, Wullwye NR, Kybeyan, Myalla NR, Bobundara NR, Dangelong NR, Kydra, Dalgety, Maffra, Nimmitabel, Ironmungy NR, Numbla Vale, Holts Flat, Brown Mtn, Bungarby, Jincumbilly, Gunning Grach, Jimenbuen, Bukalong, Ando, Cathcart, Bibbenluke, South Bukalong, Tingaringi, Tombong, Cambalong, Quidong NR, Corrowong, Bombala, Coolumbooka NR, Maharatta, Rocky Hall, Delegate, Craigie, Mila, Bondi Gulf NR, Platts, Bendoc, Bendoc Upper, Rockton, Nungatta, Coopracambra National Park, Chandlers Creek, Wroxham, Mt Buckle, Timbillica, Nadgee Nature Reserve, Cape Howe

Peelwood, Limerick, Fullerton, Abercrombie River Nat Pk, Thalaba, Binda, Golspie, Yalbraith, Laggan, Richlands, Taralga, Historic Town, Wombeyan Caves, Myrtleville, Roslyn, Bannaby, Tarlo River Nat Pk, Chatsbury, Woodhouselee, Greenwich Park, Tarlo, Brayton, Canyonleigh, Kingsdale, Towrang, Marulan, Tallong, Big Merino, GOULBURN, Tirranaville, Bungonia, Bungonia State Con Area, Komungla, Bamarang NR, Inveralochy, Windellama, Lake Bathurst, Boro, Jerralong NR, Nadgigomar NR, Doughboy, Charleyong, Tomboy, Tallaganda NP, Hoskinstown, Rossi, Braidwood, Mongarlowe, Jinglemoney, Yarbor Peak, Yanunbunbeyan NP, Ballalaba, Majors Creek, Araluen, Monga, Clyde Mtn, Monga NP, Toggannoggera, Araluen NR, Jingera, Burnt School NR, Strike-a-Light NR, Anembo, Jerangle, Great Dividing Range, Tallaganda NP, Wyanbene Caves, Granmeir, Hanging Rock, Fairfield, Deua National Park, Bendethera Caves, Snowball, Gourock NP, Badja Swamps NR, Badja, Nerrigundah, Belowra, Eurobodalla, Wagonga, Gulaga Nat Park, Wadbilliga National Park, Wandella, Yowrie, Kooraban Nat Park, Cobargo, Verona, Brogo, Brogo Res, South East Forests Nat Pk, Numbugga, Bemboka, Pipers Lookout, Morans Crossing, Cheese Heritage Ctr, Bega, Candelo, Kalaru, Wolumla, Wyndham, Pambula, Lochiel, Greigs Flat, Burragate, Egan Peaks NR, Nethercote, Towamba, Pericoe, Mt Imlay Nat Pk, Boydtown, Kiah, Narrabarba

Kanangra-Boyd Nat Park, Blue Mtns Nat Park, Blue Mountains Nat Park, Old Silver Mining Town, Nattai, Yerranderie, Camden, The Oaks, Campbelltown, Picton, Thirlmere, Thirlmere Lakes NP, Nattai Nat Park, Appin, Bargo, Tahmoor, Cataract Res, Pheasants Nest, Bullio, Bullio Road Tunnel NR, High Range, Colo Vale, Tugalong, Joadja, Bargo Wilderness Area, Berrima, Historic Village, Mittagong, Bowral, Moss Vale, Bradman Museum, Macquarie Pass NP, WOLLONGONG, Corrimal, Bulli, Mt Keira Lookout, Port Kembla, Dapto, Warilla, Lake Illawarra, Shell harbr, Sutton Forest, Exeter, Fitzroy Falls, Robertson, Jamberoo, Bundanoon, Paddys River, Wingello, Morton National Park, Bombo, Kiama, Kangaroo Valley, Bendeela, Lake Yarrunga, Tallowa Dam, Cambewarra Range NR, Cambewarra Lookout, Berry, Gerringong, Black Pt, Gerroa, Seven Mile Bch NP, Jaspers Brush, Bomaderry, Nowra, Yalwal, HMAS Albatross, Shoalhaven Heads, Comerong Is. NR, Greenwell Point, Culburra Bch, Ettrema Wilderness Area, Parma Ck NR, Parma Falls Ck, Wollumboola, Jervis Bay NP, Jerrawangala Nat Park, Beecroft Hd, Bees Nest NR, Huskisson, Currarong, Wandandian, Bewong, Tomerong, Vincentia, Jervis Bay, Lighthouse, Pt Perpendicular, Booderee Nat Park, Tianjara Falls, Sassafras, Nerriga, St Georges Basin, Sussex Inlet, Jervis Bay Marine Park, Swan Lake, Cudmirrah, Conjola, Conjola Nat Park, Yatte Yattah, Bendalong, Lake Conjola, Narrawallee, Narrawallee Creek NR, Mollymook, Milton, Pigeon House, Kings Point, Ulladulla, Warden Head, Burrill Lake, Meroo NP, Bimberamala NP, Brooman, Termeil, Lake Tabourie, Shallow Crossing, Bawley Point, Murramarang Aboriginal Area, Kioloa, East Lynne, Pebbly Beach, Durras Water, Durras, Cullendulla Creek NR, Nelligen, Murramarang National Park, Long Beach, Batemans Bay, Batehaven, Malua Bay, Mogo, Tomakin, Mossy Point, Broulee, Moruya Heads, Moruya, Congo, Batemans Marine Park, Eurobodalla, Bergalia, Coila Creek, Turlinjah, Bingi Point, Coila Lake, Tuross Head, Tuross Lake, Bodalla, Potato Point, Eurobodalla National Park, Brou Lake, Dalmeny, Kianga, Narooma, Montague Is Nature Res, Central Tilba, Tilba Tilba, Cape Dromedary, Mystery Bay, Wallaga Lake, Wallaga Lake Heights, Bermagui, Bermagui South, Quaama, Murrah Lake, Biamanga Nat Pk, Bunga, Wapengo, Mimosa Rocks, Bithry Inlet, Tanja, Tathra, Maritime Museum, Bournda National Park, Wallagoot Lake, Tura Beach, Merimbula, Aquarium, Pambula Beach, Haycock Point, Ben Boyd Nat Park, Killer Whale Museum, Eden, Twofold Bay, Boyds Tower, Edrom, Saltwater Creek, Ben Boyd Nat Park, Wonboyn Lake, Bittangabee Bay, Green Cape Lighthouse, Disaster Bay, Ranger Station, Newtons Beach

Shoalhaven Coast · Eurobodalla Coast · Sapphire Coast

TASMAN SEA

VICTORIA

For more details on this area, see Hema's South East New South Wales Map

0 10 20 30 40 50km

N

© Hema Maps Pty Ltd

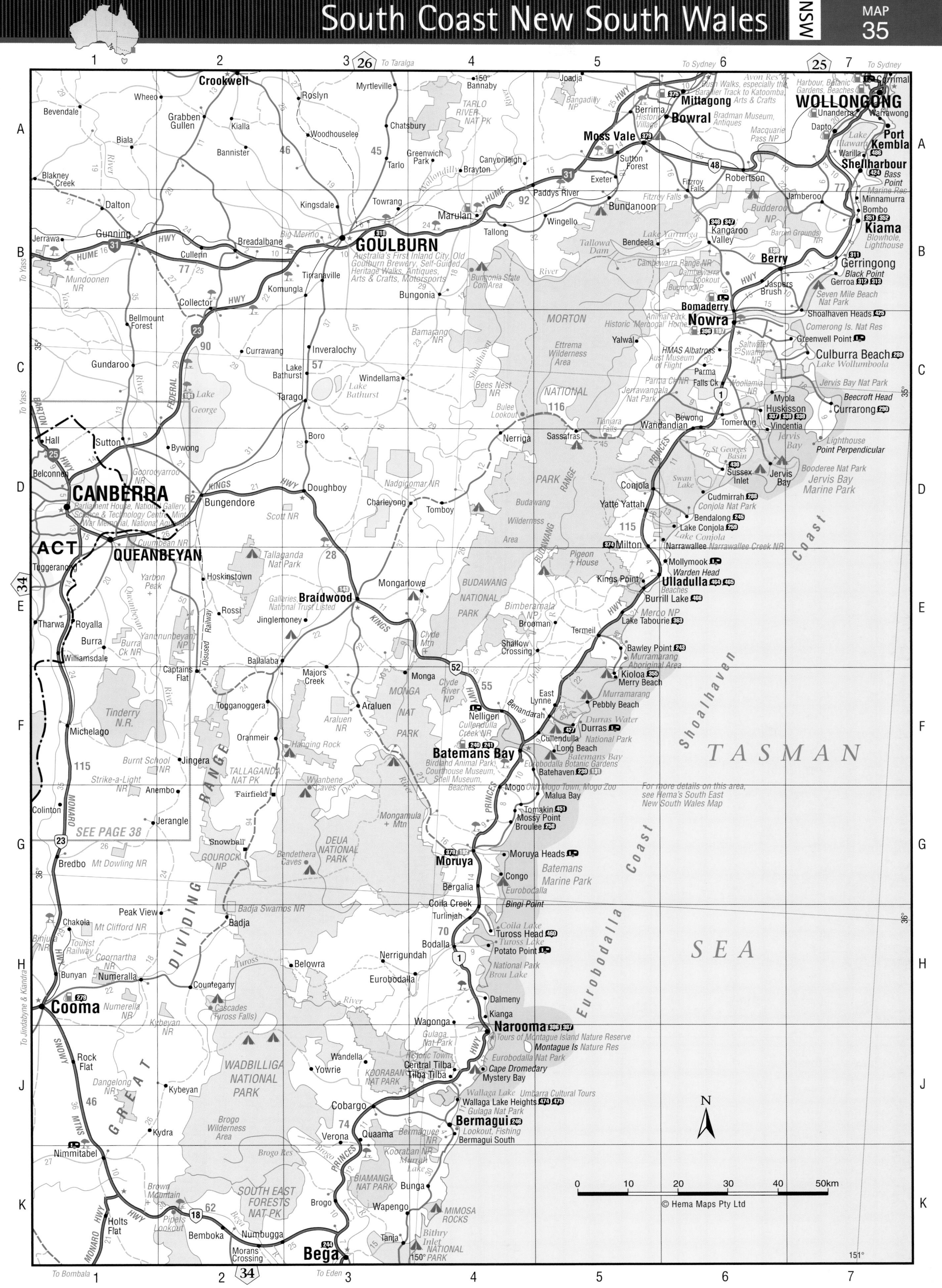

South Coast New South Wales
NSW
MAP 35
To Taralga
To Sydney
To Sydney
Crookwell
Wheeo
Bevendale
Grabben Gullen
Kialla
Roslyn
Woodhouselee
Myrtleville
Chatsbury
Bannaby
TARLO RIVER NAT PK
Joadja
Bangadilly NP
Berrima
Mittagong
Bowral
Bradman Museum, Antiques
Bush Walks, especially the Barallier Track to Katoomba, Arts & Crafts
Moss Vale
Sutton Forest
Exeter
Macquarie Pass NP
Robertson
WOLLONGONG
Corrimal
Harbour, Botanic Gardens, Beaches
Unanderra
Warrawong
Dapto
Port Kembla
Lake Illawarra
Warilla
Shellharbour
Bass Point Marine Res
Biala
Bannister
Greenwich Park
Canyonleigh
Brayton
Tarlo
Blakney Creek
Dalton
Kingsdale
Towrang
Marulan
Paddys River
Wingello
Tallong
Fitzroy Falls
Bundanoon
Budderoo NP
Jamberoo
Minnamurra
Bombo
Kiama
Blowhole, Lighthouse
Barren Grounds NR
Jerrawa
Gunning
Breadalbane
Cullerin
Big Merino
GOULBURN
Australia's First Inland City, Old Goulburn Brewery, Self-Guided Heritage Walks, Antiques, Arts & Crafts, Motorsports
Tallowa Dam
Lake Yarrunga
Bendeela
Kangaroo Valley
Berry
Gerringong
Black Point
Gerroa
Seven Mile Beach Nat Park
Mundoonen NR
To Yass
Collector
Komungla
Tirranaville
Bungonia
Bungonia State Con Area
Cambewarra Range NR
Cambewarra Lookout
Bugong NP
Bomaderry
Jaspers Brush
Shoalhaven Heads
Bellmount Forest
Animal Park, Historic 'Meroogal' Homes
Nowra
MORTON
Comerong Is. Nat Res
Greenwell Point
Gundaroo
Currawang
Inveralochy
Bamarang NR
Ettrema Wilderness Area
Yalwal
HMAS Albatross Aust Museum of Flight
Saltwater Swamp NR
Culburra Beach
Lake Wollumboola
Lake George
Lake Bathurst
Windellama
Tarago
Bees Nest NR
NATIONAL
Parma Ck NR
Parma
Falls Ck
Woollamia NR
Jervis Bay Nat Park
Beecroft Head
Currarong
Mypla
Huskisson
Vincentia
Jerrawangala Nat Park
Bulee Lookout
Tianjara Falls
Wandandian
Bewong
Tomerong
BARTON
Hall
Sutton
Bywong
Boro
Nerriga
Sassafras
St Georges Basin
Jervis Bay
Lighthouse
Point Perpendicular
Belconnen
Gooroooyarroo NR
CANBERRA
Parliament House, National Gallery, Science & Technology Centre, Mint, War Memorial, National Aquarium
Bungendore
Doughboy
Nadgigomar NR
Charleyong
Tomboy
PARK
RANGE
Conjola
Swan Lake
Sussex Inlet
Jervis Bay
Booderee Nat Park
Jervis Bay Marine Park
Budawang
Wilderness
Area
Yatte Yattah
Cudmirrah
Conjola Nat Park
Bendalong
Lake Conjola
ACT
QUEANBEYAN
Cumbean NR
Scott NR
Tallaganda Nat Park
Toggeranong
Pigeon House
Milton
Narrawallee
Narrawallee Creek NR
Mollymook
Warden Head
Coast
Hoskinstown
Yarbon Peak
Galleries, National Trust Listed
Braidwood
Mongarlowe
BUDAWANG NATIONAL PARK
Kings Point
Ulladulla
Beaches
Burrill Lake
Tharwa
Royalla
Rossi
Jinglemoney
Bimberamala NP
Brooman
Termeil
Meroo NP
Lake Tabourie
Burra
Burra Ck NR
Yanununbeyan NP
Disused Railway
Clyde Mtn
Shallow Crossing
Bawley Point
Murramarang Aboriginal Area
Williamsdale
Captains Flat
Ballalaba
Majors Creek
Monga
Clyde River NP
Kioloa
Merry Beach
Shoalhaven
Tinderry N.R.
Togganoggera
Araluen
MONGA NAT PARK
East Lynne
Benandarah
Murramarang
Pebbly Beach
Michelago
Oranmeir
Araluen NR
Nelligen
Cullendulla Creek NR
Durras Water
Durras
Cullendulla
National Park
Long Beach
Hanging Rock
Batemans Bay
Birdland Animal Park, Courthouse Museum, Shell Museum, Beaches
Batemans Bay
Eurobodalla Botanic Gardens
Batehaven
TASMAN
Burnt School NR
Jingera
TALLAGANDA NAT PK
Strike-a-Light NR
Anembo
'Fairfield'
Wyanbene Caves
Mogo
Old Mogo Town, Mogo Zoo
Malua Bay
For more details on this area, see Hema's South East New South Wales Map
Colinton
MONARO
SEE PAGE 38
Jerangle
Mongamula Mtn
Tomakin
Mossy Point
Broulee
Bredbo
Mt Dowling NR
'Snowball'
GOUROCK NP
Bendethera Caves
DEUA NATIONAL PARK
Moruya
Moruya Heads
Congo
Batemans Marine Park
Eurobodalla
Bergalia
Coila Creek
Bingi Point
Turlinjah
Peak View
Badja Swamps NR
Badja
DIVIDING
Chakola
Mt Clifford NR
Bimjula NR
Tourist Railway
Coila Lake
Tuross Head
Tuross Lake
Bodalla
Potato Point
SEA
Coornartha NR
Belowra
Nerrigundah
National Park
Brou Lake
Bunyan
Numeralla
Countegany
Eurobodalla
Cooma
Numerella NR
Cascades (Tuross Falls)
River
Dalmeny
Kianga
To Jindabyne & Kiandra
Kybeyan NR
Wagonga
Narooma
Tours of Montague Island Nature Reserve
Montague Is Nature Res
Gulaga Nat Park
Rock Flat
WADBILLIGA NATIONAL PARK
Wandella
Historic Town
Central Tilba
Tilba Tilba
Eurobodalla Nat Park
Cape Dromedary
Mystery Bay
Yowrie
KOORABAN NAT PARK
Dangelong NR
Kybeyan
SNOWY
MTNS
GREAT
Wallaga Lake
Umbarra Cultural Tours
Wallaga Lake Heights
Gulaga Nat Park
Cobargo
Bermagui
Lookout, Fishing
Brogo Wilderness Area
Kydra
Verona
Quaama
Bermaguee NR
Bermagui South
N
Nimmitabel
Brogo Res
Kooraban NR
Murrah Lake
BIAMANGA NAT PARK
Bunga
0 10 20 30 40 50km
© Hema Maps Pty Ltd
Brown Mountain
SOUTH EAST FORESTS NAT PK
Brogo
Wapengo
MIMOSA ROCKS
Holts Flat
Pipers Lookout
Bemboka
Numbugga
Bithry Inlet
NATIONAL PARK
Tanja
Morans Crossing
Bega
To Bombala
To Eden
HUME HWY
KINGS HWY
PRINCES HWY
MONARO HWY
FEDERAL HWY

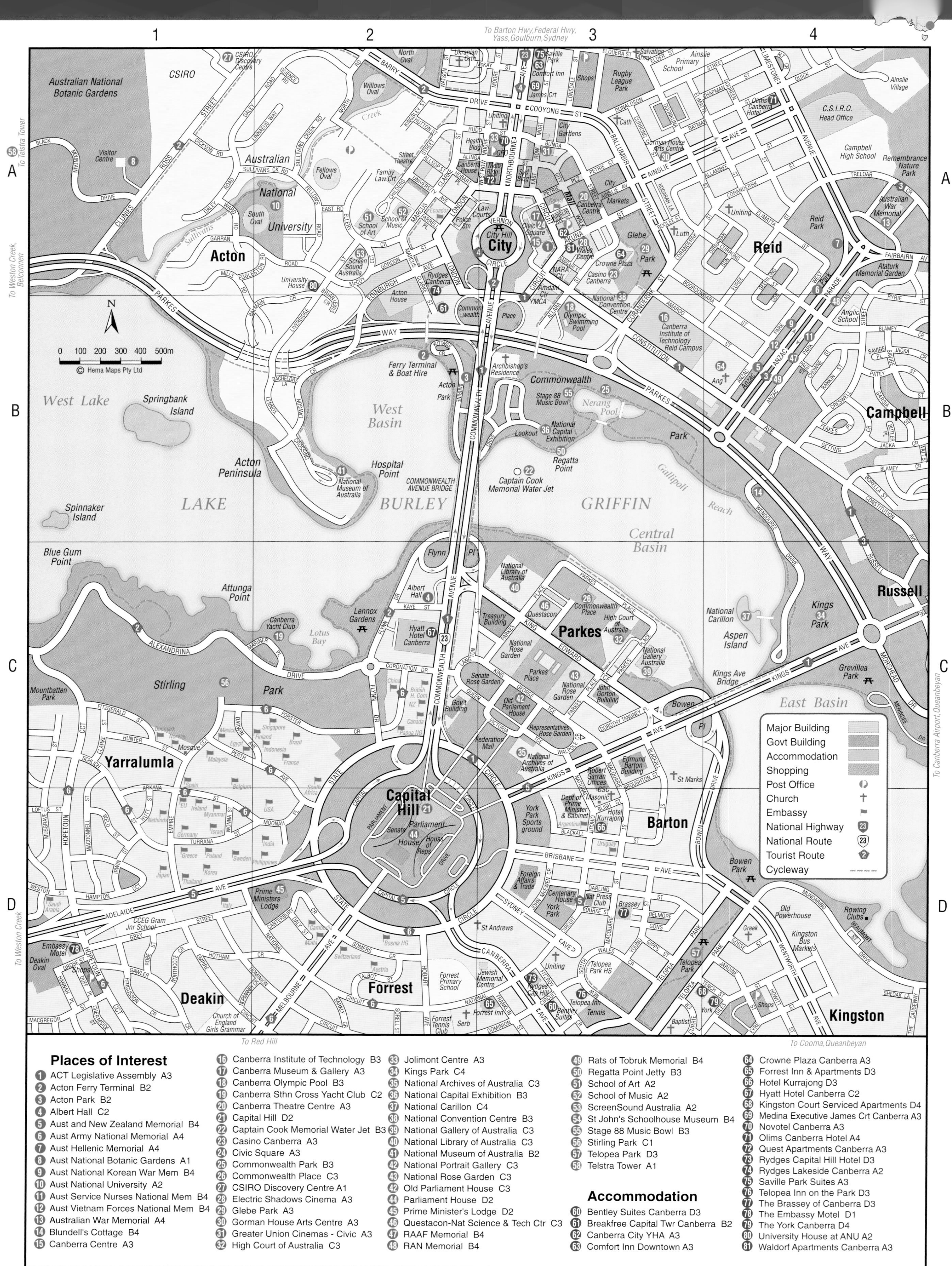
1
2
3
4
A
B
C
D
To Barton Hwy, Federal Hwy, Yass, Goulburn, Sydney
To Telstra Tower
To Weston Creek, Belconnen
To Weston Creek
To Red Hill
To Cooma, Queanbeyan
To Canberra Airport, Queanbeyan
0 100 200 300 400 500m
© Hema Maps Pty Ltd
N
Australian National Botanic Gardens
CSIRO
Australian National University
Acton
City
Reid
Campbell
Russell
Parkes
Capital Hill
Barton
Yarralumla
Deakin
Forrest
Kingston
West Lake
West Basin
Central Basin
East Basin
LAKE BURLEY GRIFFIN
Springbank Island
Spinnaker Island
Acton Peninsula
Blue Gum Point
Attunga Point
Aspen Island
Stirling Park
Commonwealth Park
Kings Park
Bowen Park
Grevillea Park
Major Building
Govt Building
Accommodation
Shopping
Post Office
Church
Embassy
National Highway
National Route
Tourist Route
Cycleway
Places of Interest
1 ACT Legislative Assembly A3
2 Acton Ferry Terminal B2
3 Acton Park B2
4 Albert Hall C2
5 Aust and New Zealand Memorial B4
6 Aust Army National Memorial A4
7 Aust Hellenic Memorial A4
8 Aust National Botanic Gardens A1
9 Aust National Korean War Mem B4
10 Aust National University A2
11 Aust Service Nurses National Mem B4
12 Aust Vietnam Forces National Mem B4
13 Australian War Memorial A4
14 Blundell's Cottage B4
15 Canberra Centre A3
16 Canberra Institute of Technology B3
17 Canberra Museum & Gallery A3
18 Canberra Olympic Pool B3
19 Canberra Sthn Cross Yacht Club C2
20 Canberra Theatre Centre A3
21 Capital Hill D2
22 Captain Cook Memorial Water Jet B3
23 Casino Canberra A3
24 Civic Square A3
25 Commonwealth Park B3
26 Commonwealth Place C3
27 CSIRO Discovery Centre A1
28 Electric Shadows Cinema A3
29 Glebe Park A3
30 Gorman House Arts Centre A3
31 Greater Union Cinemas - Civic A3
32 High Court of Australia C3
33 Jolimont Centre A3
34 Kings Park C4
35 National Archives of Australia C3
36 National Capital Exhibition B3
37 National Carillon C4
38 National Convention Centre B3
39 National Gallery of Australia C3
40 National Library of Australia C3
41 National Museum of Australia B2
42 National Portrait Gallery C3
43 National Rose Garden C3
44 Old Parliament House C3
44 Parliament House D2
45 Prime Minister's Lodge D2
46 Questacon-Nat Science & Tech Ctr C3
47 RAAF Memorial B4
48 RAN Memorial B4
49 Rats of Tobruk Memorial B4
50 Regatta Point Jetty B3
51 School of Art A2
52 School of Music A2
53 ScreenSound Australia A2
54 St John's Schoolhouse Museum B4
55 Stage 88 Music Bowl B3
56 Stirling Park C1
57 Telopea Park D3
58 Telstra Tower A1
Accommodation
60 Bentley Suites Canberra D3
61 Breakfree Capital Twr Canberra B2
62 Canberra City YHA A3
63 Comfort Inn Downtown A3
64 Crowne Plaza Canberra A3
65 Forrest Inn & Apartments D3
66 Hotel Kurrajong D3
67 Hyatt Hotel Canberra C2
68 Kingston Court Serviced Apartments D4
69 Medina Executive James Crt Canberra A3
70 Novotel Canberra A3
71 Olims Canberra Hotel A4
72 Quest Apartments Canberra A3
73 Rydges Capital Hill Hotel D3
74 Rydges Lakeside Canberra A2
75 Saville Park Suites A3
76 Telopea Inn on the Park D3
77 The Brassey of Canberra D3
78 The Embassy Motel D1
79 The York Canberra D4
80 University House at ANU A2
81 Waldorf Apartments Canberra A3

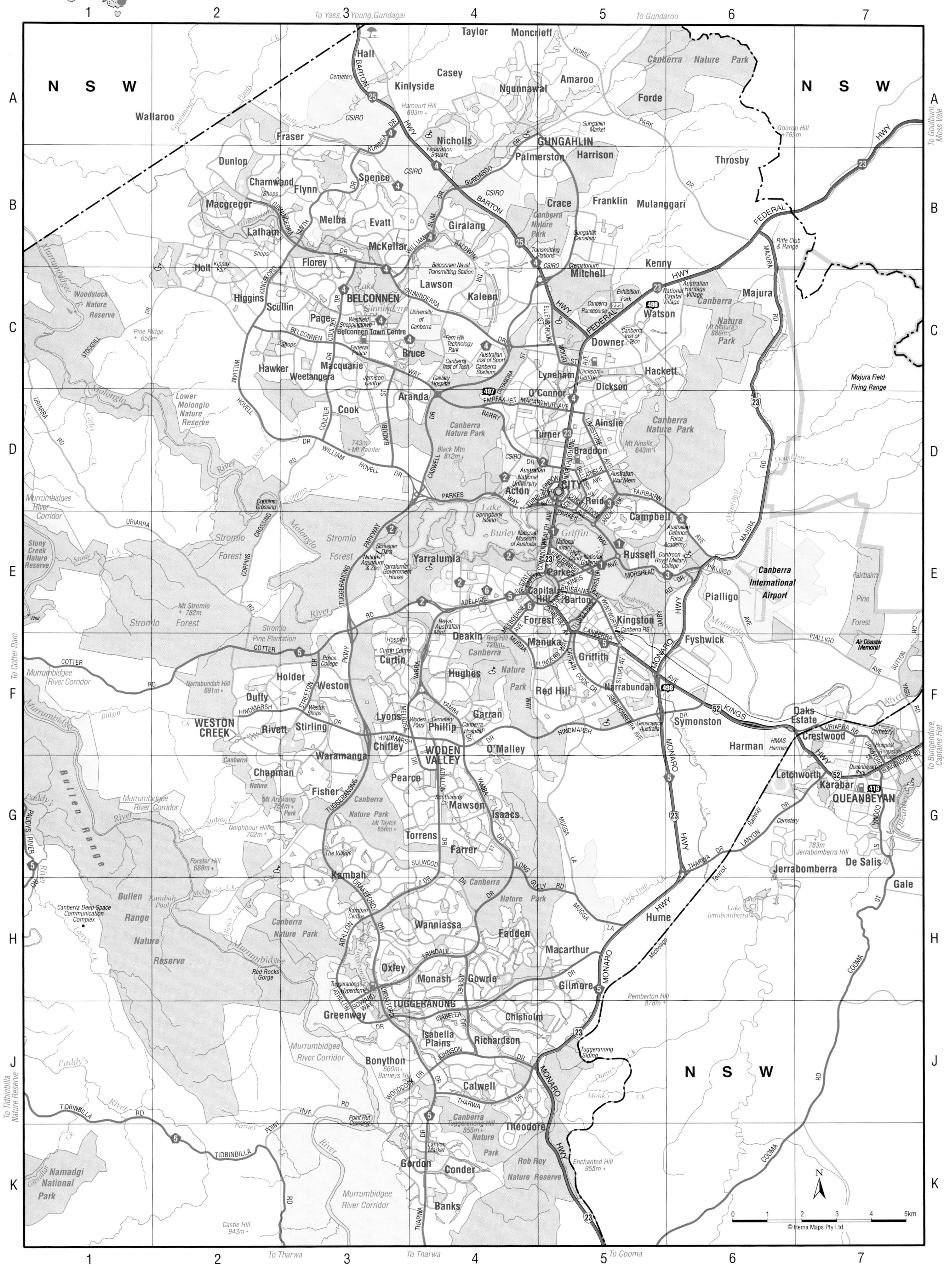

NSW

To Yass, Young, Gundagai
To Gundaroo
To Goulburn, Moss Vale
To Bungendore, Captains Flat
To Cotter Dam
To Tidbinbilla Nature Reserve
To Tharwa
To Cooma

Hall
Taylor
Moncrieff
Casey
Kinlyside
Ngunnawal
Amaroo
Forde
Canberra Nature Park
Wallaroo
Harcourt Hill 693m
CSIRO
Gungahlin Market
Gooroo Hill 765m
Fraser
Nicholls
Federation Square
GUNGAHLIN
Harrison
Palmerston
Throsby
Dunlop
Spence
Charnwood
Flynn
Macgregor
Melba
Evatt
Crace
Franklin
Mulanggari
Latham
Giralang
Gungahlin Cemetery
Rifle Club & Range
Holt
Kippax Fair
McKellar
Florey
Belconnen Naval Transmitting Station
Transmitting Stations
Crematorium
Mitchell
Kenny
Woodstock Nature Reserve
Higgins
Scullin
BELCONNEN
Lake Ginninderra
Lawson
Kaleen
Exhibition Park
National Capital Village
Australian Heritage Village
Majura
Page
Westfield Shoppingtown
Belconnen Town Centre
University of Canberra
Canberra Racecourse
Watson
Pine Ridge 656m
Fern Hill Technology Park
Downer
Canberra Inst of Tech
Mt Majura 888m
Federal Police
Bruce
Australian Inst of Sport
Canberra Stadium
Hawker
Macquarie
Weetangera
Jamison Centre
Calvary Hospital
Lyneham
Dickson Centre
Hackett
Dickson
Majura Field Firing Range
O'Connor
Lower Molonglo Nature Reserve
Aranda
Cook
Ainslie
Canberra Nature Park
Turner
743m Mt Painter
Black Mtn 812m
Braddon
Mt Ainslie 843m
Australian National University
Australian War Mem
Acton
CITY
Reid
Murrumbidgee River Corridor
Coppins Crossing
Lake Burley Griffin
Springbank Island
Campbell
Stromlo Forest
National Museum of Australia
Australian Defence Force Academy
Stony Creek Nature Reserve
Scrivener Dam
National Aquarium & Zoo
Yarralumla
Yarralumla Government House
National Library
High Court
National Gallery
Russell
Duntroon Royal Military College
Canberra International Airport
Parkes
Capital Hill
Barton
Pialligo
Mt Stromlo 782m
Royal Australian Mint
Forrest
Kingston
Canberra RS
Red Hill 720m
Deakin
Manuka
Fyshwick
Pine Plantation
Hospital
Curtin Centre
Curtin
Police College
Griffith
Air Disaster Memorial
Holder
Weston
Hughes
Narrabundah Hill 691m
Duffy
Red Hill
Narrabundah
WESTON CREEK
Rivett
Stirling
Weston Shops
Lyons
Woden Plaza
Cemetery
Phillip
Garran
Canberra Hospital
Symonston
Geoscience Australia
Oaks Estate
Crestwood
Chapman
Chifley
Waramanga
WODEN VALLEY
O'Malley
Harman
HMAS Harman
Queanbeyan Park
Fisher
Pearce
Letchworth
Karabar
QUEANBEYAN
Mt Arawang 784m
Southlands Ctr
Mawson
Isaacs
Paddys River
Bullen Range
Murrumbidgee River Corridor
Neighbour Hill 702m
Mt Taylor 856m
Torrens
Farrer
783m Jerrabomberra Hill
De Salis
The Village
Forster Hill 688m
Kambah
Jerrabomberra
Gale
Bullen Range Nature Reserve
Kambah Pool
Kambah Centre
Hume
Lake Jerrabomberra
Canberra Deep Space Communication Complex
Wanniassa
Fadden
Red Rocks Gorge
Macarthur
Oxley
Monash
Gowrie
Gilmore
Tuggeranong Hyperdome
TUGGERANONG
Pemberton Hill 878m
Greenway
Chisholm
Isabella Plains
Richardson
Bonython
660m Barneys Hill
Tuggeranong Siding
Calwell
Point Hut Crossing
Theodore
Tuggeranong Hill 855m
Lanyon Market
Gordon
Conder
Rob Roy Nature Reserve
Enchanted Hill 955m
Namadgi National Park
Banks
Castle Hill 943m

Roads: Barton Hwy, Federal Hwy, Monaro Hwy, Kings Hwy, Gundaroo Dr, Ginninderra Dr, William Slim Dr, Belconnen Way, Kingsford Smith Dr, William Hovell Dr, Coulter Dr, Caswell Dr, Parkes Way, Tuggeranong Pkwy, Cotter Rd, Adelaide Ave, Yarra Glen, Hindmarsh Dr, Athllon Dr, Drakeford Dr, Erindale Dr, Tharwa Dr, Johnson Dr, Tidbinbilla Rd, Point Hut Rd, Uriarra Rd, Pialligo Ave, Majura Rd, Canberra Ave, Jerrabomberra Ave, Mugga La, Long Gully Rd, Lanyon Dr, Cooma Rd, Sutton Rd, Yass Rd

0 1 2 3 4 5km

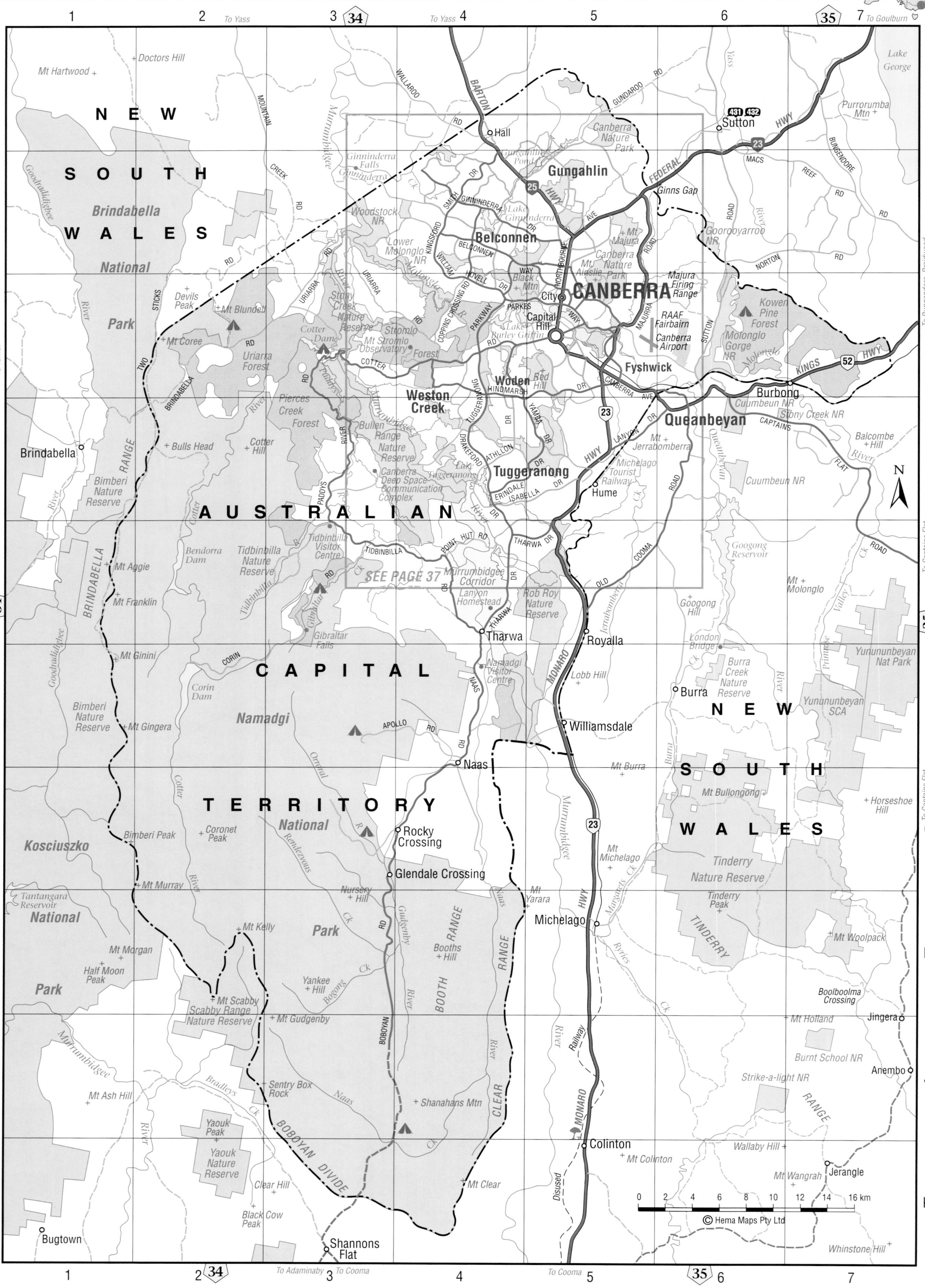

AUSTRALIAN CAPITAL TERRITORY

NEW SOUTH WALES

CANBERRA
Belconnen
Gungahlin
Woden
Weston Creek
Tuggeranong
Queanbeyan
Fyshwick
City
Capital Hill
Hall
Sutton
Burbong
Hume
Tharwa
Royalla
Williamsdale
Naas
Rocky Crossing
Glendale Crossing
Michelago
Colinton
Burra
Brindabella
Bugtown
Shannons Flat
Jingera
Anembo
Jerangle

Brindabella National Park
Namadgi National Park
Kosciuszko National Park
Tinderry Nature Reserve
Bimberi Nature Reserve
Tidbinbilla Nature Reserve
Scabby Range Nature Reserve
Yaouk Peak Nature Reserve
Canberra Nature Park
Kowen Pine Forest
Uriarra Forest
Pierces Creek Forest
Stromlo Forest
Burra Creek Nature Reserve
Yununbunbeyan Nat Park
Yununbunbeyan SCA
Googong Reservoir
Lake George
Corin Dam
Bendorra Dam
Cotter Dam
Tantangara Reservoir
Canberra Airport
RAAF Fairbairn
Majura Firing Range
Canberra Deep Space Communication Complex
Mt Stromlo Observatory
Lanyon Homestead
Namadgi Visitor Centre
Tidbinbilla Visitor Centre
Murrumbidgee Corridor
Rob Roy Nature Reserve
Bullen Range Nature Reserve
Woodstock NR
Lower Molonglo NR
Stony Creek Nature Reserve
Molonglo Gorge NR
Goorooyarroo NR
Cuumbeun NR
Stony Creek NR
Burnt School NR
Strike-a-light NR
Michelago Tourist Railway

SEE PAGE 37

Mt Hartwood, Doctors Hill, Devils Peak, Mt Blundell, Mt Coree, Bulls Head, Cotter Hill, Mt Aggie, Mt Franklin, Mt Ginini, Mt Gingera, Bimberi Peak, Coronet Peak, Mt Murray, Mt Kelly, Mt Morgan, Half Moon Peak, Mt Scabby, Mt Gudgenby, Yankee Hill, Nursery Hill, Booths Hill, Sentry Box Rock, Shanahans Mtn, Mt Clear, Mt Ash Hill, Clear Hill, Black Cow Peak, Mt Yarara, Mt Michelago, Mt Burra, Mt Bullongong, Lobb Hill, Googong Hill, London Bridge, Mt Jerrabomberra, Mt Molonglo, Balcombe Hill, Purrorumba Mtn, Horseshoe Hill, Tinderry Peak, Mt Woolpack, Mt Holland, Boolboolma Crossing, Wallaby Hill, Mt Colinton, Mt Wangrah, Whinstone Hill, Mt Majura, Mt Ainslie, Black Mtn, Red Hill, Ginns Gap, Gibraltar Falls, Ginninderra Falls

Federal Hwy, Barton Hwy, Monaro Hwy, Kings Hwy, Captains Flat Road, Cooma Road, Boboyan Rd, Naas Rd, Apollo Rd, Corin Rd, Brindabella Rd, Two Sticks Rd, Uriarra Rd, Cotter Rd, Paddys River Rd, Tidbinbilla Rd, Point Hut Rd, Tharwa Dr, Mountain Creek Rd, Wallaroo Rd, Gundaroo Rd, Macs Reef Rd, Bungendore Rd, Norton Rd, Sutton Rd, Old Cooma Rd

Murrumbidgee River, Cotter River, Goodradigbee River, Queanbeyan River, Molonglo River, Naas River, Gudgenby River, Orroral River, Yass River

BRINDABELLA RANGE, BOOTH RANGE, CLEAR RANGE, TINDERRY RANGE, BOBOYAN DIVIDE

To Yass; To Goulburn; To Tumut; To Bungendore, Braidwood; To Captains Flat; To Adaminaby; To Cooma

0 2 4 6 8 10 12 14 16 km

© Hema Maps Pty Ltd

POPULATION: 5 million
AREA: 227,416 sq km
CAPITAL CITY: Melbourne

Distances are shown in kilometres and follow the most direct major sealed route

	Ballarat	Bairnsdale	Bendigo	Echuca	Eden (NSW)	Geelong	Hamilton	Horsham	Melbourne	Mildura	Shepparton	Swan Hill	Traralgon	Wangaratta	Warrnambool
Albury	423	330	302	237	617	395	579	504	321	613	180	391	485	72	582
Ballarat		394	121	214	681	87	174	187	112	486	243	309	276	346	186
Bairnsdale			430	492	287	356	398	581	282	840	694	618	118	304	543
Bendigo				93	717	208	277	207	148	410	122	188	312	225	307
Echuca					751	284	370	300	210	376	71	154	374	160	400
Eden (NSW)						643	791	868	569	1127	694	905	405	591	830
Geelong							236	274	74	573	258	393	238	316	187
Hamilton								132	286	431	399	383	450	502	100
Horsham									299	299	329	251	463	432	232
Melbourne										558	184	336	164	242	261
Mildura											433	222	722	536	531
Shepparton												211	348	103	429
Swan Hill													500	314	385
Traralgon														406	425
Wangaratta															503

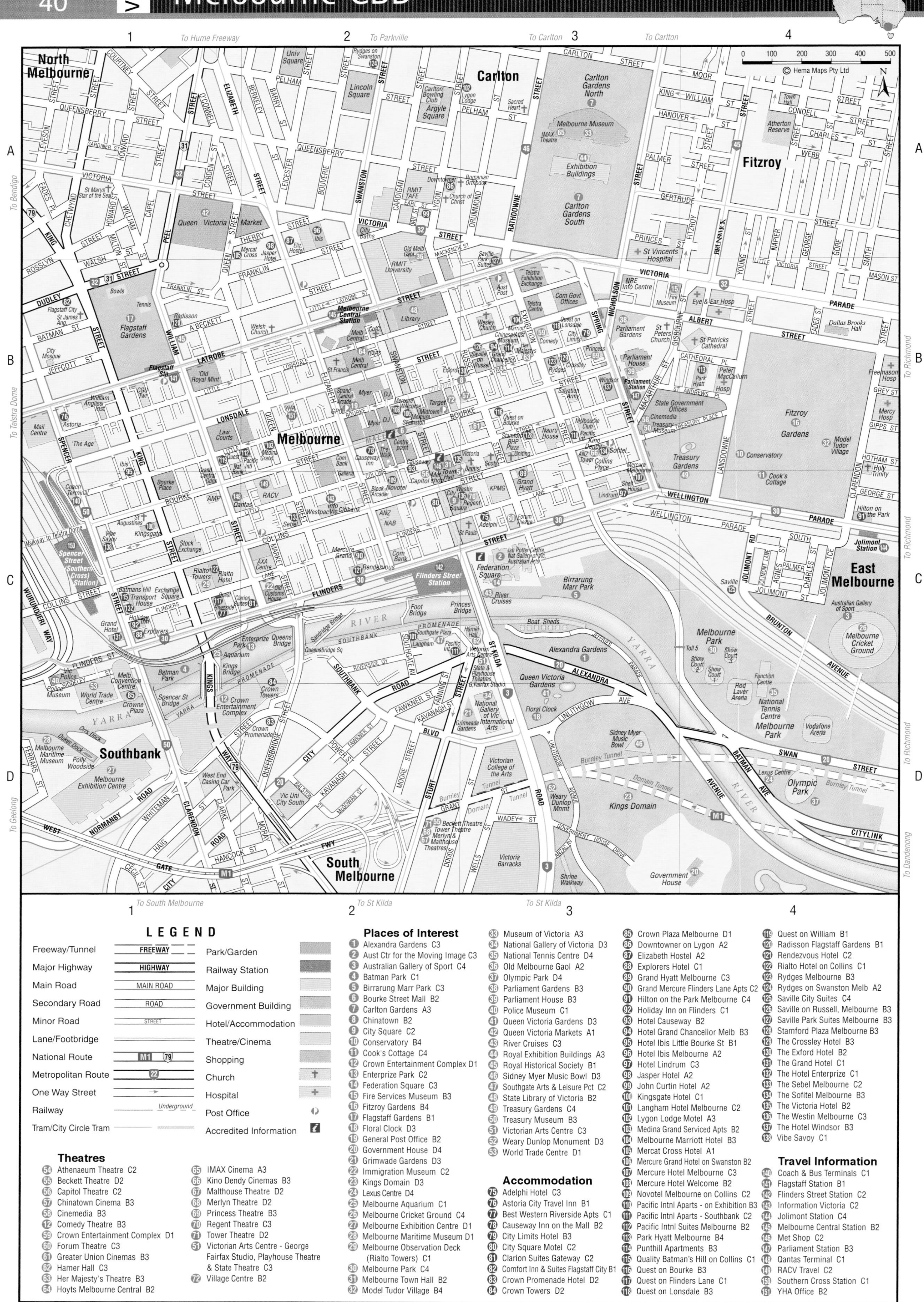

North Melbourne
Carlton
Fitzroy
Melbourne
East Melbourne
Southbank
South Melbourne
To Hume Freeway
To Parkville
To Carlton
To Bendigo
To Telstra Dome
To Geelong
To Richmond
To Dandenong
To South Melbourne
To St Kilda
© Hema Maps Pty Ltd
LEGEND
Freeway/Tunnel
Major Highway
Main Road
Secondary Road
Minor Road
Lane/Footbridge
National Route
Metropolitan Route
One Way Street
Railway
Underground
Tram/City Circle Tram
Park/Garden
Railway Station
Major Building
Government Building
Hotel/Accommodation
Theatre/Cinema
Shopping
Church
Hospital
Post Office
Accredited Information
Places of Interest
1 Alexandra Gardens C3
2 Aust Ctr for the Moving Image C3
3 Australian Gallery of Sport C4
4 Batman Park C1
5 Birrarung Marr Park C3
6 Bourke Street Mall B2
7 Carlton Gardens A3
8 Chinatown B2
9 City Square C2
10 Conservatory B4
11 Cook's Cottage C4
12 Crown Entertainment Complex D1
13 Enterprize Park C2
14 Federation Square C3
15 Fire Services Museum B3
16 Fitzroy Gardens B4
17 Flagstaff Gardens B1
18 Floral Clock D3
19 General Post Office B2
20 Government House D4
21 Grimwade Gardens D3
22 Immigration Museum C2
23 Kings Domain D3
24 Lexus Centre D4
25 Melbourne Aquarium C1
26 Melbourne Cricket Ground C4
27 Melbourne Exhibition Centre D1
28 Melbourne Maritime Museum D1
29 Melbourne Observation Deck (Rialto Towers) C1
30 Melbourne Park C4
31 Melbourne Town Hall B2
32 Model Tudor Village B4
33 Museum of Victoria A3
34 National Gallery of Victoria D3
35 National Tennis Centre D4
36 Old Melbourne Gaol A2
37 Olympic Park D4
38 Parliament Gardens B3
39 Parliament House B3
40 Police Museum C1
41 Queen Victoria Gardens D3
42 Queen Victoria Markets A1
43 River Cruises C3
44 Royal Exhibition Buildings A3
45 Royal Historical Society B1
46 Sidney Myer Music Bowl D3
47 Southgate Arts & Leisure Pct C2
48 State Library of Victoria B2
49 Treasury Gardens C4
50 Treasury Museum B3
51 Victorian Arts Centre C3
52 Weary Dunlop Monument D3
53 World Trade Centre D1
Theatres
54 Athenaeum Theatre C2
55 Beckett Theatre D2
56 Capitol Theatre C2
57 Chinatown Cinema B3
58 Cinemedia B3
59 Comedy Theatre B3
12 Crown Entertainment Complex D1
60 Forum Theatre C3
61 Greater Union Cinemas B3
62 Hamer Hall C3
63 Her Majesty's Theatre B3
64 Hoyts Melbourne Central B2
65 IMAX Cinema A3
66 Kino Dendy Cinemas B3
67 Malthouse Theatre D2
68 Merlyn Theatre D2
69 Princess Theatre B3
70 Regent Theatre C3
71 Tower Theatre D2
51 Victorian Arts Centre - George Fairfax Studio, Playhouse Theatre & State Theatre C3
72 Village Centre B2
Accommodation
75 Adelphi Hotel C3
76 Astoria City Travel Inn B1
77 Best Western Riverside Apts C1
78 Causeway Inn on the Mall B2
79 City Limits Hotel B3
80 City Square Motel C2
81 Clarion Suites Gateway C2
82 Comfort Inn & Suites Flagstaff City B1
83 Crown Promenade Hotel D2
84 Crown Towers D2
85 Crown Plaza Melbourne D1
86 Downtowner on Lygon A2
87 Elizabeth Hostel A2
88 Explorers Hotel C1
89 Grand Hyatt Melbourne C3
90 Grand Mercure Flinders Lane Apts C2
91 Hilton on the Park Melbourne C4
92 Holiday Inn on Flinders C1
93 Hotel Causeway B2
94 Hotel Grand Chancellor Melb B3
95 Hotel Ibis Little Bourke St B1
96 Hotel Ibis Melbourne A2
97 Hotel Lindrum C3
98 Jasper Hotel A2
99 John Curtin Hotel A2
100 Kingsgate Hotel C1
101 Langham Hotel Melbourne C2
102 Lygon Lodge Motel A3
103 Medina Grand Serviced Apts B2
104 Melbourne Marriott Hotel B3
105 Mercat Cross Hotel A1
106 Mercure Grand Hotel on Swanston B2
107 Mercure Hotel Melbourne C3
108 Mercure Hotel Welcome B2
109 Novotel Melbourne on Collins C2
110 Pacific Intnl Aparts - on Exhibition B3
111 Pacific Intnl Aparts - Southbank C2
112 Pacific Intnl Suites Melbourne B2
113 Park Hyatt Melbourne B4
114 Punthill Apartments B3
115 Quality Batman's Hill on Collins C1
116 Quest on Bourke B3
117 Quest on Flinders Lane C1
118 Quest on Lonsdale B3
119 Quest on William B1
120 Radisson Flagstaff Gardens B1
121 Rendezvous Hotel C2
122 Rialto Hotel on Collins C1
123 Rydges Melbourne B3
124 Rydges on Swanston Melb A2
125 Saville City Suites C4
126 Saville on Russell, Melbourne B3
127 Saville Park Suites Melbourne B3
128 Stamford Plaza Melbourne B3
129 The Crossley Hotel B3
130 The Exford Hotel B2
131 The Grand Hotel C1
132 The Hotel Enterprize C1
133 The Sebel Melbourne C2
134 The Sofitel Melbourne B3
135 The Victoria Hotel B2
136 The Westin Melbourne C3
137 The Hotel Windsor B3
138 Vibe Savoy C1
Travel Information
140 Coach & Bus Terminals C1
141 Flagstaff Station B1
142 Flinders Street Station C2
143 Information Victoria C2
144 Jolimont Station C4
145 Melbourne Central Station B2
146 Met Shop C2
147 Parliament Station B3
148 Qantas Terminal C1
149 RACV Travel C2
150 Southern Cross Station C1
151 YHA Office B2

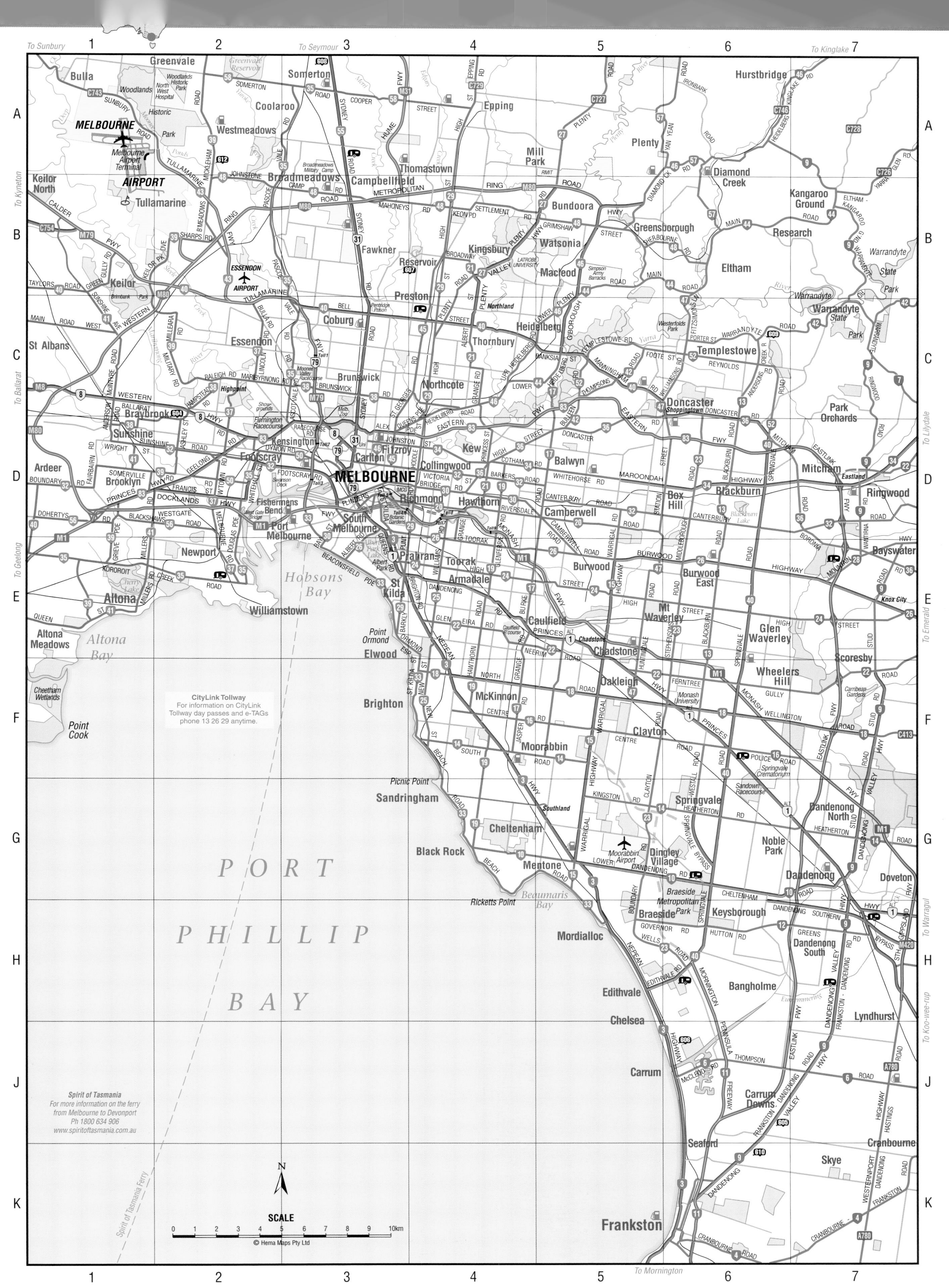
To Sunbury
To Seymour
To Kinglake
To Kyneton
To Ballarat
To Geelong
To Lilydale
To Emerald
To Warragul
To Koo-wee-rup
To Mornington
1
2
3
4
5
6
7
A
B
C
D
E
F
G
H
J
K
Greenvale
Bulla
Somerton
Coolaroo
Epping
Hurstbridge
MELBOURNE AIRPORT
Westmeadows
Plenty
Mill Park
Keilor North
Broadmeadows
Campbellfield
Thomastown
Diamond Creek
Tullamarine
Bundoora
Kangaroo Ground
Greensborough
Research
Fawkner
Kingsbury
Watsonia
Keilor
ESSENDON AIRPORT
Reservoir
Macleod
Eltham
Warrandyte
Preston
Coburg
Heidelberg
Warrandyte State Park
St Albans
Essendon
Thornbury
Templestowe
Brunswick
Northcote
Doncaster
Park Orchards
Braybrook
Sunshine
Kensington
Fitzroy
Kew
Ardeer
Footscray
Carlton
Balwyn
Mitcham
Brooklyn
MELBOURNE
Collingwood
Ringwood
Richmond
Hawthorn
Box Hill
Blackburn
Fishermens Bend
South Melbourne
Camberwell
Port Melbourne
Newport
Prahran
Toorak
Burwood
Burwood East
Bayswater
Armadale
Hobsons Bay
St Kilda
Altona
Williamstown
Mt Waverley
Glen Waverley
Altona Meadows
Altona Bay
Caulfield
Point Ormond
Elwood
Chadstone
Scoresby
Cheetham Wetlands
Oakleigh
Wheelers Hill
CityLink Tollway
For information on CityLink Tollway day passes and e-TAGs phone 13 26 29 anytime.
Brighton
McKinnon
Point Cook
Clayton
Moorabbin
Picnic Point
Sandringham
Springvale
Dandenong North
Cheltenham
Noble Park
Black Rock
Moorabbin Airport
Dingley Village
PORT PHILLIP BAY
Mentone
Dandenong
Doveton
Ricketts Point
Beaumaris Bay
Braeside Metropolitan Park
Braeside
Keysborough
Mordialloc
Dandenong South
Edithvale
Bangholme
Chelsea
Lyndhurst
Carrum
Carrum Downs
Spirit of Tasmania
For more information on the ferry from Melbourne to Devonport
Ph 1800 634 906
www.spiritoftasmania.com.au
Seaford
Cranbourne
Skye
Spirit of Tasmania Ferry
N
SCALE
0 1 2 3 4 5 6 7 8 9 10km
© Hema Maps Pty Ltd
Frankston

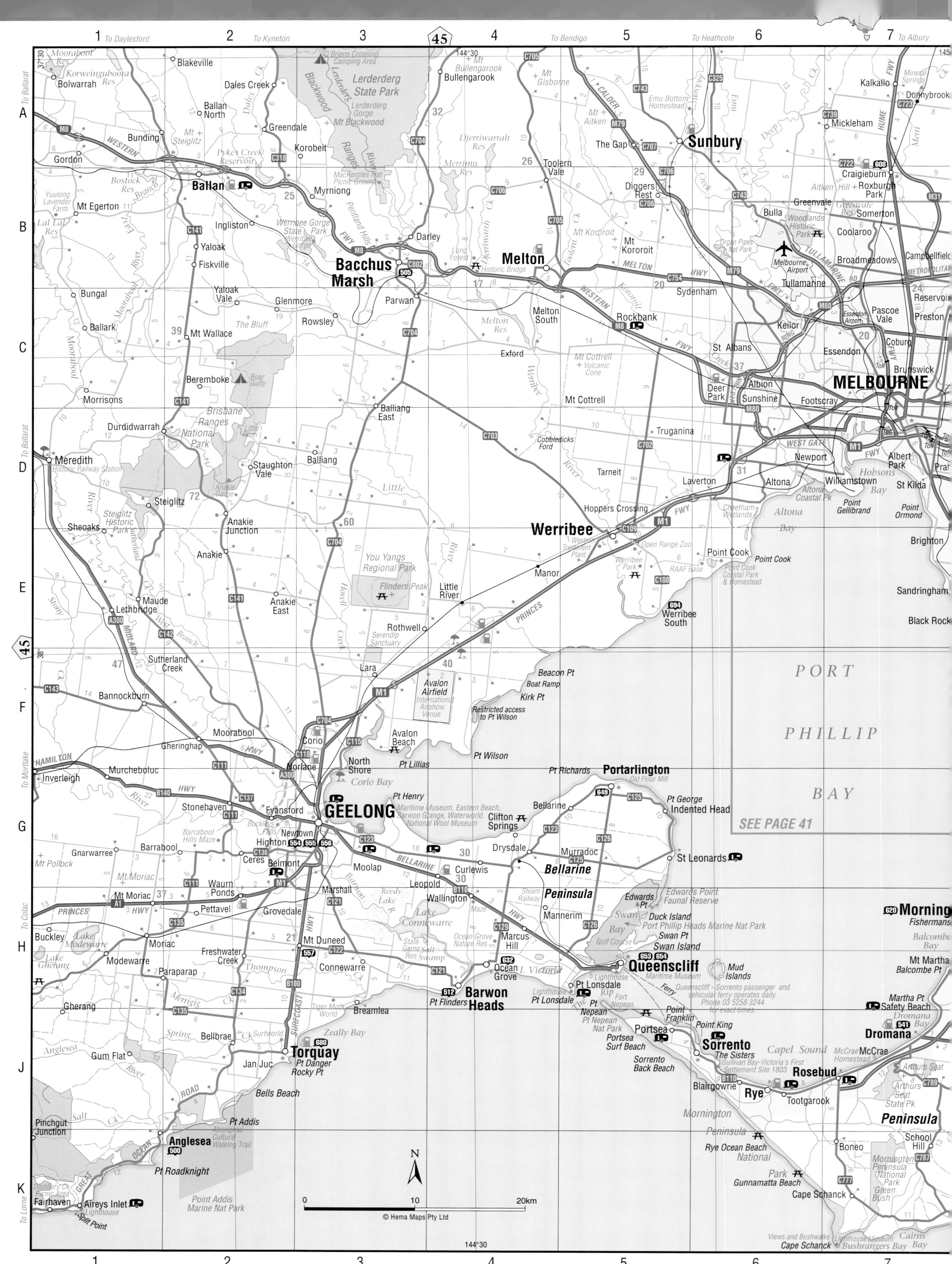
45
To Daylesford
To Kyneton
To Bendigo
To Heathcote
To Albury
To Ballarat
To Mortlake
To Colac
To Lorne
Moorabool Res
Korweinguboora Res
Bolwarrah
Blakeville
Dales Creek
Lerderderg State Park
Briens Crossing Camping Area
Lerderderg Gorge
Mt Blackwood
Bullengarook
Mt Bullengarook
Mt Gisborne
Emu Bottom Homestead
Kalkallo
Donnybrook
Ballan North
Greendale
Mt Aitken
Mickleham
Bunding
Mt Steiglitz
Korobeit
Djerriwarrah Res
The Gap
Sunbury
Gordon
Pykes Creek Reservoir
MacKenzies Flat Picnic Ground
Merrimu Res
Toolern Vale
Craigieburn
Ballan
Myrniong
Diggers Rest
Roxburgh Park
Bostock Res
Yuulong Lavender Farm
Mt Egerton
Greenvale
Greenvale Res
Somerton
Bulla
Woodlands Historic Park
Coolaroo
Lal Lal Res
Ingliston
Werribee Gorge State Park
Darley
Mt Kororoit
Kororoit
Organ Pipes Nat Park
Yaloak
Bacchus Marsh
Melton
Long Forest
Historic Bridge
Broadmeadows
Campbellfield
Fiskville
Melbourne Airport
Tullamarine
Sydenham
Bungal
Yaloak Vale
Glenmore
Parwan
Melton South
Rockbank
Pascoe Vale
Reservoir
Preston
Essendon Airport
Keilor
Ballark
The Bluff
Rowsley
Melton Res
Mt Wallace
Exford
St Albans
Coburg
Essendon
Mt Cottrell Volcanic Cone
Brunswick
Beremboke
Boar Gully
Deer Park
Albion
Sunshine
MELBOURNE
Morrisons
Balliang East
Mt Cottrell
Footscray
Brisbane Ranges National Park
Durdidwarrah
Little River
Cobbledicks Ford
Truganina
Newport
Albert Park
Meredith
Historic Railway Station
Balliang
Staughton Vale
Tarneit
Williamstown
Hobsons Bay
St Kilda
Laverton
Altona
Altona Coastal Pk
Anakie Gorge
Steiglitz
Hoppers Crossing
Cheetham Wetlands
Altona Bay
Point Gellibrand
Point Ormond
Sheoaks
Steiglitz Historic Park
Anakie Junction
Werribee
Western Treatment Plant
Open Range Zoo
Brighton
Anakie
You Yangs Regional Park
Point Cook
Manor
Werribee Park
RAAF Base
Point Cook Coastal Park & Homestead
Sandringham
Flinders Peak
Little River
Maude
Lethbridge
Anakie East
Werribee South
Black Rock
Rothwell
Serendip Sanctuary
Sutherland Creek
Lara
Avalon Airfield International Airshow Venue
Beacon Pt
Boat Ramp
Kirk Pt
PORT PHILLIP BAY
Bannockburn
Restricted access to Pt Wilson
Moorabool
Corio
Avalon Beach
Gheringhap
Pt Lillias
Pt Wilson
Inverleigh
Murchebolue
North Shore
Norlane
Corio Bay
Pt Richards
Portarlington
Old Flour Mill
Pt Henry
Pt George
Indented Head
Stonehaven
Fyansford
GEELONG
Maritime Museum, Eastern Beach, Barwon Grange, Waterworld, National Wool Museum
Bellarine
Clifton Springs
SEE PAGE 41
Barrabool Hills Maze
Newtown
Drysdale
Gnarwarree
Barrabool
Highton
Murradoc
St Leonards
Mt Pollock
Ceres
Belmont
Moolap
Curlewis
Bellarine Peninsula
Mt Moriac
Waurn Ponds
Leopold
Marshall
Steam Railway
Edwards Pt
Edwards Point Faunal Reserve
Mt Moriac
Pettavel
Grovedale
Wallington
Reedy Lake
Lake Connewarre
Mannerim
Swan Bay
Duck Island
Port Phillip Heads Marine Nat Park
Swan Pt
Swan Island
Golf Course
Morning
Fishermans
Buckley
Lake Modewarre
Moriac
Mt Duneed
Ocean Grove Nature Res
Marcus Hill
Balcombe Bay
Lake Gherang
Modewarre
Freshwater Creek
State Game Res
Salt Swamp
Connewarre
Ocean Grove
Lake Victoria
Queenscliff
Mud Islands
Mt Martha
Balcombe Pt
Paraparap
Lighthouse
Maritime Museum
Pt Lonsdale
Barwon Heads
Pt Flinders
Queenscliff - Sorrento passenger and vehicular ferry operates daily. Phone 03 5258 3244 for exact times.
Martha Pt
Safety Beach
Gherang
Tiger Moth World
Breamlea
Rip
Fort Nepean
Pt Nepean
Pt Nepean Nat Park
Point Franklin
Point King
Dromana
Dromana Bay
Bellbrae
Surfworld
Zeally Bay
Portsea
Portsea Surf Beach
Sorrento
The Sisters
Sullivan Bay-Victoria's First Settlement Site 1803
Capel Sound
McCrae
McCrae Homestead
Gum Flat
Jan Juc
Torquay
Pt Danger
Rocky Pt
Sorrento Back Beach
Arthurs Seat
Bells Beach
Blairgowrie
Rye
Tootgarook
Rosebud
Arthurs Seat State Pk
Pinchgut Junction
Pt Addis
Aboriginal Cultural Walking Trail
Mornington Peninsula National Park
Peninsula
Anglesea
Rye Ocean Beach
School Hill
Boneo
Pt Roadknight
Gunnamatta Beach
Mornington Peninsula National Park
Green Bush
Distillery Ck Picnic Area
Fairhaven
Aireys Inlet
Lighthouse
Split Point
Point Addis Marine Nat Park
Cape Schanck
Views and Bushwalks
Lighthouse Museum
Bushrangers Bay
Cairns Bay
0
10
20km
© Hema Maps Pty Ltd
144°30
37°30
38°
WESTERN FWY
MELTON HWY
TULLAMARINE FWY
HUME FWY
CALDER FWY
WEST GATE FWY
PRINCES FWY
MIDLAND HWY
HAMILTON HWY
BELLARINE HWY
PRINCES HWY
SURFCOAST HWY
GREAT OCEAN ROAD
METROPOLITAN RING RD
1
2
3
4
5
6
7
A
B
C
D
E
F
G
H
J
K

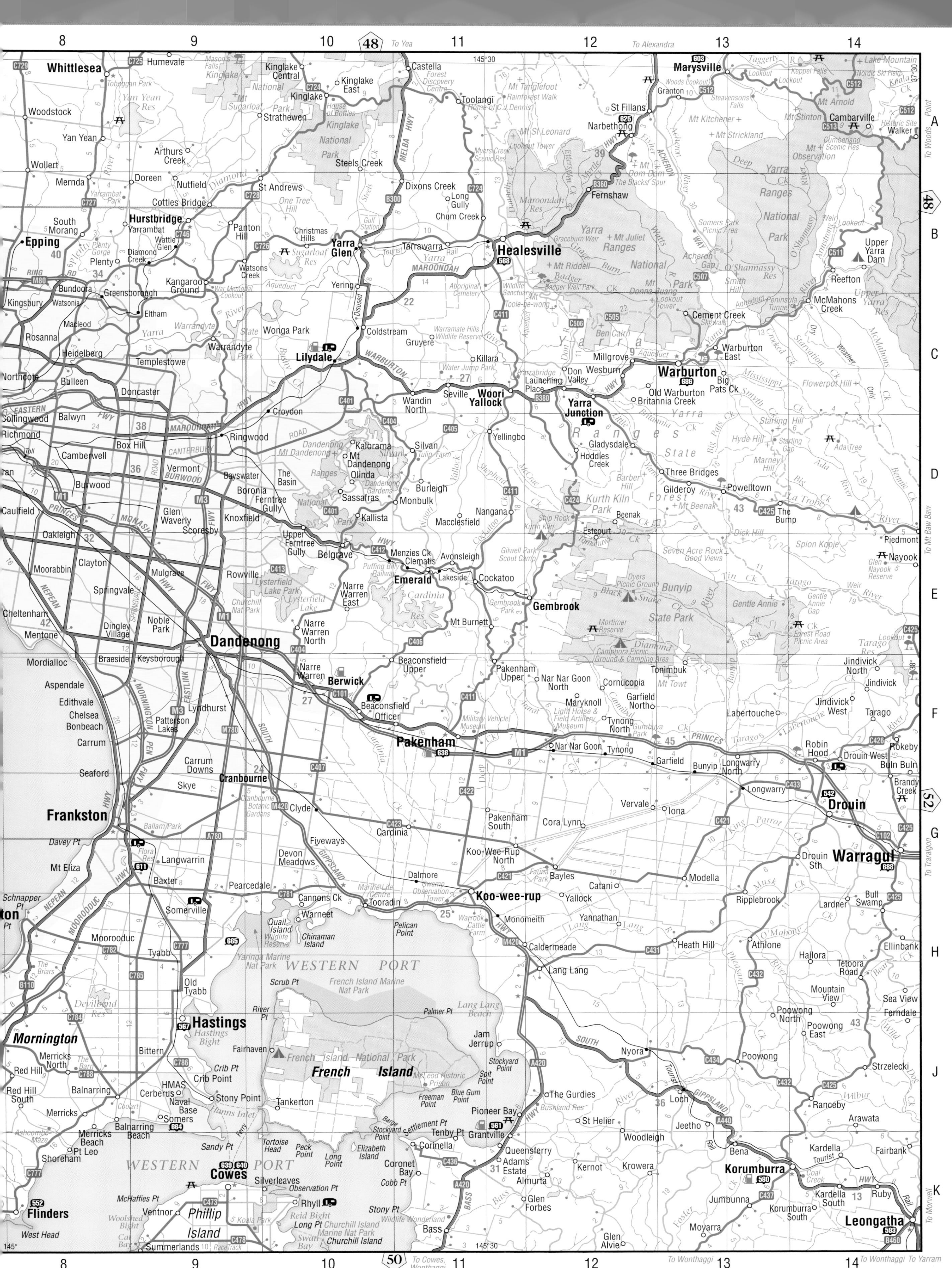

8
9
10
11
12
13
14
48
To Yea
To Alexandra
A
B
C
D
E
F
G
H
J
K
52
50
To Cowes, Wonthaggi
To Wonthaggi
To Wonthaggi To Yarram
To Woods Point
To Mt Baw Baw
To Traralgon
To Morwell
145°30
145°
37°30
38°
Whittlesea
Humevale
Kinglake Central
Kinglake East
Kinglake
Castella
Toolangi
Marysville
Lake Mountain
Woodstock
Yan Yean
Strathewen
Kinglake National Park
St Fillans
Narbethong
Granton
Cambarville
Walker
Wollert
Mernda
Arthurs Creek
Steels Creek
Mt St Leonard
Mt Dom Dom
Yarra Ranges National Park
Doreen
Nutfield
St Andrews
Dixons Creek
Long Gully
Chum Creek
Fernshaw
South Morang
Hurstbridge
Yarrambat
Cottles Bridge
Panton Hill
Christmas Hills
Epping
Wattle Glen
Diamond Creek
Plenty
Watsons Creek
Yarra Glen
Tarrawarra
Healesville
Upper Yarra Dam
Kangaroo Ground
Yering
Reefton
Bundoora
Greensborough
Kingsbury
Watsonia
Eltham
McMahons Creek
Cement Creek
Macleod
Rosanna
Heidelberg
Warrandyte
Wonga Park
Coldstream
Gruyere
Templestowe
Lilydale
Killara
Millgrove
Wesburn
Warburton
Warburton East
Northcote
Bulleen
Doncaster
Don Valley
Launching Place
Big Pats Ck
Old Warburton
Britannia Creek
Wandin North
Seville
Woori Yallock
Yarra Junction
Collingwood
Balwyn
Croydon
Richmond
Ringwood
Box Hill
Camberwell
Kalorama
Mt Dandenong
Olinda
Silvan
Yellingbo
Gladysdale
Hoddles Creek
Vermont
Bayswater
The Basin
Burwood
Boronia
Ferntree Gully
Sassafras
Burleigh
Monbulk
Three Bridges
Gilderoy
Powelltown
Caulfield
Glen Waverly
Knoxfield
Scoresby
Kallista
Macclesfield
Nangana
Kurth Kiln Park
Beenak
The Bump
Oakleigh
Upper Ferntree Gully
Belgrave
Menzies Ck
Clematis
Avonsleigh
Estcourt
Piedmont
Nayook
Moorabbin
Clayton
Mulgrave
Rowville
Emerald
Lakeside
Cockatoo
Springvale
Narre Warren East
Gembrook
Bunyip State Park
Cheltenham
Mentone
Noble Park
Dingley Village
Dandenong
Narre Warren North
Mt Burnett
Mordialloc
Braeside
Keysborough
Narre Warren
Berwick
Beaconsfield Upper
Pakenham Upper
Nar Nar Goon North
Cornucopia
Tonimbuk
Jindivick North
Jindivick
Aspendale
Edithvale
Chelsea
Bonbeach
Carrum
Lyndhurst
Patterson Lakes
Beaconsfield
Officer
Maryknoll
Garfield North
Tynong North
Jindivick West
Labertouche
Tarago
Pakenham
Nar Nar Goon
Tynong
Garfield
Bunyip
Longwarry North
Robin Hood
Drouin West
Rokeby
Buln Buln
Brandy Creek
Seaford
Carrum Downs
Cranbourne
Skye
Longwarry
Drouin
Frankston
Clyde
Pakenham South
Cora Lynn
Vervale
Iona
Cardinia
Davey Pt
Mt Eliza
Langwarrin
Fiveways
Devon Meadows
Koo-Wee-Rup North
Drouin Sth
Warragul
Baxter
Pearcedale
Dalmore
Bayles
Catani
Modella
Schnapper Pt
Somerville
Cannons Ck
Tooradin
Warneet
Koo-wee-rup
Yallock
Ripplebrook
Lardner
Bull Swamp
Quail Island
Chinaman Island
Pelican Point
Monomeith
Yannathan
Mooroduc
Tyabb
Caldermeade
Heath Hill
Athlone
Ellinbank
Lang Lang
Hallora
Tetoora Road
WESTERN PORT
French Island Marine Nat Park
Old Tyabb
Scrub Pt
Mountain View
Sea View
Ferndale
Hastings
River Pt
Palmer Pt
Lang Lang Beach
Poowong North
Poowong East
Mornington
Jam Jerrup
Merricks North
Bittern
Fairhaven
French Island National Park
French Island
Nyora
Poowong
Red Hill
Crib Pt
Crib Point
Stockyard Point
Spit Point
Strzelecki
Red Hill South
Balnarring
HMAS Cerberus
Naval Base
Stony Point
Tankerton
Freeman Point
Blue Gum Point
The Gurdies
Loch
Ranceby
Merricks
Somers
Pioneer Bay
St Helier
Jeetho
Arawata
Merricks Beach
Balnarring Beach
Pt Leo
Shoreham
Sandy Pt
Tortoise Head
Peck Point
Long Point
Elizabeth Island
Settlement Pt
Tenby Pt
Grantville
Corinella
Woodleigh
Bena
Kardella
Fairbank
WESTERN PORT
Cowes
Silverleaves
Observation Pt
Coronet Bay
Cobb Pt
Queensferry
Adams Estate
Almurta
Kernot
Krowera
Korumburra
Flinders
McHaffies Pt
Ventnor
Phillip Island
Rhyll
Stony Pt
Glen Forbes
Jumbunna
Kardella South
Ruby
Korumburra South
Woolshed Bight
Cat Bay
Reid Bight
Long Pt
Churchill Island
Marine Nat Park
Swan Bay
Bass
Moyarra
Leongatha
West Head
Summerlands
Glen Alvie

South-West Victoria

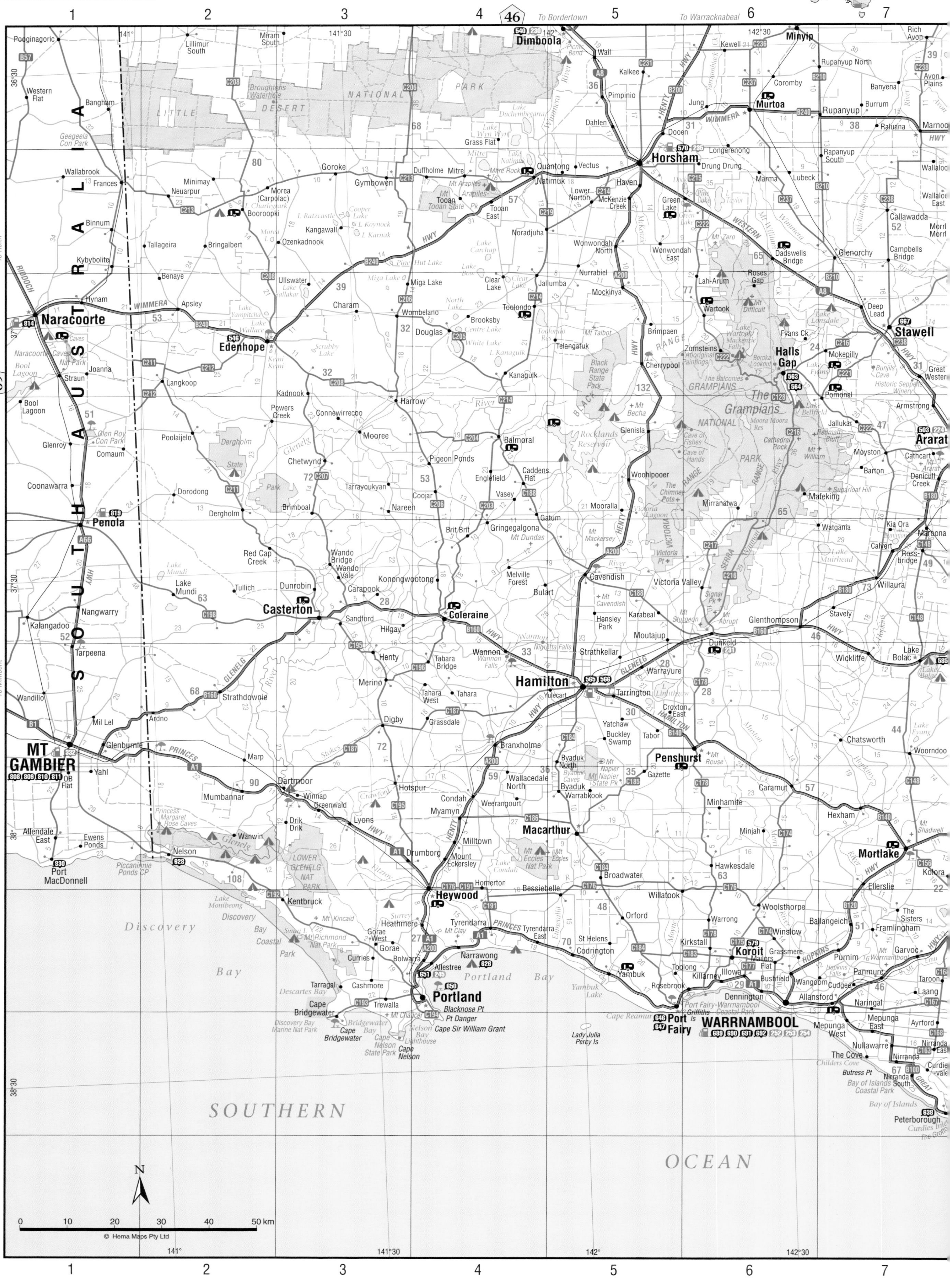

1 2 3 4 5 6 7

To Bordertown · To Warracknabeal

A: Pooginagoric, Lillimur South, Miram South, Dimboola, Wail, Kewell, Minyip, Rich Avon, Western Flat, Bangham, Little Desert National Park, Broughtons Waterhole, Lake Duchembegarra, Kalkee, Pimpinio, Jung, Murtoa, Corromby, Rupanyup North, Banyena, Avon Plains, Burrum, Rupanyup, Dahlen, Dooen, Raluana, Marnoo, Geegeela Con Park, Grass Flat, Lake Wyn Wyn

B: Wallabrook, Frances, Minimay, Neuarpur, Goroke, Morea (Carpolac), Booroopki, Gymbowen, Duffholme, Mitre, Mt Arapiles, Natimuk, Quantong, Vectus, Horsham, Longerenong, Drung Drung, Rupanyup South, Mt Toolon, Toolon State Pk, Toolon East, Lower Norton, McKenzie Creek, Haven, Green Lake, Marma, Lubeck, Wallaloo, Wallaloo East, Binnum, Tallageira, Bringalbert, Kangawall, Ozenkadnook, Noradjuha, Wonwondah North, Wonwondah East, Callawadda, Glenorchy, Campbells Bridge, Dadswells Bridge, Kybybolite, L Ratzcastle, Cooper Lake, L Koynock, L Karnak, Lake Carchap, Pine Hut Lake, Mt Zero, Morrl Morrl

C: Benayie, Hynam, Apsley, Naracoorte, Ullswater, Miga Lake, Charam, Clear Lake, Jallumba, Nurrabiel, Mockinya, Lah-Arum, Roses Gap, Wartook, Mt Difficult, Deep Lead, Stawell, Edenhope, Wombelano, Brooksby, Douglas, Toolondo, Telangatuk, Brimpaen, Zumsteins, Halls Gap, Fyans Ck, Mokepilly, Pomonal, Great Western, Joanna, Straun, Bool Lagoon, Naracoorte Caves Nat Park, Lake Wallace, Keon Keon, Scrubby Lake, White Lake, L Kanagulk, Kanagulk, Cherrypool, Mt Talbot, Black Range State Park, The Balconies, Boroka Lookout, Grampians, Bunjils Cave, Historic Seppelt Winery

D: Langkoop, Kadnook, Harrow, Powers Creek, Connewirrecoo, Mooree, Balmoral, Glenisla, Mt Becha, Rocklands Reservoir, Glenroy, Glen Roy Con Park, Poolaijelo, Comaum, Dergholm State Park, Chetwynd, Pigeon Ponds, Caddens Flat, Englefield, Woohlpooer, Moora Moora Res, Cathedral Rock, Mt William, Moyston, Cathcart, Barton, Ararat, Armstrong, Jallukar, Coonawarra, Dorodong, Tarrayoukyan, Vasey, Coojar, Nareen, Mt Arapiles, The Chimney Pots, Cave of Fishes, Cave of Hands, Mirranatwa, Mafeking, Denicull Creek

E: Penola, Dergholm, Brimboal, Gatum, Moorallla, Victoria Lagoon, Brit Brit, Gringegalgona, Mt Dundas, Mt Mackersey, Watgania, Kia Ora, Maroona, Calvert, Ross-bridge, Red Cap Creek, Wando Bridge, Wando Vale, Lake Mundi, Tullich, Dunrobin, Konongwootong, Melville Forest, Bulart, Cavendish, Victoria Valley, Victoria Pt, Serra Range, Signal Pk, Willaura, Lake Muirhead, Casterton, Carapook, Nangwarry, Sandford, Hilgay, Coleraine, Hensley Park, Karabeal, Mt Sturgeon, Mt Abrupt, Glenthompson, Stavely, Kalangadoo, Moutajup, Dunkeld

F: Tarpeena, Henty, Wannon, Wannon Falls, Nigretta Falls, Strathkellar, Warrayure, Wickliffe, Lake Bolac, Tahara Bridge, Merino, Hamilton, Tarrington, Wandillo, Strathdownie, Tahara West, Tahara, Yulecart, Croxton East, Mil Lel, Ardno, Digby, Grassdale, Yatchaw, Buckley Swamp, Tabor, Chatsworth, Woorndoo, Lake Repose, Lake Linlithgow, Mt Gambier, Glenburnie, Branxholme, Byaduk North, Mt Napier, Penshurst, Mt Rouse, Marp

G: Yahl, OB Flat, Mumbannar, Dartmoor, Hotspur, Wallacedale North, Byaduk Caves, Mt Napier State Pk, Gazette, Caramut, Winnap, Greenwald, Condah, Byaduk, Warrabkook, Minhamite, Hexham, Lyons, Myamyn, Weerangourt, Allendale East, Ewens Ponds, Drik Drik, Macarthur, Minjah, Mt Shadwell, Wanwin, Nelson, Drumborg, Milltown, Mt Eccles, Mt Eccles Nat Park, Mortlake, Port MacDonnell, Piccaninnie Ponds CP, Princess Margaret Rose Caves, Lower Glenelg Nat Park, Mount Eckersley, Lake Condah, Broadwater, Hawkesdale, Ellerslie, Kolora

H: Kentbruck, Heywood, Homerton, Bessiebelle, Willatook, Woolsthorpe, Lake Monibeong, Discovery Bay, Discovery Bay Coastal Park, Mt Kincaid, Surrey, Heathmere, Tyrendarra, Mt Clay, Tyrendarra East, Orford, Warrong, Ballangeich, The Sisters, Framlingham, Swan Lake, Mt Richmond Nat Park, Gorae West, Gorae, St Helens, Kirkstall, Koroit, Winslow, Grassmere, Codrington, Garvoc, Purnim, Mt Warrnambool, Curries, Bolwarra, Narrawong, Yambuk, Toolong, Killarney, Illowa, Mailors Flat, Bushfield, Wangoom, Panmure, Taroon, Allestree, Portland Bay, Hopkins Falls, Cudgee, Laang, Tarragal, Cashmore, Descartes Bay, Portland, Yambuk Lake, Rosebrook, Dennington, Allansford, Naringal

J: Cape Bridgewater, Trewalla, Blacknose Pt, Pt Danger, Mt Chaucer, Cape Sir William Grant, Cape Reamur, Port Fairy, Griffiths Is, Port Fairy-Warrnambool Coastal Park, Warrnambool, Mepunga West, Mepunga East, Ayrford, Discovery Bay Marine Nat Park, Bridgewater Bay, Cape Nelson State Park, Cape Nelson, Nelson Bay Lighthouse, Lady Julia Percy Is, Nullawarre, Nirranda East, The Cove, Childers Cove, Nirranda, Butress Pt, Nirranda South, Bay of Islands Coastal Park, Bay of Islands, Curdievale, Peterborough, Curdies Inlet, The Grotto

SOUTHERN OCEAN

SOUTH AUSTRALIA

Highways: Wimmera Hwy, Western Hwy, Henty Hwy, Glenelg Hwy, Hamilton Hwy, Princes Hwy, Hopkins Hwy, Riddoch Hwy, Great Ocean Rd

Scale: 0 10 20 30 40 50 km

To Keith · To Millicent

141° · 141°30 · 142° · 142°30 · 36°30 · 37° · 37°30 · 38° · 38°30

A B C D E F G H J K

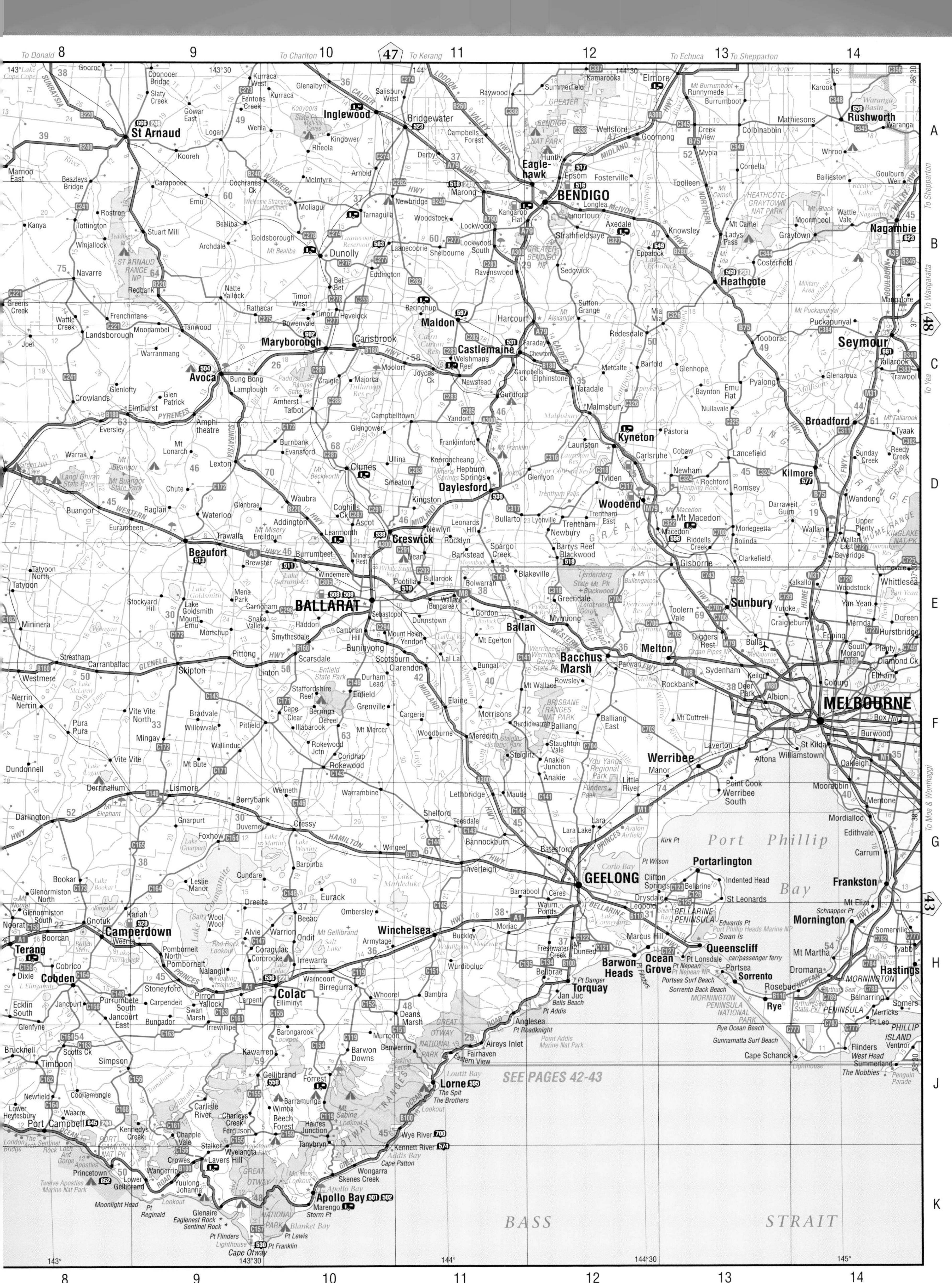

To Donald
8
9
To Charlton
10
47
To Kerang
11
12
To Echuca
13
To Shepparton
14
A
B
C
D
E
F
G
H
J
K
Gooroc
Coonooer Bridge
Slaty Creek
Kurraca West
Kurraca
Fentons Creek
Glenalbyn
Salisbury West
Inglewood
Bridgewater
Raywood
Kamarooka
Summerfield
Elmore
Mt Burrumboot
Runnymede
Burrumboot
Karook
Rushworth
Waranga Basin
Waranga
Mathiesons
Colbinabbin
Creek View
Wellsford
Goornong
St Arnaud
Gowar East
Logan
Wehla
Kingower
Rheola
Campbells Forest
Derby
Marnoo East
Kooreh
Arnold
McIntyre
Eaglehawk
Huntly
Epsom
BENDIGO
Fosterville
Myola
Cornella
Toolleen
Whroo
Bailieston
Goulburn Weir
Beazleys Bridge
Carapooee
Cochranes Ck
Emu
Moliagul
Newbridge
Marong
Longlea
Junortoun
Axedale
Knowsley
Mt Camel
Heathcote-Graytown Nat Park
Moormbool
Wattle Vale
Nagambie
Kanya
Rostron
Tottington
Stuart Mill
Archdale
Bealiba
Goldsborough
Tarnagulla
Dunolly
Laanecoorie
Woodstock
Lockwood
Lockwood South
Kangaroo Flat
Strathfieldsaye
Eppalock
Ladys Pass
Graytown
Winjallock
St Arnaud Range NP
Navarre
Redbank
Eddington
Shelbourne
Ravenswood
Sedgwick
Costerfield
Heathcote
Mangalore
Greens Creek
Natte Yallock
Timor West
Bet Bet
Baringhup
Sutton Grange
Mia Mia
Wattle Creek
Frenchmans
Rathscar
Bowenvale
Timor
Havelock
Maldon
Harcourt
Redesdale
Puckapunyal
Seymour
Landsborough
Moonambel
Tarnwood
Maryborough
Carisbrook
Castlemaine
Faraday
Chewton
Tooborac
Joel
Warranmang
Welshmans Reef
Moolort
Metcalfe
Barfold
Glenhope
Pyalong
Glenaroua
Tallarook
Trawool
Avoca
Bung Bong
Lamplough
Craigie
Majorca
Joyces Ck
Newstead
Campbells Ck
Elphinstone
Taradale
Baynton
Emu Flat
Glenlofty
Crowlands
Glen Patrick
Amherst
Talbot
Guildford
Malmsbury
Nullavale
Broadford
Elmhurst
Pyrenees
Eversley
Amphi theatre
Campbelltown
Yandoit
Mt Tallarook
Tyaak
Glengower
Franklinford
Kyneton
Pastoria
Warrak
Mt Lonarch
Burnbank
Evansford
Lauriston
Carlsruhe
Cobaw
Lancefield
Reedy Creek
Sunday Creek
Lexton
Clunes
Ullina
Kooroocheang
Hepburn Springs
Newham
Rochford
Kilmore
Chute
Smeaton
Daylesford
Glenlyon
Tylden
Romsey
Buangor
Raglan
Waubra
Kingston
Woodend
Wandong
Mt Buangor State Park
Waterloo
Glenbrae
Coghills Ck
Ascot
Bullarto
Lyonville
Trentham
Trentham East
Mt Macedon
Darraweit Guim
Upper Plenty
Wallan
Eurambeen
Addington
Learmonth
Leonards Hill
Newlyn
Newbury
Macedon
Monegeetta
Kinglake Nat Pk
Trawalla
Ercildoun
Creswick
Rocklyn
Spargo Creek
Barrys Reef
Blackwood
Riddells Creek
Bolinda
Wallan East
Beveridge
Beaufort
Brewster
Burrumbeet
Miners Rest
Dean
Barkstead
Gisborne
Clarkefield
Humevale
Tatyoon North
Tatyoon
Windemere
Pootilla
Bullarook
Blakeville
Lerderderg State Pk
Whittlesea
Kalkallo
Woodstock
Stockyard Hill
Mena Park
BALLARAT
Bolwarrah
Greendale
Sunbury
Yan Yean
Lake Goldsmith
Carngham
Sebastopol
Wallace
Bungaree
Gordon
Myrniong
Toolern Vale
Yuroke
Doreen
Mininera
Mount Emu
Snake Valley
Haddon
Cambrian Hill
Mount Helen
Yendon
Dunnstown
Ballan
Craigieburn
Mernda
Hurstbridge
Mortchup
Smythesdale
Buninyong
Mt Egerton
Melton
Diggers Rest
Bulla
Epping
South Morang
Plenty
Diamond Ck
Streatham
Carranballac
Glenelg
Pittong
Scarsdale
Lal Lal
Bacchus Marsh
Parwan
Sydenham
Keilor
Eltham
Westmere
Skipton
Linton
Scotsburn
Clarendon
Durham Lead
Bungal
Rowsley
Rockbank
Deer Park
Albion
Coburg
Nerrin Nerrin
Staffordshire Reef
Enfield
Mt Wallace
MELBOURNE
Vite Vite North
Bradvale
Cape Clear
Berringa
Grenville
Elaine
Cargerie
Morrisons
Brisbane Ranges Nat Park
Balliang
Balliang East
Mt Cottrell
Box Hill
Pura Pura
Mingay
Willowvale
Pitfield
Illabarook
Dereel
Mt Mercer
Woodburne
Meredith
Durdidwarrah
Staughton Vale
Laverton
Burwood
Wallinduc
Rokewood Jctn
Coridhap
Rokewood
Steiglitz
Anakie Junction
You Yangs Regional Park
Werribee
Altona
Williamstown
St Kilda
Oakleigh
Dundonnell
Vite Vite
Mt Bute
Anakie
Manor
Point Cook
Werribee South
Moorabbin
Derrinallum
Lismore
Werneth
Warrambine
Lethbridge
Maude
Little River
Mentone
Darlington
Mt Elephant
Berrybank
Duverney
Cressy
Shelford
Teesdale
Lara
Mordialloc
Gnarpurt
Foxhow
Hamilton
Wingeel
Bannockburn
Lara Lake
Avalon Airfield
Edithvale
Port Phillip
Kirk Pt
Batesford
Carrum
Bookar
Barpinba
Inverleigh
Pt Wilson
Portarlington
Leslie Manor
Cundare
Corio Bay
Glenormiston North
Eurack
Barrabool
GEELONG
Clifton Springs
Indented Head
Bellarine
Bay
Frankston
Dreeite
Ceres
Drysdale
St Leonards
Noorat
Glenormiston South
Gnotuk
Kariah
Wool Wool
Ombersley
Waurn Ponds
Leopold
Bellarine Peninsula
Mt Eliza
Schnapper Pt
Beeac
Winchelsea
Moriac
Edwards Pt
Port Phillip Heads Marine NP
Swan Is
Mornington
Somerville
Boorcan
Camperdown
Alvie
Warrion
Mt Gellibrand
Ondit
Armytage
Buckley
Freshwater Creek
Mt Duneed
Marcus Hill
Queenscliff
Terang
Weerite
Pomborneit North
Pomborneit
Coragulac
Corrorooke
Irrewarra
Salt Lake
Wurdiboluc
Bellbrae
Barwon Heads
Ocean Grove
Pt Lonsdale
car/passenger ferry
Pt Nepean
Pt Nepean NP
Portsea
Sorrento
Mt Martha
Tyabb
Dixie
Cobrico
Cobden
Nalangil
Stoneyford
Pirron Yallock
Colac
Warncoort
Birregurra
Pt Danger
Torquay
Jan Juc
Bells Beach
Portsea Surf Beach
Sorrento Back Beach
Dromana
Hastings
Rosebud
Mornington
Ecklin South
Jancourt
Purrumbete South
Jancourt East
Carpendeit
Swan Marsh
Larpent
Elliminyt
Whoorel
Bambra
Pt Addis
Mornington Peninsula National Park
Rye
Arthurs Seat State Pk
Balnarring
Peninsula
Somers
Merricks
Pt Leo
Glenfyne
Bungador
Irrewillipe
Deans Marsh
Anglesea
Pt Roadknight
Point Addis Marine Nat Park
Rye Ocean Beach
Gunnamatta Surf Beach
Phillip Island
Ventnor
Bucknell
Scotts Ck
Barongarook
Murroon
Benwerrin
Great Otway National Park
Aireys Inlet
Fairhaven
Eastern View
Cape Schanck
Flinders
West Head
Summerland
The Nobbies
Penguin Parade
Timboon
Simpson
Kawarren
Barwon Downs
Gellibrand
Forrest
Loutit Bay
Lorne
The Spit
The Brothers
SEE PAGES 42-43
Newfield
Cooriemungle
Barramunga
Wimba
Lower Heytesbury
Waarre
Carlisle River
Charleys Creek
Ferguson
Beech Forest
Haines Junction
Mt Sabine
Otway Ranges
Port Campbell
Kennedys Creek
Chapple Vale
Wye River
London Arch
The Sentinel
Loch Ard Gorge
Port Campbell Nat Pk
Stalker
Wyelangta
Tanybryn
Kennett River
Addis Bay
Cape Patton
12 Apostles
Princetown
Crowes
Lavers Hill
Wangerrip
Wongarra
Skenes Creek
Twelve Apostles Marine Nat Park
Lower Gellibrand
Yuulong
Johanna
Apollo Bay
Marengo
Storm Pt
Moonlight Head
Pt Reginald
Glenaire
Eaglenest Rock
Sentinel Rock
Blanket Bay
Pt Flinders
Lighthouse
Pt Franklin
Pt Lewis
Cape Otway
BASS
STRAIT
To Shepparton
To Wangaratta
To Yea
To Moe & Wonthaggi
48
43
143°
143°30
144°
144°30
145°

North-West Victoria

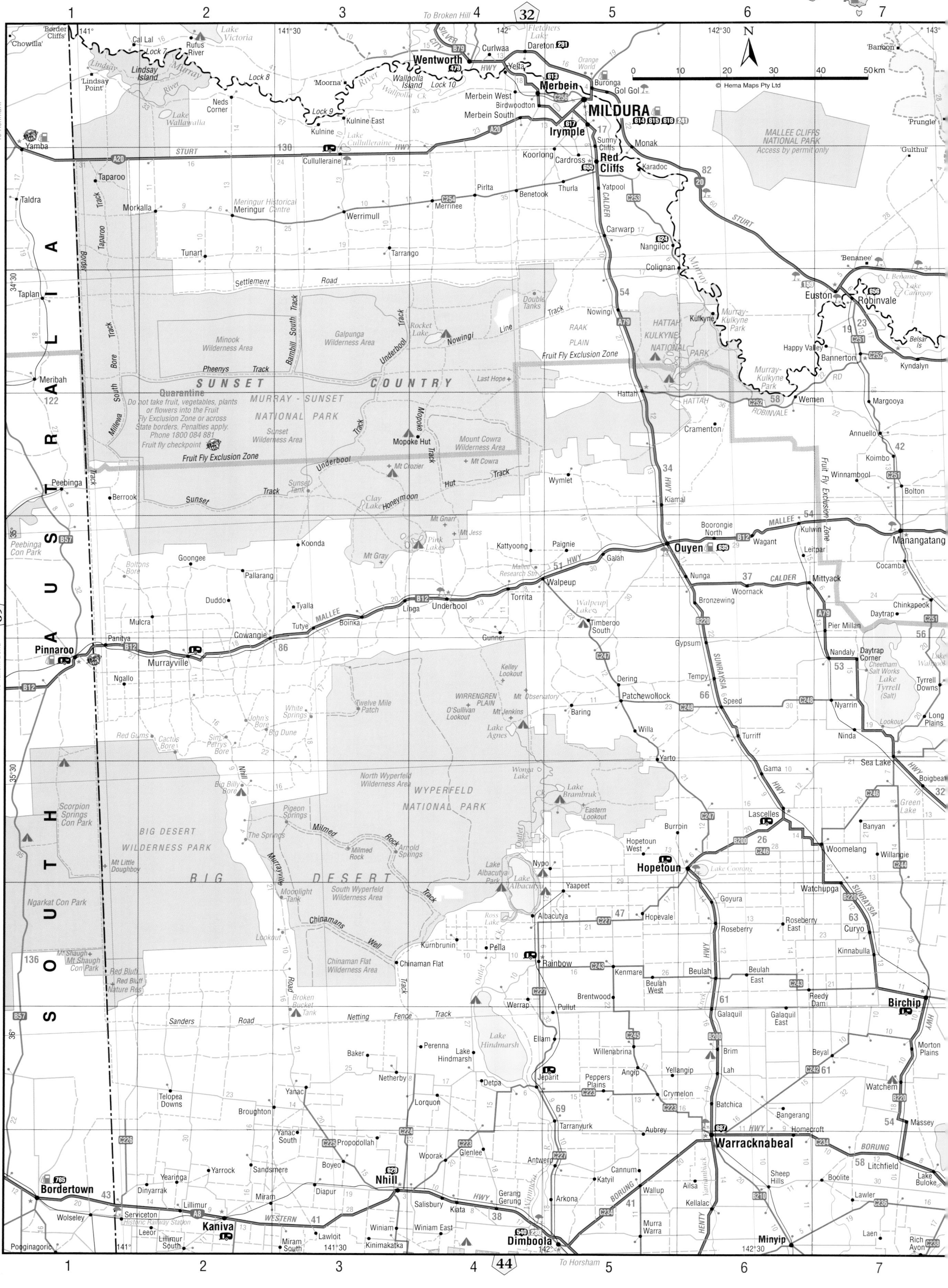

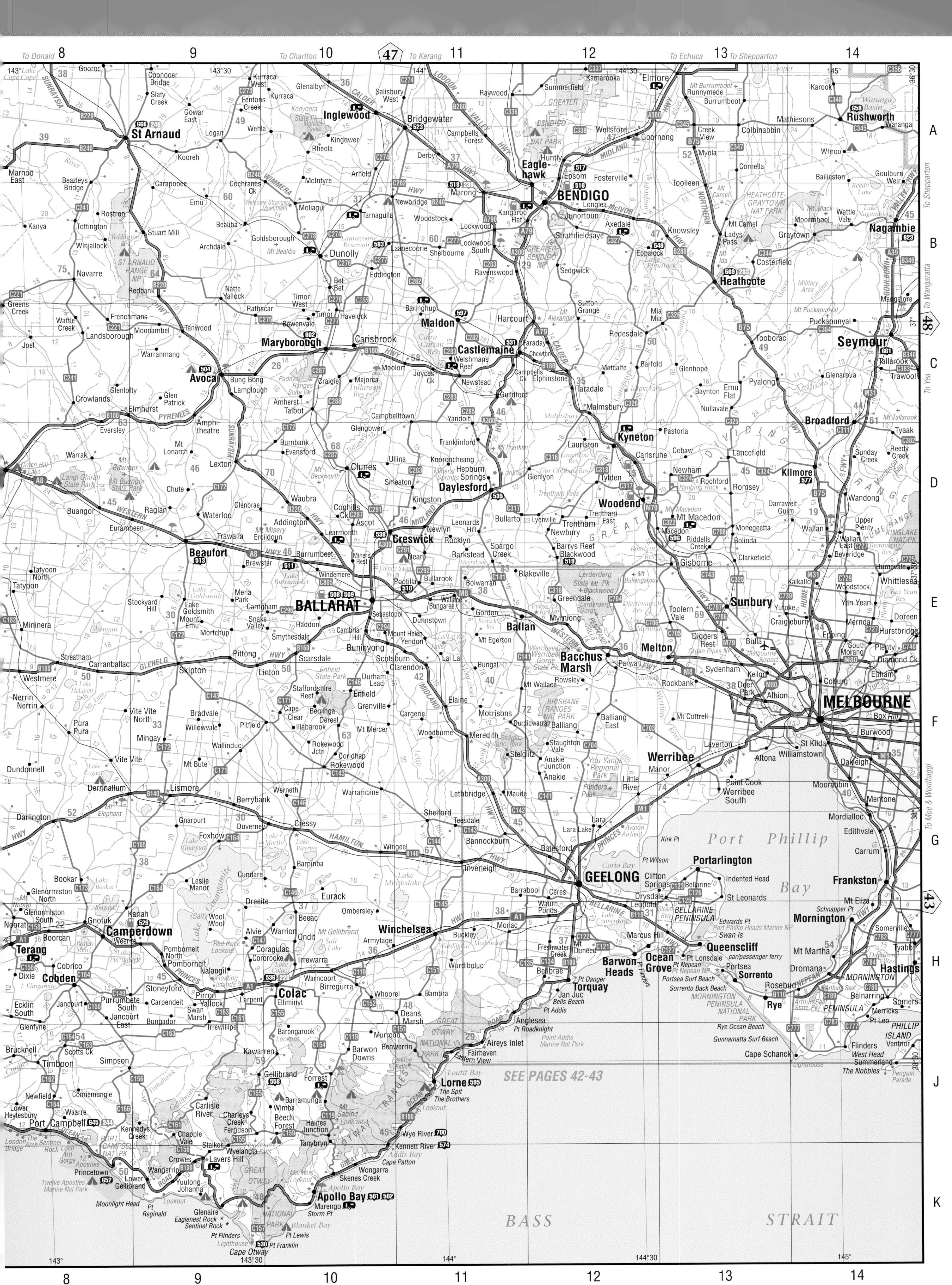

To Donald
To Charlton
47
To Kerang
To Echuca
To Shepparton
8
9
10
11
12
13
14
A
B
C
D
E
F
G
H
J
K
St Arnaud
Inglewood
Bridgewater
Eaglehawk
BENDIGO
Elmore
Rushworth
Nagambie
Heathcote
Seymour
48
Maryborough
Avoca
Maldon
Castlemaine
Dunolly
Kyneton
Broadford
Kilmore
Daylesford
Creswick
Clunes
Woodend
Beaufort
BALLARAT
Ballan
Bacchus Marsh
Melton
Sunbury
MELBOURNE
Werribee
GEELONG
Camperdown
Terang
Cobden
Colac
Winchelsea
Torquay
Lorne
Apollo Bay
Queenscliff
Sorrento
Rye
Frankston
Mornington
Hastings
43
Port Phillip Bay
BASS STRAIT
SEE PAGES 42-43
To Wangaratta
To Yea
To Moe & Wonthaggi

North-West Victoria

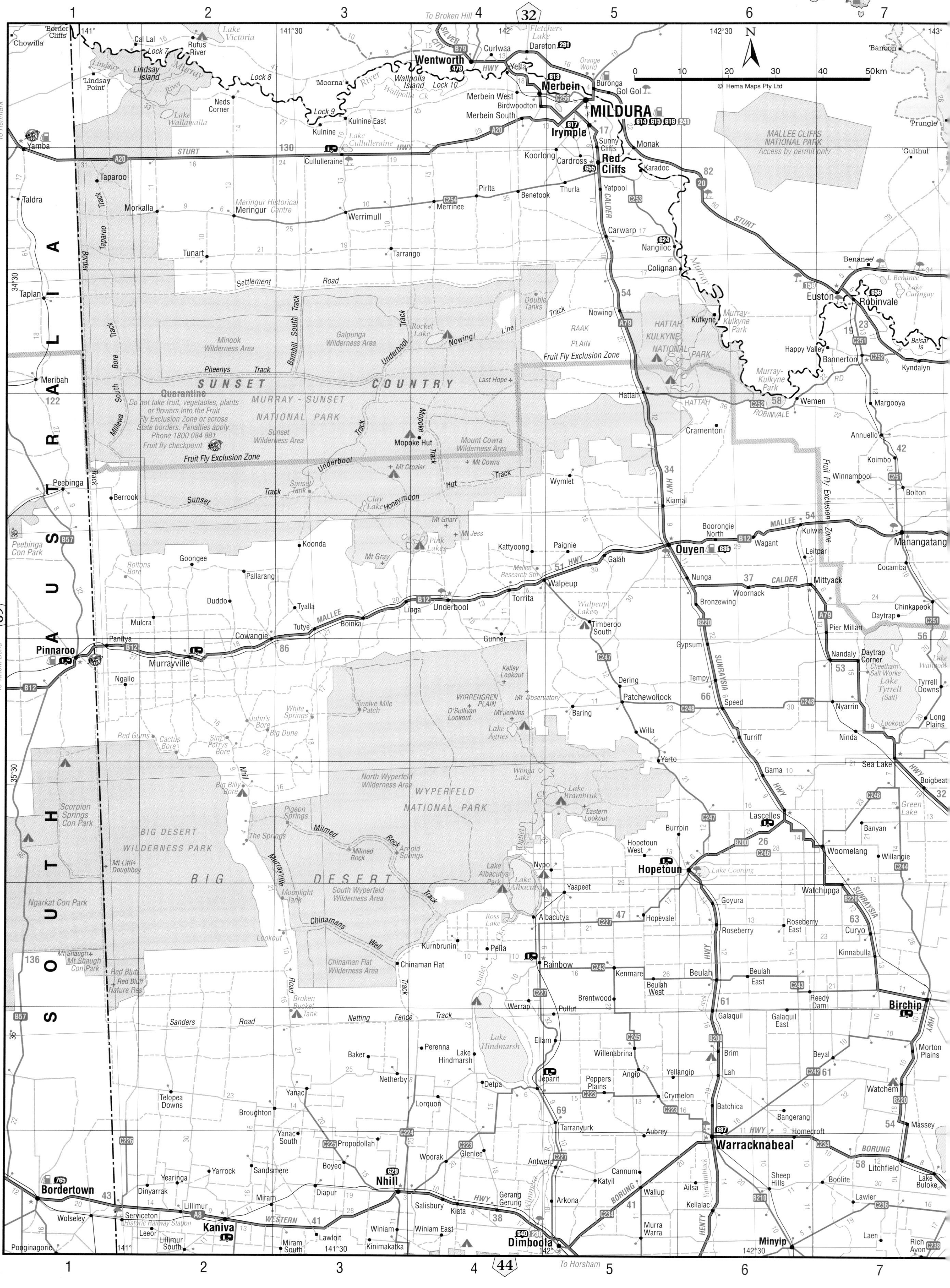

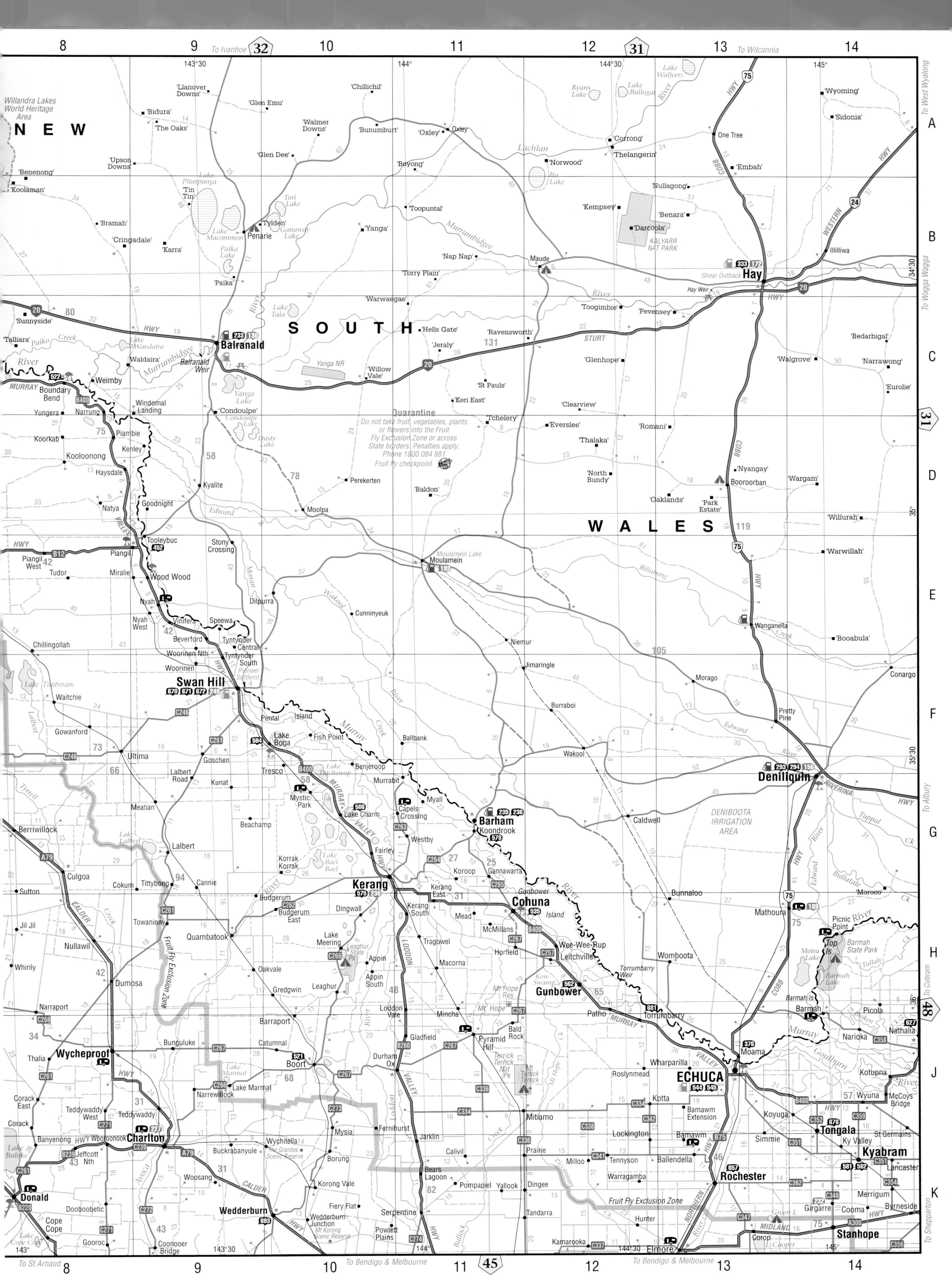

8
9
To Ivanhoe
32
10
11
12
31
13
To Wilcannia
14
143°30
144°
144°30
145°
To West Wyalong
Willandra Lakes World Heritage Area
NEW
SOUTH
WALES
'Llanover Downs'
'Bidura'
'The Oaks'
'Glen Emu'
'Chillichil'
'Walmer Downs'
'Bunumburt'
'Oxley'
Oxley
'Glen Dee'
'Upson Downs'
'Boyong'
Lachlan
'Norwood'
Ita Lake
Ryans Lake
Lake Bullogal
Lake Waljeers
River
'Corrong'
'Thelangerin'
One Tree
'Wyoming'
'Sidonia'
'Embah'
COBB
HWY
WESTERN
'Benenong'
'Koolaman'
Lake Pitarpunga
'Tin Tin'
Tori Lake
'Tylden'
Penarie
Lake Macommon
Ganawary Lake
Paika Lake
'Paika'
'Bramah'
'Cringadale'
'Karra'
'Yanga'
'Toopuntal'
Murrumbidgee
'Nap Nap'
'Torry Plain'
Maude
'Kempsey'
'Darcoola'
KALYARR NAT PARK
'Benara'
'Nullagong'
Illilliwa
Shear Outback
Hay
Hay Weir
34°30
To Wagga Wagga
'Sunnyside'
'Talliara'
Paiko Creek
Lake Wandaira
Balranald
Balranald Weir
Lake Tala
'Warwaegae'
'Hells Gate'
'Ravensworth'
STURT
'Toogimbie'
'Pevensey'
'Jeraly'
'Glenhope'
'Bedarbigal'
'Walgrove'
'Narrawong'
'Eurolie'
River
Weimby
Waldaira
Yanga NR
'Willow Vale'
'St Pauls'
MURRAY
Boundary Bend
Yungera
Narrung
Windomal Landing
'Condoulpe'
Condoulpe Lake
Yanga Lake
'Keri East'
Quarantine
Do not take fruit, vegetables, plants or flowers into the Fruit Fly Exclusion Zone or across State borders. Penalties apply. Phone 1800 084 881
Fruit fly checkpoint
'Tchelery'
'Everslee'
'Clearview'
'Romani'
'Thalaka'
Koorkab
Piambie
Kenley
Kooloonong
Haysdale
Dusty Lake
'North Bundy'
'Nyangay'
Booroorban
'Wargam'
Kyalite
Perekerten
'Baldon'
'Oaklands'
'Park Estate'
Natya
Goodnight
Moolpa
Edward
'Willurah'
35°
Tooleybuc
Stony Crossing
Moulamein Lake
Moulamein
Billabong
'Warwillah'
Piangil West
Piangil
Tudor
Miralie
Wood Wood
Wakool
Nyah
Nyah West
Vinifera
Speewa
Dilpurra
Cunninyeuk
Wanganella
Creek
Chillingollah
Beverford
Tyntynder Central
Woorinen Nth
Tyntynder South
Woorinen
Pioneer Settlement
Niemur
Jimaringle
'Booabula'
Lake Timboram
Swan Hill
Waitchie
Pental
Island
Morago
Conargo
Burraboi
Pretty Pine
Lalbert
Gowanford
Lake Boga
Fish Point
Murray
Ballbank
Edward
Ultima
Goschen
Wakool
Tresco
Lake Tutchewop
Benjeroop
Murrabit
Deniliquin
RIVERINA
35°30
To Albury
Lalbert Road
Kunat
Mystic Park
Lake Charm
Capels Crossing
Myall
Barham
Koondrook
Caldwell
DENIBOOTA IRRIGATION AREA
Tuppal
Berriwillock
Meatian
Beachamp
Westby
Lake Lalbert
Lalbert
Korrak Korrak
Lake Bael Bael
Fairley
Gannawarra
Koroop
Culgoa
Cannie
Kerang
Cohuna
Gunbower Island
Bunnaloo
Moroco
Billabong
Sutton
Cokum
Tittybong
Budgerum
Budgerum East
Kerang East
Mead
Mathoura
Picnic Point
Jil Jil
Towaninny
Dingwall
Kerang South
McMillans
Wee-Wee-Rup
Top Is
Barmah State Park
Nullawil
Quambatook
Lake Meering
Leaghur State Pk
Tragowel
Horfield
Leitchville
Womboota
Moira Lake
Tullah
Whirily
Oakvale
Appin
Appin South
Macorna
Kow Swamp
Gunbower
Torrumbarry Weir
Barmah Lake
Dumosa
Fruit Fly Exclusion Zone
Gredgwin
Leaghur
Mt Hope Res
Mt Hope
Barmah Is
Barmah
Picola
36°
To Cobram
Narraport
Loddon Vale
Mincha
Patho
Torrumbarry
Nathalia
Barraport
Bald Rock
Narioka
Wycheproof
Bunguluke
Catumnal
Gladfield
Pyramid Hill
Moama
Goulburn
Thalia
Boort
Durham Ox
Terrick Terrick Nat Pk
Wharparilla
Lake Marmal
Roslynmead
ECHUCA
Kotupna
Narrewillock
Lake Marmal
Mt Hope
Corack East
Teddywaddy West
Teddywaddy
Kotta
Wyunu
McCoys Bridge
Corack
Charlton
Mysia
Fernihurst
Jarklin
Mitiamo
Lockington
Bamawm Extension
Bamawm
Koyuga
Tongala
Ky Valley
St Germains
Simmie
Banyenong
Wooroonook
Lake Buloke
Jeffcott Nth
Buckrabanyule
Wychitella
The Granites Scenic Reserve
Borung
Calivil
Prairie
Milloo
Tennyson
Ballendella
Kyabram
Lancaster
Bears Lagoon
Pompapiel
Yallook
Dingee
Warragamba
Rochester
Donald
Woosang
Korong Vale
Fruit Fly Exclusion Zone
Merrigum
Byrneside
Dooboobetic
Cope Cope
Wedderburn
Fiery Flat
Wedderburn Junction
Mt Korong Scenic Reserve
Serpentine
Tandarra
Hunter
Girgarre
Cooma
Green L
MIDLAND
Stanhope
Lake Cope Cope
Gooroc
Coonooer Bridge
Powlett Plains
Kamarooka
Elmore
Corop
L Cooper
To Shepparton
143°
143°30
144°
144°30
145°
To St Arnaud
To Bendigo & Melbourne
45
To Bendigo & Melbourne
A
B
C
D
E
F
G
H
J
K
48

North-East Victoria

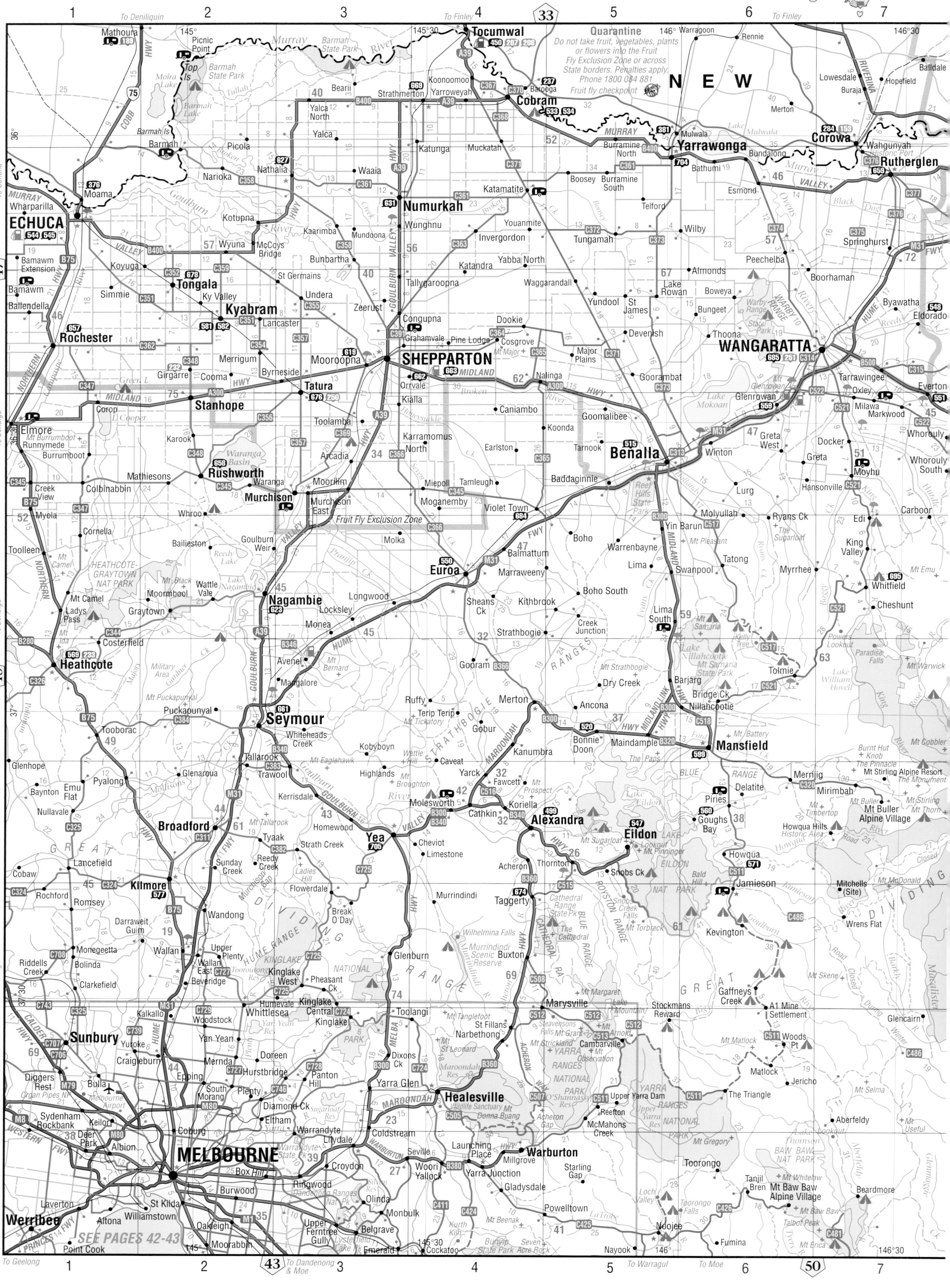

Quarantine
Do not take fruit, vegetables, plants or flowers into the Fruit Fly Exclusion Zone or across State borders. Penalties apply. Phone 1800 084 881
Fruit fly checkpoint

Fruit Fly Exclusion Zone

NEW SOUTH WALES

Tocumwal
Cobram
Yarrawonga
Corowa
Wahgunyah
Rutherglen
Echuca
Moama
Numurkah
Tongala
Kyabram
Rochester
Shepparton
Mooroopna
Tatura
Stanhope
Rushworth
Murchison
Nagambie
Heathcote
Seymour
Euroa
Benalla
Wangaratta
Mansfield
Alexandra
Eildon
Yea
Broadford
Kilmore
Sunbury
Whittlesea
Healesville
Warburton
Melbourne
Werribee

To Deniliquin
To Finley
To Cohuna
To Bendigo
To Ballarat
To Geelong
To Dandenong & Moe
To Warragul
To Moe
SEE PAGES 42-43

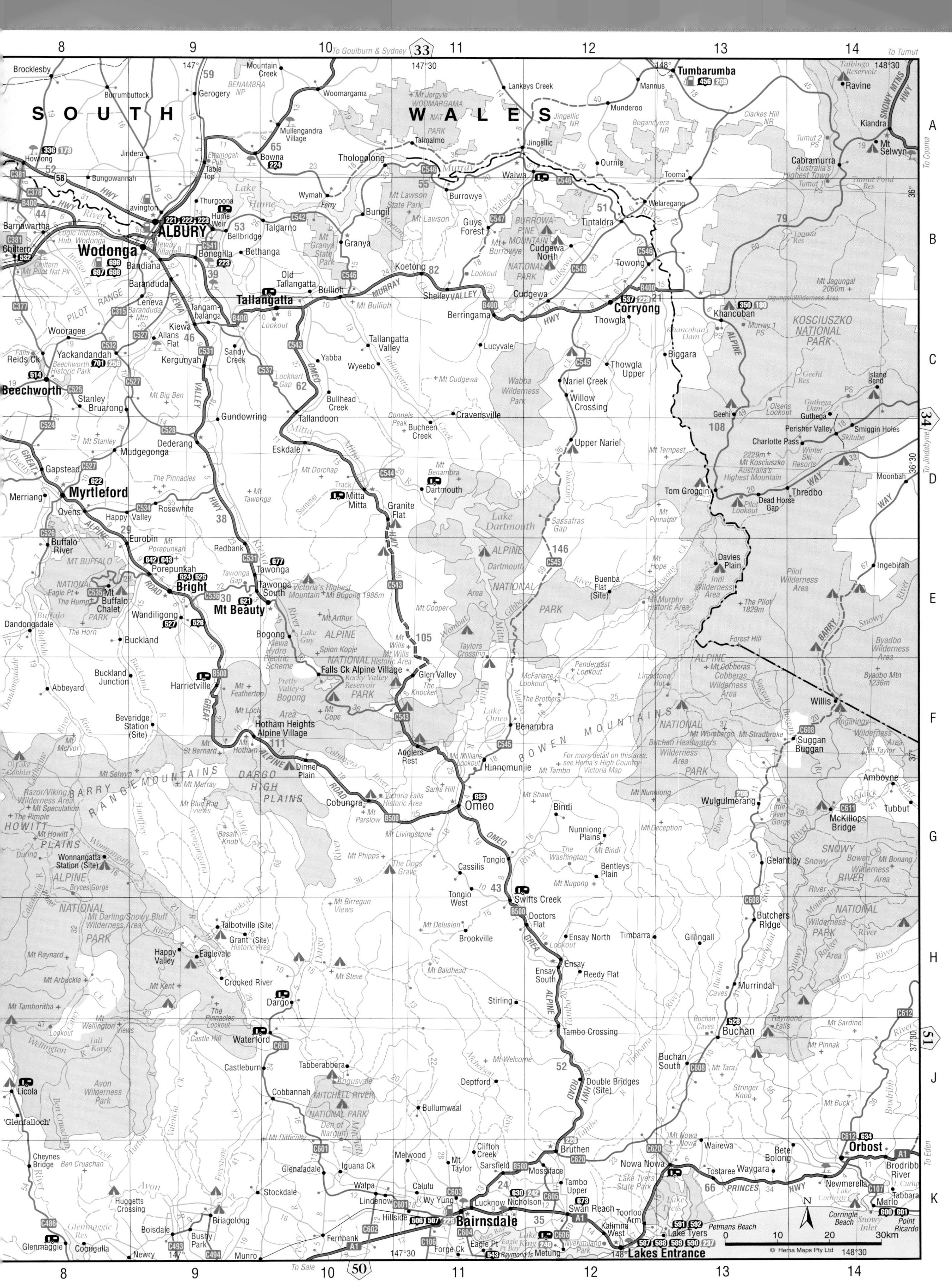

8
9
10
11
12
13
14
To Goulburn & Sydney
33
To Tumut
147°
147°30
148°
148°30
SOUTH
WALES
A
B
C
D
E
F
G
H
J
K
Brocklesby
Burrumbuttock
Mountain Creek
Gerogery
BENAMBRA NP
Woomargama
Mt Jergyle
WOODMARGAMA NAT PARK
Lankeys Creek
Mannus
Tumbarumba
Talbingo Reservoir
Ravine
SNOWY MTNS HWY
Mullengandra Village
Jingellic NR
Munderoo
Bogandyera NR
Clarkes Hill NR
Kiandra
Howlong
Jindera
Bowna
Talmalmo
Tholoqolong
Jingellic
Ournie
Tumut 2 PS
Mt Selwyn
To Cooma
Bungowannah
Table Top
Lake Hume
Murray
Walwa
Tooma
Cabramurra
Australia's Highest Town
Tumut 1 PS
Tumut Pond Res
36°
Barnawartha
Lavington
Thurgoona
Hume Weir
Wymah
Ferry
Mt Lawson State Park
Burrowye
Welaregang
Chiltern
ALBURY
Talgarno
Bungil
Mt Lawson
Guys Forest
BURROWA-PINE MOUNTAIN NATIONAL PARK
Tintaldra
Tooma Res
Wodonga
Logic Industry Hub, Wodonga
Bonegilla
Bellbridge
Bethanga
Mt Granya State Park
Granya
Mt Burrowye
Cudgewa North
Chiltern Mt Pilot Nat Pk
Bandiana
Towong
Barandudo
Old Tallangatta
Koetong
Lookout
Mt Jagungal 2060m
Leneva
Baranduda Mtn
Tallangatta
Bullioh
Shelley
MURRAY VALLEY
Cudgewa
Corryong
Jagungal Wilderness Area
PILOT RANGE
Kiewa
Tangambalanga
Mt Bullioh
Berringama
Thowgla
Khancoban
KOSCIUSZKO NATIONAL PARK
Wooragee
Allans Flat
Lookout
Khancoban Dam
Murray 1 PS
Yackandandah
Beechworth Historic Park
Kergunyah
Sandy Creek
Tallangatta Valley
Lucyvale
Biggara
Reids Ck
Yabba
Wyeebo
Thowgla Upper
Nariel Creek
Geehi Res
Island Bend
Beechworth
Stanley
Bruarong
Mt Big Ben
Lockhart Gap
Mt Cudgewa
Wabba Wilderness Park
Willow Crossing
Olsens Lookout
Guthega Dam
Guthega
Gundowring
Bullhead Creek
Tallandoon
Connels Peak
Cravensville
Geehi
Perisher Valley
Smiggin Holes
Skitube
Mt Stanley
Dederang
Mudgegonga
Mitta
Eskdale
Bucheen Creek
Upper Nariel
Mt Tempest
Charlotte Pass
2229m Mt Kosciuszko Australia's Highest Mountain
Winter Ski Resorts
To Jindabyne
34
Gapstead
The Pinnacles
Mt Dorchap
Mt Benambra
Dartmouth
Moonbah
36°30
Merriang
Myrtleford
Mt Tawonga
Mitta Mitta
Granite Flat
Tom Groggin
Thredbo
Pilot Lookout
Dead Horse Gap
Ovens
Happy Valley
Rosewhite
Lake Dartmouth
Sassafras Gap
Mt Pinnabar
Eurobin
Mt Porepunkah
Buffalo River
MT BUFFALO
Redbank
ALPINE
Dartmouth
Davies Plain
Ingebirah
Porepunkah
Tawonga Gap
Tawonga
Mt Hope
Buenba Flat (Site)
Indi Wilderness Area
Pilot Wilderness Area
NATIONAL PARK
Eagle Pt
The Hump
Mt Buffalo Chalet
Bright
Tawonga South
Victoria's Highest Mountain
Mt Bogong 1986m
Area
Mt Murphy Historic Area
The Pilot 1829m
Wandiligong
Mt Beauty
Mt Cooper
Dandongadale
Mt Arthur
The Horn
Buckland
Bogong
Lake Guy
Kiewa Hydro Electric Scheme
105
Mt Wills
Taylors Crossing
Forest Hill
Byadbo Wilderness Area
Spion Kopje
Historic Area
Pendergast Lookout
Buckland Junction
Harrietville
Falls Ck Alpine Village
Rocky Valley Reservoir
Glen Valley
The Knocker
McFarlane Lookout
Limestone Hut
Mt Cobberas
Cobberas Wilderness Area
Byadbo Mtn 1236m
Abbeyard
Mt Feathertop
Pretty Valley
Bogong
Mt Cope
The Brothers
Willis
Beveridge Station (Site)
Mt Loch
Hotham Heights Alpine Village
Lake Omeo
Benambra
BOWEN MOUNTAINS
Mt Wombargo
Mt Stradbroke
Suggan Buggan
Ingaringy Wilderness Area
Mt McIvor
Mt St Bernard
Mt Hotham
Anglers Rest
Mt Millians Lookout
Hinnomunjie
For more detail on this area, see Hema's High Country Victoria Map
Buchan Headwaters Wilderness Area
Mt Taylor
37°
Lake Cobbler
Mt Selwyn
Dinner Plain
DARGO HIGH PLAINS
Mt Tambo
Amboyne
Razor/Viking Wilderness Area
Mt Speculation
BARRY RANGE MOUNTAINS
Mt Murray
Mt Blue Rag
Sams Hill
Victoria Falls Historic Area
Omeo
Mt Shaw
Mt Nunniong
Wulgulmerang
Tubbut
The Pimple
HOWITT PLAINS
Mt Howitt
Cobungra
Mt Parslow
Bindi
Little River Gorge
McKillops Bridge
Basalt Knob
Mt Livingstone
Nunniong Plains
Mt Deception
Wonnangatta Station (Site)
Mt Phipps
The Washington
Mt Bindi
Tongio
Gelantipy
SNOWY RIVER NATIONAL PARK
Mt Bonang
Bryces Gorge
The Dogs Grave
Cassilis
Bentleys Plain
Bowen Ck Wilderness Area
Mt Nugong
Tongio West
Swifts Creek
Mt Birregun Views
Mt Darling/Snowy Bluff Wilderness Area
Doctors Flat
Butchers Ridge
Talbotville (Site)
Mt Delusion
Brookville
Ensay North
Timbarra
Gillingall
Grant (Site) Historic Area
Lookout
Mt Reynard
Happy Valley
Eaglevale
Ensay
Ensay South
Reedy Flat
Mt Baldhead
Mt Arbuckle
Crooked River
Mt Steve
Mt Kent
Murrindal
Buchan Caves
Stirling
Dargo
Mt Tamboritha
The Pinnacles Lookout
Mt Wellington Views
Raymond Falls
Mt Sardine
Buchan
Tali Karng
Castle Hill
Waterford
Tambo Crossing
Buchan Caves
Mt Pinnak
37°30
51
Castleburn
Tabberabbera
Angusvale
Mt Welcome
Buchan South
Mt Tara
Licola
Avon Wilderness Park
Deptford
Double Bridges (Site)
Stringer Knob
MITCHELL RIVER NATIONAL PARK
Cobbannah
Mt Buck
Den of Nargun
Bullumwaal
'Glenfalloch'
Mt Difficulty
Mt Nowa Nowa
Wairewa
Bete Bolong
Orbost
Cheynes Bridge
Ben Cruachan
Melwood
Mt Taylor
Clifton Creek
Bruthen
Nowa Nowa
Tostaree
Waygara
Brodribb River
Iguana Ck
Sarsfield
Mossiface
Lake Tyers State Park
To Eden
Glenaladale
Walpa
Calulu
Tambo Upper
Stockdale
Wy Yung
Newmerella
Lake Corringle
Curlip
Huggetts Crossing
Lindenow
Lucknow
Nicholson
PRINCES HWY
Tabbara
Marlo
Corringle Beach
Snowy Inlet
Point Ricardo
Hillside
Bairnsdale
Swan Reach
Toorloo Arm
Lake Tyers
Petmans Beach
Boisdale
Briagolong
Bushy Park
Fernbank
Eagle Pt
Eagle Pt Bay
Lake King
Metung
Kalimna West
Glenmaggie
Coongulla
Newry
Munro
Forge Ck
Raymond Is
Lakes Entrance
0
10
20
30km
© Hema Maps Pty Ltd
To Sale
50

South-East Victoria

To Benalla 1 2 3 To Wangaratta 4 49 5 To Tallangatta 6 To Corryong 7

146°30 147° 147°30 148°

For more detail on this area see Hema's High Country-Victoria Map

A

Mt Battery, Mansfield, To Yea, Burnt Hut Knob, The Pinnacle, Mt Cobbler, Lake Cobbler, Mt Stirling Alpine Resort, Mt Selwyn, Mt St Bernard, Dinner Plain, Anglers Rest, Mt Millers Lookout, Hinnomunjie, Mt Tambo, Buchan Wilderness, ALPINE, BLUE RANGE, Delatite, Merrijig, Mirimbah, The Monument, Mt Stirling, Razor/Viking Wilderness Area, Mt Speculation, The Pimple, BARRY RANGE MOUNTAINS, Mt Murray, DARGO HIGH PLAINS, GREAT ALPINE, Cobungra, Cobungra River, Victoria Falls Historic Area, Sams Hill, Omeo, Mt Shaw, Bindi, Mt Nunniong, Pires, Mt Buller, Mt Timbertop, Mt Buller Alpine Village, Mt Thorn, Mt Blue Rag views, Mt Parslow, Mt Livingstone, ROAD, Nunniong Plains, Mt Deception, Howqua Hills Historic Area, HOWITT, Mt Howitt, Basalt Knob, 30 Mile Ck, Wongungarra, Humffray R, Mt Bindi, The Washington, Mt Phipps, OMEO

B

Howqua, Closed, PLAINS, Wonnangatta Station (Site), Wonnangatta, Tongio, Cassilis, The Dogs Grave, Bentleys Plain, Jamieson, Mitchells (Site), Mt McDonald, DIVIDING, ALPINE, Bryces Gorge, NATIONAL, Mt Darling/Snowy Bluff Wilderness Area, Crooked R, Mt Birregun Views, Tongio West, Swifts Creek, Mt Nugong, Kevington, Wrens Flat, Goulburn, PARK, Caledonia R, Talbotville (Site), Grant (Site) Historic Area, Mt Delusion, Doctors Flat, Brookville, Ensay North, Timbarra, GREAT, Mt Reynard, Happy Valley, Eaglevale, Dargo, Mt Baldhead, Ensay, Lookout, Reedy Flat, Ensay South

C

Mt Skene, Closed, During, Mt Arbuckle, Mt Kent, Crooked River, Mt Steve, Gaffneys Creek, A1 Mine Settlement, Macalister, Mt Tamboritha, Mt Wellington Views, The Pinnacles Lookout, Dargo, Stirling, Glencairn, Lookout, Tali Karng, Wellington, Castle Hill, Waterford, Tambo Crossing, Mt Matlock, Woods Pt, Castleburn, Tabberabbera, Mt Welcome, Timbarra, Matlock, Jericho, Licola, Avon Wilderness Park, Angusvale, Cobbannah, Deptford, Double Bridges (Site), MITCHELL RIVER, Nicholson

D

The Triangle, YARRA RANGES NATIONAL PARK, Mt Selma, Glenfalloch, Ben Cruachan, Valencia Ck, NATIONAL PARK, Den of Nargun, Bullumwaal, Aberfeldy, Mt Useful, Mt Difficulty, Lake Thomson, Mt Gregory, BAW BAW NAT PARK, Cheynes Bridge, Ben Cruachan, Turton, Freestone Ck, Clifton Creek, Mt Taylor, Bruthen, Mt Nowa Nowa, Toorongo, Tanjil Bren, Mt Whitelaw, Mt Baw Baw Alpine Village, Beardmore, Avon, Glenaladale, Iguana Ck, Melwood, Sarsfield, Mossiface, Nowa Nowa, Tambo Upper, Lake Tyers State Park, Mt Baw Baw, Huggetts Crossing, Stockdale, Walpa, Lindenow, Calulu, Wy Yung, Lucknow, Nicholson, Swan Reach, Toorloo Arm, To Cambarville

E

Fumina, Talbot Peak, Mt Erica, Glenmaggie Res, Boisdale, Briagolong, Hillside, Bairnsdale, Kalimna West, Lakes Tyers, Tyers, Rawson, Walhalla Historic Area, Glenmaggie, Seaton, Coongulla, Newry, Bushy Park, Munro, Fernbank, Eagle Pt, Eagle Pt Bay, Jones Bay, Lake King, Nyerimilang Park, Forge Ck, Raymond Is, Metung, Paynesville, Lakes Entrance, Erica, Coopers Creek, Thomson, Heyfield, Tinamba, Maffra, Stratford, HWY, Hill End, Moondarra State Pk, Moondarra, Cowwarr, River, Goon Nure, Bengworden, Meerlieu, Wattle Pt, Lake Victoria, THE LAKES NATIONAL PARK, Willow Grove, Mt Tanjil, Blue Rock Lake, Moondarra Res, Toongabbie, Nambrok, Bundalaguah, Airly, Clydebank, Hollands Landing, Loch Sport, Mile, Beach

F

Tyers Park, Glengarry, West Sale Aerodrome, Cobains, Marlay Point, Lake Wellington, Seacombe, MOE, Yallourn North, Tyers, La Trobe, Kilmany, Wurruk, Sale, RAAF Base, The Heart, Gippsland Lakes Coastal Park, Ninety, Yallourn, TRARALGON, PRINCES, Rosedale, Longford, Lake Coleman, Lake Reeve, Trafalgar, Holey Plains State Park, Paradise Beach, Golden Beach, MORWELL, Driffield, HYLAND, Merriman, Willung, Stradbroke West, Childers, Thorpdale, Hazelwood, Churchill, Loy Yang, Traralgon Sth, Gormandale, The, To Melbourne

G

Yinnar, Powers Hill Lookout, Little Monkey Ck, Stradbroke, Boolarra, Yinnar South, MORWELL NAT PARK, Mt Tassie Lookout, Carrajung, RIDGE, The Honeysuckles, Seaspray, Mirboo Nth, Budgeree, Balook, TARRA-BULGA NAT PARK, HWY, Giffard, Ninety Mile Beach Marine Nat Park, Mardan, Mirboo, GRAND, RIDGE, Tarra, Won Wron, Darriman, Lake Denison, Jack Smith Lake, To Leongatha

H

Dumbalk North, Dumbalk, Ryton, Turtons Falls, Mt Fatigue, Hiawatha Falls, Jack River, Devon North, Greenmount, Woodside, Woodside Beach, Wonyip, Yarram, Albert, Reeves Beach, SOUTH, Binginwarri, Alberton, GIPPSLAND, Foster, Agnes Falls, Toora, Tarraville, St Margaret Is, Manns Beach, McLoughlins Beach, Welshpool, Port Franklin, Barrys Beach, Port Welshpool, Sunday Is, Port Albert, Clonmel Is, Little Snake Is, Snake Is, Corner Inlet Marine & Coastal Park, Corner Inlet, Nooramunga Marine & Coastal Park, To Leongatha

J

Shallow Inlet, Yanakie, Duck Pt, Yanakie Beach, Granite Is, Corner Inlet MNP, Mt Hunter, Mt Margaret, Bennison Is, Sandy Pt, Shallow Inlet M & C Park, Mt Roundback, Wilderness Area, Johnny Souey Pt, WILSONS PROMONTORY, Wilsons Promontory Marine Park, Wilsons Promontory Marine Park, Mt Vereker

K

Tongue Point, Mt Leonard, Wilsons Promontory, Sparkes Lookout, NATIONAL PARK, Sealers Cove, Horn Pt, Tidal River, Norman Bay, Views, Mt Wilson, Brown Head, Oberon Bay, Mt Oberon, Cape Wellington, Waterloo Bay, Glennie Group, Mt Norgate, Mt Boulder, Wilsons Promontory Marine National Park, South Peak, South West Point, Lighthouse, Anser Group, Wattle Is, South Point

37°30 38° 38°30 39°

146°30 147° 147°30 148°

1 2 3 4 5 6 7

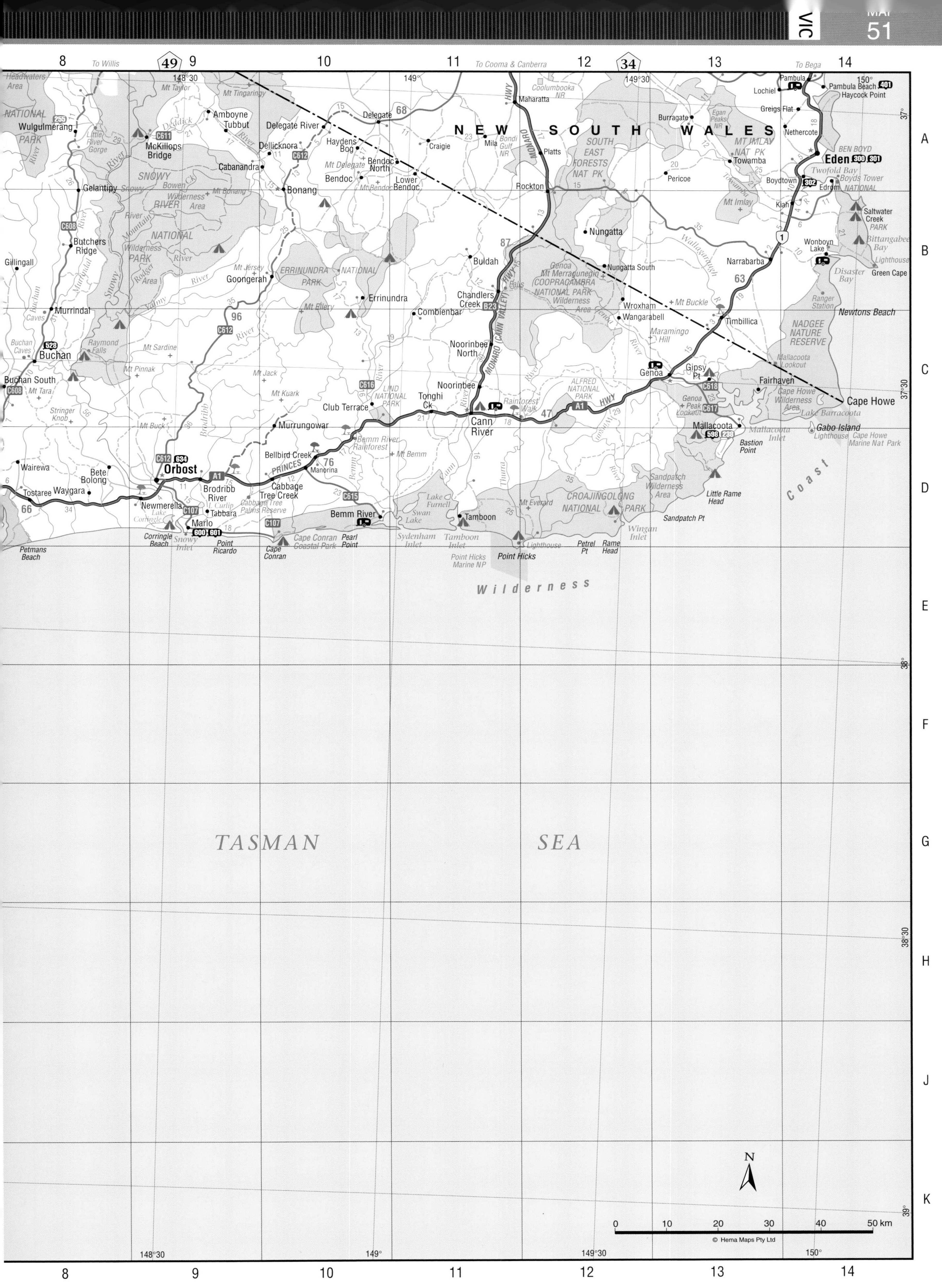
NEW SOUTH WALES
TASMAN SEA
Orbost
Eden
Cann River
Mallacoota
Genoa
Bonang
Delegate
Buchan
Cape Howe
Gabo Island
Point Hicks
Marlo
Bemm River
Tamboon
Errinundra
Goongerah
Noorinbee
Noorinbee North
Chandlers Creek
Wangarabell
Wroxham
Timbillica
Narrabarba
Nungatta
Bendoc
Club Terrace
Murrungowar
Cabbage Tree Creek
Newmerella
Tostaree
Waygara
Bete Bolong
Wairewa
Buchan South
Murrindal
Gelantipy
Wulgulmerang
McKillops Bridge
Amboyne
Tubbut
Dellicknora
Cabanandra
Delegate River
Combienbar
Buldah
Tonghi Ck
Bellbird Creek
Manorina
Brodribb River
Tabbara
Corringle Beach
Point Ricardo
Cape Conran
Pearl Point
Sydenham Inlet
Tamboon Inlet
Petrel Pt
Rame Head
Wingan Inlet
Sandpatch Pt
Little Rame Head
Bastion Point
Mallacoota Inlet
Lake Barracoota
Fairhaven
Gipsy Pt
Wonboyn Lake
Green Cape
Disaster Bay
Newtons Beach
Kiah
Boydtown
Edrom
Towamba
Pericoe
Burragate
Nethercote
Greigs Flat
Lochiel
Pambula
Pambula Beach
Haycock Point
Rockton
Platts
Mila
Craigie
Maharatta
SNOWY RIVER NATIONAL PARK
ERRINUNDRA NATIONAL PARK
CROAJINGOLONG NATIONAL PARK
COOPRACAMBRA NATIONAL PARK
SOUTH EAST FORESTS NAT PK
MT IMLAY NAT PK
BEN BOYD NATIONAL
NADGEE NATURE RESERVE
LIND NATIONAL PARK
ALFRED NATIONAL PARK
Cape Conran Coastal Park
Point Hicks Marine NP
Cape Howe Marine Nat Park
Cape Howe Wilderness Area
PRINCES HWY
MONARO (CANN VALLEY) HWY
Wilderness Coast
© Hema Maps Pty Ltd
0 10 20 30 40 50 km

West Gippsland Region, Victoria

MELBOURNE
Healesville
Warburton
Dandenong
Frankston
Mornington
Hastings
Cowes
Koo-wee-rup
Drouin
Warragul
MOE
Trafalgar
Korumburra
Leongatha
Wonthaggi
Inverloch
Foster
Wilsons Promontory

Kalkallo, Woodstock, Whittlesea, Humevale, Kinglake Central, Kinglake, Toolangi, Yuroke, Craigieburn, Yan Yean, Mernda, Doreen, Epping, Hurstbridge, Panton Hill, Bulla, South Morang, Plenty, Diamond Ck, Eltham, Keilor, Coburg, Warrandyte, Albion, Box Hill, Burwood, Ringwood, Croydon, Lilydale, Coldstream, Yarra Glen, Dixons Ck, St Kilda, Williamstown, Altona, Oakleigh, Moorabbin, Mentone, Mordialloc, Edithvale, Carrum, Upper Ferntree Gully, Belgrave, Olinda, Monbulk, Emerald, Cockatoo, Gembrook, Berwick, Beaconsfield, Pakenham, Nar Nar Goon, Tynong, Garfield, Bunyip, Longwarry, Lyndhurst, Cranbourne, Clyde, Pearcedale, Mt Eliza, Somerville, Tyabb, Tooradin, Warneet, Mt Martha, Dromana, Rosebud, Rye, Balnarring, Merricks, Somers, Flinders, Cape Schanck, Stony Pt, Tankerton, Rhyll, Ventnor, Summerland, Newhaven, San Remo, Corinella, Grantville, Bass, Almurta, Kernot, Woolamai, Anderson, Kilcunda, Dalyston, Archies Ck, Dudley, Cape Paterson, Harmers Haven, Seville, Woori Yallock, Launching Place, Yarra Junction, Millgrove, Gladysdale, Starling Gap, Powelltown, Marysville, Narbethong, St Fillans, Cambarville, Stockmans Reward, Woods Pt, Matlock, Jericho, A1 Mine Settlement, The Triangle, Upper Yarra Dam, Reefton, McMahons Creek, Toorongo, Tanjil Bren, Mt Baw Baw Alpine Village, Noojee, Nayook, Fumina, Neerim, Neerim South, Jindivick, Labertouche, Rokeby, Buln Buln, Hill End, Willow Grove, Darnum, Yarragon, Ellinbank, Seaview, Childers, Thorpdale, Driffield, Yinnar, Boolarra, Mirboo Nth, Budgeree, Mirboo, Mardan, Hallston, Wooreen, Strzelecki, Mt Eccles, Ranceby, Poowong, Poowong East, Nyora, Loch, Bena, Woodleigh, Krowera, Jumbunna, Glen Alvie, Kongwak, Leongatha South, Koonwarra, Dumbalk, Dumbalk North, Meeniyan, Tarwin, Stony Creek, Buffalo, Pound Ck, Tarwin Middle, Tarwin Lower, Tarwin Meadows, Venus Bay, Fish Ck, Toora, Port Franklin, Waratah Nth, Waratah Bay, Walkerville Nth, Walkerville Sth, Liptrap, Cape Liptrap, Sandy Pt, Yanakie, Tidal River, Iona, Cora Lynn, Bayles, Catani, Modella, Ripplebrook, Yannathan, Athlone, Lang Lang, Drouin Sth

Port Phillip Bay, Western Port Bay, French Island, Phillip Island, Mornington Peninsula, Bass Strait, Corner Inlet, Waratah Bay, Anderson Inlet

© Hema Maps Pty Ltd

TASMANIA Key Map

POPULATION: 500,000
AREA: 68,401 sq km
CAPITAL CITY: Hobart

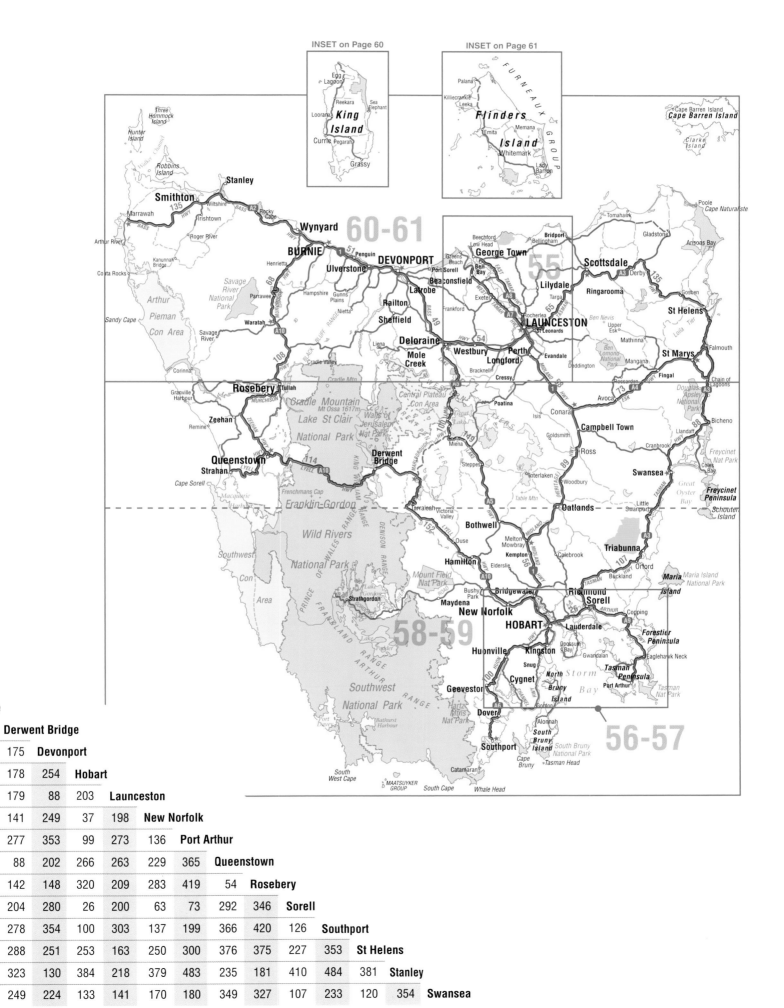

	Burnie	Derwent Bridge	Devonport	Hobart	Launceston	New Norfolk	Port Arthur	Queenstown	Rosebery	Sorell	Southport	St Helens	Stanley	Swansea
Burnie														
Derwent Bridge	226													
Devonport	51	175												
Hobart	305	178	254											
Launceston	139	179	88	203										
New Norfolk	300	141	249	37	198									
Port Arthur	404	277	353	99	273	136								
Queenstown	163	88	202	266	263	229	365							
Rosebery	109	142	148	320	209	283	419	54						
Sorell	331	204	280	26	200	63	73	292	346					
Southport	405	278	354	100	303	137	199	366	420	126				
St Helens	302	288	251	253	163	250	300	376	375	227	353			
Stanley	79	323	130	384	218	379	483	235	181	410	484	381		
Swansea	275	249	224	133	141	170	180	349	327	107	233	120	354	

Distances are shown in kilometres and follow the most direct major sealed route

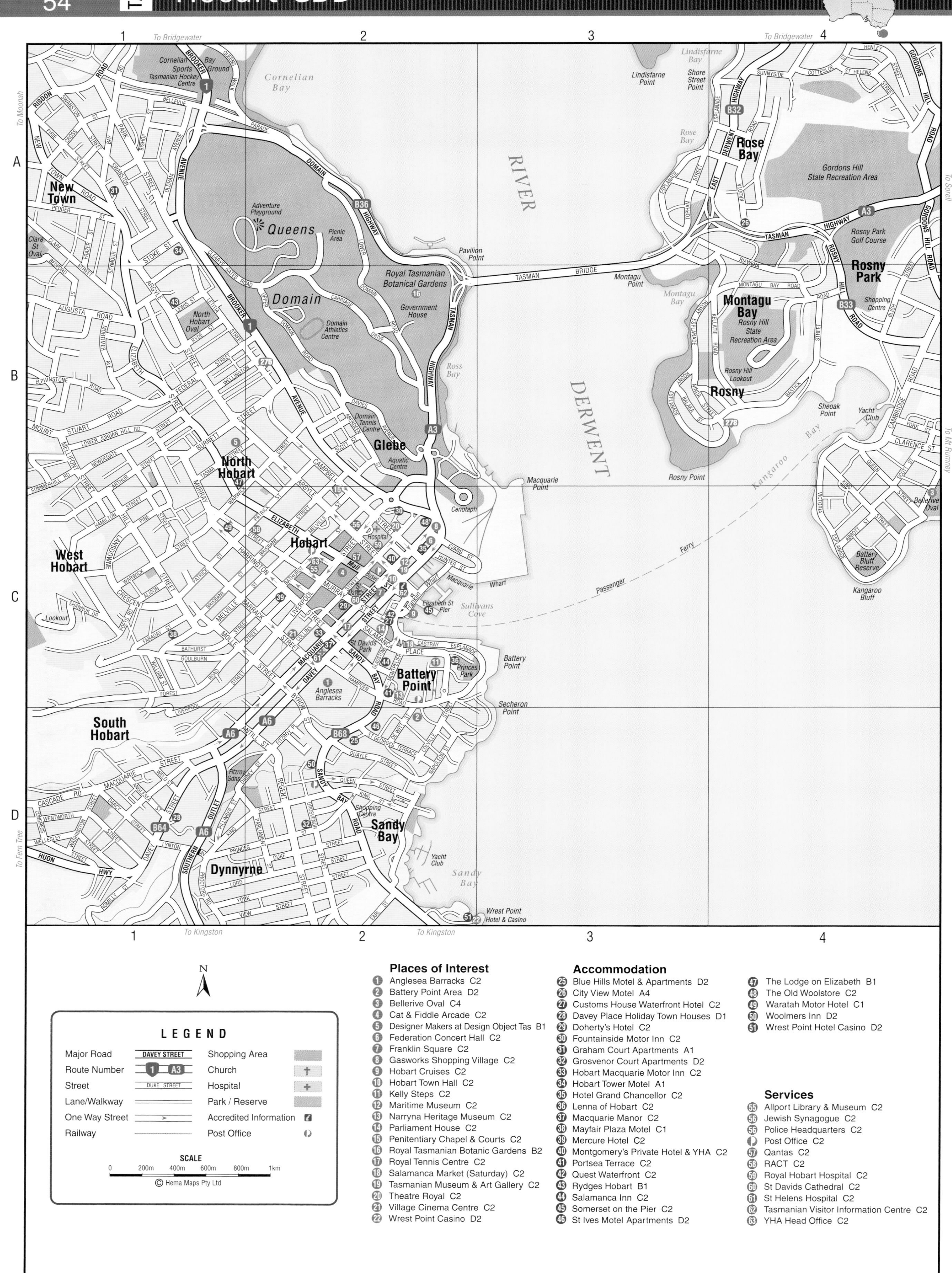
To Bridgewater
To Moonah
To Sorell
To Mt Rumney
To Fern Tree
To Kingston
New Town
North Hobart
West Hobart
Hobart
South Hobart
Glebe
Battery Point
Sandy Bay
Dynnyrne
Rose Bay
Rosny Park
Montagu Bay
Rosny
Queens Domain
Royal Tasmanian Botanical Gardens
Government House
Cornelian Bay
RIVER DERWENT
Sullivans Cove
Kangaroo Bay
Wrest Point Hotel & Casino
Places of Interest
1 Anglesea Barracks C2
2 Battery Point Area D2
3 Bellerive Oval C4
4 Cat & Fiddle Arcade C2
5 Designer Makers at Design Object Tas B1
6 Federation Concert Hall C2
7 Franklin Square C2
8 Gasworks Shopping Village C2
9 Hobart Cruises C2
10 Hobart Town Hall C2
11 Kelly Steps C2
12 Maritime Museum C2
13 Narryna Heritage Museum C2
14 Parliament House C2
15 Penitentiary Chapel & Courts C2
16 Royal Tasmanian Botanic Gardens B2
17 Royal Tennis Centre C2
18 Salamanca Market (Saturday) C2
19 Tasmanian Museum & Art Gallery C2
20 Theatre Royal C2
21 Village Cinema Centre C2
22 Wrest Point Casino D2
Accommodation
25 Blue Hills Motel & Apartments D2
26 City View Motel A4
27 Customs House Waterfront Hotel C2
28 Davey Place Holiday Town Houses D1
29 Doherty's Hotel C2
30 Fountainside Motor Inn C2
31 Graham Court Apartments A1
32 Grosvenor Court Apartments D2
33 Hobart Macquarie Motor Inn C2
34 Hobart Tower Motel A1
35 Hotel Grand Chancellor C2
36 Lenna of Hobart C2
37 Macquarie Manor C2
38 Mayfair Plaza Motel C1
39 Mercure Hotel C2
40 Montgomery's Private Hotel & YHA C2
41 Portsea Terrace C2
42 Quest Waterfront C2
43 Rydges Hobart B1
44 Salamanca Inn C2
45 Somerset on the Pier C2
46 St Ives Motel Apartments D2
47 The Lodge on Elizabeth B1
48 The Old Woolstore C2
49 Waratah Motor Hotel C1
50 Woolmers Inn D2
51 Wrest Point Hotel Casino D2
Services
55 Allport Library & Museum C2
56 Jewish Synagogue C2
56 Police Headquarters C2
Post Office C2
57 Qantas C2
58 RACT C2
59 Royal Hobart Hospital C2
60 St Davids Cathedral C2
61 St Helens Hospital C2
62 Tasmanian Visitor Information Centre C2
63 YHA Head Office C2
LEGEND
Major Road
Route Number
Street
Lane/Walkway
One Way Street
Railway
Shopping Area
Church
Hospital
Park / Reserve
Accredited Information
Post Office
SCALE
0 200m 400m 600m 800m 1km
© Hema Maps Pty Ltd

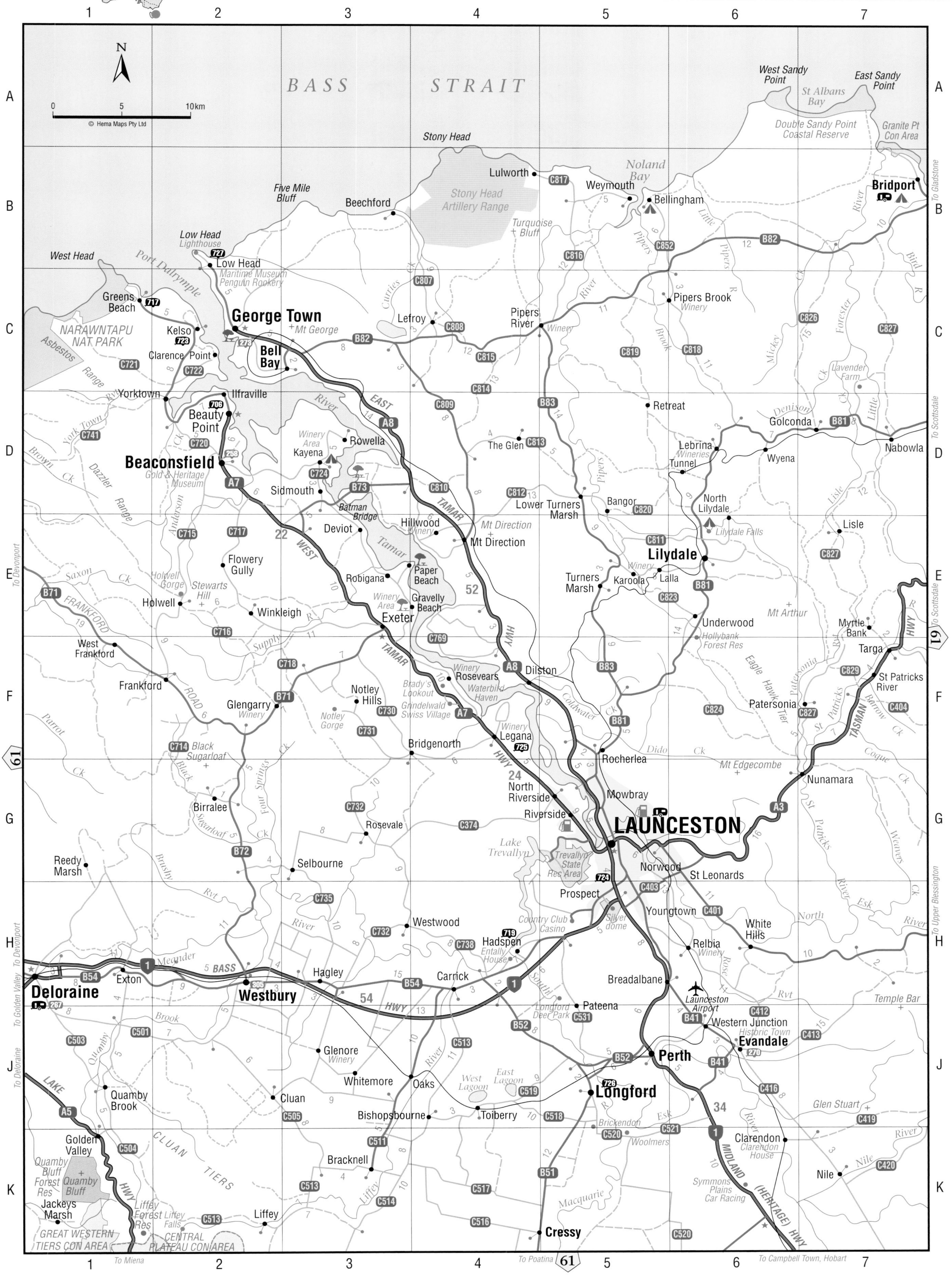
BASS STRAIT
0 5 10km
© Hema Maps Pty Ltd
N
West Sandy Point
East Sandy Point
St Albans Bay
Double Sandy Point Coastal Reserve
Granite Pt Con Area
Stony Head
Stony Head Artillery Range
Lulworth
Noland Bay
Weymouth
Bellingham
Bridport
To Gladstone
Five Mile Bluff
Beechford
Turquoise Bluff
Low Head Lighthouse
Low Head
Maritime Museum
Penguin Rookery
West Head
Port Dalrymple
Greens Beach
Kelso
George Town
Mt George
NARAWNTAPU NAT PARK
Asbestos Range
Clarence Point
Bell Bay
Lefroy
Pipers River
Pipers Brook
Winery
Yorktown
Ilfraville
Beauty Point
Beaconsfield
Gold & Heritage Museum
Retreat
Golconda
Nabowla
Lebrina
Wineries
Tunnel
Wyena
Lavender Farm
To Scottsdale
Rowella
Kayena
The Glen
Sidmouth
Batman Bridge
Deviot
Hillwood
Mt Direction
Lower Turners Marsh
Bangor
North Lilydale
Lilydale Falls
Lisle
Flowery Gully
Holwell Gorge
Stewarts Hill
Holwell
Winkleigh
Robigana
Paper Beach
Gravelly Beach
Exeter
Turners Marsh
Karoola
Lalla
Lilydale
Underwood
Hollybank Forest Res
Mt Arthur
Myrtle Bank
Targa
St Patricks River
West Frankford
Frankford
Glengarry
Notley Hills
Notley Gorge
Brady's Lookout
Grindelwald Swiss Village
Rosevears
Waterbird Haven
Dilston
Legana
Paterosnia
Black Sugarloaf
Bridgenorth
Rocherlea
Mt Edgecombe
Nunamara
Birralee
North Riverside
Riverside
Mowbray
Rosevale
LAUNCESTON
Lake Trevallyn
Trevallyn State Rec Area
Norwood
St Leonards
Reedy Marsh
Selbourne
Prospect
Youngtown
Westwood
Country Club Casino
Silverdome
White Hills
Hadspen
Entally House
Relbia
Deloraine
Exton
Westbury
Hagley
Carrick
Breadalbane
Launceston Airport
Temple Bar
Longford Deer Park
Pateena
Western Junction
Historic Town
Evandale
Glenore
Whitemore
Oaks
West Lagoon
East Lagoon
Perth
Longford
Quamby Brook
Cluan
Bishopsbourne
Toiberry
Brickendon
Woolmers
Glen Stuart
Golden Valley
Quamby Bluff Forest Res
Quamby Bluff
CLUAN TIERS
Bracknell
Clarendon
Clarendon House
Nile
Symmons Plains Car Racing
Jackeys Marsh
Liffey Forest Res
Liffey Falls
Liffey
GREAT WESTERN TIERS CON AREA
CENTRAL PLATEAU CON AREA
Cressy
To Miena
To Poatina
To Campbell Town, Hobart
To Devonport
To Golden Valley
To Deloraine
To Upper Blessington
MIDLAND (HERITAGE) HWY
TASMAN HWY
BASS HWY
LAKE HWY
WEST TAMAR HWY
EAST TAMAR HWY
FRANKFORD ROAD

Hobart Region, Tasmania

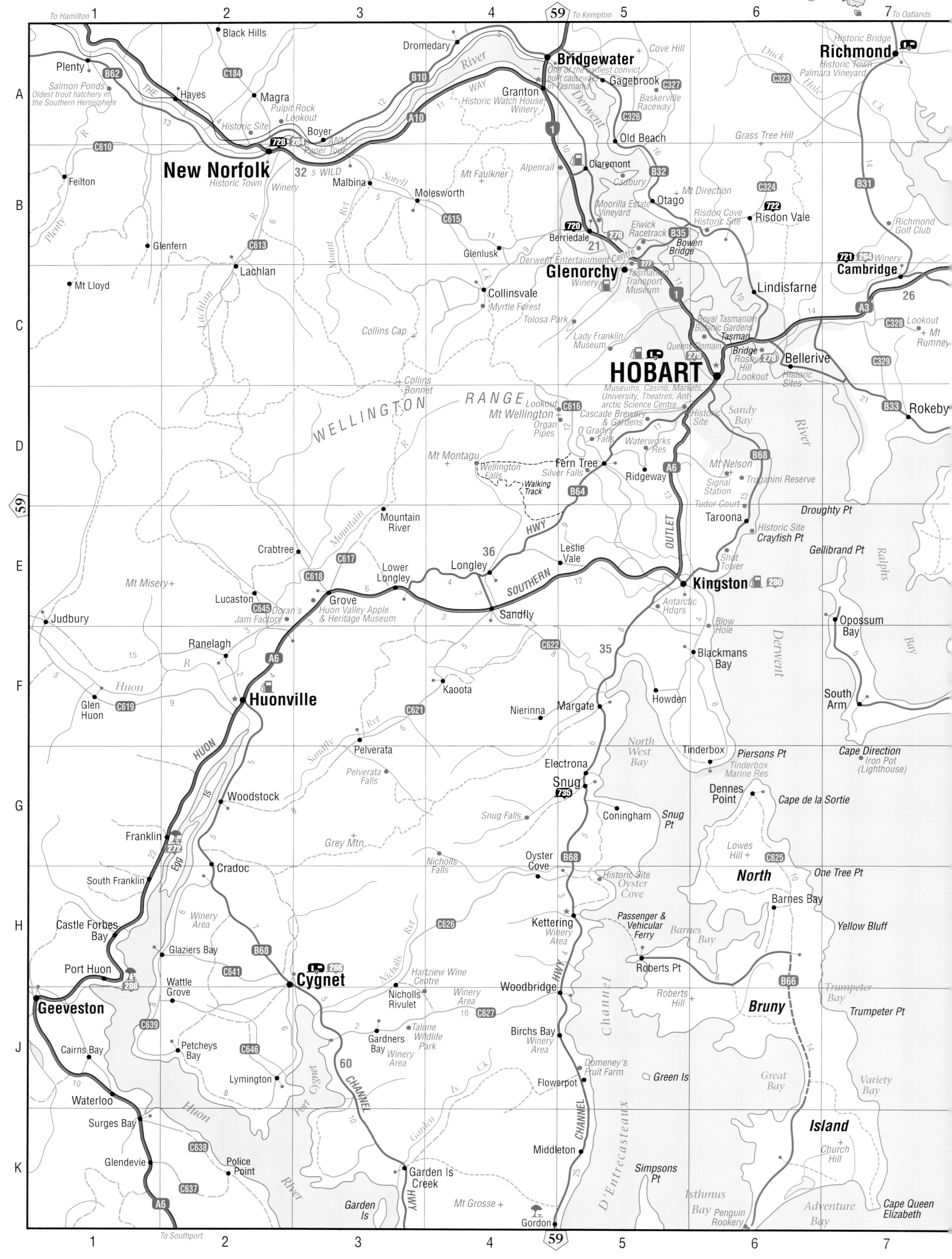

To Hamilton 1 2 3 4 59 To Kempton 5 6 7 To Oatlands

A

Black Hills
Dromedary
Bridgewater
One of the earliest convict built causeways in Tasmania
Cove Hill
Historic Bridge
Richmond
Historic Town
Palmara Vineyard
Plenty
B62
Salmon Ponds
Oldest trout hatchery in the Southern Hemisphere
THE
Hayes
C184
Magra
Pulpit Rock Lookout
B10
River
WAY
Granton
Historic Watch House
Winery
Gagebrook
C327
Baskerville Raceway
Duck
C323
Hole
Ck
Historic Site
Boyer
ANM Paper Tour
728
284
A10
1
Derwent
C326
Old Beach
Grass Tree Hill

B

C610
New Norfolk
Historic Town
Winery
32 WILD
Malbina
Sorell
Mt Faulkner
Alpenrail
Claremont
Cadbury
B32
Feilton
Molesworth
Moorilla Estate Vineyard
Otago
Mt Direction
C324
B31
Risdon Cove Historic Site
722
Risdon Vale
C615
Elwick Racetrack
B35
Bowen Bridge
720
Berriedale
276
21
Richmond Golf Club
Plenty
Glenfern
C613
Lachlan
Mount Rvt
Glenlusk
Derwent Entertainment Centre
721
264
Winery
Cambridge

C

Mt Lloyd
Lachlan
Collinsvale
Myrtle Forest
Glenorchy
Winery
277
Tasmanian Transport Museum
Lindisfarne
26
A3
Tolosa Park
Royal Tasmanian Botanic Gardens
Tasman
C328
Lookout
Mt Rumney
Collins Cap
Lady Franklin Museum
Queens Domain
Bridge
Rosny Hill Lookout
278
Bellerive
275
HOBART
C329
Historic Sites
Collins Bonnet

D

WELLINGTON RANGE
Lookout
Mt Wellington
C616
Museums, Casino, Markets, University, Theatres, Antarctic Science Centre
B33
Rokeby
Cascade Brewery & Gardens
Historic Site
Sandy Bay
River
Organ Pipes
O'Grady's Falls
Waterworks Res
Mt Montagu
Wellington Falls
Fern Tree
Silver Falls
Ridgeway
B68
Mt Nelson
Walking Track
A6
Signal Station
Truganini Reserve
B64
Tudor Court
Droughty Pt
Mountain River
HWY
Taroona

E

Mountain
Crabtree
C617
OUTLET
Historic Site
Crayfish Pt
36
Leslie Vale
Shot Tower
Gellibrand Pt
Ralphs
C618
Lower Longley
Longley
SOUTHERN
Kingston
280
Mt Misery
Lucaston
Grove
C645
Doran's Jam Factory
Huon Valley Apple & Heritage Museum
Sandfly
Antarctic Hdqrs
Blow Hole
Opossum Bay
Judbury

F

Ranelagh
C622
35
Blackmans Bay
Derwent
Bay
15
R
Huon
A6
Huonville
Kaoota
Glen Huon
C619
C621
Margate
Howden
South Arm
Nierinna
Rvt
Sandfly
Pelverata
North West Bay
Tinderbox
Piersons Pt
Tinderbox Marine Res
Cape Direction
Iron Pot (Lighthouse)
HUON

G

Pelverata Falls
Electrona
Is
Snug
735
Dennes Point
Cape de la Sortie
Woodstock
Snug Falls
Coningham
Snug Pt
Franklin
272
Grey Mtn
Lowes Hill
C625
Egg
Nicholls Falls
Oyster Cove
B68
North
One Tree Pt
South Franklin
Cradoc
Historic Site
Oyster Cove

H

Winery Area
Rvt
C626
Passenger & Vehicular Ferry
Barnes Bay
Barnes Bay
Castle Forbes Bay
Kettering
Winery Area
Yellow Bluff
Glaziers Bay
B68
HWY
Roberts Pt
Port Huon
288
C641
Cygnet
266
Hartzview Wine Centre
B66
Trumpeter Bay
Wattle Grove
Nicholls
Woodbridge
Channel

I

Geeveston
Nicholls Rivulet
Winery Area
C627
Roberts Hill
Bruny
Trumpeter Pt
C639
Gardners Bay
Talune Wildlife Park
Birchs Bay
Winery Area

J

Cairns Bay
Petcheys Bay
C646
Winery Area
60
Domeney's Fruit Farm
Green Is
Great Bay
Variety Bay
Lymington
Port Cygnet
CHANNEL
Flowerpot
Waterloo
Huon
Is
Garden
Ck

K

Surges Bay
CHANNEL
D'Entrecasteaux
Island
C638
Church Hill
Glendevie
Police Point
Garden Is Creek
Middleton
Simpsons Pt
River
C637
A6
Garden Is
HWY
Mt Grosse
Gordon
Isthmus Bay
Penguin Rookery
Adventure Bay
Cape Queen Elizabeth

1 To Southport 2 3 4 59 5 6 7

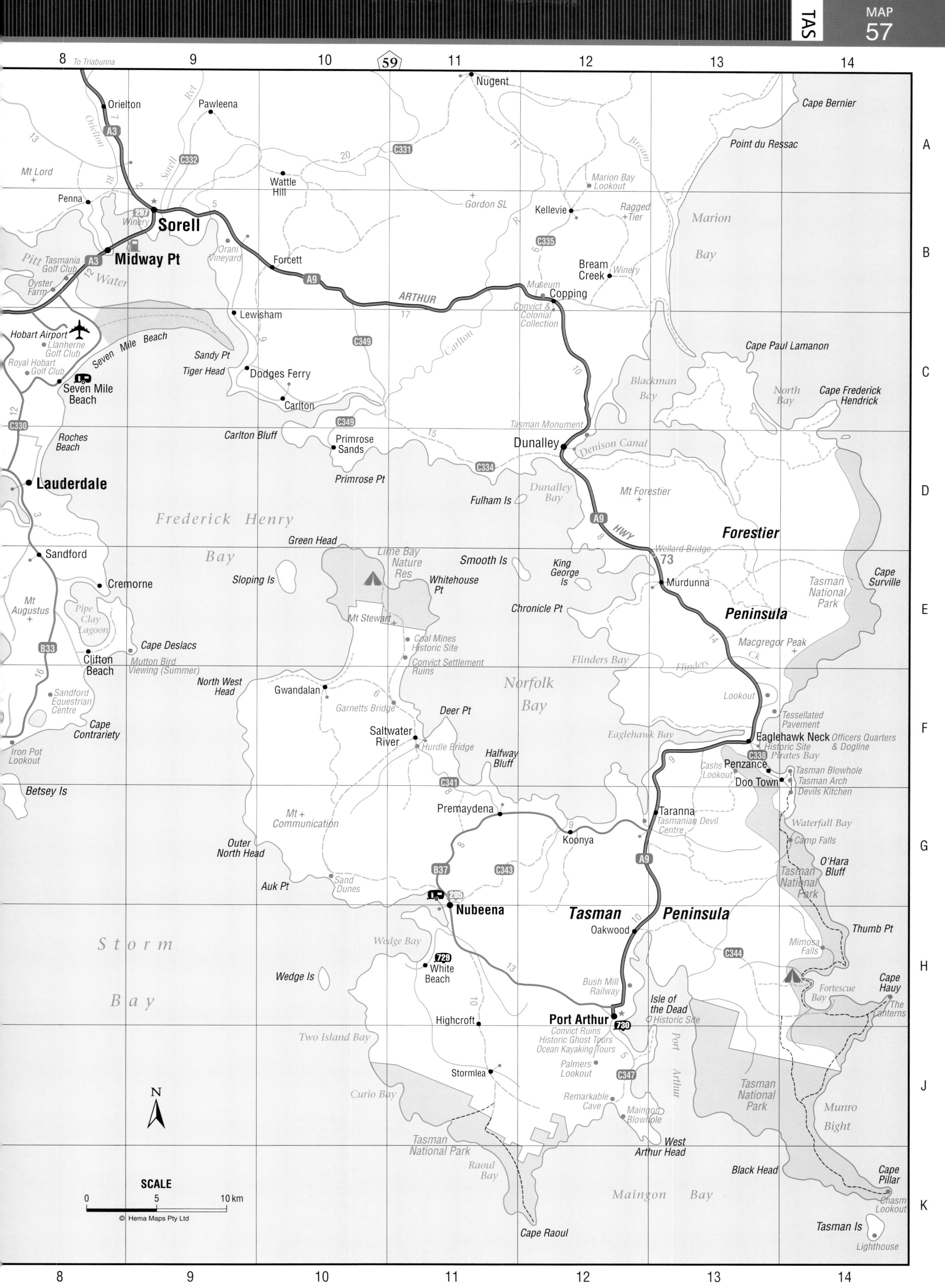
To Triabunna
59
Orielton
Pawleena
Nugent
Cape Bernier
Point du Ressac
Mt Lord
Wattle Hill
Marion Bay Lookout
Penna
Sorell
Gordon SL
Kellevie
Ragged Tier
Marion Bay
Winery
Midway Pt
Orani Vineyard
Forcett
Bream Creek
Pitt Water
Tasmania Golf Club
Oyster Farm
ARTHUR
Museum
Copping
Convict & Colonial Collection
Lewisham
Hobart Airport
Llanherne Golf Club
Seven Mile Beach
Sandy Pt
Tiger Head
Dodges Ferry
Cape Paul Lamanon
Royal Hobart Golf Club
Carlton
Blackman Bay
North Bay
Cape Frederick Hendrick
Tasman Monument
Roches Beach
Carlton Bluff
Primrose Sands
Dunalley
Denison Canal
Lauderdale
Primrose Pt
Mt Forestier
Fulham Is
Dunalley Bay
Frederick Henry Bay
HWY
Forestier
Green Head
Lime Bay Nature Res
Smooth Is
King George Is
Wellard Bridge
Sandford
Cape Surville
Sloping Is
Whitehouse Pt
Murdunna
Cremorne
Tasman National Park
Mt Augustus
Pipe Clay Lagoon
Mt Stewart
Chronicle Pt
Peninsula
Coal Mines Historic Site
Macgregor Peak
Cape Deslacs
Clifton Beach
Mutton Bird Viewing (Summer)
Convict Settlement Ruins
Flinders Bay
North West Head
Norfolk Bay
Gwandalan
Lookout
Sandford Equestrian Centre
Garnetts Bridge
Deer Pt
Tessellated Pavement
Cape Contrariety
Saltwater River
Eaglehawk Bay
Eaglehawk Neck
Officers Quarters & Dogline
Historic Site
Pirates Bay
Iron Pot Lookout
Hurdle Bridge
Halfway Bluff
Cashs Lookout
Penzance
Tasman Blowhole
Tasman Arch
Doo Town
Devils Kitchen
Betsey Is
Premaydena
Taranna
Tasmanian Devil Centre
Waterfall Bay
Mt Communication
Koonya
Camp Falls
Outer North Head
O'Hara Bluff
Auk Pt
Sand Dunes
Nubeena
Tasman Peninsula
Storm Bay
Oakwood
Thumb Pt
Wedge Bay
Mimosa Falls
White Beach
Wedge Is
Bush Mill Railway
Cape Hauy
Fortescue Bay
Isle of the Dead
Historic Site
The Lanterns
Port Arthur
Highcroft
Convict Ruins
Historic Ghost Tours
Ocean Kayaking Tours
Two Island Bay
Palmers Lookout
Stormlea
Curio Bay
Remarkable Cave
Maingon Blowhole
Munro Bight
West Arthur Head
Raoul Bay
Black Head
Cape Pillar
Maingon Bay
Chasm Lookout
Cape Raoul
Tasman Is
Lighthouse
SCALE
0 5 10 km
© Hema Maps Pty Ltd

Southern Tasmania
To Burnie
60
SOUTHERN
OCEAN
Rosebery
Tullah
Zeehan
Queenstown
Strahan
Derwent Bridge
Strathgordon
Tarraleah
Wayatinah
Bronte Park
Granville Harbour
Trial Harbour
Renison Bell
Williamsford
Dundas
Gormanston
Linda
Lynchford
Regatta Pt
Lowana
Macquarie Hds
Cape Sorell
Sophia Pt
Macquarie Harbour
Liberty Pt
Sloop Pt
George Pt
Sarah Is
Birthday Bay
Varna Bay
Hibbs Bay
Point Hibbs
Spero Bay
Endeavour Bay
Christmas Cove
High Rocky Pt
Low Rocky Pt
Elliott Bay
Nye Bay
Elliott Pt
Mulcahy Bay
Brier Holme Head
Mt Hean
Svenor Pt
Wreck Bay
James Kelly Basin
Payne Bay
North Head
Pt St Vincent
Breaksea Is
Port Davey
Bathurst Harbour
Hilliard Head
Stephens Bay
Mutton Bird Is
Melaleuca Ranger Office & Bird Observatory
Mt Melaleuca
Window Pane Bay
Cox Bight
Mt Karamu
South West Cape
Telopea Pt
Cox Bluff
Red Pt
Louisa Bay
Havelock Bluff
Ile du Golfe
De Witt Is
Flat Witch Is
Walker Is
MAATSUYKER GROUP
Maatsuyker Is
Lighthouse
CRADLE MOUNTAIN LAKE ST CLAIR NATIONAL PARK
PART OF WORLD HERITAGE AREA
FRANKLIN - GORDON WILD RIVERS NATIONAL PARK
PART OF WORLD HERITAGE AREA
SOUTHWEST CONSERVATION AREA
SOUTHWEST NATIONAL PARK
PART OF WORLD HERITAGE AREA
WALLS OF JERUSALEM NATIONAL PARK
GRANITE TOR CON AREA
CENTRAL PLATEAU CONSERV
DU CANE RANGE
CHEYNE RANGE
KING WILLIAM RANGE
PRINCE OF WALES RANGE
DENISON RANGE
FRANKLAND RANGE
ARTHUR RANGE
WENTWORTH HILLS
Mt Ossa
Mt Pelion West
Mt Pelion East
Cathedral Mtn
Mt Jerusalem
Eldon Peak
Eldon Bluff
High Dome
Mt Gould
Mt Olympus
Pyramid Mtn
Mt Hugel
Mt Rufus
Mt Gell
Mt Alma
Mt Arrowsmith
Mt King William I
Mt King William II
Mt King William III
Guelph Basin
Frenchmans Cap
Victoria Pass
Mt Owen
Mt Huxley
Mt Lyell
Mt Sedgwick
Mt Jukes
Mt Darwin
Mt Sorell
Darwin Dam
Crotty Dam
Mt McCall
Kelly Basin
Heritage Landing
Goodwins Peak
Mt Humboldt
Reeds Peak
Mt Lee
Innes Pk
Mt Lewis
Lake Gordon
Gordon Dam
Serpentine Dam
Teds Beach
Mt Sprent
McPartlan Pass
Adamsfield
Frodshams Pass
Mt Wedge
Mt Bowes
Mt Mueller
Mt Field West
Clear Hill
Wyids Craig
Double Peak
Lake Pedder
Mt Solitary
Mt Anne
Mt Eliza
Lake Judd
Scotts Peak Dam
Edgar Dam
Mt Hesperus
Mt Orion
West Portal
Federation Peak
Ripple Mtn
Mt Norold
Mt Rugby
Moulters Inlet
Mt Counsel
Mt Louisa
Castle Hill
Lake Rowallan
Lake Murchison
Lake Pieman
Lake Plimsoll
Lake Margaret
Lake Burbury
L. Rolleston
Montezuma Falls
Mt Read
Mt Murchison
Mt Dundas
Mt Zeehan
Mt Agnew
Henty Dunes
Ocean Beach
Henty Glacial Moraine
Nelson Falls
Franklin River Nature Trail
Creepy Crawly Nature Trail
Butlers Gorge PS
Mt Hobhouse
Liapootah PS
Forty Lakes
Lake Augusta
Lake King William
Derwent
Gordon River
Franklin
Crossing
Old
Arthur Plains
Lake Will
Barn Bluff
Murchison Dam
Mackintosh Dam
Victoria Peak
Bastyan PS,Dam
Anthony PS
Mt Read
Mt Selina
LYELL HWY
MURCHISON HWY
ZEEHAN HWY
GORDON RIVER ROAD
Overland Walking Track
SWCA
A10
B27
B28
B24
B61
C249
C248
C251
C252
C601
C602
C603
C604
C607
C171
C172
145°
145°30
146°
146°30
42°
42°30
43°
43°30
A B C D E F G H J K
1 2 3 4 5 6 7
N
0 10 20 30 40 km
© Hema Maps Pty Ltd

To Devonport, Launceston
To Launceston
61
To St Marys
To St Marys, St Helens
HOBART
New Norfolk
Bridgewater
Richmond
Sorell
Kingston
Huonville
Geeveston
Dover
Southport
Cygnet
Snug
Campbell Town
Oatlands
Bothwell
Hamilton
Triabunna
Swansea
Bicheno
Port Arthur
Tasman Peninsula
Forestier Peninsula
Freycinet Peninsula
Maria Island
Schouten Island
Bruny Island
Storm Bay
TASMAN SEA
SEE PAGES 56-57

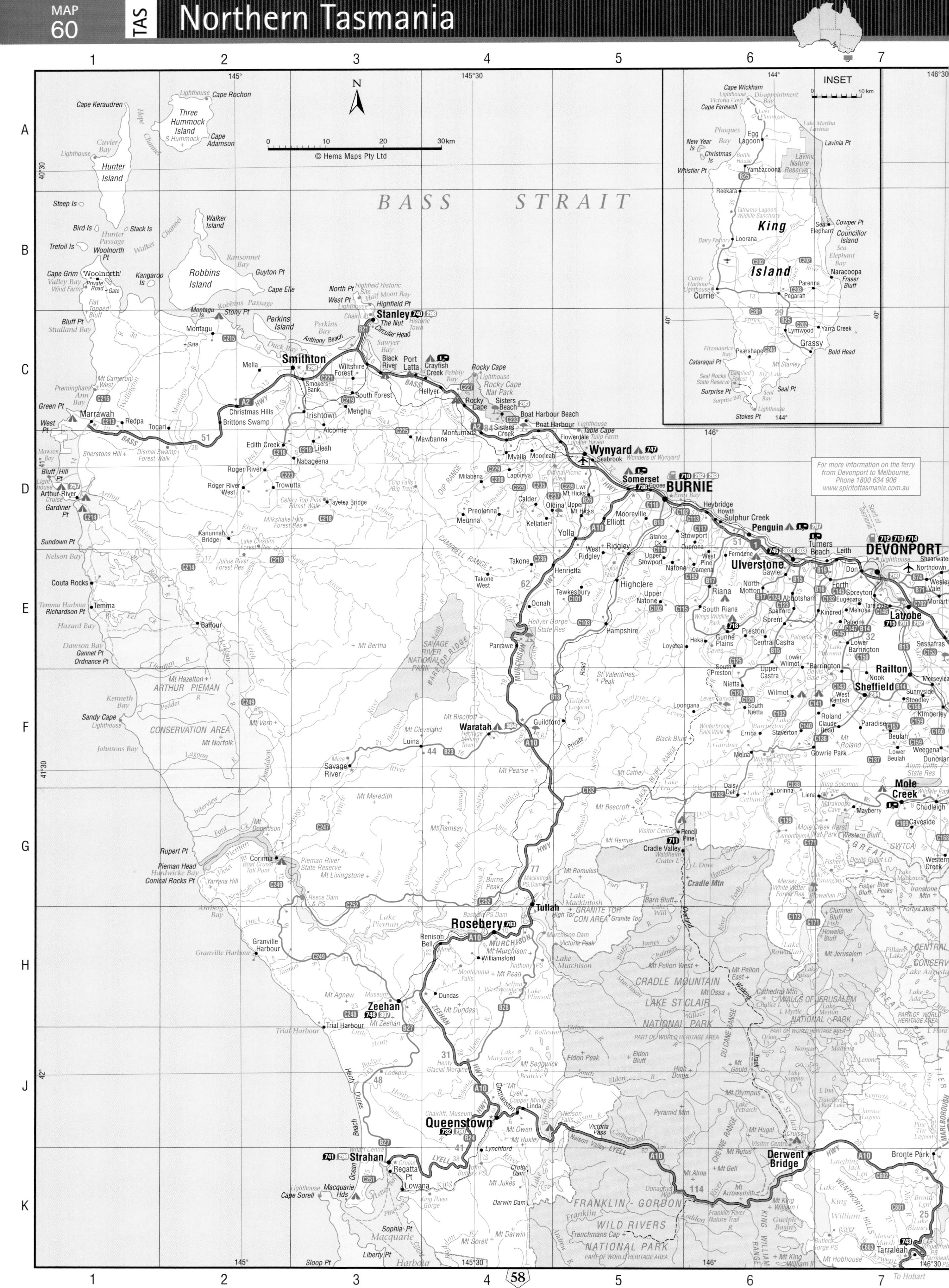
Northern Tasmania
BASS STRAIT
© Hema Maps Pty Ltd
INSET
King Island
For more information on the ferry from Devonport to Melbourne, Phone 1800 634 906 www.spiritoftasmania.com.au
Hunter Island
Three Hummock Island
Robbins Island
Walker Island
Cape Grim
Stanley
Smithton
Marrawah
Wynyard
Somerset
BURNIE
Penguin
Ulverstone
DEVONPORT
Latrobe
Railton
Sheffield
Mole Creek
Waratah
Tullah
Rosebery
Zeehan
Queenstown
Strahan
Derwent Bridge
Yolla
Riana
Currie
Grassy
Naracoopa
ARTHUR PIEMAN CONSERVATION AREA
SAVAGE RIVER NATIONAL PARK
CRADLE MOUNTAIN LAKE ST CLAIR NATIONAL PARK
FRANKLIN - GORDON WILD RIVERS NATIONAL PARK
WALLS OF JERUSALEM NATIONAL PARK
Cradle Mtn
Macquarie Harbour
Sophia Pt
Liberty Pt
Sloop Pt
Bronte Park
Tarraleah
To Hobart
58

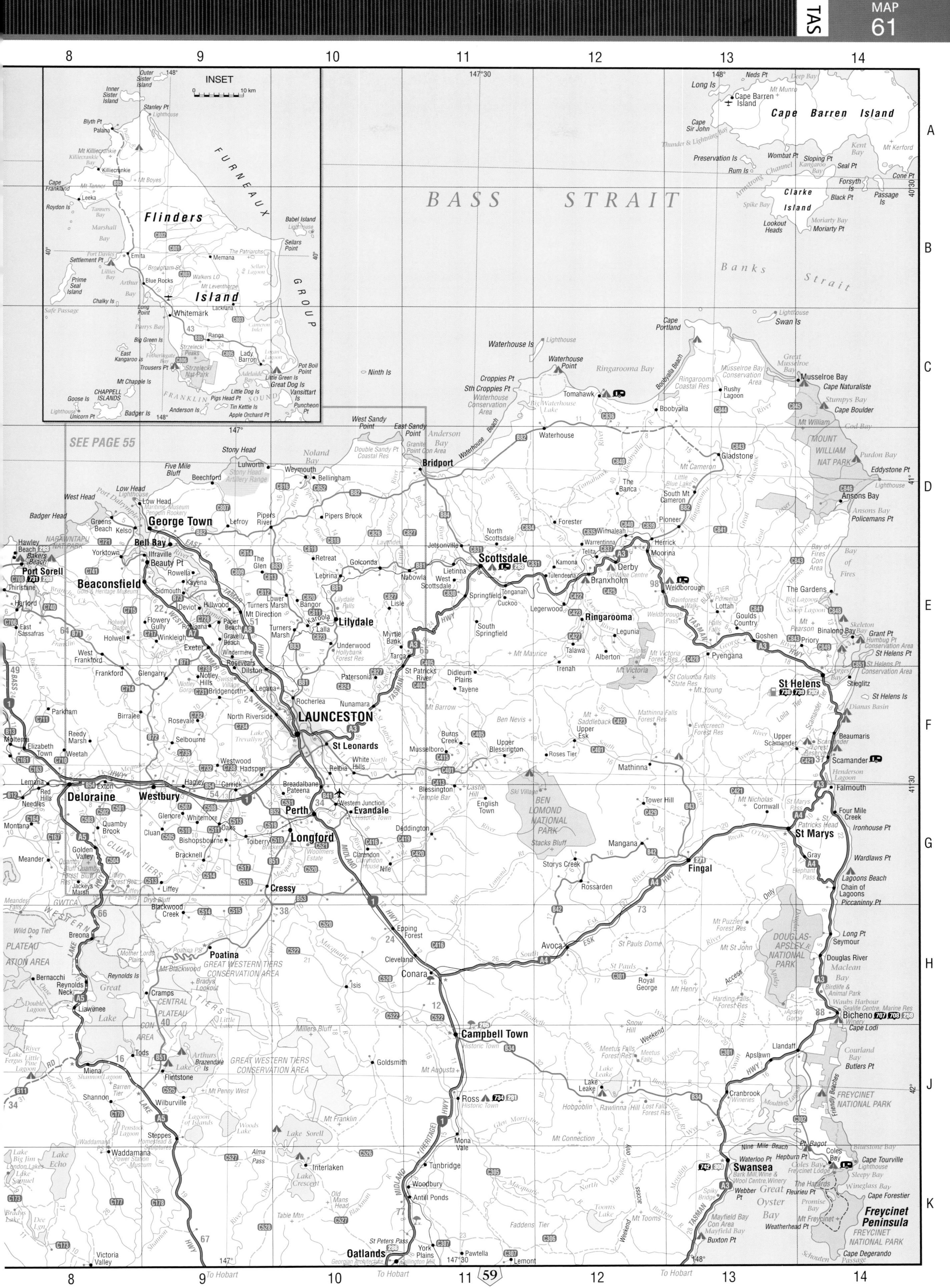
INSET
FURNEAUX GROUP
Flinders Island
Outer Sister Island
Inner Sister Island
Stanley Pt
Blyth Pt
Palana
Mt Killiecrankie
Killiecrankie
Cape Frankland
Leeka
Roydon Is
Marshall Bay
Babel Island
Sellars Point
The Patriarchs
Settlement Pt
Emita
Memana
Prime Seal Island
Chalky Is
Blue Rocks
Whitemark
Lackrana
Long Point
Big Green Is
East Kangaroo Is
Strzelecki Peaks
Ranga
Lady Barron
Trousers Pt
Mt Chappell Is
CHAPPELL ISLANDS
Goose Is
Badger Is
Pigs Head Pt
Little Dog Is
Great Dog Is
Vansittart Is
Pot Boil Point
Puncheon Pt
Anderson Is
Tin Kettle Is
Apple Orchard Pt
Unicorn Pt
FRANKLIN SOUND
BASS STRAIT
Cape Barren Island
Long Is
Cape Barren Island
Neds Pt
Deep Bay
Mt Munro
Cape Sir John
Preservation Is
Rum Is
Wombat Pt
Sloping Pt
Kent Bay
Mt Kerford
Seal Pt
Cone Pt
Armstrong Channel
Clarke Island
Forsyth Is
Black Pt
Passage Is
Spike Bay
Lookout Heads
Moriarty Bay
Moriarty Pt
Banks Strait
Swan Is
Cape Portland
Waterhouse Is
Waterhouse Point
Ringarooma Bay
Ninth Is
Croppies Pt
Sth Croppies Pt
Waterhouse Conservation Area
Tomahawk
Boobyalla
Rushy Lagoon
Musselroe Bay
Cape Naturaliste
Cape Boulder
Mt William
MOUNT WILLIAM NAT PARK
Eddystone Pt
Ansons Bay
Policemans Pt
Gladstone
Waterhouse
SEE PAGE 55
West Sandy Point
East Sandy Point
Anderson Bay
Bridport
Stony Head
Noland Bay
Five Mile Bluff
Lulworth
Weymouth
Beechford
Bellingham
Low Head
West Head
Badger Head
George Town
Lefroy
Pipers River
Pipers Brook
Greens Beach
Kelso
Bell Bay
Hawley Beach
Port Sorell
Beaconsfield
Yorktown
Ilfraville
Beauty Pt
Rowella
Kayena
Retreat
Golconda
Lebrina
Nabowla
Jetsonville
Scottsdale
Lietinna
West Scottsdale
North Scottsdale
Forester
Winnaleah
Pioneer
The Banca
South Mt Cameron
Herrick
Moorina
Derby
Branxholm
Weldborough
Tulendeena
Kamona
Springfield
Tonganah
Cuckoo
Legerwood
Ringarooma
Lottah
Goulds Country
Goshen
Pyengana
Binalong Bay
The Gardens
Grant Pt
Humbug Pt
St Helens Pt
St Helens
Stieglitz
Beaumaris
Scamander
Upper Scamander
Falmouth
Thirlstane
Harford
East Sassafras
Sidmouth
Hillwood
Deviot
Flowery Gully
Holwell
Rosevears
Exeter
Winkleigh
Lower Turners Marsh
Turners Marsh
Mt Direction
Bangor
Karoola
Lilydale
Lalla
Underwood
Myrtle Bank
Targa
Legunia
Talawa
Alberton
Mt Victoria
Trenah
South Springfield
Mt Maurice
West Frankford
Frankford
Glengarry
Dilston
Notley Hills
Bridgenorth
Legana
Rocherlea
Patersonia
Nunamara
St Patricks River
Didleum Plains
Tayene
Parkham
Birralee
North Riverside
LAUNCESTON
Rosevale
Reedy Marsh
Elizabeth Town
Weetah
Selbourne
St Leonards
White Hills
Relbia
Burns Creek
Musselboro
Upper Blessington
Ben Nevis
Mt Saddleback
Upper Esk
Roses Tier
Mathinna
Mt Young
Westwood
Hadspen
Carrick
Hagley
Deloraine
Westbury
Exton
Red Hills
Needles
Montana
Breadalbane
Pateena
Perth
Western Junction
Evandale
Blessington
English Town
Castle Hill
BEN LOMOND NATIONAL PARK
Stacks Bluff
Tower Hill
Cornwall
Mt Nicholas
St Patricks Head
St Marys
Four Mile Creek
Ironhouse Pt
Quamby Brook
Cluan
Glenore
Whitemore
Oaks
Bishopsbourne
Toiberry
Longford
Deddington
Clarendon
Nile
Meander
Golden Valley
Bracknell
Liffey
Cressy
Storys Creek
Rossarden
Mangana
Fingal
Gray
Wardlaws Pt
Lagoons Beach
Chain of Lagoons
Piccaninny Pt
Jackeys Marsh
Blackwood Creek
Breona
Epping Forest
Cleveland
Conara
Avoca
St Pauls Dome
Mt St John
DOUGLAS-APSLEY NATIONAL PARK
Long Pt
Seymour
Douglas River
Maclean Bay
Poatina
GREAT WESTERN TIERS CONSERVATION AREA
Bernacchi
Reynolds Neck
Cramps
Liawenee
Great Lake
Isis
Royal George
Mt Henry
Bicheno
Waubs Harbour
Cape Lodi
Campbell Town
Snow Hill
Millers Bluff
Tods
Miena
Arthurs Lake
Goldsmith
Mt Augusta
Apslawn
Llandaff
Courland Bay
Butlers Pt
Flintstone
Shannon
Wilburville
Mt Penny West
Ross
Lake Leake
Hobgoblin
Rawlinna
Cranbrook
FREYCINET NATIONAL PARK
Steppes
Lake Sorell
Mt Franklin
Mona Vale
Mt Connection
Nine Mile Beach
Pt Bagot
Coles Bay
Cape Tourville
Sleepy Bay
Waddamana
Lake Echo
Interlaken
Lake Crescent
Tunbridge
Woodbury
Antill Ponds
Swansea
Waterloo Pt
Hepburn Pt
Webber Pt
Great Oyster Bay
Fleurieu Pt
Wineglass Bay
Cape Forestier
Freycinet Peninsula
Mayfield Bay
Buxton Pt
Mt Tooms
Tooms Lake
Faddens Tier
Table Mtn
Victoria Valley
St Peters Pass
Oatlands
York Plains
Pawtella
Lemont
Weatherhead Pt
Mt Freycinet
Cape Degerando
Schouten Passage
To Hobart

SOUTH AUSTRALIA Key Map

POPULATION: 1.6 million
AREA: 983,482 sq km
CAPITAL CITY: Adelaide

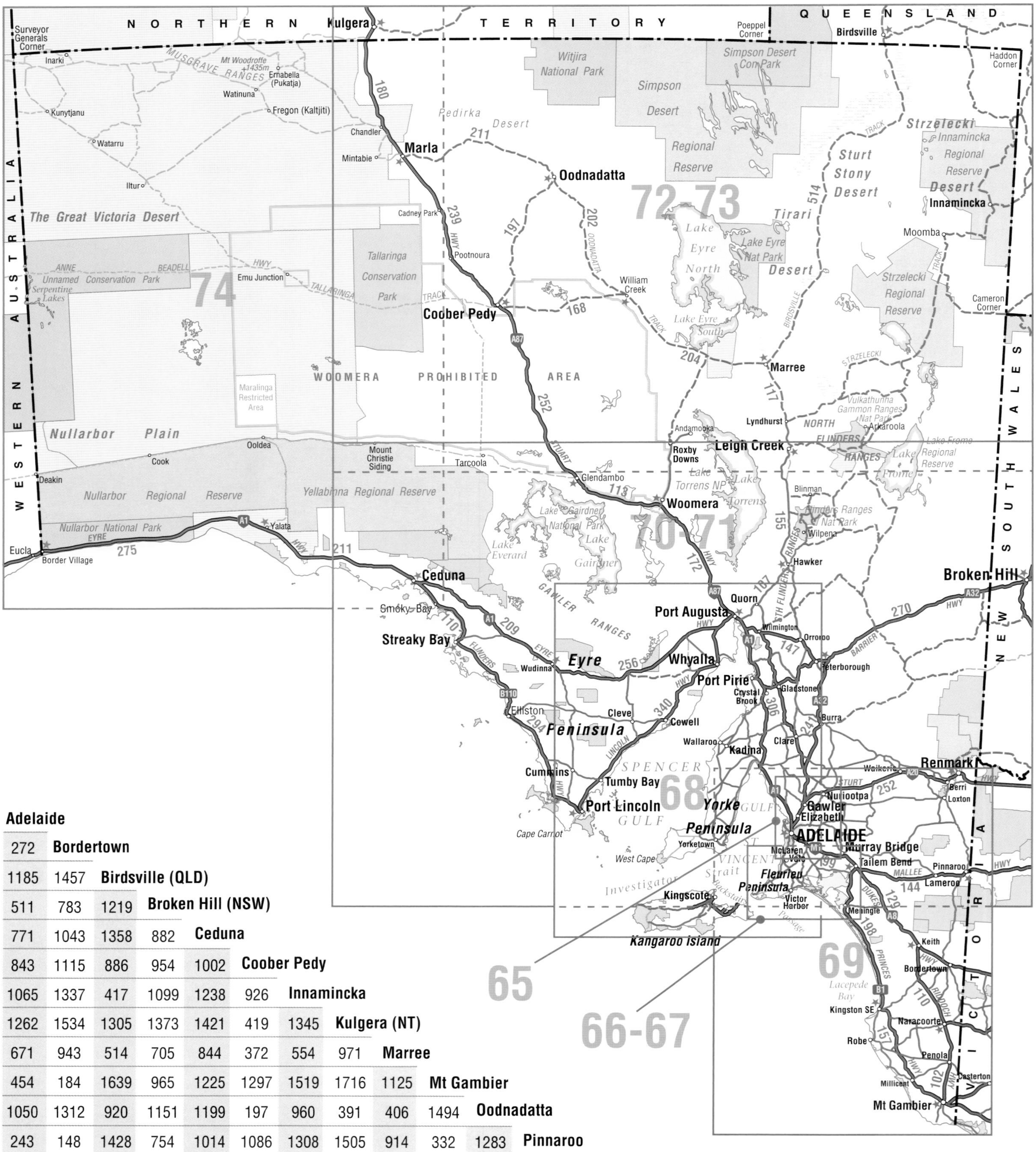

	Adelaide	Bordertown	Birdsville (QLD)	Broken Hill (NSW)	Ceduna	Coober Pedy	Innamincka	Kulgera (NT)	Marree	Mt Gambier	Oodnadatta	Pinnaroo	Port Augusta	Port Lincoln	Renmark
Bordertown	272														
Birdsville (QLD)	1185	1457													
Broken Hill (NSW)	511	783	1219												
Ceduna	771	1043	1358	882											
Coober Pedy	843	1115	886	954	1002										
Innamincka	1065	1337	417	1099	1238	926									
Kulgera (NT)	1262	1534	1305	1373	1421	419	1345								
Marree	671	943	514	705	844	372	554	971							
Mt Gambier	454	184	1639	965	1225	1297	1519	1716	1125						
Oodnadatta	1050	1312	920	1151	1199	197	960	391	406	1494					
Pinnaroo	243	148	1428	754	1014	1086	1308	1505	914	332	1283				
Port Augusta	306	578	893	417	465	537	773	956	379	760	734	549			
Port Lincoln	646	918	1233	757	404	877	1113	1296	719	1100	1074	889	340		
Renmark	252	298	1234	560	897	969	1114	1388	720	368	1166	150	432	772	
WA-SA Border Village	1257	1529	1844	1368	486	1488	1724	1970	1330	1711	1685	1500	951	890	1383

Distances are shown in kilometres and follow the most direct major sealed route where possible

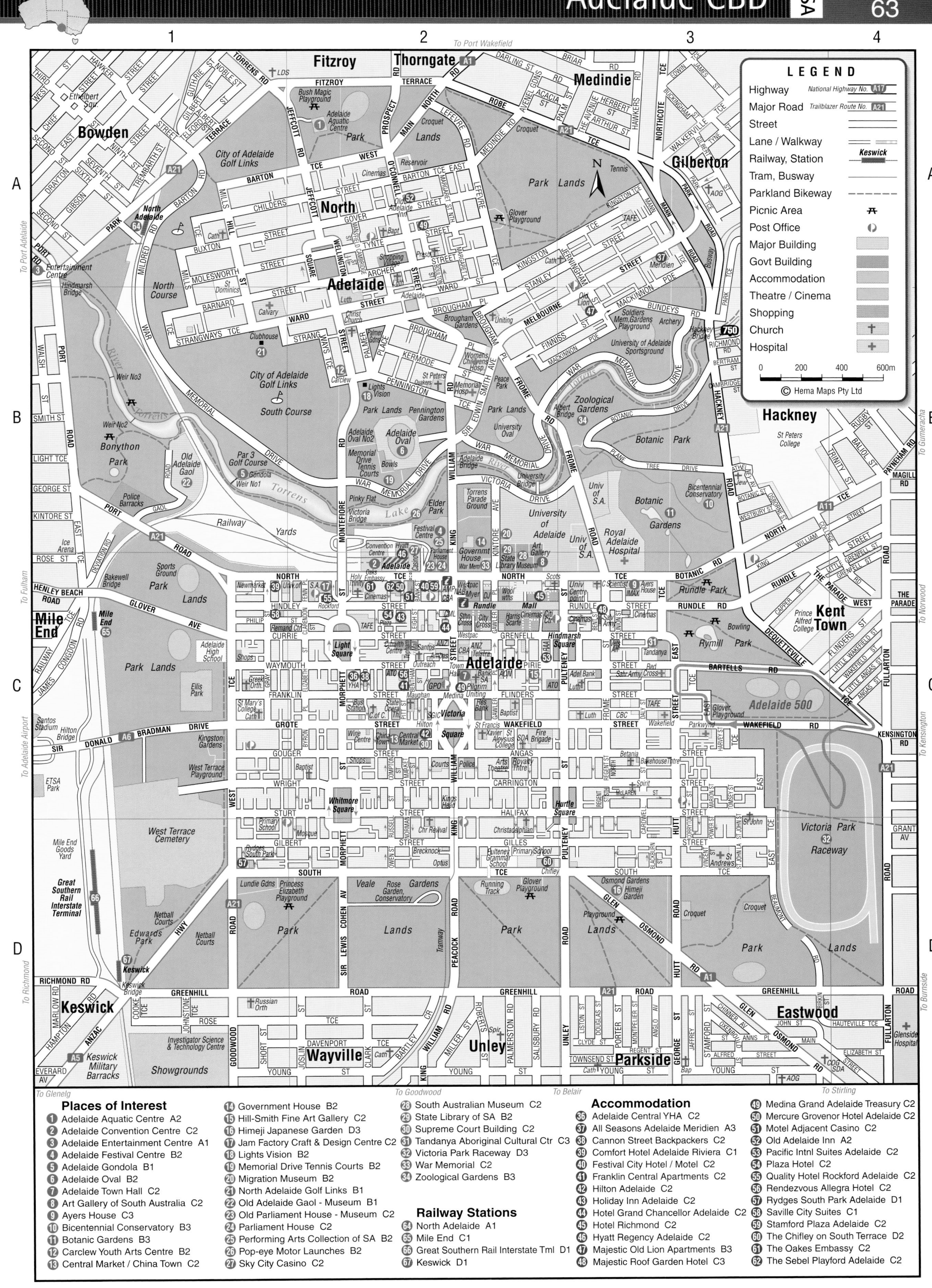
1
2
3
4
A
B
C
D
Fitzroy
Thorngate
Medindie
Gilberton
Bowden
North Adelaide
Adelaide
Hackney
Kent Town
Mile End
Keswick
Wayville
Unley
Parkside
Eastwood
City of Adelaide Golf Links
Park Lands
North Course
South Course
Botanic Park
Botanic Gardens
Zoological Gardens
Victoria Park Raceway
Adelaide 500
Railway Yards
Lake Torrens
West Terrace Cemetery
Showgrounds
Keswick Military Barracks
Victoria Square
Light Square
Hindmarsh Square
Hurtle Square
Whitmore Square
Rundle Mall
Royal Adelaide Hospital
University of Adelaide
Adelaide Oval
Great Southern Rail Interstate Terminal
To Port Wakefield
To Port Adelaide
To Fulham
To Adelaide Airport
To Richmond
To Glenelg
To Goodwood
To Belair
To Stirling
To Burnside
To Kensington
To Norwood
To Gumeracha
LEGEND
Highway — National Highway No. A17
Major Road — Trailblazer Route No. A21
Street
Lane / Walkway
Railway, Station — Keswick
Tram, Busway
Parkland Bikeway
Picnic Area
Post Office
Major Building
Govt Building
Accommodation
Theatre / Cinema
Shopping
Church
Hospital
0 200 400 600m
© Hema Maps Pty Ltd
Places of Interest
1 Adelaide Aquatic Centre A2
2 Adelaide Convention Centre C2
3 Adelaide Entertainment Centre A1
4 Adelaide Festival Centre B2
5 Adelaide Gondola B1
6 Adelaide Oval B2
7 Adelaide Town Hall C2
8 Art Gallery of South Australia C2
9 Ayers House C3
10 Bicentennial Conservatory B3
11 Botanic Gardens B3
12 Carclew Youth Arts Centre B2
13 Central Market / China Town C2
14 Government House B2
15 Hill-Smith Fine Art Gallery C2
16 Himeji Japanese Garden D3
17 Jam Factory Craft & Design Centre C2
18 Lights Vision B2
19 Memorial Drive Tennis Courts B2
20 Migration Museum B2
21 North Adelaide Golf Links B1
22 Old Adelaide Gaol - Museum B1
23 Old Parliament House - Museum C2
24 Parliament House C2
25 Performing Arts Collection of SA B2
26 Pop-eye Motor Launches B2
27 Sky City Casino C2
28 South Australian Museum C2
29 State Library of SA B2
30 Supreme Court Building C2
31 Tandanya Aboriginal Cultural Ctr C3
32 Victoria Park Raceway D3
33 War Memorial C2
34 Zoological Gardens B3
Railway Stations
64 North Adelaide A1
65 Mile End C1
66 Great Southern Rail Interstate Tml D1
67 Keswick D1
Accommodation
36 Adelaide Central YHA C2
37 All Seasons Adelaide Meridien A3
38 Cannon Street Backpackers C2
39 Comfort Hotel Adelaide Riviera C1
40 Festival City Hotel / Motel C2
41 Franklin Central Apartments C2
42 Hilton Adelaide C2
43 Holiday Inn Adelaide C2
44 Hotel Grand Chancellor Adelaide C2
45 Hotel Richmond C2
46 Hyatt Regency Adelaide C2
47 Majestic Old Lion Apartments B3
48 Majestic Roof Garden Hotel C3
49 Medina Grand Adelaide Treasury C2
50 Mercure Grosvenor Hotel Adelaide C2
51 Motel Adjacent Casino C2
52 Old Adelaide Inn A2
53 Pacific Intnl Suites Adelaide C2
54 Plaza Hotel C2
55 Quality Hotel Rockford Adelaide C2
56 Rendezvous Allegra Hotel C2
57 Rydges South Park Adelaide D1
58 Saville City Suites C1
59 Stamford Plaza Adelaide C2
60 The Chifley on South Terrace D2
61 The Oakes Embassy C2
62 The Sebel Playford Adelaide C2

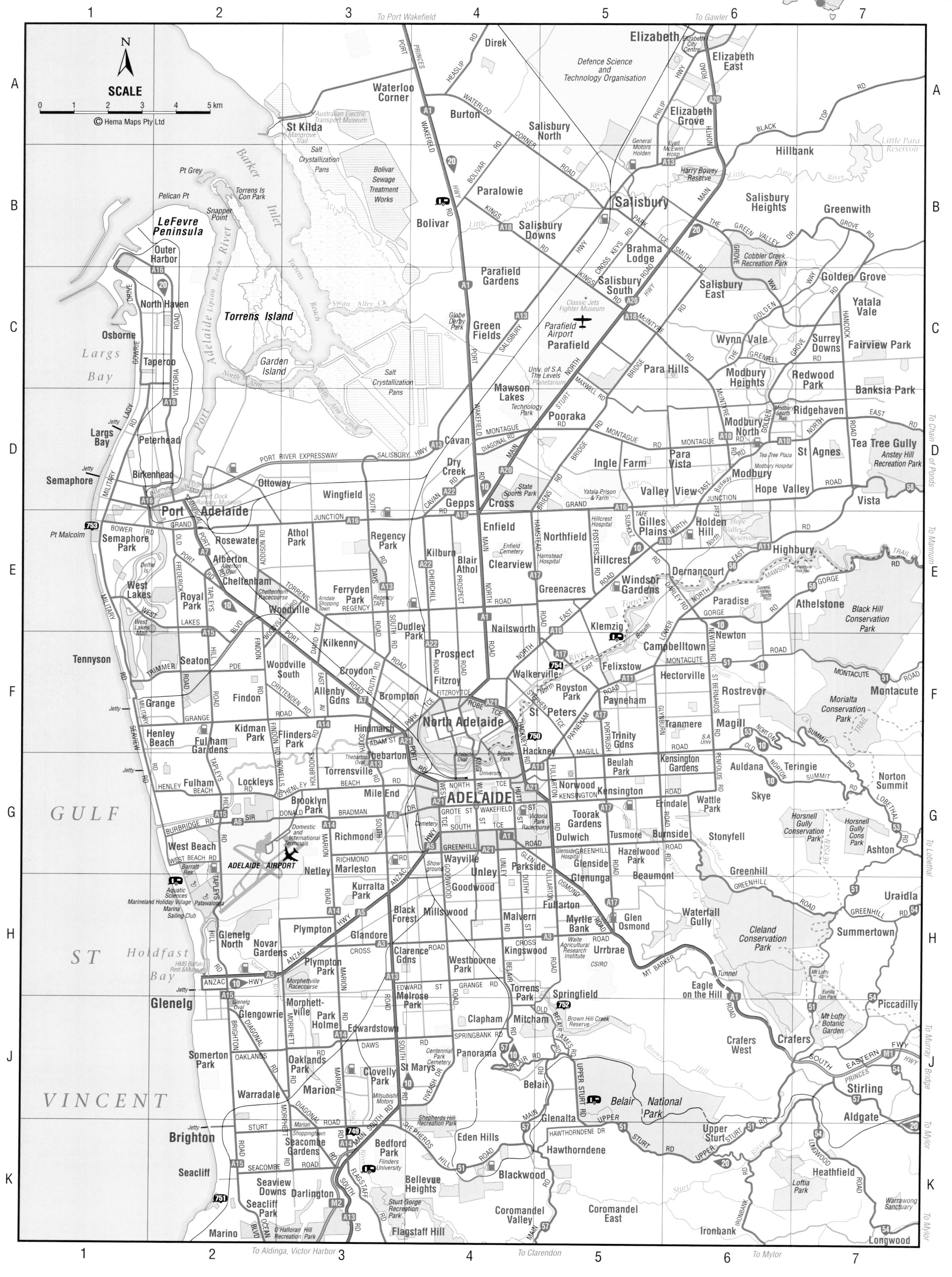

Adelaide Throughroads

SCALE
0 1 2 3 4 5 km
© Hema Maps Pty Ltd

To Port Wakefield
To Gawler
To Chain of Ponds
To Mannum
To Lobethal
To Murray Bridge
To Mylor
To Aldinga, Victor Harbor
To Clarendon

Direk
Elizabeth
Elizabeth East
Elizabeth Grove
Defence Science and Technology Organisation
Waterloo Corner
Burton
St Kilda
Salisbury North
Hillbank
Little Para Reservoir
Pt Grey
Pelican Pt
Barker Inlet
Torrens Is Con Park
Snapper Point
LeFevre Peninsula
Bolivar Sewage Treatment Works
Salt Crystallization Pans
Paralowie
Bolivar
Salisbury
Salisbury Downs
Salisbury Heights
Greenwith
Harry Bowey Reserve
Outer Harbor
Brahma Lodge
Cobbler Creek Recreation Park
Parafield Gardens
Salisbury South
Salisbury East
Golden Grove
North Haven
Torrens Island
Yatala Vale
Osborne
Largs Bay
Garden Island
Green Fields
Parafield Airport
Parafield
Wynn Vale
Surrey Downs
Fairview Park
Taperoo
Para Hills
Modbury Heights
Redwood Park
Banksia Park
Mawson Lakes
Pooraka
Ridgehaven
Largs Bay
Peterhead
Modbury North
Tea Tree Gully
Anstey Hill Recreation Park
Cavan
Dry Creek
Para Vista
St Agnes
Semaphore
Birkenhead
Ingle Farm
Modbury
Ottoway
Wingfield
Gepps Cross
Valley View
Hope Valley
Vista
Port Adelaide
Enfield
Gilles Plains
Holden Hill
Pt Malcolm
Semaphore Park
Rosewater
Athol Park
Regency Park
Northfield
Hillcrest
Highbury
Alberton
Kilburn
Blair Athol
Clearview
Windsor Gardens
Dernancourt
West Lakes
Cheltenham
Royal Park
Ferryden Park
Greenacres
Paradise
Athelstone
Black Hill Conservation Park
Woodville
Dudley Park
Nailsworth
Klemzig
Newton
Tennyson
Seaton
Kilkenny
Prospect
Campbelltown
Woodville South
Croydon
Walkerville
Felixstow
Hectorville
Rostrevor
Montacute
Grange
Findon
Allenby Gdns
Brompton
Fitzroy
Royston Park
Payneham
St Peters
Morialta Conservation Park
Henley Beach
Fulham Gardens
Kidman Park
Flinders Park
Hindmarsh
North Adelaide
Trinity Gdns
Tranmere
Magill
Thebarton
Hackney
Beulah Park
Kensington Gardens
Auldana
Teringie
Fulham
Lockleys
Torrensville
Mile End
Norwood
Kensington
Skye
Norton Summit
Brooklyn Park
ADELAIDE
Toorak Gardens
Erindale
Wattle Park
West Beach
Richmond
Dulwich
Tusmore
Burnside
Stonyfell
Horsnell Gully Conservation Park
Ashton
ADELAIDE AIRPORT
Netley
Marleston
Wayville
Unley
Parkside
Glenside
Hazelwood Park
Beaumont
Greenhill
Uraidla
Kurralta Park
Goodwood
Glenunga
Fullarton
Black Forest
Millswood
Malvern
Myrtle Bank
Glen Osmond
Waterfall Gully
Summertown
Plympton
Glandore
Glenelg North
Novar Gardens
Clarence Gdns
Kingswood
Urrbrae
Cleland Conservation Park
Plympton Park
Westbourne Park
Torrens Park
Springfield
Eagle on the Hill
Glenelg
Glengowrie
Morphettville
Melrose Park
Park Holme
Clapham
Mitcham
Piccadilly
Crafers West
Crafers
Edwardstown
Panorama
Somerton Park
Oaklands Park
Clovelly Park
St Marys
Stirling
Warradale
Marion
Belair
Belair National Park
Aldgate
Glenalta
Brighton
Eden Hills
Hawthorndene
Upper Sturt
Seacombe Gardens
Bedford Park
Heathfield
Seacliff
Blackwood
Seaview Downs
Darlington
Bellevue Heights
Loftia Park
Seacliff Park
Coromandel Valley
Coromandel East
Marino
Flagstaff Hill
Ironbank
Longwood

GULF ST VINCENT
Holdfast Bay

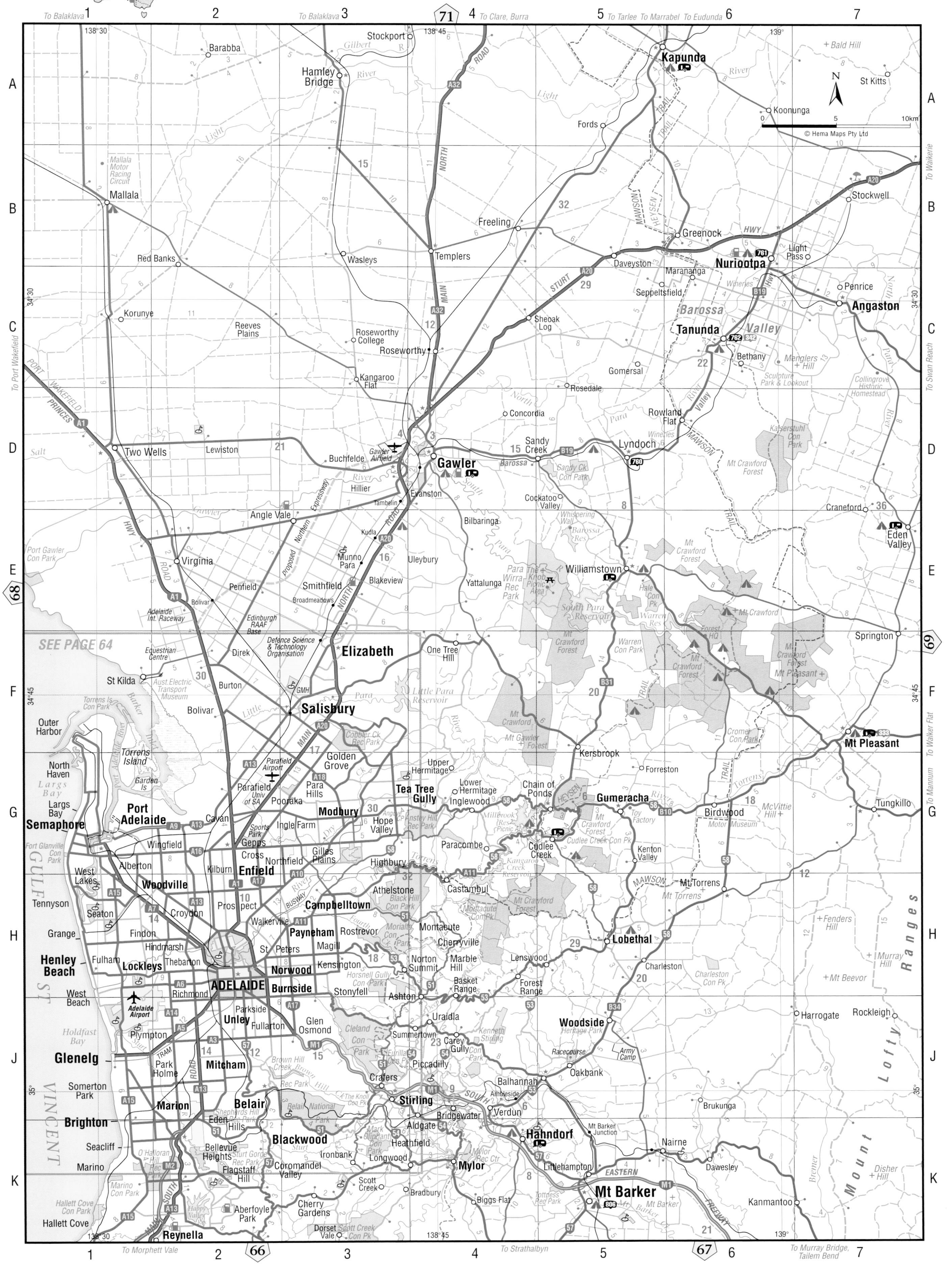

Adelaide Region, South Australia

To Balaklava 1 2 To Balaklava 3 71 4 To Clare, Burra 5 To Tarlee To Marrabel To Eudunda 6 7

138°30 138°45 139°

Barabba
Stockport
Gilbert R
Hamley Bridge
River
Kapunda
River
Bald Hill
St Kitts
Koonunga
0 5 10km
© Hema Maps Pty Ltd
Fords
Light
ROAD
A32
NORTH
TRAIL
HEYSEN
MAWSON
Light
Mallala Motor Racing Circuit
Mallala
15
16
32
A20
Stockwell
To Waikerie
Freeling
Greenock
HWY
Templers
Wasleys
Daveyston
Light Pass
Red Banks
Nuriootpa
761
STURT
29
Marananga
Seppeltsfield
Wineries
Penrice
B19
Angaston
34°30
Korunye
Reeves Plains
Sheoak Log
Barossa
Tanunda
762
342
Valley
Roseworthy College
Roseworthy
12
A32
MAIN
Bethany
Menglers Hill
Sculpture Park & Lookout
Collingrove Historic Homestead
To Port Wakefield
To Swan Reach
PORT WAKEFIELD
PRINCES
A1
Kangaroo Flat
Gomersal
Rosedale
22
Concordia
North Para
Rowland Flat
Valley
Wineries
Kaiserstuhl Con Park
Salt
Two Wells
Lewiston
21
Buchfelde
Gawler Airfield
Gawler
15
Sandy Creek
B19
Lyndoch
760
MAWSON
Mt Crawford Forest
Barossa
Sandy Ck Con Park
River
Hillier
Evanston
Tambelin
Gawler
Angle Vale
Proposed Northern Expressway
Cockatoo Valley
Whispering Wall
Barossa Res
Bilbaringa
8
Craneford
36
Eden Valley
Port Gawler Con Park
HWY
ROAD
Virginia
Kudla
A20
Munno Para
16
Uleybury
Mt Crawford Forest
TRAIL
68
Penfield
Smithfield
Blakeview
Para Wirra Rec Park
The Knob Picnic Area
Yattalunga
Williamstown
Hale Con Pk
Warren Res
Mt Crawford
A1
Bolivar
Broadmeadows
NORTH
South Para Reservoir
Adelaide Int. Raceway
Edinburgh RAAF Base
Defence Science & Technology Organisation
Mt Crawford Forest
Forest HQ
Springton
69
SEE PAGE 64
Elizabeth
One Tree Hill
Warren Con Park
Mt Crawford Forest
Equestrian Centre
Direk
Mt Crawford Forest
St Kilda
Aust.Electric Transport Museum
30
Burton
GMH
B31
Mt Pleasant
34°45
Little Para Reservoir
20
Torrens Is Con Park
Barker
Para
River
TRAIL
Outer Harbor
Bolivar
Little
Salisbury
Mt Crawford
Mt Gawler Forest
Cromer Con Park
Mt Pleasant
333
To Walker Flat
Torrens Island
A20
Cobbler Ck Rec Park
Kersbrook
MAIN
17
Golden Grove
North Haven
Largs Bay
Garden Is
A13
Parafield Airport
Upper Hermitage
Forreston
To Mannum
Largs Bay
A18
Para Hills
Tea Tree Gully
Lower Hermitage
Chain of Ponds
Gumeracha
Torrens
River
18
McVittie Hill
Tungkillo
Semaphore
Port Adelaide
Parafield
Univ of SA
Pooraka
Inglewood
58
HEYSEN
B10
Birdwood
Motor Museum
A9
A13
Cavan
Modbury
30
Millbrook Res Picnic Area
Toy Factory
Fort Glanville Con Park
Wingfield
Ingle Farm
Hope Valley
Anstey Hill Rec Park
Mt Crawford Forest
Sports Park
Gepps Cross
Paracombe
Cudlee Creek
Cudlee Creek Con Pk
Kenton Valley
A16
Gilles Plains
West Lakes
Alberton
Kilburn
Enfield
A17
Northfield
Highbury
Torrens
Kangaroo Creek Reservoir
MAWSON
Mt Torrens
12
Woodville
A10
Castambul
Mt Torrens
Tennyson
A15
10
Athelstone
Black Hill Con Park
Mt Crawford Forest
Ranges
Seaton
A7
Croydon
Prospect
BUSWAY
Campbelltown
Montacute Con Pk
Fenders Hill
Grange
14
Findon
Walkerville
Payneham
Rostrevor
Morialta Con Park
Montacute
Lobethal
Hindmarsh
Magill
Cherryville
29
Henley Beach
Fulham
Lockleys
Thebarton
St Peters
18
Norton Summit
Marble Hill
Lenswood
Charleston
Murray Hill
Kensington
Norwood
Horsnell Gully Con Park
Basket Range
20
Charleston Con Pk
Mt Beevor
West Beach
A6
Richmond
ADELAIDE
Burnside
Stonyfell
Ashton
Forest Range
Adelaide Airport
A14
Parkside
A17
Harrogate
Rockleigh
Holdfast Bay
Plympton
A5
Unley
Fullarton
Glen Osmond
Cleland Con Park
Uraidla
Kenneth Stirling
Woodside
Heritage Park
Summertown
23
Carey Gully
Glenelg
TRAM
14
Mitcham
12
15
Brown Hill Creek
Piccadilly
Racecourse
Army Camp
Lofty
Park Holme
Crafers
Oakbank
Somerton Park
ROAD
A13
Rec Park
Brownhill
The Knoll Con Pk
Balhannah
35°
Marion
Belair
Belair National Park
Stirling
M1
SOUTH
Ambleside
53
Verdun
Brukunga
A15
Brighton
Shepherds Hill
Bridgewater
Eden Hills
Aldgate
Hahndorf
Mt Barker Junction
Nairne
Seacliff
Bellevue Heights
Sturt Gorge Rec Park
Blackwood
Mark Oliphant Con Park
Heathfield
Ironbank
Longwood
Mylor Rec Ctr
Dawesley
Marino
O'Halloran Hill Rec Park
Flagstaff Hill
Coromandel Valley
Mylor
Littlehampton
EASTERN
Disher Hill
Mount
Marino Con Park
Scott Creek
8
Tottness Rec Park
Mt Barker
806
FREEWAY
M1
Kanmantoo
Hallett Cove Con Park
Hallett Cove
Happy Valley Res
Aberfoyle Park
Cherry Gardens
Bradbury
Biggs Flat
Mt Barker
Bremer
A15
Dorset Vale
Scott Creek Con Pk
21
Reynella
138°30
138°45
139°

1 To Morphett Vale 2 66 3 4 To Strathalbyn 5 67 6 To Murray Bridge, Tailem Bend 7

A B C D E F G H J K

GULF ST VINCENT

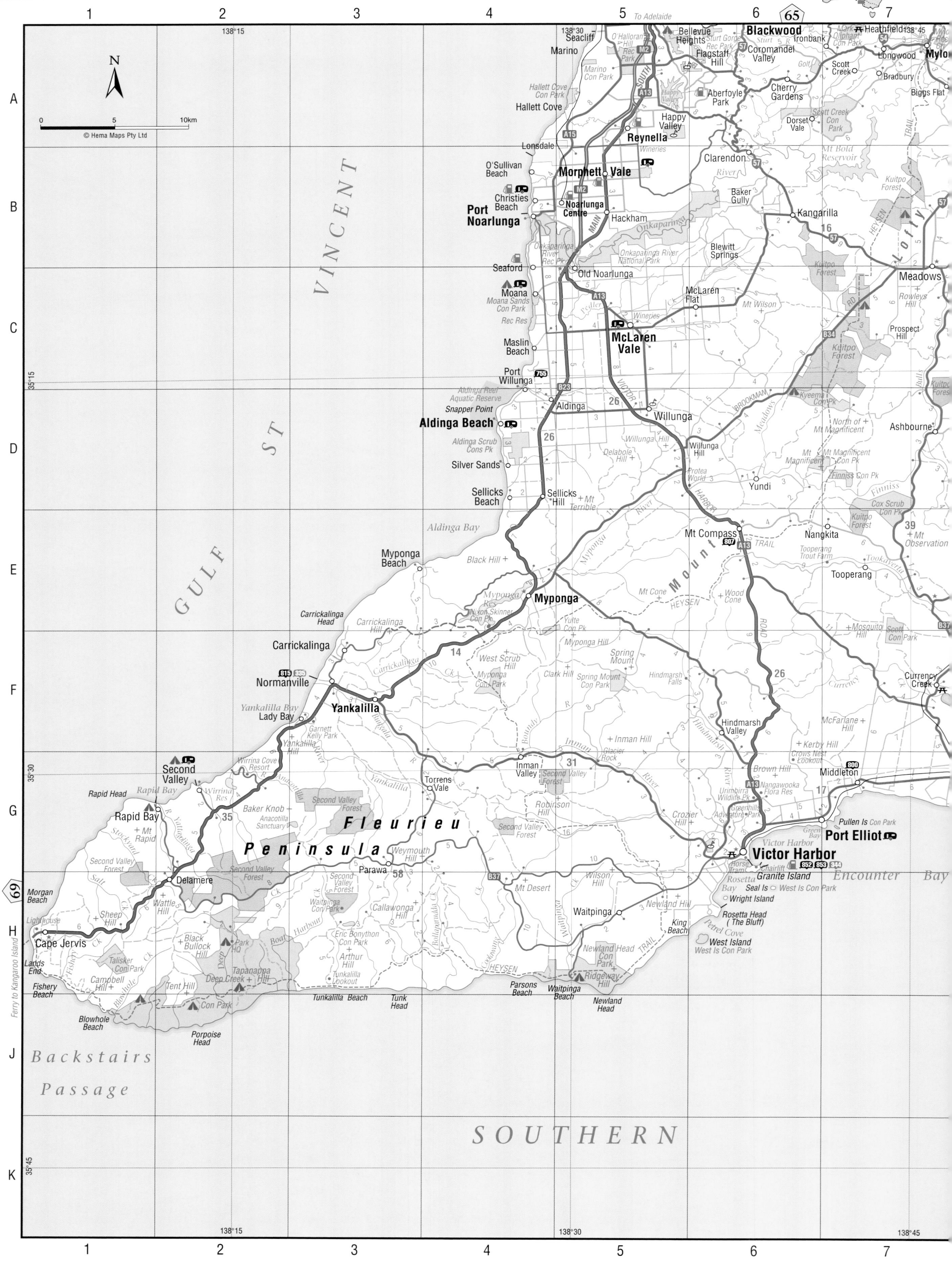

N
0 5 10km
© Hema Maps Pty Ltd
138°15
138°30
138°45
35°15
35°30
35°45
To Adelaide
65
69
GULF ST VINCENT
Backstairs Passage
SOUTHERN
Encounter Bay
Aldinga Bay
Fleurieu Peninsula
Seacliff
Marino
Bellevue Heights
Blackwood
Ironbank
Heathfield
Mylor
Coromandel Valley
Flagstaff Hill
Longwood
Scott Creek
Bradbury
Biggs Flat
Marino Con Park
Hallett Cove Con Park
Hallett Cove
Aberfoyle Park
Cherry Gardens
Happy Valley
Dorset Vale
Scott Creek Con Park
Reynella
Lonsdale
O'Sullivan Beach
Morphett Vale
Clarendon
Mt Bold Reservoir
Kuitpo Forest
Christies Beach
Port Noarlunga
Noarlunga Centre
Hackham
Baker Gully
Kangarilla
Onkaparinga River Rec Pk
Onkaparinga River National Park
Blewitt Springs
Seaford
Old Noarlunga
Meadows
Moana
Moana Sands Con Park
Rec Res
McLaren Flat
Mt Wilson
Rowleys Hill
Prospect Hill
McLaren Vale
Maslin Beach
Port Willunga
Aldinga Reef Aquatic Reserve
Snapper Point
Aldinga
Willunga
Kyeema Con Pk
Aldinga Beach
Aldinga Scrub Cons Pk
North of Mt Magnificent
Ashbourne
Willunga Hill
Delabole Hill
Silver Sands
Mt Magnificent
Mt Magnificent Con Pk
Protea World
Finniss Con Pk
Yundi
Sellicks Beach
Sellicks Hill
Mt Terrible
Cox Scrub Con Pk
Mt Compass
Nangkita
Mt Observation
Myponga Beach
Black Hill
Tooperang Trout Farm
Tooperang
Myponga
Myponga Res
Nixon Skinner Con Pk
Mt Cone
Wood Cone
Carrickalinga Head
Carrickalinga Hill
Yulte Con Pk
Myponga Hill
Mosquito Hill
Scott Con Park
Carrickalinga
West Scrub Hill
Spring Mount
Normanville
Myponga Con Park
Clark Hill
Spring Mount Con Park
Hindmarsh Falls
Currency Creek
Yankalilla Bay
Lady Bay
Yankalilla
Garnett Kelly Park
Yankalilla Hill
Hindmarsh Valley
McFarlane Hill
Inman Hill
Kerby Hill
Crows Nest Lookout
Glacier Rock
Second Valley
Wirrina Cove Resort
Inman Valley
Second Valley Forest
Brown Hill
Middleton
Rapid Head
Rapid Bay
Wirrina Res
Torrens Vale
Nangawooka Flora Res
Urimbirra Wildlife Pk
Robinson Hill
Greenhills Adventure Park
Baker Knob
Anacotilla Sanctuary
Crozier Hill
Pullen Is Con Park
Mt Rapid
Port Elliot
Victor Harbor
Weymouth Hill
Horse Tram
Chairlift
Granite Island
Parawa
Second Valley Forest
Delamere
Mt Desert
Wilson Hill
Rosetta Bay
Seal Is
West Is Con Park
Wright Island
Morgan Beach
Wattle Hill
Waitpinga Con Park
Callawonga Hill
Newland Hill
Waitpinga
Rosetta Head (The Bluff)
Sheep Hill
Lighthouse
Cape Jervis
Black Bullock Hill
Park HQ
Eric Bonython Con Park
Arthur Hill
King Beach
Petrel Cove
West Island
West Is Con Park
Lands End
Talisker Con Park
Newland Head Con Park
Campbell Hill
Tapanappa Hill
Deep Creek
Tunkalilla Lookout
Fishery Beach
Tent Hill
Ridgeway Hill
Ferry to Kangaroo Island
Con Park
Tunkalilla Beach
Tunk Head
Parsons Beach
Waitpinga Beach
Newland Head
Blowhole Beach
Porpoise Head
HEYSEN TRAIL

To Adelaide
To Mannum
To Karoonda
To Keith, Pinnaroo
To Coonalpyn
To Kingston SE
Hahndorf
Littlehampton
Mt Barker
Nairne
Dawesley
Kanmantoo
Pallamana
Mypolonga
Monarto
Murray Bridge
Army Field Firing Range
Monarto Zoological Park
Echunga
Wistow
Callington
Monarto South
Rabila
Long Is Con Pk
Lookout
Swanport
Bell Landing
Monteith
Flaxley
Bonython Hill
Greenhill
Macclesfield
Monarto Con Park
Hartley
Woodchester
Paris Creek
Jarman Landing
Woods Point
Old Tailem Town
Ferries-McDonald Con Park
Brinkley
Bulls Creek
Bletchley
Tailem Bend
Strathalbyn
Jervois
Belvidere
Langhorne Creek
Wineries
Giles Hill
Tailem Bend Forest Res
Wellington East
Marina
Boggy Lake
Mosquito Point
Angus Plains
Sandergrove
Wellington
Ferry
Pelican Lagoon
Dog Lake
Toldérol Pt
Toldérol Game Res
Finniss
Milang
Pomanda Pt
Lake Alexandrina
Low Pt
Currency Creek Game Res
Goolwa
Bridge
Clayton
Point Sturt
Raukkan
Narrung
Point Malcolm
Poltalloch
Ashville
Marina
Hindmarsh Island
Point McLeay
Aboriginal Reserve
Barrage
The Narrows
Mt Misery
Long Is
Sir Richard Peninsula
Mundoo Is
Mud Islands Game Res
Reedy Is
Nurra Nurra
Albert Hill
Ewe Is
Mud Is
Murray Mouth
Tauwitchere Is
Reedy Point
Loveday Bay
Pelican Point
Salt Lagoon Is Con Park
Waltowa Swamp
Lake Albert
Rumply Point
PRINCES HWY
Coorong
Mark Point
Younghusband Peninsula
The Coorong National Park
Mulbin Yerrok Pt
Meningie
Meningie Hill
Long Point
Warringee Point
Aboriginal Reserve
OCEAN
Mt Sandy
Noonameena
Robs Point

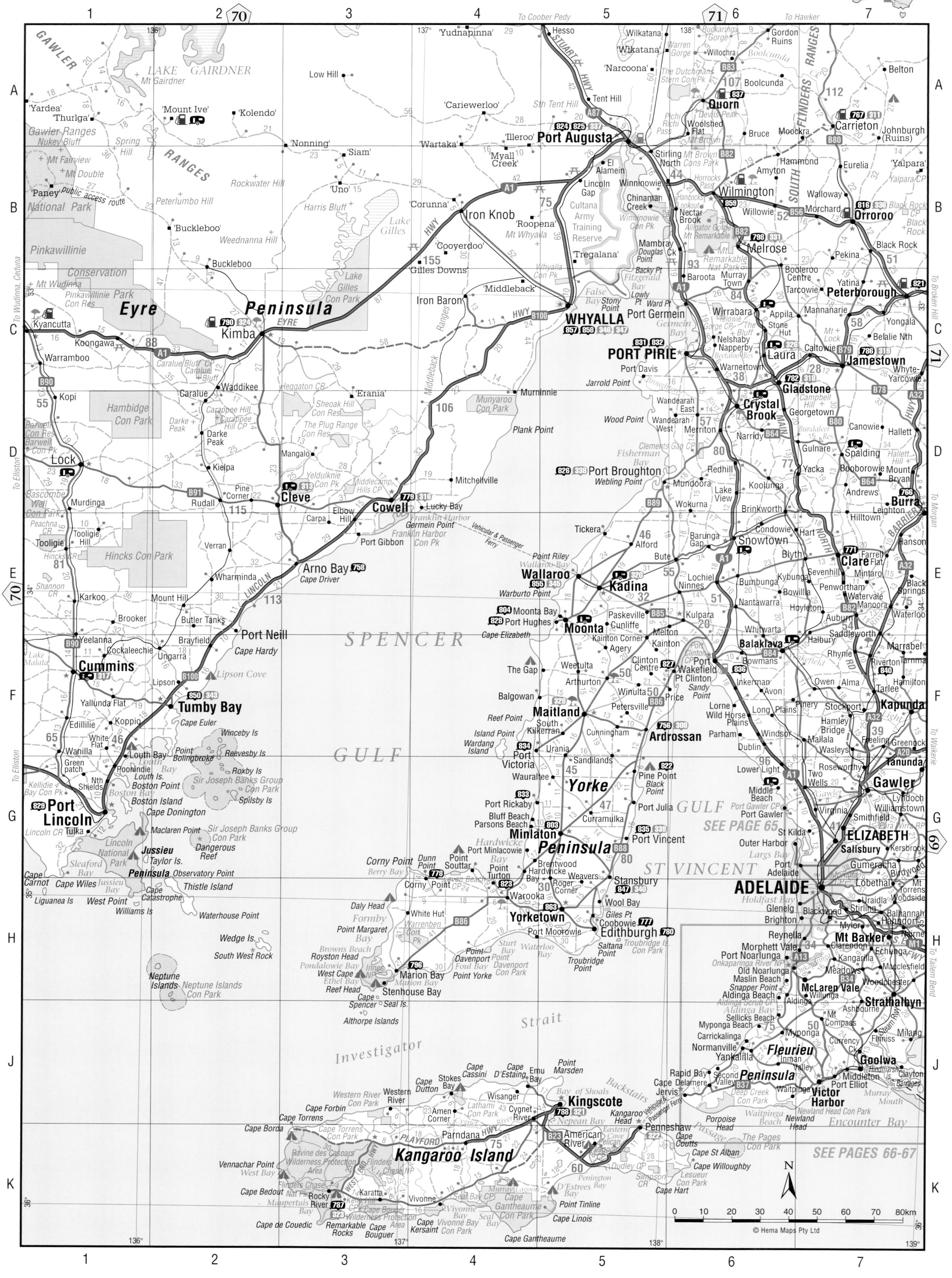

Central South Australia

Gawler Ranges
Lake Gairdner
Gawler Ranges National Park
Pinkawillinie Conservation Park
Eyre Peninsula
Kimba
Whyalla
Port Augusta
Port Pirie
Iron Knob
Quorn
Wilmington
Melrose
Orroroo
Peterborough
Jamestown
Gladstone
Crystal Brook
Laura
Port Germein
Port Broughton
Cleve
Cowell
Arno Bay
Port Neill
Tumby Bay
Cummins
Lock
Port Lincoln
Lincoln National Park
Spencer Gulf
Wallaroo
Kadina
Moonta
Maitland
Ardrossan
Yorke Peninsula
Minlaton
Port Vincent
Edithburgh
Yorketown
Marion Bay
Stenhouse Bay
Investigator Strait
Gulf St Vincent
Clare
Burra
Balaklava
Port Wakefield
Kapunda
Gawler
Elizabeth
Adelaide
Mt Barker
Strathalbyn
McLaren Vale
Fleurieu Peninsula
Victor Harbor
Goolwa
Encounter Bay
Kingscote
Penneshaw
American River
Parndana
Kangaroo Island
Flinders Chase National Park
Backstairs Passage
SEE PAGE 65
SEE PAGES 66-67

0 10 20 30 40 50 60 70 80km

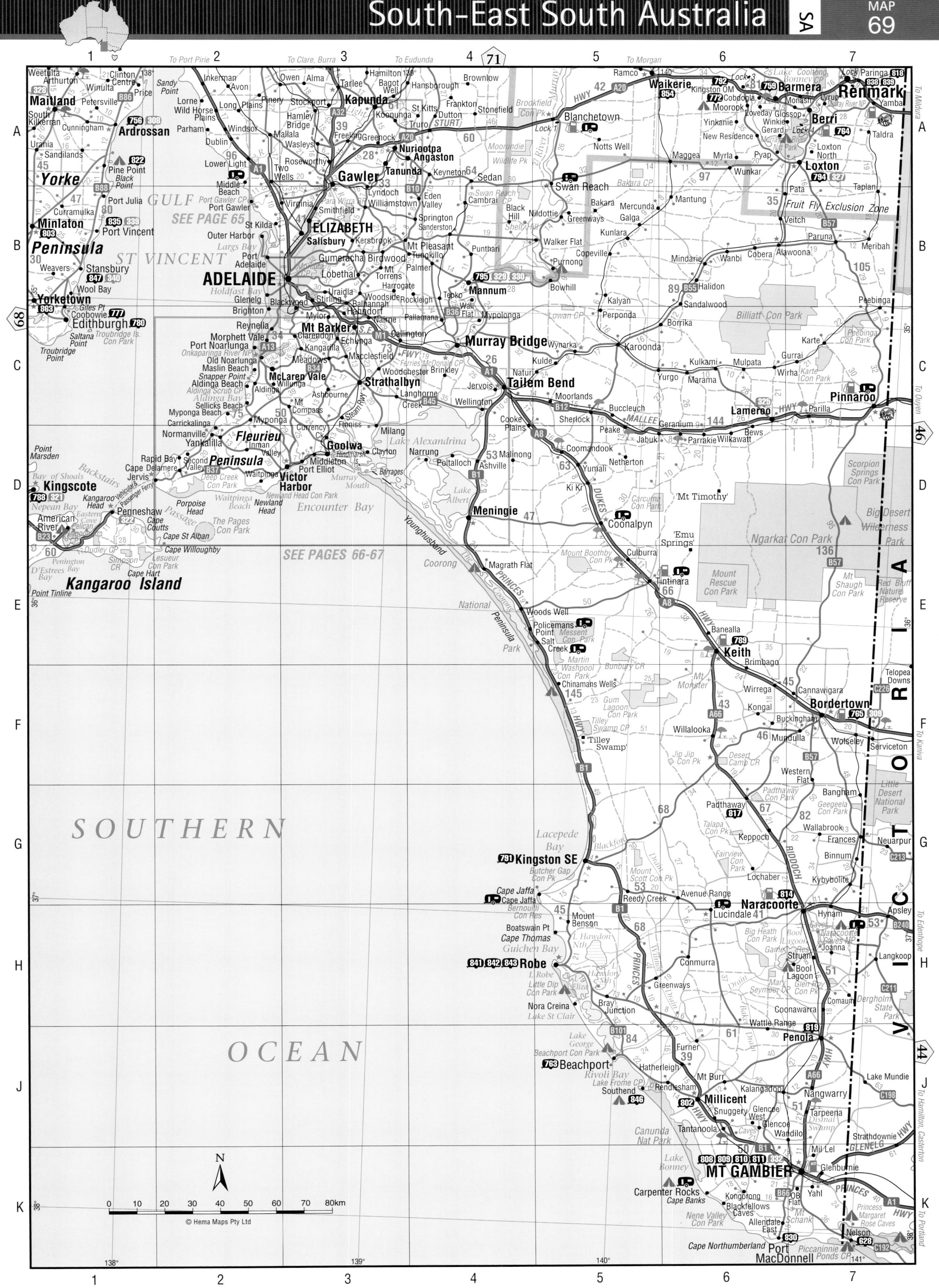
To Port Pirie
To Clare, Burra
To Eudunda
To Morgan
To Mildura
To Ouyen
To Kaniva
To Edenhope
To Hamilton, Casterton
To Portland
Maitland
Ardrossan
Yorke
Peninsula
Minlaton
Port Vincent
Stansbury
Yorketown
Edithburgh
GULF
ST VINCENT
SEE PAGE 65
ADELAIDE
Gawler
ELIZABETH
Salisbury
Kapunda
Nuriootpa
Angaston
Tanunda
Mt Barker
Murray Bridge
Mannum
Tailem Bend
Strathalbyn
McLaren Vale
Goolwa
Victor Harbor
Fleurieu
Peninsula
Kingscote
Kangaroo Island
Penneshaw
American River
Encounter Bay
SEE PAGES 66-67
Lake Alexandrina
Meningie
Coorong
National
Park
Waikerie
Barmera
Renmark
Berri
Loxton
Blanchetown
Swan Reach
Fruit Fly Exclusion Zone
Karoonda
Pinnaroo
Lameroo
Coonalpyn
Tintinara
Keith
Bordertown
Ngarkat Con Park
Big Desert Wilderness Park
Kingston SE
Lacepede Bay
Naracoorte
Robe
Beachport
Penola
Millicent
MT GAMBIER
Port MacDonnell
Cape Northumberland
SOUTHERN
OCEAN
VICTORIA
© Hema Maps Pty Ltd
0 10 20 30 40 50 60 70 80km

Central-East South Australia

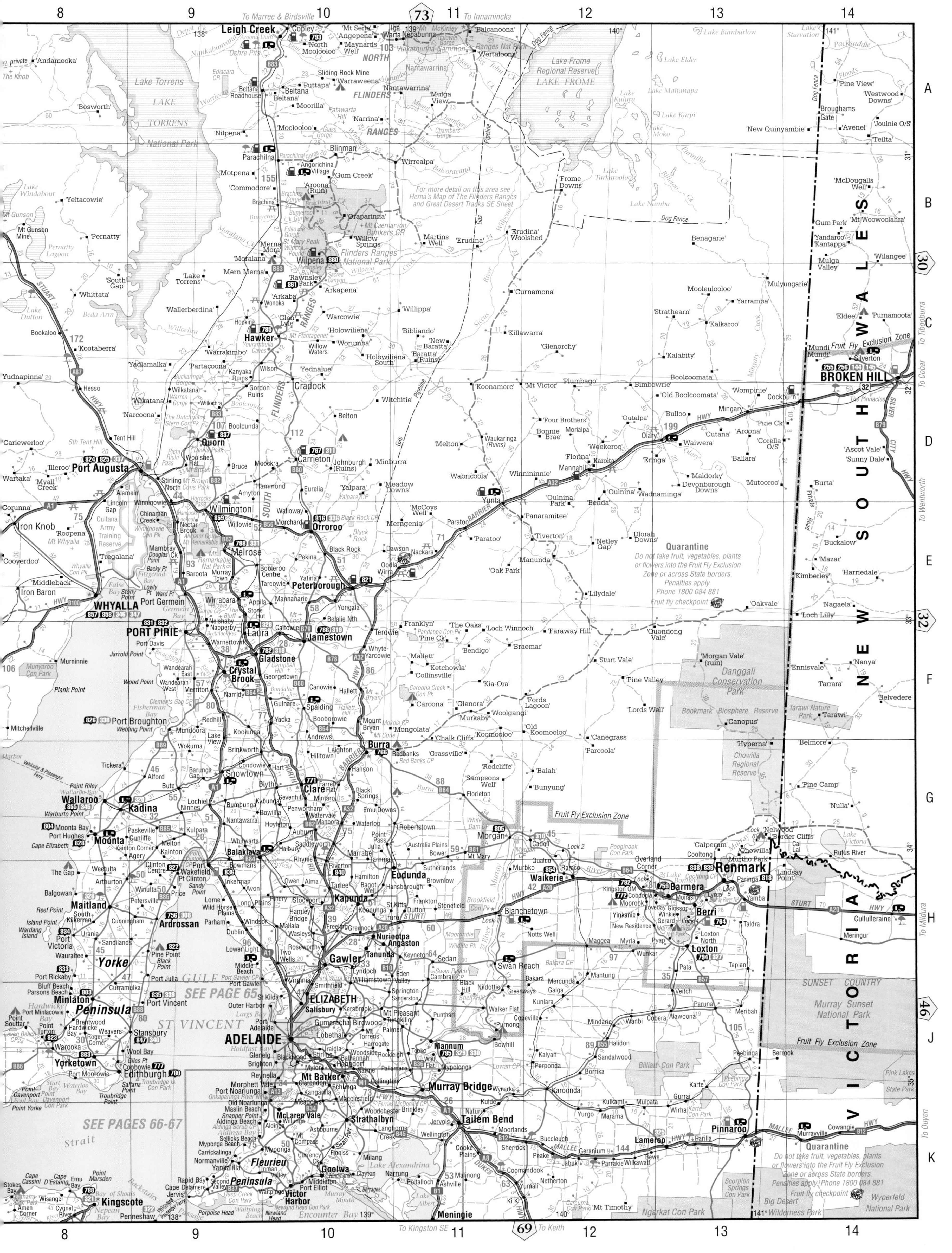

8 9 10 11 12 13 14

To Marree & Birdsville — 73 — To Innamincka

Leigh Creek · Copley · Lyndhurst · Beltana · Parachilna · Blinman · Hawker · Wilpena · Quorn · Port Augusta · Wilmington · Orroroo · Peterborough · Melrose · Whyalla · Port Pirie · Jamestown · Gladstone · Crystal Brook · Laura · Port Broughton · Burra · Clare · Kadina · Wallaroo · Moonta · Maitland · Ardrossan · Minlaton · Yorketown · Edithburgh · Kapunda · Eudunda · Gawler · Elizabeth · ADELAIDE · Mt Barker · Murray Bridge · Mannum · Tailem Bend · Strathalbyn · McLaren Vale · Goolwa · Victor Harbor · Kingscote · Meningie · Morgan · Waikerie · Barmera · Renmark · Berri · Loxton · Pinnaroo · Lameroo · Yunta · Mannahill · Olary · Cockburn · BROKEN HILL · Silverton

Lake Torrens National Park · LAKE TORRENS · Lake Frome Regional Reserve · LAKE FROME · FLINDERS RANGES · NORTH FLINDERS RANGES · Flinders Ranges National Park · Danggali Conservation Park · Bookmark Biosphere Reserve · Chowilla Regional Reserve · Murray Sunset National Park · SUNSET COUNTRY · Billiatt Con Park · Ngarkat Con Park · Wyperfeld National Park · Big Desert Wilderness Park · Scorpion Springs Con Park

Yorke Peninsula · Fleurieu Peninsula · GULF ST VINCENT · Investigator Strait · Encounter Bay

NEW SOUTH WALES · VICTORIA

For more detail on this area see Hema's Map of The Flinders Ranges and Great Desert Tracks SE Sheet

Quarantine
Do not take fruit, vegetables, plants or flowers into the Fruit Fly Exclusion Zone or across State borders.
Penalties apply.
Phone 1800 084 881
Fruit fly checkpoint

Fruit Fly Exclusion Zone · Dog Fence

SEE PAGE 65
SEE PAGES 66-67

To Tibooburra · To Cobar · To Wentworth · To Mildura · To Ouyen · To Kingston SE · 69 · To Keith

A B C D E F G H J K

8 9 10 11 12 13 14

North-East South Australia

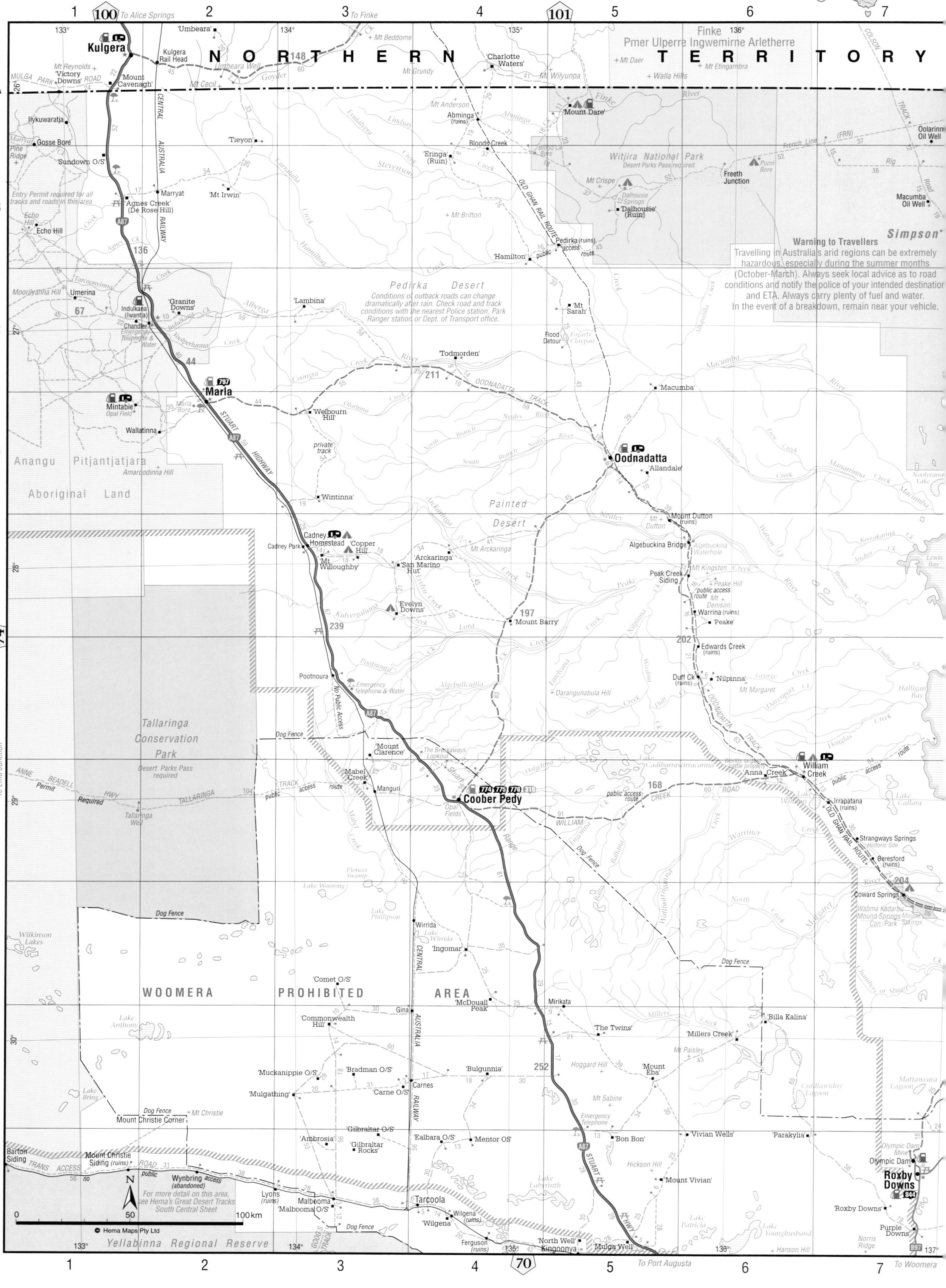

NORTHERN TERRITORY

Warning to Travellers

Travelling in Australia's arid regions can be extremely hazardous, especially during the summer months (October-March). Always seek local advice as to road conditions and notify the police of your intended destination and ETA. Always carry plenty of fuel and water. In the event of a breakdown, remain near your vehicle.

Conditions of outback roads can change dramatically after rain. Check road and track conditions with the nearest Police station, Park Ranger station or Dept. of Transport office.

Entry Permit required for all tracks and roads in this area

For more detail on this area, see Hema's Great Desert Tracks South Central Sheet

Kulgera
Kulgera Rail Head
'Umbeara'
Umbeara Well
'Mount Cavenagh'
'Victory Downs'
Mulga Park Road
Ilykuwaratja
Gosse Bore
'Sundown O/S'
Marryat
'Agnes Creek' (De Rose Hill)
Echo Hill
'Tieyon'
'Mt Irwin'
Central Australia Railway
Stuart Highway
'Charlotte Waters'
Mt Wilyunpa
Abminga (ruins)
Bloods Creek
'Eringa' (Ruin)
'Mount Dare'
Finke
Pmer Ulperre Ingwemirne Arletherre
Witjira National Park
Desert Parks Pass required
Mt Crispe
'Dalhousie' (Ruin)
Dalhousie Springs
Freeth Junction
French Line (FRN)
Rig Road
Oolarinna Oil Well
Macumba Oil Well
Simpson
Old Ghan Rail Route
Pedirka (ruins)
'Hamilton'
Pedirka Desert
'Lambina'
Umerina
Indulkana (Iwantja)
Chandler
'Granite Downs'
'Mt Sarah'
Flood Detour
'Todmorden'
Oodnadatta Track
'Macumba'
Marla
Mintabie
Marla Bore
Wallatinna
'Welbourn Hill'
Oodnadatta
'Allandale'
Anangu Pitjantjatjara Aboriginal Land
Amarcodinna Hill
'Wintinna'
Painted Desert
Mount Dutton (ruins)
Algebuckina Bridge
Cadney Homestead
Cadney Park
'Copper Hill'
'Mt Willoughby'
'Arckaringa'
Mt Arckaringa
'San Marino Hut'
Peak Creek Siding
'Evelyn Downs'
'Mount Barry'
Warrina (ruins)
'Peake'
Edwards Creek (ruins)
Pootnoura
Duff Ck (ruins)
'Nilpinna'
Darangunabula Hill
Tallaringa Conservation Park
Desert Parks Pass required
Dog Fence
'Mount Clarence'
'Mabel Creek'
Manguri
Coober Pedy
Opal Fields
The Breakaways Lookout
William Creek
'Anna Creek'
Irrapatana (ruins)
Strangways Springs Historic Site
Beresford (ruins)
Coward Springs
Wabma Kadarbu Mound Springs Con Park
Anne Beadell Hwy
Tallaringa Well
Wilkinson Lakes
Wirrida
'Ingomar'
WOOMERA PROHIBITED AREA
'Comet O/S'
'McDouall Peak'
Mirikata
Gina
'Commonwealth Hill'
'The Twins'
'Billa Kalina'
'Millers Creek'
'Muckanippie O/S'
'Bradman O/S'
'Bulgunnia'
'Mount Eba'
Hoggard Hill
Carnes
'Carne O/S'
'Mulgathing'
Mt Sabine
Mount Christie Corner
'Ambrosia'
'Gilbraltar O/S'
'Gilbraltar Rocks'
'Ealbara O/S'
'Mentor OS'
'Bon Bon'
'Vivian Wells'
'Parakylia'
Barton Siding
Mount Christie Siding (ruins)
Trans Access Road
Wynbring (abandoned)
Lyons (ruins)
Malbooma
'Malbooma O/S'
Tarcoola
Wilgena (ruins)
'Wilgena'
'Mount Vivian'
Olympic Dam
Roxby Downs
'Roxby Downs'
Purple Downs
Ferguson (ruins)
'North Well'
Kingoonya
Mulga Well
Yellabinna Regional Reserve
To Alice Springs
To Finke
To Port Augusta
To Woomera
To Emu Junction

0 50 100 km

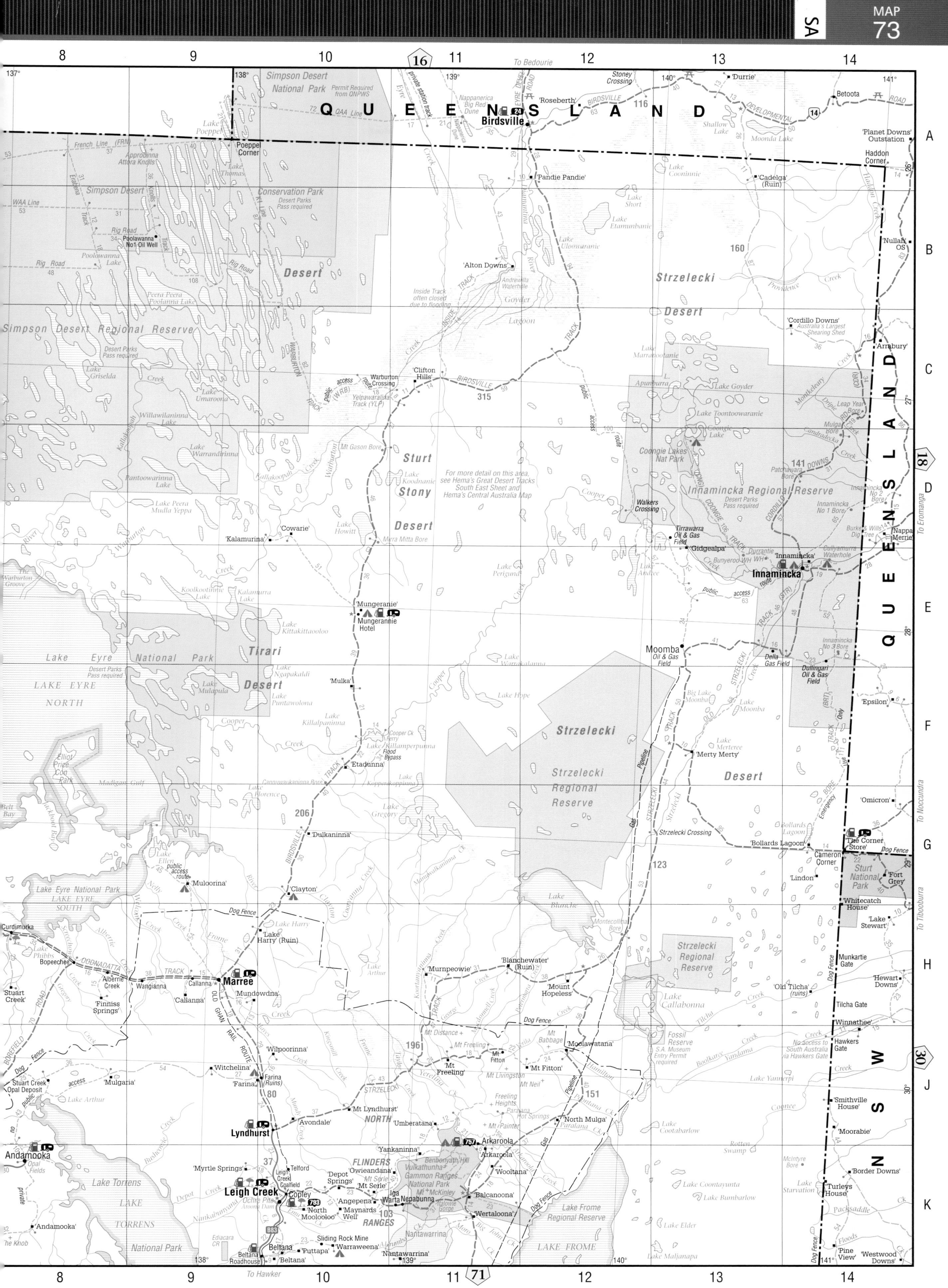
SA
MAP
73
QUEENSLAND
NSW
To Bedourie
To Eromanga
To Noccundra
To Tibooburra
To Hawker
Simpson Desert National Park
Permit Required from QNPWS
Birdsville
'Roseberth'
Nappanerica Big Red Dune
Stoney Crossing
'Durrie'
Betoota
'Planet Downs' Outstation
Haddon Corner
Lake Poeppel
Poeppel Corner
Approdinna Attora Knolls
French Line (FRN)
QAA Line
WAA Line
Rig Road
Poolawanna No1 Oil Well
Poolawanna Lake
Simpson Desert Conservation Park
Desert Parks Pass required
Simpson Desert Regional Reserve
Desert
Peera Peera Poolanna Lake
Lake Griselda
Lake Umaroona
Willawilaninna Lake
Lake Warrandirinna
Pantoowarinna Lake
Lake Peera Mudla Yeppa
'Pandie Pandie'
Lake Cooninnie
'Cadelga' (Ruin)
Lake Short
Lake Etamunbanie
Lake Ulowaranie
'Alton Downs'
Andrewilla Waterhole
Goyder Lagoon
Inside Track often closed due to flooding
Strzelecki Desert
'Nullan OS'
Providence Creek
'Cordillo Downs' Australia's Largest Shearing Shed
'Arrabury'
Lake Marradootanie
L. Apanburra
Lake Goyder
Lake Toontoowaranie
Coongie Lake
Coongie Lakes Nat Park
Leap Year Bore
Mulga Bore
Patchawarra Bore
Innamincka Regional Reserve
Innamincka No 2 Bore
Innamincka No 1 Bore
Burke & Wills Dig Tree
'Nappa Merrie'
Walkers Crossing
Tirrawarra Oil & Gas Field
'Gidgealpa'
Durrantie WH
Bunyeroo WH
Cullyamurra Waterhole
'Innamincka'
Innamincka
Warburton Crossing
'Clifton Hills'
Yelpawaralina Track (YLP)
Birdsville Track
Mt Gason Bore
Sturt Stony Desert
Lake Koodnanie
Lake Howitt
For more detail on this area, see Hema's Great Desert Tracks South East Sheet and Hema's Central Australia Map
Mirra Mitta Bore
'Cowarie'
'Kalamurina'
The Warburton Groove
Koolkootinnie Lake
Kalamurra Lake
Lake Kittakittaooloo
'Mungeranie'
Mungerannie Hotel
Lake Perigundi
Lake Andree
Moomba
Moomba Oil & Gas Field
Della Gas Field
Dullingari Oil & Gas Field
Innamincka No 3 Bore
Lake Eyre National Park
LAKE EYRE NORTH
Tirari Desert
Lake Ngapakaldi
Lake Mulapula
Lake Puntawolona
'Mulka'
Lake Killalpaninna
Lake Warrakalanna
Lake Hope
Big Lake Moomba
Lake Moomba
'Epsilon'
Cooper Ck Ferry
Lake Killamperpunna
Flood Bypass
'Etadunna'
Elliot Price Con Park
Madigan Gulf
Belt Bay
Jackboot Bay
Cannuwaukaninna Bore
Lake Kopperamanna
Lake Florence
Lake Gregory
'Dulkaninna'
Strzelecki Regional Reserve
Lake Merteree
'Merty Merty'
Strzelecki Desert
'Omicron'
Bollards Lagoon
'Bollards Lagoon'
Strzelecki Crossing
The Corner Store
Cameron Corner
Dog Fence
'Lindon'
Sturt National Park
'Fort Grey'
Lake Ellen
'Muloorina'
LAKE EYRE SOUTH
'Clayton'
Lake Blanche
Montecollina Bore
'Whitecatch House'
'Lake Stewart'
Curdimurka
Lake Phibbs
Bopeechee
Lake Harry
'Lake Harry' (Ruin)
Oodnadatta Track
Alberrie Creek
Wangianna
Callanna
'Callanna'
Marree
'Mundowdna'
'Finniss Springs'
'Stuart Creek'
Lake Arthur
'Murnpeowie'
'Blanchewater' (Ruin)
'Mount Hopeless'
Strzelecki Regional Reserve
Lake Callabonna
Munkartie Gate
'Hewart Downs'
'Old Tilcha' (ruins)
Tilcha Gate
'Winnathee'
Hawkers Gate
No access to South Australia via Hawkers Gate
Old Ghan Rail Route
Mt Distance
Mt Freeling
Mt Babbage
'Moolawatana'
Fossil Reserve S.A. Museum Entry Permit required
'Wilpoorinna'
'Witchelina'
Farina (Ruins)
'Farina'
'Mulgaria'
Stuart Creek Opal Deposit
Lake Arthur
Mt Fitton
'Mt Fitton'
'Mt Freeling'
Mt Livingston
Mt Neil
Freeling Heights
Paralana Hot Springs
Lake Yannerpi
'Smithville House'
Mt Lyndhurst
'Mt Lyndhurst'
NORTH FLINDERS RANGES
'Avondale'
Lyndhurst
'Umberatana'
Mt Painter
'North Mulga'
Lake Cootabarlow
Rotten Swamp
'Moorabie'
Arkaroola
'Arkaroola'
'Yankaninna'
Andamooka
Opal Fields
'Myrtle Springs'
Telford
Leigh Creek Coalfield
'Depot Springs'
'Owieandana'
Mt Serle
'Mt Serle'
Benbonyathe Hill
Vulkathunha-Gammon Ranges National Park
Mt McKinley
'Wooltana'
Lake Coontayunta
Lake Bumbarlow
McIntyre Bore
Lake Starvation
'Border Downs'
Lake Torrens
LAKE TORRENS
Lake Torrens National Park
Leigh Creek
Ochre Pits
Aroona Dam
Copley
'North Moolooloo'
'Angepena'
'Maynards Well'
Iga Warta
Nepabunna
Italowie Gorge
'Balcanoona'
'Wertaloona'
Lake Frome Regional Reserve
LAKE FROME
Lake Elder
Lake Maljanapa
'Turleys House'
Packsaddle
'Andamooka'
Ediacara CR
Beltana
Beltana Roadhouse
'Beltana'
'Puttapa'
Sliding Rock Mine
'Warraweena'
Nantawarrina
'Nantawarrina'
Floods Ck
'Pine View'
'Westwood Downs'
137°
138°
139°
140°
141°
26°
27°
28°
29°
30°
8
9
10
11
12
13
14
A
B
C
D
E
F
G
H
J
K

Western South Australia

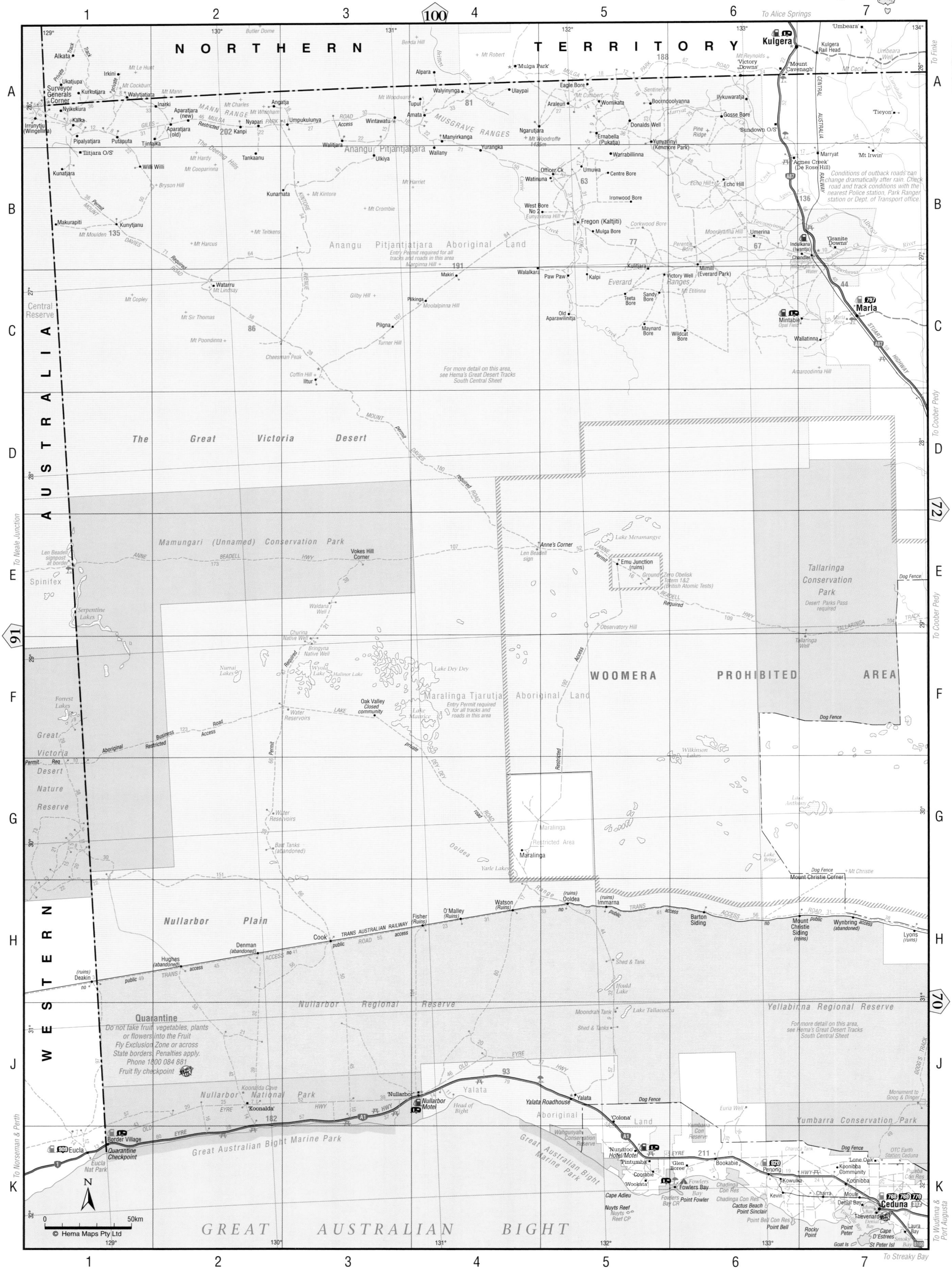

POPULATION: 2 million
AREA: 2,529,875 sq km
CAPITAL CITY: Perth

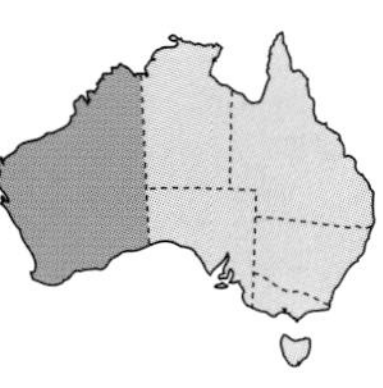

Distances are shown in kilometres and follow the most direct major sealed route where possible

1401	2020	411	1564	939	3610	1977	805	835	483	1315	342	2618	**Albany**
3101	615	2245	1051	1676	1063	845	2197	1942	2589	1462	2427	**Broome**	
1585	1832	182	1376	751	3422	1748	774	606	667	1086	**Bunbury**		
2338	867	904	985	819	2457	662	1460	480	1625	**Carnarvon**			
918	1994	721	1538	1069	3584	2169	392	1145	**Esperance**				
1822	1347	424	964	339	2937	1142	980	**Geraldton**					
904	1602	592	1146	677	3192	1786	**Kalgoorlie**						
2690	259	1566	631	1256	1849	**Karratha**							
4096	1610	3240	2046	2671	**Kununurra**								
1597	1081	569	625	**Mt Magnet**									
2050	456	1194	**Newman**										
1434	1650	**Perth**											
2506	**Port Hedland**												
WA-SA Border Village													

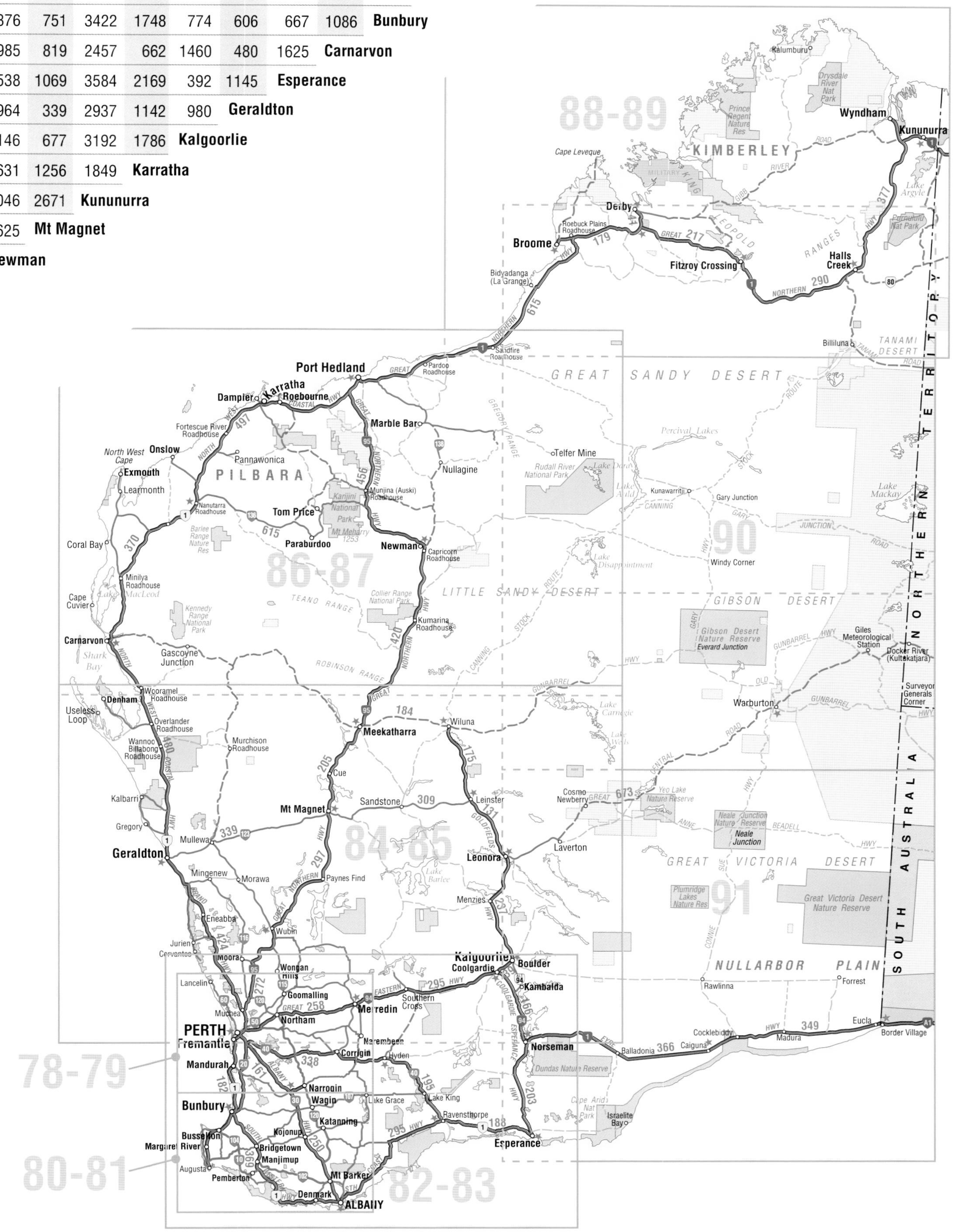

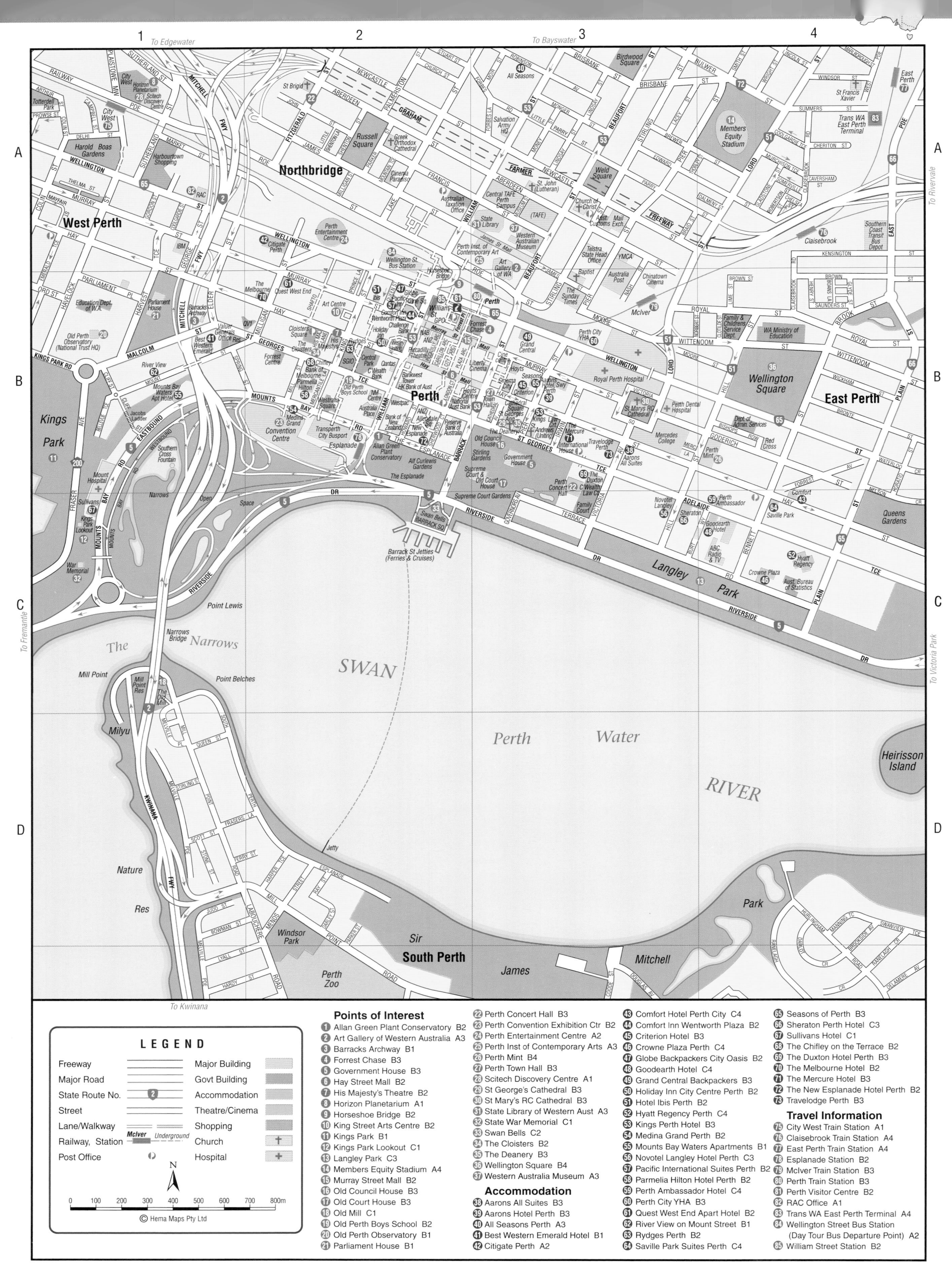

1
2
3
4
A
B
C
D
To Edgewater
To Bayswater
To Rivervale
To Victoria Park
To Fremantle
To Kwinana
West Perth
Northbridge
Perth
East Perth
Kings Park
Wellington Square
Langley Park
SWAN
Perth Water
RIVER
The Narrows
Heirisson Island
South Perth
Perth Zoo
Windsor Park
Sir James Mitchell Park
Mill Point
Point Lewis
Point Belches
Milyu Nature Res
Barrack St Jetties (Ferries & Cruises)
LEGEND
Freeway
Major Road
State Route No.
Street
Lane/Walkway
Railway, Station
McIver
Underground
Post Office
Major Building
Govt Building
Accommodation
Theatre/Cinema
Shopping
Church
Hospital
N
0
100
200
300
400
500
600
700
800m
© Hema Maps Pty Ltd
Points of Interest
1 Allan Green Plant Conservatory B2
2 Art Gallery of Western Australia A3
3 Barracks Archway B1
4 Forrest Chase B3
5 Government House B3
6 Hay Street Mall B2
7 His Majesty's Theatre B2
8 Horizon Planetarium A1
9 Horseshoe Bridge B2
10 King Street Arts Centre B2
11 Kings Park B1
12 Kings Park Lookout C1
13 Langley Park C3
14 Members Equity Stadium A4
15 Murray Street Mall B2
16 Old Council House B3
17 Old Court House B3
18 Old Mill C1
19 Old Perth Boys School B2
20 Old Perth Observatory B1
21 Parliament House B1
22 Perth Concert Hall B3
23 Perth Convention Exhibition Ctr B2
24 Perth Entertainment Centre A2
25 Perth Inst of Contemporary Arts A3
26 Perth Mint B4
27 Perth Town Hall B3
28 Scitech Discovery Centre A1
29 St George's Cathedral B3
30 St Mary's RC Cathedral B3
31 State Library of Western Aust A3
32 State War Memorial C1
33 Swan Bells C2
34 The Cloisters B2
35 The Deanery B3
36 Wellington Square B4
37 Western Australia Museum A3
Accommodation
38 Aarons All Suites B3
39 Aarons Hotel Perth B3
40 All Seasons Perth A3
41 Best Western Emerald Hotel B1
42 Citigate Perth A2
43 Comfort Hotel Perth City C4
44 Comfort Inn Wentworth Plaza B2
45 Criterion Hotel B3
46 Crowne Plaza Perth C4
47 Globe Backpackers City Oasis B2
48 Goodearth Hotel C4
49 Grand Central Backpackers B3
50 Holiday Inn City Centre Perth B2
51 Hotel Ibis Perth B2
52 Hyatt Regency Perth C4
53 Kings Perth Hotel B3
54 Medina Grand Perth B2
55 Mounts Bay Waters Apartments B1
56 Novotel Langley Hotel Perth C3
57 Pacific International Suites Perth B2
58 Parmelia Hilton Hotel Perth B2
59 Perth Ambassador Hotel C4
60 Perth City YHA B3
61 Quest West End Apart Hotel B2
62 River View on Mount Street B1
63 Rydges Perth B2
64 Saville Park Suites Perth C4
65 Seasons of Perth B3
66 Sheraton Perth Hotel C3
67 Sullivans Hotel C1
68 The Chifley on the Terrace B2
69 The Duxton Hotel Perth B3
70 The Melbourne Hotel B2
71 The Mercure Hotel B3
72 The New Esplanade Hotel Perth B2
73 Travelodge Perth B3
Travel Information
75 City West Train Station A1
76 Claisebrook Train Station A4
77 East Perth Train Station A4
78 Esplanade Station B2
79 McIver Train Station B3
80 Perth Train Station B3
81 Perth Visitor Centre B2
82 RAC Office A1
83 Trans WA East Perth Terminal A4
84 Wellington Square Bus Station
(Day Tour Bus Departure Point) A2
85 William Street Station B2

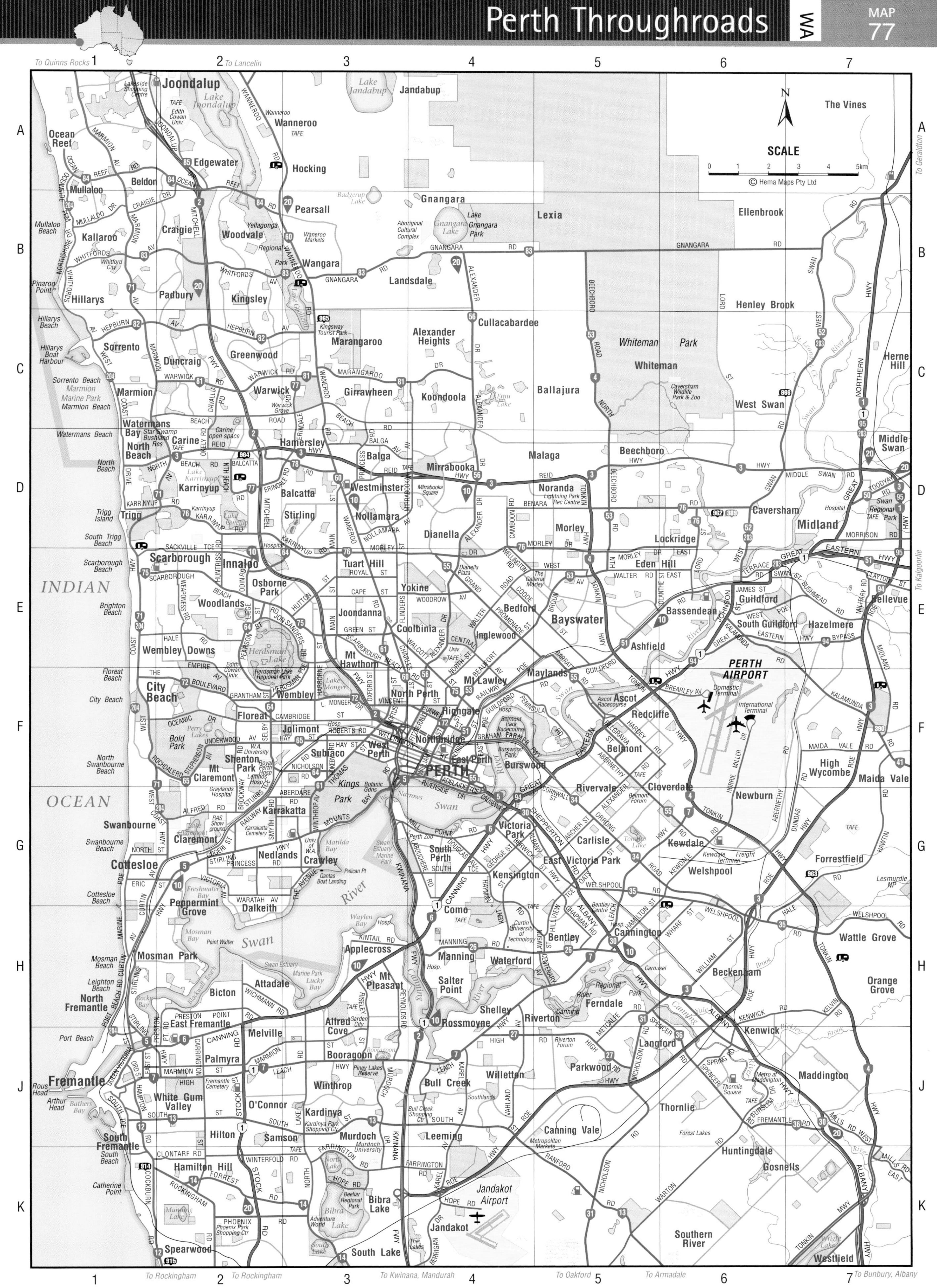
To Quinns Rocks
To Lancelin
To Geraldton
To Kalgoorlie
To Rockingham
To Rockingham
To Kwinana, Mandurah
To Oakford
To Armadale
To Bunbury, Albany
SCALE
0 1 2 3 4 5km
© Hema Maps Pty Ltd
N
INDIAN
OCEAN
Joondalup
Lake Joondalup
Lake Jandabup
Jandabup
Wanneroo
Ocean Reef
Edgewater
Hocking
The Vines
Beldon
Mullaloo
Pearsall
Gnangara
Lake Gnangara
Lexia
Ellenbrook
Mullaloo Beach
Kallaroo
Craigie
Woodvale
Yellagonga Regional Park
Wangara
Landsdale
Pinaroo Point
Hillarys
Padbury
Kingsley
Henley Brook
Hillarys Beach
Hillarys Boat Harbour
Sorrento
Duncraig
Greenwood
Marangaroo
Alexander Heights
Cullacabardee
Whiteman Park
Whiteman
Sorrento Beach
Marmion Marine Park
Marmion Beach
Marmion
Warwick
Girrawheen
Koondoola
Ballajura
Caversham Wildlife Park & Zoo
West Swan
Herne Hill
Watermans Beach
Watermans Bay
Carine
Hamersley
Balga
Mirrabooka
Malaga
Beechboro
Middle Swan
North Beach
Karrinyup
Balcatta
Westminster
Nollamara
Noranda
Caversham
Midland
Trigg Island
Trigg
Stirling
Dianella
Morley
Lockridge
South Trigg Beach
Scarborough
Innaloo
Tuart Hill
Eden Hill
Scarborough Beach
Osborne Park
Yokine
Guildford
Bellevue
Brighton Beach
Woodlands
Joondanna
Bedford
Bayswater
Bassendean
South Guildford
Hazelmere
Coolbinia
Inglewood
Ashfield
Wembley Downs
Herdsman Lake
Mt Hawthorn
Mt Lawley
Maylands
PERTH AIRPORT
Domestic Terminal
International Terminal
Floreat Beach
City Beach
Wembley
North Perth
Ascot
Redcliffe
Floreat
Jolimont
Highgate
Bold Park
Northbridge
Belmont
Subiaco
West Perth
High Wycombe
North Swanbourne Beach
Shenton Park
Mt Claremont
PERTH
East Perth
Burswood
Maida Vale
Kings Park
Rivervale
Cloverdale
Newburn
Karrakatta
Swan River
Swanbourne
Victoria Park
Carlisle
Claremont
Nedlands
Crawley
South Perth
Kewdale
Forrestfield
Swanbourne Beach
Cottesloe
Kensington
East Victoria Park
Welshpool
Lesmurdie NP
Cottesloe Beach
Peppermint Grove
Dalkeith
Como
Wattle Grove
Mosman Park
Applecross
Manning
Waterford
Bentley
Cannington
Mosman Beach
Leighton Beach
North Fremantle
Bicton
Attadale
Mt Pleasant
Salter Point
Shelley
Riverton
Ferndale
Beckenham
Orange Grove
Port Beach
East Fremantle
Alfred Cove
Rossmoyne
Melville
Kenwick
Palmyra
Booragoon
Langford
Parkwood
Fremantle
Rous Head
Arthur Head
Winthrop
Bull Creek
Willetton
Maddington
White Gum Valley
O'Connor
Kardinya
Thornlie
Hilton
Samson
Murdoch
Leeming
Canning Vale
South Fremantle
South Beach
Hamilton Hill
Huntingdale
Gosnells
Catherine Point
Bibra Lake
Jandakot Airport
Jandakot
Spearwood
South Lake
Southern River
Westfield
Phoenix Park Shopping Ctr
Manning Lake

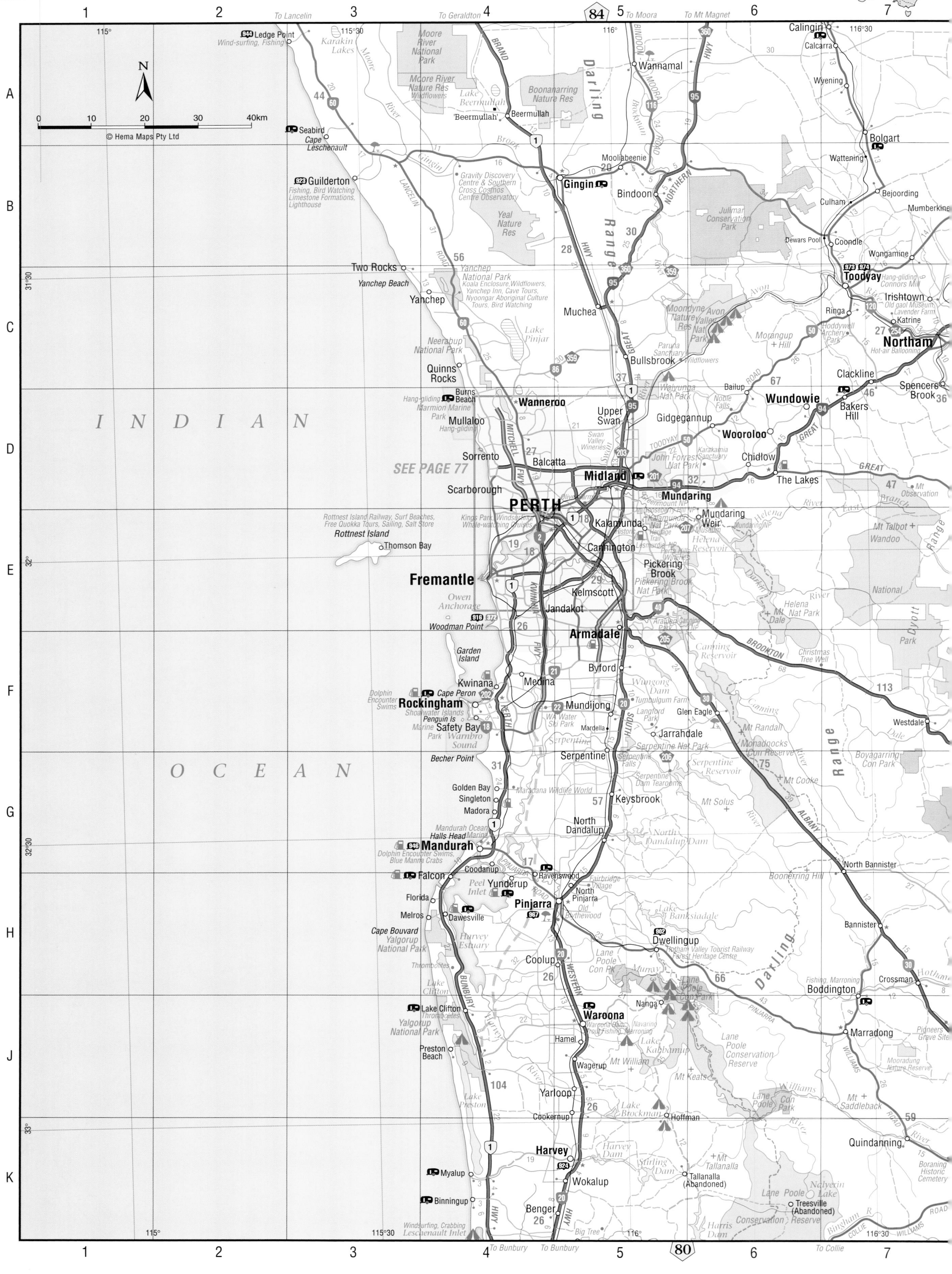

Perth Region, Western Australia

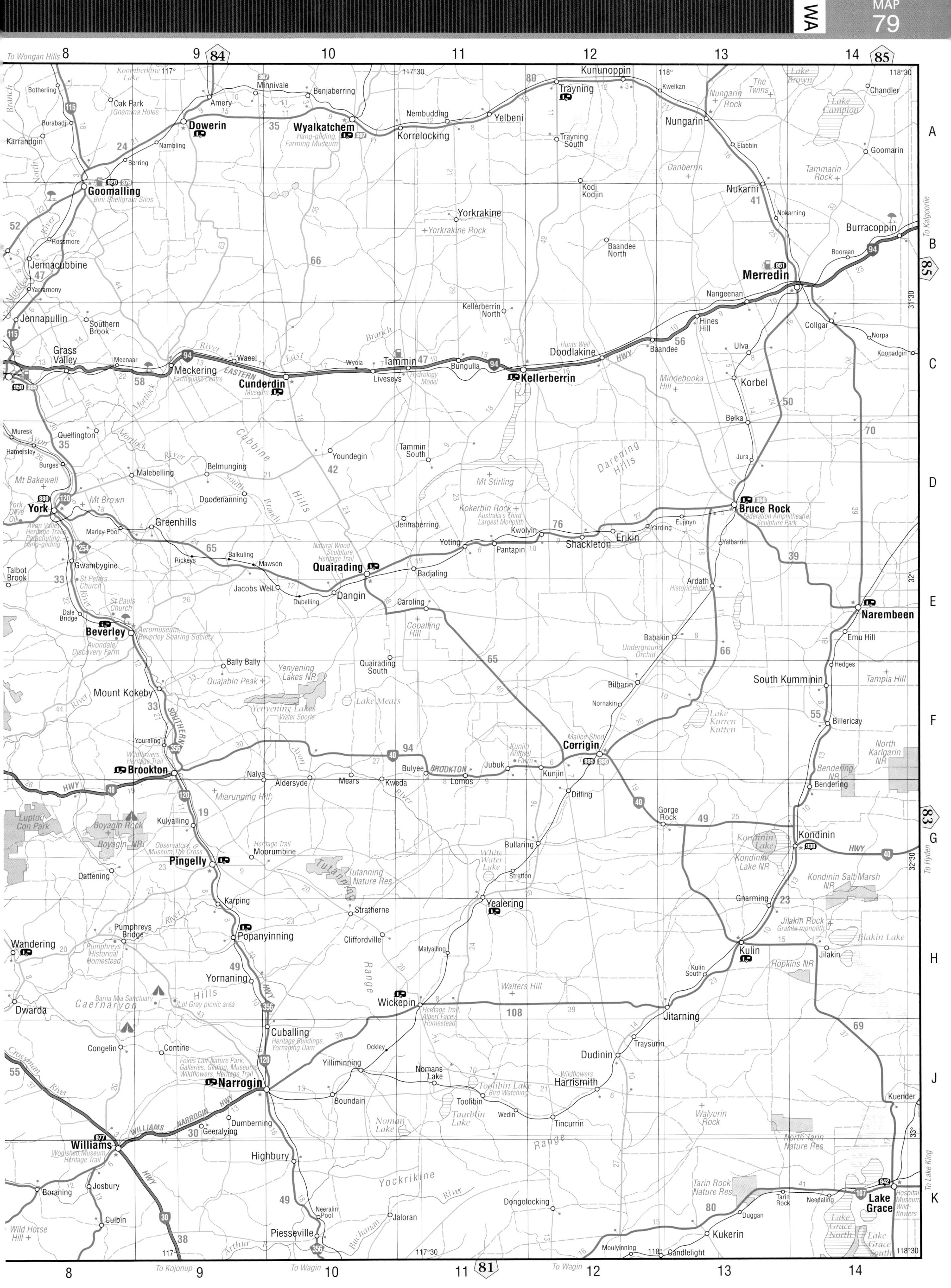
Goomalling
Dowerin
Wyalkatchem
Trayning
Kununoppin
Nungarin
Merredin
Burracoppin
Kellerberrin
Tammin
Cunderdin
Meckering
Doodlakine
Bruce Rock
York
Beverley
Quairading
Narembeen
Corrigin
Brookton
Pingelly
Kondinin
Kulin
Yealering
Wickepin
Jitarning
Dudinin
Harrismith
Narrogin
Williams
Highbury
Piesseville
Kukerin
Lake Grace
Cuballing
Popanyinning
Wandering
Dwarda
To Wongan Hills
To Kalgoorlie
To Hyden
To Lake King
To Kojonup
To Wagin

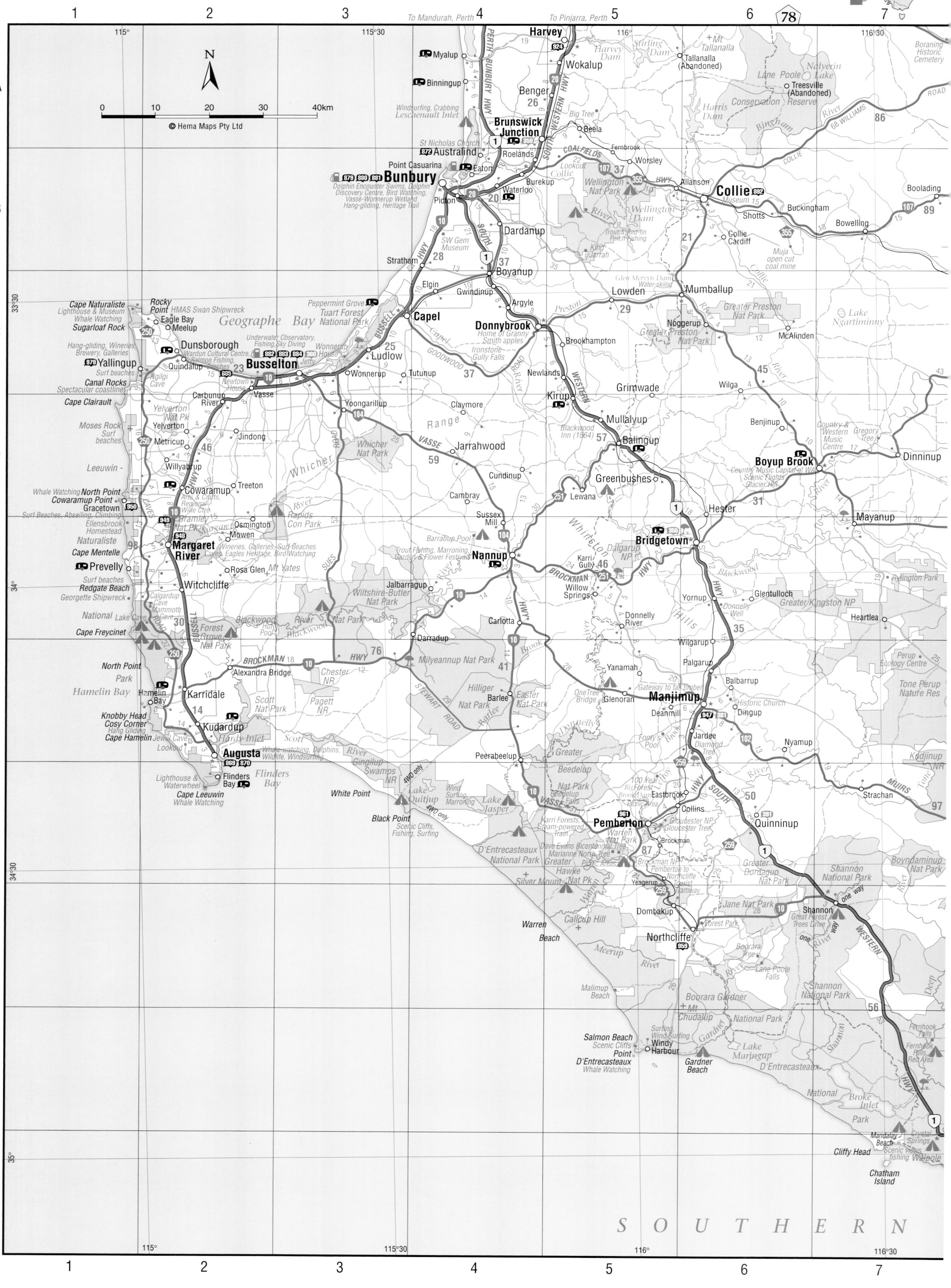

To Mandurah, Perth
To Pinjarra, Perth
78

© Hema Maps Pty Ltd

0 10 20 30 40km

Harvey
Myalup
Binningup
Wokalup
Harvey Dam
Stirling Dam
Mt Tallanalla
Tallanalla (Abandoned)
Lane Poole
Nalyerin Lake
Treesville (Abandoned)
Conservation Reserve
Harris Dam
Benger
Windsurfing, Crabbing
Leschenault Inlet
Brunswick Junction
Big Tree
Beela
St Nicholas Church
Australind
Roelands
Coalfields
Fernbrook
Worsley
Point Casuarina
Bunbury
Eaton
Dolphin Encounter Swims, Dolphin Discovery Centre, Bird Watching, Vasse-Wonnerup Wetland Hang-gliding, Heritage Trail
Waterloo
Burekup
Lookout
Collie
Wellington Nat Park
Wellington Dam
Allanson
Collie
Museum
Boolading
Buckingham
Bowelling
Shotts
Picton
Dardanup
Trout & Redfin Perch Fishing
King Jarrah
Collie Cardiff
Muja open cut coal mine
SW Gem Museum
Stratham
Boyanup
Glen Mervyn Dam Water-skiing
Lowden
Mumballup
Greater Preston Nat Park
Lake Ngartiminny
Elgin
Gwindinup
Argyle
Capel
Donnybrook
Home of Granny Smith apples
Noggerup
McAlinden
Ironstone Gully Falls
Brookhampton
Cape Naturaliste Lighthouse & Museum Whale Watching
Sugarloaf Rock
Rocky Point
HMAS Swan Shipwreck
Eagle Bay
Meelup
Geographe Bay
Peppermint Grove
Tuart Forest National Park
Dunsborough
Underwater Observatory, Fishing, Sky Diving
Wonnerup House
Hang-gliding, Wineries, Brewery, Galleries
Wardun Cultural Centre, Salmon Fishing
Ludlow
Yallingup
Surf beaches
Quindalup
Busselton
Jetty
Canal Rocks
Spectacular coastlines
Ngilgi Cave
Newtown House
Wonnerup
Tutunup
Newlands
Grimwade
Wilga
Cape Clairault
Carbunup River
Vasse
Yoongarillup
Claymore
Kirup
Yelverton Nat Pk
Yelverton
Range
Mullalyup
Benjinup
Moses Rock
Surf beaches
Metricup
Jindong
Whicher Nat Park
Blackwood Inn (1864)
Balingup
Country & Western Music Centre
Gregory Tree
Leeuwin -
Vasse
Jarrahwood
Boyup Brook
Dinninup
Country Music Capital of WA
Scenic Flights Glacier Hill
Willyabrup
Whicher
Cundinup
Greenbushes
Whale Watching
North Point
Cowaramup Point
Gracetown
Cowaramup
Treeton
Cambray
Lewana
Surf Beaches, Abseiling, Climbing
Ellensbrook Homestead
Arts & Crafts, Regional Wine Ctre
Bramley Nat Pk
Osmington
Mowen
River Rapids Con Park
Sussex Mill
Hester
Mayanup
Naturaliste
Barrabup Pool
Bridgetown
Cape Mentelle
Margaret River
Wineries, Galleries, Surf Beaches Caves, Eagles Heritage, Bird Watching
Trout Fishing, Marroning, Garden & Flower Festivals
Nannup
Dalgarup NP
Prevelly
Rosa Glen
Mt Yates
Karri Gully
Brockman
Willow Springs
Glentulloch
Surf beaches
Redgate Beach
Witchcliffe
Jalbarragup
Wiltshire-Butler Nat Park
Ryllington Park
Georgette Shipwreck
Calgardup Cave
Mammoth Cave
Yornup
Donnelly Well
Greater Kingston NP
National
Lake Cave
Forest Grove Nat Park
Blackwood
Nat Park
Carlotta
Donnelly River
Heartlea
Cape Freycinet
Darradup
Hills
Wilgarup
Milyeannup Nat Park
Palgarup
Perup Ecology Centre
North Point
Park
Alexandra Bridge
Chester NR
Yanamah
Hamelin Bay
Hamelin Bay
Karridale
Hilliger Nat Park
Barlee
Easter Nat Park
Balbarrup
Tone Perup Nature Res
Gateway to tall timber
Scott Nat Park
Pagett NR
Stewart Road
One Tree Bridge
Glenoran
Manjimup
Historic Church
Dingup
Knobby Head
Cosy Corner
Hang Gliding
Cape Hamelin
Kudardup
Deanmill
Jewel Cave
Lookout
Hardy Inlet
Scott
Fonty's Pool
Jardee
Nyamup
Augusta
Whale-watching, Dolphins, Wildlife, Windsurfing
River
Diamond Tree
Kodjinup NR
Peerabeelup
Greater
Gingilup Swamps NR
4WD only
Beedelup Nat Park
Beedelup Falls
Lighthouse & Waterwheel
Flinders Bay
Flinders Bay
Cape Leeuwin
Whale Watching
White Point
Lake Quitjup
Wind Surfing, Marroning
Lake Jasper
100 Year Forest
Big Brook Dam
Picnic Area
Eastbrook
Strachan
Muirs
Collins
Quinninup
Black Point
Scenic Cliffs, Fishing, Surfing
Karri Forests, Steam-powered Train
Pemberton
Gloucester NP
Gloucester Tree
Warren Nat Park
Brockman
D'Entrecasteaux National Park
Dave Evans Bicentennial Tree
Marianne North Tree
Greater
Picnic Areas
Brockman NP
Pemberton to Northcliffe Forest Tramway
Greater Dordagup Nat Park
Boyndaminup Nat Park
Shannon National Park
Hawke Nat Pk
Silver Mount
Yeagerup
Warren
Jane Nat Park
Shannon
Great Forest Trees Drive
one way
Dombakup
Warren Beach
Calcup Hill
Forest Park
Northcliffe
Meerup
River
Boorara Tree
Lane Poole Falls
Western
Deep
Shannon National Park
Malimup Beach
Boorara Gardner
Mt Chudalup
National Park
Fernhook Falls
Salmon Beach
Scenic Cliffs
Point D'Entrecasteaux
Whale Watching
Windy Harbour
Surfing, Wind Surfing
Gardner Beach
Lake Maringup
D'Entrecasteaux
Fernhook Falls Rec Area
National
Broke Inlet
Park
Mandalay Beach
Crystal Springs
Scenic Views, Fishing
Walpole
Cliffy Head
Chatham Island

SOUTHERN

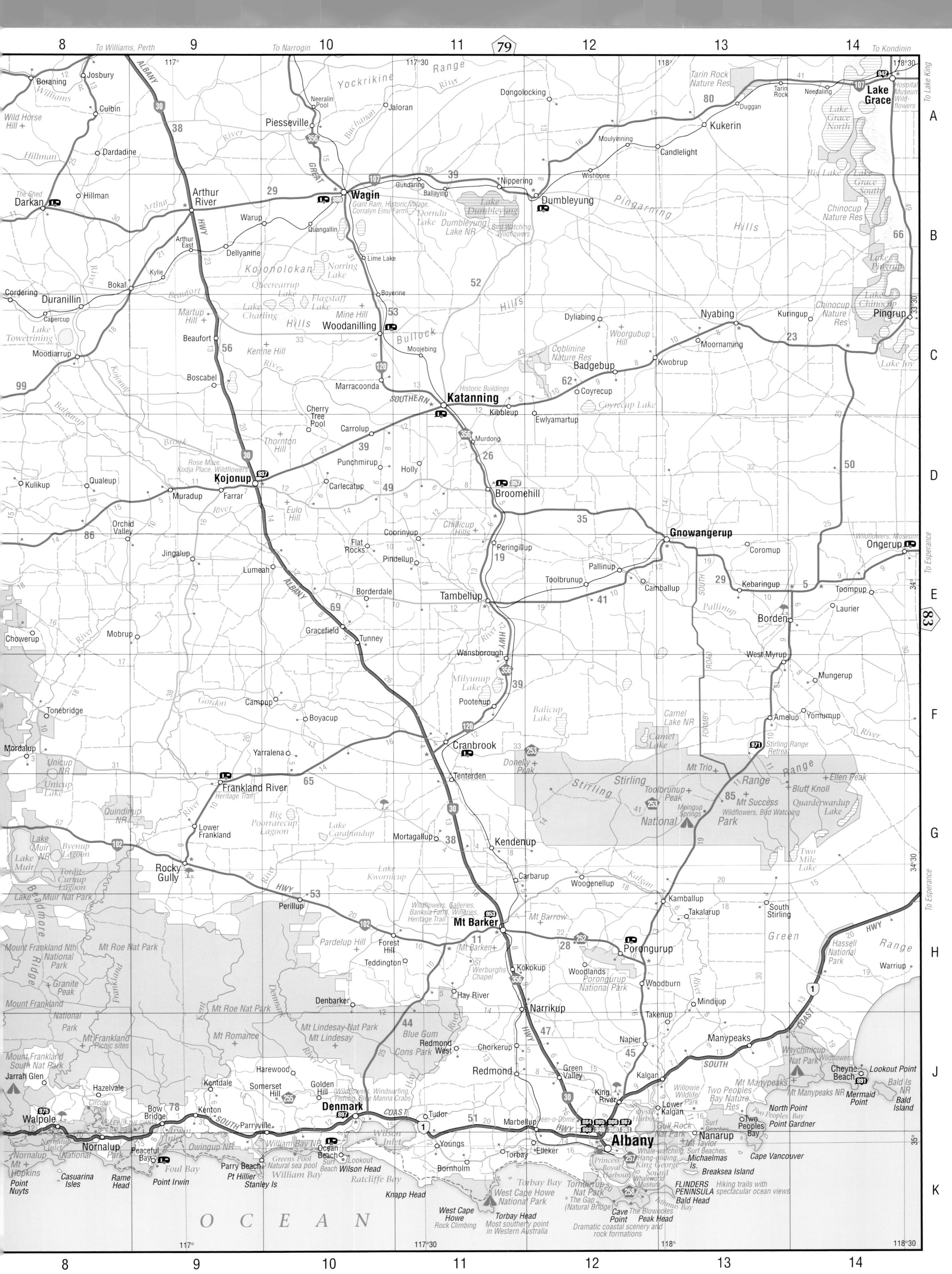
79
To Williams, Perth
To Narrogin
To Kondinin
To Lake King
117°
117°30
118°
118°30
Boraning
Josbury
Williams
Culbin
Wild Horse Hill
Hillman
Dardadine
The Shed
Darkan
Hillman
Arthur River
Arthur
Arthur East
Warup
Dellyanine
Kylie
Bokal
Cordering
Duranillin
Capercup
Lake Towerrining
Moodiarrup
Beaufort
Martup Hill
Beaufort
Boscabel
Yockrikine
Range
Neeralin Pool
Jaloran
Piesseville
Buchanan
Wagin
Giant Ram, Historic Village, Corralyn Emu Farm
Quangallin
Lime Lake
Kojonolokan
Norring Lake
Queerearrup Lake
Flagstaff Lake
Lake Charling
Hills
Mine Hill
Woodanilling
Boyerine
Bullock
Moojebing
Kenine Hill
Marracoonda
Gundaring
Ballaying
Lake Dumbleyung
Dornda Lake
Dumbleyung Lake NR
Bird Watching, Wildflowers
Nippering
Dumbleyung
Dongolocking
Moulyinning
Wishbone
Candlelight
Kukerin
Duggan
Tarin Rock Nature Res
Tarin Rock
Needaling
Lake Grace
Hospital Museum Wildflowers
Lake Grace North
Big Lake
Lake Grace South
Chinocup Nature Res
Pingarning
Hills
Lake Pingrup
Lake Chinocup
Chinocup Nature Res
Pingrup
Kuringup
Nyabing
Moornaming
Dyliabing
Woorgubup Hill
Coblinine Nature Res
Badgebup
Kwobrup
Coyrecup
Coyrecup Lake
Lake Joy
Historic Buildings
Katanning
SOUTHERN
Kibbleup
Ewlyamartup
Murdong
Cherry Tree Pool
Carrolup
Thornton Hill
Punchmirup
Holly
Brook
Rose Maze, Kodja Place, Wildflowers
Kojonup
Kulikup
Qualeup
Muradup
Farrar
River
Carlecatup
Broomehill
Eulo Hill
Orchid Valley
Coorinyup
Chillicup Hills
Flat Rocks
Pindellup
Peringillup
Gnowangerup
Coromup
Wildflowers, Museum
Ongerup
To Esperance
Jingalup
Lumeah
Pallinup
Toolbrunup
Camballup
Kebaringup
Toompup
Laurier
Borderdale
Tambellup
Pallinup
Borden
Chowerup
Mobrup
Gracefield
Tunney
Wansborough
West Myrup
Mungerup
Tonebridge
Gordon
Campup
Boyacup
Milyunup Lake
Pootenup
Balicup Lake
Camel Lake NR
Amelup
Yomumup
River
Mordalup
Unicup NR
Unicup Lake
Yarralena
Cranbrook
Donelly Peak
Camel Lake
Stirling Range Retreat
Mt Trio
Tenterden
Frankland River
Heritage Trail
Stirling
Toolbrunup Peak
Range
Ellen Peak
Bluff Knoll
Mt Success
Quaderwardup Lake
Quindinup NR
Big Poorrarecup Lagoon
Lake Caralundup
Stirling National
Meingup Springs
Park
Wildflowers, Bird Watching
Lake Muir
Lake Muir NR
Byenup Lagoon
Lower Frankland
Mortagallup
Kendenup
Two Mile Lake
Rocky Gully
Tordit-Gurrup Lagoon
Lake Muir Nat Park
Lake Kwornicup
Carbarup
Woogenellup
Kalgan
Kamballup
Takalarup
South Stirling
Perillup
Wildflowers, Galleries, Banksia Farm, Wineries, Heritage Trail
Mt Barrow
Mt Barker
Green
Range
Hassell National Park
Warriup
Mount Frankland Nth National Park
Mt Roe Nat Park
Pardelup Hill
Forest Hill
Teddington
Mt Barker
St Werburghs Chapel
Porongurup
Woodlands
Porongurup National Park
Woodburn
Kokokup
Granite Peak
Hay River
Mindijup
Mount Frankland National Park
Mt Roe Nat Park
Denbarker
Narrikup
Takenup
Mt Lindesay Nat Park
Mt Lindesay
Blue Gum
Redmond West
Cons Park
Chorkerup
Napier
Manypeaks
Mt Frankland Picnic sites
Mt Romance
Mount Frankland South Nat Park
Redmond
Green Valley
Kalgan
Waychinicup Nat Park
Wildflowers
Lookout Point
Cheyne Beach
Bald Is NR
Mermaid Point
Bald Island
Jarrah Glen
Harewood
Hazelvale
Kentdale
Somerset Hill
Golden Hill
Wildflowers, Windsurfing, Fishing, Blue Manna Crabs
Denmark
King River
Mt Manypeaks
Mt Manypeaks NR
Two Peoples Bay Nature Res
Willowie Wildlife Park
North Point
Two Peoples Bay
Point Gardner
Lower Kalgan
Bow Bridge
Kenton
Parryville
Tudor
Marbellup
Walpole
Nornalup
Peaceful Bay
William Bay NP
Ocean Beach
Wilson Inlet
Youngs
Elleker
Albany
Gull Rock Nat Park
Surf Beaches
Mt Taylor
Nanarup
Nornalup National Park
Mt Hopkins
Point Nuyts
Casuarina Isles
Rame Head
Owingup NR
Foul Bay
Point Irwin
Parry Beach
Greens Pool
Natural sea pool
William Bay
Pt Hillier
Stanley Is
Lookout
Surf Beach
Wilson Head
Ratcliffe Bay
Bornholm
Torbay
Princess Royal Harbour
Whale-watching, Surf Beaches, Hang-gliding
King George Sound
Whaleworld Museum
Michaelmas Is.
Breaksea Island
Cape Vancouver
Torbay Bay
Torndirrup Nat Park
The Gap (Natural Bridge)
FLINDERS PENINSULA
Hiking trails with spectacular ocean views
Bald Head
Knapp Head
West Cape Howe National Park
West Cape Howe
Rock Climbing
Torbay Head
Most southerly point in Western Australia
Cave Point
The Blowholes
Peak Head
Dramatic coastal scenery and rock formations
OCEAN
SOUTH
COAST
HWY
ALBANY
83
8
9
10
11
12
13
14
A
B
C
D
E
F
G
H
J
K

South-West Western Australia

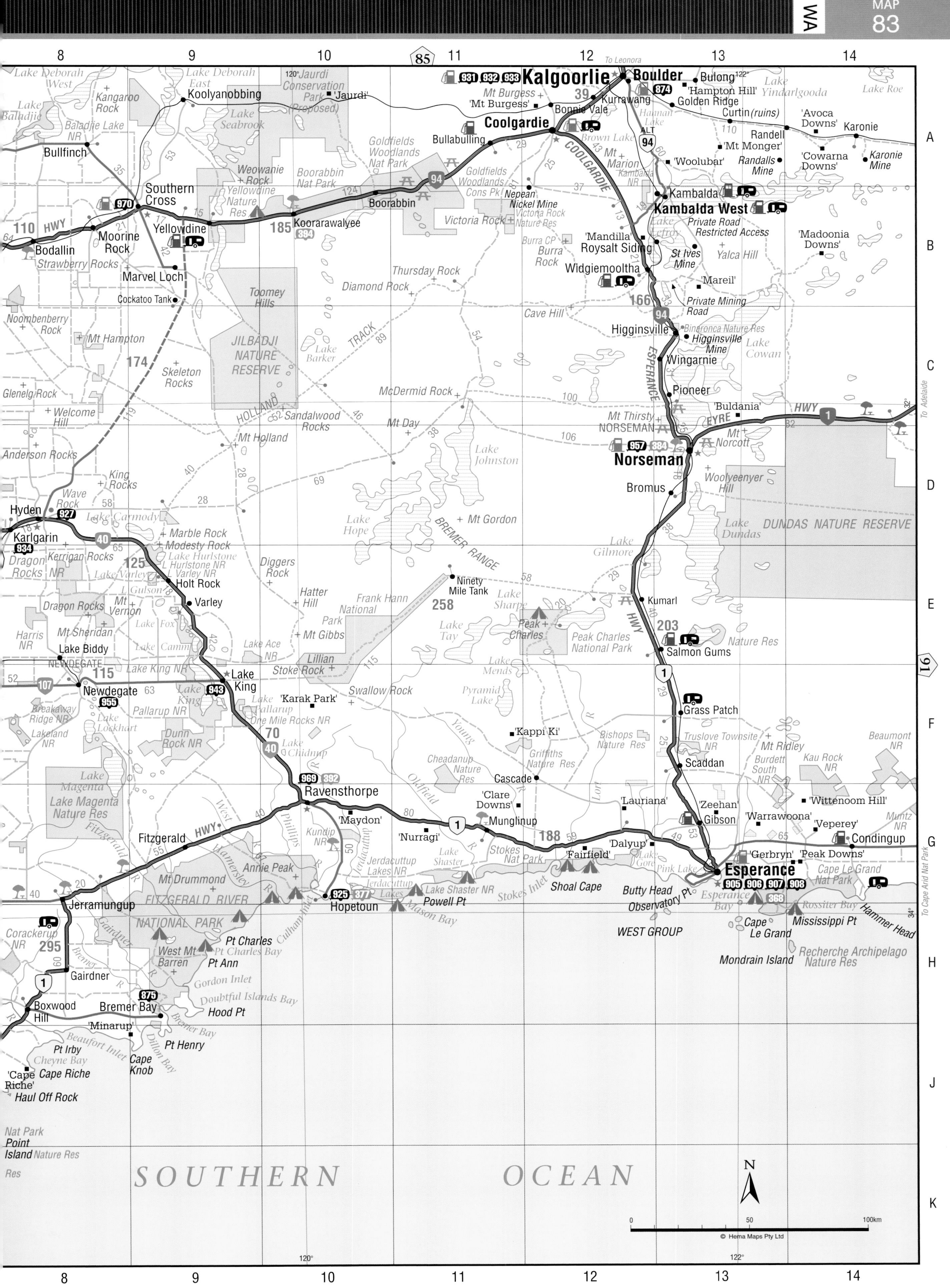
Kalgoorlie
Boulder
Bulong
'Hampton Hill'
Golden Ridge
Lake Yindarlgooda
Lake Roe
Curtin (ruins)
'Avoca Downs'
Karonie
Randell
'Mt Monger'
'Cowarna Downs'
Karonie Mine
Randalls Mine
'Woolubar'
Mt Burgess
'Mt Burgess'
Kurrawang
Bonnie Vale
Hannan Lake
Coolgardie
Bullabulling
Brown Lake
Mt Marion
Kambalda NR
Kambalda
Kambalda West
Private Road Restricted Access
'Madoonia Downs'
Yalca Hill
St Ives Mine
'Mandilla'
Roysalt Siding
Widgiemooltha
'Mareil'
Private Mining Road
Burra CP
Burra Rock
Nepean Nickel Mine
Victoria Rock Nature Res
Victoria Rock
Goldfields Woodlands Cons Pk
Goldfields Woodlands Nat Park
Boorabbin Nat Park
Boorabbin
Koorarawalyee
Jaurdi Conservation Park (Proposed)
'Jaurdi'
Lake Deborah West
Lake Deborah East
Kangaroo Rock
Koolyanobbing
Lake Baladjie
Baladjie Lake NR
Lake Seabrook
Bullfinch
Weowanie Rock
Yellowdine Nature Res
Southern Cross
Yellowdine
Bodallin
Moorine Rock
Strawberry Rocks
Marvel Loch
Cockatoo Tank
Toomey Hills
Thursday Rock
Diamond Rock
Cave Hill
Noombenberry Rock
Mt Hampton
JILBADJI NATURE RESERVE
Lake Barker
TRACK
Skeleton Rocks
Glenelg Rock
Welcome Hill
HOLLAND
Sandalwood Rocks
McDermid Rock
Mt Day
Mt Holland
Anderson Rocks
King Rocks
Lake Johnston
Higginsville
Binaronca Nature Res
Higginsville Mine
Lake Cowan
Wingarnie
ESPERANCE
Pioneer
'Buldania'
EYRE HWY
Mt Thirsty
NORSEMAN
Norseman
Mt Norcott
To Adelaide
Woolyeenyer Hill
Bromus
Lake Dundas
DUNDAS NATURE RESERVE
Lake Gilmore
Wave Rock
Hyden
Karlgarin
Lake Carmody
Lake Hope
Mt Gordon
BREMER RANGE
Marble Rock
Modesty Rock
Lake Hurlstone
L Hurlstone NR
L Varley NR
Kerrigan Rocks
Dragon Rocks NR
Lake Varley
Holt Rock
Varley
L Gulson
Diggers Rock
Ninety Mile Tank
Lake Sharpe
Kumarl
Dragon Rocks
Mt Vernon
Hatter Hill
Frank Hann National Park
Peak Charles
Peak Charles National Park
Lake Tay
Salmon Gums
Nature Res
Harris NR
Mt Sheridan
Lake Fox
Lake Camm
Lake Ace NR
Mt Gibbs
Lake Biddy
NEWDEGATE
Lake King NR
Lake King
Lillian Stoke Rock
Lake Mends
Newdegate
Breakaway Ridge NR
Pallarup NR
Lake Pallarup
One Mile Rocks NR
'Karak Park'
Swallow Rock
Pyramid Lake
Grass Patch
Lakeland NR
Lake Lockhart
Dunn Rock NR
Lake Chidnup
Young
'Kappi Ki'
Bishops Nature Res
Truslove Townsite
Mt Ridley
Beaumont NR
Lake Magenta
Lake Magenta Nature Res
Cheadanup Nature Res
Griffiths Nature Res
Cascade
Scaddan
Burdett South NR
Kau Rock NR
Ravensthorpe
Oldfield
'Clare Downs'
'Lauriana'
'Zeehan'
'Wittenoom Hill'
West
Phillips
'Maydon'
Kundip NR
Munglinup
Gibson
'Warrawoona'
'Veperey'
Muntz NR
Fitzgerald HWY
'Nurragi'
Stokes Nat Park
'Fairfield'
'Dalyup'
'Gerbryn'
'Peak Downs'
Condingup
Annie Peak
Jerdacuttup Lakes NR
Lake Shaster
Lake Gore
Pink Lake
Esperance
Cape Le Grand Nat Park
Mt Drummond
FITZGERALD RIVER NATIONAL PARK
Lake Shaster NR
Stokes Inlet
Shoal Cape
Butty Head
Observatory Pt
Esperance Bay
Rossiter Bay
Hammer Head
To Cape Arid Nat Park
Jerramungup
Hopetoun
Powell Pt
Mason Bay
Culham Inlet
Cape Le Grand
Mississippi Pt
Corackerup NR
Gairdner
Bremer
Pt Charles
Pt Charles Bay
West Mt Barren
Pt Ann
WEST GROUP
Mondrain Island
Recherche Archipelago Nature Res
Gairdner
Gordon Inlet
Doubtful Islands Bay
Boxwood Hill
Bremer Bay
Hood Pt
'Minarup'
Bremer Bay
Beaufort Inlet
Pt Irby
Cheyne Bay
Pt Henry
Dillon Bay
Cape Knob
'Cape Riche'
Cape Riche
Haul Off Rock
Point Nat Park
Island Nature Res
SOUTHERN OCEAN
N
0 50 100km
© Hema Maps Pty Ltd
120°
122°
8 9 10 11 12 13 14
A B C D E F G H J K

Central-West Western Australia

To Carnarvon

For more detail on this area, see Hema's Mid West Map

For more detail on this area, see Hema's Mid West Map

Cape Levillain, Cape Peron North, Guichenault Pt, FRANCOIS PERON NATIONAL PARK, Cape Leseur, Peron, Monkey Mia, Denham Sound, Quoin Head, Dirk Hartog Island, 'Peron', Denham, Faure Island, 'Faure', Petit Pt, Peninsula, L'Haridon Bight, HAMELIN POOL MARINE NATURE RESERVE, 'Dirk Hartog', Useless Loop (no public access), Steep Pt, Most Westerly Mainland Point, 'Nanga', Henry Freycinet Harbour, Zuytdorp Pt, 'Carrarang', Giraud Pt, 'Tamala', Zuytdorp Cliffs, Disappointment Reach

'Wahroonga', 'Meedo', 'Wooramel', Wooramel Roadhouse, 'Yaringa', 'Woodleigh', 'Carba', Overlander Roadhouse, 'Hamelin', 'Coburn', 'Meadow', Billabong Roadhouse, 'Nerren Nerren', Zuytdorp Nature Reserve, TOOLONGA NATURE RESERVE, KALBARRI NAT PARK, 'Eurardy', The Loop, Z Bend, Murchison House, Gantheaume Bay, Kalbarri, Red Bluff, Bluff Point, 'Mt View', Binnu, Shoal Point, Hutt Lagoon, Gregory, North Island, Horrocks, Wallabi Group, Houtman Abrolhos, Middle Channel, Easter Group, Zeewyk Channel, Pelsaert Group, Geelvink Channel, Coronation Beach, Geraldton, Pt Moore, Greenhough, Northampton, Yuna, Nabawa, East Yuna NR, Mullewa, Tenindewa, Wicherina, Wongoondy, Walkaway, Burma Road NR, Coalseam Con Park, Seven Mile Beach, Dongara, Pt Denison, Mingenew, Mt Lefroy, Mt Adams, Arrino, White Pt, Yardanogo NR, Cliff Head, Three Springs, Yarra Yarra Lakes, Carnamah, Illawong, Beekeepers NR, Twin Hills, Wotto NR, Tathra NP, Desperation Bay, Eneabba, Coolimba, Stockyard Gully NP, Leeman, Sth Eneabba NR, Alexander Morrison Nat Park, Capamauro NR, Coorow, Marchagee, Green Head, Lesueur Nat Park, Mt Lesueur, Pinjarrega NR, Coomallo NR, Watheroo Nat Park, Watheroo, Drovers Cave NP, Jurien Bay, Southern Beekeepers NR, Ronsard Bay, Badgingarra, Badgingarra Nat Pk, Thirsty Pt, Cervantes, Nambung Nat Park, Pinnacles, Coomberdale, 'Strathmore', Moora, Dandaragan, 'Cooljarloo', Cataby, Wanagarren Nature Res, 'Mimegarra', Wedge Is, Nilgen NR, Dide Bay, Namming Lake, Cowalla, Lancelin, Mogumber, Wannamal, Moore River Nat Pk, Ledge Pt, Breton Bay, Sea Bird, Beermullah, Guilderton, Gingin, Two Rocks, Yanchep, Yanchep NP, Muchea, Neerabup Nat Park, Quinns Rocks, Marmion Marine Pk, Wanneroo, Upper Swan, Mullaloo, Scarborough, PERTH, Rottnest Island, Fremantle, Midland, Kalamunda, Mundaring, Walyunga Nat Park, Avon Valley Nat Park, Moondyne, Bindoon, Toodyay, Wundowie, Wooroloo, Clackline, The Lakes, York, Wandoo Con Park, Greenhills, Dangin, Quairading, Northam, Grass Valley, Meckering, Cunderdin, Tammin, Doodlakine, Kellerberrin, Erikin, Shackleton

Dalwallinu, Pithara, Kalannie, Miling, Bindi Bindi, Ballidu, Wubin, Buntine, Maya, Latham, Perenjori, Morawa, Nullewa Lake, Gutha, Canna, Tardun, Pindar, Urawa NR, 'Tallering', Wurarga, Yalgoo, 'Gabyon', Wandana NR, Wongan Hills, New Norcia, Calingiri, Wyening, Bolgart, Goomalling, Dowerin, Wyalkatchem, Koorda, Cadoux, Bencubbin, Beacon, Burakin, Kulja, Mollerin NR, Trayning, Lake Wallambin, Cowcowing Lakes, Lake Hillman, Lake O'Grady, Goodlands NR, Carlyarn Rocks NR, 'Remlap', Paynes Find, 'Maranalgo', 'Ninghan', 'Mt Gibson', Mongers Lake, 'Wannarra', 'Damperwah', Mt Mulgine, Wedlhamby Lake, 'Karara', 'Warriedar', 'Kadji Kadji', 'Mellenbye', 'Thundelarra', Gnows Nest Range, 'Bunnawarra', 'Badja', 'Muralgarra', 'Mourourbra', Lake Moore, 'Bimbijy', 'Pullagaroo', 'Oudabunna', 'Wydgee', 'Burnabinmah', Cooladar Hill, 'Kirkalocka', 'Wogarno', 'Iona', 'Murrum', 'Yowergabbie', Mt Magnet, 'Boogardie', 'Noongal', Harding Range, 'Pindathuna', 'Tardie', 'Yuin', 'Mount Farmer', 'Dalgaranga', Dalgaranga Meteorite Crater, 'Jingemarra', 'Woolgorong', 'Pinegrove', 'Lake Nerramyne', 'Coolcalalya', 'Yallalong', 'New Forest', 'Billabalong', Twin Peaks, 'Murgoo', 'Mt Wittenoom', 'Meka', Mt Luke, Sanford River, PIA, 'Wooleen', 'Meeberrie', Murchison Roadhouse, 'Boolardy', Roderick River, Mt Murchison, 'Kalli', 'Muggon', 'Mt Narryer', Mt Narryer, 'Curbur', 'Manfred', 'Nookawarra', 'Talisker', 'Yalardy', Mt Rebecca, 'Byro', 'Milly Milly', 'Beringarra', Mt Hale, Murchison River, Mt Nairn, 'Gillroyd', 'Callytharra Springs', Wooramel River, 'Carey Downs', 'Coordewandy (ruins)', Mt Coordewandy, 'Yalbra', 'Innouendy', Mt Gould, 'Mt Gould', TALBOT DIVIDE, 'Mt Padbury', 'Moorarie', 'Koonmarra', 'Mileura', 'Belele', Muggabullin Swamp, Lake Austin, Cue, 'Nallan', 'Coodardy', Tuckanarra, 'Glen', 'Karbar', 'Beebyn', 'Madoonga', Weld Range, WILGIE MIA, 'Annean' (abandoned), 'Lakeside', Yalgar

NORTH WEST COASTAL HWY, BRAND HWY, GREAT NORTHERN HWY, MIDLANDS ROAD, GREAT EASTERN HWY, DARLING RANGE, GAIRDNER RANGE, HARDING RANGE

INDIAN OCEAN

SEE PAGES 78-79

0 50 100 km

To Bunbury 78 · To Albany · To Beverley 79

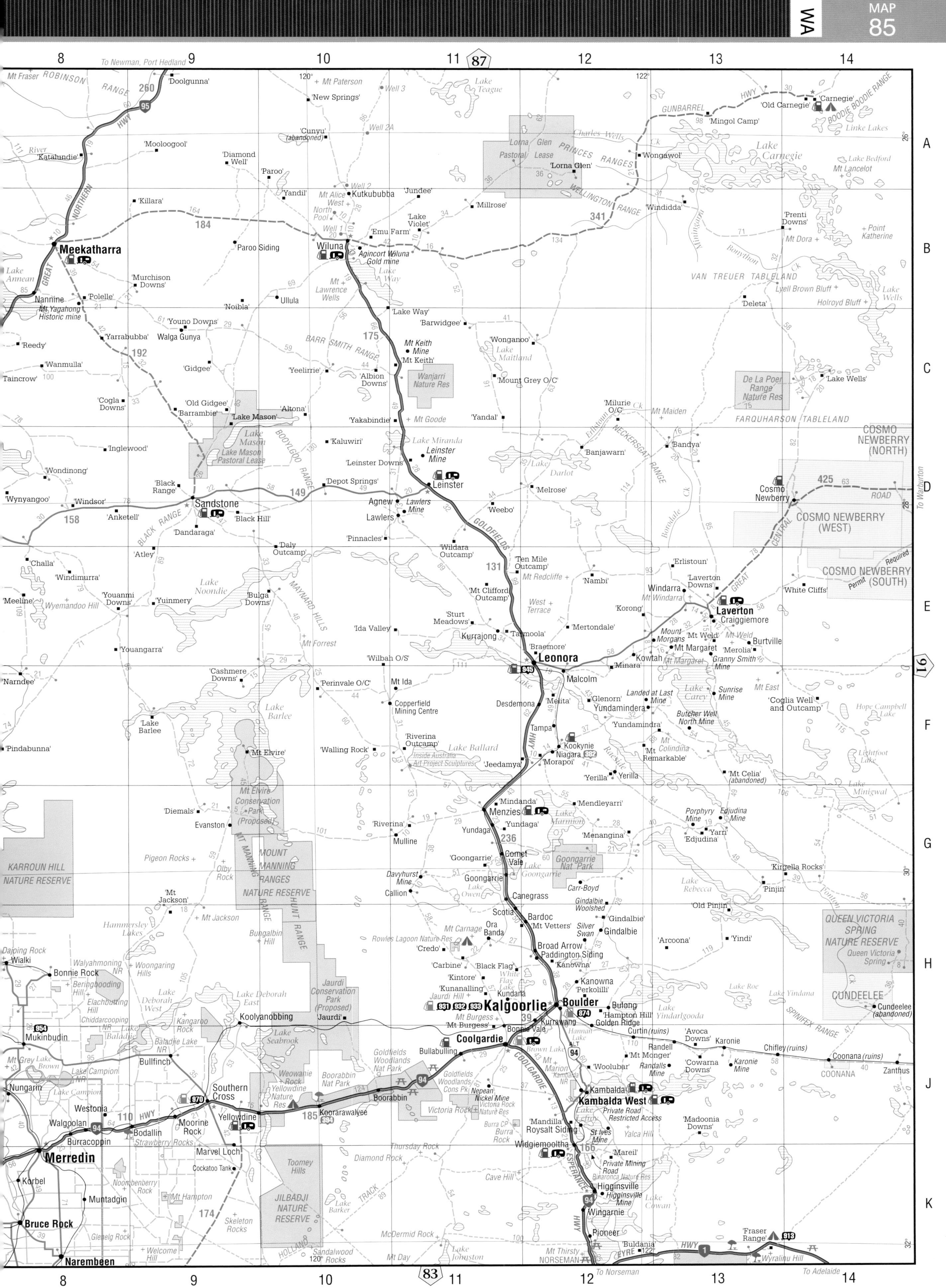
To Newman, Port Hedland
To Warburton
To Norseman
To Adelaide
Meekatharra
Wiluna
Sandstone
Leinster
Leonora
Laverton
Menzies
Kalgoorlie
Boulder
Coolgardie
Kambalda
Kambalda West
Merredin
Bruce Rock
Narembeen
Southern Cross
Norseman
Cosmo Newbery
Agnew
Lawlers
Malcolm
Kookynie
Niagara
Ora Banda
Broad Arrow
Widgiemooltha
Higginsville
Yellowdine
Bullabulling
Koolyanobbing
Bodallin
Moorine Rock
Westonia
Walgoolan
Burracoppin
Nungarin
Mukinbudin
Bonnie Rock
Bullfinch
Marvel Loch
Muntadgin
Korbel
Evanston
Mulline
Canegrass
Comet Vale
Goongarrie
Kurrawang
Coonana (ruins)
Zanthus
Karonie
Randells
Lake Carnegie
Lake Way
Lake Barlee
Lake Ballard
Lake Carey
Lake Raeside
Lake Lefroy
Lake Cowan
Lake Mason
Lake Noondie
Lake Darlot
Lake Miranda
Lake Maitland
Lake Rebecca
Lake Deborah East
Lake Deborah West
Lake Seabrook
Lake Campion
Lake Yindana
Lake Minigwal
Lake Marmion
VAN TREUER TABLELAND
FARQUHARSON TABLELAND
PRINCES RANGES
WELLINGTON RANGE
BARR SMITH RANGE
BOOYLGOO RANGE
MAYNARD HILLS
BLACK RANGE
SPINIFEX RANGE
GREAT NORTHERN HWY
GOLDFIELDS HWY
COOLGARDIE ESPERANCE HWY
GREAT CENTRAL ROAD
GUNBARREL HWY
GREAT EASTERN HWY
EYRE HWY
HOLLAND TRACK
Wanjarri Nature Res
De La Poer Range Nature Res
KARROUN HILL NATURE RESERVE
MOUNT MANNING RANGES NATURE RESERVE
Mt Elvire Conservation Park (Proposed)
Jaurdi Conservation Park (Proposed)
Goongarrie Nat Park
Goldfields Woodlands Nat Park
Boorabbin Nat Park
JILBADJI NATURE RESERVE
QUEEN VICTORIA SPRING NATURE RESERVE
COSMO NEWBERRY (NORTH)
COSMO NEWBERRY (WEST)
COSMO NEWBERRY (SOUTH)
Permit Required
CUNDEELEE
Lorna Glen Pastoral Lease
Lake Mason Pastoral Lease
Inside Australia Art Project Sculptures

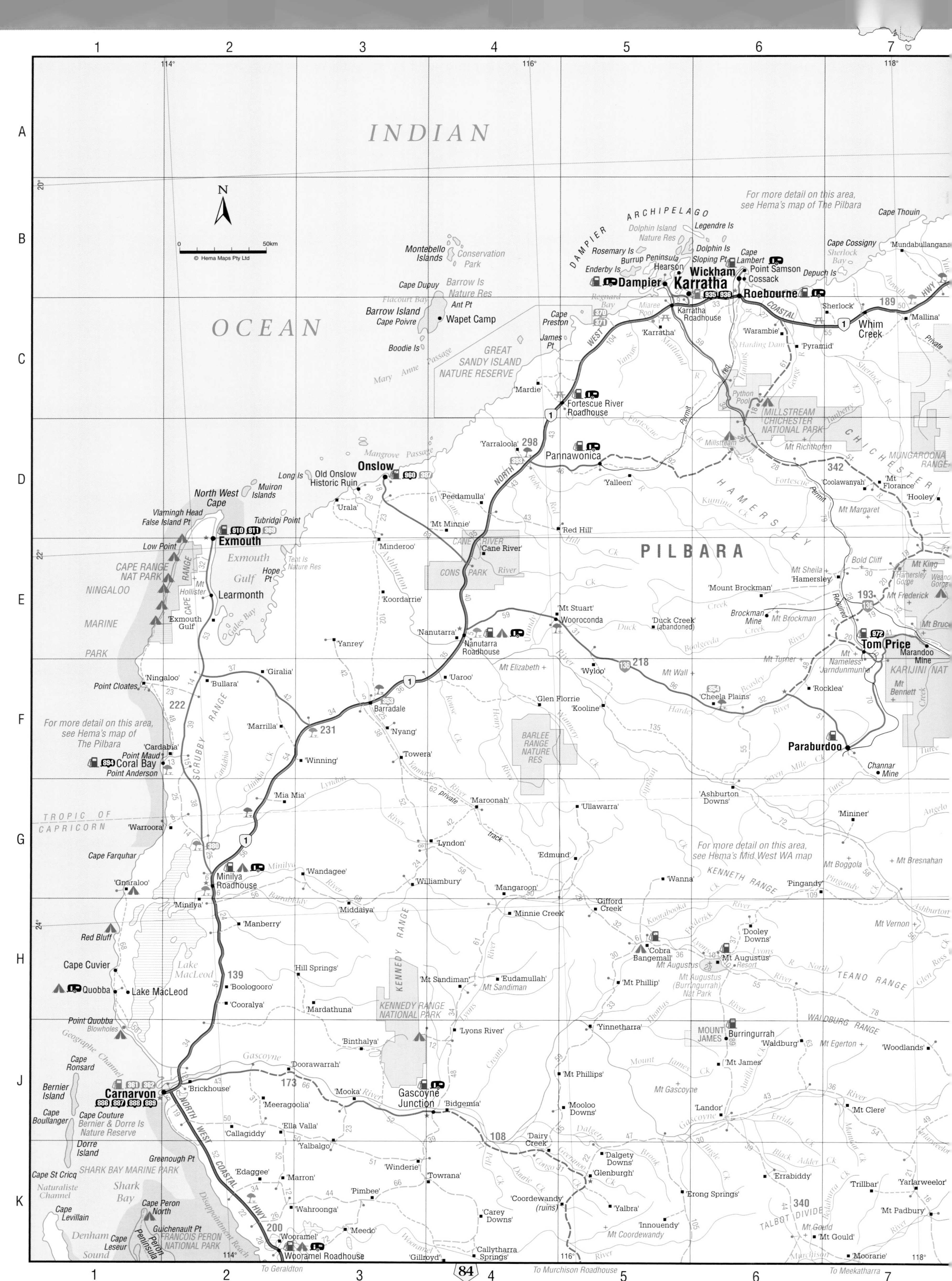

INDIAN
OCEAN
For more detail on this area, see Hema's map of The Pilbara
© Hema Maps Pty Ltd
DAMPIER ARCHIPELAGO
Dolphin Island Nature Res
Legendre Is
Rosemary Is
Burrup Peninsula
Dolphin Is
Enderby Is
Hearson
Cape Lambert
Wickham
Point Samson
Cossack
Dampier
Karratha
Roebourne
Sloping Pt
Depuch Is
Cape Thouin
Cape Cossigny
Sherlock Bay
'Mundabullangana'
Montebello Islands
Conservation Park
Cape Dupuy
Barrow Is Nature Res
Ant Pt
Flacourt Bay
Barrow Island
Cape Poivre
Wapet Camp
Boodie Is
Mary Anne Passage
GREAT SANDY ISLAND NATURE RESERVE
Cape Preston
James Pt
Regnard Bay
Miaree Pool
Karratha Roadhouse
'Karratha'
'Sherlock'
Whim Creek
'Mallina'
'Warambie'
'Pyramid'
Harding Dam
Python Pool
MILLSTREAM CHICHESTER NATIONAL PARK
Millstream
Mt Richthofen
'Mardie'
Fortescue River Roadhouse
Fortescue
'Yarraloola'
Pannawonica
'Yalleen'
Mangrove Passage
Onslow
Long Is
Old Onslow Historic Ruin
Muiron Islands
North West Cape
'Urala'
'Peedamulla'
Vlamingh Head
False Island Pt
Tubridgi Point
Exmouth
Low Point
Exmouth Gulf
Hope Pt
Tent Is Nature Res
CAPE RANGE NAT PARK
NINGALOO MARINE PARK
Mt Hollister
Learmonth
'Exmouth Gulf'
Gales Bay
'Mt Minnie'
'Minderoo'
CANE RIVER CONS PARK
'Cane River'
'Red Hill'
PILBARA
HAMERSLEY
CHICHESTER
MUNGAROONA RANGE
'Coolawanyah'
'Mt Florance'
'Hooley'
Mt Margaret
Bold Cliff
Mt King
Hamersley Gorge
Weano Gorge
Mt Sheila
'Hamersley'
Mt Frederick
'Mount Brockman'
'Koordarrie'
'Mt Stuart'
Wooroconda
'Duck Creek' (abandoned)
Brockman Mine
Mt Brockman
Mt Bruce
'Nanutarra'
Nanutarra Roadhouse
'Yanrey'
Tom Price
Marandoo Mine
Mt Nameless
Jarndunmunha
Mt Turner
KARIJINI NAT
Mt Bennett
Mt Elizabeth
'Wyloo'
Mt Wall
'Rocklea'
'Ningaloo'
Point Cloates
'Bullara'
'Giralia'
'Uaroo'
'Glen Florrie'
'Kooline'
'Cheela Plains'
Barradale
'Marrilla'
'Nyang'
BARLEE RANGE NATURE RES
Paraburdoo
Channar Mine
For more detail on this area, see Hema's map of The Pilbara
'Cardabia'
Point Maud
Coral Bay
Point Anderson
SCRUBBY RANGE
'Winning'
'Towera'
'Mia Mia'
'Maroonah'
'Ullawarra'
'Ashburton Downs'
'Mininer'
TROPIC OF CAPRICORN
'Warroora'
'Lyndon'
'Edmund'
For more detail on this area, see Hema's Mid West WA map
Mt Boggola
Mt Bresnahan
Cape Farquhar
Minilya Roadhouse
'Wandagee'
'Williambury'
'Wanna'
KENNETH RANGE
'Pingandy'
'Gnaraloo'
'Minilya'
'Middalya'
'Mangaroon'
'Minnie Creek'
'Gifford Creek'
'Manberry'
Red Bluff
KENNEDY RANGE
'Dooley Downs'
Mt Vernon
Cape Cuvier
Lake MacLeod
'Hill Springs'
'Boologooro'
'Cooralya'
'Mt Sandiman'
Mt Sandiman
'Eudamullah'
Cobra Bangemall'
Mt Augustus
'Mt Augustus'
Mt Augustus Resort
Mt Augustus (Burringurrah) Nat Park
'Mt Phillip'
TEANO RANGE
Quobba
'Mardathuna'
KENNEDY RANGE NATIONAL PARK
Point Quobba
Blowholes
Geographe Channel
'Lyons River'
'Yinnetharra'
MOUNT JAMES
Burringurrah
WALDBURG RANGE
'Waldburg'
Mt Egerton
'Woodlands'
Cape Ronsard
'Binthalya'
'Doorawarrah'
'Mt James'
Bernier Island
Carnarvon
'Brickhouse'
'Mooka'
Gascoyne Junction
'Bidgemia'
'Mt Phillips'
Mt Gascoyne
'Mt Clere'
Cape Boullanger
Cape Couture
Bernier & Dorre Is Nature Reserve
'Meeragoolia'
'Mooloo Downs'
'Landor'
'Callagiddy'
'Ella Valla'
'Dairy Creek'
Dorre Island
'Yalbalgo'
'Dalgety Downs'
Greenough Pt
Cape St Cricq
SHARK BAY MARINE PARK
'Edaggee'
'Marron'
'Winderie'
'Towrana'
'Glenburgh'
'Errabiddy'
'Trillbar'
'Yarlarweelor'
Naturaliste Channel
Shark Bay
'Pimbee'
'Coordewandy' (ruins)
'Erong Springs'
Cape Levillain
Cape Peron North
'Wahroonga'
'Carey Downs'
'Yalbra'
TALBOT DIVIDE
'Mt Padbury'
Guichenault Pt
FRANCOIS PERON NATIONAL PARK
Denham
Cape Lesueur
Peron Peninsula
'Wooramel'
'Meedo'
'Innouendy'
Mt Coordewandy
Mt Gould
'Mt Gould'
Sound
Wooramel Roadhouse
'Gillroyd'
'Callytharra Springs'
'Moorarie'
To Geraldton
To Murchison Roadhouse
To Meekatharra

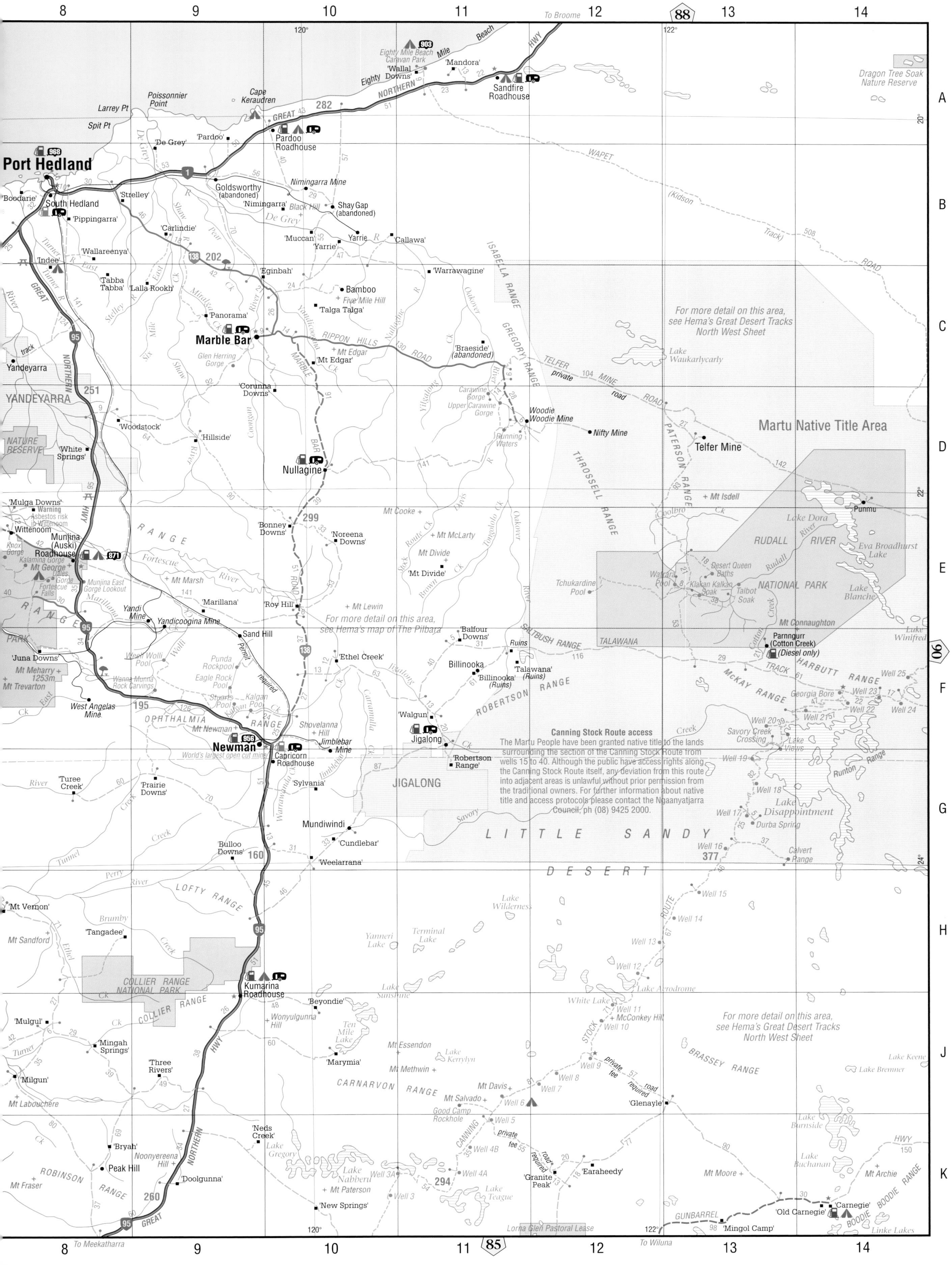
To Broome
88
Dragon Tree Soak Nature Reserve
Eighty Mile Beach Caravan Park
903
'Wallal Downs'
Eighty Mile Beach
'Mandora'
Sandfire Roadhouse
NORTHERN HWY
Cape Keraudren
Poissonnier Point
Larrey Pt
Spit Pt
GREAT
282
Pardoo Roadhouse
'Pardoo'
'De Grey'
968
Port Hedland
South Hedland
'Boodarie'
'Pippingarra'
'Strelley'
Goldsworthy (abandoned)
Nimingarra Mine
'Nimingarra'
Shay Gap (abandoned)
WAPET
(Kidson
Track)
ROAD
De Grey
'Carlindie'
'Muccan'
'Yarrie'
Yarrie
'Callawa'
'Wallareenya'
'Indee'
138
202
'Eginbah'
'Warrawagine'
ISABELLA RANGE
'Tabba Tabba'
'Lalla Rookh'
Bamboo
Five Mile Hill
'Talga Talga'
'Panorama'
Marble Bar
RIPPON HILLS ROAD
Mt Edgar
'Mt Edgar'
'Braeside' (abandoned)
GREGORY RANGE
For more detail on this area, see Hema's Great Desert Tracks North West Sheet
Lake Waukarlycarly
TELFER MINE ROAD
private road
Yandeyarra
YANDEYARRA
251
Glen Herring Gorge
'Corunna Downs'
Carawine Gorge
Upper Carawine Gorge
Woodie Woodie Mine
Nifty Mine
Martu Native Title Area
Telfer Mine
PATERSON RANGE
THROSSELL RANGE
NATURE RESERVE
'Woodstock'
'Hillside'
'White Springs'
Running Waters
Nullagine
MARBLE BAR ROAD
'Mulga Downs'
Warning Asbestos risk in Wittenoom
Wittenoom
Munjina (Auski) Roadhouse
871
'Bonney Downs'
299
Mt Cooke
Mt Isdell
Punmu
Lake Dora
RUDALL RIVER NATIONAL PARK
Eva Broadhurst Lake
'Noreena Downs'
Mt McLarty
Mt Divide
'Mt Divide'
Desert Queen Baths
Watrara Pool
Klakan Kalkan Soak
Talbot Soak
Tchukardine Pool
Lake Blanche
Kalamina Gorge
Mt George
Dales Gorge
Fortescue Falls
Munjina East Gorge Lookout
Mt Marsh
Fortescue River
'Marillana'
'Roy Hill'
Mt Lewin
For more detail on this area, see Hema's map of The Pilbara
Mt Connaughton
Lake Winifred
Yandi Mine
Yandicoogina Mine
Sand Hill
'Balfour Downs'
SALTBUSH RANGE
TALAWANA
Parnngurr (Cotton Creek)
(Diesel only)
HARBUTT RANGE
TALAWANA TRACK
McKAY RANGE
Mt Meharry 1253m
Mt Trevarton
'Juna Downs'
West Wolli Pool
Wanna Munna Rock Carvings
Punda Rockpool
Eagle Rock Pool
Stuarts Pool
Kalgan Pool
Permit required
'Ethel Creek'
Billinooka
'Billinooka' (Ruins)
'Talawana' (Ruins)
ROBERTSON RANGE
Georgia Bore
Well 25
Well 23
Well 22
Well 24
West Angelas Mine
195
OPHTHALMIA RANGE
Mt Newman
956
Newman
World's largest open cut mine
Capricorn Roadhouse
Shovelanna Hill
Jimblebar Mine
'Walgun'
Jigalong
'Robertson Range'
Canning Stock Route access
The Martu People have been granted native title to the lands surrounding the section of the Canning Stock Route from wells 15 to 40. Although the public have access rights along the Canning Stock Route itself, any deviation from this route into adjacent areas is unlawful without prior permission from the traditional owners. For further information about native title and access protocols please contact the Ngaanyatjarra Council, ph (08) 9425 2000.
Well 20
Well 21
Savory Creek Crossing
Lake Views
Well 19
Runton Range
Well 18
'Turee Creek'
'Prairie Downs'
Sylvania'
JIGALONG
Lake Disappointment
Well 17
Durba Spring
Mundiwindi
'Cundlebar'
LITTLE SANDY DESERT
Well 16
377
Calvert Range
'Bulloo Downs'
160
'Weelarrana'
LOFTY RANGE
Well 15
'Mt Vernon'
Lake Wilderness
CANNING STOCK ROUTE
Well 14
'Tangadee'
Mt Sandford
Yanneri Lake
Terminal Lake
Well 13
COLLIER RANGE NATIONAL PARK
Well 12
Lake Aerodrome
Kumarina Roadhouse
Lake Sunshine
White Lake
Well 11
McConkey Hill
Well 10
'Beyondie'
COLLIER RANGE
Wonyulgunna Hill
'Mulgul'
Ten Mile Lake
For more detail on this area, see Hema's Great Desert Tracks North West Sheet
'Mingah Springs'
Mt Essendon
Lake Kerrylyn
BRASSEY RANGE
'Marymia'
Mt Methwin
Lake Keene
Lake Bremner
'Three Rivers'
Well 9
private fee required road
'Milgun'
CARNARVON RANGE
Well 8
Mt Davis
Well 7
Well 6
Mt Salvado
'Glenayle'
Mt Labouchere
Good Camp Rockhole
Well 5
'Neds Creek'
Lake Burnside
Lake Gregory
Well 4B
private fee road required
HWY 150
'Bryah'
Noonyereena Hill
Lake Buchanan
Peak Hill
NORTHERN HWY
Well 4A
Lake Teague
'Earaheedy'
Mt Moore
Mt Archie
ROBINSON RANGE
Well 3A
294
'Granite Peak'
BOODIE BOODIE RANGE
'Doolgunna'
Lake Nabberu
Mt Paterson
Well 3
Mt Fraser
260
'New Springs'
GUNBARREL
'Old Carnegie'
'Carnegie'
GREAT
Lorna Glen Pastoral Lease
'Mingol Camp'
Linke Lakes
To Meekatharra
85
To Wiluna
90
120°
122°
20°
22°
24°
8 9 10 11 12 13 14
A B C D E F G H J K

INDIAN
OCEAN
For more detail on this area, see Hema's map of The Kimberley
BUCCANEER ARCHIPELAGO
KING SOUND
BEAGLE BAY
Broome
Derby
Cape Leveque
One Arm Pt
Lombadina
Beagle Bay
Cable Beach
Gantheaume Point
Roebuck Bay
Roebuck Plains Roadhouse
Willare Bridge Roadhouse
Curtin Air Base
Mowanjum
Pandanus Park
Camballin
Looma
Bidyadanga
Port Smith Caravan Park
Eighty Mile Beach Caravan Park
Sandfire Roadhouse
Cape Villaret
Cape Bossut
Cape Jaubert
Coulomb Point Nature Reserve
Dragon Tree Soak Nature Reserve
EDGAR RANGES
YAMPI TRAINING AREA
Lacepede Islands
HEYWOOD ISLANDS
Koolan
Cockatoo
GREAT NORTHERN HWY
To Port Hedland
© Hema Maps Pty Ltd

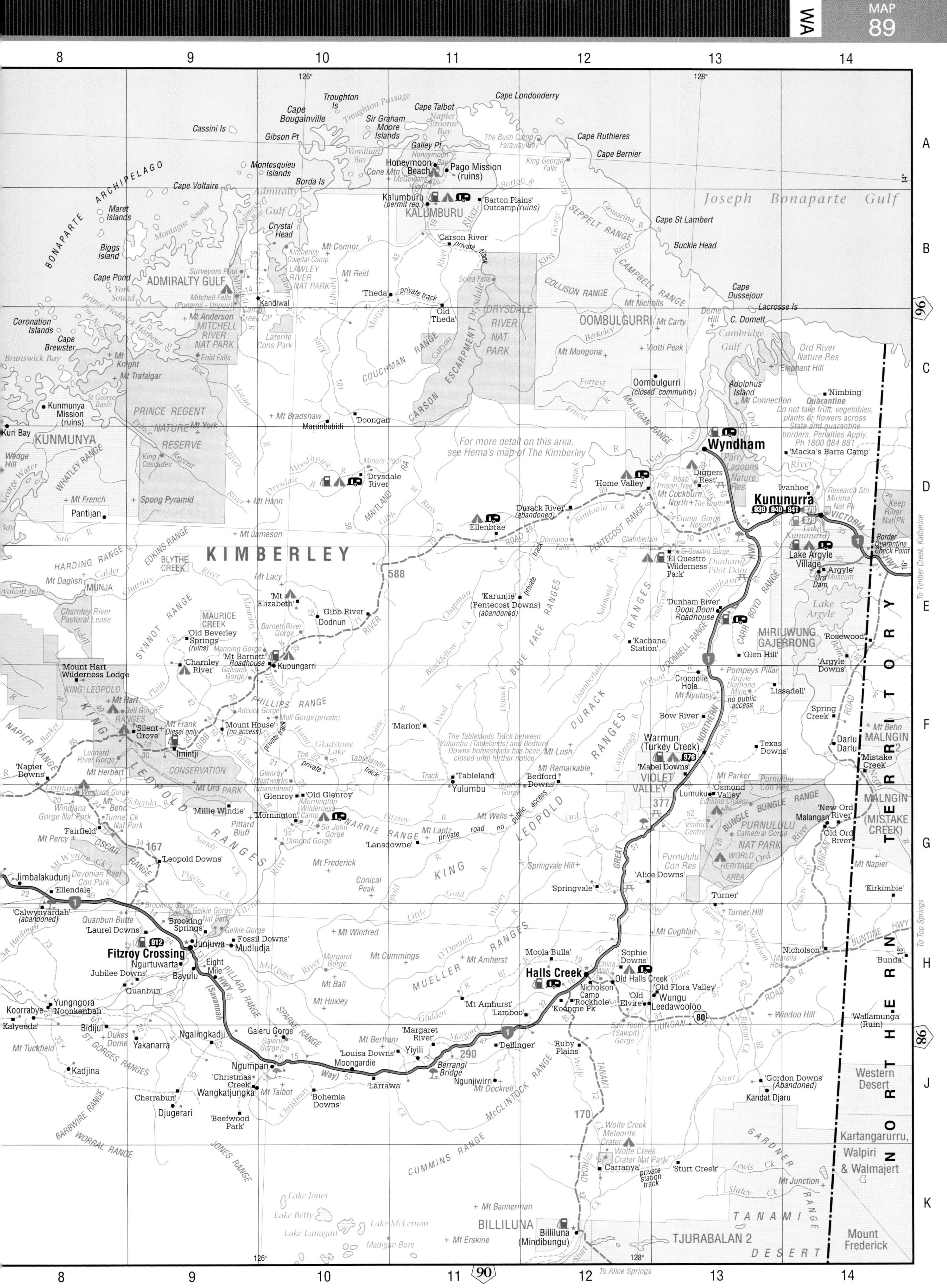WA
MAP 89
Joseph Bonaparte Gulf
BONAPARTE ARCHIPELAGO
KIMBERLEY
Troughton Is
Cape Londonderry
Cape Talbot
Cape Bougainville
Sir Graham Moore Islands
Cassini Is
Gibson Pt
Galley Pt
Cape Ruthieres
Cape Bernier
Montesquieu Islands
Honeymoon Beach
Pago Mission (ruins)
Cape Voltaire
Borda Is
Kalumburu (permit req.)
KALUMBURU
'Barton Plains' Outcamp (ruins)
Maret Islands
Crystal Head
Cape St Lambert
Biggs Island
Buckie Head
Cape Pond
ADMIRALTY GULF
Mt Connor
Mt Reid
'Carson River'
COLLISON RANGE
Cape Dussejour
Lacrosse Is
Kandiwal
'Theda'
'Old Theda'
DRYSDALE RIVER NAT PARK
OOMBULGURRI
Coronation Islands
Cape Brewster
Mt Anderson
MITCHELL RIVER NAT PARK
Mt Carty
C. Domett
Cambridge Gulf
Brunswick Bay
Mt Knight
Mt Trafalgar
Mt Mongona
Viotti Peak
Ord River Nature Res
Elephant Hill
COUCHMAN RANGE
CARSON ESCARPMENT
Oombulgurri (closed community)
Adolphus Island
Mt Connection
'Nimbing'
Quarantine
Do not take fruit, vegetables, plants or flowers across State and quarantine borders. Penalties Apply. Ph 1800 084 881
Kunmunya Mission (ruins)
PRINCE REGENT NATURE RESERVE
Mt York
Mt Bradshaw
Marunbabidi
'Doongan'
Kuri Bay
KUNMUNYA
For more detail on this area, see Hema's map of The Kimberley
Wyndham
'Macka's Barra Camp'
Wedge Hill
WHATLEY RANGE
King Cascades
'Drysdale River'
'Home Valley'
Diggers Rest
Parry Lagoons Nature Res
Ivanhoe
Mt Cockburn North
Kununurra
Mt French
Spong Pyramid
Mt Hann
'Durack River' (abandoned)
Emma Gorge Resort
Keep River Nat Pk
Pantijan
'Ellenbrae'
PENTECOST RANGE
Mt Jameson
HARDING RANGE
EDKINS RANGE
BLYTHE CREEK
Oomaloo Falls
El Questro Wilderness Park
Lake Argyle Village
Border Quarantine Check Point
Mt Daglish
MUNJA
Mt Lacy
588
'Argyle'
Walcott Inlet
'Mt Elizabeth'
'Gibb River'
Dodnun
'Karunjie' (Pentecost Downs) (abandoned)
BLUE FACE RANGES
'Dunham River'
Doon Doon Roadhouse
Lake Argyle
Charnley River Pastoral Lease
MAURICE CREEK
'Old Beverley Springs' (ruins)
Barnett River Gorge
Manning Gorge
'Kachana Station'
MIRIUWUNG GAJERRONG
'Rosewood'
'Mount Hart Wilderness Lodge'
'Charnley River'
'Mt Barnett' Roadhouse
Kupungarri
SYNNOT RANGE
'Glen Hill'
'Argyle Downs'
Pompeys Pillar
KING LEOPOLD
Mt Hart
PHILLIPS RANGE
Crocodile Hole
Mt Nyulasy
'Lissadell'
no public access
Adcock Gorge
Moll Gorge (private)
Bell Gorge
RANGES
Mt Frank Diesel only
'Mount House' (no access)
'Marion'
'Bow River'
'Spring Creek'
Silent Grove
Imintji
Gladstone Lake
DURACK RANGES
Warmun (Turkey Creek)
Mt Behn
MALNGIN
Darlu Darlu
NAPIER RANGE
Lennard River Gorge
The Tablelands Track between Yulumbu (Tablelands) and Bedford Downs homesteads has been closed until further notice
Mt Lush
'Texas Downs'
'Mistake Creek'
'Napier Downs'
Mt Herbert
CONSERVATION
'Tableland'
Yulumbu
Mt Remarkable
'Bedford Downs'
'Mabel Downs'
Mt Parker
Purnululu Con Res
Windjana Gorge
Mt Ord
PARK
'Glenroy'
'Old Glenroy'
Mornington Wilderness Camp
VIOLET VALLEY
377
Lumuku
'Osmond Valley'
Echidna Chasm
BUNGLE BUNGLE RANGE
'New Ord River'
Malangan
MALNGIN (MISTAKE CREEK)
Windjana Gorge Nat Park
Tunnel Ck Nat Park
'Millie Windie'
'Mornington'
Pittard Bluff
Mt Wells
Mt Laptz
private road no public access
Visitors Centre
PURNULULU NAT PARK
Cathedral Gorge
'Old Ord River'
'Fairfield'
Mt Percy
OSCAR RANGE
167
'Leopold Downs'
NARRIE RANGE
Sir John Gorge
Dimond Gorge
'Lansdowne'
LEOPOLD
WORLD HERITAGE AREA
Mt Napier
NORTHERN TERRITORY
Jimbalakudunj
Devonian Reef Con Park
'Ellendale'
Mt Frederick
KING
Springvale Hill
Conical Peak
'Alice Downs'
Purnululu Con Res
'Springvale'
'Kirkimbie'
'Calwynyardah' (abandoned)
Brooking Gorge
Geikie Gorge Nat Park
'Turner'
Turner Hill
Quanbun Butte
'Laurel Downs'
Brooking Springs
Geikie Gorge
Mt Winifred
Mt Coghlan
Fitzroy Crossing
Junjuwa
'Fossil Downs'
Mudludja
Mt Cummings
O'Donnell RANGES
'Moola Bulla'
'Sophie Downs'
'Nicholson'
BUNTINE HWY
To Top Springs
'Bunda'
Ngurtuwarta
'Jubilee Downs'
Eight Mile
Bayulu
Margaret Gorge
Mt Amherst
Halls Creek
China Wall
Old Halls Creek
'Old Flora Valley'
Quanbun
Mt Ball
MUELLER RANGES
Nicholson Camp
Rockhole
'Old Elvire'
Wungu
Leedawooloo
Yungngora
'Noonkanbah'
PILLARA RANGE
Mt Huxley
'Mt Amhurst'
'Lamboo'
Koongie Pk
Windoo Hill
'Wallamunga' (Ruin)
Koorrabye
Kalyeeda
Bidijul
Dukes Dome
Ngalingkadji
Galeru Gorge
SPARKE RANGE
Mt Bertram
'Margaret River'
Saw Tooth (Sawpit) Gorge
DUNGAN
80
'Ruby Plains'
Mt Tuckfield
Yakanarra
'Louisa Downs'
Yiyili
Moongardie
290
'Dellinger'
ST GEORGES RANGES
Ngumpan
Berrangi Bridge
'Gordon Downs' (Abandoned)
Kadjina
'Christmas Creek'
Wangkatjungka
Mt Talbot
'Larrawa'
Ngunjiwirri
Mt Dockrell
McCLINTOCK RANGE
TANAMI
Kandat Djaru
Western Desert
'Cherrabun'
Djugerari
'Bohemia Downs'
170
'Beefwood Park'
BARBWIRE RANGE
WORRAL RANGE
JONES RANGE
Wolfe Creek Meteorite Crater
Wolfe Creek Crater Nat Park
GARDNER RANGE
Kartangarurru, Walpiri & Walmajert
CUMMINS RANGE
'Carranya'
private station track
'Sturt Creek'
Lewis Ck
Mt Junction
Lake Jones
Lake Betty
Lake Lanagan
Lake McLernon
Madigan Bore
Mt Bannerman
BILLILUNA
Billiluna (Mindibungu)
Mt Erskine
TANAMI DESERT
TJURABALAN 2
Mount Frederick
To Alice Springs
To Timber Creek, Katherine
96
90
126°
128°
14°
16°
18°
8
9
10
11
12
13
14
A
B
C
D
E
F
G
H
J
K

Central Western Australia

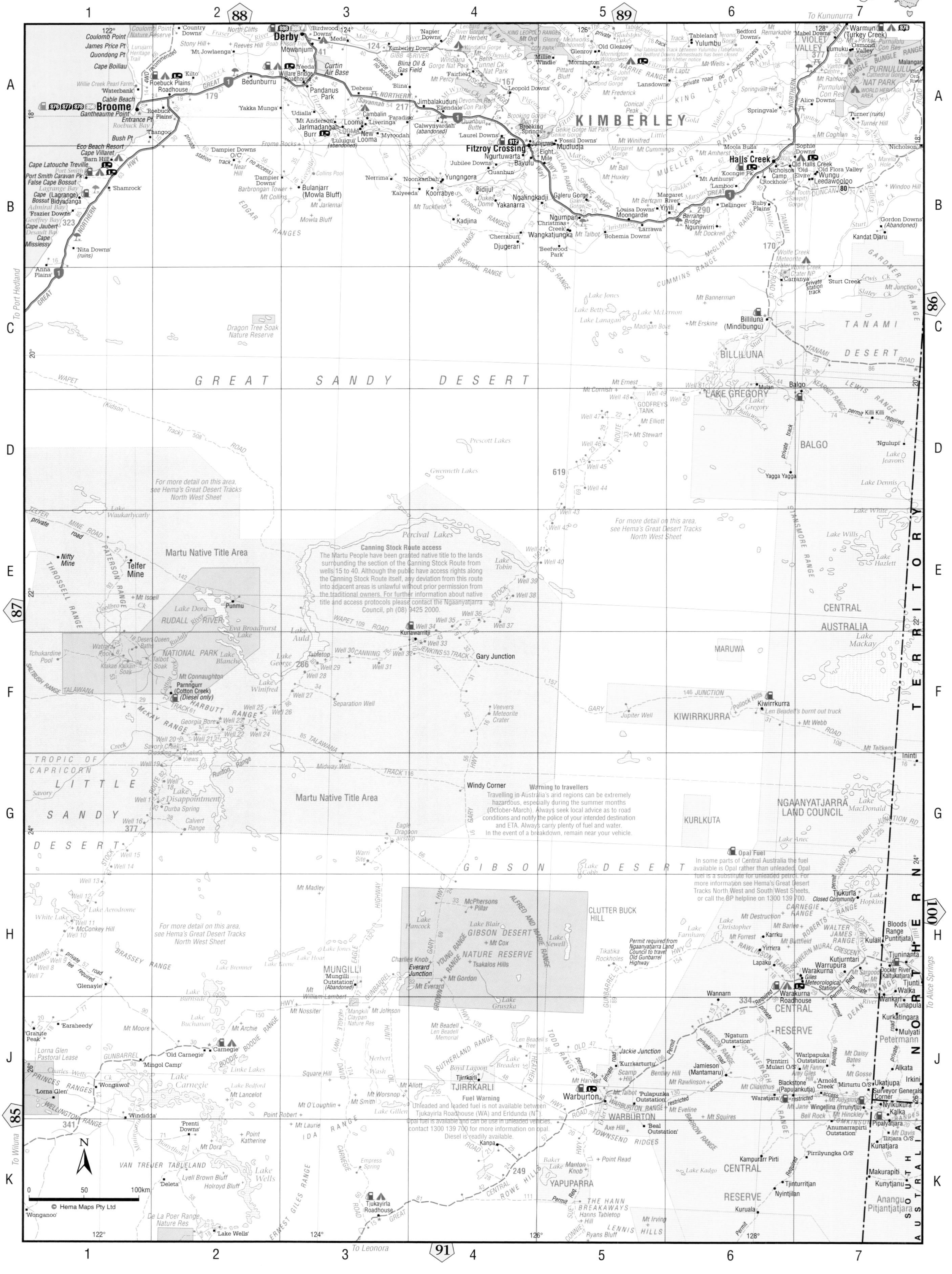

For more detail on this area, see Hema's Great Desert Tracks North West Sheet

Martu Native Title Area

Canning Stock Route access

The Martu People have been granted native title to the lands surrounding the section of the Canning Stock Route from wells 15 to 40. Although the public have access rights along the Canning Stock Route itself, any deviation from this route into adjacent areas is unlawful without prior permission from the traditional owners. For further information about native title and access protocols please contact the Ngaanyatjarra Council, ph (08) 9425 2000.

Warning to travellers

Travelling in Australia's arid regions can be extremely hazardous, especially during the summer months (October-March). Always seek local advice as to road conditions and notify the police of your intended destination and ETA. Always carry plenty of fuel and water. In the event of a breakdown, remain near your vehicle.

Opal Fuel

In some parts of Central Australia the fuel available is Opal rather than unleaded. Opal fuel is a substitute for unleaded petrol. For more information see Hema's Great Desert Tracks North West and South West Sheets, or call the BP helpline on 1300 139 700.

Permit required from Ngaanyatjarra Land Council to travel Old Gunbarrel Highway

Fuel Warning

Unleaded and leaded fuel is not available between Tjukayirla Roadhouse (WA) and Erldunda (NT). Opal fuel is available and can be use in unleaded vehicles, contact 1300 139 700 for more information on opal. Diesel is readily available.

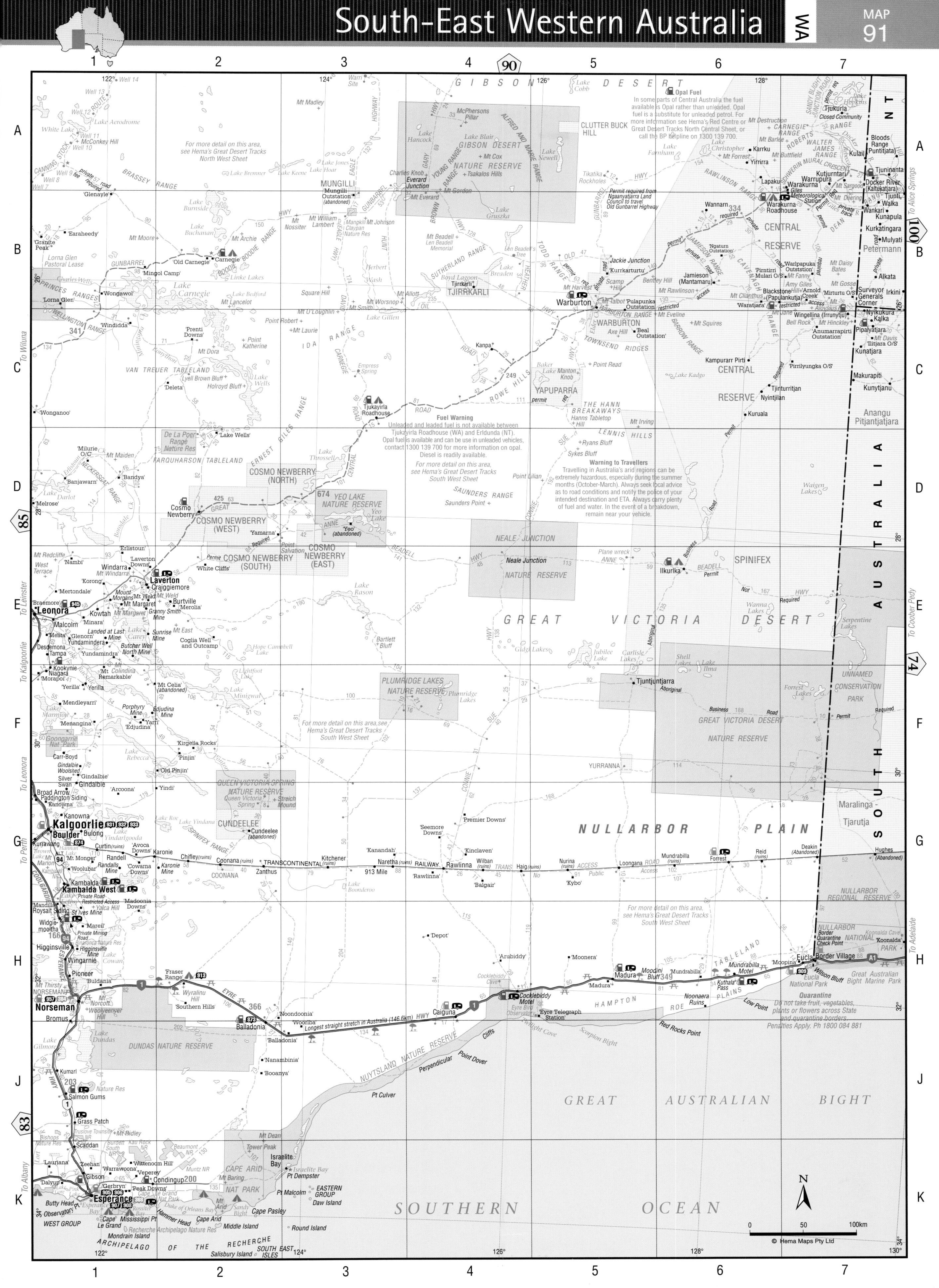
South-East Western Australia
WA
MAP 91
GIBSON DESERT
Opal Fuel
In some parts of Central Australia the fuel available is Opal rather than unleaded. Opal fuel is a substitute for unleaded petrol. For more information see Hema's Red Centre or Great Desert Tracks North Central Sheet, or call the BP helpline on 1300 139 700.
CLUTTER BUCK HILL
For more detail on this area, see Hema's Great Desert Tracks North West Sheet
GIBSON DESERT NATURE RESERVE
MUNGILLI
CENTRAL RESERVE
Warburton
WARBURTON
TJIRRKARLI
YAPUPARRA
Tjukayirla Roadhouse
Fuel Warning
Unleaded and leaded fuel is not available between Tjukayirla Roadhouse (WA) and Erldunda (NT). Opal fuel is available and can be used in unleaded vehicles, contact 1300 139 700 for more information on opal. Diesel is readily available.
For more detail on this area, see Hema's Great Desert Tracks South West Sheet
Warning to Travellers
Travelling in Australia's arid regions can be extremely hazardous, especially during the summer months (October-March). Always seek local advice as to road conditions and notify the police of your intended destination and ETA. Always carry plenty of fuel and water. In the event of a breakdown, remain near your vehicle.
COSMO NEWBERRY (NORTH)
COSMO NEWBERRY (WEST)
COSMO NEWBERRY (SOUTH)
COSMO NEWBERRY (EAST)
YEO LAKE NATURE RESERVE
NEALE JUNCTION NATURE RESERVE
SPINIFEX
Ilkurlka
Laverton
Leonora
GREAT VICTORIA DESERT
PLUMRIDGE LAKES NATURE RESERVE
For more detail on this area, see Hema's Great Desert Tracks South West Sheet
Tjuntjuntjara
GREAT VICTORIA DESERT NATURE RESERVE
UNNAMED CONSERVATION PARK
QUEEN VICTORIA SPRING NATURE RESERVE
CUNDEELEE
Kalgoorlie
Boulder
NULLARBOR PLAIN
Maralinga - Tjarutja
TRANSCONTINENTAL RAILWAY
Rawlinna
Kambalda West
Norseman
DUNDAS NATURE RESERVE
Balladonia
Caiguna
Cocklebiddy Motel
Madura
Mundrabilla Motel
Eucla
Border Village
NULLARBOR REGIONAL RESERVE
NULLARBOR NATIONAL PARK
Quarantine
Do not take fruit, vegetables, plants or flowers across State and quarantine borders. Penalties Apply. Ph 1800 084 881
Longest straight stretch in Australia (146.6km)
NUYTSLAND NATURE RESERVE
GREAT AUSTRALIAN BIGHT
SOUTHERN OCEAN
CAPE ARID NAT PARK
Esperance
ARCHIPELAGO OF THE RECHERCHE
SOUTH AUSTRALIA
NT
0 50 100km
© Hema Maps Pty Ltd

NORTHERN TERRITORY Key Map

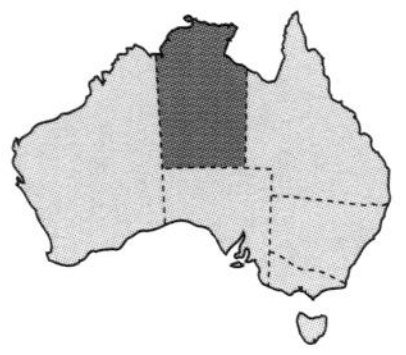

POPULATION: 215,000
AREA: 800,642 sq km
CAPITAL CITY: Darwin

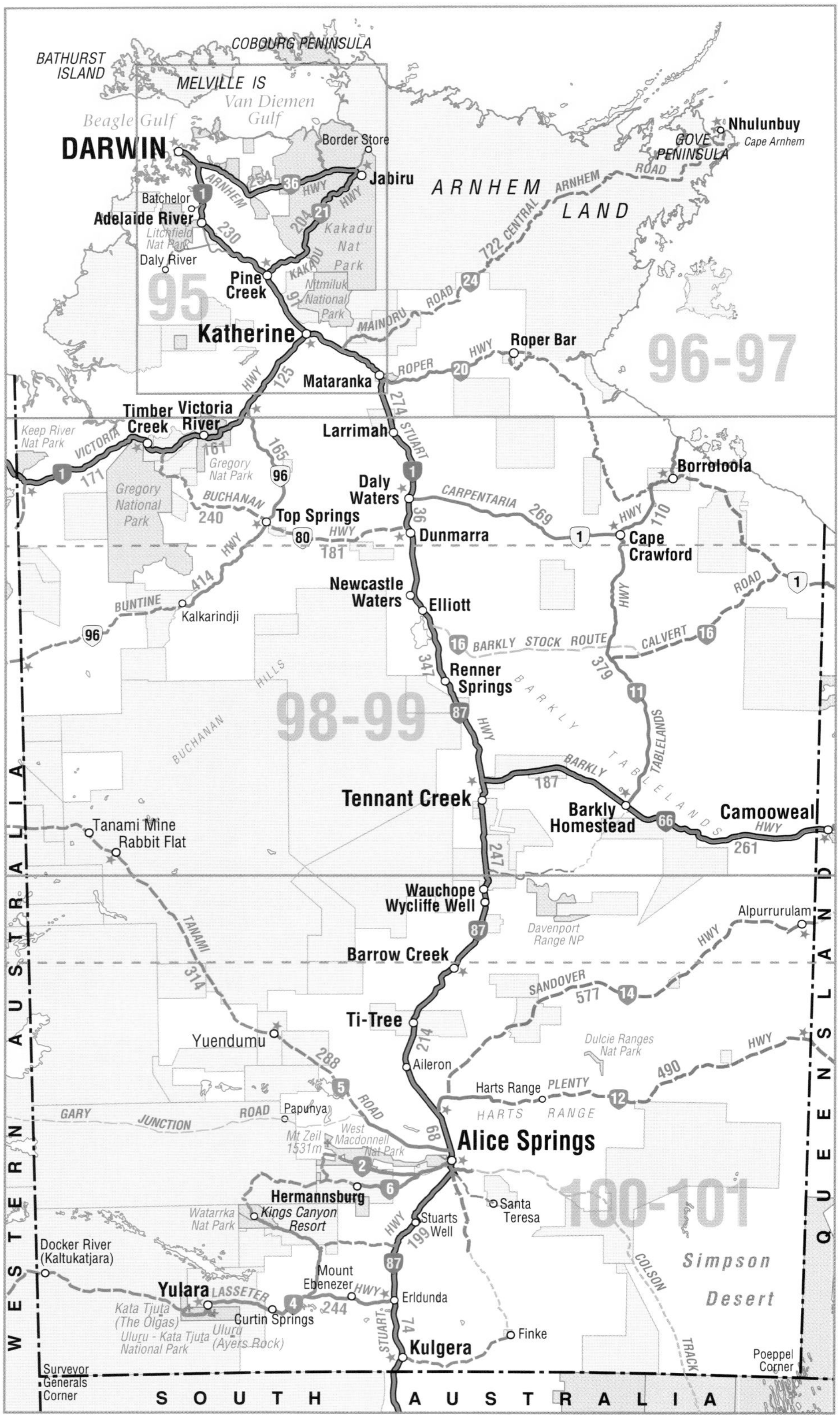

	Nhulunbuy	Mataranka	Kununurra (WA)	Kulgera	Katherine	Jabiru	Halls Creek	Darwin	Camooweal (QLD)	Borroloola	Barrow Creek	Ayers Rock	Alice Springs
Ayers Rock													443
Barrow Creek												725	282
Borroloola											923	1648	1205
Camooweal (QLD)										750	695	1420	977
Darwin									1418	974	1217	1942	1499
Halls Creek								1192	1556	1184	1336	1497	1054
Jabiru							1166	254	1392	948	1191	1916	1473
Katherine						295	871	321	1097	653	896	1621	1178
Kulgera					1451	1746	1327	1772	1250	1478	555	318	273
Kununurra (WA)				1685	513	808	358	834	1435	1063	1234	1855	1412
Mataranka			618	1346	105	400	974	426	992	548	791	1516	1073
Nhulunbuy		725	1235	2071	722	1017	1593	1043	1717	1273	1516	2241	1798
Tennant Creek	1293	568	1011	778	673	968	1132	994	472	700	223	948	505

Distances are shown in kilometres and follow the most direct major sealed route where possible

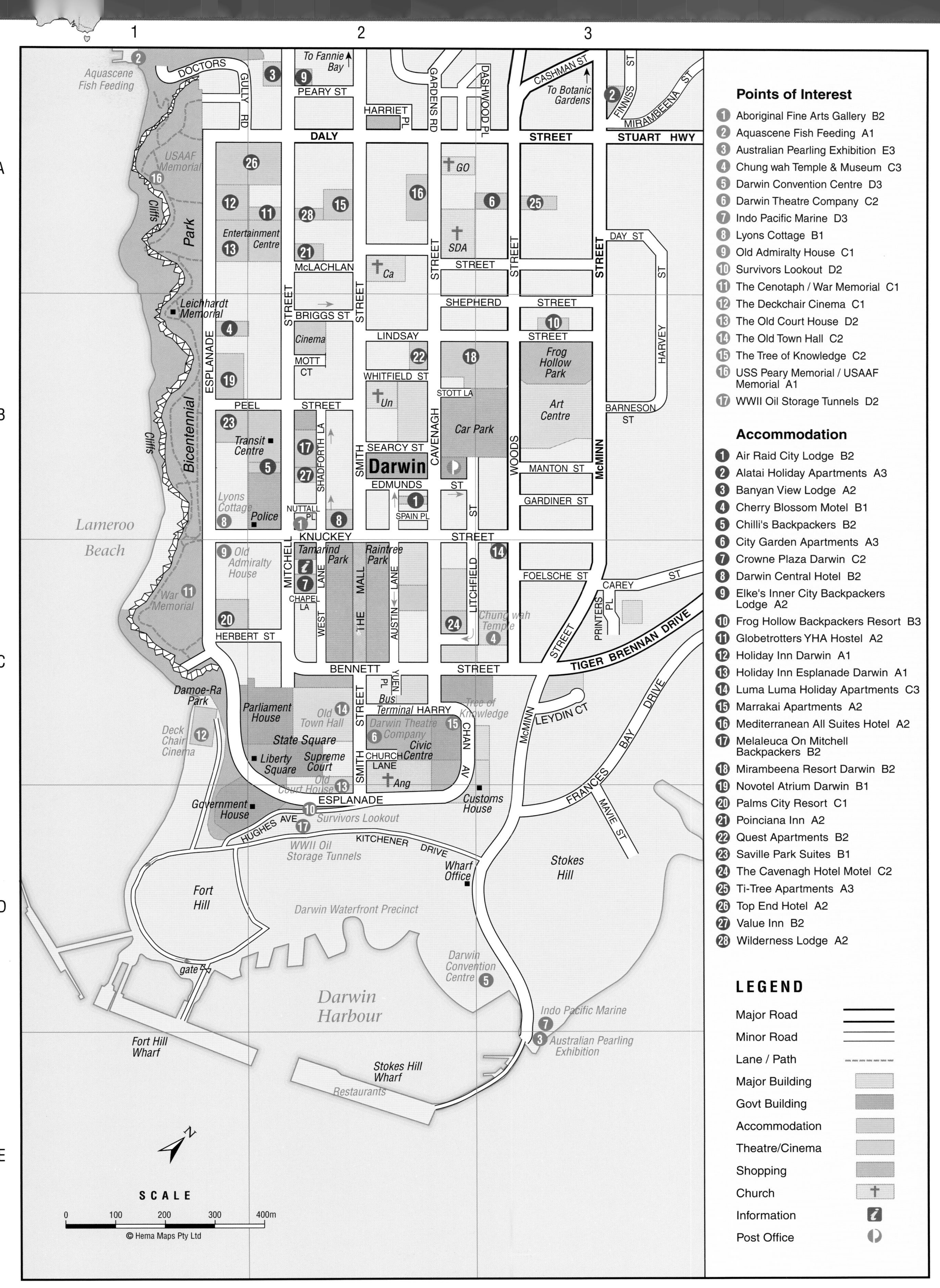

1
2
3
A
B
C
D
E
Points of Interest
1 Aboriginal Fine Arts Gallery B2
2 Aquascene Fish Feeding A1
3 Australian Pearling Exhibition E3
4 Chung wah Temple & Museum C3
5 Darwin Convention Centre D3
6 Darwin Theatre Company C2
7 Indo Pacific Marine D3
8 Lyons Cottage B1
9 Old Admiralty House C1
10 Survivors Lookout D2
11 The Cenotaph / War Memorial C1
12 The Deckchair Cinema C1
13 The Old Court House D2
14 The Old Town Hall C2
15 The Tree of Knowledge C2
16 USS Peary Memorial / USAAF Memorial A1
17 WWII Oil Storage Tunnels D2
Accommodation
1 Air Raid City Lodge B2
2 Alatai Holiday Apartments A3
3 Banyan View Lodge A2
4 Cherry Blossom Motel B1
5 Chilli's Backpackers B2
6 City Garden Apartments A3
7 Crowne Plaza Darwin C2
8 Darwin Central Hotel B2
9 Elke's Inner City Backpackers Lodge A2
10 Frog Hollow Backpackers Resort B3
11 Globetrotters YHA Hostel A2
12 Holiday Inn Darwin A1
13 Holiday Inn Esplanade Darwin A1
14 Luma Luma Holiday Apartments C3
15 Marrakai Apartments A2
16 Mediterranean All Suites Hotel A2
17 Melaleuca On Mitchell Backpackers B2
18 Mirambeena Resort Darwin B2
19 Novotel Atrium Darwin B1
20 Palms City Resort C1
21 Poinciana Inn A2
22 Quest Apartments B2
23 Saville Park Suites B1
24 The Cavenagh Hotel Motel C2
25 Ti-Tree Apartments A3
26 Top End Hotel A2
27 Value Inn B2
28 Wilderness Lodge A2
LEGEND
Major Road
Minor Road
Lane / Path
Major Building
Govt Building
Accommodation
Theatre/Cinema
Shopping
Church
Information
Post Office
Darwin
Aquascene Fish Feeding
DOCTORS
GULLY RD
To Fannie Bay
PEARY ST
HARRIET PL
GARDENS RD
DASHWOOD PL
CASHMAN ST
To Botanic Gardens
FINNISS ST
MIRAMBEENA ST
DALY
STREET
STUART HWY
USAAF Memorial
Cliffs
Park
Bicentennial
Entertainment Centre
McLACHLAN
BRIGGS ST
STREET
SHEPHERD
DAY ST
HARVEY
Leichhardt Memorial
ESPLANADE
Cinema
MOTT CT
LINDSAY
WHITFIELD ST
STOTT LA
Frog Hollow Park
Art Centre
Car Park
BARNESON ST
PEEL
Transit Centre
SHADFORTH LA
SEARCY ST
SMITH
CAVENAGH
WOODS
McMINN
MANTON ST
GARDINER ST
EDMUNDS
SPAIN PL
NUTTALL PL
Lyons Cottage
Police
Lameroo Beach
KNUCKEY
Old Admiralty House
MITCHELL
Tamarind Park
Raintree Park
THE MALL
WEST LANE
AUSTIN LANE
LITCHFIELD
FOELSCHE ST
CAREY ST
PRINTERS PL
CHAPEL LA
War Memorial
Chung wah Temple
HERBERT ST
BENNETT
TIGER BRENNAN DRIVE
YUEN PL
Bus Terminal
HARRY CHAN AV
Tree of Knowledge
LEYDIN CT
Damoe-Ra Park
Parliament House
Old Town Hall
Darwin Theatre Company
Civic Centre
State Square
Deck Chair Cinema
Liberty Square
Supreme Court
CHURCH LANE
Ang
Old Court House
Customs House
FRANCES BAY DRIVE
MAVIE ST
Government House
ESPLANADE
Survivors Lookout
HUGHES AVE
KITCHENER DRIVE
WWII Oil Storage Tunnels
Wharf Office
Stokes Hill
Fort Hill
Darwin Waterfront Precinct
Darwin Convention Centre
gate
Darwin Harbour
Indo Pacific Marine
Australian Pearling Exhibition
Fort Hill Wharf
Stokes Hill Wharf
Restaurants
GO
SDA
Ca
Un
N
SCALE
0
100
200
300
400m
© Hema Maps Pty Ltd

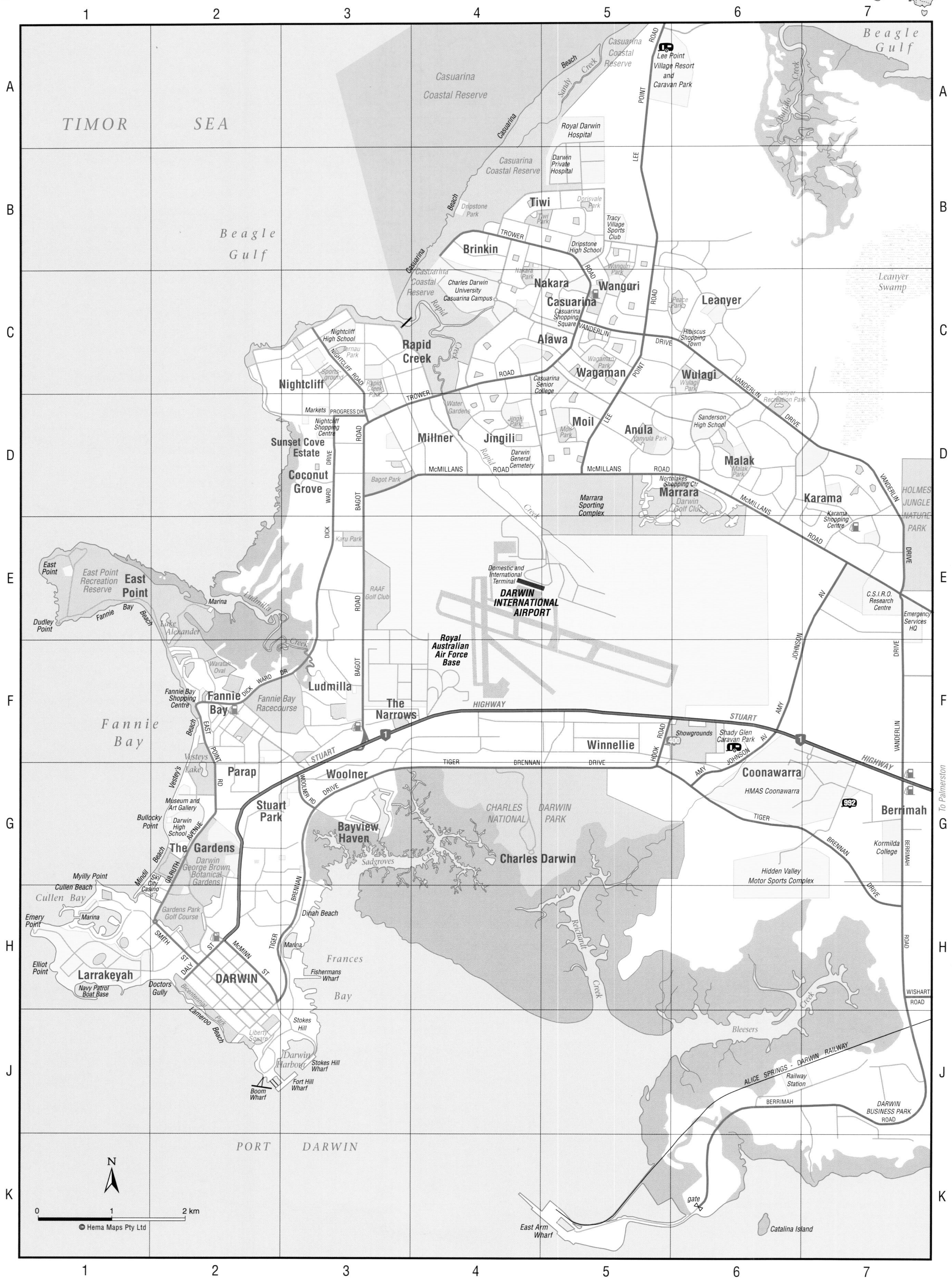

1 2 3 4 5 6 7

A B C D E F G H J K

TIMOR SEA

Beagle Gulf

Casuarina Coastal Reserve

Casuarina Beach

Sandy Creek

Lee Point Village Resort and Caravan Park

LEE POINT ROAD

Royal Darwin Hospital

Darwin Private Hospital

Dripstone Park

Tiwi

Dorisvale Park

Tiwi Park

Tracy Village Sports Club

Dripstone High School

TROWER

Brinkin

Nakara

Nakara Park

Wanguri

Wanguri Park

Charles Darwin University Casuarina Campus

Casuarina

Casuarina Shopping Square

Peace Park

Leanyer

Leanyer Swamp

Buffalo Creek

Hibiscus Shopping Town

VANDERLIN DRIVE

Nightcliff High School

Ternau Park

NIGHTCLIFF ROAD

Rapid Creek

Alawa

Wagaman

Wagaman Park

Wulagi

Wulagi Park

Leanyer Recreation Park

Sports-ground

Nightcliff

Rapid Creek Park

TROWER ROAD

Casuarina Senior College

Markets

PROGRESS DR

Nightcliff Shopping Centre

Water Gardens

Jingili Park

Moil

Moil Park

Anula

Anula Park

Sanderson High School

Sunset Cove Estate

Millner

Jingili

Darwin General Cemetery

Malak

Malak Park

McMILLANS ROAD

Bagot Park

Coconut Grove

Nightcliff Shopping Ctr

Marrara

Darwin Golf Club

Marrara Sporting Complex

Karama

Karama Shopping Centre

HOLMES JUNGLE NATURE PARK

DICK WARD DRIVE

BAGOT ROAD

Karu Park

East Point

East Point Recreation Reserve

Domestic and International Terminal

DARWIN INTERNATIONAL AIRPORT

RAAF Golf Club

C.S.I.R.O. Research Centre

Emergency Services HQ

Dudley Point

Fannie Bay

Marina

Ludmilla Creek

Lake Alexander

Royal Australian Air Force Base

AMY JOHNSON AV

VANDERLIN DRIVE

Waratah Oval

Fannie Bay Shopping Centre

Fannie Bay Racecourse

Ludmilla

The Narrows

STUART HIGHWAY

Showgrounds

Shady Glen Caravan Park

HOOK ROAD

Winnellie

EAST POINT RD

Vesteys Lake

Vestey's Beach

Parap

TIGER BRENNAN DRIVE

Woolner

WOOLNER RD

Coonawarra

HMAS Coonawarra

To Palmerston

Museum and Art Gallery

Bullocky Point

Darwin High School

GILRUTH AVENUE

Stuart Park

Bayview Haven

CHARLES DARWIN NATIONAL PARK

Berrimah

Charles Darwin

Kormilda College

BERRIMAH ROAD

Mindil Beach

Sky City Casino

The Gardens

Darwin George Brown Botanical Gardens

Sadgroves Creek

Hidden Valley Motor Sports Complex

Myilly Point

Cullen Beach

Cullen Bay

Emery Point

Marina

Gardens Park Golf Course

Dinah Beach

Reichardt Creek

SMITH ST

DALY ST

McMINN ST

Frances Bay

Marina

Elliot Point

Larrakeyah

Navy Patrol Boat Base

Doctors Gully

DARWIN

Fishermans Wharf

Bay

WISHART ROAD

Bicentennial Park

Lameroo Beach

Liberty Square

Stokes Hill

Bleesers Creek

Darwin Harbour

Stokes Hill Wharf

ALICE SPRINGS - DARWIN RAILWAY

Railway Station

Boom Wharf

Fort Hill Wharf

BERRIMAH

DARWIN BUSINESS PARK ROAD

PORT DARWIN

N

0 1 2 km

gate

East Arm Wharf

Catalina Island

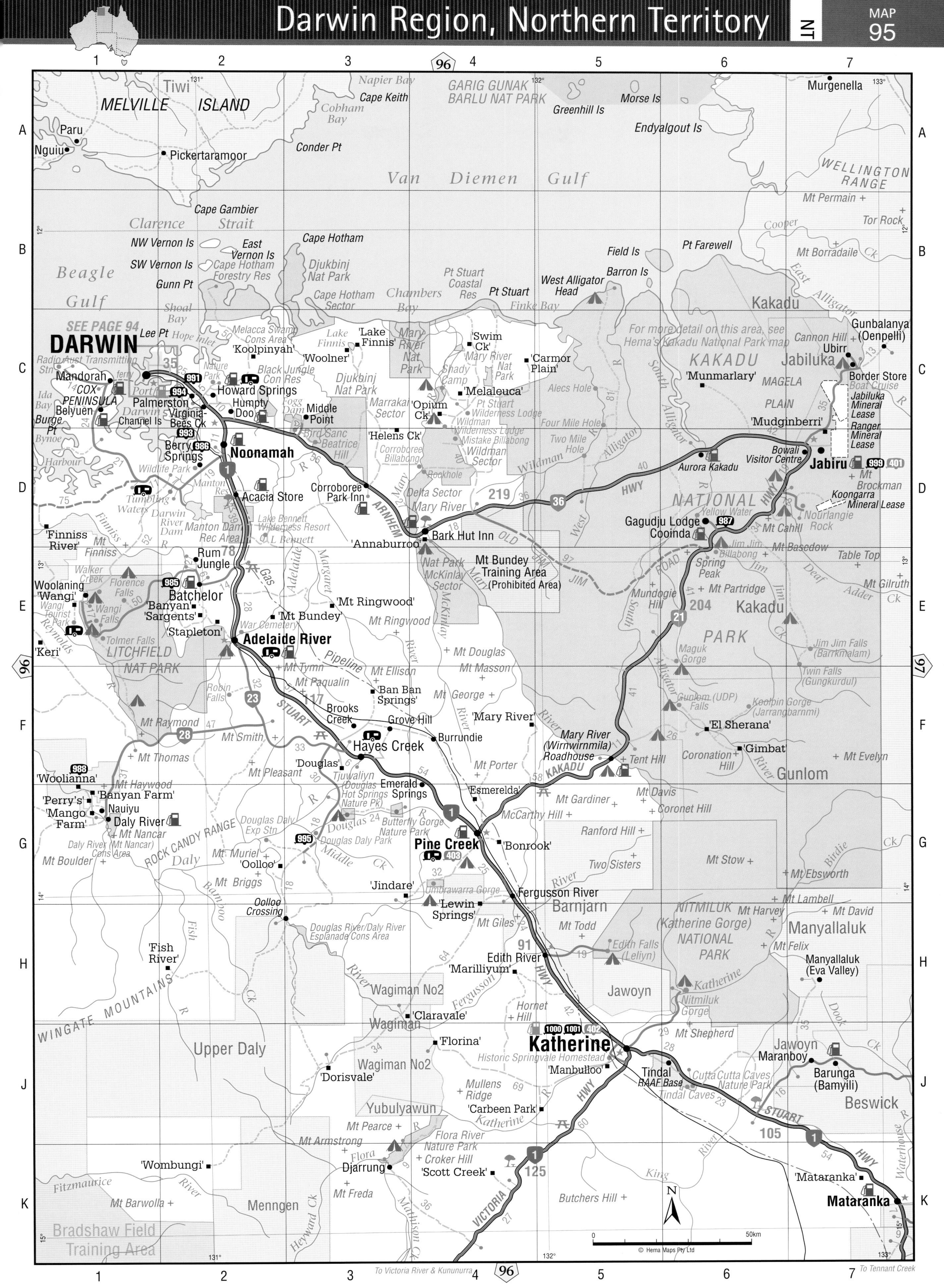

DARWIN
Noonamah
Batchelor
Adelaide River
Hayes Creek
Pine Creek
Katherine
Jabiru
Mataranka
MELVILLE ISLAND
Van Diemen Gulf
Clarence Strait
Beagle Gulf
KAKADU NATIONAL PARK
LITCHFIELD NAT PARK
NITMILUK (Katherine Gorge) NATIONAL PARK
SEE PAGE 94
For more detail on this area, see Hema's Kakadu National Park map
To Victoria River & Kununurra
To Tennant Creek
© Hema Maps Pty Ltd

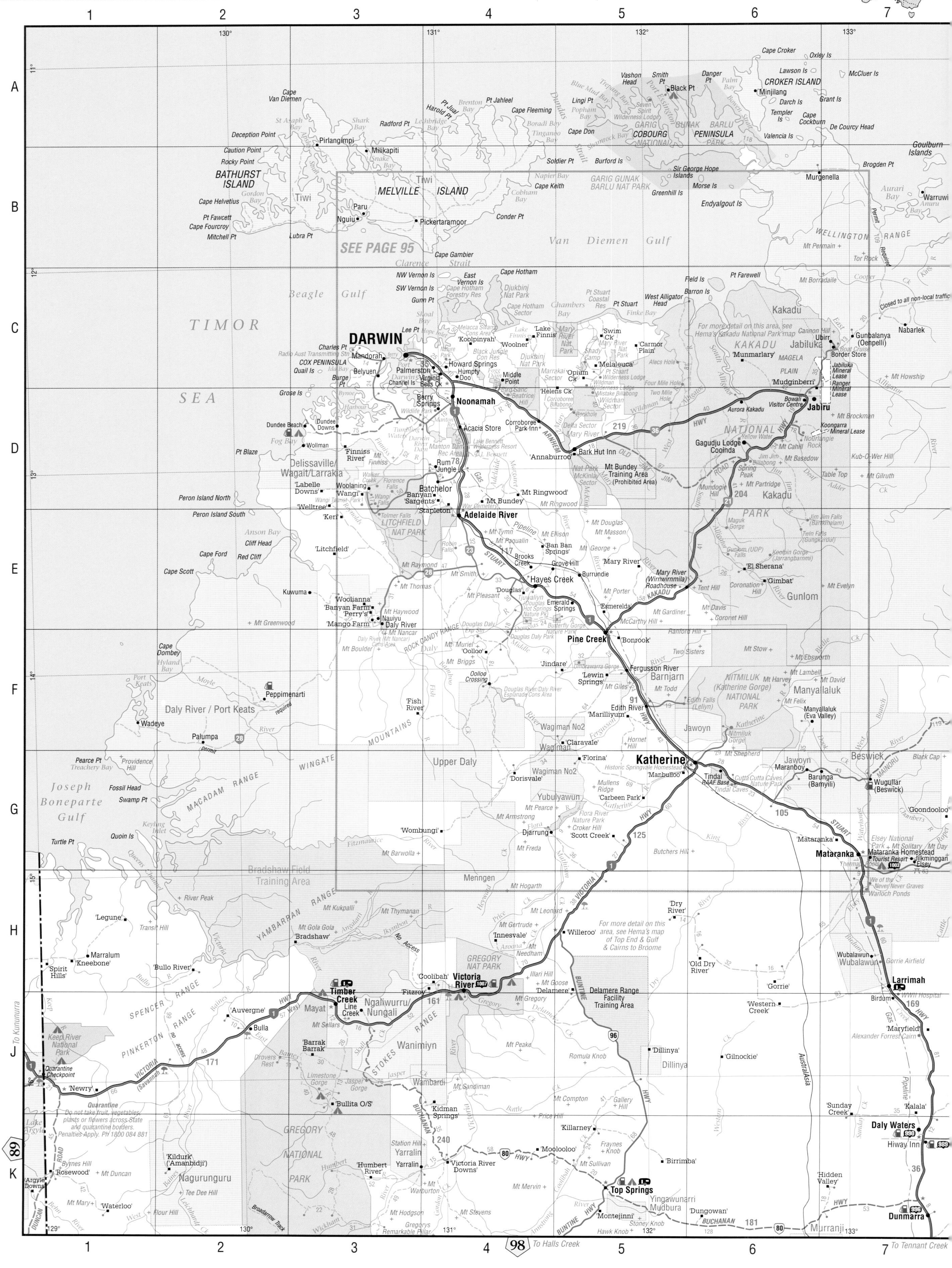

SEE PAGE 95

Cape Croker, Oxley Is, Lawson Is, McCluer Is, CROKER ISLAND, Minjilang, Darch Is, Grant Is, Templer Is, Cape Cockburn, De Courcy Head, Valencia Is, Goulburn Islands, Brogden Pt, Murgenella, Aurari Bay, Warruwi

Vashon Head, Smith Pt, Black Pt, Danger Pt, Palm Bay, Bowen Strait, Seven Spirit Wilderness Lodge, GARIG GUNAK BARLU COBOURG PENINSULA NATIONAL PARK, Port Essington, Trepang Bay, Blue Mud Bay, Lingi Pt, Popham Bay, Cape Don, Shoalrock Bay, Burford Is, Soldier Pt, Sir George Hope Islands, Morse Is, Endyalgout Is, Greenhill Is, GARIG GUNAK BARLU NAT PARK, Napier Bay, Cape Keith, Dundas Strait

Cape Van Diemen, St Asaph Bay, Shark Bay, Radford Pt, Pt Jahleel, Brenton Bay, Pt Jual, Harold Pt, Lethbridge Bay, Cape Fleeming, Boradi Bay, Tinganoo Bay, Deception Point, Pirlangimpi, Milikapiti, Snake Bay, Caution Point, Rocky Point, BATHURST ISLAND, Tiwi, MELVILLE ISLAND, Gordon Bay, Cape Helvetius, Paru, Nguiu, Pickertaramoor, Cobham Bay, Conder Pt, Pt Fawcett, Cape Fourcroy, Mitchell Pt, Lubra Pt

Van Diemen Gulf, Cape Gambier, Clarence Strait, Cape Hotham, NW Vernon Is, SW Vernon Is, East Vernon Is, Cape Hotham Forestry Res, Djukbinji Nat Park, Gum Pt, Beagle Gulf, TIMOR SEA, Cape Hotham Sector, Chambers Bay, Pt Stuart Coastal Res, Pt Stuart, West Alligator Head, Finke Bay, Field Is, Barron Is, Pt Farewell, WELLINGTON RANGE, Mt Permain, Tor Rock, Mt Borradaile, Closed to all non-local traffic

DARWIN, Lee Pt, Charles Pt, Mandorah, Radio Aust Transmitting Stn, COX PENINSULA, Quail Is, Belyuen, Palmerston, Howard Springs, Humpty Doo, Virginia, Bees Ck, Channel Is, Middle Point, Burge Pt, Grose Is, 'Koolpinyah', 'Woolner', 'Lake Finniss', Mary River Nat Park, 'Swim Ck', 'Carmor Plain', 'Melaleuca', Djukbinji Nat Park, Marrakai Sector, 'Opium Ck', Shady Camp, Pt Stuart Wilderness Lodge, Wildman Wilderness Lodge, 'Helens Ck', Corroboree Billabong, Alecs Hole, Four Mile Hole, Two Mile Hole

For more detail on this area, see Hema's Kakadu National Park map

Kakadu, KAKADU, 'Munmarlary', MAGELA PLAIN, Jabiluka, Ubirr, Cannon Hill, Border Store, Gunbalanya (Oenpelli), Nabarlek, 'Mudginberri', Jabiluka Mineral Lease, Ranger Mineral Lease, Mt Howship, Bowali Visitor Centre, Jabiru, Aurora Kakadu, Mt Brockman, Koongarra Mineral Lease, Nourlangie Rock, Gagudju Lodge Cooinda, Yellow Water, Mt Cahill, Jim Jim Billabong, Mt Basedow, Kub-O-Wer Hill, Table Top, Mt Gilruth, Spring Peak, Mt Partridge, Mundogie Hill, NATIONAL PARK

Noonamah, Berry Springs, Wildlife Park, Dundee Beach, Dundee Downs, Fog Bay, Wollman, Acacia Store, Corroboree Park Inn, Bark Hut Inn, 'Annaburroo', Mary River, Wildman Sector, Mt Bundey Training Area (Prohibited Area), Delta Sector, Pt Blaze, 'Finniss River', Mt Finniss, Manton Dam Rec Area, Lake Bennett Wilderness Resort, Rum Jungle, Delissaville/ Wagait/Larrakia, 'Labelle Downs', Woolaning, 'Wangi', Batchelor, 'Banyan', 'Sargents', Stapleton, 'Welltree', 'Mt Ringwood', 'Mt Bundey', War Cemetery, Peron Island North, Peron Island South, 'Keri', Adelaide River, LITCHFIELD NAT PARK, Tolmer Falls, Wangi Falls, Florence Falls, Walker Creek

Anson Bay, Cliff Head, Cape Ford, Red Cliff, Cape Scott, 'Litchfield', Mt Tymn, Mt Paqualin, Mt Ellison, Mt Douglas, Mt Masson, Robin Falls, 'Ban Ban Springs', Mt George, Brooks Creek, Grove Hill, 'Mary River', Mary River Roadhouse (Wirnwirnmila), Burrundie, Hayes Creek, Mt Raymond, Mt Smith, Mt Thomas, Kuwuma, 'Woolianna', 'Banyan Farm', 'Perry's', Mt Haywood, Nauiyu, Daly River, 'Mango Farm', 'Douglas', Mt Pleasant, Tjuwaliyn (Douglas) Hot Springs Nature Park, Emerald Springs, Mt Porter, 'Esmerelda', Mt Gardiner, Mt Davis, Coronet Hill, Tent Hill, 'El Sherana', 'Gimbat', Coronation Hill, Gunlom, Mt Evelyn, Jim Jim Falls, Twin Falls, Gunlom (UDP) Falls, Koolpin Gorge, PARK, Kakadu

Mt Greenwood, Mt Nancar, Daly River (Mt Nancar) Cons Area, Mt Boulder, ROCK CANDY RANGE, Douglas Daly Exp Stn, Douglas Daly Park, Butterfly Gorge Nature Park, McCarthy Hill, Pine Creek, 'Bonrook', Ranford Hill, Two Sisters, Mt Stow, Mt Ebsworth, Mt Muriel, 'Oolloo', Mt Briggs, Oolloo Crossing, 'Jindare', Umbrawarra Gorge, 'Lewin Springs', Mt Giles, Fergusson River, Barnjarn, NITMILUK (Katherine Gorge) NATIONAL PARK, Mt Harvey, Mt Lambell, Mt David, Manyallaluk, Mt Todd, Edith Falls (Leliyn), Mt Felix, Manyallaluk (Eva Valley), Edith River, 'Marrilliyum', Jawoyn, Nitmiluk Gorge

Cape Dombey, Hyland Bay, Moyle, Port Keats, Peppimenarti, Daly River / Port Keats, Wadeye, Palumpa, 'Fish River', MOUNTAINS, Douglas River/Daly River Esplanade Cons Area, Wagiman No2, Wagiman, 'Claravale', Hornet Hill

Pearce Pt, Treachery Bay, Providence Hill, WINGATE, Joseph Bonaparte Gulf, Fossil Head, Swamp Pt, MACADAM RANGE, Upper Daly, 'Florina', Katherine, Historic Springvale Homestead, 'Manbulloo', 'Dorisvale', Wagiman No2, Tindal, RAAF Base, Cutta Cutta Caves Nature Park, Tindal Caves, Jawoyn, Maranboy, Barunga (Bamyili), Beswick, Wugullar (Beswick), Black Cap, Mullens Ridge, 'Carbeen Park', Yubulyawun, Mt Pearce, Flora River Nature Park, Croker Hill, 'Scott Creek', Djarrung, Mt Armstrong, Mt Freda, 'Wombungi', Keyling Inlet, Quoin Is, Turtle Pt, Fitzmaurice, Mt Barwolla, King, Butchers Hill, 'Goondooloo', 'Mataranka', Mataranka, Elsey National Park, Mt Solitary, Mataranka Homestead Tourist Resort, Jilkmingan, Elsey, Thermal Pools, We of the Never Never Graves, Warloch Ponds

Bradshaw Field Training Area, Queens Channel, Mennqen, Mt Hogarth, River Peak, Mt Kukpalli, YAMBARRAN RANGE, Mt Thymanan, Mt Gola Gola, 'Bradshaw', No Access, 'Legune', Transit Hill, Mt Leonard, Mt Gertrude, 'Innesvale', Mt Needham, Aroona, 'Willeroo', 'Dry River'

For more detail on this area, see Hema's map of Top End & Gulf & Cairns to Broome

'Old Dry River', Wubalawun, Gorrie Airfield, Larrimah, WWII Hospital, Birdum, 'Gorrie'

'Marralum', 'Kneebone', 'Spirit Hills', 'Bullo River', SPENCER RANGE, GREGORY NAT PARK, 'Coolibah', Timber Creek, 'Fitzroy', Victoria River, Illari Hill, Mt Goose, 'Delamere', Delamere Range Facility Training Area, BUNTINE HWY, Mayat, Line Creek, Ngaliwurru/Nungali, Mt Gregory, 'Western Creek', 'Auvergne', Mt Sellars, PINKERTON RANGE, no access, Bulla, Keep River National Park, Quarantine Checkpoint, 'Barrak Barrak', Drovers Rest, Wanimiyn, STOKES RANGE, Mt Peake, Romula Knob, 'Dillinya', Dillinya, 'Gilnockie', 'Maryfield', Alexander Forrest Cairn, Limestone Gorge, Jasper Gorge, Wambardi, Mt Sandiman, 'Newry', 'Bullita O/S', 'Kidman Springs', Mt Compton, Gallery Hill, Price Hill, AustralAsia, 'Sunday Creek', 'Kalala', Daly Waters, Hiway Inn, To Kununurra, Lake Argyle

Quarantine
Do not take fruit, vegetables, plants or flowers across State and quarantine borders. Penalties Apply. Ph 1800 084 881

GREGORY NATIONAL PARK, 'Kildurk' ('Amanbidji'), Byrnes Hill, 'Rosewood', Mt Duncan, 'Argyle Downs', Nagurunguru, Tee Dee Hill, Mt Mary, 'Waterloo', Flour Hill, Broadarrow Track, Station Hill, Yarralin, 'Humbert River', Mt Warburton, 'Victoria River Downs', 'Mooloolooo', Fraynes Knob, Mt Sullivan, 'Killarney', 'Birrimba', 'Hidden Valley', Mt Mervin, Top Springs, Yingawunarri Mudbura, 'Dungowan', Mt Hodgson, Mt Stevens, Gregorys Remarkable Pillar, 'Montejinni', Hawk Knob, Stoney Knob, Murranji, Dunmarra, DUNCAN ROAD, BUCHANAN HWY, VICTORIA HWY, STUART HWY, ARNHEM HWY, KAKADU HWY

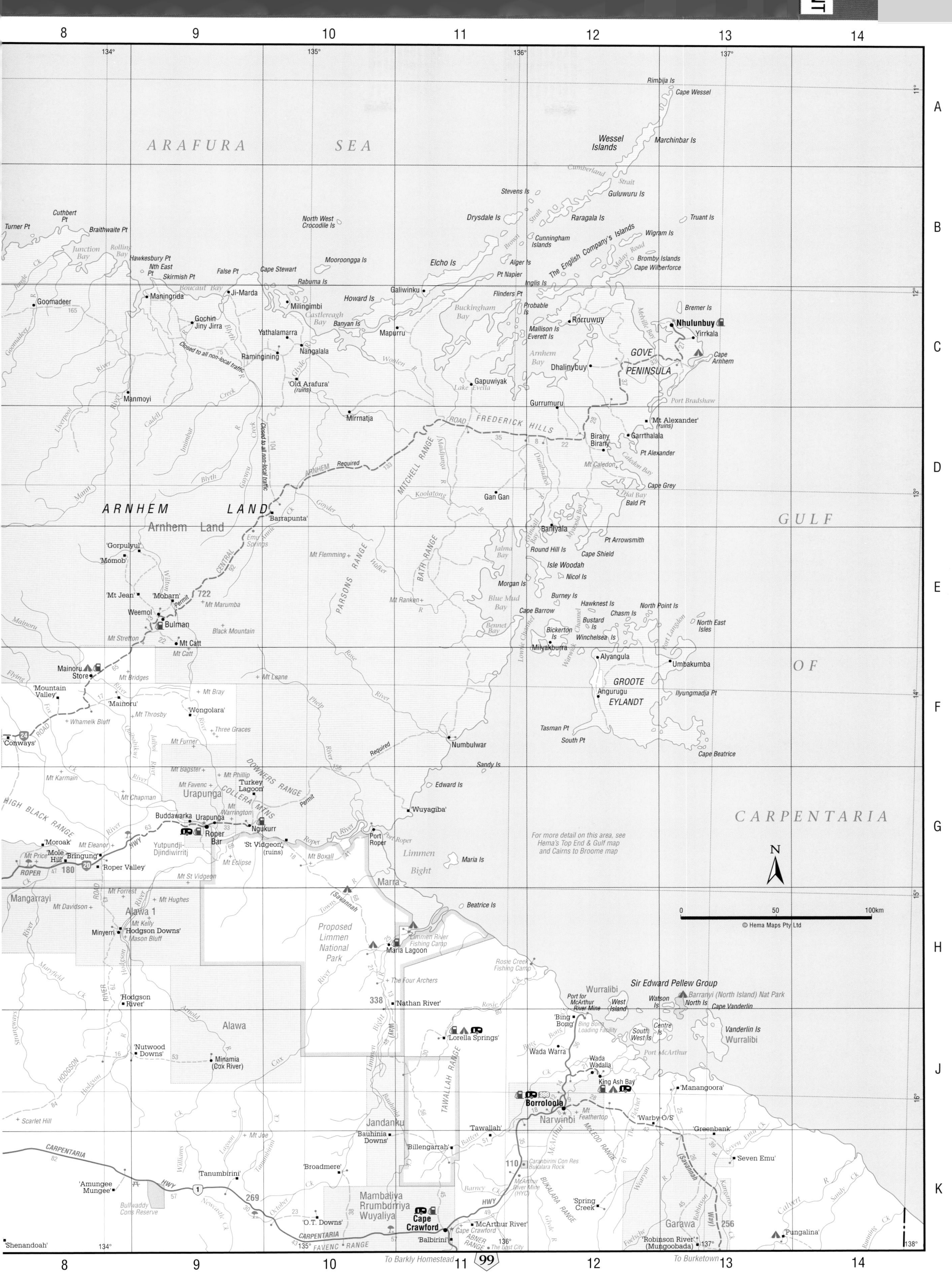

ARAFURA SEA
GULF OF CARPENTARIA
ARNHEM LAND
Arnhem Land
Wessel Islands
Rimbija Is
Cape Wessel
Marchinbar Is
Cumberland Strait
Stevens Is
Guluwuru Is
Drysdale Is
Raragala Is
Truant Is
Cunningham Islands
The English Company's Islands
Wigram Is
Bromby Islands
Cape Wilberforce
Alger Is
Pt Napier
Inglis Is
Elcho Is
Galiwinku
Flinders Pt
Probable Is
Mallison Is
Everett Is
Rorruwuy
Bremer Is
Nhulunbuy
Yirrkala
Cape Arnhem
GOVE PENINSULA
Dhalinybuy
Arnhem Bay
Port Bradshaw
Gurrumuru
Gapuwiyak
Lake Evella
Buckingham Bay
Howard Is
Mapurru
Banyan Is
North West Crocodile Is
Mooroongga Is
Cape Stewart
Rabuma Is
Milingimbi
Castlereagh Bay
Yathalamarra
Nangalala
Ramingining
Closed to all non-local traffic
'Old Arafura' (ruins)
Mirrnatja
Cuthbert Pt
Turner Pt
Braithwaite Pt
Junction Bay
Rolling Bay
Hawkesbury Pt
Nth East Pt
Skirmish Pt
False Pt
Boucaut Bay
Ji-Marda
Maningrida
Goomadeer
Gochin Jiny Jirra
Manmoyi
Liverpool
Mann
Blyth
FREDERICK HILLS
ROAD
CENTRAL ARNHEM
Required
Permit
MITCHELL RANGE
BATH RANGE
PARSONS RANGE
'Mt Alexander' (ruins)
Garrthalala
Birany Birany
Pt Alexander
Mt Caledon
Caledon Bay
Cape Grey
Trial Bay
Bald Pt
Gan Gan
Koolatong
Baniyala
Pt Arrowsmith
Round Hill Is
Cape Shield
Isle Woodah
Nicol Is
Jalma Bay
Morgan Is
Blue Mud Bay
Burney Is
Hawknest Is
Chasm Is
North Point Is
North East Isles
Cape Barrow
Bennet Bay
Bickerton Is
Bustard Is
Winchelsea Is
Milyakburra
Alyangula
Umbakumba
GROOTE EYLANDT
Angurugu
Ilyungmadja Pt
Tasman Pt
South Pt
Cape Beatrice
'Barrapunta'
Goyder
Emu Springs
'Gorpulyul'
'Momob'
Mt Flemming
Walker
'Mt Jean'
'Mobarn'
722
Mt Marumba
Mt Ranken
Weemol
Bulman
Black Mountain
Mt Stretton
Mt Catt
Mainoru Store
Mt Bridges
Mt Leane
'Mountain Valley'
'Mainoru'
Mt Bray
'Wongolara'
Mt Throsby
Whamelk Bluff
Three Graces
'Conways'
Mt Furner
Numbulwar
Sandy Is
Edward Is
'Wuyagiba'
Mt Karmain
Mt Bagster
Mt Phillip
Mt Favenc
DOWNERS RANGE
COLLERA MTNS
Urapunga
Turkey Lagoon
Mt Chapman
HIGH BLACK RANGE
Mt Warrington
Buddawarka
Urapunga
Roper Bar
Ngukurr
'Moroak'
Mt Eleanor
Yutpundji-Djindiwirritj
'St Vidgeon' (ruins)
Port Roper
Limmen Bight
Maria Is
For more detail on this area, see Hema's Top End & Gulf map and Cairns to Broome map
'Mole Hill'
Mt Price
'Bringung'
ROPER
180
'Roper Valley'
Mt Eclipse
Mt Boxall
Mt St Vidgeon
Mangarrayi
Mt Forrest
Mt Hughes
Mt Davidson
Alawa 1
Mt Kelly
Minyerri
'Hodgson Downs'
Mason Bluff
Marra
Beatrice Is
Proposed Limmen National Park
Limmen River Fishing Camp
Maria Lagoon
Rosie Creek Fishing Camp
The Four Archers
'Hodgson River'
338
'Nathan River'
Alawa
'Lorella Springs'
'Nutwood Downs'
Minamia (Cox River)
Sir Edward Pellew Group
Barranyi (North Island) Nat Park
Wurralibi
Port for McArthur River Mine
West Island
Watson Is
North Is
Cape Vanderlin
'Bing Bong'
Bing Bong Loading Facility
South West Is
Centre Is
Vanderlin Is
Wurralibi
Port McArthur
Wada Warra
Wada Wadalla
King Ash Bay
TAWALLAH RANGE
Borroloola
Narwinbi
Mt Feathertop
'Manangoora'
'Warby O/S'
'Greenbank'
'Seven Emu'
Jandanku
Scarlet Hill
Mt Joe
'Bauhinia Downs'
Tawallah
'Billengarrah'
110
Caranbirini Con Res
Bukalara Rock
McARTHUR RANGE
BUKALARA RANGE
CARPENTARIA HWY
'Broadmere'
Tanumbirini
'Amungee Mungee'
Bullwaddy Cons Reserve
269
Mambaliya Rrumburriya Wuyaliya
Cape Crawford
'O.T. Downs'
'McArthur River'
McArthur River Mine (HYC)
'Spring Creek'
Garawa
256
'Pungalina'
'Balbirini'
Cape Crawford
ABNER RANGE
The Lost City
FAVENC RANGE
'Robinson River' (Mungoobada)
'Shenandoah'
To Barkly Homestead
To Burketown
0 50 100km
© Hema Maps Pty Ltd

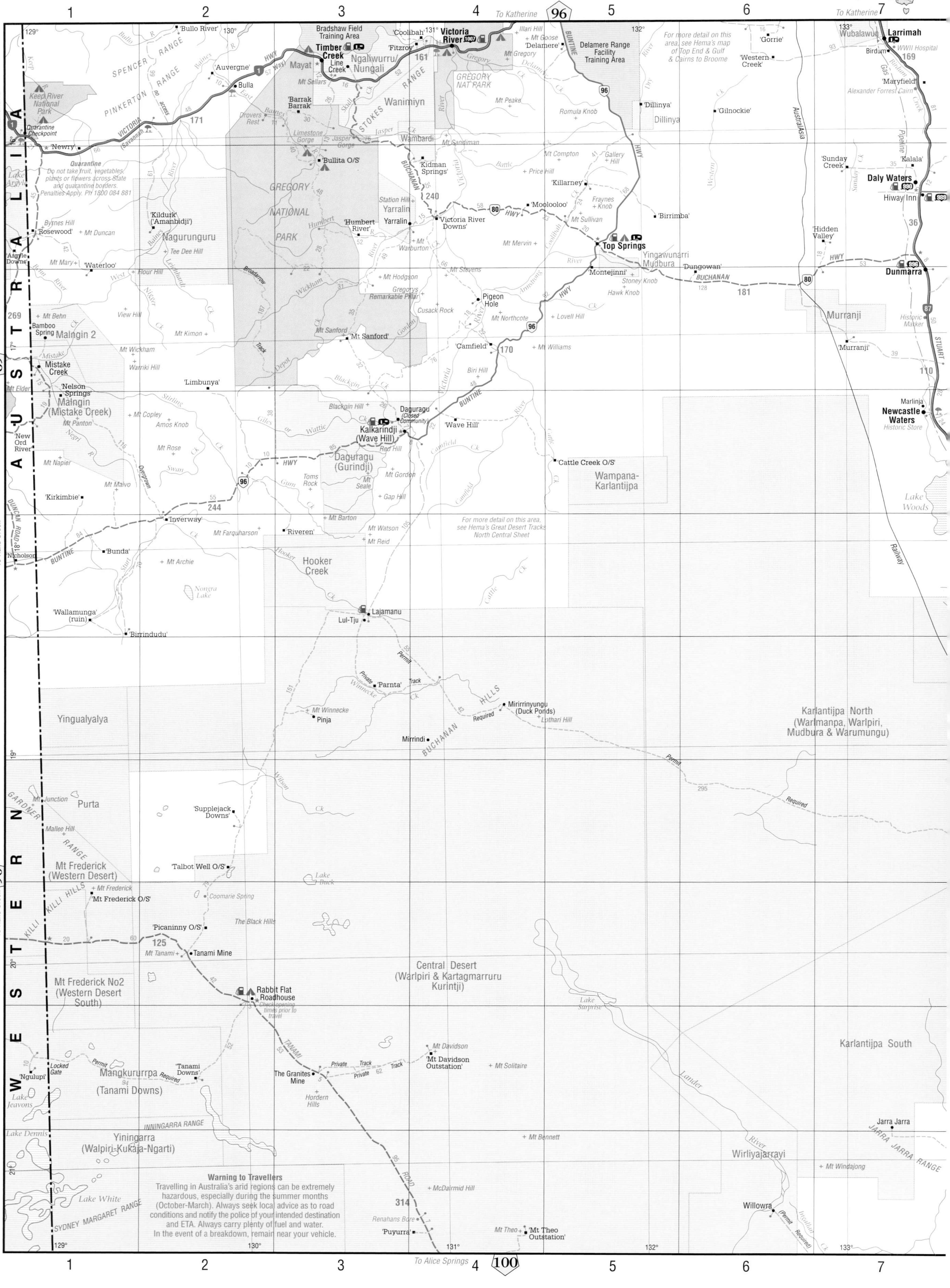

Central Northern Territory

Quarantine
Do not take fruit, vegetables, plants or flowers across State and quarantine borders. Penalties Apply. Ph 1800 084 881

For more detail on this area, see Hema's map of Top End & Gulf & Cairns to Broome

For more detail on this area, see Hema's Great Desert Tracks North Central Sheet

Warning to Travellers
Travelling in Australia's arid regions can be extremely hazardous, especially during the summer months (October-March). Always seek local advice as to road conditions and notify the police of your intended destination and ETA. Always carry plenty of fuel and water. In the event of a breakdown, remain near your vehicle.

Timber Creek
Victoria River
Larrimah
Daly Waters
Dunmarra
Top Springs
Newcastle Waters
Kalkarindji (Wave Hill)
Lajamanu
Rabbit Flat Roadhouse
Tanami Mine
Keep River National Park
Gregory National Park
Delamere Range Facility Training Area
Bradshaw Field Training Area
Hooker Creek
Central Desert (Warlpiri & Kartagmarruru Kurintji)
Karlantijpa North (Warlmanpa, Warlpiri, Mudbura & Warumungu)
Karlantijpa South
Mt Frederick (Western Desert)
Mt Frederick No2 (Western Desert South)
Mangkururrpa (Tanami Downs)
Yiningarra (Walpiri-Kukaja-Ngarti)
Wirliyajarrayi
Wampana-Karlantijpa
Yingualyalya
Purta
Murranji
Dillinya
Wanimiyn
Nagurunguru
Malngin (Mistake Creek)
Daguragu (Gurindji)
Ngaliwurru/Nungali

WESTERN AUSTRALIA

To Katherine · To Kununurra · To Halls Creek · To Alice Springs

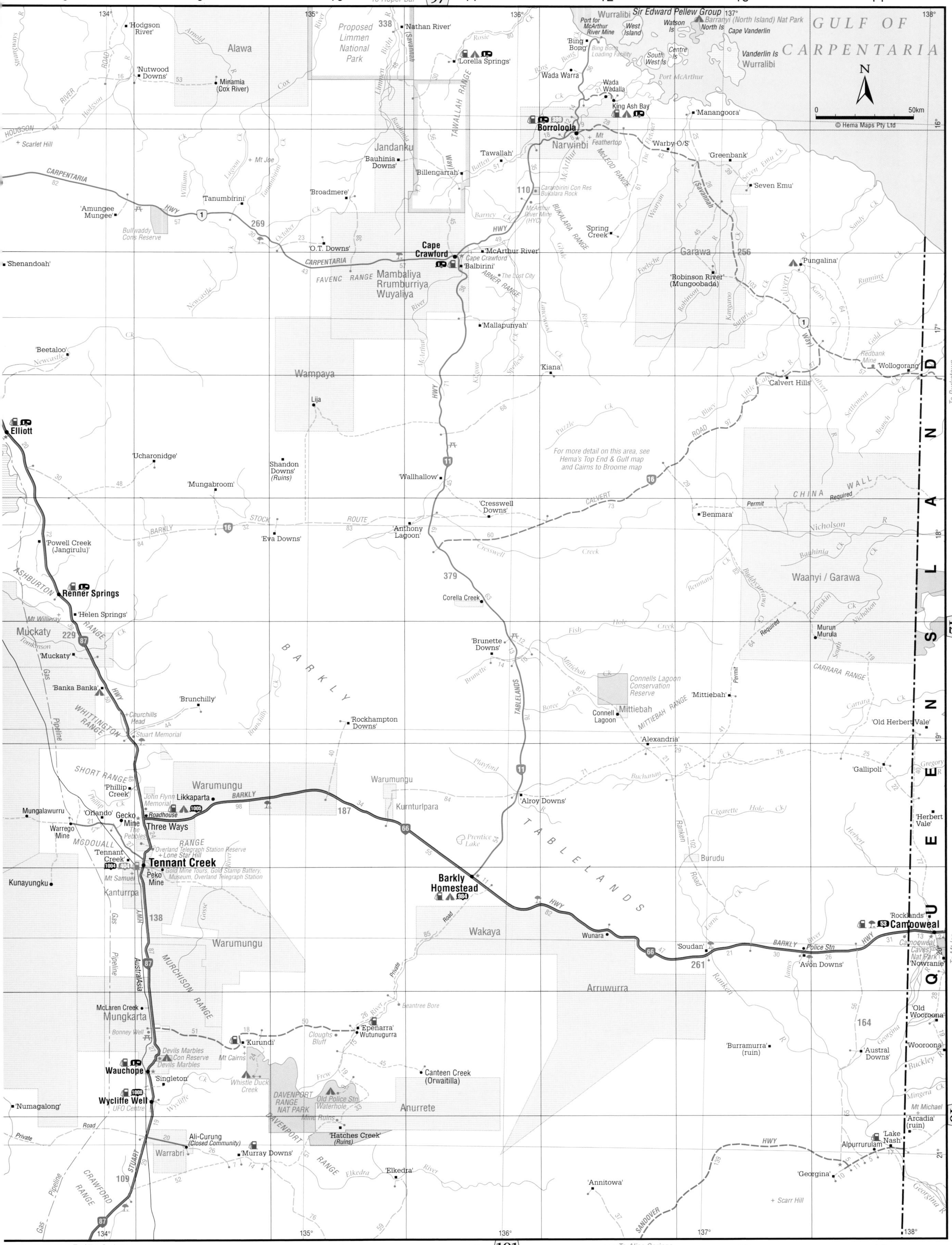

8 9 10 To Roper Bar 97 11 12 13 14

GULF OF CARPENTARIA

Sir Edward Pellew Group
Wurralibi
Port for McArthur River Mine
West Island
Barranyi (North Island) Nat Park
North Is
Cape Vanderlin
Watson Is
Centre Is
South West Is
Vanderlin Is
Wurralibi
'Bing Bong'
Bing Bong Loading Facility
Port McArthur
'Wada Warra'
Wada Wadalla
King Ash Bay
'Manangoora'
© Hema Maps Pty Ltd
0 50km

'Hodgson River'
Alawa
'Nutwood Downs'
Minamia (Cox River)
Proposed Limmen National Park
338
'Nathan River'
'Lorella Springs'
Tawallah Range
Jandanku
'Bauhinia Downs'
'Billengarrah'
'Tawallah'
Borroloola
Narwinbi
Mt Feathertop
'Warby O/S'
'Greenbank'
'Seven Emu'
Hodgson River
Scarlet Hill
Mt Joe
Carpentaria Hwy
'Amungee Mungee'
Bullwaddy Cons Reserve
'Tanumbirini'
269
'Broadmere'
110
Caranbirini Con Res
Bukalara Rock
McArthur River Mine (HYC)
Bukalara Range
McLeod Range
'Spring Creek'
Garawa
256
'O.T. Downs'
Cape Crawford
'McArthur River'
Cape Crawford
'Balbirini'
The Lost City
Abner Range
Favenc Range
Mambaliya Rrumburriya Wuyaliya
'Robinson River' (Mungoobada)
'Pungalina'
'Shenandoah'
'Mallapunyah'
'Beetaloo'
Wampaya
'Kiana'
Redbank Mine
'Wollogorang'
'Calvert Hills'
To Burketown
Lija
Elliott
For more detail on this area, see Hema's Top End & Gulf map and Cairns to Broome map
'Ucharonidge'
Shandon Downs' (Ruins)
'Mungabroom'
'Wallhallow'
Calvert Road
China Wall
Permit Required
'Cresswell Downs'
'Benmara'
Barkly Stock Route
'Eva Downs'
'Anthony Lagoon'
'Powell Creek (Jangirulu)'
Nicholson R
Ashburton Range
Renner Springs
379
Waanyi / Garawa
'Helen Springs'
Corella Creek
Mt Willieray
Muckaty
229
'Muckaty'
'Brunette Downs'
Murun Murula
Barkly
Carrara Range
'Banka Banka'
Connells Lagoon Conservation Reserve
Mittiebah
'Mittiebah'
Mittiebah Range
'Brunchilly'
Churchills Head
Whittington Range
Stuart Memorial
'Rockhampton Downs'
Connell Lagoon
Tablelands Hwy
'Alexandria'
'Old Herbert Vale'
Short Range
Warumungu
'Phillip Creek'
John Flynn Memorial
Likkaparta
Warumungu
Kurnturlpara
'Gallipoli'
Mungalawurru
'Orlando'
Gecko Mine
Roadhouse
Three Ways
187
'Alroy Downs'
Warrego Mine
The Pebbles
McDouall Range
Overland Telegraph Station Reserve
Lone Star Hill
Tablelands
'Herbert Vale'
'Tennant Creek'
Tennant Creek
Gold Mine Tours, Gold Stamp Battery, Museum, Overland Telegraph Station
Prentice Lake
Burudu
Kunayungku
Mt Samuel
Peko Mine
Kanturrpa
Barkly Homestead
138
Wakaya
'Rocklands'
Camooweal
Warumungu
Wunara
'Soudan'
261
Barkly Hwy
Police Stn
Camooweal Caves Nat Park
'Nowranie'
To Mt Isa
'Avon Downs'
Murchison Range
Arruwurra
Queensland
McLaren Creek
Mungkarta
Beantree Bore
'Old Wooroona'
164
Bonney Well
'Epenarra' Wutunugurra
Cloughs Bluff
'Kurundi'
Devils Marbles Con Reserve
Devils Marbles
Mt Cairns
'Burramurra' (ruin)
'Austral Downs'
'Wooroona'
Wauchope
'Canteen Creek (Orwaitilla)
'Singleton'
Whistle Duck Creek
Davenport Range Nat Park
Old Police Stn Waterhole
Wycliffe Well
UFO Centre
Anurrete
Mt Michael
'Numagalong'
Mine Ruins
'Arcadia' (ruin)
Davenport Range
'Hatches Creek' (Ruins)
Ali-Curung (Closed Community)
'Lake Nash'
Alpurrurulam
Warrabri
'Murray Downs'
'Georgina'
Crawford Range
109
Stuart Hwy
'Elkedra'
'Annitowa'
Scarr Hill
Sandover Hwy
Georgina R

8 To Alice Springs 9 10 11 101 12 To Alice Springs 13 14

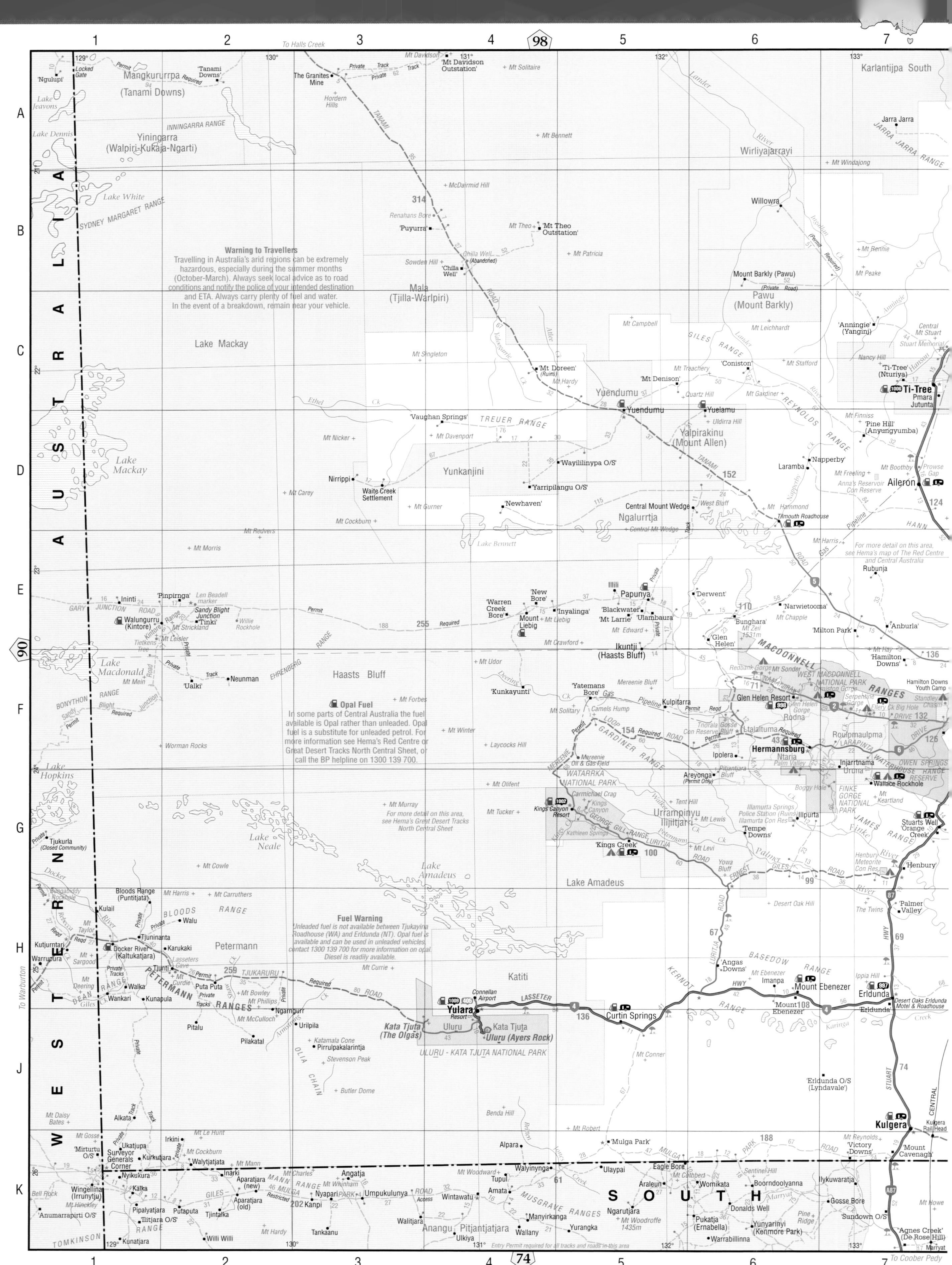
1
2
3
4
5
6
7
98
74
90
A
B
C
D
E
F
G
H
J
K
To Halls Creek
To Coober Pedy
To Warburton
Warning to Travellers
Travelling in Australia's arid regions can be extremely hazardous, especially during the summer months (October-March). Always seek local advice as to road conditions and notify the police of your intended destination and ETA. Always carry plenty of fuel and water. In the event of a breakdown, remain near your vehicle.
Opal Fuel
In some parts of Central Australia the fuel available is Opal rather than unleaded. Opal fuel is a substitute for unleaded petrol. For more information see Hema's Red Centre or Great Desert Tracks North Central Sheet, or call the BP helpline on 1300 139 700.
Fuel Warning
Unleaded fuel is not available between Tjukayirla Roadhouse (WA) and Erldunda (NT). Opal fuel is available and can be used in unleaded vehicles, contact 1300 139 700 for more information on opal. Diesel is readily available.
For more detail on this area, see Hema's Great Desert Tracks North Central Sheet
For more detail on this area, see Hema's map of The Red Centre and Central Australia
Entry Permit required for all tracks and roads in this area
W E S T E R N A U S T R A L I A
S O U T H
Mangkururrpa (Tanami Downs)
Yiningarra (Walpiri-Kukaja-Ngarti)
Mala (Tjilla-Warlpiri)
Lake Mackay
Lake White
SYDNEY MARGARET RANGE
INNINGARRA RANGE
The Granites Mine
'Mt Davidson Outstation'
Karlantijpa South
Jarra Jarra
JARRA JARRA RANGE
Wirliyajarrayi
Willowra
Mount Barkly (Pawu)
Pawu (Mount Barkly)
'Puyurru'
'Mt Theo Outstation'
'Chilla Well'
Yuendumu
Yuelamu
Yalpirakinu (Mount Allen)
TREUER RANGE
Yunkanjini
Nirrippi
Waite Creek Settlement
'Newhaven'
Central Mount Wedge
Ngalurrtja
Tilmouth Roadhouse
Ti-Tree
Aileron
Napperby
Laramba
'Anningie' (Yanginj)
'Coniston'
'Mt Denison'
REYNOLDS RANGE
GILES RANGE
TANAMI ROAD
Lake Bennett
Ininti
Walungurru (Kintore)
'Pinpirnga'
Sandy Blight Junction
Tinki
GARY JUNCTION ROAD
Papunya
Ilili
'Warren Creek Bore'
'New Bore'
Mount Liebig
'Inyalinga'
Ikuntji (Haasts Bluff)
Haasts Bluff
'Derwent'
'Narwietooma'
'Bunghara'
'Milton Park'
'Anburla'
'Glen Helen'
Lake Macdonald
'Ualki'
Neunman
EHRENBERG RANGE
BONYTHON RANGE
'Kunkayunti'
'Yatemans Bore'
Kulpitarra
MACDONNELL RANGES
WEST MACDONNELL NATIONAL PARK
Glen Helen Resort
Rodna
Hermannsburg
Ntaria
Ltalaltuma
Roulpmaulpma
Injartnama
Uruna
Wallace Rockhole
FINKE GORGE NATIONAL PARK
Ipolera
Areyonga
MERENIE LOOP ROAD
GARDINER RANGE
WATARRKA NATIONAL PARK
Kings Canyon Resort
Urrampinyu Iltjiltjarri
'Kings Creek'
GEORGE GILL RANGE
LURITJA ROAD
ERNEST GILES ROAD
Lake Amadeus
Lake Neale
Lake Hopkins
Tjukurla (Closed Community)
Tempe Downs
Illpurta
Stuarts Well
'Orange Creek'
JAMES RANGE
'Henbury'
'Palmer Valley'
Bloods Range (Puntitjata)
BLOODS RANGE
Kulail
Walu
Tjuninanta
Docker River (Kaltukatjara)
Karukaki
Petermann
Kutjuntari
Warrupura
Tjunti
Puta Puta
PETERMANN RANGES
TJUKARURU ROAD
Walka
Wankari
Kunapula
DEAN RANGE
Ngarnpurr
Pitalu
Urilpila
Pilakatal
Pirrulpakalarintja
Katiti
Yulara
Connellan Airport
Kata Tjuta (The Olgas)
Uluru
Kata Tjuta
Uluru (Ayers Rock)
ULURU - KATA TJUTA NATIONAL PARK
LASSETER HWY
Curtin Springs
'Angas Downs'
Imanpa
Mount Ebenezer
'Mount Ebenezer'
BASEDOW RANGE
Erldunda
Desert Oaks Erldunda Motel & Roadhouse
'Erldunda O/S' (Lyndavale')
STUART HWY
Kulgera
Kulgera Rail Head
'Victory Downs'
'Mount Cavenagh'
'Mulga Park'
Alpara
Alkata
'Mirrturtu O/S'
Ukatjupa
Surveyor Generals Corner
Kurkutjara
Irkini
Walytjatjata
Inarki
Angatja
Wingellina (Irrunytju)
Nyikukura
Kalka
Pipalyatjara
Ilitjara O/S
Aparatjara (new)
Aparatjara (old)
Putaputa
Tjintalka
Willi Willi
Kunatjara
'Anumarrapirti O/S'
TOMKINSON RANGE
MANN RANGE
Nyapari
Kanpi
Umpukulunya
Tankaanu
Wintawatu
Walitjara
Amata
Tupul
Walyinynga
MUSGRAVE RANGES
Manyirkanga
Wallany
Ulkiya
Anangu Pitjantjatjara
Ngarutjara
Yurangka
Ulaypai
Eagle Bore
Araleun
Womikata
Boorndoolyanna
Donalds Well
Pukatja (Ernabella)
Yunyarinyi (Kenmore Park)
Warrabillinna
Ilykuwaratja
Gosse Bore
Sundown O/S
'Agnes Creek' (De Rose Hill)
Marryat
MULGA PARK ROAD
129°
130°
131°
132°
133°
22°
23°
24°
25°
26°

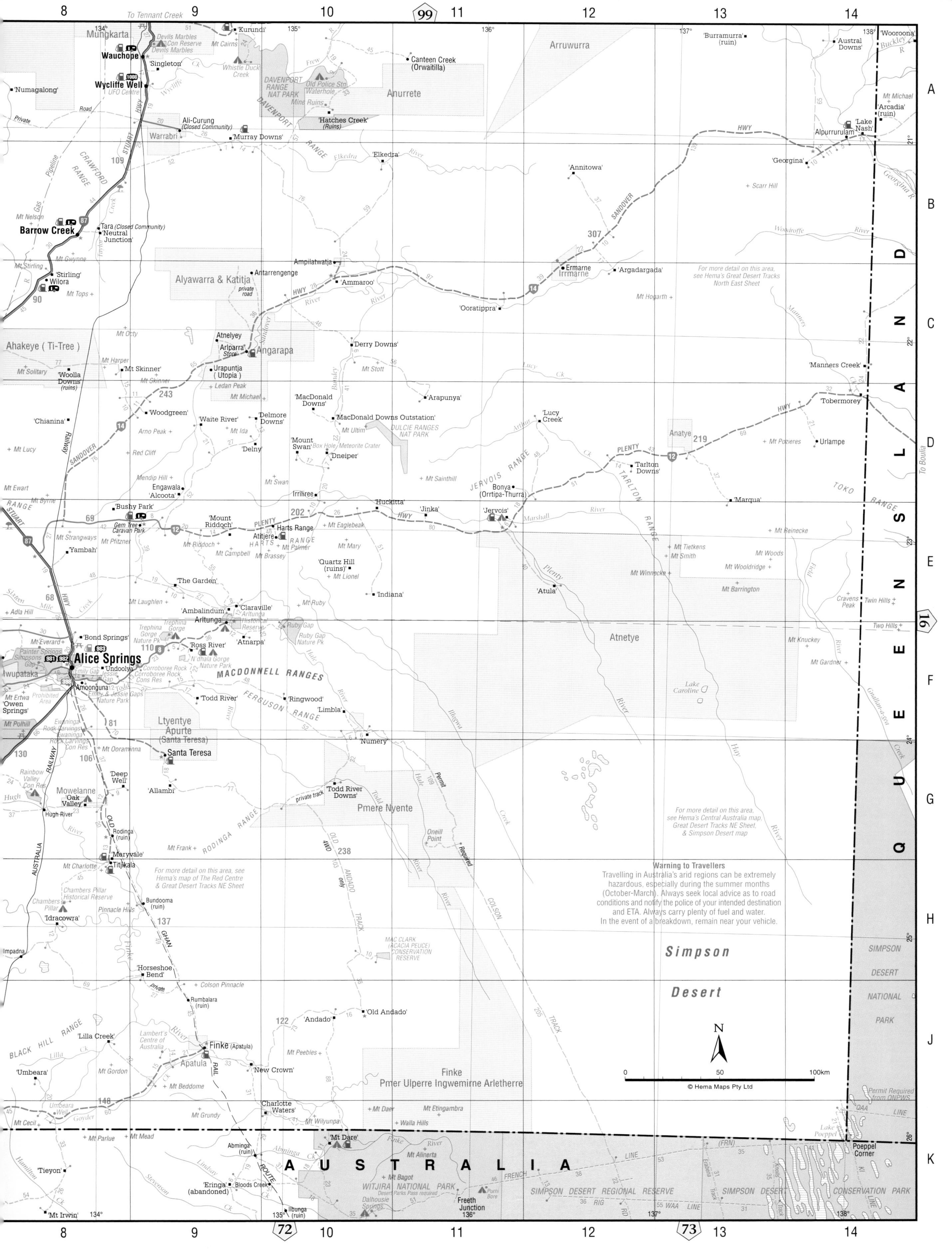

8 9 10 11 12 13 14

A B C D E F G H J K

To Tennant Creek
Mungkarta
Wauchope
Devils Marbles Con Reserve
Devils Marbles
'Kurundi'
Mt Cairns
Whistle Duck Creek
'Singleton'
Wycliffe Well
UFO Centre
'Numagalong'
Ali-Curung (Closed Community)
Warrabri
'Murray Downs'
DAVENPORT RANGE NAT PARK
Old Police Stn
Waterhole
Mine Ruins
'Hatches Creek' (Ruins)
DAVENPORT RANGE
Canteen Creek (Orwaitilla)
Anurrete
Arruwurra
'Burramurra' (ruin)
'Austral Downs'
'Wooroona'
Buckley R
Mt Michael
'Arcadia' (ruin)
'Lake Nash'
Alpurrurulam
'Georgina'
Georgina R
'Elkedra'
Elkedra River
'Annitowa'
+ Scarr Hill
CRAWFORD RANGE
STUART HWY
Gas Pipeline
Mt Nelson
Barrow Creek
Tara (Closed Community)
'Neutral Junction'
SANDOVER HWY
Woodroffe River
Mt Stirling
Mt Gwynne
'Stirling'
Wilora
Mt Tops
Alyawarra & Katitja
private road
Antarrengene
Ampilatwatja
'Ammaroo'
Ermarne
Irrmarne
'Argadargada'
For more detail on this area, see Hema's Great Desert Tracks North East Sheet
Mt Hogarth
'Ooratippra'
Manners
Mt Octy
Ahakeye (Ti-Tree)
Atnelyey
Arlparra Store
Angarapa
'Derry Downs'
Mt Harper
'Mt Skinner'
Mt Solitary
'Woolla Downs' (ruins)
Mt Skinner
Urapuntja (Utopia)
Ledan Peak
Mt Michael
Mt Stott
Lucy Ck
'Manners Creek'
'Tobermorey'
'MacDonald Downs'
'Arapunya'
'Woodgreen'
'Chianina'
'Waite River'
'Delmore Downs'
'MacDonald Downs Outstation'
Mt Ultim
DULCIE RANGES NAT PARK
'Lucy Creek'
Anatye
PLENTY HWY
'Urlampe'
Mt Pozieres
Arno Peak
Mt Ida
'Delny'
'Mount Swan'
Box Hole Meteorite Crater
'Dneiper'
Mt Lucy
Railway
Red Cliff
JERVOIS RANGE
'Tarlton Downs'
TARLTON RANGE
Mt Sainthill
To Boulia
Mendip Hill
Mt Swan
Engawala
'Alcoota'
Mt Ewart
Irrilirree
Bonya (Orrtipa-Thurra)
'Marqua'
TOKO RANGE
Mt Byrne
RANGE STUART
'Bushy Park'
Gem Tree Caravan Park
'Mount Riddoch'
Huckitta
'Jinka'
'Jervois'
Marshall River
Harts Range
Atitjere
HARTS RANGE
Mt Eaglebeak
Mt Strangways
Mt Pfitzner
'Yambah'
Mt Riddoch
Mt Campbell
Mt Palmer
Mt Brassey
Mt Mary
Mt Tietkens
Mt Smith
Mt Reinecke
Mt Woods
Mt Winnecke
Mt Wooldridge
'Quartz Hill' (ruins)
Mt Lionel
'The Garden'
'Indiana'
Plenty
'Atula'
Mt Barrington
Sixteen Mile Creek
Mt Laughlen
Adla Hill
Mt Ruby
'Ambalindum'
'Claraville'
Arltunga
Arltunga Historical Reserve
Cravens Peak
Twin Hills
Two Hills
Trephina Gorge Nature Pk
Trephina Gorge
Ruby Gap
Ruby Gap Nature Pk
'Atnarpa'
Atnetye
Mt Knuckey
Mt Everard
'Bond Springs'
Painter Springs
Simpsons Gap
Alice Springs
'Ross River'
N'dhala Gorge Nature Park
Mt Gardner
'Undoolya'
Emily Gap
Jessie Gap
Corroboree Rock Cons Res
Iwupataka
Amoonguna
Emily & Jessie Gaps Nature Park
MACDONNELL RANGES
Mt Ertwa
Prohibited Area
'Owen Springs'
'Todd River'
FERGUSON RANGE
'Ringwood'
'Limbla'
Lake Caroline
Mt Polhill
Ewaninga Rock Carvings
Ltyentye Apurte (Santa Teresa)
Santa Teresa
'Numery'
Illogwa
Mt Oorarninna
Rainbow Valley Con Res
Mowelanne
'Oak Valley'
Hugh River
'Deep Well'
'Allambi'
'Todd River Downs'
private track
Pmere Nyente
Permit Required
Hale River
Hay River
For more detail on this area, see Hema's Central Australia map, Great Desert Tracks NE Sheet, & Simpson Desert map
Rodinga (ruin)
RODINGA RANGE
Mt Frank
Oneill Point
OLD ANDADO TRACK
4WD only
'Maryvale'
Titjikala
Mt Charlotte
For more detail on this area, see Hema's map of The Red Centre & Great Desert Tracks NE Sheet
Chambers Pillar Historical Reserve
Chambers Pillar
Pinnacle Hills
Bundooma (ruin)
'Idracowra'
GHAN
COLSON TRACK
Impadna
MAC CLARK (ACACIA PEUCE) CONSERVATION RESERVE
Simpson Desert
SIMPSON DESERT NATIONAL PARK
'Horseshoe Bend'
private
Colson Pinnacle
Rumbalara (ruin)
'Old Andado'
'Andado'
BLACK HILL RANGE
'Lilla Creek'
Lambert's Centre of Australia
Finke (Apatula)
Apatula
Mt Peebles
'Umbeara'
Mt Gordon
Mt Beddome
'New Crown'
Finke
Pmer Ulpiere Ingwemirne Arletherre
Umbeara Well
Goyder
Mt Cecil
Mt Grundy
'Charlotte Waters'
Mt Wilyunpa
Mt Dare
Mt Etingambra
Walla Hills
Permit Required from ONPWS
QAA LINE
Lake Poeppel
Poeppel Corner
Mt Parlue
Mt Mead
'Mt Dare'
Finke River
Mt Allnerta
Abminga (ruin)
Abminga Ck
SOUTH AUSTRALIA
Mt Bagot
WITJIRA NATIONAL PARK
Desert Parks Pass required
Dalhousie Springs
Purni Bore
FRENCH LINE
Freeth Junction
SIMPSON DESERT REGIONAL RESERVE
RIG RD
WAA LINE
SIMPSON DESERT CONSERVATION PARK
K1 LINE
Hamilton
'Tieyon'
Lindsay
Stevenson
'Eringa' (abandoned)
Bloods Creek
ROUTE
Ilbunga (ruin)
'Mt Irwin'
QUEENSLAND

Warning to Travellers

Travelling in Australia's arid regions can be extremely hazardous, especially during the summer months (October-March). Always seek local advice as to road conditions and notify the police of your intended destination and ETA. Always carry plenty of fuel and water. In the event of a breakdown, remain near your vehicle.

N

0 50 100km

A

B

Bellbird Park QLD 7 C8
Bellbrae VIC 42 J2 45 H12
Bellbridge VIC 49 B9
Bellbrook NSW 29 H11
Bellenden Ker QLD 13 D13 14 G6
Bellerive TAS 56 C6 59 F11
Bellevue WA 77 E7
Bellevue Heights SA 64 K4 65 K2 66 A6
Belli Park QLD 5 B8
Bellingen NSW 29 G12
Bellinger River Nat Park NSW 29 G12
Bellingham TAS 55 B5 61 D10
Bellmere QLD 5 G8
Bellmount Forest NSW 34 C3 35 C1
Belltrees NSW 27 B9
Belmont NSW 23 D6 27 F10
Belmont QLD 3 F6
Belmont VIC 42 G2
Belmont WA 77 F5
Belmore NSW 22 G4 25 E11
Belmunging WA 79 D9
Beloka NSW 34 H2
Belowra NSW 34 G4 35 H3
Belrose NSW 25 B11
Belsar Island VIC 46 C7
Beltana SA 71 A10 73 K10
Beltana Roadhouse SA 71 A10 73 K10
Belton SA 68 A7 71 D10
Belvidere SA 67 D9
Belyando Crossing QLD 10 E5 17 B14
Belyuen NT 95 C1 96 C3
Bemboka NSW 34 H4 35 K2
Bemm River VIC 51 D10
Ben Boyd Nat Park NSW 34 J5 51 A14
Ben Bullen NSW 26 F6
Ben Halls Gap Nat Park NSW 27 A9
Ben Lomond NSW 29 F9
Ben Lomond Nat Park TAS 61 G12
Bena NSW 33 D13
Bena VIC 43 K13 52 F5
Benalla VIC 48 D5
Benambra VIC 49 F11
Benambra Nat Park NSW 33 J12 49 A9
Benandarah NSW 34 E6 35 F5
Benaraby QLD 11 J11
Benarkin QLD 4 F2
Benarkin Nat Park QLD 4 D3 9 E11
Benaye VIC 44 C2
Bencubbin WA 82 A6 84 H7
Bendalong NSW 34 D6 35 D6
Bendeela NSW 26 K7 34 C6 35 B5
Bendemeer NSW 29 H8
Bendering WA 79 G14
Bendering Nature Res WA 79 F14
Bendick Murrell NSW 26 J3 34 A2
Bendidee Nat Park QLD 9 H8 28 A7
Bendigo VIC 45 B12
Bendoc VIC 34 K3 51 A10
Bendoc North VIC 51 A11
Bendoc Upper VIC 34 K3
Bendolba NSW 27 D10
Beneree NSW 26 G4
Benetook VIC 32 F3 46 B4
Benger WA 78 K4 80 A4
Bengerang NSW 8 K6
Bengworden VIC 50 E5
Beni NSW 26 C4
Beninbi Nat Park QLD 9 C10
Benjaberring WA 79 A10
Benjeroop VIC 47 F10
Benjinup WA 80 D6
Benlidi QLD 10 K2 17 G11
Bennet Bay NT 97 E11
Bennison Island VIC 50 J1
Benowa QLD 7 G12
Bensville NSW 23 J5
Bentinck Island QLD 12 D3
Bentley NSW 29 B13
Bentley WA 77 H5
Bentleys Plain VIC 49 G12 50 B7
Benwerrin VIC 45 J10
Berajondo QLD 11 K12
Berala NSW 25 D10
Berambing NSW 24 B5 26 G7
Berat QLD 6 G2
Beremboke VIC 42 C2
Beresfield NSW 23 B6 27 E10
Beresford SA 72 G7
Bergalia NSW 34 F5 35 G4
Bergen QLD 4 J1
Bergins Pocket QLD 4 A7
Berkeley Vale NSW 23 H5
Berkshire Park NSW 25 C8
Bermaguee Nature Res NSW 34 H5 35 J4
Bermagui NSW 34 H5 35 J4
Bermagui South NSW 34 H5 35 J4
Bernacchi TAS 59 A8 61 H8
Bernier & Dorre Island Nature Res WA 86 J1
Bernier Island WA 86 J1
Bernouilli Con Reserve SA 69 H4
Berowra NSW 22 A4 25 B10
Berowra Heights NSW 22 A5
Berowra Valley Regional Park NSW 22 A4 25 B10
Berowra Waters NSW 25 A10
Berri SA 32 F1 69 A7 71 H13
Berridale NSW 34 G2
Berriedale TAS 56 B5
Berrigan NSW 33 J10
Berrilee NSW 25 B10
Berrima NSW 26 K7 34 B6 35 A5
Berrimah NT 94 G7
Berring WA 79 A8
Berringa VIC 45 F10
Berringama VIC 49 C11
Berriwillock VIC 32 J5 47 G8
Berrook VIC 32 H1 46 D1 71 J13
Berry NSW 34 C7 35 B6
Berry Bay SA 68 G3
Berry Springs NT 95 D2 96 D4
Berrybank VIC 45 G9
Berwick VIC 43 F10 52 D3
Bessiebelle VIC 44 H4
Bet Bet VIC 45 B10
Beta QLD 10 H4 17 F13
Bete Bolong VIC 49 K14 51 D8
Bethanga VIC 49 B9
Bethania QLD 3 K6
Bethany SA 65 C6
Bethungra NSW 26 K1 33 G14
Betoota QLD 16 J5 18 C3 73 A14
Betsey Island TAS 57 G8 59 G11
Beulah TAS 60 F7
Beulah VIC 32 K4 46 H6
Beulah East VIC 46 H6
Beulah Park SA 64 G5
Beulah West VIC 46 H5
Bevendale NSW 26 K4 34 B3 35 A1
Beverford VIC 32 H6 47 E9
Beveridge VIC 45 E14 48 H2
Beveridge Station (site) VIC 49 F9
Beverley WA 79 E8 82 D4
Beverly Hills NSW 22 G4 25 E11
Bewong NSW 34 D6 35 C6
Bews SA 69 D6 71 K12
Bexhill NSW 29 B13
Bexley NSW 25 E11
Beyal VIC 46 J7
Biala NSW 26 K4 34 B3 35 A1
Biamanga Nat Park NSW 34 H5 35 K3
Biarra QLD 4 H4
Bibbenluke NSW 34 J3
Biboohra QLD 13 D12 14 E3
Bibra Lake WA 77 K3
Bicheno TAS 59 A14 61 H14
Bickerton Island NT 97 E12
Bicton WA 77 H2
Biddaddaba QLD 7 G10
Biddon NSW 26 A4 28 K2
Bidgeemia NSW 33 J11
Bidijul WA 89 J8 90 B4
Bidyadanga (Lagrange) WA 88 J3 90 B1
Big Bush Nature Res NSW 33 F13
Big Desert Wilderness Park VIC 32 J2 46 G2 69 D7 71 K14
Big Green Island TAS 61 C9
Big Heath Con Park SA 69 H6
Big Pats Creek VIC 43 C13
Bigga NSW 26 H4 34 A3
Biggara VIC 49 C13
Biggenden QLD 9 B11
Biggs Flat SA 65 K4 66 A7
Biggs Island WA 89 B8
Bilambil NSW 7 J13 29 A14
Bilbarin WA 79 F12
Bilbaringa SA 65 E4
Bilgola NSW 25 A12
Billabong Roadhouse WA 84 C3
Billericay WA 79 F14
Billiatt Con Park SA 32 H1 69 C6 71 J13
Billiluna (Mindibungu) WA 89 K12 90 C6
Billimari NSW 26 G3
Billinga QLD 7 H13
Billinooka WA 87 F11
Billinudgel Nature Res NSW 29 B14
Billinudgell NSW 29 B14
Billys Creek NSW 29 F11
Biloela QLD 11 J10
Bilpin NSW 24 B5 27 G8
Bilwon QLD 14 D3
Bilyana QLD 13 F13
Bimberamala Nat Park NSW 34 E6 35 E4
Bimberi Nature Res NSW 38 D1
Bimbi NSW 26 H2 33 E14
Binalong NSW 26 K3 34 B2
Binalong Bay TAS 61 E14
Binaronca Nature Res WA 83 C13 85 K12 91 H1
Binbee QLD 10 B6
Binda NSW 26 J5 34 A4
Bindango QLD 8 E4
Bindarri Nat Park NSW 29 G12
Bindi VIC 49 G12 50 A7
Bindi Bindi WA 84 H5
Bindoon WA 78 B5 82 B3 84 J5
Bingara NSW 28 E7
Bingera Nat Park QLD 9 A11
Bingil Bay QLD 13 E13 14 K7
Binginwarri VIC 50 H2
Binguy NSW 28 D6
Binjour QLD 9 B10
Binjura Nature Res NSW 34 G3 35 H1
Binna Burra QLD 7 J11 9 H13 29 A13
Binnaway NSW 26 A5 28 K4
Binnaway Nature Res NSW 26 A5 28 K4
Binningup WA 78 K4 80 A4 82 F2
Binnu WA 84 D3
Binnum SA 44 B1 69 G7
Binya NSW 33 F11
Birany Birany NT 97 D12
Birchip VIC 32 K5 46 H7
Birchs Bay TAS 56 J4 59 H10
Bird Island TAS 60 B1
Birdsville QLD 16 K4 18 C1 73 A11
Birdum NT 96 J7 98 A7
Birdwood NSW 27 A12 29 K11
Birdwood SA 65 G6 68 G7 69 B3 71 J10
Birdwoodton VIC 32 F3 46 A4
Biriwal Bulga Nat Park NSW 27 A12 29 K10
Birkdale QLD 3 F7 7 B11
Birkenhead SA 64 D1
Birnam Range QLD 7 F10
Birralee QLD 10 C6
Birralee TAS 55 G2 61 F8
Birrego NSW 33 H12
Birregurra VIC 45 H10
Birri Lodge QLD 12 C3
Birriwa NSW 26 C5
Birrong NSW 22 F2
Birru QLD 6 C6
Bishops Nature Res WA 83 F12 91 J1
Bishopsbourne TAS 55 J3 61 G9
Bittern VIC 43 J9
Black Andrew Nature Res NSW 34 C2
Black Bulga State Con Area NSW 27 C11
Black Forest SA 64 H3
Black Hill SA 69 B4 71 J11
Black Hill Con Park SA 64 E7 65 H3
Black Hills TAS 56 A2 59 F9
Black Jungle Con Res NT 95 C2 96 C4
Black Mountain NSW 29 G9
Black Mountain Nat Park QLD 13 B12 15 K6
Black Point NT 96 A5
Black Range State Park VIC 44 C5
Black River TAS 60 C3
Black Rock SA 68 B7 71 E10
Black Rock VIC 41 G4 42 E7
Black Rock Con Park SA 68 B7 71 E10
Black Springs NSW 26 H6
Black Springs SA 68 E7 71 G10
Black Swamp NSW 29 C11
Blackall QLD 10 J3 17 G12
Blackalls Park NSW 23 D6
Blackbraes Nat Park QLD 10 A1 13 H10
Blackbull QLD 12 F7
Blackburn VIC 41 D6
Blackbutt QLD 4 E2 9 F11
Blackdown Tableland Nat Park QLD 11 H8
Blackfellows Caves SA 69 K6
Blackheath NSW 24 D4 26 G7
Blackmans Bay TAS 56 F6 59 G10
Blacksmith Island QLD 11 C8
Blacksmiths NSW 23 D6
Blackstone (Papulankutja) WA 90 J6 91 B6
Blacktown NSW 22 D1 25 D9
Blackville NSW 26 A7
Blackwater QLD 11 H8
Blackwater Mine QLD 10 H7
Blackwood SA 64 K4 65 K3 66 A6 68 H7 69 B3 71 J10
Blackwood VIC 45 E12
Blackwood Creek TAS 59 A9 61 H9
Blackwood Nat Park QLD 10 D5 17 B14
Blackwood River Nat Park WA 80 E2
Bladensburg Nat Park QLD 17 D9
Blair Athol QLD 10 F6
Blair Athol SA 64 E4
Blairgowrie VIC 42 J6
Blakehurst NSW 22 H4 25 E11
Blakeview SA 65 E3
Blakeville VIC 42 A2 45 E11
Blakney Creek NSW 26 K4 34 B3 35 A1
Blanchetown SA 69 A5 71 H11
Bland NSW 26 H1 33 E13
Blandford NSW 27 B9
Blanket Flat NSW 26 J4 34 A3
Blaxland NSW 24 D6 27 G8
Blaxlands Ridge NSW 24 A7
Blayney NSW 26 G5
Blenheim QLD 6 C4
Blessington TAS 61 G11
Bletchley SA 67 C10
Blewitt Springs SA 66 B6
Bli Bli QLD 5 C10
Bligh Park NSW 25 C8
Blighty NSW 33 J9
Blina Oil & Gas Field WA 88 G7 90 A3
Blinman SA 71 B10
Bloods Creek SA 72 A4 101 K9
Bloods Range (Puntitjata) NT 90 H7 91 A7 100 H1
Bloomfield QLD 13 B12
Bloomsbury QLD 10 C7
Blow Clear NSW 26 E1 33 C14 33 E13
Blue Bay NSW 23 G6
Blue Gum Con Park WA 81 J11
Blue Lake Nat Park QLD 7 B13 9 G14
Blue Mountains Nat Park NSW 24 C5 26 H7 34 A5
Blue Mud Bay NT 97 E11
Blue Rocks TAS 61 B9
Bluewater QLD 13 H14
Bluewater Springs Roadhouse QLD 10 A3 13 H13
Bluff QLD 11 H8
Bluff Beach SA 68 G4
Bluff River Nature Res NSW 29 C10
Blyth SA 68 E6 71 G10
Blythdale QLD 8 E5
Boambee NSW 29 G13
Boat Harbour TAS 60 D4
Boat Harbour Beach TAS 60 C4
Bobadah NSW 31 K12 33 A12
Bobbin Head NSW 22 A5 25 B10
Bobin NSW 27 B12
Bobundara Nature Res NSW 34 H3
Bodalla NSW 34 G5 35 H4
Bodallin WA 83 B8 85 J9
Bodangora NSW 26 D4
Boddington WA 78 H7 82 E4
Bogan Gate NSW 26 E1 33 C14
Bogandyera Nature Res NSW 33 K14 34 F1 49 A12
Bogangar NSW 29 A14
Bogantungan QLD 10 H5
Bogee NSW 26 E7
Boggabilla NSW 8 J7 28 B6
Boggabri NSW 28 H5
Boggy Lake SA 67 D12
Boginderra Hills Nature Res NSW 26 J1 33 F13
Bogolong Creek NSW 26 H2 33 E14
Bogong VIC 49 E10
Boho VIC 48 E5
Boho South VIC 48 E5
Boigbeat VIC 46 G7
Boinka VIC 32 H2 46 E3
Boisdale VIC 49 K9 50 E4
Bokal WA 81 B8
Bokarina QLD 5 D10
Bolgart WA 78 A7 82 B4 84 J6
Bolinda VIC 45 D13 48 H1
Bolivar SA 64 B4 65 E2 65 F2
Bolivia NSW 29 D10
Bolivia Hill Nature Res NSW 29 D10
Bollanolla Nature Res NSW 29 H12
Bollon QLD 8 H2
Bolton VIC 32 H5 46 D7
Bolton Point NSW 23 D6
Boltons Beach Con Area TAS 59 D13
Bolwarra NSW 23 A5
Bolwarra VIC 44 H3
Bolwarrah VIC 42 A1 45 E11
Bomaderry NSW 34 C7 35 B6
Bombala NSW 34 J3
Bombo NSW 27 K8 34 B7 35 B7
Bomera NSW 26 A6 28 K5
Bonalbo NSW 9 K12 29 B12
Bonang VIC 34 K2 51 A10
Bonaparte Archipelago WA 89 B8
Bonbeach VIC 43 F8
Bondi NSW 22 F7 25 D12
Bondi Gulf Nature Res NSW 34 K3 51 A11
Bondi Junction NSW 22 F6
Bonegilla VIC 33 K12 49 B9
Boneo VIC 42 K7
Bongaree QLD 5 G11 9 F13
Bongil Bongil Nat Park NSW 29 G13
Bonnells Bay NSW 23 E5
Bonnet Bay NSW 22 J3
Bonnie Doon VIC 48 F5
Bonnie Rock WA 85 H8
Bonnie Vale WA 83 A12 85 J11
Bonny Hills NSW 27 A13
Bonnyrigg NSW 25 E9
Bonogin QLD 7 H12
Bonshaw NSW 9 K9 29 C8
Bonville NSW 29 G12
Bonya (Orrtipa-Thurra) NT 101 D12
Bonython ACT 37 J3
Booborowie SA 68 D7 71 F10
Boobyalla TAS 61 C12
Booderee Nat Park ACT 34 D7 35 D7
Boodie Island WA 86 C3
Boodjamulla (Lawn Hill) Nat Park QLD 12 G2
Boogan QLD 14 J6
Booie QLD 4 B1
Bookabie SA 70 C1 74 K6
Bookaloo SA 71 C8
Bookar VIC 45 G8
Booker Bay NSW 23 J5
Bookham NSW 34 C2
Bookin QLD 12 K6 16 A6
Bool Lagoon SA 44 D1 69 H7
Booloading WA 80 B7
Boolaroo NSW 23 C6
Boolarra VIC 50 G1 52 F7
Boolba QLD 8 H4
Boolburra QLD 11 H9
Boolcunda SA 68 A6 71 D9
Booleroo Centre SA 68 C6 71 E10
Booligal NSW 33 E8
Boolite VIC 46 K7
Boomi NSW 8 J6 28 B4
Boomi Nature Res NSW 28 B4
Boomi West Nature Res NSW 28 B4
Boonah QLD 6 G7 9 H12
Boonanarring Nature Res WA 78 A4 82 B3 84 J5
Boonanghi Nature Res NSW 29 J11
Boonarga QLD 9 E8
Boondall QLD 3 B5 5 K10 7 A10
Boondooma QLD 9 D10
Boonmoo QLD 13 D12 14 F1
Boonoo Boonoo NSW 29 C10
Boonoo Boonoo Nat Park NSW 9 K11 29 B11
Boonooroo QLD 9 C13
Booraan WA 79 B14
Boorabbin WA 83 B10 85 J10
Boorabbin Nat Park WA 83 A10 85 J10
Booragoon WA 77 J3
Booragul NSW 23 D6
Booral NSW 27 D11
Boorara Gardner Nat Park WA 80 H6
Boorcan VIC 45 H8
Boorganna Nature Res NSW 27 A12
Boorhaman VIC 48 C6
Boorindal NSW 31 E11
Boorndoolyanna SA 74 A5 100 K6
Boorongie North VIC 32 H4 46 E6
Booroolong Nature Res NSW 29 G9
Booroopki VIC 44 B2
Booroorban NSW 33 G8 47 D13
Boorowa NSW 26 J3 34 B2
Boort VIC 32 K6 47 J10
Boosey VIC 48 B5
Booti Booti Nat Park NSW 27 C13
Booyal QLD 9 B11
Bopeechee SA 73 H8
Boppy Mount NSW 31 H11
Borallon QLD 6 B7
Borambil NSW 26 B6
Borambola NSW 33 H14
Boraning WA 79 K8 81 A8
Borda Island WA 89 A10
Borden WA 81 E13 82 H7
Border Island QLD 11 B8
Border Ranges Nat Park NSW 7 K8 9 J12 29 A12
Border Store NT 95 C7 96 C7
Border Village SA 74 K1 91 H7
Borderdale WA 81 E10
Bordertown SA 46 K1 69 F7
Boree NSW 26 F4
Boree QLD 17 A10
Boree Creek NSW 33 H12
Boreen Point QLD 9 D13
Bornholm WA 81 K11
Boro NSW 34 D4 35 D3
Boronga Nature Res NSW 28 B5
Boronia VIC 43 D9
Boronia Heights QLD 3 K4
Boroobin QLD 5 E8
Bororen QLD 11 J11
Borrika SA 69 C6 71 J12
Borroloola NT 97 J12 99 A12
Borung VIC 47 K10
Boscabel WA 81 C9
Bossley Park NSW 25 E9
Bostobrick NSW 29 G11
Boston Bay SA 68 G1
Boston Island SA 68 G1 70 H6
Botany NSW 22 H6 25 E12
Botany Bay NSW 22 H5 25 E12
Botany Bay Nat Park NSW 22 J6 25 E12 27 H9
Botherling WA 79 A8
Bothwell TAS 59 D9
Boucaut Bay NT 97 C9
Bouddi Nat Park NSW 23 J6 27 G10
Boulder WA 83 A12 85 H12 91 G1
Bouldercombe QLD 11 H10
Boulia QLD 16 E4
Boundain WA 79 J10
Boundary Bend VIC 32 G5 47 C8
Bountiful Island QLD 12 D4
Bourke NSW 31 E10
Bournda Nat Park NSW 34 J5
Bow NSW 26 C7
Bow Bridge WA 81 J9
Bowden SA 63 A1
Bowelling WA 80 B7 82 F4
Bowen QLD 10 B7
Bowen Mountain NSW 24 B6
Bowen Park NSW 26 F4
Bowenfels NSW 24 C2
Bowenvale VIC 45 C10
Bowenville QLD 9 F10
Bower SA 71 G11
Boweya VIC 48 C6
Bowhill SA 69 B5 71 J11
Bowillia SA 68 E6 71 G9
Bowling Alley Point NSW 27 A9 29 K8
Bowling Green Bay QLD 10 A5
Bowling Green Bay Nat Park QLD 10 A5
Bowman QLD 11 F9
Bowmans SA 68 F6 71 H9
Bowna NSW 33 K13 49 A10
Bowning NSW 26 K4 34 C2
Bowral NSW 26 K7 34 B6 35 A6
Bowraville NSW 29 H12
Box Hill NSW 25 C8
Box Hill VIC 41 D6 43 D9 45 F14 48 K2 52 B2
Boxwood Hill WA 83 H8
Boyacup WA 81 F10
Boyagarring Con Park WA 78 G7
Boyagin Nature Res WA 79 G8 82 D4
Boyanup WA 80 C4 82 G3
Boydtown NSW 34 K5 51 A14
Boyeo VIC 46 K3
Boyer TAS 56 A3 59 F10
Boyerine WA 81 C10
Boyland QLD 7 F10
Boyndaminup Nat Park WA 80 G7
Boyne Island QLD 11 J11
Boynedale QLD 11 J11
Boyup Brook WA 80 D7 82 G4
Bracalba QLD 5 G8
Brachina SA 71 B10
Bracken Ridge QLD 3 A4 5 J9
Brackendale NSW 29 J9
Bracknell TAS 55 K3 61 G9
Bradbury NSW 25 G9
Bradbury SA 65 K4 66 A7
Braddon ACT 37 D5
Bradvale VIC 45 F9
Braefield NSW 27 A8 28 K7
Braeside QLD 6 K1
Braeside VIC 41 H5 43 F8
Brahma Lodge SA 64 B5
Braidwood NSW 34 E5 35 E3
Bramble Bay QLD 3 A5 5 J10
Bramfield SA 70 F4
Bramley Nat Park WA 80 E2
Brampton Island QLD 11 C8
Brampton Islands Nat Park QLD 11 C8
Bramston Beach QLD 13 E13 14 G6
Bramwell Junction QLD 15 D2
Brandon QLD 10 A5
Brandy Creek VIC 43 G14
Branxholm TAS 61 E12
Branxholme VIC 44 F4
Branxton NSW 23 A3 27 D10
Brawlin NSW 26 K2 33 G14 34 B1
Bray Junction SA 69 H5
Bray Park NSW 7 K12
Braybrook VIC 41 C1
Brayfield SA 68 F2 70 G6
Brays Creek NSW 7 K11
Brayton NSW 26 K6 34 B5 35 A4
Brazendale Island TAS 59 B9 61 J9
Breadalbane NSW 34 C4 35 B2
Breadalbane TAS 55 H5 61 G10
Break O'Day VIC 48 H3
Breakaway Ridge Nature Res WA 83 F8
Breakfast Creek NSW 26 D6 26 J3 34 A2
Breaksea Island TAS 58 J5
Bream Creek TAS 57 B12 59 F12
Breamlea VIC 42 H3
Bredbo NSW 34 F3 35 G1
Breelong NSW 26 B4
Breeza NSW 28 J6
Bremer Bay WA 83 H9
Bremer Island NT 97 C13
Brendale QLD 3 A3
Brentwood SA 68 G5 71 J8
Brentwood VIC 46 H5
Breona TAS 59 A8 61 H8
Breton Bay WA 84 J4
Bretti NSW 27 B11
Bretti Nature Res NSW 27 B11
Brewarrina NSW 31 D12
Brewer NSW 33 D11
Brewster VIC 45 E9
Briaba QLD 10 C6
Briagolong VIC 49 K9 50 D4
Bribbaree NSW 26 H1 33 F14
Bribie Island QLD 5 F10 9 F13
Bribie Island Nat Park QLD 5 F10 5 G11 9 F13
Bridge Creek VIC 48 F6
Bridgeman Downs QLD 3 B3
Bridgenorth TAS 55 F4 61 F9
Bridgetown WA 80 E5 82 H3
Bridgewater SA 65 J4
Bridgewater TAS 56 A5 59 F10
Bridgewater VIC 45 A11
Bridport TAS 55 B7 61 D11
Brigalow QLD 9 E9
Bright VIC 49 E9
Brighton QLD 3 A4 5 J10
Brighton SA 64 K2 65 K1 68 H6 69 C2 71 J10
Brighton TAS 59 F10
Brighton VIC 41 F3 42 E7
Brighton-Le-Sands NSW 22 H5 25 E11
Brightview QLD 6 B5
Brightwaters NSW 23 E6
Brim VIC 46 J6
Brimbago SA 69 F6
Brimboal VIC 44 D3
Brimpaen VIC 44 C5
Brindabella NSW 34 D2 38 D1
Brindabella Nat Park NSW 34 D2 38 B1
Brinerville NSW 29 G11
Bringalbert VIC 44 B2
Bringelly NSW 25 F8
Brinkin NT 94 B4
Brinkley SA 67 C12 69 C4 71 K11
Brinkworth SA 68 D6 71 G9
Brisbane QLD 2 B2 3 E4 7 B9 9 G13
Brisbane Forest Park QLD 3 D1 4 J7 7 A8
Brisbane Ranges Nat Park VIC 42 D2 45 F12
Brisbane Water Nat Park NSW 23 J4 27 G9
Brit Brit VIC 44 E4
Britannia Creek VIC 43 C12
Brittons Swamp TAS 60 C2
Brixton QLD 10 H2 17 E11
Broad Arrow WA 85 H12 91 G1
Broad Sound QLD 11 F9
Broad Sound Island Nat Park QLD 11 E9
Broadbeach QLD 7 G13 9 H14
Broadford VIC 45 C14 48 G2
Broadmarsh TAS 59 E9
Broadmeadows SA 65 E3
Broadmeadows VIC 41 B3 42 B7
Broadmount QLD 11 H10
Broadwater NSW 9 K13 29 C14
Broadwater QLD 4 B2
Broadwater VIC 44 G5
Broadwater Nat Park NSW 9 K13 29 C14
Brocklehurst NSW 26 C3
Brocklesby NSW 33 J12 49 A8
Brockman WA 80 G5
Brockman Mine WA 86 E6
Brockman Nat Park WA 80 G5 82 J3
Brodribb River VIC 49 K14 51 D9
Brogo NSW 34 H5 35 K3
Broke NSW 23 C1 27 E9
Broken Bay NSW 23 K5 25 A12 27 G9
Broken Hill NSW 30 J2 32 A2 71 C14
Bromby Islands NT 97 B12
Bromelton QLD 7 F9
Brompton SA 64 F3
Bromus WA 83 D13 91 H1
Bronte NSW 25 D12
Bronte Park TAS 58 C7 60 K7
Bronzewing VIC 32 H4 46 E6
Brookdale NSW 33 H12
Brooker SA 68 E1 70 G6
Brookfield NSW 27 D11
Brookfield QLD 3 E1 7 B8
Brookfield Con Park SA 69 A4 71 H11
Brookhampton WA 80 C5
Brooking Gorge Con Park WA 89 H9 90 A4
Brooklands QLD 7 E9
Brooklyn NSW 23 K4 25 A11
Brooklyn VIC 41 D1
Brooklyn Park SA 64 G3
Brooks Creek NT 95 F3 96 E4
Brooksby VIC 44 C4
Brookstead QLD 9 G10
Brookton WA 79 F9 82 D5
Brookvale NSW 22 D6 25 C12
Brookville VIC 49 H11 50 B6
Brooloo QLD 4 B7 9 E12
Brooman NSW 34 E6 35 E5
Broome WA 88 G4 90 A1
Broomehill WA 81 D11 82 G6
Brooms Head NSW 29 E13
Brooweena QLD 9 C11
Broughton VIC 46 J2
Broughton Island NSW 27 D12
Broula NSW 26 H3

C

Catamaran TAS 59 K9
Catani VIC 43 G12 52 E4
Cataract Nat Park NSW 29 B11
Cathcart NSW 34 J4
Cathcart VIC 44 D7
Cathedral Beach QLD 9 B13
Cathedral Range State Park VIC 48 H5
Cathedral Rock Nat Park NSW 29 G10
Catherine Field NSW 25 F8
Catherine Hill Bay NSW 23 E6
Cathkin VIC 48 G4
Cathundral NSW 26 B1 31 J14
Cattai NSW 25 A8
Cattai Nat Park NSW 25 A8 27 G9
Catumnal VIC 47 J10
Caulfield VIC 41 E5 43 D8
Cavan NSW 34 C3
Cavan SA 64 D4 65 G2
Caveat VIC 48 F4
Cavendish VIC 44 E5
Caversham WA 77 D6
Caves Beach NSW 23 E6
Caveside TAS 60 G7
Cawarral QLD 11 G10
Cawdor NSW 25 G8
Cawongla NSW 29 B13
Cecil Park NSW 25 E9
Cecil Plains QLD 9 G9
Cedar Bay Nat Park QLD 13 B12
Cedar Brush NSW 23 F4
Cedar Creek QLD 5 J8 7 E11
Cedar Grove QLD 7 F10
Cedar Point NSW 29 B13
Cedarton QLD 5 E8
Ceduna SA 70 C2 74 K7
Cement Creek VIC 43 C13
Central Castra TAS 60 E6
Central Mangrove NSW 23 G4
Central McDonald NSW 23 H2
Central Mount Wedge NT 100 D5
Central Plateau Con Area TAS 58 A7 59 A9 60 H7
Central Tilba NSW 34 G5 35 J4
Centre Bore SA 74 B5
Centre Island NT 97 J13 99 A13
Ceratodus QLD 9 B9
Ceres NSW 26 C2
Ceres VIC 42 G2 45 G12
Cervantes WA 84 H4
Cessnock NSW 23 C3 27 E10
Chadinga Con Res SA 70 C1 74 K6
Chadstone VIC 41 E5
Chaelundi Nat Park NSW 29 F11
Chaelundi State Con Area NSW 29 F11
Chain of Lagoons TAS 61 G14
Chain Of Ponds SA 65 G5
Chain Valley Bay NSW 23 E6
Chakola NSW 34 G3 35 H1
Chalky Island TAS 61 B8
Chambers Bay NT 95 B4 96 C5
Chambers Flat QLD 7 D10
Chambers Pillar Historical Res NT 101 H8
Chambigne Nature Res NSW 29 E12
Champagny Island WA 88 C7
Chandada SA 70 E4
Chandler QLD 3 F7 7 B10
Chandler SA 72 C2 74 B7
Chandler WA 79 A14
Chandlers Creek VIC 34 K3 51 B11
Channar Mine WA 86 F7
Channel Island NT 95 C1 96 C3
Chapel Hill QLD 3 F2 7 B9
Chapman ACT 37 G2
Chappell Islands TAS 61 C8
Chapple Vale VIC 45 J9
Charam VIC 44 C3
Charbon NSW 26 E6
Charles Darwin NT 94 G4
Charles Darwin Nat Park NT 94 G4
Charleston SA 65 H5
Charleston Con Park SA 65 H6
Charlestown NSW 23 C6
Charleville QLD 17 K13 19 D13
Charleyong NSW 34 D5 35 D3
Charleys Creek VIC 45 J9
Charlotte Pass NSW 34 H1 49 D14
Charlton VIC 47 K9
Charlwood QLD 6 G6
Charmhaven NSW 23 F6
Charnwood ACT 37 B2
Charra SA 70 C2 74 K7
Charters Towers QLD 10 B4 13 J13
Chasm Island NT 97 E12
Chatsbury NSW 26 K6 34 B5 35 A3
Chatswood NSW 22 D5 25 C11
Chatswood West NSW 22 D5
Chatsworth NSW 29 D13
Chatsworth VIC 44 F7
Cheadanup Nature Res WA 83 F11
Cheepie QLD 19 E11
Cheetams Flats NSW 24 D2
Chelmer QLD 3 F3
Chelsea VIC 41 H5 43 F8
Cheltenham NSW 22 C3 25 C10
Cheltenham SA 64 E2
Cheltenham VIC 41 G4 43 E8
Cherbourg QLD 9 D11
Cherbourg Nat Park QLD 4 A1 9 C11
Chermside QLD 3 C4 5 K9 7 A9
Chermside West QLD 3 C3
Cherry Gardens SA 65 K3 66 A6
Cherry Tree Hill NSW 29 D8
Cherry Tree Pool WA 81 D10
Cherrybrook NSW 22 C3 25 C10
Cherrypool VIC 44 C5
Cherryville SA 65 H4
Cheshunt VIC 48 E7
Chester Hill NSW 25 D10
Chester Nature Res WA 80 F3
Chesterton Range Nat Park QLD 8 D2
Chetwynd VIC 44 D3
Cheviot VIC 48 G4
Cheviot Island QLD 11 E10
Chewko QLD 14 E3
Chewton VIC 45 C12
Cheyne Bay WA 83 J8
Cheyne Beach WA 81 J14 82 J7
Cheynes Bridge VIC 49 K8 50 D3
Chichester NSW 27 C10
Chiddarcooping Nature Res WA 82 A7 85 H8
Chidlow WA 78 D6
Chifley ACT 37 F3
Chifley NSW 25 E12
Chifley WA 85 J13 91 G2
Childers QLD 9 B11
Childers VIC 50 F1 52 E7
Childowlah NSW 34 C2
Chillagoe QLD 13 D11
Chillagoe-Mungana Caves Nat Park QLD 13 D11
Chilli Beach QLD 15 E4
Chillingham NSW 7 K11 29 A13
Chillingollah VIC 32 H5 47 E8
Chiltern VIC 33 K12 49 B8
Chiltern - Mt Pilot Nat Park VIC 33 K12 49 B8
Chinaman Creek SA 68 B5 71 E9
Chinaman Flat VIC 32 K3 46 H3
Chinaman Island VIC 43 H10
Chinamans Wells SA 69 F5
Chinbi QLD 17 B10
Chinchilla QLD 9 E8
Chinderah NSW 7 J13 29 A14
Chinghee Creek QLD 7 J9
Chinkapook VIC 32 H5 46 E7
Chinocup Nature Res WA 81 B14 82 F7
Chipping Norton NSW 25 E10
Chisholm ACT 37 J4
Chittaway Point NSW 23 G5
Chorkerup WA 81 J11
Chorregon QLD 17 D10
Chowerup WA 81 E8
Chowilla Reg Res SA 32 E1 71 G13
Christies Beach SA 66 B4
Christmas Creek QLD 7 H9
Christmas Hills TAS 60 C2
Christmas Hills VIC 43 B10
Christmas Island TAS 60 A6
Chudleigh TAS 60 G7
Chum Creek VIC 43 B11
Church Point NSW 22 A7 25 B11
Churchill VIC 50 G2
Churchill Island VIC 43 K10
Churchill Island Marine Nat Park VIC 43 K10 52 F3
Churchill Nat Park VIC 43 E9 52 C3
Chute VIC 45 D9
City Beach WA 77 F2
Clackline WA 78 C7 82 C4 84 K6
Clairview QLD 11 F9
Clandulla NSW 26 E6
Clapham SA 64 J4
Clare QLD 10 B5
Clare SA 68 E7 71 G10
Claremont TAS 56 B5 59 F10
Claremont WA 77 G2
Clarence NSW 24 B3
Clarence Gardens SA 64 H3
Clarence Point TAS 55 C2
Clarence Strait NT 95 B2
Clarence Town NSW 27 D11
Clarendon NSW 24 B7
Clarendon SA 66 B6 68 H7 69 C3 71 J10
Clarendon TAS 55 K6 61 G10
Clarendon VIC 45 F11
Clareville NSW 25 A12
Clarina QLD 12 E6
Clarke Island TAS 61 B13
Clarkefield VIC 45 E13 48 H1
Clarkes Hill Nature Res NSW 33 K14 34 F1 49 A13
Claude Road TAS 60 F7
Claverton QLD 19 F13
Clayfield QLD 3 D4
Claymore WA 80 D4
Clayton SA 67 G9 68 J7 69 D3 71 K10
Clayton VIC 41 F5 43 E8
Clear Island Waters QLD 7 G12
Clear Lake VIC 44 C4
Clear Mountain QLD 3 A1
Clear Ridge NSW 33 E13
Clearview SA 64 E4
Cleland Con Park SA 64 H6 65 J3
Clematis VIC 43 E11
Clements Gap Con Park SA 68 D6 71 F9
Clermont QLD 10 G6
Cleve SA 68 D3 70 G7
Cleveland QLD 7 B11
Cleveland TAS 59 A10 61 H11
Cliffordville WA 79 H10
Clifton NSW 25 H11
Clifton QLD 6 F1 9 H10
Clifton Beach QLD 13 D12 14 D5
Clifton Beach TAS 57 E8 59 G11
Clifton Creek VIC 49 K11 50 D6
Clifton Gardens NSW 22 E6
Clifton Springs VIC 42 G4 45 G12
Clinton SA 68 F6 71 H9
Clinton Centre SA 68 F5 69 A1 71 H9
Clintonvale QLD 6 G2
Cloncurry QLD 12 K5 16 A4
Clonmel Island VIC 50 H3
Clontarf NSW 22 E6 25 C12
Clothiers Creek NSW 7 K13
Clouds Creek NSW 29 F11
Clovelly NSW 25 D12
Clovelly Park SA 64 J3
Cloverdale WA 77 G6
Cluan TAS 55 J3 61 G9
Club Terrace VIC 51 C10
Clump Mountain Nat Park QLD 14 K7
Clunes NSW 29 B14
Clunes VIC 45 D10
Clybucca NSW 29 J12
Clyde VIC 43 G10 52 D3
Clyde River Nat Park NSW 34 E5 35 F4
Clydebank VIC 50 E4
Coal Creek VIC 43 K14
Coal Point NSW 23 D6
Coalcliff NSW 25 H11
Coaldale NSW 29 D12
Coalseam Con Park WA 84 F4
Coalstoun Lakes QLD 9 C11
Cobains VIC 50 E4
Cobaki NSW 7 J13
Cobar NSW 31 H10
Cobargo NSW 34 G5 35 J3
Cobark NSW 27 B10
Cobaw VIC 45 D13 48 G1
Cobbadah NSW 28 F7
Cobba-da-mana QLD 9 J9 29 A8
Cobbannah VIC 49 J10 50 C4
Cobbity NSW 25 F8
Cobbler Creek Rec Park SA 65 F3
Cobbora NSW 26 C5
Cobby Cobby Island QLD 7 D12
Cobden VIC 45 H8
Cobdogla SA 69 A6 71 H12
Cobera SA 69 B6 71 J12
Cobham Bay NT 95 A3
Coblinnie Nature Res WA 81 C12
Coboco NSW 26 B3
Cobourg Peninsula NT 96 A5
Cobram VIC 33 K10 48 A4
Cobrico VIC 45 H8
Cobungra VIC 49 G10 50 A5
Coburg VIC 41 C3 42 C7 45 F14 48 K2 52 B1
Cocamba VIC 46 E7
Cocata Con Park SA 70 F5
Cocata Con Res SA 70 F5
Cochranes Creek VIC 45 B9
Cockaleechie SA 68 F1 70 G6
Cockatoo VIC 43 E11 48 K4 52 C4
Cockatoo WA 88 D6
Cockatoo Island WA 88 D6
Cockatoo Tank WA 83 B9 85 K9
Cockatoo Valley SA 65 D5
Cockburn SA 30 K1 32 A1 71 D14
Cockermouth Island QLD 11 C9
Cockle Creek TAS 59 K9
Cocklebiddy Motel WA 91 H4
Coconut Grove NT 94 D3
Cocoparra Nat Park NSW 33 F11
Cocoparra Nature Res NSW 33 E11
Codrington VIC 44 H5
Coen QLD 15 H3
Coffin Bay SA 70 H5
Coffin Bay Nat Park SA 70 H5
Coffs Harbour NSW 29 G13
Coghills Creek VIC 45 D10
Cohuna VIC 32 K7 47 H11
Coila Creek NSW 34 F5 35 G4
Cokum VIC 47 G9
Colac VIC 45 H10
Colbinabbin VIC 45 A13 48 D1
Coldstream VIC 43 C10 48 K3 52 B3
Coleambally NSW 33 G10
Colebee NSW 25 C8
Colebrook TAS 59 E10
Coledale NSW 25 J11 27 J8
Coleraine VIC 44 E4
Coles Bay TAS 59 C14 61 K14
Coleyville QLD 6 E6
Colignan VIC 32 G4 46 B5
Colinroobie NSW 33 F12
Colinton NSW 34 F3 35 G1 38 K5
Colinton QLD 4 F4
Collarenebri NSW 28 D2
Collaroy NSW 22 C7 25 B12
Collector NSW 34 C4 35 B2
Collerina NSW 31 D12
Colley SA 70 E4
Collgar WA 79 C14
Collie NSW 26 A2
Collie WA 80 B6 82 F3
Collie Cardiff WA 80 B6
Collier Bay WA 88 D7
Collier Range Nat Park WA 87 H9
Collingullie NSW 33 H12
Collingwood VIC 41 D4 43 D8
Collins WA 80 G6
Collins Island QLD 11 F10
Collinsvale TAS 56 C4 59 F10
Collinsville QLD 10 C6
Colly Blue NSW 26 A7 28 K5
Colo NSW 23 K1 24 A7
Colo Heights NSW 27 F8
Colo Vale NSW 26 J7 34 B6
Colton QLD 9 B12
Colton SA 70 F4
Columboola QLD 9 E8
Colyton NSW 25 D8
Comara NSW 29 H11
Comaum SA 44 D1 69 H7
Combaning NSW 26 J1 33 F14
Combara NSW 28 J1
Combienbar VIC 51 C11
Combo Waterhole Con Park QLD 16 B7
Combogolong NSW 28 G1
Comboyne NSW 27 A12
Come-By-Chance NSW 28 G1
Comerong Island Nature Res NSW 34 C7 35 C7
Comet QLD 10 H7
Comet Vale WA 85 G11
Comleroy Road NSW 24 B6
Commodore Heights NSW 23 K5 25 A11
Como NSW 22 J3 25 F11
Como WA 77 H4
Conara TAS 59 A11 61 H11
Conargo NSW 33 H9 47 F14
Concord NSW 22 E4 25 D11
Concordia SA 65 D4
Condah VIC 44 G4
Condamine QLD 8 E7
Condell Park NSW 25 E10
Conder ACT 37 K4
Condingup WA 83 G14 91 K1
Condobolin NSW 33 C13
Condong NSW 7 K13 29 A14
Condowie SA 68 E6 71 G9
Cone Bay WA 88 E6
Coneac State Con Area NSW 27 B11
Congelin WA 79 J8
Congewai NSW 23 D3
Congo NSW 34 F6 35 G4
Congupna VIC 48 C3
Conimbla NSW 26 G3
Conimbla Nat Park NSW 26 H3
Coningham TAS 56 G5
Coniston NSW 25 K10
Conjola NSW 34 D6 35 D5
Conjola Nat Park NSW 34 D7 35 D6
Conmurra SA 69 H6
Connell Lagoon NT 99 F12
Connells Lagoon Con Res NT 99 F12
Connells Point NSW 22 H4
Connemurra NSW 26 A6 28 K5
Connewarre VIC 42 H3
Connewirrecoo VIC 44 D3
Conoble NSW 33 C8
Conondale QLD 4 D7 9 E12
Conondale Nat Park QLD 4 D6 9 E12
Contine WA 79 J9
Conway Beach QLD 11 C8
Conway Nat Park QLD 11 C8
Coober Pedy SA 72 G4
Coobowie SA 68 H5 69 C1 71 J8
Coochiemudlo Island QLD 7 C12
Coochin Creek QLD 5 E10
Coodanup WA 78 G4
Cooee TAS 60 D5
Coogee NSW 22 G6 25 D12
Coojar VIC 44 D4
Cook ACT 37 D3
Cook SA 74 H3
Cookamidgera NSW 26 F2
Cookardinia NSW 33 J13
Cooke Plains SA 69 C4 71 K11
Cookernup WA 78 J5
Cooks Gap NSW 26 C6
Cooktown QLD 13 A12 15 K7
Coolabah NSW 31 G12
Coolabunia QLD 9 E11
Coolac NSW 33 G14 34 C1
Cooladdi QLD 19 E12
Coolah NSW 26 B6
Coolah Tops Nat Park NSW 26 B7
Coolamon NSW 33 G13
Coolana QLD 6 B6
Coolangatta QLD 7 H14 9 H14 29 A14
Coolaroo VIC 41 A2 42 B7
Coolatai NSW 28 D7
Coolbaggie Nature Res NSW 26 B3
Coolbinia WA 77 E4
Coolgardie WA 83 A12 85 J11
Coolimba WA 84 G3
Coolmunda Dam QLD 9 J9 29 A8
Coolongolook NSW 27 C12
Cooloolabin QLD 5 B9
Cooltong SA 32 F1 71 G13
Cooltong Con Park SA 69 A7 71 H13
Coolum Beach QLD 5 B10 9 E13
Coolumbooka Nature Res NSW 34 J3 51 A12
Coolup WA 78 H4 82 E3
Cooma NSW 34 G3 35 H1
Cooma VIC 47 K14 48 C2
Coomallo Nature Res WA 84 H4
Coomandook SA 69 D5 71 K11
Coomba NSW 27 C12
Coombabah QLD 7 F12
Coombabah Lake QLD 7 F12
Coombah NSW 32 C2
Coomberdale WA 84 H5
Coomera QLD 7 E12 9 H13
Coomera Island QLD 7 E12
Coominya QLD 4 K5 6 A5 9 G11
Coonabarabran NSW 28 J3
Coonalpyn SA 69 D5
Coonamble NSW 28 H1
Coonana WA 85 J14 91 G2
Coonawarra NT 94 G6
Coonawarra SA 44 D1 69 H7
Coondle WA 78 B7
Coongee VIC 32 H2
Coongie Lake SA 18 F3 73 D13
Coongie Lakes Nat Park SA 73 D13
Coongoola QLD 19 G13
Coongulla VIC 49 K8 50 E3
Coonooer Bridge VIC 45 A9 47 K9
Cooperabung Creek Nature Res NSW 29 K12
Coopernook NSW 27 B13
Coopers Creek VIC 50 E2
Coopers Plains QLD 3 G4
Cooplacurripa NSW 27 A11
Coopracambra Nat Park VIC 34 K3 51 B12
Coorabakh Nat Park NSW 27 B12
Coorabie SA 74 K5
Cooran QLD 9 D12
Cooranbong NSW 23 E5 27 F10
Cooranga North QLD 9 E10
Cooriemungle VIC 45 J8
Coorinyup WA 81 E11
Coornartha Nature Res NSW 34 G3 35 H1
Coorong Nat Park SA 67 H10 69 E4
Coorow WA 84 G5
Cooroy QLD 5 A9 9 E12
Coorparoo QLD 3 F4
Cootamundra NSW 26 K2 33 G14 34 B1
Coothalla QLD 19 E13
Cooya QLD 14 B3
Cooyal NSW 26 D6
Cooyar QLD 9 F11
Copacabana NSW 23 J6
Cope Cope VIC 47 K8
Copeland Tops State Con Area NSW 27 B11
Copeton Dam NSW 29 E8
Copeville SA 69 B5 71 J12
Copley SA 71 A10 73 K10
Copmanhurst NSW 29 E12
Coppabella QLD 10 E7
Copperfield QLD 10 G6
Copperfield Mining Centre WA 85 F11
Copperhannia Nature Res NSW 26 H4
Copping TAS 57 B12 59 F12
Cora Lynn VIC 43 G12 52 D4
Corack VIC 47 J8
Corack East VIC 47 J8
Corackerup Nature Res WA 83 H8
Coragulac VIC 45 H9
Coraki NSW 9 K13 29 C13
Coral Bay WA 86 F1
Coral Coast QLD 9 A12 11 K13
Coral Sea QLD 13 A14
Coramba NSW 29 G12
Cordalba QLD 9 B11
Cordering WA 81 C8
Coreen NSW 33 J11
Corella Creek NT 99 E11
Corfield QLD 17 C9
Coridhap VIC 45 F10
Corinda QLD 3 G3
Corindi Beach NSW 29 F13
Corinella VIC 43 K11 52 F3
Corinna TAS 60 G2
Corio VIC 42 F3
Cornella VIC 45 A13 48 E1
Corner Inlet VIC 50 J1 52 H7
Cornucopia VIC 43 F12
Cornwall TAS 61 G13
Cornwallis NSW 24 B7
Corny Point SA 68 H4 70 J7
Corobimilla NSW 33 G11
Coromandel East SA 64 K5
Coromandel Valley SA 64 K4 65 K3 66 A6
Coromby VIC 44 A6
Coromup WA 81 E13
Coronation Beach WA 84 E3
Coronation Islands WA 89 C8
Coronet Bay VIC 43 K11
Corop VIC 47 K13 48 D1
Cororooke VIC 45 H9
Corowa NSW 33 K11 48 A7
Corridgery NSW 26 F1 33 D14
Corrigin WA 79 F12 82 D6
Corrimal NSW 25 K10 27 J8 34 B7 35 A7
Corroboree Park Inn NT 95 D3 96 D4
Corroboree Rock Con Res NT 101 F9
Corrowong NSW 34 J2
Corryong VIC 33 K14 49 C12
Cosgrove VIC 48 C4
Cosmo Newberry WA 91 D2
Cosmo Newbery WA 85 D13
Cossack WA 86 B6
Costerfield VIC 45 B13 48 F1
Cottage Point NSW 25 B11
Cottan-Bimbang Nat Park NSW 27 A12 29 K10
Cottesloe WA 77 G1
Cottles Bridge VIC 43 B9
Couchy Creek Nature Res NSW 29 A13
Cougal NSW 7 K9 29 A13
Coulomb Point Nature Res WA 88 F4 90 A1
Coulson QLD 6 F7
Coulston Park QLD 11 E8
Coulta SA 70 H5
Councillor Island TAS 60 B7
Countegany NSW 34 G4 35 H2
Courabyra Nature Res NSW 33 J14
Couta Rocks TAS 60 E1
Coutts Crossing NSW 29 E12
Cowabbie West NSW 33 F12
Cowan NSW 25 A10
Cowan Cowan QLD 5 H12
Cowangie VIC 32 H2 46 E2 71 K14
Cowaramup WA 80 D2 82 G2
Coward Springs SA 72 H7
Cowcowing Lakes WA 82 A5 84 J7
Cowell SA 68 D3 70 G7
Cowes VIC 43 K9 52 F3
Cowley QLD 13 E13
Cowley Beach QLD 14 J7
Cowper NSW 29 E13
Cowra NSW 26 H3
Cowwarr VIC 50 E3
Cox Peninsula NT 95 C1 96 C3
Cox Scrub Con Park SA 66 D7
Coyrecup WA 81 C12
Crab Island QLD 15 C1
Crabtree TAS 56 E2 59 G9
Crace ACT 37 B5
Cracow QLD 9 B8
Cradle Mountain - Lake St Clair Nat Park TAS 58 A5 60 H5
Cradle Valley TAS 60 G5
Cradoc TAS 56 H2 59 H9
Cradock SA 71 C10
Crafers SA 64 J6 65 J3
Crafers West SA 64 J6
Craiggiemore WA 85 E13 91 E1
Craigie NSW 34 J3 51 A11
Craigie VIC 45 C10
Craigie WA 77 B2
Craigieburn VIC 42 B7 45 E14 48 J2 52 A1
Craiglie QLD 13 C12 14 B4
Cramenton VIC 32 G4 46 D6
Cramps TAS 59 A9 61 H9
Cramsie QLD 10 H1 17 E10
Cranbourne VIC 41 K7 43 G9 52 D3
Cranbrook TAS 59 B13 61 J13
Cranbrook WA 81 F11 82 H6
Cranebrook NSW 24 C7
Craneford SA 65 D7
Cranley QLD 6 B1
Crater Lakes Nat Park QLD 14 G4
Craven NSW 27 C11
Cravensville VIC 49 C11
Crawfordville NSW 23 C3
Crawley WA 77 G3
Crayfish Creek TAS 60 C4
Creek Junction VIC 48 E5
Creek View VIC 45 A13 48 D1
Cremorne NSW 22 E6 25 D12
Cremorne TAS 57 E8 59 G11
Crescent Head NSW 29 J12
Cressy TAS 55 K5 61 G10
Cressy VIC 45 G10
Crestmead QLD 3 K5 7 D10
Crestwood NSW 37 F7
Creswick VIC 45 D11
Crib Point VIC 43 J9
Croajingolong Nat Park VIC 51 D12
Crocodile Hole WA 89 F13
Croftby QLD 6 H6
Croker Island NT 96 A6
Cromer Con Park SA 65 F6
Cronulla NSW 22 K5 25 F12
Crooble NSW 28 C6
Crooked River VIC 49 H9 50 B4
Crookwell NSW 26 K5 34 B4 35 A2
Croppa Creek NSW 28 C6
Crossdale QLD 4 H6
Crossman WA 78 H7
Crow Mountain NSW 28 G7
Crowdy Bay Nat Park NSW 27 B13
Crowes VIC 45 K9
Crowlands VIC 45 C8
Crows Nest NSW 22 E5
Crows Nest QLD 4 J2 9 F11
Crows Nest Nat Park QLD 4 J2 9 F11
Croxton East VIC 44 F5
Croydon QLD 12 F7
Croydon SA 64 F3 65 H2
Croydon VIC 43 C10 48 K3 52 B3
Crusoe Island QLD 7 D13
Crymelon VIC 46 J5
Cryon NSW 28 F2
Crystal Brook SA 68 D6 71 F9
Crystal Creek NSW 7 J12
CSA Mine NSW 31 H10
Cuballing WA 79 J10 82 E5
Cubbaroo NSW 28 F3
Cuckoo TAS 61 E11
Cudal NSW 26 F3
Cudgee VIC 44 H7
Cudgegong NSW 26 E6
Cudgen NSW 7 J14 29 A14
Cudgen Lake NSW 7 K14
Cudgen Nature Res NSW 29 A14
Cudgera Creek NSW 7 K13 29 A14
Cudgewa VIC 33 K14 49 B12
Cudgewa North VIC 49 B12
Cudlee Creek SA 65 G5
Cudlee Creek Con Park SA 65 G5
Cudmirrah NSW 34 D6 35 D6
Cudmore Nat Park QLD 10 G4 17 D13
Cue WA 84 C7
Culbin WA 79 K8 81 A8
Culburra NSW 34 C7
Culburra SA 69 E5
Culburra Beach NSW 35 C7
Culcairn NSW 33 J12
Culgoa VIC 32 J5 47 G8
Culgoa Floodplain Nat Park QLD 8 K1 31 B12
Culgoa Nat Park NSW 8 K1 31 C12
Culgoora NSW 28 F4
Culham WA 78 B7
Cullacabardee WA 77 C4
Cullen Bay NT 94 H1
Cullen Bullen NSW 24 A1 26 F6
Cullendulla NSW 34 E6 35 F5
Cullendulla Creek Nature Res NSW 34 E5 35 F4
Cullerin NSW 34 C4 35 B2
Cullulleraine VIC 32 F2 46 B3 71 H14
Cumborah NSW 31 D14
Cummins SA 68 F1 70 H5
Cumnock NSW 26 E3
Cundare VIC 45 G9
Cundeelee WA 85 H14 91 G2
Cunderdin WA 79 C10 82 C5 84 K7
Cundinup WA 80 D4
Cungena SA 70 D4
Cunliffe SA 68 E5 71 G9
Cunnamulla QLD 19 H12
Cunnawarra Nat Park NSW 29 H10
Cunningham SA 68 F5 69 A1 71 H9
Cunningham Islands NT 97 B12
Cunninyeuk NSW 32 H7 47 E10
Cuprona TAS 60 D6
Curacoa Island QLD 13 G14

F

G

H

I

Ingalba Nature Res NSW 33 F13
Ingebirah NSW 34 H2
Ingebyra NSW 49 E14
Ingham QLD 13 G13
Ingle Farm SA 64 D5 65 G3
Ingleburn NSW 25 F9
Inglegar NSW 31 H14
Ingleside NSW 22 B6 25 B11
Inglewood QLD 9 J9 29 A8
Inglewood SA 65 G4
Inglewood VIC 45 A10
Inglewood WA 77 E4
Inglis Island NT 97 B12
Ingliston VIC 42 B2
Ingoldsby QLD 6 D3
Ininti NT 90 G7 100 E1
Injarrtnama NT 100 F7
Injinoo QLD 15 B2
Injune QLD 8 C4
Inkerman QLD 10 A6
Inkerman SA 68 F6 69 A2 71 H9
Inman Valley SA 66 G4 68 J6 69 D2 71 K10
Innaloo WA 77 E2
Innamincka SA 18 G3 73 E14
Innamincka Reg Res SA 18 F3 73 D13
Inner Sister Island TAS 61 A8
Innes Nat Park SA 68 H3 70 K7
Innisfail QLD 13 E13 14 H7
Innisplain QLD 7 H9
Innot Hot Springs QLD 13 E12 14 J2
Interlaken TAS 59 C10 61 K10
Inveralochy NSW 34 C4 35 C3
Inverell NSW 29 E8
Invergordon VIC 48 B4
Inverleigh VIC 42 G1 45 G11
Inverloch VIC 52 G5
Inverramsay QLD 6 G3
Investigator Group Con Park SA 70 G3
Investigator Strait SA 68 J3
Iona VIC 43 G13 52 D5
Ipolera NT 100 F6
Ipswich QLD 6 C7 9 G12
Iredale QLD 6 C2
Irishtown TAS 60 C3
Irishtown WA 78 C7
Irkini NT 74 A1 90 J7 91 B7 100 K2
Iron Baron SA 68 C4 71 E8
Iron Knob SA 68 B4 71 E8
Iron Range QLD 15 F3
Iron Range Nat Park QLD 15 E4
Ironbank SA 64 K6 65 K3 66 A6
Ironbark Nature Res NSW 28 G7
Irondale NSW 24 B1
Ironmungy Nature Res NSW 34 H2
Ironwood Bore SA 74 B5
Irrapatana SA 72 G7
Irrewarra VIC 45 H10
Irrewillipe VIC 45 J9
Irrilitee NT 101 D10
Irrunytju (Wingellina) WA 74 A1
Irvinebank QLD 13 E12 14 G2
Irymple VIC 32 F3 46 A5
Isaacs ACT 37 G4
Isabella NSW 26 H5
Isabella Plains ACT 37 J4
Isis TAS 59 A10 61 H10
Isis Junction QLD 9 B12
Isisford QLD 10 J1 17 G11
Isla Gorge Nat Park QLD 8 B7
Island Bend NSW 34 G2 49 C14
Island Lagoon SA 70 B7
Isle of the Dead TAS 57 H13
Isle Woodah NT 97 E12
Israelite Bay WA 91 K3
Ivanhoe NSW 32 C7
Iveragh QLD 11 J11
Ivory Creek QLD 4 G4

J

Jaaningga Nature Res NSW 29 H12
Jabiru NT 95 D7 96 D6
Jabuk SA 69 D5 71 K12
Jack River VIC 50 H2
Jack River Nat Park QLD 13 A11 15 J6
Jackadgery NSW 29 E11
Jackeys Marsh TAS 55 K1 61 G8
Jackie Junction WA 91 B5
Jackson QLD 8 E6
Jacobs Well QLD 7 E12
Jacobs Well WA 79 E10
Jalbarragup WA 80 E3
Jallukar VIC 44 D7
Jallumba VIC 44 C4
Jalma Bay NT 97 E11
Jaloran WA 79 K10 81 A10
Jam Jerrup VIC 43 J11
Jamberoo NSW 27 K8 34 B7 35 B7
Jambin QLD 11 J10
Jamboree Heights QLD 3 G2
Jamestown SA 68 C7 71 F10
Jamieson VIC 48 H6 50 B1
Jamieson (Mantamaru) WA 90 J6 91 B6
Jamisontown NSW 24 D7
Jan Juc VIC 42 J2 45 H12
Jancourt VIC 45 H8
Jancourt East VIC 45 H8
Jandabup WA 77 A4
Jandakot WA 77 K4 78 E5
Jandowae QLD 9 E9
Jane Nat Park WA 80 H6
Jannali NSW 22 J3
Japoon QLD 14 J6
Japoon Nat Park QLD 13 E13 14 J5
Japoonvale QLD 13 E13 14 J6
Jaraga QLD 10 B6
Jardee WA 80 F6
Jardine River Nat Park QLD 15 C2
Jardine Valley QLD 10 C1 17 A10
Jarklin VIC 47 K11
Jarlmadangah-Burr WA 88 H6 90 A3
Jarman Landing SA 67 C14
Jarra Jarra NT 98 J7 100 A7
Jarrah Glen WA 81 J8
Jarrahdale WA 78 F5 82 D3
Jarrahwood WA 80 D4 82 D3
Jasper Nature Res NSW 27 A12 29 K11
Jaspers Brush NSW 34 C7 35 B6
Jaurdi Con Park WA 83 A10 85 H10
Jeetho VIC 43 J13
Jeffcott North VIC 47 K8
Jennaberring WA 79 D11
Jennacubbine WA 79 B8
Jennapullin WA 79 C8
Jenolan Caves NSW 24 F2 26 H6
Jeogla NSW 29 H10
Jeparit VIC 46 J5
Jerangle NSW 34 F4 35 G2 38 K7
Jerdacuttup Lakes Nature Res WA 83 G10
Jericho QLD 10 H4 17 F13
Jericho TAS 59 D10
Jericho VIC 48 J6 50 C1 52 A7
Jerilderie NSW 33 H10
Jerrabomberra NSW 37 G7
Jerralong Nature Res NSW 34 D5
Jerramungup WA 83 G8
Jerrawa NSW 34 C3 35 B1
Jerrawangala Nat Park NSW 34 C6 35 C6
Jerrys Plains NSW 27 D9
Jerseyville NSW 29 J12
Jervis Bay NSW 34 D7 35 D6
Jervis Bay Nat Park NSW 34 C7 35 C7
Jervois SA 67 D14 69 C4 71 K11
Jetsonville TAS 61 D11
Jigalong WA 87 F11
Jil Jil VIC 32 K5 47 H8
Jilakin WA 79 H14
Jilbadji Nature Res WA 83 C9 85 K10
Jilkminggan NT 96 G7
Jilliby NSW 23 G5
Ji-Marda NT 97 C9
Jimaringle NSW 32 H7 47 F11
Jimbalakudunj WA 89 G8 90 A4
Jimblebar Mine WA 87 F10
Jimboomba QLD 7 E10 9 H12
Jimbour QLD 9 F9
Jimenbuen NSW 34 J2
Jimna QLD 4 C5 9 E12
Jincumbilly NSW 34 H3
Jindabyne NSW 34 H2
Jindalee QLD 3 G2 7 B9
Jindera NSW 33 K12 49 A9
Jindivick VIC 43 F14 52 D6
Jindivick North VIC 43 F14
Jindivick West VIC 43 F14
Jindong WA 80 D2
Jingalup WA 81 E9
Jingellic NSW 33 K14 49 A12
Jingellic Nature Res NSW 33 K14 49 A12
Jingera NSW 34 F4 35 F2 38 J7
Jingili NT 94 D4
Jinglemoney NSW 34 E4 35 E3
Jip Jip Con Park SA 69 F6
Jitarning WA 79 H13 82 E6
Joadja NSW 26 K7 34 B6 35 A5
Joadja Nature Res NSW 26 J7 34 B6
Joanna SA 44 C1 69 H7
Joel VIC 45 C8
Jogo QLD 14 H6
Johanna VIC 45 K9
John Forrest Nat Park WA 78 D5 82 C3 84 K5
Johnburgh SA 68 A7 71 D10
Johns River NSW 27 B13
Johnstown QLD 4 A2
Jolimont WA 77 F3
Jondaryan QLD 9 G10
Jones Gully QLD 4 H1
Joondalup WA 77 A2
Joondanna WA 77 E3
Josbury WA 79 K8 81 A8
Joseph Banks (Round Hill Head) Con Park QLD 11 J12
Joseph Bonaparte Gulf NT WA 89 B13 96 G1
Josephville QLD 7 G9
Joycedale QLD 10 H4 17 F13
Joyces Creek VIC 45 C11
Jubilee Vale QLD 4 G1
Jubuk WA 79 F11
Judbury TAS 56 E1 59 G9
Jueburra QLD 16 B4
Jugiong NSW 34 C1
Julatten QLD 13 C12 14 C3
Julia SA 71 G10
Julia Creek QLD 12 K7 16 A7
Julimar Con Park WA 78 B6
Jumbunna VIC 43 K13 52 F5
Junabee QLD 6 J2
Junction Bay NT 97 B8
Junction View QLD 6 E3
Jundah QLD 17 H9 19 A8
Junee NSW 33 G13
Junee Nat Park QLD 11 G8
Junee Reefs NSW 26 K1 33 G13
Jung VIC 44 A6
Junjuwa WA 89 H9 90 A4
Junortoun VIC 45 B12
Junuy Juluum Nat Park NSW 29 G11
Jura WA 79 D13
Jurema QLD 10 G6
Jurien Bay WA 84 H4
Jussieu Bay SA 68 H1
Jussieu Peninsula SA 68 G2
Juugawaarri Nature Res NSW 29 H12

K

Kaarimba VIC 48 B3
Kaban QLD 13 E12 14 H3
Kabelbara QLD 10 G6
Kabra QLD 11 H10
Kadina SA 68 E5 71 G8
Kadjina WA 89 J8 90 B4
Kadnook VIC 44 C3
Kadungle NSW 26 D1 33 B13
Kagaru QLD 7 E9
Kaimkillenbun QLD 9 F10
Kainton SA 68 F5 71 G9
Kainton Corner SA 68 F5 71 G9
Kairi QLD 13 D12 14 F4
Kaiserstuhl Con Park SA 65 D7
Kajabbi QLD 12 J4
Kajuligah Nature Res NSW 33 B8
Kakadu Nat Park NT 95 C6 96 D6
Kalamunda WA 78 E5 82 C3 84 K5
Kalamunda Nat Park WA 78 E5 82 C3 84 K5
Kalang NSW 29 G12
Kalangadoo SA 44 E1 69 J6
Kalannie WA 84 H6
Kalarka QLD 11 F9
Kalaru NSW 34 J5
Kalbar QLD 6 F6 9 H12
Kalbarri WA 84 D2
Kalbarri Nat Park WA 84 C2
Kaleen ACT 37 C4
Kaleentha NSW 32 B5
Kalgan WA 81 J12
Kalgoorlie WA 83 A12 85 H12 91 G1
Kalimna West VIC 49 K12 50 E7
Kalka SA 74 A1 90 J7 91 C7 100 K1
Kalkallo VIC 42 A7 45 E14 48 J2 52 A1
Kalkarindji (Wave Hill) NT 98 D3
Kalkee VIC 44 A5
Kallangur QLD 5 J9
Kallaroo WA 77 B1
Kallista VIC 43 D10
Kalorama VIC 43 D10
Kalpi SA 74 C5
Kalpowar QLD 9 A10 11 K11
Kalumburu WA 89 B11
Kalvarr Nat Park NSW 33 F8
Kalyan SA 69 B5 71 J12
Kalyarr Nat Park NSW 47 B12
Kamarah NSW 33 F12
Kamarooka VIC 45 A12 47 K12
Kambah ACT 37 G3
Kambalda WA 83 B13 85 J12 91 G1
Kambalda Nature Res WA 83 A12 85 J12 91 G1
Kambalda West WA 83 B13 85 J12 91 G1
Kamballup WA 81 H13
Kamber NSW 26 A3 28 K2
Kamma QLD 14 E5
Kamona TAS 61 E12
Kampurarr Pirti WA 90 K6 91 C6
Kanagulk VIC 44 C4
Kanangra-Boyd Nat Park NSW 24 G3 26 H6 34 A5
Kandanga QLD 4 A7 9 D12
Kandat Djaru WA 89 J13 90 B7
Kandiwal WA 89 B10
Kandos NSW 26 E6
Kangarilla SA 66 B6 68 H7 69 C3 71 J10
Kangaroo Flat SA 65 C3
Kangaroo Flat VIC 45 B11
Kangaroo Ground VIC 41 B7 43 B9
Kangaroo Island QLD 7 D12
Kangaroo Island SA 68 K4 69 E1
Kangaroo Island TAS 60 B1
Kangaroo Point QLD 2 C4
Kangaroo Valley NSW 26 K7 34 C7 35 B6
Kangarooby NSW 26 G3
Kangawall VIC 44 B3
Kangy Angy NSW 23 G5
Kaniva VIC 46 K2
Kanmantoo SA 65 K6 67 A10
Kanowna WA 85 H12 91 G1
Kanpa WA 90 K4 91 C4
Kanpi SA 74 A2 100 K3
Kanumbra VIC 48 F4
Kanunnah Bridge TAS 60 D2
Kanwal NSW 23 G6
Kanya VIC 45 B8
Kanyaka Ruins SA 71 C9
Kaoota TAS 56 F4 59 G10
Kapinnie SA 70 G5
Kapunda SA 65 A6 68 F7 69 A3 71 H10
Karabar NSW 37 G7
Karabeal VIC 44 E5
Karadoc VIC 32 F4 46 B5
Karama NT 94 D7
Karana Downs QLD 7 B8
Karanja TAS 59 E9
Karara QLD 9 H10 29 A9
Karatta SA 68 K3
Karawatha QLD 3 J5
Karawinna VIC 32 F3
Kardella VIC 43 K14
Kardella South VIC 43 K14
Kardinya WA 77 J3
Kareela NSW 22 J3 25 F11
Kareeya Power Station QLD 14 J4
Kariah VIC 45 H8
Karijini Nat Park WA 86 F7
Kariong NSW 23 J5
Karkoo SA 68 E1 70 G5
Karlgarin WA 83 D8
Karonie WA 83 A14 85 J13 91 G2
Karonie Mine WA 83 A14 85 J13 91 G2
Karook VIC 45 A14 48 D2
Karoola TAS 55 E5 61 E10
Karoon QLD 10 C2 17 A11
Karoonda SA 69 C5 71 J12
Karping WA 79 H9
Karragarra Island QLD 7 C12
Karrakatta WA 77 G2
Karramomus North VIC 48 D4
Karrandgin WA 79 A8
Karratha WA 86 B5
Karratha Roadhouse WA 86 C5
Karridale WA 80 F2 82 H2
Karrinyup WA 77 D2
Karrku WA 90 H6 91 A6
Karroun Hill Nature Res WA 85 G8
Kars Springs NSW 27 B8
Karte SA 32 H1 69 C7 71 J13
Karte Con Park SA 32 H1 69 C7 71 K13
Karuah NSW 27 D11
Karuah Nature Res NSW 27 D11
Karukaki NT 100 H2
Karumba QLD 12 E5
Karween VIC 32 F2
Katamatite VIC 33 K10 48 B4
Katandra VIC 48 B4
Katanning WA 81 C11 82 G5
Katherine NT 95 J5 96 G5
Katoomba NSW 24 D4 26 G7
Katrine WA 78 C7
Kattyong VIC 32 H3
Kattyoong VIC 46 E4
Katunga VIC 33 K10 48 A4
Katyil VIC 46 K5
Kau Rock Nature Res WA 83 F14 91 K1
Kawana Waters QLD 5 D10
Kawarren VIC 45 J10
Kayena TAS 55 D3 61 E9
Kearsley NSW 23 C4
Kebaringup WA 81 E13
Kedron QLD 3 C4 5 K10 7 A10
Keep River Nat Park NT 89 D14 96 J1 98 A1
Keera NSW 28 F7
Keilor VIC 41 B1 42 C6 45 F13 48 J1 52 B1
Keilor North VIC 41 B1
Keirbar NSW 23 B3
Keith SA 69 E6
Kellalac VIC 46 K6
Kellatier TAS 60 D4
Kellerberrin WA 79 C12 82 C6 84 K7
Kellerberrin North WA 79 C11
Kellevie TAS 57 B12 59 F12
Kellidie Bay Con Park SA 68 G1 70 H5
Kelly Hill Con Park SA 68 K3
Kellys Creek NSW 26 H3
Kellyville NSW 22 B1 25 C9
Kelmscott WA 78 E5 82 D3
Kelso TAS 55 C2 61 D8
Kelvin NSW 28 H6
Kelvin Grove QLD 2 A2 3 E3
Kembla Heights NSW 25 K10
Kemps Creek NSW 25 E8
Kempsey NSW 29 J12
Kempton TAS 59 E10
Kendall NSW 27 B13
Kendenup WA 81 G11 82 J6
Kenebri NSW 28 H3
Kenilworth QLD 4 C7 9 E12
Kenley VIC 47 D9
Kenmare VIC 32 K4 46 H5
Kenmore QLD 3 F2 7 B9
Kenmore Hills QLD 3 F2
Kennedy QLD 13 F13
Kennedy Range Nat Park WA 86 H3
Kennedys Creek VIC 45 J8
Kenneth Stirling Con Park SA 65 J4
Kennett River VIC 45 K11
Kenny ACT 37 B5
Kennys Creek NSW 26 J4 34 B3
Kensington NSW 25 D12
Kensington SA 64 G5 65 H3
Kensington VIC 41 D3
Kensington WA 77 G4
Kensington Gardens SA 64 G6
Kent Island QLD 14 J7
Kent Town SA 63 C3
Kentbruck VIC 44 H3
Kentdale WA 81 J9
Kenthurst NSW 22 B2
Kentlyn NSW 25 G9
Kenton WA 81 J9
Kenton Valley SA 65 G5
Kentucky NSW 29 H9
Kentville QLD 6 B5
Kenwick WA 77 J6
Keperra QLD 3 D2 5 K9 7 A9
Keppel Bay Islands Nat Park QLD 11 G11
Keppel Sands QLD 11 H10
Keppoch SA 69 G6
Kerang VIC 32 J7 47 G10
Kerang East VIC 47 H11
Kerang South VIC 47 H11
Kerein Hills NSW 33 B12
Kergunyah VIC 49 C9
Kernot VIC 43 K12 52 F4
Kerrabee NSW 26 D7
Kerrisdale VIC 48 G3
Kerriwah NSW 31 K13 33 B13
Kerrs Creek NSW 26 E4
Kerry QLD 7 H9
Kersbrook SA 65 G5 68 G7 69 B3 71 J10
Keswick SA 63 D1
Kettering TAS 56 H5 59 H10
Kevin SA 70 C1 74 K6
Kevington VIC 48 H6 50 B1
Kew NSW 27 B13
Kew VIC 41 D4
Kewarra Beach QLD 14 D4
Kewdale WA 77 G6
Kewell VIC 44 A6
Keyneton SA 69 A4 71 H11
Keysborough VIC 41 H6 43 F9
Keysbrook WA 78 G5
Khancoban NSW 33 K14 34 G1 49 C13
Khappinghat Nature Res NSW 27 C13
Khatambuhl Nature Res NSW 27 B11
Kholo QLD 6 B7
Ki Ki SA 69 D5 71 K11
Kia Ora VIC 44 E7
Kiacatoo NSW 33 C12
Kiah NSW 34 K5 51 B14
Kialla NSW 26 K5 34 B4 35 A2
Kialla VIC 48 D3
Kiama NSW 27 K8 34 C7 35 B7
Kiamal VIC 32 H4 46 D5
Kiandra NSW 34 F2 49 A14
Kianga NSW 34 G5 35 H4
Kianga QLD 11 K9
Kiata VIC 46 K4
Kibbleup WA 81 C11
Kidaman Creek QLD 4 C7
Kidman Park SA 64 F2
Kidston QLD 13 G10
Kielpa SA 68 D2 70 F6
Kiewa VIC 49 C9
Kikoira NSW 33 D12
Kilburn SA 64 E4 65 G2
Kilcoy QLD 4 F6 9 F12
Kilcunda VIC 52 G4
Kilkenny SA 64 F3
Kilkivan QLD 9 D11
Killabakh NSW 27 B12
Killabakh Nature Res NSW 27 B12
Killara NSW 22 D5 25 C11
Killara VIC 43 C11
Killarney QLD 6 K4 9 J11 29 A11
Killarney VIC 44 H6
Killarney Heights NSW 22 D6 25 C11
Killarney Nature Res NSW 27 C11
Killarney Vale NSW 23 H6
Killcare NSW 23 J5 27 G9
Killi Killi WA 90 D7
Killiecrankie TAS 61 A8
Killingworth NSW 23 C5
Kilmany VIC 50 F3
Kilmore VIC 45 D14 48 G2
Kimba SA 68 C2 70 E6
Kimberley TAS 60 F7
Kimbriki NSW 27 B12
Kimburra QLD 10 C3 13 K12
Kin Kin QLD 9 D12
Kinalung NSW 30 K3 32 A3
Kinchega Nat Park NSW 30 K3 32 B3
Kinchela Creek NSW 29 J12
Kincumber NSW 23 J5
Kindee NSW 27 A12 29 K11
Kindred TAS 60 E7
King Ash Bay NT 97 J12 99 A12
King George Island TAS 57 E12
King Island QLD 15 H5
King Island TAS 60 B6
King Leopold Ranges Con Park WA 89 F8 90 A4
King River WA 81 J12
King Sound WA 88 F6
King Valley VIC 48 E7
Kingaroy QLD 9 E10
Kingfisher Bay QLD 9 B13
Kingfisher Islands WA 88 D7
Kinglake VIC 43 A10 48 J3 52 A3
Kinglake Central VIC 43 A10 48 H3 52 A3
Kinglake East VIC 43 A10
Kinglake Nat Park VIC 43 A10 45 D14 48 H3 52 A3
Kinglake West VIC 48 H3
Kingoonya SA 70 A5 72 K5
Kingower VIC 45 A10
Kings Cross NSW 21 C3 25 D12
Kings Langley NSW 22 C1
Kings Plains Nat Park NSW 29 E9
Kings Point NSW 34 E6 35 E5
Kingsborough QLD 13 D12 14 E1
Kingsbury VIC 41 B4 43 C8
Kingscliff NSW 7 J14 9 J14 29 A14
Kingscote SA 68 J5 69 D1 71 K8
Kingsdale NSW 26 K6 34 B4 35 B3
Kingsford NSW 22 G6 25 D12
Kingsholme QLD 7 E11
Kingsley WA 77 B2
Kingston ACT 36 D4 37 E5
Kingston QLD 3 K5 7 C10
Kingston TAS 56 E6 59 G10
Kingston VIC 45 D11
Kingston OM SA 69 A6 71 H12
Kingston SE SA 69 G5
Kingstown NSW 29 G8
Kingsvale NSW 26 J2 34 B1
Kingswood NSW 24 D7
Kingswood SA 64 H4
Kinimakatka VIC 46 K3
Kinlyside ACT 37 A3
Kinnabulla VIC 46 H7
Kinrara Nat Park QLD 13 G12
Kioloa NSW 34 E6 35 F5
Kipper QLD 4 J4
Kirkstall VIC 44 H6
Kirrama Nat Park QLD 13 F13
Kirramingly Nature Res NSW 28 E5
Kirrawee NSW 22 J3
Kirup WA 80 D5 82 G3
Kital QLD 6 G2
Kitchener NSW 23 C4
Kitchener WA 91 G3
Kithbrook VIC 48 E5
Kiwirrkurra WA 90 F6
Kleinton QLD 4 K1 6 A1
Klemzig SA 64 E5
Knapp Creek Con Park QLD 6 H7
Knight Island QLD 11 D9
Knorrit Flat NSW 27 B11
Knowsley VIC 45 B13
Knoxfield VIC 43 D9
Koah QLD 14 D4
Kobyboyn VIC 48 F3
Kodj Kodjin WA 79 B12
Kodjinup Nature Res WA 80 F7
Koetong VIC 33 K13 49 B11
Kogan QLD 9 F8
Kogarah NSW 22 H4
Koimbo VIC 32 H5 46 D7
Kojonup WA 81 D9 82 G5
Kokokup WA 81 H11
Kokotungo QLD 11 J9
Koloona NSW 28 E7
Kolora VIC 44 G7
Komungla NSW 34 C4 35 B3
Kondalilla Nat Park QLD 5 C8
Kondinin WA 79 G14 82 D7
Kondinin Lake Nature Res WA 79 G13
Kondinin Salt Marsh Nature Res WA 79 G14
Kongal SA 69 F6
Kongorong SA 69 K6
Kongwak VIC 52 G5
Konongwootong VIC 44 E3
Konupa QLD 10 K1 17 H10 19 A10
Kookaburra NSW 29 J11
Kookynie WA 85 F12 91 F1
Koolamarra QLD 12 J4
Koolan WA 88 D6
Koolan Island WA 88 D6
Koolewong NSW 23 J5
Koolgera Con Res SA 70 D4
Kooloonong VIC 32 G5 47 D8
Kooltandra QLD 11 G9
Koolunga SA 68 D6 71 F9
Koolyanobbing WA 83 A9 85 H9
Koombooloomba QLD 13 E12 14 K4
Koombooloomba Dam QLD 14 K4
Koonadgin WA 79 C14
Koonda VIC 32 H2 46 E3 48 D5
Koondoola WA 77 C4
Koondrook VIC 32 J7 47 G11
Koongawa SA 68 C1 70 F6
Koonibba SA 70 C2 74 K7
Koonibba Community SA 70 C2 74 K7
Koonoomoo VIC 48 A4
Koonunga SA 65 A6 69 A3 71 H10
Koonwarra VIC 52 G6
Koonya TAS 57 G12 59 G12
Kooraban Nat Park NSW 34 G5 35 J3
Kooraban Nature Res NSW 35 K3
Kooragang NSW 23 B7
Kooragang Nature Res NSW 27 E11
Kooralbyn QLD 7 G8
Koorarawalyee WA 83 B10 85 J10
Koorawatha NSW 26 H3
Koorawatha Nature Res NSW 26 H3 34 A2
Koorboora QLD 13 E11
Koorda WA 82 A5 84 J7
Koorebang Nature Res NSW 27 A12 29 K11
Kooreh VIC 45 A9
Kooringal QLD 5 K13 7 A13
Koorkab VIC 32 G5 47 D8
Koorlong VIC 32 F3 46 B5
Kooroocheang VIC 45 D11
Koorrabye WA 89 H8 90 B4
Kootingal NSW 29 J8
Koo-wee-rup VIC 43 H11 52 E4
Koo-Wee-Rup North VIC 43 G11
Kooyong State Con Area NSW 29 D13
Kooyoora State Park VIC 45 A10
Kopi SA 68 D1 70 F5
Koppio SA 68 F1 70 H6
Korbel WA 79 C13 82 C7 85 K8
Koreelah Nat Park NSW 6 J5 29 A11
Koriella VIC 48 G4
Korobeit VIC 42 A3
Koroit VIC 44 H6
Korong Vale VIC 47 K10
Koroop VIC 47 G11
Korora NSW 29 G13
Korrak Korrak VIC 47 G10
Korrelocking WA 79 A11
Korumburra VIC 43 K13 52 F5
Korumburra South VIC 43 K13
Korunye SA 65 C1
Kosciuszko Nat Park NSW 33 K14 34 G1 38 G1 49 C14
Kotta VIC 47 J12
Kotupna VIC 47 J14 48 B2
Koukandowie Nature Res NSW 29 F12
Koumala QLD 11 E8
Koumala South QLD 11 E8
Kowanyama QLD 12 A7 15 K1
Kowguran QLD 8 D7
Kowrowa QLD 14 D4
Kowtah WA 85 E12 91 E1
Kowulka SA 70 C1 74 K6
Koyuga VIC 47 J13 48 B1
Krambach NSW 27 C12
Kroombit Tops Nat Park QLD 11 J11
Krowera VIC 43 K12 52 F5
Kudardup WA 80 F2 82 H1
Kudla SA 65 E3
Kuender WA 79 J14
Kuitpo Forest SA 66 C7
Kukerin WA 79 K13 81 A13 82 F7
Kulail NT 100 H1
Kulail WA 90 H7 91 A7
Kulde SA 69 C5 71 K11
Kulgera NT 72 A1 74 A6 100 J7
Kulgera Rail Head NT 72 A2 74 A7 100 J7

Lorne SA 68 F6 69 A2 71 H9
Lorne VIC 45 J11
Lorquon VIC 46 J4
Lostock NSW 27 C10
Lota QLD 3 E7 7 B11
Lottah TAS 61 E13
Loughnan Nature Res NSW 33 D10
Louisville TAS 59 E12
Louth NSW 31 F9
Louth Bay SA 68 F1 70 H6
Louth Island SA 68 G1 70 H6
Loveday SA 69 A6 71 H13
Loveday Bay SA 67 H11
Lovett Bay NSW 22 A7
Low Head TAS 55 B2 61 D9
Low Hill SA 68 A3 70 D7
Low Isles QLD 14 A4
Lowan Con Park SA 69 C5 71 J11
Lowana TAS 58 C3 60 K3
Lowden WA 80 C5 82 G3
Lowdina TAS 59 E11
Lower Barrington TAS 60 E7
Lower Beechmont QLD 7 G11
Lower Belford NSW 23 A2
Lower Bendoc VIC 51 A11
Lower Beulah TAS 60 F7
Lower Bucca NSW 29 F13
Lower Creek NSW 29 H11
Lower Cresswell QLD 4 G5
Lower Frankland WA 81 G9
Lower Gellibrand VIC 45 K9
Lower Glenelg Nat Park VIC 44 G3
Lower Hawkesbury NSW 23 J3
Lower Hermitage SA 65 G4
Lower Heytesbury VIC 45 J8
Lower Hunter Valley Vineyards NSW 23 B2
Lower Kalgan WA 81 J13
Lower Light SA 68 G6 69 A2 71 H9
Lower Longley TAS 56 E3
Lower Mangrove NSW 23 J3
Lower Marshes TAS 59 D10
Lower Molonglo Nature Res ACT 37 D2 38 B4
Lower Mookerawa NSW 26 E4
Lower Mount Hicks TAS 60 D5
Lower Mount Walker QLD 6 D5
Lower Norton VIC 44 B5
Lower Portland NSW 23 K1 25 A8
Lower Turners Marsh TAS 55 D5 61 E10
Lower Wilmot TAS 60 E6
Lowesdale NSW 33 K11 33 K11 48 A7
Lowlands NSW 24 B7 33 C9
Lowmead QLD 11 K12
Lowood QLD 6 B6 9 G12
Lowther NSW 24 D2
Loxton SA 69 A7 71 H13
Loxton North SA 32 G1 69 A7 71 H13
Loy Yang VIC 50 F2
Loyetea TAS 60 E5
Lubeck VIC 44 B6
Lucas Heights NSW 22 J2 25 F10
Lucaston TAS 56 E2 59 G9
Lucinda QLD 13 G14
Lucindale SA 69 H6
Lucknow NSW 26 F4
Lucknow VIC 49 K11 50 D6
Lucky Bay SA 68 D4 70 G7
Lucky Flat NSW 28 G4
Lucyvale VIC 49 C11
Luddenham NSW 24 E7
Ludlow WA 80 C3 82 G2
Ludmilla NT 94 F3
Lue NSW 26 D6
Lugarno NSW 25 E10
Luina TAS 60 F3
Lul-Tju NT 98 E3
Lulworth TAS 55 B4 61 D9
Lumeah WA 81 E10
Lumuku WA 89 G13 90 A7
Lunawanna TAS 59 J10
Lune River TAS 59 J9
Lupton Con Park WA 79 G8 82 D4
Lurg VIC 48 D6
Lurnea NSW 25 E9
Luscombe QLD 7 E11
Lutwyche QLD 3 D4
Lymington TAS 56 J2 59 H9
Lymwood TAS 60 C6
Lynchford TAS 58 C4 60 K4
Lyndbrook QLD 13 E11
Lyndhurst NSW 26 G4
Lyndhurst SA 73 J10
Lyndhurst VIC 41 H7 43 F9 52 D3
Lyndoch SA 65 D5 68 G7 69 A3 71 H10
Lyneham ACT 37 C5
Lyons ACT 37 F3
Lyons SA 70 A3 72 K3 74 H7
Lyons VIC 44 G3
Lyonville VIC 45 D12
Lyrup SA 32 F1 69 A7 71 H13
Lysterfield Lake Park VIC 43 E10 48 K3
Lytton QLD 3 D6 5 K10 7 A10

M

Ma Ma Creek QLD 6 C3
Maaroom QLD 9 C13
Maatsuyker Group TAS 58 K7
Maatsuyker Island TAS 58 K7
Mabuiag Island QLD 15 A2
Mac Clark (Acacia Peuce) Con Res NT 101 H10
Macalister QLD 9 F9
Macarthur ACT 37 H5
Macarthur VIC 44 G4
Macclesfield SA 67 B8 68 H7 69 C3 71 J10
Macclesfield VIC 43 D11
Macedon VIC 45 D13
Macgregor ACT 37 B2
MacGregor QLD 3 G5 7 C10
Machans Beach QLD 14 D5
Mackay QLD 11 D8
MacKenzie QLD 3 G6
Macksville NSW 29 H12
Maclean NSW 29 D13
Macleay Island QLD 7 C12
Macleod VIC 41 B5 43 C8
Macorna VIC 32 K7 47 H11
Macquarie ACT 37 C3
Macquarie Fields NSW 25 F9
Macquarie Marshes Nature Res NSW 31 F13
Macquarie Pass Nat Park NSW 27 K8 34 B7 35 A6
Macquarie Plains TAS 59 F9
Macrossan QLD 10 B4 13 J14
Macumba Oil Well SA 72 B7
Maddarr WA 88 E6
Maddington WA 77 J7
Madora WA 78 G4
Madura WA 91 H5
Mafeking VIC 44 D6
Maffra NSW 34 H3
Maffra VIC 50 E4
Maggea SA 69 A6 71 H12
Magill SA 64 F6 65 H3
Magnetic Island QLD 13 G14
Magnetic Island Nat Park QLD 13 G14
Magra TAS 56 A2 59 F9
Magrath Flat SA 69 E4
Maharatta NSW 34 J3 51 A11
Maianbar NSW 25 F11
Maida Vale WA 77 F7
Maidenwell QLD 9 E10
Mailors Flat VIC 44 H6
Maimuru NSW 26 J2 34 A1
Main Beach QLD 7 F13
Main Creek NSW 27 C11
Main Range Nat Park QLD 6 F4 9 H11 29 A11
Maindample VIC 48 F5
Mainoru Store NT 97 F8
Mairjimmy NSW 33 J10
Maitland NSW 23 A5 27 E10
Maitland SA 68 F5 69 A1 71 H8
Maitland Vale NSW 23 A4
Major Plains VIC 48 C5
Majorca VIC 45 C10
Majors Creek NSW 34 E5 35 F3
Majura ACT 37 C6
Makiri SA 74 C4
Makowata QLD 11 K12
Makurapiti SA 74 B1 90 K7 91 C7
Malaan Nat Park QLD 13 E12 14 H4
Malabar NSW 22 H6
Malaburra WA 88 F6
Malaga WA 77 D5
Malak NT 94 D6
Malanda QLD 13 E13 14 G4
Malangan WA 89 G14 90 A7
Malar QLD 4 B1
Malbina TAS 56 B3 59 F10
Malbon QLD 16 B5
Malbooma SA 70 A3 72 K3
Malcolm WA 85 F12 91 E1
Maldon NSW 25 H8
Maldon VIC 45 C11
Malebelling WA 79 D9
Maleny QLD 5 D8 9 E12
Maleny Nat Park QLD 4 C7
Malinong SA 69 D4 71 K11
Mallacoota VIC 51 C13
Mallala SA 65 B1 68 F7 69 A2 71 H10
Mallanganee NSW 29 C12
Mallanganee Nat Park NSW 9 K12 29 C12
Mallee Cliffs Nat Park NSW 32 F4 46 A6
Mallison Island NT 97 C12
Malmsbury VIC 45 C12
Malua Bay NSW 34 F6 35 G5
Malvern SA 64 H4
Malvernton QLD 10 J2 17 G12
Malyalling WA 79 H11
Mamboo QLD 10 H5 17 F14
Mambray Creek SA 68 B5 71 E9
Mammoth Mines QLD 12 J3
Manangatang VIC 32 H5 46 E7
Mandagery NSW 26 F3
Mandalong NSW 23 E5
Mandorah NT 95 C1 96 C3
Mandurah WA 78 G4 82 E2
Mandurama NSW 26 G4
Mangalo SA 68 D3 70 F7
Mangalore QLD 19 E13
Mangalore TAS 59 E10
Mangalore VIC 45 B14 48 F3
Mangana TAS 61 G12
Mangkili Claypan Nature Res WA 90 J3 91 B3
Mangoplah NSW 33 H13
Mangrove Creek NSW 23 H3
Mangrove Creek Dam NSW 23 G2
Mangrove Mountain NSW 23 H3 27 F9
Manguri SA 72 G3
Manildra NSW 26 F3
Manilla NSW 28 H7
Maningrida NT 97 C9
Manjimup WA 80 F6 82 H3
Manly NSW 22 D7 25 C12 27 H9
Manly QLD 3 D7 7 B11
Manly Vale NSW 22 D6 25 C12
Manly West QLD 3 E7
Manmoyi NT 97 C8
Mann River Nature Res NSW 29 E10
Mannahill SA 71 D12
Mannanarie SA 68 C7 71 E10
Mannerim VIC 42 H4
Mannering Park NSW 23 E6
Manning WA 77 H4
Manns Beach VIC 50 H3
Mannum SA 69 B4 71 J11
Mannus NSW 33 J14 49 A12
Manobalai Nature Res NSW 27 C8
Manoora SA 68 E7 71 G10
Manor VIC 42 E4 45 F13
Manorina VIC 51 D10
Manowar Island QLD 12 C3
Mansfield QLD 3 G5
Mansfield VIC 48 F6 50 A1
Manton Dam Rec Area NT 95 D2 96 D4
Mantung SA 69 B6 71 H12
Manuka ACT 37 F5
Manumbah Mill QLD 4 A4
Manumbar QLD 4 A3 9 D11
Many Peaks QLD 11 K11
Manyallaluk (Eva Valley) NT 95 H7 96 F6
Manyirkanga SA 74 A4 100 K4
Manypeaks WA 81 J13 82 J7
Manyung QLD 9 D11
Mapleton QLD 5 C8 9 E12
Mapleton Falls Nat Park QLD 5 C8
Mapoon QLD 15 D1
Mapurru NT 97 C10
Maralinga SA 74 G4
Marama SA 69 C6 71 K12
Marananga SA 65 C6
Maranboy NT 95 J7 96 G6
Marandoo Mine WA 86 E7
Marangaroo WA 77 C3
Marathon QLD 17 A9
Marathon South QLD 17 A9
Maraylya NSW 25 B8
Marayong NSW 25 C9
Marbellup WA 81 J11
Marble Bar WA 87 C9
Marble Hill SA 65 H4
Marble Island QLD 11 E10
Marburg QLD 6 B6 9 G12
Marchagee WA 84 G5
Marchinbar Island NT 97 A12
Marcoola QLD 5 C10
Marcus Beach QLD 5 A10
Marcus Hill VIC 42 H4 45 H12
Mardan VIC 50 G1 52 F7
Mardella WA 78 F5
Mareeba QLD 13 D12 14 E3
Marengo VIC 45 K10
Maret Islands WA 89 B8
Margaret River WA 80 E2 82 H1
Margate QLD 5 J10
Margate TAS 56 F5 59 G10
Margooya VIC 32 G5 46 D7
Maria Creek Nat Park QLD 14 K7
Maria Island NT 97 G11
Maria Island TAS 59 F13
Maria Island Nat Park TAS 59 E13
Maria Lagoon NT 97 H10
Maria Nat Park NSW 29 J12
Mariala Nat Park QLD 17 K12 19 C11
Marian QLD 11 D8
Marimo QLD 16 A5
Marino SA 64 K2 65 K1 66 A5
Marino Con Park SA 65 K1 66 A5
Marion SA 64 J3 65 J2
Marion Bay SA 68 H4 70 K7
Mark Oliphant Con Park SA 65 K3 66 A7
Marks Point NSW 23 D6
Markwood VIC 48 D7
Marla SA 72 D2 74 C7
Marlborough QLD 11 G9
Marlee NSW 27 B12
Marleston SA 64 G3
Marley Pool WA 79 D8
Marlinja NT 98 D7
Marlo VIC 49 K14 51 D9
Marma VIC 44 B6
Marmion WA 77 C1
Marmion Marine Park WA 84 K4
Marmor QLD 11 H10
Marnoo VIC 44 A7
Marnoo East VIC 45 A8
Marong VIC 45 B11
Maroochy River QLD 5 C9
Maroochydore QLD 5 C10 9 E13
Maroon QLD 6 H7
Maroona VIC 44 E7
Maroota NSW 23 K2
Maroota South NSW 23 K2 25 A9
Maroubra NSW 22 G6 25 E12
Marp VIC 44 F2
Marraba QLD 16 A4
Marrabel SA 68 F7 71 G10
Marracoonda WA 81 C10
Marradong WA 78 J7 82 E4
Marralum NT 96 H1
Marramarra Nat Park NSW 23 K3 25 A10 27 G9
Marrangaroo NSW 24 B2
Marrangaroo Nat Park NSW 24 C2
Marrar NSW 33 G13
Marrara NT 94 D6
Marrawah TAS 60 C1
Marraweeny VIC 48 E4
Marree SA 73 H9
Marrickville NSW 25 D11
Marryat SA 72 B2 74 B7 100 K7
Marsden NSW 26 G1 33 E13
Marsden QLD 3 K5 7 D10
Marsden Park NSW 25 C8
Marsfield NSW 22 D4 25 C10
Marshall VIC 42 H3
Marshdale NSW 27 D11
Martin Washpool Con Park SA 69 E5
Martindale NSW 27 D8
Martinsville NSW 23 E4
Marton QLD 13 A12
Marulan NSW 26 K6 34 C5 35 B4
Marunbabidi WA 89 C10
Marvel Loch WA 83 B9 85 K9
Mary Kathleen QLD 12 K4 16 A4
Mary River (Wirnwirnmila) Roadhouse NT 95 F5 96 E5
Mary River Nat Park NT 95 C4 96 C5
Mary Seymour Con Park SA 69 H6
Maryborough QLD 9 C12
Maryborough VIC 45 C10
Maryfarms QLD 13 C12
Maryknoll VIC 43 F12
Maryland NSW 23 C6
Maryland Nat Park NSW 29 A10
Marysville VIC 43 A13 48 H5 52 A5
Maryvale NSW 26 D4
Maryvale QLD 6 G3
Mascot NSW 22 G5 25 D11
Maslin Beach SA 66 C4 68 H6 69 C2 71 K9
Massey VIC 46 J7
Masthead Island QLD 11 H12
Matakana NSW 33 C10
Mataranka NT 95 K7 96 G7
Mataranka Homestead NT 96 G7
Matcham NSW 23 H5
Matheson NSW 29 E9
Mathiesons VIC 45 A14 48 D2
Mathinna TAS 61 F12
Mathoura NSW 33 K8 47 H13 48 A1
Matlock VIC 48 J6 50 C1 52 A7
Matong NSW 33 G12
Matraville NSW 22 H6 25 E12
Maude NSW 32 F7 47 B12
Maude VIC 42 E1 45 G11
Maudsland QLD 7 F12
Maupertuis Bay SA 68 K3
Mawbanna TAS 60 D3
Mawson ACT 37 G4
Mawson WA 79 E9
Mawson Lakes SA 64 C4
Maxwelton QLD 13 K8 17 A8
Maya WA 84 G6
Mayanup WA 80 E7 82 G4
Mayberry TAS 60 G7
Maybole NSW 29 F9
Maydena TAS 59 F8
Mayfield NSW 23 B7
Mayfield Bay Con Area TAS 59 C13 61 K13
Maylands WA 77 F5
Maynard Bore SA 74 C5
Mayrung NSW 33 J9
Maytown QLD 13 B10
Mazeppa Nat Park QLD 10 F5
McAlinden WA 80 C6
McCluer Island NT 96 A7
McCoys Bridge VIC 47 J14 48 B2
McCrae VIC 42 J7
McCullys Gap NSW 27 C9
McDowall QLD 3 C3
McGraths Hill NSW 25 B8
McKellar ACT 37 B3
McKenzie Creek VIC 44 B5
McKillops Bridge VIC 49 G14 51 A9
McKinlay QLD 16 B6
McKinnon VIC 41 F4
McLaren Creek NT 99 J8
McLaren Flat SA 66 C6
McLaren Vale SA 66 C5 68 H7 69 C2 71 K10
McIntyre VIC 45 A10
McMahons Creek VIC 43 C14 48 J5 52 B5
McMahons Reef NSW 26 K3 34 B2
McMasters Beach NSW 23 J6
McMillans VIC 47 H11
McPhail NSW 26 D2
Mead VIC 47 H11
Meadow Flat NSW 26 G6
Meadows SA 66 C7 68 H7 69 C3 71 K10
Meandarra QLD 8 F7
Meander TAS 61 G8
Meandu Creek QLD 4 D1
Mears WA 79 F10
Meatian VIC 47 G9
Mebbin Nat Park NSW 7 K10 9 J13 29 A13
Meckering WA 79 C9 82 C5 84 K6
Medina WA 78 F4
Medindie SA 63 A3
Medlow Bath NSW 24 D4
Medowie NSW 23 A7
Meeandah QLD 3 D5
Meekatharra WA 85 B8
Meelup WA 80 C2
Meenaar WA 79 C8
Meeniyan VIC 52 G6
Meerawa QLD 14 F6
Meerlieu VIC 50 E5
Megalong NSW 24 E4
Megan NSW 29 G12
Mekaree QLD 10 K2 17 G11
Melacca Swamp Con Area NT 95 C2 96 C4
Melawondi QLD 4 A6
Melba ACT 37 B3
Melbourne VIC 40 B2 41 D3 42 C7 45 F14 48 K2 52 B1
Meldale QLD 5 G10
Mella TAS 60 C2
Melros WA 78 H4
Melrose NSW 33 B12
Melrose SA 68 B6 71 E9
Melrose TAS 60 E7
Melrose Park SA 64 J4
Melsonby (Gaarraay) Nat Park QLD 13 A11 15 J6
Melton SA 68 E5 71 G9
Melton VIC 42 B4 45 E12
Melton Mowbray TAS 59 D10
Melton South VIC 42 C4
Melville WA 77 J2
Melville Bay NT 97 C12
Melville Forest VIC 44 E4
Melville Island NT 95 A1 96 B3
Melville Range Nature Res NSW 28 J6
Melwood VIC 49 K11 50 D5
Memana TAS 61 B9
Memerambi QLD 9 D10
Mena Creek QLD 14 J6
Mena Park VIC 45 E9
Menai NSW 22 J2 25 F10
Menangle NSW 25 G8
Menangle Park NSW 25 G8
Mendooran NSW 26 B4
Mengha TAS 60 C3
Menindee NSW 30 K4 32 B4
Meningie SA 67 J13 69 D4 71 K11
Mentone VIC 41 G5 43 E8 45 G14 52 C2
Menzies WA 85 G11
Menzies Creek VIC 43 E11
Mepunga East VIC 44 J7
Mepunga West VIC 44 J7
Merah North NSW 28 F4
Merbein VIC 32 F3 46 A5
Merbein South VIC 32 F3 46 A4
Merbein West VIC 46 A4
Mercunda SA 69 B5 71 J12
Merebene NSW 28 H3
Meredith VIC 42 D1 45 F11
Merewether NSW 23 C7
Meribah SA 32 G1 46 C1 69 B7 71 J13
Merimbula NSW 34 J5
Merinda QLD 10 B7
Meringandan QLD 9 G10
Meringur VIC 32 F2 46 B2 71 H14
Merino VIC 44 F3
Merivale QLD 14 G4
Mermaid Beach QLD 7 G13
Mernda VIC 43 B8 45 E14 48 J2 52 A2
Meroo Nat Park NSW 34 E6 35 E5
Merredin WA 79 B14 82 B7 85 K8
Merriang VIC 49 D8
Merriangaah Nature Res NSW 34 H3
Merricks VIC 43 J8 45 H14 52 F2
Merricks Beach VIC 43 K8
Merricks North VIC 43 J8
Merrigum VIC 47 K14 48 C2
Merrijig VIC 48 G6 50 A1
Merrimac QLD 7 G12
Merrinee VIC 32 F3 46 B4
Merriot Nature Res NSW 27 B10
Merriton SA 68 D6 71 F9
Merriwa NSW 26 C7
Merriwagga NSW 33 E10
Merry Beach NSW 35 F5
Merrygoen NSW 26 B5
Merrylands NSW 22 E2 25 D10
Merryvale QLD 6 E6
Merrywinebone NSW 28 E2
Merseylea TAS 60 F7
Merton NSW 33 K11 48 A6
Merton VIC 48 F4
Messent Con Park SA 69 E5
Messines QLD 29 B10
Metcalfe VIC 45 C12
Methul NSW 33 G13
Metricup WA 80 D2
Metung VIC 49 K12 50 E7
Meunna TAS 60 D4
Mia Mia VIC 45 C13
Miallo QLD 13 C12 14 B3
Miami QLD 7 G13
Miandetta NSW 31 H12
Miara QLD 9 A11 11 K12
Michaelmas and Upolu Cays Nat Park QLD 13 C13
Michaelmas Cay Nat Park QLD 14 C6
Michelago NSW 34 E3 35 F1 38 H5
Mickleham VIC 42 A7
Middingbank NSW 34 G2
Middle Beach SA 68 G6 69 A2 71 H9
Middle Brother Nat Park NSW 27 B13
Middle Camp NSW 23 E6
Middle Dural NSW 22 A2
Middle Island QLD 11 E10
Middle Island WA 91 K2
Middle Lagoon WA 88 E4
Middle Park QLD 7 B9
Middle Point NT 95 C3 96 C4
Middle Swan WA 77 D7
Middlecamp Hills Con Park SA 68 D3 70 F7
Middlemount QLD 10 G7
Middleton QLD 16 D6
Middleton SA 66 G7 68 J7 69 D3 71 K10
Middleton TAS 56 K5 59 H10
Midge Point QLD 11 C8
Midkin Nature Res NSW 28 D5
Midland WA 77 D7 78 D5 82 C3 84 K5
Midway Point TAS 57 B8 59 F11
Miena TAS 59 B8 61 J8
Miepoll VIC 48 D4
Miga Lake VIC 44 C4
Mil Lel SA 44 F1 69 K7
Mila NSW 34 J3 51 A11
Milabena TAS 60 D4
Milang SA 67 E10 68 J7 69 D3 71 K10
Milawa VIC 48 D7
Milbrulong NSW 33 H12
Milchomi NSW 28 G2
Mildura VIC 32 F3 46 A5
Mile End SA 63 C1 64 G3
Miles QLD 8 E7
Milford QLD 6 G7
Milguy NSW 28 D6
Milikapiti NT 96 B3
Miling WA 84 H5
Milingimbi NT 97 C10
Mill Park VIC 41 A4
Millaa Millaa QLD 13 E13 14 H4
Millaroo QLD 10 B5
Millbank NSW 29 H11
Millchester QLD 10 B4 13 J14
Miller NSW 25 E9
Millers Forest NSW 23 A6
Millers Point NSW 21 A1
Millfield NSW 23 D3 27 E9
Millgrove VIC 43 C12 48 K4 52 B4
Millicent SA 69 J6
Millie NSW 28 E4
Millmerran QLD 9 H9
Millner NT 94 D4
Milloo VIC 47 K12
Millstream Chichester Nat Park WA 86 C6
Millstream Falls Nat Park QLD 14 J3
Millswood SA 64 H4
Millthorpe NSW 26 G4
Milltown VIC 44 G4
Milparinka NSW 30 D2
Milperra NSW 22 G2 25 E10
Milton NSW 34 D6 35 D5
Milton QLD 7 B9
Milvale NSW 26 J2 33 F14
Milyakburra NT 97 F12
Milyeannup Nat Park WA 80 F4
Milyu Nature Res WA 76 D1
Mimili (Everard Park) SA 74 C6
Mimosa Rocks Nat Park NSW 34 H5 35 K4
Minamia (Cox River) NT 97 J9 99 A9
Mincha VIC 47 H11
Mindarie SA 69 B6 71 J12
Minden QLD 6 B6
Mindijup WA 81 H13
Miners Rest VIC 45 E10
Minerva QLD 10 J6
Minerva Hills Nat Park QLD 10 J6
Mingary SA 71 D13
Mingay VIC 45 F9
Mingela QLD 10 B4 13 J14
Mingenew WA 84 F4
Mingoola QLD 29 C9
Minhamite VIC 44 G6
Mini Moxham QLD 14 E2
Minilya Roadhouse WA 86 G2
Minimay VIC 44 B2
Mininera VIC 45 E8
Minjah VIC 44 G6
Minjary Nat Park NSW 33 H14 34 D1
Minjilang NT 96 A6
Minlaton SA 68 G5 69 B1 71 J8
Minmi NSW 23 C6
Minnamurra NSW 27 K8 35 B7
Minnie Water NSW 29 E13
Minnipa SA 70 E4
Minnivale WA 79 A9
Minore NSW 26 C3
Mintabie SA 72 D1 74 C6
Mintaro SA 68 E7 71 G10
Minto NSW 25 F9
Minyerri NT 97 H8
Minyip VIC 44 A6 46 K6
Miralie VIC 32 H5 47 E9
Miram VIC 46 K2
Miram South VIC 44 A3 46 K3
Miranda NSW 22 J4 25 F11
Mirani QLD 11 D8
Mirannie NSW 27 D10
Mirboo VIC 50 G1 52 F7
Mirboo North VIC 50 G1 52 F7
Miriam Vale QLD 11 J12
Mirikata SA 72 H5
Mirima Nat Park WA 89 D14
Mirimbah VIC 48 G7 50 A2
Mirirrinyungu (Duck Ponds) NT 98 F4
Miriwinni QLD 13 E13 14 G6
Mirrabooka QLD 19 F13
Mirrabooka WA 77 D4
Mirranatwa VIC 44 D6
Mirrindi NT 98 F4
Mirrnatja NT 97 D10
Mirrool NSW 33 F12
Missabotti NSW 29 H12
Mission Bay QLD 14 D6
Mission Beach QLD 13 E13
Misson Beach QLD 14 K7
Mistake Creek NT 98 C1
Mitakooki QLD 16 A4
Mitcham SA 64 J4 65 J2
Mitcham VIC 41 D7
Mitchell ACT 37 C5
Mitchell QLD 8 D3
Mitchell - Alice Rivers Nat Park QLD 12 A7 15 K2
Mitchell River Nat Park VIC 49 J10 50 C5
Mitchell River Nat Park WA 89 C9
Mitchells (site) VIC 48 H7 50 B1
Mitchellville SA 68 D4 71 F8
Mitchelton QLD 3 D2
Mitiamo VIC 47 J12
Mitre VIC 44 B4
Mitta Mitta VIC 49 D10
Mittagong NSW 26 K7 34 B6 35 A6
Mittyack VIC 32 H4 46 E6
Moa Island QLD 15 A2
Moama NSW 33 K8 47 J13 48 B1
Moana SA 66 C4
Moana Sands Con Park SA 66 C4
Moana Sands Rec Res SA 66 C4
Mobrup WA 81 E8
Mockinya VIC 44 C5
Modbury SA 64 D6 65 G3
Modbury Heights SA 64 C6
Modbury North SA 64 C6
Modella VIC 43 G13 52 E5
Modewarre VIC 42 H1

Moe VIC 50 F1 52 D7
Moganemby VIC 48 D4
Moggill QLD 3 H1 7 C8
Mogo NSW 34 F6 35 G4
Mogriguy NSW 26 C3
Mogumber WA 82 A3 84 J5
Moil NT 94 D5
Moina TAS 60 F6
Mokepilly VIC 44 C7
Mokola Con Park SA 71 F10
Mole Creek TAS 60 G7
Mole Creek Karst Nat Park TAS 60 G7
Mole River NSW 9 K10 29 C9
Molesworth TAS 56 B3 59 F10
Molesworth VIC 48 G4
Moliagul VIC 45 B10
Molka VIC 48 E3
Molle Islands Nat Park QLD 11 B8
Mollerin Lake WA 84 H7
Mollerin Nature Res WA 84 H7
Mollymook NSW 34 D6 35 E6
Molong NSW 26 F4
Molonglo Gorge Nature Res ACT 38 C6
Moltema TAS 61 F8
Molyullah VIC 48 D6
Mona Vale NSW 22 B7 25 B12 27 G9
Mona Vale TAS 59 C11 61 J11
Monadnocks Con Res WA 78 F6 82 D3
Monak NSW 32 F4 46 A5
Monarto SA 67 A11
Monarto Con Park SA 67 B11
Monarto South SA 67 B11
Monarto Zoological Park SA 67 A11
Monash ACT 37 H4
Monash SA 69 A7 71 H13
Monbulk VIC 43 D11 48 K3 52 C3
Moncrieff ACT 37 A4
Mondrain Island WA 83 H14 91 K1
Monduran Dam QLD 9 A11 11 K12
Monea VIC 48 E3
Monegeetta VIC 45 D13 48 H1
Monga NSW 34 E5 35 F4
Monga Nat Park NSW 34 E5 35 F3
Mongarlowe NSW 34 E5 35 E4
Mongers Lake WA 84 F6
Monkerai Nature Res NSW 27 C11
Monkey Mia WA 84 A2
Monkeycot Nature Res NSW 27 B10
Monogorilby QLD 9 D9
Monomeith VIC 43 H11
Monsildale QLD 4 D5
Montacute SA 64 F7 65 H4
Montacute Con Park SA 65 H4
Montagu TAS 60 C2
Montagu Bay TAS 54 B4
Montagu Island TAS 60 C2
Montague Island NSW 34 G6 35 J4
Montague Island Nature Res NSW 34 G6 35 J4
Montague Sound WA 89 B9
Montana TAS 61 G8
Monteagle NSW 26 J2 34 A1
Montebello Islands WA 86 B4
Montebello Islands Con Park WA 86 B4
Montefiores NSW 26 D4
Monteith SA 67 B14 67 C13
Monterey NSW 22 H5 25 E11
Montesquieu Islands WA 89 A10
Montgomery Islands WA 88 D7
Monto QLD 9 A9 11 K11
Montumana TAS 60 D4
Montville QLD 5 D8 9 E12
Mooball NSW 9 J14 29 A14
Mooball Nat Park NSW 7 K13 9 J13 29 A14
Moockra SA 68 A7 71 D10
Moodiarrup WA 81 C8
Moodlu QLD 5 G8
Moogara TAS 59 F9
Moogerah QLD 6 G6
Moogerah Peaks Nat Park QLD 6 G6
Moojebing WA 81 C11
Moolap VIC 42 G3
Mooliabeenie WA 78 B5
Mooloolaba QLD 5 D10 9 E13
Mooloolah QLD 5 D9
Mooloolah River Nat Park QLD 5 D10
Moolort VIC 45 C11
Moolpa NSW 32 H6 47 D10
Moomba SA 18 H2 73 E13
Moombooldool NSW 33 F12
Moombra QLD 4 J5
Moona Plains NSW 29 J10
Moonambel VIC 45 C9
Moonan Flat NSW 27 B9
Moonaran NSW 28 H7
Moonbah NSW 34 H2 49 D14
Moonbi NSW 29 J8
Moonda Lake QLD 16 K5 18 C3 73 A13
Moondarra VIC 50 E1
Moondarra State Park VIC 50 E1 52 D7
Moondyne Nature Res WA 78 C6 82 B3 84 K5
Moonee Beach NSW 29 G13
Moonee Beach Nature Res NSW 29 G13
Mooney Mooney NSW 23 K4 25 A11
Moonford QLD 9 A9 11 K11
Moongardie WA 89 J10 90 B5
Moongobulla QLD 13 G14
Moonie QLD 9 G8
Moonlight Flat SA 70 E4
Moonta SA 68 E5 71 G8
Moonta Bay SA 68 E5 71 G8
Moora WA 82 A3 84 H5
Moorabbin VIC 41 F5 43 E8 45 G14 48 K2 52 C2
Moorabool VIC 42 F2
Mooradung Nature Res WA 78 J7
Mooralla VIC 44 D5
Moore QLD 4 E4 9 F11
Moore Creek NSW 28 J7
Moore Park QLD 9 A12 11 K13
Moore River Nat Park WA 78 A4 82 B2 84 J5
Moore River Nature Res WA 78 A4 84 J5
Moorebank NSW 22 G1 25 E10
Mooree VIC 44 D3
Mooreville TAS 60 D5
Moorilim VIC 48 D3
Moorina TAS 61 E12
Moorine Rock WA 83 B8 85 J9
Moorland NSW 27 B13
Moorlands SA 69 C5 71 K11
Moorleah TAS 60 D4
Moormbool VIC 45 B14 48 E2
Moornaming WA 81 C13
Moorooduc VIC 43 H8
Moorook SA 69 A6 71 H12
Moorooka QLD 3 G4
Mooroongga Island NT 97 B10
Mooroopna VIC 48 C3
Moorrinya Nat Park QLD 10 D2 17 B11
Moorumbine WA 79 G9
Moorundie Wildlife Park SA 71 H11
Mootai NSW 23 D3
Mopoke Hut VIC 32 G3
Morago NSW 47 F13
Moranbah QLD 10 E6
Morangarell NSW 26 J1 33 F14
Morans Crossing NSW 34 H4 35 K2
Morawa WA 84 F5
Morayfield QLD 5 G9
Morchard SA 68 B7 71 E10
Mordalup WA 81 F8
Mordialloc VIC 41 H5 43 F8 45 G14 52 D2
Morea (Carpolac) VIC 44 B2
Moree NSW 28 D5
Morella QLD 17 E10
Moresby QLD 13 E13 14 J7
Moresby Range Nat Park QLD 14 H7
Moreton Bay QLD 3 A6 5 J11 9 F13
Moreton Bay Marine Park QLD 7 A12 9 F14
Moreton Island QLD 5 H12 9 F14
Moreton Island Nat Park QLD 5 H12 9 F14
Moreton Telegraph Station QLD 15 E2
Morgan SA 71 G11
Morgan Con Park SA 71 G11
Morgan Island NT 97 E11
Moriac VIC 42 H1 45 H11
Morialpa SA 71 D12
Morialta Con Park SA 64 F7 65 H3 68 G7 69 B3 71 J10
Moriarty TAS 60 E7
Morisset NSW 23 E5 27 F10
Morisset Park NSW 23 E6
Morkalla VIC 32 F2 46 B2
Morley WA 77 D5
Morna Point NSW 27 E11
Morningside QLD 3 E5
Mornington VIC 42 H7 45 H14 52 E2
Mornington Island QLD 12 C3
Mornington Peninsula VIC 43 J8 45 H14 52 E2
Mornington Peninsula Nat Park VIC 42 K7 45 H13 52 F1
Morongla Creek NSW 26 H3
Mororo Creek Nature Res NSW 29 D13
Morpeth NSW 23 A5
Morphett Vale SA 66 B5 68 H6 69 C2 71 J10
Morphettville SA 64 J3
Morri Morri VIC 44 B7
Morrisons VIC 42 C1 45 F11
Morrisons Lake Nature Res NSW 32 C7
Morse Island NT 95 A5 96 B6
Mortagallup WA 81 G11
Mortchup VIC 45 E9
Mortdale NSW 25 E11
Mortlake VIC 44 G7
Morton Nat Park NSW 34 C6 35 C5
Morton Plains VIC 32 K5 46 J7
Morundah NSW 33 G11
Moruya NSW 34 F5 35 G4
Moruya Heads NSW 34 F6 35 G4
Morven NSW 33 J13
Morven QLD 8 D2
Morwell VIC 50 F2
Morwell Nat Park VIC 50 G2
Moselle QLD 13 K9 17 A9
Mosman NSW 22 E6 25 C12
Mosman Park WA 77 H1
Moss Vale NSW 26 K7 34 B6 35 A5
Mossgiel NSW 33 D8
Mossiface VIC 49 K12 50 D6
Mossman QLD 13 C12 14 B3
Mossy Point NSW 34 F6 35 G4
Moulamein NSW 32 H7 47 E11
Moule SA 70 C2 74 K7
Moulyinning WA 79 K12 81 A12
Mount Aberdeen Nat Park QLD 10 B6
Mount Adolphus Island QLD 15 B2
Mount Alford QLD 6 G6
Mount Annan NSW 25 G8
Mount Arapiles - Tooan State Park VIC 44 B4
Mount Archer Nat Park QLD 11 H10
Mount Augustus (Burringurrah) Nat Park WA 86 H6
Mount Barker SA 65 K5 67 A9 68 H7 69 C3 71 J10
Mount Barker WA 81 H11 82 J6
Mount Barker Junction SA 65 K5
Mount Barkly (Pawu) NT 100 B6
Mount Barney Nat Park QLD 6 J7 9 J12 29 A12
Mount Bauple Nat Park QLD 9 C12
Mount Baw Baw Alpine Village VIC 48 K6 50 D1 52 C7
Mount Beau Brummell Con Park QLD 6 E4
Mount Beauty VIC 49 E9
Mount Benson SA 69 H5
Mount Beppo QLD 4 H5
Mount Berryman QLD 6 D4
Mount Binga Nat Park QLD 9 F11
Mount Boothby Con Park SA 69 E5
Mount Brown Con Park SA 68 B6 71 D9
Mount Bryan SA 68 D7 71 F10
Mount Buangor State Park VIC 45 D8
Mount Buffalo Chalet VIC 49 E8
Mount Buffalo Nat Park VIC 49 E8
Mount Buller Alpine Village VIC 48 G7 50 A2
Mount Burnett VIC 43 E11
Mount Burr SA 69 J6
Mount Bute VIC 45 F9
Mount Camel VIC 45 B13 48 E1
Mount Carbine QLD 13 C12 14 B2
Mount Catt NT 97 E9
Mount Chapple Island TAS 61 C8
Mount Chinghee Nat Park QLD 7 J9
Mount Christie Corner SA 72 J2 74 H7
Mount Christie Siding SA 72 K1 74 H7
Mount Claremont WA 77 F2
Mount Clifford Nature Res NSW 34 G3 35 H1
Mount Clunie Nat Park NSW 6 J5 9 J12 29 A11
Mount Colah NSW 22 B4 25 B10
Mount Colliery QLD 6 J4
Mount Colosseum Nat Park QLD 11 J12
Mount Compass SA 66 E6 68 J7 69 C3 71 K10
Mount Cook Nat Park QLD 13 A12 15 K6
Mount Coolon QLD 10 D5
Mount Coolum QLD 5 C10
Mount Coolum Nat Park QLD 5 B10
Mount Coot-tha QLD 3 E2 7 B9
Mount Cotton QLD 7 C11
Mount Cottrell VIC 42 C5 45 F13
Mount Crawford Forest SA 65 F6
Mount Crosby QLD 7 B8
Mount Cuthbert Mine QLD 12 J4
Mount Damper SA 70 E4
Mount Dandenong VIC 43 D10
Mount Dangar QLD 10 B7
Mount David NSW 26 H5
Mount Direction TAS 55 E4 61 E9
Mount Dowling Nature Res NSW 34 F3 35 G1
Mount Druit NSW 25 D8
Mount Drummond SA 70 H5
Mount Duneed VIC 42 H3 45 H12
Mount Dutton SA 72 E5
Mount Ebenezer NT 100 H6
Mount Eccles VIC 52 F6
Mount Eccles Nat Park VIC 44 G4
Mount Eckersley VIC 44 G4
Mount Egerton VIC 42 B1 45 E11
Mount Eliza VIC 43 G8 45 H14 52 E2
Mount Elvire Con Park (Proposed) WA 85 G9
Mount Emu VIC 45 E9
Mount Ernest Island QLD 15 A2
Mount Etna Caves Nat Park QLD 11 G10
Mount Field Nat Park TAS 59 E8
Mount Fitton SA 73 J11
Mount Frankland Nat Park WA 81 H8 82 J4
Mount Gambier SA 44 F1 69 K7
Mount Garnet QLD 13 E12 14 J2
Mount George NSW 27 B12
Mount Gipps NSW 30 J2 32 A2
Mount Glorious QLD 4 J7
Mount Gordon QLD 12 J3
Mount Granya State Park VIC 33 K13 49 B10
Mount Gravatt QLD 3 G5 7 B10
Mount Grenfell Historic Site NSW 31 H9
Mount Gunson Mine SA 71 B8
Mount Hawthorn WA 77 E3
Mount Helen VIC 45 E11
Mount Hill SA 68 E2 70 G6
Mount Hope NSW 33 C10
Mount Hope SA 70 G5
Mount Hope Res VIC 47 H11
Mount Hopeful Con Park QLD 11 H10
Mount Hunter NSW 25 G8
Mount Hyland Nature Res NSW 29 F11
Mount Hypipamee Nat Park QLD 13 E12 14 G3
Mount Ida WA 85 F11
Mount Imlay Nat Park NSW 34 K4 51 A13
Mount Irvine NSW 24 B5
Mount Isa QLD 12 K3 16 A3
Mount Jerusalem Nat Park NSW 9 J13 29 B14
Mount Kaputar Nat Park NSW 28 F6
Mount Keith Mine WA 85 C11
Mount Kelly Mine QLD 12 J3
Mount Kokeby WA 79 F9
Mount Kororoit VIC 42 B5
Mount Kuring-gai NSW 22 A5 25 B10
Mount Larcom QLD 11 H11
Mount Lawley WA 77 F4
Mount Lawson State Park VIC 33 K13 49 B11
Mount Leura Con Park QLD 10 H6
Mount Leyson Mine QLD 10 B4 13 J14
Mount Liebig NT 100 E4
Mount Lindesay Nat Park WA 81 J10
Mount Lion NSW 29 A13
Mount Lloyd TAS 56 C1 59 F9
Mount Lonarch VIC 45 D9
Mount Macedon VIC 45 D13
Mount Mackay Nat Park QLD 13 F13 14 K6
Mount Mackenzie Nature Res NSW 29 C10
Mount Magnet WA 84 D7
Mount Magnificent Con Park SA 66 D7
Mount Manning Ranges Nature Res WA 85 G10
Mount Manypeaks Nature Res WA 81 J14
Mount Margaret WA 85 E13 91 E1
Mount Martha VIC 42 H7 45 H14 52 E1
Mount Martin Nat Park QLD 11 D8
Mount Mary SA 71 G11
Mount Mee QLD 4 G7
Mount Mercer VIC 45 F10
Mount Molloy QLD 13 C12 14 C3
Mount Morgan QLD 11 H10
Mount Morgans WA 85 E13 91 E1
Mount Moriac VIC 42 H1
Mount Mort QLD 6 E5
Mount Napier State Park VIC 44 G5
Mount Nathan QLD 7 F11
Mount Nebo QLD 5 K8 7 A8
Mount Neville Nature Res NSW 29 D12
Mount Nothofagus Nat Park NSW 6 K6 29 A12
Mount O'Connell Nat Park QLD 11 G9
Mount Olive NSW 27 D9
Mount Ommaney QLD 3 G2
Mount Ossa QLD 11 D8
Mount Ossa Nat Park QLD 11 D8
Mount Oxide Mine QLD 12 H3
Mount Perry QLD 9 B10
Mount Perry Con Park QLD 7 D8
Mount Pikapene Nat Park NSW 9 K12 29 C12
Mount Pleasant QLD 4 H7
Mount Pleasant SA 65 F7 69 B3 71 J10
Mount Pleasant WA 77 H3
Mount Pritchard NSW 22 G1 25 E9
Mount Remarkable Nat Park SA 68 B6 71 E9
Mount Rescue Con Park SA 69 E6
Mount Richmond Nat Park VIC 44 H3
Mount Roe Nat Park WA 81 H8
Mount Royal Nat Park NSW 27 C9
Mount Russell NSW 28 E7
Mount Samaria State Park VIC 48 F6
Mount Samson QLD 5 J8
Mount Scott Con Park SA 69 G5
Mount Seaview NSW 27 A11 29 K10
Mount Seaview Nature Res NSW 27 A12 29 K10
Mount Selwyn NSW 34 F1 49 A14
Mount Seymour TAS 59 D11
Mount Shaugh Con Park SA 32 K1 46 H1 69 E7
Mount Stanley QLD 4 C3
Mount Stirling Alpine Resort VIC 48 G7 50 A2
Mount Sturt QLD 6 J3
Mount Surprise QLD 13 F11
Mount Sylvia QLD 6 D3
Mount Tamborine QLD 7 F11
Mount Tarampa QLD 6 A5
Mount Taylor VIC 49 K11 50 D6
Mount Thorley NSW 23 A1
Mount Torrens SA 65 H6 68 H7 69 B3 71 J10
Mount Vernon NSW 25 E8
Mount Victoria NSW 24 C3 26 G7
Mount View NSW 23 C3
Mount Vincent NSW 23 C5
Mount Walker QLD 6 E5
Mount Wallace VIC 42 C2 45 F12
Mount Walsh Nat Park QLD 9 C11
Mount Warning Nat Park NSW 7 K11 9 J13 29 A13
Mount Waverley VIC 41 E6
Mount Webb Nat Park QLD 13 A12 15 J6
Mount Wedge SA 70 F5
Mount White NSW 23 J4
Mount Whitestone QLD 6 C3
Mount Whitfield Con Park QLD 14 D5
Mount William Nat Park TAS 61 D14
Mount Wilson NSW 24 B4 26 G7
Mount Windsor Nat Park QLD 13 C12 14 A1
Mount Worth State Park VIC 52 E6
Mount Yarrowyck Nature Res NSW 29 G8
Mountain Creek NSW 33 J13 49 A10
Mountain Creek QLD 5 D10
Mountain River TAS 56 E3 59 G10
Mountain View VIC 43 H14
Moura QLD 11 K9
Mourilyan QLD 13 E13 14 H7
Mourilyan Harbour QLD 13 E13 14 H7
Moutajup VIC 44 E5
Mowanjum WA 88 G6 90 A3
Mowbray TAS 55 G5
Mowbray Nat Park QLD 14 B3
Mowbray Park NSW 24 H7
Mowen WA 80 E2
Moyarra VIC 43 K13
Moyhu VIC 48 D7
Moyston VIC 44 D7
Muchea WA 78 C5 82 C3 84 K5
Muckadilla QLD 8 E4
Muckatah VIC 33 K10 48 A4
Mud Island QLD 5 K11
Mud Island SA 67 G10
Mud Islands VIC 42 H6
Mud Islands Game Res SA 67 G10
Mudamuckla SA 70 D3
Mudgee NSW 26 D5
Mudgeeraba QLD 7 G12 9 H13
Mudgegonga VIC 49 D8
Mudjarn Nature Res NSW 34 D1
Mudjimba QLD 5 C10
Mudludja WA 89 H9 90 B5
Muiron Islands WA 86 D2
Mukinbudin WA 82 A7 85 J8
Mulan WA 90 C6
Mulanggari ACT 37 B5
Mulbring NSW 23 C5 27 E10
Mulcra VIC 32 H2 46 E2
Mulga Bore SA 74 B5
Mulgildie QLD 9 A9 11 K11
Mulgoa NSW 24 E7
Mulgowie QLD 6 D4
Mulgowrie NSW 26 J4 34 A3
Mulgrave NSW 25 C8
Mulgrave VIC 43 E9
Mullaley NSW 28 J5
Mullaloo WA 77 A1 78 D4 82 C2 84 K5
Mullalyup WA 80 D5
Mullaway NSW 29 F13
Mullengandra Village NSW 33 K13 49 A10
Mullengudgery NSW 31 J13
Mullewa WA 84 E4
Mulline WA 85 G11
Mullion Creek NSW 26 F4
Mullumbimby NSW 9 J13 29 B14
Mulpata SA 69 C6 71 K12
Mulurulu Lake NSW 32 C6
Mulwala NSW 33 K11 48 A6
Mulyandry NSW 26 G2 33 D14
Mulyati NT 90 J7 91 B7
Mumballup WA 80 C6 82 G3
Mumbannar VIC 44 G2
Mumberkine WA 78 B7
Mumbil NSW 26 D4
Mumbleberry Lake QLD 16 G2
Mummel Gulf Nat Park NSW 27 A11 29 K9
Mummel Gulf State Con Area NSW 27 A11 29 K10
Mummulgum NSW 9 K12 29 C12
Mumu QLD 17 A10
Mundaring WA 78 D5 82 C3 84 K5
Mundaring Nat Park WA 78 E6
Mundaring Weir WA 78 E6
Mundarlo NSW 33 H14
Munderoo NSW 33 K14 49 A12
Mundijong WA 78 F5 82 D3
Mundiwindi WA 87 G10
Mundoo Island SA 67 G9
Mundoona VIC 48 B3
Mundoonen Nature Res NSW 34 C3 35 B1
Mundoora SA 68 D6 71 F9
Mundowey NSW 28 H7
Mundrabilla WA 91 G6
Mundrabilla Motel WA 91 H6
Mundubbera QLD 9 C10
Mundulla SA 69 F7
Mungalawurru NT 99 G8
Mungallala QLD 8 D3
Mungana QLD 13 D11
Mungar QLD 9 C12
Mungaroona Range Nature Res WA 86 D7
Mungerannie Roadhouse SA 73 E10
Mungeriba NSW 26 C2
Mungeribar NSW 31 K14 33 A14
Mungerup WA 81 F14
Munghorn Gap Nature Res NSW 26 D6
Mungindi NSW 8 K5 28 C3
Mungkan Kandju Nat Park QLD 15 G2
Munglinup WA 83 G11
Mungo Brush NSW 27 D12
Mungo Nat Park NSW 32 E5
Mungunburra QLD 10 B3 13 K13
Mungungo QLD 9 A9 11 K11
Munjina (Auski) Roadhouse WA 87 E8
Munmorah State Con Area NSW 27 F10
Munno Para SA 65 E3
Munro VIC 49 K9 50 E4
Muntadgin WA 82 C7 85 K8
Muntz Nature Res WA 83 G14 91 K2
Munyaroo Con Park SA 68 D4 71 F8
Muogamarra Nature Res NSW 25 A10 27 G9
Muradup WA 81 D9
Muralug QLD 15 B2
Murarrie QLD 3 E6
Murbko SA 71 H11
Murcheboluc VIC 42 G1
Murchison VIC 48 D3
Murchison East VIC 48 D3
Murchison Roadhouse WA 84 C5
Murdinga SA 68 D1 70 G5
Murdoch WA 77 J3
Murdong WA 81 D11
Murdunna TAS 57 E13 59 G12
Muresk WA 79 D8
Murga NSW 26 F3
Murgenella NT 95 A7 96 B6
Murgon QLD 9 D10
Murninnie SA 68 D4 71 F8
Muronbung NSW 26 C4
Murphys Creek QLD 6 B2 9 G11
Murra Warra VIC 46 K5
Murrabit VIC 32 J7 47 G11
Murradoc VIC 42 G5
Murramarang Nat Park NSW 34 E6 35 F5
Murrami NSW 33 F11
Murrawal NSW 26 A5 28 K4
Murray - Sunset Nat Park VIC 32 G2 46 D3 71 J14
Murray Bridge QLD 6 J2
Murray Bridge SA 67 A13 69 C4 71 J11
Murray River Nat Park SA 32 F1 69 A7 71 H13
Murray Town SA 68 C6 71 E9
Murray Upper Nat Park QLD 13 F13
Murray-Kulkyne Park VIC 32 G4 46 C6
Murrayville VIC 32 J2 46 F2 71 K14
Murrigal QLD 13 F13
Murrin Bridge NSW 33 C11
Murrindal VIC 49 H13 51 B8
Murrindindi VIC 48 H4
Murringo NSW 26 J3 34 A2
Murroon VIC 45 J10
Murrumbateman NSW 34 C3
Murrumburrah NSW 26 K2 34 B1
Murrungowar VIC 51 C10
Murrurundi NSW 27 B8
Murtoa VIC 44 A6
Murun Murula NT 99 F14
Murweh QLD 19 E13
Murwillumbah NSW 7 K13 9 J13 29 A14
Musselboro TAS 61 F11
Musselroe Bay Con Res TAS 61 C13
Muswellbrook NSW 27 C9
Mutarnee QLD 13 G14
Mutawintji Nat Park NSW 30 H4
Mutawintji Nature Res NSW 30 G4
Mutchilba QLD 13 D12 14 F2
Mutdapilly QLD 6 D7
Muttaburra QLD 10 F1 17 D11
Muttama NSW 33 G14 34 C1
Mutton Bird Island TAS 58 J5
Mutton Hole Wetlands Con Park QLD 12 E6
Myall VIC 47 G11
Myall Lakes Nat Park NSW 27 D12
Myalla TAS 60 D4
Myalla Nature Res NSW 34 H3
Myalup WA 78 K4 80 A4 82 F2
Myamyn VIC 44 G4
Myaoola Bay NT 97 D12
Mylestom NSW 29 G12
Mylor SA 65 K4 66 A7 68 H7 69 C3 71 J10
Mylor Rec Centre SA 66 A7
Mylor Recreation Centre SA 65 K4
Myola NSW 35 C6
Myola VIC 45 A13 48 D1
Mypolonga SA 67 A13 69 C4 71 J11
Myponga SA 66 E4 68 J7 69 C2 71 K10
Myponga Beach SA 66 E3 68 J6 69 C2 71 K9
Myponga Con Park SA 66 F4
Myrla SA 69 A6 71 H12
Myrniong VIC 42 B3 45 E12
Myrrhee VIC 48 E6
Myrtle Bank SA 64 H5
Myrtle Bank TAS 55 E7 61 E10
Myrtle Scrub NSW 27 A11 29 K10
Myrtleford VIC 49 D8
Myrtletown QLD 3 C6
Myrtleville NSW 26 K6 34 B5 35 A3
Mysia VIC 47 J10
Mystery Bay NSW 34 G5 35 J4
Mystic Park VIC 47 G10
Myubee QLD 16 B4

N

N'dhala Gorge Nature Park NT 101 F9
Naas ACT 38 F4
Nabageena TAS 60 D3
Nabarlek NT 96 C7
Nabawa WA 84 E3
Nabiac NSW 27 C12
Nabowla TAS 55 D7 61 E11
Nackara SA 71 E11
Nadgee Nature Res NSW 34 K5 51 C14
Nadgigomar Nature Res NSW 34 D5 35 D3
Nagambie VIC 45 B14 48 E2
Nagoorin QLD 11 J11
Nailsworth SA 64 E4
Nairana Nat Park QLD 10 E5 17 B14
Nairne SA 65 K6 67 A9 68 H7 69 C3 71 J10
Nakara NT 94 C5
Nala TAS 59 D11
Nalangil VIC 45 H9
Nalinga VIC 48 C4
Nalya WA 79 F10
Namadgi Nat Park ACT 34 E3 37 K1 38 F2
Nambling WA 79 A9
Nambour QLD 5 C9 9 E13
Nambrok VIC 50 E3
Nambucca Heads NSW 29 H12
Nambung Nat Park WA 82 A1 84 H4
Namming Nature Res WA 82 A2 84 J4
Nana Glen NSW 29 F12
Nanango QLD 4 C1 9 E11
Nanarup WA 81 K13 82 K7
Nandaly VIC 32 H4 46 F7
Nanga WA 78 J5
Nangalala NT 97 C10
Nangana VIC 43 D11
Nangar Nat Park NSW 26 F3
Nangeenan WA 79 B13
Nangiloc VIC 32 G4 46 B5
Nangkita SA 66 E7
Nangur Nat Park QLD 9 D11
Nangus NSW 33 H14
Nangwarry SA 44 E1 69 J7
Nannine WA 85 B8
Nannup WA 80 E4 82 H3
Nantawarra SA 68 E6 71 G9
Nanutarra Roadhouse WA 86 E4
Napier WA 81 J12
Napier Bay NT 95 A3
Napier Broome Bay WA 89 A11
Napperby SA 68 C6 71 F9
Napranum QLD 15 E1
Nar Nar Goon VIC 43 F12 52 D4
Nar Nar Goon North VIC 43 F12
Naracoopa TAS 60 B7
Naracoorte SA 44 C1 69 H7
Naracoorte Caves Nat Park SA 44 C1 69 H7
Naradhan NSW 33 D11
Narangba QLD 5 H9
Narara NSW 23 H5
Narawntapu Nat Park TAS 55 C1 61 D8
Narbethong VIC 43 A12 48 J4 52 A4
Nardoo QLD 19 G13
Nareen VIC 44 D3
Narellan NSW 25 G8
Narellan Vale NSW 25 G8
Narembeen WA 79 E14 82 C7 85 K8
Naretha WA 91 G3
Nariel Creek VIC 49 C12
Naringal VIC 44 H7
Narioka VIC 47 J14 48 B2
Narooma NSW 34 G5 35 J4
Narrabarba NSW 34 K5 51 B13
Narrabeen NSW 22 C7 25 B12
Narrabri NSW 28 G5
Narrabri West NSW 28 G5
Narrabundah ACT 37 F5
Narraburra NSW 26 J1 33 F14
Narran Lake NSW 31 D13
Narran Lake Nature Res NSW 31 D13
Narrandera NSW 33 G11
Narraport VIC 32 K5 47 H8
Narrawa NSW 26 J4 34 B3

Narrawallee NSW 34 D6 35 D6
Narrawallee Creek Nature Res NSW 35 D6
Narraweena NSW 22 C7 25 C12
Narrawong VIC 44 H4
Narre Warren VIC 43 F10
Narre Warren East VIC 43 E10
Narre Warren North VIC 43 E10
Narrewillock VIC 47 J9
Narridy SA 68 D6 71 F9
Narrien Range Nat Park QLD 10 G5 17 D14
Narrikup WA 81 H12 82 J6
Narrogin WA 79 J10 82 E5
Narromine NSW 26 C2
Narrung SA 67 G11 69 D4 71 K11
Narrung VIC 32 G5 47 C8
Narrungar SA 70 B7
Nashdale NSW 26 F4
Nathalia VIC 33 K9 47 J14 48 B3
Nathan QLD 3 G4
Natimuk VIC 44 B4
National Park TAS 59 F8
Natone TAS 60 E5
Nattai NSW 24 H6 26 H7 34 A6
Nattai Nat Park NSW 24 J6 26 J7 34 A6
Nattai State Rec Park NSW 24 H6
Natte Yallock VIC 45 B9
Natural Bridge QLD 7 J11
Naturi SA 69 C5 71 K11
Natya VIC 32 H5 47 D8
Nauiyu NT 95 G1 96 E3
Navarre VIC 45 B8
Nayook VIC 43 E14 48 K5 52 C6
Nea NSW 28 J6
Neale Junction WA 91 E4
Neale Junction Nature Res WA 91 D4
Nearie Lake Nature Res NSW 32 D3
Neath NSW 23 C4
Nebo QLD 10 E7
Nectar Brook SA 68 B6 71 E9
Nedlands WA 77 G2
Neds Corner VIC 32 F2 46 A2
Needaling WA 79 K14 81 A14
Needles TAS 61 G8
Neerabup Nat Park WA 78 C4 82 C2 84 K4
Neeralin Pool WA 79 K10 81 A10
Neerim VIC 52 C6
Neerim South VIC 52 D6
Neilrex NSW 26 A5
Nelia QLD 13 K8 16 A7
Nelligen NSW 34 E5 35 F4
Nelshaby SA 68 C6 71 E9
Nelson NSW 25 C9
Nelson VIC 44 G2 69 K7
Nelson Bay NSW 27 E11
Nelsons Plains NSW 23 A6
Nembudding WA 79 A11
Nemingha NSW 28 J7
Nene Valley Con Park SA 69 K6
Nepabunna SA 71 A11 73 K11
Nepean Bay SA 68 J5
Nepean Nickel Mine WA 83 B12 85 J11
Neptune Islands SA 68 H2 70 K6
Neptune Islands Con Park SA 68 H2 70 K6
Nerang QLD 7 F12 9 H13
Neranwood QLD 7 H12
Nerriga NSW 34 D5 35 D4
Nerrigundah NSW 34 G5 35 H3
Nerrin Nerrin VIC 45 F8
Nest Hill Nature Res NSW 33 J13
Netherby VIC 46 J3
Nethercote NSW 34 J5 51 A14
Netherdale QLD 10 D7
Netherton SA 69 D5 71 K12
Netley SA 64 G3
Neuarpur VIC 44 B2 69 G7
Neumgna QLD 4 E1
Neunman NT 100 F2
Neurea NSW 26 D4
Neurum QLD 4 F7
Neutral Bay NSW 22 E6
Nevertire NSW 25 G3 26 B1 31 J14
Neville NSW 26 G5
Nevilton QLD 6 E1
New Angledool NSW 8 K3 31 B14
New Beith QLD 7 D9
New England Nat Park NSW 29 G11
New Farm QLD 3 E4 7 B10
New Italy NSW 29 D13
New Looma WA 88 H7 90 A3
New Mollyann NSW 26 A5 28 K3
New Norcia WA 82 A3 84 J5
New Norfolk TAS 56 B2 59 F9
New Residence SA 69 A6 71 H12
New Town TAS 54 A1
New Year Island TAS 60 A6
Newbridge NSW 26 G5
Newbridge VIC 45 B11
Newburn WA 77 G6
Newbury VIC 45 D12
Newcastle NSW 23 C7 27 E11
Newcastle Waters NT 98 D7
Newdegate WA 83 F8
Newell QLD 13 C12 14 B3
Newfield VIC 45 J8
Newham VIC 45 D13
Newhaven VIC 52 F3
Newland Head Con Park SA 66 H5 68 J7 69 D2 71 K10
Newlands WA 80 C5
Newlands Mine QLD 10 D6
Newlyn VIC 45 D11
Newman WA 87 F9
Newmarket QLD 3 D3
Newmerella VIC 49 K14 51 D9
Newnes NSW 26 F7
Newnes Junction NSW 24 B3
Newport NSW 22 A7 25 B12
Newport VIC 41 E2 42 D6
Newry VIC 49 K8 50 E3
Newry Islands Nat Park QLD 11 C8
Newrybar NSW 29 B14
Newstead QLD 3 E4
Newstead VIC 45 C11
Newton SA 64 F6
Newton Boyd NSW 29 E11
Newtown NSW 22 F5
Newtown VIC 42 G2
Ngadang Nature Res NSW 34 H2
Ngalingkadji WA 89 J9 90 B5
Ngallo VIC 46 F1
Ngambaa Nature Res NSW 29 H12
Ngarkat Con Park SA 32 K1 46 H1 69 D6 71 K13
Ngarngurr NT 100 J2
Ngarutjara SA 74 A4 100 K5
Nguiu NT 95 A1 96 B3
Ngukurr NT 97 G9
Ngulin Nature Res NSW 27 A10 29 K9
Ngumpan WA 89 J9 90 B5
Ngunjiwirri WA 89 J11 90 B6
Ngunnawal ACT 37 A4
Ngurtuwarta WA 89 H9 90 B4
Nhill VIC 46 K3
Nhulunbuy NT 97 C13
Niagara WA 85 F12 91 F1
Niagara Park NSW 23 H5
Niangala NSW 29 K8
Nicholls ACT 37 A4
Nicholls Rivulet TAS 56 J3 59 H10
Nicholson VIC 49 K11 50 D6
Nicholson Camp WA 89 H12 90 B6
Nicol Island NT 97 E12
Nicoll Scrub Nat Park QLD 7 H13
Niemur NSW 32 H7 47 E11
Nierinna TAS 56 F4 59 G10
Nietta TAS 60 F6
Nifty Mine WA 87 D12 90 E1
Night Island QLD 15 F4
Nightcap Nat Park NSW 9 J13 29 B13
Nightcliff NT 94 C3
Nildottie SA 69 B5 71 J11
Nile TAS 55 K7 61 G10
Nilgen Nature Res WA 82 A2 84 J4
Nillahcootie VIC 48 F6
Nimaru QLD 19 D13
Nimbin NSW 9 J13 29 B13
Nimingarra Mine WA 87 B10
Nimmitabel NSW 34 H3 35 K1
Nimmo Nature Res NSW 34 G2
Ninda VIC 46 F7
Nindigully QLD 8 H5 28 A2
Ninety Mile Beach Marine Nat Park VIC 50 G4
Ninety Mile Tank WA 83 E11
Ningaloo Marine Park WA 86 E1
Ningi QLD 5 G10
Ninnes SA 68 E6 71 G9
Ninth Island TAS 61 C10
Nippering WA 81 B11
Nirranda VIC 44 J7
Nirranda East VIC 44 J7
Nirranda South VIC 44 J7
Nirrippi NT 100 D3
Nitmiluk (Katherine Gorge) Nat Park NT 95 H6 96 F6
Nixon Skinner Con Park SA 66 E4
Noah Beach QLD 13 B12
Noarlunga Centre SA 66 B5
Nobby QLD 6 E1 9 H10
Nobbys Creek NSW 7 J12
Noble Park VIC 41 G6 43 E9
Noccundra QLD 18 G7
Nocoleche Nature Res NSW 30 D7
Noggerup WA 80 C6 82 G3
Nokarning WA 79 B13
Nollamara WA 77 D3
Nomans Lake WA 79 J11
Nombinnie Nature Res NSW 33 C10
Nome QLD 10 A5 13 H14
Nonda QLD 13 K8 17 A8
Nongra Lake NT 98 E2
Noogoora QLD 6 B7
Noojee VIC 48 K5 52 C6
Nook TAS 60 F7
Noonamah NT 95 D2 96 D4
Noonameena SA 67 K12
Noondoo QLD 8 J4 28 A1
Noorat VIC 45 H8
Noorinbee VIC 51 C11
Noorinbee North VIC 51 C11
Noosa Heads QLD 5 A10 9 D13
Noosa Nat Park QLD 5 A10 9 D13
Noosaville QLD 5 A10
Nora Creina SA 69 H5
Noradjuha VIC 44 B4
Norah Head NSW 23 G6 27 F10
Noranda WA 77 D5
Noraville NSW 23 G6
Nords Wharf NSW 23 E6
Norlane VIC 42 F3
Normanby Island QLD 14 F7
Normanhurst NSW 25 C10
Normanton QLD 12 E6
Normanville SA 66 F2 68 J6 69 D2 71 K9
Nornakin WA 79 F12
Nornalup WA 81 K8 82 K4
Norpa WA 79 C14
Norseman WA 83 D13 91 H1
North Adelaide SA 63 A2 64 F4
North Arm QLD 5 B9
North Bannister WA 78 G7
North Beach WA 77 D1
North Bondi NSW 25 D12
North Bourke NSW 31 E10
North Bruny Island TAS 56 H6 59 H10
North Dandalup WA 78 G5
North East Island QLD 11 E10
North East Isles NT 97 E13
North Fremantle WA 77 H1
North Goonyella QLD 10 E7
North Goonyella Mine QLD 10 E6
North Haven NSW 27 B13
North Haven SA 64 C2 65 G1
North Hobart TAS 54 B1
North Ipswich QLD 6 C7
North Isis QLD 9 B11
North Island NT 97 H13 99 A13
North Island WA 84 E2
North Johnstone QLD 14 G4
North Karlgarin Nature Res WA 79 F14 82 D7
North Keppel Island QLD 11 G11
North Lilydale TAS 55 D6
North Maclean QLD 7 D9
North Molle Island QLD 11 B8
North Motton TAS 60 E6
North Parkes Mine NSW 26 E2 33 C14
North Perth WA 77 F4
North Pinjarra WA 78 H5
North Point Island NT 97 E12
North Richmond NSW 24 B7
North Riverside TAS 55 G4 61 F9
North Rothbury NSW 23 A3
North Ryde NSW 22 D4 25 C11
North Scottsdale TAS 61 D11
North Shields SA 68 G1 70 H6
North Shore VIC 42 F3
North Solitary Island NSW 29 F13
North St Ives NSW 25 C11
North Star NSW 9 K8 28 C6
North Stradbroke Island QLD 5 K13 7 B13 9 G14
North Sydney NSW 22 E5 25 D11
North Tamborine QLD 7 F11
North Tarin Nature Res WA 79 J14
North Toowoomba QLD 6 B1
North Turramurra NSW 22 C5
North West Cape WA 86 D2
North West Crocodile Island NT 97 B10
North West Island QLD 11 H12
North Willoughby NSW 22 D6
North Wollongong NSW 25 K10
Northam WA 78 C7 82 C4 84 K6
Northampton WA 84 E3
Northbridge NSW 22 E6
Northbridge WA 76 A2 77 F4
Northcliffe WA 80 H6 82 J3
Northcote VIC 41 C4 43 C8
Northdown TAS 60 E7
Northfield SA 64 E5 65 G2
Northumberland Islands QLD 11 D9
Northumberland Islands Nat Park QLD 11 D9
Northville NSW 23 C6
Norton Summit SA 64 G7 65 H4
Norval Park QLD 11 K12
Norwood SA 64 G5 65 H3
Norwood TAS 55 G5
Notley Hills TAS 55 F3 61 F9
Notts Well SA 69 A5 71 H12
Novar Gardens SA 64 H2
Nowa Nowa VIC 49 K13 50 D7
Nowendoc NSW 27 A11 29 K9
Nowendoc Nat Park NSW 27 A10 29 K9
Nowingi VIC 32 G3 46 C5
Nowley NSW 28 F3
Nowra NSW 34 C7 35 C6
Nubeena TAS 57 H11 59 H12
Nudgee QLD 3 C5 5 K10 7 A10
Nudgee Beach QLD 3 B5 5 K10
Nuga Nuga Nat Park QLD 8 A5 10 K7
Nugent TAS 57 A11 59 F12
Nukarni WA 79 B13
Nulkaba NSW 23 C3
Nullagine WA 87 D10
Nullamanna NSW 29 E8
Nullarbor Motel SA 74 J4
Nullarbor Nat Park SA 74 J2 91 H7
Nullarbor Reg Res SA 74 J3 91 G7
Nullavale VIC 45 C13 48 G1
Nullawarre VIC 44 J7
Nullawil VIC 32 K5 47 H8
Nullewa Lake WA 84 F5
Number One NSW 27 B11
Numbla Vale NSW 34 H2
Numbugga NSW 34 H4 35 K2
Numbulwar NT 97 F11
Numeralla NSW 34 G4 35 H1
Numerella Nature Res NSW 35 H1
Numinbah NSW 7 J11
Numinbah Nature Res QLD 29 A13
Numinbah Valley QLD 7 H11
Numurkah VIC 33 K9 48 B3
Nunamara TAS 55 G7 61 F10
Nundah QLD 3 C4
Nundle NSW 27 A9 29 K8
Nunga VIC 32 H4 46 E6
Nungarin WA 79 A13 82 B6 85 J8
Nungatta NSW 34 K4 51 B12
Nungatta South VIC 51 B12
Nunjikompita SA 70 D3
Nunniong Plains VIC 49 G12 50 A7
Nunnyah Con Res SA 70 C3
Nurina WA 91 G5
Nurinda QLD 4 F4
Nuriootpa SA 65 B6 69 A3 71 H10
Nurrabiel VIC 44 B5
Nurrai Lakes SA 74 F2
Nutfield VIC 43 B9
Nuyts Archipelago Con Park SA 70 D2
Nuyts Reef Con Park SA 74 K5
Nuytsland Nature Res WA 91 J3
NW Vernon Island NT 95 B2 96 C4
Nyabing WA 81 C13 82 G7
Nyah VIC 32 H6 47 E9
Nyah West VIC 32 H6 47 E9
Nyamup WA 80 F6
Nyapari SA 74 A2 100 K3
Nyarrin VIC 46 F7
Nyerimilang State Park VIC 50 E7
Nyikukura SA 74 A1 90 J7 91 C7 100 K1
Nyintjilan WA 90 K6 91 C6
Nymagee NSW 31 J11 33 A11
Nymboi-Binderay Nat Park NSW 29 F12
Nymboi-Binderay State Con Area NSW 29 G12
Nymboida NSW 29 F12
Nymboida Nat Park NSW 29 E11
Nyngan NSW 31 H13
Nyora NSW 33 J10
Nyora VIC 43 J12 52 E5
Nypo VIC 32 J3 46 G4

O

O'Connell NSW 26 G6
O'Connor ACT 37 D5
O'Connor WA 77 J2
O'Halloran Hill Rec Park SA 65 K2 66 A5
O'Malley ACT 37 F4
O'Malley SA 74 H4
O'Reillys QLD 9 H13 29 A13
O'Sullivan Beach SA 66 B4
Oak Beach QLD 13 C12 14 C4
Oak Creek Nature Res NSW 34 C2
Oak Forest QLD 14 D4
Oak Park WA 79 A8
Oak Valley SA 74 F3
Oakbank SA 65 J5
Oakey QLD 9 G10
Oakey Creek NSW 26 A6 28 K4
Oakhampton NSW 23 A5
Oakhurst NSW 25 C8
Oaklands NSW 33 J11
Oaklands Park SA 64 J3
Oakleigh VIC 41 F5 43 E8 45 F14 48 K2 52 C2
Oaks TAS 55 J4 61 G9
Oaks Estate ACT 37 F7
Oakvale VIC 47 H9
Oakville NSW 25 B8
Oakwood NSW 29 E8
Oakwood TAS 57 H12 59 H12
Oaky Creek Mine QLD 10 G7
Oasis Roadhouse QLD 13 G11
Oatlands NSW 25 D10
Oatlands TAS 59 D10 61 K10
Oatley NSW 25 E11
OB Flat SA 44 G1 69 K7
Oban NSW 29 F10
Oberne NSW 33 J14
Oberon NSW 24 E1 26 G6
Obi Obi QLD 5 C8
Obley NSW 26 D3
Ocean Beach WA 81 K10
Ocean Grove VIC 42 H4 45 H12
Ocean Reef WA 77 A1
Ocean Shores NSW 29 B14
Ocean View QLD 5 H8
Ockley WA 79 J10
Offham QLD 19 G13
Officer VIC 43 F10
Officer Creek SA 74 B5
Ogmore QLD 11 F9
Olary SA 71 D13
Old Adaminaby NSW 34 F2
Old Aparawilinitja SA 74 C5
Old Bar NSW 27 C13
Old Beach TAS 56 A5 59 F10
Old Bonalbo NSW 29 B12
Old Bowenfels NSW 24 C2
Old Grevillia NSW 29 A12
Old Halls Creek WA 89 H12 90 B6
Old Junee NSW 33 G13
Old Koreelah NSW 6 K5
Old Noarlunga SA 66 C5 68 H6 69 C2 71 J10
Old Onslow Historic Ruin WA 86 D3
Old Silkwood QLD 14 J6
Old Tyabb VIC 43 H9
Old Warburton VIC 43 C13
Old Warrah NSW 27 A8
Oldina TAS 60 D4
Olinda NSW 26 E7
Olinda VIC 43 D10 48 K3 52 C3
Olio QLD 17 C9
Olive Island Con Park SA 70 E3
Olympic Dam SA 72 K7
Ombersley VIC 45 H10
Omeo VIC 49 G11 50 A6
Ondit VIC 45 H10
One Arm Point WA 88 E5
One Mile Rocks Nature Res WA 83 F10
One Tree NSW 33 F8 47 A13
One Tree Hill SA 65 F4
One Tree Island QLD 11 H12
Ongerup WA 81 E14 82 G7
Onkaparinga River Nat Park SA 66 B5 68 H6 69 C2 71 J10
Onkaparinga River Rec Park SA 66 B4
Onslow WA 86 D3
Oodla Wirra SA 71 E11
Oodnadatta SA 72 D5
Oolambeyan Nat Park NSW 33 G9
Oolarinna Oil Well SA 72 A7
Ooldea SA 74 H5
Oolloo Crossing NT 95 H2 96 F4
Ooma North NSW 26 G2 33 D14
Oombulgurri WA 89 C13
Oombunghi QLD 14 E6
Oonah TAS 60 E4
Oondooroo QLD 17 C9
Oorindi QLD 12 K6 16 A6
Ootann QLD 13 E11
Ootha NSW 33 C13
Opalton QLD 17 E8
Ophir NSW 26 F5
Opossum Bay TAS 56 E7 59 G11
Ora Banda WA 85 H11
Oran Park NSW 25 F8
Orange NSW 26 F4
Orange Grove WA 77 H7
Orangeville NSW 24 G7
Oranmeir NSW 34 E4 35 F2
Orbost VIC 49 K14 51 D9
Orchard Hills NSW 25 D8
Orchid Beach QLD 9 A13 11 K14
Orchid Valley WA 81 D8
Ord QLD 14 H1
Ord River Nature Res WA 89 C14
Orford TAS 59 E12
Orford VIC 44 H5
Organ Pipes Nat Park VIC 42 B6 45 E13 48 J1
Orielton TAS 57 A8 59 F11
Orkabie QLD 11 E9
Ormeau QLD 7 E11
Ormiston QLD 7 B11
Orpheus Island Nat Park QLD 13 G14
Orroroo SA 68 B7 71 E10
Orrvale VIC 48 C3
Osborne NSW 33 H12
Osborne SA 64 C1
Osborne Mine QLD 16 C5
Osborne Park WA 77 E2
Osborne Well NSW 33 J10
Osmington WA 80 E2
Osterley TAS 59 D8
Otago TAS 56 B5 59 F10
Otford NSW 25 H11
Ottaba QLD 4 H4
Ottoway SA 64 D2
Oura NSW 33 H13
Ourimbah NSW 23 H5 27 F10
Ournie NSW 33 K14 49 A12
Ouse TAS 59 D8
Outer Harbor SA 64 B2 65 F1 68 G6 69 B2 71 J10
Outer Sister Island TAS 61 A9
Ouyen VIC 32 H4 46 E6
Ovens VIC 49 D8
Overland Corner SA 71 H12
Overland Telegraph Station Reserve NT 99 G9
Overlander Roadhouse WA 84 B3
Owen SA 68 F7 69 A3 71 H10
Owen Springs Reserve NT 100 F7
Owens Gap NSW 27 B8
Owingup Nature Res WA 81 K9 82 K5
Oxenford QLD 7 F12
Oxford Falls NSW 22 C6 25 B11
Oxley ACT 37 H3
Oxley NSW 32 F7 47 A11
Oxley QLD 3 G2 7 B9
Oxley VIC 48 D7
Oxley Island NT 96 A6
Oxley Wild Rivers Nat Park NSW 29 H10
Oyster Bay NSW 25 E11
Oyster Cove TAS 56 G4 59 H10
Ozenkadnook VIC 44 B3

P

Pacific Palms NSW 27 D12
Packsaddle NSW 30 F3
Padbury WA 77 B2
Paddington NSW 21 D3 25 D12
Paddington QLD 3 E3
Paddington Siding WA 85 H12 91 G1
Paddys Ranges State Park VIC 45 C10
Paddys River NSW 26 K7 34 B6 35 B5
Padstow NSW 22 H3 25 E10
Padstow Heights NSW 22 H3
Padthaway SA 69 G6
Padthaway Con Park SA 69 G6
Page ACT 37 C3
Pagett Nature Res WA 80 F3
Pagewood NSW 25 E12
Pago Mission WA 89 A11
Paignie VIC 32 H3 46 E5
Pains Island QLD 12 D2
Pakenham VIC 43 F11 52 D4
Pakenham South VIC 43 G11
Pakenham Upper VIC 43 F11
Palana TAS 61 A8
Palarang NSW 34 J3
Palen Creek QLD 7 J8
Palgarup WA 80 F6
Pallamallawa NSW 28 D6
Pallamana SA 67 A12 69 C4 71 J11
Pallara QLD 3 J3
Pallarang VIC 32 H2 46 E2
Pallarenda QLD 10 A5 13 H14
Pallarup Nature Res WA 83 F9
Pallinup WA 81 E12
Palm Beach NSW 23 K5 25 A12 27 G9
Palm Beach QLD 7 H13
Palm Cove QLD 13 D13 14 D5
Palm Grove NSW 23 H4
Palmdale NSW 23 H5
Palmer SA 69 B4 71 J11
Palmer River Roadhouse QLD 13 C11
Palmers Oakey NSW 26 F6
Palmerston ACT 37 B5
Palmerston NT 95 C2 96 C3
Palmgrove Nat Park QLD 8 A6 11 K8
Palmvale NSW 7 K13
Palmview QLD 5 D10
Palmwoods QLD 5 D9
Palmyra WA 77 J2
Paloona TAS 60 E7
Paluma QLD 13 G13
Paluma Range Nat Park QLD 10 A4 13 G13
Palumpa NT 96 F2
Pambula NSW 34 J5 51 A14
Pambula Beach NSW 34 J5 51 A14
Pandanus Park WA 88 G6 90 A3
Pandappa Con Park SA 71 F11
Panitya VIC 32 H1 46 F1
Panmure VIC 44 H7
Pannawonica WA 86 D5
Pannikin Island QLD 7 C12
Panorama SA 64 J4
Pantapin WA 79 E11
Pantijan WA 89 D8
Panton Hill VIC 43 B9 48 J3 52 A3
Paper Beach TAS 55 E4 61 E9
Pappinbarra NSW 27 A12 29 K11
Papunya NT 100 E5
Para Hills SA 64 C5 65 G3
Para Vista SA 64 D6
Para Wirra Rec Park SA 65 E4 68 G7 69 B3 71 J10
Paraburdoo WA 86 F7
Parachilna SA 71 B10
Paracombe SA 65 G4
Paradise SA 64 E6
Paradise TAS 60 F7
Paradise Beach VIC 50 F5
Paradise Point QLD 7 E13
Parafield SA 64 C5 65 G2
Parafield Gardens SA 64 C4
Paralowie SA 64 B4
Parap NT 94 G2
Paraparap VIC 42 H2
Paratoo SA 71 E11
Parattah TAS 59 D10
Parawa SA 66 G3
Pardoo Roadhouse WA 87 A10
Parenna TAS 60 B6
Parham SA 68 F6 69 A2 71 H9
Parilla SA 69 C7 71 K13
Paringa SA 32 F1 69 A7 71 H13
Paris Creek SA 67 C8
Park Holme SA 64 J3 65 J2
Park Orchards VIC 41 C7
Park Ridge QLD 7 D10
Parkes ACT 36 C3 37 E5
Parkes NSW 26 F2 33 C14
Parkham TAS 61 F8
Parkhurst QLD 11 H10
Parkinson QLD 3 J4
Parkside SA 63 D3 64 G4 65 J2
Parkville NSW 27 B9
Parkwood QLD 7 F12
Parkwood WA 77 J5
Parma NSW 34 C6 35 C6
Parma Creek Nature Res NSW 35 C6
Parnabal QLD 11 H8
Parndana SA 68 K4
Parnngurr (Cotton Creek) WA 87 F13 90 F2
Paroo Siding WA 85 B9
Paroo-Darling Nat Park NSW 30 G6
Parrakie SA 69 D6 71 K12
Parramatta NSW 22 E2 25 D10 27 H9
Parrawe TAS 60 E4
Parry Beach WA 81 K9
Parry Lagoons Nature Res WA 89 D13
Parryville WA 81 J9
Parsons Beach SA 68 G4 71 J8
Partridge Island TAS 59 J10
Paru NT 95 A1 96 B3
Paruna SA 32 G1 69 B7 71 J13
Parwan VIC 42 C3 45 F12
Pascoe Vale VIC 42 C7
Paskeville SA 68 E5 71 G9
Passage Island TAS 61 A14
Pastoria VIC 45 D13
Pata SA 69 B6 71 H13
Patchewollock VIC 32 J4 46 F5
Pateena TAS 55 J5 61 G10
Paterson NSW 27 D10
Patersonia TAS 55 F6 61 F10
Patho VIC 33 K8 47 H12
Patonga NSW 23 K5 25 A11
Patterson Lakes VIC 43 F9
Paupong NSW 34 H2
Paupong Nature Res NSW 34 H2
Paw Paw SA 74 C5
Pawleena TAS 57 A9 59 F11
Pawtella TAS 59 C11 61 K11
Paxton NSW 23 D3 27 E9
Payne QLD 10 G1 17 E10
Payneham SA 64 F5 65 H3
Paynes Crossing NSW 23 D1 27 E9
Paynes Find WA 84 F7
Paynesville VIC 50 E6
Peaceful Bay WA 81 K9
Peachester QLD 5 E8
Peachna Con Res SA 68 E1 70 G5
Peak Charles Nat Park WA 83 E12
Peak Creek Siding SA 72 E5
Peak Crossing QLD 6 E7
Peak Downs Mine QLD 10 F7
Peak Hill NSW 26 D2
Peak Hill WA 87 K8
Peak Range Nat Park QLD 10 F6
Peak View NSW 34 F4 35 H1
Peake SA 69 D5 71 K12
Peakhurst NSW 22 H3
Pearce ACT 37 G3
Pearcedale VIC 43 G9 52 E3
Pearl Beach NSW 23 K5 25 A11
Pearsall WA 77 B3
Pearshape TAS 60 C6
Pearson Isles SA 70 G3

Peats Ridge NSW 23 H4 27 F9
Pebbly Beach NSW 34 E6 35 F5
Pechey QLD 4 J2
Pedirka SA 72 B5
Pee Dee Nature Res NSW 29 H11
Peebinga SA 32 H1 46 D1 69 B7 71 J13
Peebinga Con Park SA 32 H1 46 E1 69 C7 71 J13
Peechelba VIC 48 B6
Peel NSW 26 F5
Peel Island QLD 7 B12
Peelwood NSW 26 J5 34 A4
Peerabeelup WA 80 F4
Peery Lake NSW 30 F6
Pegarah TAS 60 B6
Pekina SA 68 B7 71 E10
Peko Mine NT 99 H9
Pelaw Main NSW 23 B4
Pelham TAS 59 E9
Pelican Lagoon Con Park SA 68 K5 69 D1
Pelican Waters QLD 5 E10
Pella VIC 32 K3 46 H4
Pelorus Island QLD 13 G14
Pelsaert Group WA 84 F2
Pelton NSW 23 C3
Pelverata TAS 56 G3 59 G10
Pemberton WA 80 G5 82 J3
Pembrooke NSW 27 A13 29 K12
Penarie NSW 32 F6 47 B9
Pencil Pine TAS 60 G5
Pender Bay WA 88 E5
Penfield SA 65 E2
Penguin TAS 60 D6
Penguin Island WA 78 F4
Penington Bay SA 68 K5
Penna TAS 57 B8 59 F11
Pennant Hills NSW 22 C3 25 C10
Penneshaw SA 68 K5 69 D1 71 K9
Penola SA 44 E1 69 J7
Penong SA 70 C1 74 K6
Penrice SA 65 C7
Penrith NSW 24 D7 27 H8
Penshurst VIC 44 F5
Pental Island VIC 47 F10
Pentland QLD 10 C2 13 K12 17 A12
Penwortham SA 68 E7 71 G10
Penzance TAS 57 F13
Peppermint Grove WA 77 G2
Peppers Plains VIC 46 J5
Peppimenarti NT 96 F2
Peranga QLD 9 F10
Percival Lakes WA 90 E4
Percy Isles QLD 11 E10
Percy Isles Nat Park QLD 11 E10
Peregian Beach QLD 5 B10
Perekerten NSW 32 H7 47 D10
Perenjori WA 84 F5
Perenna VIC 46 J4
Perforated Island SA 70 H4
Pericoe NSW 34 K4 51 A13
Perillup WA 81 H10
Peringillup WA 81 E11
Perisher NSW 34 G1 49 D14
Perkins Island TAS 60 C2
Pernatty Lagoon SA 71 B8
Peron Island North NT 96 D2
Peron Island South NT 96 E2
Perponda SA 69 C5 71 J12
Perseverance QLD 4 K2 6 A2
Perth TAS 55 J5 61 G10
Perth WA 76 B2 77 F4 78 D4 82 C3 84 K4
Perthville NSW 26 G5
Petcheys Bay TAS 56 J2 59 H9
Peterborough SA 68 C7 71 E10
Peterborough VIC 44 J7
Peterhead SA 64 D2
Peters Island QLD 10 A6
Petersville SA 68 F5 69 A1 71 H9
Petford QLD 13 E12 14 G1
Petina SA 70 D3
Petrie QLD 5 J9 9 F12
Petrie Terrace QLD 2 B1
Pettavel VIC 42 H2
Pheasant Creek VIC 48 H3
Pheasants Nest NSW 27 J8 34 A7
Phegans Bay NSW 23 J5
Phillip ACT 37 F4
Phillip Bay NSW 25 E12
Phillip Island VIC 43 K9 45 J14 52 F2
Phillott QLD 19 H13
Phils Creek NSW 26 J4 34 A3
Phosphate Hill Mine QLD 16 C4
Piallamore NSW 29 J8
Piallaway NSW 28 J6
Pialligo ACT 37 E6
Piambie VIC 32 G5 47 D8
Piangil VIC 32 H5 47 E9
Piangil West VIC 47 E8
Piccadilly SA 64 J7 65 J4
Piccaninnie Ponds Con Park SA 44 G1 69 K7
Pickanjinnie QLD 8 E5
Pickering Brook WA 78 E5
Pickering Brook Nat Park WA 78 E5
Pickertaramoor NT 95 A2 96 B3
Picnic Point NSW 33 K9 47 H14 48 A2
Picola VIC 47 H14 48 A2
Picton NSW 25 H8 27 J8 34 A7
Picton WA 80 B4 82 F3
Pidna Nat Park QLD 4 E1
Piedmont VIC 43 E14
Piednippie SA 70 E3
Pieman River State Res TAS 60 G3
Pier Millan VIC 32 H4 46 E7
Pierces Creek QLD 4 H2
Piesseville WA 79 K10 81 A10 82 F5
Pigeon Hole NT 98 C4
Pigeon Ponds VIC 44 D4
Piggabeen NSW 7 H13
Pikedale QLD 9 J10 29 B9
Pilakatal NT 100 J2
Pilgna SA 74 C3
Pilkinga SA 74 C4
Pillar Valley NSW 29 E13
Pilliga NSW 28 G2
Pilliga Nature Res NSW 28 H4
Pilton QLD 6 E2
Pimba SA 70 B7
Pimpama QLD 7 E12
Pimpinio VIC 44 A5
Pinchgut Junction VIC 42 K1
Pindar WA 84 E4
Pindellup WA 81 E11
Pine Clump NSW 28 K1 31 H14
Pine Corner SA 68 D2 70 F6
Pine Creek NT 95 G4 96 F5
Pine Hill QLD 10 H5 17 F14
Pine Lodge VIC 48 C4
Pine Peak Island QLD 11 E10
Pine Point SA 68 G5 69 A1 71 H9
Pine Ridge NSW 27 A8 28 K6
Pinelands QLD 4 J1
Pinery SA 68 F7 69 A2 71 H10
Piney Range NSW 26 H2 33 E14
Pingaring WA 82 E7
Pingelly WA 79 G9 82 E5
Pingrup WA 81 C14 82 G7
Pinja NT 98 F3
Pinjarra WA 78 H5 82 E3
Pinjarra Hills QLD 3 G1
Pinjarrega Nature Res WA 84 G4
Pink Lakes State Park VIC 71 J14
Pinkawillinie Con Park SA 68 B1 70 E5
Pinkawillinie Con Res SA 68 C1 70 E5
Pinkenba QLD 3 D6
Pinnacle QLD 10 D7
Pinnaroo SA 32 H1 46 F1 69 C7 71 K13
Pioneer TAS 61 D13
Pioneer WA 83 C13 85 K12 91 H1
Pioneer Bay VIC 43 J11
Pipalyatjara SA 74 A1 90 J7 91 C7 100 K1
Pipers Brook TAS 55 C6 61 D10
Pipers Flat NSW 24 B1
Pipers River TAS 55 C4 61 D9
Pipon Island QLD 15 H5
Piries VIC 48 G6 50 A1
Pirlangimpi NT 96 A3
Pirlta VIC 32 F3 46 B4
Pirrinuan QLD 9 F9
Pirron Yallock VIC 45 H9
Pirrulpakalarintja NT 100 J3
Pitalu NT 100 J2
Pitarpunga Lake NSW 32 F6 47 B9
Pitfield VIC 45 F9
Pithara WA 84 H6
Pitt Town NSW 25 B8
Pitt Water TAS 57 B8
Pittong VIC 45 E9
Pittsworth QLD 9 G10
Plainland QLD 6 C4
Planchonella Nature Res NSW 28 C7
Platts NSW 34 J3 51 A12
Pleasant Hills NSW 33 J12
Plenty TAS 56 A1 59 F9
Plenty VIC 41 A5 43 B8 45 E14 48 J2 52 B2
Plumpton NSW 25 D8
Plumridge Lakes Nature Res WA 91 F4
Plympton SA 64 H3 65 J1
Plympton Park SA 64 H3
Pmara Jutunta NT 100 C7
Poatina TAS 59 A9 61 H9
Poeppel Corner NT QLD SA 16 K1 73 A9 101 K14
Point Addis Marine Nat Park VIC 42 K2 45 J12
Point Arkwright QLD 5 B10
Point Bell Con Res SA 70 D1 74 K6
Point Clare NSW 23 J5
Point Cook VIC 42 E6 45 F13 48 K1
Point Davenport Con Park SA 68 H4 71 J8
Point Hicks Marine Nat Park VIC 51 E11
Point Leo VIC 43 K8 45 H14 52 F2
Point Lonsdale VIC 42 H5 45 H13
Point Lookout QLD 7 A14 9 G14
Point Nepean Nat Park VIC 45 H13
Point Pass SA 71 G10
Point Samson WA 86 B6
Point Souttar SA 68 G4 71 J8
Point Stuart Coastal Res NT 95 B4 96 C5
Point Turton SA 68 G4 71 J8
Pokataroo NSW 28 D2
Pokolbin NSW 23 B3 27 E9
Police Point TAS 56 K2 59 H9
Policemans Point SA 69 E4
Poltalloch SA 67 G13 69 D4 71 K11
Pomborneit VIC 45 H9
Pomborneit North VIC 45 H9
Pomona QLD 5 A8 9 D12
Pomonal VIC 44 D7
Pompapiel VIC 47 K11
Pondalowie Bay SA 68 H3
Pontville TAS 59 E10
Poochera SA 70 E4
Pooginagoric SA 44 A1 46 K1
Pooginook Con Park SA 71 G12
Poolaijelo VIC 44 D2
Poolawanna No. 1 Oil Well SA 73 B9
Poona QLD 9 C13
Poona Nat Park QLD 9 C12
Pooncarie NSW 32 D4
Poonindie SA 68 G1 70 H6
Pooraka SA 64 D5 65 G3
Pootenup WA 81 F11
Pootilla VIC 45 E11
Pootnoura SA 72 F3
Poowong VIC 43 J13 52 E5
Poowong East VIC 43 J14 52 E5
Poowong North VIC 43 J13
Popanyinning WA 79 H9 82 E5
Popiltah Lake NSW 32 C3
Popran Nat Park NSW 23 H4 27 F9
Porcupine Gorge Nat Park QLD 10 C1 13 K11
Porepunkah VIC 49 E9
Pormpuraaw QLD 12 A6 15 J1
Porongurup WA 81 H12 82 J6
Porongurup Nat Park WA 81 H12 82 J6
Porphyry Mine WA 85 G13 91 F1
Port Adelaide SA 64 E2 65 G1 68 G6 69 B2 71 J10
Port Albert VIC 50 H3
Port Alma QLD 11 H10
Port Arthur TAS 57 H12 59 H12
Port Augusta SA 68 A5 71 D9
Port Botany NSW 22 H6
Port Broughton SA 68 D5 71 F9
Port Campbell VIC 45 J8
Port Campbell Nat Park VIC 45 J8
Port Clinton Con Park SA 68 F6 71 G9
Port Darwin NT 94 J2
Port Davis SA 68 C5 71 F9
Port Denison WA 84 F3
Port Douglas QLD 13 C12 14 B4
Port Elliot SA 66 G7 68 J7 69 D3 71 K10
Port Fairy VIC 44 J5
Port Fairy - Warrnambool Coastal Park VIC 44 H6
Port Franklin VIC 50 H1 52 H7
Port Gawler SA 68 G6 69 B2 71 J9
Port Gawler Con Park SA 65 E1 68 G6 69 B2 71 H9
Port Germein SA 68 C5 71 E9
Port Gibbon SA 68 E3 70 G7
Port Hacking NSW 22 K4
Port Hedland WA 87 B8
Port Hughes SA 68 E5 71 G8
Port Huon TAS 56 H1 59 H9
Port Jackson NSW 22 E7
Port Julia SA 68 G5 69 B1 71 H9
Port Kembla NSW 25 K11 27 K8 34 B7 35 A7
Port Kenny SA 70 E4
Port Latta TAS 60 C3
Port Lincoln SA 68 G1 70 J6
Port MacDonnell SA 44 G1 69 K6
Port Macquarie NSW 27 A13 29 K12
Port Melbourne VIC 41 D3
Port Minlacowie SA 68 G4 71 J8
Port Moorowie SA 68 H5 71 J8
Port Neill SA 68 E2 70 G6
Port Noarlunga SA 66 B4 68 H6 69 C2 71 J10
Port Phillip Bay VIC 42 F6 45 G13 52 D1
Port Phillip Heads Marine Nat Park VIC 42 H5 45 H13
Port Pirie SA 68 C5 71 F9
Port Rickaby SA 68 G4 71 H8
Port Roper NT 97 G10
Port Sorell TAS 61 E8
Port Stewart QLD 15 H4
Port Victoria SA 68 F4 71 H8
Port Vincent SA 68 G5 69 B1 71 J9
Port Wakefield SA 68 F6 71 H9
Port Welshpool VIC 50 H2
Port Willunga SA 66 C4
Portarlington VIC 42 G5 45 G13
Porters Retreat NSW 24 J1 26 H6
Portland NSW 26 F6
Portland VIC 44 H4
Portland Bay VIC 44 H4
Portland Roads QLD 15 E4
Portsea VIC 42 J5 45 H13
Possession Island Nat Park QLD 15 B2
Potato Point NSW 34 G5 35 H4
Potts Point NSW 21 B4
Pottsville NSW 7 K14 9 J14 29 A14
Pound Creek VIC 52 G5
Powelltown VIC 43 D13 48 K5 52 C5
Powers Creek VIC 44 D3
Powlathanga QLD 10 B4 13 J13
Powlett Plains VIC 47 K10
Poynter Island QLD 11 E9
Prahran VIC 41 E4 42 D7
Prairie QLD 10 C1 13 K11 17 A11
Prairie VIC 47 K12
Precipice Nat Park QLD 8 B7
Premaydena TAS 57 G11 59 G12
Premer NSW 26 A6 28 K5
Prentice Lake NT 99 G11
Preolenna TAS 60 D4
Preservation Island TAS 61 A13
Preston QLD 6 C1
Preston TAS 60 E6
Preston VIC 41 C1 42 C7
Preston Beach WA 78 J4 82 E2
Pretty Beach NSW 23 J5
Pretty Gully NSW 29 B11
Pretty Pine NSW 33 J8 47 F13
Prevelly WA 80 E1 82 H1
Price SA 68 F6 69 A1 71 H9
Price Island SA 70 H5
Priestdale QLD 3 H6
Prime Seal Island TAS 61 B8
Primrose Sands TAS 57 D10 59 G11
Prince Frederick Harbour WA 89 C9
Prince of Wales Island QLD 15 B1
Prince Regent Nature Res WA 89 C9
Princess Charlotte Bay QLD 15 H5
Princetown VIC 45 K8
Princhester QLD 11 G9
Princhester Con Park QLD 11 G9
Priors Pocket QLD 3 H1
Priory TAS 61 E14
Probable Island NT 97 C11
Propect Hill SA 66 C7
Propodollah VIC 46 K3
Proserpine QLD 10 C7
Prospect NSW 22 E1 25 D9
Prospect SA 64 F4 65 H2
Prospect TAS 55 H5
Proston QLD 9 D10
Prubi QLD 17 C9
Prudhoe Island QLD 11 D9
Pt Nepean Nat Park VIC 42 J5
Pucawan NSW 33 F13
Pucawan Nature Res NSW 33 F13
Puckapunyal VIC 45 C14 48 F2
Pudman Creek NSW 26 K4 34 B3
Pukatja (Ernabella) SA 100 K6
Pullabooka NSW 26 G1 33 E14
Pullen Island SA 66 G7
Pullen Island Con Park SA 66 G7
Pullenvale QLD 7 B8
Pulletop Nature Res NSW 33 E10
Pullut VIC 46 J5
Pumphreys Bridge WA 79 H8
Punchbowl NSW 22 G3 25 E10
Punchmirup WA 81 D10
Punmu WA 87 E14 90 E2
Punthari SA 69 B4 71 J11
Pura Pura VIC 45 F8
Pureba Con Park SA 70 C3
Pureba Con Res SA 70 C3 74 K7
Purfleet NSW 27 B12
Purga QLD 6 D7
Purlewaugh NSW 28 K4
Purnim VIC 44 H7
Purnong SA 69 B5 71 J11
Purnululu Con Res WA 89 F13 90 A7
Purnululu Nat Park WA 89 G13 90 A7
Purrumbete South VIC 45 H8
Puta Puta NT 100 H2
Putaputa SA 74 A1 100 K2
Putty NSW 27 E8
Pyalong VIC 45 C13 48 G1
Pyap SA 69 A6 71 H13
Pyengana TAS 61 E13
Pygery SA 70 E5
Pymble NSW 22 C5 25 C11
Pymurra QLD 12 K5 16 A5
Pyramid Hill VIC 32 K7 47 J11
Pyramul NSW 26 E5

Q

Quaama NSW 34 H5 35 J3
Quail Island NT 96 C3
Quail Island QLD 11 F9
Quail Island VIC 43 H10 52 E3
Quairading WA 79 E10 82 C5 84 K7
Quairading South WA 79 E10
Quakers Hill NSW 25 C9
Qualco SA 71 G12
Qualeup WA 81 D8
Quambatook VIC 32 K6 47 H9
Quambone NSW 31 G14
Quamby QLD 12 K5
Quamby Brook TAS 55 J1 61 G8
Quanda Nature Res NSW 31 J12
Quandialla NSW 26 H1 33 E14
Quangallin WA 81 B10
Quantong VIC 44 B5
Quarram Nature Res WA 82 K4
Queanbeyan NSW 34 D3 35 D1 37 G7 38 D6
Queen Victoria Spring Nature Res WA 85 H14 91 G2
Queens Lake Nature Res NSW 27 A13
Queenscliff NSW 25 C12
Queenscliff VIC 42 H5 45 H13
Queensferry VIC 43 K11
Queenstown TAS 58 B4 60 J4
Queerah QLD 14 E5
Quellington WA 79 D8
Quidong Nature Res NSW 34 J3
Quilberry QLD 19 F13
Quilpie QLD 19 E10
Quinalow QLD 9 F10
Quindalup WA 80 C2
Quindanning WA 78 K7 82 F4
Quindinup Nature Res WA 81 G8 82 H5
Quinninup WA 80 G6
Quinns Rocks WA 78 C4 82 C2 84 K4
Quipolly NSW 27 A8 28 K7
Quirindi NSW 27 A8 28 K7
Quobba WA 86 H1
Quoin Island NT 96 G1
Quondong NSW 30 K3 32 A3
Quorn SA 68 A6 71 D9
Quorrobolong NSW 23 D4

R

Rabbit Flat Roadhouse NT 98 H2
Rabbit Island QLD 11 C8
Rabila SA 67 B13
Rabuma Island NT 97 B10
Raby NSW 25 F9
Raby Bay QLD 7 B11
Raglan QLD 11 H11
Raglan VIC 45 D9
Railton TAS 60 F7
Rainbow VIC 32 K3 46 H5
Rainbow Beach QLD 9 C13
Rainbow Valley Con Res NT 101 G8
Raine Island QLD 15 D5
Raleigh NSW 29 G12
Raluana VIC 44 A7
Ramco SA 69 A5 71 H12
Raminea TAS 59 J9
Ramingining NT 97 C10
Ramornie Nat Park NSW 29 E12
Ramsay QLD 6 D1
Ramsgate NSW 25 E11
Ranceby VIC 43 J14 52 F5
Rand NSW 33 J12
Randalls Mine WA 83 A13 85 J13 91 G1
Randell WA 83 A13 85 J13 91 G1
Randwick NSW 22 G6 25 D12
Ranelagh TAS 56 F2 59 G9
Ranga TAS 61 C9
Rangal QLD 11 H8
Rangelands QLD 17 C9
Rankins Springs NSW 33 E11
Rannes QLD 11 J9
Rannock NSW 33 G13
Ransome QLD 3 E7
Rapanyup South VIC 44 B7
Rapid Bay SA 66 G1 66 G1 68 J6 69 D2 71 K9
Rapid Creek NT 94 C4
Rapids Con Park WA 80 E3
Rappville NSW 29 C12
Raragala Island NT 97 B12
Rathdowney QLD 7 H8 9 H12 29 A12
Rathmines NSW 23 D6
Rathscar VIC 45 C9
Raukkan SA 67 G11
Ravensbourne QLD 4 K2 6 A2
Ravensbourne Nat Park QLD 4 K3 6 A3 9 G11
Ravensdale NSW 23 F4
Ravenshoe QLD 13 E12 14 J4
Ravensthorpe WA 83 G10
Ravenswood QLD 10 B5 13 J14
Ravenswood VIC 45 B11
Ravenswood WA 78 H4
Ravensworth NSW 27 D9
Ravine NSW 34 F1 49 A14
Rawbelle QLD 9 A9 11 K11
Rawdon Creek Nature Res NSW 27 A13 29 K12
Rawdon Vale NSW 27 C10
Rawlinna WA 91 G4
Rawson VIC 50 E2
Raymond Island VIC 50 E6
Raymond Terrace NSW 23 A6 27 E10
Raywood VIC 45 A12
Razorback Nature Res NSW 26 H5 34 A4
Recherche Archipelago Nature Res WA 83 H14 91 K1
Red Bluff Nature Res VIC 69 E7
Red Banks SA 65 B2
Red Banks Con Park SA 71 G11
Red Bluff Nature Res VIC 32 K2 46 H1
Red Cap Creek VIC 44 E2
Red Cliffs VIC 32 F3 46 B5
Red Hill ACT 37 F5
Red Hill QLD 2 A1 3 E3 7 A9
Red Hill VIC 43 J8
Red Hill South VIC 43 J8
Red Hills TAS 61 G8
Red Range NSW 29 E10
Red Rock NSW 29 F13
Redbank VIC 45 B9 49 E9
Redbank Plains QLD 7 C8
Redbanks SA 71 G11
Redcliffe QLD 5 J10 9 F13
Redcliffe WA 77 F5
Redesdale VIC 45 C12
Redfern NSW 22 F6 25 D11
Redhead NSW 23 D7
Redhill SA 68 D6 71 F9
Redland Bay QLD 7 C11 7 C12 9 G13
Redlynch QLD 13 D13 14 D4
Redmond WA 81 J11 82 K6
Redmond West WA 81 J11
Redpa TAS 60 C1
Redwood Park SA 64 C7
Reedy Creek QLD 7 H12
Reedy Creek SA 69 G5
Reedy Creek VIC 45 D14 48 G2
Reedy Dam VIC 32 K4 46 H7
Reedy Flat VIC 49 H12 50 B7
Reedy Island SA 67 G10
Reedy Marsh TAS 55 G1 61 F8
Reef Hills Regional Park VIC 48 D5
Reefton NSW 33 F13
Reefton VIC 43 B14 48 J5 52 B5
Reekara TAS 60 B6
Reeves Plains SA 65 C2
Reevesby Island SA 68 F2 70 H6
Regatta Point TAS 58 C3 60 K3
Regency Park SA 64 E3
Regents Park NSW 22 F2 25 D10
Regents Park QLD 3 K4
Regentville NSW 24 D7
Regnard Bay WA 86 C5
Reid ACT 36 A4 37 D5
Reid WA 91 G6
Reid River QLD 10 A5 13 J14
Reids Creek VIC 49 C8
Reids Flat NSW 26 J4 34 A3
Relbia TAS 55 H6 61 F10
Rendlesham SA 69 J6
Renison Bell TAS 58 A4 60 H4
Renmark SA 32 F1 69 A7 71 H13
Renner Springs NT 99 E8
Rennie NSW 33 K11 48 A6
Research VIC 41 B6
Reservoir VIC 41 B4 42 C7
Retreat TAS 55 D5 61 E10
Retro QLD 10 G6
Revesby NSW 22 H3 25 E10
Reynella SA 65 K2 66 A5 68 H6 69 C2 71 J10
Reynolds Island TAS 59 A8 61 H8
Reynolds Neck TAS 59 A8 61 H8
Rheban TAS 59 E13
Rheola VIC 45 A10
Rhodes NSW 25 D10
Rhyll VIC 43 K10 52 F3
Rhyndaston TAS 59 D11
Rhynie SA 68 F7 71 G10
Riana TAS 60 E6
Rich Avon VIC 44 A7 46 K7
Richardson ACT 37 J4
Richlands NSW 26 J6 34 A5
Richlands QLD 3 H2
Richmond NSW 24 B7 27 G8
Richmond QLD 13 K9 17 A9
Richmond SA 64 G3 65 H2
Richmond TAS 56 A7 59 F11
Richmond VIC 41 D4 43 D8
Richmond Range Nat Park NSW 9 J12 29 B12
Rickeys WA 79 E9
Riddells Creek VIC 45 E13 48 H1
Ridgehaven SA 64 D7
Ridgelands QLD 11 G10
Ridgeway TAS 56 D5
Ridgley TAS 60 E5
Rifle Creek QLD 16 A4
Rimbanda QLD 17 D10
Rimbija Island NT 97 A13
Ringa WA 78 C7
Ringarooma TAS 61 E12
Ringarooma Coastal Res TAS 61 C13
Ringwood VIC 41 D7 43 D9 48 K3 52 B3
Ripley QLD 7 D8
Ripplebrook VIC 43 H13 52 E5
Risdon Vale TAS 56 B6 59 F10
Rita Island QLD 10 A6
River Heads QLD 9 B13
Riverhills QLD 3 G1
Riverside TAS 55 G5
Riverside Mine QLD 10 E6
Riverstone NSW 25 C8
Riverton SA 68 F7 71 H10
Riverton WA 77 H5
Rivervale WA 77 G5
Riverview QLD 7 C8
Riverwood NSW 22 H3 25 E10
Rivett ACT 37 F2
Roadvale QLD 6 F7
Rob Roy Nature Res ACT 37 K4 38 E5
Robbins Island TAS 60 B2
Robe SA 69 H5
Roberts Point TAS 56 H5
Robertson NSW 27 K8 34 B7 35 A6
Robertson QLD 3 G4
Robertstown SA 71 G11
Robigana TAS 55 E3 61 E9
Robin Hood VIC 43 F14
Robina QLD 7 G12
Robinvale VIC 32 G5 46 C7
Rochedale QLD 3 G6 7 C10
Rochedale South QLD 3 H6
Rocherlea TAS 55 F5 61 F10
Rochester VIC 47 K13 48 C1
Rochford VIC 45 D13 48 H1
Rock Flat NSW 34 G3 35 J1
Rockbank VIC 42 C5 45 F13 48 K1
Rockdale NSW 22 H4 25 E11
Rockhampton QLD 11 H10
Rockingham WA 78 F4 82 D2
Rocklands Reservoir VIC 44 D5
Rocklea QLD 3 G3 7 B9
Rockleigh SA 65 J7 69 B4 71 J10
Rockley NSW 26 G5
Rocklyn VIC 45 D11
Rocksberg QLD 5 G8
Rockton NSW 34 K3 51 A12
Rockvale NSW 29 G10
Rocky Cape TAS 60 C4
Rocky Cape Nat Park TAS 60 C4
Rocky Creek NSW 28 F6
Rocky Crossing ACT 38 G4
Rocky Glen NSW 28 J4
Rocky Gully WA 81 G9 82 J5
Rocky Hall NSW 34 J4
Rocky Hill QLD 4 E1
Rocky Island QLD 12 C3
Rocky River NSW 29 H9
Rocky River SA 68 K3
Rodds Bay QLD 11 J11
Rodinga NT 101 G8
Roebourne WA 86 B6
Roebuck Bay WA 88 H4
Roebuck Plains Roadhouse WA 88 G4 90 A2
Roelands WA 80 B4
Roger Corner SA 68 H5 71 J8
Roger River TAS 60 D2
Roger River West TAS 60 D2
Rokeby TAS 56 D7 59 G11
Rokeby VIC 43 F14 52 D6
Rokewood VIC 45 F10
Rokewood Junction VIC 45 F10
Roland TAS 60 F7
Rollands Plains NSW 27 A13 29 K12
Rolleston QLD 10 J7
Rolling Bay NT 97 B8
Rollingstone QLD 13 G14
Roma QLD 8 E5
Romsey VIC 45 D13 48 H1
Ronsard Bay WA 84 H3
Rookhurst NSW 27 B11
Rooty Hill NSW 25 D8
Ropely QLD 6 C4
Roper Bar NT 97 G9
Rorruwuy NT 97 C12
Rosa Glen WA 80 E2
Rosanna VIC 43 C8
Rose Bay NSW 25 D12
Rose Bay TAS 54 A4
Rosebank NSW 29 B14
Roseberry VIC 32 K4 46 H6
Roseberry East VIC 46 H6
Rosebery TAS 58 A4 60 H4
Rosebrook NSW 23 A4
Rosebrook VIC 44 H5

Turkey Beach QLD 11 J12
Turlinjah NSW 34 F5 35 H4
Turner ACT 37 D5
Turners Beach TAS 60 E7
Turners Marsh TAS 55 E5 61 E10
Turon Nat Park NSW 26 F6
Turondale NSW 26 F5
Tuross Head NSW 34 F6 35 H4
Tuross Lake NSW 34 G6
Turramurra NSW 22 C4 25 C10
Turrawan NSW 28 G5
Turriff VIC 46 F6
Turtle Group Nat Park QLD 15 J6
Turtle Head Island QLD 15 B3
Tusmore SA 64 G5
Tutanning Nature Res WA 79 G10 82 D5
Tutunup WA 80 C4
Tutye VIC 32 H2 46 E3
Tweed Heads NSW 7 H14 9 H14 29 A14
Twelve Apostles Marine Nat Park VIC 45 K8
Twelve Mile NSW 26 D5
Two Mile Flat NSW 26 D5
Two Peoples Bay WA 81 J13 82 K7
Two Peoples Bay Nature Res WA 81 J13 82 K7
Two Rocks WA 78 C3 82 B2 84 K4
Two Wells SA 65 D1 68 G7 69 A2 71 H10
Twofold Bay NSW 34 K5 51 A14
Twyford QLD 13 C12
Tyaak VIC 45 D14 48 G2
Tyabb VIC 43 H9 45 H14 52 E2
Tyagarah Nature Res NSW 29 B14
Tyagong NSW 26 H2 34 A1
Tyalgum NSW 7 K11 9 J13 29 A13
Tyalgum Creek NSW 7 K10
Tyalla VIC 32 H2 46 E3
Tycannah NSW 28 E5
Tyenna TAS 59 F8
Tyers VIC 50 F2
Tygalgah NSW 7 J13
Tylden VIC 45 D12
Tylerville QLD 7 J8
Tyndale NSW 29 E13
Tynong VIC 43 F12 52 D4
Tynong North VIC 43 F12
Tyntynder Central VIC 32 H6 47 E9
Tyntynder South VIC 32 H6 47 F9
Tyrendarra VIC 44 H4
Tyrendarra East VIC 44 H4
Tyringham NSW 29 G11
Tyrrell Downs VIC 32 J5 46 F7

U

Uarbry NSW 26 B6
Ubirr NT 95 C7
Ubobo QLD 11 J11
Ukatjupa NT 90 J7 100 K1
Uki NSW 7 K12 9 J13 29 A13
Ulamambri NSW 28 J4
Ulan NSW 26 C6
Ulandra Nature Res NSW 26 K2 33 G14
Ulaypai SA 74 A4 100 K5
Uleybury SA 65 E4
Ulidarra Nat Park NSW 29 G13
Ulidia NSW 29 B12
Ulinda NSW 26 A5 28 K4
Ulkiya SA 74 B3 100 K4
Ulladulla NSW 34 E6 35 E6
Ullina VIC 45 D10
Ullswater VIC 44 C3
Ullula WA 85 B10
Ulmarra NSW 29 E13
Ulong NSW 29 G12
Ultima VIC 32 J6 47 F8
Ultimo NSW 21 D1
Uluru - Kata Tjuta Nat Park NT 100 J4
Ulva WA 79 C13
Ulverstone TAS 60 E6
Umagico QLD 15 B2
Umbakumba NT 97 F13
Umerina SA 72 C1 74 B6
Umina NSW 23 J5
Umpukulunya SA 74 A3 100 K3
Umuwa SA 74 B5
Unanderra NSW 25 K10 35 A7
Undara Volcanic Nat Park QLD 13 F11
Undera VIC 48 C3
Underbool VIC 32 H3 46 E4
Underwood QLD 3 H5
Underwood TAS 55 E6 61 E10
Undina QLD 12 K6 16 A5
Ungarie NSW 33 D12
Ungarra SA 68 F2 70 G6
Ungo QLD 10 K1 17 H10
Unicup Nature Res WA 81 F8 82 H4
Unley SA 63 D2 64 G4 65 J2
Unnamed Con Park SA 74 E2 91 F7
Upolu Cay Nat Park QLD 14 C6
Upper Bingara NSW 28 F7
Upper Blessington TAS 61 F11
Upper Bowman NSW 27 B11
Upper Caboolture QLD 5 H8
Upper Castra TAS 60 F6
Upper Colo NSW 24 A7
Upper Coomera QLD 7 F11
Upper Durogy NSW 7 J13
Upper Esk TAS 61 F12
Upper Ferntree Gully VIC 43 E10 48 K3 52 C3
Upper Freestone QLD 6 H3
Upper Hermitage SA 65 G4
Upper Horton NSW 28 F6
Upper Kedron QLD 3 D1
Upper Manilla NSW 28 H7
Upper McDonald NSW 23 H1
Upper Mount Gravatt QLD 3 G5
Upper Mount Hicks TAS 60 D5
Upper Myall NSW 27 C12
Upper Nariel VIC 49 D12
Upper Natone TAS 60 E5
Upper Orara NSW 29 G12
Upper Pilton QLD 6 F2
Upper Plenty VIC 45 D14 48 H2
Upper Rollands Plains NSW 29 K11
Upper Scamander TAS 61 F13
Upper Spring Creek QLD 6 F2
Upper Stone QLD 13 G13
Upper Stowport TAS 60 E5
Upper Sturt SA 64 K6
Upper Swan WA 78 D5 82 C3 84 K5
Upper Tallebudgera QLD 7 J12
Upper Tenthill QLD 6 C3
Upper Yarra Dam VIC 43 B14 48 J5 52 B6
Uraidla SA 64 H7 65 J4 69 B3 71 J10
Uralla NSW 29 H9
Urana NSW 33 H11
Urandangi QLD 16 C1
Urangeline NSW 33 J12
Urangeline East NSW 33 J12
Urania SA 68 F5 69 A1 71 H8
Uranquinty NSW 33 H13
Urapunga NT 97 G9
Urapuntja (Utopia) NT 101 C9
Urawa Nature Res WA 84 E4
Urbenville NSW 9 J12 29 A12
Uriadla SA 68 H7
Urilpila NT 100 J3
Urlampe NT 16 D1 101 D14
Urlip NSW 7 J12
Urrbrae SA 64 H5
Urunga NSW 29 G12
Useless Loop WA 84 B1
Utah Lake NSW 31 E8
Uxbridge TAS 59 F9

V

Vacy NSW 27 D10
Vale View QLD 6 C1
Valencia Island NT 96 A6
Valentine NSW 23 D6
Valley Heights NSW 24 D6
Valley View SA 64 D5
Van Diemen Gulf NT 95 A4 96 B5
Vanderlin Island NT 97 J13 99 A13
Vandyke Creek Con Park QLD 10 J6
Vansittart Bay WA 89 A10
Vansittart Island TAS 61 C10
Varley WA 83 E9
Vasey VIC 44 D4
Vasse WA 80 C2
Vaucluse NSW 22 F7 25 D12
Vectus VIC 44 B5
Veitch SA 69 B6 71 J13
Venman Bushland Nat Park QLD 3 J7 7 C11
Ventnor VIC 43 K9 45 J14 52 F2
Venus Bay SA 70 F4
Venus Bay VIC 52 H5
Venus Bay Con Park SA 70 F3
Venus Bay Con Res SA 70 E3
Verdun SA 65 J4
Verdure QLD 14 G1
Veresdale QLD 7 F9
Vermont VIC 43 D9
Verona NSW 34 H5 35 J3
Verona Sands TAS 59 H10
Verran SA 68 E2 70 G6
Vervale VIC 43 G12
Victor Harbor SA 66 G6 68 J7 69 D3 71 K10
Victoria Park WA 77 G4
Victoria Point QLD 7 C12
Victoria River NT 96 H4 98 A4
Victoria Rock Nature Res WA 83 B11 85 J11
Victoria Valley TAS 59 D8 61 K8
Victoria Valley VIC 44 E5
Victory Well SA 74 C5
Villawood NSW 22 F2
Villeneuve QLD 4 F6
Vincentia NSW 34 D7 35 C6
Vineyard NSW 25 C8
Vinifera VIC 32 H6 47 E9
Violet Town VIC 48 D4
Virginia QLD 3 C5 4 H2
Virginia SA 65 E2 68 G7 69 B3 71 H10
Virginia-Bees Creek NT 95 C2 96 C4
Vista SA 64 D7
Vite Vite VIC 45 F8
Vite Vite North VIC 45 F9
Vivonne SA 68 K4
Vivonne Bay SA 68 K4
Vivonne Bay Con Park SA 68 K4
Vokes Hill Corner SA 74 E3
Vulkathunha-Gammon Ranges Nat Park SA 71 A11 73 K11

W

Waaia VIC 48 B3
Waarre VIC 45 J8
Wabba Wilderness Park VIC 49 C11
Wabma Kadarbu Mound Springs Con Park SA 72 H7
Wacol QLD 3 H1 7 C9
Wada Wadalla NT 97 J12 99 A12
Wada Warra NT 97 J12 99 A12
Wadbilliga Nat Park NSW 34 G4 35 J2
Waddamana TAS 59 C8 61 K8
Waddi NSW 33 G10
Waddikee SA 68 C2 70 F6
Wadeye NT 96 F1
Waeel WA 79 C9
Wagaman NT 94 C5
Wagant VIC 32 H4 46 E6
Wagerup WA 78 J5
Wagga Wagga NSW 33 H13
Waggabundi QLD 12 H3
Waggarandall VIC 48 C5
Wagin WA 81 B10 82 F5
Wagonga NSW 34 G5 35 H4
Wahgunyah VIC 48 B7
Wahgunyah Con Res SA 74 K5
Wahroonga NSW 22 C4 25 C10
Waikerie SA 69 A5 71 H12
Wail VIC 44 A5
Wairewa VIC 49 K13 51 D8
Waitchie VIC 32 J5 47 F8
Waite Creek Settlement NT 100 D3
Waitpinga SA 66 H5 68 J6 69 D2 71 K10
Waitpinga Con Park SA 66 H3
Wakefield NSW 23 D5
Wakool NSW 33 J8 47 F12
Walalkarra SA 74 C4
Walang NSW 26 G6
Walbundrie NSW 33 J12
Walcha NSW 29 J9
Walcha Road NSW 29 J8
Waldegrave Island Con Park SA 70 F4
Walebing WA 82 A3 84 H5
Walga Gunya WA 85 C9
Walgett NSW 28 F1 31 E14
Walgoolan WA 82 B7 85 J8
Walhalla VIC 50 E2
Walitjara SA 74 A3 100 K3
Walka NT 90 H7 91 B7 100 H1
Walkamin QLD 13 D12 14 F3
Walkaway WA 84 F3
Walker VIC 43 A14
Walker Flat SA 69 B5 71 J11
Walker Island TAS 58 K6 60 B2
Walkers Crossing SA 73 D12
Walkerston QLD 11 D8
Walkerville SA 64 F4 65 H2
Walkerville North VIC 52 H6
Walkerville South VIC 52 J6
Wall Flat SA 69 B4 71 J11
Walla Walla NSW 33 J12
Wallabadah NSW 27 A8 28 K7
Wallabadah Nature Res NSW 27 A9 28 K7
Wallabi Group WA 84 E2
Wallabrook SA 44 B1 69 G7
Wallaby Island QLD 12 A6 15 G1
Wallace VIC 45 E11
Wallace Rockhole NT 100 G7
Wallacedale North VIC 44 G4
Wallacia NSW 24 E7 27 H8
Wallaga Lake Heights NSW 34 G5 35 J4
Wallal QLD 19 E13
Wallalong NSW 23 A5
Wallaloo VIC 44 B7
Wallaloo East VIC 44 B7
Wallamba Nature Res NSW 27 C12
Wallan VIC 45 D14 48 H2
Wallan East VIC 45 D14 48 H2
Wallangarra NSW 9 K10 29 C10
Wallangra NSW 28 D7
Wallany SA 74 B4 100 K4
Wallarah Nat Park NSW 27 F10
Wallaroo NSW 37 A2
Wallaroo SA 68 E5 71 G8
Wallaroo Bay SA 68 E5
Wallaroo Nature Res NSW 27 D11
Wallatinna SA 72 D2 74 C7
Wallaville QLD 9 A11
Wallendbeen NSW 26 K2 33 G14 34 B1
Wallerawang NSW 24 B1 26 F7
Walleroobie NSW 33 F12
Walli NSW 26 G4
Wallinduc VIC 45 F9
Wallingat Nat Park NSW 27 C12
Wallington VIC 42 H4
Wallon QLD 6 C7
Walloway SA 68 B7 71 E10
Wallpolla Island VIC 46 A3
Walls of Jerusalem Nat Park TAS 58 A6 60 H6
Wallsend NSW 23 C6 27 E10
Wallumbilla QLD 8 E6
Wallundry NSW 26 J1 33 F14
Wallup VIC 46 K5
Walmer NSW 26 D3
Walmesty Bay WA 89 B9
Walpa VIC 49 K10 50 D5
Walpeup VIC 32 H3 46 E5
Walpole WA 81 J8 82 K4
Walpole-Nornalup Nat Park WA 81 K8 82 K4
Waltara NSW 25 C10
Walu NT 100 H2
Walungurru (Kintore) NT 100 E1
Walwa VIC 33 K14 49 A12
Walyahmoning Nature Res WA 85 H8
Walyinynga SA 74 A4 100 K4
Walytjatjata NT 74 A1 100 K2
Walyunga Nat Park WA 78 C5
Wamberal NSW 23 H6
Wamberal Lagoon Nature Res NSW 27 G10
Wambool Nature Res NSW 26 G6
Wamboyne NSW 33 D13
Wammuta QLD 16 B4
Wamoon NSW 33 F11
Wamuran QLD 5 G8 9 F12
Wamuran Basin QLD 5 G8
Wanaaring NSW 30 D7
Wanagarren Nature Res WA 82 A1 84 J4
Wanbi SA 69 B6 71 J12
Wandana Nature Res WA 84 D4
Wandandian NSW 34 D6 35 C6
Wandearah East SA 68 D6 71 F9
Wandearah West SA 68 D6 71 F9
Wandella NSW 34 G5 35 J3
Wandering WA 79 H8 82 E4
Wandiligong VIC 49 E9
Wandilo SA 44 F1 69 J6
Wandin North VIC 43 C11
Wando Bridge VIC 44 E3
Wando Vale VIC 44 E3
Wandoan QLD 8 D7
Wandong VIC 45 D14 48 H2
Wandoo Con Park WA 82 D4 84 K6
Wandoo Nat Park WA 78 E7
Wandsworth NSW 29 F9
Wangan QLD 14 H6
Wanganella NSW 33 H8 47 E13
Wangara WA 77 B3
Wangarabell VIC 51 C12
Wangaratta VIC 48 C6
Wangary SA 70 H5
Wangerrip VIC 45 K9
Wangetti QLD 13 C12 14 C4
Wangi Wangi NSW 23 E6
Wangkatjungka WA 89 J9 90 B5
Wangoom VIC 44 H6
Wanguri NT 94 C5
Wanilla SA 68 F1 70 H5
Wanjarri Nature Res WA 85 C11
Wankari NT 90 H7 91 B7 100 H1
Wanko QLD 19 E13
Wannamal WA 78 A5 82 B3 84 J5
Wannarn WA 90 H6 91 B6
Wanneroo WA 77 A3 78 D4 82 C2 84 K5
Wanniassa ACT 37 H4
Wannon VIC 44 F4
Wanora QLD 6 B6
Wansbeck QLD 4 A1
Wansborough WA 81 F11
Wantabadgery NSW 33 H14
Wanwin VIC 44 G2
Wapengo NSW 34 H5 35 K3
Wapet Camp WA 86 C4
Wappinguy NSW 26 C7
Waragai Creek Nature Res NSW 29 E13
Warakurna WA 90 H7 91 A7
Warakurna Roadhouse WA 90 H7 91 B6
Waramanga ACT 37 G3
Warana QLD 5 D10
Waranga VIC 45 A14 48 D2
Waratah NSW 23 C6
Waratah TAS 60 F4
Waratah Bay VIC 52 H6
Waratah North VIC 52 H6
Warburn NSW 33 F10
Warburton VIC 43 C13 48 K4 52 B5
Warburton WA 90 J5 91 B5
Warburton East VIC 43 C13
Warby Range State Park VIC 48 C6
Ward Island SA 70 G3
Wardang Island SA 68 F4 71 H8
Wardell NSW 29 C14
Wards Mistake NSW 29 F10
Wards River NSW 27 C11
Warialda NSW 28 D7
Warianna QLD 17 B10
Warilla NSW 27 K8 34 B7 35 A7
Warkton NSW 26 A5 28 K3
Warkworth NSW 27 D9
Warmun (Turkey Creek) WA 89 F13 90 A7
Warncoort VIC 45 H10
Warneet VIC 43 H10 52 E3
Warner Vale NSW 23 G5
Warners Bay NSW 23 C6
Warnertown SA 68 C6 71 F9
Warooka SA 68 H4 71 J8
Waroona WA 78 J5 82 E3
Warra QLD 9 E9
Warra Nat Park NSW 29 F10
Warrabah Nat Park NSW 28 G7
Warrabillinna SA 74 B5 100 K6
Warrabkook VIC 44 G5
Warracknabeal VIC 46 K6
Warradale SA 64 J2
Warraderry NSW 26 G2
Warragamba NSW 24 F7 27 H8
Warragamba VIC 47 K12
Warragoon NSW 33 K11 48 A6
Warragul VIC 43 G14 52 D6
Warrah Creek NSW 27 B8
Warrak VIC 45 D8
Warrambine VIC 45 G10
Warramboo SA 68 C1 70 F5
Warrandyte VIC 41 C7 43 C9 48 K3 52 B2
Warrandyte State Park VIC 41 B7 43 C9 48 K3 52 B2
Warranmang VIC 45 C9
Warranulla NSW 27 C11
Warrapura WA 91 A7
Warrawee NSW 25 C10
Warrawenia Lake NSW 32 D3
Warrawong NSW 35 A7
Warrayure VIC 44 F5
Warreah QLD 10 C2 13 K11 17 A11
Warrego Mine NT 99 G8
Warrell Creek NSW 29 H12
Warren NSW 26 A1 31 J14
Warren Con Park SA 65 F5
Warren Nat Park WA 80 G5 82 J3
Warrenbayne VIC 48 E5
Warrenben Con Park SA 68 H4 70 J7
Warrentinna TAS 61 D12
Warriewood NSW 25 B11
Warrigal QLD 10 C2 13 K12 17 A12
Warrill View QLD 6 E6
Warrimoo NSW 24 D6
Warrina SA 72 E6
Warrion VIC 45 H10
Warriup WA 81 H14
Warrnambool VIC 44 J6
Warro Nat Park QLD 9 A10 11 K12
Warrong VIC 44 H6
Warroo NSW 26 F1 33 D13
Warrow SA 70 H5
Warrumbungle NSW 28 J2
Warrumbungle Nat Park NSW 28 J3
Warrupura WA 90 H7 100 H1
Warruwi NT 96 B7
Wartburg QLD 11 K12
Wartook VIC 44 C6
Warup WA 81 B9
Warwick QLD 6 J2 9 H11 29 A10
Warwick WA 77 C2
Warwick Farm NSW 22 G1
Wasaga QLD 15 B2
Washpool Nat Park NSW 29 D11
Wasleys SA 65 B3 68 F7 69 A3 71 H10
Watagan NSW 23 E3
Watagans Nat Park NSW 23 D4 27 E9
Watalgan QLD 11 K12
Watanobbi NSW 23 G5
Watarrka Nat Park NT 100 G5
Watarru SA 74 C2
Watchem VIC 46 J7
Watchupga VIC 32 K4 46 H7
Waterfall NSW 25 G10 27 J9
Waterfall Gully SA 64 H6
Waterford VIC 49 J10 50 C4
Waterford WA 77 H4
Waterhouse TAS 61 D12
Waterhouse Con Area TAS 61 C11
Waterhouse Island TAS 61 C11
Waterloo SA 68 E7 71 G10
Waterloo TAS 56 J1 59 H9
Waterloo VIC 45 D9
Waterloo WA 80 B4
Waterloo Bay SA 68 H5
Waterloo Corner SA 64 A3
Watermans Bay WA 77 C1
Watervale SA 68 E7 71 G10
Watgania VIC 44 E7
Watheroo WA 84 H5
Watheroo Nat Park WA 84 H5
Watinuna SA 74 B5
Watson ACT 37 C5
Watson SA 74 H4
Watson Island NT 97 H13 99 A13
Watson Oil Field QLD 18 H6
Watsonia VIC 41 B5 43 C8
Watsons Bay NSW 22 E7 25 D12
Watsons Creek NSW 29 H8
Watsons Creek VIC 43 B9
Watsons Creek Nature Res NSW 29 H8
Wattamolla NSW 25 G11
Wattamondara NSW 26 H3
Wattening WA 78 B7
Wattle Creek VIC 45 C8
Wattle Flat NSW 26 F6
Wattle Glen VIC 43 B9
Wattle Grove NSW 25 E10
Wattle Grove TAS 56 J2 59 H9
Wattle Grove WA 77 H7
Wattle Hill TAS 57 A10 59 F11
Wattle Island VIC 50 K1
Wattle Park SA 64 G6
Wattle Point VIC 50 E6
Wattle Range SA 69 J6
Wattle Vale VIC 45 B14 48 E2
Waubra VIC 45 D10
Wauchope NSW 27 A13 29 K12
Wauchope NT 99 J8 101 A8
Waukaringa SA 71 D11
Wauraltee SA 68 G4 71 H8
Waurn Ponds VIC 42 H2 45 H12
Wavell Heights QLD 3 C4
Waverley NSW 22 F7 25 D12
Wayatinah TAS 58 D7
Waychinicup Nat Park WA 81 J14 82 J7
Waygara VIC 49 K13 51 D8
Wayville SA 63 D2 64 G4
Weabonga NSW 29 J8
Weavers SA 68 G5 69 B1 71 J8
Webbs NSW 26 C2
Webs Creek NSW 23 J1
Wedderburn NSW 25 G9
Wedderburn VIC 47 K10
Wedderburn Junction VIC 47 K10
Weddin Mountains Nat Park NSW 26 H2 33 E14
Wedge Island SA 68 H2 70 J6
Wedge Island TAS 57 H10
Wedge Island WA 82 A1 84 J4
Wedge Islands TAS 59 H11
Wedin WA 79 J11
Wednesday Island QLD 15 B2
Wee Jasper NSW 34 D2
Wee Jasper Nature Res NSW 34 D2
Wee Waa NSW 28 F4
Weegena TAS 60 F7
Weelhamby Lake WA 84 F6
Weemelah NSW 28 C3
Weemol NT 97 E9
Weerangourt VIC 44 G4
Weerite VIC 45 H8
Weetah TAS 61 F8
Weetaliba NSW 26 A5 28 K4
Weetalibah Nature Res NSW 26 B5
Weetangera ACT 37 C3
Weethalle NSW 33 E12
Weetulta SA 68 F5 69 A1 71 H8
Wee-Wee-Rup VIC 47 H12
Wehla VIC 45 A9
Weilmoringle NSW 8 K1 31 C12
Weimby NSW 32 G5 47 C8
Weipa QLD 15 E1
Weismantels NSW 27 C11
Weitalaba QLD 11 J11
Weja NSW 33 D12
Welaregang NSW 33 K14 49 B12
Weldborough TAS 61 E13
Welford Lagoon QLD 17 H10 19 A9
Welford Nat Park QLD 17 H9 19 A8
Wellesley Islands QLD 12 C4
Wellingrove NSW 29 E9
Wellington NSW 26 D4
Wellington SA 67 E13 69 C4 71 K11
Wellington East SA 67 D14
Wellington Nat Park WA 80 B5 82 F3
Wellington Point QLD 7 B11
Wellsford VIC 45 A12
Wellstead WA 82 J7
Welshmans Reef VIC 45 C11
Welshpool VIC 50 H2
Welshpool WA 77 G6
Wembley WA 77 F3
Wembley Downs WA 77 E2
Wemen VIC 32 G4 46 D6
Wentworth NSW 32 F3 46 A4
Wentworth Falls NSW 24 D5 26 G7
Werakata Nat Park NSW 27 E10 23 B3
Weranga QLD 9 F8
Werneth VIC 45 G10
Werombi NSW 24 F7 27 H8
Werrap VIC 46 H4
Werribee VIC 42 E4 45 F13 48 K1
Werribee Gorge State Park VIC 42 B3 45 E12
Werribee South VIC 42 E5 45 G13
Werrikimbe Nat Park NSW 29 J10
Werrimull VIC 32 F2 46 B3
Werrington NSW 25 D8
Werris Creek NSW 28 K7
Wesburn VIC 43 C12
Wesley Vale TAS 60 E7
Wessel Islands NT 97 A12
West Angelas Mine WA 87 F8
West Bay SA 68 K2
West Beach SA 64 G2 65 H1
West Bore No. 2 SA 74 B5
West Cape SA 68 H3
West Cape Howe Nat Park WA 81 K11 82 K6
West End QLD 2 D1 3 E3 7 B10
West Frankford TAS 55 F1 61 E8
West Gosford NSW 23 H5
West Group WA 83 H12 91 K1
West Hill QLD 11 E8
West Hill Island QLD 11 E9
West Hill Nat Park QLD 11 E9
West Hobart TAS 54 C1
West Hoxton NSW 25 E9
West Island NT 97 H12 99 A12
West Island QLD 15 B1
West Island SA 66 H6
West Island Con Park SA 66 H6
West Kentish TAS 60 F7
West Killara NSW 25 C11
West Lakes SA 64 E1 65 H1
West MacDonnell Nat Park NT 100 F7
West Myrup WA 81 F13
West Pennant Hills NSW 22 C2
West Perth WA 76 A1 77 F3
West Pine TAS 60 E6
West Pymble NSW 22 D4 25 C10
West Ridgley TAS 60 E5
West Ryde NSW 22 E4
West Scottsdale TAS 61 E11
West Swan WA 77 C6
West Wallsend NSW 23 C5
West Wyalong NSW 33 E13
Westbourne Park SA 64 H4
Westbury TAS 55 H2 61 G9
Westby VIC 32 J7 47 G11
Westdale WA 78 F7
Western Creek TAS 60 G7
Western Flat SA 44 A1 69 F7
Western Junction TAS 55 J6 61 G10
Western Port VIC 43 H10
Western River SA 68 J3 70 K7
Western River Con Park SA 68 J3 70 K7
Westerway TAS 59 E8
Westfield WA 77 K7
Westgate QLD 19 D13
Westmar QLD 8 H6
Westmead NSW 22 E2
Westmeadows VIC 41 A2
Westmere VIC 45 F8
Westminster WA 77 D3
Weston ACT 37 F3
Weston NSW 23 B4
Weston Creek ACT 37 F2 38 D4
Westonia WA 82 B7 85 J8
Westwood QLD 11 H9
Westwood TAS 55 H4 61 F9
Wetherill Park NSW 25 D9
Weyba Downs QLD 5 A10
Weymouth TAS 55 B5 61 D10
Whale Beach NSW 23 K5 25 A12
Wharminda SA 68 E2 70 G6
Wharparilla VIC 47 J13 48 B1
Whealbah NSW 33 E9
Wheelers Hill VIC 41 F6
Wheeo NSW 26 K5 34 B4 35 A2
Wherrol Flat NSW 27 B12
Whetstone QLD 9 J9 29 A8
Whicher Nat Park WA 80 D3
Whidbey Isles Con Park SA 70 J4
Whiltshire-Butler Nat Park WA 80 E3
Whiltwarta SA 68 E6
Whim Creek WA 86 C7
Whiporie NSW 29 D13
Whirily VIC 47 H8
White Beach TAS 57 H11 59 H12
White Cliffs NSW 30 G5
White Dam Con Park SA 71 G11
White Flag Lake WA 85 H11

White Flat SA 68 F1 70 H6
White Gum Valley WA 77 J2
White Hills TAS 55 H6 61 F10
White Hut SA 68 H4 70 J7
White Lake WA 87 J12
White Mountains Nat Park QLD 10 C2 13 K12 17 A11
White Rock QLD 14 E5
Whitefoord TAS 59 D11
Whiteheads Creek VIC 48 F3
Whiteman WA 77 C5
Whitemark TAS 61 C9
Whitemore TAS 55 J3 61 G9
Whitewood QLD 17 B10
Whitfield VIC 48 E7
Whitsunday Group QLD 11 B8
Whitsunday Island QLD 11 B8
Whitsunday Islands Nat Park QLD 11 B8
Whittingham NSW 23 A1
Whittlesea VIC 43 A8 45 E14 48 J2 52 A2
Whitton NSW 33 F11
Whitwarta SA 71 G9
Whoorel VIC 45 H10
Whorouly VIC 48 D7
Whorouly South VIC 48 D7
Whroo VIC 45 A14 48 D2
Whyalla SA 68 C5 71 E8
Whyalla Con Park SA 68 C5 71 E8
Whyte Island QLD 3 D7 5 K11 7 A11
Whyte-Yarcowie SA 68 C7 71 F10
Wialki WA 85 H8
Wiangaree NSW 9 J12 29 B13
Wicherina WA 84 E4
Wickepin WA 79 H11 82 E6
Wickham WA 86 B6
Wickliffe VIC 44 F7
Widden NSW 26 D7
Wide Bay QLD 9 C13
Widgelli NSW 33 F11
Widgiemooltha WA 83 B12 85 J12 91 H1
Widgiewa NSW 33 H11
Wigram Island NT 97 B12
Wigton Island QLD 11 C9
Wilandspey Con Park QLD 10 E4 17 B14
Wilban WA 91 G4
Wilberforce NSW 25 B8
Wilburville TAS 59 B9 61 J9
Wilby VIC 48 B6
Wilcannia NSW 30 H5
Wild Duck Island QLD 11 E9
Wild Horse Plains SA 68 F6 69 A2 71 H9
Wildcat Bore SA 74 C6
Wilga WA 80 C6
Wilgarup WA 80 F6
Wilgena SA 70 A4 72 K4
Wilkatana SA 68 A5 71 D9
Wilkawatt SA 69 D6 71 K12
Wilkie Island QLD 15 G4
Wilkinson Lakes SA 72 H1 74 F6
Willa VIC 46 F5
Willalooka SA 69 F6
Willandra Lakes World Heritage Area NSW 32 D5
Willandra Nat Park NSW 33 C8
Willangie VIC 46 G7
Willara Crossing NSW 19 K10 30 C7
Willare Bridge Roadhouse WA 88 G6 90 A3
Willatook VIC 44 H5
Willaura VIC 44 E7
Willawarrin NSW 29 J11
Willawong QLD 3 H3 7 C9
Willbriggie NSW 33 F11
Willenabrina VIC 46 J5
Willetton WA 77 J4
Willi Willi SA 74 B1 100 K2
Willi Willi Nat Park NSW 29 J11
William Bay WA 81 K10 82 K5
William Bay Nat Park WA 81 K10 82 K5
William Creek SA 72 G6
Williams WA 79 K8 82 F5
Williams Island SA 68 H1 70 J6
Williamsdale ACT 35 E1
Williamsdale NSW 34 E3 38 F5
Williamsford TAS 58 A4 60 H4
Williamstown SA 65 E5 68 F7 69 B3 71 J10
Williamstown VIC 41 E2 42 D7 45 F14 48 K2 52 C1
Williamtown NSW 23 A7 27 E11
Willis VIC 34 J1 49 F14
Willmot NSW 25 C8
Willochra SA 68 A6 71 D9
Willow Crossing VIC 49 C12
Willow Grove VIC 50 E1 52 D7
Willow Springs WA 80 E5
Willow Tree NSW 27 A8
Willow Waters SA 71 C10
Willowbank QLD 6 D6
Willowie SA 68 B6 71 E9
Willowra NT 98 K6 100 B6
Willows QLD 10 H6
Willows Gemfield QLD 10 H6
Willowvale QLD 6 H2
Willowvale VIC 45 F9
Willung VIC 50 F3
Willunga SA 66 D4 68 H7 69 C2 71 K10
Willunga Hill SA 66 D6
Willyabrup WA 80 D2
Wilmington SA 68 B6 71 E9
Wilmot TAS 60 F6
Wilora NT 101 C8
Wilpena SA 71 B10
Wilson SA 71 C10
Wilson Island QLD 11 H12
Wilsons Downfall NSW 29 B10
Wilsons Promontory VIC 50 K1 52 J7
Wilsons Promontory Marine Nat Park VIC 50 K2 52 J7
Wilsons Promontory Nat Park VIC 50 K1 52 J7
Wilton NSW 25 J8
Wiltshire TAS 60 C3
Wiluna WA 85 B10
Wimba VIC 45 J10
Wiminda NSW 28 E1
Winbin QLD 19 E11
Winburndale Nature Res NSW 26 F6
Winceby Island SA 68 F2 70 H6
Winchelsea VIC 45 H11
Winchelsea Island NT 97 E12
Windamere Dam NSW 26 E6
Windarra WA 85 E13 91 E1
Windellama NSW 34 C5 35 C3
Windemere VIC 45 E10
Windera QLD 9 D10
Windermere TAS 61 E9
Windeyer NSW 26 E5
Windjana Gorge Nat Park WA 89 G8 90 A4
Windomal Landing NSW 47 C9
Windorah QLD 17 J8 18 B7
Windsor NSW 25 B8 27 G8
Windsor QLD 3 D4
Windsor SA 68 F6 69 A2 71 H9
Windsor Downs NSW 25 C8
Windsor Downs Nature Res NSW 25 C8 27 G8
Windsor Gardens SA 64 E5
Windurong NSW 26 A3 28 K2
Windy Corner WA 90 G4
Windy Harbour WA 80 J5 82 J3
Winfield QLD 11 K12
Wingala NSW 22 D7
Wingarnie WA 83 C13 85 K12 91 H1
Wingeel VIC 45 G10
Wingellina (Irrunytju) WA 90 J7 91 C7 100 K1
Wingello NSW 26 K7 34 C6 35 B5
Wingen NSW 27 B9
Wingen Maid Nature Res NSW 27 B8
Wingfield SA 64 D3 65 G2
Wingham NSW 27 B12
Winiam VIC 46 K3
Winiam East VIC 46 K4
Winjallock VIC 45 B8
Winkie SA 69 A7 71 H13
Winkleigh TAS 55 E2 61 E9
Winmalee NSW 24 D6
Winnaleah TAS 61 D12
Winnambool VIC 32 H5 46 D7
Winnap VIC 44 G3
Winnellie NT 94 F5
Winninowie SA 68 B5 71 E9
Winninowie Con Park SA 68 B5 71 E9
Winnungra NSW 33 D12
Winslow VIC 44 H6
Winston Hills NSW 22 D2 25 C9
Wintawatu SA 74 A3 100 K4
Winthrop WA 77 J3
Winton QLD 17 D9
Winton VIC 48 D6
Winulta SA 68 F5 69 A1 71 H9
Winwill QLD 6 C3
Winya QLD 4 F6
Wirha SA 69 C6 71 K13
Wirra Wirra QLD 13 G10
Wirrabara SA 68 C6 71 E9
Wirraminna SA 70 B6
Wirrega SA 69 F6
Wirrida SA 72 H4
Wirrimah NSW 26 J3 34 A1
Wirrinya NSW 26 G1 33 E14
Wirrulla SA 70 D4
Wisanger SA 68 J4 71 K8
Wisemans Ferry NSW 23 J2 27 G9
Wishart QLD 3 G5
Wishbone WA 81 A12
Wistow SA 67 B9
Witchcliffe WA 80 E2 82 H1
Withcott QLD 6 B2
Withersfield QLD 10 H6
Witjira Nat Park SA 72 B5 101 K10
Witta QLD 5 G4
Wittenbra NSW 28 J3
Wittenoom WA 87 E8
Wivenhoe Pocket QLD 6 A6
Wiyarra QLD 6 J3
Woden ACT 38 C4
Woden Valley ACT 37 F4
Wodonga VIC 33 K12 49 B8
Woggoon Nature Res NSW 33 C12
Wokalup WA 78 K5 80 A5 82 F3
Woko Nat Park NSW 27 B11
Wokurna SA 68 D6 71 G9
Wolfdene QLD 7 E11
Wolfe Creek Crater Nat Park WA 89 K12 90 C6
Wolfram QLD 13 D12
Wolfram Camp QLD 14 E1
Wollar NSW 26 C6
Wollemi Nat Park NSW 24 A4 26 D7
Wollert VIC 43 A8
Wollman NT 96 D3
Wollombi NSW 23 D2 27 E9
Wollomombi NSW 29 G10
Wollondilly River Nature Res NSW 26 J6 34 B5
Wollongong NSW 25 K10 27 K8 34 B7 35 A7
Wollumbin Nat Park NSW 29 A13
Wollun NSW 29 H9
Wolseley SA 46 K1
Wolselley SA 69 F7
Wolumla NSW 34 J5
Wolvi QLD 9 D12
Wombarra NSW 25 H11
Wombat NSW 26 J2 34 B1
Wombat Creek State Con Area NSW 29 D12
Wombelano VIC 44 C3
Womboota NSW 33 K8 47 H13
Womikata SA 74 A5 100 K6
Won Wron VIC 50 G3
Wonboyn Lake NSW 34 K5 51 B14
Wondai QLD 9 D10
Wondalga NSW 33 J14 34 D1
Wondecla QLD 14 G3
Wondul Range Nat Park QLD 9 H9
Wonga Beach QLD 13 C12 14 A3
Wonga Park VIC 43 C10
Wongalara Lake NSW 30 H7
Wongaling Beach QLD 14 K7
Wongamine WA 78 B7
Wongan Hills WA 82 A4 84 J6
Wongarbon NSW 26 C4
Wongarbon Nature Res NSW 26 C4
Wongarra VIC 45 K10
Wongawallan QLD 7 E11
Wongianna SA 73 H9
Wongoondy WA 84 F4
Wongwibinda NSW 29 G10
Wonnangatta Station (site) VIC 49 G8 50 A3
Wonnerup WA 80 C3
Wonoka SA 71 C10
Wonthaggi VIC 52 G4
Wonwondah East VIC 44 B5
Wonwondah North VIC 44 B5
Wonyip VIC 50 H2
Woobera QLD 16 B4
Wood Wood VIC 32 H6 47 E9
Woodanilling WA 81 C10 82 G5
Woodberry NSW 23 B6
Woodbine QLD 6 E3
Woodbridge TAS 56 J4 59 H10
Woodburn NSW 9 K13 29 C13
Woodburn WA 81 H12
Woodburne VIC 45 F11
Woodbury TAS 59 C11 61 K11
Woodchester SA 67 C9 68 H7 69 C3 71 K10
Woodenbong NSW 6 K6 9 J12 29 A12
Woodend NSW 33 J12
Woodend VIC 45 D12
Woodford NSW 24 D5
Woodford QLD 5 F8 9 F12
Woodford Island Nature Res NSW 29 E13
Woodgate QLD 9 B12
Woodhill QLD 7 F9
Woodhouse QLD 10 B5
Woodhouselee NSW 26 K5 34 B4 35 A3
Woodie Woodie Mine WA 87 D11
Woodlands QLD 6 C4
Woodlands WA 77 E2 81 H12
Woodlands Historic Park VIC 42 B6
Woodleigh VIC 43 K12 52 F4
Woodman Point WA 78 E4
Woodpark NSW 25 D9
Woodridge QLD 3 J5 7 C10
Woods Point SA 67 C14
Woods Point VIC 48 J6 50 C1 52 A7
Woods Reef NSW 28 G7
Woods Well SA 69 E4
Woodsdale TAS 59 D11
Woodside SA 65 J5 68 H7 69 B3 71 J10
Woodside VIC 50 H3
Woodstock NSW 26 G4
Woodstock QLD 10 A5 13 H14
Woodstock TAS 56 G2 59 G9
Woodstock VIC 43 A8 45 B11 45 E14 48 J2 52 A2
Woodstock Nature Res ACT 37 C1 38 B3
Woodvale WA 77 B2
Woodville NSW 23 A5 27 D10
Woodville SA 64 E3 65 H2
Woodville South SA 64 F3
Woody Bay QLD 5 G11
Woody Island QLD 9 B13 14 A4
Woody Point QLD 5 J10
Woogenellup WA 81 G12
Woogoompah Island QLD 7 E12
Woohlpooer VIC 44 D5
Wool Bay SA 68 H5 69 B1 71 J8
Wool Wool VIC 45 H9
Woolamai VIC 52 F4
Woolaning NT 95 E1 96 D3
Woolbrook NSW 29 J8
Woolgarlo NSW 34 C2
Woolgoolga NSW 29 F13
Wooli NSW 29 F13
Woollahra NSW 25 D12
Woollamia Nature Res NSW 34 D7 35 C6
Woolloomooloo NSW 21 C3
Woolner NT 94 G3
Woolnorth TAS 60 B1
Woolomin NSW 29 K8
Woolooga QLD 9 D11
Woolooma NSW 27 B9
Woolooware NSW 22 K4
Woolshed Flat SA 71 D9
Woolshet Flat SA 68 A6
Woolsthorpe VIC 44 H6
Woomargama NSW 33 K13 49 A10
Woomargama Nat Park NSW 33 K13 49 A11
Woombye QLD 5 C9
Woomelang VIC 32 J4 46 G7
Woomera SA 70 B7
Woongoolba QLD 7 D12
Woonigan QLD 16 B4
Woonona NSW 25 J10
Woorabinda QLD 11 J8
Wooragee VIC 49 C8
Woorak VIC 46 K4
Wooramel Roadhouse WA 84 A2 86 K3
Wooreen VIC 52 F6
Woori Yallock VIC 43 C11 48 K4 52 B4
Woorim QLD 5 G11
Woorinen VIC 32 H6 47 F9
Woorinen North VIC 47 E9
Woornack VIC 32 H4 46 E6
Woorndoo VIC 44 F7
Wooroconda WA 86 E5
Wooroloo WA 78 D6 82 C3 84 K5
Wooroolin QLD 9 D11
Wooroonook VIC 47 K8
Wooroonooran Nat Park QLD 13 D13 14 G5
Woosang VIC 47 K9
Wootha QLD 5 D8
Wootton NSW 27 C12
Woowonga Nat Park QLD 9 B11
Worongary QLD 7 G12
Woronora NSW 22 J3
Woroon Nat Park QLD 9 D10
Worsley WA 80 B5
Wotto Nature Res WA 84 G4
Wowan QLD 11 J9
Woy Woy NSW 23 J5
Wreck Island QLD 11 H12
Wrens Flat VIC 48 H7 50 B2
Wright Island SA 66 H6
Wroxham VIC 34 K4 51 B12
Wubalawun NT 96 H7
Wubin WA 84 G6
Wudinna SA 70 E5
Wugullar (Beswick) NT 96 G7
Wujal Wujal QLD 13 B12
Wulagi NT 94 C6
Wulgulmerang VIC 49 G13 51 A8
Wullwye Nature Res NSW 34 H2
Wumalgi QLD 11 F9
Wunara NT 99 H12
Wundowie WA 78 D6 82 C3 84 K5
Wunghnu VIC 48 B3
Wungu WA 89 H13 90 B7
Wunkar SA 69 A6 71 H12
Wurarga WA 84 E5
Wurdiboluc VIC 45 H11
Wurruk VIC 50 F4
Wurtulla QLD 5 D10
Wuruma Dam QLD 9 B9
Wutan QLD 15 F1
Wutul QLD 9 F10
Wutunugurra NT 99 J10
Wy Yung VIC 49 K11 50 D6
Wyalkatchem WA 82 B5 84 J7
Wyalong NSW 33 E13
Wyan NSW 29 C12
Wyandra QLD 19 F13
Wyanga NSW 26 D2 31 K14 33 B14
Wyangala NSW 26 H4
Wybong NSW 27 C8
Wycarbah QLD 11 H10
Wycheproof VIC 32 K5 47 J8
Wychitella VIC 47 K10
Wycliffe Well NT 99 J8 101 A8
Wye River VIC 45 J11
Wyee NSW 23 F5 27 F10
Wyee Point NSW 23 E6
Wyeebo VIC 49 C10
Wyelangta VIC 45 K9
Wyena TAS 55 D6
Wyening WA 78 A7
Wylie Creek NSW 29 B11
Wylkatchem WA 79 A10
Wymah NSW 33 K13 49 B10
Wymlet VIC 32 H3 46 D5
Wynarka SA 69 C5 71 J11
Wynbring SA 72 K2 74 H7
Wyndham NSW 34 J4
Wyndham WA 89 D13
Wynn Vale SA 64 C6
Wynnum QLD 3 D7 7 A11
Wynyard TAS 60 D5
Wyola WA 79 C10
Wyola Lake SA 74 F3
Wyoming NSW 23 H5
Wyong NSW 23 G5 27 F10
Wyong Creek NSW 23 G5
Wyongah NSW 23 G6
Wyperfeld Nat Park VIC 32 J3 46 G4 71 K14
Wyrallah NSW 29 C13
Wyrrabalong NSW 23 G6
Wyrrabalong Nat Park NSW 27 F10
Wyuna VIC 47 J14 48 B2

Y

Yaamba QLD 11 G10
Yaapeet VIC 32 K3 46 H5
Yabba VIC 49 C10
Yabba North VIC 48 B4
Yabba Vale QLD 4 A7
Yabbra Nat Park NSW 9 J12 29 B11
Yabulu QLD 10 A4 13 H14
Yacka SA 68 D7 71 F10
Yackandandah VIC 49 C8
Yagga Yagga WA 90 D6
Yagoona NSW 25 E10
Yahl SA 44 G1 69 K7
Yakanarra WA 89 J9 90 B4
Yalamurra QLD 19 E12
Yalata SA 74 J5
Yalbarrin WA 79 D13
Yalboroo QLD 10 C7
Yalbraith NSW 26 J6 34 A5
Yalca VIC 48 A3
Yalca North VIC 48 A3
Yalgogrin NSW 33 E12
Yalgogrin South NSW 33 F12
Yalgoo WA 84 E6
Yalgorup Nat Park WA 78 H3 82 E2
Yalkula QLD 14 C3
Yallambie NSW 23 E2
Yallaroi NSW 9 K8 28 C6
Yalleroi QLD 10 J3 17 F13
Yallingup WA 80 C1 82 G1
Yallock VIC 43 H12
Yallook VIC 47 K11
Yallourn VIC 50 F1
Yallourn North VIC 50 F1 50 F1
Yallunda Flat SA 68 F1 70 H6
Yaloak VIC 42 B2
Yaloak Vale VIC 42 C2
Yalpara Con Park SA 68 B7 71 D10
Yalwal NSW 34 C6 35 C5
Yam Island QLD 15 A2
Yamala QLD 10 H7
Yamanto QLD 6 C7
Yamba NSW 29 D13
Yamba SA 32 F1 46 B1 69 A7 71 H13
Yambacoona TAS 60 A6
Yamboyna QLD 10 H6
Yambuk VIC 44 H5
Yampi Sound WA 88 D6
Yan Yean VIC 43 A8 45 E14 48 J2 52 A2
Yanac VIC 46 J3
Yanac South VIC 46 K3
Yanakie VIC 50 J1 52 H7
Yanamah WA 80 F5
Yanchep WA 78 C4 82 C2 84 K4
Yanchep Nat Park WA 78 C4 82 B2 84 K5
Yanco NSW 33 G11
Yanco Glen NSW 30 J2
Yandaran QLD 9 A11 11 K12
Yanderra NSW 25 K8
Yandeyarra WA 87 C8
Yandi Mine WA 87 E9
Yandicoogina Mine WA 87 E9
Yandina QLD 5 B9 9 E12
Yandoit VIC 45 C11
Yanga Nature Res NSW 32 G6 47 C10
Yangan QLD 6 H3
Yango NSW 23 E2
Yaninee SA 70 E5
Yankalilla SA 66 F3 68 J6 69 D2 71 K9
Yankalilla Bay SA 66 F2
Yanna Ridge QLD 19 E13
Yannathan VIC 43 H12 52 E4
Yanneri Lake WA 87 H10
Yantabulla NSW 31 C8
Yantara Lake NSW 30 E3
Yantbangee Lake NSW 30 F6
Yanununbeyan Nat Park NSW 34 E4 35 E2
Yaouk NSW 34 F2
Yaouk Nature Res NSW 34 F2 38 K2
Yaraka QLD 10 K1 17 H10 19 A10
Yarck VIC 48 G4
Yardanogo Nature Res WA 84 G4
Yarding WA 79 D12
Yaringa Marine Nat Park VIC 43 H9 52 E3
Yarle Lakes SA 74 G4
Yarloop WA 78 J5 82 E3
Yarra Creek TAS 60 C7
Yarra Glen VIC 43 B10 48 J3 52 A3
Yarra Junction VIC 43 C12 48 K4 52 B4
Yarra Ranges Nat Park VIC 43 B12 48 J5 50 D1 52 A5
Yarra Yarra Lakes WA 84 G5
Yarrabah QLD 13 D13 14 D6
Yarrabandai NSW 26 F1 33 C13
Yarrabin NSW 26 D5
Yarragon VIC 52 E6
Yarralena WA 81 F10
Yarralin NT 96 K3 98 B3
Yarralumla ACT 36 C1 37 E4
Yarram VIC 50 H2
Yarramalong NSW 23 G4
Yarraman NSW 26 A7 28 K5
Yarraman QLD 4 E1 9 E11
Yarrambat VIC 43 B9
Yarramony WA 79 B8
Yarranderie NSW 24 J4
Yarranderie Rec Park NSW 24 J5
Yarrangobilly NSW 34 E2
Yarrara VIC 32 G2
Yarras NSW 27 A12 29 K11
Yarravel Nature Res NSW 29 J12
Yarrawonga VIC 33 K10 48 B5
Yarriabini Nat Park NSW 29 H12
Yarrie WA 87 B10
Yarringully Nature Res NSW 29 C13
Yarrock VIC 46 K2
Yarroweyah VIC 48 A4
Yarrowitch NSW 29 K10
Yarrowyck NSW 29 G8
Yarto VIC 32 J4 46 F5
Yarwun QLD 11 H11
Yass NSW 34 C3
Yatala QLD 7 D11
Yatala Vale SA 64 C7
Yatchaw VIC 44 F5
Yathalamarra NT 97 C10
Yathong Nature Res NSW 31 K10 33 B10
Yatina SA 68 C7 71 E10
Yatpool VIC 32 F3 46 B5
Yattalunga SA 65 E4
Yatte Yattah NSW 34 D6 35 D5
Yawalpa QLD 7 E12
Yea VIC 48 G3
Yeagurup WA 80 G5
Yeal Nature Res WA 78 B4 82 B3 84 J5
Yealering WA 79 G11 82 E6
Yearinan NSW 28 J3
Yearinga VIC 46 K2
Yednia QLD 4 D5 9 E12
Yeelanna SA 68 F1 70 G5
Yeerongpilly QLD 3 F3
Yelarbon QLD 9 J8 28 B7
Yelbeni WA 79 A11
Yeldulknie Con Park SA 68 D3 70 F7
Yellabinna Reg Res SA 70 A2 72 K2 74 J7
Yellagonga Regional Park WA 77 B2
Yellangip VIC 46 J5
Yellingbo VIC 43 D11
Yellowdine WA 83 B9 85 J9
Yellowdine Nature Res WA 83 B9 85 J10
Yelta VIC 32 F3 46 A4
Yelverton WA 80 D2
Yelverton Nat Park WA 80 D2
Yenda NSW 33 F11
Yendon VIC 45 E11
Yengo Nat Park NSW 23 E1 27 E9
Yennora NSW 25 D10
Yenyening Lakes Nature Res WA 79 F10 82 D5
Yeo Lake Nature Res WA 91 D3
Yeo Yeo NSW 26 K2 33 F14
Yeoval NSW 26 D3
Yeppoon QLD 11 G11
Yerilla WA 85 F12 91 F1
Yering VIC 43 B10
Yerong Creek NSW 33 J12
Yeronga QLD 3 F3
Yerranderie NSW 26 J7 34 A6
Yerrinbool NSW 25 K8
Yetholme NSW 26 G6
Yetman NSW 28 B7
Yilliminning WA 79 J10
Yin Barun VIC 48 E5
Yinkanie SA 69 A6 71 H12
Yinnar VIC 50 G1 52 E7
Yinnar South VIC 50 G1
Yirrirra WA 90 H6 91 A6
Yirrkala NT 97 C13
Yiyili WA 89 J11 90 B6
Yokine WA 77 E4
Yolla TAS 60 D5
Yomumup WA 81 F14
Yongala SA 68 C7 71 E10
Yoogali NSW 33 F11
Yoongarillup WA 80 D3
York WA 79 D8 82 C4 84 K6
York Plains TAS 59 C11 61 K11
York Sound WA 89 B8
Yorke Peninsula SA 68 G5 69 A1
Yorketown SA 68 H5 69 B1 71 J8
Yorkeys Knob QLD 13 D13 14 D5
Yorklea NSW 29 C13
Yorkrakine WA 79 B11
Yorktown TAS 55 D1 61 E8
Yornaning WA 79 H9 82 E5
Yornup WA 80 E6
Yoting WA 79 E11
You Yangs Reg Park VIC 42 E3 45 F12
Youanmite VIC 48 B4
Youndegin WA 79 D10
Young NSW 26 J2 34 A1
Younghusband Peninsula SA 67 H10 69 D4
Youngs WA 81 K11
Youngtown TAS 55 H5
Youraling WA 79 F9
Yowah QLD 19 H11
Yowie Bay NSW 22 K4
Yowrie NSW 34 G5 35 J3
Yuelamu NT 100 D6
Yuendumu NT 100 D5
Yukan QLD 11 E8
Yulara NT 100 J4
Yuleba QLD 8 E6
Yulecart VIC 44 F5
Yulte Con Park SA 66 E5
Yuluma NSW 33 H11
Yulumbu WA 89 G11 90 A6
Yumali SA 69 D5 71 K11
Yumbarra Con Park SA 70 C2 74 K7
Yumbarra Con Res SA 74 K6
Yuna WA 84 E4
Yundaga WA 85 G11
Yundamindera WA 85 F12 91 E1
Yunderup WA 78 H4 82 E3
Yundi SA 66 D6
Yundool VIC 48 C5
Yungaburra QLD 13 D12 14 F4
Yungera VIC 47 C8
Yungngora WA 89 H8 90 B4
Yunta SA 71 E11
Yunununbeyan Nat Park NSW 38 F7
Yunununbeyan State Con Area NSW 38 F7
Yunyarinyi (Kenmore Park) SA 74 A5 100 K6
Yurangka SA 74 B4 100 K5
Yuraygir Nat Park NSW 29 E13
Yuraygir State Con Area NSW 29 F13
Yurgo SA 69 C5 71 K12
Yuroke VIC 45 E13 48 J1 52 A1
Yurol QLD 5 A8
Yuulong VIC 45 K9

Z

Zagai Island QLD 15 A2
Zanthus WA 85 J14 91 G2
Zeehan TAS 58 A3 60 H3
Zeerust VIC 48 C3
Zillmere QLD 3 B4
Zinifex Century Mine QLD 12 G2
Zumsteins VIC 44 C6
Zuytdorp Nature Res WA 84 C2

List of Abbreviations

CBD	–	Central Business District
Con Area	–	Conservation Area
Con Park	–	Conservation Park
Nat Park	–	National Park
Nature Res	–	Nature Reserve
Rec Park	–	Recreation Park
Reg Res	–	Regional Reserve
Res	–	Reserve

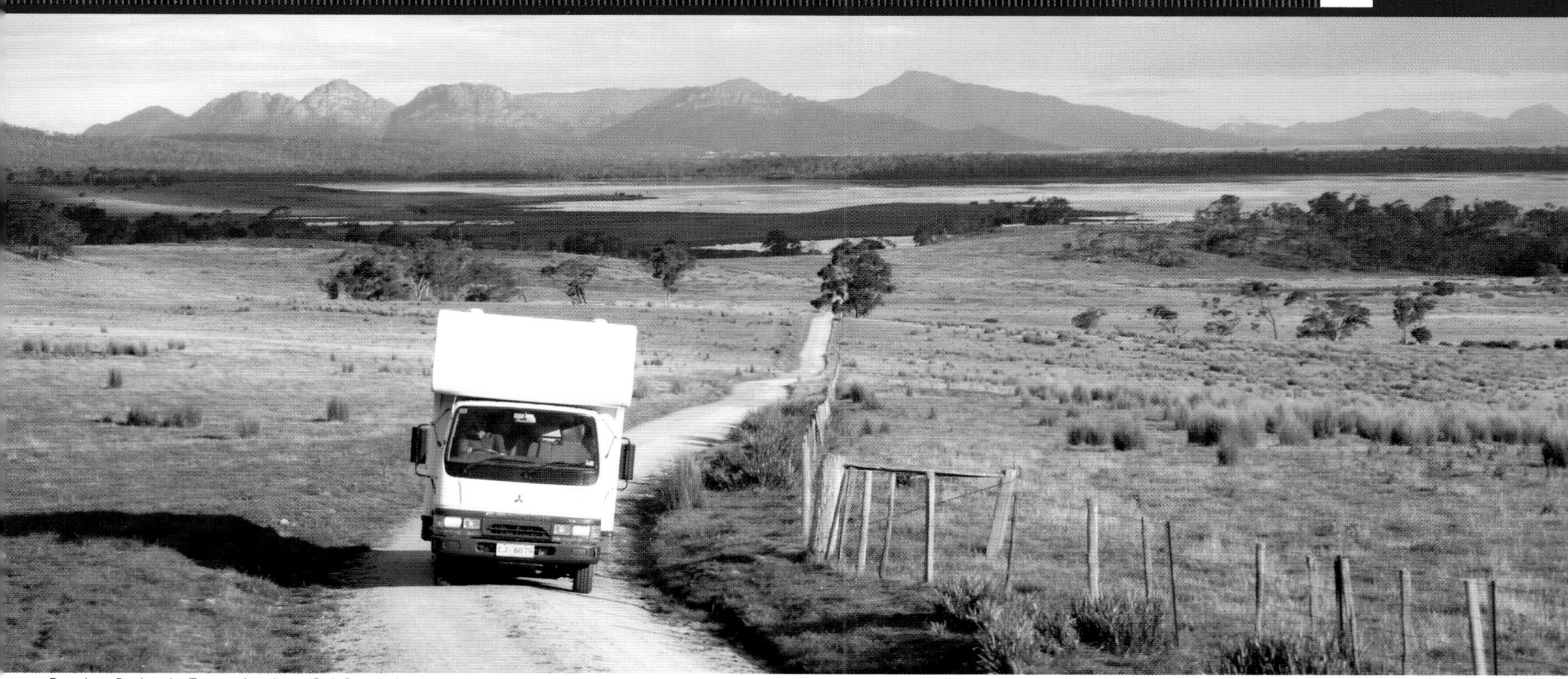

Freycinet Peninsula, Tasmania photo: Rob Boegheim

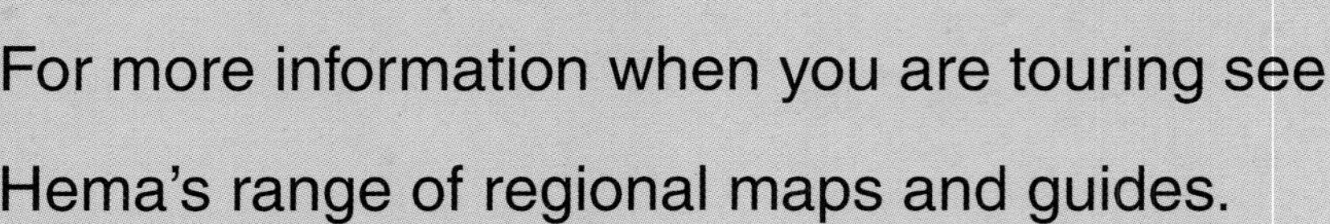

For more information when you are touring see Hema's range of regional maps and guides.

Regional maps

- Cape York
- Regions
- Atherton Tableland
- Barrington Tops NP
- Blue Mountains NP & Towns
- Cairns to Cooktown
- Cape York
- Central Australia
- Central East NSW
- Central Queensland
- East Gippsland & the Sapphire Coast
- Flinders Ranges
- Fraser Island
- Girraween, Bald Rock & Sundown NPs
- Great Desert Tracks Map Pack
- Great Desert Tracks - NC Sheet
- Great Desert Tracks - NE Sheet
- Great Desert Tracks - NW Sheet
- Great Desert Tracks - SC Sheet
- Great Desert Tracks - SE Sheet
- Great Desert Tracks - SW Sheet
- Great 4WD Destinations Map Pack
- High Country - Victoria
- Hunter Valley & Wineries
- Kakadu NP
- Kimberley
- Lakefield NP
- Lamington NP
- Mackay and Whitsundays
- Margaret River Region & Southern Forests WA
- Mid West WA
- North East NSW
- North Queensland
- North Stradbroke Island
- Outback NSW
- Pilbara and Coral Coast
- Purnululu NP - Bungle Bungle
- Queensland's Outback
- Red Centre
- Simpson Desert
- Snowy - Kosciuszko
- South East NSW
- South East QLD
- South West WA
- Sunshine Coast
- Top End and Gulf
- Tropical North QLD
- Victoria - East and West
- Wide Bay - Burnett
- Wollemi NP

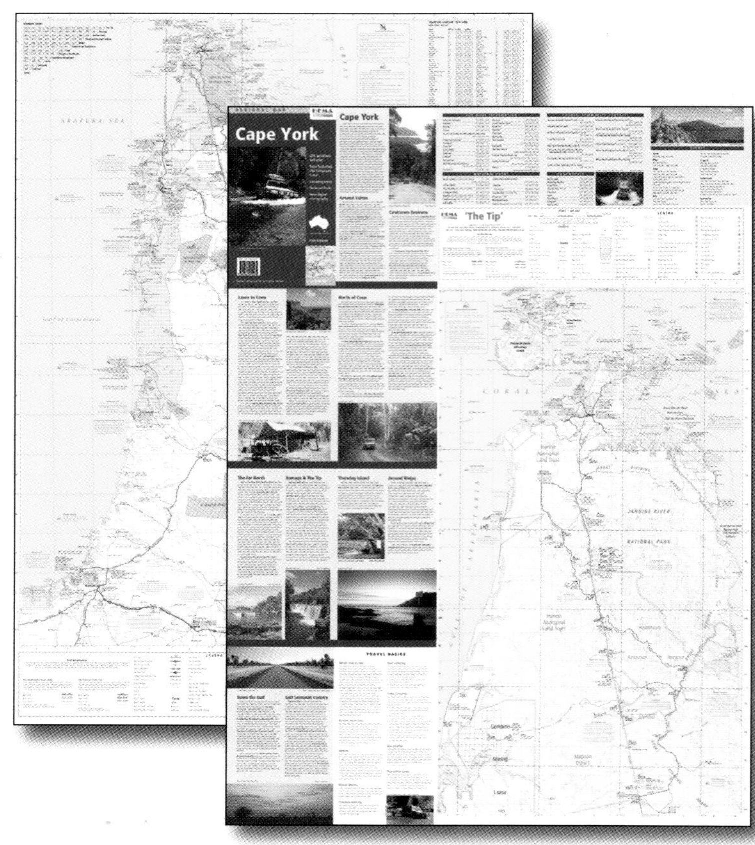

Guides

- Cape York
- Fraser Island
- Great Desert Tracks
- The Kimberley
- The Outback Way
- South West WA
- Tasmania
- Top End & Gulf
- Tropical North QLD
- WA 4WD Top 50

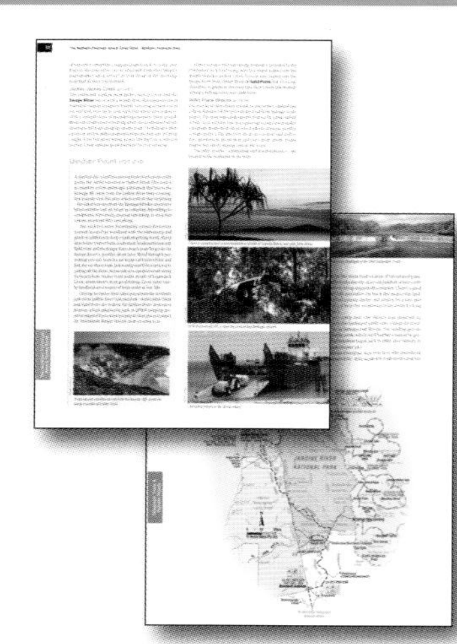

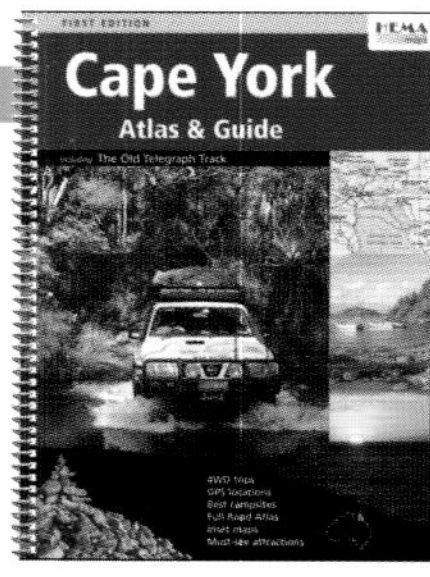

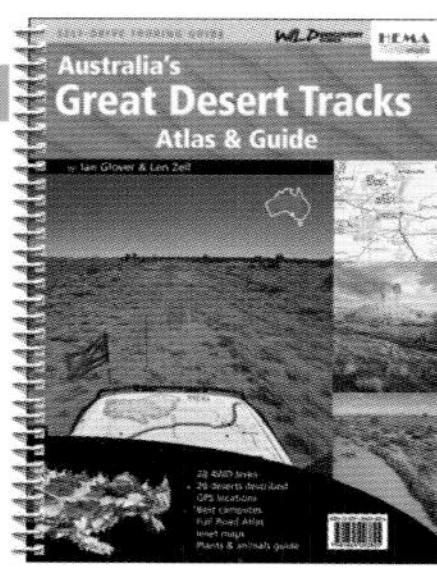

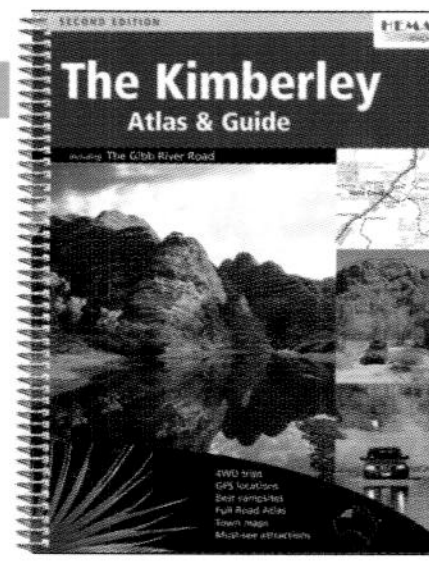

www.hemamaps.com